mypoliscilab™

Where participation leads to action!

MyPoliSciLab is a state-of-the-art, interactive, and instructive online solution for introducing students to American Government. Designed to amplify and supplement a traditional lecture course or completely administer an online course, MyPoliSciLab combines multimedia — simulations, videos, news feeds and archives, quizzes and tests — to make teaching and learning more effective and fun!

WHAT STUDENTS ARE SAYING ABOUT ONLINE EXAMS AND QUIZZES

> I love it. I keep trying until I get a perfect grade and after a couple times you know the content like the back of your hand!

> I liked being able to view the results of the quizzes immediately instead of having to wait for them to be graded by the instructor.

WHAT STUDENTS ARE SAYING ABOUT ONLINE ACTIVITIES

> The activities were my favorite part of the course. They took a different approach to an interesting subject, and made it more applicable to real-life situations. This made the subject seem even more real than before.

> I think they are a great tool to get students to interact with the material in a way you couldn't really do in class.

ONE PLACE.
Everything your students need to succeed.

MyPoliSciLab is a state-of-the-art, interactive, and instructive online solution for your American Government course.

❯❯ Pre-Test, Post Test, and Chapter Exam
For each chapter of the printed textbook, students will navigate through a pre-test, post-test, and a full-chapter exam — all fully integrated with the online E-Book so students can assess, review, and improve their understanding of the material in each chapter.

❯❯ Chapter Review
For each chapter, students will find additional resources such as a complete study guide, learning objectives, and a summary.

❯❯ E-Book
Matching the exact layout of the printed textbook, the E-Book contains multimedia icons in the margins that launch a wealth of exciting resources.

❯❯ The *New York Times* Online Feed & The *New York Times* Search by Subject™ Archive
Both provide free access to the full text of The *New York Times* and articles from the world's leading journalists of the *Times*. The online feed provides students with updated headlines and political news on an **hourly** basis.

❯❯ Online Administration
Instructors can easily track students' work on the site and monitor their progress on each activity. The *Instructor Gradebook*, which now includes upgraded functionality, provides maximum flexibility for allowing instructors to sort by student, activity, or to view the entire class in spreadsheet view.

❯❯ Research Navigator™
This database provides thousands of articles from journals as well as popular periodicals, such as *Newsweek* and *USA Today*, that give students and professors access to scholarly and topical content from a variety of sources.

❯❯ Interactive Activities
Students will find over 100 simulations, interactive timelines, videos, comparative exercises, and more — all integrated with the online E-Book through icons that appear in the margins. Now fully updated with brand-new activities!

SIMULATION Students are given a role to play — such as congress member, lobbyist, or police officer — so they can experience the challenges and excitement of politics firsthand.

TIMELINE With an abundance of media and graphics, students can step through the evolution of an aspect of our political system.

VISUAL LITERACY Students interpret and apply data about intriguing political topics. Each activity begins with an interactive primer on reading graphs and charts.

PARTICIPATION Bringing the importance of politics home, these activities appear as three types: 1) Debates, 2) Surveys, and 3) "Get Involved" activities.

COMPARATIVE Students compare the U.S. political system to those of other countries.

CONTINUOUSLY UPDATED MULTIMEDIA MAPPED TO CHAPTER CONTENT

NEW FEATURES

Student Polling
Updated weekly with timely, provocative questions, this new feature allows students to participate in nationwide polls on hot topics. Students are asked to vote on questions such as "Should flag burning be permitted?" Results of student responses around the country are immediately displayed.

PoliSci News
PoliSci News contains 1) an online feed from The *New York Times* that is updated hourly, 2) an exclusive *New York Times* database that allows students to browse by subject area or search for a specific topic, and 3) PoliSci News Review — a series of articles selected by a political science professor that recap the previous week's most important political events and are followed by quizzes.

Roundtable Discussion Video Clips
Video clips consist of three professors discussing important concepts covered in the text. Key concepts such as campaign finance reform and critical questions such as "Is Federalism Dead?" are discussed from a wide range of perspectives and viewpoints — providing students with a balanced review of key course material. Each discussion is accompanied by critical thinking prompts, multiple choice questions, and a transcript for reference.

Debate Video Clips
Offering lively, challenging debates from two sides of an issue, these clips feature two professors discussing hot-button issues and answering pressing questions such as "Did George Bush steal the election?" Each discussion is accompanied by critical thinking prompts, multiple choice questions, and a transcript for reference.

INSTRUCTOR: WE CAN HELP YOU EASILY INTEGRATE THESE AMAZING ASSETS INTO YOUR COURSE...HOW?

Author's Choice
With so many incredible activities to assign, we have asked our authors to hand select one or two activities that best complement or amplify each chapter. You have the work done for you in easy-to-use, pre-packaged MyPoliSciLab assignments. If you only have time to assign and complete one activity for the chapter, the Author's Choice designation makes it easy!

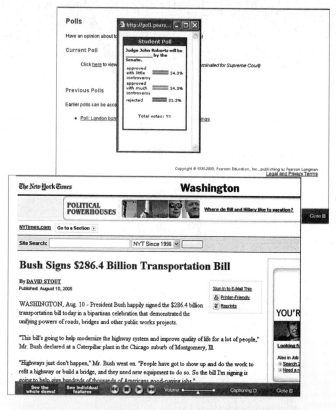

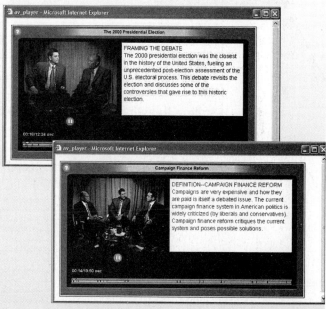

Go to **MyPoliSciLab.com** to see a sample chapter!

Student Survey Results

Recently, Longman Publishers conducted a nationwide survey of students to determine just how useful they find MyPoliSciLab and its individual features. The sample included hundreds of students from both 2-year and 4-year schools. Students were asked to add a value between 1 and 5 to the following elements of MyPoliSciLab and here's how they responded.

The results are impressive. Not only do they show that students find MyPoliSciLab to be an effective supplement, but they show how each specific feature of MyPoliSciLab enhances students' learning experience and engages them with the course material. See for yourself!

Very low learning value →   Very high learning value

	1	2	3	4	5	4s & 5s
Online Quizzes	1.3%	1.3%	8.8%	26.8%	61.9%	88.7%
Chapter Exams	0.8%	5.0%	8.4%	18.4%	67.4%	85.8%
Debate Videos	2.2%	3.5%	15.8%	27.6%	50.9%	78.5%
Roundtable Videos	3.0%	3.0%	16.5%	32.0%	45.5%	77.5%
Chapter Activities	0.9%	5.2%	16.5%	23.9%	53.5%	77.4%
Online E-Book	5.4%	8.3%	15.1%	17.6%	53.7%	71.2%
PS News Review	5.0%	4.5%	23.2%	23.2%	44.1%	67.3%
Homepage Updates	8.0%	11.7%	16.9%	23.9%	39.4%	63.4%
Polling Questions	7.6%	9.0%	27.0%	20.9%	35.5%	56.4%

WHAT STUDENTS ARE SAYING ABOUT ONLINE E-BOOK

"It helped a lot, especially since you could magnify the words. Also, it was great to be able to type in a key word and see exactly where it appears in the text."

WHAT STUDENTS ARE SAYING ABOUT ROUNDTABLE VIDEOS

"All videos were fantastic and allowed each topic to be discussed from each viewpoint but was kept objective by the moderator."

WHAT STUDENTS ARE SAYING ABOUT POLISCI NEWS

"I really liked this feature. I don't get a chance to catch up on political news very often, so this was very helpful."

WHAT STUDENTS ARE SAYING ABOUT POLLING QUESTIONS

"The polling questions are fun. Sometimes I was very surprised at other students' responses."

The New American Democracy

FIFTH EDITION

Morris P. Fiorina
Stanford University

Paul E. Peterson
Harvard University

Bertram Johnson
Middlebury College

William G. Mayer
Northeastern University

PEARSON
Longman

New York • Boston • San Francisco • London •
Toronto • Sydney • Tokyo • Singapore • Madrid • Mexico City •
Munich • Paris • Cape Town • Hong Kong • Montreal

Editor in Chief: Eric Stano
Development Editor: Barbara A. Conover
Senior Marketing Manager: Elizabeth Fogarty
Supplements Editor: Brian Belardi
Production Manager: Savoula Amanatidis
Project Coordination, Text Design, and Electronic Page Makeup: Electronic Publishing Services, Inc.
Cover Design Manager: Wendy Ann Fredericks
Cover Designer: Kay Petronio
Cover Photo: Copyright © Bettman/Corbis. All Rights Reserved.
Senior Manufacturing Buyer: Alfred C. Dorsey
Printer and Binder: Courier Corporation—Kendalville
Cover Printer: Phoenix Color Corporation

For permission to use copyrighted material, grateful acknowledgment is made to the copyright holders on pp. 701–702, which are hereby made part of this copyright page.

Library of Congress Cataloging-in-Publication Data

The new American democracy / Morris P. Fiorina ... [et al.]. -- 5th ed.
    p. cm.
  Includes bibliographical references and index.
  ISBN 0-321-41614-7
  1. Democracy--United States--Textbooks. 2. United States--Politics and government--Textbooks. I. Fiorina, Morris P.

  JK1726.N45 2007
  320.473--dc22

                                        2006039213

Please visit our website at http://www.ablongman.com

ISBN 0-321-41614-7 (The New American Democracy, Fifth Edition)

ISBN 0-321-43007-7 (The New American Democracy, Alternate Fifth Edition)

ISBN 0-321-52201-7 (The New American Democracy, Great Questions in Politics, Sandbox Edition)

ISBN 0-205-55096-7 (The New American Democracy, Ala Carte Edition)

2 3 4 5 6 7 8 9 10—CRK—09 08 07

Dedication

To George Cole, John Kessel, Wayne Merrick, and other members of the Allegheny College Political Science Department, circa 1966

To Harding C. Noblitt, Concordia College

To Richard Keiser and Steven Schier, Carleton College

And to the Friars at Fenwick High School

In appreciation for their teaching excellence

✩ ✩ ✩ ✩

BRIEF CONTENTS

DETAILED CONTENTS

CHAPTER 6   Individual Participation   149

CHAPTER 9   The Media   233

PART 4   THE GOVERNMENT

CHAPTER 12   The Congress and Its Work   331

PART 5   CIVIL LIBERTIES AND CIVIL RIGHTS

CHAPTER 16   Civil Liberties   457

CHAPTER 17   Civil Rights   491

PART 6   PUBLIC POLICY

CHAPTER 18   Domestic Policy   521

Appendices

TO THE STUDENTS

This text grew out of a decade of Morris Fiorina and Paul Peterson teaching the introductory American government course together. As we listened to each other's lectures each year, we noticed that our course was evolving into one whose underlying theme was different from the themes that could be found in other American government textbooks. Specifically, elections and their repercussions gradually became the primary connecting thread that tied together our lectures and discussions. In part, this emphasis reflected our own backgrounds and interests. Morris Fiorina has devoted his professional career to the study of elections—both narrowly, in the sense of why people vote the way they do, and more broadly, in the sense of how elections affect politicians, political institutions, and the policies they produce. Paul Peterson began his career with a focus on citizen participation in the War on Poverty and later studied the way the federal system limited what local officials could do. In recent years, he has examined the ways elections shape government response to budget deficits, welfare needs, race relations, educational issues, and the changing foreign policy environment.

It was not just our own research interests, however, that brought election issues to the fore. Both of us attempt to keep our lectures connected to present-day government and politics, and as a reflection of a changing reality, we found our lectures increasingly infused with the connections between elections and the work of government. From experience we know that students are keenly aware of the way elections affect the strategies of politicians and the decisions of policymakers, as well as a great many other things that happen in government. As a result, we have written a different kind of American government textbook, one that gives a central place to elections and their consequences.

Level and Tone of This Textbook

Some educators think that today's students are less proficient in certain skills and less motivated than were students of a generation ago. Our view is that you may be different from those earlier students, but being different does not mean that you are any less capable. In fact, you also have skills that were nonexistent years ago. (We bet that on average you are better at surfing the Internet than your professors!) As for motivation, that is something not purely your responsibility. It is our job as teachers to make the material as stimulating to you and as relevant to your lives as possible. Our premise is that undergraduate students are fully capable of understanding information and analyses that are clearly expressed. For this reason, this book emphasizes meaning and significance. It contains considerable interpretation in addition to the essential facts.

We do not shy away from controversy. Some individuals in American higher education would protect students from intellectual discomfort. The consequences of such beliefs include well-intentioned efforts to place some subjects and arguments outside the boundaries of classroom discussion. We do not agree with this approach. Our view is that politics is fundamentally about conflict. People have conflicting interests and, even more seriously, conflicting values. Politics is the nonviolent resolution of such conflicts. People can settle their disagreements and rise above their dislikes through political deliberation, or they can choose weapons, as so many have over the course of human history.

We believe that you need to learn to engage in such political deliberation. Within the bounds of civil discourse, you should be challenged, even at times provoked. Education proceeds by defending one's viewpoints and by learning to understand those of others. Thus, in the chapters that follow, we consider arguments that some of you may find uncomfortable. In the realm of education, a better, clearer understanding supersedes all other values.

Although the study of American politics is far more than the study of current events, a book that emphasizes the importance of elections can make its points come to life by placing them in the context of contemporary politics. This fifth edition is a careful revision of the fourth edition, updated to include information about important recent events such as the ongoing war in Iraq, the arrival of a new era in international politics, the latest Supreme Court decisions, and, of course, the dramatic 2006 campaigns and elections that put the Democrats back in control of Congress. Of course, these stories—like politics generally—continue to evolve, and we hope this text provides you with the information you need to understand future developments.

Specific Features

This fifth edition has a number of specific features, many related to our elections theme, designed to stimuate critical thinking, engage you, and help you understand the chapter material. We call your attention to the following:

- Each chapter introduces you to the subject matter with an **opening vignette** on a high-interest issue or incident. Some vignettes are classics from American history, while others are based on current events. Examples include a discussion of the politics of Hurricane Katrina (Chapter 3—Federalism: Division of Power Among National, State, and Local Governments); national reaction to "suspect" minorities in the wake of wars (Chapter 4—American Political Culture); discussion of the 2006 congressional elections and their impact on the Bush agenda; and an analysis of "the battle that wasn't"—the appointment of John Roberts to the Supreme Court (Chapter 15—The Courts).
- Many chapters contain an **International Comparison** box that compares a feature of American government with a similar feature in other countries. These boxes will give you a better understanding of the strengths and limitations of American democracy by letting you think about real alternatives, not just unattainable ideals. The feature box in Chapter 2 looks at the making of a constitution in Iraq; and in Chapter 4 compares citizenship requirements in Europe to those in the United States; in Chapter 14 it discusses the issue of political versus professional bureaucrats; while in Chapter 18 it illustrates the differences in student learning and expenditures between the United States and several European countries and Japan.

- You are given an opportunity to exercise your own critical thinking by considering a **Democratic Dilemma** in some chapters. Are there instances in which democratic values are in conflict? Will policy changes or institutional reforms actually achieve the goals their proponents claim? This box presents arguments pro and con, poses questions, and invites students to grapple with them. Some examples: in Chapter 6 the reflection on whether voters can speak for those who abstain; in Chapter 13 the discussion as to whether divided government is bad; and in Chapter 16 the query as to whether campus speech codes unduly restrict free speech.

- To illustrate the book's focus on electoral forces, some chapters include a box entitled **Election Connection**, describing the relationship between elections and institutions or policies. For instance, in Chapter 4 the box describes Republican efforts to court Hispanic voters, and in Chapter 6 it discusses the use of earmarking by members of Congress to help them get reelected.

- **Critical thinking questions** accompany figures, photographs, and boxes to provoke discussion and thought about the issues at hand and to connect this material to the text discussion it complements or amplifies.

- Each chapter includes full **marginal definitions** for key terms that are boldfaced in the text and included in the end-of-book Glossary.

- At the end of each chapter, we include an **On the Web** feature to direct readers to Web sites where they can find more information on the topics discussed.

- Also, included at the end of each chapter are a **Chapter Summary**, **Key Terms** (alphabetized at the end of the chapter, with page references), and annotated **Suggested Readings**.

- Throughout the text, icons appearing in the margins refer readers to a Web site available with this text, **MyPoliSciLab.** Each icon appears next to a particular topic and indicates that a simulation, visual literacy exercise, interactive timeline, participation activity, comparative government exercise, video roundtable discussion, or video debate related to that topic exists on the site. Activities bring the concepts to life, help the reader better understand the topics presented in the text, provide feedback and assessments, and make learning interactive and fun. See the front pages of this text for more information on this exciting, interactive, and valuable resource that is available at no additional charge when bundled with a new copy of the text.

In addition, we've expanded a feature from the fourth edition, "Voices of the Permanent Campaign"—renaming it "**Election Voices**"—which further emphasizes the election theme. Each follows a related chapter or a set of related chapters.

Based on important current events, each of the ten Election Voices presents a thought-provoking issue and then illustrates how that issue plays out in today's election-driven political environment. Every Election Voices feature includes a brief review of the issue at hand, consideration of opposing viewpoints, references to pertinent Web sites, and critical thinking questions. For example, the new Election Voices that follows Chapter 4 discusses the complex issue of immigration; also new is the Election Voices following Chapter 10, which considers the pros and cons of a national primary to nominate presidential candidates. Chapter 14 is followed by an updated feature on the politics of Homeland Security; an updated discussion of the Arab-Israeli conflict follows Chapter 20. We are confident that each Election Voices feature will stimulate students' intellect, drive home the relevance of the text's material, and help foster lively, thoughtful debates.

New to This Edition

The text has been carefully revised since its fourth edition. This fifth edition includes substantive rewrites, extensively revised features, and the inclusion of the latest information and examples on key topics, such as:

- The 2006 congressional campaigns and elections that heralded the return of divided government
- The concern about terrorism and governmental steps to combat it
- The complexities of immigration—legal and illegal
- The latest developments in the area of campaign finance
- The latest Supreme Court decisions concerning federalism, civil liberties, and other issues, including discussion of the decisions
- The civil rights of Latinos, Asian Americans, and gays and lesbians

New Versions of *The New American Democracy*

With the fifth edition, for the first time, Longman is offering *The New American Democracy* in three versions: the comprehensive edition (20 chapters), the alternate edition (17 chapters, excluding chapters devoted to public policy), and the "Great Questions in Politics" edition—a new option that allows your professor to build and customize one's own book.

By choosing to create a "Great Questions in Politics" edition, your professor can use any of the chapters from *The New American Democracy* and combine them with any of the chapters from the books in Longman's prestigious and popular "Great Questions in Politics" series. Those books include:

- *Culture War? The Myth of a Polarized America,* Second Edition (Morris P. Fiorina, Samuel J. Abrams, and Jeremy C. Pope)
- *A Divider, Not a Uniter: George W. Bush and the American People* (Gary C. Jacobson)
- *Governing by Campaigning: The Politics of the Bush Presidency* (George C. Edwards III)
- *Is Voting for Young People?* (Martin P. Wattenberg)
- *Seven Sins of American Foreign Policy* (Loch K. Johnson)
- *Congressional Travels: Places, Connections, and Authenticity* (Richard F. Fenno, Jr.)

Your instructor merely needs to visit **www.ablongman.com/FiorinaGreatQuestions** to build a book perfectly designed to meet course needs. Once the chapters are selected, your professor can view their seamlessly customized book online within minutes, and within days they will receive a complimentary desk copy printed for their review.

Supplements for Students of Qualified College Adopters

- **MyPoliSciLab** Longman's state-of-the-art, interactive online solution for your course. Available in CourseCompass, Blackboard, and WebCT—or as a Web site free of these course management systems—MyPoliSciLab offers students a wealth of simulations, interactive exercises, videos, weekly polls, hourly news feeds, and assessment tools—integrated with an online E-book version of this text. For each chapter of the text, students will navigate through a pre-test, post-test, chapter review, and a full-chapter exam, so they can assess, review, and improve their understanding of the concepts within the chapters. See the advertisement at the front of this book for more information.

- **Companion Web Site (www.longmanamericangovernment.com).** This online study site includes: Practice tests with feedback (multiple-choice, true/false, and fill-in-the-blank); Web links, Flash Cards, and more.

- **Research Navigator and Research Navigator Guide.** Research Navigator is a comprehensive Web site comprising three exclusive databases of credible and reliable source material for research and for student assignments: EBSCO's ContentSelect Academic Journal Database, the *New York Times* Search-by-Subject Archive, "Best of the Web" Link Library, and *Financial Times* Article Archive and Company Financials. The site also includes an extensive help section. The Research Navigator Guide provides your students with access to the Research Navigator Web site and includes reference material and hints about conducting online research. **Available at no additional charge to qualified college adopters.**

- *New York Times* **Discount Subscription.** A 10-week subscription for only $20. Contact your local Allyn & Bacon/Longman representative for more information.

- *You Decide! Current Debates in American Politics,* **2007 Edition.** Edited by John T. Rourke, University of Connecticut, this exciting debate-style reader is updated annually and examines provocative issues in American politics *today.* The topics have been selected for their currency, importance, and student interest, and the pieces that argue various sides of a given issue come from recent journals, congressional hearings, think tanks, and periodicals. (ISBN: 0-321-43016-6)

- *Divided Government* **(Longman Classics in Political Science)** by Morris P. Fiorina. This reissued, authoritative text on political parties in the U.S. features a foreword by David R. Mayhew of Yale University. Fiorina's classic book reviews the historical evolution of political parties and explores the consequences of divided government for the policy process. (ISBN: 0-321-12184-8)

- *Voices of Dissent: Critical Readings in American Politics,* **Seventh Edition.** Edited by William F. Grover, St. Michael's College, and Joseph G. Peschek, Hamline University, this collection of critical essays goes beyond the debate between mainstream liberalism and conservatism to fundamentally challenge the status quo. Available at a discount when ordered packaged with this text.

- *American Government: Readings and Cases,* **Seventeenth Edition.** Edited by Peter Woll, Brandeis University, this longtime best-selling reader provides a strong, balanced blend of classic readings and cases that illustrate and amplify important concepts in American government, alongside extremely current selections drawn from today's issues and literature. Available at a discount when ordered packaged with this text. (ISBN: 0-321-47314-0)

- *Ten Things That Every American Government Student Should Read.* Edited by Karen O'Connor, The American University. We asked American government instructors across the country to vote for 10 things beyond the text that they believe every student should read and put them in this brief and useful reader. Available at no additional cost when ordered packaged with the text. (ISBN: 0-205-28969-X)

- *Choices: An American Government Database Reader.* This customizable reader allows instructors to choose from a database of more than 300 readings to create a reader that exactly matches their course needs. Go to **www.pearsoncustom.com/database/choices.html** for more information.

- **Discount Subscription to *Newsweek* Magazine.** Students receive 12 issues of *Newsweek* at more than 80 percent off the regular price. An excellent way for students to keep up with current events.
- **Penguin-Longman Value Bundles.** Longman offers 25 Penguin Putnam titles at more than a 60 percent discount when packaged with any Longman text. This unusual offer is a wonderful way to enhance students' understanding of concepts in American government. Please go to **www.ablongman.com/penguin** for more information.
- *Writing in Political Science,* **Third Edition, by Diane Schmidt.** Takes students step-by-step through all aspects of writing in political science. Available at a discount when ordered packaged with any Longman textbook. (ISBN: 0-321-21735-7)
- *Texas (Longman State Politics Series),* **Fourth Edition, by Debra St. John.** A 90-page primer on state and local government and issues in Texas. Available at no additional cost when shrink-wrapped with text (ISBN: 0-321-38456-8).
- *California (Longman State Politics Series),* **Fourth Edition, by Pamela Fiber.** A 70-page primer on state and local government and issues in California. Available at no additional cost when shrink-wrapped with text (ISBN: 0-321-42764-5).
- *Florida (Longman State Politics Series),* **by George A. Gonzalez.** A 50-page primer on state and local government and issues in Florida. Available at no additional cost when shrink-wrapped with text. (ISBN: 0-321-42763-7)
- *Georgia (Longman State Politics Series),* **by Said L. Sewell and F. Carl Walton.** A 70-page primer on state and local government issues in Georgia. Available at no additional cost when shrink-wrapped with text (ISBN: 0-321-42765-3).

Great Questions in Politics   Written by some of the most influential scholars and thinkers in political science, each book in this series examines a major question in American politics, offers a new perspective on our political system, and challenges conventional wisdom and prevailing attitudes. Package any of the Great Questions in Politics books with The New American Democracy and receive a 10 percent discount.

- *Culture War? The Myth of a Polarized America,* Morris. P. Fiorina, Stanford University; Samuel J. Abrams, Harvard University; and Jeremy C. Pope, Stanford University (ISBN: 0-321-36606-9). This text combines polling data with a compelling narrative to debunk commonly believed myths about American politics—particularly the claim that Americans are deeply divided in their fundamental political views.
- *Governing by Campaigning: The Politics of the Bush Presidency,* 2007 Edition, George C. Edwards III, Texas A&M University (ISBN: 0-205- 52962-3). This brief volume, by one of the foremost experts on the presidency, explores how the Bush administration has attempted sweeping changes in public policy—without broad support for doing so—by taking its case to the American public more than any other president in history.

- *A Divider, Not a Uniter: George W. Bush and the American People: The 2006 Election and Beyond,* Gary C. Jacobson, University of California, San Diego (ISBN: 0-205-52974-7.) This brief, engaging book is rich in data and analyzes the reasons the public is so divided along party lines about George W. Bush.

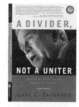

- *Is Voting for Young People?* with New Postscript on New Forms of Citizen Engagement, Martin P. Wattenberg, University of California, Irvine (ISBN: 0-205-51807-9). This accessible, provocative, and brief book explores the reasons the young are less and less likely to follow politics and vote in the United States, as well as many other established democracies, and suggests ways of changing that.

- *Seven Sins of American Foreign Policy,* Loch K. Johnson, University of Georgia (ISBN: 0-321-41585-X). This brief, accessible book by renowned intelligence and foreign policy expert, Loch Johnson, examines seven major shortcomings—"sins"—in American foreign policy over several administrations that have generated pervasive negative attitudes toward the United States, cost us friendship and support, and impaired our ability to advance our international interests.

- *Congressional Travels: Places, Connections, and Authenticity,* Richard F. Fenno Jr., University of Rochester (ISBN: 0-321-47071-0). This book argues that authenticity—knowing what a representative is like in his or her district and looking beyond mere roll-call voting—contributes significantly to understanding the full body of work done by our members of Congress. It further posits, by recounting Fenno's life's work, that the best way to gain a sense of authenticity is to do what Fenno is most famous for—making multiple trips and spending a great deal of time observing representatives at home, with their constituents, in their districts.

TO OUR COLLEAGUES

The chapters that follow speak directly to students in down-to-earth language. In this preface we address their teachers, our colleagues, in more professional terms, about the reasons we decided to write this text.

More than a generation ago, one of the leading political scientists of the century, Robert Dahl, published a textbook entitled *Pluralist Democracy in the United States.* Dahl was the acknowledged leader of the pluralist school of American political science, which viewed American politics as a collection of arenas in which leaders of organized interest groups bargained over the substance of public policies, with public officials involved both as brokers and as representatives of broader societal interests. Political institutions, in turn, were viewed as regularized bargaining arenas in which leaders were constrained by formal rules. *Groups, bargaining*, *leaders*, and *representation* were the operative terms for understanding American politics.

American politics has changed a good deal since Dahl wrote. Indeed, Dahl himself notes a number of these changes:

> Without intending to do so, over the past thirty years or so Americans have created a new political order. Although it retains a seamless continuity with the order it has displaced, in its present form it constitutes something so new that journalists, commentators, scholars, and ordinary citizens are still struggling to understand it.

Dahl argues that this new political order is more fragmented and more plebiscitary than the old one. The proliferation of interest groups combined with the deterioration of traditional party organizations has strengthened divisive forces and weakened unifying ones. Such political developments, along with social and technological changes, have exposed public officials to popular pressures more than in the past. As a consequence, Dahl contends, representation and deliberation have suffered. He worries that these changes might create "a pseudo-democratic facade on a process manipulated by political leaders to achieve their own agendas."

Another leading political scientist of Dahl's generation, Gabriel Almond, weighs in with similar sentiments:

> Television and radio have largely preempted the print media and the primary opinion leaders . . . . Domestic and international events are brought into the living room with powerful visual and emotional impact—a telepopulism that constrains and distorts public policy. The deliberative processes of politics are diluted and heated by this populism, and by "instant" public opinion polls based on telephone samples.

Although we do not agree with every particular of these indictments, they serve to emphasize that something has happened to American government since the days when an earlier generation of scholars characterized it as a pluralist democracy. For better or for worse, it has become something closer to a popular democracy. In the pages that follow, we describe the forces that have brought about these changes as well as their impact on contemporary politics, institutions, and policies. But, we are getting ahead of ourselves here.

Each year as we considered the range of texts available for the introductory American government course, we decided that available books, however worthy, did not match our views. In the first place, many gave less emphasis than we would like to topics that are essential parts of contemporary American politics—elections, most obviously, but also closely related topics such as public opinion, political participation, and the media. Second, in many texts the role of prime mover implicitly is assigned to the courts, whereas we see electoral context as an important influence on judicial activity and judicial outcomes. Third, contemporary textbooks typically separate the study of elections from other major headings: constitutional fundamentals, bureaucratic politics, the courts, and the formation of public policies. As James Stimson comments:

> In our texts, public opinion is a chapter or two. The various branches of government are usually a chapter each. And the connection between what the public wants and what the government does is on the page fold between them. Public opinion is conceptualized as a set of measures and processes that do not speak to government. Governing institutions are studied in a manner, which doesn't deny public opinion influence, but doesn't permit its active study. When citizens of Washington, DC, could not vote, the analogy was complete; all opinion was outside the beltway, all government was inside.

This book breaks down the artificial and unfortunate separation identified by Stimson. Rather than discuss public opinion in one self-contained chapter, political participation in a second, and elections in a third, then move on to a series of institutional and policy chapters, we give public opinion and electioneering their due in individual chapters devoted to those topics, but we continue to trace their effects on other political and institutional processes, culminating in discussions of why American public policies have the shape they do. Thus, the chapters of this text bear the familiar titles, but they are linked by an extended discussion of the pervasiveness of electoral influences in the new American democracy.

When we began writing the first edition of this book almost 15 years ago, we knew that our argument for the contemporary dominance of electoral forces would meet with some resistance. Most of the developments we described were fairly recent, and we understood that some colleagues might not see as sharp a break with the pre-1960s era as we did. But the passing of the years has lessened the novelty of our argument. Under the "horse race" presidencies of Bill Clinton and George W. Bush, the line between electioneering and governing all but disappeared, as the techniques of the campaign moved to the very pinnacle of government. Under George W. Bush, political adviser Karl Rove became a symbol of the permanent campaign, dividing his time between offering advice to the president and such tasks as selecting Republican precinct coordinators for the 2004 race and plotting strategy for the 2006 midterm elections. After the Democrats won control of Congress in 2006, Rahm Emanuel (D-IL) declared "It's time for the endless campaign to stop and the hard work of governing to begin." We doubt this distinction is viable. Our view that contemporary American politics is a "permanent campaign" is now common. In fact, the Pew Charitable Trusts recently organized a consortium of public-policy think tanks to study the permanent campaign—how it has affected the range of American institutions and the policy process, with what consequences, and whether a line between electioneering and governing might once again be drawn. This fifth edition now lies squarely in the mainstream of thinking about American politics.

We emphasize that to say that public opinion, political campaigns, and elections are of great import is to offer neither a celebrationist nor a cynical interpretation of American politics. On the one hand, the shift to a more popular democracy is associated with a greater role for previously disadvantaged voices in the population. As the scramble to register new voters in 2004 illustrates, those who had been left out in the past can now exercise electoral power. On the other hand, the shift to a more popular democracy grants greater access to special interests and limits opportunities for reflective consideration of the long-range consequences of policy choices. But there is no reason to rush to a critical judgment. Future generations of scholars can judge whether the new order does more or less to advance the welfare of the American people than the old one.

Nor should our emphasis on elections suggest a focus on anything so narrow as what happens on Election Day or in the campaigns that precede it. When we say that elections play a dominant role, we are thinking not only of their direct effects, but also of the indirect ways in which they affect the thinking of interest groups, parties, and public officials—both elected and appointed. It is not so much elections themselves as their anticipation that provides so much of the motive power in contemporary political life in the United States.

Finally, we understand that our colleagues will be understandably skeptical of any attempt to squeeze the study of American government into any single thematic frame—even one defined as broadly as our understanding and interpretation of electoral influence. The subject matter of American government is voluminous, and an introductory course must touch on its many aspects. We do not believe that elections explain all that needs to be known about all aspects of American government and politics. Our general approach is to consider the incentives at work in any situation. If electoral incentives are often a major force, they certainly are not the only one. Some leaders risk their reputations with the public for the good of the country. Some act out of ideological commitments, regardless of their electoral consequences. Some realize that foreign policies must take into account the interests of nations throughout the world. Where these and other non-electoral factors are important, we recognize that fact and proceed accordingly. The result is a book that is more focused than most American government texts, but not one that forces the whole subject into a single theme.

In sum, we do not believe this book could or should have been written even as recently as a generation ago. For although elections have always been central to American politics, we believe, with Dahl, that American politics became significantly more plebiscitary in the late twentieth century. The contributing factors are widely recognized. Transformations in the process of nominating and electing candidates produced an individualistic politics in which each candidate forms his or her own organization rather than relying on a common party organization. Transformations in communications technology—survey research, phone, fax, and the Internet—made it possible for politicians to learn the political impacts of their decisions almost instantaneously. Transformations in the media generated a seemingly insatiable demand for news material—a demand often satisfied by stories about political conflict. In this context, interest groups mushroomed, polls and primaries proliferated, and the permanent campaign arrived on the scene. Older concepts used to characterize pluralist politics—groups, bargaining, leaders, and representation—are still important, but a full and accurate account of American politics today must also include careful consideration of the roles played by the media, polls, and campaigns and elections.

Approach and Organization

This book cuts across the old categories that characterize existing American government texts: historical development, political "inputs," institutions, and policy "outputs." Although we discuss all these aspects of American politics, we approach them in a more integrated manner. Following are a few illustrations of our approach:

- Contemporary practices are compared and contrasted with those existing in earlier periods, making the historical material more relevant to today's readers.
- Chapters on so-called political inputs focus on the choices of individuals, groups, parties, and the media as a response to the incentives they face.
- Analyses of Congress, the presidency, the bureaucracy, and the judiciary do not just describe the main institutions of government, but also show how elections shape the behavior of officeholders within these institutions.
- Civil liberties and civil rights are treated not simply as the result of judicial decisions, but also as the product of popular mobilization and other electoral forces. These chapters are placed at the end of the book, instead of at the beginning as part of the historical foundations of American government, in order to highlight the extent to which basic constitutional rights are themselves shaped by public opinion and electoral outcomes.
- Discussions of public policies do not just list policy problems or classify types of policies, but show how elections in particular and politics in general shape the way policies are addressed and adopted.

Finally, the book offers a critical but fair picture of American government and politics. Any objective observer must recognize that American government and politics have numerous shortcomings. We point out many of them and explain why they exist. But throughout the text we show that, judged against realistic standards, American politics and government are not nearly as blameworthy as the evening news and tabloid shows often suggest.

Instructor Supplements for Qualified College Adopters

- **Companion Web Site (www.longmanamericangovernment.com).** This study web site provides a wealth of resources for students and instructors using *The New American Democracy,* Fifth Edition. Students will find the site serving as a useful, online study guide with practice tests, Web links, flash cards, and a variety of other learning tools.
- **Instructor's Resource Center (www.ablongman.com/IRC).** Instructors have access to the Instructor's Manual, PowerPoint® slides, and teaching links via a link

to the Instructor's Resource Center Web site. Contact your local Allyn & Bacon/Longman representative for an access code.

- *Digital Media Archive for American Government.* This cross-platform CD-ROM for instructors contains hundreds of images, maps, audio and video clips ready for classroom presentation or downloading into PowerPoint or any other presentation software (ISBN: 0-321-27068-1).

- **Instructor's Manual.** Prepared by Cecilia Manrique of the University of Wisconsin–La Crosse, each chapter of this resource manual contains a Chapter Overview, Key Concepts and Objectives, Chapter Outline, Terms for Review, and Teaching Suggestions. (ISBN: 0-205-53247-0)

- **Test Bank with Practice Tests.** This test bank, prepared by Cecilia Manrique of University of Wisconsin–La Crosse, contains hundreds of multiple-choice, true/false, short answer, and essay questions, all accompanied by an answer key. (ISBN: 0-205-53302-7)

- **TestGen-EQ Computerized Testing System.** This flexible, easy-to-use computer test bank includes all the test items in the printed test bank. The software allows you to edit existing questions and add your own items. Tests can be printed in several formats and can include figures such as graphs and tables. (ISBN: 0-205-51955-5)

- **Text-Specific Transparency Acetates.** Transparencies drawn from figures in *The New American Democracy*, made available for showing in a classroom. (ISBN: 0-205-51954-7)

- **Longman American Government Video Archive.** These videos from a broad range of sources include famous debates, speeches, political commercials, and congressional hearings. The archive also includes series such as "Eyes on the Prize" and "The Power Game." Ask your Longman sales representative for more information.

See page xxvii, To the Students, for a list of student supplements and information on new versions of this text.

ACKNOWLEDGMENTS

We want to thank the many people who helped us with the preparation of this book. Our deepest gratitude goes to the many undergraduate students whose questions forced us to refine our thinking about American government over the past 10 years. We also thank numerous cohorts of teaching fellows for their perceptive comments, questions, and criticisms. We are also especially grateful to Bruce Nichols, who first argued with us the need for a new-century approach to the introductory text on American government. The Center for Advanced Study in the Behavioral and Social Sciences provided generous support for Paul E. Peterson's work on the first edition of the text during his academic year there.

Harding Noblitt of Concordia College read the entire first edition manuscript in search of errors of fact and interpretation, saving the authors much embarrassment. In addition, portions were read by Danny Adkison, Sue Davis, Richard Fenno, Gary Jacobson, Barry Rabe, and Chris Stamm, whose comments helped with fact checking. We especially appreciate John Ferejohn and the undergraduate students at Stanford University who took his course and tested an early draft of the entire manuscript, and Jay Greene and his students at the University of Texas at Austin who used subsequent page proofs. Larry Carlton supplied important factual material. Research assistance was provided by Ted Brader, Jay Girotto, Donald Lee, Jerome Maddox, Kenneth Scheve, Sean Theriault, and Robert Van Houweling—as well as William Howell who, in addition to making many other contributions, helped write the regulatory policy section in Chapter 18. Rebecca Contreras, Alison Kommer, Shelley Weiner, and Sarah Peterson provided staff assistance. Bert Johnson wishes to thank his American Politics students at Carleton College and Middlebury College, as well as professors Sharon Navarro, Kanishkan Sathasivam, Steven Schier, and Kim Smith for their helpful suggestions. William Mayer would like to thank his wife, Amy Logan, for making sure he had time to do his share of the revisions.

We would like to extend our special thanks to Martin West of Harvard University and Jeremy Pope and Sam Abrams at Stanford University for the multitude of tasks they undertook to see this fifth edition into publication, and improved upon the fourth.

In the course of writing this book, we benefited from the advice of many instructors across the country. We deeply thank all the following, but we are especially grateful for the expert advice of Stephen Ansolabehere, Richard Fenno, John Ferejohn, Bonnie Honig, William Mayer, and Diana Owen.

The following are reviewers who assisted in the preparation of the second, third, and fourth editions of the text: Danny M. Adkison, Oklahoma State University; Donald P. Aiesi, Furman University; Michael Bailey, Georgetown University; Gordon Bennett, University of Texas; Mark Berger, State University of New York at Stony Brook; William Bianco, Penn State University; Nancy Bond, Ranger College; Chris W. Bonneau, University of Pittsburgh; Michael Caldwell, University of Illinois, Urbana–Champaign; Thomas A. Chambers, Golden West College; Mark A. Cichock, University of Texas at Arlington; Louis DeSipio, University of Illinois,

Urbana–Champaign; Richard E. Dunn, College of Charleston; Audrey Haynes, University of Georgia; Christine Fastnow, University of Michigan; Eric Herzik, University of Nevada; Jon Hurwitz, University of Pittsburgh; Robert Jacobs, Central Washington University; Carlos Juarez, Hawaii Pacific University; David Leal, State University of New York at Buffalo; Brad Lockerbie, University of Georgia; William Lyons, University of Tennessee; Cecilia Manrique, University of Wisconsin, La Crosse; Madhavi McCall, San Diego State University; William P. McLauchlan, Purdue University; Michael E. Meagher, University of Missouri, Rolla; Charles Menifield, Murray State University; David S. Meyer, City College of New York; Sarah Miller, Lourdes University; Timothy Nokken, University of Houston; John H. Parham, Minnesota State University; Curt Reithel, University of Wisconsin, La Crosse; Mankato; James A. Rhodes, Luther College; Beth Rosenson, University of Florida; Todd M. Schaefer, Central Washington University; Theodore M. Vestal, Oklahoma State University; Shirley Anne Warshaw, Gettysburg College; Linda Faye Williams, University of Maryland; Jeremy Zilber, College of William and Mary.

The following are reviewers who assisted in the preparation of this fifth edition: Bruce Unger, Randolph–Macon College; Alan Arwine, University of Illinois; Mark Blitz, Claremont McKenna College; Kelechi Kalu, University of Northern Colorado; Terrence Casey, Rose-Hulman Institute of Technology; Beth Rosenson, University of Florida; Christopher Housenick, Pennsylvania State University; Fred Slocum, Minnesota State University; Joe Gershtenson, Eastern Kentucky University; Brian Brox, Tulane University; and Anna Harvey, New York University.

M. P. F.
P. E. P.
B. J.
W. G. M.

ABOUT THE AUTHORS

Morris P. Fiorina

Morris P. Fiorina is Wendt Professor of Political Science and Senior Fellow of the Hoover Institution at Stanford University. He received a B.A. from Allegheny College in Meadville, Pennsylvania, and a Ph.D. from the University of Rochester. Before moving to Stanford, he taught at the California Institute of Technology and Harvard University.

Fiorina has written widely on American government and politics, with special emphasis on representation and elections. He has published numerous articles and five books: *Representatives, Roll Calls, and Constituencies; Congress—Keystone of the Washington Establishment; Retrospective Voting in American National Elections; The Personal Vote: Constituency Service and Electoral Independence* (coauthored with Bruce Cain and John Ferejohn); and *Divided Government*. He has served on the editorial boards of a dozen journals in the fields of political science, economics, law, and public policy, and from 1986 to 1990, he served as chairman of the Board of Overseers of the American National Election Studies. He is a member of the National Academy of Sciences and is a Wendt Family Professor of Political Science.

In his leisure time, Fiorina favors physical activities, including hiking, fishing, and sports. Although his own athletic career never amounted to much, he was a successful youth baseball coach for 15 years. Among his most cherished honors is a plaque given by happy parents on the occasion of an undefeated Babe Ruth season.

Paul E. Peterson

Paul E. Peterson is the Henry Lee Shattuck Professor of Government and Director of the Center for American Political Studies at Harvard University. He received his B.A. from Concordia College in Moorhead, Minnesota, and his Ph.D. from the University of Chicago.

Peterson is an author or editor of twenty books and numerous articles on federalism, urban politics, race relations, and public policy, including studies of education, welfare, and fiscal and foreign policy. He received the Gladys Kammerer Award from the American Political Science Association for his book, *School Politics, Chicago Style* (1976) and the Woodrow Wilson Award for his book *City Limits* (Chicago, 1981). In 1996 his book *The Price of Federalism* (Brookings, 1995) was given the Aaron Wildavsky Award for the best book on public policy. He is a member of the American Academy of Arts and Sciences.

It is not only when writing a textbook that Peterson makes every effort to be as accurate as possible. On the tennis courts, he always makes correct line calls and has seldom been heard to hit a wrong note when tickling the ivories.

Bertram Johnson

Bert Johnson teaches political science at Middlebury College in Middlebury, Vermont. He received his B.A. from Carleton College and his Ph.D. from Harvard University.

Johnson has written on federalism, intergovernmental relations, and campaign finance. When not investigating new ideas about American politics, he can be found exploring prime rock climbing spots throughout the United States.

William G. Mayer

William G. Mayer is an associate professor of political science at Northeastern University in Boston, having received his B.A. and his Ph.D. from Harvard University. He is the author of six books and numerous articles on such topics as public opinion, political parties, voting and elections, media and politics, and the presidential nomination process. More importantly, he is married to Amy Logan and the father of two children, Natalie and Thomas. He also teaches Sunday School to kindergartners at St. Jude's Catholic Church in Waltham, Massachusetts.

CHAPTER 1

✮ ✮ ✮ ✮ ✮ ✮ ✮ ✮ ✮ ✮

Democracy in the United States

CHAPTER OUTLINE

The Permanent Campaign Goes into Overtime

George W. Bush became president of the United States in one of the most closely contested elections in American history—and also one of the most controversial. Bush actually received several hundred thousand fewer votes than the man he defeated. He squeaked out a victory only because of the Electoral College, a 200-year-old method of selecting the chief executive (see Chapter 10). Bush picked up 271 out of 538 electoral votes.

Nor was Bush's victory simply a matter of old-fashioned rules giving him a bit of luck. The vote margin in Florida was so razor-thin that state law required a protracted and highly contentious recount that was not resolved until a Supreme Court ruling ended the vote counting (see Chapter 15). Bush's ascension to the presidency therefore was not widely accepted as legitimate.

Voters were polarized over the Bush presidency, with roughly half disapproving of the new chief executive. Bush could not take the American public for granted if he wanted to be a viable president. Despite promises that he would make "decisions based upon principle, not based upon polls or focus groups," Bush had to stay in campaign mode and constantly weigh policy choices for their likely political consequences. The White House reportedly polled voters twice a month.[1]

Bush brought to the Oval Office a clever political operative named Karl Rove. Rove became Bush's domestic adviser but his true role, observers concluded, was to serve as chief political strategist. Rove reportedly played a significant role in public policies. For example, many observers attributed Bush's decision to halt Navy bombing on the Puerto Rican island of Viecques and his proposal to grant amnesty to as many as 3 million illegal Mexican immigrants to Rove's ambition to attract more of the Hispanic vote.[2]

Bush received a huge burst in popularity after the 9/11 terrorist attacks. Indeed, his job approval ratings reached unprecedented levels. But Bush's father had attained similarly impressive ratings during the Gulf War without being able to win reelection. The younger Bush knew that his newfound popularity would fade. He moved quickly against two nations thought to harbor terrorists—Afghanistan and Iraq—and his administration sent upbeat images and messages back to the American people (see Chapter 5). Bush also worked quickly to set up a new homeland security apparatus, a dramatic change in the federal bureaucracy (see pp. 421–424).

Numerous other White House policy decisions seemed to reflect political calculations. Bush agreed to raise barriers against foreign steel, contrary to Republican free-trade principles, in apparent recognition that the party needed votes in steel-producing states. Bush reluctantly caved in to farm-state demands for large agricultural subsidies, shoring up the rural vote (see Chapter 12). Bush and his congressional allies never stopped campaigning for reelection.

Nor were the Democrats sleeping during this time. Many liberals expected that anger about the nature of Bush's victory would mobilize Democrats four years later and sweep Bush out of office after only one term. Commentators began speculating on likely Democratic candidates before Bush entered the Oval Office. Nine Democratic candidates had entered the presidential race by early 2003, only halfway into Bush's term. U.S. Sen. John Kerry of Massachusetts, the eventual nominee, was already dropping by key nomination states.

After Kerry won the nomination, his former rivals began working for his victory. New campaign finance reforms had weakened the ability of the national parties to fund hard-hitting campaign ads on behalf of their candidates. Into this void appeared new organizations—called "527 Committees"—that would collect political donations and independently run ads to influence the election (see p. 324). Anti-Bush 527 committees attracted the most money.

Senator Kerry, meanwhile, strove to connect with campaign audiences. He smiled a lot, took vacations that showed off his athleticism, and named a youthful running mate, Senator John Edwards of North Carolina. He sharpened his political positions, which had evolved from the intricacies of congressional politics, so that they would be easier to communicate. When Kerry's spunky wife seemed too outspoken, their large brood of well-mannered children traveled the country to campaign.[3]

Overall, it was a presidential campaign of great energy, some positive, some negative. The American voter could hardly feel neglected. Two well-funded and capable presidential candidates had spent years wooing them, offering plans and proposals, passion and promises (see Chapter 6). Americans turned out to vote at a rate not seen since the crisis year of 1968.

The 2004 election produced a temporary hiatus in presidential campaigning that lasted for about four months. By the early spring of 2005, however, several major Democrats, including John Kerry, John Edwards, and Hillary Clinton, were clearly starting to position themselves for the 2008 campaign. With Bush constitutionally prohibited from running for a third term, a number of Republicans were also testing the waters.

It was the new American democracy at work.

MAKING THE CONNECTION

The 2004 election illustrates important features of contemporary American democracy and how it differs from democratic practice elsewhere. The campaign was long and drawn out. Huge sums of money were spent. The mass media were deeply involved in the process. Some of the candidates' policy positions reflected their personal commitments and party principles, while others played to public opinion as revealed through the polls.

Elections underlie many of the most important developments in American government at the beginning of the twenty-first century. Indeed, the central theme of this book is that elections are the key to understanding contemporary American democracy. Not only are elections more important in the United States than in other democracies, but they are more important today than they were in most earlier periods of our history.

In this chapter we address why elections have attained more importance in the United States than in other democracies, how minorities exert influence in a system based on majority rule, and why American politics has become a "permanent campaign" in recent years. In addition, we discuss whether it matters that Americans governments are freely elected rather than chosen in some other way. And, finally, we consider whether elections produce a reasonably good government.

Elections in America

More than in any other democracy, politics in the United States is driven by electoral influences. To avoid any misunderstanding, we emphasize three points at the outset. First, our notion of electoral influence is very broad. We refer not just to what happens on Election Day or even just to what goes on during the formal campaigns. Rather, when we write about the importance of elections, we include the anticipation of and the preparation for future elections—what we call the permanent campaign. (You can learn more about the permanent campaign on pages 11–16.) Looking ahead to the next election affects what presidents propose, what they sign, and what they veto; what Congress passes and what it kills; whom groups support and whom they oppose; whom and what the media cover and whom and what they ignore. Just as the winner of an Olympic event may have been determined on the training fields years earlier, so the outcomes of elections may be determined far in advance of the actual campaigns by the anticipatory actions of candidates, groups, contributors, the media, and other political actors.

Second, when we emphasize the importance of elections, we are not making a naïve claim that "the people" rule. On the contrary, elections are not always accurate expressions of popular preferences. Elections give more power to some groups than to others. Sometimes elections allow special interests to block actions desired by the majority. And even if every election reflected the preferences of a majority, leaders elected by different majorities at different times might deadlock. Elections can be tremendously important without necessarily giving the public what it wants. Whether elections are truly representative and whether they generally work to produce good government are questions that spark debate and disagreement.

Finally, to say that elections are a key ingredient in American democracy—even *the* key ingredient—is not to deny that other elements are important as well. Elections are part of a very complicated political system. They are closely bound up with the historical evolution of American government, the political behavior of Americans, the workings of the country's basic institutions, and the policies that the governmental process generates. All of these topics receive thorough treatment in the chapters that follow.

Because Americans take elections so much for granted, we begin by calling attention to the sheer amount of electioneering that occurs in the United States.

Half-a-Million Elected Officials

The United States has more elections that choose more officials for public offices than any other country on Earth. Unbelievable as it may seem, more than half-a-million people in the United States are elected officials, about 1 for every 500 Americans. If all these elected officials lived in one place, the population would exceed that of Cleveland.[4]

National elections, in which voters choose the officials of the federal government, are held every two years. These important elections determine the president, the vice president, 100 senators, and 435 members of the House of Representatives. Although national elections get most of the media's attention, hundreds of thousands of elections occur at other levels of government.

In *state elections* the citizens of the 50 states choose their state public officials. Voters elect the governor and the state legislature in every state, and in nearly all states they elect a handful of other statewide offices such as the lieutenant governor, the treasurer, the state's attorney general, and the auditor. Finally, voters in some states elect state railroad and public utility commissioners.

The number of elections explodes when we move to *local elections*, in which officials for all governments below the state level are chosen. Voters in cities elect mayors and city councils. Voters in the more than 3,000 counties elect sheriffs, county treasurers, and county boards, among other officials. Voters select the membership of 90 percent of the nation's 16,000 school boards, as well as numerous officials responsible for the governance of towns, villages, and special districts.

Even the judicial system, which is often viewed as insulated from political pressure, is permeated by elections. In 37 states, voters elect at least some judges.[5] Altogether, Americans elect more than 1,000 state judges and about 15,000 county, municipal, and other local judges and officers of the court.[6] Moreover, in recent years judges have been increasingly subject to **recall elections**, in which dissatisfied citizens try to remove incumbents from office during their terms.

recall election
Attempt to remove an official from office before completion of the term.

Nominating Candidates and Deciding Issues

Although half-a-million elected officials sounds like a lot, there are far more elections than there are elected officials. First, many officials must win two elections before they can take office. In the **primary election**, each party chooses a nominee who then squares off against the other parties' nominees in the **general election**. In *nonpartisan elections,* where candidates do not run with party labels, primaries are sometimes used to narrow the field of candidates. A place on the primary ballot is open to anyone who has the supporters to gather the required number of signatures and the money to pay the filing fees.

Second, to the extensive list of elections that choose officeholders, we must add those elections in which the people directly decide public issues. In 27 states and the District of Columbia, citizens express themselves by voting on initiatives, referenda, or both. An **initiative** is a proposed law or amendment to a state constitution placed on the ballot in response to a citizen petition. A **referendum** is a law or state constitutional amendment that is proposed by a legislature or other elected body but goes into effect only if approved by a specified majority of voters. Often lumped together as **propositions**, initiatives and referenda enable citizens to bypass or overrule elected officials and decide budgets, taxes, laws, and amendments to state constitutions directly.[7] Some states, such as California, frequently have more propositions on the ballot than elected offices to be filled.

Americans have become accustomed to the frequency and variety of elections, but observers from other countries are struck by Americans' repeated trips to the polling places. (See *International Comparison*, p. 6.) Noted British analyst Anthony King argues that "American exceptionalism"—the distinctive shape of American

primary election
Preliminary election that narrows the number of candidates by determining who will be the nominees in the general election.

general election
Final election that selects the office holder.

initiative
Proposed laws or state constitutional amendments placed on the ballot via citizen petition.

referendum
A law or state constitutional amendment that is proposed by a legislature or city council but does not go into effect unless the required majority of voters approve it.

proposition
A shorthand reference to an initiative or a referendum.

Conan the Usurper

Arnold Schwarzenegger first made his name in Hollywood in 1981 as Conan, a barbarian who vanquished his enemies and seized a throne. More than two decades later, the charismatic Republican seized another high office—the governorship of California—through the relatively peaceful means of a recall election.

The Initiative
and Referendum

INTERNATIONAL COMPARISON

Elections in Other Democracies

In contrast to Americans, many of whom can vote more than a dozen times for scores of candidates and issues in any given four-year period, citizens of other democracies vote for fewer offices and vote less frequently. Consider Great Britain, which elected Tony Blair Prime Minister in 1997 and re-elected him in 2001 and 2005. In each of these elections, Britons voted for only one person—a candidate for Parliament. Between these two elections, Britons voted on only two other occasions, for only two offices—their local councilor and their representative to the European Community. Most of the other European democracies vote more often than Britain does but far less often than does the United States.

The United States even looks peculiar when compared to our North American neighbors. In Mexico a presidential election is held every six years. Congressional elections are held every three years. Some Mexican states hold state and municipal elections at the same time as congressional elections, and others hold them at a different time. But at most a Mexican citizen votes four times in a four-year period: in presidential, congressional, state, and municipal elections.

In Canada, too, provincial and municipal elections may or may not be coordinated with national elections. If the elections are not so coordinated, a Canadian votes at most three times (national, provincial, and municipal) in a four-year period, except for an occasional referendum, such as Québec's vote on secession in 1995. Canadian officials are well aware of the contrast between the two systems. Former Prime Minister Jean Chrétien ruffled some American feathers when he commented that "In your system, you guys campaign for 24 hours [a day] every [day for] two years. You know, politics is one thing, but we have to run a government."[a]

[a] David Shribman, "In Canada, the Lean Season," *Boston Globe*, May 23, 1997: p. A3.

---

democracy when seen from an international perspective—arises not from our culture or from our institutions, as many have argued, but rather from the multitude and frequency of our elections. King observes that

> Americans take the existence of their elections industry for granted. Some like it; some dislike it; most are simply bored by it. But they are all conscious of it, in the same way that they are conscious of Mobil, McDonald's, *Larry King Live*, Oprah Winfrey, the Dallas Cowboys, the Ford Motor Company, and all the other symbols and institutions that go to make up the rich tapestry of American life. In a meaningful sense, America is about the holding of elections.[8]

Government and Politics

Ironically, although Americans choose hundreds of thousands of their public officials in elections, and although they use initiatives and referenda to make specific policy decisions, many Americans are frustrated by government. As illustrated in Figure 1.1, despite an increase in confidence in recent years, Americans do not trust government as much as they did in the early 1960s. Citizens believe that government costs too much, delivers too little, and wastes their tax dollars. They think politics is needlessly contentious and often corrupt. Many are unenthusiastic about major-party presidential candidates such as George Bush and John Kerry and yearn for new leaders—though the record also indicates that when fresh faces and unconventional candidates do run for office, their "freshness" wears off quickly and they are soon perceived to be no better than the "usual crowd." Many Americans are suspicious of the established TV networks and major newspapers and turn to alternative information providers such as talk show hosts and cable television comics. Many are frustrated with existing political processes and support radical reforms such as constitutional amendments to limit the number of terms elected officials may serve.[9]

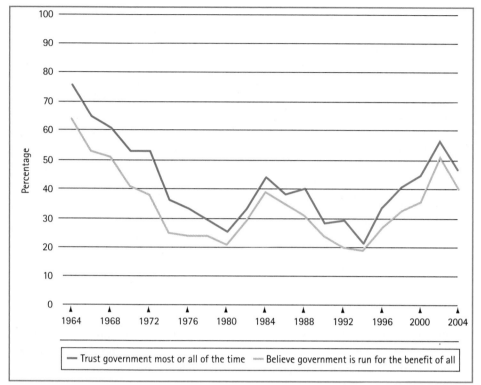

FIGURE 1.1

Americans Are More Skeptical of the National Government than in the Early 1960s

Note: **The second question was not asked in 1986.**

SOURCE: The American National Election Studies, University of Michigan.

Political Corruption

To some extent, suspicion of government is healthy. By their very nature, governments threaten human liberty. The great German sociologist Max Weber defined **government** as the institution in society holding a "monopoly of the legitimate use of physical force."[10] Government is the only institution that *legally* can appropriate people's property (by taxing them and by invoking eminent domain), restrict their movements (by imprisoning them or prohibiting certain kinds of behavior), and even take their lives (by executing them). As George Washington put it a century before Weber, "Government is not reason, it is not eloquence—it is force."[11]

Because government has the power to coerce, people have good reasons to distrust and fear it. Those who participate in politics generally do so because they want to see the powers of government used for some particular purpose. At times the purposes are noble, as when Abraham Lincoln drafted soldiers to fight to save the Union. At times the purposes are less honorable, as when Richard Nixon tried to use the Internal Revenue Service to punish his political critics. Most of the time, the purposes are mixed. John Kerry offers a good example. No one would deny that he entered politics partly to satisfy his personal ambitions, which had been on display since high school.[12] But only his most bitter enemies would deny that he also hoped his leadership could improve the nation.

Because governmental power is fearsome and the motives of those who use it are mixed, citizens understandably do not trust it. Why, then, do we have governments at all? Do we really need them? When campaigning for president, Jimmy Carter professed that "All I want is . . . to have a nation with a government that is as good and honest and decent and competent and compassionate and as filled with love as are the American people."[13] These are admirable sentiments, but with all due respect to the former president, government is necessary precisely because such qualities are often

government

The institution in society that has a "monopoly of the legitimate use of physical force."

One Man's Good Government

When campaigning for president, Jimmy Carter said, "All I want is . . . to have a nation with a government that is as good . . . as are the American people."

• *How good would such a government be?*

missing from human behavior. As another former president, James Madison, put it earlier, "If men were angels, no government would be necessary."[14]

Governments are designed less for the times when people agree—when they are decent and compassionate and filled with love—than for the times when they disagree. No matter who you are, what you believe, what you want, or how you behave, it is an unfortunate fact of life that some of your fellow citizens dislike you for exactly those reasons. People can settle their disagreements and rise above enmity through peaceful political means, or they can kill each other, as Americans did in the Civil War and as so many peoples of the world have done before and since.

The great political theorist Thomas Hobbes made the most basic case for government and politics. A world without government, he said, would be nothing less than "a war of all against all." Life would be "nasty, brutish and short."[15] Government is not a perfect solution to human conflicts, so citizens *should* be suspicious of its powers. But government is the best solution for human conflicts that human beings have yet contrived and civilized life is unimaginable without it. Of course, that still leaves an important question: What *kind* of government?

Types of Government

British author Samuel Johnson once commented that "I would not give half a guinea to live under one form of government rather than another. It is of no moment to the happiness of an individual."[16] Johnson's comment is silly—at best. Lives can be terribly damaged or greatly improved, depending on the type of government under which people live. Twenty-three centuries ago, Aristotle classified governments into three general types: government by one person, government by the few, and government by the many. Although others have proposed more complex classifications, Aristotle's simple scheme remains a useful place to begin our study of government.

Government by One Person

Historically, pharaohs, emperors, kings, tsars, and other monarchs ruled by hereditary right or religious appointment (although, like modern dictators, they usually needed the support of an army or police force as well). The quality of government by a single ruler depends on who is in charge. The ruler can put the welfare of the people first, last, or anywhere in between. But placing the coercive power of government in the hands of one person requires unlimited trust in that person, and no one is so deserving. As another political theorist, Lord Acton, observed in the nineteenth century, "power tends to corrupt and absolute power corrupts absolutely." In the twentieth century alone, millions of people died at the hands of rulers who gained near-absolute power—tyrants such as Germany's Hitler, the Soviet Union's Stalin, China's Mao, and Cambodia's Pol Pot.

Government by the Few

aristocracy
Government by a few leaders made eligible by birthright.

oligarchy
Government by a few who gain office by means of wealth, military power, or membership in a single political party.

Government by the few is called **aristocracy** if leaders are chosen by birth or **oligarchy** if leaders are chosen on the basis of wealth, military power, or membership in a political party. Aristocracies ruled many countries in the past, but in the modern world birthright no longer seems an acceptable justification for ruling over others. Oligarchies still exist, however. The most important one governs China, where a small group of Communist Party leaders has remained in power since 1946. Oligarchies have some advantages over dictatorships; to a limited extent, members of the oligarchy can check and balance each other. But here, too, power tends to corrupt, as the few take advantage of their position to acquire wealth at the expense of the rest of society.

Government by the Many

Government in which all citizens share power is called **democracy**. The word derives from the Greek word *demos,* which means "people." In its purest form, **direct democracy**, all citizens participate directly in making government decisions. In Aristotle's time, direct democracy was practical because citizenship was limited to free adult men with property, who in many Greek cities numbered no more than a few thousand. Direct democracy still exists in a few small New England towns where community decisions are made at town meetings in which all residents can participate.

Direct democracy is not practical in large countries such as the United States. Even with such modern communications as cable television, fax, e-mail, and the Internet, every citizen cannot participate in every governmental decision. People would have to spend their entire lives attending meetings, deliberating, and voting in order to decide all the questions that come up.

Because direct democracy is impractical in the modern world, government by the many generally takes the form of **representative democracy**, an *indirect* form of democracy in which citizens choose *representatives* who decide what government does. Free elections are the key feature of representative democracy, as its opponents well understand. Soviet dictator Joseph Stalin once commented, "The disadvantage of free elections is that you can never be sure who is going to win them."[17]

Although they generally agree on the importance of free elections, political theorists disagree about many other aspects of representative democracy.[18] As shown in Table 1.1, most of the arguments can be summarized by distinguishing between two general types or models of representative democracy, the popular model and the responsible model.

In the popular model of democracy, citizens take an active role in government. Popular democracy strives to be as open and responsive as representative democracy can be. Elections express the *popular will,* thus providing elected officials with *mandates*—instructions from the voters to adopt specific policies. In order for elections to work this way, citizens must be well informed about public issues, and they must engage in **prospective voting**. That is, they must look to the future while voting, taking into

Government by One Person

Pol Pot murdered millions of his fellow Cambodians all in the name of progress.

democracy

System in which governmental power is widely shared among the citizens, usually through free and open elections.

direct democracy

Type of democracy in which ordinary people are the government, making all the laws themselves.

representative democracy

An indirect form of democracy in which the people choose representatives who determine what government does.

prospective voting

Voting on the basis of a candidate's policy promises for the future.

TABLE 1.1	
Two Models of Democracy	
The Popular Model	The Responsible Model
Elections determine policies.	Elections determine leaders.
Citizens vote prospectively.	Citizens vote retrospectively.
Direct democracy is preferred.	Representative democracy is preferred.
Popular participation is necessary for effective democracy.	Clear accountability of leaders is necessary for effective democracy.
Democratic politics should advance the civic education of citizens.	Democratic politics should produce effective governance.

account each candidate's campaign promises. Each election becomes an occasion to decide the direction of public policies.

Those who favor the popular model say that democracy is more than a mechanical process for producing outcomes; it is also an educational forum in which individuals become better citizens by participating in democratic deliberation. Through participation, the public can reach consensus and make better decisions. Thus, popular democracy is expected to produce both better citizens and better policies. The process of participation transforms "private into public," "conflict into cooperation."[19]

Critics say that popular democracies are inefficient and can even be dangerous if uninformed citizens vote for poor public policies. These critics favor instead the responsible model of democracy, in which citizens play a more passive role. Citizens choose public officials but do not tell them what to do. Elected officials have the responsibility to govern and must answer to the people for the decisions they make. In this model, elections are occasions on which citizens grant or deny *popular consent* rather than grant or deny popular mandates. According to the responsible model, citizens need not be particularly well informed because they engage in **retrospective voting**, looking more to the past than to the future. In other words, they decide whether incumbents have done a good or a bad job. If the voters approve, they reelect incumbents; if the voters disapprove, they vote in a new group of leaders.

Critics of the responsible model say that it is hardly democracy at all.[20] In fact, critics sometimes refer to the responsible model as "elitist democracy" because elites— those who hold office, manage the parties, and lead the interest groups—dominate the political process. Those who favor the responsible model concede that it gives ordinary citizens a modest role—but they claim that direct popular participation in government is unnecessary, or even harmful, because people often are poorly informed.

Popular and Responsible Democracy in the United States

In the real world, of course, pure types do not exist; every real-world democracy has both popular and responsible features. Yet democracies differ in the degree to which they tend toward one or the other model. Britain, for example, more closely resembles the responsible model. British voters elect members of Parliament, but in the normal five-year period between elections, the governing party has great freedom to undertake independent action—including fairly radical action such as nationalizing or denationalizing entire industries, or going to war.

The United States has always been a more popular democracy than its European counterparts. When the French scholar Alexis de Tocqueville visited the United States during the 1830s, he was astounded by the extent of popular participation. "It must be seen to be believed," he exclaimed to his fellow French citizens. "No sooner do you set foot on American ground than you are stunned by a kind of tumult . . . . Almost the only pleasure an American knows is to take part in the government and discuss its measures."[21]

From the earliest days of the republic, the principles of popular democracy were an important part of American politics. "Where annual elections end, there slavery begins," said the second president, John Adams, arguing that citizens must have frequent opportunities to instruct and judge their representatives.[22] The third president, Thomas Jefferson, wanted to "divide the country into wards," so that "free men could control their own political destinies."[23]

retrospective voting
Voting on the basis of the past performance of the incumbent politician.

Self-Government

The framers believed that rules written down on paper, which they called *parchment barriers,* were no guarantee of good government. Words alone would not prevent elected officials from abusing power, especially if unscrupulous officeholders were backed by a majority of voters. The framers thought that tyranny could best be prevented by "buttressing" constitutional rules with something firmer: a system of checks and balances that divided power among different representatives chosen in different elections.[24] Each office in the national government was assigned a separate **constituency**—a set of people entitled to vote for the holder of that office—and office holders were to be chosen by these different constituencies at different times. In this way, the framers constructed a responsible democracy, even while including many popular features. Leaders have the interest and capacity to resist both popular passions and attempts by would-be tyrants to seize power.

constituency
Those legally entitled to vote for a public official.

The New American Democracy

When the Constitution was adopted, a small proportion of Americans had the right to participate in politics, but American politics has evolved in the direction of greater popular participation. Over the course of two centuries, more and more of the population have gained full rights of citizenship, the connection between representatives and the public has become increasingly direct, national institutions have become more open to popular influence, and the number and frequency of elections (coupled with the more extensive campaigning that accompanies them) have increased. These trends have accelerated dramatically in recent decades—to the extent that it is no exaggeration to title this book *The New American Democracy.*

The Permanent Campaign

The new American democracy is marked by a **permanent campaign**.[25] On the surface, this term means that campaigning literally never ends: The next election campaign begins as soon as the last one has finished, if not before. The dust from the 2002 elections had barely settled before discussion turned to which party would win control of the Senate in 2004. And even before the 2004 presidential campaign had run its course, pundits were speculating about who would run for president in 2008.

The deeper meaning of the term *permanent campaign* is that the line between campaigning and governing has disappeared. To some extent governing becomes a part of the campaign; in effect, it is a campaign strategy. Every action undertaken—or not undertaken—by the 108th Congress (2003–2004) was viewed as a potential issue in the upcoming presidential campaign. At its worst, the permanent campaign can be harmful. According to Professor Hugh Heclo, campaign values corrupt the governmental process: Public officials sacrifice the long-term good for short-term electoral advantage, they adopt adversarial rather than collaborative mindsets, and they abandon deliberation and education in favor of persuasion and selling.[26] Nevertheless, officials who are constantly concerned with pleasing voters are relatively likely to be responsive ones.

At least seven developments have contributed to the permanent campaign: the separation of election days, the decay of party organizations, the spread of primary elections, advances in mass communications, the explosion of interest groups, the prolifer-

permanent campaign
Condition that prevails when the next election campaign begins as soon as the last has ended and the line between electioneering and governing has disappeared.

TABLE 1.2

SEVEN KEY DEVELOPMENTS HAVE CONTRIBUTED TO THE PERMANENT CAMPAIGN

Development	Effect
Separate election days for federal, state, and local elections	Increased number of elections, shortened time between elections
Spread of primary elections	Increased number of elections, shortened time between elections
Decay of traditional party organizations	Candidates must build individualized, personal campaign organizations almost from scratch
Rise of mass communication	Candidates may communicate directly with voters, but their mistakes are easily publicized
Profusion of interest groups	Elected officials constantly being watched and mistakes quickly publicized
Proliferation of polls	Provide constant feedback about potential election outcomes
Role of campaign money	Elected officials must spend more time fundraising

ation of polling, and the increasing need for money (see Table 1.2). Together these factors have moved American democracy in a significantly more popular direction.

Separation of Elections   Imagine that all public officials were elected on the same day and served the same four-year term of office. There would be a long span of time between electoral contests during which no one had to think much about campaigning. Most other democracies are closer to this hypothetical scenario than to the electoral chaos that exists in the United States.

A century ago, American officials usually *were* elected on the same day. A graduate student named Woodrow Wilson wrote in 1885 that "This is preeminently a country of frequent elections, and few states care to increase the frequency by separating elections of state from elections of national functionaries."[27] In Wilson's time, citizens of most states cast votes simultaneously for president, senator, representative, governor, mayor, state representative and state senator, city council, and so forth. In a few states today, voters still fill most offices on the same day, but the trend in the past half-century has been to separate election days.[28] Most Americans now turn out to vote for president at one general election, for governor at another, and for mayor at another still. Primary elections, as well as those for local offices, are held earlier in the election year. Initiatives and referenda may be scheduled on yet other occasions.

Thus, Americans today are called to the polls repeatedly. Rather than our imaginary Election Day held every four years, a conscientious citizen in California, for example, generally has to go to the polls on 16 separate occasions in each four-year presidential election cycle. As election dates have proliferated, electioneering has become a pervasive feature of American politics. There is some campaign going on somewhere, nearly all the time. There is very little "quiet time" during which there are no campaigns.

Decay of Party Organizations   Many political scientists think political parties are essential to the workings of representative democracy. Although we cannot always detect clear differences between Republicans and Democrats, the two parties give voters a choice by offering different political philosophies. The Republican Party leans in a conservative direction, generally favoring smaller government, lower taxes, less regu-

Already Running?
As early as 2003, many political observers were speculating about a 2008 presidential run for Democratic Senator Hillary Clinton of New York.

• *How do you think the permanent campaign changes the way prospective presidential candidates behave in office?*

lation of business activity, and greater support for traditional family values. The Democratic Party leans in a liberal direction, usually favoring a strong federal government, more extensive social programs, more regulation, and legal accommodation for alternative lifestyles. Because party positions on issues shift only gradually, parties give continuity and familiarity to political life, making it easier for voters to make choices.

A century ago, many state and local party organizations were powerful, disciplined structures that could mobilize large numbers of voters on Election Day. Public officials relied on the parties to conduct their campaigns when election time rolled around. But governmental reforms and various social changes killed off these types of organizations (see Chapter 8). As a consequence, today's parties do not deliver the vote for all the candidates running under their label. Instead, elected officials must build individual organizations and develop *personal* constituencies to achieve election and reelection.[29] Such personalized support is less reliable than the partisan support shared by numerous candidates in earlier eras.[30] Thus, incumbents today must constantly campaign to maintain their base of electoral support.

Spread of Primaries   In most countries, small groups of party leaders select candidates for office. A century ago this was the standard procedure in the United States as well. Candidates were picked in "smoke-filled rooms" by party "bosses." To eliminate the corruption and unresponsiveness that often accompanied such deal making, reformers passed laws giving voters the right to select party nominees in primary elections.

Although they came into being about a century ago, primaries did not become a significant part of the presidential nominating process until after World War II. The first presidential candidate who owed his nomination in any significant degree to winning primaries was Dwight D. Eisenhower, elected in 1952. As late as 1968, the Democratic nominee, Hubert Humphrey, did not enter a single primary.

Primaries contribute substantially to today's permanent campaign. Whereas in 1968 fewer than 20 states held presidential primaries, now the number is more than 40. Primaries shorten the time between one election and the next. Behind-the-scenes planning for the presidential election of 2004 began in 2001, and the campaign was well under way by mid-2003, more than six months before the primaries began and only two and a half years into George W. Bush's first term. Nor is the permanent campaign limited to the campaign for the White House. Some members of the House of Representatives face primaries more than six months before their two-year terms end. On April 9, 1996, for example, a Texas Republican was defeated in a primary, scarcely 15 months after he had taken the oath of office.

Rise of Mass Communications   Technological progress also has helped to make campaigns continuous. Today's candidates constantly work to get their names in the papers and their faces on television. Moreover, cheap phone rates, fax, and e-mail give more opportunities for citizens and politicians to talk to each other. Dozens of cable television channels enable candidates to communicate with small, specialized audiences. C-SPAN provides continuous coverage of congressional debates, giving people outside Washington a chance to observe public officials directly. Radio talk shows have increased in popularity. Candidate and interest-group Web sites have proliferated. Conversation on the Internet, although often conspiratorial and inaccurate, is perhaps the fastest-growing mode of political communication.

Democracy and
the Internet

The effects of technological change have been intensified by changes in the culture of the mass media. The demand for content has been greatly increased by 24-hour news services. Any move a politician makes might end up on television, and virtually every move a prominent politician makes is now evaluated for its political motivations and its electoral implications. Partly as a consequence of the media's insatiable appetite for news, the distinction between public and private life has eroded. The financial and medical histories of elected officials are treated as public knowledge, and reporters ask candidates almost any question imaginable, no matter how tasteless or unrelated to politics and government. Democratic presidential candidate John Kerry's Vietnam War service came under particularly close scrutiny during the 2004 election, even though he was a decorated war hero. As one communications professor put it, "We like to know the character of a candidate."[31]

Profusion of Interest Groups   The personal organizations that today's candidates construct to support them through the permanent campaign are based in large part on the numerous interest groups that have formed during the past generation. Many of the newer groups are spin-offs of the social movements of the 1960s (the antiwar, civil rights, women's, and environmental movements) which cut across and compete with traditional economic interests. Computer technology has played a role in the formation of other kinds of groups. In the snail-mail era, it was far more difficult for small economic interests even to locate each other, let alone to organize. Today, interest groups can monitor the actions of elected officials electronically and then post information on their Web sites or send blanket e-mails to their members.

The most recent development is for interest groups to run critical ads well before a campaign ever begins. For example, a group calling itself the Club for Growth ran a series of advertisements criticizing four moderate Republican senators who seemed poised to vote against President Bush's tax cut proposals in 2003.[32] Two of these senators would not have to face voters formally for another three years, but for them the campaign was already under way.

Proliferation of Polls   Polling contributes to the permanent campaign. When an issue or problem arises, politicians no longer wonder about the state of public opinion—the newspapers and TV channels report it within days or sometimes hours. Even if elected officials wanted to make decisions without thinking about their political implications, it would be difficult to do so: They are bombarded with information about political implications at every turn. As Figure 1.2 shows, the media have made public opinion a much more important part of their coverage both by sponsoring polls and by incessant reporting of polling results.

Leaders always have been concerned about public opinion, of course. In the closing days of the Constitutional Convention in 1787, George Washington proposed a major change in the representational scheme for the House of Representatives so that the new Constitution would stand a better chance of being ratified by the elected state conventions. Abraham Lincoln waited for a military victory before he issued the Emancipation Proclamation abolishing slavery in the Confederate states, so that a happy northern public would be more inclined to support it. Politicians traditionally are portrayed as having their "ear to the ground" and their "finger to the wind." Until the introduction of modern

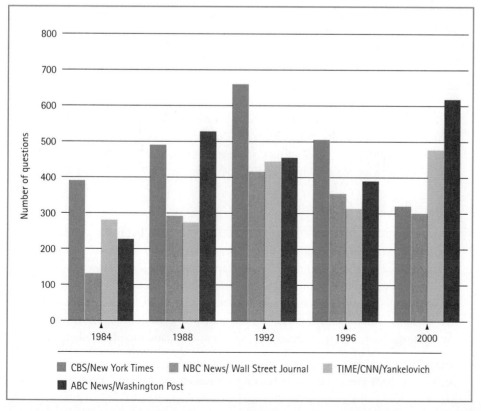

FIGURE 1.2

Today's Media Conduct Their Own Polls

Bars represent the number of questions, mentioning one or both of the major-party presidential candidates, that were asked by various media-sponsored polls.

SOURCE: Compiled by authors from Lexis-Nexis database.

Number of questions

1984   1988   1992   1996   2000

■ CBS/New York Times   ■ NBC News/ Wall Street Journal   ■ TIME/CNN/Yankelovich
■ ABC News/Washington Post

polling in the 1930s, however, beliefs about the state of public opinion were only guesses. As we will see in Chapter 5, polls have their own set of problems and limitations, but they undoubtedly *seem* more precise and scientific and, therefore, difficult to ignore.

Rising Campaign Costs   Campaigning today is expensive. Polls, political consultants, and TV ads cost a great deal of money. As Figure 1.3 shows, the total costs of election campaigns have increased dramatically in the past three decades. Campaigns for the House of Representatives, for example, were more than three times more expensive in 2002 than in 1976, even after adjusting for inflation.[33]

Although elections may occur only every two, four, or six years, the quest for money is continuous. Nearly all governors serve four-year terms, but current estimates are that incumbents in large states must raise an average of $50,000 *every week of their terms* to fund their campaign for reelection.[34] U.S. senators serve six-year terms, but most contemporary observers believe that the Senate today is just as electorally sensitive as the House.[35] One reason is that Senate races are expensive; on average, senators must raise more than $15,000 every week of their six-year terms to run for reelection. Thus, the effect of the six-year term has been partially offset by the constant quest for money.

Minorities and Elections

American democracy may have moved in a popular direction, but majorities do not get their way consistently. Elections by themselves do not guarantee that all citizens exert equal influence on the government. On the contrary, it is easy to show how special-interest groups and other numerical minorities influence elections, and to cite examples of how elected officials sometimes act contrary to popular wishes. The factors that give such minorities an advantage include unequal participation, the nominating process, single-issue voters, unequal campaign resources, and misinformed citizens.

Voter Participation   In nearly all elections, most people do *not* vote (see Chapter 6). Even in the 2004 presidential election, only 59 percent of the adult population voted.

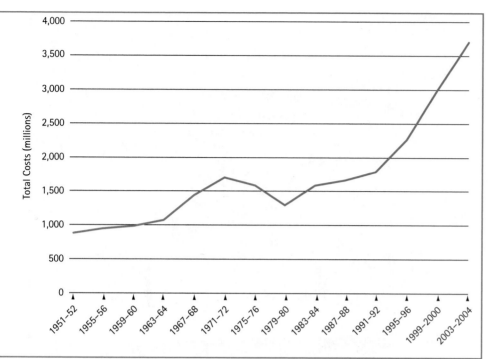

FIGURE 1.3

The Total Costs of American Elections Have Increased Dramatically in the Last Five Decades

Note: All figures have been adjusted for inflation in terms of 2001 CPI constant dollars.

SOURCES: Common Cause, the Center for Responsive Politics; and respective volumes of Herbert E. Alexander, *Financing the 1951–1952* [and 1955–2000 vols.] *Election* (Washington, DC: CQ Press).

Only 36 percent voted in the 2002 congressional elections. Turnout rates in other elections are much lower—even under 10 percent in some local elections!

One vote does not count for much, but collectively the vote is an important political resource. The simple fact is that groups of people who vote at higher rates have more influence. For example, older people vote more frequently than the young or the poor.[36] Not surprisingly, programs for the elderly are much better funded than programs that serve the young and the needy. Turnout is not the only explanation, of course, but elected officials naturally tend to pay greater heed to the demands of frequent voters than to those of people who do not bother to vote.

SIMULATION

How to Satisfy Aunt Martha

Nominating Candidates   Although primary elections were intended to enhance popular control, only party members can vote in these elections in many states, and the turnout for primaries everywhere is much lower than for general elections. Those who vote in primaries are usually more involved and more committed than citizens who do not vote. Republican primary voters tend to be more conservative than the typical American, and Democratic primary voters tend to be more liberal. To win primary elections, candidates have a strong incentive to take positions that appeal to the typical Democratic or Republican primary voter, even though these positions will not seem very centrist to the people who vote in general elections. As a result, elections may give middle-of-the-road Americans a choice between two unappealing candidates.

Single-Issue Voters   Suppose that there is a small group of voters—say, 5 percent of the electorate—that is single-mindedly obsessed with one particular issue. The issue may be abortion or gun control or farm policy—whatever the precise subject, it is the only issue that these voters take into account when deciding how to vote. Suppose further

single-issue voter

Voter who cares so deeply about some particular issue that a candidate's position on this one issue determines his or her vote.

Playing Hooky

In 2004, despite massive get-out-the-vote efforts and higher turnout than usual, people aged 18–29 barely increased their voting rates outside of the swing states.

• *Why don't young people vote?*

that the rest of the electorate—the other 95 percent—don't care much about this issue—in particular, that it doesn't carry much weight in determining their votes.

In a situation such as this, candidates have a strong incentive to give in to the small group and endorse their favored policy position—even if it sharply conflicts with the opinion of the overwhelming majority. Such a strategy won't win the candidates a lot of votes, of course, but at least it won't cost any votes—and in a close election, 5 percent can spell the difference between victory and defeat.

How many groups and issues resemble the circumstances just described is difficult to say. What is clear is that many interest groups try to convince candidates that their issue fits the profile: that they speak for thousands or millions of energized voters, who are just waiting to punish any candidate or officeholder who refuses to toe the line.

Campaign Resources As we have noted, modern campaigns increasingly rely on expensive hired help: consultants, pollsters, and other campaign professionals. Higher-level campaigns that rely on TV advertising are especially expensive. Consequently, the first job nearly every candidate faces is raising money. Moreover, even in today's technologically advanced world, campaigns also require workers. This is particularly true of lower-level campaigns. Volunteers circulate petitions, stuff envelopes, knock on doors, make phone calls, stage rallies and other photo ops, and drive voters to the polls. Thus, paradoxically, a candidate who wants to win an election may, in order to acquire various kinds of essential campaign resources, take positions that are out of sync with those of the typical voter.

A few paragraphs earlier, we observed that the level of voter turnout in American elections is rather modest, even in the best of circumstances. But when it comes to political participation, voting is as good as it gets. Almost every other form of participation—including giving money, attending campaign rallies, even displaying a campaign bumper sticker or yard sign—is generally performed by fewer than 10 percent of the adult population. Everything we have said about the unrepresentative nature of voters applies with even more force to campaign donors and volunteers. Single-issue voters are also likely to be overrepresented within the ranks of campaign activists.

Uninformed or Misinformed Citizens   Most Americans are not highly attentive to politics (see Chapter 5). Politics often seems remote from people's everyday interests and concerns, and political controversies often are complicated and confusing. Moreover, nearly all of the players in politics present information and arguments that are biased; they are like opposing lawyers trying to win a lawsuit. Even the media exhibit well-known biases, as we discuss in Chapter 9. Thus, there are frequent opportunities to manipulate public opinion and elections.

Majorities and Elections

Although single-issue voters and other kinds of special interests at times wield disproportionate influence, such groups lose much of their clout when a clear majority of the voters take a strong interest in a highly visible subject. For example, Americans hold moderate views on the abortion issue (see Chapter 5). Thus, the Democratic Congresses of 1990–1994 did not pass the "Freedom of Choice Act," strongly supported by pro-choice forces, nor did more recent Republican Congresses adopt a constitutional amendment to outlaw abortion, as pro-life forces urgently sought.

Local Politics

Candidates for local office can rarely afford expensive television advertising. Here, the father of a candidate volunteers his time.

• *Does a lack of media attention (and money to buy attention) mean that such races are unimportant?*

Moreover, majorities have the potential to be powerful even when the public is uninformed about or unaware of an issue. Elected officials realize that the media spotlight might suddenly shine into what seemed to be a dark corner. Additionally, challengers pore over the incumbent's record, searching for unpopular votes cast, positions taken, or statements made. If found, such matters become campaign issues. Most of the time, incumbents think twice before taking actions in back rooms if those actions cannot be defended once the doors are opened.[37]

Thus, elected officials cannot routinely take positions contrary to those of their constituents and expect to escape the wrath of the electorate indefinitely. Because leaders are never sure which issues will become central to election campaigns, they tend to be cautious in handling all of them. Hence, the power of minorities is limited by the potential threat that the majority will become aroused. Ordinarily, majorities rule not so much because they actively articulate their views but because public officials anticipate majority opinion long before it asserts itself.

Reform?

The United States pays a price for the pervasiveness of its elections. Continuous electioneering creates a governmental system that is unattractive in many respects. Scandals—real and trumped up—are common; inefficiency and stalemate are widespread; important problems are ignored; and effective actions are delayed or compromised into ineffectiveness.[38]

Even though many citizens understandably are frustrated by American government, we should view proposals for radical reform cautiously. In particular, reforms often call for further movement toward popular democracy—more opportunities for constituencies to influence government, such as more elections (primaries, initiatives and referenda, recalls), more opportunities to exert popular pressure (open public meetings, electronic town halls), or more power for elected officials (oversight of independent boards and commissions). Americans apparently believe, with John Dewey, that "The cure for the ailments of democracy is more democracy."[39]

Such reforms overlook the tremendous popular pressure that political leaders are already under. Indeed, some scholars argue that popular influence on government may be part of the problem, not the solution.[40] Each public official answers to a somewhat different constituency. If all constituencies were similar, representatives would find it easier to reach agreement. But America is a diverse country, and the constituencies of elected officials reflect that diversity. People have conflicting interests and (even more important) conflicting values. Even if hundreds of officials were personally in agreement, which is unlikely, their views of governmental programs and policies often would conflict because they have an **electoral incentive**—the desire to be elected and reelected—that compels them to represent the views of their different constituencies. It is impossible to reach decisions without resolving differences generated by these constituencies. Political leaders must either persuade their opponents or bargain for their support.

Reforms that shift American politics in a still more popular direction may make problems worse rather than solving them. Louder demands from an increasingly diverse public will only make problem solving more elusive. If reformers are to be effective, they must take into account the electoral incentives that public officials face, and either iden-

You Are the Director of Development for the City of Los Angeles, California

electoral incentive

Desire to obtain or retain elected office.

tify reforms that permit negotiation, bargaining, and compromise or actually change the political system so that agreement is easier to reach. All too often, reformers forget that fact and substitute good intentions and rosy scenarios for realistic analysis.

Benefits of an Electoral Democracy: A Pretty Good Government

As mentioned earlier, an irony of the new American democracy is that although citizens have more opportunities than ever before to influence their government, they have been growing increasingly unhappy with it. In our view, a significant part of the sour national mood is difficult to justify on the basis of objective conditions. Serious problems and unresolved conflicts obviously exist, but there is more that is right with the United States than political commentators may suggest. Too often, critics apply unrealistic standards of evaluation.

An old maxim states that "the best is the enemy of the good." Any policy or institution falls short when judged against some abstract standard of perfection. Perfection does not exist in the real world, but the wish for perfection in politics makes people unhappy with their government and their leaders. The search for perfection causes harm when people abandon the "pretty good" for something worse. As the great American judge Learned Hand once commented, "even though counting heads is not an ideal way to govern, it is at least better than breaking them."[41]

If American politics and government are so blameworthy, why are the governments of so many new democracies adopting institutions similar to those found in the United States? And why, throughout history and continuing today, have so many people left family and country behind to start over in the United States? Historically, most countries have posted border guards to keep people in; the United States has them to keep people out!

Across the entire sweep of human history, most governments have been controlled by one or a few. Many were tyrannical: A government that did not murder and rob its subjects was about as good a government as people could hope for. Nor are tyrannical governments just a matter of ancient history. Only a bare majority of the world's population today lives under governments that can reasonably be considered democratic, and in the twentieth century, governments caused the deaths of 170 million people, *not including wars.*[42] In recent years Americans have watched in horror as civil war or genocide has erupted in Iraq, Afghanistan, Sudan, Northern Ireland, Cambodia, Azerbaijan, Bosnia, Rwanda, Burundi, Chechnya, Albania, Zaire, Kosovo, East Timor, and Sierra Leone. Official tyranny—and worse—remains a contemporary reality.

VIDEO DEBATE

American Democracy and Human Rights

To be sure, Americans should not set too low a standard for their political life. No one would seriously argue that Americans should be satisfied just because their country has not dissolved into warring factions. But Americans should have realistic standards for evaluating their political system. Critics selectively cite statistics showing that the United States is worse than Germany in one respect, worse than Japan in another respect, worse than Sweden in some other respect, and so on. But can one conclude with confidence that any other government of a large country works better? Probably not. This judgment should not discourage us from continuing to strive for a better government, but it should remind us that we are striving for levels of achievement never yet attained by real governments responsible for large populations. Only when comparing the United States with other countries do we see that American democracy, for all its faults, has extraordinary strengths as well.

Defenders of democracy often cite Winston Churchill's remark that "democracy is the worst form of government except all those other forms that have been tried."[43] Churchill's observation applies with special force to the new American democracy, which carries this form of government toward its popular extreme. Citizens in the United States enjoy rights and privileges that citizens in other lands only dream of. Not only can American citizens vote more often, but Americans also can speak their minds more freely, find out more easily what their government is doing, and deal with a government less likely to discriminate against them on the basis of race, religion, gender, social status, sexual preference, or anything else.

Citizens of the United States have enjoyed a government that has a better record than most at protecting them against foreign aggression while usually avoiding unwise involvement in foreign conflicts. On average, citizens of the United States are wealthier than citizens of any other comparably large country. They are better housed, better fed, and better clothed. Compared with residents of most other countries, they enjoy better communications, a superior national transportation system, better medical services, and safer working conditions. Their physical environment is more protected against degradation. Even the large fiscal deficits that have caused political controversies since the 1980s compare favorably to the deficits of most other industrial countries. The United States, for all its problems, has as good a government as exists anywhere, and a better one than most.

Of course, the United States is not the best at everything. Economic inequality and poverty rates are higher in the United States than in countries with comparable living standards. More homeless people are visible on our city streets than in other industrialized countries—a sign that the safety net has gaping holes (although it may also be a sign that poor people in the United States move about more freely than the poor of other nations).[44] More people lack access to adequate medical care than in other developed democracies (though for those who do have access, the quality of American medical care is superior to that in any other country). More people are murdered and more are imprisoned in the United States than in almost any other industrialized country. Just why the United States does poorly at some things and well at others will be considered in the pages that follow.

In coming chapters, we trace the effects of the permanent campaign through the institutions and processes that make up American government, finishing with the policies that government produces. The remainder of Part 1 discusses the Constitution, the federal system, and the underlying cultural predispositions that provide the foundations for the country's political life. Part 2 examines the people, groups, parties, and news media that constitute the elements of electoral politics. Part 3 looks closely at contemporary campaigns and elections. Part 4 turns to the central political institutions: Congress, the presidency, the bureaucracy, and the courts. Part 5 discusses civil liberties and civil rights—not in the standard way, as the foundations of democratic politics, but as rights and privileges that democratic politics regularly changes. Finally, Part 6 treats a broad range of important public policies, domestic and foreign.

COMPARATIVE

Comparing Political
Landscapes

Chapter Summary

Elections are a more prominent part of democracy in America than in other countries because there are so many elective offices in the United States, because terms of office generally are shorter, and because Americans select candidates in primaries and vote directly on propositions as well. If free elections are the essence of democracy—of government by the people—as democratic theorists believe, then politics in the United States is indisputably democratic.

American democracy is more open to popular influence today than ever before. It is characterized by a permanent campaign. Changing technologies helped bring this situation about, especially developments in mass communications and public-opinion polling. Institutional changes also contributed, especially the weakening of political parties, the proliferation of primary elections, and the separation of election days. Social changes, such as the

explosion of organized interests, also played a role. And the increased need for money has contributed to the permanent campaign. Electoral considerations are never far from the minds of elected officials.

When weighing the costs and benefits of this movement toward a more popular democracy, it is not easy to decide which way the balance tips. Pervasive elections and electioneering change the way the government does business: It is more difficult to plan for the long run, and it seems harder to find acceptable compromises. Yet the advantages of more widespread participation are clear as well. The needs of once-excluded groups now are given at least some consideration. Citizens' concerns quickly become public issues. Imperfect as they are, American political institutions are still the envy of much of the world.

Key Terms

aristocracy, p. 8
constituency, p. 11
democracy, p. 9
direct democracy, p. 9
electoral incentive, p. 20
general election, p. 5

government, p. 6
initiative, p. 5
oligarchy, p. 8
permanent campaign, p. 11
primary election, p. 5
proposition, p. 5

prospective voting, p. 9
recall election, p. 4
referendum, p. 5
representative democracy, p. 9
retrospective voting, p. 10
single-issue voter, p. 17

Suggested Readings

Of General Interest

Blumenthal, Sidney. *The Permanent Campaign.* New York: Simon & Schuster, 1982. Describes the electioneering side of the new American democracy.

Bok, Derek. *The Trouble With Government.* Cambridge, MA: Harvard University Press, 2001. Comprehensive analysis of the pros and cons of modern government in the U.S.

Downs, Anthony. *An Economic Theory of Democracy.* New York: Harper, 1957. Seminal theoretical discussion of how elections shape the activities of voters, candidates, parties, and interest groups.

King, Anthony. *Running Scared: Why Politicians Spend More Time Campaigning Than Governing.* New York: Free Press, 1996. Provocative study by a British political scientist who shows how elections shape contemporary American politics.

Morone, James A. *The Democratic Wish.* New York: Basic Books, 1990. Brilliant historical analysis that shows how Americans have long tried to cure the ills of democracy by extending citizen participation.

Stanley, Harold, and Richard Niemi. *Vital Statistics on American Politics 2005–2006.* Washington, DC: CQ Press, 2006. Indispensable source of facts and figures about American government and politics.

Focused Studies

Chubb, John, and Paul Peterson, eds. *Can the Government Govern?* Washington, DC: The Brookings Institution, 1989. Collection of essays on problems of governing a democracy that is moving in the popular direction.

Cronin, Thomas. *Direct Democracy: The Politics of Initiative, Referendum, and Recall.* Cambridge, MA: Harvard University Press, 1989. Takes a generally positive view of direct democracy in the United States.

Dahl, Robert. *Who Governs?* New Haven, CT: Yale University Press, 1961. Although it is a study of politics in New Haven, Connecticut, this classic shows more generally how elections shape power and influence.

Lowi, Theodore. *The End of Liberalism.* New York: Norton, 1969. Classic study of the way in which special interests have gained power over government.

Schier, Steven E. *By Invitation Only: The Rise of Exclusive Politics in the United States.* Pittsburgh: University of Pittsburgh Press, 2000. Argues that parties, interest groups, and candidates have switched in recent years from broad-based mobilization of voters to targeted "activation" of select portions of the public.

On the Web

The Internet allows citizen activists, interest groups, and government agencies to disseminate more and more political information. Given that elections are the main focus of this textbook, here are four sites that can help citizens make sense of the vast amount of information in elections.

www.dnet.org
www.vote-smart.org
The Democracy Network and Project Votesmart are excellent, nonpartisan resources for learning about federal candidates' positions and records of public service. The Votesmart surveys of candidate positions (NPAT) are especially helpful for determining where your representatives stand on the issues.

www.fec.gov
The Federal Election Commission is responsible for monitoring federal elections. Its site links to candidate and interest-group financial filings, analysis of recent spending and fund-raising in elections, and descriptions of current campaign-finance law.

www.tray.com
Political Moneyline is a private watchdog organization that links to much the same information as the FEC, though in a somewhat more user-friendly—and opinionated—fashion. It is particularly useful for finding donors to campaigns and how much they donated.

CHAPTER 2

★ ★ ★ ★ ★ ★ ★ ★ ★ ☆

Establishing a Constitutional Democracy

The First National Election

Although the United States Constitution is revered today, many Americans were skeptical of the document when it emerged from the secretive Constitutional Convention in September 1787. Those who supported the new plan were by no means assured of success, and they achieved victory only because they provided strong leadership, mobilized voters, sidestepped obstacles, and crafted powerful arguments in favor of ratifying (approving) the document.

In 1787 and 1788, in what might be called the first U.S. national election, voters chose delegates to ratification conventions in each of the 13 states. If 9 of the 13 states approved the proposed constitution, its supporters asserted, it would become the law of the land. In newspaper editorials, debates, and public rallies, the **Federalists** (page 27), those who wrote and campaigned for ratification of the Constitution, clashed with opponents, who called themselves **Anti-Federalists** (page 27). Each side argued that its position was in the best interests of the voters.

Anti-Federalists appealed to voters' suspicions about the structure of the new system. They claimed that a strong national government would lead to suppression of the rights of states and of individual citizens. In Virginia the eminent American patriot Patrick Henry sounded the alarm. "I conceive the republic to be in extreme danger," he warned. "Here is a revolution as radical as that which separated us from Great Britain. . . . [O]ur rights and privileges are endangered, and the sovereignty of the States [shall] be relinquished. . . . The rights of conscience, trial by jury, liberty of the press, all pretensions to human rights and privileges, are rendered insecure, if not lost. . . . "[1]

Like Henry, many opponents of ratification claimed to represent the interests of average people. Some wrote anonymous pamphlets and editorials under humble pseudonyms such as "A Federal Farmer," "A Son of Liberty," "A Citizen," and "A Countryman."[2] Federalists, while never conceding that the plan was bad for common farmers, appealed to different concerns of the voters, stressing that the new system would resolve costly economic conflicts among states and would enable the United States to negotiate more effectively with foreign countries.

Without a strong union, Alexander Hamilton of New York argued, even as minor an issue as payment of the nation's Revolutionary War debt could lead to disaster.

States would disagree about who should bear the burden of repayment, while impatient foreign creditors might decide to make war on the young country: "The citizens of the States interested would clamour, foreign powers would urge for the satisfaction of their just demands; and the peace of the States would be hazarded to the double contingency of external invasion and internal contention."[3]

With energy and organization on their side, the Federalists easily won the first rounds in the ratification struggle. Conventions in four of the smaller states (Delaware, New Jersey, Georgia, and Connecticut) ratified the document by an overwhelming vote within four months of its signing in September 1787.[4] Influenced by elder statesman Ben Franklin's prestige and some strong-arm tactics, Pennsylvania also quickly approved. Massachusetts signed on as well, after Federalists promised to add a Bill of Rights. By the end of 1788, Federalists

---

TABLE 2.1

VOTING OF DELEGATES AT CONSTITUTIONAL RATIFYING CONVENTIONS

Article VII of the Constitution provided that "The Ratifications of the Conventions of nine States, shall be sufficient for the Establishment of this Constitution."

- *Why do you think the founders settled on 9 states instead of all 13? Or just 7?*

State	Date	"Yes" Votes/"No" Votes
Delaware	Dec. 7, 1787	30/0
Pennsylvania	Dec. 11, 1787	46/23
New Jersey	Dec. 18, 1787	38/0
Georgia	Jan. 2, 1788	26/0
Connecticut	Jan. 9, 1788	128/40
Massachusetts	Feb. 6, 1788	187/168
Maryland	Apr. 26, 1788	63/11
South Carolina	May 23, 1788	149/73
New Hampshire	June 21, 1788	57/47
Virginia	June 25, 1788	89/79
New York	July 26, 1788	30/27
North Carolina	Nov. 21, 1789	194/77
Rhode Island	May 29, 1790	34/32

Source: Lauren Bahr and Bernard Johnson, eds., *Collier's Encyclopedia*, Vol. 7 (New York: P. F. Collier, 1992), p. 239.

had persuaded 11 of the 13 states to ratify the Constitution, and in February 1789, Revolutionary War hero George Washington was elected president. North Carolina ratified later that year. Rhode Island, which had refused even to send delegates to the Constitutional Convention, finally gave its grudging approval on May 29, 1790 (see Table 2.1).

At the time the Constitution was adopted, the United States was not a modern democracy. For example, only male property owners ("freeholders") could vote in the election of delegates to most ratifying conventions. Yet the provisions in the Constitution had to win the approval of a wide variety of these voters. Those who wrote the Constitution had to be sensitive to regional differences, immediate governmental needs, and inherited political traditions. In this sense, the Constitution was not the product of a secretive meeting of men in Philadelphia but was, rather, the work of all those who voted in the first national election. As James Madison, a key participant in the Constitutional Convention, said years later, "Whatever veneration might be entertained for the body of men who formed our Constitution, . . . it was nothing more than the draft of a plan, nothing but a dead letter, until life and validity were breathed into it by the voice of the people, speaking through the several State Conventions."[5]

MAKING THE CONNECTION

In this chapter, we consider the circumstances surrounding the drafting of the Constitution, the basic governing document of the United States. We also review the historical background leading up to its approval, as well as several key problems and many significant successes associated with the document over the centuries since it went into effect.

Before thinking about the ways in which the Constitution affects modern U.S. politics, however, it is important to remember that its authors drafted the document to win the support of the electorate in the late 1780s. Representatives at special state conventions were charged with accepting or rejecting the Constitution, and the voters who elected them were guided by their own practical interests, as well as by commonly accepted political theories and the colonial experience. In the pages that follow, you will learn about these interests, theories, and experiences in greater detail. Finally, you will learn about how well the Constitution has stood the test of time, and how it can be changed.

The Colonial and Revolutionary Era

When delegates to the state conventions debated the Constitution in 1787, they drew lessons from nearly two centuries of colonial history. Beginning in the 1600s, European settlers had brought with them political theories and methods of governance that later colonists adapted and extended on the basis of their own needs and experiences. In this section, we review the nature of early colonial political systems, discuss how democratic ideals spread before and during the Revolution, and describe the state of political thought at the dawn of U.S. independence.

The Colonial Experience with Democracy

Although the United States would become the world's first large, stable democracy of the modern era, colonists first arrived as part of a failed business venture. In 1584 the British "Virgin Queen" Elizabeth granted Sir Walter Raleigh the right (a "charter") to explore and colonize a portion of the New World. Raleigh's own attempts to establish

Constitution
Basic governing document of the United States.

Federalists
Those who wrote and campaigned on behalf of ratification of the Constitution.

Anti-Federalists
Those who opposed ratification of the Constitution.

divine right

Doctrine that says God selects the sovereign for the people.

royal colony

Colony governed by the king's representative with the advice of an elected assembly. See *proprietary colony.*

a permanent colony came to nothing, although he succeeded in naming his territory "Virginia," after his benefactress. Years later, the Virginia Company, a group of investors who had inherited Raleigh's charter, made another attempt to found a profitable settlement. This colony, named Jamestown after King James, who had succeeded Elizabeth in 1603, was notable because it was there, in 1619, that settlers elected the first representative assembly on American colonial territory. Any semblance of self-government was short-lived, however, because in 1624 James reclaimed the territory from the now-bankrupt Virginia Company.[6] Like most monarchs at the time, James claimed to rule by **divine right**, a doctrine stating that God selects the sovereign for the people. Virginia became a **royal colony**, one governed by the king's representative with the assembly's advice.

A small group of religious dissenters, now remembered as the Pilgrims, intended to sail to Virginia in 1620. After their ship, the *Mayflower*, was blown off course and arrived in what today is Provincetown, Massachusetts, the Pilgrims found that they lacked a clear governmental framework. Rejecting the divine right of kings, they believed that individuals should decide both religious and political matters for themselves. Their first political decision is still revered as the very beginning of the democratic experiment in America. Before leaving the ship, the Pilgrims signed the **Mayflower Compact**, the first document in colonial America in which the people gave their expressed consent to be governed. The Pilgrims promised to "covenant and combine ourselves together into a civil Body Politick, for our better Ordering and Preservation." The principle that government resulted from the people's consent was thus established from the very beginning of colonial settlement.[7]

Mayflower Compact

First document in colonial America in which the people gave their expressed consent to be governed.

Governance of the Colonies   As European settlement spread across the eastern shores of the North American continent, so did issues of politics and governance. Many colonies were initially organized as **proprietary colonies**, governed either by a prominent English noble or by a company. Settlements organized by companies, such as the Jamestown colony, were founded almost exclusively for economic gain, including the search for gold. But several of the most successful colonies, such as the Pilgrims' settlement in Massachusetts and the Maryland colony established for Catholics by Lord Baltimore, were founded as havens for the practice of particular religious beliefs. The more economically motivated of the proprietary colonies often ran into political difficulties and were eventually reorganized as royal colonies, like Virginia. On the eve of the Revolution, 9 of the 13 had become royal colonies.

proprietary colony

Colony governed either by a prominent English noble or by a company. See *royal colony.*

In both proprietary and royal colonies, power was divided between the governor (appointed by either the proprietor or the king) and a two-chamber legislature. The **colonial assembly** was the lower legislative chamber elected by male property owners in the colony. The **colonial council** was the upper legislative chamber appointed by British officials, upon the recommendation of the governor.

colonial assembly

Lower legislative chamber elected by male property owners in a colony.

colonial council

Upper legislative chamber whose members were appointed by British officials on the recommendation of the governor.

Governors could veto any legislation passed by the legislature, but usually, instead of vetoing legislation, they maintained support in the assembly by means of their **patronage** power—the power to hand out jobs and benefits. Governors appointed their political supporters as sheriffs, judges, justices of the peace, militia officers, magistrates, and clerks. In Massachusetts, for example, 71 percent of the members of the 1763 assembly were simultaneously justices of the peace, giving "the Governors vast Influence."[8]

patronage

Appointment of individuals to public office in exchange for their political support. Widely practiced in the eighteenth and nineteenth centuries and continues to present day.

Although the governors' patronage influenced colonial assemblies, the assemblies held the power to levy taxes. They used this key authority to broaden their influence, often obtaining financial control of the salaries of the governor and his appointed officials.[9] The men elected to assemblies were usually esteemed members of the community. For example, Thomas Jefferson won both public respect and election to the Virginia assembly after persuading his fellow farmers to work together and clear the Rivanna River, making it navigable for their common benefit.[10] As the power of the elected colonial assemblies grew, the colonial councils appointed by the governors lost prestige and authority, gradually becoming little more than advisory bodies.

Voting Qualifications   Although the assemblies were gaining control over colonial affairs, they were not democratic in the modern sense of the word. Women, slaves, and indentured servants were excluded from the voting rolls from the very beginning. Even male white voters usually had to meet property qualifications: In Virginia they had to own 25 acres and a house. In Maryland and Pennsylvania, voters needed to be worth 50 acres or 40 pounds. And in Connecticut, prospective voters not only had to own property, but also had to demonstrate that they were "civil in conversation."[11] By 1750 these and other restrictions denied the vote to as much as one-quarter to one-half of the male population.[12]

Spread of Democratic Ideals During the Revolutionary War

The democratic practices that evolved during the colonial period were reinforced by the struggle for independence.[13] Liberties that the colonists had taken for granted now had to be defended against the fearsome power of the British king. The revolutionary struggle was set in motion with opposition to a tax, swelled into a question of rights and representation, and finally led to a Declaration of Independence cast in language that would shape American politics for centuries to come.

Taxation Without Representation   The revolutionary movement would eventually become a struggle for citizen rights and liberties, but it began as a tax revolt. Because military expenses were rising, the British government decided to ask the colonists to pay the cost of keeping troops in the colonies—troops that were needed to defend against potential attacks by both Indian tribes and French and Spanish soldiers. In 1765 the British government announced its intention to impose a **stamp tax**, which required that people purchase a small stamp to be affixed to pamphlets, playing cards, dice, newspapers, marriage licenses, and other legal documents. To the British, the stamp tax seemed reasonable—after all, colonial taxes were lower than those the British themselves paid. But to the colonists, who had never before paid a direct tax, it was an outrageous imposition by King George III on a free people.

Colonial leaders opposed what they called **taxation without representation**, the levying of taxes by a government in which the people are not represented by their own elected officials. To organize their protest, nine colonies sent delegates to a **Stamp Act Congress** in New York, which became the first political organization that brought together leaders from throughout the colonies.

The Stamp Act Congress gave clear expression to the American demand for representative government. One of its resolutions boldly proclaimed "that the only Representatives of the People of these Colonies are Persons chosen therein by

stamp tax
Passed by Parliament in 1765, it required people in the colonies to purchase a small stamp to be affixed to legal and other documents.

taxation without representation
Levying of taxes by a government in which the people are not represented by their own elected officials.

Stamp Act Congress
A meeting in 1765 of delegates from nine colonies to oppose the Stamp Act; the first political organization that brought leaders from several colonies together for a common purpose.

themselves, and that no Taxes . . . can be Constitutionally imposed on them, but by their respective Legislature."[14] In Boston, a group of citizens calling themselves the Sons of Liberty decided to enforce the resolutions of the Stamp Act Congress. They hung in effigy the city's proposed tax collector and then looted his home—and that of the lieutenant governor for good measure. As violence spread throughout the colonies, some frightened tax collectors resigned their positions, others refused to take their places, and colonial assemblies banned the importation of English goods, making homespun clothes fashionable. Patrick Henry, who was one of the more outspoken members of the Virginia assembly, shouted, "Caesar had his Brutus; Charles the First his Cromwell; and George the Third [here the speaker of the assembly cried "Treason!"] may profit by their example. If this be treason, make the most of it." In the face of a tax revolt inspired by rhetoric that compared King George with rulers who were overthrown and killed, the Stamp Act became unenforceable, and within a year Parliament repealed the legislation.[15]

The British ignored the American demands for representation. They also unwisely replaced the stamp tax with a tax on tea, arousing passions even further. Colonists were urged on by such leaders as John Hancock and Samuel Adams, who began calling themselves **Patriots**, a political group defending American liberties against British infringements. In 1773 many Patriots organized the Boston Tea Party, a nighttime foray in which protesters disguised as American Indians dumped chests of tea into the city's harbor. Outraged at this lawlessness, Parliament punished the Bostonians by shutting down democratic institutions in the Massachusetts colony. It withdrew the colony's charter, closed its colonial assembly, banned town meetings, blockaded Boston's harbor, and strengthened the armed garrison stationed in the city.

The Continental Congresses   The Patriots responded in 1774 by organizing the **First Continental Congress**, the first quasi-governmental institution that spoke for nearly all the colonies. Attended by delegates from 12 of the colonies, the Continental Congress issued a statement of rights and called for a boycott of British goods, a measure the Patriots hoped would hurt the British economy. In Massachusetts, Patriots assembled guns and trained volunteers in military exercises.

To put down the rising insurrection, British soldiers marched from Boston Harbor on April 19, 1775, in search of weapons hidden in the nearby countryside. Warned by Boston silversmith Paul Revere that British Redcoats were approaching, 600 Patriots at Concord fired shots that poet Ralph Waldo Emerson would later write were "heard round the world." Certainly, word of the shots spread rapidly throughout the colonies, even to the Virginia assembly, where Patrick Henry cried, "Give me liberty, or give me death." Delegates from all 13 colonies soon journeyed to Philadelphia to participate in the **Second Continental Congress**, the political authority that, beginning in 1775, directed the struggle for independence. On July 4, 1776, the Continental Congress issued a **Declaration of Independence**, the document asserting the political independence of the United States of America from Great Britain. For seven long years the Patriots valiantly fought the British soldiers. Many **Tories**, colonists who opposed independence, lost their property and were imprisoned or chased from the colonies; some 80,000 fled to London, Nova Scotia, or the West Indies. In 1783 the British recognized American independence in the Treaty of Paris.

Patriots
Political group defending colonial American liberties against British infringements.

First Continental Congress
The first quasi-governmental institution that spoke for nearly all the colonies (1774).

Second Continental Congress
Political authority that directed the struggle for independence beginning in 1775.

Declaration of Independence
Document signed in 1776 declaring the United States to be a country independent of Great Britain.

Tories
Those colonists who opposed independence from Great Britain.

Theory of Rights and Representation

The democratic experiment had officially begun, the new nation having committed itself to government by the people. Americans transformed colonial practice into a political doctrine stating that if governments are to be legitimate, they must be headed by leaders who have been chosen in elections.

No single document better expresses the democratic spirit that animates American politics than the Declaration of Independence. Written mainly by Thomas Jefferson, the document both denounced King George III and expressed the country's commitment to certain democratic principles. The Declaration asserts that God gave people the rights to "life, liberty, and the pursuit of happiness." People create governments so that these fundamental rights may be preserved and protected. If a government fails to safeguard these rights, however, the people may and should abolish the old government and create a new one. (See Appendix 1 for the full text of the Declaration of Independence.)

The Declaration of Independence "epitomizes and summarizes" a train of political thought that originated in England.[16] By the time of the Revolution, political thinkers who influenced the Patriots had long discarded the notion that kings had a God-given right to rule. In place of divine right stood three principles:

1. Government arises from the consent of the governed.
2. Power should be divided among separate institutions.
3. Citizen rights must be protected.

Each of these principles would shape the writing of the Constitution.

Leviathan

Thomas Hobbes (1588–1679) thought that humans are by nature warlike and selfish. His treatise *Leviathan* held that the only way to maintain human society was for individuals to consent to rule by a single, all-powerful leader or government.

• *Do you think that people are basically selfish? If so, does democracy function in spite of, or because of, this basic selfishness? How did Locke modify Hobbes's theory?*

separation of powers

A system of government in which different institutions exercise different components of governmental power.

Consent of the Governed   As early as 1651, Thomas Hobbes, England's greatest political theorist, said that kings governed not by divine right but by the consent of the governed. People form a government because without a government, they live in a chaotic state of nature in which there is a "war of all against all." Without a government, everyone must resort to violence simply to avoid being a victim. Life becomes "solitary, poor, nasty, brutish and short." Hobbes argued that only a sovereign king with absolute power can prevent the war of all against all. If power is divided among more than one person, conflict among them becomes inevitable.[17] As a result, people consent to be governed by one all-powerful ruler.

Separation of Powers   Hobbes was ruthlessly logical. Accept his premise that individuals are selfish and shortsighted, and his conclusion that the people readily consent to be ruled by an absolute sovereign seems almost inevitable. But the English, more pragmatic than consistent, shunned Hobbes's uncompromising defense of absolute kingly power. Instead, John Locke's ideas became popular. Writing in 1690, Locke agreed with Hobbes that government arises from the consent of the people, but Locke did not think it was necessary for this power to be concentrated in the hands of one absolute and all-powerful ruler.[18] Instead, Locke argued that governmental power took several different forms, each requiring a different institution. A country's founders should create a **separation of powers**, a system of government in which different institutions exercise the various components of governmental power. Locke thought each institution should be constituted as follows:

1. *Legislative power*, the making of law, to be exercised by an assembly with two chambers, the upper chamber consisting of the aristocracy and the lower chamber chosen by the people.
2. *Executive power*, the enforcement of law, to be exercised by a single person, often a king.

Nearly 60 years after Locke's writings, the French philosopher Charles de Secondat, Baron de Montesquieu, added a third institution:

3. *Judicial power,* the application of law to particular situations, exercised by independent judges.

Great political theorists often come to conclusions that differ very little from existing governmental practice. So it was with Locke, who set forth a theory that closely resembled English government. England had a legislature or parliament consisting of two chambers: the House of Lords (representing the aristocracy) and the House of Commons (representing the people). Executive power was exercised by the king. The House of Lords appointed the judges.

Cynics have said that the English discovered Locke's wisdom before he set it down on paper. More accurately, Locke's genius consisted of making theoretical sense of English practice, giving the English an enlightening way of thinking about a government that had evolved haphazardly over many centuries.

Citizen Rights and Representation   Not long after Locke wrote, British practice changed. Power, instead of being separated among the three branches, was concentrated in a small group of ministers drawn from Parliament but appointed by the king.

These ministers, who owed their livelihoods to the monarch, were reluctant to be critical of the king's wishes.[19]

This system provoked intense opposition from a group known as **Whigs**, who attacked it as hopelessly corrupt and developed a counter-theory of citizen rights and representation. To the Whigs, a formal division of powers was not enough to ensure the security of the people. After all, in Great Britain, powers were divided in principle, but concentrated in practice. Instead, Whigs argued, citizens themselves should be given increased power over the government. The most important political thinker among the Whigs was James Harrington. In place of parliamentary control over a large nation, Harrington favored small self-governing republics (small cities governed by virtuous citizen leaders), each of which would protect the freedoms of its own citizens. In place of officeholders beholden to the king, he called for the election of virtuous citizens for short periods of time. In place of an aristocracy of birth, he said ordinary citizens should choose leaders from the most noble among them.[20]

Whig criticism of the British government made sense to many American colonists. The rough equality of colonial America stood in sharp contrast to the court intrigues in London. Colonial leaders thought of themselves as a natural aristocracy distinct from the inherited nobility in Britain. The more Parliament imposed taxes and interfered in colonial affairs, the more apparent became English corruption. The more the English government insisted on the ultimate sovereignty of the king, the more obvious it became to Americans that taxation without representation was illegitimate.

The Whig theory of rights and representation took its most forceful and popular form in *Common Sense*, written by Thomas Paine, a native Englishman who had immigrated to the colonies.[21] Filled with heated rhetoric and widely read among Patriots in the months before the Declaration of Independence, the book declared kingship to be "the most bare-faced falsity ever imposed on mankind." Instead of contributing to peace, as Hobbes had claimed, a hereditary monarchy "makes against it." Peaceful government is better achieved by representatives "who . . . have the same concerns at stake" as the people. If elections were frequent, representatives would establish a "common interest with every part of the community."

Still, the Whigs and their American followers were not modern-day democrats. Although they advanced a more participatory doctrine of rights and representation than previous theorists, they believed that only male property owners had the necessary virtues to be good citizens. Aside from philosopher and poet Alexander Pope, who blithely observed that "Most women have no characters at all," few theorists of the era took the time to explain why women could not be full citizens. But such views were so widespread that English author Mary Wollstonecraft, writing in 1787, the year the Constitution was drafted, was moved to lament, "It would be an endless task to trace the variety of meannesses, cares, and sorrows into which women are plunged by the prevailing opinion that they were created rather to feel than reason."[22]

Only many years later would the theory of rights and representation come to include women, the propertyless, former slaves, and other previously excluded groups.

Government After Independence

Independence had been won, but the hard work of governance lay ahead. The Revolution had united the colonies in one cause, but it remained to be seen whether

Whigs
Political opposition in eighteenth-century England that developed a theory of rights and representation.

Articles of Confederation
The first (1781–1789) basic governing document of the United States and forerunner to the Constitution.

there was cause enough to keep them united in the absence of the British threat. The new states were slow to reorganize their own governments during the war years, and the loose confederation plan that the Second Continental Congress had assembled remained in place after the Treaty of Paris ended the conflict. But changes were afoot in two arenas. First, participation in government began to broaden. And second, the **Articles of Confederation**, the first basic governing document of the United States and forerunner of the Constitution, proved increasingly unsatisfactory as a governing system for the new nation.

Broadening Participation

The Patriots gave voice to sweeping participatory ideals during the seven years they fought for independence from England. During the war the colonies, now calling themselves "states," constructed governments of their own. For the most part, the 13 new states kept their colonial institutions much as they were, except "with Parliament and the King left out."[23] But the pace of democratization began to accelerate. Eight of the 13 states eased the property qualifications for voters, and five lowered them for candidates for the lower house of the state legislature.[24] The percentage of state legislators who had great wealth declined, giving new political opportunities to those from more modest backgrounds. Ten states required that governors be elected annually, and six limited the number of terms they could serve.[25]

Some leaders believed that the Whig theory of the rights of man should apply to women. In a letter to her Patriot husband, Abigail Adams proposed giving women their rights and liberties as well: "In the new code of laws . . . I desire you would remember the ladies, and be more generous and favorable to them than your ancestors . . . . If . . . attention is not paid to the ladies we are determined to foment a rebellion, and will not hold ourselves bound by any laws in which we have no voice, or representation." But many of those who espoused Whig theory were unwilling to come to terms with all of its implications. Even Abigail Adams's husband, John, who became the nation's second president, argued against making changes in voting qualifications. "[T]here will be no end of it," he said. "Women will demand a vote; lads from twelve to twenty-one will think their rights not enough attended to; and every man, who has not a farthing, will demand an equal voice."[26]

A League of Friendship
The Articles of Confederation, proposed in 1775, were finally ratified in 1781—eight years before the Constitution. Those eight years were marked by government instability.

• *How does the Constitution differ from the Articles of Confederation?*

The Articles of Confederation (1781–1789)

The new country needed, above all, a sense of national unity. In one of its more inspired decisions, the Second Continental Congress helped bring the nation together during the war by appointing George Washington, a Virginia plantation owner, as commander of a continental army—even though most soldiers initially came from northern colonies.

Washington's leadership was important, but tough constitutional decisions also needed to be made. The idea of creating a national government was so foreign to the colonial experience that it took the Continental Congress nearly five years after declaring independence to write and win ratification for the country's first constitution, the Articles of Confederation. In the meantime, the Continental Congress did its best to govern by means of its own cumbersome procedures.

Provisions of the Articles   Ratified in 1781, the Articles of Confederation amounted, in its own words, to little more than a "firm league of friendship" in which "each state retains its sovereignty, freedom and independence." The Articles granted the Congress only limited powers. Although it could declare war, it could raise an army only by requesting states to provide soldiers. Congress could not tax citizens directly; instead, it had to rely on voluntary contributions from the states. The Continental Congress could coin money, but it could not prevent states from also doing so. As a result, the country was flooded with many different currencies. Congress could negotiate tariffs with other countries, but so could each state. Most significant, Congress could not prevent states from interfering with interstate commerce. In fact, states imposed trade barriers on one another. New York, for example, taxed New Jersey cabbage and Connecticut firewood.[27]

Articles of
Confederation

Members of the Congress were elected annually by state legislatures. Each state, no matter how large or small, was equally represented. On all important issues, a super-majority of 9 states (out of 13) had to agree before action could be taken. Even if this supermajority could agree on a policy, individual states frequently ignored Congress's wishes. This prompted a frustrated Alexander Hamilton to point out that national laws were "in practice . . . mere recommendations which the States observe or disregard at their option."[28]

The Articles of Confederation did not create a system of divided powers along the lines Locke had envisioned. Instead, the Congress wielded all national powers, such as they were. There was no independent executive. A congressional Committee of the States could make decisions between meetings of Congress, but this was an unwieldy body because each state had representation. Again, 9 of the 13 delegates had to agree before the committee could take action. States exercised most judicial functions, except that disputes between states were settled by ad hoc panels of judges selected by Congress. Congress could amend the Articles only with the approval of all the state legislatures.

Government Under the Articles   Members of Congress almost immediately recognized the problems with the Articles. Virginia delegate James Madison became convinced that a new constitution was necessary after he discovered that it was impossible for Congress to keep states from issuing their own money. National leaders watched helplessly as trade among the states was impeded by quarreling over the relative worth of the coins of New York, Pennsylvania, and Virginia.

Commercial problems were frustrating, but new threats to civil order made it clear that the Articles had difficulty even keeping the peace. **Shays' Rebellion**, an armed uprising in western Massachusetts in 1786 led by Revolutionary War captain Daniel Shays, was especially disruptive. A group of impoverished, back-country farmers, unable to pay their taxes or mortgages, tried to intimidate state courts into forgiving their debts. Because it took months to suppress the rebellion, many prominent leaders felt that this episode proved that state governments were too weak. Even more embarrassing was an incident in which a group of ex-soldiers from the continental army descended on Congress in 1783, demanding their rightful back pay. Members of the Congress appealed to the State of Pennsylvania for help, but when none was forthcoming, they fled to Princeton College in New Jersey.

Threats from foreign countries were disturbing as well. The British disputed the boundary between its Canadian colonies and the United States. Also, the British navy

Shays' Rebellion
Uprising in western Massachusetts in 1786 led by Revolutionary War captain Daniel Shays.

Debtors Revolt

Scuffles broke out in western Massachusetts during Shays' Rebellion, when poor farmers and Revolutionary War veterans joined in an uprising.

• *How did this rebellion influence the writing of the Constitution?*

FIGURE 2.1

Map of Competing Claims

This map shows only some of the competing claims being made in North America in 1787. Because the British had a superior navy, the United States was, in a sense, surrounded by foreign powers.

• *How did this threat influence the debates over the Constitution?*

Source: Edgar B. Wesley, *Our United States: Its History in Maps* (Chicago: Denoyer-Geppert Co., 1965), p. 37.

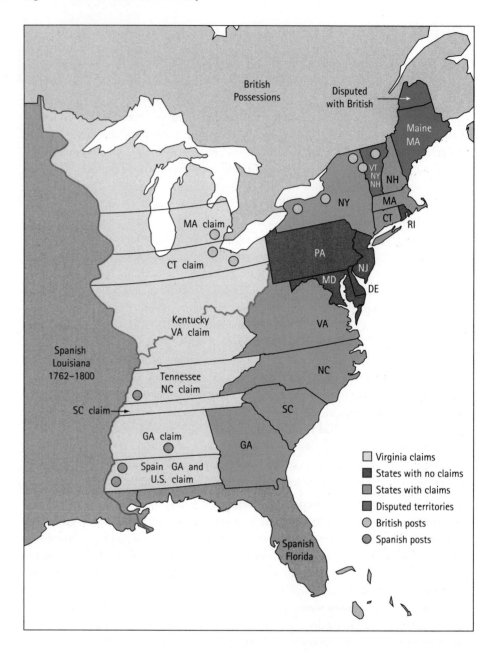

routinely intercepted American ships and dragooned U.S. sailors into service, claiming that anyone who spoke English must be British unless he could prove otherwise. Spain, in possession of Florida and the lands west of the Mississippi River, claimed large segments of what are today the states of Mississippi and Alabama (see Figure 2.1). Even France, a Revolutionary War ally, blocked U.S. trade with its islands in the West Indies and demanded repayment of money advanced during the Revolution. Congress found it difficult to resolve these disputes, because it could not prevent individual states from undermining congressionally-appointed diplomats by engaging in independent negotiations with foreign countries.

Drafting and Adopting a New Constitution

In light of the fragility of the American government in the 1780s, it is remarkable that the end of that decade produced a document that has, for the most part, remained intact for more than 200 years. No less a figure than James Madison pronounced it "a miracle" that agreement on a new constitution was reached at all.[29] In this section we review the key events that led to this agreement and discuss the major components of the Constitution itself. We then turn to the important debates between Federalists and Anti-Federalists that set the stage for ratification.

The Constitutional Convention

None felt the deficiencies in the Articles more keenly than George Washington and James Madison. An avid speculator in land west of the Appalachian Mountains, Washington was frustrated by the inability of the states to work together to build canals and roads that would help develop the country's interior. Madison despaired at Congress's inability to raise money.

Alexander Hamilton, Madison, and other reformers met to discuss needed constitutional reforms in 1786 at what became known as the **Annapolis Convention**, but inasmuch as they represented only five states, they were unable to propose major constitutional changes. Later that year, however, in the aftermath of Shays' Rebellion, Madison persuaded Congress to ask each state legislature to elect delegates to a convention in Philadelphia for the "sole and express purpose of revising the Articles of Confederation."[30] Every state legislature but Rhode Island's agreed to do so. Rhode Islanders were fearful that any revisions in the Articles would reduce the powers of their small state.

Annapolis Convention
1786 meeting to discuss constitutional reform.

For the most part, states sent political leaders who favored major constitutional change; most of those opposed to changing the Articles stayed away. Patrick Henry, when asked to be a delegate, refused, saying he "smelt a rat." True, 10 delegates abandoned the convention before the Constitution was completed, and another three refused to sign the resulting document, but the great majority of those in Philadelphia agreed that the national government needed to be strengthened.

VIDEO ROUNDTABLE

Intent of the Framers

The delegates to the Constitutional Convention did not constitute a cross section of the population. The people who met in Philadelphia were bankers, merchants, plantation owners, and speculators in land west of the Appalachians.[31] Yet the delegates had not gone to Philadelphia just to protect the interests of their social class. They believed the country as a whole needed a stronger government that could provide political stability, effectively mediate conflicts among the states, and defend the nation from foreign threats.[32]

Nor did delegates agree on all issues. Each owed allegiance to the state legislature that had elected him, and these local ties inevitably led to conflicts. Two divisions were paramount. Delegates from states with large populations often found themselves disagreeing with delegates from smaller states. And delegates from southern slave states opposed those from northern states, whose economies did not depend on slavery.

These differences were less apparent during the opening weeks of the convention, when a spirit of unity and reform filled the Philadelphia hall. But as the four-month convention progressed, differences among the delegates emerged, and compromises had to be reached to produce a document that could be ratified.[33]

The Virginia Plan   Delegates made three important decisions at the very beginning of the convention:

- Hold discussions behind closed doors. If debates were held in public, disagreements could be exploited by Anti-Federalists.
- Write an entirely new constitution instead of simply following Congress's instruction to suggest amendments to the Articles of Confederation.
- Use the **Virginia Plan** as the basis for initial discussions.

Virginia Plan

Constitutional proposal supported by convention delegates from large states.

The Virginia Plan, which would win the support of most delegates from the larger states, had been prepared by Madison (with Washington's active involvement) prior to the gathering in Philadelphia. It proposed massive changes in the design and powers of the national government, creating a separation of powers along the lines that Locke had recommended. To win popular support for the new constitution, the Virginia Plan called for ratification by state convention delegates "expressly chosen by the people."[34]

Instead of a one-chamber Congress like that of the Articles, Madison proposed two chambers. The lower chamber—the future House of Representatives—would be elected by the voters. The upper chamber—the future Senate—would be nominated by state legislatures and elected by the lower house.

The Virginia Plan changed representation in Congress dramatically from the pattern that prevailed under the Articles of Confederation. Instead of each state's having one vote, the number of both representatives and senators would depend on a state's population. In short, Virginia, Pennsylvania, and other more populous states would have much more power under this plan than under the Articles.

The Virginia Plan also gave the national government vast powers far beyond those enjoyed by the old Congress. The new Congress could legislate on all matters that affected "the harmony of the United States" and could negate "all laws passed by the several states."[35] It could also use force to ensure that states fulfilled their duties.

According to the Virginia Plan, the weak executive power under the Articles was to be replaced by a president chosen by Congress. A Supreme Court would have the authority to resolve disputes among individuals from different states, something that could not be done under the Articles of Confederation. The Virginia Plan received strong support from two of the most populous states, Virginia and Pennsylvania, as well as from states that expected to grow rapidly in population in the next few years, North Carolina, South Carolina, and Georgia.

The New Jersey Plan   Delegates from smaller states, especially New Jersey and Delaware, were uneasy about the Virginia Plan. About two weeks into the convention, these states offered an alternative design prepared by New Jersey's William Paterson that became known as the **New Jersey Plan**, the small-state proposal for constitutional reform (see Table 2.2).

New Jersey Plan

Small-state proposal for constitutional reform.

The New Jersey Plan also separated powers into three branches, but instead of creating a House and Senate, it kept a one-chamber Congress in which each state had a single vote. It also envisioned a more limited national government. Unlike the Virginia Plan, it did not grant Congress general legislative power. Instead it gave Congress specific powers, including the power to levy taxes on imported goods, the power to compel states to pay their share of taxes, and the power to regulate "trade & commerce with foreign nations" and among the states. The judicial branch could hear only specific types of cases, such as those involving treaties or foreigners.[36]

TABLE 2.2	
THE VIRGINIA AND NEW JERSEY PLANS	

The differences between the Virginia Plan and the New Jersey Plan illustrate the disagreements between large and small states at the time of the convention.

- *Why were both large and small states willing to accept the Connecticut Compromise?*

Virginia Plan (favored by larger states)	New Jersey Plan (favored by smaller states)
Key Difference	
Each state is represented in proportion to its population.	Every state has the same number of representatives in Congress.
Other Differences	
Congress has general power.	Congress has only limited, defined powers.
Supreme Court settles disputes among individuals.	Judiciary settles only certain disputes (for example, those involving foreigners).

Despite these limitations, the New Jersey Plan still granted the national government power far in excess of what existed under the Articles. The plan's supporters were not so much opposed to a stronger government as afraid that the big states would control such a government. As one delegate observed at the time, "Give New Jersey an equal vote, and she will dismiss her scruples, and concur in a National system."[37]

The Connecticut Compromise   The convention nearly collapsed when a majority of the delegates rejected the New Jersey Plan. Representatives from the small states considered walking out of the convention, which would have killed all hope of successful ratification. The large states flirted with the idea of forming their own union and then using economic pressure to force the small states to join. To calm these unsettled waters, Benjamin Franklin proposed beginning each session with prayer, although the idea was rejected on the grounds that no money was available to pay a chaplain.

To temper the debate, the convention turned the most divisive issues over to a committee controlled by moderates. This committee came back with a split-the-difference compromise offered by delegates from the medium-sized state of Connecticut. Proposing a Congress along the lines we know today, the **Connecticut Compromise** called for a House proportionate to population and a Senate in which all states were represented equally (see Figure 2.2). Small states were placated by their strong representation in the Senate; large states took comfort in the requirement that representation in the House of Representatives be proportionate to a state's population.

Connecticut Compromise
Constitutional Convention proposal that created a House proportionate to population and a Senate in which all states were represented equally.

A Government of Separated Powers

Once the delegates accepted the Connecticut Compromise, they found it relatively easy to broker other differences between the Virginia and New Jersey Plans. Following the Virginia Plan, they created a government with three branches—legislative, executive, and judicial—dividing powers among them. But in a step consistent with the New Jersey Plan, they limited the powers of all three branches.

Congress   Echoing the New Jersey Plan, the convention delegates gave Congress a number of specific powers, including the powers to tax, coin money, regulate commerce, declare war, and maintain an army (see Table 2.3). But to address the concerns

FIGURE 2.2

The Connecticut
Compromise

• *On the basis of the pie charts
shown here, why do you think
Connecticut was the state that
proposed the compromise?*

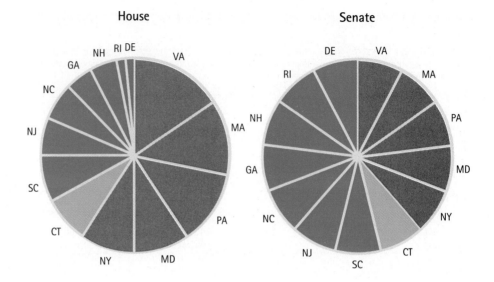

House

Senate

necessary and proper clause
Says Congress has the power to
"make all laws which shall be
necessary and proper for carrying
into Execution" its other powers.

of the proponents of the Virginia Plan, they included the **necessary and proper clause**, which says that Congress has the power to "make all laws which shall be necessary and proper for carrying into Execution" its other powers. What is the definition of *necessary and proper?* Some delegates thought it meant only what was absolutely essential. Others thought it meant anything convenient and useful. The phrasing was ambiguous enough that all delegates could interpret the language to their own liking.

The delegates were also influenced by the Whig theory on rights and representation that had proved so powerful during the Revolutionary War. Following Whig theory, the Constitution said that members of the House of Representatives were to be

TABLE 2.3

THE CONSTITUTION AND THE ARTICLES OF CONFEDERATION COMPARED

Many provisions of the Constitution directly address the failures of the Articles of Confederation.

• *Are there problems with the previous system that were not addressed by the Constitution?*

• *Why do you think these problems were not addressed?*

Weaknesses of the Articles of Confederation	How They Are Addressed in Constitution
Congress could not levy taxes.	Congress has power to levy taxes (Article I, Section 8).
States could restrict commerce among states.	States cannot regulate commerce without the consent of Congress (Article I, Section 10).
States could issue their own currency.	States are prohibited from coining money (Article I, Section 10).
Executive was not independent of Congress.	An independently elected president holds the executive power (Article II).
There was no national judicial system.	The Supreme Court was created, and Congress was granted the power to establish lower federal courts (Article III, Section 1).
Amendments to Articles had to have unanimous approval of states.	Large majorities are necessary to amend the Constitution, but there are several different ways to do so (Article V).

chosen by the voters and were to be subject to reelection every two years. Still, the convention came closer to creating a responsible democracy than a popular one (see Chapter 1). It departed from the Whig theory by not establishing a limit on the number of terms that a member could serve. The delegates modified Whig theory even further in regard to the Senate. Senators were to be elected not by voters but by state legislatures, and they would serve six-year terms of office.

The delegates settled on a delicate political solution to the question of voter qualifications. They said states could establish their own requirements, provided that anyone eligible to vote for the lower chamber of the state legislature must also be allowed to vote in elections for the House of Representatives. This arrangement avoided changing state voting requirements but still guaranteed the vote to everyone already eligible. The open-ended language also permitted a gradual, state-by-state extension of the right to vote to many who were excluded from the electorate in 1787.

The Executive   Some analysts have claimed that many convention delegates secretly harbored a desire to create an executive who had powers comparable to those of a British king.[38] The delegates, however, were too practical to treat such an idea seriously—except for Alexander Hamilton, who actually made a proposal along these lines. They knew that voters would reject out of hand a Constitution that threatened the return of anyone comparable to King George.

Instead, the Constitution keeps presidential power under tight congressional control. The president is made commander in chief of the armed forces, but only Congress can declare war. Presidents can call Congress into session and speak to Congress, but they cannot dismiss Congress or prevent it from meeting. Presidents are given the power to veto legislation, but Congress can override a presidential veto with a two-thirds vote of each chamber. (See Chapter 13 for a full discussion of how the constitutional system shapes the relationship between Congress and the president.)

Other presidential powers can be exercised only with senatorial **advice and consent**—support for a presidential action by a designated number of senators. For example, the president can sign treaties with foreign countries, but treaties can take effect only if two-thirds of the Senate approves. Also, the president can appoint both judges and executive branch officers, but appointees must be confirmed by a **majority** (50 percent plus one) of the Senate.

advice and consent
Support for a presidential action by a designated number of senators.

majority
Fifty percent plus one.

The impeachment clause makes clear the president's ultimate dependence on political support from Congress. The House of Representatives can impeach the president for "Treason, Bribery, or other high Crimes and Misdemeanors." If impeached, the president is tried in the Senate. If convicted by a two-thirds vote, the president is removed from office. Although no president has ever been removed in this way, in 1999 Bill Clinton was tried but not convicted, in 1974 Richard Nixon chose to resign in the face of almost certain impeachment and conviction, and in 1868 Andrew Johnson avoided conviction by only one vote.

The Electoral College   Although the Constitution sharply checked presidential power, delegates to the Constitutional Convention still expected the president to be a powerful political figure. As a consequence, they debated at great length on the method of presidential selection. Once again, the dispute divided the big states from the small ones. If the president were chosen by popular vote, big states would prevail because most people lived in big states. If the choice were made by the House of

electoral college

Those chosen to cast a direct vote for president by a process determined by each state.

Explore Your
State Constitution

judicial review

Court authority to declare laws null and void on the grounds that they violate the Constitution.

Representatives, big states would once again dominate. If the choice resided in the Senate, the small states would have extra clout.

The delegates finally agreed on a compromise that created the **electoral college**—those electors chosen to cast a direct vote for president by a process determined by each state. The electoral college is part of a complicated two-stage procedure that remains in effect today. The first stage involves selection of the electoral college and gives an advantage to larger states. Each state chooses the same number of electors as it has senators and representatives in Congress. For example, Texas now has 34 electoral votes, because it elects 2 senators and 32 representatives. (In addition, as a result of the passage of the Twenty-Third Amendment, the District of Columbia casts three electoral votes.) If a candidate receives a majority of the electoral votes, that person is elected president.

If no candidate receives a majority in the electoral college, the action moves to the House of Representatives. In this stage, smaller states have an advantage, because each state delegation has a single vote.

The Constitution does not require that the members of the electoral college be chosen by the voters. Instead, the manner of selecting electors was left up to the states. Constitutional silence on this key matter was not an accident. Some delegates thought the president should be elected by the people; others felt this could lead to mob rule. The Constitutional Convention compromised on the question, as it did on so many, by leaving the issue up to the states. Not until 1864 did the last state, South Carolina, give voters the power to vote directly for its electors (though by the 1820s, electors were chosen by the voters in the great majority of states).[39]

Some think the electoral college compromise has proved to be less of a success than the Connecticut Compromise. For example, in four elections (1824, 1876, 1888, and 2000), the candidate who won the most popular votes was not selected president. Some scholars favor eliminating the electoral college altogether, on the theory that the candidate receiving the most popular votes should win the election. Others think that the electoral college, for all its faults, helps to maintain the two-party system and provides representation for both the states and the people.

The Judicial Compromise   Most convention delegates thought the country needed a Supreme Court to adjudicate conflicts between the states. They also found it fairly easy to agree that justices should be nominated for lifetime positions by the president and confirmed by a majority of the Senate.

The delegates differed over whether the Supreme Court needed lower federal courts to assist it. Advocates of the Virginia Plan wanted lower federal courts because state courts "cannot be trusted with the administration of the National Laws."[40] Advocates of the New Jersey Plan said the state courts were sufficient and protested that "the people will not bear such innovations" as a national court system.[41] The delegates compromised on the issue by leaving it to Congress to decide whether lower federal courts were needed. The first Congress created a system of lower federal courts, whose essentials remain intact today. The court system is described in Chapter 15.

The delegates also seem to have disagreed on whether the Supreme Court should be given the power of **judicial review**, court authority to declare laws null and void on the grounds that they violate the Constitution. Although Madison's account of the debate over judicial review is sketchy, many delegates, it seems, favored judicial review as a check on the power of state legislatures. Yet there is no record of anyone having risen to its defense when two delegates opposed judicial review. Although scholars have puzzled over the relative silence at the convention about an issue that would loom large in later years, this lack of debate is probably best explained by political expediency. Judicial review had provoked controversy in North Carolina and Rhode Island, and convention delegates avoided the issue because taking a clear position might have jeopardized ratification.

Instead of explicitly providing for judicial review, convention delegates inserted into the Constitution an ambiguous phrase that has become known as the **supremacy clause**, which says the Constitution is the "supreme Law of the Land," to which all judges are bound. To some, this phrase simply told state judges to be mindful of the Constitution when interpreting state laws. To others, it gave the Supreme Court the power to declare both state and federal laws unconstitutional. The issue was not settled until 20 years later, when, as we shall see in Chapter 15, the Supreme Court interpreted the supremacy clause as giving the Court the power of judicial review over both federal and state laws.

supremacy clause
Part of the Constitution that says the Constitution is the "supreme Law of the Land," to which all judges are bound.

Compromising on the Issue of Slavery   The delegates never seriously contemplated eliminating slavery under the Constitution, although one delegate contended that it was their moral duty to do so. Many delegates were slave owners themselves, and the convention participants knew that southern states would not ratify the Constitution if it abolished slavery. The debate over slavery took other forms instead. Northerners wanted to end the international slave trade. Most southerners argued that the slave trade, however despicable, was necessary to fuel economic growth in unsettled parts of the South. The two sides compromised by agreeing not to abolish the slave trade for 20 years. Abiding by this provision, Congress waited until 1808 before taking that step.

Northern delegates did not want to count slaves when figuring state representation in the House of Representatives. Southerners thought they should be counted. The two sides came up with the expedient, if disreputable, **three-fifths compromise**, which counted each slave, for purposes of representation, as "three-fifths" of a person. One sign that this was a delicate arrangement is that the three-fifths clause identified slaves not as such but as "other persons." Not until after the Civil War did the Fourteenth Amendment repeal the three-fifths clause.

three-fifths compromise
Constitutional provision that counted each slave as three-fifths of a person when calculating representation in the House of Representatives; repealed by the Fourteenth Amendment.

North and South also split over tariffs. Northerners wanted to give Congress the right to impose tariffs on imports; southerners were afraid this provision would be used to protect northern manufacturing at southern expense. In exchange for the three-fifths compromise, southerners agreed to let Congress impose tariffs on foreign goods.

The Bill of Rights

The delegates to the Constitutional Convention made one mistake so serious that it nearly ruined their chances of securing ratification: They failed to include within the Constitution clauses that clearly protected the liberties of the people. It is surprising that the delegates to the Philadelphia Convention, who otherwise showed excellent political judgment, made such a serious political miscalculation. Ever since the Revolutionary War, the Whig concept of rights and representation had been central to American constitutional thinking. Quite apart from the Declaration of Independence, with its ringing endorsement of the "right to life, liberty, and the pursuit of happiness," the Virginia assembly—also in 1776—had passed a Bill of Rights protecting free speech, the right of the propertied to vote, the right to a trial by jury, the right not to be compelled to testify against oneself, and other civil liberties.[42] Many other states had similar provisions in their constitutions or statutes. Yet at the Constitutional

Convention, when South Carolina's Charles Pinckney offered a motion to guarantee freedom of the press, a majority voted the proposal down—on the grounds that regulation of speech and press was a state responsibility.[43]

The convention majority may have been technically correct, but they failed to appreciate how powerfully the demand for the protection of civil liberties would resonate with the voters. To win popular acceptance, the Constitution needed to contain an explicit expression of the Whig theory of rights and representation that the country had taken to heart during the Revolutionary War. When it failed to do so, Thomas Jefferson, author of the Declaration of Independence, wrote to Madison from his diplomatic post in Paris, arguing that a Bill of Rights was necessary and appropriate.

Bill of Rights

The first 10 amendments to the Constitution, which protect individual and state rights.

Eventually, the Federalists recognized their mistake. To win ratification in Massachusetts, Virginia, and New York, they promised to enact, as a series of amendments to the Constitution, a **Bill of Rights** that would guarantee civil liberties. Two states, North Carolina and Rhode Island, wanted to make sure the Federalists made good on their promise. Although they probably would have ratified the Constitution at some point simply to avoid becoming isolated, they withheld their approval until after the first Congress fulfilled the Federalist promise to add a Bill of Rights (see Table 2.4). The Bill of Rights, which comprises the first 10 amendments to the Constitution, has played such a central role in the country's constitutional development that all of Chapter 16, on civil liberties, is devoted to it.

The Anti-Federalist–Federalist Debate

Although the absence of a Bill of Rights gave Anti-Federalists powerful ammunition for their assault on the Constitution during the ratification campaign, their critique of

Each State a Pillar

At the time of this cartoon's publication, only 11 states had ratified the Constitution. The cartoonist eagerly awaited North Carolina ("Rise it will") and Rhode Island ("The foundation good—it may yet be saved") joining the new Union.

• *Why was Rhode Island the last state to ratify the Constitution?*

TABLE 2.4
KEY CIVIL LIBERTIES PROTECTED BY THE BILL OF RIGHTS

Responding to criticism by Anti-Federalists, proponents of the Constitution agreed to add a Bill of Rights soon after ratification.

* *Why is a Bill of Rights important in a democracy?*
* *What rights can you think of that are not in the Bill of Rights but should be?*

Freedom of speech, press, and assembly (Amendment I)

Free exercise of religion (Amendment I)

Right to bear arms (Amendment II)

Protection against soldiers being quartered in private homes (Amendment III)

Home security against unreasonable searches and seizures (Amendment IV)

Cannot be deprived of life, liberty, or property without due process of law (Amendment V)

Cannot be forced to testify against oneself (Amendment V)

Trial by jury (Amendments VI and VII)

No cruel or unusual punishment (Amendment VIII)

Assurance that people retain other rights not explicitly stated (Amendment IX)

Powers not delegated to national government are retained by states or people (Amendment X)

the document was more broadly based. Drawing on the Whig theory of rights and representation, which valued decentralized, popular government, they attacked the Constitution for laying the groundwork for a national tyranny. They said the shift in power from the states to the national government took power from the people. The number of representatives in Congress was too small to include a wide variety of citizens from all parts of the United States. In essence, presidents could become kings, because they could be reelected again and again for the rest of their lives. The reelection of senators and representatives would create a political aristocracy.[44]

Three Federalists—Alexander Hamilton, James Madison, and John Jay—wrote a series of newspaper columns to answer these Anti-Federalist arguments. Now known as the **Federalist Papers**, these essays are generally regarded as the finest essays on American political theory ever written.[45] The authors argued that tyranny could come from either outside or inside the country. The external danger came from European countries, which were eager to divide the new nation so that each section could be controlled. The Constitution would help prevent such divisions by creating a stronger national government that could defend the country.

Threats to liberty could also come from factions inside the country seeking to impose their will on others. The greatest threat to liberty came from a majority faction, because it could so easily impose its will on minorities. There were several ways of preventing majority factions from arising, or, if they did arise, of preventing them from tyrannizing over the rights of others. The authors of the *Federalist Papers* said that the large size of the new nation would help to prevent majority factions from arising because of the "greater variety of parties and interests" that a bigger nation would necessarily include.[46] The Constitution would prevent majority tyranny by creating a system of **checks and balances**, a division of governmental power among

You Are
James Madison

Federalist Papers

Essays that were written in support of the Constitution's ratification and have become a classic argument for the American constitutional system.

checks and balances

Constitutional division of power into separate institutions, giving each institution the power to block the actions of the others.

James Madison
(1751–1836), left, and
Alexander Hamilton
(1755–1804), Authors of
the *Federalist Papers*
•   *How did the Federalists
respond to the Anti-Federalist
claim that the new constitution
would produce tyranny?*

The American System
of Checks and Balances

separate institutions, giving each institution the power to block the actions of the others. In the first place, power was split between the states and a national government. Then, at the national level, power was divided among three branches: legislative, executive, and judicial. Finally, the legislative branch was divided into two chambers, a Senate and a House of Representatives. Each was elected in a different way, which would make it more difficult for any momentary majority to seize total power.

In retrospect, the Federalists seem to have had the better argument. The Federalists had a plan for the future; the Anti-Federalists had little to offer but the unsatisfactory status quo. When the Anti-Federalists claimed that the Constitution stripped the people of their rights and liberties, they relied on the not very convincing argument that the government of any large nation was likely to trample the liberties of the people. The writers of the *Federalist Papers* analyzed the situation more accurately; by creating a system of checks and balances that divided power into different branches and different levels, and by grounding each level in separate elections, they hoped to ensure that the ambitions of one group of politicians would restrain those of other groups. (See Appendix III and IV for two *Federalist Papers* that explain this argument in more detail: Federalist 10 and Federalist 51.)

Amendments to the Constitution

The delegates to the Constitutional Convention, realizing that the document they were writing was not perfect and that unforeseen circumstances could arise, considered ways in which the Constitution might be amended. Small states wanted to require unanimous consent of state legislatures. Big states felt that a unanimity rule would lead to stagnation and protracted conflict. Southern states were afraid that slavery would be endangered if amendments could be made easily.

To obtain agreement, Convention delegates designed a complicated formula that allowed amendment by any one of four different procedures, as shown in Figure 2.3. The simplest and most frequently used way to amend the Constitution requires a two-thirds vote in both houses of Congress and then ratification by three-quarters of the state legislatures. Of the 27 amendments to the Constitution, 26 have been enacted by

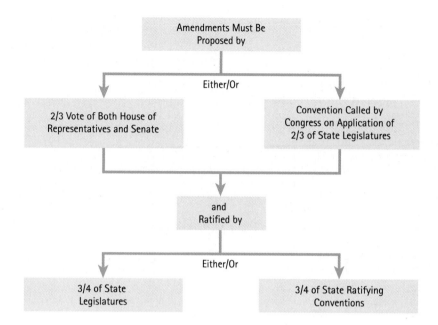

FIGURE 2.3

Amending the
Constitution:

A Two-Stage Process

• *Why did the founders make
the amendment process so
complicated?*

You Are Proposing
a Constitutional
Amendment

this procedure. On one occasion, the amendment that repealed prohibition, the state legislatures were bypassed in favor of state ratifying conventions attended by delegates chosen by the voters (the same procedure used to ratify the Constitution itself).

Amending the Constitution requires such overwhelming majorities that only 17 amendments have been enacted since ratification of the Bill of Rights—less than one amendment every 12 years. Thousands of amendments have been proposed over the decades, but nearly all have failed to win approval. The hurdles a proposed amendment must jump are so high that even popular amendments that have the endorsement of both political parties are not necessarily approved. For example, many people thought that the Equal Rights Amendment, which said that men and women had "equality of rights under the law," would win approval in the 1970s. The amendment received overwhelming support in both houses of Congress and was quickly ratified by 34 states. But when the proposed amendment became intertwined with abortion and other disputed issues, it failed to win ratification by the final three state legislatures necessary to provide the required three-quarters approval.[47]

The single kind of amendment that seems capable of jumping the high hurdles needed to achieve adoption is one that extends democratic electoral practices. Despite the complicated procedures that are in place, many amendments since the Bill of Rights have tightened the electoral connection well beyond what was originally envisioned by the Constitution—by broadening the electorate, by extending civil liberties, or by making more direct the connections between leaders and voters. Five amendments specifically extended the suffrage to citizens previously excluded from voting: African Americans, women, young people (ages 18–21), residents of the District of Columbia, and those unwilling or unable to pay a poll tax. Other amendments have corrected procedural deficiencies thought to be inconsistent with democratic practice. (See the *Election Connection* box on the next page.)

The History
of Constitutional
Amendments

ELECTION CONNECTION

Amendments to the Constitution Have Extended Liberties and Tightened the Election Connection

Amendment	Year Ratified	Provision
XIII	1865	Abolishes slavery.
XIV	1868	Defines "citizens" to include African Americans. Guarantees citizens the right of due process and equal protection before state law. Removes the three-fifths compromise from the Constitution.
XV	1870	Extends suffrage to African Americans.
XVII	1913	Institutes direct election of senators. Up to this point, senators had been selected by state legislatures.
XIX	1920	Extends suffrage to women.
XXII	1951	Imposes two-term limit on presidents, an idea discussed but not implemented by the founders.
XXIII	1961	Extends presidential suffrage to residents of the District of Columbia; grants the District three electoral votes in presidential elections.
XXIV	1964	Abolishes taxes on voting, which had barred many African Americans from the polls.
XXVI	1971	Extends suffrage to 18-year-olds.

The Constitution: An Assessment

The debate over the Constitution did not end with its ratification in 1788. The influential historian Charles Beard wrote in 1913 that the Constitution represented a victory for the propertied classes against the masses of the people.[48] Beard pointed out that wealthy people wrote the document and that only people with property were allowed to vote in the ratification campaign. But modern-day historians Bernard Bailyn and Gordon Wood see it as moving the country toward the ideals of citizen rights and representation that motivated the revolutionary patriots.[49] In their view, the Whig ideals that spurred the war of independence were given practical expression in the Constitution.

A Step Backward?

Both sides of this debate probably overstated their cases. The adoption of the Constitution consolidated changes in citizen participation and representation that had already taken place in many states. The adoption of the Constitution did not broaden the right to vote, but neither did it further restrict it. The Constitution divided powers that had been lodged in a single representative body under the Articles of Confederation, but each of the new entities—House, Senate, Congress, and the courts—was ultimately grounded in the people. Senators were elected by the legislatures of each state, but the members of each state legislature were chosen in popular elections. Presidents were chosen by electors, but the electors were chosen according to state rules, which since the 1830s have almost always called for direct elections by the voters. Judges were appointed for life, but they were selected by the president and confirmed by the Senate. If the U.S. government under the Constitution was a limited, responsible democracy in 1789, a more popular democracy evolved within the framework the Constitution set forth, although it took a Civil War to incorporate all races into the democratic process.

There remains much in the Constitution to criticize. The powers of the Supreme Court are poorly defined. The electoral college, while praised by some for representing both states and people, is criticized by others as a haphazard contraption that has more than once failed to work well. Many important issues are papered over with vague, ambiguous wording.

Certain clauses in the Constitution are especially disturbing to the modern eye. Written by 55 prosperous gentlemen, the document falls far short of expressing contemporary democratic ideals. The Constitution explicitly permitted the slave trade to continue until 1808, even though many delegates thought it an evil practice. Nothing was done to extend voting rights to women, indentured servants, slaves, youths, or those without property. Until the Bill of Rights was added, the Constitution said nothing about basic freedoms of speech, religion, and assembly, which are now taken for granted.

You Are Attempting to Revise the California State Constitution

But we cannot judge eighteenth-century decisions by twenty-first-century principles. Most of what we see as flaws was written into the Constitution not to frustrate later generations but to get the votes needed to achieve ratification. Delegates compromised on the issue of slavery because that was the only way to get the support of voters in both northern and southern states. Even when slavery made its way into the Constitution, references to the practice were so vague and oblique that reasonable people could disagree on the Constitution's aim. Famed abolitionist and escaped slave Frederick Douglass even argued that "If that Constitution had dropped down to us from the blue over-hanging sky, and we had read its contents, there [is] not a man who could reasonably suppose it was intended to sanction and support the slave system, but on the contrary . . . everything in it was intended to support justice and equality between man and man."[50]

The Constitution says nothing about the right to vote, because every state had its own voting rules. Had the Constitution proposed changing them, the states would have seen such provisions as violations of their sovereignty. The procedures for electing the president were designed to reduce conflicts between large and small states. The one big mistake the convention could most certainly have avoided—neglecting to include a Bill of Rights—was corrected by the first Congress.

If we want to censure the Constitution for its undemocratic features, we must first criticize the limits on suffrage imposed by state voting laws inherited from the colonial period. Historians estimate that only 20 percent of the electorate and 5 percent of the adult population voted.[51] The country was no longer ruled by King George III, but it was hardly a full-fledged democracy. The Constitution was written to win the support of the white, male, property-owning population. That it could do so—and still leave open the possibility for greater democratization in the centuries to come—is to the honor, not the discredit, of those who met in Philadelphia.

Achievements

Although it is easy to disparage the Constitutional Convention for what it failed to achieve, the delegates wrote a document that contributed to the solution of two of the most immediate and pressing problems facing the United States under the problematic Articles of Confederation. First, it created a unified nation capable of defending American sovereignty from foreign threats. True, the United States would fight an unsuccessful war against Britain in 1812. But the Constitution kept the country from disintegrating at a time when Britain, France, and Spain were all looking for a piece of the action in the New World. Instead of falling prey to European ambitions, the United

States profited from European divisions by seizing, in 1803, the opportunity to make the Louisiana Purchase, which doubled the size of the country. This land was eventually incorporated into the Union as new member states.

Second, the new Constitution facilitated the country's economic development by outlawing the separate state currencies and state tariffs that had proliferated under the Articles. As a result, trade among states flourished, and the United States grew into an economic powerhouse more rapidly than any had expected.

The Constitution also created a presidency that was first filled by George Washington, the country's most beloved political leader. His great prestige gave the national government the additional strength it needed to overcome the many difficulties the new nation encountered.

The Constitution Today

Democracy
and the Internet

In addition to solving immediate problems, the Constitution created a framework that facilitated an ever more popular democratic experiment. The document's durable but peaceful division of power, in which one branch can check another, would have surprised Thomas Hobbes, who said that a country could avoid chaos only by vesting power in a sovereign king. If a constitution separates powers into many parts and each part represents a different set of interests, then liberty can be preserved by giving minorities the opportunity to protect themselves from tyrannical majorities. The many compromises at the Constitutional Convention produced this kind of separation of powers that set competing interests against one another. The interests of big states, small states, northerners, southerners, commercial entrepreneurs, farmers, property owners, and debtors were all woven into the constitutional fabric.

In the two centuries that followed, the main lines of conflict have changed. People no longer worry much about divisions between big and small states or differences between commerce and agriculture. The country today has quite different ethnic, gender, cultural, income, and generational issues to resolve. But the Constitution still gives the many different groups and interests clear opportunities to voice their concerns.

Constitutional Ambiguity: A Virtue   The very ambiguities embedded in the Constitution have also been a plus. Written as compromises among conflicting interests, such vague phrases as "necessary and proper" and "supreme Law of the Land" have had the elasticity necessary to accommodate powerful social and political forces that the founders could not have anticipated. Over the centuries, the Supreme Court has interpreted ambiguous constitutional phrases in ways that have allowed the Constitution to remain relevant to the issues of the day. In subsequent chapters we shall discuss ways in which the compromises of 1787 have been redefined and given new meaning in response to changing political circumstances.

The Constitution's extraordinary adaptability over a prolonged period of time testifies to the framers' stunning accomplishment. Although the United States is often thought of as a relatively new country, its governing arrangements have remained intact for much longer than those in most other countries. Of all the great industrial democracies, only the British system comes close to enjoying basic governing arrangements that date back as far as those of the United States. And even the democratic features of British government are newer than those of the United States. Not until 1867 did most British men get the right to vote.

INTERNATIONAL COMPARISON

Constitution-Making in Iraq

After the U.S.-led overthrow of Saddam Hussein's government in 2003, Iraqis were faced with the daunting task of setting up a democratic system of government. After a brief period of rule by a U.S. administrator and an appointed "governing council," Iraqis set to work in spring 2004 to create a lasting constitution. They came up with a system that was similar in many respects to that of the United States. It included protections of fundamental rights, as well as a federal system of government, for example. As in the case of the U.S. Constitution, the Iraqi constitution had to secure the approval of voters, which it did in October 2005. Despite superficial similarities between the United States and Iraqi constitutions, however, the situation in Iraq is very different from that which faced the U.S. in its early days. Each of these differences may affect whether the constitution ultimately succeeds or fails.

1. The U.S. Constitution was written by revolutionary leaders who had won the country's independence. In Iraq, a dictatorship was overthrown by an outside power. Some Iraqis also questioned whether exiles who had not been in the country for years should be included in the process of rebuilding the nation.

2. George Washington was revered as a military hero. There is no such consensus choice for a leader in Iraq. Ayad Allawi, leader of Iraq's interim government, lost the presidency after the first Iraqi election in 2005.

3. In the United States, brief uprisings such as Shays' Rebellion, while alarming, were quickly quelled. In Iraq, an ongoing anti-U.S. insurgency has sought to disrupt the reconstruction efforts.

4. While there were religious and cultural differences in the early United States, the authors of the constitution were willing to compromise on them. In Iraq, religious differences between Sunni and Shiite Muslims, as well as cultural differences between Kurds and other Iraqis, were so intense as to threaten the stability of the new government.

5. In the early United States, women were excluded from politics. In Iraq, the 2005 constitution prohibits gender discrimination, although many women worried that this guarantee would be weakened by traditional interpretations of religious law.

- *In light of the experience in Iraq, do you believe that the success of the United States constitution was mostly due to careful planning or mostly due to favorable circumstances?*

Source: Ellen Knickmeyer, "Iraqi Women See Little But Darkness," *Washington Post*, October 15, 2005, p. A14.

Most other countries have much newer constitutions. Iraq struggled with drafting a new constitution in 2004 (see the accompanying *International Comparison*). The latest Russian constitution was adopted in 1993. The current Spanish constitution was approved in 1978, the French constitution dates back only to 1958, the Danish to 1953, and the German, Italian, and Japanese constitutions to the late 1940s.

Comparing Constitutions

The Stain of Slavery Despite everything positive that can be said for the Constitution, the stain of slavery remains indelible. The Constitution validated the slave trade and stated that each slave could be counted as three-fifths of a person. The Constitution also explicitly required free states to return escaped slaves to the place from which they had fled.

Dividing and checking concentrations of power prevented the tyranny of the majority. But it also prevented a majority from undoing the tyranny of slavery. By denying the national government the capacity to bring slavery peacefully to an end, separation of powers helped perpetuate the slave system at a time when the practice was disappearing throughout the rest of the world. Perhaps it is too much to ask of any constitution that it provide the tools for resolving what had become an intractable problem. Perhaps it was, as Abraham Lincoln once said, only providential that "every drop of blood drawn with the lash shall be paid by another drawn with the sword."[52] It is not easy to imagine how the delegates to the Constitutional Convention could have designed a constitution that would have both freed slaves and won ratification by the voters of 1788.

Chapter Summary

The colonists who settled the eastern coast of North America established incomplete but meaningful rules of democracy through such institutions as the Mayflower Compact and elected colonial assemblies. These democratic institutions were reinforced by the spread of philosophical ideals during the Revolutionary War. Of critical importance was the concept that legitimate governments get their power from the consent of the governed. This principle formed the basis for the U.S. Constitution.

The Constitution was written to rectify difficulties the country experienced under the Articles of Confederation. The national government could not raise its own army, levy its own taxes, or regulate commerce among the states. Many leaders believed the country was too weak to fend off potential threats from Britain, Spain, and France.

When drafting a new Constitution designed to address needs unmet by the Articles of Confederation, the delegates to the Constitutional Convention designed a new basic law acceptable to the voters who were asked to ratify it. As a result, they prepared a document built both on their own colonial experience and on political theories popular at the time. They also incorporated many of the ideals expressed during the revolutionary struggle against King George III.

The Constitution curbed the powers of state governments, gave Congress additional authority, created a presidency of limited powers, and established a Supreme Court as the head of the judicial system. By dividing power between the states and the national government and by further dividing the power of the national government among the legislative, executive, and judicial branches, the Constitution provided an enduring system of limited government well designed to protect the liberties of the citizens.

To win ratification of the Constitution by voters in all parts of the country, the delegates to the Constitutional Convention had to reach many compromises. Congress was given not general power but a set of specific powers, along with the capacity to do anything "necessary and proper" to carry out these specific powers. Differences of opinion between delegates from big and small states were resolved by creating a Senate that gave equal representation to all states and a House of Representatives wherein states were represented in proportion to their population. Presidents were selected via a complicated two-stage system, which included a cumbersome electoral college arrangement. The Supreme Court was neither given nor denied the power of judicial review. Differences between the North and South were settled via a compromise: preserving the slave trade for 20 years and counting each slave as three-fifths of a person for purposes of representation.

The convention delegates erred in not including a Bill of Rights in the Constitution. But during the ratification campaign, Anti-Federalists insisted on, and the Federalists finally agreed to, 10 amendments to the Constitution that became known as the Bill of Rights. Although the procedures for amending the Constitution are complicated, 17 additional amendments have been approved since the Bill of Rights was drafted, and 13 of these have shifted American democracy in a popular direction.

Key Terms

advice and consent, p. 41
Annapolis Convention, p. 37
Anti-Federalists, p. 27
Articles of Confederation, p. 34
Bill of Rights, p. 44
checks and balances, p. 45
colonial assembly, p. 28
colonial council, p. 28
Connecticut Compromise, p. 39
Constitution, p. 27
Declaration of Independence, p. 30
divine right, p. 28

electoral college, p. 42
Federalist Papers, p. 45
Federalists, p. 27
First Continental Congress, p. 30
judicial review, p. 42
majority, p. 41
Mayflower Compact, p. 28
necessary and proper clause, p. 40
New Jersey Plan, p. 38
Patriots, p. 30
patronage, p. 28
proprietary colony, p. 28

royal colony, p. 28
Second Continental Congress, p. 30
separation of powers, p. 32
Shays' Rebellion, p. 35
Stamp Act Congress, p. 29
stamp tax, p. 29
supremacy clause, p. 43
taxation without representation, p. 29
three-fifths compromise, p. 43
Tories, p. 30
Virginia Plan, p. 38
Whigs, p. 33

Suggested Readings

Of General Interest

Dahl, Robert. *How Democratic Is The American Constitution?* New Haven: Yale University Press, 2003. A critical look at the Constitution from one of the country's most eminent political scientists.

The Federalist Papers. New York: Signet Classic (New American Library), 2003. Powerful defense of the proposed constitution by Alexander Hamilton, James Madison, and John Jay under the pseudonym Publius.

Johnson, Michael P. *Reading the American Past, Selected Historical Documents, Volume I* (to 1877) and *Volume II* (from 1865). New York: Bedford/St. Martin's, 2004 (Volume I) and 2002 (Volume II). Collection of key primary documents in American history.

McCullough, David. *1776.* New York: Simon & Schuster, 2005. Readable account of one key year of the Revolutionary War.

Rakove, Jack. *Original Meanings: Politics and Ideas in the Making of the Constitution.* New York: Random House, 1996. Pulitzer Prize-winning examination of the ideologies and political factors behind the drafting of the Constitution.

Storing, Herbert J., ed. *The Anti-Federalist.* Chicago: University of Chicago Press, 1986. Selection of Anti-Federalist writings.

Focused Studies

Bailyn, Bernard. *The Origins of American Politics.* New York: Knopf, 1968. Identifies the sources of the American Revolution in colonial thought and practice.

Beard, Charles A. *An Economic Interpretation of the Constitution of the United States.* New York: Free Press, 1913. Interprets the writing of the Constitution as an effort by the wealthy to protect their property rights.

Elkins, Stanley, and Eric McKitrick. *The Age of Federalism.* New York: Oxford University Press, 1993. Authoritative account of political life during the first decade after the adoption of the Constitution.

Hartz, Louis. *The Liberal Tradition in America.* New York: Harcourt, 1955. A difficult but rewarding book that describes the distinctive quality of the American political tradition.

Roche, John P. "The Founding Fathers: A Reform Caucus in Action." *American Political Science Review* 55 (December 1961): 799–816. Identifies the election connection at the Constitutional Convention.

Wood, Gordon S. *The Radicalism of the American Revolution.* New York: Knopf, 1992. Portrays the unleashing of a democratic ideology during the struggle for independence.

On the Web

In this chapter, we examined the events that led to the drafting of the U.S. Constitution and the political struggles surrounding its ratification.

www.archives.gov/national_archives_experience/constitution.html
The text of the Constitution appears in the Appendix, and a high-resolution digital picture of the document itself is available at the National Archives and Records Administration Web site.

www.earlyamerica.com
The early American colonists brought with them traditional European ideas and forms of government. They also developed new ways of thinking by adapting these concepts to their own new world experiences. To learn more about the colonists, visit the Web site.

www.utm.edu/research/iep/l/locke.htm
www.utm.edu/research/iep/h/hobbes.htm
To learn more about one of the major political theories that influenced colonial thought, see the Internet Encyclopedia of Philosophy entries on John Locke and Thomas Hobbes.

www.pbs.org/ktca/liberty/
For a comprehensive account of the Revolutionary War, including timelines, accounts of battles, and biographies of key figures, see the companion Web site to the PBS *Liberty!* series on the American Revolution.

www.yale.edu/lawweb/avalon/federal/fed.htm
The Avalon Project at Yale Law School provides a transcription of all 85 *Federalist Papers*, which can be searched by keyword.

www.usconstitution.net/constam.html
www.usconstitution.net/constamfail.html
As this chapter shows, the Constitution has been repeatedly amended, but this is a difficult and time-consuming process. To view a list of proposed amendments to the Constitution, go to the Web site. You can also go to see a list of amendments that did not make it through the approval process.

Election Voices

The Politics of the Death Penalty

Excessive bail shall not be required, nor excessive fines imposed, nor cruel and unusual punishments inflicted.

—Constitution, Amendment VIII

THE ISSUE

Is the death penalty a just and legitimate punishment for the most heinous of crimes? Or is it an unworkable violation of the Constitution's ban on "cruel and unusual punishment"?

Timothy McVeigh Does the example of Timothy McVeigh demonstrate that the death penalty is justified?

Background

In drafting his proposed bill of rights in 1789, James Madison relied in many respects on previous such declarations. In the case of what would become the Eighth Amendment, he lifted text almost verbatim from the English Bill of Rights of a century earlier, which said, "[E]xcessive bail ought not to be required, nor excessive fines imposed; nor cruel and unusual punishments inflicted." That pronouncement had been drafted in response to the reign of the widely hated King James II, whose enemies were sometimes "hanged, cut down before death, disemboweled, beheaded, and hacked to pieces."[1] For those who wonder what the founders meant by "cruel and unusual," this gruesome punishment would surely fit the bill.

But what about the modern death penalty? Although the number of people executed in the United States is lower now than it was in the 1930s, it has increased since the 1970s, when several Supreme Court decisions made it clearer what kinds of capital-punishment statutes would survive legal scrutiny (see Figure 1). As of 2006, 38 states provide for a penalty of death for the most serious crimes, and criminals may be sentenced to death under federal law for crimes such as treason, grave drug offenses, terrorism, and, under extreme circumstances, murder.[2] In 2005, 60 convicted criminals were put to death, and about 3,400 prisoners sat on "death row," awaiting execution.[3]

Proponents of the death penalty argue that capital punishment is the best way to deter heinous crimes. As George W. Bush put it, "I support the death penalty because I believe, if administered swiftly and justly, capital punishment is a deterrent against future violence and will save other innocent lives."[4] Proponents also claim that it offers closure to victims or their relatives. After serial killer Ted Bundy was executed in 1989, the father of one of his victims said "People said I even looked different. It took the black cloud out of my perspective."[5] Similarly, when Timothy McVeigh received his death sentence in 2001 for killing 168 people in the Oklahoma City bombing, few observers shed tears, and many surviving victims and family members expressed relief.

But opponents argue that although it is perhaps not so abhorrent as the excesses of James II, the modern death penalty constitutes cruel and unusual punishment. One of the most eloquent critics of the death penalty, Supreme Court Justice William Brennan, argued that "the state, even as it punishes, must treat its citizens in a manner consistent with their intrinsic worth as human beings—a punishment must not be so severe as to be degrading to human dignity."[6]

In recent years, some anti-death-penalty groups have achieved success with a more practical approach, focusing on allegedly flawed state death penalty systems. Legislatures and governors in Maryland, Illinois, and New Jersey have halted the use of the death penalty, at least temporarily, in the face of evidence that poor and minority defendants are more likely to

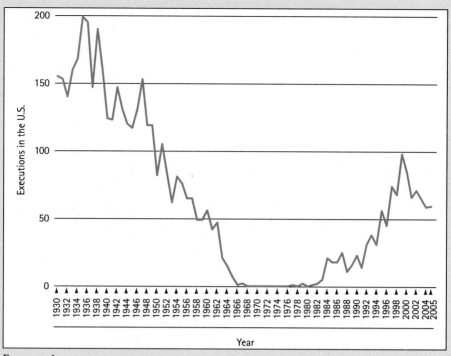

FIGURE 1

Executions in the U.S. 1930–2005

• *Why do you think executions were more common in the 1930s than today?*

Source: U.S. Department of Justice, Bureau of Justice Statistics, *Capital Punishment 2004* (November 2005).

be wrongly convicted.[7] "The death penalty is typically about the poor, victims of child abuse, [and] people who had bad attorneys," said one expert. "If the only people on death row were the Bundys and McVeighs, the whole debate would be very, very different."[8]

The Death Penalty and Elections

Sensing that a majority of the public supports capital punishment, most politicians adopt that perspective as well. Both Bill Clinton and George W. Bush presided over controversial executions as governors of their respective states during their campaigns for president, and the Bush administration's Justice Department made a clear effort to increase the use of the federal death penalty.[9] Large majorities of voters continue to be in favor of the death penalty for murder (see Figure 2).

Opposing Viewpoints on the Death Penalty

Against the Death Penalty

Opponents of capital punishment make two types of arguments. The first is that the death penalty in any form is fundamentally immoral:

"We oppose capital punishment not just for what it does to those guilty of horrible crimes but for what

it does to all of us as a society. Increasing reliance on the death penalty diminishes all of us and is a sign of growing disrespect for human life. We cannot overcome crime by simply executing criminals, nor can we restore the lives of the innocent by ending the lives of those convicted of their murders. The death penalty offers the tragic illusion that we can defend life by taking life."

—United States Conference of Catholic Bishops, "A Good Friday Appeal to End the Death Penalty," April 2, 1999

A second argument is that the death penalty, as applied, violates civil rights and liberties by being levied against certain groups more than others:

"Minorities and the poor often cannot pay for adequate and competent [legal] representation. They cannot afford 'dream teams' who negotiate with prosecutors to eliminate the possibility of a death sentence before a trial begins . . . . Innocent people are often unable to adequately address their legal problems with definitive evidence of their innocence."

—Rep. Jesse L. Jackson Jr. (D-IL), *CQ Researcher*, November 16, 2001

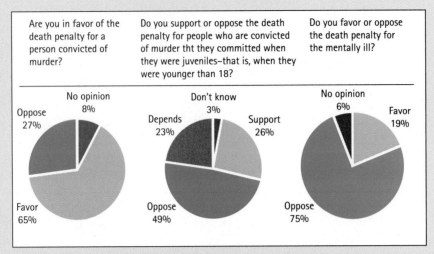

Are you in favor of the death penalty for a person convicted of murder?

Oppose 27%

No opinion 8%

Favor 65%

Do you support or oppose the death penalty for people who are convicted of murder tht they committed when they were juveniles–that is, when they were younger than 18?

Depends 23%

Don't know 3%

Support 26%

Oppose 49%

Do you favor or oppose the death penalty for the mentally ill?

No opinion 6%

Favor 19%

Oppose 75%

FIGURE 2

Most Americans Favor the Death Penalty, with Reservations

• *Should public opinion about the death penalty influence how the Supreme Court rules on the issue?*

Sources: Pew Research Center Poll, March 8–12, 2006; ABC News Poll, December 10–14, 2003; and Gallup Poll, May 6–9, 2002.

For the Death Penalty

Death penalty critics do not have a monopoly on moral argument. Defenders of capital punishment appeal to justice as well:

> "If a man steals your bicycle and society allows him to keep and ride around on that bicycle, most of us would find that profoundly unjust. Why, then, is it just to allow everyone who steals a life to keep his own? . . . [A]llowing all murderers to keep their lives diminishes the worth of human life. The way society communicates what it thinks about a crime is by the punishment it metes out."
>
> —Dennis Prager, "Death Penalty Guards What Is Valued Most," *Milwaukee Journal–Sentinel*, June 9, 2001

They also argue that practical problems with state and federal systems are of minor significance and are being overcome:

> "With the average time consumed by appeals between sentencing and execution now at about 10 years, and with the arrival of DNA testing . . . , the likelihood of wrongful executions is less than ever . . . . Compelled to administer justice in an imperfect world, we should not allow a utopian yearning for perfect certainty to render us moral eunuchs."
>
> —Eugene H. Methvin, "Death Penalty Is Fairer Than Ever," *Wall Street Journal*, May 10, 2000

What Do Americans Believe?

A majority of Americans appear to agree, more or less, with the voter who advised one pollster, "I'll tell you where I stand on the death penalty: right next to the switch!"[10] In 2006, 65 percent of Americans said that they favored the death penalty for those convicted of murder, and this number has remained high for many years.[11]

Nevertheless, when pollsters ask voters more complex questions, Americans' positions seem more conditional. Fully three-quarters of respondents oppose the death penalty for the mentally ill, and nearly half say they oppose the death penalty for minors (see Figure 2).

Is the Death Penalty Constitutional?

In 1972 the Supreme Court ruled in *Furman v. Georgia* that the death penalty, as it was then being applied in the states, violated the Constitution's guarantee against cruel and unusual punishment. The decision was confusing because each justice wrote a separate opinion, but the view of the majority seemed to be that existing death penalty laws were too likely to be unfairly applied across racial and income groups.[12]

States struggled for several years to rewrite their laws, and in the meantime they refrained from executing criminals, as Figure 1 illustrates. Then, in 1976, the Court ruled that a new Georgia law that included procedural safeguards against arbitrary executions did not violate the Constitution.[13] Since then, states have modeled their systems on this law, and the use of capital punishment has increased.

In 2002 and 2005 the Supreme Court issued three important rulings on capital punishment that have altered the way states administer the death penalty, but did not diverge from majority public opinion on the issue. First, in 2002 it ruled that juries—not judges—must be responsible for deciding whether to apply the death penalty in any given case. Second, that same year it declared that the execution of mentally retarded criminals constitutes cruel and unusual punishment. Third, in 2005 the Court banned the death penalty for those who committed crimes when they were under 18.[14] In the latter two cases, the Court cited evidence that a "national consensus" existed that the death penalty was a "disproportionate punishment" for minors and the mentally ill.[15]

What Do You Think?

1. Should the constitutional guarantee of no cruel and unusual punishment protect criminals from being executed, or does it apply only to sadistic violence such as that practiced by James II?

2. What standard should officials use to determine what constitutes cruel and unusual punishment?

3. Regardless of which position you take on the death penalty, which types of arguments are more convincing to you—moral arguments or practical arguments? Why?

4. Is the Supreme Court shaping public opinion on this question, or is public opinion affecting court decisions?

The death penalty is a subject of heated national debate. To conscientiously investigate this controversial issue and the arguments for and against, be sure to go to the Web sites of both those groups that are in favor of the death penalty and those groups that are opposed. In your opinion, which Web site(s) presents the most convincing argument?

[1]Barry Latzer, Death Penalty Cases: Leading U.S. Supreme Court cases on Capital Punishment (Boston, MA: Butterworth-Heinemann, 1998), p. 2.

[2]"Facts About the Death Penalty," Death Penalty Information Center, May 12, 2006, http://www.deathpenaltyinfo.org/FactSheet.pdf, accessed May 25, 2006; for more details on the federal death penalty, see *The Federal Death Penalty System: A Statistical Survey, 1988–2000* (Washington, DC: U.S. Department of Justice, September 12, 2000), available at http://www.usdoj.gov/dag/pubdoc/dpsurvey.html, accessed July 15, 2002.

[3]Amnesty International, "Facts and Figures About the Death Penalty," March 2002, available at http://web.amnesty.org/pages/deathpenalty-facts-eng, accessed May 25, 2006.

[4]Quoted in John Aloysius Farrell, "Lethal Dilemma: Five of the Prisoners Scheduled for Execution in Texas Early Next Year Will Highlight Gov. George W. Bush's Death Penalty Role," *Boston Globe,* December 19, 1999: p. A1.

[5]Lois Romano, " 'It Took the Black Cloud Out'; Families of Murder Victims Find Some Peace After Executions," *Washington Post,*August 8, 1996: p. A19.

[6]*Gregg v. Georgia,* 428 U.S. 153 (1976).

[7]Maryland halted executions from 2002 to 2003; Illinois from 2000 to the present (2006), New Jersey in 2006. See "Uncertain Justice: Efforts to Determine Whether a State has Executed an Innocent Man Reflect the Country's Growing Unease with Capital Punishment," *Houston Chronicle,* January 24, 2006, p. B8.

[8]Michael Radelet, quoted in Michael Kranish, "McVeigh Case Defies Views on Death in General, Support for Executions Down," *Boston Globe,* June 11, 2001:p. A1.

[9]J. M. Lawrence, "AG Death Penalty Push Adds Up to Trouble," *Boston Herald,* October 17, 2004.

[10]Farrell.

[11]Gallup poll, June 2, 2004.

[12]*Furman v. Georgia,* 408 U.S. 238 (1972).

[13]*Gregg v. Georgia.*

[14]The three cases were: *Ring* v. *Arizona* 536 U.S. 584 (2002) (juries, not judges must decide on death penalty); *Atkins* v. *Virginia* 536 U.S. 304 (2002) (execution of mentally ill prohibited); and *Roper* v. *Simmons* 543 U.S. 551 (2005) (death penalty for minors prohibited).

[15]Quotes are from *Roper* v. *Simmons* 543 U.S. 551

CHAPTER 3

★ ★ ★ ★ ★ ★ ★ ★ ★ ★ ★

Federalism: Division of Power Among National, State, and Local Governments

CHAPTER OUTLINE

The Politics of Katrina

"I have no idea where my 2-year-old son is," Nicole Williams, a new arrival to Houston's Astrodome, was trying to enlist the help of the media. On her tee-shirt she had written "Please help me find my family." Not long before, she explained, she and four relatives had gathered with thousands of other displaced New Orleans residents at the interchange of Interstate 10 and Causeway Boulevard for evacuation. After she boarded a bus bound for Texas, Williams realized to her dismay that her family would not be allowed to join her. Nor did state troopers allow her to disembark. Now, like countless other victims of Hurricane Katrina, she had to cope not only with the consequences of the winds and floods, but also with a haphazard and disorganized federal, state, and local government response.[1]

Hurricane Katrina roared ashore near New Orleans on August 29, 2005. The scale of the disaster that followed in Louisiana, Mississippi, and Alabama is difficult to comprehend. At least 1,300 people lost their lives,[2] 1.5 million were displaced, hundreds of thousands were thrown out of work, and estimates of property damage approximated $100 billion.[3]

Government at all levels had fair warning that such an event was possible. For years, experts had called attention to the fact that New Orleans, with many below-sea-level neighborhoods protected by an elaborate system of levees and canals, was particularly vulnerable to a large hurricane. Disappearing wetlands in the Mississippi delta had left the city even more exposed to the devastation that a major storm could bring.[4] Walter Maestri, a local emergency management official, said in 2001 that "Even though I have to plan for it, I don't even want to think about the loss of life a huge hurricane would cause."[5]

The 2005 storm was devastating, but what shocked most Americans was the seeming incapacity of all levels of government to respond to the calamity. For days, chaos and lawlessness gripped the city as thousands of increasingly desperate disaster victims waited for rescue in the Superdome, at the city Convention Center, at the I-10 cloverleaf, in hospitals and nursing homes, and on the roofs of their houses. Whatever plans each level of government had made for such a contingency seemed to be dependent on another level of government's bearing most of the burden. New Orleans Mayor Ray Nagin said

that city had hoped to "Get people to higher ground and have the feds and the state airlift supplies to them—that was the plan, man."[6] Louisiana Governor Kathleen Blanco argued that the state lacked capacity to respond without significant federal assistance. As her chief of staff put it, "This was a bigger natural disaster than any state could handle by itself, let alone a small state and a relatively poor one."[7] Still, Congressional investigators found that state and local governments were too slow to evacuate, had inadequate plans for sheltering evacuees, and suffered from poor coordination and communication.[8]

The federal government's own curiously flat-footed response compounded the problem. The Federal Emergency Management Agency (FEMA), which had recently made a difficult transition to the new Department of Homeland Security, was slow to realize how serious the disaster was, and its bureaucratic requirements held up the arrival of trailers, helicopters, and rescue personnel to the affected area.[9] President Bush himself appeared to have received poor advice in the disaster aftermath, and FEMA director Michael Brown had not even received the required training to act as a federal "incident management" coordinator.[10] For his part, Brown (who was fired in the wake of the disaster) blamed the delayed response on bickering between the state and the city. "I very strongly, personally regret," Brown told Congress, "that I was unable to persuade Governor Blanco and Mayor Nagin to sit down, get over their differences and work together."[11]

Disaster planning and response have always been a joint effort between all levels of government. States and cities serve as critical "first responders" in times of crisis, but their limited resources mean that they must work smoothly with the national government and rely on federal largesse when they are overwhelmed. Hurricane Katrina shook the faith of the public and many policymakers that this process was working effectively. As Senator Susan Collins (R–ME) put it, "If our system did such a poor job when there was no enemy . . . how would the federal, state and local governments have coped with a terrorist attack that provided no advance warning and that was intent on causing as much death and destruction as possible?"[12]

MAKING THE CONNECTION

In this chapter we consider the divisions of authority between states and the federal government, called federalism, as well as the divisions of responsibility between states and cities. A disaster such as Hurricane Katrina highlights many important questions about how different levels of government function and interact. In the pages that follow, you will learn about how the contemporary debate over federalism relates to historical debates, from the time of the ratification of the Constitution, to the Civil War, to major Supreme Court rulings in the twentieth century. You will also learn how Congress influences the nature of federalism through its power to spend money, and how electoral forces and political conflicts have shaped American federalism.

The Federalism Debate: It's New But It's Old

Federalism is defined in terms of **sovereignty**—that is, fundamental governmental authority. **Federalism** divides sovereignty between at least two different levels. In the United States, the fundamental units are the national government and the state governments, and each has the power to act independently of the other. For a democratic government to be called a federal system, each fundamental level of government must have:

1. Its own set of elected officials;
2. Its own capacity to raise revenues by means of taxation;
3. Independent authority to pass laws regulating the lives of its citizens.

Local governments, such as cities, counties, towns, and school districts, are also important institutions of government in the United States, but they are not fundamental units in the U.S. federal system in the same way that the national and state governments are. According to a long-standing legal doctrine known as **Dillon's rule** (after the nineteenth-century Iowa judge John Dillon), local governments are, in legal terms, mere "creatures of the state." A state legislature can, at any time, alter the boundaries of any local government, expand or narrow its power, or abolish it altogether. Because local governments are by law secondary, we set them aside for the moment and begin by discussing the relationships between states and the federal government.

Federalism in Context

As a principle of government, federalism has had a dubious history. Simón Bolívar, the great fighter for Venezuelan independence, once observed, "Among the popular and representative systems of government, I do not approve of the federal system: It is too perfect; and it requires virtues and political talents much superior to our own."[13] Like Bolívar, many political leaders have been skeptical that federalism would work in practice, a position that has led the vast majority of countries in the world to have **unitary governments**, in which all authority is held by a single, national government. In unitary arrangements, regional and local governments are simply administrative outposts of the national government. In Britain, for example, Parliament has the power

sovereignty
Fundamental governmental authority.

federalism
Division of sovereignty between at least two different levels of government.

Dillon's rule
Legal doctrine that local governments are mere creatures of the state.

unitary government
System under which all authority is held by a single, national government.

Great Britain and the United States: Unitary and Federal Governments

In Great Britain, which has a unitary government, the national government (Parliament) can reorganize regional and local governments whenever it wishes. In 1998, to put into effect a peace agreement reached between warring factions within the Catholic and Protestant communities in Northern Ireland, the British Parliament reorganized the government of Northern Ireland, granting it an autonomous assembly. Parliament has also created assemblies for Scotland and Wales. But Parliament, if it so desires, can at any time eliminate the regional governments of Wales, Scotland, and Northern Ireland, and it can pass legislation to override their policies. As it is, the new assemblies have power only over such "secondary" policy areas as health, agriculture, education, local government, and economic development. The Parliament of Wales has endured particular ridicule for spending inordinate amounts of time on inconsequential matters such as the location of member seats in the chamber (an issue that occasioned a tumultuous floor debate in July 2003). As the presiding officer put it, "What is the point of getting up in the morning, cleaning my teeth, washing and shaving, if you go to work in an institution like this?"

• *In the United States, which has a federal system of government, Congress cannot change the constitutional powers of states, reorganize state government, or change state boundaries without the state's consent. In your view, what are the advan-*

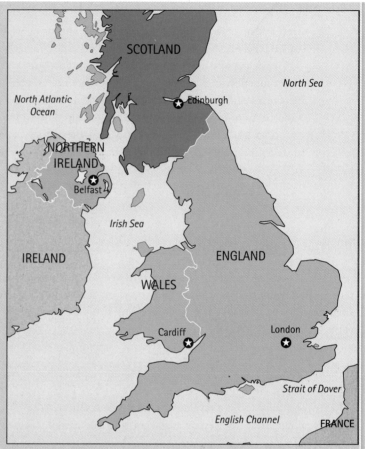

Britain: A Unitary Government
Regional and local boundaries can be changed by the British national government at any time.

tages and disadvantages of a federal system with regard to (1) political accountability, (2) efficient administration, and (3) cultural identity?

Source: Alison Rowat, "Giving New Voice to the Valleys; The Welsh traditionally treat devolution with a kind of jokey contempt. Can the Assembly change that?" *The Herald* (Glasgow), April 30, 2004, p. 13.

to abolish all local governments, a power it has often used to redesign the country's municipal and county governments. Even though Britain has granted some powers to local Scottish and Northern Irish parliaments, it could abolish or override these parliaments at any time. (See the accompanying *International Comparison*.)

Despite its unpopularity elsewhere, federalism proved to be essential to the founding and growth of the United States. The authors of the Constitution provided for a strong central government, but they preserved the sovereignty of the existing states to help win the ratification debate. As the United States added new territories in later decades, federalism allowed these territories to enter the union in an orderly way. Finally, because states are able to make their own policies, federalism has helped the

United States adapt to different cultural and economic conditions. As early as the 1830s, the keen French observer of American politics Alexis de Tocqueville noted, "One can hardly imagine how much [the] division of sovereignty contributes to the well-being of each of the states that compose the Union. In these small communities . . . all public authority [is] turned toward internal improvements."[14]

Comparing Federal and Unitary Systems

Long before federalism had gained international respectability, Americans had reached almost universal agreement on its worth. But the exact distribution of powers between the national and state governments has been a subject of great conflict over the course of the nation's history. Individual protagonists in this debate have often made forceful arguments based on fundamental principles of governance. But the larger political divisions over these issues have reflected the practical consequences of the distribution of power for policy and for elections. Political parties have gradually altered their positions over time as their bases of electoral strength and their policy concerns have shifted from national to local and back again.

Federalism and the Ratification of the Constitution

THE CONSTITUTION, TENTH AMENDMENT: *"The powers not delegated to the United States by the Constitution, nor prohibited by it to the States, are reserved to the States respectively, or to the people."*

The earliest debate over federalism divided the Federalists and the Anti-Federalists at the time the Constitution was being ratified. The Federalists (some say they should have been called Nationalists) were especially concerned with the military strength and economic vitality of the United States as a whole.[15] They favored a strong national government, arguing that centralized power was needed to overcome rivalries among the states and to defend the nation against foreign powers. The Anti-Federalists included many who were suspicious of the potential threat of national power to the independence of states and localities.[16] They wanted to limit the power of the central government, fearing that a powerful national government would trample the liberties of the people.

The Constitution represents a compromise between these competing groups. To appease the Federalists, who wanted a weak national government, the Constitution denied Congress a general legislative power, instead giving it only specific, delegated powers, such as the powers to levy taxes and to regulate interstate commerce. It also gave states independent authority, such as the responsibility for appointing officers in the militia (today known as the National Guard). In addition, it guaranteed existing state boundaries, saying that no state can be stripped of its territory or divided into parts without its consent. The Anti-Federalists also won (as part of the Bill of Rights) the Tenth Amendment, which reserved to the states and to the people all powers not delegated to the federal government.

To satisfy the Federalists, the Constitution gave Congress, in addition to its delegated powers, the authority to undertake all activities "necessary and proper" to carry out its enumerated powers. It also enacted a **supremacy clause** stating that national laws "shall be the supreme Law of the Land . . . any Thing in the . . . Laws of any State to the Contrary notwithstanding," a statement that comes close to saying (yet does not quite say) that only the national government is truly sovereign. Table 3.1 summarizes the allocation of powers between the national and state governments.

supremacy clause

Constitutional provision that says the laws of the national government "shall be the supreme Law of the Land."

TABLE 3.1
CONSTITUTIONAL DIVISION OF POWER BETWEEN NATIONAL AND STATE GOVERNMENTS

• *Why are both the national government and the state governments given vague grants of power (in the necessary and proper clause) and why are states given the right to exercise powers not granted to the national government?*

Powers Granted to the National Government	Powers Granted to the State Governments
Conduct foreign affairs	
Raise armies and declare war	Maintain state militias (the National Guard)
Regulate imports and exports	
Regulate interstate commerce	Regulate commerce within the state
Regulate immigration and naturalization	
Establish and operate federal court system	Establish and operate state court systems
Levy taxes	Levy taxes
Borrow money	Borrow money
Coin money	
Provide for the general welfare	
Make laws "necessary and proper" to accomplish the above tasks	Exercise powers not granted to the national government

Evolution of the Federalism Debate

Because the authors of the Constitution compromised on many of the differences between Federalists and Anti-Federalists, the issues raised at the time of the ratification campaign have never disappeared from American politics. Instead, the shape of American federalism has fluctuated over the course of American history, as the events in Figure 3.1 illustrate.

The driving force behind this fluctuation in the meaning of federalism has been political conflict between those who would benefit most from centralized power and those who would benefit most from local control. As the issues of the day changed, the coalitions favoring national power and local power shifted along with them. Changes in control of Congress and the presidency often have had direct and immediate effects on the federal system.

Political conflict over the meaning of federalism has also often found its way to the Supreme Court, as the federal government, states, and individuals have engaged in legal battles, hoping that the courts will validate friendly interpretations of the Constitution. Supreme Court decisions have had a fundamental impact because the Supreme Court has the power of **judicial review**, the authority to declare laws null and void on the grounds that they violate the Constitution (see Chapter 15). When the Supreme Court declares a law of Congress unconstitutional, it not only limits congressional power but also often expands the arena in which states are considered sovereign. When the Supreme Court declares state laws unconstitutional, their decisions often have the reverse effect—expanding national power at the expense of state sovereignty. In the pages that follow, we shall see how political conflict, elections, and the Supreme Court have often altered the shape of federalism.

SIMULATION

You Are a
Federal Judge

judicial review

Court authority to declare laws null and void on the grounds that they violate the Constitution.

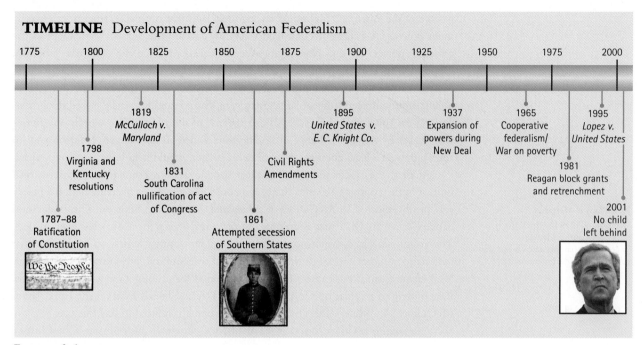

FIGURE 3.1

Development of American Federalism

Nationally elected leaders, state legislators, and courts have all shaped the evolution of American federalism.

Dual Sovereignty and Nullification

Much of the legal debate over federalism, both historical and contemporary, concerns the doctrine of **dual sovereignty**, which says that both the national and state governments have final authority over their own policy domains. As a legal and political doctrine, dual sovereignty is an American invention that challenges Thomas Hobbes's powerful argument stating there could be only one sovereign (see Chapter 2). If governmental power is divided, Hobbes said, the competing sovereigns will inevitably come into conflict with one another, driving the country into a state of civil war.

The authors of the *Federalist Papers* defended dual sovereignty by turning Hobbes's argument on its head. Whereas Hobbes said that divided sovereignty would lead to war, they argued that ensuring the division of power was the best way of preserving liberty. If power is concentrated in any one place, it can be used to crush individual liberty. Even in a democracy a **tyranny of the majority** (a suppression of rights by those voted into power by the majority) may arise—and that is the worst kind of tyranny because it is stifling, complete, and seemingly legitimate. Dividing power between the national and state governments reduces the possibility that any single majority will be able to control all centers of governmental power.

Dual-sovereignty theory was an entrenched part of constitutional understanding during the first decades after the adoption of the Constitution. Some supporters of states' rights thought state sovereignty so complete that they propounded the doctrine of **nullification**, which says that state legislatures can invalidate acts of Congress that threaten state or individual liberties. States first used this doctrine in 1798 in response to the

dual sovereignty
A theory of federalism saying that both the national and state governments have final authority over their own policy domains.

tyranny of the majority
Suppression of rights imposed by those voted into power by a majority.

nullification
A doctrine that says that states have the authority to declare acts of Congress unconstitutional.

passage of the Alien and Sedition Acts, national laws that outlawed criticism of government officials. A Federalist-controlled Congress enacted the legislation to suppress the
growing power of the Democratic–Republican Party, led by Thomas Jefferson.
Opposition newspaper editors were imprisoned, and even Vermont Congressman
Matthew Lyon was arrested and prosecuted under these laws. Invoking the doctrine of
nullification, outraged Jeffersonian legislators in Virginia and Kentucky passed resolutions
voiding the law within their states. Their defense of the right of free speech was praise-
worthy, yet by using the theory of nullification to defend free speech, Jefferson and his
allies proposed a legal doctrine that, six decades later, would help tear the country apart.

At first, the doctrine of nullification had no serious consequences for national
unity. On the contrary, the idea that states could undermine or overrule national policy
was firmly rejected in ***McCulloch v. Maryland***, a sweeping Supreme Court decision
handed down in 1819 that is among the most important the Court has ever made.[17]
The issue involved a dispute over the Bank of the United States, an institution that
national commercial interests thought was vital to economic prosperity but that many
local farmers, small businesses, and debtors blamed for causing a recent financial crisis.
Responding to popular opinion, the state of Maryland levied a tax on the bank. James
McCulloch, an officer of the bank's Maryland branch, refused to pay this tax.

A unanimous Court found in favor of McCulloch. In his opinion, Chief Justice
John Marshall dismissed Maryland's argument that the national government possessed
only those powers delegated to it by the sovereign states. Individual citizens, not the
states, were the source of national power, he wrote. "The government of the Union
. . . is, emphatically and truly, a government of the people. In form and in substance,
it emanates from them." Because the people were the source of the central government's authority, a state could not override a national law. Although Marshall admitted that Maryland's tax was not a direct attempt to negate a law, as the Virginia and
Kentucky resolutions had been, he said it was still unconstitutional because the "power
to tax involves the power to destroy."[18] If a state government could tax a federal
agency, then states could undermine the sovereignty of the federal government, just
as if they had asserted that a national law was null and void. In declaring this state law
unconstitutional, Marshall cast profound doubt on the power of the states to nullify
acts of Congress.

Despite the McCulloch decision, the doctrine of nullification was not dead. The
issue next arose shortly after the tumultuous 1828 election of Andrew Jackson as president. His vice-president, John Calhoun, formerly a senator from South Carolina, claimed
that states had the power to nullify federal laws. A controversy developed over a tariff (a
tax on imports) that northern manufacturers favored as a way of protecting the region's
industries from foreign competition. Southerners opposed the tariff, because they wanted
to sell their cotton to Europe and buy cheap manufactured products in return.

After winning the 1832 state legislative elections, Calhoun's supporters in South
Carolina called a special convention, which declared the tariff null and void in the state.
The state even threatened to secede from the Union if the federal government tried to
collect the tariff by force. President Jackson prepared to use the U.S. Army and Navy
to crush the dissidents, but cooler heads prevailed. Congress passed a lower tariff less
objectionable to southern interests, and South Carolina agreed to pay it.

Although the tariff was an important issue for the South, an even more important
and less tractable issue was slavery. Afraid that northerners would abolish slavery, south-

McCulloch v. Maryland
Decision of 1819 in which the
Supreme Court declared
unconstitutional the state's power to
tax a federal government entity.

**VISUAL
LITERACY**

Federalism and
Regulations

ern leaders continued to espouse the doctrine of nullification as well as the right to secede peacefully from the Union. The issue came to a head with the election of Abraham Lincoln in 1860. Lincoln was the candidate of the new Republican Party, which opposed the extension of slavery into the western territories and favored its eventual abolition. Seeing the Republicans as a direct challenge to slavery, white southerners invoked what they saw as their right of secession, and the United States experienced what Hobbes had most feared: a war between competing sovereigns. South Carolina, the state that had precipitated the tariff crisis, was the first to secede. Only after half a million soldiers had died and the southern countryside had been laid to waste was the doctrine of nullification finally repudiated. After the Civil War, it was clear that whatever dual sovereignty meant, it did not mean that state legislatures could declare null and void the decisions of the federal government.

The Supreme Court and the Meaning of Dual Sovereignty

Once the doctrine of nullification had been laid to rest, it was up to the federal courts, not state legislatures, to decide the constitutional meaning of dual sovereignty. For more than 60 years following the Civil War, the Supreme Court generally defended the sovereignty of the states against national power. While the war had settled the issue of whether states could secede, the Court preserved state autonomy in such areas as economic regulation and, distressingly, racial segregation (see Chapter 17). In the 1930s, after a political battle that threatened to change the structure of the Supreme Court, the Court began to side most often with those who argued for broader national authority. The Court soon interpreted the Constitution's commerce clause and necessary and proper clause, which define the boundaries of national power, as allowing much more federal intervention into areas that were previously the domains of the states. Since the mid-1990s, however, a more conservative Court has used a series of key cases to reassert states' rights under these clauses. The Court has also invoked the doctrine of state sovereign immunity, found in the Eleventh Amendment, to expand state authority in the federal system.

Federalism and the Supreme Court

The Commerce Clause and the Court-Packing Episode

CONSTITUTION, ARTICLE I: *"Congress shall have power . . . to regulate commerce . . . among the several states."*

In 1932, Democrat Franklin D. Roosevelt defeated Republican incumbent Herbert Hoover in a bitter presidential election that foreshadowed a period of expansion of federal power. Campaigning in the midst of the Great Depression, Roosevelt promised to use the power of the federal government to make the country prosperous again. He and his Democratic Party allies in Congress enacted a series of governmental policies known as the **New Deal**, a wide array of programs that expanded the power of the federal government for the purposes of stimulating economic recovery and creating a national safety net for those in need. Many Republicans opposed these New Deal policies, arguing that they violated long-standing principles of federalism.

A majority of the Supreme Court, appointed by previous presidents, felt that the Court was duty-bound to reject much of Roosevelt's New Deal. In several key cases, the Court struck down New Deal legislation because, in the Court's view, it exceeded

New Deal

Programs created by the Franklin Roosevelt administration that expanded the power of the federal government for the purpose of stimulating economic recovery and establishing a national safety net.

commerce clause

Constitutional provision that gives Congress power to regulate commerce "among the states."

the power of the national government under the Constitution's **commerce clause**, which gives Congress the power to regulate commerce among the states.

The courts have generally distinguished interstate (between-state) commerce, which Congress may regulate, from intrastate (within-state) commerce, which only the states can regulate. In the nineteenth century, intrastate commerce was defined as including all commerce that did not overtly cross state lines. Thus, for example, the Supreme Court in 1895 said, in *United States v. E. C. Knight Co.*, that Congress could not break up a monopoly that had a nationwide impact on the price of sugar, because the company that enjoyed the monopoly refined its sugar solely within the state of Pennsylvania.[19] The fact that the sugar was to be sold nationwide was said to be only "incidental" to its production.

The Supreme Court used this distinction to invalidate several key components of the New Deal. In the critical case of *Schechter Poultry Corp. v. U.S.*, for example, the Court declared unconstitutional the National Recovery Administration's regulation of economic activity inside individual states (see page 435 in Chapter 15). In trying to regulate the manner in which animals were slaughtered and sold within states, said the Court, Congress had gone beyond its authority to regulate interstate commerce.[20]

Democrats were furious at this and other decisions that restricted their ability to enact programs that they saw as necessary to combat the Depression. Roosevelt mocked the Court for using an outdated "horse-and-buggy definition of interstate commerce."[21] Never before had federalism placed the Supreme Court in such direct conflict with the president and Congress.

After his landslide reelection victory in 1936, Roosevelt believed he had the public mandate he needed to move against the Court. Early the following year, he surprised Congress with a proposal to add up to six new justices, one for each sitting justice older than 70. The resulting larger Court would be more efficient and more effective, argued the president. And—of course—it would be dominated by Roosevelt appointees. "The people are with me," FDR confidently told visitors to the White House.[22]

Many politicians and members of the public were uneasy with the president's proposal. They worried that the sudden increase in the size of the Court would upset the separation of powers between the branches of government. Roosevelt's court-packing scheme met stern opposition in Congress and was killed in the Senate Judiciary Committee.

Although Roosevelt lost the battle, he won the war. Less than two months after he announced his court-packing plan, Chief Justice Charles Evans Hughes and Justice Owen Roberts, who had previously voted to restrict federal power, changed their views. This time the issue involved the recently passed Wagner Act, a New Deal law that protected union organizers. Despite the fact that the new law regulated activities within a state, a Court majority, in a 5 to 4 vote, declared it constitutional. Chief Justice Hughes declared: "When industries organize themselves on a national scale, . . . how can it be maintained that their industrial labor relations constitute a forbidden field into which Congress may not enter?"[23] Relations between employers and their workers, once said to be local, were now found to be part of interstate commerce.

The change of heart by Hughes and Roberts has been called "the switch in time that saved nine." In fact, the court-packing episode both illustrates the Court's susceptibility to political pressure and represents a critical shift in the dominant conception of federalism. With new appointments to the Court by President Roosevelt, the definition of interstate commerce continued to expand. In 1942 a farmer violated crop quotas imposed under New Deal legislation by sowing 23 acres of wheat. The Court ruled the quota law a constitutional regulation of interstate commerce, even though the farmer was feeding all the wheat to his own livestock. The Court reasoned that the farmer, by not buying wheat and instead producing his own, was depressing the worldwide price of grain.[24] With such an expansive definition of interstate commerce, hardly anything could be characterized as simply local or beyond the scope of Congress to regulate.

This broad interpretation of the commerce clause remained unquestioned until 1995. That year, the Supreme Court considered the constitutionality of the Gun Free School Zones Act. Enacted in response to public concerns about high crime rates, this law made it a federal crime to carry unauthorized weapons near a public school.

In *U.S. v. Lopez*, a case involving a young man with no criminal record who foolishly brought a .38 caliber handgun to school, the Court said that Congress did not have the power to enact this law. State governments, said the Court, had the authority to regulate this type of activity. "We do not doubt," wrote Chief Justice Rehnquist, "that Congress has authority . . . to regulate numerous commercial activities that . . . affect the educational process. That authority, though broad, does not include the authority to regulate each and every aspect of local schools."[25]

Since *Lopez*, the Supreme Court has been more willing to place limits on Congress's ability to intervene in state and local affairs. In 2000, for example, the Court invalidated a law that gave victims of domestic violence the power to sue their attackers in federal courts. Gender motivated violence, the Court ruled, had little or nothing to do with interstate commerce.[26] The Court still has allowed Congress to regulate broadly when the activities at issue have something to do with commerce, however. For example, in 2005 the Supreme Court allowed Congress to override state laws allowing the use of medicinal marijuana, on the grounds that marijuana cultivation, like wheat cultivation, has "a substantial effect on supply and demand in the national market."[27]

VIDEO DEBATE

Contemporary Federalism

Marijuana—A Medical Necessity or an Illegal Drug?

This 67-year-old former paratrooper smokes medical marijuana at his home, in order to ease the pain of spinal cancer. He says that smoking the drug helps him sleep at night, has restored his appetite, and has reduced his need for expensive prescription drugs.

• *Should states or the federal government regulate drugs like marijuana?*

Necessary and Proper Clause

CONSTITUTION, ARTICLE I: *"Congress shall have power . . . to make all laws which shall be necessary and proper for carrying into Execution the . . . Powers vested by this Constitution in the government of the United States."*

necessary and proper clause

Constitutional clause that gives Congress the power to take all actions that are "necessary and proper" to the carrying out of its delegated powers. Also known as the elastic clause.

The delegated powers of Congress include those items specifically mentioned in the Constitution, such as the power to tax, borrow money, and establish a currency. The **necessary and proper clause** gives Congress the authority to "make all laws which shall be necessary and proper for carrying to execution" its delegated powers. Justice John Marshall first analyzed the words *necessary and proper* in the same decision that challenged the doctrine of nullification, *McCulloch v. Maryland.* Maryland argued that Congress had no authority to establish a national bank, because a bank was not *necessary* for Congress to carry out its delegated power to coin money; it was only a *convenient* way of doing so. But Justice Marshall rejected such an interpretation as annihilating Congress's ability to select an appropriate means to carry out a task.

"Let the end be legitimate," Marshall said. "Let it be within the scope of the Constitution, and all means which are appropriate, which are plainly adapted to that end, which are not prohibited, but consistent with the letter and spirit of the Constitution, are constitutional."[28] Since this decision, the courts have generally found that almost any means selected by Congress are "necessary and proper." As a result, the necessary and proper clause has come to be known as the *elastic clause*: Over the centuries it has been stretched to fit almost any circumstance.

Even though an elastic interpretation of the necessary and proper clause has given Congress broad powers, the Supreme Court said in 1992 that these powers are not without limit. Adding its voice to the rising political concern in Congress over increasing federal power, the Supreme Court, in *New York v. U.S.*, declared that Congress cannot give direct orders to states. Though discussed in the arcane language of dual sovereignty, this case involved one of the most modern of political issues: the disposal of radioactive waste.

Disposal of radioactive waste—even so-called "low-level" waste from medical research, radiation detection equipment, and cleaning materials in power plants—has become a particularly concerning political problem. Millions of cubic feet of such waste needs to be buried someplace where it cannot be disturbed for thousands of years.[29] The problem has become an elected official's nightmare: Something needs to be done, and there is no way of doing it without making some people extremely angry. Easily alarmed at the very word *radioactive,* citizens organize protests and demonstrations whenever a near-by area is mentioned as a potential radioactive dump. Everyone knows the stuff has to go somewhere, but everyone also says, "Not In My Back Yard." This is generally known as the *NIMBY problem.*

NIMBY problem

Everyone wants the problem solved, but "Not In My Back Yard."

After stewing fitfully over the NIMBY problem for several years, Congress discovered a politically painless solution: It required each state either to find an adequate burial site for its waste or to become legally responsible for any damages the waste might cause. Rather than making tough decisions themselves, Congress decided to place an unfunded mandate on governors and state legislatures.

As a result, the debate over domestic radioactive waste shifted to the states. In no state was the issue more hotly debated than in New York. Often, when state officials identified a potential dump, angry voters ran them off the site and burned them in effigy.[30] Under the pressure of the federal law, New York state officials decided to ignore the opposition and dump the waste in Cortland and Allegany Counties. But the elected boards for the two counties, to keep faith with county voters, filed a suit claiming that the federal law was unconstitutional. Justice Sandra Day O'Connor, writing for the majority of the Supreme Court, said Congress could not force states or local governments to bury their nuclear waste; such direct orders to a state violated its sovereignty.[31]

With the radioactive waste case, the old doctrine of dual sovereignty was clearly revived. All doubts seemed to vanish in 1997 when the Supreme Court invalidated a portion of a national gun control law that required local police to check the backgrounds of gun buyers. If such a law were allowed to stand, said the Court, it would "compromise the structural framework of dual sovereignty."[32] Even though the Court has marked out a new direction for American federalism, many observers now believe further movement in this direction will be slowed by the terrorist attacks of September 11, 2001, which underlined the need for a strong national government. Others argue that new appointees John Roberts and Samuel Alito are naturally sympathetic to dual sovereignty.

State Sovereign Immunity

CONSTITUTION, ELEVENTH AMENDMENT: *"The Judicial power of the United States shall not be construed to extend to any suit in law or equity, commenced or prosecuted against one of the United States . . . "*

The necessary and proper clause and the commerce clause give power to the national government, but the Eleventh Amendment, ratified in 1795, explicitly restricts it. Since the mid-1990s, the Supreme Court has used the Eleventh Amendment to reinforce, and in some cases expand, the concept of **state sovereign immunity**, a doctrine that says that states cannot be sued under federal law by private parties.

Whereas cases involving state sovereign immunity may seem arcane and technical, they can have wide-reaching implications because private lawsuits are sometimes the main means by which certain laws are enforced. For example, the Indian Gaming Regulatory Act of 1988 established rules for states to negotiate gambling regulations with local Native American tribes. If states negotiated in "bad faith," the act gave Indians the right to sue. But the Supreme Court said in 1996 that this portion of the act was unconstitutional.[33]

Similarly, the Americans With Disabilities Act of 1990 allowed disabled employees to sue their employers if they were mistreated because of their disabilities. But when breast cancer sufferer Patricia Garrett sued her employer—the state of Alabama—charging discrimination, the Supreme Court ruled that her lawsuit, too, was invalid. Because of their immunity, "[s]tates are not required . . . to make special accommodations for the disabled," wrote Chief Justice Rehnquist in his 2001 opinion.[34]

In 2002, the Court ruled that a cruise line could not seek relief from the Federal Maritime Commission on a complaint that one of its ships was denied a berth by the state-owned port of Charleston, South Carolina. In his majority opinion, Justice Thomas argued that South Carolina had a right to conduct its business free of federal interference, saying that "Dual sovereignty is a defining feature of our constitutional blueprint."[35]

state sovereign immunity
Legal doctrine, based on the Eleventh Amendment, that says states cannot be sued under federal law by private parties.

The doctrine of state sovereign immunity has the potential to create a broad range of independent power for states, but the Court is far from unanimous on its usefulness. Each major case on the issue since 1996 has divided the justices on a vote of 5 to 4, and some have written angry dissents. In 2003, the Court found that the Eleventh Amendment did not exempt states from being sued under the Family and Medical Leave Act, a law that requires employers to grant up to 12 weeks of unpaid leave to employees caring for a new child or seriously ill relative. Because the law was designed to ensure the civil rights of women (see Chapter 16), the Court found that Congress was within its constitutional authority to enact the law. The fate of the doctrine of state sovereign immunity may hinge on future presidential appointments to the Supreme Court.

Cooperative Federalism

marble-cake federalism
The theory that all levels of government can work together to solve common problems. Also known as *cooperative federalism*.

The commerce clause, the necessary and proper clause, and the doctrine of state sovereign immunity work to define the boundaries between the domains of the states and of the federal government. These provisions therefore establish a constitutional basis for dual sovereignty. The congressional power to tax and spend, on the other hand, provides the constitutional basis for what has become known as the theory of **cooperative federalism**, or **marble-cake federalism**. According to this theory, first propounded by political scientist Morton Grodzins, all levels of government should—and in fact do—perform all governmental functions together. Because the Supreme Court has established a broad interpretation of Congress's spending power, the most serious political conflicts over national powers to tax and spend have occurred not in courtrooms, but in Congress and the state legislatures. These battles have often revolved around the nature of federal grants to state and local governments.

Spending Clause

> CONSTITUTION, ARTICLE I: *"Congress shall have power . . . to lay and collect taxes, duties, imposts and excises, to pay the debts and provide for the . . . general welfare of the United States."*

spending clause
Constitutional provision that gives Congress the power to collect taxes to provide for the general welfare.

The **spending clause** grants Congress the power to collect taxes to provide for the general welfare. The New Deal Supreme Court considered the meaning of this clause when it ruled on the constitutionality of the social security program for senior citizens, which was enacted in 1935. A taxpayer challenged the program on the grounds that tax dollars were being spent for the specific welfare of the elderly, not for the general welfare. But the Supreme Court, now in tune with Roosevelt's enlarged conception of federal power, said it was up to Congress, not the Court, to decide whether any particular program was for the general welfare. "[T]he discretion belongs to Congress," said the Court, "unless the choice is clearly wrong."[36] So far, the Court has never found Congress "clearly wrong."

Not only did the Supreme Court refuse to restrict the purposes for which Congress could tax and spend money, but it also conceded to Congress the right to attach any reasonable regulation to the money it spends. In 1984 Congress provided a grant to state governments for highway maintenance but withheld some of the funding unless states raised the drinking age from 18 to 21. South Dakota challenged the constitutionality of this mandate on the grounds that teenage drunkenness had only a remote connection to road repair. The Supreme Court rejected this argument.[37] State sovereignty was not violated, the Court concluded, because any state could choose not to accept the money. The regulation proved effective, inasmuch as every state has now accepted its full share of federal dollars and has raised its drinking age to 21.

The congressional power to tax and spend has remained one of the broadest federal powers, because it allows Congress to attach whatever regulations it deems appropriate to the money it gives to states. Nevertheless, it is not beyond the realm of possibility that the Supreme Court could restrict this authority in its future decisions. In the South Dakota case, Chief Justice Rehnquist pointed out that "the spending power is of course not unlimited," and several judges have argued that the Court should begin to narrow its interpretation of the spending clause to safeguard some "sovereign rights" of the states.[38]

A Government of Shared Functions   Political scientist Morton Grodzins criticized proponents of dual sovereignty for viewing government as a layer cake, each level independent of and separate from the others.[39] He pointed out that Congress has established many programs in which the agencies established to operate them must work together with other levels of government, combining and intertwining their functions to such an extent that the intergovernmental system resembles a marble cake.

In all policy realms, Grodzins said, one finds many levels of government working together on similar tasks. For example, in the area of disaster planning and response, the national Federal Emergency Management Agency (FEMA) must coordinate its efforts with state offices of emergency preparedness as well as with local first responders such as police departments and rescue squads. As the Katrina case shows, this can often be difficult, but according to Grodzins, all levels of government should work together for three reasons:

1. Cooperative federalism is democratic. The involvement of all levels of government ensures that many different interests in society are represented.
2. Compromises are reached among officials elected by different constituencies. Federal officials listen to state and local officials, because the latter have influence with members of Congress. Similarly, state officials listen to community leaders, because to stay in office state legislators must pay attention to local needs.
3. Professional administrators have similar training and values, no matter what level of government they work for. Law enforcement officials have numerous things in common, whether they work for the FBI or the local police. Most educational administrators, whether federal, state, or local, were once schoolteachers.

The 1964 election of Lyndon Johnson, together with an overwhelming Democratic majority in Congress, provided an opportunity to test more fully Grodzins's theory of cooperative federalism. Over the next few years, Congress passed a broad range of legislation that greatly enlarged the number, size, and complexity of **intergovernmental grants,** programs funded in part by the federal government but administered by state and local governments. State and local governments are often required to provide matching funds for a program in order to receive the grant. The typical "match" is 50 percent of total costs, but it can be as much as 90 percent or as little as 10 percent. Intergovernmental grants have become a key feature of the federal system. In 1930 only $97.1 million was spent on intergovernmental grants to local governments.[40] As Figure 3.2 on page 78 indicates, by 1962 grants to state and local governments had grown to $51.9 billion, and by 1982 they had more than tripled to $175.5 billion. (Unless otherwise indicated, all amounts in this chapter are in 2005 dollars.)

intergovernmental grant
Grant from the national government to a state or local government.

Growth in the number and size of intergovernmental grants was facilitated by their popularity with most members of Congress. Many found they could profit handsomely from new projects begun in their home districts. As Senator Barry Goldwater said, "I don't care what the piece of equipment is—or how bad it is—if it's done in his state, the senator has to stand up and scream for it."[41] Such grants are often criticized as mere **pork barrel projects**—special legislative benefits targeted toward the constituents of particular members of Congress that have little or no general value.

Most grants are, of course, well received by the city or town lucky enough to get the money, and this goodwill can improve the chances of reelection for the members of Congress responsible for the grants. "I make no excuses for the fact that, representing the district that I do, I can get dollars for specific programs," said Representative José Serrano, Democrat of New York City.[42] In 2005, public interest groups criticized thousands of grants targeted at individual states and districts that were included in a major transportation bill. Funding for several bridges in Alaska came under severe scrutiny, especially when media reports indicated that one of them would connect a tiny town to a small island at the cost of $223 million.[43] Alaska's congressional delegation fought hard for the bridges, despite the negative publicity. Finally, the state's senators and representative agreed to a sort of compromise: the money would still go to Alaska, but could be used for any purpose—not just the controversial bridges.[44]

Categorical Grants

In the 1960s and 1970s, the theory of cooperative federalism was particularly well suited to the Democratic Party. It fit well with the Democrats' philosophy, and it was not difficult to pursue as a policy, because Democrats usually controlled Congress. Many Democrats saw federal grants as vehicles that could help the country address needs that state and local governments had long ignored. To ensure that funds were properly used, Democrats generally favored **categorical grants**—grants that include regulations that specify how the money is to be spent. Although some of these categorical grants fund basic government services, such as the construction of transportation and sanitation infrastructure, most have had social welfare purposes. Categorical grants provide compensatory education for those coming from disadvantaged backgrounds, fund special educational programs for the disabled, and train the unemployed. They provide housing for low- and moderate-income groups and food stamps for the poor. Such grants also subsidize rapid-transit operations to help reduce commuting costs.

The **War on Poverty**, a wide-ranging set of programs designed to enhance the economic opportunity of low-income citizens, became the most famous and controversial of all categorical grant programs. It was one of a series of initiatives by President Lyndon Johnson, dubbed the **Great Society**, that aimed to address social ills among the nation's poor, elderly, and minority communities. Enacted in 1964 at the height of the civil rights movement, the War on Poverty legislation required politicians and administrators not only to assist poor Americans, but to involve them in the policy making process as much as possible.

Several accomplishments of the War on Poverty remain evident more than four decades later. The popular Head Start program for preschoolers anticipated and paved the way for a nationwide system of child care and nursery school programs. Job Corps, a residential education and training program, paid off in better wages and employment

pork barrel projects
Special legislative benefits targeted toward the constituents of particular members of Congress.

categorical grants
Federal grants to a state and/or local government that impose programmatic restrictions on the use of funds.

War on Poverty
One of the most controversial of the Great Society programs, designed to enhance the economic opportunity of low-income citizens.

Great Society
Series of programs enacted under President Lyndon Johnson, designed to address social ills in the nation's poor, elderly, and minority communities.

prospects. Most notably, these antipoverty programs incorporated many minority leaders into the political process. From the ranks of the warriors on poverty emerged many minority mayors, state legislators, and members of Congress elected in the 1980s and 1990s.

Despite these achievements, the War on Poverty is better remembered for the warring factions that it generated than for its substantive results. An annual budget of just $24.3 billion was simply not capable of financing a "war" against poverty. In addition, efforts to coordinate local social services suffered from repeated dismal failures. Finally, most of the job search, worker readiness, summer job, and other short-term training programs had only limited long-term benefits.

The main political objection to the War on Poverty, however, was its emphasis on community mobilization. In many cities, poverty warriors antagonized local agencies and elected officials by encouraging protests, demonstrations, legal action, and minority electoral involvement. Local officials questioned why federal monies should be used to fund political opposition. Some blamed the program for the wave of civil violence that swept through American cities in the two years following its adoption. In 1974, Republican President Richard Nixon, who had campaigned against the War on Poverty, persuaded Congress to transfer its most popular components to other agencies and to shut down the remainder.

Head Start

More than four decades after the War on Poverty launched a variety of such initiatives, Head Start remains one of the most visible and successful early-intervention programs for disadvantaged preschoolers.

Problems of Implementation

The War on Poverty was only one of many categorical grant programs associated with the Great Society which came under tough scrutiny from those who studied their **implementation**—the way in which grant programs are actually administered at the local level. These arguments are important because they continue to be made about grant programs today. Public policy scholars gave three reasons for doubting that many intergovernmental grants were as effective as Grodzins had said:[45]

implementation
The way in which grant programs are administered at the local level.

1. National and local officials, serving different constituencies, often block and check one another, making it impossible to get much done. In 2004, for example, New Jersey's governor issued an order prohibiting companies with state contracts from contributing to state and local political campaigns. This reform measure broke federal transportation rules, which (in an effort to keep overall costs low) require state recipients of national grants to allow anyone—even campaign contributors—to bid for contracts. New Jersey risked losing $350 million in transportation grants. After a costly court battle, the state relented, withdrawing its policy.[46]

2. When many participants are involved, delays and confusion are almost inevitable. A 2004 study of Homeland Security grant money found that more than 80 percent of the $6.3 billion appropriated for terrorism preparedness had not yet been used—months or even years after it had been authorized by law.[47] As Massachusetts Governor Mitt Romney put it, "The standard grant process and purchasing procedures that exist in our country at all levels of government don't work terribly well if your objective is speed."[48]

3. Federal policy makers often raise unrealistic expectations by using exaggerated rhetoric, thereby guaranteeing disappointment. It was a mistake to equate the mid-1960s poverty programs with a "war" when only limited resources were available.

Three Levels of Government

President G.W. Bush confers with New Orleans Mayor Ray Nagin and Louisiana Governor Blanco several weeks after Hurricane Katrina devastated the city and its environs.

• *When time is of the essence, can all levels of the federal government cooperate effectively?*

These implementation theorists may have exaggerated the difficulty of getting different governments to cooperate. Most implementation studies focused on problems that federal grant programs had experienced during their first two or three years. Other studies have shown that many administrative problems diminished with the passage of time. For example, at first the federal compensatory education program stigmatized disadvantaged students by separating them from their classmates in order to make sure that federal funds were concentrated on the most needy. But once administrators determined that this requirement was counterproductive to education, they eliminated it.[49] As the Hurricane Katrina episode shows, however, sometimes different levels of government do not have the luxury of time. Under such circumstances, it makes sense to pay attention to the criticisms lodged by the implementation theorists.

Block Grants

Despite these more positive findings from recent research, the criticisms of categorical grants proved influential. To simplify federal policy, Congress replaced many categorical grants with **block grants**, intergovernmental grants with a broad set of objectives, a minimum of federal restrictions, and maximum discretion for local officials. Table 3.2 illustrates the difference between categorical and block grants and gives some examples of each.

The surge toward block grants has had three distinct waves, each prompted by Republican victories in national elections. Republicans were naturally hostile to categorical grants because many of these grants funded programs that Republicans had opposed in the first place and believed were unnecessary or counterproductive in prac-

block grants

Federal grants to a state and/or local government that impose minimal restrictions on the use of funds.

TABLE 3.2		
CATEGORICAL GRANTS AND BLOCK GRANTS: SOME EXAMPLES		
Type of Grant	Restrictions on Use of Funds	Examples
Categorical grant	Significant	Food stamps (created 1971): Provides funds to states and localities to supply food to eligible low-income residents.
		Medicaid (created 1965): Provides health insurance to low-income and disadvantaged citizens.
Block grant	Minimal	Housing and Community Development Block Grant (created 1974): Provides funds to states and localities for general development purposes.
		Temporary Assistance to Needy Families (created 1996): Provides funds to states to design and implement their own welfare programs.

tice. The first wave of block grants began after President Nixon won election to the White House in 1968. The most comprehensive, **general revenue sharing**, gave state and local governments a share of federal tax revenues to be used for any purpose whatsoever. During this first wave, block grants did not replace categorical grants so much as supplement them. To win support for general revenue sharing and other block grants, Nixon was forced to agree to continue many of the categorical programs that Democrats in Congress favored. As a consequence, the total size of the intergovernmental grant program continued to grow throughout the administrations of Nixon and Gerald Ford. By the late 1970s, as the top line in Figure 3.2 shows, they cost more than $186 billion.

general revenue sharing
The most comprehensive of block grants, which gives money to state and local governments to be used for any purpose whatsoever.

The second wave of block grants came after Ronald Reagan's 1980 defeat of Democrat Jimmy Carter. President Reagan's administration, unlike the Nixon administration, enjoyed a Republican majority in the Senate. Reagan succeeded in converting a broad range of categorical grants in education, social services, and community development to block grants and public health programs. During this second wave, the new block grants not only had fewer restrictions than the older categoricals,[50] but their funding levels also were reduced to comply with the administration's overall policy of "shrinking government." The amount spent on block grants fell from about $112 billion in 1977 to only $76.8 billion in 1998, and most of this reduction occurred in the early 1980s. General revenue sharing was eliminated in 1985, and the community development block grant, a major grant program for cities across the country, was cut from $9.2 billion in 1980 to $5.3 billion in 2005.[51]

The third wave of block grants took place after the congressional election of 1994, when Republicans captured control of Congress. Earlier block grant initiatives had not touched large social programs, such as Medicaid and Aid to Families with Dependent Children (AFDC). But in 1996 Congress transformed the AFDC program, commonly called "welfare," into a block grant that gave states broad discretion over the way monies could be used (see Chapter 18). Congress also tried to transform the Medicaid low-income health insurance program into a block grant, but this change was forestalled by President Clinton's veto. As a result, expenditures on categorical grants have continued to rise (see Figure 3.2).

FIGURE 3.2

Growth and Change in Federal Grants to States and Localities

Expenditures for categorical grants continue to rise, whereas expenditures for block grants have remained stable in recent years.

• *Why do you think expenditures for block grants have not increased?*

Note: Totals exclude defense expenditures. Deriving precise estimates of block and categorical grants is difficult. Here we have employed grants used mainly for developmental purposes as a proxy for block grants, and grants used mainly for redistributive purposes as a proxy for categorical grants.

Sources: Paul E. Peterson, *The Price of Federalism* (Washington, DC: The Brookings Institution, 1995), chap. 5; and U.S. Bureau of the Census, *Federal Aid to the States for Fiscal Year 1998*, U.S. Bureau of the Census, *Federal Aid to the States for Fiscal Year 2002*, U.S. Bureau of the Census, *Federal Aid to the States for Fiscal Year 2003*.

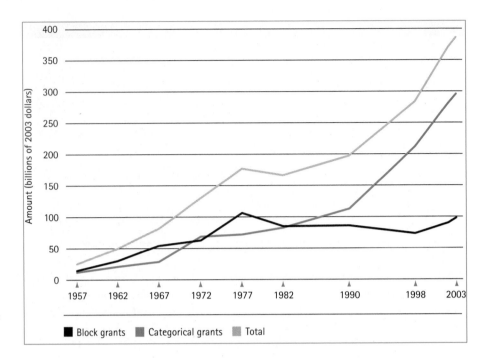

Since the 1994 election, the debate over categorical and block grants has become a matter of intense political conflict. Each side can make a compelling case for its point of view. (See *Democratic Dilemma*, page 80.) Perhaps the best argument against both categorical and block grants is that even though they are often defended as a way of equalizing resources across the country,[52] federal grants in fact do not have this effect. Instead, wealthier states often receive more federal dollars than poorer states. Figure 3.3 shows that on average, the 10 richest states in the country get much more money from block grants, per resident, than other states.

Perhaps the best argument in favor of federal grants is that they are necessary to maintain properly funded social programs. Federal categorical grants, such as Medicaid, food stamps, and other social welfare programs are especially important, because states, when not subject to federal regulation, try to shift to other states the burden of serving the needy, the sick, and the poor. Fearful of migration from other places, many states feel pressured to offer fewer benefits than their neighbor states and thus create a vicious cycle of cuts that President Clinton called a "race to the bottom." Between 1970 and 1993, welfare benefits in the average state fell by 42 percent.[53] From 1998 to 2005, in the wake of the reform of welfare that allowed states more flexibility, overall spending remained stable, but the number of people receiving welfare shrank by about 40 percent.[54] Whether a race to the bottom is responsible for these changes is unclear, but one study of state TANF programs found that "welfare policies are created in an extremely politicized environment," with state officials reacting strongly to constituent pressures and resource constraints.[55]

Although the debate over grants has polarized between those in favor of a wide variety of intergovernmental grants and those opposed to all of them, the most sensible solutions may lie somewhere in the middle. In areas where state and local govern-

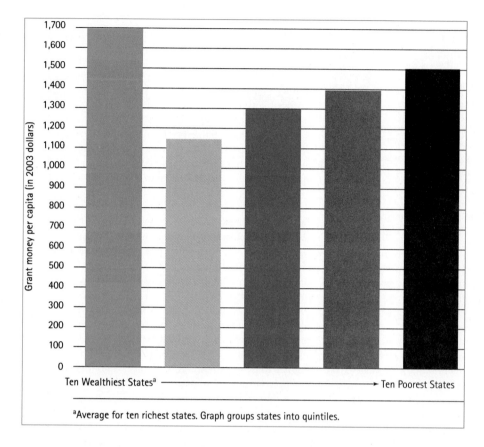

FIGURE 3.3

Richer States Get More Per Capita Aid

Richer states get as much or more grant money than poorer states from the federal government, controlling for population.

• *Is this unfair, or do rich states deserve more because they pay more to the federal government in taxes?*

Note: State "wealth" defined as Gross State Product per capita.

Sources: Calculated by authors from U.S. Bureau of the Census, Federal Aid to the States for Fiscal Year 2003, September 2004, Table 1; Statistical Abstract of the United States, 2004–2005, Table 17; Statistical Abstract of the United States 2006, Table 654.

ments have traditionally concentrated their efforts, including transportation, sanitation, and education, it may be appropriate to keep the federal role to a minimum, because states and localities can be expected to provide these services whether they receive federal aid or not. But in other areas, such as Medicaid and food stamps, it may be important to establish federal standards so that states do not "race to the bottom." In 1996 Congress and the president in fact found it possible to reach compromises at this middle position. They made the biggest cuts in traditional programs. They also changed the AFDC program into a block grant welfare program. But the largest social programs, Medicaid and food stamps, remain federally funded categorical programs.[56]

The Contemporary Debate

With the presidency of George W. Bush and consolidation of control in Congress, Republicans have modified their long-standing opposition to increased federal regulation of intergovernmental grants. Although in the past Republicans had opposed categorical grant programs, they now favored such grants when they required states and cities to spend money in ways that Republicans preferred. In 2001 President Bush enthusiastically signed into law a new education reform (the "No Child Left Behind" Act) that required all states, in exchange for federal dollars, to test students annually so

DEMOCRATIC DILEMMA

Categorical or Block Grant: Which Is Better?

The intense debate over categorical and block grants strikes at the heart of how broad we understand federalism to be. Because of the restrictions Congress places on their use, categorical grants reserve more power for the national government. Block grants, on the other hand, relinquish more responsibility to the states.

A supporter of block grants might make the following arguments against categorical grants, and in favor of block grants:

1. Categoricals are inefficient. Federal regulations tie the hands of state and local governments, who have a better understanding of local conditions. Categorical grants for public housing—designed with urban areas in mind—may be tied to inflexible regulations that are impractical for rural states, such as Montana and Idaho.
2. Categoricals create powerful interest groups. Categorical grants typically contain restrictions that focus services on specific groups. These groups support powerful lobbies that perpetuate unnecessary policies.
3. Categoricals impose unfunded mandates. Federal funds do not cover the full cost of the rules that accompany them. In effect, this forces states to raise the extra money through taxes. By forcing states to raise and spend this money, categorical grants sap their independence.
4. Block grants allow states and localities the freedom to effectively address local needs. It is difficult to assess how best to use money from the distance of Washington, D.C. Block grants allow state and local officials—those who have the most detailed knowledge of local problems—to use the money as they see fit.

A supporter of categorical grants might make the following arguments:

1. Categoricals are necessary to achieve national purposes. For example, many environmental problems are national in scope. If a state does not clean up its radioactive waste or allows its factories to spew smoke into the air, the resulting pollution can spread far beyond its own boundaries. The federal government needs to attach regulations to its grants to ensure that all states comply with the effort to achieve national policy goals.
2. If grants are not categoricals that include regulations, states will "race to the bottom." Federal supervision of Medicaid, food stamps, and other welfare programs is especially important, because states, when not subject to federal regulation, often try to lower the benefits they make available, hoping that the needy and sick will move to other states.
3. Block grants are wasteful. If the federal government provides the money, it has every right and responsibility to make sure the funds are used for federal purposes. Block grants are a dream for local politicians—"free" money to be spent however they want without being held accountable to local taxpayers. When money is "free," it is likely to be wasted.
4. Block grants are simply the first step toward eliminating needed federal programs. After a program has been converted from a categorical to a block grant, its constituency is less well defined and it becomes harder to sustain the program's political base of support. Once the states are in charge of making policy decisions, it is easier for the federal government to abandon responsibility for the program altogether.

• *Which of these points makes the most sense to you? Why? Which position do you find more persuasive?*

that their educational progress could be monitored. Certain penalties are scheduled for those schools that fail to keep up. Four years later, Bush proposed changing the Community Development Block Grant program into a series of categorical grants that would be targeted toward particular development initiatives.[57]

unfunded mandates
Federal regulations that impose burdens on state and local governments without appropriating enough money to cover costs.

The parties also appear to have modified their positions on **unfunded mandates**, the imposition of federal regulations on state and local governments without the appropriation of enough money to cover their cost. By 1993, mostly Democratic congresses had enacted countless mandates.[58] For example, state and local governments had to ensure equal access to public facilities by disabled persons but were given little money to cover the new construction costs. Clean-air legislation asked state and local governments to reduce air pollution but skimped on the funding necessary to do the job.[59] Medicaid required expanded services for low-income recipients, but for many states the law funded only half the cost of the program.[60]

Critics of unfunded mandates had high hopes that after the 1994 elections, mandates would be a thing of the past. That year, Republican candidates campaigned in favor of governmental **devolution**, the return of governmental responsibilities to state and local governments. But Republican lawmakers soon proved that they were not immune to the practice. The Bush education bill required states and school districts to set standards, but critics said it provided little money to help them do so. After 2001 new antiterrorism rules also placed severe strain on state and local governments, as law enforcement officials were required to step up their monitoring of potential terrorist targets around the country. With the shoe on the other foot, Democrats began complaining about unfunded mandates. "I find it ironic [that] . . . the party that talks about being opposed to unfunded mandates is giving us a very significant unfunded mandate," said West Virginia Governor Robert Wise, a Democrat, about the education program.[61] Republican Senator Lamar Alexander—a former Tennessee governor—lamented, "The conservatives are just as bad as liberals at passing new programs and expecting someone else to pay for it."[62]

Whether they are Democrats or Republicans, members of Congress have strong incentives to impose mandates on state and local governments, and to leave them unfunded. When a mandate is imposed, members of Congress get the credit for helping constituents. When it is left unfunded, Congress, safe at a distance, evades the taxpayers' wrath.

Local Government

State and local governments now play a more prominent role in the federal system than they have for several decades. Even before the most recent devolution, a large proportion of all domestic government expenditure was paid for by taxes raised by state and local governments. This pattern, shown in Figure 3.4, is in keeping with long-standing American traditions. Nearly a century ago, the British scholar James Bryce identified the key role played by local governments in the American federal system:

devolution
Return of governmental responsibilities to state and local governments.

Is Federalism Dead and Should It Be?

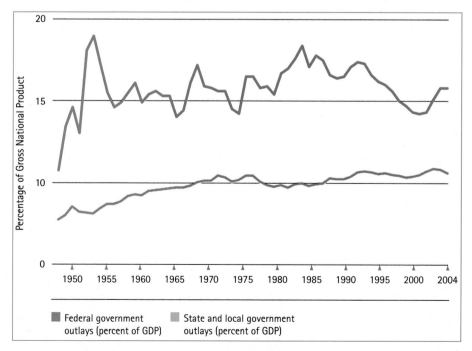

FIGURE 3.4

Domestic Expenditure of Governments

State and local governments spend almost as much as the national government does.
• *Why did national government spending increase relative to state and local spending in the 1970s?*
Note: Figures on national government spending do not include "off budget" items or defense expenditures; figures on state and local government expenditures do not include expenditures funded by federal grants.

Source: Office of Management and Budget, *United States Budget for Fiscal Year 2006,* Historical Tables, Table 15.3.

Federal government outlays (percent of GDP) State and local government outlays (percent of GDP)

> It is the business of a local authority to mend the roads, to clean out the village well or to provide a new pump, to see that there is a place where straying beasts may be kept till the owner reclaims them, to fix the number of cattle each villager may turn out on the common pasture, [and] to give each his share of timber cut in the common woodland.[63]

The nature of the work has been modernized since Bryce observed it, but the basic functions remain much the same. Local governments maintain roads; take care of parks; provide police, fire, and sanitation services; run the schools; and perform many other functions that affect the everyday lives of citizens.

The Number and Types of Local Governments

Comparing State and Local Governments

In sheer numbers, local governments constitute an overwhelming and growing presence; there were more than 74,000 in 2002, up from about 46,000 in 1942 (see Figure 3.5).[64] There are several different major types of local governments, each of which has responsibilities that vary from state to state. Though the basic unit in most states is the county, not all counties are alike. In some states they manage school systems, welfare programs, local roads, sanitation systems, a sheriff's office, and an array of other governmental activities. In other states they have hardly any duties. Many counties are divided into townships—there are 16,500 of them nationwide—whose duties generally include local road maintenance and other small-scale activities.

As the population has become concentrated in urban areas, the total number of municipalities—cities, suburbs, and towns—has increased to nearly 20,000. In most states, these municipal governments have assumed many of the responsibilities once performed by counties.

States, counties, and municipalities have also created an extraordinary array of special districts—more than 35,000 in all. Each special district has responsibility for only one or a few specific governmental functions. Such governments are unique in that they overlap the boundaries of other local governments, sometimes spanning many different municipal jurisdictions. As Figure 3.5 shows, special districts account for most of the increase in the number of local governments over the last 50 years. Some special districts run schools, others manage parks, and still others administer transportation systems or garbage collection.[65] Even as humble a task as mosquito abatement can be the responsibility of a special district.

Local Elections

Most local governments are run by elected officials, although special district heads are sometimes appointed by other local governments. In the United States as a whole, the total number of elected local officials approaches half-a-million people. Despite the large number of local elections, actual rates of citizen participation in them are surprisingly low. When a particularly colorful candidate runs for mayor, or when ethnic or racial issues are raised, large numbers of voters can show up at the polls, but much of the time the local electorate is no more than half the size of the presidential electorate.[66] Like many features of local government, local election dates and procedures are held according to state-set rules, a fact underscored when Louisiana Governor Kathleen Blanco postponed a New Orleans election for more than two months after Hurricane Katrina created a raft of logistical difficulties.[67]

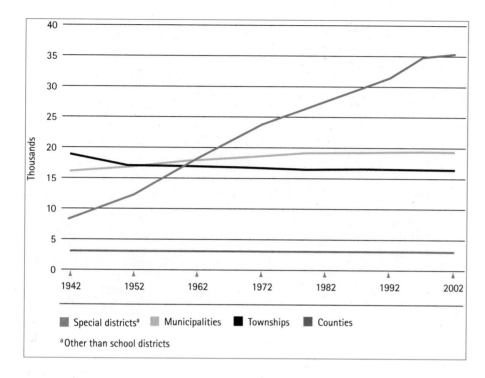

FIGURE 3.5

Number of Local
Governments, 1942–2002

• *Why do you think the number
of special districts has increased so
much over the last 50 years?*

Source: U.S. Bureau of the Census,
Statistical Abstract of the United States, 2006,
Table 415.

Under ordinary circumstances, the near invisibility of local elections helps to reduce local participation rates.[68] The sheer number of elected officeholders often makes local government elections confusing to many voters. Newspaper coverage is haphazard. Local governments frequently hold elections at times that coincide with neither state nor national elections, which further reduce turnout rates.[69] When asked about the hotly contested 2001 Los Angeles mayoral race, one potential voter gave a typical response: "I don't really care too much. All I know is that there is a lot of bashing going on. One guy was like the D.A. or something like that and the other guy worked for him . . . I don't know."[70]

Surprisingly, local governments also oversee the administration of national elections. This local responsibility became a key issue in the close 2000 presidential election, when some voters in Palm Beach County, Florida, claimed that the county's confusing ballot design had led them to vote for the wrong candidate. The following summer, a nationwide commission of state and local election officials asked the federal government to provide procedural guidelines and standards—but not mandates—to prevent such confusion from occurring again.[71] The result, the 2002 "Help America Vote Act" (HAVA), provided $3.1 billion in grants to localities to update their voting machines. As in the case of many grant programs, however, critics of HAVA complained of delays, intergovernmental conflicts, and unfunded mandates. As one California county clerk, preparing for a June 2006 election, put it, "We are in limbo, we are in uncertainty, and we are getting more frustrated by the day."[72]

Popularity of Local Government

One might think that this diverse, complicated, only half-democratic, and seemingly irrational system could not possibly succeed. Yet local government remains very popu-

A Local Election

Three young supporters hold signs endorsing a Hispanic candidate on election day.

• *Why are local governments popular with voters?*

lar. According to one survey, fully 70 percent of Americans express "a great deal" or "a fair amount" of "trust and confidence" in their local government, while the public divided about 50–50 on a similar assessment of the national government.[73]

One explanation for the apparent popularity of local government, despite the low profile of its elections, is the ability of people to "vote with their feet"—that is, to move from one community to another—if they are unhappy with their local government. Americans are a mobile people: More than 15 percent move each year.[74] Every local government has to remember that if it is inefficient or unresponsive, its city or town will suffer a decline in population and property values. As a result, most local governments have good reason to be mindful of their constituents' needs, despite low voting rates.

The wide variety of local governments also gives people a choice. Some people favor sex education programs and condom distribution in school; others do not. Some people think refuse collection should be publicly provided; others prefer to recycle their own garbage. Some people think police protection should be intensive; others think an intrusive police presence violates the civil liberties of citizens. By giving people a choice, the diversity of local governments reduces conflict and enhances citizen satisfaction.

Limits on Local Government

For all the strengths of local governments, they often do not have the resources to meet the needs of the poor, the sick, and the disabled. If a local government tries to provide substantial services to the needy, it runs the risk of attracting more poor people and driving away those who are better off. For example, in the early 1990s, Framingham, Massachusetts, provided a broad range of social services to disadvantaged residents, including group homes for recovering drug and alcohol abusers, halfway houses for juvenile offenders, counseling centers, and other programs for the poor. Although the programs were well administered, the growing number of clients provoked complaints from town leaders that the community was becoming "a magnet for everyone else's problems." Complaining that taxpayers were being asked to foot the bill for the education, security, and fire protection of low-income nontaxpayers, one candidate appealed effectively to local voters by insisting, "We can't afford this anymore."[75] Most other cities agree; local governments nationwide spend only about 10.5 percent of their budgets on social programs, compared to around 24 percent for the state governments and about 60 percent for the federal government.[76] (But such is the variety of local governments that one can find exceptions to this as to any other rule. San Francisco and New York City, for example, provide a broad range of social services for needy groups.)

Local governments also compete with one another to attract businesses. Although such competition usually has positive benefits in that it keeps local governments sensitive to the community's economic needs, sometimes the competition can get out of hand. With state help, one county in Kentucky outbid its neighbors for a Canadian steel mill employing 400 people. It ended up costing the state $350,000 for every job created. Such bidding wars have spread across the country. As one Michigan official put it, "Right now, all we are doing is eating each other's lunch. At some stage we have to start thinking about dinner."[77]

In other cases, cities compete to secure or retain professional sports teams. In 1995 Cleveland Browns owner Art Modell abruptly decided to move the football team to Baltimore, which had promised him a new stadium, permanent seat licenses, and other financial incentives. Baltimore's mayor and Maryland's governor participated in the negotiations for the team and helped announce the move. Meanwhile, Cleveland officials were incensed. Mayor Michael White likened the move to "a kick in the teeth."[78] Undaunted, the city of Cleveland worked with major financial backers to bring professional football back to the city, this time as an expansion team. In 1999 the expansion Cleveland Browns played their first season in a brand new $283 million stadium.

You Are a
Restaurant Owner

State Government

When the Constitution was written, the design of the federal government was adapted from that which existed in many states. Thus, it is not surprising that the basic organization of most state governments bears a strong resemblance to that of the national government. Just as Congress has the Senate and the House of Representatives, the legislatures in all states except Nebraska have an upper and a lower chamber (Nebraska has only one). All states have multi-tiered court systems roughly comparable to that of the federal system. And every state has an independently elected **governor**, the state chief executive whose responsibilities roughly parallel those of the president.

State governments vary in many important ways, however. State legislatures vary greatly in size. Most lower houses have around 100 representatives, but in Alaska, Delaware, and Nevada they have as few as 40 members each, whereas in New Hampshire, with a similarly small population, the lower house includes 400 legislators. Some state governments hold their elections in even-numbered years, in conjunction with federal races; others do not. In some states, state administrative officers from the secretary of state to the attorney general are elected, whereas in other states, the governor appoints these officials.

governor
State chief executive whose responsibilities roughly parallel those of the president.

laboratories of democracy
Doctrine that state and local governments contribute to democracy by providing places where experiments are tried and new theories tested.

State policies vary as well. State governments may serve as **laboratories of democracy**—places where experiments are tried and new theories about government are tested. If successful, an experiment may be copied by other states or by the national government. If it fails, the experiment is soon abandoned. For example, scholars have shown that states are more likely to establish state lotteries if their neighbors have their own lottery programs.[79] There is also significant state-by-state variation in the legality of assisted suicide, the rules governing a woman's access to an abortion, and social welfare policies. In South Dakota most consumer fireworks are permitted, but in Georgia even sparklers are against the law. In Nevada gambling is legal, but in Idaho it is a misdemeanor.

Some scholars believe the reason for many of these differences lies in variations in state political cultures. Citizens from different backgrounds and historical traditions form governments and elect officials that reflect these traditions. Minnesota and Massachusetts voters, for example, hold more positive views toward active government than do voters in Texas or Florida.[80] It is no surprise, then, that Minnesota and Massachusetts have governments larger than those in other states, with more responsibilities.[81]

State Elections

Despite policy differences among states, state elections bear a strong resemblance to national elections. The same two political parties—Republican and Democratic—are the dominant competitors in nearly all state elections. For many decades following the Civil War, the party of Lincoln, the Republicans, dominated the North, whereas the South was solidly Democratic. These regional patterns of party dominance have broken down in recent years as a result of the civil rights movement and population shifts. Republicans now often win as many southern elections as Democrats do. A new trend toward competitive politics and divided government has developed in most states. Democrats have had the advantage in state legislative races; Republicans have more often elected governors. The voters may like it this way: Each party can act as a check on the other, and government does not drift to either political extreme.[82]

Variation in State Government Responsibilities

The size and range of state responsibilities have grown dramatically in recent decades. As a percentage of GNP, state expenditures increased by more than 60 percent between 1960 and 2003. States bear heavy responsibilities for financing elementary and secondary education, as well as for funding state colleges and universities. They maintain state parks, highway systems, and prisons. They manage welfare and Medicaid programs that serve low-income populations. They give grants to local governments to help pay for police, fire, and other basic governmental services.

The amount spent on government services varies from state to state. For one thing, wealthier states spend much more on public services. In 2003 the state and local governments in the 10 richest states spent an average of $5,861 per person on public services, whereas in the 10 poorest states they spent, on average, about $4,900.[83] Many liberals say these differences in spending for education, health, and other public services are inequitable and should be rectified by federal grants. Many conservatives say that it is only to be expected that wealthier people will spend more on public services,

Explaining
Differences
in State Laws

just as they spend more for clothes, houses, and cars. In any case, federal grants have done very little, if anything, to reduce interstate fiscal inequalities.

Expenditures are also affected by elections. Each party has its favorite type of public service. The more often Democrats are elected to the legislature, the higher the expenditure for social services. The more Republicans who win, the higher the expenditure for traditional government services.[84]

Recent Developments at the State Level

In recent years, state governments have evolved in several important ways. State political institutions have become more modern, the role of governors has grown, and states have begun to develop their own economic policies.

State Financial Crisis   After a decade of rising budgets and a booming economy, state and local governments suffered greatly from a serious financial crisis prompted by the recession of 2001. As most states drafted their 2002 and 2003 budgets, they faced significant shortfalls due to declining tax revenues and increasing governmental responsibilities. In June 2003, the executive director of the National Governor's Association declared that the budget crisis was the worst for the states since the War of 1812.[85] Local governments suffered too, as states reduced aid to their cities to help fill the budget gaps. Many voters blamed politicians for these budget woes, just as in national elections economic problems often harm the president's reelection chances. Most memorably, Democratic Governor Gray Davis of California, whose state faced a $38 billion budget shortfall in 2003, lost a special recall election to actor-turned-politician Arnold Schwarzenegger.

Governors

The degree to which governors manage to cope with economic crises successfully may have broad repercussions for national politics. Being governor of a medium-sized or large state has historically been one of the best ways to position oneself for national office. Four of the last five U.S. presidents have been governors, and former governors have been major candidates in every presidential election campaign since 1976. George W. Bush's popularity as governor of Texas, coupled with the advantages of a well-known family name, quickly catapulted him into the presidential limelight. In 2004 Democratic presidential candidate and former Vermont governor Howard Dean reminded voters that his state was one of the few that did not face a budget shortfall during the 2002–2003 crisis.[86]

Reapportionment and Professionalization   When the state constitutions were written, many of them included provisions freezing the boundaries of their legislative districts. In many other states, legislatures did not bother to change district boundaries to reflect shifts in population. Because the country became more urbanized in the first half of the twentieth century, by the early 1960s these rigid district boundaries meant that rural areas were grossly over-represented in state legislatures. Soon legal challenges brought these issues before the Supreme Court. In 1962 and 1964, the Court ruled that states must regularly redraw their districts so that all districts have similar numbers of residents,[87] a process known as **reapportionment**. In the wake of these decisions, turnover in state legislatures rose significantly as they became more representative. In the longer term, the reapportionment requirements have sparked regular partisan battles

reapportionment
Redrawing of electoral district lines to reflect population changes.

in many states, as Democrats and Republicans compete to draw district boundaries in ways most favorable to their party.[88]

After the 2000 census, reapportionment battles began again in earnest. A Colorado state representative complained that his state's reapportionment process had been "submerged in a morass of partisan haranguing."[89] A local official in Louisiana protested that his constituents were "being shifted around like the red-headed stepchild."[90] In the most extreme case, 51 Democratic legislators in the state of Texas fled the state in 2003 in an effort to prevent Republicans from passing a redistricting plan that would deliver more U.S. House seats to the GOP. Without the 51 legislators present, the House did not have enough members to conduct business legally. As the Democrats huddled at the Holiday Inn in Ardmore, Oklahoma, just beyond the reach of Texas state troopers, the standoff drew national attention. A network news correspondent described the situation as "like an old Western: a band of outlaws headed for Oklahoma with the Texas Rangers hot in pursuit."[91] After a second walkout and three special sessions of the legislature, Texas lawmakers finally passed the Republican plan. By 2006, the Supreme Court had agreed to hear a challenge to the districting plan, and a minor scandal erupted when media reports indicated that career bureaucrats at the Justice Department had wanted to reject the districting plan as discriminatory but were over-ruled by their political-appointee superiors.[92]

Not all politicians were unhappy with their state's reapportionment process, however. "I believe [the new apportionment plan] gives us control for the next 10 years," said Pennsylvania's state House Republican Leader John Perzel. "I'm very very happy. I'm ecstatic."[93]

As state government has become more complicated, state legislatures have also become more professional. Scholars associate higher legislative "professionalization" with lower turnover rates, higher salaries, more staff, and longer sessions. In 2006 California's legislature was among the most modern. Its members remained in session throughout the year, receiving $110,880 in salary, retirement benefits, and handsome per diem expense pay, as well as the services of a full-time staff. By contrast, Wyoming paid its legislators only $125 dollars a day and limited its legislative sessions to a maximum of 40 working days in odd-numbered years and 20 days in even-numbered years.[94]

During the 1990s, voters reacted against the professionalization of state government, as many states limited the terms of legislators, cut their staffs, and reduced their salaries and benefits. In the eyes of one expert, this trend has produced "a crumbling of legislative power" in which "the legislature is becoming a less than equal branch of government."[95] Term limit laws are now on the books in 15 states, including California, Michigan, Florida, and Colorado, but the trend to limit legislative terms appears to have slowed.[96]

State Economic Action   In the nineteenth century, state governments played an active role in their states' economies, granting charters to private corporations and investing their resources to assist in the development of key industries. After the New Deal, the federal government became predominant, and states relaxed their economic roles. Then, toward the end of the twentieth century, many states again became more active players in their economic development. States especially hard-hit by a decline in manufacturing jobs and by economic recessions sought to reinvigorate their business climate through tax incentives and active recruitment of firms from out of state.

States with large economies and significant international exports, such as California and Texas, have arranged frequent trade missions to countries such as

Mexico, Japan, and Canada. When Arnold Schwarzenegger won election as governor in 2003, one of his first meetings was with Mexico's secretary of foreign affairs.[97] Ohio Governor Bob Taft claimed that a trade mission he led to Europe in fall 2005 led to more than 500 new jobs and $160 million in investment for his state.[98]

Chapter Summary

Federalism divides sovereignty between the states and the national government. Its existence in the United States is the result of a compromise between Constitutional Convention delegates who believed that a strong national government was necessary to preserve stability, and those who feared that centralized power would lead to tyranny.

Because the federal structure was a compromise, the Constitution does not clearly define the powers of the federal and state governments. As a result, the nature of American federalism has changed in response to electoral forces and Supreme Court decisions. Much of the debate over federalism has revolved around the meaning of dual sovereignty. The most extreme interpretation of dual sovereignty, the doctrine of nullification, was rejected with the end of the Civil War.

The power of the states was further eroded with the election of Franklin Roosevelt and the enactment of New Deal legislation that greatly enhanced the power of the federal government. Three provisions in the Constitution facilitated the expansion of federal power: the necessary and proper clause, the commerce clause, and the spending clause. The state sovereignty amendment has recently been used to restrict its expansion.

With the election of strong Democratic majorities in the 1960s, there emerged a new theory of federalism known as cooperative or marble-cake federalism, which holds that all levels of government can and should work together. In accordance with this theory, many new federal grants were given to state and local governments. The majority of these grants were categorical in nature; they contained restrictions that specified how the money should be spent. In response to criticism of the implementation of categorical grants, Republican leaders called for their replacement with block grants that have few federal mandates or restrictions. The two parties remain divided over the merits of categorical and block grants, although disagreements over these topics have shifted as Republicans gained the upper hand in Congress and the presidency.

Despite the expansion of federal power, state and local governments remain vital components of the federal system. Nearly half the domestic expenditures of the government are paid for with state and local tax dollars. Even though few citizens participate in local elections, local governments are the most popular of all governmental levels, in part because people can "vote with their feet"—that is, they can choose to live in the local community they like best.

State governments can play key roles in economic development, and governors are often well positioned to seek the presidency. Despite legal and structural variation, partisan battles on the state level can resemble those on the national level, as legislatures become more professional and voters increasingly choose "divided government" wherein neither party dominates all policy making.

Key Terms

block grants, p. 76
categorical grants, p. 74
commerce clause, p. 68
cooperative federalism, p. 72
devolution, p. 81
Dillon's rule, p. 61
dual sovereignty, p. 65
federalism, p. 61
general revenue sharing, p. 77
governor, p. 85
Great Society, p. 74

implementation, p. 75
intergovernmental grant, p. 73
judicial review, p. 64
laboratories of democracy, p. 86
marble-cake federalism, p. 72
McCulloch v. Maryland, p. 66
necessary and proper clause, p. 70
New Deal, p. 67
NIMBY problem, p. 70
nullification, p. 65

pork barrel projects, p. 74
reapportionment, p. 87
sovereignty, p. 61
spending clause, p. 72
state sovereign immunity, p. 71
supremacy clause, p. 63
tyranny of the majority, p. 65
unfunded mandates, p. 80
unitary government, p. 61
War on Poverty, p. 74

Suggested Readings

Of General Interest

Conlan, Timothy. *From New Federalism to Devolution: Twenty-Five Years of Intergovernmental Reform*. Washington, DC: The Brookings Institution, 1998. Excellent analysis of changing federal policy.

Dahl, Robert. *Who Governs?* New Haven, CT: Yale University Press, 1961. Classic study of local politics in New Haven.

Dye, Thomas R. *American Federalism: Competition Among Governments*. Lexington, MA: D.C. Heath, 1990. Comprehensive account of the way state and local governments work.

Nivola, Pietro S. *Tense Commandments: Federal Prescriptions and City Problems*. Washington, DC: The Brookings Institution, 2002. Argues that national prescriptions and mandates are restricting cities' ability to respond to local needs.

Peterson, Paul E. *The Price of Federalism*. Washington, DC: The Brookings Institution, 1995. Contrasts the responsibilities of national, state, and local governments.

Riker, William H. *Federalism: Origin, Operation, Significance*. Boston: Little, Brown, 1964. Theoretical treatise on federalism.

Focused Studies

Berman, David R. *Local Government and the States: Autonomy, Politics, and Policy*. Armonk, NY: M.E. Sharpe, 2003. Interesting account of the relationships between cities and states.

Elazar, Daniel. *American Federalism: A View from the States*. New York: Harper & Row, 1984. Discussion of various regional political cultures in the United States.

Elkins, Stanley, and Eric McKitrick. *The Age of Federalism*. New York: Oxford University Press, 1993. Account of the first decades of the federal system under the Constitution.

Fiorina, Morris, *Divided Government*. New York: Macmillan, 1992. Explains why control of many state governments is divided between the Democratic and Republican parties.

Grodzins, Morton. *The American System: A New View of Government in the United States*. Chicago: Rand McNally, 1966. Classic study of cooperative federalism.

Pressman, Jeffrey L., and Aaron Wildavsky. *Implementation*. 3rd ed. Berkeley: University of California Press, 1973. Readable, fascinating account of the implementation of a federal program in Oakland, California.

Smith, Jean E. *John Marshall: Definer of a Nation*. New York: Henry Holt, 1996. Excellent biography of the chief justice who helped define American federalism.

On the Web

State and local governments have formed a variety of organizations to make their voices heard on the federal level.

www.nlc.org

www.ncsl.org

www.nga.org

The National League of Cities, the National Conference of State Legislatures, and the National Governor's Association provide information and policy priorities for state and local governments.

http://newfederalism.urban.org/

The Urban Institute's "Assessing the New Federalism" project provides a variety of studies on the impact of recent devolutionary programs.

www.federalismproject.org

The American Enterprise Institute's Federalism Project advocates devolution of more rights and responsibilities to the states.

CHAPTER 4

☆ ☆ ☆ ☆ ☆ ☆ ☆ ☆ ☆ ☆

American Political Culture

CHAPTER OUTLINE

A Hard Test for American Diversity

On September 11, 2001, the United States suffered the most serious act of terrorism in its history. Followers of Muslim fanatic Osama bin Laden hijacked four jetliners, crashing two into New York City's World Trade Center, another into the Pentagon, and a fourth into a remote Pennsylvania field. Almost 3,000 people died on this horrible day.

All 19 of the terrorists came from Middle Eastern countries. In the aftermath of the attacks a few Americans chose to express their grief and anger by committing violent acts against people of Middle Eastern background living in the United States. Some incidents were as minor as bullying at school recess. Others were fatal. A Sikh was gunned down in a deadly instance of mistaken identity. A Yemeni father of eight was shot and killed within sight of the American flag hanging in the window of his shop. In all, Arab Americans suffered an estimated 270 violent assaults within a month of 9/11. Five resulted in death.[1] In 2001, California alone recorded 73 official hate crimes against people perceived to be Arabs (compared to three the year before). More than half of these were violent.[2]

These hostile acts, however, were carried out by a relatively small number of Americans acting on their own; none were official government actions. True, there were calls for the adoption of anti-Arab policies. Survey respondents overwhelmingly endorsed special airport security checks for those of Middle Eastern background, a majority favored requiring Arabs to carry special identification cards, and more than a third supported placing them under "special surveillance."[3] But the official response fell far short of such demands.

Within two months of 9/11 the United States invaded Afghanistan and overthrew the Taliban regime that had given refuge to Osama bin Laden. Within another year the Bush administration decided that the United States should invade Iraq and overthrow Saddam Hussein, which it did in the spring of 2003. At the time of this writing American forces have been fighting in the Middle East for three years.

Government policy has changed as a result of this ongoing conflict. Security in airports has become more intrusive and, some critics charge, more discriminatory.[4] States have tightened their screening of applicants for driver's licenses and other government documents.[5] Federal officials have slowed the rate at which foreigners receive permission to visit the United States, have required the fingerprinting of applicants, and have reversed years of neglect by tracking down those who had overstayed their visas. Federal officials have asked colleges to ensure that international students have their paperwork in order. They have required more than 80,000 males from 25 mostly Middle Eastern countries to register at U.S. immigration offices. And law-enforcement officers have seized hundreds of foreigners, from U.S. Army privates to pizza delivery boys, for minor legal violations that they previously had ignored.[6]

Although some critics believe that such government actions are excessive, the domestic response to the Middle Eastern conflict pales in comparison to policies adopted during previous American wars. Two generations ago, when the Japanese attacked Pearl Harbor, the government rounded up 120,000 Americans of Japanese ancestry—citizens and noncitizens alike—and held them for up to three years in internment camps. Detainees often lost their property and their jobs.[7] A generation earlier, after the United States entered World War I, German Americans experienced a variety of official abuses—some jurisdictions passed laws prohibiting the use of the German language.[8] And social pressures were so great that some immigrants abandoned their family names to hide their ethnic origin.[9] In short, compared to historical experience, contemporary attacks on Arab Americans have been relatively isolated and discrimination has been relatively mild.

Perhaps even more striking is the amount of effort that many Americans have devoted to dampening hostility toward Arab Americans. For every legislator who worried about Arabs running "all the convenience stores across the country," many more increased their outreach to Arab American constituents who felt vulnerable as a result of the backlash. President Bush called for unity and told Americans that Islam is a

Border Protections Increased After 9/11

peaceful religion. The American media also showed little inclination to stir up ethnic hatreds, as they had during previous crises. Instead, journalists documented the injustices caused by new government policies and ran stories conveying a simple message: that the country's immigrant communities were filled with loyal Americans.

It is all too easy to take this reaction for granted. "Of course Arabs can be good Americans," you might be thinking. "What does Americanism have to do with race or religion?" Such a distinction makes perfect sense in the United States, but it would be far from obvious in most other countries. Carl Friedrich, a professor who immigrated to the United States from Germany in the 1930s, once wrote that "To be an American is an ideal, while to be a Frenchman is a fact."[10] Friedrich was pointing out that, in most of the world, **citizenship** is indeed defined by ethnicity. Either you are German or you are not (see *International Comparison,* page 94).

MAKING THE CONNECTION

The values held by a nation's people shape their political system. These core beliefs are more fundamental than the opinions citizens might hold about particular issues or public officials (see Chapter 5). They reflect a broad orientation toward how government should and should not operate, a set of expectations about how it should treat them and how it should treat others. These assumptions define what leaders consider possible and what they rule out as unacceptable. Because such broad expectations are rather durable—a long-lasting tradition not unlike cultural preferences for certain foods or certain clothing—scholars often refer to them as the nation's **political culture**.

As this chapter will show, America's political culture stands out for the extent to which it defines the nation. It is unusually uniform, given the large land mass it unites and the varied population it integrates, and it distinguishes the United States from other advanced democracies. When you finish reading the chapter, therefore, you should understand why other U.S. citizens would accept that Arab-American Muslims could belong to the same nation as they do. More generally, you should be able to formulate an answer to the following questions:

• What core beliefs set Americans apart from citizens elsewhere?

• What influences caused these values to develop and spread?

• How have they stayed strong after more than 200 years?

• Do immigrants threaten America's political culture?

INTERNATIONAL COMPARISON

Citizenship in Europe and the United States

Any child born in the United States is a U.S. citizen. A child born outside the United States is a U.S. citizen if either parent is a U.S. citizen and that parent has lived in the United States for 10 years—including two years after the age of 14. Legal immigrants can become "naturalized" citizens after five years of residence: They must learn English, demonstrate knowledge of American history and government, renounce their previous citizenship, and swear allegiance to the Constitution and laws of the United States. Naturalized citizens may not serve as U.S. president, because of a constitutional prohibition, but otherwise they have the same rights and privileges as native citizens.

Practices in other countries differ greatly. In Germany, for example, citizenship historically has been based on ethnicity. The constitution of the new German republic created after World War II carried over a 1913 law defining a German as "a refugee or expellee of German stock or as the spouse or descendant of such a person." As a consequence, Eastern European and Russian residents whose ancestors left Germany centuries ago can migrate to Germany today and quickly assume the rights and privileges of citizenship (as can Americans of German descent if they can make a case for hardship). But the children of Turkish "guest workers," born in Germany and speaking German as their first language, typically face major bureaucratic obstacles to becoming citizens because they are not Germans by blood.

Political cultures that emphasize ethnicity struggle with the challenges of immigration. In Germany, the government attempted to liberalize immigration laws in 1999, but the proposals met strong resistance. A compromise reduced the residency requirement before an immigrant was eligible for citizenship from 15 years to 8 years and granted citizenship to any child born in Germany whose parents had resided there for eight years or longer. Meanwhile, France contains the largest Muslim population of any European country. Ethnic tensions in 2004 led to a popular government crackdown on religious head coverings that obviously targeted the Islamic *hajib* or head scarf—a religion-based regulation similar to one that the U.S. Supreme Court declared unconstitutional in a 1993 case called *Hialeah v. Lukumi Babalu*. And in the autumn of 2005 Muslim youths rioted for two weeks in nearly 300 cities and towns, throwing France into crisis. Although many of the rioters were citizens, by all accounts immigrants and their children are not treated as full members of the French polity.

---

citizenship
Status held by someone entitled to all the rights and privileges of a full-fledged member of a political community.

political culture
Collection of beliefs and values about the justification and operation of a country's government.

9-11-2001

Americans: A Contradictory People?

Americans are more ethnically and religiously diverse than the citizens of other democracies. Most long-lasting multicultural countries have been ruled by authoritarian regimes that suppressed cultural divisions, as in the Austro-Hungarian and Soviet empires. By contrast, most of the world's multicultural democracies have not lasted long—Yugoslavia being one recent, especially tragic, example. The United States is the exception, an unusual example of diverse people coexisting peacefully under a long-lasting democratic government.[11]

At the same time, many foreign observers point to a striking consistency in political beliefs across the United States, a consistency that seems at odds with the cultural diversity. More frequently than in other democracies, Americans agree on fundamentals and share basic assumptions about the nature of a good society; they value liberty, individual responsibility, equality, and religious faith. On first hearing, this claim strikes many students as exaggerated, if not wrong. The United States certainly has its share of political conflict. Republicans and Democrats clash angrily in the halls of government. Liberals and conservatives argue noisily in the media. But the range of disagreement historically is narrower than that found in other democracies, which may contain political parties hoping to restore a royal family to the throne, to establish an official church, or to create a "dictatorship of the proletariat." Beliefs considered valid in other cultures fall outside the mainstream in the United States.

How might such a contradiction arise? How does an ethnically and religiously heterogeneous society develop a political culture more homogeneous than most? To answer this question, we must know more about both the makeup of the American population and the core beliefs that Americans share. The next section therefore considers the diversity produced by new immigrants continuously arriving in the United States. The section that follows it discusses the philosophy that unifies American beliefs and values.

Social Diversity

In "Federalist 2," John Jay described Americans as a "united people" who were "descended from the same ancestors, speaking the same language, professing the same religion, attached to the same principles of government, very similar in their manners and customs." Here Jay was exaggerating American unity—a campaign tactic aimed at downplaying divisions that threatened ratification of the U.S. Constitution. In fact, no "united people" colonized the so-called New World.

The Dutch settled New York, and Swedes and Germans settled along the Delaware River. The French were present on the northern and western borders, and a small Spanish population lived in the South. The British were most numerous, of course, but they were not all of a kind. Religious dissenters called Puritans settled in New England, but Virginia's colonists remained loyal to the Church of England. Maryland was a grant to Lord Baltimore, who welcomed his fellow Catholics, and Pennsylvania accepted Quakers, who were unwelcome almost everywhere else. Moreover, after 1700, British immigration came increasingly from Scotland, Wales, and Ireland, rather than from England.

Indentured servants—who made up half the population of Pennsylvania, New York, and New Jersey—included thousands of Germans, Scandinavians, Belgians, French, and Swiss. And these were only the voluntary immigrants; the involuntary immigrants—slaves—who made up about 20 percent of the population, were from Africa. (Native Americans, whose numbers had been decimated by wars and disease, were viewed as separate nations altogether.) Historians estimate that on the eve of the American Revolution, only 50 percent of the population of the colonies was English.[12]

Students may react skeptically to this description of colonial diversity: a bunch of European Christians is your idea of diversity? Today, debates over **multiculturalism** do not revolve around whether Catholics and Calvinists should get along, or whether the British should tolerate the Dutch. Instead, we debate whether people with nontraditional lifestyles should enjoy the same rights and privileges as those who follow more traditional moral codes, or we struggle to formulate policies that will give people of color the same chances in life that the white majority has. But notions of diversity are relative to time and place. A few centuries ago, Protestants and Catholics looked upon each other with no more understanding (and possibly with less) than that with which a Christian might look upon a Muslim today—and the cultural distance between them often turned deadly.

The grandparents of some of the framers of the American Constitution may have been alive during the Thirty Years War (1618–1648), when northern European Christians raped, tortured, and murdered each other on a monumental scale over religious differences. The conflict claimed the lives of one-third of the population of what

multiculturalism
The idea that ethnic and cultural groups should maintain their identity within the larger society and respect one another's differences.

is now Germany. Near the end of that period, Puritan dissenters from the Church of England fought against Royalist defenders of church and crown in the English Civil War (1642–1653). Ultimately, the king and the archbishop both lost their heads. For perhaps the most appalling contradiction of the misconception that northern European Christians were all alike, consider the St. Bartholomew's Day Massacre that preceded the Thirty Year's War. Over the course of several weeks French Catholics moved methodically from door to door and farm to farm, killing 30,000 French Calvinists with swords, axes, and crude firearms.

Relative to other countries, and to the times, America has always been diverse. The national motto imprinted on the United States seal and on several coins, *E Pluribus Unum* ("out of many, one"), explicitly recognizes our diversity. It is a key ingredient of the nation's historical experience. In fact, the existence of distinct ethnic and religious groups and their desire to preserve some part of their distinctiveness underlie much of the history of political conflict in America. The contemporary debates over immigration, multiculturalism, and related issues show an unfortunate ignorance of American history. For that reason we should take a brief look at our past.

A Nation of Immigrants Then

After the successful campaign for ratification of the Constitution, the new federal government maintained the status quo policy of unrestricted immigration—if you could get here, you could come. Of course, not everyone was happy about such open borders. One of the most cosmopolitan Americans of the time, Benjamin Franklin, expressed his resentment of Germans in various letters:

> Why should *Pennsylvania,* founded by the *English,* become a colony of Aliens, who will shortly be so numerous as to Germanize us instead of our Anglifying them, and will never adopt our Language or Customs any more than they can acquire our Complexion? [emphasis in original].[13]

Despite such misgivings, land was plentiful, and labor scarce. The quicker the territory could be populated, the sooner economic development would follow. Immigration gradually increased, until by mid-century immigrants from England, Ireland, and Germany were arriving in numbers as high as 400,000 per year. Irish immigration became a major political issue. Many Protestants feared that Irish Catholics would put allegiance to the Pope above loyalty to the United States and that they might even plot to overthrow the government. Cartoonists of the period depicted the Irish as dark, hairy, ape-like people. In the 1854 elections, the anti-Catholic "Know-Nothing" party won 43 seats in the House of Representatives, almost a fifth of the chamber at the time. (The party's name came from its secret password, "I know nothing about it.")

Immigration increased considerably in the 1860s and continued at a high rate until World War I. In the 1860s and 1870s, the first of an eventual half-million French Canadians crossed the northeastern border of the United States, and several million Scandinavians joined a continuing stream of English, Irish, and Germans (see Figure 4.1). Political conflict in the late nineteenth century frequently was "ethno-cultural."[14] In the Midwest and much of the East, the Republican base lay in native Protestant communities, whereas the Democrats sank deep roots in the immigrant Catholic communities. Politics revolved around such issues as the prohibition or regulation of

ST. PATRICK'S DAY 1867.

RUM.   BRUTAL ATTACK ON THE POLICE. "THE DAY WE CELEBRATE!"   IRISH RIOT.   BLOOD.

Bigotry on St. Patrick's
Day c.1867
Thomas Nast portrays the Irish
(celebrating a national holiday) as
violent, ape-like brutes that riot
and attack the police.

• *Would you be likely to see
such a cartoon today? How would
racism be expressed today?*

alcohol, public funding of parochial schools, bilingual schools (mostly German, but French in New England), and Sunday "blue laws"—laws that restricted commercial and recreational activities on Sundays. German Lutherans were an important "swing" group in some midwestern states; they generally voted Republican but cultural conflict some-times swung them to the Democratic side. In Wisconsin, for example, the Republicans lost only two statewide elections between 1858 and 1890. One came after the party raised liquor license fees; the second, after it passed a measure requiring English language instruction in the schools.[15]

The Chinese were the first Asians to immigrate on a significant scale. More than 20,000 Chinese participated in the California Gold Rush, which began in 1849. (Only two-thirds of the "forty-niners" were Americans, and only two-thirds of the Americans were white; large numbers of Cherokee Indians and African Americans panned for gold.[16]) More than 100,000 Chinese laborers helped build the western links of the transcontinental railroads. At first these newcomers were viewed positively as peaceful, hard-working (and cheap) labor. Soon, however, a virulent backlash set in. During the congressional debate on the Chinese Exclusion Act of 1882, California Senator John Miller characterized the Chinese as

> machine-like . . . of obtuse nerve, but little affected by heat or cold, wiry, sinewy, with muscles of iron; . . . automatic engines of flesh and blood; . . . patient, stolid, unemotional, and persistent, with such a marvelous frame and digestive apparatus that they can dispense with the comforts of shelter and . . . grow fat on less than half the food necessary to sustain life in the Anglo Saxon.

How could white Californians (even in the nineteenth century!) compete with such immigrants? In the eyes of Senator Miller, they couldn't:

> The experiment now being tried in California is to subject American free labor to competition with Chinese servile labor, and so far as it has gone, it has put in progress the displacement of American laborers, and the substitution of Chinese for white men.

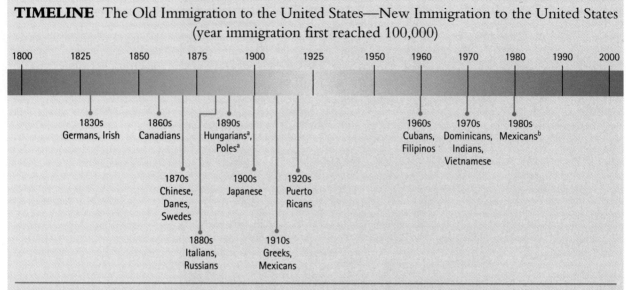

TIMELINE The Old Immigration to the United States—New Immigration to the United States (year immigration first reached 100,000)

1800   1825   1850   1875   1900   1925   1950   1960   1970   1980   1990   2000

1830s
Germans, Irish

1860s
Canadians

1890s
Hungarians[a],
Poles[a]

1960s
Cubans,
Filipinos

1970s
Dominicans,
Indians,
Vietnamese

1980s
Mexicans[b]

1870s
Chinese,
Danes,
Swedes

1900s
Japanese

1920s
Puerto
Ricans

1880s
Italians,
Russians

1910s
Greeks,
Mexicans

[a] Estimated because immigrants from the Austro-Hungarian Empire were not separately classified before World War I.

[b] Mexican immigration first reached 100,000 in the 1910s. However, in terms of new immigration, Mexican immigration peaked in the 1980s with over 1.65 million immigrants to the United States.

FIGURE 4.1

Immigration to the United States

The quantity and origin of immigrants to the United States have changed sharply over time.
* *Why might interest in emigrating to the United States rise and fall?*

Sources: Stephanie Bernado, *The Ethnic Almanac* (Garden City, NY: Doubleday, 1981): 22–140; The U.S. Immigration and Naturalization Service (http://www.ins.gov).

> The process will continue if permitted until the white laborer is driven out into other fields, or until those who remain in the contest come down to the Chinese level.[17]

Such charges were as common then as now: Cheap foreign labor will undercut the standard of living of "real" Americans—a charge that has repeatedly been leveled at immigrants through the decades.

Beginning in the 1880s the character of immigration changed, as millions of people from southern and eastern Europe followed their northern and western European predecessors. Once again, these new arrivals were viewed as threatening by many "real" Americans, who by now believed that pre-1880 immigrants "were drawn from the superior stocks of northern and western Europe, while those who came later were drawn from the inferior breeds of southern and eastern Europe."[18] A best-selling book by Madison Grant of the American Museum of Natural History, published in 1916, reflects the sentiments of the time. Grant charged that European governments were unloading on the United States "the sweepings of their jails and asylums." He described new immigrants as "the weak, the broken, and the mentally crippled of all races drawn from the lowest stratum of the Mediterranean basin and the Balkans, together with hordes of the wretched, submerged populations of the Polish ghettoes."[19]

Reflecting widespread popular concern, a government commission was established in 1907 to study the immigration situation. Three years later, the U.S. Immigration

Commission issued an immense report. The following observations, lifted from that report, illustrate how Americans of the time period viewed outsiders, and also how quick they were to prejudge entire immigrant groups:

[Greeks]: "There is no doubt of their nimble intelligence. They compete with the Hebrew race as the best traders of the Orient."

[Southern Italian]: "excitable, impulsive, highly imaginative, impracticable . . . an individualist having little adaptability to high organized society."

[Persian]: "is rather brilliant and poetical than solid in temperament. Like the Hindu he is more eager to secure the semblance than the substance of modern civilization."

[Poles]: "are more high strung than are the most of their neighbors. In this respect they resemble the Hungarians farther south."

[Romanians]: "more emotional than the Slav, less stolid and heavy than the Bulgarian."

[White Russians]: "are said by travelers to be a distinctly weaker stock than the Great Russians and less prepossessing in appearance."

[Serbo-Croatians]: 19th century "savage manners" persist, "illiteracy is prevalent and civilization at a low stage . . . ."[20]

Such ethnic stereotyping displays official insensitivity on a scale undreamed of today. No one should ever think that the American "melting pot" in any way resembled Mr. Rogers' neighborhood—a community of harmony and love.

Not all opposition to immigration reflected ethnic or religious bigotry. Some opposed further immigration for economic or political reasons. Union leaders feared that continued immigration would undercut the bargaining power of workers. And, in fact, American business did encourage immigration as a source of cheap labor. The Progressives, a reformist political movement, opposed further immigration because they viewed immigrants as the foundation of corrupt urban political machines (see Chapter 8). The Progressives believed that shutting off immigration would shut off the supply of uninformed, ignorant voters whom the machines could manipulate.

For many reasons, then, anti-immigration sentiment grew. After two decades of agitation, a national literacy test was adopted in 1917 (as we shall see in Chapter 17, such a device had earlier been used to disfranchise African Americans and poor whites in the South). Supporters of the test did not disguise their motives. The noted Massachusetts senator Henry Cabot Lodge observed that the test "will bear most heavily on the Italians, Russians, Poles, Hungarians, Greeks, and Asiatics, and very lightly, or not at all upon English-speaking emigrants or Germans, Scandinavians, and French."[21]

Contrary to what Senator Lodge believed, many would-be immigrants knew how to read—or learned to do so quickly—so stronger legislation was needed to close the door. A series of laws passed in the 1920s restricted immigration both quantitatively (the total was limited) and qualitatively (quotas gave northern and western Europeans preference over people from other areas).[22] The Japanese and other Asians were added to the Chinese as groups that were excluded altogether. By 1930 the era of the open door had ended, although Mexicans continued to enter the southwestern states to work in American agriculture (joining those who had been incorporated when Mexico ceded a substantial part of its territory to the United States), and after World War II Puerto Ricans in significant numbers emigrated to New York City. But, before the United States closed its doors to immigrants, more than 35 million people had left hearth and home to come to America. These immigrants and their children made a major contribution to the growth of the United States from a country of about 10 million inhabitants in 1820 to one of more than 100 million in 1920.

Restrictions on immigration were part of a general reactionary movement that broke out after World War I. During the "Red Scare," immigrants were persecuted as carriers of Bolshevik, anarchist, and other subversive foreign ideologies. In the 1920s anti-Catholic and anti-Jewish sentiments energized the second Ku Klux Klan; it counted 25–30 percent of the adult male Protestant population in its membership.[23] Not surprisingly, the 1928 Democratic presidential nomination of Catholic Al Smith caused a virulent reaction.[24]

In the 1930s discrimination against Catholics and Jews was still widespread. Indeed, not until the 1950s did Ivy League universities eliminate informal quotas on admissions of Jewish students. Gradually, however, ethno-cultural tensions died down. The cumulative effects of economic depression, World War II, revulsion at the Holocaust, and the Cold War led to a general reduction in ethnic and racial tensions that lasted approximately a generation. However, this short period from the early 1930s to the mid-1960s, during which ethnic and religious issues were relatively dormant, was the exception, not the norm. From the founding through the 1930s, the kinds of issues now discussed under the heading of multiculturalism were an important part of American politics.

A Nation of Immigrants Now

The Immigration Act of 1965 abandoned the national-quotas system favoring northern Europeans, opening the door to the largest surge of immigration since the 1900s.

Small Family-Owned Businesses Have Often Provided Immigrants with an Entry Point into the American Economy

A Korean flower shop in the East Village of New York City, one of many markets throughout the city that are owned and run by Korean immigrants.

Illegal Immigrants: An Emerging Political Power?

In 2004, illegal immigrants held rallies throughout the country to demand increased access to government benefits and services routinely available to citizens and legal immigrants, such as driver's licenses. As the cartoon indicates, not everyone was delighted with this development.

Immigration from Latin America and the West Indies increased rapidly. In addition, hundreds of thousands of new immigrants from Vietnam, Korea, Cambodia, India, Iran, the Philippines, and other countries became the first numerically significant Asian groups to arrive since the Japanese in the early years of the twentieth century (review Figure 4.1).

In the 1990s the absolute number of immigrants—about 9 million—was higher than in any previous decade, although it was lower as a proportion of the population than it had been at the turn of the century. Three million came from Mexico, Central America, and the Caribbean, and nearly as many from Asia. Nearly half a million came from South America and almost 200,000 from Africa. These figures include only legal immigrants; an estimated 11 million people now live in the United States illegally.[25]

Figure 4.2 depicts the result of this newest wave of immigration. Euro-whites are now less than three-quarters of the population. And Hispanics, the largest newer immigrant group, now surpass African Americans as the nation's largest minority group. The Census Bureau projects that the population of European origin will fall to less than 60 percent by 2030. In many large cities, whites of European origin are already a minority. These dramatic changes underlie contemporary debates over issues such as bilingual education and the provision of social services to immigrants.

Understanding
Who We Are

Immigration as a Contemporary Issue

In 1994, California voters overwhelmingly passed Proposition 187, an initiative that denied state services to illegal immigrants and their children. Although the proposition was struck down by the courts, the question of eligibility for governmental services has

FIGURE 4.2

U.S. Population by Race and Ethnicity, 2005 and 2030

The two fastest-growing population groups are Asians and Hispanics. The Census Bureau projects that this will result in a significant shift in the composition of the American population over the next two decades.

Source: U.S. Census Bureau, www.census.gov.

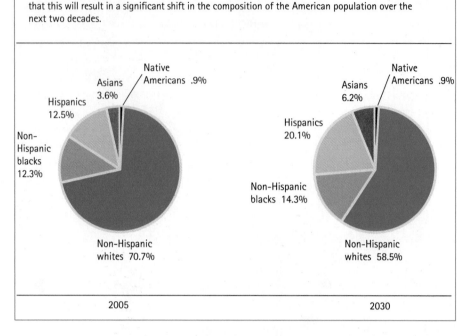

The two fastest-growing population groups are Asians and Hispanics. The Census Bureau projects that this will result in a significant shift in the composition of the American population over the next two decades.

2005

Native Americans .9%
Asians 3.6%
Hispanics 12.5%
Non-Hispanic blacks 12.3%
Non-Hispanic whites 70.7%

2030

Native Americans .9%
Asians 6.2%
Hispanics 20.1%
Non-Hispanic blacks 14.3%
Non-Hispanic whites 58.5%

The Debate Over Immigration

remained on the national agenda ever since. Welfare reforms enacted in 1996 denied legal immigrants access to food stamps, a law that remained in effect until it was reversed in 2003. President Bush's 2004 proposal to grant amnesty to undocumented Mexicans working in the United States failed to pass; it was opposed by Democrats with labor union ties as well as by Republicans who considered the proposal a reward for lawbreakers. At the present time immigration remains a contentious issue in Congress. (See *Election Voices: Immigration* at the end of this chapter.)

Much of the contemporary debate over immigration would sound familiar to Americans of earlier eras. Does providing services to immigrants impose a burden on native citizens? Do immigrants take jobs from native workers? Do hard-working immigrant entrepreneurs drive "native" shopkeepers out of business? As we have seen, such fears are not new, but historical analogies are never perfect. In some significant respects immigration today differs from that of the past.

First, in contrast to earlier periods in American history, immigrants are not entering an economy hungry for unskilled labor. There is no exploding railroad industry to absorb today's immigrants as it absorbed the Irish and the Chinese. No expanding steel industry hires recruiters in Latin America to recruit laborers as it hired recruiters in Poland and Italy. The American economy is moving away from manufacturing to a globally integrated service and information economy. Many Americans, especially those who lack technical skills, are disadvantaged by the transition. Research indicates that competition from immigrants undercuts the wages of low-skilled Americans who already are struggling to make ends meet.[26]

Second, there are geographical and jurisdictional mismatches between the costs and benefits of immigration. A large majority of the new immigrants have settled in a few states such as California, New York, Texas, Florida, New Jersey, and Illinois. Although most studies conclude that immigrants contribute to economic growth and pay nearly as much in taxes as they consume in government services, most of the taxes paid by immigrants are federal income and social security taxes that go to the national government rather than directly to the states where immigrants concentrate.[27] In addition, within states, the localities are responsible for providing educational and social services to new immigrants, although they do not directly receive the taxes immigrants pay. Disparities such as these focus the costs of immigration much more narrowly than the benefits. Heavy immigration forces local and state governments to cut services, raise taxes, and beg for money from higher levels of government, options that elected officials naturally view as unpleasant.

Finally, whereas late-nineteenth-century law barred persons "likely to become a public charge," the immigration law adopted in 1965 gives preference to those with relatives already in the country: more than two-thirds of all immigrants in recent years have entered the country on family preferences.[28] In consequence, a higher proportion of dependent persons—especially older people—are admitted now than in previous eras. Thus, current U.S. immigration policy admits fewer taxpayers and more people in need of services than did earlier laws that gave first preference to productive workers. Even if immigrants as a group pay as much in taxes as they consume in services, many American taxpayers ask why they should admit *anyone* likely to be dependent on government programs?

Of course, appropriate changes in public policy could address these economic reasons why some Americans oppose immigration. However, some Americans would still oppose immigration because they regard it as a different sort of risk, not an economic risk but one that threatens the American political culture. They believe that immigrants who speak different languages, believe in different religions, and practice different customs threaten American unity. Samuel Huntington, for example, claims that today's immigrants lack the Anglo-Protestant values that constitute the American identity.[29] Such critics urge the United States to close the door before too much *pluribus* destroys the *unum*.[30] To evaluate such fears, we need to understand the American identity that some fear is at risk.

Philosophical Unity

From the French visitor Alexis de Tocqueville in the 1830s to the Swede Gunnar Myrdal in the 1940s, foreign observers have claimed that Americans share basic values. These fundamental beliefs usually are described as *liberal*—but to political philosophers the term means something very different from its meaning in current politics.[31] Classical **liberalism** is a philosophy that emerged in Europe as medieval thought disintegrated in the religious wars of the seventeenth century. It sought to free individuals from a society structured by heredity and religious privilege, and to empower them at the expense of the nobility and the clergy. Roughly speaking, liberal thinkers wanted people to make political and religious choices for themselves. Modern-day American conservatives, who champion keeping government out of economic decisions, and modern-day American liberals, who champion keeping government out of moral decisions, both have roots in a "liberal" political philosophy.

Focusing on individuals rather than groups gave liberal thinkers a unique perspective on society and government. They did not view people as a product of their society, a view that goes back to the Greeks. Rather, they considered society a product of the individuals who made it up. The writings of the "social contract" theorists, such as Thomas Hobbes, John Locke, and Jean-Jacques Rousseau, contain the purest expression of this perspective. These philosophers tried to imagine what human life would be like in a natural state,

liberalism
A philosophy that elevates and empowers the individual as opposed to religious, hereditary, governmental, or other forms of authority.

without society or government, so that they could deduce why people would create political institutions in the first place. That is, their approach started from an assumption that people can exist as isolated beings. They imagined government as nothing more than a creation of the individuals who chose to develop it, an agreement much like a contract in which both rulers and ruled accept certain rights, duties, and obligations.

Locke deduced a string of political principles from such assumptions. First, individuals have basic rights—life, liberty, and property—that precede the existence of government and that government therefore may not violate. Second, individuals are equal under the law; there are no distinctions based on heredity or religion. Third, to safeguard rights, government must be limited. Fourth, government is instrumental—not an end in itself but a means to the end of ensuring people's rights. Fifth, when a government threatens rights or fails to protect citizens, they may replace it with another.

The preceding principles should have a familiar ring. American colonists read social-contract theorists such as Locke in the years before rebelling against England. Thomas Jefferson encapsulated the spirit of classical liberalism in the Declaration of Independence:

> **We hold these truths to be self-evident: That all men are created equal, that they are endowed by their Creator with certain inalienable Rights, that among these are Life, Liberty, and the Pursuit of Happiness.**
>
> **That to secure these rights Governments are instituted among Men, deriving their just powers from the consent of the governed;**
>
> **That whenever any Form of Government becomes destructive of these ends, it is the Right of the People to alter or to abolish it, and to institute new Government, laying its foundation on such principles and organizing its powers in such form, as to them shall seem most likely to effect their Safety and Happiness.**

These eloquent sentences capture the five tenets of liberal philosophy: political equality, rights, instrumental government, limited government, and the right to rebel. The Constitution and its Bill of Rights followed on this liberal tradition by laying out in detail the rights of citizens, the limits on government, and rules for changing leaders that would make future rebellion unnecessary.

To some degree, philosophers and historians have exaggerated the extent to which all Americans share such a coherent political philosophy. Many writers refer to the American "creed" and the American "ethos." Terms such as these suggest a more unified and well-defined set of beliefs than actually exists. In fact, at the time of the American Revolution, liberalism coexisted with a rival, civic republican tradition.[32] According to Gordon Wood, **civic republicanism** placed more emphasis on the welfare of the community relative to the rights of the individual.[33] Called "communitarian" today, this tradition faded over time but certainly has not disappeared—as illustrated by President John F. Kennedy's famous exhortation: "Ask not what your country can do for you; ask what you can do for your country!"

Skeptics also point out that the rights and privileges exalted in the liberal tradition extended only so far. In particular, they did not extend to the Native American tribes that were destroyed by the American settlers, and they did not extend fully to African Americans until a century after the Civil War. Full rights and privileges did not extend to women until even later.[34] And the rights of other minority groups such as homosexuals remain matters of political disagreement today. But even if the "liberal tradition" has been less than all-encompassing, there is plenty of evidence that Americans tend to agree on certain basic "liberal" principles and that Americans differ in systematic ways from the citizens of other democracies.

civic republicanism
A political philosophy that emphasizes the obligation of citizens to act virtuously in pursuit of the common good.

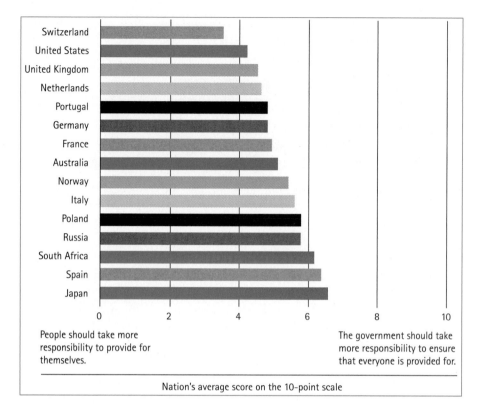

FIGURE 4.3

Americans Emphasize
Individual Responsibility
More Than People
Elsewhere

Source: The World Values Survey, 2005.

American Individualism

Perhaps the most striking way in which Americans differ from people elsewhere lies in the balance they strike between individual responsibility on the one hand and governmental responsibility on the other. International surveys consistently find that Americans lean more toward the side of individual responsibility than do citizens of other democracies. For example, Figure 4.3 compares the responses of citizens of 15 democracies to a question about individual versus government responsibility for the welfare of individuals. While all countries display a mixture of viewpoints, on average we Americans favor self-reliance more than do the citizens of 13 of the other democracies; only the Swiss exceed us.

Other recent surveys show that Americans are much less supportive of government efforts to reduce inequality than are people elsewhere. As shown in Figure 4.4, just over a quarter of Americans support government policies to reduce income inequality, whereas majorities in Germany, Britain, and various other democracies support it. Americans are suspicious of governmental power and skeptical about governmental competence, attitudes that reinforce their emphasis on individual responsibility. As one scholar comments, "the distinctive aspect of the American creed is its antigovernment character. Opposition to power and suspicion of government as the most dangerous embodiment of power are the central themes of American political thought."[35] If people fundamentally doubt the motives and capabilities of government, they can hardly be expected to grant it expansive powers and responsibilities. Moreover, Americans believe that individual responsibility works, that hard work and perseverance pay off. People elsewhere are less likely to see personal effort as a sure means to better one's life, and therefore are less likely to be optimistic about getting ahead (see Figure 4.5.)

FIGURE 4.4

Americans Are Less Supportive of Government Actions to Reduce Economic Inequality than Are People Elsewhere

Source: Ladd, The American Ideology (1994), p. 75.

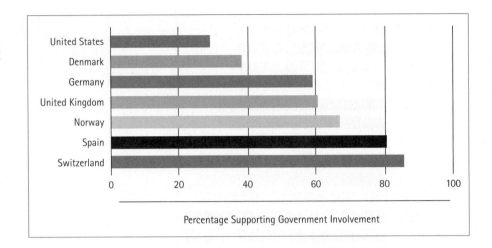

Percentage Supporting Government Involvement

One of the most striking features of the American belief in individual responsibility is that it is not closely tied to the actual social and economic circumstances in which Americans find themselves. We might think those at the bottom of the economic ladder to be far less individualistic and optimistic than those at the top, but that expectation is wrong. Even the very poorest Americans reject a government-guaranteed income, and only the very poorest believe that the government should reduce income differences. There is little or no relationship between income and belief in the benefits of hard work: majorities of the poorest Americans subscribe to this belief, just as do similar majorities of the most affluent.[36]

Other studies reveal that poor Americans are as likely as more affluent ones to embrace the "work ethic" and equally likely to take personal responsibility for their condition.[37] The poor dislike the progressive income tax almost as much as the rich (see Chapter 19).[38] Perhaps the most powerful illustration of American individualism lies in the attitudes of minorities. African Americans clearly share less in the American dream than do whites.

FIGURE 4.5

Americans Are More Optimistic About Their Chances of Getting Ahead Than People Elsewhere

Note: On a 1–10 scale of "How much freedom of choice and control you feel you have over the way your life turns out," the reported percentages are a summation of the three most positive responses.

Source: The World Values Survey, 2005.

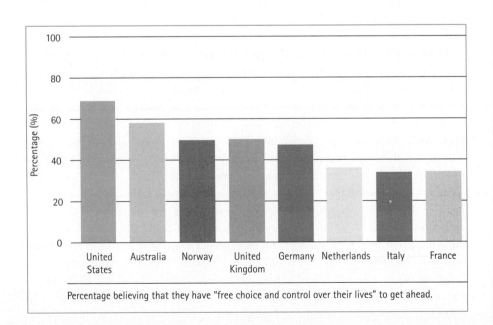

Percentage believing that they have "free choice and control over their lives" to get ahead.

On average, they earn less, work in less prestigious occupations, and suffer discrimination in many forms. It comes as a surprise, then, that they are almost as likely as whites to embrace the individualist ethic (see Figure 4.6). In sum, even those Americans who are faring poorly in an individualist social order still support its basic premises.[39]

The Tension Between Individualism and Equality

The findings on American individualism raise an important question: What about equality? Liberal philosophy places great importance on equality, and writers in the liberal tradition typically mention it just after liberty. Yet great inequalities exist in the United States. For example, not only is there a large gulf between the incomes of the poor and rich, but the gulf actually has increased since the early 1970s. Nevertheless, most Americans do not demand that such income inequality be eliminated or even lessened.

At one time there was no incompatibility between liberty and equality. Indeed, Tocqueville and other early-nineteenth-century visitors were struck by the extent of social and economic equality in the United States. Liberty and equality were thought to be complementary in the sense that free people would use their liberty to achieve economic success, and an economically secure middle class would use its resources to promote liberty. After the Civil War, however, economic development weakened the association between liberty and equality. The Industrial Revolution produced great concentrations of private wealth on the one hand and masses of low-wage workers on the other. Under such conditions, liberty and equality became detached.

Nevertheless, radical movements such as socialism have made little headway in the United States. American reform movements typically have focused on reducing economic inequality without attacking the foundations of the economic system that generates it. At first glance this limited demand for change might suggest that Americans actually do not value equality very much, but the more likely explanation for this apparent inconsistency is that America's political culture supports only a limited kind of equality. Liberalism emphasized equality before the law, regardless of heredity or religious faith or personal connections; it did not demand economic equality. It guaranteed freedom to

You Are the Leader
of Concerned Citizens
for World Justice

What Are American
Civic Values?

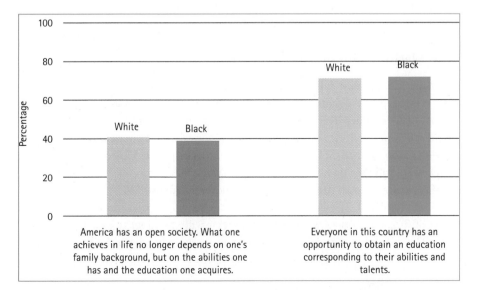

FIGURE 4.6

Even Racial Minorities Share the Individualist Values of the Larger Society

Source: The General Social Survey, 2004.

pursue happiness; it did not promise that everyone would achieve happiness. Most Americans regard economic inequality as not only inevitable but also generally fair—those who produce more for society deserve to receive more, even if they get rich. Majorities therefore reject aggressive government action to erase such inequalities.

Today, it is customary to talk about this distinction in terms of the difference between **equality of opportunity** and **equality of condition**. Americans strongly support equality of opportunity: Everyone should have a fair chance. After the competition starts, though, may the best person win! Americans just as strongly reject attempts to bring about equality of condition, because that may involve rewarding people who are undeserving at the expense of those who work harder. Survey data probing attitudes about affirmative action reflect this distinction. Americans favor affirmative action for women and minorities when the survey questions are clear that equal opportunity is the goal. For example, one study found that

> Ninety-four percent agree that "Our society should do what is necessary to make sure that everyone has an equal opportunity to succeed."

> Seventy-nine percent agree that "After years of discrimination, it is only fair to set up special programs to make sure that women and minorities are given every chance to have equal opportunities in employment and education."

But Americans just as strongly oppose affirmative action when the survey questions indicate that equality of outcome is the goal:

> Eighty-six percent don't think "blacks and other minorities should receive preference in college admissions to make up for past inequalities."

> Eighty percent don't think "blacks and other minorities should receive preference in hiring to make up for past inequalities."[40]

As far as most Americans are concerned, equality of opportunity should be enough. The rest is up to the individual. This belief also shows up in government policy. As social critics have pointed out, the United States spends a smaller proportion of its national income on social welfare than most other democracies—and spends especially little on the young (see Chapter 18). But the United States historically has spent a larger proportion of its national income on education than other democracies. Education is not "welfare." It is a means to create equal opportunity, a way for individuals to improve their skills and become better economic competitors. That idea fits with American core values.[41]

One Nation, Under God?

The American political culture stands out in one other notable way, one that is seemingly at odds with its emphasis on individualism: Americans are more religious than the citizens of most other democracies. Americans are more likely to believe in God, to attend religious services, and to report that religion plays an important role in their lives—far more so than citizens in the countries that originally settled the colonies (see Figure 4.7). And they do not separate their religious beliefs from their politics: a majority of Americans report that they will not vote for an atheist.[42]

The prevalence of religious faith goes back to the nation's founding, of course. Many of the original settlers were people seeking the freedom to practice their religion. These deeply religious people sought to escape persecution by the established churches of Europe. Furthermore, the nation periodically has replenished its store of

equality of opportunity
The notion that individuals should have an equal chance to advance economically through individual talent and hard work.

equality of condition
The notion that all individuals have a right to a more or less equal part of the material goods that society produces.

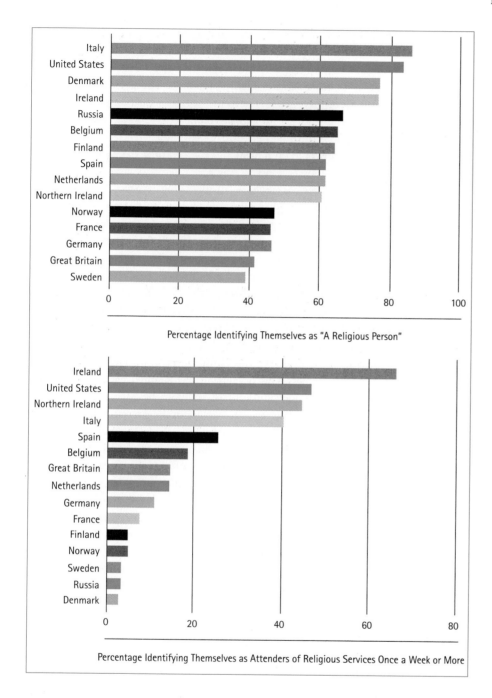

FIGURE 4.7
Americans Are More
Religious Than People
Elsewhere

Source: The World Values Survey, 2005.

religious energy through great spiritual "awakenings" that wash over the country: the First Great Awakening in the 1730s and 1740s, the second around 1800 and into Jackson's presidency (1828–1836), the third starting in the 1890s and lasting about two decades.

While church and state institutions are separate in the United States (with early exceptions, such as the Congregational Church, which was the established church of

Church
and State

Connecticut until 1818 and of Massachusetts until 1833), religion and politics have seldom been separate. Church leaders cannot impose laws on American citizens and punish them for immoral behavior, as they can in some countries. Nevertheless, foreign observers agree that American politics is highly moralistic. Throughout history, religiously motivated Americans have attempted to use government to improve the character of their fellow citizens—that is, "to legislate morality"—more so than people in other democracies. At various times and places, laws have restricted recreational activities on Sundays, prohibited people from drinking, and censored the books and magazines people can read or the movies they can watch.

The continued importance of religion in the United States puzzles many observers. The nation's historical origins alone cannot explain it. After all, numerous forces have changed American society since the founding: westward expansion, the Industrial Revolution, immigration, and great wars, to name a few. Moreover, churches are not publicly supported in the United States. Some other democracies have an "established" church, an official religion that is subsidized by the state. The Anglican Church is the established church in Great Britain, the Catholic Church in Italy, the Lutheran Church in Norway, and the Eastern Orthodox Church in Greece. In the United States, no religious institution receives direct government support.

Furthermore, religiosity does not seem to fit well with American values. Christian faith, for example, may impose various burdens on members, in particular, an obligation to help their fellow human beings. This orientation seems somewhat at odds with a political culture that emphasizes individualism. In addition, by calling Americans to reflect on spiritual matters, religion also seems to clash with the American reputation for practicality. Americans stereotypically focus on problem solving, on material success. They are supposed to show a trust in logic, in science, in technology, in the evidence before their eyes (a way of thinking that philosophers call "positivism"). How can we explain the robustness of religious faith in a country with no established church, with a reputation for individualism, and with a people known for their hard-headed pragmatism?

The answer is that religion and the liberal tradition are more compatible than it first appears. Some argue that just as the liberal tradition encourages economic entrepreneurship, so it encourages religious entrepreneurship as well. Church leaders know that they do not have a captive audience, as in countries with established churches. They compete to retain the loyalty of their existing "customers" and adapt their "product" to the changing interests and values of potential new customers. Thus, contemporary churches provide services and activities (youth clubs, sports clubs, and even singles clubs) that people value. Just as the free market in economics encourages economic enterprise, a free market in religion may encourage religious enterprise.

The result of all this religious enterprise is a greater *supply* of religion in the United States. Think of the wide assortment of religions, denominations, branches, and sects. This rich range of options makes it easier for a person to find a comfortable match with some religion in America than in other countries, where citizens typically have a much smaller range of choices. If an American does not like one religion, there are numerous others from which to choose, and exceptionally hard-to-please worshippers can always start their own churches, which a fair number of people do—just Google "house church" and look at what comes up. Thus, Americans may be more involved with religion than people in other countries because, stimulated by competition, American religion offers them more reasons to be.

Perhaps the most intriguing explanation for the persistence of religiosity in the United States has been proposed by Robert Booth Fowler, who argues that there is a greater *demand* for religion in the United States. Fowler argues that the liberal tradition and religiosity do not conflict. In fact, just the opposite is true—the liberal tradition creates a deep need for religion. People steeped in the liberal tradition jealously guard their rights and hold themselves personally responsible for their successes and failures. They create a society characterized by social and geographic mobility and by rapid social and economic change.

Fowler believes that many people find life in such a society precarious, or at least somewhat lonely. He sees religion as filling a gap in American life. Whereas citizens in communal cultures already feel part of something bigger than themselves, individualism leaves Americans with a greater need for a religious dimension in their lives:

> Religion has aided liberalism by being a *refuge* from liberalism . . . . [I]t provides an escape from liberal culture, a place of comfort where individualism, competition, this-worldly pragmatism, and relentless rationalism do not hold sway. In a liberal country with liberal citizens, religion is a place where one can come home . . . and *then* emerge refreshed for the battles of life in the liberal world.[43]

If true, this argument would explain the periodic occurrence of religious awakenings. They should result whenever the prosperity created by individualism draws Americans too far from the spiritual ideals that many of them hold.[44] People eventually begin to wonder whether there is something more to life than money and success. Others are troubled by the self-serving behavior of their fellow individualists. Thus people turn to religion as an alternate avenue to personal satisfaction and as a means of correcting the destructive behavior of others.

Some observers believe that the United States is in the middle of its fourth great awakening, for reasons similar to those implied by Fowler's theory. They suggest that Evangelical Protestantism surged in the 1980s as a reaction to the excesses of the 1960s, a period of great economic growth during which the baby boomers—the individualistic "me generation"—came of age. Such sweeping historical claims are impossible to prove. Nevertheless, the last several decades only reinforce an indisputable feature of the American political culture: Along with individualism and belief in equality of opportunity, religiosity is a long-standing trait of the American public.

Why a Liberal Political Culture?

The time has now come to answer the question posed at the start of this chapter: How can we explain the apparent inconsistency between a population that is strikingly heterogeneous in its ethnic, racial, and religious composition but surprisingly homogeneous in the beliefs and values that make up its political culture?

Traditional Explanations of American Liberalism

Early American colonists tended to come from the European "middle class." They usually were not poor peasants, but they also were not rich nobles. They were largely the very merchants, professionals, and artisans among whom liberal ideas had flourished, and they carried their political philosophy with them to North America, where they found little to contradict it. According to scholar Louis Hartz, the key to understanding America is that it lacked a feudal tradition. There was no hereditary aristocracy or established church to defend or to resist, nor was there an oppressed peasant class that might revolt.[45] In short, the United States took form among a white population for whom classical liberalism could be taken as "self-evident."

Others argue that perhaps as important as what the United States lacked, is what it had: in particular, a great deal of land. North America was a sparsely populated continent over which the United States steadily expanded.[46] Some historians suggest that the frontier operated like a social safety valve: Rather than revolt against intolerable conditions, the only option in the settled countries of Europe, struggling Americans found it easier to pack up their belongings, move west, grab some land (often from Mexico or an indigenous tribe), and start again.

A plentiful supply of land and a scarcity of labor meant that ambitious individuals could and did succeed. Social conditions in the new country therefore reinforced the individualistic values that early settlers brought with them. And with little competition from alternative value systems, a liberal political order and a market economy thrived. Generations of radical critics of American society have sadly asked, "Why no socialism in America?"[47] Many complex philosophical and historical answers have been offered, but the simplest answer is that Americans never saw much need for socialism. Under the conditions that prevailed, individual effort usually was enough to provide an acceptable life for most people; they did not require governmental solutions (let alone revolutionary ones).

Still, questions remain. The frontier was officially closed more than a century ago, and labor shortages have not been of much concern for more than half a century. So even if social conditions in the nineteenth century reinforced the beliefs and values of

Major Technological Innovations That Have Changed the Political Landscape

the early settlers, how relevant is that today? Slaves freed after the Civil War certainly had little experience with liberty or equality. Moreover, the millions of immigrants who arrived after the Civil War were not from liberal societies. Most of them came from authoritarian states with established churches and had lived their lives in communal peasant societies that *did* have feudal traditions. What is the basis for *their* adherence to the individualist values of the liberal tradition?

Perhaps the answer lies in a process of **political socialization** that continues to instill liberal values long after the initial basis for those values—social equality, an unsettled land, a frontier—eroded. Certainly, material conditions are not the only factor that determines how people think and view the world. Different cultures socialize their children into different ways of thinking and different ways of viewing the world, even under similar material circumstances. Beginning in the family and continuing in schools, religious institutions, and other organizations, societies instill certain values and patterns of thinking in their members. Thus, the explanation for the persistence of the liberal tradition could be simple: Socialization perpetuates a consensus established in the eighteenth century, a consensus that so dominated the schools and other social institutions that it was able to integrate the children of slaves as well as tens of millions of immigrants.

Many scholars find such an explanation insufficient. For one thing, one of the principal means by which immigrants were integrated into American society was through the efforts of political parties, particularly the urban machines discussed in Chapter 8. The machines were interested in controlling government; to do that they had to win elections, and immigrant votes counted just as much as those of the native-born. Thus the machines organized each arriving group: In some eastern cities the Democrats gained an edge by organizing the Irish, the Republicans then countered by organizing the Italians, and so on. But the urban machines did not embody liberal, individualist values. On the contrary, the machines were something of an anomaly in the larger American political culture; they were collectivist and clannish—with an emphasis on obedience and loyalty, not on independence. Because machine politics and immigration are closely associated in American history, we might expect political socialization to have pushed immigrants in a direction different from the liberal tradition.

political socialization

The set of psychological and sociological processes by which families, schools, religious organizations, communities, and other societal units inculcate beliefs and values in their members.

Renewing the Tradition

Immigration is a difficult process that tends to attract people with a greater sense of individualism and independence than found among those who stay in their home countries.

Newer Explanations

Researchers skeptical of cultural explanations of how classical liberalism has survived over the centuries despite the influx of millions of diverse people from different traditions have proposed alternative explanations. In a provocative argument Sven Steinmo suggests that the belief that liberal ideas shape American government and politics is an oversimplification; rather, the reverse is also true—the government and politics of the United States recreate liberal ideas.[48] Specifically, Steinmo argues that American government is so fragmented and decentralized that it rarely acts in a positive way to improve society. Often it is "gridlocked" or unable to act, and when it does act, its actions reflect deals among special interests. In consequence, successive generations of Americans learn the same basic lesson: Rely on yourself because you cannot rely on government, and best keep government limited because it will usually act in support of special interests. Given their institutions, Americans would have learned this lesson whether they were originally liberal individualists or not. Steinmo's key insight is that, once established, institutions that originally *reflected* particular values may come to *generate* those values.

More recently, scholars have begun to advance the argument that social diversity and the liberal tradition never contradicted each other in the first place. Rather than posing a threat to American traditions, in fact, the flow of diverse peoples to America may have reinforced and strengthened American traditions. How could that be the case? The answer lies in what statistical analysts refer to as *self-selection*. With the notable exception of African Americans, immigrants came to the United States voluntarily. True, many came when crops failed, when they could not find work, or when they faced political persecution at home. Emigration under such circumstances might not seem to have occurred by choice, *but not everyone chose to emigrate.* Only a small fraction of the potential immigrants—less than 1 percent—actually left their own countries. Furthermore, not all of them chose to stay in the United States; about a third of immigrants eventually returned to their home countries.

What kind of person would have been most likely to travel to a new country, leaving family, friends, and village behind? Remember that immigration through most of history was not a matter of taking a train to Dublin, Frankfurt, or Rome and catching a flight to New York or Chicago. Before the Civil War, the journey usually took months, as immigrants walked to a port and then suffered through a long, miserable journey below deck on a sailing ship. Even after the Civil War, when the steamship shortened the ocean voyage and the railroad shortened the journey overland, it still took weeks. Many (if not most) of the people who booked passage knew that they would never see their relatives or their homes again.[49] What kind of people made such a decision?

In all probability the people who immigrated already were—relative to their own societies—unusually individualistic. They were more motivated to break free from the traditions of their communities. They were more ambitious, more willing to run risks in the hope of bettering themselves—in Hartz's words, more likely to possess "the spirit which repudiated peasantry and tenantry."[50] Prejudiced as it was, even the Immigration Commission in 1911 conceded that "emigrating to a strange and distant country, although less of an undertaking than formerly, is still a serious and relatively difficult matter, requiring a degree of courage and resourcefulness not possessed by weaklings of any class."[51] In short, even if they had never heard of the liberal tradition, immigrants already embodied much of its spirit.

Given this independent spirit, immigration and the diversity it produced never were a threat to American values. On the contrary, successive waves of immigrants rejuvenated those values. People who were willing to endure hardships, eager to work hard, and convinced that they could have a better life were compatible with the American way of life. There is no reason to believe that today's immigrants are any different. They too have left homes and families. They have endured hardships to come to a new land with a different culture and language. In some extreme cases, they have risked life and limb to emigrate, as did the "boat people" of southeast Asia—who braved pirates, sharks, and storms—and the Cubans who swam from rafts to the Florida coast. Such people display a kind of individual initiative that can rightly be considered "American," regardless of their nationality.

Arguments such as the preceding suggest that the fears of people such as Huntington are misplaced. Huntington worries that the processes of assimilation that imposed Anglo-Protestant values on earlier immigrants will not work on the new waves of Catholic—especially Latino—immigrants. The ideology of multiculturalism has made American elites reluctant to encourage immigrants to adopt American values, and the contiguity of the U.S. to Mexico and Latin America make Spanish-speaking immigrants reluctant to cut their ties with their ancestral homes. But one does not have to be Anglo or Protestant to have the kinds of values that Huntington believes define the American identity.

Indeed, most non-Anglo, non-Protestants who immigrate to the United States probably have a greater commitment to such values than some Anglo-Protestants who have lived here for generations. One reason that scholars such as Huntington go astray is that they pay too much attention to the writing and rhetoric of unrepresentative ethnic activists and have too little contact with the great mass of immigrants. As we will note repeatedly in the chapters that follow, the leaders of interest groups generally have more extreme views than the people they claim to represent. For every activist demanding the preservation of a separate cultural identity (or reuniting the American Southwest with Mexico!), there are thousands of ordinary immigrants working hard so that they and their children can enjoy the benefits of life in America.

In fact, systematic evidence strongly suggests that the Mexican laborers, Korean grocers, and Middle Eastern service-station operators are today's successors to the Irish laborers, Italian grocers, and Jewish shopkeepers of generations past. One widely noted study reports that on the basis of standard measures of assimilation (citizenship, home ownership, English acquisition, and intermarriage), today's immigrants "overwhelmingly do what immigrants have always done: slowly, often painfully, but quite assuredly, embrace the language, cultural norms and loyalties of America."[52] Other studies suggest that the use of English as a principal language is occurring *more* rapidly among the children of today's immigrants than in the past.[53] And educational and economic progress among Latinos is occurring faster than among earlier European immigrants.[54]

Similarly, in the less tangible realm of beliefs and values, de la Garza's surveys find that the children of Puerto Rican immigrants hold values almost indistinguishable from those native English speakers in similar socioeconomic conditions.[55] His studies of Mexican immigrants reach very similar conclusions.[56] Earlier Gallup surveys found that immigrants, even those who have been in the country 10 years or less, are virtually indistinguishable from native-born Americans—both in their beliefs about economic opportunity and in their general attitudes toward assimilation.[57]

In sum, the evidence is mounting that American society today is evolving along a path that it has followed in the past. Ethnic, racial, and religious diversity does not imply disagreement on basic values. Although the process has never been easy, Americans seem to be working their way through today's conflicts in much the same way that earlier generations did. All in all, today's diversity is more likely to reinforce than to undermine the American political culture.

Chapter Summary

For more than two centuries, the United States has been a study in contrasts. On the one hand, this country always has been socially diverse, containing a wider array of ethnic and religious groups than most other lands. On the other hand, the diverse citizenry of the United States has long shown a higher level of agreement on fundamental political principles than is found in other democracies. These fundamental principles grew out of a classical liberal philosophy that stresses the rights and liberties of individuals.

Native-born citizens have always feared that immigration was a threat to the distinctly American political culture. Much of today's multiculturalism debate is reminiscent of debates that have taken place throughout American history. Yes, recent immigrants want to maintain some part of their cultural distinctiveness; so did previous waves of immigrants. Yes, "native citizens" worry that the new immigrants are too different to fit easily into American society; so did native-born Americans a century ago. Such fears have proved unfounded in the past, and they probably will prove unfounded in the future. Immigrants reinforce rather than weaken the spirit of individualism in the United States. The very fact of their immigrating suggests that they possess the ambitious, individualistic outlook that is such a distinctive part of the American political culture.

Key Terms

citizenship, p. 94
civic republicanism, p. 104
equality of condition, p. 108

equality of opportunity, p. 108
liberalism, p. 103
multiculturalism, p. 95

political culture, p. 94
political socialization, p. 113

Suggested Readings

Of General Interest

Fuchs, Lawrence. *The American Kaleidoscope: Race, Ethnicity, and the Civic Culture.* Hanover, NH: University Press of New England, 1990. Dispassionate discussion of the problems and prospects of contemporary immigrants and African Americans. Prefers "kaleidoscope" to "melting pot" as a metaphor for the history of ethnicity in America.

Huntington, Samuel. *Who Are We? The Challenges to America's National Identity.* New York: Simon & Schuster, 2004. Controversial argument that Latino immigration threatens America's "Anglo-Protestant" values.

Lipset, Seymour Martin. *American Exceptionalism.* New York: Norton, 1996. An examination of the American political culture by an eminent senior scholar who has spent much of his career studying it.

Portes, Alejandro, and Ruben G. Rumbaut. *Immigrant America: A Portrait.* Berkeley, CA: University of California Press, 1997. A sympathetic account of the post-1965 wave of immigration. Like much contemporary writing, it exaggerates the differences between immigration today and that of a century ago.

Focused Studies

Borjas, George. *Heaven's Door: Immigration Policy and the American Economy.* Princeton, NJ: Princeton University Press, 1999. Argues

that immigration has hurt the poorest native-born workers, especially African Americans. Calls for restricting immigration and limiting it to better-educated and more highly skilled people.

Hartz, Louis. *The Liberal Tradition in America.* New York: Harcourt, 1955. A classic, if impenetrable, discussion of the liberal tradition. Argues that the absence of feudalism allowed liberal ideas to spread without resistance in the United States.

Kleppner, Paul. *The Cross of Culture.* New York: Free Press, 1970. This example of the "ethno-cultural" school of political history provides a detailed account of political conflict in the Midwest from the rise of the Republican Party to the end of the nineteenth century.

Heclo, Hugh, and Wilfred McClay, eds. *Religion Returns to the Public Square.* Baltimore: Johns Hopkins University Press, 2003. Informative essays on various aspects of the relationship between religion and politics in the contemporary United States.

Simon, Julian. *The Economic Consequences of Immigration.* 2nd ed., Ann Arbor, MI: University of Michigan Press, 1999. Argues that the U.S. economy would benefit from an increase in legal immigration.

On the Web

Anyone with an interest in diversity can find it on the Internet.

http://uscis.gov
The Department of Homeland Security's Web site on immigration and naturalization explains the naturalization process for aspiring citizens and provides statistical reports on the history of immigration to the United States.

www.cic.gc.ca
www.immi.gov.au
www.germany-info.org
Information on the immigration laws of some other countries (Canada, Australia, and Germany, respectively) can be found at these Web sites.

www.diversityinc.com
DiversityInc.com tries to take advantage of American diversity. Sponsored by several major corporations and public interest

organizations, the site provides original content on many subgroups of the American population, with a particular focus on the advantages of diversity in the workplace.

www.academicinfo.net
Academia has responded to the call for more diversity by promoting new areas of study, including women's studies, African-American studies, and gay and lesbian studies. The Academic Information Gateway contains bibliographies and guides for these subjects. Of course, these specific subpopulations—and any others you can think of—are represented by many interest groups or clubs, most of them with Web sites. A good search engine can find hundreds of pages, illustrating the diversity of the Internet.

Election Voices

The Immigration Issue

Background

In the spring of 2006 political conflict over immigration, an issue that had agitated the United States since its foundation, once again boiled over. The central issue concerned "illegal" or "undocumented," or "unauthorized" immigrants, and particularly Mexicans, who account for the largest share of the currently estimated 10 to 12 million unauthorized immigrants. A few months earlier, House Republicans had passed an "enforcement-only" bill that would have made unauthorized entry into the country a felony (later amended to a criminal misdemeanor), provided for more than 700 miles of border fencing to keep people out, and imposed stiff penalties on employers who hire illegal immigrants. Some Republican hard-liners also tried to end "birthright citizenship"—automatic citizenship to children born in the United States—if their parents were not citizens or legal immigrants.

Most Democrats and some Republicans support a plan closer to what President Bush had previously proposed, often called "enforcement-plus." Such a plan would provide stricter border controls, but also allow undocumented immigrants to stay in the country and take advantage of a legal path to eventual citizenship. The Senate took up the

Support for immigration rights Demonstrators march through downtown Chicago in May 2006 as part of a nationwide action to show both support for immigration reform and opposition to legislation that would criminalize the actions of an estimated 11 million illegal immigrants.

subject of immigration in the spring with rival plans representing the enforcement-only and enforcement-plus points of view.

In April immigrants' rights groups staged several demonstrations whose large turnout surprised many people, including the organizers. On May 1, a holiday, "megamarches" were held in a number of American cities. More than a million people took part.

The Issues

The issues today are reminiscent of, but arguably more complex than those of the past. On the economic side, some studies conclude that immigrants are a net benefit to the economy; others, that they are a net cost. Few studies, however, contend that the net benefits or costs are large compared to major government programs such as Medicare and Social Security.[1] Of course, benefits and costs accrue to or fall on individuals, not on an abstract "national economy." Here the arguments become quite complex. Economists point out that not all immigrants are alike: skilled immigrants are a significant net gain to the economy, but unskilled immigrants depress the wages of low-skilled native workers.[2] Those sympathetic to immigration retort that low-skilled immigrants only take jobs Americans would not take. As one chicken industry executive commented, "Reality speaks and it says that, absent Hispanic workers, we could not process chicken."[3] But that argument brings the objection that without competition from low-skilled foreigners, wages might be high enough that Americans would take jobs in agriculture and service industries that they currently shun. Higher wages, however, would raise prices for consumers. Finally, other commentators point out that whatever the national costs and benefits, these fall differently on government jurisdictions: state and local jurisdictions spend a lot more on social services for immigrants—education, police, medical care—than they receive in taxes.[4]

There is a cultural side to the debate as well, especially because today's immigrants include such a high proportion of Spanish speakers. Some immigration opponents worry that the greater homogeneity of today's immigrants has overwhelmed the processes of assimilation that worked in the past. If so, the new immigrants will become a large subpopulation of alienated "outsiders," and eventually the Southwest could become "Mexifornia."[5] In the recent protest marches, some participants carried Mexican flags, stoking these fears. Other observers consider such fears to be exaggerated, pointing to evidence that today's immigrants want to be part of the United States, not separate from it. Under new laws, for example, Mexicans in the U.S. can register to vote in Mexico, but few do so.[6] Organizers in Los Angeles rented a 2,000-seat audito-

rium for a rally attended by top Mexican officials and politicians; only 30 people showed up. Los Angeles mayor Antonio Villaraigosa, whose parents were immigrants, explained: "Most of us don't want to go back to Mexico and we don't want any part of this country reverting to Mexico. We know we are a lot better off being Americans."[7]

A final complicating factor is security. Americans in the nineteenth century worried about Jesuit revolutionaries and terrorists. Americans today worry about Al Qaeda or other terrorists who might smuggle in chemical, biological, or nuclear weapons. Indeed, fear of Osama Bin Laden seems somewhat more well-founded than fear of Mexican Catholicism and of the Pope.

Immigration and Electoral Politics

The immigration issue splits both parties, although the political disagreement appears greater among Republicans.[8] Democrats are traditionally favorable to ethnic minorities, but low-skilled Americans who compete directly with low-skilled immigrants tend to be Democrats. Moreover, many local and state Democratic elected officials are on the firing line: their constituents are exposed daily to new immigrants and they are responsible for providing public services to people who pay relatively little in state and local taxes. In response, the Democratic governors of Arizona and New Mexico have declared states of emergency.

Republicans are split into several factions. Many in the business wing of the party, such as the chicken industry executive quoted earlier, are sympathetic to immigration as a source of plentiful and cheap labor. Republicans of a libertarian stripe are in favor of immigration as a matter of principle. But many Republicans worry about the threats to national security and others about threats to American culture. Still others believe as a matter of principle that people who enter the country without legal authorization should not be rewarded, especially ahead of those who patiently wait in line. All in all, the Republican Party includes every viewpoint on the issue, from most liberal to most conservative.

Many Republican politicos are concerned about the electoral danger immigration poses for their party.[9] On the one hand, there are votes to be won by responding to popular concerns. But on the other hand, President Bush and some other Republicans have been engaged in a long-term project to bring Hispanic voters into the Republican Party, arguing that Hispanics are an entrepreneurial, culturally conservative constituency that should look favorably on the Republican Party. Thus, short-term electoral gains risk alienating a large and growing bloc that eventually might become middle-class Americans.

What Do Americans Believe?

As they typically do, most Americans occupy a middle ground on the immigration issue, agreeing neither with the most strident critics of immigration, nor with its most ardent defenders. Rather, showing their characteristic pragmatic streak, Americans agree with parts of the case made by each side and with parts of the solutions offered by each side. Table 1 shows a sampling of the numerous public opinion polls on this subject. Americans overwhelmingly agree that illegal immigration is out of control,

and that in principle it is unfair to grant rights to illegal immigrants while those who follow the law wait in line. Consistent with those who argue about the benefits and costs of immigration, Americans disagree on whether immigrants are a net boon or burden, and on whether illegal immigrants contribute more to the country than they cost in services (the latter numbers fluctuate considerably depending on wording of the questions). About as many Americans support such strong policy proposals as building a fence along the U.S.-Mexico border and abolishing birthright citizenship as oppose these proposals.

On the other hand, unfair or not, and with costs and benefits unclear, Americans agree with defenders of immigration that it is simply unrealistic to think about deporting, or even punishing, the unauthorized immigrants

TABLE 1	
PUBLIC OPINION ON IMMIGRATION	
Is illegal immigration out of control? (USA Today/Gallup, April 7–9, 2006)	Yes: 81%
Fair to grant rights to illegal immigrants while others wait in line for legal entry? (Fox News/Opinion Dynamics, April 4–5, 2006)	Unfair: 81%
Immigration helps U.S. more than it hurts? (NBC News/Wall Street Journal April 21–24, 2006)	Helps More: 45% Hurts More: 45%
Illegal immigrants mostly make a contribution to American society or mostly a drain? (AP/IPSO, March 28–30, 2006)	Contribution: 51% Drain: 42%
Illegal immigrants provide more benefits to the nation by doing work Americans don't want to do, or cost more because they don't pay taxes and they use public services? (Fox News/Opinion Dynamics, April 4–5, 2006)	Provide benefits: 22% Cost more: 65%
Build a wall or fence along the border from Texas to California? (Fox News/Opinion Dynamics, April 4–5, 2006)	Favor: 47% Oppose:48%
Birthright citizenship? (Fox News/Opinion Dynamics, April 4–5, 2006)	Yes: 45% No: 48%
If you had to choose:	
Deport illegal immigrants	35%
Allow to stay if they meet certain conditions (NBC News/Wall Street Journal April 21–24, 2006)	61%
Which comes closest to your view?	
Deport all illegal immigrants	18%
Allow to stay for limited time	17%
Allow to stay and eventually become citizens (NBC News/Wall Street Journal April 21–24, 2006)	63%
Providing food, shelter, or medical care to an illegal immigrant should be a criminal offense?	Should: 27% Should not: 67%

SOURCE: PollingReport.com (accessed May 3, 2006). (Question wordings are paraphrases, not exact.)

already here—let alone those who aid them, as some member of Congress have proposed. Thus, American public opinion seems generally supportive of the "enforcement-plus" plans under consideration. Americans agree that illegal immigration is a serious problem, and that it must be stopped, but that those already here should be offered a path toward eventual status as legal residents or U.S. citizens.

What Do You Think?

1. Should the federal government take strong measures such as building fences and walls to secure the country's borders?

2. Should the principle of obeying the law be subordinated to the practical difficulties of doing anything about the illegal immigrants already here?

3. Should illegal immigrants be eligible for public services such as schools and medical care?

4. Should children born in the United States automatically be citizens, even if their parents are illegal immigrants?

5. Although immigration has traditionally been considered a responsibility of the federal government, some states have begun to act on their own to curb illegal immigration. For example, the Arizona legislature has considered proposals to construct its own border fence, to fine employers who hire undocumented workers, and to check the citizenship of anyone stopped for a traffic offense.[10] Given the differential impact of illegal immigration on the country, should the states be free to deal with the problem as they see fit?

[1]Studies by the Center for Immigration Reform often report costs: www.cis.org/topics/costs.html.

[2]Carolyn Lockhead, "Economists Support Entry of Educated Foreigners," San Francisco Chronicle, April 26, 2006: A4

[3]Quoted in Peter Slevin, "Town's-Eye View of Immigration Debate," Washington Post, April 3, 2006: A01.

[4]Peter Brown, "Immigration Costs More than Thought," Orlando Sentinel, October 14, 2005.

[5]Mexifornia: A State of Becoming (New York: Collier, 2004).

[6]Oscar Avila and Hugh Dellios, "Mexican Expatriate Voter Drive Comes up Far Short," Chicago Tribune, January 13, 2006.

[7]Thomas Elias, ""Lack of Attendance at Forum Speaks Volumes," The Unon.com, December 9, 2005.

[8]Peter Brown, "Democrats are Split on Immigration, Too," RealClearPolitics, April 3, 2006. Mort Kondracke, "Bush Must Talk Sense to Republicans on Immigration, RealClearPolitics, January 10, 2006.

[9]Ruth Marcus, "The GOP Walks a Border Tightrope," Washington Post, March 29, 2006: A19.

[10]T. R. Reid, "Hill Impasse Spurs States to Tackle Illegal Immigration," Washington Post, May 3, 2006: A01.

CHAPTER 5

★ ★ ★ ★ ★ ★ ★ ★ ☆

Public Opinion

CHAPTER OUTLINE

Public Opinion and War

Contrary to the impression we might get from popular mythology, American wars have often been controversial among our citizens. The War of 1812, the Mexican War, the Civil War, World War I, Korea, Vietnam—all provoked substantial domestic opposition. Indeed, World War II may have been the only war in American history in which the country was united in its determination to fight the war through to victory.

Given that background, it should have come as no surprise that, as President George W. Bush tried to prepare the nation for an invasion of Iraq in late 2002 and early 2003, the American public was divided about whether such a war was necessary or desirable. In every major prewar poll that was taken on the subject, a majority of Americans supported taking military action against Saddam Hussein, but a sizable minority always opposed military action. ABC News and the *Washington Post*, for example, asked this question eight times between January and mid-March, 2003: "Would you favor or oppose having U.S. forces take military action against Iraq to force Saddam Hussein from power?" On average, 64 percent were in favor, 32 percent opposed.

As is often the case, once the fighting started on March 20, Americans closed ranks behind the military effort. Surveys conducted in late March and April found

Antiwar Protests Can Both Express and Change Public Opinions About the War

Iraqi war veterans join with anti-war protestors in late 2005, as they wait for the presidential motorcade to arrive with George W. Bush for a dedication ceremony at the Ronald Reagan Presidential Library.

that about three-fourths of the public supported the war, while just 20 percent opposed it. Polls also showed that 70 percent of Americans approved of the way Bush was handling the situation in Iraq.

FIGURE 5.1

Wartime Presidents, Father and Son

George H. W. Bush's extraordinarily high approval rating declined steadily after the media shifted its focus to the economy (rather than Desert Storm). His son, George W. Bush, saw an enormous jump in approval rating after September 11, 2001. It subsequently eroded, but not before the 2002 elections, when the Republicans gained in both the House and the Senate.

Source: Gallup Organization

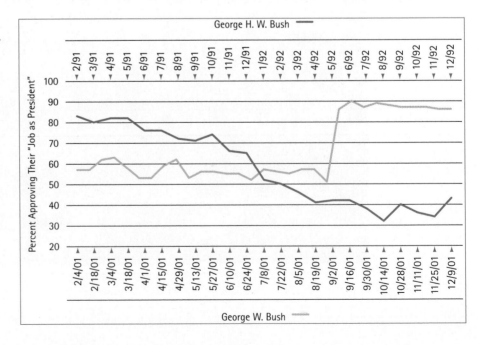

Had the war in Iraq ended the same way that the 1991 Gulf War did, with a clear U.S. victory followed by rapid withdrawal of American forces, there is little doubt that the second Gulf War would be regarded today as one of the signal achievements of George Bush's presidency. But the war didn't end with such a clear-cut victory. Though U.S. forces captured Baghdad on April 9, 2005, pacifying and rebuilding Iraq has proved to be vastly more difficult than defeating Saddam Hussein's army.

In a classic study of American public attitudes about the wars in Vietnam and Korea, political scientist John Mueller showed that opposition to both wars mounted in direct proportion to the number of U.S. casualties.[1] Slowly but steadily, the same thing has occurred in Iraq. The day Baghdad fell Gallup found that 76 percent of the American public said that it was "worth going to war." By January 2006, a narrow majority of Americans took the opposite position: 52 percent said the Iraq war had not been worth fighting (see Figure 5.1) and only about 40 percent of the public approved of President Bush's performance on the war.

Still, although the American public was increasingly dissatisfied with and pessimistic about the war, they were not ready to withdraw U.S. troops and leave Iraq to its fate. In a Pew Research Center poll conducted in early January 2006, the sample split exactly in half: 48 percent wanted to "keep military troops in Iraq until the situation has stabilized" and 48 percent wanted to "bring [U.S.] troops home as soon as possible." Moreover, of those who favored troop withdrawals, only 29 percent wanted to "remove all troops from Iraq immediately"; 67 percent said that the withdrawal should be "gradual over the next year or two."

MAKING THE CONNECTION

In the era of the permanent campaign, public opinion probably is more important than it has ever been.[2] Certainly, modern politicians have more information about it than ever before—but the role that public opinion plays in determining what government does continues to be complicated and unpredictable. As the polling data on the Iraq war show, many Americans may come to regret a policy that they themselves endorsed when the crucial decisions were being made. In this chapter we define public opinion and explain how it is formed. We then explain how public opinion is measured—and often mismeasured. We discuss some important characteristics of public opinion. Finally we consider the gap that sometimes exists between public opinion and public policy in our democracy.

What Is Public Opinion?

Public opinion is the aggregation of people's views about issues, situations, and public figures. Although conceptions of democracy differ (see Chapter 1), public opinion is an essential element of all of them—either determining policy outcomes directly or setting the bounds within which elected officials must operate when they choose public policies.

Political scientist V. O. Key, Jr., captures the importance of public opinion when he defines it as "those opinions held by private persons which governments find it prudent to heed."[3] Democratic governments find it "prudent" to heed the opinions of private persons, of course, because of elections. Note that, in Key's conception, public opinion need not be actively expressed. Even if public opinion is silent, or "latent," public officials may act or fail to act because they fear arousing it. This is the so-called law of anticipated reactions, whereby public opinion influences government even though it does so indirectly and passively.[4] When we say, "Public opinion wouldn't stand for that," we are referring to this latent, constraining function of public opinion.

public opinion
The aggregation of people's views about issues, situations, and public figures.

War, Peace, and Public Opinion

Sources of Public Opinion

If public opinion is nothing more than the aggregated opinions of individual people, the first step in understanding public opinion is to figure out where individuals get their political ideas. Most of the sources of political attitudes fall into several broad categories. These categories are not mutually exclusive; often they overlap.

Socialization

socialization
The end result of all the processes by which social groups give individuals their beliefs and values.

Are You a Liberal
or a Conservative?

People learn political beliefs and values in their families, schools, communities, religious institutions, and workplaces—a process called **socialization**. Sometimes socialization occurs directly and explicitly, as when schools teach citizenship and patriotism. Catholic doctrine condemns abortion, and church-going Catholics are indeed less accepting of abortion than are mainline Protestants and Jews.[5] Most fundamentalist Protestant churches officially condemn homosexuality, and rank-and-file members are indeed less tolerant of homosexuality than are mainline Protestants.[6] Labor unions typically endorse Democratic candidates, and union members are indeed more Democratic in their voting than other blue-collar workers.[7]

Sometimes socialization occurs indirectly, when someone observes or imitates others—a form of socialization that is no less powerful for being unplanned. Children begin to form political attitudes at an early age. Research carried out in the 1950s and 1960s usually concluded that the single most important socializing agent was the family (although a few scholars argued that schools carried more weight).[8] Within the family, studies generally found that the mother was most important; she spent more time with the children. Not surprisingly, then, studies have found that many children will identify themselves as Democrats or Republicans well before they have any idea what the parties stand for.[9] Older children are especially likely to share the party affiliation of their parents.[10] Different socializing agents may be dominant today, however, because of changes in American family life. Increases in single parenthood and in the divorce rate have left many children in one-parent families. Moreover, the proportion of mothers who work outside the home has doubled since the 1960s; even some children in two-parent families may spend more time with service providers such as nannies, teachers, and coaches than with the members of their household.

Personal Experiences

Although people form many of their attitudes in childhood, political views continue to develop over the course of a lifetime. Childhood socialization can be modified or even reversed by adult experiences. The horrors of the Great Depression focused many Americans on the importance of economic issues and, after the depression lifted, cemented their loyalty to the Democratic Party. On the other hand, the stagflation of the 1970s left a younger generation of Americans disenchanted with the Democrats and later encouraged their identification with the Republican Party of Ronald Reagan. The ill-fated war in Vietnam made many people skeptical about getting U.S. troops involved in foreign wars.

Not all experiences are historical ones that change entire generations. Some life experiences differ from person to person within a single generation, perhaps because of the place in which one lives or the groups one chooses to join. Life experiences may differ because of how a community treats different sorts of people: men vs. women, young people vs. the elderly, the poor vs. the affluent, or people of minority races, the handicapped, fat people, short people, and innumerable other categories. Varying life experiences can profoundly influence not only how we think about specific parties or policy proposals, but also how we feel about fundamental concepts such as fairness, authority, freedom, or justice.

Self-Interest

Public policies seldom affect everyone equally. Usually some people will benefit from a policy proposal and others will suffer. Some people profit from a political party's initiatives; others do not. Ordinary citizens show a rather impressive ability to determine where their bread is buttered, as the old saying puts it, when they approach public affairs.[11]

Voters do not always behave in a fashion that directly benefits them. People rarely abandon their party loyalties, for example, simply because one candidate or one policy position contradicts their personal tastes. Nevertheless, people's interests often determine where they stand in a political debate.[12] For example, blue-collar workers are more sensitive to a rise in unemployment that throws them out of work, and professionals and managers are more sensitive to a rise in inflation that drives up interest rates and depresses the overall business climate. Women working outside the home, who must balance the conflicting demands of home and workplace, are more supportive of gender equality than are stay-at-home mothers.[13]

Education

Although schools are socializing agents and one's training certainly affects self-interest, education belongs in something of a separate category—especially higher education. In general, education is associated with a somewhat more tolerant outlook. Highly educated people are especially tolerant of minority groups and practices.[14] Apparently, values emphasized in higher education predispose college graduates to think about political issues differently; they are more likely to accept people different from them and practices different from theirs (see Figure 5.2). They are also more likely to view political involvement as a duty to carry out rather than as a chore to be avoided. And higher education is associated with a greater sense of **political efficacy** (the belief that the citizen can make a difference by acting politically).

Political
Knowledge

political efficacy
The belief that one can make a difference in politics by expressing an opinion or acting politically.

Reference Groups

Members of various social groups often differ significantly in the opinions they hold (Figure 5.3). Weekly churchgoers show more hostility to homosexuality than those less religiously involved. African Americans endorse government involvement in health care at a higher level than whites customarily do. Women support banning pornography at much higher rates than men do. To a certain extent, group differences likely result from the same sources of public opinion that we have already discussed: different interests, life experiences, forms of socialization, and levels of schooling. Churches may socialize members to believe that homosexuality is wrong, for example. African Americans may be more likely to need improved health care, or they may be more likely to witness cases in which someone lacks adequate care. Women may be socialized against consuming pornography, leaving them little reason to support keeping it legal.

On the other hand, individuals may look to the groups of which they are a part to determine where they ought to stand in a political debate. Even if their experiences or their interests push them to oppose a proposed law, they may become friendlier toward it if they notice that people like them tend to be supporters. Individuals are

FIGURE 5.2

Higher Education Is
Associated with Greater
Tolerance of Diversity

Individuals with a college education are less likely to express
negative feelings toward
Hispanics, blacks, and gays.

Source: American National Election Study,
2004

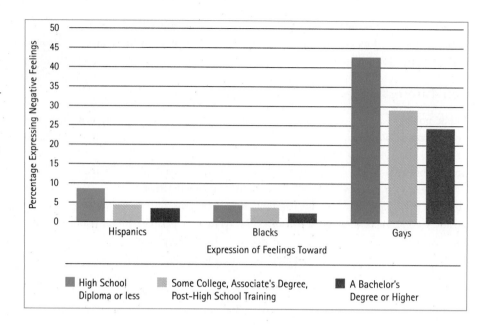

especially likely to stick with their reference group when they identify closely with its
fate, or if they tend to hear about public affairs through word of mouth, from the
perspective of other group members. Some groups even attempt to enforce solidarity,
as when union members disparage "scabs" who cross their picket lines or African
Americans dismiss those who break ranks as "Uncle Toms." In short, the pushes and
pulls of group identity can shape people's political attitudes beyond what one might
expect given the other influences on their thinking.

The Media

In recent years, many people have expressed a fear that public opinion is increasingly
shaped by the mass media. This substantial issue is steeped in controversy (see Chapter
9). Suffice it to say that under some circumstances the media can sway public opinion,
while under other circumstances the media are surprisingly ineffectual. Overall, little
evidence supports the worst fears of media critics. For example, an extensive study of
opinion change during a presidential campaign found that, in the aggregate, TV and
newspaper exposure had only marginal effects on preexisting views.[15] And, more
generally, despite the overwhelmingly negative coverage that President Bill Clinton
received during the Monica Lewinsky scandal, his job performance ratings scarcely
budged. At best, the media represent only one influence on public opinion out of many.

Measuring Public Opinion

For most of the nation's history, figuring out what voters wanted was more art than
science. Politicians attended public gatherings, scanned influential newspapers, or
consulted with powerful local officials to gauge the popular mood. Often they made
mistakes and paid the price on Election Day.

Estimating public attitudes requires much less guesswork in modern times. A
whole industry has sprung up dedicated to contacting individuals, asking them questions, and collecting the responses. Firms range from specialized campaign-consulting
operations to highly reputable research and marketing companies (such as Gallup,

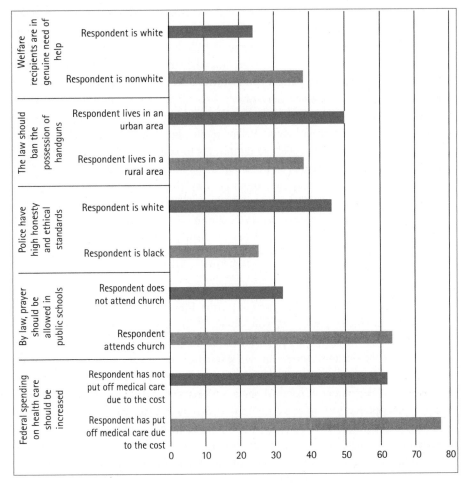

FIGURE 5.3

Examples of Group Differences in Public Opinion

People with different life experiences hold different views about politics.

Source: Calculated from the National Election Studies and the Gallup Poll Cumulative Index.

Roper, and Chilton). Sometimes these companies divulge their poll results to the media. So do various academic institutions and nonprofit foundations that conduct intensive surveys on particular public-affairs issues. Media corporations, meanwhile, have formed alliances to survey public opinion for their own news coverage (examples include CBS News/*New York Times* and ABC News/*Washington Post*).[16]

As a result, the United States is now awash in polling data. Almost every day brings the release of some new poll that reports how the president rates or what the public thinks about some hot policy issue or how the next election will turn out. For example, when pollsters are interested in learning what the public thinks about the president, the most frequently used question is what is usually called the presidential approval question: "Do you approve or disapprove of the way [president's name] is handling his job as president?" This question was invented by the Gallup Poll, which asked it about 15 times a year during the 1950s and 1960s. About once every three and a half weeks, in other words, new data would be made public that claimed to show the latest ebbs and flows in Eisenhower, Kennedy, or Johnson's popularity. By 2005, in contrast, this question was asked in 183 separate polls—one every two days—by more than 20 different survey organizations.[17]

Sampling Error

Americans sometimes express doubt about the reliability of all these opinion polls. They recognize that surveys rarely report the exact truth. Part of the problem with opinion polls

sampling error
The error that arises in public opinion surveys as a result of relying on a representative, but small, sample of the larger population.

You Are a
Polling Consultant

selection bias
The error that occurs when a sample systematically includes or excludes people with certain attitudes.

is that even properly administered surveys contain **sampling error**—chance variation that results from using a small sample to estimate the characteristics of a larger population. People may not think about the problem in such technical terms, but they understand the idea intuitively. If you flip a coin, you expect that the chance of having it come up heads is the same as the chance of having it come up tails—which is why it is a fair method for deciding who gets to go first in a game or who gets the last piece of pie. If you flip a coin 10 times, though, you would not be shocked by a result other than five heads and five tails. Coin tosses will vary by chance alone. Polling results also contain such sampling error. A survey of randomly selected people can tip this way or that through the luck of the draw.

The variability that results from sampling error makes people suspicious about polls. "I refuse to believe," they sometimes protest, "that the opinions of 1,500 people can speak for a nation of 220 million adults." This skepticism is unjustified, however. A properly administered survey of national opinion should not require more than 1,500 people (nor would increasing the number of participants do anything to redeem an *improperly* designed or administered survey). A small sample of people can mirror a much larger population reasonably well.

Furthermore, statistical theory provides a means to determine how reliable a given survey should be, at least as regards sampling error. If every reader of this book flipped a penny 1,500 times, 95 percent of you would fall somewhere between 705 and 795 heads—that is, between 47 and 53 percent—within 3 points of the average. Bigger deviations are possible but they will occur rarely, one time out of 20. Similarly, the answers provided by a random sample of 1,500 Americans on any political question would fall within 3 percentage points of national opinion 95 percent of the time. That is a statistical fact. It is what pollsters mean when they report that their survey has a "margin of error" of 3 percent. The natural variation caused by taking a random sample therefore does not explain most instances of misleading survey results. Two other sources of inaccuracy—selection bias and measurement error—usually account for misleading survey results.

Selection Bias

Survey researchers use a bewildering variety of techniques to ensure that their samples will mirror the larger population. However, the trait that unites most sampling methods is that they are devised to avoid **selection bias**—distortion caused when a method systematically includes or excludes people with certain types of attitudes. Surveys that fail to guard against selection bias usually offer nothing of value; results they report will not be *representative* of the larger population. For example, if we were to poll attendees at a hockey game, a heavy-metal concert, or even a political-science lecture, the results would say very little about public opinion because these events attract audiences that differ from other Americans in politically relevant ways.

Perhaps it seems obvious that the political attitudes held by heavy-metal fans would reveal little about national opinion. Yet real-life organizations regularly conduct polls just as likely to induce selection bias. Interest groups and magazines conduct mail surveys. Their samples are not representative, because their members and readers differ from the population at large. Moreover, those who bother to fill out and return the questionnaires are a biased sample of those who receive the survey—they are people who care more than others about the subject of the poll. The same is true for call-in surveys conducted by radio and TV stations. These may be good ways of generating audience interest, but they have little or no scientific value.

THE WIZARD OF ID   **parker and hart**

Polling Wizardry

Surveys often provide inaccurate results because of errors in measurement, such as when the options available to respondents do a poor job of capturing the actual range of opinions. Pollsters who wish to avoid biased research must shape the wording of their questions carefully.

By permission of John L. Hart FLP, and Creators Syndicate, Inc.

The latest craze is online surveys, but few such polls take adequate care to ensure a proper sample. Most tap only the opinions of people with existing World Wide Web connections who happen to find their way to the poll site and who have their own motivations for taking part in the exercise—hardly a representative group. The problem with Internet polls was highlighted by a mildly embarrassing experience suffered by the Democratic National Committee (DNC) in January 2000. At that time, the DNC Web site offered a weekly opinion feature. One question noted that the United States anticipated a large budget surplus and asked people to vote for one of two ways to use the surplus:

> "saving Social Security, strengthening Medicare, and paying down the debt," or "implementing George W. Bush's $1.7 trillion risky tax scheme that overwhelmingly benefits the wealthy."

Surprisingly, when the results were tabulated, 72 percent of the respondents favored "risky" tax cuts for "the wealthy"—mischievous Republicans monitoring the opposition had swamped the Democrats' poll![18] This amusing episode graphically illustrates the problem with allowing a sample to determine itself.

In a scientific poll, the investigator must control who is included in the sample and who is not. Pollsters typically select sampling methods that somehow choose participants *randomly,* with minimal differences from person to person in the chance of being picked. For example, telephone polls customarily rely on "random-digit dialing," in which a computer randomly selects some portion of the number being called. People with unlisted telephone numbers may be surprised and irritated when they answer their phone and hear a pollster, but no one has given out their personal information—the computer has found them by chance.

Not all selection bias results from flaws in the sampling method. Even if pollsters devise an approach that avoids favoring some sorts of people over other sorts, potential respondents still control whether to participate in the survey. In a typical telephone poll, more than half the original sample either never answers the phone or refuses to be interviewed.[19] Research shows that, as a result, survey samples tend to contain too few men, whites, young adults, and wealthy people.[20] Although pollsters try to adjust their numbers to compensate for unequal rates of participation, they may not succeed at eliminating the bias. In 1996, pre-election polls overestimated Bill Clinton's margin over Robert Dole. Some conservative commentators claimed that the error occurred because pro-Democratic groups were more likely than pro-Republican groups to respond to the polls.[21]

Some tools for exploring public opinion do not seek to eliminate selection bias. Researchers using these tools care less about getting a representative sample than they do about reaching a complex and detailed understanding of certain kinds of people. For example, political consultants increasingly rely on **focus groups**, small groups of people brought together to talk about issues or candidates at length and in depth. These groups are too small to provide good estimates of public opinion, but they are useful for testing the appeal of ads, terms, slogans, symbols, and so forth. For example, focus group research led Republicans to advocate social security *personal* accounts rather than *private* accounts, and Democrats to warn about *climate change* rather than *global warming*.

focus groups

Small groups used to explore how ordinary people think about issues and how they react to the language of political appeals.

Measurement Error

Media accounts of poll results routinely report sampling error. They also often describe the method for gathering the sample, and may even report the rate of participation among the people interviewers contacted. If sampling error and selection bias were the only two sources of inaccuracy in opinion polls, an attentive reader could judge their reliability fairly well. Unfortunately, sampling is a relatively unimportant source of error in most professional surveys. Various kinds of **measurement error** are much more troublesome.

measurement error

The error that arises from attempting to measure something as subjective as opinion.

An individual's opinion is not an objective fact like the length of a stick. Ask 10 people to measure a stick, and, if a ruler is handy, they will all do it about the same way. Unless they are careless, all 10 will report approximately the same length. Opinions do not have such obvious physical properties; they are intangible. No obvious tool, such as a ruler, exists to measure them (although pollsters do sometimes settle on particular questions that they like to ask repeatedly).

Answers to survey questions can vary dramatically depending on how a question is asked. For example, poll responses vary according to the choices provided.[22] People tend to give more consistent answers to questions that allow graduated responses (agree strongly, agree somewhat, neither agree nor disagree, disagree somewhat, disagree strongly) than to either/or questions (agree/disagree). More people will choose a "don't know" or "not sure" answer when it is explicitly offered to them than will volunteer such an answer when it is not offered. Survey responses also depend on the larger context. People respond differently if earlier questions in a survey prompt them to think along certain lines, or if the interviewer lists arguments on each side of an issue before asking about it. People also respond differently when surveyed after significant social, economic, or political developments than when surveyed beforehand.[23]

Opinions are particularly hard to pin down when citizens are unfamiliar with an issue. Just to take one example: A flurry of public opinion polls taken in the summer of 2001 probed whether citizens supported federal funding of embryonic stem cell research. Most Americans had not given much thought to this technical question, nor did pollsters have an established way to ask about it. Not surprisingly, polls reported anywhere from 24 percent to 70 percent in favor of the funding.[24] Sampling error certainly did not produce this much variability.

The wording of survey questions may be the most important source of measurement error. Even if people have fairly fixed opinions, the answers they provide pollsters will depend on exactly what they think a question is asking. Question wording may (1) confuse respondents, (2) prompt respondents to think about an issue in a certain way, or (3) oversimplify complex social issues. Let's consider examples of each problem.

Confusing Questions: The Holocaust Poll Fiasco   Germany's Nazi leaders executed millions of innocent civilians during World War II. Although they targeted gypsies, homosexuals, and Poles—among others—Nazi officials put most of their genocidal efforts into exterminating European Jews. They shipped Jewish men, women, and children to concentration camps within Nazi-controlled territory, where victims either were worked to death or were executed outright. Careful research indicates that at least 5 million Jews died as a result of the Holocaust, including almost the entire Jewish populations of Czechoslovakia, Poland, and the Baltic states. Aside from a fringe group of conspiracy theorists, who deny that such large-scale genocide really took place, scholars uniformly count the Holocaust as one of the worst horrors in a global war filled with tragedy.

Just before the opening of the Holocaust Memorial Museum in Washington, D.C., a respected commercial polling organization called Roper Starch Worldwide tried to determine whether Holocaust deniers were making headway among the American public. Roper's survey, commissioned by the American Jewish Committee, produced some distressing results. It indicated that 22 percent of the American public believed it "possible the Nazi extermination of the Jews never happened" and that another 12 percent were unsure.

The news media jumped on the story. Editorialists in particular pondered what might be wrong with the American public that they would give such shocking survey responses. Had anti-Semitism grown so strong that a third of Americans embraced the views of the lunatic fringe? Was the educational system failing so miserably that, just 50 years after World War II, the American public could have forgotten one of the best-documented tragedies of that global crisis? What did the Holocaust poll say about the American people?

Very little, it turned out. Social scientists knowledgeable about prejudice and public opinion were immediately suspicious of the poll findings, which contradicted other research on American attitudes. The Gallup organization—a Roper business competitor—soon demonstrated that the Roper poll was seriously in error because it had asked a confusing question. The exact wording of Roper's question was:

> **Does it seem possible, or does it seem impossible to you that the Nazi extermination of the Jews never happened?**

One of the first rules of survey research is to keep questions clear and simple. The Roper question fails that test because it contains a double negative (*impossible . . . never happened*)—a grammatical construction long known to confuse people.

Gallup conducted a new poll in which half of the sample was asked the Roper question with the double negative and the other half an alternative question:

> **Does it seem possible to you that the Nazi extermination of the Jews never happened, or do you feel certain that it happened?**

Embarrassed by a Poll

The opening of the Holocaust Memorial Museum was accompanied by a polling embarrassment that underscored the necessity of keeping public-opinion-poll questions clear and simple.

• *Why might a person have answered yes to the following: "Does it seem possible, or does it seem impossible to you that the Nazi extermination of the Jews never happened?"*

This change in the question's wording may seem minor, but it made a great deal of difference. In the half of the sample that was asked the Roper question, one-third of the respondents again replied that it was possible the Holocaust never happened or that they were unsure, but in the half that were asked Gallup's alternative question, less than 10 percent of the sample were Holocaust doubters. The whole episode had been the product of a simple verbal mistake.[25] Nothing was wrong with the Roper sample, as verified by Gallup when it asked Roper's question. Rather, Roper asked a poorly constructed question that produced an inaccurate measurement.

Leading Questions: The Welfare Policy Mystery   What looks like minor variation in question wording can elicit significantly different answers. Such an error is especially likely when questions use emotionally or politically "loaded" terms. A classic example comes from the policy area of government spending on the poor. Consider the following survey question:

> We are faced with many problems in this country, none of which can be solved easily or inexpensively. I'm going to name some of these problems and for each one I'd like you to tell me whether you think we're spending too much money, too little money, or about the right amount.[26]

When the public was asked about "welfare," the responses showed that a large majority of Americans believed that too much was being spent:

Too little: 13%
About right: 25%
Too much: 62%

Conservatives might interpret such a poll to mean that Americans want to slash aid to the poor. But when the *same people* in the *same poll* were asked about "assistance to the poor," a similarly large majority responded that too little was being spent:

Too little: 59%
About right: 25%
Too much: 16%

Liberals could use the poll to argue that welfare spending should rise.

Although *welfare* and *assistance to the poor* may appear to mean the same thing—welfare is the policy used to provide assistance to poor families—the terms evidently tap into different attitudes. *Welfare* carries negative connotations; it seems to prompt people to think of lazy and undeserving recipients—the stereotypical welfare cheats. But *assistance to the poor* does not evoke these negative stereotypes. Careless (or clever) question wording can produce contradictory findings on a major public issue. Reputable survey organizations work constantly to identify and eliminate loaded questions.

Oversimplified Questions: Public Opinion on Abortion   In 1973, the Supreme Court handed down its *Roe v. Wade* decision, striking down any restrictions on a woman's right to terminate a pregnancy in the first trimester and limiting restrictions on that right in the second trimester. The *Webster* decision in 1989 and the *Casey* decision in 1992 further refined the court's position. Most Americans long ago decided where they stood on the abortion issue. Indeed, when the *same* survey question is repeated over time, public opinion is strikingly constant. Yet support for abortion rights varies widely from one poll question to another—prompting both pro-choice and pro-life spokespersons to claim that a majority of Americans support their position. Unless the laws of arithmetic fail to hold in the case of this issue, one side or both must be wrong, but neither side makes up its figures. How can this be?

As with welfare policy, part of the inconsistency comes from the use of leading questions.[27] One *Los Angeles Times* poll conducted at about the time of the *Webster* decision asked,

> **Do you think a pregnant woman should or should not be able to get a legal abortion, no matter what the reason?**

By a heavy margin (57 percent to 34 percent), Americans said no. As pro-life spokespersons claimed, Americans were pro-life. Should Democratic campaign consultants have advised their clients to flip-flop to the pro-life side? Well, probably not. A few months later, a CBS News/*New York Times* survey asked,

> **If a woman wants to have an abortion, and her doctor agrees to it, should she be allowed to have an abortion or not?**

By more than a 2:1 margin (58 percent to 26 percent), Americans said yes. As the pro-choice spokespersons claimed, America had a pro-choice majority. Should Republican campaign consultants have advised their clients to flip-flop to the pro-choice side?

Which poll was right? Probably neither. Upon close examination, both survey questions are suspect. Each contains words and phrases that predispose people to answer in one direction. The first question uses the phrase "no matter what the reason." If forced to choose yes or no unconditionally, some generally pro-choice people will say no, believing that some circumstances are just not sufficiently serious to justify abortion.

The CBS/*NYT* question leans in the opposite direction. A doctor's approval suggests a considered decision based on medically justifiable grounds. Some generally pro-life people might agree to abortion in such a case.

In addition, Americans distinguish between the morality of behavior and the legality of behavior. A 2003 poll asked people whether they agreed or disagreed with the stark claim that "abortion is the same thing as murdering a child." Americans were evenly split (46 percent agreed, 46 percent disagreed).[28] Similarly, a plurality or majority of Americans thinks that "abortion is morally wrong."[29] On the other hand, majorities of Americans favor keeping abortion legal, and comfortable majorities support *Roe. v. Wade*.[30] Thus, individualistic Americans favor freedom of choice, especially when it involves preventing government interference. Many Americans who are troubled—even deeply troubled—by abortion nonetheless will not support making it illegal.

As opinions on abortion are especially likely to change depending on the way pollsters ask about the issue, the use of leading questions may be insufficient to explain the volatility. More likely, opinions on abortion are too complex for pollsters to capture in a single, simple question. Evidence that pollsters often oversimplify the abortion issue appears in surveys taken by the National Opinion Research Center, which use a more complex question. The NORC question reads as follows:

Please tell me whether or not you think it should be possible for a pregnant woman to obtain a legal abortion if

1. the woman's health is seriously endangered?
2. she became pregnant as a result of rape?
3. there is a strong chance of serious defect in the baby?
4. the family has low income and cannot afford any more children?
5. she is not married and does not want to marry the man?
6. she is married and does not want any more children?

As Figure 5.4 shows, after moving in a liberal direction in the late 1960s, opinion stabilized at the time of the 1973 *Roe v. Wade* decision, stayed remarkably constant for two decades, and then moved a bit in a conservative direction in the late 1990s. These trends across time vary much less than responses do across circumstances, showing that Americans are pragmatic, not ideological, when it comes to abortion. They favor the right to choose in general, but not an unconditional right to choose in every circumstance. Different people draw a line at different points.

In the late 1990s, some pro-life groups began to focus media attention on a procedure called "partial-birth abortion," in which the fetus is destroyed after it has been partially delivered. Pictures and verbal descriptions of this process, disseminated by pro-life groups, are gruesome. The publicity surrounding this particularly distressing form of abortion probably explains why support for pro-choice positions declined during the period (review Figure 5.4). Majorities of Americans have consistently registered opposition to the procedure. The debate over partial-birth abortion reminded Americans of the conditions under which they opposed abortion rights, underscoring the fact that most Americans hold complicated opinions about when abortion should and should not be legal.

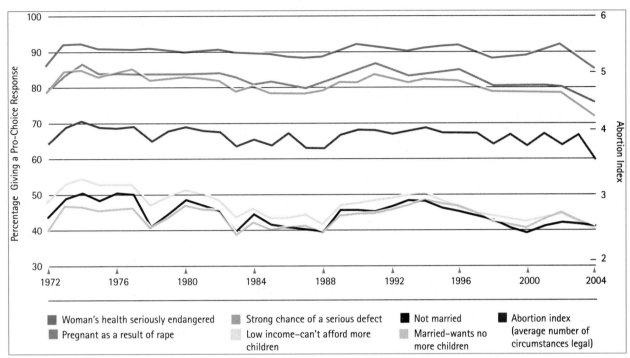

FIGURE 5.4

Popular Attitudes Toward Abortion Have Been Remarkably Stable Since *Roe v. Wade* (1973)

Note: Respondents who answered "don't know" are included in the calculation.

Source: Calculated by Sam Abrams from the General Social Survey 1972–2004 Cumulative Data File.

Figure 5.5 shows this complexity in a different way. It indicates that very few Americans hold absolute positions on abortion; only a fifth want abortion "always illegal" and only a quarter wish to keep it "always legal." The majority of Americans hold a more complicated set of preferences that would make abortion legal in some circumstances and illegal in others. Thus, although opinion on abortion has been stable over time—indicating that it is not the result of haphazard poll responses—it does not accommodate the oversimplified questions that pollsters customarily ask about it.

One final point should be made about public opinion polls. Though it is easy to identify problems with polls and to provide examples of biased samples and loaded questions, one major thing needs to be said in their favor: As a way of measuring and monitoring public opinion, systematic sample surveys are far better than any of the alternatives. For all kinds of reasons, both practical and moral, elected officials and political activists need timely, reliable information about the state of public opinion: what issues the public cares about, how the public assesses officials' current performance, the themes and policies the public favors or opposes. And, though polls are not a foolproof way of answering such questions, they do provide a considerably more accurate picture of the public mind than we might get by, for example, listening to talk radio or holding town meetings or reading letters sent in by constituents. The solution to bad or misleading surveys is not to abandon polls, but to learn how to interpret them correctly and to use them carefully.

FIGURE 5.5

Americans Tend to Favor
Abortion Rights, but with
Restrictions

Note: N = 1,001 adults nationwide. Margin of error +/- 3.

Source: CNN/*USA Today*/Gallup Poll

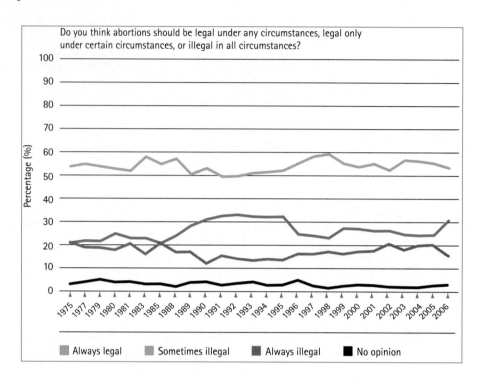

Characteristics of Public Opinion

Why should the results of measuring public opinion be so sensitive to *how* it is measured? The characteristics of public opinion often make it very hard to obtain reliable measurements.

Public Opinion Is Uninformed

On many issues, people have little or no information. The extent of popular ignorance
is most apparent when surveys pose "factual" questions. As shown in Figure 5.6, only
a third of adults over age 36 could identify the political party controlling their state
legislatures in 2003. Less than a quarter could identify the speaker of the U.S. House
of Representatives; more than a third could not even identify the political party in
charge. Young adults are even less knowledgeable.

Elections are not SAT tests, of course; it is not necessary to know the answers to
all sorts of factual questions in order to vote intelligently. But widespread ignorance
extends beyond such factual questions to important matters of government and public
policy. During the 1995 federal government shutdown, 40 percent of Americans were
unaware that the Republicans controlled both houses of Congress (and 10 percent did
not know that the president was a Democrat). By more than a 2:1 margin, Americans
believed—absolutely wrongly—that the federal government spent more on foreign aid
than on Medicare. In fact, the United States was spending four times as much on
Medicare as on foreign aid and the ratio was rising.[31]

Upon learning the full extent of popular ignorance, some politically involved
students react critically, jumping to the conclusion that ordinary Americans are lazy and

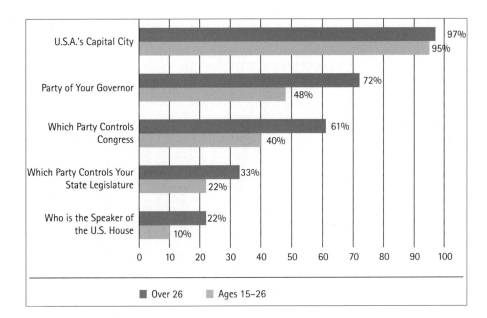

FIGURE 5.6

Americans Are Not Very
Knowledgeable About the
Specifics of American
Government

Young people know even less
about government than relatively
ill-informed older Americans.

Source: Representative Democracy in
America Project, 2003.

irresponsible people who fall far short of the democratic ideal. Such reactions are understandable, but unjustified. Many people fall short of the ideal, but it is the ideal that is unjustified. The simple fact is that most people have little time for politics. They work hard to take care of life's necessities, such as paying bills, caring for families, and nurturing personal relationships—leaving little time or energy to read the *New York Times* or watch C-SPAN. Nor do Americans stand out for their inattentiveness to public affairs. Citizens in other countries lack political and historical knowledge as well. A British Gallup poll, for example, found that only 40 percent of Britons knew that the United States once was part of their empire![32]

Those who criticize ordinary citizens for their lack of attention to public affairs often have jobs that enable them to stay informed with little effort. For example, political conversation is a common diversion on college campuses; professors and students find it easy to stay informed. Likewise, the jobs of many journalists involve following politics: If they are not informed, they are not doing their job. If everyone worked in a university or for the news media, we would all be much better informed. But most people do not—a fact that social critics tend to overlook.

The general point is that gathering, digesting, and storing information is neither effortless nor free; it is costly. For most Americans, bearing such **information costs** brings them few immediate benefits[33] Citizens doubt that they can make much difference when civil war rages in Somalia. When faced with a costly activity that has no clear benefit, many of them quite rationally decide to minimize their costs. Thus, from a logical standpoint, the puzzle is not that so many Americans are ill informed; rather, the puzzle is that as many are as well informed as they are.[34]

Information costs do not fall equally heavily on all people. Education makes it easier to absorb and organize information; thus it comes as no surprise that more-educated Americans are better informed than less-educated ones (see Figure 5.7). In addition, the benefits of information are not the same for all people on all issues. Most people will be better informed on issues that directly affect their lives or livelihoods. Teachers are

Comparing
Public Opinion

information cost

The time and mental effort required
to absorb and store information,
whether from conversations, personal
experiences, or the media.

FIGURE 5.7

Higher Education Is
Strongly Associated with
Greater Knowledge of
Politics and Government

Source: Data are taken from Michael Delli
Carpini and Scott Keeter, *What Americans
Know About Politics and Why It Matters*
(New Haven: Yale University Press, 1997:
189).

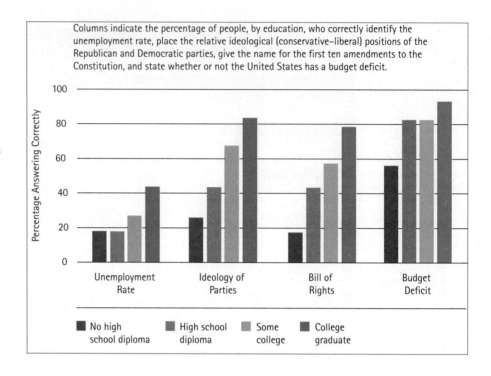

Columns indicate the percentage of people, by education, who correctly identify the unemployment rate, place the relative ideological (conservative–liberal) positions of the Republican and Democratic parties, give the name for the first ten amendments to the Constitution, and state whether or not the United States has a budget deficit.

issue public
Group of people particularly affected
by, or concerned with, a specific issue.

especially knowledgeable about school operations and budgets. Auto workers have strong views on foreign imports. Farmers keep track of proposals to change agricultural subsidies. Such **issue publics** are different from the great majority of citizens in that they find relevant information particularly valuable and can gather it more cheaply.[35]

Of course, some people will bear information costs even when they get little direct benefit from doing so. They may feel a duty as citizens to be informed, so they stay attuned to public affairs because they believe it is the "right thing" to do. Other people follow public affairs because they find it intrinsically interesting just as some follow baseball or art. For such people, following public affairs is a recreational activity. Probably most citizens know as much as they do because they enjoy staying informed, not because they derive any tangible benefit from doing so.[36]

Many of the Opinions Expressed in Polls Are Not Strongly Held

Elected officials and other political activists often use poll results as proof that the public approves of their actions and policies. Yet even when survey data appear to support such claims, there is considerable evidence that many of the responses registered in public opinion surveys are not very strongly held: respondents do give the answers recorded, but they are not firmly committed to them.

A group of researchers at the University of Cincinnati asked a sample of local residents the following question: "Some people say that the 1975 Public Affairs Act should be repealed. Do you agree or disagree with this idea?" Thirty-three percent of those interviewed took a position on this matter (16 percent agreed, 17 percent disagreed)—which is noteworthy because there was, in fact, no such act. In other words, 33 percent of the sample claimed to have an opinion on a completely fictitious issue.[37]

Spending Time with Friends

Many Americans have little time or energy to devote to staying informed after a busy day working and tending to their families and personal relationships. They prefer to spend their remaining time on leisure and light entertainment.

How do we explain such an anomalous finding? The answer says much about both the nature of public opinion and the peculiarities of the survey interview situation. Unlike most activists, most ordinary citizens do not have well-defined, clearly thought out opinions on numerous different policy issues. Nothing in their daily lives requires them to. Yet, when a survey interviewer calls them up on the phone or shows up at their door and asks them questions about such issues, they wish to be cooperative and they are reluctant to admit ignorance. Hence, they invent opinions on the spot. Such responses are often called "non-attitudes" or "doorstep opinions."

A measure of the prevalence of such doorstep opinions comes from using screen or filter questions in public opinion surveys—phrases or sentences added on at the beginning or end of survey questions in order to exclude those who do not know about an issue or do not have a clear position. In a poll conducted by the University of Chicago, half of the sample was asked this question: "In general, do you think the courts in this area deal too harshly or not harshly enough with criminals?" The other half of the sample was asked a similar but slightly different question: "In general, do you think the courts in this area deal too harshly or not harshly enough with criminals, or don't you have enough information about the courts to say?" In the first case, 7 percent of those interviewed said they weren't sure or didn't have an opinion. For the second question, 29 percent chose the "no opinion" response. In short, the number of "no opinion" responses jumped by 22 percentage points just because the question made it a little easier to take this position.[38]

Public Opinion Is Not Ideological

Another characteristic of public opinion that makes it easy to misinterpret is that even when people have reasonably firm views on issues, those views usually are not closely connected to one another. In short, most Americans are not ideological.

An **ideology** is a system of principles that ties together a person's views on a wide range of particular issues. For example, if you are told that Representative Smith is a

ideology

System of beliefs in which one or more organizing principles connect the individual's views on a wide range of issues.

political elite
Activists and officeholders who are deeply interested in, and knowledgeable about, politics.

mass public
Ordinary people for whom politics is a peripheral concern.

"liberal" Democrat, you can guess that Smith is pro-choice on abortion, favors gun control, and supports a strong government role in health care. Conversely, if you are told that Representative Jones is a "conservative" Republican, you might guess that she is pro-life, opposes gun control, and thinks that health care should be left to the private sector as much as possible. Such assumptions will usually be right. The reason is that **political elites**—people who are deeply involved in politics, whether as activists or as officeholders—tend to have well-structured ideologies that bind together their positions on different policy issues.

Ordinary citizens are another matter. People with little direct involvement in politics—a group traditionally called the **mass public**—usually are not ideological.[39] Their views on specific issues do not cluster together like those of elites, nor do their evaluations of party leaders or of political groups.[40] Rather than believe consistently in either activist or minimal government, citizens favor government spending in some areas but oppose it in others. They like some Democratic politicians but dislike others. They favor toleration for some groups in some situations, but not for other groups in other situations.

Even when the standards for ideological thinking are rather low, the evidence indicates that few people follow conventional political ideologies. For example, *when given the option,* one-quarter to one-third of the population will not classify themselves on a liberal–conservative scale, and another one-quarter put themselves exactly in the middle: "moderate, middle of the road."[41] Furthermore, many Americans are unaware of the ideologies held by the people they elect. During the 2004 campaign, for example, only two-thirds of those polled considered the Republicans the more conservative of the two parties (one-sixth thought the Democrats were).[42]

Here again, there is a tendency to disparage regular citizens. Critics assume that ordinary Americans form their political attitudes haphazardly because their preferences do not follow conventional patterns. Although that certainly is true of some, it is not necessarily true of most, for ideologies are *social* constructions. Personal views aside, can anyone explain why a person who prefers lower taxes and a strong military necessarily should oppose abortion but not the death penalty and should support strip-club regulations but not gun control? Such issue positions may go together when people polarize across an ideological divide—that is, when they view the political world as a struggle between liberals and conservatives and adopt the many views that characterize their side—but no comprehensive political philosophy ties all these issue positions together. Indeed, ideologies change over time.[43] Rather than criticize normal nonideological citizens, maybe we should criticize political elites for slavishly conforming to a laundry list of policy preferences that have no logical connection to each other.

Whether you regard ideological thinking as good or bad, however, you should bear one point in mind. Because they presume that ideological thinking is the norm, party and issue activists, media commentators, and many public officials will conclude too much on the basis of opinion polls and voting returns. Support for one variety of government action may indicate nothing about support for another, seemingly similar government action. Support for a candidate's position on one issue may suggest little or nothing about that candidate's "mandate" to act on seemingly related issues. The nonideological nature of public opinion means that elites often hear more than the voters are saying.

Public Opinion Is Inconsistent

Given that people often have not thought about issues, and given that most of them do not think ideologically, it is not surprising that the public sometimes sends contradictory messages. For example, in 1980, when Ronald Reagan defeated Jimmy Carter and the Republicans made striking gains in Congress, many observers interpreted the election results as a "resurgence of conservatism" or a "turn to the right" in American politics. In fact, the data were confusing.[44]

Polls reported that large majorities of the citizenry felt that the federal government was spending too much money and doing too much regulating. Popular sentiments such as these seemed to explain Reagan's victory. But the same polls asked the *same people* which domestic programs they favored cutting and which areas of business activity they favored deregulating. Surprisingly, pluralities—and often majorities—felt that most domestic activities deserved *higher* funding or warranted *more* regulation. Their sentiments about particular spending reductions and regulatory changes did not match the principles they claimed to endorse. Americans were inconsistent.

Findings such as these are not unusual. In recent decades, the American people have never delivered a clear mandate either for the Republicans to cut and retrench or for the Democrats to tax and expand.[45] After the Republicans took control of Congress in 1994, for example, most Americans wanted to balance the budget but opposed cutting expensive entitlement programs that accounted for much of the budget deficits. Early in his administration President George W. Bush pushed a tax-cut plan that a plurality of voters supported at the same time that they endorsed increasing spending on social security and education.[46] Such contradictory views may be amusing—they recall the old maxim that "everybody wants to go to heaven but nobody wants to die"—but they confuse political debate. One consequence of inconsistent public preferences was the gridlock and deficits of the 1980s and 1990s. Both parties could refuse to compromise, citing public opinion polls that supported what they wished to do.

Why is public opinion so inconsistent? Ignorance explains some of the contradictions. People think that the federal budget lavishes money on unpopular programs such as "welfare" and foreign aid, even though such policies account for relatively little federal spending. They also believe that government agencies waste so much money that elected leaders could slice funding without harming essential services. Citizens therefore unrealistically expect painless budget cuts.

Not all examples of inconsistency reflect inaccurate information, however. People oppose amending the Constitution but they endorse numerous amendment proposals. They support various fundamental rights, but not for groups they oppose.[47] As Figure 5.8 shows, most citizens favor free speech "for all"—but half would prevent a member of their most disliked group from giving a speech. They favor freedom of the press and freedom of assembly—with "reasonable" exceptions. And they believe in the separation of church and state—but favor prayer in schools. In short, citizens are so consistently inconsistent when applying general principles to specific cases that explanations other than ignorance must be at work.

Some social critics contend that Americans are hypocrites. Americans pay lip service to fine-sounding principles, but they do not really believe in these values. They abandon them whenever it is convenient to do so. We authors have a more positive

FIGURE 5.8
Americans Tend to
Endorse General Principles
but Make Numerous
Exceptions to Them

Source: Data are taken from John Sullivan,
James Piereson, and George Marcus,
Political Tolerance and American Democracy
(Chicago: University of Chicago Press,
1982).

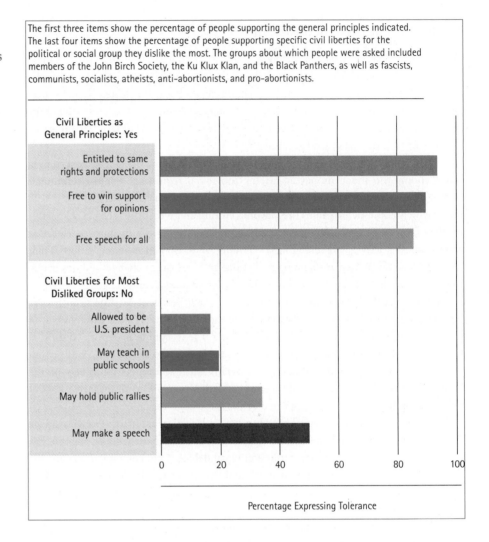

The first three items show the percentage of people supporting the general principles indicated. The last four items show the percentage of people supporting specific civil liberties for the political or social group they dislike the most. The groups about which people were asked included members of the John Birch Society, the Ku Klux Klan, and the Black Panthers, as well as fascists, communists, socialists, atheists, anti-abortionists, and pro-abortionists.

interpretation. Law professors, newspaper editors, and political activists tend to view rights inflexibly—as rules that government officials must respect at all times. Once leaders start making exceptions, they can water down rights until they provide no protection whatsoever. Few Americans accept such an absolutist perspective, though. They tend to be more practical, to be pragmatists. Rights are good things, but at times they conflict with other values.[48]

Most citizens are prepared to make trade-offs on a case-by-case basis,[49] relaxing rights when they threaten to produce "unreasonable" outcomes that violate "common sense." Yes, free speech is a good thing—but perhaps not enough to justify allowing Nazi rallies in a neighborhood where Holocaust survivors live. Yes, people should be treated equally—but perhaps historically disadvantaged groups should receive some special consideration when they apply for college as a way to erase social differences. Yes, police should follow proper procedures—but murderers should not necessarily go free just because police violated some technical point of law. To adults familiar with life's complexities, the realm of real-world politics has to be flexible. They may feel no contradiction in treating rights more as guidelines rather than as ironclad rules.[50]

Just What Is Permitted?

Americans are supportive of free speech in general, but many are willing to restrict hate groups.

• *If rights are considered as part of a trade-off, rather than as inalienable rights, what will the consequences be for the substance of those rights? What sorts of limits on extreme groups are permissible? For instance, is it fair to allow the individuals shown here to march, but not in a town filled with Holocaust survivors?*

Governing by Public Opinion?

Public Opinion and Leadership

Never before have American politicians had so much information about public opinion. Indeed, critics regularly complain that politics and government today are "poll-driven." As we have seen, however, given the characteristics of public opinion, trying to measure and interpret it is far from an exact science. At times it is more like reading tea leaves! Furthermore, even when public opinion is fairly clear, there is no guarantee that policy makers will follow it. Political scientists have tried to determine if public opinion influences policy, and if so, when it does or does not do so.

The Power of Public Opinion

Public opinion may be uninformed, nonideological, and inconsistent—but these flaws do not mean elected officials can ignore it. The public as a whole generally possesses enough information about the political system to understand the choices voters need to make. For example, the public at large understands that the Democrats are to the left of the Republicans on most issues.[51] Moreover, even within the same party, the public knew that Ronald Reagan was farther to the right than Richard Nixon and that George McGovern was farther to the left than Jimmy Carter. Political scientist James Stimson has shown that, when numerous survey questions are analyzed together, researchers can find distinct shifts in the general direction or "mood" of the public. For example, after analyzing hundreds of questions, he found that the electorate in fact did shift to the right in the years leading up to Ronald Reagan's election.[52]

In the same vein, noted political scientists Benjamin Page and Robert Shapiro have argued that, viewed *collectively,* the public is reasonably "rational." Analysis of thousands of poll questions asked repeatedly over more than a 40-year period shows that in the aggregate, public opinion is far more stable than the opinions of individual members of

The Irrational Public?

The inconsistencies in public opinion may suggest that voters are buffoons who think that government can provide anything they want. However, what seems like inconsistency may grow from the public's desire to avoid extremes and seek a practical balance between competing principles.

© Creators Syndicate

BY LUCKOVICH FOR THE ATLANTA CONSTUTUTION

the public. When it does shift, public opinion generally reacts to new events and conditions in natural ways. For example, when federal spending goes up, public preferences for continued increases go down, an effect that indicates some broad public recognition of the direction in which government policy has moved.[53]

Given the stability and sensibility of overall public opinion, elected officials usually feel compelled to give voters what they want. Page and Shapiro confirm that American policies follow public opinion. When trends in opinion are clearly moving in one direction, public policy generally follows. The more pronounced the trend in opinion, the more likely policy is to follow it.[54] Such findings show that an often uninformed, nonideological, and inconsistent public still will influence the direction of public policy.

Why can a limited public nonetheless guide the behavior of their government? The answer lies in the distinction between individuals and aggregates. Even if particular voters have little grasp of public affairs, as a group they may be much more capable—with the process of aggregation canceling out individual error and enabling the general public preference to emerge. Think of a grade school orchestra. Individually, the young musicians are so unsteady that it is difficult to identify the tune each is playing, but put them all together and the audience can make out "Twinkle, Twinkle Little Star." So it is with public opinion. On some issues and at some times, public opinion and public policy may not be closely aligned, but looking at the general direction of public policy over the long run reveals that it tends to follow public opinion.

The Limits of Public Opinion: Gun Control

Policy makers may consider voter preferences when they shape policy, but the public does not always get what it wants. Even if individual politicians are highly responsive to public opinion, the system as a whole need not be. The Columbine shootings provide a stark illustration. On April 20, 1999, two deranged students at Columbine High School in Colorado killed a teacher and 12 of their schoolmates and wounded more than 20 others. The killers used two shotguns, a semi-automatic pistol, and a semi-automatic rifle in their murderous spree. This was the fourth high-profile school shooting in the United States in little more than a year. Whether because of the cumulative impact or the sheer scale of the rampage, the Columbine tragedy energized elected officials.

Gun Control

In the Senate, a juvenile-crime bill had been going nowhere fast. Anti-gun legislators decided to use this bill as a vehicle for passing new gun control measures, sensing that the Columbine shootings might allow them to get a bill through the law-making process. They proposed an amendment to the bill that tightened restrictions on sales at gun shows. In a highly publicized climax to the renewed debate, the Senate adopted the amendment only after Vice-President Al Gore cast a tie-breaking vote (under the Constitution, the vice-president votes when the Senate is tied). By much wider margins, the Senate adopted other provisions mandating trigger locks or lock boxes with every handgun sale, outlawing imports of high-capacity ammunition clips, and raising the age at which juveniles could buy handguns and assault weapons. The amended bill easily passed the Senate.

In the House, Republican leaders agreed that the aroused state of public opinion required some response. Speaker Dennis Hastert (R-IL) commented, "This is one of those rare times when the national consensus demands that we act." He promised that the House would pass a gun control measure.[55] But the issue was now thoroughly entangled in partisan politics. Vice-President Gore believed that his highly visible gun control stance would aid his 2000 presidential bid, and congressional Democrats hoped to use the issue to take over Congress. The key target group was suburban voters—especially women, whom polls showed to be more in favor of gun control than were men.[56] To appeal to them, Democrats framed the issue as one of protecting children by restricting access to guns.

The Democrats were not united, however. A senior Democrat, John Dingell of Michigan, was an avid hunter and a former National Rifle Association board member. Dingell worked with Republican leaders to develop an amendment that would soften the Senate's gun-show restrictions. Forty-five Democrats followed Dingell, helping pass the alternative provision. Then, angry liberals who believed the weakened legislation did not go far enough joined angry conservatives who felt it still went too far. Together, they defeated the bill. Gun control was dead!

At first glance, this story seems to be one of irresponsible or even corrupt behavior by the Congress. The story line offered by the media was simple: Public opinion counted less than the campaign contributions and arm twisting of the NRA. Certainly the media interpretation was correct in one respect: The U.S. public favors limits on guns. As Figure 5.9 indicates, large majorities favor the specific provisions—background checks, trigger locks, restrictions on magazine size—that were part of the rejected bill. Different polls showed a high degree of agreement on these questions. How, then, could representatives of the people fail to pass gun control? The answer has two parts, one institutional, the other behavioral.

Institutionally, a member of the House represents a congressional district of approximately 630,000 people. The national distribution of opinion is of little importance to members of Congress. What counts is the distribution of opinion in their home districts,

FIGURE 5.9

Most Americans Support
Gun Control Proposals

Source: "Bear Arms—But More
Regulation," *Public Perspective,* June/July
1999: 34.

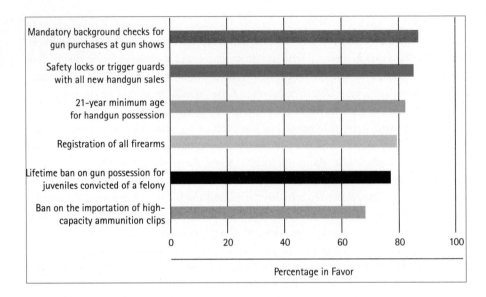

especially among the voters who elected them. Many of these district electorates differ significantly from the country as a whole. Opinion on gun control varies according to whether someone lives in an urban or a rural environment, for example, with rural residents far more supportive of gun rights. Not surprisingly, therefore, 81 percent of the representatives from rural districts voted for Dingell's amendment, including a majority of rural Democrats (see Figure 5.10).[57] Although no detailed study is available, it is likely that many representatives who voted against gun control voted in accordance with the sentiments of voting majorities *in their districts.*

Still, given the extremely high level of support for the gun-control provisions, it is also likely that some representatives did vote against district preferences. Was this the NRA at work? To some extent, perhaps. But remember that interest-group endorsements and campaign contributions don't vote. There have to be voters in the district who will act on the group's support. That is the second part of the explanation for the failure of gun control. Behaviorally, supporters of gun control feel less strongly about it than do opponents. As Democratic Minority Leader Richard Gephardt (D-MO) conceded, "The 80 percent that are for gun safety just aren't for it very much. They're not intense."[58]

Indeed, although most polls registered a high level of support for gun control after Columbine, the same polls indicated that the public did not regard it as one of the more important issues facing the country. Gun control ranked relatively low compared to issues such as social security, health care, Medicare, and education. One national poll had gun control twelfth in importance as a voting issue in the next election.[59] Not many supporters of gun control are intense, single-issue voters (if they vote at all), but opponents of gun control are classic single-issue voters. Indeed, Representative Dingell pointed out that popular support for gun control was at least as high earlier in the decade as it was after Columbine. Despite that fact, Democrats lost their congressional majority in 1994 in part because of the party's support for the ban on assault weapons.

Why are gun-control supporters less intense about the issue than its opponents are? Part of the explanation seems to be cultural. Guns are an important part of rural culture, especially in the South and West.[60] For many rural voters, guns are not alien and frightening mechanical devices as they may seem to suburban voters; rather, guns

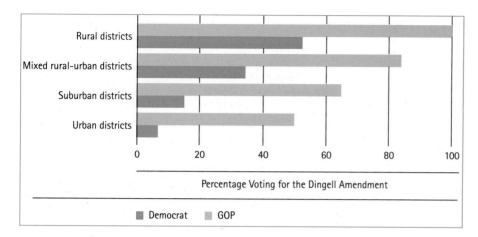

FIGURE 5.10

Rural Members Are Far More Opposed to Gun Control Than Urban Members

Source: Don Carney, "Beyond Guns and Violence: A Battle of House Control," CQ Weekly, June 19, 1999; and Roll Call Votes, pp. 1496–1497.

are a standard part of everyday life. As former Senator Alan Simpson of Wyoming likes to joke during dinner speeches, "Where I come from, people think gun control means how steady can you hold your rifle." Such voters view gun control laws as government interference with their way of life, an attack on their values.

By contrast, gun-control supporters see restricting guns as little more than one method to reduce violence. They have relatively low expectations for gun control, believing that dangerous criminals will find ways to get around restrictive laws.[61] It is hard to feel passionate about laws that would have such a minor impact. Gun-control supporters are so doubtful about the effectiveness of restrictions that they seldom retaliate against elected officials who stand on the other side. They lack intensity. Thus, this example illustrates the imperfect connection between aggregate public opinion and national public policy.

Chapter Summary

Public opinion is at the core of democratic politics. For the people to "rule," their opinions must translate into public laws and policies. However, measuring public opinion is an inexact science at best. Sample design and question wording make interpreting opinion polls very tricky. And on many issues—among them abortion—the public truly does not have an answer that is easily quantified.

Even when public opinion seems relatively clear, governing by opinion poll may not be a good idea. Citizens tend to be uninformed, so polling data may not represent firmly held opinions. Preferences can change with little notice, and the public may not connect two issues that elected officials consider clearly related. Thus, leaders often misinterpret poll results. Politicians who respond too quickly to short-term fluctuations in the polls may get into political trouble.

Rather, public opinion exerts its influence largely through the calculations of officials who try to anticipate what they must do to win reelection. Clearly, elected officials will hesitate to defy the will of an aroused public—but they pay more attention to the wishes of their own voters than they do to the wishes of the American public as a whole.

Key Terms

focus groups, p. 130
ideology, p. 139
information cost, p. 137
issue public, p. 138

mass public, p. 140
measurement error, p. 130
political efficacy, p. 125
political elite, p. 140

public opinion, p. 123
sampling error, p. 128
selection bias, p. 128
socialization, p. 124

Suggested Readings

Of General Interest

Asher, Herbert. *Polling and the Public: What Every Citizen Should Know*, 6th ed. Washington: CQ Press, 2004. Good introductory discussion of how polls are conducted and how to interpret them.

Mayer, William. *The Changing American Mind: How and Why American Public Opinion Changed Between 1960 and 1988*. Ann Arbor: University of Michigan Press, 1992. Masterful survey of the changing contours of public opinion over the past generation, with careful dissection of the sources of opinion change.

Page, Benjamin, and Robert Shapiro. *The Rational Public*. Chicago: University of Chicago Press, 1992. Prize-winning study of public opinion from the 1930s to the 1990s. The authors argue that, viewed as a collectivity, the public is rational, however imperfect the individual opinions that members of the public hold.

Schuman, Howard, and Stanley Presser. *Questions and Answers in Attitude Surveys*. New York: Sage Publications, 1996. A comprehensive study of the effects of question wording, form, and context on survey results.

Focused Studies

Cook, Elizabeth, Ted Jelen, and Clyde Wilcox. *Between Two Absolutes: Public Opinion and the Politics of Abortion*. Boulder, CO: Westview, 1992. Although more than a decade old, this careful, disinterested description and explanation of American attitudes toward abortion is still accurate today.

Geer, John. *From Tea Leaves to Opinion Polls*. New York: Columbia University Press, 1996. Thoughtful consideration of a democratic dilemma: Do politicians lead public opinion or follow it? Concludes that rational leaders always follow on salient issues but often lead on less salient ones.

Jacobs, Lawrence, and Robert Shapiro. *Politicians Don't Pander: Political Manipulation and the Loss of Democratic Responsiveness*. Chicago: University of Chicago Press, 2000. Provocative argument that today's politicians follow their own strongly held preferences and that polls are only a tool used to determine how best to frame the positions that the politicians personally favor.

Schuman, Howard, Charlotte Steeh, and Lawrence Bobo. *Racial Attitudes in America: Trends and Interpretations*. Cambridge, MA: Harvard University Press, 1985. Thoughtful examination of racial attitudes. The authors find that Americans have come to accept principles of equal treatment but remain quite divided on government policies designed to bring about racial equality.

Stimson, James. *Public Opinion in America: Moods, Cycles, and Swings*. Boulder, CO: Westview Press, 1991. Statistically sophisticated examination of American public opinion from the 1960s to the 1990s. The author finds that public opinion was moving in a conservative direction in the 1970s, but reversed direction around the time of Reagan's election.

Zaller, John. *The Nature and Origins of Mass Opinion*. New York: Cambridge University Press, 1992. An influential reinterpretation of public opinion findings that argues that people do not have fixed opinions on many subjects. Rather, their responses reflect variable considerations stimulated by the question and the context.

On the Web

Academic organizations archive a great deal of public opinion data on political and social topics.

www.aapor.org

www.ropercenter.uconn.edu

www.norc.uchicago.edu

Some of the best sites are the American Association for Public Opinion Research, the Roper Center, and the National Opinion Research Center. The AAPOR site links to the best scholarly journal of public opinion, *Public Opinion Quarterly*. The world's largest collection of public opinion data can be found at the Roper Center for Public Opinion Research. This collection includes a huge amount of commer-cial and academic poll data. The Roper Center's service—iPoll—requires subscription, but your university may be able to help you gain access. The National Opinion Research Center site contains the 23 General Social Surveys (GSS) carried out since 1972.

www.pollingreport.com

The Polling Report summarizes recent media polls from major media outlets such as CNN/Gallup and the *New York Times*, among others. This site will have more current information than the academic sites, but because news organizations polling about trendy issues sometimes use inconsistent or inadequately tested question wordings, the findings are more subject to question and interpretation.

CHAPTER 6

Individual Participation

CHAPTER OUTLINE

Getting Out the Vote in 2004

On Election Day 2004 the Republican and Democratic Parties devoted an extraordinary amount of effort and resources to turning out their voters. In most modern campaigns, the parties have concentrated on persuading the undecideds. The "get-out-the-vote" effort has generally been regarded as a secondary concern.

The roots of this reversal in emphasis go back to the 2000 election. George Bush led Al Gore in the polls through all of October, but ultimately lost the popular vote to Gore. This last-minute surprise, Bush's advisors believed, was due to the failure of the Republican Party to get its voters to the polls as effectively as the Democrats had. In addition, looking ahead to 2004, Republican strategists felt that most voters had formed strong impressions of President Bush; hence, the number of voters in the middle—the so-called swing voters—would be unusually small. Under these conditions victory would likely go to whichever party could mobilize its supporters more effectively.

The upshot was a Republican "72-Hour Plan," a detailed get-out-the-vote plan that would be implemented during the final three days of the campaign. The Republican National Committee field-tested the plan in a few states during the 2002 midterm elections, and then set the full program in motion in 2004, painstakingly setting up an extensive, grass-roots field organization in every major state that was expected to be competitive. In Ohio, for example, the 2000 Gore campaign had 16 paid staffers, supplemented by 22,000 volunteers, and was never organized at the precinct level. By contrast, in August of 2004 the *Columbus Dispatch* reported that the Bush organization already had 45 full-time staffers, 58,000 volunteers, and a chairperson in each of Ohio's 12,132 precincts.[1]

The Republican get-out-the-vote drive was organized and implemented by their national and state party organizations. The Democrats, in contrast, largely "outsourced" their voter turnout effort, relying on the volunteers and organizational capabilities of labor unions and liberal activist groups such as MoveOn.org and America Coming Together. Whoever was providing the muscle, the result was, according to a *New York Times* report on the morning of the election, "the most expensive and successful voter drive in history." Both Democrats and Republicans claimed to have a million volunteers. The Republicans said they had contacted 18 million voters; the Democrats said they had made 23 million phone calls and knocked on 8 million doors. (As the *Times* also noted, these numbers were "impossible to verify.")[2]

What effect did all this reputed work have on the actual voting? The answer remains uncertain. In 2004, 60.7 percent of the eligible electorate voted, the highest turnout in 36 years and 6.4 percentage points higher than turnout in 2000. But it is unclear how much the party field organizations had to do with this surge. A significant portion of the increase no doubt reflected the emotion and energy generated by the controversy over the war in Iraq and other issues. Even in the "non-battleground" states, which were conceded to one candidate or the other and thus saw little organizational activity, turnout increased by 5.4 percent.[3]

Moreover, whatever the contribution of the various factors, the simple fact remains that despite a close election, hotly contested issues, and a massive get-out-the-vote effort, 40 percent of eligible Americans sat out the election. Even under highly favorable conditions, U.S. voter turnout still lagged well behind the levels routinely recorded in other democracies.

MAKING THE CONNECTION

Many Americans are concerned about turnout levels in the United States, because voting is widely regarded as the fundamental form of democratic participation. Indeed, in modern democracies, voting is the *only* form of participation for the bulk of the population. About one-third of Americans report having signed a petition, and a similar number claim to have contacted a government official at one time or another, but fewer make financial contributions to a party or candidate, and substantially fewer attend a political meeting or rally, or work in a campaign.

For most people, then, failure to vote means failure to participate at all. And if a bare majority—or even fewer people—vote, how representative are the public officials they elect, and how legitimate are the actions these officials take? Not very, some answer. Benjamin Barber charges that, "In a country where voting is the primary expression of citizenship, the refusal to vote signals the bankruptcy of democracy."[4]

Should Americans worry about the dismal rate of voter participation in their country's elections? Answering that question requires a close look at the historical, personal, and institutional reasons why many Americans fail to vote and whether other forms of participation can substitute for voting. This chapter provides the background necessary to analyze the state of political participation in America. In the pages that follow we first recount how the **franchise**—or right to vote—spread in the United States. Then we address two general questions: why is turnout lower in the United States than in other democracies, and why did turnout decline in the United States during the last third of the twentieth century? Then we consider whether Americans have developed alternate forms of participation that compensate for their failure to turn out on Election Day. With that background, we can reach a clearer understanding of whether low participation levels threaten the legitimacy of American government.

A Brief History of the Franchise in the United States

franchise
The right to vote.

For a document that was proclaimed in the name of "we the people" and that guaranteed to every state "a republican form of government," the Constitution said remarkably little about who would be allowed to vote. The only clause in the original document that mentioned voting was in Article I, section 2. "Electors" for the House of Representatives were to have the "Qualifications requisite for Electors of the most numerous Branch of the State Legislature." Thus, voter eligibility was left with the states, who could set pretty much any standards they wanted, as long as they applied those same standards to the lower houses of their own state legislatures.

In the early days of the republic most states limited the franchise to white male property-holders. Although restrictions varied from state to state and were unevenly enforced, property qualifications gradually were eliminated, but most states restricted the franchise to taxpayers until the 1850s.[5] Moreover, not all voter qualifications were economic. Until the 1830s, a few states limited voting to those who professed belief in a Christian god. Not until the eve of the Civil War could it be said that the United States had universal white male **suffrage** (another term for the right to vote).[6]

suffrage
Another term for the right to vote.

Voting Rights in the Amendment Process

Between the Civil War and 1971 a series of constitutional amendments gradually expanded electoral access until today most Americans over 18 years of age hold the legal right to vote in federal elections.

Demonstrating for Women's Suffrage

The suffragists put considerable pressure on President Woodrow Wilson to support the Nineteenth Amendment, even though women initially received the franchise in only a few western states.

• *How did that increase the pressure on politicians to support an amendment to the Constitution?*

The Fifteenth Amendment to the Constitution, adopted in 1870, extended the franchise to black males. Within a few decades, though, violence, intimidation, and other discriminatory procedures disenfranchised African Americans in many states (see Chapter 17). Black men could not exercise their voting rights in many parts of the South until the 1960s, when the Voting Rights Act reestablished federal oversight of southern elections. The result was a sharp increase in voting among African Americans.

Women's suffrage also progressed slowly.[7] The first state that allowed women to vote in national elections, Wyoming, did not do so until 1890. Eleven other states had expanded the franchise to women by 1916. Most were western states, where frontier conditions often required women to be more independent than those living on or near the eastern seaboard. The suffrage movement won its crowning victory in 1920 when the Nineteenth Amendment granted women voting rights in every state.[8]

A small extension of the franchise occurred in 1961 when the Twenty-third Amendment to the Constitution was ratified. This amendment granted residents of the District of Columbia the right to vote for presidential electors. By law (if not in practice), all mentally competent, law-abiding Americans of voting age now had the right to vote for president. (The District of Columbia still lacks representation in the U.S. Senate, and its delegate to the House of Representatives may not vote on legislation.)

The next and, to date, the last constitutional extension of the franchise came in 1971 with the adoption of the Twenty-sixth Amendment, which lowered the official voting age to 18.[9] Prior to the amendment, the federal Constitution did not guarantee voting rights to those under 21 (although individual states could use a lower limit). During the Vietnam War, however, Americans began to ask why people old enough to die on a foreign battlefield were not old enough to vote for the officials who sent them to war.[10] Support for lowering the voting age grew until Republican President Richard Nixon announced his backing for a constitutional amendment, even though many Republicans feared it would help the Democrats.

In sum, the trend over the course of American history has been steady expansion of the franchise (see Figure 6.1). Today most adult U.S. citizens may vote if they wish.

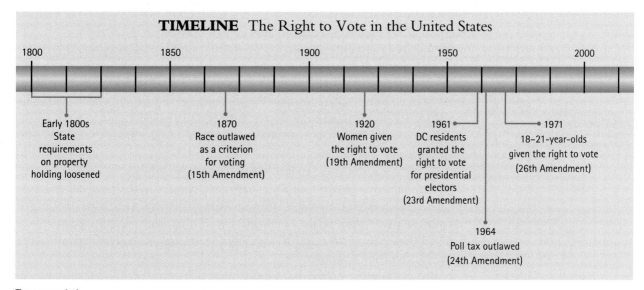

FIGURE 6.1

The Right to Vote in the United States Has Been Steadily Expanded

The right to vote in the United States has been a story of continual, if uneven, expansion.

• *Can still more groups be enfranchised? Which ones?*

Convicted felons are not eligible in many states, but some critics argue that even this restriction ought to be abolished because it falls especially heavily on African Americans. One-eighth of the black male voting age population is ineligible to vote, and this proportion rises to one-third in states such as Alabama and Florida.[11] Others have argued, presumably tongue-in-cheek, that voting rights should be expanded to include children, perhaps by giving extra weight to the choices of their parents.[12]

How Voting Rights Spread

The separate states extended the suffrage in different ways at different times. During times of war, for example, a disenfranchised group usually could expect to receive the suffrage in at least some states as a reward for their military service—a process that opened the door for immigrants, for those who did not own property or pay taxes, and for young adults who were considered "old enough to fight, old enough to vote."[13] Once a group gained voting rights in one state, however, national candidates and political parties seeking their support had an incentive to support similar expansions in other states. Electoral pressures, therefore, often caused voting rights to spread quickly, a dynamic that was most apparent in the case of women's suffrage.

Woodrow Wilson won the three-way 1912 presidential election with only 42 percent of the popular vote. At that time, he had avoided taking a clear position on women's suffrage because many of his fellow Democrats opposed it. They believed that women would vote against labor unions, against liquor interests, and against machine politicians—all key Democratic constituencies. Southern Democrats worried, moreover, that granting voting rights to women would encourage African Americans to demand voting rights as well. Nevertheless, by 1916 when Wilson was running for reelection, women had gained the right to vote in 12 states, including California (1910) and Illinois (1913). The president signaled his support for women's suffrage by promising to vote for a related referendum in New Jersey, his home state.

Wilson's change of heart reflected the fact that his Republican opponent in 1916, Charles Evans Hughes, supported a constitutional amendment to let women vote. Had Hughes won every state with women's suffrage, their electors would constitute one-third of an Electoral College majority. Wilson's political position was precarious and he could not afford to surrender the West to Hughes, so he adopted a moderate stance on women's suffrage. In the election Wilson carried 10 of the 12 states where women could vote and narrowly won.

World War I stalled the suffrage movement temporarily. As victory approached, however, suffragists pressed hard for congressional passage of the proposed constitutional amendment. The National American Women's Rights Association encouraged women to write letters, make campaign contributions, and use other conventional political strategies, while more militant suffragists engaged in confrontational tactics such as protests and demonstrations.

Because women's suffrage soon looked inevitable, politicians fearful of being left behind jumped on the bandwagon. Congress approved the suffrage amendment and sent it to the states, which ratified the provision within three years—in time for women in all 48 states to vote in the 1920 presidential election. Interestingly, the United States was far ahead of most of the world in granting full rights of citizenship to women. France did not allow women to vote until 1945, and the last Swiss canton did not enfranchise women until 1990![14]

Why People Participate: Costs and Benefits

Voting rights have steadily expanded in the United States, but extending the franchise does not lead automatically to increased turnout. Even in presidential elections, as much as half the potential electorate stays home. After the election, some editorialists criticize the nonvoters for being lazy while others criticize the candidates for being uninspiring—but the question of why eligible voters abstain is more complicated than newspaper editorials usually imply.[15]

Voting is costly. If you are paid by the hour and you take time off in order to vote, you lose a portion of your wages. Even if you have flexible hours and can leave work early or arrive late, you may do less work on Election Day if you take the time to vote. Moreover, not all costs are tangible. You may have to wait in long lines to be able to vote before or after work. In 2004, people at some polling places were still waiting in line to vote hours after the polls were supposed to have closed. The time you spend at the voting precinct is time that you may not spend on other activities, some of which may seem more fulfilling. For some people with little information about politics, the entire voting situation can be uncomfortable; staying home enables them to avoid the discomfort. If you are surprised that such seemingly small considerations could lower turnout, consider that turnout generally falls when the weather is rainy or temperatures are extreme.[16]

There also are benefits to voting, of course. The most obvious is logically the least important: the possibility that your vote might swing an election. Your vote determines an electoral outcome only if it creates or breaks a tie.[17] Otherwise, you could stay home and the election would come out the same way. The chance that a single voter will swing a state or national election in this way is infinitesimally small. In the 1996 presidential election, which attracted the lowest turnout rate of any presidential election in the twentieth century, almost 100 million Americans voted. In the 1998 elections for the U.S. House of Representatives, which featured the lowest midterm election turnout in half a century, an average of 141,000 citizens voted in each congressional race. Given numbers such as these, a desire to determine who wins the election cannot realistically be an important motivation for turning out. From a purely individualistic standpoint, the puzzle is not that turnout is so low in the United States but, rather, that turnout is as high as it is.

Late in the nineteenth century, when turnout levels were especially high (usually more than 75 percent outside the South), some voters had a compelling reason to show up at the polls: They were paid to do so. Historians estimate that the going price of a vote in New York City elections could soar as high as $25 in particularly competitive circumstances (as expressed in current dollars).[18] Material rewards are a much rarer benefit of voting today, but direct payments for voting (sometimes called "walking-around money") still exist here and there, mainly in the poorer areas of eastern cities. Citizens also may be motivated to vote in elections because the outcome can directly affect their material interests. For example, government employees vote at higher rates than people employed in the private sector, other things being equal—especially in low-turnout local elections.[19]

Today, however, most of the individual motivations for voting are not material but psychological. Some people feel a civic duty to vote. They avoid guilt by showing up at the polls. Americans are highly individualistic, though, so they are not especially prone to place much emphasis on civic duty (see Chapter 4). Perhaps the most compelling benefit of voting is the pleasure it can bring. Some Americans take satisfaction in expressing their preference for a candidate or an issue position, much as they might enjoy cheering for an athletic team.[20] Psychological benefits are an important incentive for voting. Whereas your vote makes no difference unless it affects the outcome, you receive the psychological benefits regardless of the closeness of an election. Indeed, voters may take even more satisfaction when they can be part of a political team that wins big, much as sports teams gain in popularity when they enjoy a particularly good season.

Another reason people vote goes beyond simple individual motivations. Sometimes people participate in elections because they have been encouraged to vote by others who have personal incentives to increase turnout. **Voter mobilization** consists of the efforts of parties, groups, and activists to turn out their potential supporters. Campaign workers provide baby sitters and rides to the polls, thereby reducing the individual costs

voter mobilization
The efforts of parties, groups, and activists to encourage their supporters to turn out for elections.

DILBERT: © Scott Adams/reprinted by permission of United Features Syndicate, Inc.

of voting. They apply social pressure by contacting citizens who haven't voted and reminding them to do so. Various groups and social networks to which individuals belong also exert social pressures, encouraging the feeling that a citizen has a responsibility to vote. Although pressures and benefits such as these may seem small, remember that the costs of voting are relatively small as well.

Armed with some understanding of the general reasons why people vote or fail to vote, we can now address an important question raised in the introduction to this chapter: Why do Americans vote at lower levels than citizens in other countries?

International Comparisons of Voter Turnout

Comparing
Voting and
Elections

Americans vote at much lower rates than people in most other countries, even countries such as Italy whose citizens are exceedingly cynical about politics (see Table 6.1). That being said, procedures for calculating turnout differ from country to country. These differences systematically lower American turnout figures relative to those in other democracies.

Turnout would seem to be simple enough to measure. The U.S. Census Bureau calculates official turnout in presidential elections as:

Number of people voting for president / Number of people in the voting-age population

This definition seems straightforward, but it lowers American turnout as much as 5 percent relative to other countries.

TABLE 6.1

AMERICANS ARE LESS LIKELY TO VOTE THAN THE CITIZENS OF OTHER DEMOCRACIES

The following figures represent the average turnout (in percentages) in elections to the lower house of the legislature or parliament in 37 countries, 1945–2005.

Australia (23)★	95	Venezuela (11)	80	Bulgaria (4)	71
Belgium (19)	93	Greece (18)	80	Latvia (5)	70
Austria (17)	91	Israel (16)	80	Japan (22)	69
Italy (15)	90	Brazil (14)	78	Hungary (4)	69
Luxembourg (13)	89	Costa Rica (14)	77	United States (14)★★	55
Iceland (17)	89	Finland (16)	76	Estonia (5)	66
New Zealand (20)	89	Portugal (11)	76	Lithuania (3)	62
Malta (15)	88	United Kingdom (16)	75	India (13)	59
Netherlands (18)	87	France (16)	75	Russia (3)	58
Denmark (23)	86	Canada (18)	74	Switzerland (15)	56
Sweden (18)	86	Spain (8)	74	Poland (5)	50
Germany (15)	85	Czech Republic (5)	73		
Norway (15)	80	Ireland (16)	73		

★ Number of elections.

★★ Presidential years only

Source: Calculated from International Institute for Democracy and Electoral Assistance data.

ELECTION CONNECTION

Nonvoters Who Actually Turned Out

The contest over Florida's 2000 presidential election returned focused media attention on the large number of attempted votes that never appear in an official tally. As the Bush and Gore camps jockeyed to influence the recount, their legal battle mostly revolved around which unrecorded votes should be counted the second time around.

Floridians who turned out on Election Day 2000 were counted as nonvoters for a variety of reasons. Some failed to communicate a preference, either because their ballot confused them or because they neglected to indicate a choice clearly on the ballot. Others communicated a preference but the voting machines failed to register it. These were the undervotes. Some accidentally voted more than once, either selecting more than one presidential candidate or recording both a regular vote and a write-in vote. These were the overvotes. The whole situation was especially confusing because Florida counties used a variety of voting technologies, from paper ballots to sophisticated machines, with widely differing rates of undervotes and overvotes.

In the aftermath of the Florida fiasco, state voting officials, election scholars, and a small army of "blue-ribbon" commissions undertook a wide-ranging search for the "perfect voting technology." Yet while everyone agreed that punch card ballots were too error prone, there was no clear consensus on what to replace them with. Many experts favored "touch screen" machines, similar to the ATMs (automatic teller machines) that most people use today to do their banking.

Yet others argued that, however well they worked in the lab, in real-world settings touch screens often broke down, were intimidating to many elderly voters, and, because they left no hard, paper record of the individual votes, greatly increased the likelihood of vote fraud.

By all indications, the 2004 election was much less troublesome than that of 2000. Yet much of the difference may simply reflect the fact that 2004 had a more decisive final result. Though the election was close by historical standards, no states essential to Bush's victory were won by just a few hundred votes as in 2000. Some controversy developed in Ohio, particularly over counting 155,000 provisional ballots, which were given to voters whose names could not be located on local registration lists. But, for all the difficulties, the final result in that state was never in doubt: Bush carried Ohio by 118,000 votes. Bush won two other states much more narrowly: Iowa by 10,000 votes and New Mexico by 6,000. But he could have lost both states and still had a majority in the Electoral College. As one election law scholar noted several days after the election, "If it was Iowa or New Mexico that held the balance [in the electoral college], we would be in litigation now."

• *Whose responsibility is it to make sure that a vote is recorded properly? Is it the voter's problem, or do election officials have a special obligation to correct for voter mistakes that lead to overvotes and undervotes?*

• *Reformers often demand uniform elections technologies because they fear that some voters will suffer if resources vary. But do the virtues of uniformity outweigh the costs of developing a system that might be easier to manipulate wholesale?*

Why? Consider the numerator of the ratio. If, believing that all the candidates are bums, you do not vote for president, you are not counted as having voted. Election officials in many jurisdictions also ignore frivolous write-in votes (actual examples from U.S. elections: Rambo, ZZ Top, Batman). In contrast, the French have a long tradition wherein alienated voters scribble an offensive suggestion across their ballots (the English translation has initials "F. Y."). French election officials count such ballots, whereas most American officials would not.[21] Vote-counting machines, meanwhile, occasionally fail to register a person's vote (see the accompanying *Election Connection*). Technically speaking, these are all examples of **undervotes:** although you cast your ballot, you are not counted. Alternatively, if you vote for more than one candidate, your ballot is classified as an **overvote** and you again are not included when officials compute the turnout rate. Procedures differ in other countries and U.S. procedures lower turnout figures by a couple of percentage points per election.[22]

undervotes

Ballots that indicate no choice for an office (e.g., for president in 2000), whether because the voter abstained or because the voter's intention could not be determined.

overvotes

Ballots that have more than one choice for an office (e.g., for president in 2000), whether because the voter voted for more than one candidate or wrote in a name as well as making a mark.

voting-age population
All people in the United States over the age of 18, including those who may not be legally eligible to vote.

Factors that affect the denominator of the ratio are more significant. The **voting-age population,** or VAP, refers to the number of people over the age of 18, a number that includes some groups legally ineligible to vote: felons, people confined to mental or correctional institutions, and (most important) noncitizens. Counting the entire VAP rather than only the eligible VAP lowers U.S. turnout figures by another 3 percent.[23] And this underestimate is growing because ineligible adults such as felons and immigrants make up an increasing proportion of the voting-age population.[24]

Personal Costs and Benefits: Registration

Far more important than the inclusion of ineligible felons and noncitizens in the U.S. voting age population is that other countries use an entirely different denominator in their turnout calculations. Their denominator is the registered population. More than 30 percent of the American VAP has not registered. When turnout is measured as the number voting among **registered voters**, U.S. figures jump into the middle range of turnout in industrial democracies.

registered voters
Those legally eligible to vote who have registered in accordance with the requirements prevailing in their state and locality.

Registration is automatic in most of the world. It is the responsibility of the central government, like maintaining social security records in the United States. Because virtually everyone who is eligible is registered, turnout rates are essentially the same whether they are measured as a percentage of the voting-age population or as a percentage of those registered. American practice differs in making registration entirely the responsibility of the individual (although the difficulty of registering varies from state to state, and reforms have made registration easier in recent years). Some statistical simulations suggest that liberalizing state voting laws could boost national turnout about 9 percentage points higher than it is at present.[25]

Dropping individual registration requirements would not eliminate the participation gap between the United States and other industrialized democracies, however. A few states have no registration or allow registration at the polling stations on Election Day. In these states turnout is higher than the national norm, but it still falls well below the levels in many European countries.[26] Similarly, the national government enacted a proposal to ease registration requirements in 1993. Customarily called the "motor voter" law, it required states to allow people to register to vote when they renewed driver's licenses and car registrations, among other things. Research suggests that such reforms had little impact.[27]

In sum, requiring voter registration does raise the individual costs of participating for Americans, but it is not the only reason for lower U.S. turnout levels.

Personal Costs and Benefits: Compulsion

The personal registration system makes voting relatively costly in the United States. By contrast, some countries attach costs to *nonvoting*. Would you believe that voting is compulsory in many countries? In Australia and Belgium, for example, nonvoters are subject to fines. Greek electoral law provides for imprisonment of nonvoters for up to 12 months, although that penalty is never applied. Other democracies do penalize nonvoters, at least sometimes. Australian law allows for fines of up to $50 for not voting (without a valid excuse), and estimates are that 4 percent of nonvoters pay fines. In Italy, nonvoters are not fined, but "Did Not Vote" is stamped on

Voto Latino Launches in New York City

Latin music duo Nina Sky at a press conference for Voto Latino, the campaign to encourage Latino/a youth to participate in the voting process.

their identification papers, threatening nonvoters with the prospect of unsympathetic treatment at the hands of public officials should they get into trouble or need help with a problem. Italian nonvoters also have their names posted on community bulletin boards. Turnout in democracies with compulsory voting is almost 15 percent higher than in democracies without it.[28] American turnout figures would undoubtedly increase greatly if people were compelled to vote, although such a policy shift might not solve the fundamental problem posed by low electoral interest (see *Democratic Dilemma*, next page).

Compulsory
Voting

Other Personal Costs and Benefits

Several additional institutional variations raise the costs of voting for Americans. Elections in America traditionally are held on Tuesdays, an ordinary workday. In most of the rest of the world, either elections are held on Sundays or election days are proclaimed official holidays. Italian workers receive free train fare back to their place of registration, which is usually their hometown. In effect, the government subsidizes family reunions.

Some observers argue that turnout in the U.S. is low because Americans are called on to vote so often (see Chapter 1).[29] In most European countries, citizens vote only a few times in a four-year period: once for a member of parliament, once for a representative to the European Union, and perhaps once for a small number of local officials. In contrast, Americans vote for numerous national, state, and local officials—usually twice, once in a primary or caucus, and once in a general election. They also may vote for numerous ballot propositions or in a recall election. Moreover, these elections typically occur at different times. Some commentators have suggested, not completely tongue-in-cheek, that turnout in the United States should be calculated as the percentage who vote at least once during a four-year period. Some find it telling that the only European country where voters are called

DEMOCRATIC DILEMMA

Can Voters Speak for Those Who Abstain?

After the 2004 elections, some disgruntled Democrats grumbled about the legitimacy of the election results. Although George Bush won a clear if narrow majority of the popular vote—51 percent, to 48 percent for Kerry—turnout was a bit shy of 61 percent of the voting-age population. To the losers, this meant that about 31 percent of the eligible electorate (0.51 x .61) had voted for Bush. Can less than a third of the electorate consent for a nation?

After the 1992 elections, the situation was reversed. Disgruntled Republicans complained that Bill Clinton had received only 43 percent of the popular vote. With a total turnout of 58 percent, this meant that only a quarter of the eligible electorate had endorsed Clinton.

By ignoring the preferences of nonvoters, the United States treats them as though they had consented to the election outcome—certainly a dubious assumption to make as a general matter. Although some people are content whatever happens, many nonvoters presumably would have voted for the loser had they bothered to vote. Others did not vote precisely because the choices offered did not satisfy them, so their abstention hardly implies contentment with or support for the outcome.

One proposed solution for abstentions is compulsory voting—requiring people to turn out. Compulsory voting does not resolve questions of majority consent, however. If nearly everyone turns out, then by definition the winner receives a majority—but the vote could include people who cast votes only to avoid punishment and not because they actually wished to express consent for the elected leader. Forcing people to vote removes the right to sit out an election and wait for a candidate worthy of one's support.

- *Is voting a duty that comes with the privileges of citizenship? Or are there circumstances in which a citizen might have a duty not to vote?*

- *Should the United States have compulsory voting, as do numerous other democracies? Why or why not?*

upon to vote frequently, Switzerland, has a turnout rate comparable to that in the United States.

Finally, some states use voter registration lists to select people for jury duty. The fear of losing a day's work, or more if a trial is extended (think of the Michael Jackson trial!), probably is sufficient to motivate some citizens to forfeit their right to vote. One study concluded that, in such jurisdictions, turnout could be as much as 5 to 10 percent lower than it otherwise would be.[30] Voters in other jurisdictions also sometimes avoid registering because they believe—wrongly—that they might end up with jury duty as a result.

All in all, both intentionally and incidentally, American practices raise the costs of voting relative to those in other countries. When some citizens understandably react to those costs by failing to vote, editorialists criticize them for their lack of public spirit.

Mobilization and Turnout

Not only do Americans face higher costs for voting and lower costs for nonvoting, but they also have less help to meet these costs. The chief mobilizing agent in modern democracies is the political party. Parties have incentives to mobilize their supporters; indeed, they have often undertaken that task with excessive enthusiasm, as when urban machines cast fraudulent votes on behalf of the dead or reported more votes for their candidates than there were residents in their cities. Political scientists Steven Rosenstone and Mark Hansen observe that

[P]arty mobilization underwrites the costs of political participation. Party workers inform people about upcoming elections, tell them where and when they can register and vote, supply them with applications for absentee ballots, show them the locations of campaign headquarters, and remind them of imminent rallies and meetings. Campaigns drop by to pick up donations, telephone reminders on the day of the election, and drive the lazy, the harried, the immobile, and the infirm to the polls.[31]

Certainly it is no accident that American turnout levels peaked in the late nineteenth century, when the efficiency of American parties was at a maximum and their ethics at a minimum. During this period the patronage system was in full bloom. With hundreds of thousands of government jobs at stake in elections, the parties had little trouble motivating workers, not to mention their relatives and friends. And, unconstrained by conflict-of-interest or sunshine (open-government) laws, the parties were quite willing to do whatever it took to gain or keep control of government.

American parties have declined since the nineteenth century, at least as mobilizing agents (see Chapter 8). Voters are not as attached to them as in the past, and the parties have less in the way of inducements to turn out the faithful.[32] Progressive reforms instituted around a century ago undercut the mobilizing resources once enjoyed by political parties. The personal registration system discouraged voter fraud. Primary elections weakened the parties' control of nominations for office. Civil-service reforms took away much of the patronage that parties once used to buy loyalty. A significant part of the reason why turnout in the late twentieth century was lower in the United States than in other democracies is that parties generally were stronger and more active elsewhere than here.

Political parties are not the only mobilizing agent in democracies. Interest groups and associations also bring supporters to the polls (see Chapter 7). However, these organizations are not so deeply rooted in American politics as their counterparts elsewhere. Unions and churches form the very foundation of some political parties in Europe, but the same is not true in the United States. Thus, here too, Americans receive less support from collective political actors than do citizens in other democracies.

Several analysts have dissected statistically the difference in turnout levels between the United States and other countries.[33] All other things equal, American turnout should actually be somewhat higher than turnout in Europe because of higher educational levels and American civic attitudes that encourage popular participation. But other things are far from equal. Bingham Powell, for example, estimates that differences in electoral institutions (especially registration systems) depress American turnout between 10 and 15 percent relative to Europe. Weaker mobilization efforts depress turnout by about 10 percent. In sum, it costs Americans more to vote and they receive less support for voting than do citizens in most other countries.

Why Has American Turnout Declined?

For many people the turnout problem is not only that levels in the United States are lower than in other advanced democracies but also that turnout fell during the past generation. Figure 6.2 shows that turnout in presidential elections dropped between 1960 and 1988, and hit a half-century low in 1996. In off-year elections, turnout declined more erratically, but it is significantly lower now than a generation ago.[34]

Turnout in the United
States Seldom Reaches
1960s Levels

• *What are the causes of
declining turnout? Why the
difference between presidential and
off-year elections?*

Source: The Committee for the Study of
the American Electorate.

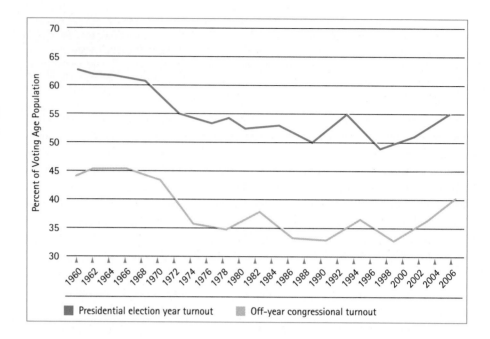

The decline in turnout is especially puzzling because developments late in the twentieth century led to an expectation of *rising* turnout. First, court decisions, federal legislation such as the Voting Rights Act, and the Twenty-fourth Amendment to the Constitution have removed numerous institutional and procedural impediments to voting and thus reduced the personal costs. Legal changes abolished poll taxes and literacy tests, shortened state and local residency requirements, simplified registration, permitted bilingual ballots, and eased the procedures for absentee voting. Such reforms were especially effective in the South, where they helped to overcome the terrible legacy of racial discrimination. Figure 6.3 shows how turnout among African Americans in the South increased sharply between 1960 and 1968.

Second, socioeconomic change should have raised turnout in the post-1964 period. True, the potential electorate was getting younger as the baby boom generation came of age, which should have lowered turnout—because young people traditionally vote at lower levels than older people. But that effect should have been more than offset by rising educational levels. Education is the single strongest predictor of turnout. Higher educational levels produce a keener sense of civic duty and help people deal with the complexities of registering and voting. Ruy Teixeira estimates that, other things being equal, the net effect of socioeconomic changes should have been to *raise* national turnout by about 4 percent.[35]

What, then, explains the decline in turnout? There is not so much agreement on why voting has declined over time as there is on the explanation of turnout differences between the United States and other democracies (where, as we have seen, registration and political parties dominate the answer). Several factors clearly have contributed to the decline in American turnout, but their precise importance is a matter of debate.

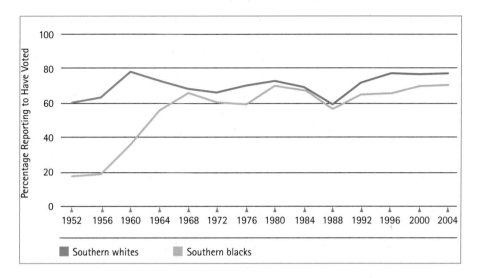

FIGURE 6.3

The Civil Rights Revolution Opened Southern Politics to African Americans

The turnout gap between African American and white voters narrowed as a result of the civil rights movement of the 1950s and 1960s.

• *Given that politicians respond to voters, how did this narrowed gap matter for public policy changes?*

Source: National Election Studies: http://electionstudies.org/nesguide/nesguide.htm.

Declining Personal Benefits

One reason why the decline in voting costs did not increase voting is that the benefits of voting may have declined at an even faster rate. Studies show that despite higher educational levels, Americans are little, if any, better informed about politics today than a generation ago.[36] Generally, they are less interested in public affairs and in political campaigns and don't believe that government is as responsive as in times past.[37] Thus, they may not see as much riding on their decisions as in years past, and they may get less intrinsic satisfaction from supporting an admired candidate or party. On the other hand, these less interested and knowledgeable citizens report that they care more about who wins, so overall, their feelings are difficult to characterize.

One political factor that has lowered the benefits of voting is that elections have become less competitive. As we discuss in Chapter 11, the advantage of incumbency in congressional elections increased greatly after the mid-1960s. A similar process occurred more slowly in state legislative elections. A number of presidential elections in the 1970s and 1980s were landslides and gubernatorial elections became less competitive as well. When candidates win by large margins, the notion that one's vote actually makes a difference must seem more outlandish than ever. Nor do blowout elections provide much incentive for campaign organizations to get out the vote. Rosenstone and Hansen find that in states with competitive gubernatorial campaigns, turnout is 5 percent higher, other things being equal.[38] Notably, turnout increased dramatically in 2004, when both the presidential election and a handful of Senate elections were especially close.

Declining Mobilization

Statistical studies suggest that personal costs and benefits account for less than half of the decline in turnout. The larger part of the decline reflects the decreased mobilization efforts of parties, campaigns, and social movements since the turbulent 1960s.

As the 2004 election showed, parties still are active, of course. But the media advertising that plays so important a role in modern campaigns probably is not a good substitute for the pound-the-pavement, doorbell-ringing workers who used to dominate campaigns. Voters may be motivated by the coaxing of a campaign worker standing at the front door or telephoning late in the afternoon of Election Day, but those same voters may not be motivated by an impersonal TV spot urging them to vote.[39] Thus, a change in style from labor-intensive to high-tech campaigning after the advent of television may have indirectly contributed to declining turnout. That conclusion is supported by the increase in turnout in 2004 when the parties returned to the old methods of voter mobilization, such as phone calls and personal visits from politically active neighbors.[40]

Declining Social Connectedness

compositional effect

A shift in the behavior of a group that arises from a change in the group's composition, not from a change in the behavior of individuals in the group.

You might interpret a turnout line trending downward to mean that any given citizen is less likely to vote today than a generation ago. Political scientist Warren Miller showed that such an interpretation is incorrect.[41] The decline in voter turnout is what social scientists call a **compositional effect**—a shift that results from a change in group composition rather than a change in the behavior of individuals already in the group. Older Americans learned to vote at high rates when they were young and they continue to do so. The turnout rates of middle-aged Americans (the baby boomers), by contrast, were lower when they entered the electorate and remain at that lower level. The turnout rates of succeeding generations are lower still. Thus, turnout is declining because of the simple fact that older Americans accustomed to voting at high rates are dying and being replaced by younger nonvoters.[42] Robert Putnam argues that the younger generation is less likely to participate in other ways as well.[43]

social connectedness

The degree to which individuals are integrated into society—families, churches, neighborhoods, groups, and so forth.

Why are younger adults less connected to the political world? Stephen Knack suggests that common thinking about voting is misconceived.[44] Rather than voting being the fundamental political act, voting may be a form of social behavior. People will vote when they are integrated into their communities through connections such as extended families, neighborhoods, religious organizations, and other social units. These forms of **social connectedness** are common among older Americans, who grew up in a simpler time when Americans were less mobile, more religious, and more trusting of their fellow citizens. Younger Americans have grown up in a highly mobile, worldly society where cynicism about their fellow citizens is widespread. They may not feel the social connections that prompt individuals to participate in political life.

This argument can be taken too far, however. Arguments based on social connectedness often sound like nostalgia for the "good old days," which frequently were not so good to those who experienced them firsthand. After all, many social ties are built on exclusion, on a sense of being right while outsiders are wrong. Young people may stay out of politics because they have less desire to impose their will on others. As *Newsweek* columnist Fareed Zakaria writes, "Today's young . . . are less sure that they have the grand solutions for society's problems."[45] Younger adults also often experience their own forms of connectivity, such as through Internet news groups or chat rooms. These "electronic communities" may not be as satisfying emotionally as real-life ties, but there is no reason they must be apolitical—especially because many of them link people with fairly similar personal interests, perhaps more similar than the interests of family or traditional organizations.

Nevertheless, a body of research does support looking to social explanations for the generational gap in voter participation. Voting is related to altruistic behavior such as giving blood, donating to charities, and doing volunteer work.[46] Turnout also is related to social connectedness. Even relying on such crude indicators as marriage rates, home ownership, church attendance, and length of residence in a community, studies find that decreased social connectedness accounts for as much as one-quarter of the decline in election turnout.[47] Along the same lines, although turnout is not related to trust in *government,* it is significantly related to trust in *people.*[48]

Who Votes and Who Doesn't?

Low voting rates probably would not stimulate as much discussion as they do if all social and economic groups in America voted at the same rate. But people differ in their ability to bear the costs of voting, in the strength of their feeling that voting is a duty, and in how often they are the targets of mobilization. Consequently, as Figure 6.4 indicates, turnout rates differ considerably across social and economic groups.[49]

Highly educated people are significantly more likely to vote than people with little formal education. Education instills a stronger sense of duty and gives people the knowledge, analytic skills, and self-confidence to meet the costs of registering and voting. Over and above education, income also matters. The wealthy are more likely to vote than the poor. Affluence, too, usually reflects a set of skills and personal characteristics that help people overcome barriers to voting.

Voting Turnout: Who Votes?

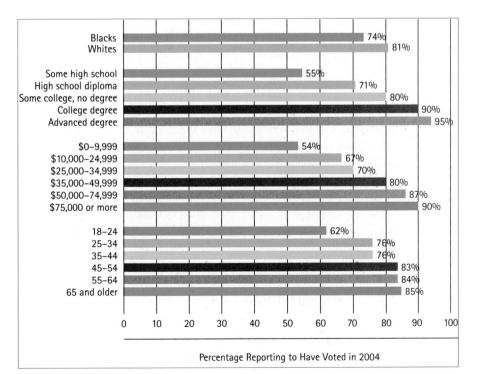

FIGURE 6.4

Do Social and Economic Differences Influence Public Policy?

• *What appears to be the strongest predictor that someone will vote? Do these differences make a difference for public policy?*

Source: National Election Study, 2004. http://electionstudies.org/nesguide/nesguide.htm.

Studies of turnout in the 1970s concluded that, once disadvantages in education and income were factored out and their younger age was considered, African Americans were at least as likely to vote as whites.[50] But more recent research finds that blacks are somewhat less likely to vote than whites, even taking into account differences in income and educational levels.[51] Other minorities, such as Latinos and Asians, still face language barriers, although the situation is gradually improving.[52]

Turnout increases with age, until very old age when the trend reverses. People presumably gain experience as they age—experience that makes it easier for them to overcome any barriers to voting. They also become more socially connected, as well as more settled down in a life situation that clarifies their political preferences.

Importantly, these relationships between socioeconomic characteristics and turnout are consistently stronger in the United States than in other democracies. Indeed, in some countries there is almost no relationship between education and income on the one hand and voting on the other.[53] The explanation is that parties elsewhere are much more effective at mobilizing their supporters. In particular, European Social Democratic parties do a better job of getting their less advantaged potential voters to the polls than does the Democratic Party in the United States.

Is Low Turnout a Problem?

Given who votes and why, should the relatively low turnout rate in the United States be a cause for concern? Quite a few answers have been offered on both sides of this question. To a considerable degree, these differing views hinge on different beliefs about people's motives for voting. We will briefly sketch three arguments on each side of the debate.

Three Arguments Why Low Turnout Is Not a Problem

A Conservative (With a Small "C") Argument Many people concerned about low turnout implicitly assume that high turnout indicates enthusiasm about politics and commitment to making the political order work. Maybe not. Some skeptics suggest that high turnout may indicate tension or conflict, even a belief that losing is unacceptable. They cite the experience of Austria and Germany as their democratic governments crumbled and the Fascist parties took power in the 1930s.[54] Turnout in those elections reached very high levels, but this mobilization probably reflected disillusionment and desperation more than commitment and enthusiasm. More recently, Anthony King observes that the highest British turnouts occur in Northern Ireland, the home of centuries-old religious strife.[55] The 2004 U.S. presidential election is a less extreme case in point. Turnout rose, but did this increase indicate a healthier political system? On the contrary, by many indications people were frustrated and upset with their government, either its war on terrorism or its neglect of "moral values." Similarly, "angry white males" reportedly drove up turnout in 1994. Generalizing from examples such as these, some commentators conclude that low turnout indicates contentment, not alienation. Therefore, low U.S. turnout levels are reassuring—a sign of political health, not disease.

An Elitist Argument On average, nonvoters are less educated than voters. Studies also show them to be less informed, less interested in politics, and less concerned about

VIDEO ROUNDTABLE

Participation and the Young

it. Given these facts, some writers argue that the quality of electoral decisions is higher if no special effort is made to increase turnout. For example, David Reisman once remarked, "Bringing sleepwalkers to the polls simply to increase turnout is no service to democracy."[56] Columnist George Will provides a more succinct example of this elitist point of view: "Smaller is smarter."[57] According to this argument, high turnout would bring lots of uninformed voters to the polls. Such individuals might be more likely to be swayed by demagogues or to vote on the basis of narrow self-interest. Of course, such arguments assume that nonvoters would remain ignorant, unconcerned, and subject to manipulation even after they decided to vote. If, instead, the process of turning people out to vote also informed them and raised their interest in politics, their preferences might well change.

You Are an
Informed Voter

A Cynical or Radical Argument   Some radicals contend that it is not the nonvoters but the voters who are a cause for concern. According to this viewpoint, elections do not matter—they are charades. The real decisions in American are made behind the scenes by power elites far from the popular arena.[58] The country actually is run by small cabals of bankers and financiers, or the heads of large corporations, or a military-industrial complex. If so, voting is merely a symbolic act. It makes the masses feel they have a say in how they are governed. Turnout doesn't matter because elections don't matter in the United States.

This is the one argument about the implications of low turnout that the evidence cannot support. Elections matter a great deal—in some cases, probably too much. They have an enormous impact on public policies that directly affect the quality of American life. The country is simply too large and diverse for any single interest to control the levers of power by itself.

Three Arguments Why Low Turnout Is a Problem

Voters Are Unrepresentative   The most obvious concern arising from low turnout is that the electorate is unrepresentative. The electorate is wealthier, whiter, older, and better educated than the population. Such an electorate is more Republican and more conservative than the population at large. Consequently, elections are biased, and public policies adopted by the winners are correspondingly biased. But plausible as the argument seems, research suggests that it is overstated. Numerous studies have compared the policy views and the candidate preferences of voters and nonvoters. Typically, they differ little. Some studies have even found that contrary to the usual expectation, the conservative candidate at times was more popular among nonvoters (Ronald Reagan in 1984, for example).[59]

Given differences in voting rates across social groups, why do the preferences of nonvoters and voters differ so little? Minorities and the poor vote less often than whites and the affluent, but the differences are only matters of degree. Yes, blacks are less likely to vote than whites, but only about one-eighth of all the nonvoters are black. Similarly, the more highly educated are more likely to vote, but 25 percent of nonvoters have some college education. Nonvoters are not all poor, uneducated members of minority groups. Plenty of nonvoters are affluent, well educated, and white—especially those who do not vote because they have recently moved residences (according to the U.S. Census Bureau, nearly one in five Americans moves during the two-year interval between national elections).

Minority Voting
Signs in both Korean and English encourage Korean Americans to register to vote.

Moreover, few groups are as one-sided in their political inclinations as African Americans, who vote about 8:1 Democratic. If turnout among most other groups were to increase, the Democrats would get somewhat more than half the additional votes, but the Republicans would get a fair proportion as well. Teixeira provides a striking illustration of these points. According to his calculations, if all the Hispanics and African Americans in the country had voted in 1988 at levels 10 percent *higher* than whites, and all the white poor had voted at levels 10 percent *higher* than the white rich, the Democratic candidate, Michael Dukakis, would still have lost by two and a half million votes.[60] In sum, it is doubtful that plausible increases in turnout would produce a sea change in American politics—unless joining the political system produced a sharp change in the political outlook of former nonvoters.

Interestingly, one grouping that is seriously underrepresented in the electorate gets little attention: independents. Those who feel some form of allegiance to one of the major parties—either party—are substantially more likely to vote than those who lack party commitments. In 2004, for example, about 85 percent of Republicans and 80 percent of Democrats told pollsters they had voted (some were lying, of course), but only 54 percent of independents claimed to have voted.[61]

Low Turnout Reflects a "Phony" Politics   This argument emphasizes the character of political issues in contemporary politics. Social critics charge that low turnout among working-class Americans reflects a party system that fails to address "real" issues of concern to such people. What are real issues? Basically, they are economic issues: jobs, health care, housing, income distribution, and education. What the United States has is two upper middle-class parties obsessed with "phony" issues: flag burning, gun control, abortion, school prayer, capital punishment, gay rights, evolution. (Political scientists refer to such issues as **social issues** to distinguish them from pocketbook worries and other practical personal concerns.)

Public opinion data support this criticism in some respects. A Gallup poll from April 2004 asked respondents what they considered the most important problem faced by the United States. Economic issues topped the list; 43 percent of respondents mentioned unemployment, the economy's overall performance, or some other economic worry. Another 39 percent selected the war in Iraq or terrorism as the nation's most important problem. Very few people listed the hot-button issues that dominated much of the campaign debate, such as guns or gay marriage.[62] The result may be that the minority of voters concerned with social issues are more motivated to vote than the majority with economic or foreign policy concerns.

Low Turnout Discourages Individual Development   The final claim is in some respects a counterargument to the elitist argument that low turnout is not a problem. Classical political theorists from Aristotle to John Stuart Mill emphasized that democracy has an important educational component. Participation in democratic politics stimulates individual development. Because participants become better citizens, they take politics to a higher level. Low turnout therefore signifies a lost opportunity to improve both the nonparticipants and politics itself.

Some analysts doubt that political participation is such an ennobling experience. Attending an intensive face-to-face political event such as a school board or city council meeting might improve a citizen. Pulling a few levers in a voting booth is unlikely

social issues
Issues (such as abortion, obscenity, gay rights, capital punishment, gun control, and prayer in schools) that reflect personal values more than economic interests.

to do so.[63] But the argument makes a valid point: Voting may affect not only who wins and what they do but also the voters themselves—what manner of people they are and what they want.

Evaluating the Arguments

There is considerable disagreement about whether low turnout in the United States is a problem and, if so, how serious a problem it is. Well-intentioned and well-informed people disagree and offer persuasive arguments in support of their positions. Our view is that nonvoters and voters have diverse motives. Some nonvoters are content whereas others are alienated, and the same goes for voters. High turnout can indicate either high approval of the political order or serious dissatisfaction with it. Nonvoters don't have much political information, but neither do many voters—so raising turnout will not "dumb down" the electorate very much. Low turnout does make the actual electorate somewhat less representative than the potential electorate, but not nearly so much as critics often assume. Some potential voters undoubtedly are discouraged by a politics that discusses social issues of little relevance for them, but other citizens turn out to vote precisely because of their concern with such issues. And, although participation fosters citizen development, we doubt that the impersonal act of casting a vote will foster it very much. In short, we find some validity in each of the arguments presented above. We reject in its entirety only the argument that elections don't matter. Low turnout is a cause for concern, yes; a cause for despair, no.

Beyond the Voting Booth

One reason that low voter turnout should not cause Americans to fear for their nation's future is that citizens often participate actively outside of the voting booth. As we discuss in the next chapter, many Americans join groups which are very active in politics. Moreover, even as individuals, many Americans participate in ways other than voting. As Figure 6.5 shows, although Americans vote at lower rates than citizens of Austria, Germany, the United Kingdom, and the Netherlands, they are significantly more likely to work in campaigns, contact public officials, or volunteer for work in their communities. They also attend political meetings at a fairly high rate.

The Prepared
Voter Kit

Americans participate actively in other ways as well, some that require a great commitment to candidates or causes, and others that take citizens outside the bounds of conventional politics. For example, an estimated one-quarter of Americans contribute money to political campaigns, judging from a survey analysis conducted by Sidney Verba and his associates. Around 14 percent attend local board meetings. Six percent of their survey respondents even admitted engaging in some form of political protest.[64] All of these sorts of activities require much greater sacrifice from participants than the simple act of voting, yet Americans make such sacrifices at higher rates than citizens elsewhere.

Why would alternate forms of participation be so popular? Ironically, for many of the same reasons that voter turnout is so low.

- The frequency of elections in the United States opens up many opportunities for campaign involvement. Americans also have more opportunities to contact public officials and attend government board meetings, because the U.S. has so

FIGURE 6.5

Americans Participate in Ways More Demanding Than Voting

• *Why might Americans not vote at rates as high as citizens of other democracies and yet participate at higher rates than others in relatively more demanding ways?*

Source: Adapted from Sidney Verba, Kay Lehman Schlozman, and Henry Brady, *Voice and Equality* (Cambridge, MA: Harvard University Press, 1995), p. 70.

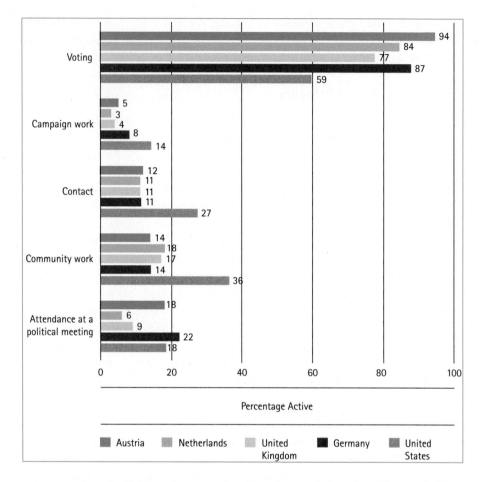

many elected officials and so many boards and commissions (see Chapter 1). Even if Americans are less likely to take advantage of any particular participatory opportunity, the sheer number of openings makes for a higher level of political participation than in other countries where opportunities are more limited. Indeed, as American elections have increased in frequency and as governmental bodies have increased in number, some studies have found increases in some kinds of campaign participation.[65]

• Our individualistic political culture may suppress the sense of civic duty that promotes voter turnout. But the political culture's emphasis on rights and liberties encourages Americans to contact their public officials and to protest government actions. In contrast, the political cultures of most other democracies are more deferential to authority and discourage ordinary citizens from taking as active a role in politics as in the United States. Citizens elsewhere are less likely to protest government decisions—and when they do, their governments are more likely to ignore them.

• In the United States candidates construct numerous personal organizations, many of whose members are temporary. In other countries a small cadre of committed party workers shoulders most of the burden of campaigning year in and year out. "Occasional activists" drift in and out of political campaigns in America, depending on whether particular candidates or issues arouse their enthusiasm.[66] As a result, overall involvement in campaign activity brings in a wider variety of individuals.

- The United States gained independence through revolution, and protests have remained a regular feature of American politics ever since. In the 1850s militant abolitionists fought slavery so aggressively that their actions resembled what we today call terrorism, as when John Brown and his abolitionist supporters seized a federal arsenal. Similarly, in the 1900s Carrie Nation waged her battle against Demon Liquor by invading taverns carrying an axe, which she used to bust open casks of beer and whiskey. In the 1960s the civil rights movement fought for racial equality using marches, sit-ins, and boycotts. Direct action may not always be healthy for democracy. When a political movement resorts to taunting police and throwing rocks, one columnist suggests, "it is trying to achieve, through intimidation and scare tactics, what it has not been able to get through legislation."[67] Nevertheless, protests are as American as apple pie.

Protests aside, American participation outside the voting booth suggests a healthier political system than the turnout rates alone might imply. Americans would not donate their money, their time, and their energy to a political system that only grappled with "phony" politics or that failed to include its citizens in the political community. Of course, those who engage in alternate forms of participation may be just as unrepresentative as voters are. Indeed, they likely are more so. But most of the legal barriers to voting—such as registration laws, election scheduling, fear of jury duty, and disenfranchisement caused by a felony conviction—would not apply to these alternative avenues of participation. The availability of a wide variety of options, each with its own costs and benefits, provides some reassurance that most citizens who entirely abstain from political life do so because they prefer not to get involved.

Often Americans do not speak to their elected officials directly. Rather, they join organizations that can communicate with government on their behalf. These interest groups mobilize their members to participate: soliciting their signatures for petitions, their contributions for fundraising drives, their attendance at group meetings, and so forth. Organized groups also can be an encouragement for unconventional (or contentious) forms of participation: protests, demonstrations, and civil disobedience. Far more groups and associations are active in American politics than are found in other countries. These provide extensive opportunities for participation. We treat interest groups at length in the next chapter.

Political Protest

The war on terrorism, and especially the war in Iraq, has resulted in increased levels of unconventional political participation.

Chapter Summary

Popular participation in democratic elections is the essence of democracy. But in most elections, a majority of the American electorate stays away from the polls. Only in presidential elections does a majority usually turn out—and usually a bare majority at that. When it comes to participation in more demanding ways, far fewer people get involved.

American turnout levels are significantly lower than in other modern democracies, and they are lower than they have been in the recent past. The international difference is not hard to explain. In many ways the United States makes voting more costly than it is in other countries: Registration is left to the individual, voting is less convenient, and citizens are called on to vote much more often. In addition, mobilizing agents such as parties and unions are weaker in the United States than in other modern democracies, so Americans get less encouragement to vote from larger organizations.

The 2004 elections saw a dramatic increase in voter turnout, to levels not seen since the late 1960s. Nonetheless, the recent experience in America has been low levels of participation, despite reforms that have lowered the costs of voting and educational levels that have gone up. Americans seem less interested in politics and less inclined to think that voting makes a difference. The reasons are a matter of much debate. Nevertheless, nonvoters differ from each other more, and from voters less, than is usually presumed.

Key Terms

compositional effect, p. 164

franchise, p. 151

overvotes, p. 157

registered voters, p. 158

social connectedness, p. 164

social issues, p. 168

suffrage, p. 151

undervotes, p. 157

voter mobilization, p. 155

voting-age population, p. 158

Suggested Readings

Of General Interest

Keyssar, Alexander. *The Right to Vote.* New York: Basic Books, 2000. A comprehensive history of the evolution of the suffrage in America.

Putnam, Robert. *Bowling Alone.* New York: Simon & Schuster, 2000. Monumental study of the decline of participation in social and political life. Argues that American life is less healthy because of the decline in civic engagement.

Verba, Sidney, Kay Schlozman, and Henry Brady. *Voice and Equality: Civic Volunteerism in American Politics.* Cambridge, MA: Harvard University Press, 1995. Fascinating discussion of the development of political skills in nonpolitical contexts such as churches. Strong on attention to differences involving race, ethnicity, and gender.

Wattenberg, Martin. *Is Voting for Young People?* New York: Longman, 2007. Documents the decline in voting and general political engagement among young people—not only in the United States but in other developed democracies. Calls for compulsory voting.

Focused Studies

Ansolabehere, Steven, and Shanto Iyengar. *Going Negative.* New York: Free Press, 1995. Based mostly on experiments, this important study finds that negative ads discourage moderates from voting.

Piven, Francis, and Richard Cloward. *Why Americans Still Don't Vote.* Boston: Beacon Press, 2000. This example of critical commentary on nonvoting in the United States contends that "have-nots" are systematically discouraged from voting.

Rosenstone, Steven, and John Mark Hansen. *Mobilization, Participation, and Democracy in America.* New York: Longman Classics ed., 2003. Statistical study of electoral and governmental participation from the 1950s to the 1980s, with particular emphasis on the decline in turnout.

Norris, Pippa. *Democratic Phoenix.* New York: Cambridge University Press, 2002. Comparative study of political and civic activism that questions the common belief that these are in decline.

On the Web

Lots of temporary organizations are designed to increase voter turnout (usually for a specific candidate). These are usually closely tied to or run by a specific campaign. Organizations committed to a broader vision of democracy are not nearly so common.

www.lwv.org

Perhaps the oldest and most respected of permanent organizations is the League of Women Voters, born out of the suffrage movement around the turn of the century. This nonpartisan group works to encourage informed and active participation.

www.rochester.edu/SBA

A useful summary of the suffrage movement, including its history and important documents, can be found via the University of Rochester.

www.vote-smart.org

One of the most useful sites for citizens interested in how to participate, and in information on candidates, is Project Vote Smart. It is also a nonpartisan site with a wealth of information on candidate backgrounds, positions, and records.

Election Voices

Should Voting Be Compulsory?

THE ISSUE

In reaction to America's chronically low electoral turnout, a number of analysts have concluded that the only sure remedy for this problem is to pass a law requiring all eligible Americans to vote in federal elections and imposing a small fine on those who do not. Others say that the right to vote also includes the right not to participate, and that compulsory voting laws would only compel many people who are not very interested in or informed about politics to cast ballots that they themselves do not regard as particularly meaningful.

Background

As we read in Chapter 6, the United States has the lowest voter turnout rate of any major democratic nation except Switzerland. In recent presidential elections, only slightly more than half of the eligible electorate has bothered to cast a ballot. Turnout rates at midterm elections have ranged between 35 and 40 percent. And, although turnout does occasionally increase above these levels—as it did in 2004, for example—there is no indication that America's low voter turnout is a temporary phenomenon, likely to be reversed in the next few years. If anything, studies of younger generations, who will constitute an increasingly large proportion of the U.S. electorate, indicate that they are less likely to follow news about government and politics, and therefore less likely to know or care much about these subjects, than their parents and grandparents were when they were at a similar age.[1]

For many years, the standard "solution" to these problems was to liberalize American voter registration practices. Americans voted less, the argument went, because it was much more difficult to register in the United States than in other countries. Consequently, numerous legal changes have been made over the last four decades that dramatically eased the process of voter registration. Yet all this activity has had almost no discernible effect on turnout. Though the number of registered voters has increased, most of the new registrants have not bothered to show up on Election Day. Over the last four decades, the level of U.S. voter turnout has actually decreased.

Faced with this apparently intractable problem, many commentators have concluded that the only sure way to increase voter turnout is to make it mandatory: to pass a law (or possibly a constitutional amendment) that would require all eligible citizens to cast a ballot and that would impose some kind of penalty—usually a small fine—on those who do not. Though such an arrangement is usually referred to as "compulsory voting," strictly speaking no one is actually compelled to *vote*. Rather, the law would require all citizens to show up at the polls on Election Day and receive an official ballot (or request an absentee ballot). Most people would then vote—but anyone who was repulsed by all of the available candidates or had some other principled reason for not voting could simply deposit a blank ballot into the ballot box. Exemptions presumably would be given to people who were sick on Election Day or had some other legitimate reason for being unable to get to the polls.

Though compulsory voting has never been tried in the United States, it is currently in use in a number of other democracies, including Australia, Belgium, and Luxembourg. And, as one can easily verify by examining the data in Table 6.1, all of these countries generally rank near the top in international comparisons of voter participation rates. More generally, as one political scientist has noted:

> On the basis of studies from the 1930s to the 1980s and 1990s, we know a great deal about the institutional mechanisms that can increase turnout . . . . And all of these studies . . . have found that compulsory voting is a particularly effective method to achieve high turnout—in spite of generally low penalties (comparable to a fine for parking violations), lax enforcement (more lenient than the enforcement of parking rules), and the secrecy of the ballot—which means that an actual vote cannot be compelled in the first place.[2]

Fewer and fewer young Americans are voting. Are compulsory voting laws the answer?

Political Dilemmas

The case for compulsory voting is founded on the premise that one essential element of democracy is the fundamental equality of all citizens. But this equality is violated when some citizens vote and others do not. Not only might this inequality have an effect on who gets elected; it also means that the elected officials will almost certainly pay more attention to the needs and concerns of groups with higher participation rates than to groups that generally stay at home. And the lower that voter turnout falls, the greater the likelihood that differential participation rates may have a major impact on policy outcomes. As Sidney Verba, Norman Nie, and Jae-On Kim argued some years ago, to equalize political participation, governments need to establish both a "ceiling," a prescribed maximum, and a "floor," a prescribed minimum.[3] In the case of voter participation, the ceiling is, of course, the requirement that all citizens can cast only one vote, no matter how wealthy or well-educated they are, no matter how zealously they support their candidate. Compulsory voting would make sure that a floor is also in place.

Would compulsory voting have a noticeable impact on who gets elected? As we have already noted earlier in this chapter, the general consensus of most academic work on this subject is that the policy views of voters and nonvoters are not very different. Yet, it is wrong to say that there are *no* differences between these two groups. Even 100 percent turnout rates would not have altered the results of presidential elections in landslide years such as 1972 and 1984—but they might have made a difference in close elections such as 2000 or 2004.[4]

Opponents of compulsory voting make several arguments against it. Voting, they contend, is a right—and inherent in every right is a person's capacity to decide not to exercise it. The right to free speech also entails the right to keep silent if one chooses. The right to an attorney means that one can also waive that right. Forcing people to go to the polls every two or four years—even if they leave the ballot blank—is thus a violation of each person's right not to participate in an election.

On a more pragmatic level, opponents of compulsory voting question the desirability of pushing people to vote when they themselves appear to place little value on that act. There is, in this respect, a very important difference between the predicament of the contemporary nonvoter and the situation that confronted women before 1920 or African Americans in the South prior to the mid-1960s. Many women and blacks clearly *did* want to vote, but they were legally prohibited from doing so. Most nonvoters today, by contrast, almost certainly could vote if they wanted to. They just don't seem to think that it is worth the effort. If people place such a limited value on their candidate preference, what exactly do we gain by pushing them into the voting booths?

What Does the Public Believe?

Because it is such an unfamiliar idea, and because it runs against the traditional American concept of rights, there is, at present, remarkably little popular support for compulsory voting proposals. In June 2004, in the only survey question we know of that deals specifically with this issue, ABC News asked a national sample, "In a few countries every eligible citizen is required by law to vote in national elections. Those who don't have a good excuse for not voting are subject to a small fine. Do you think this would be a good law or a poor law to have

in this country?" Only 21 percent of respondents said it was a good law (i.e., favored compulsory voting), versus 72 percent who thought it a poor law.

Thus, there is little chance that compulsory voting will be adopted in the United States over next few years. Yet, as advocates of compulsory voting have noted, many other intrusions into what were once believed to be private decisions are now sanctioned by law and widely endorsed by public opinion, because supporters worked hard to point out the advantages of such laws and thus changed public attitudes.[5] Were a significant number of political scientists and civic groups to decide that compulsory voting is the only way to deal with the country's chronic turnout problem, perhaps, in time, a majority of Americans might come to share this belief.

How Have the Courts Ruled?

Any law that attempted to establish compulsory voting would almost certainly be challenged in the courts—but, because nothing like compulsory voting currently exists, it is difficult to say how courts would decide such a case. The most basic challenge would concern whether the right to vote—which the U.S. Supreme Court has repeatedly recognized as enjoying substantial constitutional protection—also includes the right not to vote; and whether the latter right is violated by a law that compels every eligible voter to go to the polls.

Were compulsory voting to be instituted by federal statute, the law might also be challenged on federalism grounds: Does the Constitution give the federal government the right to regulate voting practices in the states? Through most of American history, it was assumed that all matters having to do with voter qualifications were under the control of state governments, save for the specific restrictions established in the Fifteenth and Nineteenth Amendments. More recently, however, the courts have argued that the clause in Article I, Section 4, that grants Congress the power to make regulations concerning the "times, places, and manner of holding [congressional] elections," in conjunction with the Fourteenth Amendment, gives the federal government substantial authority to pass laws that deal with voter eligibility and registration. Reasoning in this way, the Supreme Court upheld the National Voter Registration Act of 1993 (the so-called "Motor Voter" bill) and an earlier federal statute that had granted the right to vote to 18-, 19-, and 20-year-olds in all federal elections.

What Do You Think?

1. Is voting best thought of as a right or as a duty?

2. If a person favors one candidate but does not feel strongly enough about this preference to go to the polls, is society better off if we encourage or require such a person to vote?

3. Would compulsory voting have much effect on the outcomes of American elections? If so, which party would benefit most?

4. If voting is not made compulsory, is there any other way to ensure that such groups as young people and the poor vote in greater percentages?

[1]Arend Lijphart, "Unequal Participation: Democracy's Unresolved Dilemma," *American Political Science Review* 91 (March 1997): 2.
[2]Sidney Verba, Norman H. Nie, and Jae-On Kim, *Participation and Political Equality* (New York: Cambridge University Press, 1978).
[3]For an argument that increased voter participation would have changed the results in 2000 and in the 1994 midterm elections, see Martin P. Wattenberg, *Where Have All the Voters Gone?* (Cambridge: Harvard University Press, 2002), chap. 5.
[4]For a good argument along these lines, see Wattenberg, *Is Voting for Young People?*, 172–174. Two examples Wattenberg mentions are the laws that ban smoking in restaurants and those that require automobile passengers to wear seat belts.

CHAPTER 7

Interest-Group Participation in American Democracy

CHAPTER OUTLINE

How One Group Challenged Congress

Members of the House Education Committee were hard at work on a major bill in February 1994, when California Democrat George Miller offered what appeared to be an uncontroversial amendment.[1] Miller proposed to withhold federal grant money from school districts that employed teachers who were not officially certified in the subjects they taught. By approving the amendment committee members could claim that they had taken steps to improve teacher qualifications, without spending any additional money.

Miller's amendment carried additional political advantages for the Democrats who controlled the committee at the time. The mandate was sure to please two important Democratic constituency groups: teachers' unions and universities. Unions favor certification requirements because they reduce competition from otherwise qualified, but uncertified, teachers. Schools of education favor certification requirements because professionals, no matter how skilled, would have to complete one of their programs before being allowed to teach. But these were not the only constituencies watching.

Unbeknownst to many people, including most members of Congress at the time, between 500,000 and 1 million American children were being educated at home—many by conservative Christian parents opposed to the secular values of the educational profession. (The figure today is between 2 and 3 million.) A homeschool advocate who had been following these obscure committee proceedings contacted U.S. Representative Richard Armey (R-TX) to inquire whether the amendment would affect parents who teach their own children. Uncertain about the impact of the proposal, Armey sought the advice of the Home School Legal Defense Association. After consideration, the association's lawyers suggested that, given the tendency of the courts to interpret legislative mandates broadly, the proposal did threaten to disqualify parents educating their children at home.

The reaction was fierce and immediate. In a letter to Congress that illustrates the fevered pitch of political rhetoric today, the Home School Legal Defense Association charged that the House proposal was "the equivalent of a nuclear attack upon the homeschooling community." Employing modern communications technologies, the interest group set out to mobilize the potential constituency of homeschoolers and their sympathizers.

Electronic communications carried the warning to every corner of the United States and in a matter of days the echoes came back loud and clear. The homeschool constituency generated more than half-a-million communications, tying up Capitol Hill switchboards and overwhelming fax machines. A few days later, a second wave of electronic thunder rolled across Capitol Hill after the homeschool coalition convinced groups representing private schools that the proposed mandate threatened them too.

Many members of Congress—blithely unaware of what was going on in one of 275 House committees and subcommittees—went home for the President's Day recess and were caught in constituency firestorms. Some of them were verbally ambushed at town meetings by constituents incensed that Congress might be planning to destroy homeschools. And when members tried to reach their offices to figure out what was going on, they found the lines jammed. Armey could not get through from Texas, and other members had to call staff at their homes to learn the nature of the problem.

In the face of such an outcry, the House sounded a full retreat. Before galleries packed with homeschool advocates, the committee offered a floor amendment to kill the Miller provision and add statutory language specifically exempting homeschools from the legislation's scope. It passed 424 to 1: Representative Miller stood alone. Not fully satisfied, Armey introduced a further amendment declaring that the legislation did not "permit, allow, encourage or authorize any federal control over any aspect of any private, religious or homeschool." To be on the safe side, the House passed this amendment too, 374 to 53.

MAKING THE CONNECTION

This episode graphically illustrates all the perceived ills of interest-group democracy. It shows large organizations trying to use federal power to reduce competition and steer people into paying for training they may not need. It shows a small but intense minority able to send the nation's entire legislative branch scrambling for cover. It shows the extent to which public policies emerge from fear and political calculation rather than from careful deliberation. On the other hand, it also shows how interest groups can enhance democracy. Most citizens do not participate actively in politics as individuals, but many are associated with groups that are active. By mobilizing citizens who ordinarily are uninvolved, these interest groups can be an effective way for the public to express its will—especially now that they have adopted state-of-the-art communications technologies that keep the public informed and amplify voter concerns in Washington, D.C.

In this chapter we examine interest groups and how they influence government. First, we discuss how interest groups organize to communicate their views. Then, we consider the problems that interest groups face in mobilizing their members and how they overcome these obstacles. How interest groups try to influence government and whether they are successful in their attempts are our next concern. In the concluding section, we discuss whether interest groups contribute to or detract from democratic government.

Interest Groups in the United States

Americans are joiners, more so than the citizens of most other democracies (see Table 7.1). More than three-quarters of Americans belong to at least one group; on average they belong to two and they make financial contributions to four.[2] Many of these associations allow citizens to participate indirectly in politics because they are **interest groups**—organizations or associations of people with common interests that participate in politics on behalf of their members.

interest group

Organization or association of people with common interests that engages in politics on behalf of its members.

	TABLE 7.1	
	AMERICANS TEND TO BE JOINERS	

Of nine democracies surveyed to assess their level of group membership, only the Netherlands rivaled the United States as a nation of joiners. The Dutch, like the Americans, are particularly likely to participate in religious groups.

	Percent Belonging to No Groups	Percent Belonging to Four or More Groups
Netherlands	15	31
United States	18	19
Germany	33	8
Canada	35	16
Britain	46	9
Italy	59	4
France	61	4
Mexico	64	4
Spain	70	2

Source: Figures drawn from the World Values Surveys, 1990–1993, reported in *The Public Perspective*, April/May, 1995: 21.

A Recreational Group Turns Political

The NRA was founded shortly after the Civil War to promote marksmanship among hunters, target shooters, and gun collectors. By the mid-twentieth century, the NRA operated safety programs and trained law enforcement officers. It is now known, however, as the chief opponent of gun-control legislation. Its PAC is usually one of the top 10 contributors to congressional elections, and it employs some 80 lobbyists.

Of course, not all the groups with which people associate are political groups—many are social clubs, charities, service organizations, church groups, and so forth—but literally thousands of groups do engage in politics. Even seemingly nonpolitical groups often engage in political activity. For example, parent-teacher organizations are active in school politics. Neighborhood associations lobby about traffic, crime, and zoning policies. Hobby or recreation groups mobilize when they perceive threats to their favored activities—witness the National Rifle Association!

Growth and Development of Groups

Americans have a long-standing reputation for forming groups. In his classic book *Democracy in America,* Alexis de Tocqueville, a nineteenth-century French visitor to the United States, noted that Americans

> . . . are forever forming associations . . . . [A]t the head of any new undertaking, where in France you would find the government or in England some territorial magnate, in the United States you are sure to find an association.[3]

Perhaps Americans form groups because of some tendency in our culture stemming from our historical experiences, but several features of the American political system also have encouraged the formation of groups.[4] In particular, federalism and the separation of powers mean that there are lots of "points of access" or "pressure points" that groups can use to influence policy. In many countries, a teachers' group that opposed some major change in educational policy would have to defeat the policy in the national legislature. In the United States, a teachers' group might seek support within either chamber of Congress or from the president. And even if the new policy was written into law, its implementation could still be fought in the courts or the bureaucracy or at the state and local level.

Whatever the number and mix of reasons, the American tendency to form groups continues today. But group formation in the United States has not been a steady process; it has occurred in waves.[5] Before the Civil War, there were few national organizations. Life in general was local. The social organization of the United States was one of "island communities" with few social and economic links between them.[6] As the railroads connected the country after the Civil War, however, a national economy developed—and national associations were not far behind. The first two decades after the war saw the birth of national agricultural associations such as the Grange and of trade unions such as the Knights of Labor and the American Federation of Labor.

Another major wave of group organization occurred during the Progressive Era, roughly 1890 to 1917. Many of today's most broad-based economic associations date from that era: the Chamber of Commerce, the National Association of Manufacturers, and the American Farm Bureau Federation, for example. Other sorts of associations sprang up as well. For example, the National Association for the Advancement of Colored People (NAACP) formed as part of a strategy to promote equality for black Americans, and the National Audubon Society was established to promote conservation.

The post-1960 wave of group formation was by far the largest and the most diverse. Thousands of additional economic groups formed, but these tended to be more narrowly based than earlier ones. The American Soybean Association, the National Corn Growers Association, the Rocky Mountain Llama and Alpaca Association, and numerous other specialized organizations joined the more general agricultural associations. Similarly, in the commercial and manufacturing sectors, numerous specialized groups joined the older, more broad-based groups.

What are sometimes called "government interest groups" proliferated as older national associations of mayors, governors, teachers, and social workers were joined by newer, more specialized associations such as the National Association of State and Provincial Lotteries, the Association of State Drinking Water Administrators, and the U.S. Police Canine Association. Similarly, nonprofit groups now include all kinds of specialized occupational associations. Examples of particular relevance to likely readers of this book include the National Association of Student Financial Aid Administrators and the National Association of Graduate Admissions Professionals.

Innumerable shared-interest groups have formed in recent decades. Some groups advocate a particular political ideology. Liberal groups such as the National Organization for Women (NOW, a feminist group) and People for the American Way (a civil-liberties group) are deeply involved in politics, as are such conservative groups as the Christian Coalition (a group promoting traditional morality) and the Club for Growth (a group that advocates minimal government taxation and regulation). Self-proclaimed "citizens" groups purport to promote the interests of everyone by seeking the public good—even though their policy goals sometimes are just as controversial as those of more openly ideological groups. Examples include Common Cause (a political reform group), Greenpeace (an environmental group), the National Taxpayers' Union (an antitax and antispending group), and numerous other "watchdog" organizations, most less than a generation old. Some groups are so narrowly focused that they are known as **single-issue groups**. Well-known examples are pro-choice groups such as NARAL and pro-life groups such as Operation Rescue, which play prominent roles in debates over abortion.

Nearly every significant interest or activity in American society has groups that represent it—and under the right circumstances almost any group may become involved in politics. Associations representing hunters and fishers monitor regulations affecting natural resources. Associations representing snowmobilers and mountain bikers mobilize when government threatens to restrict their use of public lands. The American Association of Retired Persons (AARP), established in 1958, has become the largest voluntary association ever. It boasts upward of 33 million members—and is still growing! AARP is a major player whenever social security or Medicare is on the political agenda, as it will be in the years to come.

Gun Rights
and Gun Control

single-issue group
An interest group narrowly focused to influence policy on a single issue.

Interest groups proliferated during the past generation because of changes in both politics and technology. Increased government activity gave people more reasons to form groups. Businesses, for instance, organized to protect themselves from new taxes and regulations or to seek new government grants and contracts. Advances in communications technology, meanwhile, made groups easier to form. Computer databases permit the generation of all kinds of specialized mailing lists—and once they have located each other, people with common interests can communicate easily and cheaply via the Internet. Furthermore, once new groups organize, they may stimulate the formation of other groups opposed to them. The pro-life movement formed at least in part because of the activities of the pro-choice movement.[7] Similarly, ranching, mining, lumber, and sporting interests launched a "sagebrush rebellion" in reaction to the successes of the environmental movement.

The Nature and Variety of "Interest Groups"

Robert Salisbury has called attention to the variety of groups, associations, and organizations included under the term *interest groups*.[8] Some have elaborate formal organizations with membership dues, journals, meetings, conventions, and so forth; the American Medical Association is a well-known example. Others are little more than an address where sympathizers send contributions. One study found that of 83 public interest groups examined, 30 had no membership.[9]

Some associations, such as Common Cause, are "membership groups" composed of numerous private individuals who make voluntary contributions. Others are associations consisting of corporate or institutional representatives who pay regular dues; trade groups provide one example. Some large corporations maintain their own Washington offices for political reasons, as do hundreds of state, city, and county governments and even universities.

Political scientist Jack Walker estimated that almost 80 percent of the interest groups in existence in the 1980s represented professional or occupational constituencies.[10] For such groups, economic matters are of crucial concern—but because these groups are about equally divided between those representing profit-seeking constituencies and those representing public and nonprofit constituencies, they do not exert a uniform influence on government taxing and spending policies. The other 20 percent of American interest groups reflect the activities of citizens with shared political goals, including those spawned by what are called social movements: broad-based reform or protest movements that bring new issues to the agenda. The civil rights movement, the environmental movement, the women's movement, and the religious right are important contemporary examples. We shall have more to say about these later in the chapter.

Forming and Maintaining Interest Groups

That so many people belong to so many groups and associations often leads people to overlook the difficulties many groups face.[11] But consider these facts:

- There are more than 100 million women over the age of 18 in the United States. Polls indicate that more than half have feminist sympathies. But the largest feminist group, NOW, has fewer than 300,000 members.

- There are approximately 36 million African Americans in the United States, but the NAACP has only about 500,000 members—including whites.
- More than 40 million American households have at least one gun, but membership in the NRA is only about 3 million.
- Majorities of the 200+ million American adult population consistently support spending more on the environment, but the combined membership of seven large environmental groups is only about 6.5 million (even after counting multiple times those who belong to more than one organization).[12]

As these examples indicate, millions of people do *not* join or support associations whose interests they share. In many cases, groups and associations include 1 percent or less of their potential membership. Thus, common interest may be a necessary condition for joining a group, but it is far from a sufficient one.

Why, then, do people join or decline to join groups? The question is important, because the answer bears on how well or how poorly interest groups represent the American citizenry. If some kinds of interests are not fairly represented, politics may be biased, despite the existence of thousands of groups with millions of members.

Like voting, joining or supporting a group requires some investment of *resources*. It is a costly activity. Contributing money or paying dues is the most obvious example, but the time required for group activities also can be a significant cost. People who have more resources will find participation easier. Thus it is no surprise that the affluent contribute more than the poor and that two-worker families with small children participate less than people with more free time.[13] Regardless of the personal resources available, however, an individual will surrender them only if the *incentive* to do so—the expected benefit—justifies the investment.

Incentives take many forms and different groups rely on different incentives. James Q. Wilson divides incentives into three categories.[14] The first he calls *solidary*. Some people join a group for social reasons: They simply wish to associate with particular kinds of people. Religious groups and campus Greek organizations are examples. Where solidary incentives are dominant, membership in the group is an end in itself. Most such groups are nonpolitical, however—people who wish to socialize with each other usually do not need politics as an excuse. Conversely, it is unlikely that people join the National Taxpayers' Union to enjoy the company of other taxpayers, and people certainly do not send checks to such associations for social purposes!

A second category of incentives is *material*. Such incentives are economic rather than social: Some people join a group because membership confers tangible benefits. This is obviously the dominant incentive in economic groups and associations. Microsoft does not belong to various trade associations because its executives like to socialize with other computer executives—they have plenty of other opportunities to do that. Microsoft belongs because the trade associations are seen as a way of protecting and advancing corporate interests. Material incentives also play a role in some political groups. Those who join taxpayers' associations hope to reduce their taxes. Those who join groups that support government subsidies or services for people like themselves (realtors, the handicapped, the old, farmers) similarly hope to gain material benefits.

Finally, some people join groups for *purposive* reasons: People are committed to and wish to advance the group's social and political goals. They want to save the whales, to end abortion or to preserve freedom of choice, to bring about a liberal or a conservative Congress. Given that politically active groups usually publicize their purposive goals, such incentives would appear to be the dominant factor underlying the formation and persistence of most of the groups that are active in politics. Things are not so simple as they appear, however.

The Free-Rider Problem

free-rider problem

Problem that arises when people can enjoy the benefits of group activity without bearing any of the costs.

You Are an Environmental Activist

Most groups, but especially groups that rely on purposive incentives, face what is known as the **free-rider problem**: People can enjoy the benefits of group activity without bearing any of the costs. Thus, they have an incentive to "free-ride" on the efforts of others.[15] This problem arises when individuals perceive that attainment of the group goal has little relationship to their personal contribution. If you donate $20 to Greenpeace, does your contribution guarantee the survival of some identifiable baby seal? If you donate several hours of your time to march for the end of hunger, does your contribution measurably reduce the amount of malnutrition in the world? Although most well-meaning people are reluctant to admit it, in each case the truthful answer is no.

These examples have two common elements. First, on reflection, people realize that their personal impact is so small as to be unnoticeable. If you don't contribute, just as many baby seals will live or die, just as many children will starve. So if your contribution makes no difference, why contribute? The second element makes matters worse: Individuals receive the benefit whether they contribute or not. If other people manage to save some seals or reduce world hunger, you enjoy those outcomes even if you did nothing to help out. So if you get the same benefit regardless of your actions, why contribute? These two conditions are major obstacles to group formation and survival. They encourage individuals to free-ride on the contributions of others, a dynamic that prevents some interests from organizing and hinders the efforts of groups that do form.

Two considerations affect the severity of the free-rider problem. First, other things being equal, the larger the group, the greater the problem. A few neighbors can pool

A Swing and a Miss

The free-rider and other problems notwithstanding, attempts to limit the power of interest groups have not been very successful. In 2006, for example, the Senate enacted lobbying reforms that, at least in the view of this cartoonist, did little to achieve their purported goal.

their efforts to clean up a vacant lot that borders their properties. It is easy to identify those who don't show up and subject them to social pressure. It would be unthinkable, however, for a large city to rely on volunteer effort to maintain city parks. Social pressure is less effective where people do not know each other. Thus, cities pay city employees or private contractors to maintain their parks.

Second, other things being equal, the free-rider problem is more serious the greater the distance and abstractness of the benefit the group seeks to achieve. It is much easier to see one's personal impact on cleaning up a vacant lot than on cleaning up the atmosphere. It is much easier to see one's personal impact on feeding the poor in a specific locale than on reducing world hunger.

At issue here are what economists call **public goods**, as distinct from private goods. A tomato is a private good. If you consume it, others cannot. Clean air is a public good. If the air is clean, everyone benefits from breathing it. Economists believe that because free-riders can enjoy or consume public goods even if they make no contribution to their provision, such goods typically are provided at lower than optimal levels.[16]

public goods
Goods enjoyed simultaneously by a group, as opposed to a private good that must be divided up to be shared.

Economic goods can be public goods, too, so interest groups with an economic orientation also face free-rider problems. If General Motors lobbies successfully for a tariff or quota on Korean cars, Ford will enjoy the benefits (lower competition, higher prices) even if Ford did not aid GM in the lobbying effort. If members of the Corn Growers Association pool their efforts to get a higher corn subsidy, even growers who are not members of the association reap the benefit of the higher subsidy. The free-rider problem is widespread.

The most important implication of the free-rider problem for democratic politics lies in the kinds of groups best able to overcome it. Our discussion suggests that—again, other things being equal—small groups organized for narrow purposes have an organizational advantage over large groups organized for broad purposes. For example, a small number of corporations will find it relatively easy to organize an association to lobby for regulations that raise prices; the millions of consumers who buy the products the corporations sell will find it much more difficult to organize an association to lobby against such anti-competitive regulations. The free-rider problem implies that democratic politics will favor narrow "special" interests at the expense of the broader "public" interest.

Overcoming the Free-Rider Problem

On first learning about the free-rider problem, some idealists protest, "What if everyone felt that way?" Well, a great many people do; that is why so many groups mobilize such a small proportion of their potential constituencies. Still, there are groups that represent broad purposive interests. How do these groups manage to overcome the free-rider problem? History reveals a number of useful strategies.

Coercion   If members of a labor union strike for higher wages, how can they prevent nonunion workers from enjoying the results? Historically, the answer has been coercion. Social pressure and even violence have been used to compel reluctant workers to join unions or prevent them from crossing union picket lines. Because violence is costly to inflict and often brings violence in return, unions preferred to rely on a strategy of negotiating "closed shops" with management. Such agreements require workers to join the union as a condition of employment.

Milder forms of coercion are still widespread, although they are often unrecognized. For example, professional and occupational associations lobby governmental jurisdictions to hire or certify only their members, thus making membership a condition of working or practicing in that jurisdiction. In addition, such associations can coerce members indirectly through control of professional or occupational certification. Practicing law usually requires membership in the state bar. Engaging in specialized trades such as plumbing, or professions such as teaching, may require a state license or other official recognition. Such requirements reward the members of professional and occupational associations, while denying benefits to potential free-riders.

Although it has been very effective historically, coercion appears to be a declining means of overcoming the free-rider problem. Society no longer tolerates the informal violence associated with strikes, and state governments no longer regulate many of the occupations and professions they once did. As a result, occupational interest groups have lost members and influence. The union movement in particular has fallen on hard times, its membership declining from more than one-third of the workforce to less than one-sixth.[17]

social movement

Broad-based demand for government action on some problem or issue, such as civil rights for blacks and women or environmental protection.

Social Movements   At times people do not think individualistically, as they do when they free-ride. In these instances, large numbers of people get swept up in a social cause. Such **social movements**—broad-based demands for government action on a problem or issue—have a long history in American politics. The abolitionist movement is one of the best known. Dedicated to ending slavery, the abolitionists forced the issue onto the national agenda. Their activism played a role in the political upheaval of the 1850s and, ultimately, in the outbreak of the Civil War. Other nineteenth-century social movements included the Populist and labor movements in the 1880s and 1890s and the women's suffrage movement, which culminated in passage of the Nineteenth Amendment in 1920.

The civil rights movement is probably the best-known example of a social movement in modern times. As discussed in Chapter 17, the massive demonstrations of the 1960s evolved from a few sit-ins and boycotts in the 1950s. The movement culminated with the adoption of landmark federal legislation: the Civil Rights Act of 1964 and the Voting Rights Act of 1965.

Other movements soon followed. On April 22, 1970, Earth Day marked the sudden eruption of an environmental movement. Within the year, the United States had an Environmental Protection Agency and a Clean Air Act. The women's movement took off at about the same time, flexing its muscle in the 1972–1982 campaign for ratification of the Equal Rights Amendment (ERA), which succeeded in 35 states, 3 short of the three-fourths majority needed to adopt a constitutional amendment (see Chapter 17).[18] On the other side of the political spectrum, the ranks of the religious right swelled in the late 1970s and contributed to Ronald Reagan's presidential victories in the 1980s and to the Republican congressional resurgence in the 1990s.[19] The movement supports constitutional amendments to outlaw abortion and allow prayer in schools, but, like the feminists, the religious right has been unable as yet to achieve constitutional change. Social movements build on emotional or moral fervor. Many of those active within such movements dedicate themselves to what they see as a higher cause. When individuals think more collectively than individually, they may ignore the considerations that normally would lead them to free-ride. Still, social movements typically mobilize only small proportions of the population. Some people can be induced to think in moral or collective terms, but not many. Moreover, most people cannot sustain political passions for long, especially once demands for reform get bogged down in the tedious details of legislation and bureaucratic regulations. Thus, a social movement has a tendency to "run down" as its emotional basis subsides. For a social movement to exert long-term influence, it must find a way to "institutionalize" itself—to spin off organized groups and formal associations that will continue to work for its political goals. At that point, it faces the same free-rider problem as any other organized interest.

Increasing the Perceived Impact   As was noted earlier, the free-rider problem occurs because most people do not believe that their own contribution of time or money will have any noticeable impact on a particular issue or problem area. In an attempt to overcome this obstacle, groups may reformulate their appeals in order to suggest that even small contributions will have a measurable, concrete impact. For example, the United Nations Children's Fund (UNICEF) tries to raise money in order to deal with such problems as malnutrition, disease, and inadequate housing, especially as they affect the lives of children. Of course, most potential contributors are unlikely to believe that a contribution of $10 or $25 will have any real effect on a large, abstract problem such as "world hunger." Hence, UNICEF has, for many years, solicited money by specifically claiming that even small amounts of money will produce clear, concrete results. In May 2006, one UNICEF-affiliated organization urged visitors to its website to contribute to immunization programs by noting that:

- $1.20 can immunize a woman and her newborn against tetanus.
- $17 can immunize a child against the six major childhood diseases.
- $60 can provide enough vaccine to immunize 60 children against polio.[20]

Similarly, one of the authors of this textbook contributes money to a group that tries to combat poverty in various Third World countries. But instead of dwelling on the general problem of poverty or each person's moral duty to help the less fortunate, this group pairs up each contributor with a particular child in a poverty-stricken area, encourages the contributor and child to exchange letters, and emphasizes that most of the money contributed will help pay for better nutrition, housing, and health care in the specific area where the child lives.[21]

Selective Benefits   Many groups that work to achieve collective goods also provide their members with valuable private goods. Professional associations publish journals and magazines that contain occupationally useful information but restrict subscriptions to members. Trade associations inform their members—and only their members—about important technological advances. Agricultural associations provide their members—and only their members—with the latest information about new varieties of crops and new growing methods. In short, people, corporations, and institutions may join associations less to support the collective goods that the association supports than for the specific private goods that the association provides—selectively—to members: its **selective benefits**.

The American Association of Retired Persons (AARP) offers the most notable example of this strategy for overcoming the free-rider problem. For a mere $12.50 per year, members gain access to the world's largest mail-order pharmacy (where volume buying keeps prices low); low-cost auto, health, and life insurance; discounts on hotels,

selective benefits
Side benefits of belonging to an organization, which are limited to contributing members of the organization.

airfares, and car rentals; and numerous other benefits. Even a senior citizen who disagrees with the political positions of AARP finds it hard to forgo membership!

Selective benefits are not limited to direct economic ones or to information that indirectly produces economic benefits. Anything that people like and that can be selectively provided may be a selective benefit. Some environmental groups produce magazines full of beautiful pictures, organize outings and activities, rate outdoor clothing and equipment, and so forth. These and other benefits of membership often are sufficient to induce people to pay the modest amounts that membership requires. In short, what seems to be the principal reason for a group's existence may not be the principal reason why many people belong.

Patrons and Political Entrepreneurs   Discussions of the free-rider problem typically reflect a bottom-up notion of how groups form. The implicit assumption is that individual people, corporations, or institutions band together and form associations. Recent research, however, indicates that the process of group formation often is more top-down than bottom-up. Many groups owe their existence to a **political entrepreneur**, an individual or a small number of individuals who take the lead in setting up and operating the group.[22]

In the first place, some individuals, institutions, or corporations are so influential that they do not face the free-rider problem. Their contributions to a group effort are not futile; they make a measurable difference. Large corporations also can have a large stake in the health of their industries. Their share of any group benefit is so great that they are not likely to consider political gains to be a public good. Microsoft, for example, has its own Washington office staffed by paid employees. When the interests of software manufacturers are at risk, Microsoft may be willing to mobilize its team of lobbyists to protect the industry even if smaller firms free-ride. Sometimes a large firm will bear most of the costs to support an industry association, which gives the appearance of a broad base of support. Ralston-Purina in the feed industry is an example.

Similarly, a rich individual with a deep commitment to the group goal may be able to make a difference. Your $20 contribution to Greenpeace may have no measurable impact, but if you are in a position to give a million dollars, you can probably save some seals. Foundations also support interest groups with grants and contracts. The W. Alton Jones Foundation and the Ford Foundation give millions of dollars a year to environmental groups.[23] Similarly, conservative foundations help to fund the Wise Use Movement, which opposes traditional environmental groups.

In the second place, political entrepreneurs often set up and maintain a group for their own reasons. Their motives are varied. Some feel so strongly about a goal that they are willing to let others free-ride on them. We call such people either fanatical or dedicated, depending on whether we sympathize with their goals. An ascetic lawyer, Ralph Nader, did more than anyone else to organize the consumer movement and has devoted his life to it. Candy Lightner formed Mothers Against Drunk Driving after a man on bail from his third drunken-driving charge killed her daughter. Ross Perot founded and subsidized his own political party. Many (though not all) such individuals have passed up opportunities to parlay their visibility into riches or political office, and this restraint suggests that their commitment to broader goals is genuine.

Of course, some political entrepreneurs do have ulterior motives. They may be aspiring politicians who see an opportunity to use new groups as the basis of future

political entrepreneurs

People willing to assume the costs of forming and maintaining an organization even when others may free-ride on them.

constituencies. Candidates for city and state offices often emerge from neighborhood associations and local protest groups. They may enjoy the celebrity or power that comes from leadership positions. They may be able to convert their fame into board appointments, consulting contracts, or book royalties. In short, self-seeking political entrepreneurs may invest their resources in interest-group organization the same way that profit-seeking business entrepreneurs invest their resources in founding companies—taking on greater personal risk than others in the hope of reaping disproportionate personal gains if they succeed.

The government itself did much to organize the new groups of the 1960s and 1970s. As the role of government expanded, federal bureaucracies needed new ways to implement programs through a decentralized federal system. One strategy was to stimulate and subsidize organizations that could be used to help develop standards and regulations, and to publicize them and carry them out. These groups were politically useful as well because they often promoted generous funding of government programs. Not surprisingly, groups and associations that receive federal funds are more than twice as likely to support expanded government activity—and, by implication, the elected officials who expand it—as groups that do not.[24]

The available evidence suggests that the top-down activities of patrons and political entrepreneurs are a more important means of overcoming the free-rider problem than the provision of selective benefits, AARP notwithstanding.[25] Wealthy individuals, government agencies, corporations, and private foundations have been important sources of support for nonprofit-sector groups, especially citizens groups. About 90 percent of the latter have received such subsidies.

How Interest Groups Influence Government

The variety of groups, associations, and institutions that make up the interest-group universe engage in a wide array of political activities. We first discuss these political activities, which include government lobbying, grassroots lobbying, electioneering and political action committees, persuading the public, direct action, and litigation. We then focus on why groups choose certain tactics over others.

Lobbying

Many interest groups attempt to influence government the old-fashioned way: by lobbying public officials. **Lobbying** consists of interest-group activities intended to influence directly the decisions that public officials make. Groups and associations draft bills for friendly legislators to introduce, testify before congressional committees and in agency proceedings, meet with elected officials and present their cases (sometimes at posh resorts where the official is the guest), and provide public officials with information. In these and other ways, group representatives try to influence those who make governmental decisions.

People who engage in lobbying are called **lobbyists**, although the term is usually reserved for those who do it as their primary job. Some lobbyists are so-called hired guns, people who will use their contacts and expertise in the service of just about anyone willing to pay their price, but some of the best known are closely associated with one party or the other. Many large groups and associations have their own staff

lobbying
Interest-group activities intended to influence directly the decisions that public officials make.

lobbyist
One who engages in lobbying.

Nursing Protest

Protest by California nurses in 2005. Nurses, teachers, firefighters, and other unionized workers demonstrated to show their discontent with Governor Schwarzenegger over a range of issues.

You Are a
Lobbyist

lobbyists. Others hire lobbyists on a part-time basis or share a lobbyist with other groups. Some groups simply have their own leaders engage in lobbying, although these individuals typically are not called lobbyists.

Lobbying to ensure favorable national policies and to prevent unfavorable ones has become a massive American industry. Spending on lobbying activities has spiraled upward; it reached $200 million per month by the end of 2005. Corporations account for the lion's share of traditional lobbying. Health-care industries alone spent $183 million during the second half of 2005. Lobbying operations vary widely in scope. The U.S. Chamber of Commerce and its Institute for Legal Reform together spent $20 million in the last half of 2005. The largest lobbying firm, Patton Boggs, reported spending $18 million. Organized labor spent a total of $13 million. Other lobbyists and lobbying groups spend almost nothing at all.[26]

There are federal and state laws that require lobbyists to register, but because of disagreement about what lobbying is and who a lobbyist is, as well as lack of enforcement, those who register are only a fraction of those engaged in lobbying.[27] For example, the Center for Responsive Politics counted approximately 20,000 registered lobbyists in Washington, but reports that the true numbers are many times higher than that.[28]

The term *lobbyist* has negative connotations; few parents dream that their child will grow up to be one. Movies, novels, and newspapers often portray lobbyists as unsavory characters who operate on the borders of what is ethical or legal—and often step across them. Although the media play up every lobbying scandal, most scholars believe that the popular image of widespread illegality is an exaggeration. Numerous conflict-of-interest laws and regulations, along with an investigative media ever on the lookout for a hint of scandal, make outright corruption in today's politics relatively rarer than in earlier eras of American history. Still, in 2006 California Rep. Randall "Duke" Cunningham, Louisiana Rep. William Jefferson, Ohio Rep. Robert Ney, and West Virginia Rep. Alan Mollohan all came under criminal investigation for corruption, once again providing support for the negative popular image of lobbyists.

Scholars believe that for the most part, lobbyists provide public officials with information and supporting arguments. They tend to deal with officials already sympathetic to their positions and to support those officials' activities. Lobbyists have little incentive to lie; to do so would destroy their credibility and undermine their future effectiveness. Of course, lobbyists are strategic actors who emphasize arguments and information favorable to their viewpoints, but they do not want to hurt their political allies by lying, concealing information, or otherwise exposing them to an embarrassing counterattack.[29] Many political scientists think that lobbyists serve a useful purpose, injecting valuable information into the legislative process. As former Senator and President John Kennedy observed,

> Competent lobbyists can present the most persuasive arguments in support of their positions. Indeed, there is no more effective manner of learning all important arguments and facts on a controversial issue than to have the opposing lobbyists present their case.[30]

With the explosive growth of interest groups during the past generation, there is undoubtedly more old-fashioned lobbying than ever before. The number of corporate and trade-association offices in Washington doubled between 1970 and 1980 and membership in the District of Columbia Bar Association more than tripled between 1973 and 1983. Registered lobbyists increased six-fold between 1960 and 1980.[31] The democratization of Congress and the expansion of government helped stimulate such developments. In 1950 a group might have to lobby only one powerful committee chair or a key staffer, but by 1980 it had to lobby numerous subcommittee chairs as well as the rank and file and many of their staff (see Chapter 12).

Lobbyists

Grassroots Lobbying

Whereas lobbying consists of attempts to influence government officials *directly*, **grassroots lobbying** consists of attempts to influence officials *indirectly* through their constituents. The homeschooling example that opened this chapter illustrates the process. A Washington association communicates with its grassroots supporters, who in turn put pressure on their elected representatives.

grassroots lobbying
Efforts by groups and associations to influence elected officials indirectly, by arousing their constituents.

Some scholars believe that grassroots lobbying has grown in importance and the effectiveness of traditional lobbying has faded. As one health care lobbyist put it,

> One of the perceptions about lobbying is that you go out drinking, and the guy's your buddy so he does you favors . . . . Those days are long gone. That sort of thing may work on tiny things like a technical amendment to a bill, but on big, important issues personal friendships don't mean a thing.[32]

One reason that friendships may not sway policy is that Congress is more decentralized than it once was. When only a few leaders need to be persuaded, a personal approach may suffice. When dozens need to be persuaded, reaching out and touching their constituents through grassroots lobbying may be more effective—especially given the advent of modern communications technology. Also, government in general is more open than in the past. It is not so easy for Washington insiders to make private deals. It is more important than ever to show that there is popular support for a group's position. Grassroots mobilization can create an image of popularity.

One of the newest innovations in grassroots lobbying is "grass-tops" lobbying.[33] In this variation, an interest group makes an ad featuring a prominent local personality—

especially one who is an important supporter of a member of Congress—and then plays the ad in the member's district. Such ads signal members in no uncertain terms that influential people back home stand behind the group's goals.

By no means should anyone think that grassroots lobbying is a new tactic, however; it has been around for a long time. In a classic study of the Anti-Saloon League (a prohibition group), Peter Odegard noted that this group had more than 500,000 names on its mailing list nearly a century ago—long before dependable long-distance telephone service, let alone computers, the fax, and e-mail![34] Influencing government officials' views by reaching out to their constituents is nothing new, but decentralized political institutions and rapid advances in communications technology have made such a strategy more attractive than ever.

Electioneering and PACs

Personal and grassroots lobbying influence the views of public officials on specific matters. One way to affect the views of public officials more generally is by influencing who gets elected in the first place. Groups have always been involved in the electoral process, supporting some candidates and opposing others—but as the role of party organizations in campaigns and elections has eroded, and as campaigns have become more expensive, groups have become more active than ever before. Electioneering is probably the fastest-growing group tactic, and a principal vehicle of this tactic is the political action committee.

political action committee (PAC)
Specialized organization for raising and contributing campaign funds.

PACs and
the Money Trails

Political action committees (PACs) are specialized organizations for raising and spending campaign funds. Many are associated with an interest group or association. They come in as many varieties as the interests they represent.[35] Some, such as the realtors' RPAC and the doctors' AMPAC, represent big economic interests. Others represent thousands of smaller interests—the beer wholesalers, for example, have SixPAC. Not all PACs represent economic interests. Supporters of Israel donate to AIPAC and NATPAC. Supporters of abortion rights send money to NARAL-PAC, while their pro-life adversaries send money to National Right to Life PAC. Pro-choice Republicans uncomfortable with the liberal positions of NARAL can give money to WISH LIST. Scores of individual politicians have established personal PACs.[36]

Like interest groups in general, PACs have enjoyed explosive growth in the past few decades. From a mere handful in 1970, they proliferated rapidly in the 1980s, as Figure 7.1 shows. Reflecting the overall contours of the interest-group system, far more PACs represent business and commercial interests than represent labor or citizen interests.

As their numbers have proliferated, PACs have played an increasingly prominent role in congressional campaign finance. (Most PACs do not get involved in presidential campaigns.) During the 2004 election cycle, 17 percent of the money contributed to Senate candidates and 36 percent of the money contributed to candidates for the House of Representatives came from political action committees.[37] Most PACs tend to give to candidates who are likely to win, in order to establish good relations and access with the people who will occupy key positions in Congress after the election. Thus, most PACs contribute to incumbents, especially to incumbent members of key committees, regardless of party. When the Democrats were in the majority in

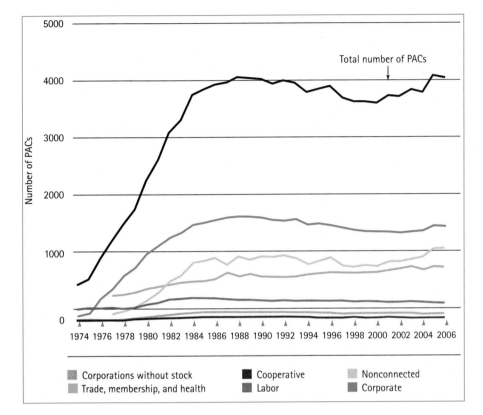

FIGURE 7.1

PACs Formed Rapidly
After the 1974 Federal
Election Campaign Act
(FECA) Reforms

Source: "FEC Issues Semi-Annual Federal
PAC Count," www.fec.gov/press/
press2006/20060223paccount (viewed
May 19, 2006).

Congress, even business PACs tended to give a very large proportion of their contributions to Democrats (see Table 7.2). Critics charged that this practice frequently affected their legislative judgment, and Democrats were not particularly anxious to adopt new campaign-finance laws that would have restricted PAC giving. When Democrats became a minority after the 1994 elections, by contrast, most business PACs started to give a lot more of their money to Republicans—and Democrats became much more favorably disposed toward regulations limiting PACs.

There is widespread public dissatisfaction with the role of PACs in campaign finance. The popular perception of campaign contributions is that they buy elections or buy support from elected officials. The PAC problem is somewhat exaggerated by the popular media, however. Most research has failed to establish a significant relationship between contributions and legislative votes.[38] PAC contributions tend to be small and are intended as a way of gaining access to public officials. Moreover, there is evidence that politicians extort PACs, pressuring them to buy tickets to fund-raisers and otherwise to make contributions as a condition of continued access. For example, a former congressional staffer told one of us the following story:

Political Action
Committees

> In our office we loved the FEC [Federal Election Commission] reports. We'd comb through
> them and list all the business groups who had contributed to our opponent. Then we'd call
> them up and say, "Hey, we noticed that you contributed to our opponent's campaign. The
> Congressman just wants you to know that there are no hard feelings. In fact, we're holding a
> fund-raiser in a few weeks; we hope you'll attend and tell us your concerns."

TABLE 7.2		
BUSINESS PAC CONTRIBUTIONS TEND TO FOLLOW POLITICAL POWER—WHEN CONTROL OF CONGRESS CHANGED, SO DID THE PATTERN OF BUSINESS CONTRIBUTIONS		
	Percentage of Contributions to Republicans Jan.–Feb. 1993 (Democratic majority)	Percentage of Contributions to Republicans Jan.–Feb. 1995 (Republican majority)
American Dental Association	27	90
American Bankers Association	52	87
American Hospital Association	53	81
Ameritech	35	79
AT&T	36	79
American Institute of CPAs	45	87
Home Builders	45	71
Realtors	75	91
RJR Nabisco	69	81
United Parcel Service	55	78

SOURCE: Jonathan Salant and David Cloud, "To the 1994 Election Victors Go the Fundraising Spoils," *Congressional Quarterly Weekly Report*, April 15, 1995: 1057.

Thus, influence runs in both directions; elected officials are not just pawns to be moved around by interest groups. Furthermore, at the risk of sounding too complacent, we suggest that reformers have not identified a clear means to keep money out of politics. In fact, the proliferation of PACs is partly an unintended consequence of a previous attempt to reform campaign finance![39]

Persuading the Public

issue advocacy
Advertising campaigns that attempt to influence public opinion on an issue.

In recent years, what has come to be called **issue advocacy** has grown in prominence: Groups conduct advertising campaigns designed to move public opinion in regard to some policy proposal. This interest-group strategy overlaps somewhat with grassroots lobbying; the homeschool story was an example of interest groups persuading ordinary Americans that congressional actions directly threatened their interests. Estimates are that about $150 million was spent on issue advocacy in the 1996 presidential campaign and $260 million during the 1998 congressional campaigns. These amounts were greatly exceeded during the 2004 campaigns: spending totaled more than $610 million, or about $475 million when state candidates and parties were excluded.[40]

Interest Groups
and Campaign Finance

Many groups communicate with citizens even when no specific legislation or regulation is at issue. Their goal is to build general support for the group and its interests so that it will be more successful in the long run. Thus, in the 1970s, the Mobil Oil Corporation began paying to have columns printed on the Op-Ed page of the *New York Times*. Sometimes these were "advocacy ads" directed specifically at a government activity or proposed law, but more often they were what are now called "infomercials"—attempts to convey information and arguments favorable to business in general and to the oil industry in particular.

Exploiting Guilt

AARP announces an advertising program designed to promote the reform of California nursing homes. The slogan, "It could be your Mom's last Home . . . " was fairly successful; their effort led to new legislation.

• *What emotions and fears are most common in interest-group appeals? Are these tactics good or bad for political discourse?*

Interest-group advocacy has become increasingly aggressive. Elected officials today rarely have the luxury of "down time" between campaigns. They never know when a group might launch an issue-advocacy campaign against them even if an election is far away. For example, during the California energy crisis in the spring of 2001, a group representing energy companies and Republicans ran attack ads against Governor Gray Davis, even though Davis was barely halfway through his term. They were attempting to "soften him up" long in advance of the Republicans' even choosing a candidate to oppose him. Davis won his reelection bid, but the critical ads may have contributed to his low popularity—which eventually resulted in a recall election that booted Davis from office.

One communications technique that is a product of modern electronic communications is **direct mail**.[41] Groups compile computerized mailing lists of people who might be favorably disposed toward their leader or cause and then send out printed material soliciting financial contributions. Often, in an attempt to scare or provoke the recipient into contributing, the mailing exaggerates the threat the group faces. Some groups depend almost completely on direct-mail fund-raising for their budgets. The citizens group Common Cause, for example, prides itself on its dependence on small contributions.[42] Once again, the rise of the Internet makes the direct-mail strategy both easier and cheaper. Tabulating who visits various Web sites makes it possible to compile e-mail lists and contact prospective supporters for a much lower cost than that of traditional "snail mail" campaigns.[43]

Finally, any group likes to have favorable media coverage for its activities and points of view. Thus, groups are always on the lookout for opportunities to get such coverage—to plant stories, to associate themselves with popular issues and candidates, and to position themselves as opponents of unpopular issues and candidates. In sum, whether we call it public relations or education, communication with a wider audience is a significant concern for many interest groups.

direct mail

Computer-generated letters, faxes, and other communications to people who might be sympathetic to an appeal for money or support.

Direct Action

direct action
Everything from peaceful sit-ins
and demonstrations to riots and
even rebellion.

Successful
Interest Groups

As noted in Chapter 2, the original 13 colonies cast off British authority in a violent revolution, the Constitutional Convention was in part stimulated by Shays' Rebellion, and the newly established federal government was tested by the Whiskey Rebellion. But these early conflicts were by no means the end of **direct action** by citizens opposed to government policies. Urban workers rioted against the Civil War draft in 1863. In the 1880s and 1890s, state or federal troops battled strikers from West Virginia to Idaho and from Michigan to Texas. In 1932, more than 20,000 veterans marched on Washington and were dispersed by federal troops.[44]

Usually, tactics such as boycotts, sit-ins, marches, and demonstrations appeal to the members of social movements. They may be too disorganized to use established means of influencing government, or they may lack access to the resources needed to exploit other political strategies. Occasionally, however, organized interest groups do take advantage of the drama of direct action. Usually they do so in combination with attempts to persuade larger constituencies. The media—TV in particular—find direct action newsworthy. (See the accompanying *Democratic Dilemma*.)

Litigation

As we shall see in detail in Chapter 17, the modern civil rights movement followed a careful legal strategy, selecting cases to litigate that eventually led to the landmark 1954 ruling *Brown v. Board of Education of Topeka, Kansas*. Drawing lessons from the success of the civil rights movement, environmentalists, feminists, advocates for the handicapped, poor people, and other groups followed suit.[45]

Litigation strategies are by no means limited to groups ordinarily thought of as liberal. In the 1970s the Pacific Legal Foundation was set up to oppose environmental protection groups. The U.S. Chamber of Commerce established a National Chamber Litigation Center to support business interests in the courts. And the religious right founded the Christian Legal Society, which focuses on issues of church and state.[46] Liberal groups continue to be more active in the courts, perhaps because they tend to find a friendlier audience among the members of the legal profession, but conservatives sometimes win important courtroom victories.

In addition to actually litigating cases, which is an expensive activity, interest groups engage in other activities intended to influence the course of litigation. Although it is improper to lobby judges directly, groups stage demonstrations in front of courthouses, generate letters and telegrams to judges, and file *amicus curiae* (a Latin term meaning "friend of the court") briefs in cases in which they are not otherwise directly involved.

Why Groups Use Particular Tactics

Different groups use different strategies or mixes of strategies. How they decide to allocate their resources depends both on their own characteristics and on the characteristics of the political situation in which they are operating.

Group Characteristics   How a group decides to deploy its resources depends on what kind of group it is, what kind of resources it has, and how much it has in the way of resources. A trade association representing profitable corporations will have a

DEMOCRATIC DILEMMA

Strange Bedfellows:
The Battle for Seattle, 1999

Politics sometimes makes for strange bedfellows. One dramatic example came in the "Battle for Seattle" in December of 1999. The World Trade Organization (WTO), an organization dedicated to removing barriers to free trade, scheduled its "millennium round" of talks in Seattle. The meetings were expected to produce further trade agreements that would be a public-relations boon to the Clinton administration, which lobbied behind the scenes to have the talks called "the Clinton round." By the time the meetings adjourned in a shambles, however, they had become a public-relations disaster. Some critics suggested that they should be remembered as the "Tear Gas Round."[a]

Ten thousand protesters disrupted the meetings, and a few ran wild in the streets of Seattle, smashing windows and looting stores. The protesters were mobilized by an extremely diverse set of groups. Labor unions claimed that trade agreements exported American jobs to low-wage countries where workers were exploited. Although often opposed to labor, some environmental groups now joined forces with unions, contending that free-trade agreements in practice operated to override domestic environmental protection laws. Both attacked the WTO as a secretive international organization that operated in the shadows and threatened American sovereignty. This sort of argument normally is made by groups on the right wing of American politics, who at various times have charged that the United Nations, the Brookings Institution, and the Trilateral Commission are fronts for international conspiracies aimed at subjugating the United States. The WTO meetings brought all these strange bedfellows together. One militia member commented on the strangeness:

> "I'll be honest—I don't really know many people like the ones here," said Butch Razey, commander of the Yakima County Militia, who attended the protest on orders from superiors in Montana. "We're willing to die for our Constitution, and the patriots are all coming out because they know this is the beginning of world government. But

Globalization Protest Garb
Not since the 1960s have Americans seen such militant protestors, obviously dressed to sharpen their message about the WTO.

> I'll be honest—this will be the first time I'll be holding hands with a bunch of tree-huggers."[b]

Wrote one observer,

> As militia members milled with black-clad anarchists and topless environmentalists . . . , it was clear that American protest had entered uncharted territory.[c]

Encouraged by their success in Seattle, leaders of environmental and labor groups have continued their collaboration against globalization and free trade.

• *Do diverse protest coalitions present any particular challenge to the major political parties?*

• *Could an anti-globalization constituency be organized into an effective third party?*

• *Does this kind of protest represent democracy working or democracy breaking down?*

[a] Charles Pope, "Will Labor–Green Alliance Succeed in 2000?" *Congressional Quarterly Weekly Report*, December 11, 1999: 2959.
[b] Charles Duhigg, "Seattle Dispatch: Means of Dissent," *The New Republic*, December 20, 1999: 14.
[c] Ibid.

Washington office with a full-time staff of experts. This gives such associations the wherewithal to maintain close personal contact with government decision makers. A mass-membership group may find grassroots lobbying a more effective use of its resources. A public-interest law firm with no citizen membership will naturally follow a litigation strategy; indeed, the group may have been formed by lawyers precisely because they wished to engage in such activities. A social movement representing a disadvantaged constituency such as the poor may find that direct action is the only means of calling attention to its cause. Wealthy groups of any size or type may find campaign contributions and media campaigns to be useful investments.

Some observers suggest that groups with a federal structure—local chapters under a national leadership—have a fund-raising advantage because contributions are solicited by people personally known to members rather than by an impersonal mailing. In addition, such groups have chapters in many communities and therefore are constituents of a large number of representatives, which may give them an advantage in grassroots lobbying. Interest groups representing realtors, doctors, and banks are good examples.

Situational Characteristics   One of the reasons why the civil rights movement adopted a litigation strategy was that more traditional strategies were unavailable. African Americans were disenfranchised in much of the South and were politically discriminated against elsewhere. In the Congresses of the 1940s and 1950s, the path of civil rights legislation was blocked by senior committee chairmen from the South. African Americans as a group were not wealthy, and they were a small minority of the population. By choosing to litigate, they made a virtue out of necessity. Then, as the movement gained support and won legal backing for its political activities, it was able to engage in direct action and later in electioneering to advance its goals further.

In contrast, an industry or corporation interested in the fine details of a bill or regulation may find it better to send an expert representative to discuss the matter with members of Congress and their staff or with regulators. Studies show that corporations spend much more on lobbying than they do on campaign contributions, probably reflecting their interest in legislative detail as opposed to their interest in the general ideological position of the legislator.[47]

Direct mail and other modern advertising and persuasion techniques were developed largely by conservative groups, probably because for 40 years Congress was controlled by Democrats who had little sympathy for their demands. Republicans have controlled the House since 1994, and the Senate for all but two years since 1994, so perhaps conservative groups now engage in more direct lobbying. Conversely, having no access to the Republican congressional leadership, liberal groups may have shifted resources to alternative methods of exerting influence.

In sum, various situational characteristics—party control of Congress and the presidency, the economic situation, the mood in the country, what the interest group seeks to achieve—interact with characteristics of interest groups to determine what mix of strategies the groups adopt.

How Influential Are Interest Groups?

Comparing
Interest Groups

The answer to this question is a matter of enormous disagreement. On the one hand, some critics believe that interest groups dominate American politics. One critic charges that the United States suffers from "demosclerosis," a condition in which interest groups clog the veins and arteries of the body politic.[48] Another claims that Americans have the best Congress money can buy.[49] Certainly the number of groups, the volume of their activities, and their massive expenditure of resources amount to strong circumstantial evidence that groups and associations are very influential in politics.

On the other hand, academic research yields less clear conclusions. Indeed, some of the most expert students of interest-group politics contend that a great deal of what groups do is canceled out.[50] There are so many groups, and so many *opposed* groups, that the efforts of one association's high-priced lobbyist only offset the efforts of another's, one group's media campaign only counteracts the effects of another's, one group's direct-mail barrage only neutralizes the effects of another's, and so on.

Even if the overall picture is ambiguous, it seems clear that changes in American politics have diminished the influence of interest groups in at least some areas. In particular, various changes have undermined the classic "subgovernments" that were described by an earlier generation of political scientists.

Subgovernments

Observers of American politics in the 1940s and 1950s often concluded that "subgovernments" dominated important areas of public policy.[51] In the idealized **subgovernment** three collective actors worked hand in hand to determine policies:

- A *congressional committee* provided an executive agency with program authorization and budgetary support,
- The *executive agency* produced outcomes favored by an interest-group constituency, and
- The *interest groups* provided the members of the congressional committee with campaign contributions and votes.

subgovernment
Alliance of a congressional committee, a bureaucratic agency, and a small number of allied interest groups that combine to dominate policy making in some specified policy area.

Subgovernments allegedly dominated critical policy areas such as agriculture, public works, and business regulation. In the most extreme cases, subgovernments were called "iron triangles" (see Chapter 14) in recognition of the difficulty faced by outsiders who wished to break into the cozy relationship uniting legislative committees, executive agencies, and interest groups.

Interest groups played a central role in this story because they were the outside actors who worked with executive and legislative officials to achieve favorable policy. Whatever their importance in the past, however, subgovernments are less important today. First, as we shall see in Chapter 12, Congress has changed. The party caucuses and leadership are stronger and the committees weaker; particular committees no longer have strangleholds on their jurisdictions.

Interest Groups
and Representation

Second, there are many more groups now, including many who oppose other groups. In particular, citizens groups representing consumers, environmentalists, and taxpayers are much more active now than they were a half-century ago. They oppose the excesses of special-interest politics and publicize their opposition.

Third, as we discuss in Chapter 9, the focus of the media has changed with time. In particular, contemporary journalists are very much on the lookout for stories of special-interest profiteering at the expense of general interests. In the spring of 1996, for example, the media helped kill an attempt by the House Agriculture Committee to aid milk producers in raising prices by quietly including a helpful regulation in the agriculture bill then under consideration. Dan Rather discussed the "attempted rip-off of the consumer" on his evening news program, and in the wake of the publicity, the attempt collapsed.[52] Iron triangles thrive when they operate behind the scenes; they melt in the glare of publicity.

Issue Networks

issue network

A loose constellation of larger numbers of committees, agencies, interest groups, and policy experts active in a particular policy area.

In the view of many scholars, subgovernments have been superseded by issue networks—bigger, broader, and much looser connections of interest groups, politicians, bureaucrats, and policy experts who have a particular interest in or responsibility for a policy area.[53] Given the enormous number and variety of interest groups today, the proliferation of legislative staff and other policy experts, and the interactions between policies in one area and those in another, issue networks are much more open than subgovernments and much less stable in their composition. Interests do not play such a central role in this new policy environment. They must compete with public officials and technical experts, as well as each other, in an effort to influence public policy.

The academic community today clearly leans toward thinking of policy environments as networks rather than as iron triangles, but not everyone agrees with this conclusion. On the one hand, some scholars suggest that even the term *network* may exaggerate the degree of organization that characterizes interest-group activity in Washington today.[54] On the other hand, some scholars emphasize that organized interests directly shape laws and regulations in new policy areas such as energy and social regulation.[55] In short, judgments about the general importance of interest groups remain as divided as ever.

Probably the safest conclusion about the power of interest groups is that influence is conditional: It ranges from weak to strong, depending on the conditions under which groups try to influence politics. Schlozman and Tierney conclude that groups are most influential when they act on low-profile issues, when they attempt to block action rather than originate it, when they are unopposed by other groups or politicians, and when they have plentiful resources.[56] Once again, the real world of American democracy is more complicated than many popular commentators suggest.

Interest Groups and Democratic Politics

Even the generic term *interest group* has a negative connotation, and terms such as *pressure group*, *vested interest*, and *special interest* have pronounced negative connotations.[57] Why do contemporary Americans hold interest groups in such low regard? After all, the Constitution protects the rights of citizens to work together to try to influence government. The First Amendment guarantees freedom of religion, speech, and the press, but it also prohibits any law abridging the "right of the people peaceably to assemble and to petition the government for a redress of grievances." Interest groups are the mechanism for exercising that right.

pluralism

A school of thought holding that politics is the clash of groups that represent all important interests in society and that check and balance each other.

Political scientists generally have not held interest groups in as low regard as ordinary citizens have. In fact, one mid-century school of thought, **pluralism**, celebrated the role of groups in American politics.[58] The pluralists believed that American politics should consist of an interplay of numerous interests. In this view, virtually everyone is represented in a dense network of groups, no single interest is dominant, and all are required to bargain and compromise. Moreover, groups exercise countervailing power; if one interest or set of interests becomes too powerful, others mobilize to counteract it. As a consequence, public policies tend to be moderate and to change incrementally. That is, the system tends to do a good job representing the broad range of interests in the country.

Pluralism is out of fashion today. Critics cite several problems with the pluralist account. We have already discussed the first, the unrepresentativeness of the interest-group universe. As critic E. E. Schattschneider once observed, "The flaw in the pluralist heaven is that the heavenly chorus sings with a strong upper-class accent."[59] Because of the free-rider problem, small special interests have an advantage over large general interests. In particular, economic groups procure narrow economic benefits at the expense of the broader population of consumers and taxpayers. This is probably one reason why the term *interest group* has negative connotations in the popular mind; people see that most groups do not represent the general interests of Americans.

Pluralism

A second objection to the pluralist account would still apply even if interest groups were more representative: The interest of the whole nation is not equal to the sum of the interests of the parts. In our discussion of public opinion, we pointed out that majorities of Americans want to cut government spending and reduce government regulation, but majorities oppose specific cuts and reductions. Thus, if Congress heeds all the wishes of individual constituencies, it will displease the country as a whole by maintaining a bigger budget and more intrusive government than a majority desires.

Trade is another example. If the government erected a system of trade barriers to protect every American industry from foreign competition, the result would be retaliation against American exports, higher prices for consumers, and slower economic growth (if not worse). As Schattschneider long ago pointed out, a Congress operating according to pluralist principles enacted just such a trade policy in 1930—the Smoot-Hawley tariff, a policy that deepened and lengthened the Great Depression.[60] Simply adding up group interests is not enough. Ideally, politics harmonizes and synthesizes particular interests and incorporates them into the general interest of the nation.

A third criticism of pluralism is that a politics dominated by interest groups distorts political discussion and (ultimately) the political process. The reason is that groups reinforce extremism and undercut moderation. Ordinary citizens have multiple attachments and affiliations, which generally serve to moderate their outlooks. A retired couple, for example, might naturally favor higher social security and Medicare expenditures. But, if they also are parents and grandparents, they might accept more modest benefits for themselves to avoid higher taxes on their children or lower government expenditures on their grandchildren's schools. Leaders of interest groups, by contrast, act in someone else's interest. Typically, they see their job as maximizing group benefits. Thus the leadership of a senior citizens group will be more supportive of higher benefits for the elderly than will many of its members. For example, AARP has been attacked as an organization composed of "tax-loving former teachers and government employees" who favor an "age-based welfare state."[61] This sharply worded attack was used by the National Taxpayers Union, an opposing interest group concerned with taxes.

This crowding out of moderate demands by more extreme ones is reinforced by the tendency of group activists and leaders to be more extreme in their views than are nonmembers or even rank-and-file members. Thus, they push their demands beyond the point where ordinary members and sympathizers would stop. Some activist supporters of the ERA suggested that it would send women into combat on the same basis as men:

TABLE 7.3		
GROUP ACTIVISTS AND LEADERS HOLD MORE EXTREME VIEWS		

Political activists are generally more extreme in their views than the people they purport to represent. For example, this table contrasts the issue disagreement between Republican and Democratic delegates to the 2004 national conventions with that between self-categorized Republicans and Democrats in the population at large. The activists differ far more than ordinary partisans do

	Delegate Difference	Identifier Difference
Government Should Do More to Solve National Problems	72	13
Cut Taxes to Improve the Economy	67	35
Make All or Most Tax Cuts Permanent	88	35
Abortion Should be Generally Available	62	32
New Anti-Terrorism Laws Excessively Restrict Civil Liberties	62	28
Extremely Important to Work Through the UN	72	35
No Legal Recognition of Gay Relationships	44	19
Government Should Do More To Promote Traditional Values	40	35

Source: Fiorina, Abrams, and Pope, *Culture War? The Myth of a Polarized America* (Longman, 2005).

"[C]ombat duty, horrendous as it might seem to all of us, must be assigned to persons on a gender-neutral basis."[62] Most American women and men preferred something less than such full equality. Environmentalists exaggerate environmental threats (see Table 7.3), while their opponents discount real threats. The minorities on the extremes of the pro-choice and pro-life debate polarize the debate and drown out the three-quarters of the population who could satisfactorily compromise on it (see Chapter 5).

In the end, the general interests of a moderate population can get lost amid the bitter fighting of intense and extreme special interests. No one can deny that groups have a useful and legitimate role to play in articulating the interests of all components of American society, but many feel that groups somehow must be constrained. One of the first pluralists, James Madison, thought factions would be limited in an extended republic that covered a wide geographical area (as he explained in "The Federalist No. 10," printed in Appendix III of this book). He did not foresee several modern developments.

First is the tremendous expansion of society that contributed to the explosion of groups. The range of interests active today probably would shock someone like Madison, who thought in terms of broad interests such as land, labor, and commerce, or debtors and creditors. Second is the prevalence of logrolling. Rather than check and balance each other, interest groups often cooperate, forming coalitions to exploit the general interests of consumers and taxpayers by getting higher prices and tax breaks.[63] Logrolling among interests is facilitated by a third development, the rise of professional politicians who, in seeking reelection, broker the group deals in return for the electoral support that interest groups provide.

But what can be done? As the critics look over the experience of democratic governments, they see only one means of controlling group demands that is both democratic and effective. Ironically, it is an institution that George Washington warned the country about—political parties, the subject of the next chapter.

Chapter Summary

Only half the American citizenry votes in presidential elections, and only small minorities engage in other forms of political participation. But most Americans participate indirectly in politics by joining groups that attempt to influence government. In fact, Americans are more likely to participate indirectly through groups than are citizens of other democracies who vote at higher levels.

In the past generation, there has been a major increase in the number of interest groups. Successful groups have found ways to overcome the free-rider problem, the tendency of people to benefit from group activity without contributing to its costs. Some of the groups rely on selective benefits that are available only to group members, whereas others depend on the efforts of dedicated or wealthy members who will bear more than a proportionate share of the costs of group maintenance.

Group characteristics and their situations lead them to adopt a variety of political strategies. Grassroots lobbying involves attempts to influence elected officials indirectly by mobilizing constituents; traditional lobbying involves attempts to influence elected officials directly by speaking personally to them. Increasingly, groups engage in electioneering—contributing money to candidates and spending money independently to elect officials sympathetic to their interests and

views. Groups also attempt to persuade or educate the public, and some resort to direct action—demonstrations, protests, and the like—to call attention to their positions. Finally, some groups end-run the political process and attempt to influence government through the courts.

Despite extensive study of interest groups, there is wide disagreement about how influential they are. In general, popular commentators view them as more powerful than do academic researchers. There is no doubt that groups engage in an incredible amount of political activity and invest a great deal of money and other resources, but it is difficult to say how effective they are. For every issue that interest groups apparently dominate, skeptics can cite another issue on which interest groups seem to be ineffectual or to offset each other's efforts.

Many social critics worry about the overall effect of interest-group activity, though. First, special interests are better represented than general interests. Second, even if that were not so, the interest of the nation as a whole is not merely the sum of the interests of the particular parts. Third, interest groups support extreme positions in political debate and thus polarize political discussion, injecting excessive conflict into the political process.

Key Terms

direct action, p. 196
direct mail, p. 195
free-rider problem, p. 184
grassroots lobbying, p. 191
interest group, p. 179
issue advocacy, p. 194

issue network, p. 197
lobbying, p. 189
lobbyist, p. 189
political action committee
   (PAC), p. 192
political entrepreneurs, p. 188

public goods, p. 185
selective benefits, p. 187
single-issue group, p. 181
social movement, p. 186
subgovernment, p. 199

Suggested Readings

Of General Interest

Baumgartner, Frank, and Beth Leech. *Basic Interests.* Princeton, NJ: Princeton University Press, 1998. Comprehensive review, critique, and synthesis of the interest-group literature.

Schattschneider, E. E. *The Semisovereign People.* New York: Holt, 1960. A delightful essay that remains timely. Argues that the pressure system of interest groups is biased and that the result is an artificially constricted range of political conflict in the United States.

Skocpol, Theda. *Diminished Democracy.* Norman, Oklahoma: University of Oklahoma Press, 2003. Describes the evolution of interest groups from mass membership associations to top-heavy organizations managed by professionals, and considers the consequences of this transformation for American democracy.

Walker, Jack. *Mobilizing Interest Groups in America.* Ann Arbor: University of Michigan Press, 1991. Explores the Washington interest-group universe. Notable for discussion of outside support for establishment of groups.

Focused Studies

Freeman, Jo, and Victoria Johnson. *Waves of Protest*. Lanham, MD: Rowman and Littlefield, 1999. Useful collection describing the social movements active since the 1960s.

Mansbridge, Jane. *Why We Lost the ERA*. Chicago: University of Chicago Press, 1986. Thoughtful discussion of the narrow failure of the women's movement to win passage of the ERA. Argues that the movement overcame the free-rider problem by emphasizing the symbolism of the ERA, a strategy that precluded compromises that would have led to passage of the amendment.

Smith, Mark. *American Business and Political Power*. Chicago: University of Chicago Press, 2000. Argues that when business interests are united they are less influential, because the issues that unite business divide the political parties and arouse public opinion.

Wright, John, *Interest Groups and Congress*. New York: Longman, 2003. Discussion of interest group politics in the contemporary Congress that puts special emphasis on the political and institutional context in which groups organize and act.

On the Web

As we have noted, the Internet has been a valuable tool for interest groups. It has reduced organization and communication costs tremendously. It is no exaggeration to say that an interest group is probably not much of an interest group until it has its own Web page. (The reverse is not true, however; it is so easy to have a Web page these days that merely possessing one does not qualify a group as an interest group.) It would take too much space to list all of the interest groups with a presence on the Web.

www.aarp.org
www.aflcio.org
www.ama-assn.org
www.sierraclub.org
www.uschamber.org
www.now.org

www.cc.org

A sample of the most important interest groups with a presence on the Web are the American Association of Retired Persons, AFL-CIO, Sierra Club, U.S. Chamber of Commerce, National Organization for Women, and Christian Coalition of America.

www.vegan.org
www.deathwithdignity.org
www.anarchy.no
www.atheists.org

A few less prominent groups, the very existence of which testifies to the power of the Internet to reduce organizational costs, are Vegan Action (pro-vegetarian lifestyle), Death With Dignity National Center (pro-assisted suicide), Anarchy.org, and American Atheists.

CHAPTER 8

★ ★ ★ ★ ★ ★ ★ ★ ★ ★

Political Parties

CHAPTER OUTLINE

A Tale of Two Conventions

A Tale of Two Conventions The Democrats and the Republicans held spectacular national conventions in the summer of 2004 to pick their presidential nominees. Both parties spent millions of dollars to kick off the general election in style—filling their convention halls with red, white, and blue banners, with thousands of balloons, and with shouting delegates wearing colorful jackets and funny hats. A series of political celebrities marched to each convention podium and gave fiery speeches to stir up the party faithful and attract uncommitted voters. It was as close as political parties get to throwing the nation a real party.

Despite all the hoopla, few Americans watched the celebration. On average, the three major television networks gave the national conventions only three hours each over a four-day span. There is little reason to believe that this limited attention left hordes of Americans clamoring for more. Only 31 percent of respondents told pollsters with the Vanishing Voter Project that they intended to watch the upcoming conventions.[1]

Voters cannot be blamed for skipping the national conventions. All the spectacle aside, the conventions offered minimal political drama. George Bush and John Kerry both had clinched their party's nominations five months earlier, after primary wins that gave each candidate a majority of his party's delegates. The vice-presidential candidates added little mystery; Kerry had named his running mate long before the convention and Bush was running with Vice President Dick Cheney again on the ticket. Nor did the events feature enough conflict to make up for the lack of surprise. Both campaigns kept a tight lid on dissident elements within the party. There were no floor fights over policy planks in the platform. No one contested the seating of any delegates. The conventions were basically long, expensive infomercials showcasing the party and its candidates.

Contrast these media events with the 1952 political conventions. That year, the three networks averaged 60 hours of convention coverage, essentially televising them from the opening gavel to the closing gavel (something only C-SPAN does now). There was no huge cable television industry in those days—if families wanted to watch TV, they had only one feasible option: the nominating conventions. Why were earlier conventions deemed so newsworthy? Basically, they made more important decisions.

At the Democratic convention of 1952, four serious rivals vied for the nomination. Senator Estes Kefauver of Tennessee, who had achieved prominence investigating organized crime and who campaigned in a coonskin cap, led on the first two ballots, but he could not secure a victory. Some minor candidates then withdrew and delegates flowed to President Truman's choice for the nomination, Governor Adlai Stevenson of Illinois. Stevenson, a northern liberal, won a narrow majority on the third ballot. Only then did Americans learn Stevenson's choice for the vice-presidential nomination: Senator John Sparkman of Alabama, whose conservatism could balance the ticket.

The Republicans had a simpler choice. Senator Robert Taft of Ohio—known as "Mr. Republican" for his long service—faced a challenge from a man who had declared his GOP affiliation less than a year earlier: General Dwight Eisenhower, a popular World War II hero. Party insiders backed Taft, but the Republicans also wished to regain the White House after a 20-year absence. When Eisenhower's supporters challenged the seating of delegates from three pro-Taft states, they won the battle. Eisenhower still failed to attain a majority on the initial vote, but minor candidates threw him enough support that he won before a second official balloting became necessary. Eisenhower then named his running mate: a young anticommunist senator from California, Richard Nixon.

Why did no one know in advance who the nominees would be? In those days there was no permanent campaign. Few states held primaries and the existing primaries selected few convention delegates. The great majority of delegates were party officials, loyalists, contributors, and influential politicians appointed by state and local party leaders. They were free to wheel and deal at the conventions, exchanging their support for promises of future political payoffs. Thus, campaigns took shape more slowly. In contrast to today's candidates, who begin organizing in the early primary states 18 months before the election, Stevenson never entered a single primary. Eisenhower was still serving as Supreme Allied Commander of NATO six weeks before winning the nomination!

Today the labels are the same as they were in 1952: "Democrats" and "Republicans." In fact, they have not changed since the nineteenth century. But the Democratic and Republican parties of 1952 looked more like those of 1852 than they resemble the parties navigating today's permanent campaign. This chapter tells the story of how and why American parties changed so radically over such a short span of time.

MAKING THE CONNECTION

All modern democracies have parties. Traditionally defined as groups of like-minded people who band together in an attempt to win control of government, political parties serve as the primary connection between ordinary citizens and the public officials they elect. They nominate candidates for office. They mobilize voters. And after elections have determined the winners, parties coordinate the actions of elected officials in the government. In this chapter we address the following questions about political parties:

- Are parties essential to democratic politics?

- How have parties shaped the political history of the United States?

- Why does the United States have only two major parties?

- How do today's parties differ from those of earlier eras?

- How influential are parties today in American politics?

What Parties Do

To political commentators in most self-governed societies, democracy is unimaginable without **political parties**. The European University Institute, a research arm of the European Community, published a four-volume study on political parties that called them "the central institutions of democratic governments," the "working mechanism" of liberal democracy.[2]

Many American professors hold similar views. Political scientist E. E. Schattschneider devoted much of his life to making the case for the vital role played by political parties. In introducing his classic work *Party Government*, he wrote, "This volume is devoted to the thesis that political parties created democracy and that modern democracy is unthinkable save in terms of the parties."[3]

For contemporary Americans, though, life without political parties is not so unthinkable. Americans rely on representative assemblies such as Congress to serve as the centerpiece of democratic government. They inhabit a political world populated by many institutions cut off from parties, such as popular initiatives, independent judges, and nonpartisan local elections. When asked directly about political parties, most Americans do not sing their praises. Indeed, surveys have shown that many Americans think government would be better without parties.[4] Could they be right, and the scholars and

political parties
Groups of like-minded people who band together in an attempt to take control of government. Parties represent the primary connection between ordinary citizens and the public officials they elect.

commentators wrong? To answer that question, this section describes both the positive and the negative functions performed by parties within the political system.

How Parties Contribute to Democratic Politics

What do parties offer to make most Europeans and some Americans think they are essential for democratic government? The general answer is that, except at the local level, a democracy that relied on the activities of individuals and interest groups would be too disorganized to operate. Politicians create parties to *organize* political life, and parties do so by carrying on a series of activities.[5]

Organizing and Operating the Government   Parties coordinate the actions of hundreds, indeed thousands, of public officials. This role is particularly noticeable in legislatures: with the exception of Nebraska, which is formally nonpartisan, every American legislature is organized on an explicitly partisan basis. The presiding officer, who generally determines the agenda (what issues get considered and when), is usually the leader of the majority party (the party that won a majority of the seats in the last election). The committee chairs, who control committee agendas and hire most committee staff, are also all members of the majority party. To a great extent, the American political system also counts on parties to help make sure that the different branches of government work together at some reasonable level of effectiveness. At each level of government, executives count on the support of their fellow partisans in the legislature, and legislators trust the information they get from their fellow partisans in the executive branch. Parties also coordinate activities across levels of government. In 1995, for example, Democratic governors convinced some Democratic members of Congress that they should support far-reaching welfare-reform proposals. Similarly, local officials appeal to their partisan allies in the state governments, and the latter appeal to their partisan allies in Congress. American government often appears disorderly, but many political scientists believe it would be absolutely chaotic without parties.

Focusing Responsibility for Governmental Action   Party labels operate much like brand names. Just as consumers might favor a reputable brand or avoid buying a brand that has sold poor merchandise in the past, voters judge Democrats and Republicans collectively.[6] The actions or performance of one leader influences the reputation of fellow party members seeking office. Parties therefore strive to fashion a record they can defend at the polls, which requires members to maintain a degree of unity. To paraphrase Ben Franklin, party members either hang together or they hang separately. President George W. Bush was able to rely on congressional support for his controversial tax-cut proposals in part because other Republicans recognized the need for his administration to create a record of accomplishment.

Developing Issues and Educating the Public   Parties engage in a continual battle for control of public offices, and they sharpen their issue positions as weapons in this struggle. They identify problems, publicize them, and advance possible solutions. Much of their motivation is adversarial, somewhat like a court proceeding in which the opposing lawyers present their cases, but the outcome of the competition can be beneficial. It generates information, educates the public, and shapes the policy agenda. Where parties are weak, as in the American South during the first half of the twentieth century, politics degenerates into a battle over personalities and private benefits rather than public issues.[7]

Synthesizing Interests   Good public policy must be more than the sum of various people's demands (see Chapter 7). Satisfying every specific interest can detract from the general interest. Also, some conflicting interests cannot be satisfied simultaneously; they require compromise. Translating societal demands into public policy therefore must go beyond simple addition to a more difficult and subtle kind of synthesizing or harmonizing. The major parties sometimes perform this critical role while trying to construct successful national coalitions. They develop platforms that offer a mix of benefits and burdens to all. When their platforms appear too focused on pleasing identifiable special interests, parties suffer electorally—as the Democrats did in 1984 and the Republicans did in 1996.

Political Parties:
State Control and
National Platforms

Recruiting and Developing Governmental Talent   There is an old adage in politics: "You can't beat somebody with nobody." Even if an elected official appears vulnerable, voters may continue to return that incumbent to office unless they are offered a plausible alternative—someone with the background and qualifications to hold the post.[8] Thus, parties are always on the lookout for promising candidates. They may make a special effort to recruit candidates who will improve the party's image, as the Republicans did in 2000 by trying to expand their pool of black candidates.[9] The parties keep track of the weak members in the opposition and bring along potential replacements from their own ranks. Like predators in the natural environment, parties help strengthen public service by weeding out the weak.

Simplifying the Electoral System   Imagine that there were no parties to winnow the field of candidates. Rather than choosing between two options for most offices, voters might be faced with a multitude of choices, each supported by a tiny slice of the electorate. Furthermore, the candidates would lack party labels, which otherwise help voters anticipate each candidate's beliefs. Neither major party is homogeneous, of course, but the labels *Democrat* and *Republican* do convey a good bit of information. As we write this book in mid-2006, we have no idea who the Democrats and Republicans will select as their presidential candidates in 2008. But we can predict, with a considerable measure of confidence, that the Democratic candidate will take the pro-choice position on abortion while the Republican candidate will be pro-life, that the Republican candidate will be more opposed to tax increases, that the Democratic nominee will be more supportive of national health insurance, and so on across a considerable range of issues. In the absence of parties, therefore, Americans would have to work much harder before knowing how to vote.

How Parties Detract from Democratic Politics

Despite the valuable organizational functions that political parties can perform, Americans are traditionally suspicious of parties and, since the end of the nineteenth century, have held them in relatively low esteem. Part of this scorn results from the fact that parties do not always perform the valuable functions of which they are capable. After all, politicians do not organize parties because they want to simplify the electoral system, recruit talent, or synthesize interests. They give structure to political life only insofar as such activities help them gain power.[10]

Thomas Jefferson nurtured the Democratic-Republican Party as a way to wrest power from the Federalists. Abraham Lincoln used the new Republican Party to

Presidential Primary Candidates

The 2004 Democratic presidential contenders offered party members a variety of ideologies and a variety of personal styles.

overthrow a Democratic majority. Theodore Roosevelt established the Bull Moose Party because he could not win the GOP nomination. Once in office, public officials work to maintain their parties because parties help them govern. Andrew Jackson used the spoils of victory to consolidate his party's majority, as did the Republicans in the aftermath of the Civil War. Franklin Roosevelt used New Deal policies to strengthen the Democratic Party in electorally critical locales.[11]

Although party leaders may view their partisan activities as furthering the public interest, their opponents seldom agree. But even voters on the winning side may be critical of parties, because party influence is a double-edged sword. Parties strong enough to perform beneficial functions are also strong enough to abuse their power. Each of the positive functions that parties can perform can be corrupted, and unfortunately, American history provides numerous such examples.

Capturing Governments and Dictating What They Do   At a certain point, coordination becomes control. A strong party that controls its members can force elected officials to stick with the desires of the leadership and ignore the wishes of voters back home (especially when candidates of the other party are equally unresponsive). At its extreme, party dominance becomes the equivalent of an elected dictatorship. In the contemporary House of Representatives, for example, both Democrats and Republicans, when they have been in the minority, have charged that the majority party was using its control of the agenda to prevent certain issues and bills from being considered and to prevent a fair vote on the minority's preferred amendments. In the early 1900s, Progressives leveled a similar charge against the urban machines that ruled many American cities. Despite facing periodic elections, the machines kept a stranglehold on elected offices through the calculated distribution of jobs, contracts, and other patronage. When private payoffs failed, they often exploited illegal methods for maintaining power—including vote fraud and police intimidation. They would even look the other way while their thugs beat up voters in strategically selected precincts.

Confusing Responsibility Because credit for good times and blame for bad times are valuable political currencies, the parties attempt to "manufacture" responsibility. Opposition members may blame the incumbent administration for events over which it had no control. Incumbents, in turn, may take credit for positive outcomes not of their making. Worse, rather than helping to solve a public problem, opposition parties may concentrate on undercutting the governing party's proposed solutions. The Republicans used this tactic with President Clinton's health-care plan in 1994, and the Democrats used it with the Republican attempt to control entitlement spending in 1995. The temptation to torpedo the other party's initiatives is especially strong when **divided government** exists—when one party holds the presidency but does not control Congress—as was the case early in George W. Bush's presidency as well as for most of the 1980s and 1990s. Under such conditions, voters are unsure how to assign responsibility for government inaction.[12]

divided government
Said to exist when a single party does not control the presidency and both houses of Congress.

Suppressing the Issues For various reasons, parties may prevent the political system from addressing new issues. The leadership of both parties may fail to appreciate new developments in society because they have grown out of touch, or they may ignore issues that threaten the internal harmony of both parties. For example, the two major parties avoided the slavery issue during the first half of the nineteenth century, when they both contained members from the North as well as the South. Today, Democratic and Republican candidates almost uniformly resist reforming programs for the elderly, promising instead to "protect Social Security and expand Medicare," because neither party wishes to risk antagonizing senior citizens. Often it takes outsiders to force an issue onto the public agenda.[13]

Dividing Society Rather than synthesize disparate interests into some larger whole, parties may do just the opposite. They may create or exacerbate social divisions as a means for gaining electoral advantage. President George Washington suggested as much two centuries ago. "The spirit of party," Washington warned during his farewell address, "agitates

Polarized Perceptions
As George Washington warned, political parties often have a vested interest in fomenting disagreement. In 2006, as this cartoon suggests, Republicans tended to underestimate the seriousness of the federal budget deficit, while Democrats frequently overstated its significance.

Celebrity Politician
Former weight-lifter/movie star Arnold Schwarzenegger touring California as he starts his successful re-election campaign in 2006.

the community with ill-founded jealousies and false alarms, kindles the animosity of one part against another, [and] foments occasional riot and insurrection."[14] Since the late 1960s, Democrats have periodically charged that Republican candidates try to inflame racial resentments (and, more recently, public feelings against homosexuals) in order to attract votes from people who might otherwise favor the Democrats. For their part, Republicans often claim that Democrats attack corporations and the wealthy in ways that are economically misleading but nevertheless appeal to poor and working class voters.

Recruiting Candidates for the Wrong Reasons   Parties usually seek candidates who can win. In competitive environments, therefore, the desire for success may prompt parties to nominate seasoned leaders or to recruit accomplished political newcomers known for their intelligence, integrity, and good judgment. On the other hand, neither experience nor ability guarantees popularity—and sometimes potential candidates are popular for reasons that have nothing to do with their aptitude at governing. Celebrities, such as entertainers and former athletes, enjoy a distinct advantage in an electoral politics driven by media and money. California Governor Arnold Schwarzenegger may be the most obvious current example, but Congress has seated movie actors (Sen. Fred Thompson), TV stars (Rep. Fred Grandy, Rep. Sonny Bono), and astronauts (Sen. John Glenn, Sen. Harrison Schmitt), as well as former stars of the NBA (Rep. Tom McMillan, Sen. Bill Bradley), the NFL (Rep. Jack Kemp), and major-league baseball (Sen. Jim Bunning). Well known? Yes. Qualified? Sometimes. In less competitive environments, meanwhile, parties may promote mediocre people characterized more by their unwavering partisanship than by their skills.

Oversimplifying the Electoral System   The voter who must choose between two candidates, one labeled Democrat and one labeled Republican, has a clearer and apparently easier choice than the voter who can choose among many candidates with no labels. But what if she doesn't like that clear but restricted choice? What if she is a pro-choice Republican or a pro-life Democrat? That's just tough. If there are only two major parties, she has only two serious alternatives. Her choice may be simple, but it also may be quite unsatisfactory.

The Balance Sheet

Given the conflict, who is correct—the scholars who champion political parties or the critics who think parties hinder democracy? Probably the safest answer is "both."

When evaluating political parties, most scholars have usually asked whether having parties is better than not having them at all. Overwhelmingly, they have concluded that it is better to have them. The functions performed by political parties are necessary for the successful operation of the political system, and scholars see no alternative institution prepared to perform those functions. They also are more likely to realize that parties inevitably act according to their political interests. They do not assume, naively, that a few legal changes suddenly will compel parties to promote the public good. Indeed, they recognize the danger of misconceived reforms, which may fail or even produce nasty unintended consequences.[15] Certainly scholars can risk becoming too complacent, confusing the way things are (which they may have devoted a lifetime to studying) with the way things ought to be. Nevertheless, they are right to value the important organizing role carried out by political parties.

Reformers focus on the failures of existing parties, the ways in which they detract from democratic government. Reformers run little risk of becoming complacent. Indeed, for many social critics, their fame and fortune depend on an ability to identify social problems. As part of this effort, reformers have publicized many real imperfections in how parties operate within the political system: abuses of power, gridlock that keeps problems unsolved, partisanship that makes political life unsavory, scandals and inefficiencies that alienate the public from their government. Certainly reformers can be too quick to demand radical change. They may not anticipate or care about the full consequences of the reforms they embrace. In particular, they do not bear the burden of identifying alternative institutions that could replace parties. Nevertheless, they are right to worry about the extent to which existing political parties undermine representation rather than promote it. As a result, the debate over party reform will continue.

Political Parties in American History

The contemporary American lack of enthusiasm for parties is somewhat ironic, given that the United States pioneered the mass parties that are an essential component of politics in modern Europe. Indeed, parties have organized American elections since the time of George Washington. At first the parties were composed of political notables who supported leaders such as Jefferson and Hamilton, and had little or no local, grass-roots organization. Such personal followings were the democratic counterparts of the "court" parties of monarchical governments—the groups of nobles who engaged in "palace intrigues" (and sometimes paid with their lives for their "treasonous" plotting).

Difference Between
Democrats and Republicans

American parties did not stay limited to national big shots for very long. During the administration of Andrew Jackson (1828–1836), the Democratic Party spread outward from Washington and downward into the grassroots, a movement soon imitated by its adversaries, the Whigs. The kinds of mass parties that were contesting American elections by the 1840s and 1850s did not become common in Europe until half a century later. As late as 1889 Lord Bryce, the famous English political commentator, could observe that, "In America the great moving forces are the parties. The government counts for less than in Europe, the parties count for more."[16] Today, of course, the first part of the statement remains true: The government counts for less than in Europe in the sense that the public sector in the United States is smaller. But the second part of Bryce's statement can be turned around: The parties also count for less than in Europe. American parties now are weaker than most of their European counterparts, and they are weaker than those of other economically developed democracies such as Japan and South Korea.

Still, above the local level, nearly all American public officials are elected as Democrats or Republicans. Unlike Europeans, Americans may not *believe* that parties are essential to democracy—but in practice parties seem to be as pervasive as in Europe. Indeed, political historians of the past generation have developed general accounts of American history organized around the concept of "party systems."[17] These accounts describe the important role the political parties, appreciated or not, have played in American history.

The Party-Systems Interpretation of American History

Political change occurs constantly. Individuals float in and out of the electorate, or from one party to another—actions that cause election results to vary—but the system as a whole usually remains fairly stable. The same people tend to vote for the same parties, and the same parties tend to win in the same places. Occasionally, however, the political system undergoes changes that are more sudden and more sweeping. Large groups may swing their support from one party to another. Republican areas can become Democratic ones, and vice versa.

realignment
Occurs when the pattern of group support for political parties shifts in a significant and lasting way.

"**Realignment**" scholars have tried to formalize the study of political change by dividing American political history into a series of distinct electoral eras, or "party systems."[18] They argue that each of these party systems is a time of general stability. In particular, four stable characteristics characterize a party system.

1. *The identities of the major parties*. While minor parties may come and go, the two major contestants for national power stay the same.
2. *The parties' relative balance of strength*. In most party systems, one party is the majority party: that is, it wins most elections. The other party comes to power only when it can capitalize on errors by or divisions within the dominant party. The years between 1876 and 1892 are, as we will see, a partial exception to this statement, when the Democrats and Republicans competed on remarkably even terms. Yet even then, the balance was stable: Neither party was able to gain a large, lasting advantage over the other.
3. *The major issues*. Parties are organized around issue disagreements. And while some issues are significant only for a very brief period of time (this is especially true in foreign policy), each party system has generally centered on one or two core concerns that are debated, in one form or another, in election after election. During the so-called New Deal party system, for example, Democrats and Republicans regularly disagreed about the role the federal government should play in regulating and controlling the national economy, with the Democrats always favoring a more extensive role for government and the Republicans invariably urging a greater reliance on private enterprise and individual initiative.
4. *The party coalitions*. Because the parties take the same relative positions on the major issues, they also tend to attract or repel the same kinds of voters. Within each party system, certain kinds of voters are reliable supporters of one party or the other, while others split their votes more evenly. This pattern means that there is considerable geographic stability from election to election: Each party has its core areas of support, while other areas are seen as contested or "battleground" regions.

critical election
Election that marks the emergence of a new, lasting alignment of partisan support within the electorate.

These stable electoral eras or party systems theoretically could dissolve rather gradually. In fact, however, party systems have ended rather suddenly. One or a very small number of **critical elections** takes place, decisively marking the end of one party system and the beginning of another. According to some scholars, these major changes in the party system, generally called realignments, take place with a surprising degree of regularity—about once every 30 years or so. Though according to most analysts the realignment is anticipated by underlying social changes that gradually make the old alignment less relevant, it is usually triggered by a crisis, such as a major depression, that divides the existing parties and increases popular interest and participation in politics. Although defining "critical elections" or "electoral eras" is a tricky business, and some scholars doubt that it is possible to do so without oversimplifying political history,[19] the party-systems interpretation nevertheless provides a useful way to remember how party competition has changed over time (see Table 8.1).

	TABLE 8.1					
THE PARTY-SYSTEMS INTERPRETATION OF AMERICAN ELECTORAL HISTORY						
	Number of Presidential Elections Won by Each Party		Number of Times Each Party Won a Majority of Seats in the House of Representatives		Number of Times Each Party Won a Majority of Seats in the Senate	
First Party System 1796–1824	Democr-Republs	7	Democr-Republs	13	Democr-Republs	13
	Federalists	1	Federalists	2	Federalists	2
Second Party System 1826–1858	Democrats	6	Democrats	13	Democrats	15
	Whigs	2	Whigs	2	Whigs	2
			Republicans	2		
Third Party System 1860–1894						
1860–1872	Republicans	4	Republicans	7	Republicans	7
	Democrats	0	Democrats	0	Democrats	0
1874–1894	Republicans	3	Democrats	8	Republicans	9
	Democrats	2	Republicans	3	Democrats	2
Fourth Party System 1896–1930	Republicans	7	Republicans	13	Republicans	15
	Democrats	2	Democrats	5	Democrats	3
Fifth Party System 1932–1966	Democrats	7	Democrats	16	Democrats	16
	Republicans	2	Republicans	2	Republicans	2
Sixth Party System 1968–???	Republicans	7	Democrats	13	Democrats	10
	Democrats	3	Republicans	6	Republicans	9

SOURCE: Compiled by the authors based on data in *Guide to U.S. Elections*, 5th ed. (Washington, D.C.: CQ Press, 2005).

The First Party System (Jeffersonian)   Most historians believe that the first party system began in the early 1790s and lasted until about 1824.[20] Though George Washington hoped to rule without parties, early in his first term a series of major controversies began to divide both Congress and Washington's own cabinet. One set of officials, centered on Treasury Secretary Alexander Hamilton, hoped to use the power of the new federal government to encourage commercial and manufacturing interests. To accomplish this, they supported such policies as the creation of a national bank, the assumption of state war debts, and a high protective tariff. Generally known as the Federalists, Hamilton and his supporters favored a broad reading of the Constitution and a foreign policy that sought closer ties with Great Britain, then the world's dominant economic power. In reaction to Hamilton's early successes, a second set of officials gradually coalesced around Secretary of State Thomas Jefferson, though James Madison, then a member of the House of Representatives, also played a prominent role in the development of this opposing coalition. Usually referred to today as the Democratic-Republicans, the Jeffersonians hoped to keep the United States a predominantly agricultural country; adopted a much narrower, "strict" reading of the Constitution; and wanted a foreign policy that was more favorable toward France than toward Great Britain. The Federalists accordingly drew their greatest support from areas with strong commercial interests, especially New England, while the Democratic-Republicans dominated the more rural and agricultural areas of the new nation.

The Federalists and Democratic-Republicans competed on relatively even terms for about eight years. In some ways, partisan competition has never been as bare-knuckled as it was early in the first party system. In 1798, when it seemed that the United States might go to war against France, the Federalists passed the Sedition Act, which imposed criminal penalties on anyone who wrote, spoke, or published "any false, scandalous, and malicious writing" against any member or branch of the federal government. As one historian has summed up the intent of this law, it equated "Republican criticism of [Federalist] policies with a traitorous loyalty to the nation's enemy."[21] All this set the stage for the presidential election of 1800, perhaps the most bitter and divisive in all of American history, in which the Federalists accused Thomas Jefferson, the Democratic-Republican candidate, of being an atheist who desired to transport the terrors of the French Revolution to American soil. In return, Jefferson's partisans accused incumbent president John Adams, the Federalist candidate, of trying to establish an American monarchy. After a tie in the electoral college, and 35 ballots in the House of Representatives, Jefferson was finally declared the victor.

Though it wasn't immediately obvious, the 1800 election marked the end of the Federalist Party as a significant force in American national government. Federalists never won another presidential election, and soon dwindled to a very small minority in both houses of Congress. Historians have identified a number of reasons for the collapse of the Federalist Party. In part, they were simply on the wrong side of the issues, supporting commercial and manufacturing interests in an overwhelmingly rural and agricultural society. The Federalists also suffered from relatively weak leadership, particularly after Alexander Hamilton, their dominant personality and leading policy spokesman, was killed in a duel in 1804. By 1816, the United States had become, in effect, a one-party nation, in which virtually every important politician and office holder considered himself a member of the Democratic-Republican Party. As a result, the years between 1816 and 1824 are often called the "Era of Good Feeling." But if this period was free from partisanship, it was not an era of particularly good government. The United States suffered its first major economic depression and also had to deal with its first major sectional crisis, as northern and southern congressmen struggled over how to deal with slavery in the territory of Missouri. (The dispute was ultimately settled by the so-called Missouri Compromise of 1820.)

The Second Party System (Jacksonian Democracy)   Parties are held together, to a large extent, by fear of the opposition. When a contemporary presidential candidate seeks to rally his own party behind him, one of his most potent appeals is the argument that, whatever his limitations and weaknesses, he is better than the candidate of the opposition party. Thus, with the Federalist Party no longer a serious contender for national power, the Democratic-Republicans also began to come apart. In the presidential election of 1824, the congressional caucus, the official nominating body of the Democratic-Republican Party, endorsed William Crawford, the Secretary of the Treasury. But with no worry that partisan disunity might elect a Federalist, three other candidates also ran for president, each of whom also claimed to be a member of the party of Jefferson and Madison.

Andrew Jackson, the only great military hero from the War of 1812, won the most popular and electoral votes, but his electoral vote total fell well short of the majority required by the Constitution. As specified in the Constitution, the choice was then made by the House of Representatives, which gave the nod to John Quincy Adams. Believing that they had been deprived of the presidency by a "corrupt bargain" between Adams and Speaker of the House Henry Clay, who was later named Secretary of State, Jackson and his supporters almost immediately began organizing for the 1828 election. Buoyed by a huge increase in turnout, Jackson won a decisive victory.

Jackson proved to be a strong but controversial president, and out of the support for and opposition to his policies came the second party system. Jackson and his supporters called themselves the Democrats. His critics were initially known as the National Republicans, but eventually settled on the name Whigs. The principal dividing line between the Democrats and the Whigs was the use of the federal government to promote national economic development, by financing such "internal improvements" as roads, bridges, and canals, using tariffs to protect infant industry from foreign competition, and rechartering a national bank. The Whigs favored such policies; the Democrats believed that these matters were better left to the states. The two parties also disagreed about the extent of presidential power, with the Democrats supporting a more vigorous and active role for the nation's chief executive. One issue that did not separate the parties was slavery. Both parties contained active opponents and strong supporters of slavery. Hence, both parties did their best to straddle the issue, generally contending that the Constitution gave the federal government no power to interfere with the institution where it already existed and otherwise trying their best to keep the issue off the congressional agenda. Those wishing to express opposition to slavery in a presidential election thus turned to third parties: the Liberty Party in 1840 and 1844, the Free Soil Party in 1848 and 1852.

Unlike the Federalists and Democratic-Republicans, the Democrats and Whigs were parties built on mass participation. Both parties had extensive grassroots organizations in every state. To coordinate their presidential campaigns, both parties developed **national nominating conventions** and national committees, institutions that are still used today. As the figures in Table 8.1 show, however, the competition was not an even one. The Democrats were the dominant party of the second party system. The only time the Whigs won the presidency was when they nominated a war hero: William Henry Harrison in 1840 and Zachary Taylor in 1848. The Democrats also won regular majorities in both the House and the Senate.

national convention
Quadrennial gathering of party officials and delegates who select presidential and vice-presidential nominees and adopt party platforms. Extension of the direct primary to the presidential level after 1968 has greatly reduced the importance of the conventions.

The Third Party System (Civil War and Reconstruction)   Try as they might, the Democrats and Whigs could not keep slavery out of national politics forever. The key sticking point was the question of how to deal with slavery in the territories that were being regularly added to the United States throughout the first half of the nineteenth century. Although the Constitution did not give the federal government any obvious way of regulating or outlawing slavery in the states, it did give Congress (in Article IV) the power "to dispose of and make all needful Rules and Regulations respecting the Territory . . . belonging to the United States." Ever since the Missouri Compromise of 1820, most Americans had regarded it as settled policy that slavery was forbidden everywhere in the Louisiana Purchase territory north of Missouri. In 1854, however, Democrats in Congress and the White House passed the Kansas-Nebraska Act, which allowed settlers to bring slaves into both of those territories.

The turmoil that followed shattered what was left of the Whig Party. Meetings and conventions, held all over the North, sought to bring together Whigs, disaffected Democrats, and Free Soil party members—everyone who was opposed to the Kansas–Nebraska policy. Over the next several years, these groups gradually coalesced into the Republican Party.

Unlike the Whigs and Democrats, the Republicans were a highly sectional party. Both of their first two presidential nominees did not win a single popular vote in 10 different southern states. They were, however, very strong throughout the North. In 1860, Abraham Lincoln won only 40 percent of the national popular vote—but he won enough northern states to win a majority in the electoral college.[22]

Third Parties

As the figures in Table 8.1 indicate, the third party system is perhaps best thought of as comprising two distinct subperiods. Between 1860 and 1872, the Republicans dominated both Congress and the presidency—but much of their success was attributable to the fact that the most Democratic region of the country, the South, had seceded from the Union. Once Reconstruction was over and federal troops were withdrawn from the former Confederate states, however, the two parties competed on remarkably even terms.[23] Of the next five presidential elections, Republicans won three and the Democrats two—but all of these elections were very close and two of the Democratic losers actually won a plurality of the popular vote. In Congress, Democrats won regular majorities in the House of Representatives while the Republicans exercised a similar dominance in the Senate.

Between 1860 and 1876, the dominant issue in American politics was the Civil War and then the Reconstruction of the South, but after 1876 economic issues took center stage. The rise of large business organizations, industrialization and its associated dislocations, and a long agricultural depression inevitably raised questions about how the national government should relate to the U.S. economy. The third party system was also the time when party organizations reached their high point. Bitter memories of the Civil War left many people committed to the party of the Union (Republicans) or the party of the rebels (Democrats), and intense electoral competition encouraged these committed citizens to vote a straight party line. Indeed, independents often were viewed contemptuously as "traitors." With feelings so strong, the parties exerted tremendous effort in campaigns, with most of that effort being devoted to the mobilization of the faithful, rather than the conversion or persuasion of the undecided.[24] Parties reached such a high level of organization in many cities that they were referred to as **machines**.[25]

machine

A highly organized party under the control of a boss, and based on patronage and control of government activities. Machines were common in many cities in the late nineteenth and early twentieth centuries.

The Fourth Party System (Industrial Republican)   Once again, the party system was unable to contain or adapt to new pressures. Partisan divisions rooted in the Civil War seemed increasingly outmoded as the United States emerged as an industrialized nation. The excesses and corruption of the urban machines spawned reform movements aimed at destroying their influence. Agricultural protest, common throughout the period, gave rise to a Populist Party that seriously challenged the major parties in the South and West.

The event that finally brought an end to the third party system was the severe depression that hit the country in the early 1890s—to that point, the worst depression in American history. The Democrats, as the party that then controlled the presidency and both houses of Congress, naturally were blamed for the country's economic crisis. Their

1896 presidential candidate, William Jennings Bryan, though a hero to many farmers and evangelical Protestants, had a style that repulsed many Catholics and urban workers. The upshot was that a small but critical segment of the nonsouthern electorate jumped from the Democratic to the Republican Party—and the Democratic Party ceased to be competitive in most areas of the North. The Democrats retained their monopoly control over southern politics and had pockets of strength in many large cities, but most elections between 1896 and 1928 resulted in Republican presidents and Republican majorities in both houses of Congress. The Democrats won the presidency only twice during the fourth party system: in 1912, when Woodrow Wilson emerged the victor in a three-way race with President William Howard Taft and ex-President Theodore Roosevelt, which split the Republican Party, and again in 1916, when Wilson was narrowly reelected on a platform of keeping the United States out of World War I.

One of the most significant political forces during this period was a loose aggregation of politicians, political activists, and intellectuals known as the **Progressives**. There were prominent Progressives in both parties; other Progressives were non-partisan and even anti-partisan. The Progressive movement drew most of its supporters from the urban middle-class, and tried to solve a host of problems connected with the industrialization and urbanization of America that occurred in the second half of the nineteenth century. The Progressives' most important legacy is the long list of political reforms they championed in an effort to "clean up" elections and government administration—initiatives and referendums, direct primaries, nonpartisan elections, voter registration systems, the Australian ballot, city managers, and the commission form of government. Though contemporary historians and political scientists generally portrayed the Progressives in very positive terms, more recent commentators have often noted a dark side to these "reforms," which often served to push ordinary citizens out of politics and made it more difficult for lower- and working-class ethnic neighborhoods to secure adequate representation.[26]

The Progressives undermined two principal resources used by political parties to maintain power: control of public employment and control of nominations. Civil service reforms begun at the national level with the Pendleton Civil Service Act of 1883 were extended wherever possible, diminishing the spoils the parties had available to distribute to their members. The **direct primary** system, which allowed voters instead of party leaders to choose nominees for office, weakened party control of nominations and hence the influence that parties could exercise over officeholders. The Progressives attacked the urban machines with demands for nonpartisan elections, and they provided tools of direct democracy such as the initiative, referendum, and recall as a way for voters to get around elected officials. The reforms targeted real corruption, but they also weakened the mobilizing agents that brought many low-income and low-status people into politics.

The Fifth Party System (New Deal)   Like its predecessor, the fourth party system was brought to an end by an economic depression—the Great Depression of the 1930s, the worst in the nation's history. In November 1930, with the Depression barely a year old, the Republicans lost 53 seats and control of the House of Representatives. The elections of 1932 swept in a Democratic Senate and, more importantly, made Franklin D. Roosevelt president, a man who was determined to fight the Depression with a much more active use of the federal government.

The Tammany Tiger

Urban political machines often appeared to threaten the nation's democratic institutions. Here, a cartoonist depicts New York City's Tammany Hall machine as a tiger.

- *Political parties may be effective at organization, but at what point does the political system become too organized?*

Progressives

Middle-class reformers of the late nineteenth and early twentieth centuries who weakened the power of the machines and attempted to clean up elections and government.

direct primary

A method of choosing party candidates by popular vote of all self-identified party members. This method of nominating candidates is virtually unknown outside the United States.

VIDEO DEBATE

Poverty and
Political Parties

The New Deal period instituted a class-based party system that resembled electoral alignments in modern European democracies. After Roosevelt's first term, the Democrats became the party of the "common" people (blue-collar workers, farmers, and minorities), while the Republicans became, more than ever, the party of business and the affluent. The former accounted for a lot more voters than the latter, leading to a period of Democratic dominance not seen since before the Civil War. Only Republican war hero Dwight Eisenhower was able to crack the Democratic monopoly, which he did in 1952 and 1956. Republicans controlled Congress for only two terms, from 1947 to 1948 and in 1953–1954.

Besides economic issues, foreign policy also occupied a prominent place on the agenda of the New Deal party system. Starting in the late 1930s, the United States had to decide whether and how to get involved in the wars that had broken out in Europe and eastern Asia, waged all-out war in both areas from 1941 to 1945, tried to set up a set of institutions that would bring peace and prosperity to the postwar world, and then found itself compelled to lead the democratic forces in a "Cold War" against the Soviet Union and China. Most of these issues, however, were handled in a relatively nonpartisan fashion, leaving politics to the domestic economic issues that favored Democrats.

But racial divisions slowly eroded the Democratic Party's electoral coalition. The New Deal coalition that Roosevelt put together in the 1930s included a remarkable diversity of groups that had in little in common except their dislike of Republicans and, to a lesser extent, a general proclivity for liberal economic policies. In particular, the Democrats drew strong support from both the white South (blacks were almost completely excluded from voting in that region) and the increasing number of northern blacks who had migrated to American cities in search of greater opportunity. After trying for a considerable period to avoid or straddle racial issues, the Democrats finally decided, at their 1948 national convention, to include in their national platform a plank calling for "full and equal political participation" and "the right to equal opportunity of employment" for all Americans. Many southern delegates walked out of the convention and later nominated Governor J. Strom Thurmond of South Carolina as the States' Rights or "Dixiecrat" candidate for president. From that point forward, the South was, at best, an uneasy partner in the Democratic electoral coalition. Though southern voters continued to elect Democrats to the House and the Senate, Republican presidential candidates were, for the first time, able to break the Democratic monopoly on the once-solid South.

The Sixth Party System   Most commentators believe that the New Deal party system is gone, but they are in less agreement about what sort of party system has replaced it—or even if one has. The electoral alignments that began to develop in the late 1960s have puzzled scholars for much of the past generation because they do not resemble realignments of the past.

What has changed since the heyday of the New Deal party system?[27] The most obvious change has been in the parties' electoral coalitions. During the New Deal—indeed, well before it—Democratic presidential candidates, no matter what their problems, could almost always count on a solid vote from the South. In Franklin Roosevelt's four presidential elections, his *worst* showing in the eleven former Confederate states was in Tennessee in 1944—and he still won more than 60 percent of the vote. Republican candidates such as Dwight Eisenhower and Richard Nixon managed to win a few southern states, such as Tennessee and Florida, but up through 1964, every Democratic presidential candidate in the twentieth century carried a majority of the southern states. Since 1968, by contrast, only one Democratic candidate—Jimmy Carter in 1976—has won a majority of southern states. Five different Democratic candidates did not carry a single southern state.

Though their geographic implications are somewhat less glaring, other important changes have also occurred in the party electoral coalitions. Whereas Republican candidates once won about a third of the black vote, now they win about one-eighth of it. Catholics have shown an increasing proclivity to vote Republican. New England, once the most solidly Republican region in the country, now gives a regular majority of its electoral votes to the Democrats.

The issue agenda has also changed. Though New Deal-type economic issues remain an important subject of debate between the parties, they have been joined by a large set of social or cultural issues—crime, abortion, gay rights, pornography, school prayer, affirmative action—that were largely absent from national politics until the mid-1960s. In addition, foreign policy has lost its consensual, nonpartisan character. Since the early 1970s, Republicans have generally advocated larger defense budgets and a more aggressive use of American military strength, while the Democrats have shown a greater preference for negotiations and the use of multilateral organizations such as the United Nations.

Perhaps the most difficult question to answer is whether and how the balance of strength between the parties has changed. Between 1968 and 1988, Republicans won five of six presidential elections, several by landslide margins, suggesting that Democratic dominance of presidential elections had come to an end and leading some commentators to predict, rather rashly, that the Republicans now had a "lock" on the electoral college. Yet Bill Clinton's triumphs of 1992 and 1996 showed that Democratic presidential candidates could also do quite well in the post-New Deal system. The disputed election of 2000 and the closely fought contest of 2004 clearly establish, at a minimum, that there is no Republican "lock" on the contemporary presidency.

Any argument that the late 1960s had ushered in a new, Republican era was further undercut by the results of congressional elections. From 1968 through 1992, the Democrats retained a pretty firm hold on Congress. The 1980 elections did bring in a Republican majority in the Senate, but it lasted only six years. That aside, Democrats seemed to have a stranglehold on Congress, particularly the House of Representatives. Many political scientists accordingly labeled the new party system as the era of "divided government," when voters would regularly elect Republican presidents and Democratic Congresses. This result occurred because of a sharp increase in **ticket-splitting**, as many Americans voted for a Republican presidential candidate and a Democratic candidate for the House and/or Senate. Yet this verdict also proved to be temporary. In 1994, the Republicans unexpectedly won majorities in both the House and the Senate, and with a brief exception in the Senate, have held onto those until 2006.

ticket splitting
Occurs when a voter votes for candidates of different parties at the same election—for example, a Republican presidential candidate but a Democratic candidate for the House of Representatives.

So what should we make of the electoral era that has held sway since 1968? As late as the mid-1980s, there were some political scientists who argued that nothing very fundamental had changed—that we were still living in the New Deal party system, albeit in an extended, "decay phase" of it.[28] But as electoral changes have accumulated, and particularly after the Republicans won control of both houses of Congress, it has been more and more difficult to defend such a claim. Instead, most contemporary analysts adhere to one of two schools of thought.

On the one hand, many scholars believe that a realignment did occur in the late 1960s and early 1970s, with 1968 generally singled out as having the best title to having been a "critical" election. The major problem with this diagnosis concerns the timing

DEMOCRATIC DILEMMA

Is Gridlock Necessarily Bad?

Political scientists traditionally have viewed "party government" as superior to a more individualistic, candidate-centered politics. From this perspective, elections should consist of cohesive parties competing for control of public offices by offering distinct policy proposals. The electorate should compare the parties' platforms, choose the one that seems best suited for the time and conditions, and give it full control of our national elective institutions—both the presidency and Congress. Such unified control would enable parties to act vigorously and efficiently when they take office, and voters would know exactly whom to credit or blame for the actions of the government.

The American parties became increasingly cohesive and programmatic beginning in the late 1960s, but voters did not follow the professors' advice. Instead, as the major parties became more distinct and more cohesive, voters increasingly split their tickets. The country entered an era when, more often than not, control of national elected institutions was split between the two parties, with the Republicans generally winning the presidency and the Democrats the Congress.

Logic might suggest that divided governments should produce gridlock (because the institutions fight rather than cooperate) and irresponsibility (because the parties blame each other for inaction). Not every researcher agrees with this supposition. Yale University political scientist David Mayhew, for example, probed the legislative record and concluded that the national government was just as likely to pass major legislation under divided government as under unified government.[a] But the bulk of the evidence does seem to reinforce the traditional belief that divided authority hampers governance. For example, influential research by James Alt and Robert Lowry shows that divided state governments adjust their budgets more slowly and are less able to avoid deficits. They also appear to be less accountable for their economic policy failures.[b]

Why don't American voters take the professional advice available to them and regularly vote to install unified governments, as they did in 2002 and 2004? Do they not realize that divided government might create gridlock? One possible explanation is that, unlike political writers inside and outside academia, the general public may not consider gridlock such a bad thing. Polls repeatedly report that majorities of Americans favor divided government. They view it as a way for one party to keep the other in check, preventing abuses of power, watching for scandalous or corrupt behavior, and vetoing the more extreme ideological indulgences of the opposition.

• *Do you think electoral politics should be guided by the clash of party ideologies and that candidates should take strong stands on the issues of the day?*

• *Do you think voters would support unified government more often if the parties nominated more middle-of-the-road candidates who offered moderate issue positions?*

• *Does a divided government make it more difficult for voters to know whom to credit or blame?*

[a] David R. Mayhew, *Divided We Govern* (New Haven: Yale University Press, 1991).

[b] James E. Alt and Robert C. Lowry, "A Dynamic Model of State Budget Outcomes Under Divided Partisan Government," *Journal of Politics* 62:4 (November 2000): 1035–1069; Alt and Lowry, "Divided Government, Fiscal Institutions, and Budget Deficits," *American Political Science Review* 88:4 (December 1994): 811–828; Lowry, Alt, and Karen E. Ferree, "Fiscal Policy Outcomes and Electoral Accountability in American States," *American Political Science Review* 92:4 (December 1998): 759–774.

---

of the key changes in electoral behavior and how extensive they were. While the late 1960s clearly did usher in a series of major changes in the general pattern of presidential voting, similar changes, as we have seen, did not occur—at least at that time—in elections for the House, Senate, state legislatures, or any other set of "sub-presidential elections." Republicans did not start to show sustained strength below the presidency until 1994; the substantial Democratic advantage in mass partisanship, as we will see in Chapter 10, did not begin to change until 1984.

There are a number of plausible ways that one can explain why the presidential-level changes took so long to trickle down through the rest of the party system.[29] But one core component of the original theory of realignment was precisely the notion that change occurred very suddenly. In the early 1930s, for example, the Democrats went from being an apparently hopeless minority to having unified control of the federal and most state governments in the span of about three years. If change occurs gradually, over a period of two or three decades, does it make sense to keep using the term realignment to describe it?

Faced with this sort of problem, other political scientists have argued that the whole theory of realignments is now outdated (indeed, may never have been valid). Electoral change undoubtedly does occur, but not in the kind of regular, thorough-going way that the proponents of realignment envision. Yet many of the scholars who pronounce realignment dead nevertheless continue to use terms such as "party system" and "electoral era" to characterize both the broad sweep of American electoral history and the changes that have occurred since the 1960s.[30] That history, in the eyes of most observers, is not merely a succession of small, unconnected changes. Some changes are more important and more lasting than others, and thus make it difficult to resist the idea that it is possible to speak of distinct periods or eras in the history of American political parties.

One key issue that divides these two schools of thought is whether one can characterize the years since 1968 in any kind of simple, unified way. And that, in turn, depends in part on what happens in the future. If the Republicans regain their hold on Congress and win the presidency in 2008, it will seem plausible to argue that we are in an electoral era dominated by the Republicans. Only time will tell.

Two-Party and Multi-Party Systems

Americans understandably regard a **two-party system** as a natural state of affairs. As the description of party systems showed, for the more than two centuries of the country's history, two major parties have dominated elections for national office, although third parties regularly arise (see Table 8.2). Several third parties, such as the Progressive Party and the Green Party, have influenced the outcomes of some American elections,

two-party system
System in which only two significant parties compete for office. Such systems are in the minority among world democracies.

			TABLE 8.2		
			THIRD PARTIES BY POPULAR SUPPORT		
Year	Candidate	Party	Popular Vote (%)	Electoral Votes	Subsequent Events
1912	T. Roosevelt	Progressive	27.4	88	Supported GOP nominee in 1916
1992	R. Perot	Independent	18.7	0	Created Reform Party, which failed.
1924	R. LaFollette	Progressive	16.6	13	Robert LaFollette died in 1925.
1968	G. Wallace	American Independent	13.5	46	Dropped from 1972 election after being maimed in assassination attempt.
1848	M. Van Buren	Free Soul	10.1	0	Supporters eventually merged with Republican Party.
1892	J.B. Weaver	Populist	8.5	22	Party supported Democratic ticket in 1896.
1996	R. Perot	Reform	8.5	0	Party collapsed in 2000 elections.
1980	J. Anderson	National Unity	6.6	0	Candidate withdrew from politics.
2000	R. Nader	Green	3.0	0	Failed to qualify for 2004 federal funding.
1948	S. Thurmond	States' Rights	2.4	38	Democrats picked slate acceptable to South in 1952.
1948	H. A. Wallace	Progressive	2.4	6	Party disappeared.

NOTE: Candidates sorted by popular vote percentage.

Third Parties
in American History

but nearly all third parties disappear.[31] Only once has a third party replaced a major party: The Republicans displaced the Whigs in the 1850s. Often third parties are a reaction to a particular problem, and they fade when the problem does. If the problem persists, the third party usually is absorbed or "co-opted" by a major party, as were the Populists in the 1890s, who joined with the Democrats.

Most democracies have multi-party systems. Americans are in a minority as far as the rest of the world is concerned. Canadians, for example, spread their votes across a number of significant alternatives—including conservative, liberal, and social democratic parties as well as a reform party and a strong regional party centered in the province of Québec. When the political system offers so many options, often no single party can win control of government; rather, two or more minority parties must ally themselves and form a coalition government based on their combined parliamentary majority. In the 2005 elections for the German Bundestag, for example, the two major parties, the Social Democrats and the Christian Democrats, each won about 36 percent of the seats. The rest of the seats were won by three smaller parties, the Greens, the Left Party, and the Free Democratic Party, each of which held between 8 and 10 percent. Because no party had a majority, this meant that after the election there was a lengthy period of negotiations, as leaders of various parties attempted to put together a coalition that could control at least half of the votes in the new Bundestag. When personal antagonisms among the party leaders ruled out some of the more obvious possibilities, the Social Democrats and Christian Democrats finally decided to govern the country through a "grand coalition" of the two major parties.

Many scholars believe that the electoral system strongly affects how many parties a country can sustain. An **electoral system** is the way in which a country's constitution or laws translate popular votes into control of public offices.[32] The United States relies almost exclusively on the **single-member, simple plurality (SMSP) system**. Elections for office take place within geographic units (states, congressional districts, cities, and so on), and the candidate who wins the most votes wins the election. When only two candidates run, one candidate will win a majority; when more than two run, a simple plurality determines the winner. This electoral system is characteristic of the "Anglo-American democracies" (England and its former colonies). It is often called the "first past the post" system: Just as in a horse race, the winner is the one who crosses the finish line first, no matter how many others are in the race or how close the finish.

In most of the world's democracies, however, the electoral system is some version (there are many variations) of **proportional representation (PR)**. In such systems, elections may (Germany) or may not (Israel) take place within smaller geographic units, but even if they do, each unit elects a number of officials, with each party winning seats in proportion to the vote it receives.

To illustrate the operation of these differing electoral systems, consider an example. In the 1992 election, the state of Minnesota had 10 electoral votes. Its popular vote was divided as follows:

Clinton: 52%

Bush: 36%

Perot: 12%

Had Minnesota divided its electoral votes on a proportional basis, Clinton would have won 5 votes, Bush 4, and Perot 1. Had the same sort of system been used everywhere

electoral system

A means of translating popular votes into control of public offices.

single-member, simple plurality (SMSP) system

Electoral system in which the country is divided into geographic districts, and the candidates who win the most votes within their districts are elected.

proportional representation (PR)

Electoral system in which parties receive a share of seats in parliament that is proportional to the popular vote they receive.

in the country, Clinton would have been the leading candidate in the electoral college—but he would have fallen far short of the majority required by the Constitution. Perot, meanwhile, would have had about 100 electoral votes—giving him and his supporters the balance of power between the two major parties and perhaps allowing them to extract policy concessions or major positions in the new administration from one of the other candidates as the price of their support.

In fact, however, the election laws in Minnesota—and in almost every other state—effectively treat the entire state as if it were a single electoral unit, with all electoral votes going to whichever candidate wins the most votes, regardless of whether or not it is a majority. Thus, the actual electoral vote cast by the Minnesota electors in 1992 was Clinton 10, Bush 0, Perot 0. Aggregated across 50 states and the District of Columbia, Clinton won a comfortable majority in the electoral college even though he received just 43 percent of the popular vote. As for Perot, who won 19 percent of the popular vote, he received not a single electoral vote.

As this example illustrates, in an SMSP electoral system, winning is everything—finishing in any position but first achieves nothing. Thus, if small parties have more in common with each other than with the largest party, they have an incentive to join together in a single opposing party to challenge the plurality winner, because dividing the opposition among more than one candidate plays into the hands of the enemy. Ordinary citizens, in turn, realize that voting for a small party is tantamount to "wasting" their vote, because such a party has no chance of coming in first.[33] Thus, they tend to support one of the two larger parties. In presidential election polls, for example, the standard pattern for third-party and independent candidates is that their share of the popular vote declines steadily the closer one gets to Election Day, as more and more voters begin to appreciate that the third-party aspirants have no real chance to win and that their votes are therefore better expended on one of the major-party candidates. In 1980, for example, John Anderson had 24 percent of the vote in mid-June, 14 percent in September, 9 percent in late October, and 7 percent in the actual election.

In PR systems, by contrast, a party wins seats in proportion to its vote (as long as it finishes above some legally defined threshold). Because it is not necessary to finish first in order to win something, party leaders have more incentive to maintain their separate organizations. And, because only votes for tiny parties fail to count, voters are not motivated to abandon smaller parties. Thus a multi-party system persists.

One other factor that affects the survival of third parties in SMSP systems is whether their votes are geographically concentrated. If they receive, say, 20 percent of the nationwide vote but it is distributed evenly across the country, they win nothing. On the other hand, if their vote is regionally concentrated so that they are the first or second party in some constituencies, they may persist indefinitely. For example, modern Canadian elections have been dominated by two major parties, the Liberals and the Progressive Conservatives, which compete nationwide and ordinarily win most of the seats in Parliament. But in recent elections, two smaller parties have established regional footholds. In the French-speaking province of Québec, the Parti Québécois is the dominant party, and in some western provinces, Reform is the strongest party.

Comparing
Political Parties

The almost exclusive use of SMSP electoral systems throughout the United States is, then, an important part of the explanation for the American two-party system. And as long as these rules persist, it is unlikely that a lasting third party will ever be established in this country. Yet there are a number of other factors that also work to the disadvantage of third-party and independent candidates and may spell the difference between victory and defeat—or a strong showing and a weak showing—in a particular contest. The election laws in most states, for example, grant automatic ballot access to every party that won some minimum percentage of the vote in the last election.[34] In practice, this means that all candidates nominated by the Democratic and Republican parties automatically get their names listed on the general election ballot. Independent and third-party candidates must generally file a petition to get on the ballot—which often requires them to collect thousands of signatures, sometimes under complex, arcane regulations. In presidential elections, federal campaign finance laws are similarly stacked in favor of the major parties. The Democrats and Republicans both have their general election campaigns paid for out of the federal treasury. Third-party candidates get no government money unless they win at least 5 percent of the vote—but not getting the money in advance makes it substantially more difficult to win 5 percent.

Patterns of media coverage also tend to hurt third-party candidates. In general, major-party candidates get far more coverage on television and in the newspapers than independents and minor-party contenders. Reporters and editors defend this practice by saying that they base their coverage on the polls and other indicators of how well the candidates are expected to do on Election Day—and because third-party candidates generally lag well behind in the polls, they therefore receive less coverage. While the media's characterization of third-party support is generally accurate, it may also be self-fulfilling. At least some third-party candidates might do quite well if they received enough coverage to make the voters aware of their candidacy—but not being affiliated with one of the major parties, they never receive that coverage and therefore never break out of their low poll numbers. Similarly, televised debates, which have played an important role in many recent campaigns, are usually restricted to the major-party candidates. There is strong evidence to show that Ross Perot's remarkable showing in the 1992 election—judged by his percentage of the popular vote, Perot was the most successful third-party candidate in 80 years—owes much to the fact that he was invited to participate in all of the debates between Bush and Clinton. In 1996, by contrast, Perot was excluded from the debates, as were Ralph Nader and Pat Buchanan in 2000.

How Strong Are American Parties Today?

Had this book been written in the 1970s, one major theme of this chapter almost certainly would have been the decline and possible death of American political parties. Though there was some disagreement about how far the trend had proceeded and what, if anything, could be done to reverse it, few political analysts contested the basic pattern. By the mid-1980s, however, second thoughts had set in. Whereas an influential book published in 1971 had been titled *The Party's Over*, less than twenty years later books appeared under the titles *The Party Goes On* and *The Party's Just Begun*.[35] How did serious students of politics arrive at such widely differing viewpoints?

Part of the answer is that people have different conceptions of what a party is.[36] In most of the world, parties are well-defined organizations. People join them in the same way they join clubs in the United States: They pay dues, receive official membership cards, go to regularly scheduled meetings, and have a right to participate in various party-sponsored activities (such as nominating candidates). In the United States, however, parties have a more nebulous existence. When Americans refer to parties, they may have in mind three distinct notions (or some combination of the three):

1. The party in the electorate: those voters who feel some kind of psychological loyalty or affiliation with the party and who will, as a result, generally vote for the party's candidates.
2. The party in government: those who have captured office under the label of the party and those who seek to do so; the party's candidates for public office and its state, local, and national officeholders.
3. The party organization: the formal machinery of the party—its leaders, committees, headquarters staff, and ward and precinct workers.

The party in the electorate is discussed more fully in Chapter 10. For now, it is enough to say that the percentage of the American adult population who have a party identification—who express a psychological tie with either the Democrats or the Republicans—did undergo a noticeable decline between about 1964 and 1974. But the significance of this decline is not as great as was initially thought, because many of the new independents seem to be "closet partisans," who will admit, if given the chance, that they feel closer to one of the major parties than the other. There is also some evidence, in recent years, that parties have recouped some of their earlier losses, and that the once-substantial rate of ticket-splitting and party defection has gone down. Unfortunately, we do not have reliable survey measures of mass partisanship from the years prior to 1952, but for the years since then, perhaps the safest conclusion is that the party in the electorate has declined somewhat, but not dramatically.

As we will see in Chapter 12, there is good reason to think that the U.S. parties in government, particularly in Congress, are stronger today than they have been at any time since the early 1900s. In 1960, political scientist and historian Clinton Rossiter famously noted that one of the most striking characteristics of American parties was "their lack of ideological or programmatic commitment . . . . [Both major parties] are creatures of compromise, coalitions of interest in which principle is muted and often even silenced. They are vast, gaudy, friendly umbrellas under which all Americans, whoever and whatever and however-minded they may be, are invited to stand for the sake of being counted in the next election."[37] Today, scarcely anyone would apply such a description to either the Democrats or the Republicans. More than at any time in the twentieth century, party labels mean something: The party under which a person comes to office says a lot about the kinds of policies he or she supports.

Deciding on
a Political Party

The Decline of Party Organizations

It is more difficult to provide a clear conclusion about the growth or decline of party organizations. Historically, the United States did not have true national party organizations. Rather, what passed for national organizations were temporary alliances of state parties and local machines that joined together every four years to work for the election of a president.

Declining
Political Parties

State and local party organizations were at their strongest about the time the Progressive movement began. The decline of American party organizations was largely a consequence of deliberate public policies the Progressives instituted. As noted earlier, the two principal resources that party organizations depend on are control of patronage and control of nominations for office. The first was gradually eliminated by regular expansions of civil service protection and, after World War II, by unionization of the public sector, which gave government workers an additional layer of insulation from partisan politics. (Presently, the largest union in the AFL-CIO is the American Federation of State, County and Municipal Employees.) The final nail in the coffin came when the U.S. Supreme Court ruled that most forms of patronage are unconstitutional, because they penalize public employees for their beliefs and associations.[38] Today the president personally controls fewer than 4,000 appointments.[39] At the height of the spoils system—and with a much smaller federal government—presidents controlled well over 100,000 appointments.[40] Similarly, governors and big-city mayors who once controlled tens of thousands of jobs now control, at most, only a few thousand—and usually far less.

Party control over nominations was greatly weakened by the spread of the direct primary, one of the most important Progressive reforms. As described in Chapter 10, the United States is the only world democracy that relies on open, popular elections to decide nominations. In all other democracies, much smaller groups of party activists and officials choose party nominees.

Deprived of their principal resources, modern American parties had few sticks and carrots to sway the behavior of members. Electoral defeat did not mean that tens of thousands of people would lose their jobs; hence they were less inclined to work for parties and support them through thick and thin. Similarly, outsiders could seek a party's nomination, and if they won, the party had no choice but to live with the fact. Controlling neither the livelihoods of ordinary voters nor the electoral fates of public officials, the party organizations atrophied.

However, political reforms do not entirely explain the weakening of American parties. Other, independent developments indirectly weakened the parties. For one thing, the communications revolution lessened the need for traditional parties. Candidates could raise funds through direct-mail appeals and then use these funds to reach voters directly by computer-generated mail and television. Technological developments have diminished the need for party workers and party support. Elections rely instead on technology and money.[41] Nor do the parties control their own TV networks, as the Christian Democrats, Social Democrats, and Communists all do in Italy.

A second development that undercut U.S. parties was the increase in mobility—social, economic, and residential—that followed World War II. Better-educated voters had less need of parties to make sense of politics and guide their behavior. In a booming economy, voters had less need of parties to help them get jobs. And as the suburbs grew, the traditional, urban-based parties came to represent an ever-smaller proportion of the population, while the new, decentralized suburbs went largely unorganized.

The Revival of Party Organizations?

Through most of their 150-year history, the national committees were the weakest level of party organization. They became active only during presidential election years, when they coordinated the efforts of independent state and city organizations. Similarly, although powerful state organizations existed in some states, in many others the state organization was only a loose confederation of local organizations. That has changed greatly in the past quarter century. By the 1980s creative politicians began to find new ways for party organizations to help them obtain and keep political power.

Most observers credit Republicans such as William Brock, chairman of the Republican National Committee (RNC) from 1976 to 1982, for leading the way to modern-day party politics. These Republican strategists raised large sums of money, passing them on to friendly candidates as well as local party organizations. They hired full-time political operatives and experts on polling, fund-raising, campaigning, and the media. They retained lawyers versed in election law and specialists skilled in computers and other technologies. Such resources were made available at low cost to Republican campaigns nationwide. By the late 1980s, there were reports of Republican congressional campaign committees actively recruiting candidates for office, a level of national intervention that would have been unthinkable a generation earlier. For their part, the Democrats eventually imitated the Republicans, especially starting with the Clinton campaign of 1992. Before the 2004 presidential election, the Democratic Party even planned to save their nominee from having to set up a campaign office in Washington, D.C.—they would provide a "nominee's room" with computers, phones, and staff space.[42]

State and local party organizations have become more active as well; indeed, there are data to suggest that the resurgence of local organizations began earlier, in the 1960s.[43] In contrast to a generation ago, most state parties have permanent headquarters, usually in the state capital, and they employ full-time directors and other staff. Many state organizations now conduct statewide polls. They, too, provide campaign aid and recruit candidates more actively than they did a few decades ago. A major study of party organization leaves no doubt that, in terms of personnel and activities, the state and local party organizations have a more tangible existence today than they did at mid-century.[44]

In sum, the national committees are active and well financed. They have been joined by senatorial and congressional campaign committees. Together these national committees have helped rejuvenate party organization at lower levels. Party increasingly matters for public officials. Republicans are increasingly conservative and Democrats increasingly liberal, both in Congress and on the stump. Competition has become less civil, with both parties "increasingly waging the political equivalent of total war" through the use of devices such as recall elections, legislative redistricting, the blocking of judicial and bureaucratic nominees favored by the other party, even impeachment. The partisan ceasefire that followed terrorist attacks in 2001 lasted only 43 days.[45]

The debate, however, is far from over. Some knowledgeable observers remain skeptical of the party-resurgence thesis. John Coleman asks whether the parties are resurgent or "just busy."[46] Others grant that the parties are more active now than in earlier decades but argue that the newer activities do not make them stronger "parties" in any traditional sense. According to these critics, the party organizations essentially have become large campaign-consulting firms, taking advantage of economies of scale to provide electioneering services to their associates.

Today's parties still do not have the control over the candidates that they had in the United States a century ago or that they have in most other democracies today. They cannot deny candidates a nomination or demand their loyalty once they are elected. If a party-recruited candidate is defeated in a primary, the party normally supports the victor, and only rarely are "rebels" in office threatened with loss of party support. In recent years, perhaps the most disloyal Republican in the U.S. Senate was Lincoln Chafee of Rhode Island. On issue after issue, Chafee votes like a Democrat. He supported affirmative action, gun control, legalized abortion, and same-sex marriage; he was the only Republican senator to vote against the nomination of Samuel Alito to

Democratic National Committee
Chairman Howard Dean
addresses party concerns
about the Bush administration
during a 2006 news conference.

the U.S. Supreme Court. In 2004, he even declined to support George W. Bush for re-election, instead writing in the name of Bush's father. Yet, when Chafee was challenged in the 2006 Republican primary by Stephen Laffey, a more mainstream Republican who is the mayor of Cranston, the National Republican Senatorial Committee actually spent money to help Chafee defeat his opponent. (The NRSC's help notwithstanding, Chafee was easily defeated in the 2000 general election.)

There are obvious reasons why the parties are so reluctant to punish officeholders who fail to toe the party line. Independence is highly valued in the United States. If a party tried to discipline a member, it would probably only ensure his or her reelection. Moreover, despite the impressive efforts of the newly constituted parties, they contribute only a fraction of the resources devoted to electioneering. Candidates create personal organizations and raise their own war chests. Contributions by the parties to members of Congress, for example, make up under 10 percent of all congressional campaign expenditures, although the amount spent "independently" is growing.

Even worse, an elected official who was punished by his own party might decide to leave the party entirely. In early 2001, for example, Republicans in the Senate talked about punishing Vermont Senator Jim Jeffords for his failure to vote for President Bush's original tax cut proposal (they never actually took any action). The White House, meanwhile, declined to invite Jeffords to a ceremony honoring a Vermont teacher as "Teacher of the Year." In response, Jeffords announced that he was leaving the Republican Party—and thus handed control of the Senate over to the Democrats for the next year and a half.

Parties Versus Interest Groups

Some political theorists believe that the power of interest groups is negatively correlated with the power of parties—that when parties are strong, groups are weak, and vice versa.[47] The argument follows from two premises: first, that parties have incentives to synthesize narrow interests in order to make the broad appeals necessary to win elections; and second, that strong parties can provide electoral resources and deliver the vote, thus freeing their candidates from dependence on interest-group resources and insulating them from interest-group reprisals.

This argument implicitly assumes two-party politics rather than multi-party politics, because in the latter, parties often make very narrow appeals. Indeed, in multi-party systems, there may be little difference between parties and large interest groups such as labor unions. But within the two-party context, the argument has considerable plausibility. As we saw in Chapter 7, interest groups proliferated in the Progressive Era, when the parties were systematically attacked by reformers, and again in the 1960s and 1970s, when American parties reached their nadir, before their recent recovery. Just as nature is said to abhor a physical vacuum, so it may be that political vacuums cannot persist. When parties do not fill them, groups or some other source of influence will.

If this argument is valid, then the real alternative to party domination of the electoral process is not popular influence but interest-group influence. Rather than reflecting the broad appeals of parties, elections will reflect the narrow views of special interests. Of course, interest groups are not the only competitors of parties in modern societies. As we will see in Chapter 9, another potential competitor is the media.

Chapter Summary

Although the Constitution makes no mention of them, political parties have been part of American politics since the colonial period. Indeed, American political history often is told in terms of "party systems," wherein each party has dependable support among particular social groups, so that elections tend to be similar within each system. At present, the United States has a party system that is less stable and more confusing than most of those systems that have preceded it.

The basic reason why parties have played such an important role in American history—as well as in the histories of all modern democracies—is that they perform organizing and coordinating functions that are essential in large-scale representative democracies. Parties coordinate the actions of numerous officeholders and focus responsibility for their actions. Parties develop issues, educate the public, and synthesize disparate interests. Parties recruit and develop governmental talent and simplify the choices of voters who would otherwise be overwhelmed by the task of choosing among numerous candidates for office.

Despite these important functions that parties perform, most Americans do not hold them in especially high regard. Parties constantly struggle for political supremacy. Thus, they act in accordance with partisan self-interest and historically have behaved dictatorially, corruptly, and divisively. The question reformers must face, however, is whether they can identify an alternative to party influence and activity.

The United States has the world's longest-lived two-party system. Parties in the United States are not so strong today as they were in earlier periods. Like other American institutions and processes, the parties have been democratized. Few "bosses" remain, party processes are open to all who register, and those elected under the party flag go their own way when it suits them or their constituents. In short, political life is especially disorganized in modern America. Despite much discussion of party decline, though, the Democratic and Republican parties continue to dominate American elections and structure governance. And, despite periodic third-party insurgencies, that dominance is likely to continue.

Key Terms

critical election, p. 214
direct primary, p. 219
divided government, p. 211
electoral system, p. 224
machine, p. 218

national convention, p. 217
political parties, p. 207
Progressives, p. 219
proportional representation (PR), p. 224

realignment, p. 214
single-member, simple plurality (SMSP) system, p. 224
ticket splitting, p. 221
two-party system, p. 223

Suggested Readings

Of General Interest

Green, John C., and Paul Herrnson, eds. *Responsible Partisanship? The Evolution of American Political Parties Since 1950.* Lawrence, KS: University Press of Kansas, 2003. Comprehensive analysis of how well the political parties have served the American electorate, spread out over essays by some of the most influential researchers on the topic.

Hershey, Marjorie Randon. *Party Politics in America.* 12th ed. New York: Longman, 2007. Probably the best current textbook on American parties and the party system.

Jewell, Malcolm E., and Sarah M. Morehouse. *Political Parties and Elections in the American States.* 4th ed. Washington, D.C.: Congressional Quarterly, 2000. Textbook on parties and elections at the subnational level.

Key, V. O. Jr. *Politics, Parties and Pressure Groups.* 5th ed. New York: Crowell, 1964. A classic text. Although dated, it can still be read both for historical interest and for theoretical observations about party politics in a democracy.

Focused Studies

Aldrich, John. *Why Parties?* Chicago: University of Chicago Press, 1995. Wide-ranging rational-choice account of how and why politicians form and transform political parties.

Layman, Geoffrey. *The Great Divide: Religious and Cultural Conflict in American Party Politics.* New York: Columbia University Press, 2001. Thorough look at the continuing importance of cultural differences in defining the major political parties.

Mayhew, David. R. *Electoral Realignments: A Critique of an American Genre*. New Haven, Conn.: Yale University Press, 2002. Recent critique of the abstract theory of electoral realignment.

Sundquist, James. L. *Dynamics of the Party System*. Rev. ed. Washington, D.C.: The Brookings Institution, 1983. History of national politics since the 1840s told from a party-systems perspective.

On the Web

www.rnc.org

www.dnc.org

Both national party committees also employ Web sites that solicit contributions, attack their opponents, and generally advocate party-advocated policies.

www.greenparty.org

www.reformparty.org

www.natural-law.org

www.lp.org

Third-parties make tremendous use of the Web. The Green Party USA, Reform Party, Natural Law Party, and Libertarian Party have the most prominent minor-party sites.

CHAPTER 9

★ ★ ★ ★ ★ ★ ★ ★ ★ ☆

The Media

The Media: 800-Pound Gorilla or 98-Pound Weakling?

More than three decades ago, hundreds of thousands of young Americans fought in the Vietnam War. More than 58,000 died, and 10 times that number were wounded. Many Americans protested against the war, and especially against the military draft—the selection system that decided who would have to fight. Their protests sometimes won sympathy with journalists, but the public response to protesters was far more negative, a striking illustration of the way people resist media messages.

As the 1968 Democratic convention drew near, activists planned to gather in Chicago and protest the impending presidential nomination of the sitting vice president. Hubert Humphrey had not entered a single primary, but his influence within the Democratic Party guaranteed that delegates would select him anyway. By 1968 most voters could not figure out exactly where Humphrey stood on the Vietnam conflict (see Chapter 10), but his previous support for the administration still angered those committed to the antiwar movement.

The level of tension that existed at that time exceeds anything familiar to observers of contemporary politics. Mayor Richard Daley and the Chicago police force fully expected widespread violence in the streets. Rumors flew among the National Guard troops and law officers stationed outside that activists might lace the convention water supply with hallucinogenic drugs or pose as cab drivers to kidnap Democratic officials.[1]

Daley refused to issue protest permits and warned that the city would deal harshly with those who spoiled the celebration. But some protest leaders were more than willing to provoke such reprisals.[2] A group calling themselves *yippies* even floated the rumor that they would fill a nearby lake with 10,000 nude bodies.[3] They never carried through on this threat, but they did help fill Chicago with roughly that number of demonstrators.

Many protestors flooded into Chicago's Grant and Lincoln parks, despite the lack of permits. They milled about on the grass, danced to provocative rock music, or chanted Buddhist mantras.[4] After some preliminary skirmishes, Daley's police finally decided to flush them out of the Parks. They bathed the assemblies with tear gas, forcing many into the streets, where more police and more

tear gas waited. The harshest confrontation occurred outside the Hilton Hotel, where the convention delegates stayed. As a mostly college-age crowd gasped and choked, armored troops formed attack wedges and surged into the crowd, flailing about with stout clubs. Other officers hid their identities and attacked news reporters.[5] Ultimately, more than 500 victims needed medical attention. An investigative commission (led by an ambitious lawyer who used the commission's report to launch a campaign for governor) later described the explosion as a "police riot."

The attacks greatly disturbed many political elites. Inside and outside the convention, public figures used the harshest rhetoric. From the podium of the convention, Senator Abraham Ribicoff of Connecticut accused Mayor Daley of using "Gestapo tactics" to quash dissent—eliciting a string of obscenities from Mayor Daley that the microphones could not pick up. Hard-bitten British reporters who had covered the civil war in Northern Ireland wrote that the Chicago police had gone berserk.[6]

Media reporters clearly sympathized with the protesters. As Tom Wicker of the *New York Times* put it, "these were our children in the streets, and the Chicago police beat them up."[7] Over the course of the evening, the media lost all semblance of balance. Longtime NBC anchor Chet Huntley condemned the police. Walter Cronkite choked back tears.

It was exactly the sort of shocked reaction that many of the protest leaders had hoped to provoke when they exposed themselves to attack. They had uncovered the bankruptcy of "the establishment," which could combat disagreement only through brute force. As tear gas floated hazily before the cameras and sirens filled the background, the news footage carried a continuous taunt from the demonstrators: "The whole world is watching, the whole world is watching."

Indeed, much of the United States *was* watching. But what neither the protesters nor the journalists realized was that most in the audience were cheering on the police! Poll results following the Democratic National Convention stunned American elites: Popular majorities believed that the Chicago police had acted appropriately. In fact, many believed that the police should have used greater force.[8]

Protesters such as those demonstrating in Chicago were familiar sights on college campuses, at public buildings such as draft offices, and in city streets. Many people had developed strong views about protesters. There was little opportunity for the media's interpretation of events in Chicago to alter such predispositions. The American people had tuned out the chatter, stared at their TVs, and rooted for the cops. So much for the awesome power of television.

MAKING THE CONNECTION

How powerful are the media, then? Are they an overwhelming force that even presidents must fear, or a lot of sound and fury that ordinary Americans ignore? The answer is that, depending on the circumstances, the media can be either of these, and everything in between. The media can have extremely powerful effects on public opinion, even to the extent of determining who wins elections and what governments do. But under other conditions, media effects are sharply limited.

We begin our analysis of the role of the media by considering how the media have attained their present position as an important political actor, and what kinds of media Americans rely on for political information. We then consider two other important issues: in what ways the media affect public opinion today, and what types of bias characterize media reports.

The relationship between the media and politics continually evolves. Politicians strive to use the media for their own ends, and the media cooperate or not, depending on the incentives they face. New developments in the political or technical realm can alter the equilibrium between these two important actors.

Development of the Mass Media

The term **mass media** refers to forms of communication that are widely affordable and technologically capable of reaching a broad audience. Such resources have existed for less than two centuries. Their development since then has shaped American democracy because politicians engage in a never-ending struggle to control the information that reaches their constituents. Information is power, and politicians contend with media organizations for control of it. In this section we trace the development of the major forms of mass media used to spread political information: print (newspapers and magazines) and broadcast (radio and television). We also look at the emergence of such new media as cable TV and the Internet. In each case we focus on control of the message: Who is responsible for the information transmitted?

When Europeans first established colonies in North America, the only technology capable of reaching a mass audience was the printing press. The first newspaper in the colonies, the *Boston News-Letter*, started publication in 1704.[9] By 1730, there were seven colonial newspapers; by 1800, there were more than 180.[10]

But these early newspapers were different from the ones we know today. Their circulation was quite limited—according to one estimate, the average newspaper in

mass media

Means of communication that are technologically capable of reaching most people and economically affordable to most.

1800 had a circulation of about 700—and came out weekly or semi-weekly. Given the technology of the time, which still relied on hand-operated presses, it was difficult to print a large number of newspapers in a short period of time. Moreover, the first papers were aimed primarily at an elite audience. Almost all papers were sold by subscription, and few people could afford them—about 5 percent of free households in 1765— although there is some evidence that the papers that were bought were passed around, read aloud, or posted in public areas.[11]

Early American newspapers did not hire reporters: The job of being a reporter, in fact, had not yet been invented. As a result, these early papers printed virtually everything they could get their hands on: official proclamations, advertisements and commercial news, letters and essays from readers, correspondence from people in other cities, news from the ships that had just arrived in port. These papers did not pursue or "dig up" stories in the way modern-day media do—a characteristic that helps explain how the Constitutional Convention of 1787 could be held behind closed doors and have virtually nothing about its deliberations appear in contemporary newspapers.

The Partisan Press and the Penny Press

The emergence and growth of political parties after the adoption of the Constitution led to a very important development in the fledgling newspaper industry: until the Civil War almost all newspapers were openly and explicitly partisan.

Today, of course, lots of major news organizations are accused of providing slanted, partisan news, an issue we consider in detail later in this chapter. But these news organizations vehemently deny such charges. By contrast, for the first 70 years or so after ratification of the Constitution, almost all American newspapers were openly affiliated with one political party or another: they announced it proudly, often at the top of their mastheads, and consciously tried to bring a partisan perspective to their writing. Most of these papers also received some kind of subsidy or patronage from the party's supporters in government.

The pattern was set very early. As soon as the division between Federalists and Democratic-Republicans started to emerge (see Chapter 8), Alexander Hamilton, the leader of the Federalists, established a newspaper to support him and his policies. The paper was called the *Gazette of the United States*, and to make sure the paper stayed in business, Hamilton, as Secretary of the Treasury, gave the paper most of the Treasury Department's printing business. In reaction, Thomas Jefferson and his followers set up their own newspaper, the *National Gazette*. Because the State Department did not have a great deal of official printing business to dispose of, Jefferson put the paper's editor, Philip Freneau, on the State Department payroll, assuring Freneau that his job "gives so little to do, as not to interfere with any other calling the person may choose."[12] As one historian has written about this period, "The distinction between the press and the party nearly vanished. It is fair to say that the most important editors in this period were actually politicians wielding newspapers."

In the early 1830s, however, a new and different form of journalism emerged: the penny press. As its name implies, one major characteristic of the penny newspapers was that each day's paper cost only one penny, compared to about six cents per copy for the more traditional, partisan papers. The reason for the lower price was that penny papers aimed at a larger, less educated, less elite audience. Technological improvements made it possible to print papers far more quickly and cheaply. There was also a growing audience for the new papers—partly because American cities were growing, partly because American politics had become more participatory and less elitist (see Chapter 6).[13]

The penny press differed from the old partisan press in a number of important ways. Its writing style was simpler and less flowery. It relied a lot more on advertising to pay the bills—and generally did not get subsidies from government. Because one could not fill a daily newspaper with enough interesting material by relying on official proclamations and letters from readers, the penny press began to hire reporters: people who would go to city hall or the national capital in Washington and send back regular reports about what was going on there. Finally, though most of the penny papers were partisan, they also claimed to be independent in the sense that they did not take orders from the parties or their leadership. During the Civil War, for example, Republican newspapers supported the general thrust of that party's policies, particularly its opposition to the spread of slavery. But many were quite critical of Lincoln and the way he was conducting the war.

Newspapers and Magazines, 1865–1920

By the end of the nineteenth century, the style of journalism practiced by the penny press had become dominant. Although most newspapers still had some kind of partisan affiliation, they increasingly relegated it (or so they claimed) to the editorial pages. Partisanship was not supposed to affect news stories.

Three Hundred Years
of American Mass Media

As large cities grew, so did newspapers. By the turn of the twentieth century, every major city in the United States had a large number of competing newspapers. Unfortunately, this competition often resulted in excesses and abuses. The 1890s and early 1900s are sometimes called the era of "yellow journalism," when many newspapers eagerly exploited scandals and any story involving sex or violence. Two of the most notorious practitioners were Joseph Pulitzer, who owned and edited the *New York World*, and William Randolph Hearst, who owned the *New York Journal*. The worst single example of their operating style occurred in 1897 and 1898, when the *World* and *Journal* gave a great deal of highly inflammatory coverage to events in Cuba, particularly the claim that Spanish saboteurs had blown up the *Maine*, an American battleship, and thereby played a major role in getting the United States to declare war against Spain.[14]

Although newspapers were clearly the dominant medium of this era, magazines were also influential. Magazines were, in a sense, the first major *national* medium. Three important magazines were founded in 1893: *McClure's*, *Cosmopolitan*, and *Munsey's*. They were later joined by *Collier's* and the *Saturday Evening Post*. There had been national magazines before these, but they had been smaller and were written for elites. The newer magazines, by contrast, were aimed at a larger national audience of middle-class, educated readers.

In the early 1900s, such magazines began to publish articles exposing political corruption and the predatory practices of large business corporations. Eventually known as "muckraking," these exposés became a major national phenomenon, attracting considerable attention and often prompting major reform movements. The muckrakers, particularly Lincoln Steffens, Ida Tarbell, and Ray Stannard Baker, were a significant part of the Progressive movement—and also were important in setting an example for future journalists. Many modern-day investigative reporters model themselves after the muckrakers.

Yellow Journalism

William Randolph Hearst's *New York Journal* went on the warpath after the explosion of the *Maine* in Cuba (ultimately leading to the Spanish-American War). Many people suspected that the Spanish were responsible, and Hearst's papers played on that fear.

• *Compare this newspaper's coverage to the coverage of the Gulf War. How is the coverage different? How is it similar?*

Radio and Television

Like many modern inventions, radio has had a complex history: It is probably inaccurate to call any one person the "inventor" of radio, but what is generally considered the first radio broadcast occurred in 1906. World War I delayed the use of radio for news, commercial, and entertainment purposes, but with the end of the war the development of radio flourished.[15]

The 1920s saw the development of three important characteristics of U.S. radio that would serve as important precedents for the future.

1. *The licensing system.* In the United States, government had never tried to regulate the newspaper industry: Anyone who wanted to establish a newspaper could do so, subject only to their ability to pay the bills. But radio was clearly different. In order for radio to work, two stations could not broadcast on the same frequency: conflicting and overlapping signals would prevent any one message from getting through in an understandable form. In one way or another, government had to bring some kind of basic order to the medium. But what role would government play?

In many European countries radio became a government-run enterprise. Broadcasting was organized and performed by government agencies, such as the British Broadcasting Corporation (BBC) in England. But the United States decided to go a different route. After a few years of indecision, Congress passed the Radio Act of 1927, which established a system that, with a few modifications, is basically still with us today—for both radio and television. The Radio Act created a Federal Radio Commission (which in 1934 became the Federal Communications Commission, or FCC) with the power to issue licenses that gave an individual or group the exclusive right to broadcast on a particular frequency. Originally, lots of licenses were granted to church groups, universities, and nonprofit organizations, but soon radio came to be dominated more and more by profit-oriented companies, who operated their stations to make money.

Censorship and the FCC

These licenses carried a number of conditions. The legislation creating the FCC established the **equal-time rule**, which said that if a station gave or sold time to a legally qualified candidate for public office, it had to make equal time available to all such candidates, on equal terms. Between 1949 and 1987, the FCC also enforced a "fairness doctrine," which required stations to air contrasting viewpoints on matters of public importance and to give public figures who had been criticized on any of the station's programs an opportunity to reply.

equal-time rule
Promulgated by the FCC, it required any station selling time to a candidate to sell time to other candidates at comparable rates.

2. *The importance of advertising.* How did radio companies make money? In England, the BBC was funded by a tax on radio receivers. In the United States, however, broadcasters paid their bills by selling commercial time to advertisers. Because advertising rates were determined by the size of the audience, this system gave broadcasters an incentive to build as large an audience as possible, which led to . . .

3. *The emergence of national networks.* After the initial novelty had worn off, radio broadcasters were faced with a major problem: What exactly should they broadcast, particularly if they wanted to attract and retain a large audience? It was not easy to fill 24 hours of airtime, particularly in smaller towns and cities that could not afford to hire high-priced talent.

The most important solution was the creation of national networks. A corporation, usually with headquarters in New York, would develop a lineup of programs that would then be sent by telephone wire to "affiliated" stations all over the country. Because FCC rules then prohibited any one entity from owning more than five stations, the network did not actually own most of the stations that ran its programs. Instead, affiliates would agree to run the programs because of the larger audience that was likely to listen to them, and, in return, they would give the network a portion of their precious advertising time. The first major network was the National Broadcasting Corporation, created by three radio manufacturers in 1926. One year later, a group called the United Independent Broadcasters established a rival network, later named the Columbia Broadcasting System (CBS). The American Broadcasting Company (ABC) began operations in 1943.

With the advent of radio it became clear that in theory, at least, it was possible to send pictures as well as sounds over the airwaves. The first public demonstration of television took place at the New York World's Fair in 1939. World War II put plans for developing television as a commercial medium on hold, but once the war was over,

television took off. In May 1949, according to a Gallup Poll, just 6 percent of Americans owned a television set—and less than half of the public had ever seen a tele-vision program. But the number of Americans who owned a TV jumped to 45 percent in 1952, and to 90 percent in 1959. In just 10 years, in short, television went from being a technological curiosity to a fixture in American homes.[16]

The Contemporary Scene

As this brief history shows, the contemporary American political system is served by a variety of media, each of which is used in distinctive ways and for somewhat differ-ent purposes.

Television When Americans hear the word "media," they think first of television: 99 percent of all U.S. households have at least one television set; and the average house-hold has four of them. The network system that had worked so well in radio migrat-ed to television, and the three major networks—ABC, CBS, and NBC—quickly came to dominate television viewing. On any given evening in the 1960s, about 90 percent of those who were watching television were likely to be tuned in to a program on one of these networks.

In recent years, however, this near-monopoly has declined dramatically. One source of new competition came when a second part of the electro-magnetic spec-trum, called UHF (for ultra-high frequency), became available for television broad-casting. Whereas television was once limited to channels 2 through 13 (which meant that even the largest cities were served by no more than four or five stations), UHF permitted broadcasting on channels 14 through 69. Initially, most of these new stations were independents that devoted most of their time to re-running old network shows and did very little original programming (and what little they did tended to be of poor quality). But, eventually, new networks were created to serve these UHF stations, such as Fox and UPN.

The other major competition to the three original networks came from cable television. Cable television actually dates back to the late 1940s, and originally it was only a means of providing better quality broadcast television to people who lived in rural areas or mountain valleys where reception was poor. In the mid-1970s, however, the deregulation of the cable industry plus the development of satellites allowed local television stations to "go national" by sending their signal to satellites that would then beam it back to hundreds of local cable companies. As more and more homes were hooked up to cable, entrepreneurs began to develop programming exclusively for cable, such as CNN, HBO, and the Weather Channel. The upshot has been a dramatic expansion in the number of stations available to most Americans. In broadcast television, even the biggest media markets are limited to about 10 or 15 stations. Cable, however, makes it possible for people to receive 30, 50, or 150 channels. By 2006, nearly two-thirds of the American population said they subscribed to cable television.

Newspapers   The development of television, along with a number of other trends in American life, had a major impact on newspapers. First, there has been a marked decline in the number of cities with more than one newspaper. In 1940, 181 American cities had competing daily newspapers. Forty years later, that number was down to 30.[17] Particularly hard hit have been afternoon and evening papers. In the 1950s and 1960s, many of the best papers in the country came out in the late afternoon or early evening; often they were purchased by commuters on their way home from work. But television made the evening newspaper a substantially less useful commodity. Whereas evening newspapers had had a total circulation of 36 million copies in 1970, by 2004 (the latest figures available) evening papers sold less than 8 million copies.[18]

Another important change affecting newspapers has been the spread of chain ownership. Increasingly, the nation's newspapers are owned by companies that own a sizable number of newspapers in cities across the country. Chain ownership is not entirely new: William Randolph Hearst, for example, at one point owned 26 daily newspapers. But where Hearst was once the exception, chain ownership is now becoming the predominant pattern. The largest single newspaper corporation is the Gannett Company, which owns *USA Today* and 89 other newspapers.

Radio   With the development of television, radio quickly lost the dominant position it had in American life in the 1930s and 1940s. Yet radio continues to be a popular medium, from which many Americans get a good deal of their news.

Indeed, one of the most noteworthy trends in American media over the last two decades has been the growth of talk radio. In 1980, about 75 stations in the United States were devoted exclusively to news and talk shows. By 2004, the number had jumped to 1,400.[19] Of course, this figure includes many nonpolitical talk shows—sports, consumer affairs, advice to the lovelorn, "shock jocks" such as Howard Stern—but much talk radio is clearly and unabashedly political. The dominant figure in the industry is Rush Limbaugh, whose three-hour show attracts about 14 million listeners every week.

The growth of talk radio is partly attributable to the development of satellites, which make it easier to broadcast a single program on hundreds of far-flung local stations. Equally important was the FCC's decision to repeal the fairness doctrine in

SIMULATION

You Are the
News Editor

1987. When the fairness doctrine was law, any figure who was attacked on a talk radio program could request an equivalent amount of *free* airtime to reply to the attack. Obviously, this ruling made stations extremely reluctant to air programs that dealt with political figures or public issues in any kind of opinionated or controversial way. It is no accident that Rush Limbaugh first began to broadcast his program to a national audience in 1988.

Magazines   Although magazines were, as we have seen, quite important in the history of American journalism, as a news source they are increasingly marginal. When Americans are asked where they get most of their news, only a tiny minority mention magazines. This is not to say that magazines are disappearing. In fact, there are a large and growing number of them. But most magazines—and particularly the best-selling ones—are not news magazines, at least not news about government and politics. The list of the best-selling magazines in the United States is headed by magazines such as *Reader's Digest*, *TV Guide*, *Better Homes and Gardens*, *National Geographic*, and *Good Housekeeping*. As of 2004, *Time* ranked eleventh on the list; *Newsweek* was number 17.[20]

The New Media

Beginning in the 1970s, a sizable number of new entrants were added to the menu of American media options. Often referred to collectively as "the **new media**," these new forms of communication were made possible by the development of new technologies. Major examples include cable television, videocassette recorders (VCRs), satellites and satellite dishes, and the Internet.

Besides their reliance on new technologies, the new media tend to have a number of shared characteristics that may have important political consequences.[21] In particular, they dramatically expand the range of options available to media consumers in the United States. Traditional broadcast television might have made three or four stations available to the typical viewer, but cable allows viewers to choose among 30 or 50 different channels. The Internet similarly allows users access to millions of different Web sites, including hundreds of newspapers and magazines and a dazzling array of specialized political sites.

One important question, however, is whether people will use their new menu of choices to seek out more political information—or to avoid it altogether. In the early days of television, it was sometimes claimed that TV had created a large "inadvertent audience" for news. Many people watched the news, not because they were really interested in it, but because they were watching TV and news was the only thing on it.[22] Today, when there are so many more options available, and remote control devices allow people to change channels without getting up, it is likely that no one watches television news unless he or she wants to. Thus, the new media may lead to a system in which a small number of political activists are better informed than ever before—while Americans in general are actually less knowledgeable about politics.[23]

Another, somewhat more controversial characteristic of the new media is that they have, to some extent, decentralized the ownership and control of media. Whereas almost all television programs were once controlled by three national networks, cable

new media
Cable and satellite TV, fax, e-mail, and the Internet—the media that have grown out of the technological advances of the past few decades.

has expanded the number of competing voices. The Internet appears to be especially "democratic," in the sense that thousands of political groups and millions of individuals have created their own Web sites and thereby gained an easily accessible portal for their viewpoints. We should not, however, overstate the diversity in new media ownership. Many of the most important cable stations are actually owned by older media corporations that have bought or created their own cable channels. Of the three largest cable news channels, CNN is now owned by Time Warner; Fox is owned by News Corp., which also owns numerous newspapers and magazines; and MS/NBC is, as its name indicates, owned by NBC. Similarly, many heavily visited political Web sites are just the Internet version of a news organization that is primarily associated with a more traditional medium, such as nytimes.com or cbs.com.

How will these new media, especially the Internet, change American politics? It is difficult to answer this question with any assurance, precisely because so many of the new media are new and many of their political applications are still being explored. As recently as 1992, neither of the major political candidates had a Web site and no pollster that we know of thought the Internet was important enough to bother asking a survey question about it. By 2000, any serious candidate for office, at every level of American government, was expected to have a Web site, and 11 percent of the adult population said they got "most of [their] news about the presidential election campaign" from the Internet.

The newest twist in Internet news coverage is the development of blogs (short for Web logs), Web sites in which people—some established journalists, others just interested amateurs—post their opinions, comment on the news, present relevant research, and so forth. In 2004, both major-party presidential candidates took the blogs seriously enough to provide links between their own Web sites and those of sympathetic bloggers. What role, if any, will the "blogosphere" play in American politics? At this point, it is simply too early to tell.

Still, we can make some general observations about the political effects of the new media. First, many of the new media require users to own, rent, or at least be capable of using some new form of technology: the Internet, satellite dishes, a cable hookup. In some cases, this will surely limit their *mass* impact, though they may still be used by political elites for various kinds of organizing and communications tasks. Yet history indicates that some kinds of technology can catch on very quickly with the American public. Television ownership, as we have already seen, jumped from 6 percent in 1949 to 90 percent in 1959. VCRs, to take a more recent example, were owned by 2 percent of American adults in 1980—but by 71 percent in 1990.[24]

Second, even after a new medium becomes available to most Americans, there remains the key question of whether they will actually use it for any kind of political purposes. In a December 2005 survey, for example, the Gallup Poll found that 51 percent of respondents said they used the Internet every day, 22 percent used it less frequently, and 27 percent said they never used it. Of the 73 percent who did use it, 45 percent said they "frequently" used it for "checking news and weather," as compared to 67 percent who frequently used it for "sending and receiving e-mail" and 18 percent for "shopping." Of all the possible uses for the Internet that Gallup tested, the lowest-rated was "reading 'blogs' or web logs," which only 9 percent said they did frequently.

Soft News vs.
Hard News

Web News

News agencies maintain Web pages that allow Americans to get world news immediately rather than waiting for the scheduled broadcast or for delivery of the daily paper.

• *How does this faster news cycle change the needs and expectations of consumers? As this outlet grows as a source, will it change what gets covered?*

On the whole, as we will see in the next section, it appears that the Internet still lags well behind television and newspapers as a source of news and information, though it has grown rapidly in recent years. But there is also some evidence to suggest that the Internet can have major effects on activists and other key political actors. In the 2000 and 2004 presidential nomination races, for example, the Internet is credited with allowing John McCain and John Kerry to raise large amounts of money in a relatively short period of time and thus to capitalize on their early victories in Iowa and/or New Hampshire. In 2002, the Internet was sometimes given credit for calling attention to a speech given by then-Senate Majority Leader Trent Lott, in which he lauded his home state of Mississippi for supporting Strom Thurmond in the 1948 election in a way that many critics thought was racist. Lott was ultimately forced to resign from the leadership. In 2004, blogs such as powerlineblog.com were given principal credit for showing that a set of memos used in a *60 Minutes* broadcast to show that George Bush had failed to fulfill his National Guard duties were actually forgeries. To date, the Internet has not turned out to be a useful vehicle for mass campaigning—but its time for this may come in the future.

What Information Sources Do Americans Rely On?

Where do Americans get most of their news? This is a surprisingly difficult question to answer. In a typical week, most of us encounter a variety of different media. We listen to the radio while driving to work, read a newspaper on the bus or in a library or coffee

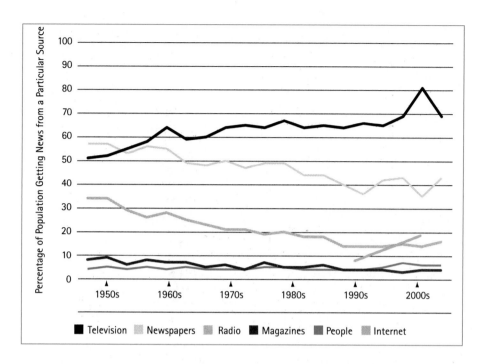

FIGURE 9.1

Changing Patterns in News Sources, by Decade: 1950s–2000s

A majority of Americans watch TV news, and almost a majority rely exclusively on the television to learn about national politics.

Source: The Roper Center and the Pew Center for the People and the Press.

shop, watch television at night, go on the Internet a number of times. We may also have conversations with family, friends, and co-workers, who tell us about what they have learned from the media, perhaps adding their own interpretations and distortions. Most people do not consciously monitor this complicated process and therefore may not be able to say exactly what they have learned from any particular source.

When public opinion surveys ask Americans where they get most of their news, they usually say "television." The single, best-known question of this type comes from the Roper Poll and was first asked in 1959, as shown in Figure 9.1. In that year, newspapers narrowly edged out television as the place where most people said they got "most of [their] news about what's going on in the world today." By 1963, however, television had pulled ahead of newspapers, and over the next three decades the margin steadily widened. Radio declined sharply between the late 1950s and the early 1970s but has held steady since then. Unfortunately, Roper stopped asking this question in 1994; but another survey question, from the Pew Center, shows where people say they got most of their news about presidential election campaigns between 1992 and 2004. As shown in Table 9.1, television is the dominant source of information, followed by newspapers and radio. The Internet, which was not even asked about in the 1992 survey, was mentioned by 21 percent of the respondents in the 2004 poll, putting it just below radio.

But there is some reason to wonder about the validity of these results. While there is no doubt that the television is turned on a lot in the typical American household—about 7 hours a day, according to some estimates—in many cases, no one is paying much attention to it. People are cleaning or cooking or doing their homework—and the TV is little more than background noise. The most eloquent testimony to how little attention people sometimes give to their television sets occurred on February 7, 1971, when a power failure on the East Side of Manhattan knocked out the transmitter on the Empire State Building, which was then used by all the TV stations in New York City. Elsewhere in the city, however, electric power was still working—which meant

TABLE 9.1

MEDIA USE TRENDS IN PRESIDENTIAL ELECTIONS, 1992–2004 (IN PERCENTAGES)

"How did you get most of your news about the presidential election campaign . . . from television, from newspapers, from radio, from magazines, or from the Internet?"

	1992	1996	2000	2004
Television	82	72	70	76
Newspapers	57	60	39	46
Radio	12	19	15	22
Magazines	9	11	4	6
Internet[a]	NA	3	11	21

[a] Option was not included in the 1992 survey. 1996 survey asked about "computer online sources."

SOURCE: Pew Research Center for the People and the Press.

that television sets still worked, even though they all had blank, soundless screens. Nevertheless, according to the Nielsen rating service, about a half million New Yorkers continued to have their television sets turned on.[25]

Whether because it is just background noise or because of inherent limitations in the medium itself, there is also a fair amount of evidence to indicate that even when people do watch television news, they do not retain or remember much of what they see. In one study conducted by researchers at the University of Michigan, interviewers located a random sample of respondents who said they had watched one of the network evening newscasts broadcast earlier that day and then asked them a series of questions about the show they had seen just one to three hours earlier. When asked how many stories they remembered from the newscast, the average respondent recalled fewer than two. Even when the interviewer provided a salient detail from each story, most people could remember the central point of that story only about a third of the time.[26]

The extent to which we get our news from television also varies from issue to issue and story to story. In a series of questions asked by the Roper Poll in 1988 (unfortunately, the questions have not been repeated since then), television clearly dominated newspapers as a source of information about presidential elections: 70 percent said they became "best acquainted with the candidates" through television, versus 20 percent who mentioned newspapers. But the two media were almost equal as a source of news about candidates for the House of Representatives, and newspapers were the more important source for "candidates running in local elections."[27]

As pollster Bud Roper has suggested, because television plays such an important role in many people's lives, there may be a kind of "halo effect" that causes people to overestimate its importance as a source of news.[28] This tendency may be reinforced by the fact that television clearly did play a major role in informing the public about certain landmark moments in American life—such as the assassination of John Kennedy or the terrorist attacks of September 11, 2001.

One final problem with almost all of the studies on this topic is their failure to recognize that "news" is not a very well-defined concept. When most social scientists use the term, they are thinking of news about important matters of political and social concern: recent developments in the Iraq war, the latest statistics on poverty and unemployment, the progress of various bills being considered by Congress. But many members of the mass public, we suspect, have a less exalted notion in mind. To them, news includes things such as yesterday's sports scores, the weather forecast, and the latest reports about Hollywood's hottest stars. In saying they became "best acquainted" with the presidential candidates on television, they may be thinking more of the candidates' looks and speaking styles than their positions on the issues.

Media Effects

Scholarly assessments of the effect of media on public opinion have gone through several distinct stages or "schools." In the 1940s many observers viewed the potential of radio as a great danger to democratic politics, for the rapid spread of radio in the 1930s coincided with the rise of fascism in Europe. Rather than a coincidence, some commentators argued that one key source of power for both Hitler and Mussolini was their ability to speak directly to their audiences. Also influential was the remarkable reaction to Orson Welles's famous "War of the Worlds" broadcast on October 30, 1938, which convinced many Americans that the planet really was being invaded by Martians and set off mass panic throughout the country.[29] The label that has sometimes been given to this school of thought was the "hypodermic model," because the capacity of the media to put ideas into people's heads was seen as so direct and powerful, it was almost like injecting drugs into a person's bloodstream.

Use of the Media by the American Public

When social scientists first started conducting systematic tests of the media's impact on mass attitudes, however, they generally found just the opposite. Particularly influential was a study called *The People's Choice*, which tracked people's reactions to the 1940 presidential campaign as it progressed in Erie County, Ohio. Contrary to their expectations, the study's authors found that most people wound up voting for the same candidate they had favored before the campaign began, that most of the voting decisions made by the initially "undecided" could be predicted in advance based on the social and demographic characteristics, and that the number of actual "conversions"— people who changed from Wilkie to Roosevelt or vice versa—was remarkably small.[30] For the next three decades or so, this became the dominant view of media effects.[31] Known as the "minimal effects school," we would almost certainly have endorsed it if we had written this textbook in the 1950s or early 1960s—if we had bothered to write about the media at all.[32] It was not until the 1970s that a younger generation of researchers really started to question the view that the media had so little effect.

Agenda Setting

The first major crack in the "minimal effects" edifice concerned a function known as "agenda setting." As Bernard Cohen memorably put it, the press "may not be successful much of the time in telling people what to think, but it is stunningly successful in telling its readers what to think *about*."[33] Or to revert to the terminology of Chapter 5, the media may not be able to change the *direction* of public attitudes, but it can change their relative *salience*. The media can induce people to focus on an issue or problem by emphasizing it and whipping up concern. The media set the agenda, even if they do not determine how issues get resolved.

Catastrophes in Third World countries, for example, largely go unnoticed unless the media—particularly television—turn their attention to such events. Famine struck

A National Canvas

Americans were shocked to learn that authorities had allowed psychological torture in Iraq's Abu Ghraib prison, such as the mock electrocution portrayed in this painting. But some observers complained that the media had abused their power to frame news stories—harping military abuses in the middle of a guerrilla war when the opposition was beheading foreigners.

CNN effect

Purported ability of TV to raise a foreign tragedy to national prominence by broadcasting vivid pictures.

agenda setting

Occurs when the media affect the issues and problems people think about, even if the media do not determine what positions people adopt.

Ethiopia in 1984, resulting in numerous front-page articles in powerful U.S. newspapers such as the *New York Times* and *Washington Post*. The Associated Press (AP) wire service carried 228 stories.[34] But it was not until television stations beamed heartrending footage into their living rooms that Americans became aware of the problem and supported governmental efforts to help.[35] Similar responses followed media coverage of tragedies in a series of countries or regions around the world—including Somalia, Rwanda, and Kosovo. Media analysts have even given government responses such as these a nickname, the **CNN effect**, after the tendency for a problem to be addressed once the Cable News Network covers it.

Agenda setting is well documented, although much of the evidence is not conclusive.[36] Say unemployment rises, the media focus heavily on unemployment, and people in growing numbers begin to think of unemployment as a major national problem. Is this agenda setting, or are both the media and the people responding to the same real conditions? Some careful studies conclude that the independent impact of the media has been exaggerated; astute government officials use the media to place problems on the national and international agendas.[37] A study of failed attempts to pass national health care plans concluded that "peaks in the volume and substantive focus of media reporting coincided with upsurges in discussions of real-world developments and fierce political debate over policy reforms."[38] Nevertheless, experimental studies that raise viewer concern about subjects *not* high on the national agenda have been able to provide some evidence of agenda setting.[39]

Priming and Framing

In the spring of 1991, following an impressive American victory in the Gulf War, President George H. W. Bush's approval ratings soared, reaching unprecedented levels. With the war's end, however, journalists turned to other stories and gradually, Bush's ratings became dependent on the nation's economic performance, which voters judged negatively.[40] He lost the 1992 election to Bill Clinton. Similarly, Bush's son enjoyed soaring popularity ratings after the 9/11 terrorist attacks. During the war in Iraq, though, media coverage dwelt on the administration's failings—including an inability to find "weapons of mass destruction" supposedly possessed by Iraq's government. Bush's ratings dropped steadily until the 2004 presidential campaign heated up, although he survived his reelection bid, and then plummeted further in 2005 and 2006. These large shifts in public opinion are striking reflections of **priming**—changing the standards that citizens use to evaluate their leaders.

By what they choose to cover, the media can prime citizens to use some standards rather than others.[41] Obviously, the media do not have full control over which criteria Americans use to evaluate their presidents. War pushes everything else off the agenda of public opinion: All other concerns seem minor when husbands and wives and sons and daughters are in danger. Thus, both the media and the public react to the reality of war. Similarly, after war ends, both turn to other concerns.

Framing and priming are related notions.[42] In Chapter 5 we explained that Americans tend to shift their opinions on abortion depending on how pollsters frame the question. How issues are framed shapes more than just survey results, however; it also molds how the public thinks about issues more generally. For example, if crime is framed as a problem that presidents can and should do something about, it is more likely to have a political impact than if it is framed as an uncontrollable by-product of social breakdown. During the 2004 campaign, John Kerry attacked President Bush for allowing corporations to shift jobs overseas. He was attempting to frame the issue of global trade in a way that reflected negatively on the president. Inducing people to think along certain lines rather than others can affect their positions on issues and their evaluations of public officials.

priming
Occurs when the media affect the standards people use to evaluate political figures or the severity of a problem.

framing
Occurs when the media induce people to think about an issue from one standpoint rather than from others.

Socialization

Many critics worry less about media persuasion of adults than about their role in socializing "impressionable youngsters." They anxiously document ways in which the mass media appear to distort reality—or at least to emphasize the seamy side of human nature—not only in news coverage but also in entertainment programs. The Henry J. Kaiser Family Foundation, for example, commissioned a survey of sex on TV. Their 2003 results indicated that one in seven shows either depicted or strongly implied an act of sexual intercourse—and about two-thirds of shows aired between 7 p.m. and 11 p.m. contained some kind of sexual content.[43]

A variety of groups, both conservative and liberal, deride the omnipresence of violent behavior on television. A study by the Parents Television Council claimed that the six biggest broadcast networks aired 534 separate violent acts during their prime-time programming in early November 2002. Most of the networks had doubled the amount of violence from four years earlier.[44] Documenting such developments in American entertainment, *Newsweek* proclaimed "The Death of Family TV" on a 2004 cover.

It is not clear how sex and violence influence American politics. They may help account for widespread concern with crime or for the increasing acceptance Americans show toward sexual practices once considered deviant. Such programming also may undermine the sense of "community" in modern life by encouraging more television watching,[45] because sex and violence seem to attract more viewers. The only clear political impact of controversial programming is that it spurs groups who demand additional broadcasting regulation. The FCC received more than 240,000 complaints about radio and TV programs in 2003. Members of Congress angrily scheduled a hearing in 2004 after the Super Bowl halftime show let viewers glimpse singer Janet Jackson's exposed breast.[46]

Some media messages may have more direct political ramifications. Government agencies come across rather poorly in popular entertainment. The renegade hero may appear on the federal payroll—such as counterterrorist agent Jack Bauer on the TV series *24* or FBI agents Mulder and Scully on the syndicated *X-Files* program—but the leadership is usually corrupt and almost always stands in the way of justice. Generally speaking, media entertainment tends to mock or disparage authority figures, a portrayal that can influence political attitudes—including the level of trust in government.[47]

Scholars have long worried about the way in which mass media portray minorities, especially African Americans. One study that probed the network news found that journalists regularly talked to black sources about crime, sports, or entertainment—but almost never about elections, economics, or foreign affairs. A related analysis of the top movies of 1996 indicated that 9 out of 10 black female characters used vulgar language, compared to fewer than a fifth of the white women. More than half of the black women committed acts of physical violence; just over a tenth of the white females did. Such portrayals reinforce negative racial stereotypes.[48] Of course, programs regularly cast blacks in positive roles—as capable doctors, artists, attorneys, or criminal profilers. Movies such as *Bedazzled* and *Bruce Almighty* have even cast black actors as God. But these "all-knowing" characters may not encourage white viewers to identify with them. They're only "means to the white characters' salvation," one cultural scholar points out, "and not ends in themselves."[49]

How Strong Are Media Effects?

Effects such as agenda setting, priming, and framing depend on both the characteristics of the audience and the nature of the information. People who are uninterested in and uninformed about politics are most susceptible to agenda setting. For example, political independents differ from partisans. Their concerns shift from one issue to another with the intensity of media coverage. Partisans, on the other hand, are inclined to think in terms of issues at the core of their party's concerns.[50]

The characteristics of the information being communicated are at least as important as the characteristics of the people receiving it. When the problem or event is far away—well beyond personal experience—the mass media provide the only information available. Their influence diminishes when information is closer to home and people have some personal basis for arriving at opinions.[51] The Vietnam War example introducing this chapter offers one illustration. During the Tet Offensive the media helped produce a backlash against President Lyndon Johnson for his administration's conduct of the war, about which journalists provided just about the only information that was available.[52] With the antiwar protests, however, TV was showing behavior about which most viewers had some personal experience (i.e., they knew young people similar to the protestors). Thus the media *can* have a major impact on public opinion, but *whether* they do so depends on both whom they are reaching and what they are covering.

Media Biases

Modern journalists purport to be objective. They are supposed to report events and describe conflicts accurately so that voters can make informed judgments. If reporters and editors usually lived up to this ideal, then media effects would not be much cause for concern. But news organizations and other media corporations represent an important player in the political system, essentially an institution with its own interests, values, and operating procedures. Many observers believe that the media do skew the news. The most common charge is that the media show political bias.

Media Bias

Ideological Bias

Conservatives first began to charge that most journalists were liberals in the 1960s. The initial response of most media organizations, not surprisingly, was to deny such charges. Over the last 30 years, however, a sizable number of studies have been conducted that interviewed samples of reporters, editors, and producers and asked them about their political attitudes and voting behavior. Without exception, these studies have shown that the original charge was true. Journalists are substantially to the left of the general adult population. The gap is relatively small on many economic issues—but huge on social and cultural issues such as abortion, gay rights, gun control, prayer in schools, and the death penalty.[53] Particularly impressive is the regularity with which media professionals—however defined—vote for the Democratic candidate for president. Since 1964, every Democratic presidential nominee has won at least 80 percent of the votes cast by journalists—even George McGovern in 1972 and Walter Mondale in 1984, who lost the elections by landslide margins.[54]

But how strongly do such personal beliefs affect the news? Conservatives often complain about the "liberal media." (See the *Democratic Dilemma* on page 254.) Even a respected nonpartisan election analyst, Charlie Cook, comments that "People who don't believe that there is a liberal or Democratic bias in the national media are kidding themselves."[55] Some studies do find evidence of partisan bias. For example, a team of researchers carefully watched tapes of the network evening news programs broadcast during the 1984 campaign. Their aim was to evaluate the **spin**—the positive or negative slant—that reporters and anchors put on their reports. They found that President Reagan got 10 seconds of bad spin for every second of good spin. In contrast, Democratic candidate Walter Mondale had a 3 to 2 ratio of good to bad spin.[56] On a less serious note, a study of the jokes told by late-night TV talk show hosts Johnny Carson and David Letterman during the 1988 campaign found that Republicans were skewered twice as often as Democrats.[57] As for the 2000 election, by mid-September George W. Bush had been the butt of 50 percent more late-night jokes than Al Gore.[58]

Although journalists do deviate from objectivity and Republicans suffer more than Democrats, lapses may not be as common as critics imply. Newspaper readers do not perceive consistently liberal viewpoints.[59] More than three-fourths of the presidential election coverage on television in 1984 had no spin at all. More recently, a study of newspaper, television, and Web coverage of the 2000 campaign during October found that Al Gore received significantly more negative coverage than George W. Bush.[60] The media tend to be hard on incumbents, losers, and those

spin
The positive or negative slant that reporters or anchors put on their reports.

caught up in scandals even when they are Democrats—as illustrated by the media-fueled scandals that plagued Bill Clinton from his initial presidential campaign until after he had left the White House. Similarly, late-night TV hosts focus on whoever offers the best material.

They may be less vocal, but critics on the left of the political spectrum also charge that the media are ideologically biased—only they see a conservative slant. Whatever the personal views of rank-and-file journalists, their publishers tend to endorse Republicans, as shown in Figure 9.2.[61] Since 1930, only Lyndon Johnson, Bill Clinton in 1992, and John Kerry have received more newspaper endorsements than their Republican opponents, although the larger urban newspapers are much more Democratic. Journalists work for profit-making enterprises reliant on corporate advertising. They often collect impressive salaries and enjoy

TABLE 9.2

TOP TALK RADIO SHOWS BY AUDIENCE SIZE AND IDEOLOGY

		Audience Size (in millions)	Political Ideology
1.	Rush Limbaugh	13.50	Conservative
2.	Sean Hannity	12.50	Conservative
3.	Michael Savage	8.25	Conservative
4.	Dr. Laura Schlessinger	7.75	Conservative
	Howard Stern	7.75	Nonideological
6.	Laura Ingraham	5.00	Conservative
7.	Neal Boortz	3.75	Libertarian
	Mike Gallagher	3.75	Conservative
9.	Jim Bohannon	3.25	Moderate
	Clark Howard	3.25	Nonpolitical (consumer)
	Bill O'Reilly	3.25	Conservative
	Doug Stephan	3.25	Nonideological
13.	Glenn Beck	2.75	Conservative
	Dr. Joy Browne	2.75	Nonpolitical (relationships)
	Jerry Doyle	2.75	Conservative
	George Noory	2.75	Nonpolitical (paranormal)
17.	Bill Bennett	2.25	Conservative
	Don Imus	2.25	Nonideological
	Kim Komando	2.25	Nonpolitical (computers)
	Michael Medved	2.25	Conservative
	Dave Ramsey	2.25	Nonpolitical (financial)
	Jim Rome	2.25	Nonpolitical (sports)
	Ed Schultz	2.25	Liberal

		Audience Size (in millions)	Political Ideology
TABLE 9.2 *(continued)*			
24.	Bob Brinker	1.75	Nonpolitical (financial)
	Tom Leykis	1.75	Nonideological
26.	G. Gordon Liddy	1.50	Conservative
	Al Franken	1.50	Liberal
28.	Tony Snow	1.25	Conservative
	Jim Cramer	1.25	Nonpolitical (financial)
	Alan Colmes	1.25	Liberal
	Mancow	1.25	Nonideological
	Randi Rhodes	1.25	Liberal
33.	Dr. Dean Edell	1.00	Nonpolitical (medical)
	Phil Hendrie	1.00	Nonideological
	Hugh Hewitt	1.00	Conservative
	Rusty Humphries	1.00	Conservative
	Lars Larson	1.00	Conservative
	Lionel	1.00	Nonideological
	Stephanie Miller	1.00	Liberal

SOURCE: Audience size figures are taken from estimates made by *Talkers* magazine and are based on an analysis of a national sample of media markets for fall 2005.

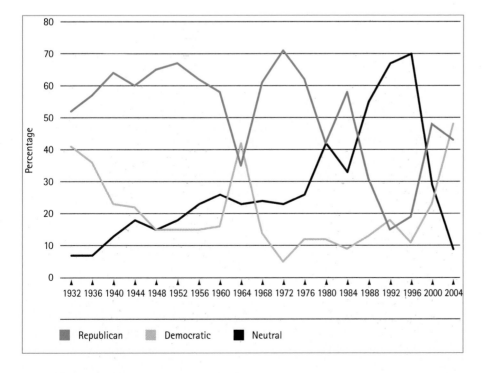

FIGURE 9.2

Newspapers Endorse Republican Presidential Candidates More Often than Democratic Candidates

SOURCE: Harold Stanley and Richard Niemi, *Vital Statistics of American Politics, 2001–2002* (Washington, DC: CQ Press, 2001), 194–195.

DEMOCRATIC DILEMMA

Talk Radio—A Conservative Answer to the Liberal Press?

Surveys repeatedly show that most of the people who work for the contemporary news media, including television, newspapers, and magazines, hold political attitudes that are far more liberal than those of the general population. But a striking exception to this pattern is talk radio. Talk radio is dominated by people who are clearly and unabashedly conservative. Every year, *Talkers* magazine, a trade publication that serves the talk radio industry, uses Arbitron figures from a national sample of media markets to compile a list of the top talk radio programs in the United States and their cumulative weekly audience. As shown in Table 9.2, conservative voices greatly outweigh liberal ones. Of the 37 programs on the most recent *Talkers* list, 16 were openly conservative—including five of the top seven. By comparison, only five of these talk-show hosts were liberal—and all were on the bottom half of the list.

To counter this conservative dominance, in 2004 a group of liberal entrepreneurs and venture capitalists created a left-wing talk network, called Air America. To date, however, Air America is still a pretty small-scale affair—at least by the standards of talk radio. The best-known of the liberal talk-show hosts is comedian Al Franken—yet as the figures in Table 9.2 indicate, Franken's weekly audience is about one-ninth the size of Rush Limbaugh's.

There are a number of reasons why conservatives dominate talk radio, but the most significant is simply that conservatives feel they have a greater need for some kind of alternative to the so-called mainstream media. Quite consistently over the past few decades, public opinion surveys have shown that a lot more Americans believe that the media have a liberal bias than believe that they are biased in the other direction.[a] In a 2003 Gallup Poll, for example, 45 percent of the respondents said that the media were too liberal, as against just 15 percent who said they were too conservative. When these results are broken down by ideology, it becomes clear that conservatives and liberals have very different attitudes toward the media. Conservatives see media as the enemy: 60 percent say the media are too liberal,

versus 9 percent who think they are too conservative. Liberals, by contrast, are not particularly upset with the media (at least, not with respect to their biases). Just 30 percent of liberals claim that the media are too conservative, while 18 percent say they are too liberal, and a plurality (50 percent) think that media get things "just about right."

As its power and prominence have grown, talk radio has, not surprisingly, become increasingly controversial. Some critics complain that talk programs and their hosts are, as a group, too shrill, partisan, and mean-spirited, inflaming their audiences with distorted and misleading information. The result, they claim, has been to make American politics increasingly rigid, nasty, and inflexible.

But a second viewpoint is also worth considering. Though the people who work for network television and the nation's major newspapers are disproportionately liberal and Democratic, the media almost never acknowledge this. Every time ABC, NBC, or CBS airs a story on abortion, the odds are overwhelming that the reporter, the producer, and the editor in charge of the program will all be pro-choice—a fact that, if more widely known, would probably help the audience better interpret the story. Yet, while the media routinely demand "full disclosure" from other newsmakers, they almost never provide the most basic information about their own backgrounds and ideologies. By contrast, radio talk show hosts are generally quite open about admitting their biases. Rush Limbaugh is a conservative and a Republican, and he says so on every program. Whatever other complaints one can lodge against Limbaugh, one cannot say that he has not warned his listeners in advance.

- *Given the current polarization of American politics, at least at the elite level, would the country be better off if we returned to something like the system that existed in the first half of the nineteenth century, where the media openly and explicitly acknowledged their biases?*

- *Instead of insisting that they are objective and that their personal beliefs and values have no effect on their reporting, should* Newsweek *and the* New York Times *admit that they are presenting "the news for and by liberals"?*

[a] For a review of the evidence, see William G. Mayer, "Why Talk Radio Is Conservative," *Public Interest*, 156 (Summer 2004): 99–100.

generous retirement benefits. Media celebrities also attract generous honoraria from corporate interests who invite them to give speeches, leading critics to call them "buckrakers" rather than muckrakers. All of these circumstances, it is alleged, exert a conservative pull.[62]

Moreover, the weakening of the dominance of the big-three networks should reduce any existing liberal bias. In particular, media observers generally agree that the increasingly popular Fox News program leans to the right; some critics have attacked it as a propaganda outlet for Republicans.[63] Local news and public-affairs programs are more likely to reflect local sentiments, so they can be more conservative than network news operations headquartered in New York, Washington, and Los Angeles. Some cable channels feature programs produced by conservative and evangelical groups. Talk radio has a conservative slant. The Internet is open to all points of view, and libertarians are especially well represented there. Columnist John Leo even notes the rise of comedy that showcases "anti-liberal humor," including *Saturday Night Live* veteran Dennis Miller, Comedy Central's Colin Quinn, and the irreverent cable TV cartoon *South Park*.[64] In short, as communications outlets grow, the mass media will be open to more points of view than were found on the airwaves in the past. But that does not mean that bias in the media is no longer a concern; other forms of bias may be more serious than the ideological kind.

Selection Bias

Periodically, frustrated citizens write to newspaper editors to complain that all their newspaper ever prints is bad news. Why not more good news? The answer is that to a considerable extent, the media *define* news as bad news.[65] A government program that works well is not news; one that is mismanaged or a failure *is* news. An elected official who is doing a good job is not newsworthy; one who is incompetent or corrupt is. Hard-working people working hard and contributing to their communities are not news; one sociopath who runs amok is. Far more pervasive than ideological bias is a bias toward the negative in the media. An emphasis on the negative is a kind of **selection principle**; reporters and editors give a skewed perception of reality based on the way they make decisions.

Media critic Larry Sabato argues that the negative tone of the media has become much more prominent in recent decades. He contends that presidents from Franklin Roosevelt to John Kennedy enjoyed the support of a press with a "lapdog" mentality. Johnson and Nixon were subjected to far greater scrutiny by a press with a "watchdog" mentality. Succeeding presidents, he maintains, suffer mean treatment from a press with a "junkyard dog" mentality.[66] Some observers believe that the negative tone of press coverage has contributed to the increased cynicism of the American public about politics and government.[67] They suggest that politics today is no worse than in previous eras—perhaps it is better—but that media treatment makes things *seem* worse.

Another selection effect is that "news" must be new, exciting, and unusual. Gradual developments and persistent conditions do not lend themselves to the kind of hit-and-run coverage favored by the contemporary media. A crisis does. Senator Jay Rockefeller of West Virginia learned this point to his dismay in 1998 when he tried to hold a press conference on health-care reform and instead faced a deluge of questions about a Clinton administration sex scandal. Exasperated, he asked, "Is there anybody here that just, almost for the practice of it, has a question about the health care of children?"[68]

The media look for heroes and villains, not for abstract social developments. This bias is particularly characteristic of TV, which is even more fast-paced than print. A frequently heard maxim to describe local TV news is "If it bleeds, it leads." TV needs dramatic events, colorful personalities, bitter conflicts, short and snappy comments (sound bites), and above all, compelling pictures. The result can be insufficient treatment of stories that do not fit the needs of the media and distorted treatment of stories to

PARTICIPATION

Are the Media Biased?

selection principle
Rule of thumb according to which stories with certain characteristics are chosen over stories without those characteristics.

make them fit those needs.[69] For example, journalists lionized Private Jessica Lynch of West Virginia after she was injured, captured, and then rescued during the war in Iraq (to the point that critics charged that reporters were helping the U.S. military fabricate "shamelessly trumped-up claims"). They paid far less attention to other members of the Army's 507th Maintenance Company, some of whom died, some of whom fought heroically, and some of whom (including another young woman, Shoshana Johnson) spent two weeks longer in captivity.

Numerous observers have pointed to such selection biases as a factor in the largest (in financial terms) policy debacle in American history—the Savings and Loan (S&L) disaster of the 1980s, with an estimated price tag of $200 billion.[70] Democrats and Republicans, Congress and the executive—all share the blame. As early as 1981, accountants, prominent economists, and a top government regulator began to issue warnings that the S&L industry was going bankrupt. The media provided only minimal coverage. Why? For one thing, the story was about financial policies that reporters found uninteresting. As one journalist commented, "It was a 'numbers' story, not a 'people' story."[71] Also, the issue was complex. Many reporters were ill-equipped to understand it, let alone to distill it into a short, simple story. The problem was particularly acute for TV, because initially the crisis offered few interesting pictures. Not until housing developments were being auctioned off for a song, S&L executives indicted, and members of Congress investigated did the media have the kind of story (and pictures) that it liked. When the government started closing insolvent S&Ls, many had been operating recklessly for years, secure in the knowledge that their losses would be covered by taxpayers. Media neglect helped add to this cost. When journalists finally did pick up the story, they distorted it. They emphasized the rare cases of fraud and corruption, even though most of the problem came from the ordinary operation of the political process: generous campaign contributions, corporate lobbying, favorable legal changes, and regulators who did not watch the industry closely.[72] Thus, the media even missed the opportunity to articulate a useful lesson that might help avoid such a problem in the future.

Some critics charge that the media desire for heroism and action—along with their desire for popularity—especially distorts the coverage of war and foreign affairs. Such criticism is not new. As early as 1966, one detractor wrote:

> Our remaining correspondents fly from earthquake to famine, from insurrection to massacre. They land running, as we were all taught to do, and they provide surprisingly good coverage of whatever is immediately going on . . . . [But] we miss anticipation, thought, and meaning. Our global coverage has become a comic book: ZAP! POW! BANG-BANG.[73]

During the war in Iraq, both the pro- and anti-war sides have complained about the slant of war reporting. In the early stages of the war, such complaints were most frequently voiced by those on the left. Many critics argued that the media were "shirking their duty" to keep an eye on government and instead had become boosters of military aggression. "Regardless of their own views on the war," according to Mark Weisbrot, co-director of the liberal Center for Economic and Policy Research, "American journalists became the Bush administration's major means of promoting it." The director-general of the British Broadcasting Corporation, meanwhile, expressed his shock at "gung-ho" war coverage, charging that reporters had "wrapped themselves in the American flag and swapped impartiality for patriotism." Beginning in about mid-2003, however, the tenor of most American war reporting became sharply more critical, leading to complaints from Republicans that the media were devoting too much attention to casualties and setbacks in Iraq and not enough to the many positive developments.

Professional Bias

A third kind of media bias arises from the demands of the journalism profession today. A few journalists are experts who work specific "beats"—the business reporter, education reporter, health reporter, Supreme Court reporter, and so on. But most reporters and journalists are generalists who lack specific substantive expertise. They operate on tight deadlines and start from scratch on many stories. Thus, on subjects more complex than scandals and conflicts, they are dependent on experts and other outside sources for information and interpretation. Ironically, despite the familiar image of the investigative reporter, studies find that reporters uncover only a small fraction of the scandals they report—probably less than one-quarter.[74] Government agencies reveal the lion's share, and they generally do so officially, not through surreptitious "leaks." Reliance on government sources can make a big difference in news coverage and helps explain why U.S. news often differs sharply from the information available in other countries. (See the *International Comparison* on the next page.)

Self Censorship
and the News

Moreover, as journalists themselves recognize, the news media have increased their emphasis on entertainment.[75] Especially in the case of TV, looks and personalities are more important today than they were a generation ago. With the growth of the new media, competitive pressures are greater than ever and have resulted in a race to the bottom, as network news becomes more like infotainment (a mixture of news and entertainment) and major newspapers become more like tabloids.

The lack of internal expertise and the competitive pressure for ratings and sales contribute to an unattractive feature of modern political coverage: "pack journalism," in which reporters unanimously decide something is the big story and attack it like wolves tearing apart wounded prey or sharks engaging in a feeding frenzy.[76] Comedian Jon Stewart prefers a different image: Small children playing soccer, all clumped together and thoughtlessly chasing a ball.[77] Normal people, observing such behavior, are puzzled by the media's pack behavior—but to journalists under great competitive pressure, there is safety in numbers. One can hardly be faulted for working on the same story as are other prominent journalists. Far better to focus on what turns out to be an overblown, inconsequential story than to "run the risk of going down in history as 'the reporter who missed the next Watergate.'"[78] Indeed, there is every indication that the "pack" mentality extends to editorial offices, where each news show or newspaper fears missing the "next big thing."

International Comparison

Al Jazeera—Questionable Sources?

As Americans tuned in during the fall of 2001 to follow the war on terrorism, they were introduced to the "The CNN of the Arab World": Al Jazeera.[a] In early 2001 Thomas Friedman of the *New York Times* had described Al Jazeera as the "freest" cable network in the Arab world even though it received significant support from the government of Qatar. Aggressive marketing, lively debate and—according to Friedman—"uncensored" news stories attracted large blocs of viewers. Al Jazeera not only styled itself after Western news organizations, but actually was allied with CNN to provide content.[b]

After the terrorist attacks of September 2001, Al Jazeera began providing CNN with video footage of Al Qaeda training camps. The network's most controversial contribution, however, was a broadcast of Osama Bin Laden speaking in a very threatening manner about the decadent West. Secretary of State Colin Powell denounced Al Jazeera's "vitriolic, irresponsible" statements. National Security Adviser Condoleezza Rice asked U.S. networks not to broadcast Bin Laden

speeches.[c] Originally heralded for its unprecedented access to news sources unavailable to American media outlets, the station increasingly faced criticism because of the perception that it had become too closely tied to those same sources. Both Middle Eastern and Western governments criticized the media outlet as biased and potentially dangerous. The First Amendment means that little can be done about Al Jazeera—besides appealing to good taste—in the U.S. context. But Islamic culture, unencumbered by a tradition of protecting dissent, may be less kind to the organization.

Al Jazeera responded to this criticism by holding back video footage of Bin Laden. But its partner CNN obtained and broadcast the footage anyway (the two organizations have since severed their relationship).[d] Al Jazeera pushed the boundaries of acceptable news coverage in the Middle East, despite its reliance on government money, but continuing controversy over the station's editorial slant illustrates how news coverage depends in part on the information sources available to journalists.

[a] T. Straus, "The CNN of the Arab World," Alternet.org, October 26, 2001.

[b] T. Friedman, "The Fast Eat the Slow," *New York Times*, February 2, 2001.

[c] Straus, "The CNN of the Arab World."

[d] Associated Press, "Arab Network Cuts Ties with CNN," February 1, 2002.

Prospects for Change

However justified, criticisms of the media's coverage of politics and government miss an important point. The news media in the United States are not part of the public education system. Rather, most are private, profit-making enterprises. As one journalist commented, "What few people recognize is that the purpose of the media is not to educate, it is to impress—to make an impression. There isn't the time or space to educate."[79]

As for complaints that their coverage falls short of what many would like to see, defenders of the media generally respond that they try to provide the kind of coverage people want, to the point of using focus groups and other measures of reader interest to serve the audience better.[80] Nonetheless, Americans are not happy with media behavior today. As Table 9.3 shows, popular evaluations of the media have declined sharply since the mid-1980s. Growing percentages of people believe that the media are unprofessional, uncaring, immoral, and even harmful to democracy.

Furthermore, media representatives have always claimed that they are more than profit-making businesses. They claim to provide an essential public service. When they publish sensitive or private information, they justify their behavior with more than a sprinkling of righteousness—using weighty terms such as "the public's right to know" or "the free flow of information in the marketplace of ideas." Such an exalted self-image may carry with it the responsibility to give the public what it needs as well as what it wants. Serving as guardians of the First Amendment may require more than 10-second sound bites. Perhaps the main hope of critics is that media executives may

Comparing
News Media

TABLE 9.3				
EVALUATIONS OF THE MEDIA HAVE WORSENED				

News organizations generally . . .

	1985 %	1999 %	2002 %	2005 %
Are moral	54	40	39	
Are immoral	13	38	36	
Care about people they report on	35	21	30	
Don't care	48	67	55	
Are highly professional	72	52	49	
Are not professional	11	32	31	
Protect democracy★	54	45	60	47
Hurt democracy★	23	38	19	33
Stand up for America		41	49	42
Too critical of America		42	35	40
Are politically biased		56	59	60
Are not politically biased		31	26	28
Pretty independent	37	23	23	21
Often influenced by powerful people and organizations	53	71	70	73
Favor one side in politics★	53	67	67	72
Deal fairly with all sides★	34	27	26	21
Get the facts straight	55	37	35	36
Stories often inaccurate	34	58	56	56
Too much attention to bad news	60	67	67	67
Report stories they should be covering	35	24	25	23
Care about how good a job they do★	79	69	78	
Don't care★	11	22	14	

★Data are derived from 2001 survey data.
SOURCE: The Pew Research Center for the People and the Press.

underestimate the average American citizen. During the 1992 presidential campaign, people in the media were stunned by the ratings earned by Ross Perot's "infomercials"—as many as 10 million households tuned in.[81] TV producers defend sound-bite journalism with the observation that the average voter has a short attention span, but Perot treated voters as intelligent adults and held the interest of many for 30 minutes with lengthy expositions accompanied by charts and figures!

The Media and Electoral Politics

The mass media play an important role in democratic politics. Ideally, they transmit information about problems and issues, helping voters make intelligent choices among the candidates who compete for their votes. Many critics feel that the general biases discussed earlier cause media coverage of elections to fall far short of the ideal.

VIDEO ROUNDTABLE

Role of the Press

Campaign Coverage

Nowhere do critics of the mass media find more to criticize than in the coverage of political campaigns. Numerous studies report that the various media biases combine to produce campaign coverage that is characterized by sins of both omission and commission (see Chapter 10).

The media provide little coverage of policy issues: the nature of social and economic problems, the contrasts among the programs that candidates advocate, and so forth. Instead, critics charge, the media devote too much attention to "character" issues that have little to do with the ability of the candidates to govern. Thus, the press dwells on whether President Bush dodged military service as a young man or whether Senator Kerry earned his military commendations in Vietnam. Such matters have some relevance, to be sure, and may provide some indication of how a candidate would govern, but reporting on such matters should not crowd out more substantive election coverage.

Not only do the media concentrate on candidates' characters at the expense of genuine policy and performance issues, but their interest primarily stems from a wish to handicap each race. Campaign coverage usually focuses on an election as though it were a horse race, reporting which candidate is leading, which candidate is dropping back, which one is coming up on the rail, what the latest polls say, who got what endorsement, and how a change in campaign personnel will affect public perceptions of the candidate. Even when the candidate announces a proposal or issue position, it is evaluated as a tactical move that can affect the candidate's standing in the larger horse race. This tendency toward "horse-race coverage" has become much more pronounced over the past generation, as the attention devoted to substance has declined.[82]

Another important characteristic of television election coverage, which is actually a recent development, is the extent to which it centers around the reporter rather than the candidates. According to a study conducted by sociologist Kiku Adatto, in 1968 the candidates were generally allowed to present their views in their own words. The average sound bite—a piece of film or video which shows the candidate speaking in his own words—lasted for 42 seconds. By 1988, the average sound bite was just 10 seconds.[83] In other words, rather than allowing the candidates to speak for themselves, journalists increasingly assumed that it was their responsibility to summarize, edit, and interpret the candidates' words. Knowing this, the candidates began to deliver speeches that reduced complex ideas and issues to one or two pithy, oversimplified sentences. And, though the networks vowed to change this aspect of their coverage, subsequent studies have shown that television sound bites have actually grown shorter—down to an average of 7.8 seconds in 2004.[84]

Observers of contemporary political campaigns are not the only ones who are critical of media coverage. The candidates themselves are critical—so much so that they are finding ways to get around the contemporary media. As noted earlier, they have started appearing on popular television programs. They also make themselves available more frequently to state and local journalists. Reporters of national stature complain that the candidates are insulating themselves from the hard questioning of seasoned journalists, but the candidates seem to enjoy the opportunity to talk about issues rather than the trivia that often dominates national news coverage. The growth of alternative news sources also gives today's candidates the means to act on such sentiments.

The Conventions

Before presidential candidates were chosen in the primaries, national conventions were important political events. Party leaders came together, made deals, hammered out a

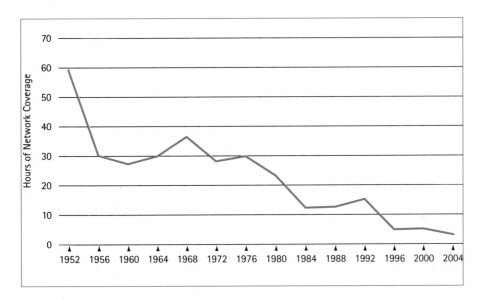

FIGURE 9.3

The Networks Increasingly
Ignore the National
Political Conventions

Note: Shows the average coverage
of each party's convention.

SOURCE: Adapted by Sam Abrams from
Harold W. Stanley and Richard G. Niemi,
Vital Statistics of American Politics
2005–2006 (Washington, DC: CQ Press,
2006), 195.

platform, nominated candidates, and (if successful) left with a unified party prepared to battle the opposition. In recognition of the importance of the conventions, CBS and NBC provided gavel-to-gavel coverage from 1956 to 1976 and regularly assigned their top anchors and reporters to the events.

The process for nominating presidential candidates was changed in 1972, in ways that removed the element of surprise from national party conventions (see Chapter 10). Since then, the conventions have not been nearly so important as in earlier eras, and media coverage has dropped accordingly (see Figure 9.3). As magazine writer Hendrik Hertzberg dryly put it, the "conventions are no longer troubled by the problem of being excessively interesting."[85] The parties now treat the conventions as huge infomercials in an attempt to take advantage of their diminishing time on the screen. Attractive speakers are slotted for prime time, and the entire convention schedule is arranged with the media in mind.

The parties showcase their candidates in hopes of producing a post-convention "bounce" upward in the polls. Recent conventions that produced large bounces for the candidates were the 2004 Republican convention (for President Bush) and the 2000 Democratic convention (for Vice President Gore).[86] Media coverage is a double-edged sword, however. If coverage emphasizes a divided party or unpopular elements of the party, it will cause the candidate to drop in the polls. The 1968 Chicago Democratic convention discussed at the beginning of this chapter is a classic example. Similarly, in 1992 Pat Buchanan gave an aggressive speech to the Republican convention that turned off many moderates.

The conventions probably will be even less important in the future. As one commentator observed after the 1996 events, "the more the party managers tried to package their message to please television, the less the major networks were interested."[87] In 1996 Ted Koppel and his *Nightline* team abandoned the Republican convention after two days, the networks cut coverage to about an hour a night, and ratings were off 25 percent from 1992. In 2000 MTV provided more convention coverage than the three major networks combined, and ABC pushed its coverage almost entirely to a program called *ABCNews Now* available on its digital channels.[88] The networks appear to be abandoning convention coverage.

The Presidential Debates

One of the high points of modern presidential campaigns is the series of debates between the two—and sometimes three—major candidates. No other campaign events earn such high ratings. In fact, more people watch the debates than vote.

The first televised debates were held during the 1960 campaign between candidates Richard Nixon and John Kennedy. One of the surprising findings in studies of the debates was that people who listened to them on the radio evaluated Nixon's performance more favorably than people who watched them on TV, an indication that visual images could have impacts different from the words with which they were associated.[89] No debates were held in 1964, 1968, or 1972, but they have been held in every election since then. Although the format and arrangements usually are matters of some controversy, debates now appear to be an institutionalized part of presidential campaigns.

Studies show that performance in the debates can sway the undecided voter. For example, in 1984 President Reagan appeared tired and confused in his first debate with Walter Mondale. His unexpectedly poor performance raised the issue of his age (then 73) and resulted in a slight drop in the polls. Knowing how important the next encounter was, Reagan came in alert, prepared, and full of good humor. He dispelled the concerns raised in the first debate and gained 4 points in the polls.[90] As in campaign coverage generally, the first question the media raise about debates is "Who won?"

Most observers agreed that President Bush blew the first debate in 2004, turning what might have been an easy race into a neck-and-neck battle. Senator John Kerry failed to press his debating advantage in the two clashes that followed—Bush held his own in the town-hall format of the second debate and Kerry seemed too tired and ill-focused to sway voters in the final showdown.

Media Coverage of Government

Media coverage of government exhibits problems and biases analogous to those evident in media coverage of campaigns. From the standpoint of the mass media, much of the routine work of government is dull—hence the media focus on what they consider more exciting.

Emphasis on the President (and Other Personalities)

The president is a single individual with personality and character. Naturally, then, he (and, one day, she) is inherently more interesting than a collectivity such as Congress or an abstraction such as the bureaucracy. The president receives the lion's share of the evening news coverage.[91] And not only does Congress play second fiddle in terms of media coverage, but coverage of the Congress has declined in recent decades.[92] The problem, of course, is that the president is only one part of the government, one with fairly limited powers (see Chapter 13). Thus, the media prime citizens to focus on the president to a degree that is out of proportion to his powers and responsibilities.

The exception to this generalization is one that proves the rule. For six months after the 1994 elections, the media virtually forgot about President Clinton as pack journalists turned their attention to House Speaker Newt Gingrich and the new Republican majority in Congress. For once, the media could represent Congress via a single personality. Now that the Republican leadership in Congress lacks a colorful personality like Gingrich, the media's former neglect of the institution has returned.

This focus of the media on personalities seems to be a universal tendency. It is similar to building military coverage around sympathetic war heroes or building sports coverage around a few outstanding superstars. An effective governmental team, like a winning sports team or a successful military unit, requires teamwork—but the media find individual heroics and failures to be more compelling stories. Unfortunately, in framing coverage in terms of individuals, the media probably discourage political entrepreneurs from building coalitions—and instead encourage them to promote themselves, to grandstand, to "hog the ball." Moreover, such media coverage primes citizens to think about government in terms of the heroic exploits and tragic failures of individuals rather than in terms of institutions and processes that are operating effectively or poorly.[93]

Emphasis on Conflict

Every time politicians make a controversial comment, they are assured of media coverage. Indeed, politicians who make the kind of inflammatory remarks the media love, and offer them up in convenient sound bites, can expect constant media attention.

In 1995, when President Clinton and Speaker Gingrich appeared on the same platform in New Hampshire and engaged in a mature discussion, citizens were receptive. Even the two rivals seemed to enjoy it. Journalists found it dull. How could they report an intelligent conversation? They would have been much more comfortable if the Speaker had leveled a serious charge or criticized the President personally in a 10-second sound bite.

Ironically, the journalistic preference for conflict can discourage politicians from doing anything really interesting. When reporters learn of an innovative proposal, the necessity to portray conflict leads them to search out the idea's likely enemies and trumpet their hostile reaction. As a result, journalists "often lead the chorus of criticism of anyone who tries to upset the apple cart. In so doing, they implicitly side with the interest groups and old-line politicians whose prerogatives are being challenged." The clamor of opposition not only immediately threatens public perception of the proposal, but also threatens the person who floated it. The would-be reformer is likely to be portrayed "as naïve and politically unsophisticated" for taking the chance.[94]

Journalists especially like conflict when it revolves around some kind of scandal. The same study that found coverage of Congress to be declining also found that the focus of coverage had changed. Policy stories outnumbered scandal stories by 13 to 1 from 1972 to the mid-1980s, but since then the ratio has plunged to 3 to 1.[95] The Clinton administration faced repeated scandals, some sexual and some financial—culminating in incessant reports of Clinton's intimate relationship with White House intern Monica Lewinsky. George W. Bush, meanwhile, faced a number of controversies that approached scandal-like proportions, including charges that his administration falsely manufactured reasons for going to war in Iraq and that his political advisers leaked the name of a CIA operative because her husband had criticized the war effort.[96] News that military police had tortured detainees in Iraq's Abu Ghraib prison also tarnished the Bush administration's image. Given media obsession with scandal and conflict, it is no wonder that politicians often try to tell journalists as little as possible. In 1998, White House spokesman Barry Toiv joked about this defense mechanism when he was late for a news briefing: "It's not easy getting up here and saying nothing. It takes a lot of preparation."[97]

Emphasis on the Negative

Media on the lookout for conflicts, scandals, and mistakes naturally emphasize the negative. What government does well is less newsworthy than what government does badly. Quiet compromises that improve public policies are less newsworthy than noisy arguments that accomplish nothing. Thus, network coverage of Congress has gone from highly negative to almost completely negative. According to one count, 3 of every 4 evaluations of Congress were negative in 1972, and that ratio rose to 9 of 10 by 1992.[98] Has Congress become that much worse, or has the change been inside the media? As mentioned earlier, even entertainment shows now portray government officials more negatively than they did a generation ago.[99]

The Response: Exaggerated Concern with the Press

Because the press has become the principal link between citizens and their government, elected officials often lose sight of the people. American politicians have long known about the political importance of the press: Witness the efforts of the early parties to establish their own newspapers. As the press became more independent and nonpartisan, politicians gradually came to understand that special efforts were needed to cultivate favorable coverage. At the presidential level, Theodore Roosevelt was perhaps the first president to have an aggressive press strategy of this type. Nearly all of his successors added new weapons to the presidential arsenal or institutionalized older ones. By the 1980s, media strategy had become a constant, almost obsessive concern of U.S. politicians, particularly those in Washington. According to a former Clinton White House official,

> When I was there, absolutely nothing was more important than figuring out what the news was going to be . . . . There is no such thing as a substantive discussion that is not shaped or dominated by how it is going to play in the press . . . . When you put together a press that is only interested in "horse race" and "inside baseball" and a White House staff that is interested only in the press, you've got the worst of both worlds.[100]

Chapter Summary

The mass media have been important players in American politics almost from the beginning. Initially small-scale and elitist, they have grown progressively more accessible to the average citizen. By most measures, television is now the most important form of mass communication—but recent technological developments have produced new media, such as cable TV and the Internet, that are weakening the traditional broadcast system.

Social science thinking about media effects on public opinion has gone through several stages or schools. Perhaps the best way to summarize the current viewpoint is that

the media can have important effects on public opinion; however, such effects are not automatic. For example, where people have strong predispositions, the effects of the mass media are limited. Also, where people have alternative sources of information, such as their personal experience, media effects are limited.

Media effects on public opinion fall into several categories. Agenda setting occurs when media coverage affects what issues or problems people think about. Priming occurs when the media encourage people to evaluate political figures in terms of one set of considerations rather than another. Framing occurs when the media present problems or issues in such a way that people are stimulated to think about them in terms of one frame of reference rather than another. The media also may change attitudes more slowly through their role in political socialization.

Frequently, critics charge the media with one or another form of bias. Surveys show that reporters and editors are more liberal and more supportive of Democrats than is the public at large, but it is less clear whether the values and opinions of journalists have a significant effect on their political coverage. Moreover, other critics charge that professional considerations lead the media in a conservative direction on economic issues.

More important than ideological biases are biases that arise from the definition of what is news, and especially what is considered good TV news. The media reflect an emphasis on the negative and an emphasis on conflict. The media focus on dramatic incidents and colorful personalities rather than on more abstract forces and developments, even where the latter are far more important. The media oversimplify complex situations and reduce complicated arguments and positions to 10-second sound bites. Such media biases are understandable. Unlike the media in many other countries, however, the U.S. media are organized and operated from the private sector. The role of the mass media in serving the public interest exists in constant tension with their role as profit-making enterprises serving their stockholders.

Key Terms

agenda setting, p. 248
CNN effect, p. 248
equal-time rule, p. 239

framing, p. 249
mass media, p. 235
new media, p. 242

priming, p. 249
selection principle, p. 255
spin, p. 251

Suggested Readings

Of General Interest

Farnsworth, Stephen J., and S. Robert Lichter. *The Nightly News Nightmare*. Lanham, MD: Rowman & Littlefield, 2003. Excellent summary of how television covered presidential campaigns between 1988 and 2000, with particularly good data on media content.

Lippmann, Walter. *Public Opinion*. New Brunswick, N.J.: Transaction Publishers, 1991. Originally published in 1922, it is still the best book ever written about the mass media.

Neumann, W. Russell. *The Future of the Mass Audience*. Cambridge, England: Cambridge University Press, 1991. Thoughtful examination of the effects of technological change on mass communications. Concludes that new media will not fragment the audience as much as many think.

Norris, Pippa. *A Virtuous Circle*. Cambridge, England: Cambridge University Press. 2000. Hugely informative survey of politics and media in advanced industrial democracies. In general, Norris takes a more sanguine view of modern developments than many critics do.

Sabato, Larry. *Feeding Frenzy*. Baltimore: Lanahan Publishers, 2000. Entertaining critique of the most extreme manifestations of "pack journalism."

Focused Studies

Hewitt, Hugh. *Blog: Understanding the Information Reformation That's Changing Your World*. Nashville, TN: Thomas Nelson, 2005. Provocative argument about the importance of blogs, written by the author of one of the most important conservative blogs.

Iyengar, Shanto, and Donald Kinder. *News That Matters*. Chicago: University of Chicago Press, 1987. An exemplary experimental study that demonstrates the existence of agenda setting and priming.

Lavrakas, Paul, and Michael Traugott, eds. *Election Polls, the News Media, and Democracy*. New York: Seven Bridges Press, 2000. Comprehensive collection of essays on election polls. Suggests that the media make a significant contribution to American democracy through election polls, properly done.

West, Darrell. *Air Wars*. 4th ed. Washington, DC: Congressional Quarterly, 2005. Readable study of the evolution and consequences of television advertising in campaigns since 1952.

On the Web

Virtually every news organization these days has a Web site.

abcnews.go.com/politics

www.cnn.com/allpolitics

www.nytimes.com/pages/politics

www.latimes.com/news/politics/

www.foxnews.com/politics/

www.washingtonpost.com

This list consists of some of the most prominent news organizations' politics Web sites. In addition to these news sites, commentary has become extremely important, particularly with respect to framing and priming issues. The editorial sections of these Web sites are also good sources for learning about elite debate and dialogue.

www.tnr.com

www.theweeklystandard.com

Magazines such as the left-of-center *New Republic* and the conservative *Weekly Standard* have become important outlets for policy ideas.

www.people-press.org

The Pew Research Center for the People and the Press conducts survey research on how the media conducts themselves. Its Web site is invaluable for understanding how the public reacts to the media.

Election Voices

Should Freedom of the Press Be Limited to Protect National Security?

THE ISSUE

Even though the First Amendment guarantees "freedom of the press," are there limits on what the media should be able to print or broadcast if a story might compromise American national security?

Background

The First Amendment to the Constitution clearly states that "Congress shall make no law . . . abridging the freedom of speech, or of the press . . . ." On its face, this seems to be a straightforward declaration. As one Supreme Court justice was fond of saying, "No law means no law." In practice, however, there is a long tradition in which courts, legislatures, and academic commentators try to carve out exceptions and qualifications to this general principle. Consult a typical textbook on constitutional law, and you will find literally hundreds of pages attempting to explain all the details and complexities of the law concerning freedom of speech and freedom of the press.[1]

One particular area of controversy concerns the duties and responsibilities of the press when it covers issues directly connected to American national security. As almost everybody concedes, secrecy is a useful, often essential attribute of decision-making in foreign policy, particularly in a time of war. But if citizens are to pass judgment on the government's performance in conducting foreign policy and prevent the abuse of governmental powers, the public must be kept informed about their country's international actions and policies. There is, in short, an unavoidable tension between secrecy and accountability when democracies conduct foreign policy, a tension that surfaces in a variety of ways.

Censorship in the Interests of National Security

Suppose that the federal government knows in advance that a newspaper will print a story that top officials in the executive branch believe will be harmful to U.S. national security. Should they be able to prevent the paper from printing the story? Should the federal government, in other words, be allowed to censor the American news media in the interests of national security?

The kind of case just described is, we should make clear, exceptional. Though top federal officials are often annoyed or outraged by what the media choose to print or broadcast, very rarely have they resorted to what is called *prior restraint*. But it has happened.

The most celebrated case of this kind was the publishing of the Pentagon Papers. In 1968, then Secretary of Defense Robert McNamara commissioned the writing of a detailed, secret history of how the United States had become involved in the Vietnam War. In 1971, a former Defense Department employee named Daniel Ellsberg leaked a copy of this still-classified history to several newspapers. In mid-June, the *New York Times* and then the *Washington Post* began publishing portions of that history, now generally known as the Pentagon Papers. Top officials in the Nixon administration—Secretary of State Henry Kissinger, in particular—believed that this publication could "result in great harm to the nation," including "the death of soldiers, the destruction of alliances, the greatly increased difficulty of negotiation with our enemies, [and] the inability of our diplomats to negotiate." Hence, they sought an injunction to prevent these newspapers from publishing any more of the Pentagon Papers. Several courts did issue a temporary injunction, which prevented the newspapers from publishing further material from the history as the case was being decided. (All newspapers complied with the court orders.)

In a 6–3 decision, however, the U.S. Supreme Court rejected the government's claim and allowed the publication to continue. A majority of the justices did not contend that prior restraint could never be justified, but the Court did say that "any system of prior restraints . . . comes to this Court bearing a heavy presumption against its constitutional validity," and that the government therefore had a "heavy burden of showing justification for . . . such a restraint." And the Nixon administration, in the Court's view, did not meet that burden.[2]

A closer call, for many commentators, occurred in 1979, when a left-wing magazine called *The Progressive* decided to print an article that explained how to build a hydrogen bomb.

267

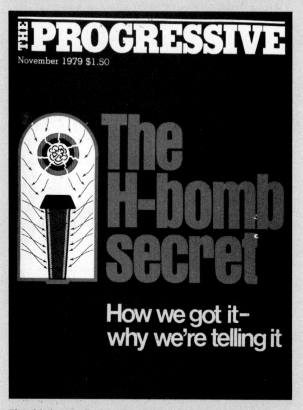

THE PROGRESSIVE

November 1979 $1.50

The H-bomb secret

How we got it— why we're telling it

Should the media be allowed to publish stories disclosing information that may endanger the country?

Claiming that the article only synthesized information from publicly available documents, the author and the publisher claimed that the article would benefit the nation "by demonstrating that open debate [about nuclear weaponry] was preferable to an oppressive and ineffective system of secrecy and classification." The federal government replied that information in the article would present an "immediate, direct, and irreparable harm" to the interests of the United States, and it submitted affidavits from various cabinet members claiming that publication of the article would increase the risk of thermonuclear proliferation. In this case, a district court ruled in favor of the government, though the case was ultimately abandoned when a lengthy letter detailing the same information was published in two newspapers.[3]

Self-Policing by the Media

The cases just described are, as we have already noted, clearly exceptional. In the more typical case, the government does not find out about the story in advance—or if it does, it simply tries to persuade the news agency not to print or broadcast it.

In other words, the decision about what might harm the nation's security, and whether that harm justifies suppressing the story, is left to the media.

An interesting case of this kind occurred in late June 2006, when the *New York Times* published a front-page story about a secret program, begun shortly after the terrorist attacks of September 11, 2001, in which counterterrorism officials had gained access to "financial records from a vast international database and examined banking transactions involving thousands of Americans and others in the United States." As the article noted, the Bush administration viewed the program as a "vital tool" in the war against terrorism, saying that it had played "a hidden role in domestic and foreign terrorism investigations . . . and helped in the capture of the most wanted [Al] Qaeda figure in Southeast Asia."

Indeed, after finding out about the investigation, administration officials made extensive efforts to persuade the paper not to publish the article, saying that "disclosure of the . . . program could jeopardize its effectiveness." But the *Times* refused to halt publication. As Bill Keller, the newspaper's executive editor, summed up his conclusion, "We remain convinced that the administration's extraordinary access to this vast repository of international financial data, however carefully targeted use of it may be, is a matter of public interest."[4]

Over the next few days, there were numerous calls for an investigation of how the *New York Times* got the story and prosecution of the executive branch officials who had leaked it to the press, but no one in the administration seriously urged that the *Times* or its reporters be punished.

Protecting Confidential Sources

Many of the stories just described—and many non-foreign policy stories as well—are obtained from reporters by so-called confidential sources: sources who ask the reporter not to disclose their identity. This is a common practice among American reporters, and though it often annoys top decision-makers (when they themselves are not the anonymous source), in most cases it does not present any particular legal dilemmas.

But suppose that the confidential source is breaking the law—as was almost certainly the case in both the Pentagon Papers and the more recent *New York Times* story. In order to prosecute the law-breaker, authorities need to find out who leaked the story—and the only way to do that, in most cases, is to ask the reporter. Should the reporter be compelled to disclose his sources to the police or prosecutors? Or does the First Amendment protect the reporter from such questioning?

The seminal Supreme Court case on this subject is *Branzburg v. Hayes*, decided in 1972. Branzburg was a reporter who wrote an article about a variety of illegal drug activities he had witnessed. Shortly thereafter, a prosecutor asked him to appear before a grand jury and identify the drug users.

Branzburg refused—and was imprisoned as a result. His attorneys argued that the use of confidential sources was often essential to news gathering; and that if reporters were required to reveal their sources, they would be "measurably deterred from furnishing publishable information, all to the detriment of the free flow of information protected by the First Amendment." But the Court ruled against Branzburg: reporters, like all other citizens, are not exempt from grand jury subpoenas.[5]

The Branzburg case, it is worth adding, only establishes that reporters do not enjoy a *constitutional* right to keep their sources secret. Partly in reaction to the Branzburg decision, more than half of the states have passed "shield" laws that provide at least a qualified privilege of confidentiality.[6]

How Have the Courts Ruled?

We should note here that the courts were a major player in almost all of the cases described above. This should come as no surprise. Whether one takes a broad or narrow view of freedom of the press, it is clear that the Constitution does pose a substantial hurdle to any legal attempts to command or regulate the press. No matter how much legislatures or executives may resent it, the final say in most such cases will inevitably be pronounced by the courts.

What Do You Think?

1. Which should be a greater concern for contemporary Americans—the threat from terrorism or the threat from secret government programs that investigate or monitor the activities of ordinary citizens?

2. Of the three court cases described in this section, in which case(s)—if any—do you agree with the final decision? On the whole, do you feel that the courts have done a good or poor job of balancing freedom of the press against the needs of national security?

3. If you were a state legislator, would you vote for a shield law that provided full or partial immunity to reporters from having to reveal their confidential sources?

4. Did the *New York Times* make the right decision in publishing its story on the administration's use of financial data to track the activities of terrorists?

On the Web

For ongoing commentary about these and other issues in journalism ethics, see the following Web sites:

www.poynter.org
www.cjrdaily.org
www.mediaresearch.org

---

[1]See, for example, Kathleen M. Sullivan and Gerald Gunther, *Constitutional Law*, 14th ed. (New York: Foundation Press, 2001), 956–1433.

[2]All quotations are taken from *New York Times Co. v. United States* 403 US 713 (1971).

[3]See *United States v. Progressive, Inc.* 467 F. Supp. 990 (W.D.Wis. 1979).

[4]The original article, which also discusses the decision to publish, is Eric Lichtblau and James Risen, "Bank Data Sifted in Secret by U.S. To Block Terrorism," *New York Times*, June 23, 2006: A1.

[5]*Branzburg v. Hayes* 408 U.S. 665 (1972).

[6]Sullivan and Gunther, *Constitutional Law*, 1410.

CHAPTER 10

★ ★ ★ ★ ★ ★ ★ ★ ★ ★

Electing the President

CHAPTER OUTLINE

The Meaning of Elections

Tension ran high in the days before the 2004 presidential election. The contest between President Bush and Sen. John Kerry looked close, "too close to call" as the journalists like to say, leaving many Americans fearful of an election fiasco resembling the one that threatened the nation's political system in 2000. Wall Street's stock market was stagnant as investors fearful of a crisis held back their funds.[1]

Opinion polls in the months before the election only added to the confusion. They gave widely varying predictions, not only from one survey organization to another, but also across different polls conducted by the same people. Even the last-minute polls gave little guidance—some put Bush ahead and some put Kerry ahead, but in every case the predicted margin of victory was so tiny that the polls were, in the words of the *Washington Post*, "meaningless in attempting to predict the outcome."

Some sources confidently predicted a Kerry victory. Polls indicated that his performance in three presidential debates impressed voters, whereas Bush's conduct in the first debate strongly alienated viewers. "The effect of Kerry's debate sweep on the core undecided and persuadable voters has already been immense," concluded United Press International. Zogby International issued a bold prediction on Election Day, that the polling trends pointed to a Kerry victory with 311 electoral votes.

Other events also seemed to be going Kerry's way. For example, signs indicated—correctly, as it turned out—that voter turnout would surge. "A huge increase is likely to favor Kerry," the *Washington Post* surmised—wrongly, as it turned out. One polling firm saw the election tilting to Kerry because they expected minority turnout to jump, not realizing that Bush's support among minorities would jump too. Polls conducted in key swing states indicated that Bush would lose in the close races necessary to keep his job.

Meanwhile, the networks had spent $10 million to establish an "exit poll," in which voters at selected precincts would be asked their choices. Democrats, including younger voters, apparently cooperated at high rates. Preliminary figures thus promised Kerry victories in the key states of Florida and Ohio.

These numbers leaked onto the Internet, which caused investors to fear an election that would take weeks to resolve. The Dow Jones Industrial Average took a nosedive late in the afternoon, and British bookmakers reported a sudden surge in bets on Kerry. Journalists reported that President Bush had expressed a "rare sense of doubt," that he "appeared subdued." Bush's British ally, Prime Minister Tony Blair, reportedly said that he had "gone to bed thinking Mr. Kerry was the next president of the United States, only to wake up to learn otherwise."

Contrast all this flurry of activity with how political scientists approached the election.[2] Using statistical models refined over several presidential elections, scholars committed themselves to predictions long before most of the remarkable campaign events took place. Some of the most sophisticated attempts at forecasting the election came out in July and August, for example, around the time of the national party conventions and long before the first presidential debate.

Of the seven forecasts, only one described the election as too close too call. The other six predicted a Bush victory. In fact, one pair of scholars predicted in August that Bush would receive 51.7 percent of the major-party vote. He received 51.5 percent. Overall, the political scientists gave much clearer and much earlier predictions than all of the pundits, and they basically got it right.

MAKING THE CONNECTION

News coverage of presidential elections typically focuses on the short-term events of election campaigns: the strategies, the personalities, the mistakes. Someone who judged American elections simply on the discussion found in newspapers, in magazines, and on the airwaves would conclude that voters make snap decisions based on short-term (if not trivial) considerations. It is hard to reconcile this story of last-minute decision making with the ability of political scientists to forecast the presidential results accurately long in advance, before all of the fluctuations in the polls and before all the campaign events that supposedly drive the outcome.

We will begin the chapter with a discussion of the nomination process, considering how presidential candidates are nominated in the United States, and how our unusual nominating process came to be. After a discussion of the pros and cons of the American nominating process, it then turns to the general election, reflecting on how the electoral college affects the nature of the campaign and how Americans vote in presidential elections. The chapter then considers why the importance of the media and the campaign is often exaggerated. It closes with a discussion of what issues and other factors have influenced the most recent presidential elections.

Nominating a Presidential Candidate

One of the major functions played by political parties, as we have seen in Chapter 8, is to simplify and clarify elections. They do this primarily by nominating candidates for public office—designating one person as the official party candidate for each office on the ballot. While parties do this for offices of all types and at all levels of government, the most important and visible nomination that the major parties make is their choice of a presidential candidate every four years.

Evolution of the Nomination Process

Though the Constitution does not explicitly say anything about how candidates for president (or for any other office) are to be nominated, the dominant understanding at the Constitutional Convention was that this function would be filled primarily by the electoral college.[3] The electors, meeting in their respective states, would scatter their votes among a large number of candidates, no one of whom would have a majority. The top five finishers in this initial balloting would thus, in effect, be "nominated," with the final choice then made by the House of Representatives. In fact, however, nothing like this scenario ever took place. In the first two presidential elections held under the Constitution, George Washington was the obvious consensus choice. By 1796, when Washington announced he would not seek a third term, both the Federalists and the Democratic-Republicans decided to nominate a presidential candidate *before* the members of the electoral college were selected. The mechanism they devised for this purpose was the congressional caucus: a meeting of each party's members in the U.S. Senate and House of Representatives. The congressional caucus was the major, though not exclusive, means for nominating presidential candidates between 1796 and 1824.

Almost from the beginning, however, the congressional caucus came under attack. Some critics felt that involving Congress in the selection of presidential candidates implicitly violated the constitutionally prescribed separation of powers. Others felt that the procedure was undemocratic, especially as it meant that any district that elected a congressman from the other party was unrepresented in the caucus deliberations. After experimenting with a number of other nominating mechanisms, by the 1840s both the Democrats and Whigs were nominating their presidential and vice-presidential candidates by national conventions. Each state party selected a number of delegates, usually at a state convention, who then met together at a central location in order to nominate the party's national ticket and adopt a short "platform" that outlined the party's positions on the most important issues of the day. It was a convention of this type that nominated, among others, Abraham Lincoln as the Republican Party presidential candidate in 1860.

In the early twentieth century, one important innovation was added to this system.[4] Spurred by the Progressive movement and its attack on corrupt party machines, a number of state legislatures required that the state parties select their national convention delegates through primary elections, rather than at state conventions. Sometimes called the "mixed system," this set of procedures was used by both the Democrats and Republicans to nominate presidential candidates between 1912 and 1968. As the name indicates, the principal virtue of this system was that it seemed to give both ordinary party voters and formal party organizations a voice in presidential nominations. Candidates who wanted to demonstrate their electoral appeal could do so by running in the primaries; but the number of primaries was sufficiently limited that party leaders still had the capacity to accept or reject the primary verdict. In 1960, for example, John Kennedy entered only seven primaries. After winning them all, he then used this showing to convince state party leaders of his electability. In 1952, by contrast, Estes Kefauver won 12 of the 13 primaries he entered—but because the Democratic leaders disliked and distrusted him, Kefauver fell well short of his party's nomination.

The Contemporary Nomination Process

Like its predecessors, however, the mixed system came under attack for being unrepresentative and undemocratic. Particularly controversial was the Democratic nomination race of 1968. With many Democratic activists outraged about the Johnson administration's conduct of the Vietnam War, two antiwar candidates, Eugene McCarthy and Robert Kennedy, won almost all of the primaries—yet the Democratic convention nevertheless gave its presidential nomination to vice-president and Johnson supporter Hubert Humphrey, who had not entered a single primary. On the second night of a remarkably bitter and divisive convention, the Democrats adopted a vaguely worded resolution that, as eventually interpreted, authorized a special commission to rewrite completely the rules the party used for selecting delegates and nominating presidents. By 1972, the rules had been so completely transformed that most political scientists treat the nomination races since then as a completely different era in nomination politics.[5] The changes, moreover, affected both parties—partly because the Republicans were anxious to show that they, too, were an open and responsive party, partly because when state legislatures rewrote their primary laws, they tended to make the changes applicable to both parties.

The central thrust of the new rules was to take a process that had been dominated by party leaders and formal party organizations and turn it into one in which almost all delegates were chosen to reflect the presidential preferences of ordinary party voters. Specifically, delegates to contemporary national conventions are chosen in three major ways:

1. *By primary election.* The most visible sign of the new system was a sharp increase in the number of presidential **primaries**, from about 17 per year in the elections of 1952–1968 to 23 in 1972, 33 in 1980, and 35 in 2004. Moreover, unlike pre-1972 primaries, the new rules generally required that delegate selection be directly tied to the presidential preference vote cast in the primaries. Much like members of the electoral college, national convention delegates were no longer elected as relatively free agents, who could go to a national convention and deliberate or bargain with other party leaders. Delegates were almost always elected in ways that made them little more than messengers, pledged to vote for a specific candidate unless that candidate withdrew and "freed" his delegates.

2. *By caucuses.* A small number of states continue to select their delegates through party-run **caucuses**. This complicated procedure generally begins with party meetings held in each town or precinct in the state. These precinct caucuses, as they are usually called, select delegates to county, congressional district, or state conventions, and it is only at these latter meetings that national convention delegates are chosen (see the *Election Connection* box on the next page).[6]

   Caucuses differ from primaries in a number of ways: They take longer, their rules are more complicated, and they generally require participants to make a public expression of their candidate preferences (rather than casting a secret ballot). Hence, they tend to have a considerably smaller turnout than primaries: Whereas the typical primary brings about 20–30 percent of the party faithful to the polls, caucuses are rarely attended by more than 1 or 2 percent of the eligible electorate. For this reason, caucuses are sometimes more susceptible to domination by extremist candidates and issue zealots, such as those that supported Jesse Jackson and Pat Robertson in 1988.

   Yet in most respects, caucuses are, as one presidential candidate described them, "the functional equivalent of a primary."[7] Like primaries, voters show up at caucuses, express their presidential preferences, and expect that national convention delegates will directly reflect those preferences. Also like primaries, caucuses are not restricted to formal party members, nor do they require participants to demonstrate that they have supported the party in the past. Virtually any voter who walks in off the street and is willing to sign a statement claiming that he or she is committed to the party or its principles can take part, with the same rights and privileges as the state party chairman or a long-time member of the state legislature.

3. *Superdelegates.* In the first several nomination contests held under the new rules, there was a severe decline in the number of Democratic elected officials and party leaders who became delegates to that party's national conventions. Hence, in 1982, the Democratic Party adopted a new set of rules under which certain kinds of party leaders—members of the U.S. House and Senate, governors, members of the national committee—became automatic or ex-officio delegates. These **superdelegates**, as they are generally known, have accounted for about one-sixth of the votes at most recent Democratic conventions. (Nothing similar exists on the Republican side.) In a closely fought nomination race, the superdelegates might hold the crucial balance of power, but with the possible exception of 1984, such an eventuality has never occurred.

primary election
Preliminary election that narrows the number of candidates by determining who will be the nominees in the general election.

caucus
Meeting of candidate supporters who choose delegates to a state or national convention.

American Electoral Rules: How Do They Influence Campaigns?

superdelegate
Certain kinds of party leaders—members of the U.S. House and Senate, governors, members of the national committee—who became automatic or ex-officio delegates.

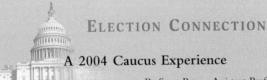

ELECTION CONNECTION

A 2004 Caucus Experience

By Scott Peters, Assistant Professor,
University of Northern Iowa

Tonight I went to the local elementary school to attend my first Democratic precinct caucus. I arrived about 15 minutes before the 6:30 p.m. start time, and was confronted with a long line of people waiting to sign in. Much to my surprise, there was no ID check, even for people who were registering on-site.

We met in the school's cafeteria, and scattered among signs telling us to eat our vegetables were campaign signs from Dean, Edwards, and Kerry. I was surprised that I didn't see any Gephardt signs. I also didn't see very many stereotypically burly union guys, whom I could peg as traditional Gephardt supporters (although there were a few senior citizens present, a group that has provided Gephardt with staunch support in the past). Other than about a half-dozen teenagers attending with their parents, there were very few people there under 30, although I did see a few young hippies wearing Kucinich stickers. The rest of the people there were middle aged, and many of them were undecided, or at least claimed to be when asked.

We had 212 people in attendance. State party procedures demand that at 7 p.m., the caucus split into preference groups—people literally walk to appointed spots in the room to demonstrate their support for a particular candidate. (It's a bit like a class splitting up to do group work, and it happens with about as much commotion, but considerably more pep.) I went to the Gephardt preference group. If influence were measured by median age, we would have been unstoppable. Unfortunately, what matters is numbers of people—if, after 30 minutes, a preference group fails to command at least 15 percent of the total number of attendees, it must disband and its members must migrate to another preference group. The magic number for our precinct was 32. After a few minutes, we had 17. The group leader started going around trying to appeal to other groups, but few of the rest of us made a similar effort. I stuck around to listen as representatives from other candidates came over to try to cherry-pick Gephardt's supporters.

The Kerry guy was very enthusiastic: "You know, Kerry's a friend of labor. He's got a 92 percent rating with AFL-CIO."

"Yeah, but he opposes the death penalty," said one 60-ish Gephardt supporter, consulting her cheat sheet with all the candidates' positions on key issues. "I don't want those criminals running around."

I eavesdropped on several conversations like this and was favorably impressed with people's knowledge of issues and desire to find a candidate they could support on issues. People were also very concerned with finding someone electable, someone who had a chance of beating Bush in November. Although along the way there was some harsh criticism of President Bush, for the most part the tone was serious but positive, and people really seemed to be having fun.

Occasionally a cheer would rise in one part of the room—it was a preference group welcoming new members who were abandoning their original choice once it became clear that it wasn't viable. First the Clark people broke up, most of them going to Kerry. Then, according to a deal the candidates had announced earlier in the day, most of the Kucinich supporters migrated over to Edwards. From what I could tell, the Edwards camp offered to give one of their county convention delegate positions to a Kucinich supporter if the group came over to Edwards. A few Kucinich people also went to Dean, which seemed to be the most natural second choice to a Kucinich supporter. Finally, the Gephardt supporters split pretty evenly between Kerry and Edwards.

When all was said and done, Edwards got 85 votes, and Kerry and Dean split the rest pretty evenly. The precinct's 13 delegates to the county convention were allotted accordingly: 5 to Edwards, and 4 each to Dean and Kerry. (The number of delegates per precinct depends, among other things, on levels of voter turnout in previous elections. One precinct near campus in which most of the residents are students, and therefore typically has very low voter turnout, was given only two delegates to the county convention despite the fact that over 200 people participated in the caucus.)

After that, the caucus broke up very quickly, a disappointment to me. One of the functions of the caucus is to propose platform planks, and I was really looking forward to observing the debate over them. But the chair of the caucus moved just to pass along all proposed planks to the county platform committee and let its members sort them out.

There was some other business the caucus had to take care of, mainly selecting various precinct officers. By my estimate, there were only about 40 people present during these discussions. The meeting ended at 8 p.m., and when I got home I turned on the TV to watch the results.

Financing Nomination Campaigns

The new delegate selection rules were not the only source of change in the presidential nomination process. In 1974, in reaction to the Watergate scandals, Congress completely rewrote the laws governing how money could be raised and spent in federal election campaigns. Prior to the passage of the Federal Election Campaign Act (FECA) of 1974, the financing of presidential campaigns was almost completely unregulated. Contributors could give as much money as they wanted and candidates could spend everything they could raise; candidates were not even required to disclose any information about their campaign finances—including who had given them the money.

The new regime established by FECA had five major features:

1. *Contribution limits.* In the original law, no one could contribute more than $1,000 to any presidential candidate. And even though the late 1970s were a time of rapid inflation, this limit remained unchanged. Finally, in 2002, the contribution limit was increased to $2,000 and indexed to inflation—that is, it will be increased every two years at the same rate that the consumer price index has increased during the same period. Though the limit for the 2008 campaign has yet to be set, it will probably be in the vicinity of $2,200.

2. *Matching funds.* To help make up for some of the money candidates lost because of the contribution limits, FECA also set up a system of federal subsidies to presidential nomination contenders. A candidate first had to demonstrate some minimum level of support, by raising $5,000 in contributions of $250 or less in 20 states. After that, every contribution of $250 or less would receive an equal amount of money in **matching funds**, paid out of the federal treasury.

3. *Spending limits.* The federal money came with strings attached, however. Candidates who accepted matching funds were also required to limit both their total spending and the amount they could spend in individual states. The overall limit was set at $10 million but was indexed to inflation; by 2004, it had increased to $37.3 million. In the first five elections held under the FECA, almost every major candidate accepted the matching funds and, thus, the spending limits. But over the last several election cycles, an increasing number of candidates have decided that the spending limits are too constraining and have thus opted to forgo federal funding. In 2004, both major-party nominees, John Kerry and George Bush, opted out of the matching fund program and then raised and spent more than $200 million—before the general election campaign had even begun. In the aftermath of that election, it was widely predicted that in 2008, almost all serious presidential candidates will reject matching funds and thus make the spending limits effectively inoperative.

4. *Self-financing.* For some candidates, there was one additional incentive to reject matching funds. When candidates accepted matching funds, they also had to agree that they would put no more than $50,000 of their own money into their campaigns. As a result of an important Supreme Court decision rendered in early 1976, however, candidates who did not take federal money could spend as much of their own money as they wanted *on their own campaign.* Historically, most presidential candidates have not been rich enough for this provision to matter, but in

matching funds
Public moneys (from $3 check-offs on income tax returns) that the Federal Election Commission distributes to primary candidates according to a pre-specified formula.

1996 multi-millionaire Steve Forbes announced that he was running for president and then poured $35 million of his own money into a six-month campaign for the Republican nomination. Although that money did not buy Forbes the nomination, it did bring him victory in two primaries and bought him a lot more visibility and attention (he was even a guest host on *Saturday Night Live*) than he would have received from a less lavishly funded effort.

5. *Disclosure requirements.* The one part of FECA that everyone seems to feel is a success is the disclosure requirements. All presidential candidates are required to file periodic reports (quarterly reports during the year before the election, monthly reports during the election year) indicating how much money they have raised and spent and, most importantly, the source of every contribution of $200 or more. Especially in the year before the election, these results are carefully monitored by the media—some pundits refer to it as "the money primary"—as an early indicator of the candidates' progress. It was these reports, for example, that first propelled Howard Dean into the national spotlight in mid-2003.

The Presidential Nomination Process in Action

How do these rules work in practice? One of the most conspicuous characteristics of contemporary presidential nomination campaigns is how long they are. In the old "mixed system," presidential candidates generally did not begin active campaigning until early in the election year itself or in the final months of the preceding year. Today, a presidential nomination race begins just a few weeks after the preceding midterm election.[8] By March of the year before the election—20 months before the general election—each party will likely have a half-dozen active presidential candidates, with a number of others seriously thinking about joining the fray. (The only exception is a party that has an incumbent president seeking reelection. Since 1980, incumbents have never faced serious opposition in their quest for renomination.)

You Are a Presidential
Campaign Consultant

This extended period of campaigning that goes on before a single primary or caucus takes place is called "the invisible primary."[9] Candidates use this period for several purposes. In part, they try out the issues and themes they hope to use to attract the voters, honing their messages and trying to get a handle on the "mood" of the electorate. A great deal of the invisible primary is also devoted to fund-raising. As a result of the FECA contribution limits, presidential aspirants can no longer fund their campaigns by calling up a handful of wealthy supporters and soliciting a few large contributions. Instead, the candidates must obtain contributions from thousands of individual donors, a task that tends to require large commitments of time from the candidate him- or herself. One former candidate has estimated that 70 percent of his time during the invisible primary was devoted to fund-raising.[10]

Finally, candidates spend a good deal of the invisible primary campaigning in a very small number of states that will hold early primaries and caucuses. Two states, in particular, have traditionally received a remarkably large share of candidate time and money and, consequently, of media attention: Iowa, which holds the first caucus, and New Hampshire, which holds the first primary.[11] Especially for a non-front-running candidate, a victory or even an unexpectedly strong showing in these two early events can endow the candidate with a key attribute known as "momentum." Momentum consists of a number of distinct but interconnected processes: the candidate get substantially more attention from the media; new funds pour into his campaign coffers; lots of voters learn about the candidate for the first time—and at least for the moment, most of the publicity is positive; other voters who already knew about the candidate but did not take him seriously now see him as a real contender for the nomination; they are also inclined to think that, by winning the primaries, he is showing his potential strength in the general election.

Iowa and New Hampshire are usually followed by a large number of major primaries and caucuses, coming in quick succession. Knowing how important the early phases of the nomination race are, more and more states have moved their primaries and caucuses forward in the calendar, generating a process that is often described as "front-loading."[12] The contest may be hotly fought for a number of weeks, but rather quickly the combination of delegate numbers, monetary pressures, and the media's incessant desire to declare a "winner" brings the nomination race to an effective conclusion. In 2000, both George W. Bush and Al Gore had clinched a first ballot nomination victory by March 14; in 2004, John Kerry achieved this milestone on March 13. Their major opponents, bowing to the inevitable, conceded the race and withdrew from the field.

Technically, a presidential aspirant does not become the official party candidate until he or she is nominated by the party's national convention, which is usually not held until July or August. But as we have already noted (see the introduction to Chapter 8), national conventions are no longer decision-making bodies. The real decision is rendered by the voters participating in the primaries and caucuses; the conventions simply count up the delegates won by each candidate months earlier, much like the meeting of the electoral college in mid-December. Instead, conventions are treated as a four-day-long advertisement for the party and its national ticket—and the media, fully aware of this, are less and less anxious to cover the conventions, thereby making them less effective as advertisements.

Strengths and Weaknesses of the Nomination Process

The contemporary presidential nomination process is now more than 30 years old. How well has it performed its basic function of narrowing the large field of presidential hopefuls down to two principal alternatives?

Perhaps the dominant goal of those who rewrote the delegate selection rules in the early 1970s was to increase the amount of popular participation in the presidential nomination process, and at one level they were clearly successful. Total turnout in presidential primaries has increased dramatically as compared to the 1950s and 1960s. Few other democracies in the world give millions of ordinary party voters such an important role in selecting their party leaders and nominating the person who, if elected, will be the most important official in the national government.[13] In most other countries, this function is performed by a relatively small number of elected officials or dues-paying, card-carrying party members.

Yet, as the Democrat's decision to create "superdelegates" testifies, not everyone is delighted with this development. While the final choice of president or prime minister should be made by the voters, some have argued, party nominations should be decided by those who have a demonstrated, long-term commitment to the party and a greater familiarity with its principles and candidates. Ordinary voters have no more business making party nominations than baseball fans have making the key personnel decisions for their favorite team. As E. E. Schattschneider, the most important defender of this position in American political science, has put it, "Democracy is not to be found in the parties but *between* the parties."[14]

Other critics have questioned just how open and egalitarian the contemporary nomination process really is. Clearly, the current system does not treat all voters equally. The voters in Iowa and New Hampshire have much more influence, and accordingly see much more of the candidates, than the voters in other states. In most recent contests, about a third of all states held their primaries after both candidates had already clinched their party's nomination.

Even in the early states, there is reason to wonder whether the contemporary nomination process really has given "power to the people" in quite the way its designers intended. As we noted in the chapters on political parties and interests groups, taking power away from one group of elites seldom empowers ordinary citizens. Other elites are more often the beneficiaries. In the case of the nomination process, many commentators fear that stripping power from party leaders and government officials may only have empowered two groups that are less representative and less accountable: political activists and the media.

political activists
People who regularly participate in politics; they are more interested in and committed to particular issues and candidates than are ordinary citizens.

Because participation in primaries and (especially) caucuses is so low, small groups of dedicated **political activists** can exert more influence in the nomination contests than they can in general elections, where turnout is much higher. In addition, it is activists who work in campaigns, donate money to candidates, and help mobilize other voters. As a result, some analysts worry that the nomination process confers an advantage on candidates who appeal to activists by taking positions far from the center of the political spectrum where the mass of Americans are located. Democratic candidates generally are more liberal, and Republican candidates generally more conservative, than the average voter. In the general election, many voters consequently feel that they are offered a choice between two relatively extreme, polarized candidates, with no one speaking up for the broad middle of the electorate.

The media are the second group that has gained influence from the nomination process. Americans must look to television, radio, and newspaper reporters—as well as commentators and editors—to interpret confusing primary and caucus developments for them. Critics complain that the press focuses too much on the "horse race": who is ahead and by how far, who is coming up on the rail, and who is fading from contention. Thomas Patterson has documented a striking shift in how the media "frame" campaigns. In the 1960s, before the primary era, media coverage was about evenly split between a policy orientation and a "game" orientation. In 1972, the first year of the new system, coverage shifted to the game frame by a proportion of 2 to 1. Since 1976, the game frame has had a 4 to 1 edge.[15] For the media, campaigns have become the political equivalent of "March Madness."

The media also tend to focus on scandals, gaffes, and campaign feuds. Critics charge that the media are more concerned with trivia and sleaze than with real questions of government policy. Of course, the media have a response to these criticisms of their behavior: Newspapers, news magazines, and television networks are profit-making enterprises that must compete for advertising dollars. They must print what sells, which is the horse race and the sleaze. What is the good of providing long, detailed policy coverage if the audience just tunes it all out?

The extent and quality of participation are not the only criteria by which to judge the presidential nomination process. Another major criticism of the current system is simply that it takes too long. In order to run for president, a potential candidate must count on devoting about two full years to the endeavor. On the one hand, this means that many plausible candidates cannot spare the time from their work in government or find the whole ordeal too exhausting and demeaning and therefore decide not to run. On the other hand, the candidates who do make the race are often compelled to ignore or give short shrift to their governing responsibilities. For example, sitting U.S. senators and representatives who run for president almost always see a sharp decline in the number of congressional roll call votes in which they participate. In 2003, for example, Senators John Edwards, Joseph Lieberman, and John Kerry, all of whom were running for president, showed up for, respectively, 61, 46, and 36 percent of the roll call votes held in the Senate that year. Because Lieberman's campaign ended early, his roll call participation rate rebounded in 2004 to 98 percent; but Kerry, as the party's nominee, took part in just 10 percent of the Senate roll call votes held during the election year. Edwards, who retired from the fray for several months and then re-entered as the party's vice presidential nominee, showed up for 41 percent of the election-year votes.[16]

Perhaps the most important question that we can ask about the presidential nomination process is: What kind of candidates does it finally nominate? Are they sufficiently representative? (Answering this question, of course, requires our deciding who the candidates are supposed to represent—all voters, party voters, or party leaders.) Are they qualified to hold the job and perform its manifold responsibilities? Unfortunately, it is very difficult to answer such questions with much assurance. There is a tendency on the part of many voters and pundits—and many political scientists—to lament the quality of recent presidents and presidential candidates. Whereas once the presidency was filled by giants such as Lincoln, Washington, and the Roosevelts, now it is occupied by men of considerably smaller stature.

These sorts of judgments, however, may tell us more about the current mood of the country and its high level of cynicism than about the reality of presidential performance. Contemporary observations and reactions are not always a good guide as to how history will regard a president. During his years in the White House, Harry Truman had very low ratings in public opinion polls and was widely regarded by commentators and congressmen as a man who was simply "out of his league": a decent, well-meaning man who had been elevated to the White House by accident and simply could not fill the ample shoes of his predecessor. Today, historians generally rate Truman to be a "near great" president. And if the old mixed system nominated Roosevelt and Truman, it also produced Warren Harding and Herbert Hoover.

One final point is worth making here. Although the designers of the contemporary presidential nomination process clearly intended to take power away from the established party leaders and increase the level of popular participation, many of the most noteworthy features of the current system were not the products of deliberate choice. Rather, they were the "unintended consequences of reform." For example, no one who wrote or approved the new delegate selection rules hoped to make the process so much longer. If anything, one of their complaints about the mixed system was that the delegate selection process in some states started too early. Yet the evidence unmistakably shows that when the new rules were implemented, presidential nomination campaigns became dramatically longer.

The general lesson, which should be committed to memory by all future reformers, is that political systems and institutions are complex creatures, and that whenever

A Ground-Breaking Choice

Vice presidential nominee Joseph Lieberman was the first Jew to run on a major-party ticket. Though defeated in the Democratic primary when he sought re-election to the Senate in 2006, Lieberman won the general election by running as an independent.

the rules are changed in a major way, the full consequences can rarely be predicted in advance. This does not mean that change should never be made, but it does suggest that change ought not be undertaken lightly or without a large measure of caution.

Who Nominates the Vice President?

Before the establishment of the contemporary nomination process, the conventions chose the vice presidential candidates as well as the presidential candidates. The choice usually was an effort to "balance" the ticket ideologically or geographically. Today, the choice of vice presidential candidates is completely in the hands of the presidential nominees, although they still attempt to choose a nominee who will improve the ticket's chances.[17] The presidential nominees simply announce their choices, and the conventions accept them, even when, as at the 1988 Republican convention, there is considerable doubt about the qualifications of the nominee. From 1960 through 1980, presidential nominees generally didn't announce their choice until after they themselves had been officially nominated, but the common practice today is to announce the decision a week or so before the start of the national convention. This was course followed by Bush and Gore in 2000 and by Kerry in 2004.

The General Election for President

Labor Day traditionally marks the start of the fall campaign, although today's nominees do not take so much of a break after the summer conventions as they did in the past. From the start of the campaign until Election Day—the first Tuesday in November—the candidates maintain an exhausting pace, and the campaign dominates the news.[18]

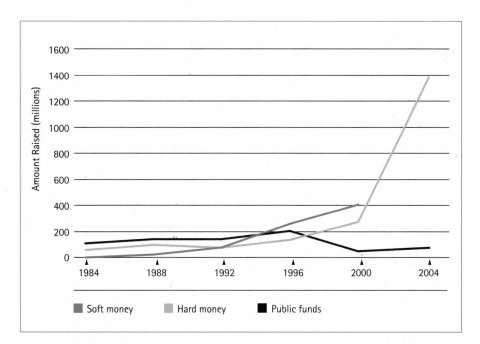

FIGURE 10.1

In the 1990s Reliance on
Soft Money in Presidential
Elections Increased
Dramatically

Public funding declined in 2000
because Bush, Forbes, and the
Republican Party declined
federal matching funds.

Source: The Federal Election Commission.
Note that the Federal Election Commission
began requiring the parties to disclose their
soft money in 1991. Figures for 1991
through 2000 are from the FEC. Figures
for the 1984 and 1988 cycles are based on
voluntary disclosures by the parties and on
published estimates.

Financing the General-Election Campaign

From the mid-1970s to the mid-1990s, presidential campaign funding was a comparatively simple proposition. Under the terms of the 1974 Federal Election Campaign Act, the general-election campaigns of the two major-party candidates were publicly funded. Very shortly after the official convention roll call vote that made their nomination official, both candidates received a large check from the federal treasury. The amount of the check was set at $20 million in the 1974 law, but was, again, indexed to inflation; by 2004, the checks sent to Bush and Kerry were worth $74.6 million. The federal money was not matching funds, as it was in the primaries: It represented, instead, all the money that the candidates were supposed to raise and spend for the general election campaign.

In the late 1980s and 1990s, however, presidential campaigns increasingly began to make use of **soft money**. Soft money is money contributed by interest groups, labor unions, and individual donors that is not subject to federal regulation. The reason why these contributions are not regulated is that the money is not given to the candidates, who are subject to FECA restrictions, but to party committees with more flexibility regarding the contributions they may accept and how they may spend them. As Figure 10.1 demonstrates, soft-money contributions to the parties exploded in the 1990s, setting off one of the campaign financing controversies that periodically erupt in the United States (see the accompanying *International Comparison* on the next page).

As a result, in 2002, Congress passed and President Bush reluctantly signed the Bipartisan Campaign Reform Act (BCRA). The central provision in this law was a ban on soft money at the national level: National committees and candidates for federal office were prohibited from soliciting, receiving, or spending any money that was not subject to federal contribution limits.[19] Yet as pre-BCRA campaign finance reformers have generally found, it is notoriously difficult to insulate the American electoral system from the influence of money. A substantial amount of the old "soft money" was

Public Campaign
Financing

soft money
Money contributed by interest
groups, labor unions, and individual
donors that is not subject to
federal regulation.

527s
Political organizations formed
primarily to influence elections
and therefore exempt from most
federal taxes.

INTERNATIONAL COMPARISON

Campaign Financing in Other Democracies

Campaign finance is rarely a major issue in democracies other than the United States. There are a number of reasons for this difference.

In the first place, much more money is spent in American elections—even relative to the size of the electorate—than in elections in other countries. For example, nationwide, the total amount spent in the 2000 U.S. elections was about $3 billion. Only Japan comes close to spending as much (relative to the size of its electorate).

One reason American campaigns are so expensive is the candidate-centered electoral system. Each candidate constructs a personal organization that funds the campaign. In contrast to the United States (and Japan), most other democracies have party-centered elections. The national party and its leaders conduct a single campaign on behalf of all the party candidates. Rather than having hundreds of individual candidates running duplicate campaigns, the parties take advantage of what economists call economies of scale.

A second reason for the high cost of American campaigns is that they are increasingly fought over the airwaves, and TV time is expensive—as are the services of the consultants, ad people, and so forth.[a] In most other democracies, candidates still rely more on the campaign work of party members than on attempting to reach voters directly through broadcasting.

One reason why campaign finance is a lesser concern in other democracies is that spending is heavily regulated. In Britain individual candidates are not permitted to buy televi-

sion or radio time! Even the parties cannot make media buys. They are limited to a small number of publicly financed addresses by national party leaders. In Germany the law requires TV networks to give the parties free airtime during campaigns, but it is illegal for candidates to buy any additional radio or TV ads.[b] If strict limits such as these were adopted in the United States, the courts would strike them down on First Amendment grounds.

Many other democracies provide at least some degree of public election financing.[c] For example, in Austria, Belgium, Denmark, Finland, Germany, Mexico, Sweden, and Turkey, the parties receive public subsidies in proportion to the number of votes they received in the last election or the number of seats they hold in parliament. In-kind subsidies, especially free media time, also are common. In the United States public financing has progressed only as far as presidential elections; attempts to extend it to Congress have failed.

In sum, candidate-centered media campaigns, the Constitution, and popular attitudes all interact to make campaign finance a more serious issue in the United States than elsewhere. Contrasts with other democracies raise a number of questions.

• *Should all legitimate candidates receive free TV time?*

• *Should all campaigns be publicly financed?*

• *Should the United States adopt a constitutional amendment that permits regulation of how much candidates can spend and what they can spend it on?*

[a] "Money and Politics," *The Economist*, February 8, 1997: 23.

[b] Charles Lane, "Kohl Train," *The New Republic*, February 14, 2000: 17.

[c] Richard Katz," Party Organizations and Finance," in *Comparing Democracies*, eds. Lawrence LeDuc, Richard Niemi, and Pippa Norris (Thousand Oaks, CA: Sage, 1996), 129–132.

simply diverted into a different type of political organization, known as 527s, after the section of the Internal Revenue Code that authorizes them. To simplify a highly complex issue, **527s** are political organizations that are formed primarily to influence elections and therefore are exempt from most federal taxes. By claiming that their primary purpose is to "influence elections in general but not any *specific* election," 527s are not subject to most of the restrictions in either FECA or BCRA.[20] According to the best study of the topic conducted to date, 527s raised $424 million in 2004—a particularly impressive figure given that their legality was in some doubt for much of the election cycle.[21] Unless new legislation is passed, it is almost certain that considerably more extensive use of 527s will be made in the 2008 elections.

Finally, a word should be said about how third-party and independent candidates finance their presidential campaigns. In a sense, they get the worst of both worlds. They are required to abide by the contribution limits: $1000 per donor from 1976–2000, $2000 per donor in 2004. Yet the vast majority of such candidates receive not a dime in federal funding. Federal law does provide some money to any third-party or independent candidate who receives 5 percent or more of the popular vote—but not having the money in advance, few third-parties have the resources to get anywhere near that figure. (Since the inauguration of public financing in 1976, only three such candidates have qualified.) The only way around this dilemma is to nominate a candidate who is wealthy enough to finance his campaign almost entirely out of his own pocket. In 1992, Ross Perot spent $65 million of his own money on his presidential campaign—and, not coincidentally, achieved the best popular-vote showing by a third-party or independent candidate in eighty years.

Spending in the General-Election Campaign

Campaign consultants oversee the expenditure of the large sums of money available to the campaigns—and they profit personally from such spending. These specialists in modern candidate-based campaigns have replaced the party leaders who supervised campaigns of earlier eras. Media consultants design the campaign ads or "spots," stage "media events" (appearances designed so that reporters get a story, not so that candidates meet voters), and schedule the candidate's time so as to maximize coverage. Derided by critics as "handlers" and "hired guns," some campaign consultants have become celebrities in recent decades. Modern campaigns also retain pollsters capable of measuring surges and slumps in candidate support.

Comparing Political Campaigns

The most important category of general-election spending is expenditures for "electronic media"—TV and radio advertising, with the lion's share going to television. Although campaign advertising is widely criticized, studies have consistently found that it is informative, in that those exposed to ads know more about the candidates and where they stand than those not exposed to ads.[22] Indeed, contrary to popular perceptions that everything is getting worse, research suggests that the issue content of ads actually has increased in recent years.[23]

Another, less positive recent trend is the tone of campaign advertising: It has grown increasingly negative.[24] Rather than make a positive case for themselves, candidates make a negative case against their opponents. However, not all negative ads are bad; pointing out the failures and flaws of an opponent is a perfectly legitimate part of the campaign.[25] But, too often, the campaign debate is filled with exaggerations, distortions, and, on occasion, outright lies.

Negative advertising seems to work, though, in the sense that people remember more of what they have seen from negative than from positive spots.[26] Candidates often succeed when they "go negative." What is good for individual candidates, of course, may have harmful consequences for the larger political process. Much of what people remember may be inaccurate, and attack ads might reduce turnout (especially among the independent, more moderate segment of the population). Candidates, then, are playing to the more committed and more extreme voters, making campaigns more polarized.[27]

The Electoral College

The Constitution stipulates that the president and vice president must be chosen by the electoral college. Under this system, each state selects a number of electors equal to the sum of its House and Senate seats. (The District of Columbia gets three votes under the terms of the Twenty-Third Amendment for a total of 538 votes nationwide.) These electors constitute the electoral college and their **electoral vote** determines who will

electoral vote

Cast by electors, with each state receiving one vote for each of its members of the House of Representatives and one vote for each of its senators.

popular vote

The total vote cast across the nation for a candidate.

Electoral College

winner-take-all voting

Any voting procedure in which the candidate with the most votes gets all of the seats or delegates at stake.

The Electoral College

become the nation's chief executive. Thus, the candidate who wins the most votes—the so-called **popular vote,** or the actual votes cast—does not necessarily become president. Rutherford Hayes in 1876, Benjamin Harrison in 1888, and George W. Bush in 2000 all became president despite coming in second in the popular vote. Depending on how one tabulates the popular votes cast in Alabama, a strong case can also be made that in 1960 John Kennedy won a majority of electoral votes even though Richard Nixon actually received more popular votes.[28] If no one receives a majority of the electoral votes, then the election is decided by the House of Representatives, as it was when John Quincy Adams defeated Andrew Jackson in 1824.

Because every state has two senators, whereas the number of House seats depends on the state's population, the electoral college gives a theoretical advantage to small states. For example, with two senators but only one seat in the House, Wyoming has three electoral votes—approximately 1 per 165,000 residents. With 2 senators but 53 seats in the House, California has 55 electoral votes, approximately 1 per 617,000 residents. In the 2004 election, if a candidate had won a plurality in each of the 40 least populated states, which together included only 43 percent of the U.S. population, he would have won a majority of the electoral college and become president. (We must add, however, that such an outcome is highly unlikely: Small and large states are spread out all over the country and have such varied interests and ideologies that there is little likelihood that a candidate will ever win all of the 40 least-populated states and no others.)

Other observers, however, believe that in practice the Electoral College has a bias in favor of large states. The reason is that almost all states assign electoral votes on a **winner-take-all** basis. Under state laws, the candidate who receives a plurality of a state's popular votes wins *all* of the state's electoral votes (except in Maine and Nebraska, which give the winner of each congressional district one electoral vote and the statewide winner the two remaining votes). Thus, a candidate who carries a large state by a tiny margin receives a windfall of electoral votes, whereas a candidate who wins small states by a landslide gets only a few. In 1996, for example, Clinton won 49 percent of the popular vote but 70 percent of the electoral vote because of the winner-take-all system.

The electoral college system has been controversial for a long time. Dozens of attempts have been made to amend the Constitution to do away with this provision. The leading alternative to the electoral college is a pure popular vote system, though proposals have also been made that would retain the electoral college but assign state electoral votes on a non-winner-take-all basis. The bottom line is that none of these attempts has succeeded; few have even come close.

The electoral college survives for a number of reasons. First, it is generally difficult to amend the Constitution, requiring two-thirds support in both houses of Congress and then ratification by three-fourths of the state legislatures. Second, small states (and sometimes, big states as well) are convinced that they derive a significant advantage from the electoral college, which makes their senators and representatives reluctant to vote for change.

Finally, the electoral college has endured because, for much of the twentieth century, the harms it allegedly produced were largely theoretical. A candidate *could* win the popular vote and then lose in the electoral college, but until 2000 that had not actually happened since 1888. (The 1960 case is somewhat more complicated and has, in any event, never been very well publicized outside of academic circles.) In the days immediately after the 2000 election, there were some signs of renewed discontent with the electoral college, but any criticisms of this type were quickly overwhelmed with complaints about how the votes were being counted (or not counted) in Florida. The anger and energy that might have been directed at the electoral college were instead focused on punch-card ballots and other voting technologies, and the electoral college ended up attracting remarkably little attention.

Voting Behavior in Presidential Elections

One impact that the electoral college clearly does have on presidential politics is its effect on how candidates allocate their personal campaign time and advertising money among the states. In general, candidates concentrate on the so-called battleground states: the states that are sufficiently close that they might plausibly be won by either candidate. By contrast, the campaigns pay much less attention to states that they cannot win and those that they are almost guaranteed to win.

Why do some states consistently support one party or the other for long periods of time? The reason is that there is considerable continuity in how citizens vote. This continuity, or "electoral inertia," not only explains why candidates know ahead of time how they will do in many states, it also explains why campaign organizations and the media generally have a limited impact on general election outcomes.

When Americans Decide

Many people decide how they will vote before the campaign begins. Typically, one-third to one-half of the electorate reports deciding how to vote *before the primaries*. This decision is easy enough for people who always vote the party line. It is also rather easy for voters who know the identity of at least one of the nominees—usually an incumbent president who seeks reelection. Another portion of the electorate reports deciding how to vote between the start of the primaries and the end of the conventions. All told, between 50 and 80 percent of the electorate report that they decided how to vote by the end of the conventions—before the fall campaign gets under way. The figure was 54 percent in 2000, when no incumbent ran, and 79 percent in 2004, when Bush was seeking reelection.[29] Hence, a large number of the electorate—typically well more than half—are not much affected by the campaign. They have already made up their minds!

How Americans Decide

How can people make up their minds before policies, programs, and personal qualifications are debated in the fall campaign? The answer is that Americans decide how to vote not only on the basis of the short-term considerations that dominate campaign coverage (the candidates and the positions they advocate) but also on the basis of longer-term considerations that arise months or years before the campaign gets under way. The considerations that determine how Americans vote fall into four general categories: party loyalties, public policies, government performance, and the qualities of the candidates.

Party Loyalties   Though pundits sometimes describe the contemporary American electorate as "disgusted with" or "turned off by" both major parties, the fact is that most Americans—about two-thirds, in fact—do feel some sort of basic psychological allegiance to either the Democrats or the Republicans. The name that is usually given to this attachment is **party identification**, or party ID for short.[30] It is measured by a question

party identification
A person's subjective feeling of affiliation with a party.

TABLE 10.1					
GROUPS DIFFER IN THEIR SUPPORT FOR THE PARTIES					
	Percentage Voting Republican				
Population Category	Bush 2004	Bush 2000	Dole 1996	Bush 1992	Bush 1988	Reagan 1984
White	58	54	46	40	59	64
Hispanic	43	31	21	25	30	37
African American	11	8	12	10	12	9
Poor (<$15,000/year)	36	37	28	23	37	45
Affluent (>$50,000/year)	56	52	48	44	62	69
Union	40	37	30	25	42	46
White Protestant	67	63	52	47	66	72
Catholic	52	47	37	35	52	54
Jewish	25	19	16	11	35	31
Big-city resident (population >500,000)	39	26	25	28	37	n/a
Suburban resident	52	49	42	39	57	61
Rural resident	59	59	46	40	55	67
Lives in the East	43	39	34	35	50	53
Lives in the Midwest	51	49	41	37	52	58
Lives in the South	58	55	46	43	58	64
Lives in the West	49	46	40	34	52	61

SOURCE: Table accompanying Marjorie Connelly, "How Americans Voted: A Political Portrait," *New York Times* Week In Review, November 7, 2004.

that asks the survey respondent, in straightforward fashion, "Generally speaking, do you usually think of yourself as a Republican, Democrat, independent, or what?"[31] This simple question is probably the most analyzed in all of political science—for it is also the best single predictor of voting behavior and many other important political attitudes.

Party ID is a long-term force that provides continuity from election to election. For example, the Civil War and Reconstruction created many "yellow dog" Democrats in the South—people who would not vote for a Republican even if the Democratic nominee were a yellow dog. Similarly, the Great Depression left many northerners intensely committed to the New Deal Democratic Party of Franklin Roosevelt. Such deeply held allegiances underlie the "party systems" discussed in Chapter 8.

Party identification explains the well-known tendencies of various groups to support candidates of one party or the other. For example, Table 10.1 shows that African Americans and Jews are heavily Democratic in their voting. Union members, urban residents, and Catholics also have traditionally been Democratic groups, although the support of union members and Catholics has fluctuated in recent decades. On the other hand, the wealthy, rural residents, southerners, and Protestants—especially evangelicals—tend to vote Republican.

At one time, party ID was considered to be much like a religious affiliation. Not only was it resistant to change, but it was also learned early in childhood and had little policy or ideological content. Just as children learn to call themselves Catholics, Jews,

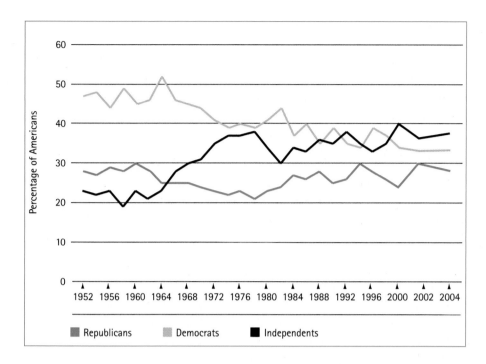

FIGURE 10.2

The Democratic Advantage
in Party Identification
Has Eroded

Source: American National Election
Studies.

or Muslims before they know the doctrines of their religion, so children learned to call themselves Democrats or Republicans before they knew what the party stood for. The traumatic events of the 1960s severely tested party loyalties, though, lessening the proportion of voters holding strong party identifications and increasing the number of independents. Thus, scholars generally recognize that party ID responds to political events and conditions, although slowly and gradually in most cases.[32]

As shown in Figure 10.2, between the 1952 and 1984 elections, more Americans consistently considered themselves Democrats than Republicans. Republican candidates such as Eisenhower and Nixon were able to win by capturing a majority of the independents and by convincing a sizable share of Democratic identifiers to defect from their party. After Reagan's reelection in 1984, however, the gap between the parties began to close. Taking into account that Republicans are more likely to vote than Democrats, today's electorate contains about equal numbers of Democrats and Republicans. For the strongest partisans, the campaign is largely irrelevant—come hell or high water, they will vote their party ID.

Public Policies   For the most politically interested voters, policies and programs are the essence of politics. There are problems and conflicts in the United States and in the world. Problems cry out for solutions and conflicts for resolution. Elections decide these solutions and resolutions. For people with this view of politics, the campaign is a long-running debate—a chance to educate the electorate about alternative paths the country might choose and to persuade voters to follow one of them.

Surprisingly, research has found that although policy concerns are important, in most elections they are not the dominant influence on voting.[33] One reason is that public policy debates often are complex, and people have limited information. To cite one extreme example, President Clinton's 1993 health care proposal was 1,342 printed pages long, and that was just one of the competing proposals! How could voters possibly be expected to have detailed views about such complex issues? Voters therefore seldom use elections as a means of giving public officials specific policy mandates. They select parties or party leaders, not policies.

Moreover, voters often are unsure where the candidates stand, because candidates equivocate and otherwise confuse voters about their positions. Research on the 1968 election, for example, found that views on U.S. policy in Vietnam (whether to escalate the war, maintain the status quo, or withdraw) were only minimally related to the presidential vote. How could that be true when intense disagreement about the war was tearing the country apart? The answer is that the positions of the candidates gave the voters little basis on which to choose. The Democratic nominee, Humphrey, supported the status quo, but he kept wavering. The Republican, Nixon, refused to reveal his position, a stance often summarized by the claim (wrongly attributed to Nixon himself) that he had a "secret plan" to end the war. In the end, befuddled voters treated the two candidates as though they supported the same policy.[34] Again, voters uncertain about what candidates believe cannot use their vote to mandate specific policies.

There are some important exceptions to the finding that public policies are not the dominant factor in most elections. Social or cultural issues, for example, occasionally do play a significant role. Candidates announce that they favor prayer in schools or that they oppose allowing same-sex unions. Such issues are "easy" for voters to process because the policy proposals and the desired outcome are one and the same: Start praying in schools, ban gay marriages.[35] Such issues are different from policy issues such as health insurance or education, where a chain of actions is required to bring about a particular outcome.[36] Social issues are as much about values held by different groups in society as they are about specific public policies. Indeed, such values often are incorporated into the party identifications of citizens. They are part of the **party images**, the associations that voters make between the parties and particular issues.[37] Voters concerned with moral issues gave overwhelming support to Republicans in 2004, for example.

A second example of issues mattering is when voters are upset about a problem and eager for government to do *something* about it. Thus, candidates talk about "getting tough on crime," "cleaning up the welfare mess," and "getting guns out of the hands of children." These are important political issues, to be sure, but often they do not involve much in the way of specific policy proposals. Voters are merely asked to choose among different priorities or between general approaches such as "soft" and "tough." Moreover, such issues at least implicitly reflect voters' unhappiness with the government *performance* that has allowed such problems to fester.

Government Performance   Real elections are a mix of considerations, but a great deal of research confirms the influence of past government performance.[38] Performance voting demands less of voters than policy voting. To make judgments about performance, voters do not have to watch C-SPAN or read the *New York Times*. Voters can judge economic conditions from their own experiences and those of their friends and neighbors. They can judge other social conditions by observing daily life in their communities, schools, and workplaces.

Voting by looking backward at performance (often called **retrospective voting**) may outweigh voting by looking forward at policy promises (often called **prospective voting**). The 1984 campaign provided a classic illustration. Public opinion surveys showed that on many issues, voters were closer to the Democratic nominee, Walter Mondale, than to President Reagan. A majority believed that tax increases were inevitable (Mondale's position), expressed skepticism about "Star Wars" (the missile defense system dear to Reagan's

party image
A set of widely held associations between a party and particular issues and values.

retrospective voting
Voting on the basis of the past performance of the incumbent administration.

prospective voting
Voting on the basis of the candidates' policy promises.

The Political Burdens of War

Recent Amertican military engagements have generally been popular when they were first launched—but become steadily more unpopular the longer they last and the more American casualties mount. By 2006, mounting public opposition to the war in Iraq was a major reason that the Republicans lost their majorities in both houses of Congress.

heart), rejected Reagan's call for further increases in defense spending, and doubted Reagan's Central America policy.[39] Nevertheless, Reagan carried 49 states. Was this overwhelming support just an expression of his winning personality? Probably not. Analysis of the election returns showed that a majority of voters approved of Reagan's performance as president, regardless of many of the specific policies he followed.

Voters hardly can be blamed for adopting shortcuts such as performance voting. The future is uncertain, the experts disagree, and time is limited, so how can one make an intelligent decision about complex policy alternatives? Moreover, candidates are not always clear about their intentions. At least good performance by government suggests competent leadership, so voters quite reasonably choose to stick with those in power when they are content.[40]

The important point to remember is that government performance is neither a long-term consideration nor a short one, but something in between. It refers to an assessment of leadership that reflects four years of activity, not something that suddenly arises when the campaign begins. Election-year campaign activity can attempt to put some "spin" on government performance, but it is difficult to make a bad economy or an unpopular war into a positive accomplishment for the incumbent administration, no matter how good the media experts and campaign consultants.

The Qualities of the Candidates   Not surprisingly, the individual candidates are the major source of change in how people vote from election to election.[41] Not since 1956, when Adlai Stevenson fought a rematch with Dwight Eisenhower, have Americans had the same choice of candidates in two presidential elections. In a country that exhorts voters to "support the person not the party," candidate quality is an extremely important influence on how people vote. Note, however, that *quality* is not

Politics Is Also a
National Pastime

Presidents often try to improve
their images by associating themselves with popular American
traditions and instututions. Here,
President Bush throws out the
ball at the opening of the baseball season in Washington.

the same thing as *personality*. Personality is overrated, especially by the losers. It is com-
forting for candidates or parties to blame failure on the foolishness of voters duped by
an opponent's sparkling personality or pleasing appearance; they would rather not
admit that voters rejected their beliefs or doubted their competence.

Even the importance of candidate quality can be exaggerated, though, because after
an election there is a tendency to downgrade the loser's personal qualities and to upgrade
the winner's. For example, after their defeat in 1996, many Republicans concluded that
Robert Dole was a terrible candidate who had run an uninspired campaign. Although
there is generally some truth to such charges, his critics seemed to forget that Dole had
been viewed much differently less than two years earlier. In the aftermath of the
Republican takeover of Congress in 1994, Dole was viewed as the "grownup" in
Washington, a mature, responsible, experienced public official who would fill the leadership vacuum, negotiate the necessary compromises, and keep the government functioning. Insider reports mentioned his quick wit and warm personality. Did Dole change in
two years? No, he was the same Dole, but losing had hurt his political reputation even
though he had taken on a popular incumbent with peace and prosperity behind him.

Al Gore provides a more recent example. After his defeat in a time of peace and
prosperity, many Democrats preferred to attribute his loss to personality flaws rather
than to his abandonment of the centrist stance that Bill Clinton had taken, or to a
popular rejection of Bill Clinton's adulterous behavior, even though research showed
those were the major reasons for Gore's loss.[42] Many in the party found it easier to
blame their messenger than to admit that the electorate had rejected their message or
the behavior of their most prominent officeholder.

There are some striking contrasts between what voters actually thought of the
candidates in a given campaign and how popular history now views the candidates. The
1960 contest between John F. Kennedy and Richard Nixon is the most vivid example.
Although historians have debunked much of the Kennedy mystique, you are probably
familiar with the Kennedy legend—the charismatic leader of a new "Camelot." In fact,
however, 1960 survey data show that Nixon was more favorably regarded as a candi-

date than Kennedy.[53] Kennedy owed his narrow victory primarily to the fact that he was a Democrat, at a time when there were more Democrats than Republicans.[44] Did the data indicate that Nixon had a more attractive personality than Kennedy? No. Nixon was viewed as more experienced and better qualified for the job. But what lives on in political folklore about the candidates may bear little resemblance to the reality of citizens' opinions when they voted.

Ronald Reagan is a more recent example. When the former president died in the summer of 2004, commentators across the political spectrum praised his winning personality and admirable character and hailed his accomplishments as president. Thousands of Americans stood in lines for hours to pass by his coffin and the spectacle of the state funeral dominated the airwaves for days. Yet, before Reagan's election in 1980, voters evaluated Jimmy Carter's personal characteristics higher than Reagan's.[45] And average presidential approval ratings during his administration were not impressive—they were slightly below the average of the 10 U.S. presidents between Truman and Clinton.[46] Memories of Reagan began to grow more positive after he left office, even before he became a victim of Alzheimer's disease. By the time he died, evaluations were considerably more positive than the views Americans had expressed at the time of his presidency. Thus, Ronald Reagan only became the beloved figure Americans remember after he had been elected and re-elected.

Finally, we should remember that what people think about the candidates is partly based on the other influences shaping their voting behavior. Most citizens with a strong Democratic party ID are going to like the Democratic candidate—any Democratic candidate. People with strong positions on certain policies probably are going to like any candidate who shares those policy commitments and to dislike any candidate who does not. People who think the president has performed very well probably are going to like him personally, although that affection is not guaranteed.

Television and
Presidential Campaigns

Limited Media Influence on Presidential Elections

The media are less influential in the general-election campaign than in the primaries. The primaries, especially the early primaries, maximize the opportunity for media influence, but in the general election, media coverage runs up against voter predispositions. These consist of party identifications that many voters hold and the impressions of government performance that voters have been forming for four (or even eight) years, not just the few months of the campaign.[47]

The importance of the campaign itself is similarly exaggerated. Contrary to what the media imply, many elections are practically "in the bag" before campaigning begins; conditions in the preceding four years and the government's response to them have determined the outcome. The 1972, 1984, and 1996 landslide reelections of incumbents are the clearest examples, but not the only ones. Political scientist James Campbell has calculated that between 1948 and 2000, the campaigns probably were decisive in 1948 and 1960, two exceedingly close elections. The campaigns may have been decisive in 1976, 1980, and 2000. In the other nine elections, the outcome was largely predetermined.[48]

Certainly campaigns do matter.[49] But campaigns are constrained by what goes on between elections. A card game provides a good analogy. Who wins a hand partly depends on the deal of the cards. No matter how skillfully you play, it may not be sufficient to overcome a bad draw. In politics, some cards are dealt years, even decades, before the election. The Democrats drew the Great Depression card in 1932 and played it

And the Winner Is . . .
Close Calls in Presidential
Elections

successfully against Republicans until after World War II. The Republicans drew the "liberal special interest" card in the 1970s and were still playing it against Democrats in 2004. Other cards have been drawn in the four years since the last election. Good economic conditions are aces dealt to the incumbent party; poor conditions are aces dealt to the opposition. The same is true for international embarrassments and costly wars.

The luck of the draw strongly affects the campaign. We praise and criticize campaigns, often forgetting that the candidates were limited in what they could do by social and economic realities. Did the fact that Michael Dukakis lost to Vice President Bush in 1988, whereas Clinton beat President Bush in 1992, indicate that Dukakis ran a poor campaign and Clinton a brilliant one? In retrospect, Dukakis surely could have done some things better and Clinton had recruited some crack advisers.[50] But Clinton's brilliant campaign probably also reflects the fact that an economic recession made the Bush administration a much wider target in 1992 than the Reagan-Bush administration had been in 1988.

The importance of the campaign in presidential elections emerges in close contests. If, on the basis of party ID and presidential performance, the race is about even when the campaign begins, then the campaign will determine the outcome by winning over the marginal, or undecided, voters. Certainly with an election as close as the ones in 2000 and 2004, almost any success, mistake, or candidate shortcoming could sway the results. Hundreds of choices "caused" the outcome. The tone of media coverage or the expertise of media advisers can win or lose the election. But the point to remember is that few elections begin as even contests. Rather, what elected officials have done between elections has largely determined the outcome.

The Contemporary Presidential Election Scene

The New Deal party system splintered in the 1960s. The racial and social turmoil created by the civil rights revolution and the war in Vietnam forced President Lyndon Johnson to withdraw from the race in 1968 and enabled Republican Richard Nixon to win two terms. It was the beginning of a Republican streak that saw them win five of the six presidential elections between 1968 and 1988. Not until the 1990s were the Democrats able to overcome the problems that first arose in the 1960s. We will survey these ups and downs in party fortunes in light of our discussion of American voting behavior in the previous section.

The 1970s and 1980s: Republican "Lock"

The so-called Republican lock on the presidency during the 1970s and 1980s reflected developments that gave Republicans a clear advantage on two of the four major factors that determine how Americans vote: performance and issues. This advantage forced Democratic candidates to defend unpopular policies and eventually eroded the long-standing Democratic advantage in party ID. Although the Democrats enjoyed a brief recovery after the Watergate scandal, the extremely narrow margin of Jimmy Carter's victory suggested the severity of the Democrats' problems. The Carter administration only retained the White House for four years, after which Republicans won three consecutive elections: 1980, 1984, and 1988. During this period, Republican performance and policies beat the Democrats on each of the major fronts in contemporary politics: economic, foreign and defense, racial, and social.

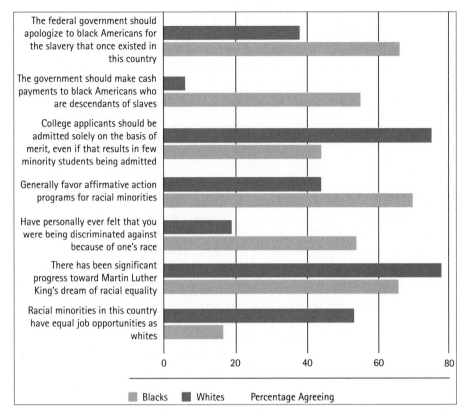

FIGURE 10.3

Blacks and Whites Differ Greatly in Their Views About Race Relations and Racial Policy

Source: "An American Dilemma" (Part II), *The Public Perspective*, February/March 1996: 20, 23, 26.

For almost half a century, Americans viewed Democrats as the party of prosperity. But in the late 1960s, an inflationary era began that economists blamed on President Johnson's attempt to wage war in Vietnam while also implementing major new domestic programs. The rising tide of inflation reached frightening levels (13 percent) under Democratic President Carter. As the party in power when economic conditions hit bottom, the Democrats took the blame.

Americans of the time also viewed Republicans as more capable in the international arena, a perception that the Vietnam War only reinforced. During the 1970s the United States faced a series of foreign challenges, and voters were not confident that the Democratic Party could deal with them. The final humiliation came in 1979 when Iranian militants seized 90 hostages from the American embassy in Tehran and held them for more than a year. This hostage crisis destroyed any remaining hope for President Carter's reelection and reinforced the popular perception that the Democrats were unable to keep America strong internationally.

Racial politics also hurt the Democrats. The exact role that racial issues played is not clear. Some believe that white support of Republican candidates grew from lingering racism.[51] Others disagree, arguing that many policies currently proposed to help minorities—such as affirmative action—are inconsistent with traditional American values.[52] Regardless, political attitudes are sharply polarized by race (see Figure 10.3). Democrats were caught in the middle of such disagreements between the white majority and the party's most loyal constituency.

Finally, social issues hurt the Democrats during this period. Starting in the 1960s, liberalism became associated in some voters' minds with controversial changes in

American life—for example, sexual permissiveness, declining religious faith, family breakdown, and violent crime. A popular reaction arose in the late 1970s in the form of the "new right," a socially conservative movement connected to evangelical religious groups. These voters swelled the Republican ranks in many elections.

The 1990s: Democratic Resurgence

In 1992 Bill Clinton was elected with 43 percent of the vote in a three-way election. Even without Ross Perot in the contest, Clinton would have won.[53] How did the Democratic Party revive? First, a recession rejuvenated the Democrats' image as the party of prosperity. The struggling economy was the foundation of Clinton's campaign. He promised to get the economy moving again, and he appealed to middle-class concerns with his support of universal health care. The end of the Cold War, meanwhile, meant that foreign threats did not distract voters from their preoccupation with the economy. With the collapse of the Soviet threat, national defense and foreign policy vanished from the list of voter concerns in 1992. Clinton also distanced himself from prominent black leaders, such as Jesse Jackson, and criticized the lyrics found in some rap music. He prayed, talked about family values, promised "to end welfare as we know it," supported capital punishment, and in other ways tried to dispel the cultural liberal image that had dogged the Democrats for a generation.

The economy grew steadily throughout Clinton's first term, and by the 1996 elections most Americans were economically optimistic—indeed, as optimistic as they had been in 1984 when they overwhelmingly reelected Republican Ronald Reagan.[54] Incumbents who run during times of economic prosperity tend to be successful, and Clinton was no exception. Clinton also increased his support among moderates through a strategy of "triangulation"—positioning himself between liberal congressional Democrats and conservative Republicans.[55] A growing gender gap also helped Clinton. Some polls reported that if only men had voted in 1996, Robert Dole would have won the election, the first time majorities of men and of women had voted for different candidates.

The gender gap is widely misunderstood. Many pundits understandably attributed the emergence of the gender gap to different male and female positions on "women's issues." On the contrary, men and women differ little in their views of abortion and issues related to equality of opportunity for women.[56] Rather, differences in voting appear to stem more from long-standing gender differences on issues of military force, the use of violence, and government activities in support of the disadvantaged (see Table 10.2).[57] There is considerable disagreement about why women and men differ on issues. Some argue that women's values are different from men's.[58] From an electoral standpoint, though, the origins of gender differences are less important than is the fact that they exist.

Perhaps most important, the Republican Congress made a serious tactical error in shutting down the government in the winter of 1995–1996, when President Clinton would not accept their budget.[59] Polls indicated that voters sided with Clinton in the dispute, probably costing Dole any chance he had of winning the 1996 election. Clinton took the position that it was necessary to reelect him in order to check and balance the Republicans in Congress. Ironically, by the end of the campaign, the Republican Party stopped seriously trying to defeat Clinton, instead running ads argu-

	Women	Men
TABLE 10.2		
WOMEN'S AND MEN'S ATTITUDES DIFFER		
Role of Government		
Consider self conservative	29%	43%
Government should provide fewer services	30	45
Poverty and homelessness are among the country's most important problems	63	44
Government should guarantee medical care for all	69	58
Favor affirmative action programs for blacks and other minority groups	53	41
Force/Violence		
American bombers should attack all military targets in Iraq, including those in heavily populated areas	37	61
Handguns should be illegal except for use by police and other authorized persons	48	28
Favor death penalty	76	82
Approve of caning the teenager in Singapore who committed acts of vandalism	39	61
Approve of the way the Justice Department took Elian Gonzalez from his Miami relatives	35	52

SOURCE: *The Public Perspective*, August/September 1996: 10–27; *The Public Perspective*, July/August 1994: 96. Gallup Tuesday Briefing, May 2, 2000.

ing that it was necessary to reelect congressional Republicans in order to check and balance the president![60]

The actions of the Republican Congress during 1995–1996 helped to widen the gender gap and reelect Bill Clinton. By adopting an approach to welfare that was viewed as punitive, by taking an aggressive stance on Medicaid and Medicare reform, and by proposing cutbacks in environmental and safety regulation—in these and similar ways, the Republicans drew attention to issues that divided men and women, naturally widening gender differences.[61] In addition, the close association between the Republican Party and the religious right probably served to widen the gender gap. Because the religious right emphasizes family values, it sometimes alienates working women, as well as those who are unmarried or divorced. The gender gap is wider among single men and women than among married men and women—a marriage gap.[62]

The 2000 Election

Prophets of doom predicted that the U.S. economy would melt down when the calendar changed from 1999 to 2000. The economy did just fine, but no one anticipated that the polity might melt down later in the year. It took five weeks to determine that Republican George W. Bush had won the presidential election. President Bush headed the first unified Republican government since 1954 (although his party temporarily lost control of the Senate when James Jeffords of Vermont left the party in May 2001).

The 2000 election underscored the difference between primary and general-election campaigns. In the primaries, hot-button issues such as abortion and gun control

George W. Bush Campaigning

Although the wealthy son of a former president, George W. Bush projects an earnestness and simplicity that help regular voters identify with him—a crucial advantage under the permanent campaign.

The 2000 Presidential Election

were prominent, but exit polls showed that such issues were of lesser importance in the general election. Gore had to back away from his primary position on guns because it was unpopular in many of the battleground states. Similarly, Bush downplayed his opposition to abortion. Instead, broad issues of concern to the great body of Americans—the economy, health care, and education—took center stage. The candidates talked long and in some detail about issues of concern to the American middle class: restructuring social security, reforming public schools, and determining what mix of taxing and spending is appropriate.

To many political scientists the 2000 election was puzzling. Given the long-standing importance of government performance to voters, most political scientists expected Al Gore to win. During the Clinton administration the country enjoyed unprecedented prosperity and relative peace. As the election approached, President Clinton's approval ratings were exceptionally high by historical standards, consumers felt optimistic about the economy, and people thought that the country was on the right track. Supposedly, incumbent administrations do not lose during times of peace and prosperity. So why did Gore lose?

Detailed statistical analysis indicates that the vote for Gore was less closely tied to the administration's record than were the votes for incumbent-party candidates in the previous seven elections.[63] Some analysts argue that Gore did not receive credit because he ran the wrong campaign. Although the effects of campaigns often are exaggerated, in this case Gore's critics may be right. Gore did not emphasize the administration's record. As one critic sarcastically observed, Gore's theme was "You've never had it so good, and I'm mad as hell about it."[64] In trying to distance himself from a scandal-plagued president, Gore may have thrown away his trump card.

Gore also paid a penalty for being seen as farther from the average voter than Bush. Although polls showed that Gore was closer to people than Bush was on specific issues such as education and social security, more people felt that Gore was too liberal than felt that Bush was too conservative.

Finally, there was the Clinton factor. Clinton's personal ratings were much lower than his job ratings, and a majority of the country agreed that the country was on the wrong track morally, whatever the state of the economy. Statistical evidence indicates that Clinton's personal ratings helped drag Gore down. Independents and even Democrats who were dismayed by Clinton's personal behavior tended to favor Bush. Whether even more swing voters would have selected Bush had Gore tied himself more closely to Clinton is a question that statistics cannot answer.

The 2004 Showdown

Polls that showed a captivatingly close race in the final days of the 2004 campaign led many media commentators to speculate that the race would again be decided in the courts or in state-level recounts. Nevertheless, the result, while not an overwhelming victory for Bush, was at least a decisive one: for the first time since 1988, the winner of the presidency amassed a clear majority (51 percent) of the popular vote. Bush's victories in key states such as Florida and Ohio, as well as Republican gains in Congress, frustrated Democrats who were convinced that economic stagnation and the Iraq war would swing undecided voters their way. In the days after the election, pundits made much of an apparent finding (based on exit polls) that significant numbers of voters based their decisions on "moral values." Some argued that Democratic candidate John Kerry ought to have placed greater emphasis on morality in his campaign speeches.

In reality, the 2004 election was not much different from past elections. Any "moral values" voters probably decided on a candidate long before Election Day. The economy, while not in great shape, was in better condition than it had been in past years when voters had thrown out incumbent presidents. The predictable criticisms of John Kerry's campaign fail to account for the fact that these and other critical factors were beyond the candidate's control.

Chapter Summary

The American nomination process is far more open than the nomination processes of other democracies. It gives rank-and-file voters more influence than in other countries where party leaders and elected officials dominate the process, and it gives "outsider" candidates a chance by enabling them to contest the early, smaller primaries and caucuses. The process begins long before the election itself and sometimes lasts months before a nominee is determined. It also heightens the influence of party issue activists and the media.

The presidential campaign is often misunderstood. It is not an independent force that determines election outcomes. Rather, the campaign itself is shaped by events and conditions in the years leading up to the election. Candidates perceived as running "good campaigns" are usually those who have good records that are easy to defend or those whose opponents have bad records that are hard to defend. Candidates who run "bad campaigns" are generally those who face uphill battles. The 2000 campaign of Al Gore, which did not try to capitalize on good government performance, may be an exception to these generalizations.

The reason why campaigns are limited in their impact is that most voters do not make up their minds on the basis of the campaign. Many of them decide well before the campaign ever begins. They do so on the basis of long-standing party identifications, evaluations of government performance, and the associations between the parties and particular values and positions. Only a minority decide how to vote late in the campaign and on the basis of the particular candidates and the particular things they say. In a case such as the 2004 election, when neither campaign makes a serious blunder, party identification, government performance, and deeper issues will determine which candidate ends up the winner.

Key Terms

caucus, p. 275
electoral vote, p. 285
527s, p. 283
matching funds, p. 277
party identification, p. 287

party image, p. 290
political activists, p. 280
popular vote, p. 286
primary election, p. 275
prospective voting, p. 290

retrospective voting, p. 290
soft money, p. 283
superdelegate 275
winner-take-all voting, p. 286

Suggested Readings

Of General Interest

Abramson, Paul, John Aldrich, and David Rohde. *Change and Continuity in the 2004 Elections.* Washington, DC: CQ Press, 2006. This quadrennial publication provides a comprehensive overview of voting behavior in national elections.

Mayer, William, ed. *The Making of the Presidential Candidates 2004.* Lanham, MD: Rowman & Littlefield, 2004. An informative collection of essays covering all facets of the contemporary nominating process.

Nelson, Michael, ed. *The Elections of 2004*. Washington, D.C.: Congressional Quarterly, 2005. This quadrennial publication by a group of knowledgeable authors complements Abramson, Aldrich, and Rohde, offering less detail about voting behavior but a broader view of the campaigns and the activities of elites.

Focused Studies

Campbell, James. *The American Campaign*. College Station, TX: Texas A&M University Press, 2000. The most comprehensive scholarly study of presidential campaigns.

Carmines, Edward, and James Stimson. *Issue Evolution: Race and the Transformation of American Politics*. Princeton, NJ: Princeton University Press, 1989. An important argument about the importance of race for realigning American politics in the 1960s.

Judis, John B., and Ruy Teixeira. *The Emerging Democratic Majority*. New York: Scribner, 2002. Interesting—and controversial—argument about various trends that the authors believe will help Democrats win most elections in the future.

Miller, Arthur, and Bruce Gronbeck, eds. *Presidential Campaigns and American Self-Images*. Boulder, CO: Westview, 1994. This collection of essays presents a balanced and sophisticated view of campaigns.

On the Web

www.multied.com/elections/

A graphical history of presidential elections can be found through MultiEducator Incorporated.

www.archives.gov/federal_register/electoral_college/

The official National Archive Web site on the electoral college answers all basic questions about procedure, and it even includes an electoral college calculator.

www.umich.edu/~nes/

Perhaps the most comprehensive source of political science data is the National Election Study Archive at the University of Michigan. The site contains a wealth of data and also many charts and figures showing changes in American politics from election to election.

www.c-span.org

Some of the best Web sites for learning about a presidential campaign are the ones set up by the candidates themselves. Of course, the official 2004 campaign Web sites are mostly down now. But you can still see the major events of that election at C-SPAN's election archives.

www.netsol.com/cgi-bin/whois/whois

In fact, if you want to search the Web to see whether any domain names are still available, you can do so here. You may want to purchase one; perhaps you could sell it to a candidate.

Election Voices

Is a National Primary the Best Way to Nominate Presidential Candidates?

"I don't care who does the electing as long as I do the nominating."

—William M. "Boss" Tweed, leader of Tammany Hall, c. 1870

THE ISSUE

Should the current presidential nomination process, in which fifty state primaries and caucuses are used to select delegates to a national convention, be replaced by a national presidential primary?

Background

Of all the major institutions and processes in contemporary American government, few have been as widely criticized as the presidential nomination process. As described in Chapter 10, the rules of the presidential nomination process were substantially rewritten in the early 1970s—and from the moment the new rules took effect, they generated a firestorm of controversy. Throughout the last several decades, political scientists, party leaders, and media pundits have regularly declared that it is time to "reform the reforms."

Of all the major proposals for restructuring the presidential nomination process, the national primary is, at once, the simplest and the most radical. It is also the oldest of the reform proposals: A national presidential primary was endorsed by the Progressive Party in their 1912 national platform and was then recommended by Woodrow Wilson in his first annual message to Congress in 1913.

As its name implies, a national primary would scrap the current system of individual state primaries and caucuses followed by a national convention. Instead, a primary election would take place in all 50 states on the same day. According to one version of the national primary plan, the winner of that election would then become his or her party's presidential candidate. In another variant, the winner would become the nominee only if he or she won at least 40 percent of the total vote. If no candidate achieved that threshold, a second, runoff election would be held between the top two finishers in the first election. In either case, a national convention would no longer play any role, even a purely formal one, in the presidential nomination process, though the parties might continue to hold one for other purposes (adopting a platform, ratifying the vice-presidential choice, rallying the party faithful, and so forth).

Political Dilemmas

According to its proponents, a national primary has several major advantages. First, it is much simpler than the current system. Instead of the complexity of 50 different state contests spread over three or four months, each with its own set of voting laws and delegate selection rules, the national primary would substitute one or at most two decisive elections, both of which, presumably, would be governed by a single system of rules.

Second, a national primary would treat all states equally. The current process, as we have seen, gives a much greater voice to states that happen to come early in the delegate selection calendar. Two states in particular, Iowa and New Hampshire, have a dramatically outsized role in selecting presidential candidates. Meanwhile, at the other end of the calendar, between a third and a half of the states hold their primaries after one candidate has already clinched the nomination and all of the major rivals have withdrawn from the race. Besides violating basic considerations of equity, it is generally conceded that both Iowa and New Hampshire are, in important ways, unrepresentative of the country as a whole. Neither state, for example, has a significant number of African Americans or a large city. In contrast, a national primary would put all states—and thus all voters—on an equal footing.

Third, as one consequence of eliminating these interstate inequalities, a national primary would almost certainly increase the number of people who participate in the presidential nomination process. Under the present system, as shown in Table 1, voter participation rates vary widely according to when a state holds its primary. In the 2000 Republican race, for example, 52 percent of the eligible electorate turned out for the New Hampshire primary on February 1. For the 17 primaries held between February 8 and March 7, when the race between George Bush and John McCain was still being actively contested, the average turnout was 26 percent. By the end of the March 7 voting, however, Bush had established such a large lead in the delegate count, and McCain was so short of money, that the race was effectively over. On March 9, McCain ended whatever suspense was left by formally announcing his withdrawal. And in the 23 primaries held after March 9, the average turnout was just 16 percent. By ensuring that all people would go to the polls while the race was still undecided, a national primary would almost certainly increase participation in all of these 23 states—and probably in most of the middle group as well.

But the national primary also has a large number of opponents. The worst aspect of a national primary, according to these critics, is that it would limit the presidential nomination process to candidates who are already well known and/or well financed. Only someone who was famous before the race began or who had an enormous amount of money to spend could run a full-scale, national campaign. Talented senators and governors from small states, who had not managed to attract the favor of the national media, would never have a realistic chance to win a presidential nomination.

For all its messiness and inequality, opponents of the national primary argue, the current system allows lesser-known candidates a better chance to compete, precisely because it does start in the two relatively small states of Iowa and New Hampshire. In these venues, lesser-known and underfinanced candidates can make their case before a smaller and more manageable audience. If they are successful there, they will then receive the additional press coverage and funding that gives them a better prospect of running a viable national campaign.

In the 2000 Republican nomination race, for example, the early front-runner was Texas governor George W. Bush, less because of his record as governor (though many Republicans admired that record) than because he was lucky enough to be

TABLE 1		
PRESIDENTIAL PRIMARY TURNOUT BY DATE, IN 1996 AND 2000		
Date	Average Turnout	(No. of States)
1996 Republican Primaries		
February 20 (New Hampshire)	42	(1)
February 24–March 2	22	(5)
March 5–26	18	(22)
April 23–June 4	14	(12)
2000 Republican Primaries		
February 1 (New Hampshire)	52	(1)
February 8–29	26	(6)
March 7	26	(11)
After March 9	16	(23)
2000 Democratic Primaries		
February 1 (New Hampshire)	40	(1)
March 7	17	(11)
After March 9	16	(22)

SOURCE: William G. Mayer and Andrew E. Busch, *The Front-Loading Problem in Presidential Nominations* (Washington, DC: Brookings Institution Press), 85.

the son of a former president. Senator John McCain of Arizona, by contrast, began the race almost entirely unknown to the national electorate, and even after almost a year of campaigning, was supported by only about 15 percent of the nation's Republicans. As a result of a great deal of personal campaigning, however, McCain won a decisive victory in the New Hampshire primary, which then made him a legitimate contender for his party's nomination. Such things would be impossible, according to most observers, under a national primary system.

Yet, supporters of the national primary might reply, is it really so bad to limit the presidential nomination process to a party's established national leaders? Critics of the current system have long deplored the fact that contemporary nomination races include so many candidates, many of whom have strikingly little previous experience in government; and that one of these little-known entities may suddenly get catapulted into the lead simply because he or she managed to gain the support of a comparative handful of voters in Iowa or New Hampshire.

For those who hold this view, the pre-eminent example is the candidacy of Jimmy Carter in 1976. By running a smart campaign, Carter won both the Iowa caucuses and the New Hampshire primary; on that basis, he achieved a burst of momentum that none of his rivals was able to stop. By early June, Carter had locked up the Democratic presidential nomination and then went on to win the general election against Gerald Ford—even though he had served just four years as the governor of Georgia and was, as even many in his own party came to concede, largely unprepared for the demands of being the nation's chief executive. There is much to be said in defense of a system that makes Carter-type candidacies less likely.

The Problem of the Zealous Minority

Depending on which specific plan is adopted, a national primary can also lead to another type of result that the current system generally avoids: the nomination of a candidate who is supported by a small but very zealous minority, but is considered unacceptable by a large segment—perhaps even a majority—of the party. The kind of situation that could easily lead to such a result is aptly illustrated by the Democratic nomination race of 1988. Through the second half of 1987, the Democratic field consisted of Jesse Jackson and six other candidates, none of whom was particularly well known outside his own state or region. Because Jackson was well known, and because he attracted strong support from blacks and a very narrow slice of white liberals, national polls that asked Democratic identifiers whom they wanted to be their party's next presidential candidate consis-

tently showed Jackson in the lead. Had a national primary been conducted at this point, it seems quite likely that Jackson would have won it, even though he probably would have received just 25 or 30 percent of the vote—and even though his presence at the head of the ticket would clearly have caused major problems for his party.

The sequential nature of the current primary system, by comparison, generally prevents this sort of problem from occurring. A fringe candidate who has the support of only 25 or 30 percent of his party's voters may win some early primaries when the rest of the vote is divided among a large number of other candidates. But, as some of these candidates demonstrate their lack of support and begin to fade or drop out, the mainstream of the party usually coalesces around a more acceptable alternative. In 1988, for example, Jesse Jackson did just fine as long as the field stayed divided. As of March 15, 1988, Jackson was actually his party's leading vote-getter in the primaries, having won 27 percent of the total vote to 25 percent for Massachusetts governor Michael Dukakis. Once Bruce Babbit, Richard Gephardt, and Paul Simon dropped out, however, the limits on Jackson's vote became obvious. In the final 14 primaries, Jackson won only once (in the District of Columbia), and lost the preference vote to Dukakis by a two-to-one margin.

It is precisely to avoid this problem that most recent national primary proposals have been structured so as to require the winner to receive some minimum percentage of the total vote (usually 40 percent) and call for a runoff election if no candidate crosses that threshold. Yet runoff elections carry problems of their own. In those states that already use runoff elections, the evidence is clear that interest and participation in the second election are usually lower than they are in the first election.[1] And because most recent national primary proposals call for the first-round primary to be held in the last half of August or the first week in September, Americans might face the routine prospect of holding three national elections over a period of just 70 days.[2]

What Does the Public Believe?

Reforms of the presidential nomination process are not, to say the least, a high-priority concern for most Americans. But when they do think about such matters, Americans have consistently expressed strong support for the national primary. On 15 occasions between 1952 and 1988, the Gallup Poll asked a national sample if they favored having "presidential candidates chosen by the voters in a nationwide primary election instead of by political party conventions as at present." On average, 67 percent of the public have supported the national primary; only 21 percent have opposed it.

What Do You Think?

1. One advantage of the national primary, according to some of its proponents, is its simplicity. Is simplicity really an advantage in the design of political institutions? Given that they created the electoral college, how might the Founders have answered this question?

2. Is there an advantage to having one or two small states lead off the delegate selection process, or would we be better off if all 50 states voted at the same time?

3. Which of the two versions of the national primary outlined above is preferable? Is it problematic if a candidate wins the presidential nomination with only 30 or 35 percent of the vote?

4. How much weight should be given to the consistent public support for a national primary?

On the Web

Though no major Web site is devoted specifically to the national primary controversy, many good sites carry detailed information on the 2008 nomination calendar.

http://www.thegreenpapers.com

http://www.gwu.edu/action/p2008

http://www.rhodescook.com

http://www.nass.org

---

[1]See Stephen G. Wright, "Voter Turnout in Runoff Elections," *Journal of Politics* 51 (May 1989): 385–96; and Charles S. Bullock III and Loch K. Johnson, *Runoff Elections in the United States* (Chapel Hill: University of North Carolina Press, 1992), chap. 6.

[2]On this last point, see James W. Davis, *U.S. Presidential Primaries and the Caucus-Convention System: A Sourcebook* (Westport, CN: Greenwood, 1977), 202–203.

CHAPTER 11

★ ★ ★ ★ ★ ★ ★ ★ ★ ★

Choosing the Congress

CHAPTER OUTLINE

Congressional Elections and the Fate of the Bush Agenda

In the weeks that followed the 2000 elections, public attention focused on the partisan battle in Florida, where the contested electoral votes would determine whether George Bush or Al Gore would be the next president. But control of the presidency was not the only tight contest in 2000. On the same day that they voted for president, Americans voted in 435 elections for the U.S. House of Representatives, and the Republicans won only nine seats more than the Democrats. Americans also voted for a U.S. senator in 33 states, and in these contests the Democrats took five seats from the Republicans; the result was a 50–50 tie between the parties! So, if Bush ultimately were declared president, he would have the support of very narrow majorities in Congress (because under Article 1 of the Constitution the vice president—who would be Dick Cheney if Bush won—breaks ties in the Senate). Conversely, if Gore were declared president, Joe Lieberman would become vice president, but the Republican governor of Connecticut would appoint a Republican to replace him (at least until a special election were held), so Gore would face narrow opposition majorities in both chambers. In either event prospects for the president's program would not appear bright.

Ultimately, George Bush became president, and Republicans controlled all three elected branches of government for the first time since 1953–54. This unified control lasted less than six months, however, because in June 2001 Sen. James Jeffords of Vermont left the Republican Party and became an independent, throwing control of the Senate back to the Democrats. Despite the divided partisan control, however, in 2001 some important legislation—a large tax cut and a major educational package—passed Congress with the help of some Democrats.

In the aftermath of 9/11 prospects for bipartisan cooperation seemed even brighter. Partisan differences waned, trust in government institutions rose, and the arrival of international terrorism made other issues seem less important. But this calm period did not last long. September 11 resurrected a set of issues—national security issues—that had been dormant since the collapse of the Soviet Union a decade earlier. And, as we discussed in Chapter 10, these were issues on which the

Republican Party had a long-standing advantage. Thus, the Bush administration and Republican congressional leaders decided to wage the 2002 Congressional elections around a campaign theme of strong defense. They portrayed the Democrats as weak on security issues, and by all indications the strategy worked: Republicans gained six seats in the House to make their majority a bit more comfortable and took back the Senate with a gain of two seats.

The first session of the 108th Congress, which sat in 2003, was the most partisan in more than five decades.[1] On roll call after roll call a unified Republican majority had its way, with the opposing Democratic minorities almost equally unified. Moreover, congressional Republicans who felt they owed their majority status to the president allowed the White House to dictate their actions to a historically unusual degree. For example, a "budget-busting" prescription drug plan was added to Medicare over the bitter private objections of many congressional Republicans because the Bush White House wished to take the issue away from the Democrats.

After the elections an emboldened Bush administration launched the invasion of Iraq. Predictions of a quick and easy victory proved over-optimistic, however, as a serious insurgency developed after the official end of the war. The conflict dragged on through 2004, casualties mounted, and President Bush's approval ratings fell. Some observers felt that the security issue now had boomeranged on the Republicans, but the administration hung tough, adopting a strategy of equating the war in Iraq with the war on terror. Still believing that their majority depended on the success of President Bush, congressional Republicans formed a unified front with the administration and once again, the strategy worked. Analysis of the 2004 election results showed that terrorism and the war were the most important issues, and the Republican advantage in this arena trumped the Democratic advantage in the economic arena.[2] In the congressional elections Republicans picked up three seats in the Senate and four in the House to make their majorities a bit more secure. By all appearances, following the administration's directives seemed to be good politics for congressional Republicans.

At first the 109th Congress acted much as the 108th did, with unified Republican and Democratic parties opposing each other. But by the summer of 2005 Republican Party unity began to fray. After seeing that President Bush's ambitious effort to restructure social security was unpopular with many of their constituents, congressional Republicans quietly buried the initiative. A few Republicans in the House and Senate spoke out critically about the situation in Iraq. Then, in the fall a storm of controversies and negative news buffeted the Bush administration. The administration's reaction to the Hurricane Katrina disaster in New Orleans was widely judged as incompetent. The president's nomination of his confidante, Harriet Myers, to the Supreme Court outraged many conservative Republicans. Government spending and pork barrel politics seemed out of control. American deaths in Iraq passed the 2,000 mark. As a result of these negative developments President Bush's approval ratings plunged.

This decline in the public standing of the Bush administration changed the relationship between the president and his party in Congress. With the 2006 election less than a year away, some members of Congress began to worry that close association with the Bush administration would cost them their seats, and even members whose own seats were safe worried that Republicans could lose control of one or both chambers of Congress. The united front that congressional Republicans had maintained for four years began to crack.[3] Some members pressed the Bush administration for a plan to withdraw troops from Iraq. Congress passed limitations on the use of torture that were strongly opposed by President Bush and Vice President Cheney. The two chambers could not agree on re-authorization of the Patriot Act that the President demanded, and eventually dissident Republicans forced the administration to compromise. On the domestic side, Republican leaders failed to gain enough votes to pass the president's budget out of a Senate committee. Environmentally sensitive Republicans in the House blocked legislation that would have allowed drilling in the Arctic National Wildlife Refuge. Similarly, some moderate Republicans rejected attempts to cut the growth of spending on social programs if tax cuts on dividends and capital gains were to be extended. A previously compliant Congress had turned balky.

Fearing for their electoral lives, some Republicans in Congress attempted to distance themselves from their president, emphasizing their incumbency status and local issues in their campaigns.

MAKING THE CONNECTION

Elections are never far from the minds of members of Congress. All members of the House of Representatives put their fates on the line every second November, and some representatives may face primary challenges as early as the spring of election years, so primary campaigns are under-way a little more than a year after members have taken the oath of office. In response to such realities, representatives campaign for reelection more or less continuously. They are Exhibit A of the permanent campaign.

Surprisingly, the situation isn't much different for senators. Although senators are elected for six-year terms, a third of them are elected every two years, so at any given time one-third of the Senate is operating with the same short time horizon as members of the House. Moreover, Senate campaigns are so expensive that the average incumbent must raise an average of just over $15,000 every week for six years—a time-consuming, psychologically draining activity that keeps all of them aware of their need to maintain political support, even if their actual reelection campaign is years away.

The great majority of congressional incumbents win reelection, but victory is rarely guaranteed. A politically damaging vote, a personal impropriety, a past association with a corrupt lobbyist, sharing the same party affiliation as an unpopular president—these and other factors can lead to the end of a political career. That simple fact strongly affects what members of Congress do, and what they are unwilling to do.

This chapter focuses on elections for the United States Congress. In the pages that follow, you will learn how Senate and House elections differ from each other and from the presidential elections we discussed in Chapter 10, what members of Congress do to get elected and reelected, and why House incumbents have a much larger incumbency advantage than Senate incumbents. You will also learn how congressional elections today differ from those held in the last third of the twentieth century. Finally, you will grapple with the long-standing question of whether 535 separate elections can select a representative Congress.

The Electoral Evolution of the Congress

The Framers of the Constitution did not expect today's Congress to operate the way it does. On the one hand, they thought that frequent elections would make the House of Representatives an unstable body whose members would come and go quickly. Madison wrote that the House should have "an immediate dependence on, and an intimate sympathy with, the people."[4] On the other hand, the Framers expected the Senate, with members elected by state legislatures for six-year terms, to be stable and electorally insulated. According to Madison, the Senate would proceed "with more coolness, with more system, and with more wisdom, than the popular branch."[5] (Remember that not until after adoption of the Seventeenth Amendment to the Constitution in 1913 did senators face popular election.)

Neither chamber developed as the Framers had anticipated. At first, the House was indeed unstable in its membership and disorderly in its operation. More than 40 percent of the members of the First Congress did not return for the Second. In fact, turnover levels often were as high as 50 percent until after the Civil War.[6] But, contrary to Madison's argument, frequent elections were not the cause of high turnover. Before the Civil War, more representatives quit than were defeated. Living conditions were unattractive after the national government moved to the uninhabited, swampy lands that became Washington, D.C. Moreover, the national government was not particularly important in the early years of the republic.[7] Many members found that they had less power in Washington than they would have in the capital cities of their home states.[8] Moreover, even those members willing to serve multiple terms sometimes were prevented from doing so by *rotation* practices, whereby a congressional district's political factions "took turns" holding the congressional seat. Abraham Lincoln, for example, was elected to the House in 1846 but stepped down after one term in accordance with local rotation agreements.[9] As a result of these various considerations, average service in the House of Representatives did not reach three terms until after 1900.

The early Senate, too, was far from being the stable, experienced body of statesmen that Madison had anticipated. In the first 10 years of the republic, more than one-third of the senators failed to serve out their terms, and until 1820 more senators resigned during their term than were denied reelection by their state legislatures. Although they had the opportunity to stay longer than members of the House, many senators chose to pass it up for the same reasons that House members went home.[10]

Today, things are much different. Congress is the world's foremost example of what political scientists call a **professional legislature**. Its members are full-time legislators

Young Representative Abraham Lincoln (Whig-IL) in 1846

professional legislature
Legislature whose members serve full-time and for long periods.

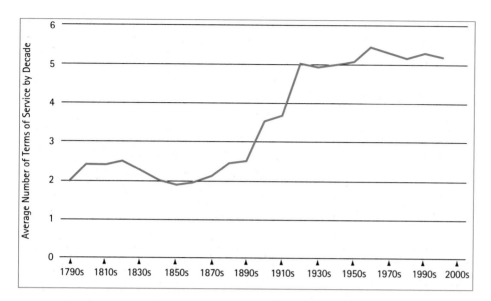

FIGURE 11.1

Congress Became a Career
in the Twentieth Century

Sources: Nelson W. Polsby, "The
Institutionalization of the U.S. House of
Representatives," *American Political Science
Review,* March 1968: 146; Norman J.
Ornstein et al., eds., *Vital Statistics on
Congress, 2001–2002* (Washington, DC:
AB Press, 2002); and the Clerk of U.S.
House of Representatives,
http://clerk.house.gov.

who stay for long periods, as shown in Figure 11.1. Relatively few members quit
voluntarily, and many intend to remain in Congress indefinitely. In fact, many people
in the United States think that the membership of Congress is *too* stable. They support
institutional changes such as term limits in order to shake up what they see as an unresponsive institution.

Claims of congressional unresponsiveness appear to clash with the general theme of
this book—that American political institutions are electorally sensitive (if not hypersensi-
tive). The explanation for this apparent contradiction is simple: contemporary members of
Congress win so often precisely *because* they are so electorally aware—they anticipate
threats to their reelection and act to avoid them. Before reviewing the evidence for this
claim, the chapter must provide some background information on congressional elections.

Reapportionment and Redistricting

How are the constituencies represented in Congress determined? In the Senate, representation is simple and unchanging. The Constitution gives every state two senators,
regardless of population, and Article 5 states that no state can be deprived of equal representation without its consent. Because less populous states will not give up their political
advantage in the Senate, equal representation in the Senate is essentially an amendment-
proof feature of American democracy (see the *Democratic Dilemma* on page 311).

Representation is considerably more complicated in the House. The Constitution
requires that a census be held every decade. After the census, the 435 seats in the House
of Representatives are apportioned among the states according to their populations—a
process called **reapportionment**. In the past half-century, northeastern and upper
midwestern states have lost more than 60 House seats to southern and southwestern
states as population has shifted from the Frostbelt to the Sunbelt.[11] Given the different
political leanings of these regions, the net effect has been to strengthen Republican
representation in the House.

Currently, seven states have such small populations that they only receive one
congressional seat, a minimum guaranteed by Article 1. After the other states learn how

You Are Redrawing
the Districts
in Your State

reapportionment

The allocation of House seats to the
states after each decennial census.

Fair Weather for Republicans

Population growth in the heavily Republican Sunbelt has outpaced that in the North, causing congressional districts to migrate southward. The Detroit area of Michigan, where this cartoon was first published, has been especially hard hit.

• *Do you think it is harder for a region to recover if it loses political power after the area has gone into decline?*

© Thompson-Detroit Free Press 2000

redistricting

Drawing new boundaries of congressional districts, usually after the decennial census.

Redistricting

gerrymandering

Drawing boundary lines of congressional districts in order to confer an advantage on some partisan or political interest.

many House seats they have received, they set to work **redistricting**—drawing the boundaries of the new districts. Congressional districts within individual states once varied widely in population, but now they must be of virtually equal population, the result of Supreme Court decisions beginning with *Wesberry v. Sanders* in 1964. Subsequent decisions have refined the standard to one of precise numerical equality (at least as indicated by census figures, which are only approximate, of course). This principle has come to be known as "one person, one vote."

It is important to remember that equal population refers to residents, not voters. Some districts contain people who turn out at very high rates, while others contain people who vote at very low rates. In 2004, for example, less than half as many people voted in some New York City districts as voted in some suburban districts. Thus, although theoretically equal, the constituencies that elect members of the House are not equal in practice. In addition, turnout in off-year congressional elections is only about two-thirds as high as turnout in presidential election years. Thus, the voting constituencies of members of the House vary greatly across both space and time. (Because states differ even more in population, Senate elections show even greater variation in the size of voter constituencies. In 2004, for example, more than 11 million people voted in the California Senate election, compared to a little more than 300,000 in the North Dakota election.)

In most states the legislature draws electoral maps, but in five states bipartisan commissions do the job, and in several others the lines are drawn by some combination of legislators and outside appointees. The redistricting process is often highly contentious, because political careers depend on which voters get placed in which districts. Charges of **gerrymandering**—drawing the lines for partisan or other political advantage—fly back and forth. Some observers believe that partisan gerrymandering, in particular, has become so outrageous that the Supreme Court should impose some limits, although this matter remains unsettled at present.

DEMOCRATIC DILEMMA

Why Not Senate Districts?

Most states have more than one U.S. representative, whom they elect from single-member districts within the states. In the early nineteenth century, a few states used multimember districts, but a federal statute in 1842 required the use of single-member districts in House elections.[a] In contrast, two U.S. senators represent each state, making states multimember districts. This feature of Senate elections is almost universally considered to be an unchangeable feature of the constitutional order.

But not everyone agrees. Terry Smith, a law professor at Fordham University, has argued that nothing in the Constitution, in the Seventeenth Amendment to the Constitution (which provides for direct election of senators), or in the debates surrounding the adoption of the Constitution or of the Seventeenth Amendment precludes the creation of Senate districts.[b] (Indeed, Smith notes that in the early decades of the nineteenth century, some states explicitly required their legislatures to choose senators from two different portions of the state and that other states did so informally well into the twentieth century.)

Smith argues that dividing states into two equally populated halves and assigning a senator to each would have a number of advantages. First, Senate constituencies would be smaller in both geographic and population terms. Therefore, senate elections would be less expensive, and the candidates' need for special-interest money would be correspondingly lower. Second, Senate districts would make the election of racial and ethnic minorities more likely. States such as New York, Illinois, and California could center one Senate district around a minority-dominated urban area (such as New York City, Chicago, or Los Angeles), which would be more likely to elect a minority than would the entire state. Furthermore, each senator would represent only half as many people as at present, allowing for closer contact with constituents.

- *Who are your two senators?*

- *Why should each state have two senators instead of one? If each had one, there would still be equal state representation in the Senate, as the Constitution guarantees.*

- *Would it be better to have just one senator represent half the number of people in your state?*

- *Is there any argument in favor of two senators running statewide, other than 200 years of tradition?*

[a] Even in the twentieth century, an entire state delegation sometimes had to run at-large (statewide) when the legislature could not agree on a redistricting plan in time for the election.

[b] Terry Smith, "Rediscovering the Sovereignty of the People: The Case for Senate Districts," *North Carolina Law Review* 75 (1996): 1–74.

The Congressional Nomination Process

The congressional nomination process is much simpler than the presidential one: nominees for the House or Senate must win at most one primary election in their state, not a sequence across many states. In a few states, party conventions can nominate candidates, but in most states the candidates are chosen in primaries. Some states hold their Senate and House primaries on the same day, and under the same rules, as their presidential primaries. Other states hold them at different times and/or under different rules.[12]

The dates of **filing deadlines** and primary elections also vary widely across states.[13] The filing deadline is the latest date on which a candidate who wishes to be on the primary ballot must file official documents with and/or pay fees to state election officials. For the 2006 elections, Illinois had the earliest filing deadline, December 19, 2005 (!), and Louisiana had the latest, August 11, 2006. The earliest primaries were held in Texas on March 7, 2006, and the latest were in Hawaii on September 23, 2006. Thus, some candidates may know the identity of their opponent as much as six months earlier than others do.

The hardest-fought primaries occur when there is an **open seat**, one without an incumbent running for reelection. If both parties have strength in the area, both will usually have competitive primaries. If one party is much stronger than the other, its primary will be hotly contested because the winner is very likely to be the next

filing deadline

The latest date on which a candidate for office may file official papers or pay required fees to state election officials.

open seat

A House or Senate race with no incumbent (because of death or retirement).

member of Congress. When incumbents run, however, they seldom lose in the primary: Indeed, they seldom face tough challenges from other members of their party. This fact does not necessarily show that primaries are unimportant; rather, it may indicate that incumbents usually are very good about keeping members of their own party satisfied, thus discouraging a strong primary challenge. In 2006, for example, only one incumbent senator—Democrat Joseph Lieberman of Connecticut—was defeated in a party primary. But Lieberman's loss sent a clear signal to every other senator in his party (and many representatives as well): Anyone who supports the war in Iraq does so at his or her peril.

Contemporary House Elections

You Are a
Professional
Campaign Manager

House elections differ from the presidential elections described in the previous chapter in a number of significant ways. One reason is that members of Congress are only *collectively* responsible for the state of the nation, whereas the president is considered *individually* responsible. For example, it is unlikely that voters will hold their representative—who is only one of 435—responsible for a national recession, but presidents regularly take the blame for slow economic times.

Another reason why House and presidential elections differ is that in presidential elections the candidates compete on a roughly equal footing. By the time the fall campaign begins both are well-known to the electorate, both have tens of millions of dollars to spend, and both have scores of supportive groups and organizations campaigning for them. In contrast, in most House elections an incumbent faces a poorly known and underfunded challenger. Because most House races are foregone conclusions, challengers cannot raise enough money to mount serious campaigns against incumbents and outside groups do not lend their support because they do not wish to waste their resources in a lost cause.

The first problem most challengers face is low visibility. Surveys show that barely a third of the citizenry can recall the name of their representative, and even fewer can remember anything he or she has done for the district. Only about one in 10 people can remember how their representative voted on a particular bill. But people know even less about challengers. So, having little information on which to base their vote, many people simply go by the "brand name," voting for the candidate of the party with which they generally sympathize. In House elections three-fourths of all voters who identify with a party typically support the House candidate with the same affiliation.[14] Given that the great majority of House districts are drawn to favor one party or the other, party-line voting will determine the winners in such **"safe seats."**

safe seat

A congressional district certain to vote for the candidate of one party.

The next problem challengers face is overcoming the advantages of incumbency. In presidential elections incumbency is a two-edged sword. A first term widely seen as successful may give the incumbent an insuperable advantage when he seeks reelection, as it did for Ronald Reagan in 1984. In contrast, a first term widely seen as unsuccessful may put an incumbent president at a great disadvantage, as when Jimmy Carter was soundly defeated for reelection in 1980. In House elections incumbency generally works in a positive direction, because, as we discuss below, it is based on considerations other than the state of the country.

Incumbency has grown in importance over the past half-century. Statistical studies of House elections show that, other things being equal, the electoral benefit of being an

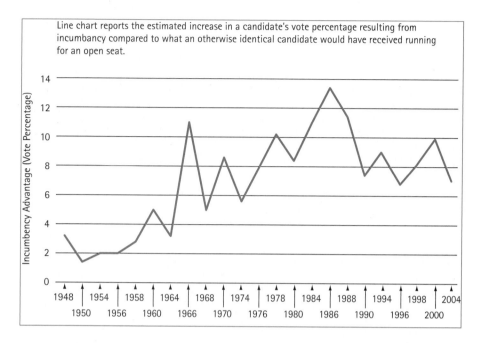

Line chart reports the estimated increase in a candidate's vote percentage resulting from incumbency compared to what an otherwise identical candidate would have received running for an open seat.

FIGURE 11.2

The Advantage of Incumbency Surged in the Mid-1960s and Peaked in the Mid-1980s

Note: The second election of each decade is not plotted because in those years decennial redistricting altered the districts of some incumbents, making incumbency advantage impossible to calculate.

Source: Calculated by Sam Abrams and Gary Jacobson using the Gelman-King method.

incumbent—that is, the **incumbency advantage**—grew from about 2 percentage points before 1960 to as high as 12 points in some late-twentieth-century elections.[15] The increase was not smooth. Rather, as shown in Figure 11.2, the incumbency advantage surged in the late 1960s, leveled off for a time, peaked in 1986, and then declined in the 1990s before creeping upward again in the most recent elections. At least five factors contributed to these trends: the weakness of political parties in the mid-twentieth century, the growth in resources available to incumbents, changes in the activities of representatives, campaign funding disparities, and more responsive incumbents.

Party Decline

Although three-fourths of all party identifiers vote for the candidate of their party, that figure dropped somewhat in the 1960s and 1970s before recovering in recent years. In addition, more voters had a party allegiance in the 1950s than did by the 1980s. When party affiliations weakened, more voters became "available," willing to vote on other less partisan bases such as the incumbent's personal characteristics and activities. Realizing that more voters now were "up for grabs," incumbents adjusted their behavior. Although their own partisan constituencies had become less secure, incumbents could provide voters with other, more personal reasons to support them. At the same time, as voters who normally might have supported the other party became more receptive to such personal appeals, incumbents began to court them. Not only did party affiliations among the voters weaken, but party organizations declined as well. Traditionally, congressional campaigns were conducted by local party organizations. As we discussed in Chapter 8, however, party organizations declined after World War II. Again, incumbents adjusted their behavior to take account of the new environment. They voted themselves resources (often called perks for "perquisites of office") that could make up for those no longer provided by party organizations.

incumbency advantage
The electoral advantage a candidate enjoys by virtue of being an incumbent, over and above his or her other personal and political characteristics.

Why Is It So Hard to Defeat an Incumbent?

Expanding Member Resources

By 1980 some observers compared members of Congress to CEOs (chief executive officers) of small businesses.[16] Each member has a Washington office and one or more district offices. The typical House member employs 18 personal staff assistants, more than 40 percent of whom are assigned to district offices.[17] Senators have even bigger staffs, although office sizes depend on each state's population. These offices have many responsibilities, but no one doubts that much of their effort is directed toward the member's reelection. Indeed, it has been said that Capitol Hill is the headquarters of 535 political machines.

Such was not always the case. In 1950 the average representative had three staff employees. And, as late as 1960, nearly a third of the representatives lacked a district office that was open when the representative was in Washington. The 1960s and 1970s were a period of great growth in congressional staff resources. Travel subsidies and other perks also expanded greatly.[18] In 1960 members were reimbursed for only three trips to their districts per year. By 1976 the number had increased to 26, and today there is no limit except the overall budget allocated to each member. Of course, before the jet plane, it was not practical for many members to go home on weekends, as they do today—many went home only once or twice a session. Improvements in transportation made it possible for members of Congress to commute, so Congress authorized the funds to support that change.[19]

frank
Name given to representatives' and senators' free use of the U.S. mail for sending communications to constituents.

Use of the **frank**—the free use of the U.S. mail for official business—has also grown. Although Congress has long subsidized communication with constituents, technological advances such as computerized mailing lists allowed members to take greater advantage of the privilege. Congressional use of the frank increased much faster than the rate of population increase or the increase in incoming mail that required answering. Not surprisingly, congressional mailings to constituents are much higher in even-numbered (election) years than in odd-numbered years.

You Are a Media Consultant to a Political Campaign

Representatives naturally take political advantage of other new technologies as well. Today, nearly all members have homepages on the Web—a development led by younger members, Republicans, and members who represent highly educated constituents.[20] Although this technology has great potential for communicating information about legislation to constituents, thus far House offices appear to be using it mostly to advertise their members.[21]

Growth in Importance of "Representative" Behavior

How did incumbents appeal to voters as partisan voting declined? You may think of members of Congress primarily as *lawmakers*. Indeed, making laws is the principal business of Congress and the major responsibility that the Constitution bestows on that body. But the official title of members of the House is *representative*, and as political scientists have long recognized, members view their job much more broadly than just writing and voting on legislation.[22] One activity that occupies a great deal of their time and effort is district service—making sure that their congressional districts get a fair share (or more) of federal programs, projects, and expenditures.[23] Some members of Congress are famous for their efforts to bring such economic benefits to their districts. Although critics of Congress often label such benefits "pork barrel spending," constituents generally approve when their representatives and senators "bring home the bacon"—and reward them at the ballot box for their successes.

Another activity to which modern representatives devote a great deal of attention is constituent assistance, usually called **casework**. Citizens, groups, and businesses frequently encounter difficulties in qualifying for government benefits or subsidies or in complying with federal regulations. When their problems are not solved through normal channels, they appeal to members of Congress for assistance. About one in six voters reports having contacted a representative for information or help with a problem. In overwhelming numbers, they report satisfactory resolution of their problems and, again, show their gratitude at the polls.[24]

District service and constituent assistance often are included together under the general rubric of **constituency service**. They share an important characteristic that sheds light on the advantage of incumbency: such activities please voters back home regardless of their party identification or ideology. Most voters are happy when federal projects and grants come to the district—roads, bridges, and community centers are neither Republican nor Democratic. Similarly, Democratic incumbents willingly help Republican businesses deal with federal regulators, and Republican incumbents willingly help Democratic constituents qualify for federal benefits. Because these activities antagonize few if any constituents—in contrast to what happens when members of Congress take positions on controversial issues—they carry significant electoral benefits but entail little if any electoral cost.

Both forms of constituency service grew in scope during recent decades. As the federal government expanded during the 1960s and 1970s, subsidizing and regulating more and more activity, the contacts of citizens, groups, and firms with the government multiplied. The opportunities for members of Congress to engage in constituency service increased correspondingly. Three times as many citizens in 1978 reported having contacted their representative for assistance as reported having done so in 1958.[25] Thus, at the same time that strength of party affiliation was declining, an expanding federal government was stimulating constituent demand for assistance that members of Congress were able and willing to provide. These activities enabled them to reinforce their own base and make inroads into that of the opposition, a tactic still important today.

casework
Efforts of members of Congress to help individuals and groups when they have difficulties with federal agencies.

constituency service
The effort by members of Congress to secure federal funding for their districts and to help constituents when they have difficulties with federal agencies.

Campaign Funds

Like presidential elections, congressional elections have become increasingly expensive: According to Federal Election Commission (FEC) reports, the average spending by a House candidate was about $680,000 in 2004. (The average spending by a Senate candidate was more than $5 million.) But congressional elections differ from presidential elections in an important respect: as Figure 11.3 shows, the gap between incumbents' spending and that of their challengers is wide and has grown wider since 1980. For many of today's reformers, the advantage of incumbency is simple and self-evident: money.

Money certainly affects candidate visibility, and congressional challengers are seriously underfunded. Nevertheless, research on the influence of money in congressional elections paints a surprisingly complex picture. Although money contributes significantly to the incumbency advantage, its contribution probably is exaggerated.

Campaign Finance Reform

FIGURE 11.3

Congressional Campaign
Funding

Source: Norman J. Ornstein, Thomas E.
Mann, and Michael J. Malbin, *Vital
Statistics on Congress, 2001–2002*
(Washington, DC: American Enterprise
Institute, 2002), 81, 87; and the Federal
Election Commission.

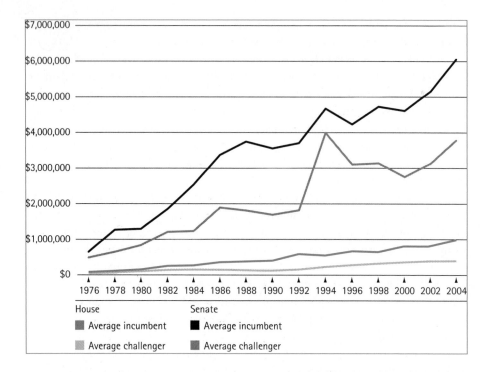

First, campaign spending has what economists call *diminishing returns*: The more a candidate spends, the less impact an additional dollar of spending can have. In particular, for an incumbent who already controls perks valued at more than $1,000,000 per year, an extra $100,000 in campaign spending has less impact than it would for a challenger who lacks such taxpayer-provided resources. Sophisticated advocates of campaign finance reform therefore oppose low limits on campaign spending. Such limits would hurt challengers, who have little name recognition, much more than incumbents, who already enjoy high visibility.[26]

Second, the surge in the incumbency advantage (in the mid-1960s) did not occur at the same time as the explosion of spending in congressional campaigns. House elections in the late 1960s and early 1970s were not nearly as expensive as they are today. Moreover, the explosive growth in political action committees (or PACs) took place *after* the adoption of campaign finance reform laws in 1974, when incumbents had already developed a significant advantage.

Finally, consider that heavy spending by an incumbent can be a sign of electoral weakness, not strength—a signal that an incumbent is in trouble.[27] For example, in 2004 the five losing incumbents on average spent $1.85 million, half a million more than their opponents and almost twice as much as spent by the average winner of an open seat.[28] They did not win by spending a lot; rather, they spent a lot because they were losing.

Some analysts believe that an important effect of incumbents' advantage in campaign funds is one that is difficult to observe, let alone measure. Because it takes so much money for a challenger to mount a serious campaign, potentially strong challengers may decide not to enter the race.[29] If the incumbent has a widely publicized million-dollar "war chest," the prospect of mounting a challenge is daunting and may scare potential opponents out of the race.[30] A challenger may have to take time off from a lucrative job, run a campaign committee deeply into debt, and even tap into personal savings to construct a campaign organization. Well-funded incumbents make taking these risks seem like a poor investment.

In recent years the topic of campaign finance reform has received enormous attention, and members of Congress have grappled with a wide variety of reform proposals. Citizens are disgusted with the present system of campaign finance and, as a result, are cynical about government in general and the Congress in particular. The problem is that the reforms likely to do the most good are the least likely to be adopted. Public financing of congressional elections, for example, would relieve candidates of the burden of fund-raising, giving them time to spend on more productive activities. It also would insulate them from the influence of special interests. But setting subsidies high enough to make challengers credible—perhaps half a million dollars in House races, not counting primaries—would no doubt require expenditures too large for a cynical public to accept (even if incumbents were ever willing to give their opposition that much funding).[31]

The Debate Over Campaign Finance Reform

All in all, the great advantage in campaign spending that incumbent representatives enjoy surely contributes to the advantage of incumbency, but it is far from the only explanation. Even if spending disparities were wiped out overnight, incumbents would still do exceptionally well.

More Responsive Incumbents

Many critics of Congress believe that there is something wrong with high rates of reelection. This is true if members' electoral success reflects the operation of some illegitimate factor—selling out to special interest groups, for example. But, as we have noted, one reason for members' success is that they work very hard at helping their constituents and at serving their districts. Another source of their success is that these legislators are extremely sensitive to the wishes of their constituents, perhaps even more so than members of Congress from earlier eras.

One reason for this increased sensitivity is that members of Congress today have more and better information about their constituents than ever before. Not only do their offices have fax machines, e-mail, Web pages—technologies undreamt of a few decades ago—but the members also physically return to their districts 30 to 50 times a year. Only a generation ago, one often heard the derisive phrase "the Tuesday-to-Thursday Club" applied to a minority of East Coast members who lived close enough to Washington to go home to their districts on Friday and return to the capitol on Monday. Today, jet transportation enables most of the Congress to belong to the Tuesday-to-Thursday club. Important legislative business is rarely scheduled for Mondays or Fridays, because so many members are traveling on those days. With members spending so much time in their districts, is it any surprise that they are highly attuned to the sentiments of constituents?

Moreover, polling is much more widespread today. Again, a generation ago only a few major interest groups ever conducted polls in congressional districts, and then usually only to gauge a candidate's chances. Today, with the growth of the survey research industry and the arrival of computer-assisted telephone interviewing, more members can afford to conduct surveys to learn the views of constituents. Today's members probably make fewer political mistakes than their predecessors did.

New Face of Leadership

The congressional election system favors incumbents and other well-connected politicians, but new political stars such as U.S. Sen. Barack Obama of Illinois do emerge from the electoral process occasionally.

Contemporary members of Congress also may have greater incentive to act in accordance with the information they have. In the modern Congress, every vote is closely watched by interest groups who rate members. Moreover, years after a vote, opponents engaged in opposition research may bring it up in a campaign. In the House, more votes are public now than a generation ago. Until 1971, many votes were cast by standing up, by voice (aye–nay), or by "tellers" (depositing colored cards in boxes)—procedures that concealed the members' individual positions. But rule changes that year made it easy to demand a roll-call vote, and the number of roll calls in an average session more than doubled. Numerous interest groups tally up the votes and score members as friends or foes of legislation of particular concern to their supporters. Challengers hire opposition researchers to pore over an incumbent's record to find even obscure votes than can be linked to a policy that proved a failure or had negative consequences. In short, more recorded votes mean more electoral danger.

Thus, members of Congress take care not to cast votes that will damage them in their districts. When party and constituency collide, party leaders generally allow constituency to trump party—except under the direst circumstances (see *Election Connection*, page 322). Today, members of Congress have enough information to know when a close association with their party or their president is electorally dangerous.

Contemporary Senate Elections

House elections differ from Senate elections almost as much as they differ from presidential elections. The importance of incumbency in House elections contrasts with its lesser importance in Senate elections. As Figure 11.4 shows, incumbent senators win more often than not, but they lose much more frequently than do representatives, and in a few elections (such as 1980) barely more than half survive. In fact, despite their six-year terms, the average length of time a senator serves is the same as the average tenure of a representative: about 11 years.[32] The more precarious position of incumbents in Senate elections reflects differences in party competition, in the information voters possess, in the quality of challengers, and in the ultimate ambitions of senators. Each of these differences makes the position of Senate incumbents less secure than that of House incumbents.

Party Competition

The two parties compete more evenly in Senate races than in House races.[33] Each senator has a state for a constituency, and in general, states are more heterogeneous than the smaller congressional districts included in them. This difference is significant because social and economic diversity provides a basis for party competition.[34] For example, an urban, heavily minority House district will be dominated by the Democrats, and a rural, white district usually will be dominated by the Republicans. If a state includes both kinds of districts, however, each party has a natural base on which to compete for the Senate seats. Only a minority of states are reliably "safe" for either party, whereas a large majority of the smaller, more homogeneous House districts are "safe" seats even without gerrymandering. Thus, part of the reason why senators lead less secure electoral lives than representatives is simply that they have larger, more diverse constituencies that are more difficult to represent.

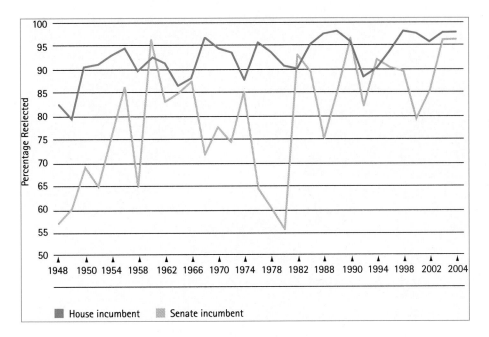

FIGURE 11.4

Representatives Get
Reelected More Often
Than Senators

Source: Harold W. Stanley and Richard G.
Nemi, *Vital Statistics on American Politics,
2005–2006* (Washington, DC: CQ Press,
2006.)

Uncontrolled Information

Senators receive much more media coverage than representatives. One study found that the average senator appeared on the network evening news 33 times over the course of a session, compared to 5 times for the average representative. Every senator had at least one appearance, whereas a quarter of the House got no coverage whatsoever.[35] Given the popular image of politicians as publicity seekers, greater media exposure might appear to benefit senators, but the source of the information is an important consideration. Nearly all the information that constituents receive about House incumbents comes *from* House incumbents—newsletters, press releases, and so forth.[36] Naturally, such information has an entirely positive slant: Representatives are not going to spread negative information about themselves! Senators also would like their constituents to receive nothing but positive information about them, but the media are not under Senate control. The media publicize controversial statements, personal embarrassments, and fights with the president and other politicians. Such coverage inevitably puts the senator in a negative light in the eyes of at least some constituents.

Better Challengers

The office of senator enjoys a higher status than the office of representative. After all, the Senate is commonly referred to as the "upper" chamber, whereas the House is referred to as the "lower" chamber (reflecting sensitive House feelings, members of Congress refer to the "other" chamber). Naturally, high-quality challengers are more willing to risk a race for prestigious Senate seats than they are for House seats. Moreover, Senate seats are much scarcer. Every two years, all 435 House seats are available, compared to 33 or 34 Senate seats; a state with 20 House seats has 60 House elections in a six-year period, but only two Senate elections. Thus, far fewer credible challengers are needed to make Senate races competitive.

Every Senator Sees a President

Hillary Clinton addresses her supporters during the 2006 campaign. Running against weak opposition, she cruised to an easy reelection victory.

The combination of greater prestige and greater scarcity attracts more Senate challengers with a serious chance of winning.[37] Senate challengers have more political experience, in terms of both campaigning and government service. They are better known and better liked than House challengers, and the funding gap between incumbents and challengers is smaller (review Figure 11.3). The combined effect of challengers who are more highly regarded and incumbents who are less highly regarded results in a limited incumbency advantage for those who sit in the Senate.

High Ambitions

Another reason why senators are associated with more controversial matters than representatives is that many of them have higher ambitions. Pundits have joked that every senator looks in the mirror and sees a president. The political system relies, of course, on ambitious office seekers putting themselves on the line.[38] But higher ambition has its risks. Senators cannot seek a presidential nomination solely on the basis of pork-barrel projects. Jockeying for national exposure requires senators to take leadership positions on controversial issues, positions that are bound to offend some constituents. Moreover, involvement with broader national and international issues leaves senators vulnerable to the charge that they are neglecting their states. Senators have been defeated partly as a result of charges that they were more interested in Africa and other far-off places than their home states.[39]

National Forces in Congressional Elections

Former Speaker of the House Thomas P. "Tip" O'Neill (D-MA) liked to say that "all politics is local." While O'Neill's maxim in part reflected the parochial politics of Massachusetts, it reminds us that even though members of Congress are national lawmakers, they are elected and reelected by people in hundreds of localities.

The ability of representatives and senators to distance themselves from party and presidential positions that are unpopular in their districts makes modern congressional elections less subject to the kinds of *national forces* that help or hurt a party's candidates across the board. Such national forces—chiefly popular reaction to wars and economic conditions—were powerful influences on congressional elections until the mid-twentieth century.[40] When a party won the presidency many of its congressional candidates would ride into office on the president's **coattails**. But coattails declined in strength at mid-century as more voters split their tickets, voting for presidential and congressional candidates of different parties. Moreover, as parties weakened and incumbency strengthened, fewer voters seemed to treat off-year elections as a means to express disappointment in the president they had elected two years before. Until 1998, in every off-year election between the Civil War and 1994 except one (1934), the party of the president lost House seats—and usually Senate seats—but that pattern has broken down in the recent mid-term elections.

coattails
Positive electoral effect of a popular presidential candidate on congressional candidates of the party.

National Forces in the 1990s: A New Era?

In the 1970s and 1980s members of the House appeared to have learned how to insulate themselves from the kinds of national forces that in earlier times had resulted in congressional turnover, but the 1994 elections challenged that conclusion. In that historic election, Democrats lost control of the House of Representatives for the first time in forty years. They suffered a 52-seat loss in the House, the largest since 1946. Coupled with an eight-seat loss in the Senate, the election results suggested that a strong national tide had swept aside the advantage of incumbency and destroyed the insulation of the Democratic Congress.

National forces clearly were more important in 1994 than in other recent elections. Nevertheless, the 1994 election did not vary from the norm of congressional insulation as much as pundits initially thought.[41] Even though incumbent losses in 1994 were severe and fell entirely on the Democratic side, 85 percent of the Democratic House incumbents who ran were reelected.

Some of the new Republicans announced that they intended to act as bold lawmakers and not engage in mundane political activities such as "bringing home the bacon." But political realities soon led them to change their minds and begin to utilize the tools of incumbency developed by the Democratic majority they ousted. There is little doubt that the Republicans saved their majority in 1996 by time-honored practices such as constituency service.[42]

The 1998 election, too, suggested that incumbency was still alive and well. In the year of the Monica Lewinsky scandal, the Democrats actually gained five seats, the first time since 1934 that the president's party had gained in a mid-term election. Despite Republican attempts to exploit the scandal, only one Democratic incumbent lost, as did four Republican incumbents, for an all-time record incumbent reelection rate of 98.5 percent. Not even a major presidential scandal disrupted congressional stability.

Congressional Elections in the 2000s: Neck and Neck

The Republicans retained their congressional majorities in the 2000 elections, but they lost a few seats in the House and for only the second time in American history there

ELECTION CONNECTION

How Not to be Reelected to Congress

After digesting the results of the 1992 congressional elections, political pundits declared that 1992 was the "year of the woman." Four new female senators were elected, and the number of women representatives rose from 28 to 47. One of the newcomers to the House of Representatives was Democrat Marjorie Margolies-Mezvinsky, commonly known as MMM. She was the first Democrat in 76 years to be elected from an affluent suburban district near Philadelphia that at the time had a 2 to 1 Republican registration edge. A well-known local newscaster, MMM jumped into the race when the Republican incumbent announced his retirement. She won the Democratic primary handily and squeaked by in the general election by less than 1 percent of the vote.

Normally, the first election is the hardest. Once in office, members embark on the permanent campaign. They behave prudently, use the advantages of incumbency to expand their support among constituents, and avoid giving potential challengers a damaging issue to run on. By following these simple rules, incumbents win reelection with very high probability. MMM violated one of these rules, and the result was a rare incumbent defeat.

Eight months after MMM's election, and 16 months before the next one, the House of Representatives held the fate of the new Clinton presidency in its hands. The final version of the president's deficit reduction plan lay before the House. A sweeping package of spending cuts and tax increases, the plan would chart the course of governmental fiscal policy for the next five years. Earlier in the year, the House and Senate had passed the Clinton plan without a single Republican vote. Differences in the two chambers' versions of the legislation had been ironed out, and now final passage was at hand. Or was it?

Again, not a single Republican in Congress would support the plan: They considered the income tax increases unacceptable. Some Democrats also opposed the plan because it included small increases in gasoline taxes as well as other elements that they disliked. Democratic leaders worked frantically to muster a majority. Speaker Thomas Foley exhorted his troops, "Tonight is the time for courage. Tonight is the time to put away the old, easy ways. Tonight is the time for responsibility. Tonight is the night to vote."[59]

President Clinton himself worked the phones, calling undecided Democrats and telling them that he had to have their vote—his presidency was at stake. For MMM, the situation was a political nightmare. She already had voted against each of Clinton's three key economic proposals, including the deficit reduction package that was now again on the floor. At the time of that earlier vote she had announced, "I promised the voters of Montgomery County that I would not vote for an across-the-board tax increase—and tonight I kept that promise."[60] Since then she had reassured her constituents that she would continue to oppose the plan. Now she was under intense pressure from the president and Democratic leaders to reverse her stand. Which would prevail, party pressure or her promise to her constituency?

At the conclusion of electronic voting, the tally stood at 216 to 216. A majority of the full house (218 of 435) is required to pass the budget. Because Pat Williams, a Democrat from Montana, had agreed to support the president if necessary, MMM, who had not yet voted, held the fate of the Clinton presidency in her hands. Surrounded by supportive Democrats and "with the demeanor of someone being marched to her own hanging," she approached the well of the House to vote for the president's budget. Gleeful Republicans chanted "Goodbye, Marjorie!"[61] MMM may have saved the Clinton presidency, but the cost was her political life.

During the 1994 campaign the Democratic congressional leadership helped MMM raise more than $1.6 million in campaign funds, and President Clinton himself came to her district to support her reelection, but money and endorsements are not enough when a representative breaks a promise and opposes the clear sentiment of her district. The Republican she defeated in 1992 returned for a rematch in the next general election. Although he raised less than two-thirds as much money as MMM did, he still won comfortably with 55 percent of the vote.

was an exact tie in the Senate. Most observers felt that the elections had no national theme, and the parties selected candidates according to their chances of victory. For example, Democratic Party committees backed some pro-life and pro-gun candidates. Only eight House incumbents lost, out of 412 who had run. As usual, senators had a rougher time; 5 of 28 were defeated.

In contrast, as we discussed in the opening paragraphs of this chapter, the congressional elections of 2002–2004 suggested that more voters approached these three elections with national issues in mind than had done so in the preceding several elections. Republicans gained seats in both the House and the Senate in 2002, despite holding the White House—for the second consecutive election voters flouted the historical norm of midterm losses for the president's party. Studies found that Republican candidates got a boost from sharing a party affiliation with President Bush, who enjoyed unusually high approval ratings after the 9/11 terrorist attacks and who campaigned vigorously in the last weeks before the elections.[43] In 2004, President Bush's victory was accompanied by additional Republican gains in both chambers, again largely attributable to voter concern with homeland security issues.

Mid-Term
Elections 2006

In 2006 a national tide appears to have run almost as strongly as it did in 1994, but in the opposite direction. As the year went on, the political conditions described in the chapter opening vignette became even more difficult for Republicans. Although the economy was in good shape by historical standards, the conflict in Iraq worsened in the late summer and fall. President Bush's approval ratings were stuck in the 35-40 percent range and by the time Congress adjourned and the campaign began in earnest, majorities of Americans had come to believe that the war had been a mistake and had not made America safer. Some polls even showed that the public now judged Democrats just as capable of dealing with the terrorist threat as Republicans—homeland security, which had been the Republican trump card in the two preceding elections, no longer gave them an edge.

Virtually everyone expected the Republicans to lose seats in both chambers, and as time went on, the expected losses mounted. Outside the South where the President remained popular, Republican candidates increasingly began to separate themselves from the president, requesting that he not campaign for them, and highlighting areas of disagreement to demonstrate their independence. (A few candidates even declined to appear with the president when he visited their states.) Some conservative thinkers published essays saying that the party deserved to lose. A significant proportion of the American public apparently agreed. In the November voting, the Democrats defeated five incumbent Republican senators and won an open seat to take control of the Senate with a 51-49 majority. The Democrats also gained about 30 seats in the House of Representatives (at the time of this writing, ten seats remain undecided) to take control of that chamber by a more comfortable margin. The 2000 elections ended divided government (p. 221); the 2006 elections brought it back.

In the immediate aftermath of the election, President Bush accepted the resignation of Defense Secretary Donald Rumsfeld, who had become a lightning rod for criticism of the war in Iraq. The new Democratic congressional leadership, Speaker of the House Nancy Pelosi and Majority Leader of the Senate Harry Reid, met with President Bush and pledged to work in bipartisan fashion to deal with the problems and challenges facing the country, but with the "invisible primary" for the 2008 presidential election (p. 278) only a few months away, the electoral pressures on both parties will be enormous. Whether these pressures will produce progress or gridlock remains to be seen.

Overall then, since 1994 national forces seem to have had more impact on congressional elections than they did in the 1970s and 1980s, although still not as great an impact as in much of American electoral history. Still, incumbents continue to do extremely well by conforming to the preferences of their own constituents. Congressional elections today illustrate both the strength of incumbency typical of elections in the 1970s and 1980s and the renewed importance of national forces that emerged in 1994.

Why Have National Forces Grown Stronger?

Although the changes represented by the 1994 elections may have been exaggerated, the evidence that has piled up since then confirms that congressional elections are more nationalized now than in Tip O'Neill's day when all politics was local. Two related developments contributed to this change. The first is more unified, and more distinct, political parties. The congressional parties are more unified today than they were a generation ago, and the differences between Republicans and Democrats are greater.[44] Thus, voters usually have a clear choice between two candidates who take distinct positions on national issues. Such clear differences are less likely to be overwhelmed by local factors or by the candidate's personal characteristics, which were more important in the preceding three decades.

The second reason lies in recent developments in campaign finance. In 2000 the parties raised nearly $500 million.[45] The parties spent much of this money on "issue advocacy," primarily TV commercials praising their own candidates or attacking the other party's candidates. Interest groups also engage in issue advocacy, often independent of the interests of the actual candidates running. In 1998, groups began running ads without the knowledge of (and sometimes in defiance of) the wishes of candidates. In a spring special election in California, for example, pro-life groups attacked the Democratic candidate even though the Republican candidate did not want to make abortion an issue in the race.[46]

Although the Bipartisan Campaign Reform Act discussed in Chapter 8 severely curtailed party issue advocacy in 2004 and 2006, the national parties now spend much more "hard money" in congressional elections. And, although party issue advocacy has been curtailed, issue advocacy by groups has filled much of the void. Numerous "527 committees" sprang up to fund independent campaign ads in the 2004 election. Most of these committees were clearly identified as either pro-Democratic or pro-Republican, although their temporary nature allowed them to fund nasty attack ads without undermining their party's reputation.

The long-term implications of truly independent spending are significant. Candidates naturally prefer to control the campaign agenda as much as possible. Both candidates may prefer that an issue not come up, either because the district is so split that neither candidate feels he or she can profit from the issue or, more innocently, because the issue is not important in their districts and unnecessarily muddies the political waters. Groups can force candidates—and voters—to address these issues.

Although many people are troubled by these developments, two things can be said in their favor. First, they help to redress the imbalance between incumbents and challengers. Parties and interest groups can inject large sums into campaigns where credible challengers are running, thus helping to offset the incumbency advantage. When Sen. Jim Bunning of Kentucky made a series of missteps in 2004, outside money helped a little-known state senator mount a credible campaign against the well-funded incumbent—although Bunning squeaked out a narrow victory in the end. Examples such as this may be one of the reasons why Congress was willing to ban soft money in 2002. Second, campaigns in which the parties and national interest groups actively participate will be more issue-oriented than those in which they are absent. Many people believe this is the way elections should be.

Do Congressional Elections Produce a Representative Body?

Members of Congress generally are well qualified. In contrast to earlier eras, today's Congress contains few political "hacks"—people lacking relevant qualifications but connected to some political influential in their home state. Of course, members today want to get reelected every bit as much as members did in the past, but current members are hard-working, well educated, bright, and personally interested in public policy. Moreover, despite such well-publicized episodes as the Abramoff scandal, today's members are less corrupt than in most previous periods of American history. Scandals are reported more commonly now than in the past, but these disclosures probably reflect changing perspectives in the media—the rise of the "junkyard dog" mentality—rather than increased corruption in the Congress.

Still, some people look at the membership of Congress and are troubled. They see a supposedly representative body that does not mirror the diversity of the United States. The Congress consists overwhelmingly of white male professionals. The 110th Congress elected in 2006 had only 70 women (16 percent of the House), 40 African Americans (9.2 percent) and 23 Hispanics (5.3 percent). The numbers in the Senate are even lower: 16 women, 2 Hispanics, and 1 African American.[47] Minnesota elected the first Muslim to Congress. As shown in Figure 11.5, the numbers have been rising in recent decades, but the rate of increase, except for the 1992 surge, has been slow.

The subject of the gender, racial, and ethnic diversity of the Congress has been a matter of considerable discussion in recent years. The concept of representation means different things to different people. For some, personal characteristics such as the gender or race of a representative are unimportant: As long as he or she is responsive to the needs of constituents, they feel well represented.[48] Others disagree. They contend that almost by definition, a male representative cannot be responsive to the needs and aspirations of women, and that white representatives cannot truly understand the needs and aspirations of African Americans and other minorities. Those who hold such views believe that Congress must be *descriptively* similar to the country in order to be a successful representative body. Still others concede that white male representatives might be able to represent women and minorities but believe nonetheless that women and minority representatives have important symbolic value. A diverse presence in the councils of government will enhance the legitimacy of government actions and provide valuable role models for women and minorities in the population.[49]

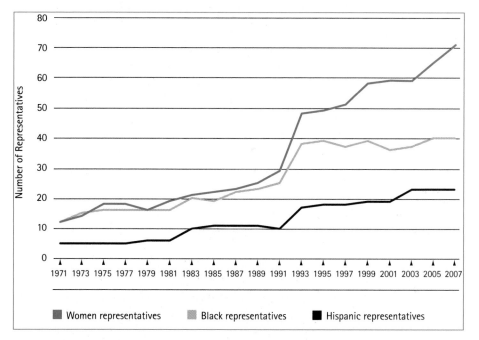

FIGURE 11.5
Women and Minority Members of Congress

Source: Library of Congress–Election Archive.

Those who believe in either the actual or the symbolic importance of diversifying the Congress are not likely to see their frustration end soon. The Congress is not like a business that hires employees or a university that admits students. Its members are chosen by millions of citizens voting independently (and secretly) in hundreds of elections. Voters can be urged to practice affirmative action, but such appeals are unlikely to be very effective—partly because most serious congressional candidates are white men, and partly because women and minorities who run face distinct disadvantages.

Women

The United States ranks near the bottom among world democracies in the proportion of women in the lower chamber of its national legislature. Indeed, politics is the major arena in which American women trail women in other countries. In terms of female membership, the U.S. House ranks above France and about the same as Belgium, Britain, and Australia, but trails other advanced democracies.[50]

Undoubtedly there are many reasons for the low proportion of women representatives in the United States, but gender prejudice does not seem to be among the major ones. Societal prejudice against women serving in public office is low and has been diminishing.[51] Probably, though, a legacy of gender discrimination continues to operate. Winning a congressional seat is usually the result of a series of successful efforts, beginning with local office or leadership in a community organization and working up the political career ladder. Along the way, the member-to-be of Congress learns the art of politics, makes valuable political allies, becomes acquainted with those who bankroll campaigns, and generally acquires the experiences, characteristics, and resources that constitute the "qualifications" that someday will make her a "credible" challenger. Women have only recently gained admission to the networks that move politicians upward to higher office; men have had a long head start. As the pool of women in state legislatures and other lower offices grows, their representation in Congress should follow.

The electoral system functioning in the United States probably contributes to the slow rate of progress. The countries with the highest proportions of women tend to have some version or another of proportional representation (PR). In such systems, party leaders submit lists of candidates who will be elected in proportion to the party's vote. Judging by the results, these lists have significant numbers of highly ranked women. Women appear less successful where they have to contend with powerful men for the same geographically defined seat.

Overall, the underrepresentation of women in Congress naturally will lessen as women's career patterns become more like those of men. Some feminists may reject this analysis, believing that women should strive to be elected as *women*, politicians with a "different voice," not because they have learned to play the electoral game in the same way men do. Because American women have a complex combination of identities, though, they are unlikely to vote as a bloc. The traditional pattern of political advancement is likely the best and fastest method available.

Minorities

The prospects for further increasing minority representation in Congress appear to be less favorable than they are for women, especially the prospects for African Americans.

The critical difference is that in ethnically diverse constituencies, **bloc voting**—in which groups vote as blocs—often occurs. When voting is racially polarized, for example, a black candidate is unlikely to win unless African Americans are a majority of the electorate. In the 103rd Congress, the first Congress after the 1990s redistricting, 32 of the 39 black members came from districts in which African Americans were in the majority, and in 5 of the remaining 7 districts, African Americans plus Latinos made up a majority. Similarly, 15 of the 17 Latino members of the 103rd Congress came from majority-Latino districts; none came from districts with a white majority. The 108th Congress elected after the 2000 census was not much different: in the 108th, 30 of 36 African American members came from majority black districts, and all 17 Hispanic members came from majority Hispanic districts.

> **bloc voting**
> Voting in which nearly all members of an ethnic or racial group vote for the same candidate or party.

Given the historical tendency toward racially polarized voting, efforts to increase minority representation in Congress have been made largely through the redistricting process. The 1982 amendments to the Voting Rights Act and subsequent court decisions required the creation of **majority-minority districts** wherever possible. In such districts, a racial or ethnic minority constitutes a majority of the population so they are able to elect a member of their group if they wish. Given the lower turnout rates that prevail among minority groups, the rule of thumb often has been to create districts with at least a 65 percent minority population (a figure that political science research suggests is unnecessarily high).[52]

> **majority-minority district**
> District in which a minority group is the numerical majority.

Efforts to create majority-minority districts—sometimes called **affirmative action redistricting**—have generated considerable controversy. Some of the districts that have been created have unusual shapes, uniting areas of different cities connected only by a highway. Such districts have provoked charges that they violate the constitutional guarantee that people will be treated equally regardless of race. In 1993 the Supreme Court ruled in *Shaw v. Reno* that majority-minority districting had limits: A district created on no basis other than to include a majority of minorities might raise constitutional questions. In later years the Court declared redistricting plans in Georgia, North Carolina, and Texas to be unconstitutional racial gerrymanders.

> **affirmative action redistricting**
> The process of drawing district lines to maximize the number of majority-minority districts.

Even racial liberals do not always support majority-minority districting. While they value the increased presence of African American and Latino representatives, research suggests that increasing descriptive representation for minorities undercuts the electoral position of the Democratic Party in surrounding districts, which are left whiter than they otherwise would be.[53] Thus, increasing the number of minorities can hurt the party that minority voters tend to support—and therefore decrease the likelihood of legislation that advances minority interests. Recognizing the partisan implications, Republican leaders often favor packing voters into majority-minority districts while Democratic leaders often oppose it. During the 1990s redistricting, in particular, the Republican Justice Department aggressively pushed the creation of minority districts.

Whatever your view of such trade-offs, there is an upper limit on the number of majority-minority districts that can possibly be created: Racial minorities by definition consist of *minorities* of people, and electoral mapmakers cannot cross state boundaries to concentrate them. Indeed, given the recent court decisions, the United States may already be near that limit. If the maximum number of majority-minority districts that can be created is little more than the number that currently exist, then the upper limit for minority representatives will be correspondingly low unless minorities can break through and win in districts where they are not numerically dominant. Thus, many people are encouraged when black incumbents win in districts that have been redrawn so that they are no longer majority African American.[54]

Another potentially negative effect of affirmative action redistricting is less obvious: It may work to marginalize minority members of Congress, particularly black representatives. The homogeneity of African American views should not be overstated.[55] Nevertheless, blacks are overwhelmingly Democratic in their allegiance, more liberal in general, and far more supportive of federal social programs in specific.[56] Representatives of such a group are correspondingly liberal. Indeed, members of the Congressional Black Caucus (CBC) are among the most liberal members of Congress, as measured by numerous interest-group ratings. But liberal records compiled as U.S. representatives may prevent African Americans from being credible challengers in gubernatorial, senatorial, and ultimately presidential elections.[57] Extremely liberal candidates (as well as extremely conservative candidates) rarely win election in a diverse constituency, regardless of race.

In sum, the subject of minority representation in Congress is a difficult one, and existing court-imposed methods of encouraging more minority representation are controversial. Each person must decide whether the gains that accrue from ensuring some level of minority representation exceed the costs. Unfortunately, those costs are highly uncertain and, to a considerable extent, subjective. Thus, people of good faith may disagree.

Elections, Parties, and Group Representation

Some of the difficulty in increasing minority representation reflects the basic fact that the single-member, simple-plurality (SMSP) electoral system is not designed to produce a descriptively representative legislative body. The SMSP system puts all minorities, racial and otherwise, at a disadvantage. If you receive fewer votes than the leading candidate—even if you get 49 percent of the vote—you win nothing. Republicans in Democratic districts and vice versa, liberals in conservative districts and vice versa, pro-lifers in pro-choice districts and vice versa—all are unrepresented when their side loses. In one sense, U.S. courts have been trying to coax a more proportional result, in terms of racial representation, from an electoral system not designed to be proportional. Not surprisingly, they have had only limited success. Recognizing these realities, some academic critics have raised questions about the electoral system itself.

Ironically, it is possible that minorities (and women) would be better represented if old-style party machines were still in existence. After all, the "balanced ticket" was a common strategy of the political party: To construct a coalition of diverse groups, the party recognized each group when they put together a slate of candidates.[58] Historians believe that because of racial prejudice, minorities generally did not fare so well as whites in the urban machines, which were based largely on white ethnic groups. But it is at least arguable that if strong local and state party organizations still existed, there would be more African Americans in government. The demise of the machines and the rise of candidate-centered politics may be an additional disadvantage imposed on African Americans.

Chapter Summary

Members of the House of Representative are reelected at very high rates—more than 90 percent in all recent elections, including the Republican landslide of 1994. Upon close examination, this high level of incumbent success does not violate the founders' intention of an electorally sensitive House. On the contrary, because representatives are so electorally sensitive, they work very hard at serving their districts, try very hard to represent constituents' policy concerns, and in general attempt to eliminate any basis for a strong challenge against them. Contrary to the charges of many critics, electoral success does not lead members of the House to be lazy and unresponsive. Rather, members are reelected *because* they are so hard-working and responsive.

Senators, too, are hard-working and responsive (probably more responsive than the Framers intended), although they do not enjoy the same electoral success as members of the House. On average, their constituencies—states—are more competitive than House districts; they face stronger challengers; and their ambitions and prominence make them the object of media coverage that they do not control and expose them to expectations and ambitions that carry risks as well as rewards.

During the last quarter of the twentieth century, the impact of national forces on congressional elections reached a historical low point. Incumbents managed to distance themselves from national leaders, de-emphasize potentially damaging issues, and emphasize their personal records. In recent elections, however, national forces have grown stronger, reflecting the greater distinctiveness of today's parties and the increased emphasis on national issues by parties and interest groups engaging in issue advocacy.

The single-member, simple-plurality electoral system provides strong incentives for representatives to be *responsive* to the wishes of majorities in their districts. But the system in no way ensures that the composition of Congress will be *descriptively representative* of the diversity of the country's population. On the contrary, if people vote as ethnic or racial blocs, the system will not elect a proportional number of ethnic and racial minorities. The courts have encouraged districting arrangements that would produce more proportional outcomes, but these efforts have met with limited success; they typically require the creation of majority-minority districts that are politically divisive. In the long run such procedures might even work against minority representation by encouraging bloc voting and promoting the election of minority representatives who have limited experience or ability attracting white votes.

For women, the problems are different, and the most promising solution—though not one that many activists want to hear—is time: As women increasingly win lower offices, the pool of qualified women candidates will inevitably expand. As the pool expands, the proportion of women candidates for Congress will increase. Otherwise, the solutions available to increase minority representation are not available for women: They are not segregated from men, so districts dominated by female voters are not feasible to draw, and women do not vote cohesively for female candidates.

Key Terms

affirmative action redistricting, p. 327
bloc voting, p. 327
casework, p. 315
coattails, p. 321
constituency service, p. 315

filing deadline, p. 311
frank, p. 314
gerrymandering, p. 310
incumbency advantage, p. 313
majority-minority districts, p. 327

open seat, p. 311
professional legislature, p. 308
reapportionment, p. 309
redistricting, p. 310
safe seat, p. 312

Suggested Readings

Of General Interest

Fenno, Richard. *Home Style*. Boston: Little, Brown, 1978. Classic study of how representatives interact with constituents, earning their trust.

Herrnson, Paul. *Congressional Elections*. 4th ed. Washington, DC: CQ Press, 2004. The most up-to-date study of congressional campaigns.

Jacobson, Gary. *The Politics of Congressional Elections*. 6th ed. New York: Longman, 2004. The definitive text on modern congressional elections.

Mayhew, David. *Congress—The Electoral Connection*. New Haven, CT: Yale University Press, 1974. Classic argument that much of congressional structure and behavior can be explained by the assumption that reelection is the most important goal of members.

Focused Studies

Brady, David. *Critical Elections and Congressional Policy Making.* Stanford, CA: Stanford University Press, 1988. Prize-winning account that ties together congressional elections, internal processes, and policy making.

Campbell, James. *The Presidential Pulse of Congressional Elections.* Lexington, KY: University of Kentucky Press, 1993. Detailed analysis of national forces operating in mid-term elections.

Cox, Gary, and Jonathan Katz. *Elbridge Gerry's Salamander.* Cambridge, England: Cambridge University Press, 2002. Definitive study of the "reapportionment revolution" of the 1960s.

Kahn, Kim, and Patrick Kenney. *The Spectacle of U.S. Senate Campaigns.* Princeton, NJ: Princeton University Press, 1999. Detailed study of how candidate strategies, media practices, and voter decisions interact in contemporary Senate campaigns.

Tate, Katherine, *Black Faces in the Mirror* (Princeton, NJ: Princeton University Press, 2003). Comprehensive discussion of racial representation in Congress, including value of majority-minority districts.

On the Web

www.cookpolitical.com

One of the most famous handicappers of congressional races is Charlie Cook. To get all of his information, you have to subscribe, but a significant portion of his analysis is available free.

www.vis.org

If you are looking for more comprehensive discussion of election politics, Voter Information Services has a host of congressional report cards and records on voting.

www.lib.umich.edu/libhome/govdocs/psusp.html

The University of Michigan also has a site that includes links to historical and present-day resources about congressional elections.

CHAPTER 12

★ ★ ★ ★ ★ ★ ★ ★ ★ ☆

The Congress and Its Work

Homeland Security Pork

The 9/11 terrorist attacks showed that America was both poorly protected from acts of terrorism and poorly prepared to deal with the aftermath of such attacks. As a result, support for federal assistance to state and local law enforcement and emergency "first responders" soared. In the first year after 9/11 federal spending on such assistance increased tenfold to $20 billion, but many Americans felt that even that amount was grossly insufficient. Democratic presidential candidate John Kerry warned that the Bush administration was not doing enough to close the "preparedness gap," and a Council on Foreign Relations study issued under the title "Drastically Underfunded, Dangerously Unprepared" called for spending $100 billion more.[1] Congress responded enthusiastically to such recommendations for more spending. Since 9/11 Congress has appropriated more than $200 billion for homeland security, including more than $50 billion in 2006.

Many expert observers are highly critical of how taxpayer dollars have been spent, however, and doubt that the billions spent have purchased much security. One would expect spending to be heavily concentrated in large population centers because the potential loss of life and the amount of property damage are much greater in heavily populated areas than in more sparsely inhabited areas. Similarly, one would expect that funds would be heavily concentrated on activities like inspecting airline and shipping cargoes and protecting nuclear power plants and critical infrastructure like bridges and tunnels. The reality is indeed different.

Rural Wyoming, for example, gets five times as many federal dollars per capita as do California and New York.[2] In fact, of the 10 cities classified by the Department of Homeland Security (DHS) as most at-risk, only Washington, D.C., (where members of Congress spend much of their time) is among the top 10 in federal assistance.

Moreover, wherever the money is spent—rural or urban—homeland security expenditures strike many observers as questionable, if not silly. Critics have pointed to scores of examples like these:

- Santa Clara County, Calif., purchased Segway scooters for its bomb squad.
- The Princeton, N.J., fire department purchased Nautilus equipment and a Bowflex machine.

- Columbus, Ohio, purchased Kevlar vests for its police dogs.
- Washington, D.C., spent money on a computerized car-towing system and a summer jobs program.
- Newark, N.J., bought air-conditioned garbage trucks.
- Converse, Texas, uses a newly purchased emergency disaster trailer to haul lawn mowers.

Additionally, federal funds went to other more worthwhile requests that were not obviously related to terrorism, such as forest fire claims in New Mexico and a federal child pornography tip line.[3] Even purchases more directly related to terrorist threats, such as chemical weapons suits for North Pole, Alaska (population about 1,600), seem to be rather low priority expenditures. What is going on?

After 9/11 Congress adopted a funding formula for homeland security spending which provided that each of the fifty states would get at least 0.75 percent of the funds. That guaranteed minimum largely explains why Wyoming, with 0.17 percent of the American population receives 0.85 percent of federal grants—five times more money than would be expected from population alone. As discussed in the preceding chapter, each state has two senators, and it is too much for us to expect politicians to stand idly by while money is being handed out to other states, when their electoral survival depends on the voters in their states.

But the guarantees to each state still leave 60 percent of the funding available for allocation on the basis of risk assessment. As the preceding examples indicate, however, something other than rational analysis seems to be at work. Much of the explanation lies in the structure of Congress. When Congress created DHS, it rolled 22 separate federal agencies into the new department. These agencies are under the jurisdiction of 88 different congressional committees and subcommittees.[4] The members of these various panels authorize the programs administered by the agencies, appropriate the funds for the programs, and oversee their operation. These activities provide numerous vantage points for members to influence where the money goes, and members take full advantage of their opportunities. Even representatives whose districts contain no plausible terrorist target demand a share of Homeland Security funds.

A Wall Goes Up
National Guard soldiers use heavy equipment to lift a section of fence in place on the U.S./Mexico border.

MAKING THE CONNECTION

Homeland Security is not an isolated example of a process gone awry. A look at agriculture policy, transportation policy, trade policy, and numerous other issue areas shows a similar picture. The electoral incentives of members of Congress lead them to structure the institution and to use the congressional process to satisfy their electoral goals. But doing so often detracts from the capacity of the institution to act in the national interest. Although individual representatives and senators may care deeply about serving the nation, they can do nothing to address societal problems if they do not remain in office. The politics of lawmaking therefore always reflect electoral considerations. Members tend to perceive political issues in terms of the needs of their own constituencies. The deals that members make can distort the purpose of legislation or make efforts to reform a public policy futile. In this chapter we will examine the workings of our most powerful, most complicated, most democratic, most electorally sensitive, but—ironically—our least respected political institution. Specifically, we will examine the party and committee organization that Congress has developed and the complex process of lawmaking. Then we will consider how the organization and operation of Congress explain the ambivalent feelings that Americans have about the institution, and why so many believe it needs reform.

Congress—The First Branch

Congress is called the first branch of government because the Constitution prescribes the powers and structure of Congress in Article I. Table 12.1 lists the powers that the Constitution gives to Congress. Historically, the most important have been the "power of the purse"—the power to tax and spend—and the "power of the sword"—the power to declare war. Additionally, through the "necessary and proper" clause, Congress has asserted broad powers over many different aspects of American life.

TABLE 12.1
THE PRINCIPAL POWERS OF CONGRESS
To levy taxes
To borrow money
To regulate commerce
To decide requirements for citizenship
To make monetary policy
To establish a postal system
To establish federal courts below the Supreme Court
To declare war
To raise an army and a navy
To call up the state militias
To make all laws that shall be necessary and proper for executing the other powers of Congress

SOURCE: U.S. Constitution, Article I.

bicameral
Containing two chambers, as does a legislature such as the U.S. Congress.

Comparing
Legislatures

Like many of the world's parliaments, Congress is **bicameral**, consisting of two chambers: an upper chamber called the Senate and a lower chamber called the House of Representatives. In other countries, the upper chamber of parliament typically has largely ceremonial duties or, at most, powers that are much weaker than those of the lower chamber. The House and the Senate possess roughly equal powers, however, which can create a certain amount of interchamber rivalry. A Speaker of the House once called the Senate "a nice quiet place where good Representatives go when they die."[5] The Senate has a quick response to such jibes: In all of American history, only one senator (Henry Clay) has given up a Senate seat to run for the House, and that was in 1811.

The legislative branch includes tens of thousands of people in addition to the 535 members of the House and Senate. The members have personal staffs that total more than 7,000 in the House and 4,000 in the Senate, and each chamber hires about a thousand staff to support its committees. Many of these staffers are clerical workers; others are policy experts who play an important role in the shaping of legislation, especially long-time staff who speak for important members. Additional staff employees support the party leaders who coordinate the flow of bills through the legislative process. All in all, about 14,000 people are employed as congressional staff.

In addition to staff employed by members and committees, thousands of others work in various support agencies of Congress. The General Accounting Office (GAO), the watchdog agency of Congress that oversees the operation of the executive branch, employs more than 3,000 people. A smaller number of people work for the Congressional Budget Office (CBO). This agency provides Congress with expert economic projections and budgetary information. In total, a broad definition of the legislative branch of government includes more than 20,000 people. Table 12.2 provides a summary listing.

The Organization of Congress

The House and Senate are not undifferentiated collections of people who sit in their seats all day debating and voting as the urge strikes them. Like other large decision-making bodies, the two chambers have evolved an extensive division of labor—the committee system—as well as a means of organizing large numbers of people to make decisions—the party leadership structure. The Constitution says nothing about either committees or parties; they developed to meet the needs of elected officials.[6] Both are more important in the House than in the Senate. Because the House is much larger, it needs to be better organized. It operates in more of a follow-the-rules fashion than the Senate, which is small enough to operate by informal coordination and negotiation.[7]

The Congressional Parties

Although parties do not dominate Congress as much as they dominate the parliaments of other democracies, they are still the principal organizing force in Congress. (See the *International Comparison* on the next page.)

Speaker of the House   The Constitution stipulates that the House shall elect a **Speaker**. In practice, members vote the party line in leadership elections, so the Speaker is always the leader of the majority party. Despite being a partisan leader, the Speaker ordinarily does not vote on legislation. Only in close contests involving matters vital to the party does the Speaker vote. In 1995, for example, even with the Republicans in control of the House for the first time in 40 years, Speaker Newt Gingrich participated in only 58 of 845 recorded votes.[8] Until the late nineteenth century, the Speaker was the only formal party leader in the House. Indeed, from the end of Reconstruction to the turn of the century, the Speaker often rivaled the president as the most powerful public official in the United States. Powerful Speakers awarded the chairmanships of important committees to their close allies, made all committee assignments, and punished disloyal members by removing them from committees on which they had previously served.[9] Moreover, as the presiding officer of the House and chairman of the Rules Committee, which determined legislative procedure, the Speaker controlled the floor.

Joseph "Boss" Cannon was the last of the great Speakers. Pushing the envelope of all the powers he had inherited, Cannon dominated the House in the first decade of the twentieth century. But times were changing. The Republican Party was split between regular and progressive wings, and maintaining party discipline led Cannon to an increasingly harsh use of his powers.[10] Dissident Republicans who chafed under the iron rule of the majority eventually joined with Democrats in a revolt that stripped the Speaker of his most important powers.[11] In 1910, rebels took away the Speaker's power to make committee assignments and removed him from the Rules Committee.[12] Procedural reforms also guaranteed ordinary members some right to have their proposals considered. A year later, after the Democrats captured the House, they stripped the Speaker of the power to make committee assignments and vested that power in the House as a whole (practically speaking, in the majority party). The office of Speaker never regained the powers removed at this time. The era of the strong Speakers was over.

TABLE 12.2	
THE LEGISLATIVE BRANCH	
Members of Congress are only a fraction of the legislative branch.	
House	
Committee	1267
Personal staff	7216
Leadership staff	179
Officers of the House staff	974
Senate	
Committee staff	910
Personal staff	4272
Leadership staff	219
Officers of the Senate staff	990
Joint Committee Staffs	104
Support Agencies	
General Accounting Office	3275
Congressional Research Service	747
Congressional Budget Office	232
Miscellaneous	
Architect	2012
Capitol police	1251

SOURCE: Norman Ornstein, Thomas Mann, and Michael Malbin, *Vital Statistics on Congress, 1999–2000* (Washington, DC: CQ Press, 2000), 129–130.

Speaker
The presiding officer of the House of Representatives; normally, the Speaker is the leader of the majority party.

Two days after the November 2006 election, President George W. Bush meets with Nancy Pelosi, the first woman to become Speaker of the House.

The Power of the Speaker of the House

INTERNATIONAL COMPARISON

Congress in a Presidential System

Most world democracies are "parliamentary" in form. Voters rarely choose the chief executive directly under such a system. Instead, voters choose representatives to the national assembly, who in turn choose ministers to execute law and policy for the nation's government. Having executives elected by the legislative branch might seem to give special influence to legislators, but in fact it makes them more dependent. They cannot afford to defect from the governing party coalition because doing so might undermine the leaders they have installed, handing political advantage to the opposition. Members of a parliament therefore usually do little more than rubber-stamp the executive's policy program. Indeed, in parliamentary systems, elected assemblies generally are not called legislatures, because they do little law making. They are called parliaments, because they do a lot of talking.

The United States is one of the exceptions, a democracy with a "presidential" form of government—a government in which the chief executive is elected directly by the people. Ironically, legislators can be more independent and therefore more influential in a presidential system. Their electoral fates are not tied as closely to the performance of the chief executive; unhappy voters can withdraw their support from a president without disrupting the membership of the legislative branch.

To highlight the legislative independence allowed by a presidential system of government, consider the Dubai Ports flap. In February 2006 an announcement that a company owned by one of the United Arab Emirates was buying the management rights at six major U.S. ports set off a congressional firestorm. That Democrats would criticize the deal came as no surprise,

but before the company ended the flap by pulling out of the deal, Senate Majority Leader Bill Frist had threatened to introduce legislation to impose a moratorium on the deal, and Speaker Dennis Hastert had announced that he would support similar legislation in the House. Some Republican committee leaders took an even more belligerent stance.[a]

These actions of Republican congressional leaders would have been unthinkable in a parliamentary system such as Britain's. Once the prime minister and cabinet decide on an important party policy, they expect virtually unanimous support from the rank-and-file in Parliament. High-ranking party members who opposed a key policy probably would be removed from their posts, assuming they did not resign voluntarily, and they might be threatened with other forms of political retribution.

One reason why the executive can impose such discipline is that, in most parliamentary systems, elections do not occur at fixed time intervals. Rather, new parliamentary elections often follow the legislative failure of a government's policy program, either because the opposition calls for a "vote of no confidence" or because the government itself chooses to dissolve Parliament and seek additional support from the nation's voters. Even if no new elections are called, the party's ministers may choose to step down if they cannot command sufficient legislative support. These various possibilities are all so dire to an executive's political allies that extreme party unity becomes the norm.

- *Do you think that members of Congress, rather than voters, should choose the president?*

- *Do you think that members of the party leadership in Congress should show greater loyalty to presidents from their party?*

- *Do you think that the president should have the constitutional power to order new elections if Congress doesn't do what he or she wants?*

In the months immediately following the 1994 elections, which brought the Republican Party to power in the House, Speaker Newt Gingrich moved boldly and decisively in a manner reminiscent of late-nineteenth-century Speakers. He elevated a few representatives to committee chairmanships even though other members had seniority over them. Some commentators explicitly likened Gingrich's behavior to that of "Boss" Cannon. But such comparisons ceased as the session wore on and the Speaker's ability to rule the House diminished.[13] When the Republicans unexpectedly lost seats in the 1998 elections, Gingrich took the fall; he resigned under pressure less than four years after some had proclaimed a "brave Newt world."

majority leader

Title used for the Speaker's chief lieutenant in the House and for the most important officer in the Senate. Each is responsible for managing the floor of his or her chamber.

Party Leadership: House   The Speaker's chief lieutenant is the **majority leader**. Chosen by the majority party caucus, majority leaders are responsible for the day-to-day work necessary to build political coalitions and enact laws: scheduling legislation;

coordinating committee activity; and negotiating with the president, the Senate, and the minority party. Unlike the Speaker, the majority leader votes on legislation. The minority party caucus elects a **minority leader** who coordinates the minority's attempts to improve or defeat majority legislation. Barbara Sinclair stresses that one important job of the leaders is to maintain "peace in the family." Different points of view flourish within parties, and it falls to the leadership to prevent minor spats and quarrels from developing into destructive feuds.[14]

Senator Harry Reid (middle), the new majority leader of the Senate, celebrates the 2006 Democratic victory with fellow Democrats Charles Schumer and Richard Durbin.

The majority and minority leaders are assisted by **whips**, who link the leadership to the party's rank-and-file. The whips communicate leadership positions and strategies to the troops, count votes, and report rank-and-file opinions back to the leadership. The whip offices are rather large, with deputy, assistant, regional, and zone whips (upward of 25 in the Democratic party, about 20 in the Republican party). Although some whips, like former Republican whip Tom DeLay, have a reputation for threats and coercion, persuasion and appeals to party loyalty probably are more important day-to-day tools of the whips.

Many party members participate in the leadership via the whip organizations. Others participate via membership in party committees such as the Democratic Steering and Policy Committee, the Republican Policy Committee, and the Republican Steering Committee. These party committees provide a forum for discussing issues and developing a party program. Occasionally they endorse legislation. When the Democrats are in the majority, the Speaker chairs the Democratic Steering and Policy Committee and appoints many of its members. Thus, this committee serves as an important lever for influencing the behavior of members in their committees. In contrast, the Republicans elect a chair of their Policy Committee and also a chair of their Steering Committee, which makes committee assignments.

Finally, Democratic members belong to their **party caucus** and Republican members belong to their **party conference**—meetings of the full party membership. These groups elect the party leadership and approve the slates of committees nominated by the Steering Committees. Sometimes they debate policies and attempt to develop party positions on policies. During President Woodrow Wilson's administration, they even adopted resolutions requiring party members to support particular policy proposals, a power that lies dormant today.

Party Leadership: Senate   Given that the Senate consists of two members from each state—an even number—some tie-breaking mechanism is necessary. The Constitution obliges by giving vice presidents authority to preside over the Senate and to cast a tie-breaking vote *when necessary*. The Constitution also provides for a **president pro tempore**, who serves as Senate presiding officer in the vice president's absence (which is nearly all the time). This office is mainly honorific, without real power. Ordinarily it goes to the most senior member of the majority party. The Senate's majority and minority leaders are the true leadership of the chamber.

Although the Senate leadership also has a structure of whips and expert staff to assist them, Senate leaders are not as strong as those in the House. They spend much of their time negotiating compromises. Indeed, one of the main jobs of Senate leaders is to hammer out **unanimous-consent agreements** acceptable to all senators with any interest in a given proposal. These agreements specify the terms of debate—the amendments that will be in order, how long they will be debated, when votes will be taken,

minority leader
Leader of the minority party who speaks for the party in dealing with the majority.

whips
Members of Congress who serve as informational channels between the leadership and the rank-and-file, conveying the leadership's views and intentions to the members and vice versa.

party caucus
All Democratic members of the House or Senate. Members in caucus elect the party leaders, ratify the choice of committee leaders, and debate party positions on issues.

party conference
What Republicans call their party caucus.

president pro tempore
President of the Senate, who presides in the absence of the vice president.

unanimous-consent agreement
Agreement that sets forth the terms and conditions according to which the Senate will consider a bill; these are individually negotiated by the leadership for each bill.

filibuster

Delaying tactic by which one or more senators refuse to allow a bill or resolution to be considered, either by speaking indefinitely or by offering dilatory motions and amendments.

cloture

Motion to end debate; requires 60 votes to pass.

Congressional
Partisanship

and so forth.[15] Such agreements are necessary because—unbelievable as it may sound—any senator can delay consideration of a bill or resolution.

The Senate has a tradition of unlimited debate: the **filibuster**. According to present rules, a senator may speak indefinitely. The only way to silence a filibuster is for the Senate to adopt a **cloture** motion ending debate, which requires the support of 60 senators. The existence of the filibuster means that a simple majority of senators is not a winning coalition. A minority of 41 can prevent the Senate from acting on a measure. Unanimous-consent agreements represent one means of avoiding time-consuming filibusters; senators agree in advance to the terms under which they will consider legislation. These agreements require true unanimity, however, so a single senator may place a hold on debate or legislation by refusing to sign on. These practices allow minorities to obstruct legislation more easily in the Senate than in the House.

Ups and Downs of the Congressional Parties   In practice it is difficult to measure party influence precisely because it often coincides with constituency sentiments and members' own views.[16] The power of congressional leadership clearly has varied over time, though, and appears to be greater now than it was for half a century after the 1910 revolt against "Boss" Cannon.

One likely reason for the growth of party power in recent decades is that congressional parties became more homogeneous in their policy preferences.[17] When party members are in agreement, leaders are likely to hold views consistent with those of the overall membership and members defer to their leaders. When party members are more diverse in their views, they are reluctant to give power to party leaders—who may act in ways objectionable, or even politically dangerous, to many of the rank-and-file.[18] As a result, institutional changes usually have followed changes in party unity (see Figure 12.1). The parties of the late nineteenth century represented distinct social groups, so Republican leaders in Congress were given great power; but they lost influence when the party divided into progressive and regular wings. When Democrats swept into power during the Great Depression, they included both northern liberals and southern moderates, so leaders remained relatively weak.[19] The social changes of the 1960s and 1970s, though, produced sharply divided parties that have grown increasingly unified and more ideologically extreme. Today's congressional parties are quite polarized. As a result, members are more willing to stick with strong leaders committed to the party's platform rather than do anything that might help the opposition.

Of course, just because a member of Congress usually agrees with the leadership does not mean that leaders will always do what the member wants. Being a leader means making tough choices. Presumably some of those choices will be objectionable to some of the party membership. Why would a member of Congress voluntarily pass decision-making authority over to leaders rather than retaining the right to "second guess" any decision?

Part of the answer is that an effective congressional party contributes to members' electoral prospects. Uninformed voters often choose among candidates on the basis of party image and performance. Members of Congress wish to be part of an effective team, not part of a team that voters consider too divided to accomplish anything. As a result, they are willing to tolerate constraints imposed by their leadership—indeed, to pass rules formalizing and strengthening such limits—because they do not wish to undermine the party's effectiveness.[20] The pressure for conformity can be especially strong when the

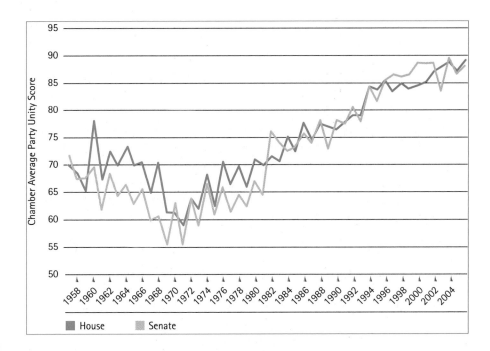

FIGURE 12.1

The Congressional Parties
Are More Unified Today
Than a Generation Ago

The graph shows the percentage
of all recorded votes on which a
majority of voting Democrats
opposed a majority of voting
Republicans. Numbers for each
year have been averaged over
each Congress.

Source: Washington, DC:
Congressional Quarterly.

president shares the member's party label. A successful president can help members
running for reelection, as President Bush did in 2002. Conversely, as the Republicans
found to their sorrow in 2006, an unsuccessful president can hurt the party. Members of
the president's party thus have an incentive to work together to help him succeed.

Another source of party influence has grown in importance in recent years: The
congressional parties are increasingly active in campaign funding. The House and
Senate campaign committees are controlled by the leadership and most members of the
leadership have established their own PACs.[21] Members who have received campaign
contributions from party leaders naturally feel some obligation to support those leaders when they have enough political flexibility to do so.

Finally, members of Congress willingly accept some party discipline because they
see it as necessary for attaining important policy goals. Every representative could imagine the perfect bill, one that would both please the voters back home and bring
national policy into perfect alignment with his or her preferences. But could the representative then turn that dream bill into law? Probably not, because every other member
would like to do the same thing. Sticking with the party's leaders increases the odds of
real change. The representative may not like every detail of legislation that party leaders will negotiate, but they can put together something better than current law—and
powerful leaders actually have the ability to get it passed.

The Committee System

Members of Congress introduce thousands of bills and resolutions every year. Since
1980, for example, 6,000 to 8,000 bills have been introduced in each two-year session
of the House of Representatives. Rather than expect everyone to master the details of
so many bills, Congress has developed a screening process. Members of each chamber
are divided up into different committees specializing in particular policy areas. Each bill

is referred to one or more committees, and the whole chamber usually only votes on legislation approved by the relevant committees. (In the House of Representatives, floor majorities can remove a proposal from a recalcitrant committee via a discharge petition, but this process requires 218 signatures and is seldom used.) Of the thousands of bills introduced each year, only 10 to 15 percent eventually pass and most of the failed bills die at the committee stage.

standing committee

Committee with fixed membership and jurisdiction, continuing from Congress to Congress.

select committee

Temporary committee appointed to deal with a specific issue or problem.

    Standing committees have fixed memberships and jurisdictions, and they continue from one Congress to another. The Appropriations, Commerce, and Foreign Relations Committees are examples. **Select committees**, by contrast, are temporary committees created to deal with specific issues. Both houses of Congress had standing committee systems in place by 1825.[22] The number of committees tends to expand until, at some point, the system is reorganized when majorities come to believe it has grown unwieldy and out of alignment with contemporary problems. The Legislative Reorganization Act of 1946 gave the committee system the shape it largely retains today, more than half a century later. In the 109th Congress (2005–2006), there were 19 standing committees in the House and 17 in the Senate (see Table 12.3). These "full" committees are subdivided into more than 150 subcommittees. There also are four "joint" committees, with membership from both houses, and a small number of select committees on special topics such as aging, national intelligence, and (in the House) homeland security.

House Committees   House committees fall into three levels of importance. The top committees are Rules, Appropriations, Ways and Means, and Commerce. The Rules Committee is the right arm of the Speaker. It controls the flow of legislation to the floor and the conditions of debate. Appropriations and Ways and Means deal with spending and taxing, broad powers that enable them to affect nearly everything government does. Commerce has extensive jurisdiction over a wide variety of policy areas. A member who serves on one of these committees ordinarily is allowed no other assignment, except that he or she is eligible to serve on the Budget Committee. Committees at the second level of importance deal with nationally significant policy areas: armed services, civil rights, agriculture, and so forth. A member ordinarily serves only on one such major policy committee and on a third-level committee of lesser importance. These less important committees include "housekeeping" committees, such as Government Reform and Oversight, and committees with narrow policy jurisdictions, such as Veterans' Affairs. The Budget Committee has a special status. Members can serve for only four years in any 10-year period, and its membership is drawn from other committees and from the leadership.

Senate Committees   The Senate committee system is simpler than that of the House; it has just major and minor committees. Like their House equivalents, Appropriations and Finance are major committees, but the Senate Rules Committee is a minor committee with nothing like the power of its House counterpart (the Senate leadership itself performs the tasks performed by the House Rules Committee). Budget is also a major committee, as is Foreign Relations, reflecting the constitutional responsibilities of the chamber in that area (advise and consent to treaties, confirm ambassadors).

    Committee power in the Senate is widely distributed: Chairs of major committees cannot chair any other committee or subcommittee, and chairs of minor committees can chair only one other panel. Each senator can serve on one minor and two major

TABLE 12.3

STANDING COMMITTEES OF THE 109TH CONGRESS

Committee	Size (party ratio)	Number of Subcommittees	Committee	Size (party ratio)	Number of Subcommittees
Senate			**House**		
Agriculture	20 (R11/D9)	4	Agriculture	46 (R25/D21)	5
Appropriations	28 (R15/D13)	12	Appropriations	66 (R37/D29)	10
Armed Services	24 (R13/D11)	6	Armed Services	62 (R34/D28)	6
Banking, Housing, and Urban Affairs	20 (R11/D9)	5	Budget	39 (R22/D17)	0
Budget	22 (R12/D10)	0	Education and Workforce	49 (R27/D22)	5
Commerce, Science, and Transportation	22 (R12/D10)	10	Energy and Commerce	57 (R31/D26)	6
Energy and Natural Resources	22 (R12/D10)	4	Financial Services	70 (R37/D32/I1)	5
Environment and Public Works	18 (R10/D8)	4	Government Reform	41 (R23/D17/I1)	7
Finance	20 (R11/D9)	5	House Administration	9 (R6/D3)	0
Foreign Relations	18 (R10/D8)	7	International Relations	50 (R27/D23)	7
Homeland/Governmental Affairs	16 (R9/D7)	3	Judiciary	40 (R23/D17)	5
Health, Education, Labor, and Pensions	20 (R11/D9)	4	Resources	49 (R27/D22)	5
Judiciary	19 (R10/D8)	8	Rules	13 (R9/D4)	2
Rules and Administration	18 (R10/D8)	0	Science	44 (R24/D20)	4
Small Business	18 (R10/D8)	0	Small Business	33 (R18/D15)	5
Veterans' Affairs	14 (R8/D6/)	0	Standards of Official Conduct	10 (R5/D5)	0
			Transportation	75 (R41/D34)	6
			Veterans' Affairs	29 (R16/D13)	4
			Ways and Means	41 (R24/D17)	6

SOURCE: Respective committee Web sites at the House homepage (www.house.gov) and the Senate homepage (www.senate.gov).

committees, and every senator gets to serve on one of the four major committees. On average, senators sit on more committees than do representatives—in part, a simple reflection of the fact that the Senate has nearly as many committees as the House with less than one-fourth as many members to staff them. But, in addition, senators represent entire states, which are typically more diverse than congressional districts; thus, they cannot afford to limit their attention to one or two subjects, as many representatives can. Holding more committee assignments creates conflicting loyalties and makes it difficult for senators to specialize in a few subjects, as many House members do. As a result, the legislative lives of senators are not so closely tied to a particular committee as are the lives of representatives.[23]

How Committees Are Formed   The committee system is formally under the control of the majority party in the chamber. Party committees nominate members for assignment and party caucuses approve those assignments. As a result, each committee has a ratio of majority to minority members at least as favorable to the majority as is the overall division of the chamber. The more important committees are stacked in favor of the majority. In the 109th Congress, for example, the Republicans had a 9 to 4 advantage over the Democrats on the House Rules Committee, a ratio far greater than their 232 to 202 edge in the chamber as a whole. In contrast, the party ratio on the less important Judiciary Committee was 23 to 17.

In practice, committees sometimes show considerable independence. Part of the reason is the traditional use of **seniority** to choose committee chairs. Under seniority, the majority-party member with the longest continuous service on the committee becomes the chair. Often called a "norm" because the use of seniority never was a formal rule, seniority became the mode of selecting Senate committee chairs in the 1880s and House chairs after the 1910 revolt and was closely followed until 1995. The practice of seniority includes the right to continued reappointment to a committee. Thus, once a member initially joins a committee, he or she automatically rises on its seniority ladder. Physically or mentally failing members sometimes are moved aside and, on occasion, the leadership or caucus rejects a nomination for chair, but the system gives committee chairs in specific, and committee members in general, a degree of independence or autonomy.

The practice of seniority began to weaken in the 1970s when Democrats removed some senior chairmen who were out of step with the caucus (including one who had addressed newly elected members as "boys and girls"). After the 1994 elections gave Republicans control of Congress for the first time in 40 years, Speaker Gingrich passed up the most senior committee member when he named the Republican chairs of Appropriations, Commerce, and Judiciary.[24] The Republican conference then adopted a three-term limit on committee chairs, which constituted a major revision of the seniority system. Senate Republicans adopted an analogous rule in 1996. Whether either chamber will revert to the old system when the Democrats regain control remains to be seen.

Committee Reforms   In the 1950s, party influence in Congress became so weak that many observers believed the chairs of the standing committees held the real power. A few of the chairs behaved autocratically, creating and abolishing subcommittees and varying subcommittee jurisdictions, monopolizing subcommittee chairmanships, controlling committee staff and budgets, and even refusing to call meetings or to consider legislation they opposed. To make matters worse, because members from safe southern seats had built up considerable seniority, many of the chairs were more conservative than the younger, mostly northern Democrats who held more liberal views.[25]

Eventually, the rank-and-file membership, operating through party caucuses, curbed the power of the standing committee chairs and injected more democracy into the committee system. Much of this effort took place in the Democratic caucus.[26] In the early 1970s, a caucus resolution limited House committee chairs to holding one subcommittee chair. A "subcommittee bill of rights" guaranteed subcommittees their permanence, jurisdictions, budgets, and staff, and made the choice of subcommittee chairs more democratic. The Senate had treated junior members somewhat better since the 1950s, but in recent decades it has moved in the same direction as the House, spreading power more evenly across the membership.

At the time many observers were unsure whether the preceding changes represented improvements. Had Congress simply decentralized power from approximately

seniority
Practice by which the majority-party member with the longest continuous service on a committee becomes the chair.

Congressional Leadership

40 standing committees to approximately 300 standing committees and subcommittees, many of them as small as eight or nine members? Had a period of "committee government" given way to a period of even more decentralized "subcommittee government"?[27] For more than a decade, political scientists debated the net impact of the reforms. Today the prevailing view is that the reforms adopted in the late 1970s to strengthen the party leadership more than offset the subcommittee reforms. The committee system today appears far more subject to party influence than it was a generation ago. An out-of-the-mainstream chair of an important committee would run a greater risk of being removed today than at any time since the revolt against "Boss" Cannon. Moreover, when the Republicans took control in 1995, their leadership acted to restrict the independence of subcommittees.

Purpose of Committees   Why does the standing committee system exist at all? Members of Congress are elected as equals. Why would a large majority give to a small minority exceptional influence in a policy area—the power to decide whether legislation should be considered, the power to shape the legislation if it is considered, and the power to review its implementation? Why not consider everything on the chamber floor (the so-called *Committee of the Whole*), where all members participate on an equal basis?

Members often use committee assignments to focus on district interests. For example, members from urban districts seek membership on committees that deal with banking, housing, or labor, whereas members from rural districts have little interest in such issues and opt instead for committees that deal with agriculture and natural resources. Members of committees like these that directly distribute government benefits are in a position to please the voters back home. Studies have documented how districts and states whose members serve on particular committees receive a disproportionate share of the projects and grants that fall within the jurisdictions of those committees.[28] This distributive process is often called **logrolling**, because it implies that members defer to their colleagues on policies they care little about in exchange for particular influence on issues that deeply matter to them.[29] Such a system can result in spending bills larded with expensive projects. An alternative interpretation is that committees primarily serve a knowledge function.[30] Members frequently are uncertain about the outcomes that policies will produce. Hence, they want some members to become experts in each subject area and share their knowledge with the broader membership. One way to encourage their hard work is to give committees disproportionate influence, subject to the condition that they do their job conscientiously and not abuse their position. Committee members can exploit their position to gain a bit extra for themselves, but only to the extent that they specialize and give the chamber useful, reliable information.

Still another theory holds that committees are the tools of the congressional parties.[31] Proponents of this partisan theory of committees argue that the party is so concerned with controlling public policy that it stacks committees with loyal members and shapes the jurisdictions of committees so that only reliable committees write and revise important legislation. Proponents of the partisan theory point out that the average ratio of majority to minority party members typically favors the majority party—sometimes by a lot.[32] And committee jurisdictions are influenced by party leaders. But there are many exceptions to these patterns. Committees sometimes behave in a bipartisan

logrolling
Colloquial term given to politicians' trading of favors, votes, or generalized support for each other's proposals.

fashion and the process of defining committee jurisdictions is extremely complicated, not clearly under the direct control of the leadership.[33]

Studies of committees are not conclusive about which of these three perspectives—distributive (or logrolling), informational, or partisan—is the best explanation for the committee system. Committees likely promote all three of these purposes as members try to balance their competing needs: to serve their local constituencies, to gain reliable information about public policy, and to accomplish partisan goals. It may also be that the type of committee matters. For instance, committees that hand out money for public projects or fund important programs seem to behave in distributive fashion. Other committees that deal with complex public policies such as environmental or telecommunications regulation may serve an informational function. Finally, some committees—such as the Rules Committee that controls the agenda and floor debate—seem dominated by the party leadership. The committee system probably reflects a mixture of the three theoretical purposes for committees, a mixture that varies over time and across committees.

Caucuses

caucus

A group within Congress, formed by members to pursue common interests.

In recent years voluntary groupings of members with common interests have become increasingly common, adding a third level of congressional organization. Usually called **caucuses**, these groupings can cross party, committee, and even chamber lines. There were nearly 300 such groups in the 109th Congress, ranging from long-standing ones such as the Congressional Black Caucus and the Northeast-Midwest Congressional Coalition, to newer ones such as the Sportsmen's Caucus, the Wine Caucus, and the End-the-Death-Tax Caucus.[34]

Caucuses are extremely varied in their concerns, their activities, and their effects. They can support the efforts of party or committee leaders but they also can pressure party or committee leaders on particular issues. Similarly, they can be a vehicle for cooperation across chambers, across parties, or across committees—or they can obstruct the proposals of chambers, parties, or committees because of some special interest they feel is being slighted or dealt with unfairly (such as wine or potatoes). Some caucuses are lavishly financed by outside interests while others subsist with modest contributions of office space, money, and staff from their members. The Sportsmen's Caucus, for example, had a 2003 budget of $860,000 provided by donations from the National Rifle Association and the sporting equipment industry.

There are few studies of caucuses and their activities as yet, but they appear to be increasingly important actors in the congressional process, another example of how congressional organization evolves to meet the needs of members in a changing political world.[35]

How a Bill Becomes a Law

SIMULATION

You Are a Member of Congress

Congress makes the laws that govern the United States. In addition to the specific legislative powers set out in Article I, the "necessary and proper" clause authorizes Congress "to make all laws which shall be necessary and proper for carrying into execution the foregoing powers, and all other powers vested by this Constitution. . . ." How do two parties in two chambers organized into over 300 committees and subcommit-

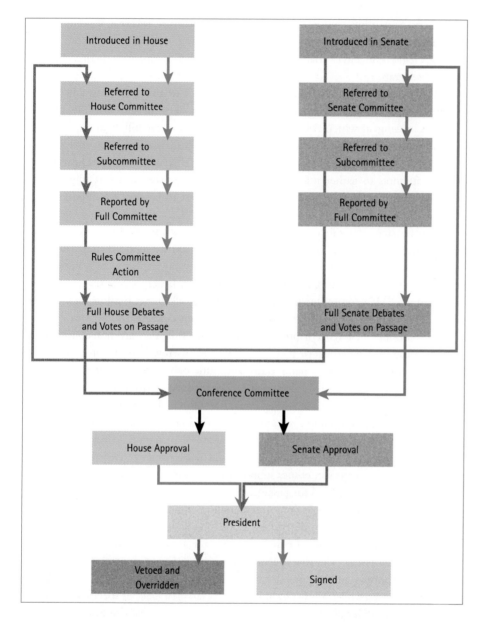

FIGURE 12.2

How a Bill Becomes a Law

Passing laws is a long and complicated process. Most bills fail to complete the journey.

tees get together and pass laws? Although no flowchart can possibly convey the complexity of getting a major bill through Congress, we will outline the process, describing the stages that important legislation goes through. Figure 12.2 lays out the general process in idealized form, but any particular bill or resolution may have a different and even more complicated history as it loops through the various stages.

As a first step, a bill or resolution is introduced by a congressional **sponsor** and one or more co-sponsors. The House Speaker or Senate presiding officer, advised by the chamber's parliamentarian (an expert on rules and procedures), refers the proposal to an appropriate committee. In some cases, sponsors are not serious but are acting only to please some constituency or interest group. If they *are* serious, they may draft their bill in such a way as to increase its chances of being referred to a friendly committee—

sponsor

Representative or senator who introduces a bill or resolution.

multiple referrals

Said to occur when party leaders give more than one committee responsibility for considering a bill.

Contemporary
Legislative Process

markup

Process in which a committee or subcommittee considers and revises a bill that has been introduced.

suspension of the rules

Fast-track procedure for considering bills and resolutions in the House; debate is limited to 40 minutes, no amendments are in order, and a two-thirds majority is required for passage.

rule

Specifies the terms and conditions under which a bill or resolution will be considered on the floor of the House—in particular, how long debate will last, how time will be allocated, and the number and type of amendments that will be in order.

often theirs. Sometimes the leadership decides on a **multiple referral**, sending the bill simultaneously to more than one committee or dividing it among several committees. Complex legislation and overlapping committee jurisdictions increase the likelihood of multiple referrals.

Once the bill goes to committee, the chair gives it to an appropriate subcommittee. Here the real work begins. If the subcommittee takes the bill seriously, the staff schedules hearings at which witnesses will speak in favor of the bill or in opposition to it. Witnesses can be other members of Congress, members of the executive branch, representatives of relevant interest groups, or ordinary citizens. Sometimes hearings are genuine attempts to gather information. More often, hearings are carefully choreographed: The subcommittee staff stacks the witness list in favor of the subcommittee chair's position.[36]

After hearings, the subcommittee begins **markup** of the bill—revising it, adding and deleting sections, and (assuming the bill enjoys majority support) preparing it for report to the full committee. The full committee may repeat the process, holding its own hearings and conducting its own markup, or it may largely accept the work of the subcommittee.[37] If a committee majority supports the bill after committee markup, the bill is nearly ready to be reported to the floor—but not quite.

Let's consider first what happens in the House. Bills that are not controversial, either because they are trivial or they have extremely narrow impact, can be called up at specified times and passed unanimously with little debate. Somewhat more important bills are considered under a fast-track procedure called **suspension of the rules**. If a two-thirds majority of those voting agrees, the bill will be considered on the floor. Debate is limited to 40 minutes, no amendments are in order, and a two-thirds majority is required for passage. There is some risk in considering a bill under suspension: Even if a majority approves of it, the bill could fail to achieve two-thirds support. Indeed, a bill's opponents sometimes support the motion to suspend the rules precisely in order to raise the threshold for passage.

Legislation that is especially important, and therefore usually controversial, goes to the Rules Committee before going to the floor. The Rules Committee, too, may hold hearings, this time on the type of **rule** it should grant. In these hearings, only members of Congress may testify. The rule specifies the terms and conditions of debate, such as how long supporters and opponents will be allowed to speak. It may prohibit any amendments (a *closed rule*), allow any amendments (an *open rule*), or specify the amendments that are in order (a *restrictive rule*). In recent years, with the rise of stronger party leadership, three-quarters of all bills that have come from the Rules Committee have been granted restrictive rules.

Some rules are unusual. For example, so-called *king of the mountain rules* allow a number of (frequently conflicting) amendments to be offered, but they specify that only the last amendment that receives a majority is adopted. Naturally, the committee orders the amendments so that the one it favors goes last. This kind of rule allows some members to play a little game with constituents. The members can vote for several conflicting amendments, thereby satisfying each of their supporters, all the while knowing that the last vote is the only one that matters.

If the Rules Committee recommends a rule, the floor then chooses to accept or reject it. In shaping the rule, the committee anticipates the limits of what the floor will accept. Thus, most rules receive approval—at which point the bill itself finally comes under consideration by the full chamber. The floor decides whether to adopt the "perfected" bill after any debate or amendment votes permitted by the rule.

The process in the Senate is a bit simpler to describe. For uncontroversial legislation, a motion to pass a bill by unanimous consent is sometimes all that is necessary. More important and controversial legislation requires the committee and party leaders to negotiate unanimous-consent agreements, which are complicated bargains analogous to the rules granted by the House Rules Committee. Assuming that such an agreement is successfully crafted and thereby avoids a filibuster, the bill eventually comes to a floor vote.

If a majority votes to adopt the bill, are we at the end of the process? Not at all. Before the bill can be sent for the president's signature, it must pass both chambers in identical form. A bill may have started in one chamber before going to the other, or it may have proceeded simultaneously through both. In either case, the House and Senate seldom pass exactly the same legislation. In fact, their versions may be in serious conflict. Unless one chamber is willing to defer to the other chamber, the two must iron out their differences. Sometimes they do so informally, but for major legislation, the usual method is that each chamber appoints representatives to a joint **conference committee** that can produce a compromise version.

In principle, each chamber's conferees are committed to the legislation approved by their colleagues, but in practice this allegiance is not likely. Conferences for some complex bills involve hundreds of members who support some parts of the bill, oppose other parts, and care little about still other parts. This complexity makes the situation ideal for bargaining. When a majority of each chamber's conferees agree to the final compromise, the bill is reported back to the parent chambers, where another floor vote in each chamber is required for passage.[38]

You may think that we have finally reached the end of the process. The bill will be sent to the president and, barring a presidential veto, will become law. Although it will formally become a law, there is no guarantee that the bill will have any effect. So far, we have been considering only the **authorization process**. All government action authorized by Congress—paying subsidies, issuing regulations, buying bombers, inspecting workplaces, whatever—also needs funding for it to be carried out.

The Constitution grants Congress the power of the purse and makes the House the lead actor: All tax bills must originate in the House, and by custom and tradition, all appropriations bills do, too. The **appropriations process** parallels the authorization process. Thirteen appropriations subcommittees in each chamber hold hearings and mark up the bill (the subcommittee chairs are commonly referred to as "the Cardinals of Capitol Hill").[39] The full committees may also do so, but they usually defer to their subcommittees. In the House, appropriations bills are privileged; they take precedence over other legislation, and a motion to take up an appropriations bill can be offered at any time. But in practice, appropriations bills, too, usually pass through the Rules Committee. Thus, appropriations subcommittees in both chambers must report spending bills, the rank-and-file in both chambers must pass them, and a conference committee must agree on every dollar before the government actually has any money to spend on the actions it has authorized.

Star Power

Actress Ashley Judd, who is global ambassador for YouthAIDS, an organization dedicated to educating and protecting young people from HIV/AIDS, testifies before the Senate Foreign Relations Committee. Judd has traveled extensively in Africa and Asia, where she had raised awareness of HIV prevention.

conference committee
Group of representatives from both the House and the Senate who iron out the differences between the two chambers' versions of a bill or resolution.

authorization process
Term applied to the entire process of providing statutory authority for a government program or activity.

appropriations process
Process of providing funding for governmental activities and programs that have been authorized.

Congressional
Term Limits

Evaluating Congress

It is easy to get so wrapped up in the details of Congress and its operations that we lose sight of the reason for our interest in the institution. The reason, of course, is that Congress is the first branch, arguably the most powerful and most important of our three branches of government. It is the branch that bears primary responsibility for representing the needs and values of the American public and for developing legislation to improve its well-being. How well does Congress meet its responsibilities?

Criticisms of Congress

The most common criticism of the congressional process should be obvious: *It is slow and inefficient.* Legislation may take months or even years to wend its way through the process, and there is much duplication of effort—both within and between the chambers. Moreover, after all is said and done, Congress often produces a compromise that leaves no one satisfied. To those who want quick, decisive action, Congress-watching is enough to put their teeth on edge. And, of course, that is what the framers intended. They wanted to ensure that laws would pass only after they had been thoroughly considered and majorities were convinced that they were needed.

But the procedural hurdles in the congressional process raise a second criticism: *The congressional process works to the advantage of policy minorities, especially those content with the status quo.* Proponents of legislation must build many winning coalitions—in subcommittee, in full committee, in appropriations committee, and on the floor, in both chambers, and perhaps in conference committee. Opponents have it much easier. A minority that controls only a single stage of the process may be able to block action. Of course, a determined majority cannot be stopped indefinitely, except by a Senate filibuster, but it can be held at bay for a long time or it can be forced to make undesirable compromises. Moreover, potential majorities sometimes decide not to act, calculating that the costs of overcoming all the obstacles are not worth the effort. Thus, the process hinders majorities who support change and helps minorities who are content to prevent change.

Two other criticisms focus on what Congress does when it acts, rather than on its failure to act. Given that members are trying to please constituencies, *they are constantly tempted to use their positions to extract constituency benefits,* even when important national legislation is at stake. President Jimmy Carter got so upset trying to deal with Congress on national energy policy that he wrote in his diary, "Congress is disgusting on this particular subject."[40] President Clinton's lobbying on behalf of the North American Free Trade Agreement (NAFTA) was likened to an "oriental bazaar," with members demanding special treatment for constituency interests or even trading their votes for concessions on unrelated issues. Many observers therefore charge that Congress defeats, distorts, and otherwise damages national interests in pursuit of its members' parochial interests. Of course, such trading of favors may simply be the price of passing any general national legislation.[41]

Finally, the nature of the congressional process is such that *sometimes the very process of passing legislation ensures that it will not work.* This is especially true of proposals that, in order to correct a social problem, would need to concentrate resources on a small portion of the population. As we discussed in the opening vignette of this chapter, members of Congress are reluctant to pass up any opportunity to deliver local benefits,

even if their district or state does not have the problem a program addresses or does not need federal money to address it. Therefore, they often pass bills that simply distribute money, rather than carefully target the problem the program is intended to solve. Consider, for example, the Economic Development Administration, created in the 1960s to subsidize the construction of infrastructure such as roads, utilities, and industrial parks in depressed areas. By the time the program was killed by the Reagan administration, *more than 80 percent of all the counties in the United States* had been classified as "economically depressed" so that they would be eligible for the federal subsidies.[42] Everyone demanded a piece of the action. Homeland security funds are only a more current and potentially far more serious example, as shown by the questionable expenditures noted at the beginning of this chapter.

Bashing the federal bureaucracy is a popular sport. Sometimes it is warranted—government programs may be poorly implemented or incompetently administered. But federal programs often fail because they were born to fail: Their enactment did not focus benefits where they would do the most good and did not concentrate resources sufficiently to have a major impact. Consequently, money is taken from some citizens and passed along to others but the nation has little to show for it. The failure does not result because government ignored the demands of voters. Quite the contrary: It results because members of Congress aggressively worked to promote the interests of their constituents.

Why Americans Like Their Members of Congress So Much More Than Congress Itself

More than people in other democracies, Americans are proud of their political institutions. They revere the Constitution, honor the law, and respect the presidency and the courts. But there is an exception to this generalization, and it is Congress. Congress is the butt of jokes. Congress has been defined as "a creature with 535 bellies, and no brain." Humorist Mark Twain once observed that "it could probably be shown with facts and figures that there is no distinctly native American criminal class except Congress."[43]

Disparaging quips like these reflect popular sentiments. As Figure 12.3 shows, Americans view their popularly elected representatives as having ethical standards well below those of most occupations. Congress as a whole also suffers from a particularly negative public image, even though it is the national government's most electorally sensitive institution.[44] Majorities of Americans doubt the competence and integrity of the legislative branch.[45]

Why, then, do members of Congress win reelection at a high rate (see Chapter 11)? Why do American voters not "throw the rascals out" and substitute better people? The answer is simple: Americans judge their own representatives by standards different

A Congressional Debate
Disrespect for Congress is nothing new, as this 1798 print of the congressional floor shows.

FIGURE 12.3

The Public Rates the
Honesty and Ethics of
Members of Congress
Lower Than Those of
Other Occupations

Source: The Gallup Poll, December 5,
2005.

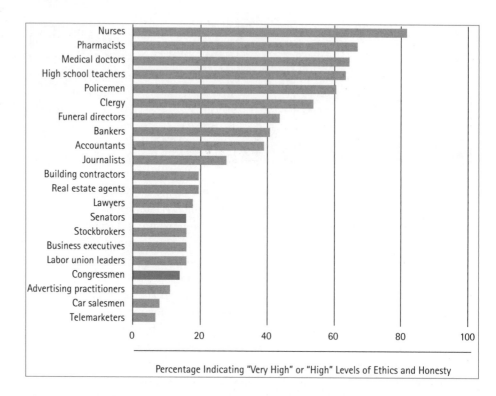

Percentage Indicating "Very High" or "High" Levels of Ethics and Honesty

from those by which they judge the collective Congress.[46] Voters like their own elected representatives. Citizens invariably rate their members of Congress far more favorably than they rate Congress as a whole, an observation that has become known as "Fenno's paradox" (after political scientist Richard Fenno, who popularized the observation).[47]

Polls show that Americans generally take a dim view of how well Congress solves national problems and meets national challenges. Congress, they believe, rarely meets its collective responsibilities. Citizens take an equally dim view of how they think Congress operates—sluggishly, conflictually, inefficiently, and sometimes corruptly. They therefore have little good to say about the institution or its membership. But citizens judge their own representatives and senators positively for doing the very things that make the collective Congress so ineffective. Members fight for what their constituents want, even if it means blocking legislation, grabbing resources needed by others, or demanding unreasonable alterations in a government program.

Voters may resent such behavior when conducted on behalf of others, but they shower electoral rewards on the public officials who do it for them. That is, they would prefer other people's representatives to be **trustees**—legislators who use their own judgment to decide what is best for the country—but demand that their own representatives serve as **delegates**—legislators who cater to the needs and views of their constituents back home regardless of what they personally believe good public policy ought to be. However, because voters everywhere demand roughly the same sort of responsiveness, members of Congress typically work as delegates to the federal government charged with getting constituents the resources they want. An old saying goes "if you want to make an omelet, you've got to break some eggs." Voters want omelets and reward legislators who deliver them to the table, but complain if their members sacrifice any local eggs to make the national omelet.

trustee

Role a representative plays when acting in accordance with his or her own best judgment.

delegate

Role a representative plays when following the wishes of those who have elected him or her.

Chapter Summary

The United States Congress is the world's most powerful legislature. It is also the most professionalized. Its members are full-time, career legislators. Congress has an extensive division of labor—the committee system—supported by an extensive party organization focused on getting bills through the difficult lawmaking process. Nevertheless, citizens hold Congress in much lower esteem than they hold their individual representatives and senators, whom they reelect regularly.

This discrepancy arises because members of Congress depend for their election on specific constituencies. They act to satisfy those constituencies, even if doing so requires behavior that may not serve the larger interest of the nation. The result is that Congress is slow and inefficient, and what emerges from the complex legislative process may not be very effective. The structure of Congress is an uneasy compromise between what it takes to get the job done and what it takes to get reelected. Frustrated voters fail to see that members of Congress have powerful electoral incentives to behave as they do. The problems they see with Congress result not from a lack of electoral responsiveness, but from an excess of it.

Key Terms

appropriations process, p. 347
authorization process, p. 347
bicameral, p. 334
caucus, p. 344
cloture, p. 338
conference committee, p. 347
delegate, p. 350
filibuster, p. 338
logrolling, p. 343

majority leader, p. 336
markup, p. 346
minority leader, p. 337
multiple referrals, p. 346
party caucus, p. 337
party conference, p. 337
president pro tempore, p. 337
rule, p 346
select committee, p. 340

seniority, p. 342
Speaker, p. 335
sponsor, p. 345
standing committee, p. 340
suspension of the rules, p. 346
trustee, p. 350
unanimous-consent agreement, p. 337
whips, p. 337

Suggested Readings

Of General Interest

Arnold, R. Douglas. *The Logic of Congressional Action.* New Haven, CT: Yale University Press, 1990. An excellent discussion of how the incentives that motivate members interact with the characteristics of public-policy problems to shape legislation.

Oleszek, Walter, and Roger Davidson. *Congress and Its Members.* 10th ed. Washington, DC: CQ Press, 2005. A readable text that relates the electoral and institutional arenas.

Ornstein, Norman, Thomas Mann, and Michael Malbin. *Vital Statistics on Congress, 2001–2002.* Washington, DC: American Enterprise Institute, 2002. This periodic compilation of congressional statistics is to Congress-watchers what *The Bill James Baseball Sourcebook* is to baseball fans.

Smith, Steven, Jason Roberts, and Ryan Vander Wielen. *The American Congress.* 3rd ed., Online Version. http://congress.wustl.edu/. A comprehensive, up-to-date, and free (!) online textbook.

Focused Studies

Adler, E. Scott. *Why Congressional Reforms Fail.* Chicago: University of Chicago Press, 2002. Historical study arguing that member desire for reelection consistently hampers efforts to reform the committee system.

Bennett, James T. *Homeland Security Scams.* Piscataway, NJ: Transaction Publishers, 2006. Popularly written highly critical account which claims Congress has turned Homeland Security into the largest pork barrel in American history.

Cox, Gary, and Mathew McCubbins. *Setting the Agenda.* New York: Cambridge University Press, 2005. Important work that shows how the majority party in Congress operates through its control of the agenda.

Hammond, Susan Webb. *Congressional Caucuses in National Policy Making.* Baltimore: Johns Hopkins Press, 2001. Discusses an increasingly important aspect of congressional organization that cuts across parties, committees, and chambers.

Oleszek, Walter. *Congressional Procedures and the Policy Process.* 6th ed. Washington, DC: CQ Press, 2003. An accessible treatment of the rules and procedures governing the congressional process.

Schickler, Eric. *Disjointed Pluralism.* Princeton, NJ: Princeton University Press, 2001. Analyzes the historical development of congressional rules and procedures.

On the Web

www.rollcall.com

Roll Call, the newspaper of Capitol Hill, is a definitive source of news on congressional affairs.

www.democrats.senate.gov

www.democrats.house.gov

www.gop.gov

These Web sites offer very current information on the partisan activities going on in Congress at any given time.

http://thomas.loc.gov

This Web site is the official source of information on Congress and has links to member offices, committee Web sites, historical documents, and (most important) the congressional record and index. The information is not always easily organized, but it is comprehensive.

www.congress.org

This Web site by Capitol Advantage is an alternative, private source of congressional information. It chronicles the daily activities of Congress in committee and on the floor and makes it easy to contact the members who represent your state or district. You can even send a hand-delivered letter.

Election Voices

An Explosion of Earmarks

THE ISSUE

Should members of Congress specify ("earmark") precisely where and on what federal money is to be spent? Or should they pass general legislation and permit experts in the federal and state bureaucracies to decide where the spending will do the most good?

Background

Pork barrel politics is almost as old as Congress itself.[1] The pejorative term refers to members' efforts to procure various benefits for their districts and states. Originally, these benefits were mostly construction projects of various kinds that brought government money and jobs to constituents—dams, roads and bridges, public buildings, military bases. But as the size and scope of government expanded, the kinds of benefits did as well until today all manner of projects, grants, and subsidies are considered part of the pork barrel.

In recent years the explosion of earmarks has aroused the ire of critics. The term has no precise meaning but it generally refers to congressional instructions that direct government activity or money to a specific project or activity in a particular location. Most such instructions are not actually included in the legislation that passes Congress, but are contained in the committee reports or the floor managers' explanatory statements that executive agencies rely on to implement the legislation.[2] Although such provisions do not have the force of law, agencies ignore them at their peril, because they must request authorization from Congress periodically and appropriations annually.

Earmarking has exploded in the past decade or so. For example, in 2005 Congress passed a transportation bill that included more than 6,300 earmarks, including nearly half a billion dollars for the notorious Alaskan "bridges to nowhere."

One bridge would have linked Ketchikan to a remote island with a population of 50 people. Another would have linked Anchorage to Port MacKenzie, a rural area with one resident.[3] Not coincidentally, Alaska representative Don Young is chair of the House Committee on Transportation and Infrastructure, and Alaska senator Ted Stevens is chair of the Senate Appropriations Committee. After a torrent of national ridicule from sources as diverse as Washington think tanks to comedian Jay Leno, the earmarks were withdrawn, but the money for Alaska was left in the bill and Alaskan officials could decide to build the bridges anyway.

Ironically, the practice of earmarking has exploded since Republicans took control of Congress in 1995, defying the popular image of Democrats as the party of big spenders. In 1991, when the Highway Program was reauthorized by a Democratic Congress, the bill contained only 538 earmarks, less than a third as many as when the Republican Congress reauthorized the program seven years later, and one-twelfth as many as when the Republican Congress reauthorized the program in 2005.[4] More broadly, the number of earmarks in annual appropriations bills rose from about 1,400 in 1995 to about 14,000 in 2005, a tenfold increase in 10 years.[5] Apparently fiscally conservative principles are no match for electoral incentives to bring home the bacon.

The more recent orgy of congressional earmarking on the "2006 Emergency Supplemental Appropriations Act for Defense, the Global War on Terror, and Hurricane Recovery" convinced many observers that Congress is out of control. Members used the occasion to direct $700 million for a "railroad to nowhere" in Mississippi. A total of $4 billion was earmarked for farm aid, most of which had nothing to do with Hurricane Katrina (for example, sugar subsidies for Hawaiian growers). More than half a billion dollars went to additional highway projects. Smaller amounts went to such seemingly nonemergency activities as grants to the Bronx College of the Arts and the Montana World Trade Center, studies of shrimp fisheries profitability, and control of riverbank erosion in California.

An Earmark or Two?
President G.W. Bush and former Speaker of the House Dennis Hastert, R–IL, lift the 1,000-page, $286.4 billion highway and mass transit bill that Bush signed into law in August 2005. The legislation includes funding for some 6,000 pet projects for lawmakers in their home districts.

The Issues

On first thought it might appear that there are no issues to discuss. Pork barrel spending in general and earmarking in particular is bad, period. But not everyone sees it that way. Probably the weakest defense of earmarks is the simple fact that relative to the federal budget the sums at stake are small potatoes. The Congressional Research Service estimates that earmarks accounted for about $53 billion in the 2004 budget.[6] To any single person, that sounds like a lot of money, but given a federal budget in 2004 that was a little more than $2 trillion, earmarks were less than 3 percent of the total. In that light, trying to reform or eliminate earmarks hardly seems worth the effort. Critics retort that wasting any amount of taxpayers' hard-earned dollars is wrong. Money could always be spent on more worth-

while programs or simply applied to the deficit to lower the burden on future generations.

A second defense of earmarking is that earmarks pave the way for legislation to pass. Even a public policy change that is highly desirable from a national standpoint generally creates losers as well as winners, and one way to induce losers to go along with the change is to compensate their constituents for losses by giving them side payments from the pork barrel.[7] Without pork barrel spending Congress would be even more gridlocked than it often is! While examples of this legislative strategy clearly exist, skeptics retort that there is no evidence that earmarks in general are used to compensate constituencies for losses from other legislation. Rather, political influence, along with party and member

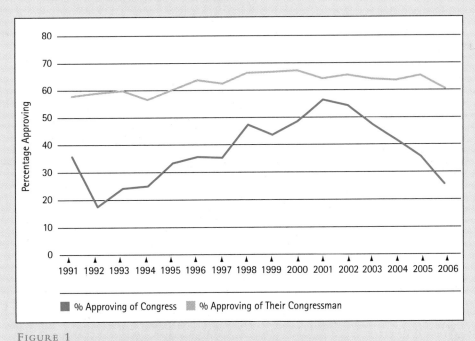

FIGURE 1

In recent years popular approval of Congress has plummeted.

SOURCE: The Gallop Organization. Those approving of their Congresspersons derives from the percent of respondents who believe that their individual Congressperson should be re-elected.

electoral concerns, appears to be a more important factor. At any rate, some critics believe that the process is so out of control today that rather than a means of passing legislation, earmarks have become the whole purpose of legislation.

Finally, members of Congress often defend their earmarking by pointing out that if they refrain from making spending decisions, those decisions will not be made by philosopher kings and queens. Rather, those decisions will be made by federal bureaucrats, state governors and legislators, state and local bureaucrats, and city mayors and councils. All of these officials are subject to political pressures as well, and the incentives they face might well lead to poorer decisions than those made by members of Congress. You can't take the politics out of politics, members say. Critics concede the point in part, but reply that the process of allocating federal money can be insulated from political pressure more than it is. Just because merit criteria can sometimes be difficult to apply doesn't mean that they should be abandoned altogether. Instead, we must work hard to design procedures to minimize political influence in the process of allocating federal funds.

What Do Americans Believe?

In recent years popular approval of Congress has plummeted (see Figure 1). At the time of this writing, only one in five Americans approves of the job Congress is doing. (After discussing some of the earmarks in the 2006 "emergency" supplemental act described above, columnist George Will wonders why even that many Americans approve.)[8] But, while approval of Congress flirts with modern lows, approval of individual members remains much higher. Fenno's paradox still lives: we like our member of Congress much more than we like Congress itself. As discussed in Chapter 12, the reason is that we reward our members for much the same activity that we condemn the Congress. To viewers of Jay Leno, the Alaskan bridges to nowhere are a congressional travesty, but to the constituents of Representative Young and Senator Stevens the bridges and associated jobs and spending are benefits stemming from the hard work of their representatives in Washington, illustrating once again the old adage that one person's waste, fraud, or abuse is another person's income. As long as constituents reward their members for activities such as earmarking, such activities will continue.

What Do You Think?

1. Should the U.S. representative from your congressional district and the senators from your state earmark legislation to benefit your district and state?

2. Some fiscal conservatives have urged the president to "stop us before we spend again" by instructing executive agencies to ignore any earmarks that are not actually written into legislation (more than 90 percent of all earmarks). Is this proposal tantamount to an unconstitutional item veto?

On the Web

Porkbusters

http://truthlaidbear.com/porkbusters/index.php

www.porkbusters.org

Citizens Against Government Waste

http://www.cagw.org

Taxpayers for Common Sense

www.taxpayer.net

[1]Pork Barrell—the state or national treasury, into which politicians and government officials dip for "pork," or funds for local projects. The phrase probably is derived from the pre-Civil War practice of periodically distributing salt pork to the slaves from huge barrels. From *Safire's New Political Dictionary* by William Safire (Random House, New York, 1993).

[2]Sandy Streeter, "Earmarks and Limitations in Appropriations Bills," *CRS Report for Congress,* December 7, 2004, 98–518.

[3]Rebecca Clarren, "A Bridge to Nowhere," http://dir.salon.com/story/news/feature/2005/08/09/bridges/index.html.

[4]Ronald Utt, "A Primer on Lobbyists, Earmarks, and Congressional Reform," The Heritage Foundation, Backgrounder #1924, April 27, 2006, 3.

[5]Ibid., 2.

[6]"Up to their Earmarks," www.washingtonpost.com/wp-dyn/content/graphic/2006/01/27/GR2006012700168.html.

[7]Diana Evans, *Greasing the Wheels* (New York: Cambridge University Press, 2004).

[8]George Will, "Many Strange 'Emergencies,' " *Newsweek*, May 8, 2006.

CHAPTER 13

★ ★ ★ ★ ★ ★ ★ ★ ★ ★

The Presidency: Powers and Practice

CHAPTER OUTLINE

Presidential Constituencies
National Constituency • Partisan Constituencies • Partisan Support in Congress

Separate Institutions Sharing Power
The Power to Inform and Persuade • The Veto Power • The Appointment Power • The Power to Recommend • The President as Chief of State • Inherent Executive Power • The Impeachment Power

Presidential Expectations and Presidential Performance
Presidential Reputations • Presidential Popularity • Great Presidents

The Presidential Agenda and the Dubai Ports Controversy

The last week of February 2006 was going to be the week when President George W. Bush would focus the country's attention on energy policy. In his nationally televised State of the Union address nearly a month earlier, Bush had announced the Advanced Energy Initiative, a program designed to help break a dependency on foreign oil that the president described as an "addiction."[1] On visits to high-tech research centers around the nation, Bush touted the new research funding and business tax credits that were part of the proposed program. "There's a lot of needless politics in Washington, D.C.," the president said. "And of all the issues, becoming less dependent on foreign sources of energy is an issue that we ought to be able to unite and show the American people we can work together to help advance the technologies that will change the world in which we live."[2]

But few elected officials in Washington were inclined to spend that week working together on energy policy. Instead, a sudden furor erupted over the sale of six major U.S. ports to a company owned by the government of the United Arab Emirates, a Middle Eastern ally of the U.S. An inter-agency task force had approved the sale of port operations in New York, New Jersey, Baltimore, New Orleans, Miami, and Philadelphia to the company,

Dubai Ports World, and the Bush administration defended the sale as a typical business transaction that posed no threat to national security.

Politicians from both political parties disagreed, arguing that foreign ownership of port operations would make the nation vulnerable to attack. "Our ports are major potential terrorist targets," said Senator Christopher Dodd (D-CT), "I strongly urge the administration to thoroughly investigate this acquisition." Senator Tom Coburn (R-OK) went further, questioning the United Arab Emirates' commitment to U.S. anti-terror policies: "Handing the keys to U.S. strategic ports to a regime that recognized the Taliban is not a sound next step in the war against terror."[3]

Only several years before, Bush and his aides might have had little trouble in muting congressional opposition, or at least in arriving at a face-saving compromise. During his first term as president, Bush achieved near-record backing from lawmakers, winning on congressional votes about 80 percent of the time.[4] But now, with the war in Iraq dragging on, the disaster of Hurricane Katrina fresh in the public mind, the president's approval rating below 40 percent, and a congressional election less than a year away, Bush could count

A Security Threat?

A cargo ship is unloaded at Maryland's Port of Baltimore, one of the half-dozen major U.S. seaports considered for take-over by a government-owned company in the United Arab Emirates.

on no such support. On the contrary, Senate Republican leader Bill Frist and Republican House Speaker Dennis Hastert hastily broke with Bush and called on him to reconsider the deal. The president threatened to veto any effort to halt the sale, but critics remained just as vocal and, as one columnist put it, "astonishingly bipartisan."[5]

By early March, Dubai Ports World realized the futility of continuing to fight and decided to give up its effort to buy the U.S. facilities. An upset President Bush

warned in a March 11 speech that the dispute could send a negative "message to our friends and allies around the world, particularly in the Middle East."[6]

Bush also spent five paragraphs of that speech talking about energy policy, but few journalists or members of Congress seemed to notice. "It's always the same story," one former administration official told a reporter. "They have a plan—an elaborate plan of the president's message day by day. But there's something in the system that has a hard time coping with the unexpected."[7]

MAKING THE CONNECTION

The contrast between President Bush's early triumphs and his frustration over the Dubai Ports controversy illustrates the pitfalls and promise of the modern presidency. At times presidents seem to have an easy time of getting what they want, but at other times their agendas get derailed unexpectedly. This inconsistency is due both to the constituency pressures they face and to the nature of their powers.

In this chapter, you will learn about the pressures on the office of the presidency and its strengths and weaknesses. The presidency is affected not only by the formal, constitutional powers of the office, but also by the relationship between the president and various constituencies. Even such factors as presidents' personalities and their place in history may figure greatly into their prospects for success.

Presidential Constituencies

Presidents often find it challenging to strike the right balance between their national constituencies, created by the general election, and their partisan constituencies, shaped by presidential primaries. Both national and partisan constituencies play a role in presidential decision making.

National Constituency

Presidents have one unique political asset: They fill a position elected by a national constituency. Only presidents can persuasively claim to speak for the country as a whole, and they can use this national constituency to powerful effect. In late 1995, after budget negotiations between the Democratic president and the Republican Congress deadlocked, much of the government was shut down for nearly a month. National parks were closed and government bills went unpaid. In the midst of the crisis, President Bill Clinton asked Congress to place the national interest above partisan objectives. Republican Speaker of the House Newt Gingrich replied by saying it was the president who should put the country's future ahead of his own. Each appealed to a national constituency, but the president, in part because he was the president, proved to be more persuasive. According to polls, most Americans sided with Clinton and blamed

Appealing to the Right

President George W. Bush speaks at the American Conservative Union Gala in Washington.

• *Why do relatively small groups, such as strong conservatives or strong liberals, wield so much power in primary elections? Unified government?*

Congress for the deadlock. One Republican strategist acknowledged the president's advantages: "We've learned that it's nearly impossible to frame the national debate from the lower chamber of the legislative branch."[8]

In early 2003, President Bush proposed a "jobs and growth" plan that had as its centerpiece a cut on the taxes that investors paid on corporate dividends. "Lower taxes and greater investment will help the economy expand," reasoned Bush in that year's State of the Union address.[9] Although Bush touted the plan as in the national interest, Democrats and liberal interest groups argued that it would be harmful to the economy and would increase the budget deficit. Democratic Senate leader Tom Daschle even pronounced the bill "dead on arrival" in that chamber.[10] Nevertheless, after a series of high-profile public appearances in states with wavering senators, Bush carried the day. Although smaller than what the president initially asked for, the $350 billion tax cut was still one of the largest in history. Once again, the president's ability to mobilize his national constituency gave him key advantages over his opponents in Congress.

Although the president's national constituency is a great political asset, it creates problems as well. Voters hold presidents responsible for many events and conditions over which they have little control. Presidents are expected to conduct foreign policy, manage the economy, administer a complex bureaucracy, promote desired legislation, respond to disasters, and address an endless variety of real and imagined social problems.[11]

Presidents are sometimes given credit for prosperity and success, but they are more often blamed when things go bad. President George H. W. Bush, for example, enjoyed foreign policy triumphs equaled by only a few of his predecessors. Most notably, in his role as **commander in chief,** the constitutional head of the U.S. armed forces, he achieved a spectacular victory in the 1991 Persian Gulf War. Yet when the economy faltered, Bush was drummed from office.

commander in chief

The president in his constitutional role as head of the armed forces.

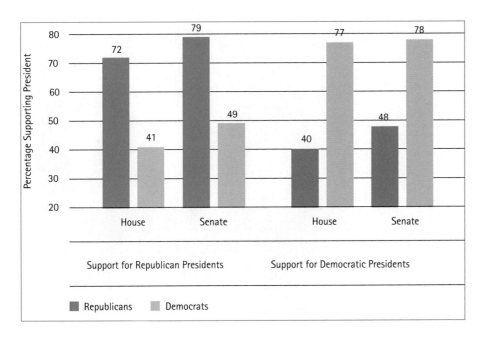

FIGURE 13.1

Partisan Support for the
President in Congress

Each party in Congress supports
its own president more often than
a president of the opposing party.

• *What do you think happens
when presidents face divided
government?*

Source: Data reflect average presidential
support scores from 1954–2005, taken from
Norman Ornstein, Thomas E. Mann, and
Michael Malbin, *Vital Statistics on Congress,
1999–2000* (Washington, D.C.: CQ Press,
2000), Table 8-2, 198–199; "Presidential
Support Background," *CQ Weekly*, January
6, 2001, 52; "Presidential Support
Background," *CQ Weekly*, January 12,
2002, 136; "Presidential Support
Background," *CQ Weekly*, December 14,
2002, 3275; "Presidential Support
Background," *CQ Weekly*, January 3, 2004,
53; "Presidential Support Background,"
CQ Weekly, January 9, 2006, 86.

Partisan Constituencies

In addition to a national constituency, presidents have a party constituency to which they must be responsive. They need to keep the support of those who work in and help finance their campaigns. If they do not satisfy their party constituency, they may encounter difficulties with the party faithful in presidential primaries.

A party constituency usually takes more extreme issue positions than does the national constituency. Presidents therefore have to find some way to balance the demands of their most ardent supporters with the more moderate concerns of the general-election voters who determine the outcome of national elections. At times, this balancing act proves unsuccessful. In 2005, President Bush angered many conservative supporters when he picked a close aide, Harriet Miers, to fill a Supreme Court vacancy. Miers's views on the constitutionality of abortion were unclear, and critics feared that she would not be a powerful conservative voice on the Court (see Chapter 15).

Partisan Support in Congress

Even if presidents can balance their national and party constituencies, they usually cannot take action on their pledges without considering their level of support in Congress. On most issues, presidents gain more support from members of their own party than from the opposition (see Figure 13.1). As a consequence, when presidents have larger majorities in Congress, they are more likely to get their proposed legislation approved.[12]

The events surrounding the first Bush tax-cut bill provide a clear illustration of the importance to presidents of a party majority in Congress. When Bush entered office in 2001, the Senate had a bare majority of Republicans, whereas the GOP had a more comfortable—though still slim—margin in the House. Because of these differences in party margins, Bush's proposed tax cuts fared differently in the two chambers. In the House, the Republican majority not only gave the president most of the tax cuts he

Presidential Success
in Polls and Congress

DEMOCRATIC DILEMMA

Is Divided Government Good or Bad?

Scholars disagree on the issue of divided government. Some see it as an unfortunate and harmful phenomenon, others as a harmless or even beneficial result of popular elections.

James Sundquist argues that divided government often prevents the government from taking necessary action because it makes it harder for the president to enact his policy agenda. "When the president sends a recommendation to the opposition-controlled Congress," says Sundquist, "the legislators are virtually compelled to reject or profoundly alter it; otherwise they are endorsing the president's leadership . . . [and] strengthening him or his party for the next election." Sundquist proposes a novel solution to this problem: four-year House terms and eight-year Senate terms, with elections coinciding with presidential elections. Sundquist claims that if the president and Congress were elected at the same time, divided government would be less likely.

Other scholars believe that the concern about divided government is unwarranted and such radical solutions unnecessary. Morris Fiorina suggests that divided government may be the result of conscious decisions by the voters to send mixed signals. If this is so, "who are we to recommend that they make a clear choice?" Perhaps voters believe that Republicans are too extreme on some issues and Democrats are too extreme on others. (For more on divided government, see Chapter 8.)

President George W. Bush and House Speaker Nancy Pelosi.

Whom do you believe?

• *Do you think divided government produces harmful gridlock? Or do you think it serves as a check against extreme action by either party?*

• *Are good policies blocked?*

• *Are bad policies prevented?*

SOURCES: James L. Sundquist, *Constitutional Reform and Effective Government* (Washington, D.C.: The Brookings Institution, 1986), 75–76, 240; and Morris Fiorina, *Divided Government* (New York: Macmillan, 1992), 128–129.

---

requested quickly, but added further tax breaks. In the Senate, Democrats and moderate Republicans combined to reduce the size of the cut by 25 percent.

Partisanship is not as pervasive in the United States as it is in many European countries. Still, political scientists have debated whether it is good or bad to have **divided government**—control of the presidency by one party and control of one or both houses of Congress by the other. (See the accompanying *Democratic Dilemma*.) In the 2002 election cycle, George W. Bush made a particularly aggressive effort to ensure unified Republican government and gain the support of his congressional partisans by becoming involved in fund-raising and candidate selection for congressional races.[13] His success in securing a Republican Congress set the groundwork for 2003 Republican victories on taxes and Medicare reform.

In the 2006 elections, many Democrats argued that if they won control over Congress, they would act as a necessary check on the president's power. As Representative Rahm Emanuel (D-IL) put it, "we're going to bring a balance to this system. Things are out of whack, whether that's on the budget front or investment front, in the areas of health care and education . . . too much concentration of power in one party has actually, in [the voters'] view, led to a lot of things that are out of balance."[14]

divided government

The control of the presidency by one party and the control of one or both houses of Congress by the other.

Separate Institutions Sharing Power

In addition to frequent partisan divisions of government, presidents also face the fundamental divisions of power between the executive and legislative branches that are written into the Constitution. Presidents can seldom force members of Congress to support them; they usually have to coax, beg, plead, and compromise to gain the necessary votes. Even when the same party controls both the presidency and Congress, presidents do not find it easy to get their proposals approved. For instance, Bill Clinton was unable to persuade a Democratic Congress to enact his health care reform proposals, and 10 years later, George W. Bush was unable to pass a Social Security reform measure through a Republican Congress.[15] More than 80 percent of the time, presidents either fail to secure passage of their major legislative agendas or must make important compromises to win congressional approval.[16] As presidential scholar Charles Jones has observed, "Presidents don't pass laws; they work with, alongside of, or against the House and Senate."[17]

When President Bush watched congressional leaders defy him on the 2006 Dubai ports deal, he was not the first president to be frustrated by Congress. Theodore Roosevelt sighed, "Oh, if I could only be president and Congress too for just ten minutes."[18] Presidents find their position particularly exasperating because they feel they have a duty to take decisive action. Facing a Republican Congress in 1995, President Clinton angrily charged congressional leaders with trying "to destroy the ability of the federal government to address the problems facing America—to move the country forward, to move the country together."[19]

Those who wrote the Constitution ensured that presidents would govern only with the help of Congress (see Table 2.3, p. 40). Most delegates to the Constitutional Convention wanted to strengthen the executive branch beyond what was provided for by the Articles of Confederation. But the founders realized that voters would never ratify a constitution that created a strong executive who might become another King George. The result is a government of "separated institutions sharing powers."[20] We now turn to the many ways in which the Constitution has shaped presidential power and practice. (Our emphasis in this chapter will be on the president's powers with respect to domestic affairs; for a discussion of foreign affairs, see Chapter 20.)

SIMULATION

Presidential Leadership:
Which Hat Do You Wear?

The Power to Inform and Persuade

PRESIDENTIAL POWER: *The President "shall from time to time give to the Congress Information of the State of the Union."*

CONGRESSIONAL CHECK: *None*

The Constitution requires presidents to give Congress information about the state of the union. Presidents have interpreted this requirement as authority to persuade Congress and the public at large to support their policies. Modern presidents rely on hundreds of speeches each year to set forth their vision of the country's future, but the most prestigious and formalized address is the **State of the Union address**, which is given annually, in late January or early February. In this speech, the president usually outlines his legislative and foreign-policy priorities for the coming year.

Early Use of Persuasion Power   The power to persuade is used much more publicly today than in times past, as Figure 13.2 illustrates. Early presidents seldom spoke

VIDEO DEBATE

Presidential Power

State of the Union address

Annual speech delivered by the president in fulfillment of the constitutional obligation of reporting to Congress on the state of the union.

FIGURE 13.2

Growth in Presidential
Speech Making

•   *Why have presidents made
more public speeches in the last 50
years?*

Note: Figures for Harding and
Franklin Roosevelt were unavailable. Estimates for Taft and
Coolidge are based on their first
year in office only. Figures on
George W. Bush are for
2001–2005.

Sources: Data on Washington through
McKinley are taken from Jeffrey Tulis, *The
Rhetorical Presidency* (Princeton, NJ:
Princeton University Press, 1987), 64. For
Theodore Roosevelt, see Robert V.
Friedenberg, *Theodore Roosevelt and the
Rhetoric of Militant Decency* (New York:
Greenwood Press, 1990). For Taft, see
*Presidential Addresses and State Papers of
William Howard Taft*, Vol. 1, 1910 (New
York: Doubleday). For Wilson, see Albert
Shaw, ed., *Messages and Papers of Woodrow
Wilson*, Vols. 1 and 2 (New York: Review
of Reviews Corporation, 1924). For
Coolidge, see Claude M. Feuss, *Calvin
Coolidge: The Man from Vermont* (Hamden,
CT: Archon Books, 1965). For Presidents
Truman through Reagan, see Roderick
Hart, *The Sound of Leadership* (Chicago:
The University of Chicago Press, 1987).
For Hoover, George H. W. Bush, Clinton,
and George W. Bush, information is taken
from *The Public Papers of the President*, vari-
ous years, and the *Weekly Compilation of
Presidential Documents*.

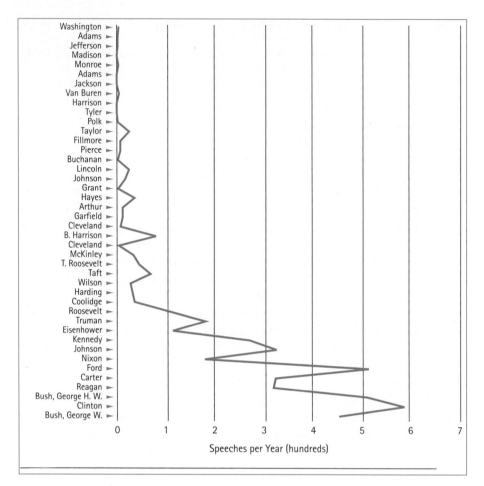

in public, and when they did, their remarks were of a general nature. To fulfill their
obligation to report on the state of the union, Thomas Jefferson and his nineteenth-
century successors sent written messages to Congress. Early presidents found other
ways of persuading Congress. Instead of using public rhetoric, Jefferson, a master
politician, invited members of Congress to the Executive Mansion (later called the
White House) for dinners at which he would persuade them to support his political
agenda.[21] Not until Woodrow Wilson addressed a joint session of both houses of
Congress in 1913 did it become a regular practice for presidents to report in person
on the state of the union.[22]

In fact, the unwritten rule against presidential rhetoric was at one time so strong
that it became a basis for presidential impeachment. President Andrew Johnson, who
succeeded to the presidency upon the assassination of Abraham Lincoln, publicly criticized specific members of Congress. In the list of impeachment charges brought
against Johnson, one seems particularly strange to modern Americans:

> That . . . Andrew Johnson, President of the United States, unmindful of the high duties of his
> office and the dignity and propriety thereof . . . did . . . deliver with a loud voice certain
> intemperate, inflammatory, and scandalous harangues, and did therein utter loud threats and
> bitter menaces . . . against Congress.

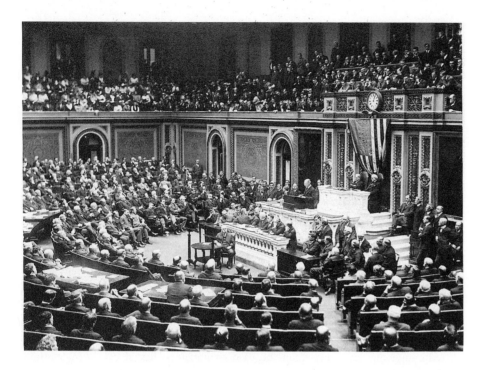

Today we would think that such a president, though perhaps not politically prudent, was merely exercising the right of free speech.[23]

Modern Persuasion Power   More than any other president, Theodore ("Teddy") Roosevelt changed the definition of what was permissible in presidential rhetoric. Roosevelt made frequent use of what he called the "**bully pulpit**" available to presidents. (*Bully* was nineteenth-century slang for "excellent.") Roosevelt suggested that, like a preacher, the president could use his position to move his "congregation"—the public—to action. He mobilized support through bold gestures, forceful speeches, presidential trips, and dramatic turns of phrase. As one historian has noted, "the number of laws [Roosevelt] inspired was certainly not in proportion to the amount of noise he emitted."[24] Yet Roosevelt's popular appeal was such that a cartoon depicting the president sparing the life of a bear cub while hunting resulted in the emergence of the term "Teddy Bear."

Presidents since Teddy Roosevelt have increasingly used the bully pulpit to persuade Congress and the public, as Figure 13.2 shows.[25] Franklin Delano Roosevelt's "fireside chats" over the radio enabled him to sidestep the print media, which he accused of being controlled by Republican publishers. John Kennedy had a compelling rhetorical style that both inspired and challenged his audience.[26]

President Reagan, the first president with experience as a professional actor, used television more effectively than any of his predecessors. He understood that there is but "a thin line between politics and theatricals."[27] As Reagan once said, "I've wondered how people in positions of this kind . . . manage without having had any acting experience."[28] Learning from Reagan's example, George W. Bush had his picture taken, on one occasion, while landing on an aircraft carrier off the coast of California, and, on another, carving a Thanksgiving turkey for U.S. troops

bully pulpit
The nature of presidential status as an ideal vehicle for persuading the public to support the president's policies.

A Popular President

Although President Theodore Roosevelt was an avid hunter, it was his decision to spare the life of a bear cub in 1902 that led to the emergence of the term "Teddy Bear."

• *How can symbolic actions such as this one increase the power of the presidential "bully pulpit"?*

in Iraq, shortly after arriving on a secret transatlantic flight. The Thanksgiving gesture proved especially popular, boosting the president's approval rating by five percentage points.

The Veto Power

PRESIDENTIAL VETO POWER: *Before any law "shall take effect," it must be "approved by" the president.*

CONGRESSIONAL CHECK: *Unless "repassed by two-thirds of the Senate and House of Representatives."*

veto power
Presidential rejection of congressional legislation. May be overridden by a two-thirds vote in each congressional chamber. Most state governors also have veto power over their legislatures.

The president's **veto power** is more concrete than is the power to inform: It gives presidents the capacity to prevent bills passed by Congress from becoming law. Before the Civil War, presidents seldom used the veto. President Washington cast only two vetoes. The average number cast by presidents between Madison and Lincoln was only a little more than four. As Figure 13.3 shows, presidents from Franklin Roosevelt on have been much more willing to use the veto power.

This presidential power to say "No" can be checked. But Congress usually fails to muster the necessary two-thirds vote in each chamber to pass an **override**, which makes the bill a law despite the president's opposition. Since the Kennedy administration, Congress has overridden approximately only 1 out of every 10 vetoes.[29] Only 2 of President Clinton's 37 vetoes were overridden.[30]

override
Congressional passage of a bill by a two-thirds vote over the president's veto.

Although the veto can seldom be used to initiate policy, it can be successfully employed as a weapon in negotiations with Congress. Before 2006, when he issued his first veto, George W. Bush went longer without issuing a veto than any president since Thomas Jefferson.[31] Still, he used the threat of the veto in negotiations with Congress over such issues as homeland security legislation, reconstruction funds for Iraq, and the Dubai ports example with which we began this chapter.[32] In the first two instances, the veto threat effectively forced Congress to reconsider its plans; in the latter case, the threat failed to deter the president's opponents.

pocket veto
Presidential veto after congressional adjournment, executed merely by not signing a bill into law.

If Congress enacts a law 10 days before it adjourns, a president may exercise a **pocket veto** by simply not signing the bill into law. Congress has no opportunity to override a pocket veto. Because these vetoes could not be overridden, President Reagan made frequent use of them to convey the impression that he was a strong president. The pocket veto strategy works only at the very end of a congressional session, however; if Congress remains in session for more than 10 days after passing a bill, the president must explicitly cast a veto to prevent the bill from becoming law. As the distinction between campaigning and governing has disappeared, Congress has remained in session virtually throughout the entire year, giving more recent presidents fewer opportunities to cast pocket vetoes.

Although Congress is sometimes able to override vetoes, it more often counters the president's veto power indirectly, by incorporating policies that presidents oppose into large bills that contain items presidents feel they must approve. When faced with such a package, the president finds it difficult to cast a veto. For example, in 2005 George W. Bush opposed a congressional ban on "cruel and inhumane treatment of prisoners," arguing that the law would unduly tie the hands of the military. But he signed the measure anyway because it was attached to an important military spending bill.[33]

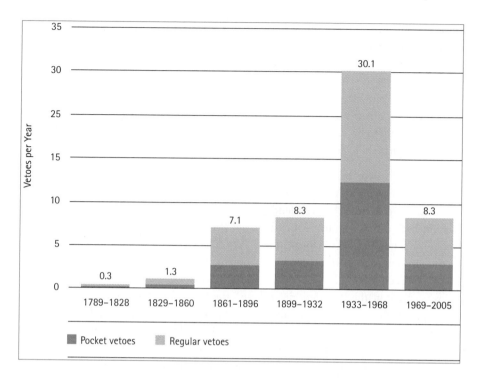

FIGURE 13.3

Trends in Presidential Use of the Veto Power

Currently presidents use the veto less than at mid-century, but more than in the 1800s.

• *Why did presidents become more assertive?*

Note: Vetoes for the two administrations of Grover Cleveland (1885–1889, 1893–1897) have been excluded from these averages because of the unusual circumstances surrounding President Cleveland's use of the veto. See Theda Skocpol, *Protecting Soldiers and Mothers* (Cambridge, MA: Harvard University Press, 1992).

Sources: Gary L. Galemore, "Presidential Vetoes, 1789–Present: A Summary Overview," Congressional Research Service Report for Congress, 98-148 GOV, November 4, 2000; and "Résumé of Congressional Activity: First Session of the One Hundred Seventh Congress," *Congressional Record Daily Digest,* January 29, 2002: D23.

Because Congress can artfully package laws in this way, many people favor giving the president the **line item veto**—the authority to negate particular provisions of a law while letting the remainder stand. The presidential line item veto has been a popular idea among congressional Republicans since the Reagan administration. In 1995, Congress passed legislation enacting a form of line item veto for the president, a measure that had President Clinton's wholehearted approval. But in 1998 the Supreme Court struck down the law as unconstitutional. In 2006, President Bush announced his support for a somewhat different version of the line item veto that proponents hoped would pass constitutional muster.[34]

line item veto

Presidential authority to negate particular provisions of a law, granted by Congress in 1996 but struck down by the Supreme Court in 1998.

The Appointment Power

PRESIDENTIAL POWER: *The president "shall appoint Ambassadors, other public Ministers and Consuls . . . and all other Officers of the United States."*

CONGRESSIONAL CHECK: *Appointments are subject to the "Advice and Consent of the Senate," which is taken to mean that a majority must approve the nomination.*

The appointment power enables presidents to appoint thousands of public officials to positions of high responsibility within their **administration**, which consists of those responsible for directing the executive branch of government.

The Cabinet   The president's **cabinet** consists of the key members of the administration. Most are heads of government departments and carry the title **secretary**. Originally, the president's cabinet had but four departments, and the secretaries met regularly with the president, giving him confidential political guidance on a broad

administration

The president and his political appointees responsible for directing the executive branch of government.

cabinet

Top administration officials; mostly heads of departments in the executive branch.

secretary

Head of a department within the executive branch.

You Are Appointing
a Supreme Court Justice

range of policies. It was in cabinet meetings, for example, that Abraham Lincoln developed his strategy for fighting the Civil War.

Over the years, government began to perform a much broader range of functions. As the number of departments grew from 4 to 14 (see Table 14.1, page 404), the cabinet lost its capacity to provide confidential advice to presidents. In President Nixon's words, "Cabinet government is a myth and won't work . . . . No [president] in his right mind submits anything to his cabinet."[35] Today the cabinet meets only occasionally, primarily for ceremonial purposes or to help the president make some kind of political statement.

The White House Staff   Many of the modern president's closest advisers are not cabinet secretaries but White House aides who deal in matters with utmost confidentiality. At one time the president's personal staff was small and informal. Abraham Lincoln had just two young assistants. Even President Franklin Roosevelt originally had only a handful of personal aides. To address organizational problems caused by the growing size of the federal government, Roosevelt in 1936 asked a committee of specialists in public administration headed by Louis Brownlow to study the issue. Saying "the President needs help," the Brownlow Committee recommended sweeping changes, including additional appointments to the president's personal staff. Brownlow said presidential staff members "should be possessed of high competence, great physical vigor, and a passion for anonymity." Although Congress rejected most of the other Brownlow recommendations, it agreed to enlarge the White House staff.[36]

Brownlow envisioned only a "small number of executive assistants," but the president's staff has steadily increased in size and complexity.[37] The number of aides has grown from 48 in 1944 to nearly 400 today.[38] Its organization is now complex enough to confuse even well-informed citizens. One basic distinction to remember is the difference between the **White House Office**, the main subject under discussion here, and the much larger **Executive Office of the President (EOP)**. Although the names make it seem as though they are much the same thing, the White House Office is just one component of the EOP, which also includes other important coordinating bodies as well as operating agencies (see Table 13.1).

In Franklin Roosevelt's day, no single person headed the White House staff. Even as late as the Carter administration, White House aides worked together as "spokes in a wheel," each having direct access to the president. But today presidents usually place one person in charge.[39] This person, the **chief of staff**, meets with the president several times a day and communicates decisions to other staff, cabinet officers, and members of Congress.

The best chiefs are usually Washington insiders. Though little acclaimed, Ronald Reagan's 1987–1988 chief, Howard Baker, was one of the most powerful and effective. A former Senate majority leader and presidential aspirant, Baker helped boost Reagan's popularity, despite the fact that the aging president himself had lost much of his former vitality. George W. Bush's first chief of staff, Andrew Card, was deputy chief of staff and later Transportation Secretary under George H. W. Bush, and had nearly two decades of experience in Washington politics when he began work at the White House in 2001. Card's successor, Josh Bolton, also had years of White House experience.

Newcomers to Washington are usually less successful. Typically, they become lightning rods—people to be blamed when things go wrong. John Sununu, former governor of New Hampshire, was forced to leave the job of chief of staff when he was

White House Office

Political appointees who work directly for the president, many of whom occupy offices in the White House.

Executive Office of the President (EOP)

Agency that houses both top coordinating offices and other operating agencies.

chief of staff

Head of White House staff. Has continuous, direct contact with the president.

TABLE 13.1

EXECUTIVE OFFICE OF THE PRESIDENT, BUDGET AND STAFF LEVELS

• *Why do you think the office of management and budget is the largest component of the EOP? (See Chapter 14.)*

	Budget (Millions)	Staff [a]
White House	207	836
Office of Management and Budget	68	484
Office of National Drug Control Policy	29	111
Office of the U.S. Trade Representative	41	212
Office of Science and Technology Policy	5	29
Office of the Vice President	5	23
Council on Environmental Quality	3	21

Note: "The White House" includes National Security Council staff, Office of Administration, Office of Policy Development, and Council of Economic Advisers, in addition to White House Office and Executive Residence.

[a] As of 2005.

SOURCE: Executive Office of the President, *Budget of the United States Government, Fiscal Year 2007,* Appendix, 1039–1048.

blamed for urging President George H. W. Bush to sign an unpopular tax increase.[40] Thomas McLarty from Arkansas resigned after early Clinton administration missteps.[41]

Although Brownlow expected White House aides to have "no power to make decisions," modern presidents have regularly used their staffs to shape their public policy proposals.[42] Within the White House staff, more than anywhere else, presidents can count on the loyalty of those around them simply because, unlike the careers of department secretaries, those of staff members are closely intertwined with that of the president.

The White House staff is more potent than ever, in part because presidents have more need than ever for political help. Presidents today need pollsters who can keep them in touch with changes in public opinion.[43] They also need assistants who can help them communicate with the media, interest groups, and members of Congress. Once a major piece of legislation arrives for consideration on the chamber floor, White House aides are in regular contact with many legislators.[44] So intense is the work inside the White House that most staff jobs demand 7-day, 100-hour workweeks. As a result, many positions go to young energetic people, and even they get tired after years on the job. By 2006, one long-time White House staffer admitted, "We're all burned out."[45]

Quite apart from the president's genuine need for lots of political help, appointment to the White House staff is an excellent way to reward loyal campaign workers. After the presidency has been won, those who worked on the campaign often expect something in return. For example, when George W. Bush became president, he appointed his chief campaign strategist Karl Rove and his campaign spokeswoman Karen Hughes to key White House posts. The White House Office is also a convenient place for the president to put campaign workers, because the president has exclusive control over appointments to his personal staff. Not even the chief of staff must be confirmed by the Senate.

Scandals in the White House Office   The highly personal and partisan nature of the White House staff can be a weakness as well as a strength. A White House full of personal friends and fellow partisans has at times so shielded the president from external criticism that the chief executive has lost touch with political reality. And sometimes staff members have used the power of the presidential office for improper—even illegal—purposes, paving the way for scandals of presidential proportions.

Scandals are hardly new to American politics. When lawmakers discovered that Abraham Lincoln's wife and her assistants outspent housekeeping funds, the president successfully pleaded with Congress to appropriate more money secretly rather than carrying out an investigation.[46] But the intensity and significance of White House scandals have escalated in recent decades.[47] In addition to the Lewinsky scandal discussed later in this chapter, two major and many more minor scandals have captured the attention of the nation and carried the potential for presidential impeachment.

The most serious was the Watergate scandal during the Nixon administration. In 1972, at the instigation of members of the White House staff, five men broke into Democratic Party headquarters at the Watergate condominium complex in Washington, D.C., apparently to obtain information on Democratic Party campaign strategies. Nixon's chief of staff, Bob Haldeman, knew that "hush money" was paid to keep the burglars from revealing White House involvement. When tapes of Nixon's own conversations indicated that the president himself had been involved in the "cover-up," the House initiated impeachment proceedings, and the president was forced to resign.

In the Iran–Contra scandal, staffers in the Reagan White House illegally sold arms to the Iranian government and gave the profits, also illegally, to a group of guerrillas known as Contras who were fighting to overthrow a left-wing government in Nicaragua. White House aides were prosecuted and some Democrats talked of impeachment, but no direct evidence implicating the president was found.

Certain factors make the White House staff particularly prone to scandal. News organizations and opposition leaders have a vested interest in uncovering a White House scandal. Any misdoing by the White House Office immediately embarrasses the president and could lead to presidential defeat, resignation, or impeachment. To guard against this propensity, George W. Bush surrounded himself with older and more experienced advisers than Clinton had relied on. The result was a more subdued, better-controlled White House staff. Said one former Clinton staffer, "If there's a mistake, staffers take the blame and insulate Bush from it. I'm not sure I could always say that about the Clinton White House."[48]

The Power to Recommend

PRESIDENTIAL POWER: *The president may recommend to Congress for "their consideration such Measures as he shall judge necessary and expedient."*

CONGRESSIONAL CHECK: *Only Congress may enact measures into law.*

The power to recommend gives the president the power of initiation—the power to set the political agenda.[19] Presidents can shut down old policy options, create new possibilities, and change the political dialogue. Bill Clinton placed major health care reform and welfare reform on the policy agenda; George W. Bush proposed tax cuts, education initiatives, and Medicare reform.

However, this power does not go unchecked. Congress can—and often does—ignore or greatly modify a presidential recommendation. Congress rejected Clinton's health care proposals and greatly modified his proposals on welfare reform. Nor is the power to initiate limited to the president. In 1994, congressional Republicans campaigned on a "Contract with America" that set the policy agenda for the next two years.

Early Use of the Power to Recommend   Presidential use of the power to recommend was exercised with great restraint in the decades preceding the Civil War.[50] Because the president was the symbol of the nation as a whole, and because the nation was divided into free and slave states, presidents dared not talk about slavery, the most important political question of the period. This principle of silence was extended to other issues as well; in general, presidents were expected to remain publicly mute on an issue once deliberations about it had begun on Capitol Hill.[51]

Modern Use of the Power to Recommend   Use of the presidential power to recommend expanded rapidly after the end of the Civil War. The country was growing swiftly, and many social and economic problems were becoming national in scope. The nation's strongest presidents have had their greatest impact not so much by making decisions as by opening up new possibilities. For example, Theodore Roosevelt made conservation a major public concern. Franklin Roosevelt called for a New Deal that would protect Americans from economic downturns and persuaded Congress to pass dozens of important bills within 100 days of his inauguration.

Timing Presidential Initiatives   Presidents make most new proposals at the very beginning of their first term. This is the time when presidential popularity is at a peak, and both Congress and the country are eager to hear what solutions the new president is bringing to the country's problems. Later in a presidency, unexpected events, the legacy of past policies, and rebellions within a president's own constituencies may make it difficult for presidents to get their message across, as the Dubai ports episode shows. As one of Lyndon Johnson's top aides noted, "You've got to give it all you can that first year . . . . You've got just one year when they treat you right . . . . You can't put anything through when half of the Congress is thinking about how to beat you."[52]

Because the beginning of a presidential term is so important, the **transition** period between the previous presidency and the new one is critical. The transition period consists of the approximately 75 days between Election Day and January 20, Inauguration Day. Incoming presidents do not yet have the burdens of office, but they have the time and resources to set the stage for a vigorous start. If the transition is well organized, this is the best of all times for building public support.

Despite the contested outcome of the 2000 election, George W. Bush enjoyed a surprisingly successful transition. Bush was able to nominate all of the members of his cabinet by Inauguration Day and won plaudits for appointing a diverse and well-qualified cabinet. However, the new president was not spared controversy. Former Missouri senator John Ashcroft barely won Senate confirmation as attorney general after many Democratic senators criticized his conservative record.[53]

The transition period is typically followed by the presidential **honeymoon**—the first several months of a presidency, when reporters are kinder than usual, Congress more inclined to be cooperative, and the public receptive to new approaches.[54] Franklin Roosevelt's successful first 100 days set the standard by which all presidential honeymoons have been judged.

Some analysts have wondered whether presidential honeymoons have gone the way of rotary-dial telephones and wooden tennis rackets. As public expectations have

transition
The period after a presidential candidate has won the November election, but before the candidate assumes office as president on January 20.

honeymoon
The first several months of a presidency, when reporters are more forgiving than usual, Congress more inclined to be cooperative, and the public receptive to new approaches.

Two Very Different Transitions

Presidents Bill Clinton and George W. Bush experienced very different transition and honeymoon periods. Clinton became bogged down with issues such as gays in the military (left), and Republicans lost control of the Senate less than four months after Bush took office. Bush had little time to prepare his administration because of the Florida election dispute.

- *What advice would you give a president who wanted to have a successful honeymoon period?*

risen and presidents have become ever more exposed to media scrutiny, chief executives can no longer count on a period of goodwill before facing determined opposition.[55] Certainly, the example of Bill Clinton's honeymoon seems to support this point of view—it hardly lasted the time it took him to traverse the Inauguration Day parade route from the Capitol to the White House. "By Memorial Day," one scholar has noted, "Clinton gave an address at the Vietnam War memorial that was met by a highly vocal and hostile crowd."[56]

President George W. Bush had a very successful honeymoon period, however, especially considering the difficult circumstances under which he became president. He avoided controversies, passed a major tax cut, and used his subdued approach to governing to his advantage. "Bush's low-key style and staying out of the vortex on a lot of these swirling issues seems to work very effectively for him," admitted one Democratic consultant.[57] The contrast between Clinton's difficult honeymoon and Bush's relatively smooth one calls into question the argument that modern honeymoon periods are doomed to failure. Planning, unity of purpose, and learning from previous mistakes may increase the chances of presidential success. As one member of Congress said, "Bush's team is extremely competent, and the fact is that makes a difference."[58]

The President as Chief of State

PRESIDENTIAL POWER: *The President "shall receive Ambassadors and other public Ministers . . . and shall Commission all the Officers of the United States."*

CONGRESSIONAL CHECK: *None.*

INTERNATIONAL COMPARISON

The Chief of State in Other Countries

In many countries the political leader and the chief of state are institutionally separated. In Great Britain, for example, the dignified chief of state is the queen. She symbolizes the unity of the nation, represents her country on formal international occasions, and presides over national holidays. The efficient aspect of British government is headed by the country's prime minister. Though powerful, prime ministers lack royal dignity. Their residence is a modest home tucked away on a small London side street.

The division of political responsibilities in Japan is much the same. The emperor of Japan is the dignified chief of state; the elected prime minister is—in ceremonial terms—nothing more than the emperor's efficient minister. Of course, the dignified queen and emperor have very little real power, but their presence as a symbol of the unity of the nation reminds people that the ministers can be ejected by the voters at any time.

In the United States, presidents are expected to combine both the efficient and the dignified aspects of government. In addition to their political and policy tasks, presidents are expected to be the symbol of national unity. When queens and emperors assemble, the United States is represented by its president. On days of national celebration, such as Independence Day and Thanksgiving, it is the president who is called upon to express national hopes and dreams. Presidents live in the White House, which, though modest by the standards of European and Japanese castles, has become an increasingly grand focal point of Washington society.

- *Do you think the dignified aspect of national leadership is necessary? What needs does it fill?*

- *What are the advantages and disadvantages of combining the efficient and dignified aspects of leadership in one person?*

In bestowing one of the very few unchecked powers granted to the president, this constitutional clause seems to say little more than that presidents may welcome visitors and administer oaths of office. Yet the words endow presidents with an invaluable political resource, the capacity to act with all the dignity countries accord their heads of state. In many countries, the political leader and the head of state are institutionally separated. (See the accompanying *International Comparison*.) In the United States, the president plays both roles.

According to Walter Bagehot, a nineteenth-century analyst of British politics, governments have both efficient and dignified aspects.[59] The **efficient aspect** of government involves the making of policy, administration of the laws, and the settling of political disputes. This is the nuts and bolts of day-to-day policy making, the kind of activity enjoyed by the Washington insider, often derisively called a "policy wonk." It is also hard work that frequently generates conflict. But government also has a **dignified aspect** that Bagehot thought equally important to its long-term effectiveness. Governments must express the unity of the people, their high moral purposes, their hopes for the future, and their capacity to defend themselves against foreign aggressors. Ceremonial occasions provide opportunities for expression of the dignified aspect of government that helps sustain public trust and loyalty.

Early American presidents were expected to play only a limited role in the efficient aspect of government so that they could enhance the dignity of the national government and serve as a unifying symbol for a far-flung country. By remaining aloof from day-to-day legislative politics, presidents tried to retain the respect and admiration of citizens throughout the nation. As presidents have become increasingly engaged in the efficient aspect of government, they have sometimes found it more difficult to maintain their dignity.

Comparing Chief Executives

efficient aspect
According to Walter Bagehot, the aspect of government that involves making policy, administering the laws, and settling disputes.

dignified aspect
According to Walter Bagehot, the aspect of government, including royalty and ceremony, that generates citizen respect and loyalty.

An Informal President

President Jimmy Carter was uncomfortable with the formal trappings of the dignified aspect of the presidency, adopting a casual style even when meeting with chiefs of state. He donned his trademark sweater for negotiations with Egyptian president Anwar Sadat.

• *Does informality detract from the president's power?*

first lady

Traditional title of the president's wife.

Presidents Richard Nixon and Ronald Reagan chose to accentuate the dignified aspect of the presidency, with markedly different results. Nixon enjoyed the pomp and circumstance of office, but as the Watergate scandal developed, many Americans began to feel that the president's vaguely royal pretensions were endangering democratic practices. Seven years after Nixon left office, Reagan worked assiduously to restore grandeur to the presidency. White House social events once again became formal affairs. The unveiling of a restored Statue of Liberty was carefully designed to celebrate the country's past and future. At the same time, Reagan withdrew from day-to-day legislative politics. By emphasizing the dignity of the office, Reagan acquired the title "the Teflon president," because bad news never seemed to stick to him.

Presidents Gerald Ford, Jimmy Carter, and Bill Clinton de-emphasized the splendor of the office. Ford adopted a folksy, informal manner that provided a noted contrast with his predecessor, Nixon. Carter wore a sweater, carried his own suitcases, and remained on a first-name basis with ordinary voters. At the same time, Carter became deeply involved in the efficient aspects of government, working late into the night on policy issues and foreign policy crises. Clinton likewise became known as a "policy wonk" who was engaged with specifics, sometimes at the expense of broader themes. After advisers warned him that this style left the public without a broad sense of what the president was fighting for, Clinton began to stress larger themes in his speeches.[60]

George W. Bush faced an agonizing conflict between the efficient and dignified aspects of the presidency on September 11, 2001. After the attacks on the World Trade Center and the Pentagon, security officials whisked Bush onto Air Force One from a Florida elementary school where he had been speaking, keeping his location secret for hours. Secret Service and military aides insisted that the president be kept safe to ensure a clear chain of command. But the nation clearly needed a dignified president to reassure the public and provide a sense of unified national response to the terrorism. Accordingly, Bush returned to the White House at 7 p.m. and delivered a televised address 90 minutes later. The symbolism of the White House address was as important as its substance. "It cannot look as if the president has been run off," said former White House official William Bennett, "or it will look like we can't defend our most important institutions."[61]

The First Lady　The historical role of the president's wife, traditionally called the **first lady**, was to reinforce the dignified aspect of the presidency. In keeping with the traditional role women have played in American society, first ladies typically hosted social events, visited the sick, promoted children's issues, and loyally stood by their husbands in times of trouble. Yet some were able to use this dignified role to make contributions that will long be remembered. Jacqueline Kennedy invigorated Washington art and culture, and restored the White House. Lady Bird Johnson committed herself to the beautification of Washington. Nancy Reagan's "Just Say No" educational program may have done more to reduce drug use than billions of dollars spent in antidrug enforcement efforts.[62]

Not all first ladies have been content to confine themselves to the dignified aspect of the presidency, however. Eleanor Roosevelt promoted civil rights and other social causes supported only off-handedly by her husband.[63] But Hillary Rodham Clinton gave the role of the first lady a dramatically new definition by participating in policy formation to a greater degree than any previous first lady. After her election to the U.S. Senate, many observers viewed her as one of the strongest candidates for the Democratic presidential nomination in 2008.

When Laura Bush became first lady in 2001, she restored to the role its traditional emphasis on reinforcing the dignified aspect of the presidency. In contrast to the overt involvement of Hillary Clinton in policy making, Laura Bush took no public stand on controversial issues. Instead, she emphasized her former career as a public school librarian by expressing support for teachers, and calling for the recruitment of additional teachers from those in business and the military who were seeking new careers.[64]

The Vice President   Traditionally, the vice president's impact on policy has been so limited that the dignity of the office suffered as well. The nation's first vice president, John Adams, wrote to his wife, "My country has in its wisdom contrived for me the most insignificant office that ever the invention of man contrived . . . . I can do neither good nor evil." Harry Truman, when vice president, allowed that the job was "about as useful as a cow's fifth teat."[65]

Jokes about the vice presidency have a basis in reality. The only formal responsibility of the office is to preside over the United States Senate and cast a vote in case of a tie. Otherwise, the vice president's duties and influence depend entirely on the will of the president. As Vice President Hubert Humphrey put it, "He who giveth can taketh away and often does."[66]

Presidents have traditionally been reluctant to delegate responsibility to vice presidents, because they constitute a potential political problem. Presidents cannot fire their vice presidents, as they can other aides. If a vice president decides to criticize the president or pursue an independent policy line, the president can do little about it. When Vice President Nelson Rockefeller pushed more liberal policies than those favored by Gerald Ford, he proved an embarrassment to the president and was not chosen to be Ford's running mate in 1976. Some analysts claim the Rockefeller controversy cost Ford his reelection.

The vice presidential selection process accentuates the potential for conflict, because vice presidents often come from a wing of the party different from that of the president.[67] An aide to John Kennedy admitted that Lyndon Johnson was picked for vice president because "he was the leader of that segment of the party where Kennedy had very little strength—the South."[68] In 2004, John Kerry of Massachusetts selected a southern senator, John Edwards of North Carolina as his running mate, hoping to secure southern votes and perhaps to add more warmth and likeability to the ticket.[69]

Even if presidents have powerful incentives to limit the vice presidential role, one can no longer dismiss vice presidents as political lightweights. For one thing, no person is more likely to become president of the United States than the vice president, who can succeed to the office through death, via resignation, or by winning the next election. Twelve of the 43 presidents of the United States held the office of vice president, and no fewer than four of the last eight presidents were vice presidents.

Perhaps because of the greater awareness that the vice president may one day gain the highest office, the role of the vice president has steadily become more powerful. George W. Bush's vice president, Richard Cheney, has been among the most powerful vice presidents in history. Cheney's Washington experience as a leading conservative in

An Aide Informs Bush of the 9/11 Attacks

President Bush insisted on returning to the White House on September 11, 2001, to fulfill his role as national leader. But security officials worried about threats to the president's person and kept his location secret for much of the day.

- *In such a crisis, how should we weigh the president's safety against the need for visible national leadership?*

the House of Representatives, as chief of staff under Gerald Ford, and as defense secretary for Bush's father made him a credible voice as Bush's top adviser. His lack of political ambition (he professed no desire for the presidency) ensured that he would not become the president's rival. Still, Cheney's advocacy of the Iraq war and his outspoken conservatism on other subjects often made him the target of administration critics. Furthermore, his chief of staff was forced to resign in 2005 after being indicted in connection with the illegal leak of the name of a CIA officer. Perhaps most embarrassing, Cheney's accidental shooting of a fellow hunter on a 2006 quail hunting trip sparked controversy when Cheney's aides did not notify the media for nearly 24 hours. As one reporter put it, "I'm not sure there is a standard protocol when the vice president shoots someone, but it's fair to say reporters prefer that news be disclosed in a timely fashion."[70]

Inherent Executive Power

PRESIDENTIAL INHERENT EXECUTIVE POWER: *"The executive power shall be vested in a President."*

inherent executive power
Presidential authority inherent in the executive branch of government, though not specifically mentioned in the Constitution.

Some scholars claim that this statement adds nothing to presidential power beyond the specific powers granted to the president. But many presidents have found in this clause the basis for a claim to additional rights and privileges. As we will see in Chapter 20, presidential claims to inherent executive power have been invoked most frequently in making foreign policy. But presidents have asserted **inherent executive power** on other occasions as well. Teddy Roosevelt placed 46 million acres of public land into the National Forest system just before signing a bill denying presidents the power to place any more land in the National Forest system.[71] After leaving office, Roosevelt admitted, "My belief was that it was not only the [president's] right but his duty to do anything that the needs of the Nation demanded unless such action was forbidden by the Constitution or by its laws."[72]

executive order
A presidential directive that has the force of law, though it is not enacted by Congress.

Executive Orders   One way in which presidents use their inherent executive powers is by issuing **executive orders**—directives that carry the weight of law even though they were not enacted by Congress. The Supreme Court ruled in 1936 that executive orders are constitutional, and since then they have increased in frequency and importance.[73] Executive orders were used by Harry Truman to desegregate the armed forces, by Lyndon Johnson to institute the first affirmative action program, by Ronald Reagan to forbid homosexuality in the military, and by George W. Bush to authorize military trials for suspected Al Qaeda terrorists. Executive orders may not run counter to congressional legislation, and they may be overturned by Congress. When President Clinton proposed to issue an executive order reversing the ban on gays in the military, the threat of congressional action reversing such an order forced the president to reach an awkward "don't ask, don't tell" compromise that distracted Clinton during his presidential honeymoon period. The use of executive orders among modern presidents has increased sharply, from about five major orders a year in the 1950s, to more than a dozen in recent years.[74]

With the Stroke of a Pen: The Executive Order over Time

executive privilege
The right of members of the executive branch to have private communications among themselves that need not be shared with Congress.

Executive Privilege   The most controversial invocation of inherent executive powers has been the doctrine of **executive privilege**—the right of the president to deny Congress information it requests on the grounds that the activities of the executive branch must be kept confidential. George Washington was the first to invoke executive privilege when he refused to provide Congress information about an ill-fated military expedition on the grounds that its "disclosure . . . would injure the public."[75] Ever since, presidents have claimed authority to withhold from Congress information on executive decision making. The Watergate scandal brought the question before the Supreme Court, which sanctioned the doctrine of executive privilege, saying that private communication among aides to the president was "fundamental to the operation of government and inextricably rooted in the separation of powers under the Constitution."[76]

The Supreme Court went on to say that although Congress could not simply demand access to any and all conversations taking place among the president's advisers, executive privilege could not be invoked to cover up criminal conduct. Communication that might be privileged under other circumstances loses that status when wrongdoing occurs. Nor can it be left to the executive branch to decide whether the communication is part of a cover-up. The disputed documents must be submitted to a court for its examination behind closed doors. When the Supreme Court examined the Watergate documents, they found sufficient evidence of criminal conduct such that President Nixon was forced to release the documents.

The Supreme Court's Watergate ruling did not halt presidents' invocation of inherent executive power, however. In 2002, Congress's General Accounting Office sued the Bush administration in an effort to obtain records of White House energy-task-force meetings. The task force, headed by Vice President Cheney, had been charged with developing the administration's energy policy the previous year, and critics suggested that failed energy company Enron had obtained undue access to the panel. The White House successfully defended itself in court, arguing that "the GAO intends to intrude into the heart of executive deliberations . . . which the law protects to ensure the candor in executive deliberations necessary for effective government."[77]

The Power to Pardon   The constitution grants the president the "Power to Grant Reprieves and Pardons for Offenses against the United States." The president may use this power at his or her discretion, with the obvious exception of cases of impeachment. Pardons have stirred major controversies throughout American history. During and after the Civil War, Presidents Lincoln and Johnson pardoned many Confederate soldiers, to the consternation of radicals in Congress. President Ford pardoned former President Nixon for any crimes committed in connection with the Watergate affair, and President Carter granted a blanket amnesty to draft resisters after the Vietnam War.

More recently, President Clinton was accused of abusing his pardon power when he pardoned an alleged tax evader whose ex-wife had donated hundreds of thousands of dollars to the Democratic Party and to Clinton's presidential library in Arkansas.

In light of the uproar surrounding this Clinton pardon, President George W. Bush took special pains to avoid using the pardon for any purpose that might border on the controversial. Bush pardoned a postal worker who had stolen $10.90 out of the mail in 1971, a Jehovah's Witness who had refused to submit to the military draft in 1957, and a man who had altered the odometer of a motor vehicle.[78]

The Impeachment Power

CONGRESSIONAL IMPEACHMENT POWER: *Presidents may be impeached by a majority of the House of Representatives for "high crimes and misdemeanors." The president is removed from office if the Senate convicts by a two-thirds vote.*

impeachment

Recommendation by a majority of the House of Representatives that a president, another official in the executive branch, or judge of the federal courts be removed from office; removal depends on a two-thirds vote of the Senate.

independent counsel

(Originally called special prosecutor.) Legal officer appointed by a court to investigate allegations of criminal activity on the part of high-ranking members of the executive branch.

Nothing makes more clear the subordination of presidents to Congress than the fact that the House of Representatives can impeach and the Senate can convict and remove presidents from office. Though seldom used, the constitutional power of **impeachment** is no dead letter. Andrew Johnson was impeached in 1868, although the Senate, by one vote, failed to convict him.[79] Richard Nixon resigned in the face of almost certain impeachment in 1974. And President Clinton's affair with Monica Lewinsky, a White House intern, led to the first impeachment and trial of a president in more than a century.

In 1994 a three-judge panel appointed Kenneth Starr as **independent counsel** with the authority to investigate charges related to the questionable Whitewater land deal in which Clinton had been involved while governor of Arkansas. Separately, an Arkansas public employee, Paula Jones, sued Clinton for sexual harassment. In 1998 the scandals merged. Starr concluded that Clinton had obstructed justice and committed perjury when, in the Jones case, he denied under oath having sexual relations with Lewinsky.

The president argued that his carefully worded denial did not constitute perjury, and the electorate seemed to take his side: Republicans lost ground in the 1998 congressional elections. But on December 19, 1998, the House voted (along mostly partisan lines) to impeach the president, making him only the second U.S. chief executive to be threatened with removal from office by Congress.

In early 1999 the Senate held its trial of the president, with Chief Justice William Rehnquist presiding. In considering their votes, most senators believed that if they were to overturn a national election by removing Clinton from office, they needed a more serious cause. After all, polls showed that two-thirds of the public still thought the president should stay.[80] On February 12, the Senate voted for acquittal.

The Clinton scandals have altered the American presidency in important respects. First, presidents are now at risk of being sued by their political opponents. Addressing the Jones case, the Supreme Court ruled that presidents can be sued for alleged wrongful conduct that is not part of their presidential duties. In its opinion, the Supreme Court said that such lawsuits were unlikely to interfere with presidential responsibilities.

Second, it has become clear that the advice presidents receive from their government attorneys is not necessarily confidential. The president's attorney claimed the right to keep conversations about Lewinsky confidential. But the courts said that conversations between government attorneys and presidents were not protected unless they involved official duties. In the future, presidents can be expected to hire private legal advisers.

Finally, some scholars have argued that the partisan nature of Clinton's impeachment is a sign that the practice is more likely to be used in the future as a political weapon. Others disagree, however, noting that the circumstances of the scandal were unique. "If Watergate was a 'long national nightmare,' " suggests one presidential scholar, the Lewinsky scandal "seems more like a drug-induced hallucination."[81]

Presidential Expectations and Presidential Performance

Presidents are expected to be strong, yet presidential powers are limited. As a result, presidents seldom satisfy the hopes and aspirations of the voting public. To sustain their reputation and effectiveness, presidents can sometimes act with Machiavellian cleverness. When Abraham Lincoln took office, seven southern states had already seceded from the Union, and were threatening a Union outpost at South Carolina's Fort Sumter. Moving while Congress was out of session, Lincoln announced that he would order the U.S. Navy to send new supplies to the fort. After Confederates fired on Sumter as supply ships neared, Lincoln blamed the South for starting the war and received overwhelming support in the North. By forcing the South's hand, Lincoln created a situation that advantaged the Union cause.[82]

Presidents in the past were frequently able to cover ruthless actions with a cloak of dignity that the role of chief of state allowed them to wear. But as the life of the president becomes more open to the media, it gets harder to keep the cloak of dignity firmly in place. As Bill Clinton put it, "It is difficult for people to function in an environment in which they feel that their character, their values, and their motives are always suspect, and where the presumption here is against them."[83]

Presidential Reputations

To meet public expectations despite their limited power, presidents need to protect their professional reputation among members of Congress and other **beltway insiders**, the politically influential people who live inside the highway that surrounds Washington, D.C.[84] Presidential reputations inside Washington are shaped by the quality of the people who serve the presidents and the frequency with which presidents win political contests. They also depend on the president's ability to let go of issues that cannot be won. As Lincoln put it, "When you have got an elephant by the hind legs and he is trying to run away, it is best to let him run."[85]

beltway insider
Person living in the Washington metropolitan area who is engaged in, or well informed about, national politics and government.

Presidential Popularity

In addition to guarding their professional reputation, presidents need to maintain their popularity with the general public. As Lincoln also shrewdly observed, "With public sentiment, nothing can fail; without it, nothing can succeed."[86] **Presidential popularity** is measured by asking the adult population how well they think the president is doing his job. Pollsters now ask the same question almost every week, so it provides a decent barometer of the public's current assessment of the president's performance.

presidential popularity
Evaluation of president by voters, usually as measured by a survey question asking the adult population how well they think the president is doing the job.

All presidents experience fluctuations in their popularity over the course of their terms. But as a general rule, presidential popularity tends to decline over time as public expectations go unfulfilled.[87] A study of the first term of eight recent presidents indicates that apart from any specific economic or foreign policy events, their popularity fell by nearly 8 points in their first year in office and by 15 points by the middle of their third year. Their popularity recovered in their fourth year, when a presidential campaign was under way, probably because at that time, presidents make special efforts to communicate positive news about their administrations. Presidents regained popularity when reelected, but once again it trailed off.[88]

George W. Bush's first term approval ratings bucked the typical pattern, perhaps because of the unique circumstances of the 9/11 terrorist attacks and the Iraq war. They surged from about 52 percent to above 80 percent in the aftermath of the attacks and remained higher than average until early 2004, when negative news from Iraq prompted a decline. In Bush's second term, his approval dropped precipitously, reaching lows of around 35 percent in early 2006.

Presidential popularity and professional reputation were at one time regarded as two quite separate phenomena. Unpopular presidents could still have the respect of beltway insiders if they husbanded their political resources carefully. But the distinction between popularity and reputation has become clouded.[89] Presidents are the focus of seemingly inexhaustible but utterly exhausting television, radio, and newspaper coverage. As soon as they have addressed one problem, they are urged to solve the next. As one commentator put it, "Getting the public's attention, particularly on a subject that the polls show is already gnawing at people, is no trick for a President . . . . The trick is holding that attention."[90]

The one kind of attention that presidents are likely to hold is the kind they don't want. When George H. W. Bush became nauseated at a state dinner in Tokyo, the embarrassing consequences were graphically reported in news headlines. President Clinton voiced exasperation over a "totally bogus story" that claimed he held up flights on a runway while getting a $200 haircut.[91] And George W. Bush endured criticism when his teenaged daughter Jenna was fined $500 for underage drinking.[92]

When these kinds of incidents cause a president's popularity to slip, weekly polling results transmit this information to beltway insiders. If the president's reputation is slipping in Washington, the news media just as quickly communicate insider opinions to the wider public. As a result, the president now has to work both the inside and the outside of the beltway at the same time.[93]

Great Presidents

Presidential
Greatness

All presidents are challenged by problems and opponents both at home and abroad, and all find it difficult to preserve both professional reputation and public popularity throughout their terms. Yet some presidents are remembered as "great presidents," because they achieve many of the objectives they set for themselves; others are seemingly unable to tackle the problems they face. Why do some succeed and others fail?

In a study of presidential character, James Barber argued that certain personality traits make for successful presidents (see Table 13.2).[94] He said that effective presidents both like their job and readily adapt their policies to changing circumstances. He called these presidents "active-positives." For Barber, Franklin Roosevelt was the ideal active-positive president. He loved his job as president, and he brought great energy to it. He changed his mind frequently, but always with an eye to solving governmental problems. Clinton also seemed to have an active-positive approach to the job.

Barber argued that most other modern presidents lacked one or the other of these two character traits. President Eisenhower brought a positive attitude, but Barber thought he was too passive. Instead of taking the initiative, he waited for others to propose solutions to problems. Barber claimed that both Lyndon Johnson and Richard Nixon brought an active-negative attitude to the job. Although both were energetic, neither could adapt to new circumstances. As a result, each pursued a policy position long after a more adaptive president would have changed course. Johnson led the country ever more deeply into the Vietnam War; Nixon tried to "cover up" Watergate misdeeds when he might have been better advised to let the problem come immediately to the surface.

TABLE 13.2		
PRESIDENTIAL CHARACTER		

	PRESIDENT HAS **HIGH** ENERGY LEVEL.	PRESIDENT HAS **LOW** ENERGY LEVEL.
PRESIDENT ENJOYS THE JOB.	**Active-Positive** Examples Thomas Jefferson Franklin Roosevelt	**Passive-Positive** Examples James Madison Dwight Eisenhower
PRESIDENT IS DISCOURAGED BY THE JOB.	**Active-Negative** Examples John Adams Lyndon Johnson	**Passive-Negative** Examples George Washington Calvin Coolidge

• *Does presidential effectiveness depend on presidential attitudes and energy?*

SOURCE: Adapted from James Barber, *The Presidential Character: Predicting Performance in the White House*, 4th ed. (Englewood Cliffs, NJ: Prentice-Hall, 1992).

Critics of Barber's schema say he placed too much emphasis on presidential activity.[95] Bill Clinton was an active policy wonk, but he was not always successful in achieving his goals. Eisenhower appeared to be passive, but presidential analyst Fred Greenstein shows that he governed with a "hidden hand."[96] Although Ike let others grab the headlines, he steered the ship from behind the scenes, staying out of controversy and preserving his popularity. Reagan was hardly an activist,[97] yet his use of the power of the dignified presidency, together with his focus on fundamental goals, made him a powerful political force.

Presidential success may depend less on personality than on the circumstances under which the newly elected come into office.[98] Presidential scholar Stephen Skowronek says that most are so hemmed in by the checks placed upon them that they simply cannot accomplish the job the public expects. As a result, presidents become "great" only when political circumstances allow them to repudiate the past and move in a sharply different direction. By rejecting the old way of doing things, they are able to discard political baggage that would limit presidential action.

Franklin Roosevelt is once again the archetypal effective president. Running for office in 1932 in the midst of the Great Depression, he declared, "these unhappy times call for . . . plans . . . that build from the bottom up and not from the top down, that put their faith once more in the forgotten man." After an election that realigned the American party system (see Chapter 8), Roosevelt pushed through a huge volume of important legislation in his first 100 days in office.

Roosevelt was not the first effective president who profited by breaking with the past (see Table 13.3). Thomas Jefferson discarded the program of John Adams and the Federalist

PARTICIPATION

Rate the
Presidents

President's Resignation

The epitome of the active-negative president, grimly determined to do his duty until the end, Richard Nixon doggedly repeats his "V for victory" sign upon leaving office on August 9, 1974.

• *Were Nixon's difficulties due to his personality?*

Party. Republican Abraham Lincoln attacked slavery. Ronald Reagan halted the growth in government that had occurred under his predecessors, saying, "Government is not the solution to our problem. Government is the problem."[99] Whether a president is able to repudiate the past successfully is somewhat beyond the president's control, however. Congress and the public must also agree that a new direction is needed.

Skowronek's model is not perfect. Many people think Theodore Roosevelt was one of the country's most successful presidents, but he did not become president through a pivotal election or at a time of crisis. And some people think other presidents—Eisenhower (for managing the Cold War) and Johnson (for initiating the Great Society)—deserve inclusion at the top of the list of presidents. But Skowronek does show that presidents are often most effective when they exercise their power to initiate new approaches. It is often left to other, less effective presidents to try to follow this lead.

If Skowronek's theory is correct, the administration of George W. Bush faces significant obstacles to success. Bush was elected by a razor-thin margin to succeed a

TABLE 13.3			
DO FAILED POLICIES AND PRESIDENTS LEAD TO THE ELECTION OF PRESIDENTS WHO SUCCEED BY REPUDIATING THE PAST?			
Year	Ineffective President	Leads to . . .	Very Successful President
1789	Articles of Confederation		George Washington
1800	John Adams		Thomas Jefferson
1828	John Q. Adams		Andrew Jackson
1860	James Buchanan		Abraham Lincoln
1932	Herbert Hoover		Franklin Roosevelt
1980	Jimmy Carter		Ronald Reagan

SOURCE: Based on Stephen Skowronek, *The Politics Presidents Make* (Cambridge, MA: Harvard University Press, 1993).

popular president from the opposing party. Moreover, many of Bush's most significant policy proposals, such as major tax cuts, are not new ideas, but are based on the agenda of a previous president: Ronald Reagan. Skowronek suggests that only one president has been successful under such circumstances: William McKinley. It is perhaps no surprise then, that Bush political adviser Karl Rove frequently cited McKinley as a role model for the Bush administration.[100]

Chapter Summary

Presidents must meet the high expectations of their national and partisan constituencies, despite the fact that Congress checks many of their most important powers.

- Presidents can initiate legislation, but Congress often rejects or substantially modifies their proposals.
- Presidents can appoint executive and judicial officers, but the Senate must approve them.
- Presidents may invoke inherent executive power, including the right of executive privilege, but Congress can impeach them.
- Although the president can veto congressional bills, Congress may override the veto by a two-thirds vote.

- Presidential leadership depends most heavily on the power of the chief executive to initiate and persuade—capacities that derive as much from the dignity of the office as from any specific clauses in the Constitution.

To achieve their goals, presidents must preserve their professional reputation and their political popularity. Because their popularity tends to slip over time, it is at the beginning of their presidency—during the transition and honeymoon periods—that they have the most capacity to initiate change. Great presidents emerge not so much because they have the right personal qualities as because they come to office when the country thinks it is time for a change.

Key Terms

administration, p. 367
beltway insider, p. 379
bully pulpit, p. 365
cabinet, p. 367
chief of staff, p. 368
commander in chief, p. 360
dignified aspect, p. 373
divided government, p. 362
efficient aspect, p. 373
Executive Office of the President
  (EOP), p. 368

executive order, p. 376
executive privilege, p. 376
first lady, p. 374
honeymoon, p. 371
impeachment, p. 378
independent counsel (originally called
  special prosecutor), p. 378
inherent executive power, p. 376
line item veto, p. 366
override, p. 366
pocket veto, p. 366

presidential popularity, p. 379
secretary, p. 367
State of the Union address, p. 363
transition, p. 371
veto power, p. 366
White House Office, p. 368

Suggested Readings

Of General Interest

Barber, James. *The Presidential Character: Predicting Performance in the White House.* 4th ed. Englewood Cliffs, NJ: Prentice-Hall, 1992. Argues that presidential character affects presidential success.

Jones, Charles. *The Presidency in a Separated System.* 2nd ed. Washington, D.C.: The Brookings Institution, 2005. Examines the role of the president under divided government.

Kernell, Samuel. *Going Public: New Strategies of Presidential Leadership.* 3rd ed. Washington, D.C.: CQ Press, 1997. Describes the increasing tendency of presidents to use popular appeals to influence legislative processes.

Nelson, Michael, ed. *The Presidency and the Political System.* 8th ed. Washington, D.C.: CQ Press, 2005. Important contemporary essays on the presidency.

Neustadt, Richard E. *Presidential Power and the Modern Presidents.* New York: Free Press, 1990. Modern classic on the limits to presidential power.

Skowronek, Stephen. *The Politics Presidents Make: Leadership from John Adams to George Bush.* Cambridge, MA: Harvard University Press, 1993. Provocative analysis of the historical development of the presidency.

Focused Studies

Korn, Jessica. *The Power of Separation: American Constitutionalism and the Myth of the Legislative Veto.* Princeton, NJ: Princeton University Press, 1996. Identifies the many ways in which power is shared between Congress and the executive.

Mayer, Kenneth. *With the Stroke of a Pen: Executive Orders and Presidential Power.* Princeton, NJ: Princeton University Press, 2001. Study of how presidents use executive orders to make policy.

Moe, Terry. "The Politicized Presidency." In *The New Direction in American Politics*, ed. John Chubb and Paul E. Peterson. Washington, D.C.: The Brookings Institution, 1985. Insightful essay on the evolution of the White House staff.

Rudalevige, Andrew. *Managing the President's Program: Presidential Leadership and Legislative Policy Formulation.* Princeton, NJ: Princeton University Press, 2002. Examines how presidents design policy initiatives.

Tulis, Jeffrey. *The Rhetorical Presidency.* Princeton, NJ: Princeton University Press, 1987. Contrasts modern presidential rhetoric with that of early presidents. Argues against a rhetorical presidency.

On the Web

www.whitehouse.gov

The official Web site of the White House offers current and historical information about U.S. presidents, as well as press releases and other policy statements.

www.thepresidency.org

Many political scientists study the factors that contribute to presidential success and failure. The Center for the Study of the Presidency publishes Presidential Studies Quarterly and showcases academic information and links.

www.archives.gov

Presidential libraries have been created for every president since Franklin Roosevelt. The National Archives and Records Administration (NARA) provides information about and links to these presidential libraries. NARA also provides a guide to presidential documents available online. These include executive orders, proclamations, speeches, and other materials.

www.vicepresidents.com

When Daniel Webster was offered the vice presidency, he famously demurred, saying "I do not propose to be buried until I am really dead." This Web site provides an online clearinghouse for information about this much-maligned post and its occupants.

Election Voices

The Politics of U.S. Energy Policy

THE ISSUE

What action should the U.S. government take to reduce dependency on foreign oil and to address environmental harms that result from the use of oil, gas, and other fossil fuels?

An Oil Refinery *Does U.S. oil dependence represent a national security risk?*

Background

Scholars of public policy often refer to "focusing events"—major episodes that draw the public's attention to problems that have long existed but have escaped widespread notice. When, in 2005, Hurricane Katrina and a later hurricane, Rita, disrupted oil rigs near Louisiana and Texas, the flow of oil from the Gulf of Mexico was interrupted and gasoline prices jumped more than 30 percent to a national average of $3.05 per gallon.[1] As commuters complained, experts made their case that the event simply highlighted the vulnerability of the nation's oil supply to unforeseen events, especially as two-thirds of that oil comes from foreign countries.[2] "If there is a silver lining in this awful cloud," said one advocate, "it's that [Katrina] reminded Americans how vulnerable we are and why we have to end our dangerous addiction to foreign oil."[3]

It is not only vulnerability of the oil supply that Katrina highlighted. The record-breaking hurricane season of 2005 also drew attention to the rising average global temperature, which has now reached a level higher than at any time within the last 400 years.[4] While it remains uncertain as to exactly how much of the increase is due to the burning of fossil fuels, most of the increase in global temperatures appears to have occurred since industrialization (which began around 1850), suggesting that the 24 billion tons of carbon dioxide (CO_2) and related pollutants produced annually by automobiles, factories, and other industrial sources around the world have caused the atmosphere to trap more solar heat than in previous eras.[5] If global warming continues at its current pace, most scientists predict that within a century habitats will undergo major changes, ice masses at the two poles will melt, and the resulting rise in sea levels will flood coastal areas worldwide. The climbing temperature warms water as well as land, and warmer

oceans induce more hurricanes such as Katrina. In the words of former vice president Al Gore, "Katrina is the first taste of a bitter cup that will be proffered to us over and over again."[6]

The United States has yet to develop a comprehensive set of policies to mitigate either the vulnerability of the country's energy supply or the rising global temperatures. The government has not ignored the problem altogether. In 1975, Congress created a strategic petroleum reserve (oil purchased on a regular basis by the government to be held for potential use in times of national crisis). It also passed two pieces of energy legislation, the first in 1992 and the second in 2005, but few believe the changes enacted were sweeping enough to be truly effective. The provisions of the 1992 act, for example, were found by a government auditing agency to be too weak to meet the law's own energy conservation goals.[7] The 2005 act offered a tax credit of up to $3,400 for those who purchased hybrid cars and trucks and provided money to businesses to develop advanced fuel-efficient (or hydrogen powered) vehicles, but did little to encourage widespread energy conservation or develop non-fossil fuel energy sources.[8]

Nor has the global warming issue been addressed in a serious way by the United States or, for that matter, the larger international community, despite unusual weather patterns, melting ice in the Arctic, and disappearing glaciers worldwide. The Kyoto Protocol on climate change, a 1997 United Nations-sponsored agreement, has been signed by more than 140 countries. Although it asks the United States, Europe, and other developed nations to reduce their emissions substantially, it places no limits on countries in the developing world, such as China and India, which are responsible for a growing proportion of the world's pollutants. In 2001, the Bush administration withdrew from participation, claiming that the treaty is unfair to U.S. industries, even though President Bush agrees that it is entirely possible that fossil fuel emissions constitute a "dangerous human interference with our climate."[9]

Energy Policy and Elections

Both global warming and the vulnerability of the nation's energy supply have the potential to become major political issues, but energy is by far the more volatile of the two. If oil supplies are disrupted and energy prices spike, the cost of transportation, heating, air conditioning, and other energy use could have a serious impact on the family budget. According to one study, the average family was paying over $1,000 more per year for gasoline in 2006 than it was in the late 1990s.[10]

When prices balloon, political leaders are tempted to look for quick fixes that seem to ameliorate the situation. During the rise in gas prices in 2005, for example, President Bush allowed the release of oil from the nation's strategic reserve, and politicians of both parties demanded investigations of alleged "price gouging." But enactment of legislation that could help move toward a longer-term solution—heavy taxes on energy usage, encouragement of nuclear energy, or comprehensive regulation of the transportation industry, for example—has been as rare as a $1.00 gallon of gas. "Congress is never at its best when it is trying to solve a long-term problem in the short term," said Representative Ellen Tauscher (D-CA).[11]

On the global warming question, Congress and the president have done even less. Political pressures to do something about climate change are less intense, even after catastrophes such as Hurricane Katrina. For one thing, it is impossible to attribute any particular weather event, no matter how serious, to global warming. Furthermore, any actions to halt global warming will be extremely costly, requiring major societal changes, and will pay off only after many years. Even then, it may be impossible to avoid significant increases in temperature levels. Finally, because climate change is a global problem, policies will be effective only if leaders engage in difficult international negotiations.

Some scholars have even begun to question whether the matter deserves the attention the issue has been given. An international group of economists including three Nobel Prize winners were asked by Danish environmentalist Bjorn Lomborg to consider how to save the most lives with the minimum amount of resources. The economists opted to fight disease and malnutrition, especially in developing countries, because much could be done with even a modest commitment of financial resources. Fighting global warming, however "would cost a colossal amount and yield distant and uncertain rewards."[12]

Opposing Viewpoints on United States Energy Policy

While global warming has yet to be tackled in a serious way, most people agree that something needs to be done about the vulner-ability of U.S. energy supplies. But there are significant disagreements about where the United States ought to focus its efforts. Some policy makers say the main thing to do is to increase the sources of supply, while others would like to do more to limit energy demand, not only because it would reduce vulnerability but also because it could mitigate the rate of global warming.

Reducing Vulnerability to Supply Interruptions

Some experts argue that U.S. policy efforts ought to focus on increasing the supply of domestic energy resources. This might include allowing additional oil rigs and refineries in previously protected areas, such as the Alaska National Wildlife Refuge (ANWR), more intensive utilization of coal resources, greater use of biological sources of energy such as ethanol (derived from corn), and, perhaps most importantly, the more extensive use of nuclear energy. They point out that the demand for energy is steadily increasing and any efforts to thwart increasing demand will have serious economic repercussions for the economy as a whole. By reducing dependence on foreign energy sources, this approach is also expected to bolster national security.

> [W]hat I believe the American people should understand is that we can put policies in place that encourage economic growth, so you've got a better standard of living, and at the same time, become less dependent on energy from overseas and protect the environment . . . .
>
> People in our country are rightly concerned about greenhouse gases and the environment, and I can understand why—I am, too . . . .
>
> For the sake of economic security and national security, the United States of America must aggressively move forward with the construction of nuclear power plants.
>
> —President George W. Bush, Remarks at Limerick Generating Station, Pottstown, Penn., May 24, 2006
>
> American demand for oil is outpacing our nation's refining capacity, adding to the increases we're all seeing at the pump . . . . We can help reverse this trend by taking common sense, responsible steps . . . to improve our nation's ability to refine crude oil . . . recognizing environmental needs and continuing to develop alternative sources of energy.
>
> —Representative Greg Waldren (R-OR), House Committee on Energy and Commerce,
> SOURCE: http://energycommerce.house.gov/108/News/06072996_1932.htm, accessed June 23, 2006

Cutting the Demand for Energy

Others argue that government should develop policies that reduce the demand for energy by encouraging conservation.

Many experts believe the best way to cut demand is by placing a higher tax on oil, gas, and other fossil fuels. (The price of gasoline in European countries can run two to three times higher than in the United States, because those countries levy a heavy tax on most energy products). But, because higher taxes are very unpopular, the United States has, up until now, tried to reduce the demand for energy through regulatory action instead. Automobile companies have been told that they must build cars and trucks that get more miles to a gallon of gas. Similarly, home energy appliances—furnaces, hot water heaters, and refrigerators—must now meet certain efficiency standards. But these regulatory actions have not been as effective as originally anticipated. As cars have become more efficient, consumers have purchased bigger cars and vans. Similarly, as it has become cheaper to heat and cool houses, consumers have purchased larger homes.

Generally speaking, most Democratic political leaders place more emphasis on energy conservation and are less supportive of efforts to encourage growth in the supply of energy. They support the Kyoto Protocol, favor tighter regulation of energy use, and oppose drilling in the ANWR. Meanwhile, most Republicans favor a greater emphasis on energy growth by lessening restrictions on oil drilling, coal mining, and the construction of nuclear plants. But the differences between the two parties may be receding, as both sides have come to realize that long-term growth will require both greater conservation and greater focus on energy supplies. This has given rise to bipartisan support for further research into alternative energy sources (wind, solar, nuclear as well as ethanol and other biomass products). But few leaders in either political party have been willing to bite the biggest energy bullet of all—a major tax increase on all gas, oil, and other fossil fuels.

> Having yet another vote on drilling in the Alaska National Wildlife Refuge (ANWR) does not constitute creative or long-range thinking about a balanced energy policy. Having yet another vote on refinery legislation that uses high oil prices as an excuse to weaken environmental protections and to give more legislative gifts to the oil industry is misguided in the extreme . . . . We can limit U.S. demand for oil by requiring automakers to use the technology that already exists to improve fuel economy . . . . And then we need to invest more in coming up with new technologies that can move us away from our dependence from gasoline. Three obvious areas that require more investment are plug-in hybrids, biofuels, and hydrogen.
>
> —Sherwood Boehlert (R–NY), Statement on Energy Policy, April 27, 2006
> SOURCE: www.house.gov/science/, accessed June 22, 2006

> We . . . need to take serious action to limit the extent of climate change by reducing our emissions. More than anything else, that will require a global technology revolution—and we need policies to make that revolution happen.
>
> . . . [W]e plainly do not have time to wait. The challenge before us requires a much more deliberate, enunciated effort to develop policies that will help push and pull climate-friendly technologies to the market. We need a guiding vision on the order of putting a person on the moon or developing a cure for cancer.
>
> —Eileen Claussen, President, Pew Center on Global Climate Change, "Climate Change: Beyond a Sideways Approach" speech at the Donald Bren School of Environmental Science and Management, January 14, 2005.
> SOURCE: www.pewclimate.org/press_room/ speech_transcripts/speech.cfm, accessed June 23, 2006

What Do Americans Believe?

Most Americans consider themselves to be environmentalists. But this consensus breaks down when they are asked whether global climate change is a serious problem, and what steps they would be willing to take to address this and other energy policy issues. As Figure 1 shows, a majority of Americans say they worry at least "a fair amount" about global warming. But as the figure also illustrates, they are less certain about what government should do to solve the nation's energy problems.

What Do You Think?

1. What is most important: increasing energy supply or limiting energy demand?

2. Is energy demand better curbed by tighter regulations or higher taxes on gas, oil, or other fossil fuels?

3. Would you be willing to pay higher prices for energy if it reduced dependence on foreign energy sources? If it would slow global warming?

4. Why has neither political party favored a tax increase on gasoline?

Web Sites on Energy Policy and Climate Change

www.heritage.org/Research/EnergyandEnvironment/

The conservative Heritage Foundation recommends increasing domestic energy supplies.

www.sierraclub.org/

The environmental group The Sierra Club argues for less reliance on oil and more international engagement on climate change.

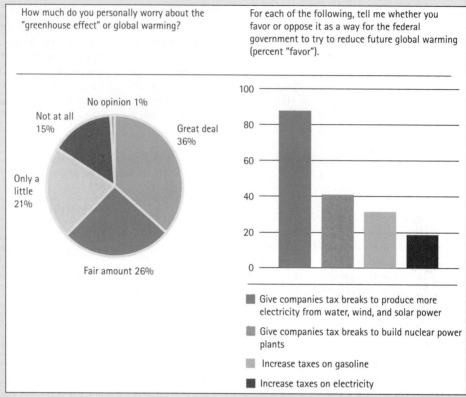

How much do you personally worry about the "greenhouse effect" or global warming?

No opinion 1%
Not at all 15%
Great deal 36%
Only a little 21%
Fair amount 26%

For each of the following, tell me whether you favor or oppose it as a way for the federal government to try to reduce future global warming (percent "favor").

■ Give companies tax breaks to produce more electricity from water, wind, and solar power

■ Give companies tax breaks to build nuclear power plants

■ Increase taxes on gasoline

■ Increase taxes on electricity

FIGURE 1

Americans Worry about Climate Change but Are Skeptical of Regulations That Would Raise Their Energy Costs

SOURCE: Gallup Poll, March 13–16, 2006; ABC News/Time/Stanford University Poll, March 9–14, 2006.

www.realclimate.org/

A site created by working climate scientists, commenting on climate-science related news.

http://energycommerce.house.gov/

http://energy.senate.gov/public/

The House Committee on Energy and Commerce and the Senate Committee on Energy and Natural Resources handle most energy-related legislation that passes through Congress.

[1]American Automobile Association data, available at www.fuelgagereport.com, accessed June 22, 2006.

[2]"Monthly Energy Review, May 2006," United States Department of Energy, Energy Information Administration, www.eia.doe.gov/emeu/mer/pdf/pages/sec1_15.pdf, accessed June 22, 2006, Table 1.7.

[3]Griff Witte, "Another Look at Fuel Efficiency," *Washington Post*, September 6, 2005: D3.

[4]Committee on Surface Temperature Reconstructions for the Last 2000 Years, National Research Council, *Surface Temperature Reconstructions for the Last 2000 Years*, (Washington, DC: National Academy of Sciences, 2006), Figure S-1.

[5]John R. Justus and Susan Fletcher, *Global Climate Change* (Washington, DC: Congressional Research Service), CRS Report for Congress IB89005, Updated May 12, 2006, 2.

[6]Geoffrey Lean, "Rita's Global Warning," *Independent on Sunday* (London), September 25, 2005: 22.

[7]Energy Policy Act of 1992: Limited Progress in Acquiring Alternative Fuel Vehicles and Reaching Fuel Goals, GAO/RCED-00-59 (Washington, DC: United States General Accounting Office, 2000).

[8]Michael Grunwald and Juliet Eilperin, "Energy Bill Raises Fears About Pollution, Fraud," *Washington Post*, July 30, 2005: A1.

[9]"President Announces Clear Skies and Global Climate Change Initiatives," www.whitehouse.gov/news/releases/2002/02/20020214-5.html, accessed June 23, 2006.

[10]Mark Cooper, Research Director, Consumer Federation of America, "Testimony Before the United States Senate Committee on Commerce, Science, and Transportation," May 23, 2006, 2.

[11]Mark Sandalow, "Congress Full of Sound and Fury on Energy Policy as Time Runs Out," *San Francisco Chronicle*, May 6, 2006: A4.

[12]"How to Save the World: Bolton v. Gore," *The Economist*, June 22, 2006: 38.

CHAPTER 14

⭐⭐⭐⭐⭐⭐⭐⭐⭐⭐

The Bureaucracy

CHAPTER OUTLINE

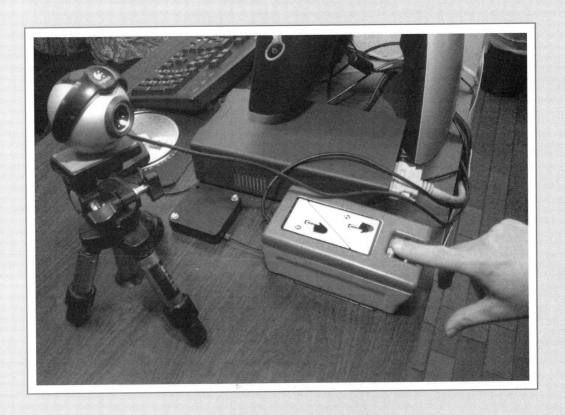

Organizing for Homeland Security

The unprecedented terrorist attacks of September 11, 2001, provoked feelings of shock, anger, and vulnerability that many Americans had never before experienced. But in the aftermath of the attacks, some channeled their reaction into a much more familiar argument: U.S. government agencies had failed to do their jobs well.

Even those loyal to these agencies agreed that they had botched the key task of protecting Americans from attacks from abroad. One former Federal Bureau of Investigation (FBI) official called the incident "the greatest counterterrorism screw-up in U.S. history." The National Security Agency (NSA), the Central Intelligence Agency (CIA), and the FBI "are all tasked with getting this kind of information," he argued. "Billions and billions of dollars are spent on this. And if we can't get it, there's something very very wrong."[1]

Nine days after the attacks, George W. Bush moved to reform the way these agencies conducted the business of domestic security. In doing so, the president moved to implement the recommendations of a blue-ribbon commission that in February 2001 had called for greater coordination and planning among dozens of government organizations. The Bush plan was different from that of the commission in one respect, however: Whereas the panel had called for "a significant organizational redesign"—namely, a new cabinet-level agency charged with securing the U.S. from terrorism[2]—Bush was initially much more modest. He created a new White House Office of Homeland Security, headed by former Pennsylvania governor Tom Ridge.

Ridge, with his small staff of 100 operating from a corner of the executive mansion, was expected to coordinate the activities of agencies as diverse as the FBI in the Justice Department, the U.S. Customs Service in the Treasury Department, the Federal Aviation Administration (FAA) in the Transportation Department, and the Federal Emergency Management Agency (FEMA), an independent entity. Each of these agencies—and dozens of others that the Homeland Security office was supposed to keep track of—had separate budgets, separate directors, and separate organizational cultures. One national security expert likened Ridge's task to "getting a 40-mule team to be pulling in the right direction."[3] In his public appearances, Ridge admitted that the job was as difficult as "building the transcontinental railroad, fighting World War II, or putting a man on the moon."[4]

In the ensuing weeks, Ridge often appeared to be overshadowed by other administration officials. When authorities discovered that the deadly disease anthrax had been mailed to members of Congress and media outlets, Secretary of Health and Human Services Tommy Thompson took center stage. When a would-be terrorist was arrested after attempting to set off a bomb hidden in his shoes on a transatlantic flight, FBI officials in Boston fielded media inquiries. And Transportation Secretary Norman Mineta was charged with ensuring that aviation screening met tough new federal standards. Ridge's most visible accomplishment was his invention of a color-coded national terrorism alert system. But even under this system it was the attorney general—not Ridge—who would decide when to raise or lower the nation's state of alert.

After eight and one-half months of trying to manage the domestic security apparatus from the White House, and as members of Congress and the public expressed alarm at new revelations about pre-9/11 intelligence failures, the president admitted he needed to do more. In June 2002, Bush asked Congress to create a cabinet-level Department of Homeland Security that would have direct authority over nearly 170,000 government workers from eight departments. The Border Patrol, the Coast Guard, the Transportation Security Administration, and even the Secret Service moved to the new organization as part of the largest federal government shakeup in more than 50 years. In a televised address to explain his reversal of course on this issue, Bush admitted that a more effective, unified structure was needed: "Right now, as many as a hundred different government agencies have some responsibilities for homeland security, and no one has final accountability."[5]

Years after its creation, experts are still debating about whether the Department of Homeland Security has lived up to expectations (see Election Voices, p. 421). But at least the Homeland Security secretary has had more authority than did a White House Homeland Security director.

MAKING THE CONNECTION

Thomas Ridge was not the first presidential appointee to find it difficult to coordinate the departments and agencies of the federal government. Agency officials feel threatened by changes in their job descriptions, and Congress is also wary of such efforts. As one member of Congress observed, "We all know that the toughest things in Washington are the turf wars . . . . No [congressional] committee likes their authority cut back."[6]

The FBI, CIA, FAA, and FEMA are all part of the federal bureaucracy. Bureaucracies are hierarchical organizations of officials with responsibility for specific tasks. They are essential to government action but are often criticized as being inefficient or too large. In this chapter, we discuss how bureaucracies have developed and describe how they fit into modern American politics. In particular, we address the role that bureaucracy plays in government, and consider the problems that impede its performance. We review the history of the bureaucracy, with an eye to how historic reforms and reorganizations have changed our bureaucracy. And finally, we consider how Congress and the president influence the bureaucracy, and how the bureaucracy itself is organized.

The Role of the Bureaucracy

Bureaucracies are essential if government is going to provide the programs and services the public expects. Laws become effective only when a government agency enforces them. Without some kind of organization, governments cannot build roads, operate schools, put out fires, fight wars, distribute social security checks, or do the thousands of other things Americans demand from their government.

As the range of governmental responsibilities has grown, the number of bureaucrats in the United States has also increased. The most growth has occurred at state and local levels, where the vast majority of civilian government workers are employed, including school teachers, police officers, and sanitation workers (see Figure 14.1). In addition, many private contractors perform tasks paid for by government agencies. Although the number of employees who work directly for the federal government is smaller, we shall focus most of our attention on federal bureaucracies, because their policies and regulations are far-reaching and their impact is felt throughout the country.

The **agency**, also known as the office or bureau, is the basic organizational unit of the federal government. It is the entity specifically assigned by Congress to carry out a task. There are hundreds of agencies within the federal government, but most are grouped under one of 15 **departments**—collections of federal agencies that report to a secretary who serves in the president's cabinet. However, there are nearly 100 independent agencies or government corporations that are free-standing entities reporting either to the president or to a supervisory board.[7] The Central Intelligence Agency and the Environmental Protection Agency are examples of independent agencies. Finally, there are around three dozen **government corporations**—a particular type of independent organizations created by Congress to fulfill functions related to business.[8] Examples of government corporations include the Federal Deposit Insurance Corporation, which insures bank deposits, and the National Railroad Passenger

bureaucracy
Hierarchical organization designed to perform a particular set of tasks.

Department of Homeland Security

agency
Basic organizational unit of federal government. Also known as *office* or *bureau*.

department
Organizational unit into which many agencies of the federal government are grouped.

government corporation
Independent organization created by Congress to fulfill functions related to business.

FIGURE 14.1

Government Employment, 1946–2003

The number of state and local employees has increased, but the number of federal employees has remained about the same.

• *Why do you think employment at the federal level has remained stable, despite budget increases and new government programs?*

Note: Federal government employment figures include civilians only. Military employment figures include only active-duty personnel.

Sources: U.S. Bureau of the Census, *Historical Statistics of the United States: Colonial Times to 1970* (Washington, DC: GPO, 1975), 1100, 1141; *Statistical Abstract of the United States, 1999*, Tables 534 and 578; *Statistical Abstract of the United States, 2006*, Tables 451, 480, 496.

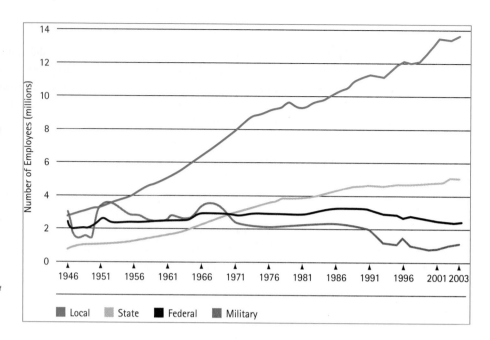

Corporation, which runs Amtrak. Figure 14.2 illustrates how the federal bureaucracy is organized.

Bureaucracies can have great influence over policy because of their **administrative discretion**, the power to interpret their legislative mandates. Congress can enact general rules, but it cannot anticipate every circumstance, nor can it apply

administrative discretion

Power to interpret a legislative mandate.

FIGURE 14.2

The Federal Bureaucracy Consists of Departments, Independent Agencies, and Government Corporations

★Top managers include an executive director, managing director, chief financial officer, chief administrative law judge, and general counsel.

★★As a government corporation, OPIC is self-funded rather than government-funded.

Sources: United States Government Manual 2005–2006 (Washington, DC: GPO, 2005), structure of Department of Agriculture and NTSB; www.opic.gov, structure and budget of OPIC; Office of Personnel Management, Federal Civilian Employment and Payroll by Branch, Selected Agency, and Area, November 2005, www.opm.gov/feddata/html/2005/november/table9.asp, accessed March 26, 2006, employment figures for all agencies; Office of Management and Budget, Budget of the United States Government, Fiscal 2007, budget figures for Agriculture and NTSB.

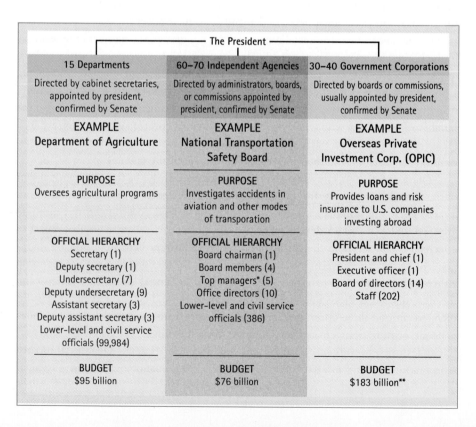

these rules to every individual case. Congress may decide to provide benefits to the disabled, but it is up to a bureaucrat (in this case, an official within the Social Security Administration) to apply the rules that decide whether a particular disability precludes employment.[9] Congress may decide to give loans to college students from families of moderate income, but it is up to a bureaucrat (in this case, an officer within the Department of Education) to interpret and apply the rules that determine what family resources count as income.

The Bureaucracy Problem

If bureaucracies exist to address public demands for programs and services, it might seem as if it should be easy to design effective government agencies. An ideal bureaucracy would be organized so that it could achieve the public's wishes most efficiently. Selection of people hired to work in the bureaucracy would be based on their ability to do the job. Each would report to his or her superior via a clear chain of command, and ultimate authority would be exercised by the head of the bureau. Agency staff would supply each worker with the materials necessary to get the job done. The ideal is best exemplified by soldiers on parade, marching together in synchronized formation. When all works perfectly, bureaucracies exhibit unity, focus, and power.[10]

The Changing Face
of the Federal Bureaucracy

Although the ideal bureaucracy has tremendous potential, many forces inhibit perfection. Some of the most significant flaws reflect the demands imposed on government bureaucrats through democratic elections: They often work under impossible expectations or debilitating limits. Other flaws are inherent in all bureaucracies: They are slow to change, they tend to expand, and the quality of their performance is difficult to measure. Taken together, these factors create what is known as the bureaucracy problem.[11]

Impossibility of Tasks

Most governmental tasks are difficult to accomplish. If they were easy, someone other than the government would have undertaken the job! Not only can agency objectives be complicated, but goals themselves often remain vague and indefinite.[12] Americans expect schools to teach their children—but many people disagree about what exactly should be taught. Commuters expect transportation agencies to achieve smoothly flowing traffic— but to avoid all bottlenecks in most large cities, construction crews would have to turn to pavement much that citizens now value for other purposes. The Environmental Protection Agency is charged with protecting the environment from pollutants—but nearly all human activity increases pollution in some way. Because their responsibilities are so complicated and the limits of their objectives are seldom well defined, bureaucracies are often blamed for problems even if they do the best possible job.

Difficulty Measuring Performance

It is often difficult to measure the performance of government bureaucracies.[13] In 2003, for example, many Californians criticized the U.S. Forest Service because its firefighters failed to stem the initial spread of the devastating Cedar Fire near San Diego that destroyed more than 2,000 homes and caused 14 deaths. Forest Service officials argued that their response had been timely, however, and that they had done the best they could under the worst of possible circumstances.[14] Because it is hard to measure the performance of most government bureaucracies, it is difficult for supervisors, elected officials, and the public to tell whether work is being performed carefully and promptly. If officials are unsure how to gauge a bureaucracy's performance, they will have trouble trying to improve it. As a result, bureaucracies often have a reputation for inefficiency.

Expansionary Tendencies

Once they are created to address a problem, bureaucracies generally try to expand so they can address it better. Government agencies almost always feel they need more money, more personnel, and more time to perform their tasks effectively.[15] Bureaucrats experience policy problems up close, and are under a lot of pressure to solve these problems, so they often sincerely believe that they need more resources. But because they focus on specific issues, they can lose sight of the big picture. Congress cannot grant unlimited funds to every bureaucracy that wants them; trade-offs and choices have to be made.

There is nothing new about this debate between bureaucrats and Congress. "You may blame the War Department for a great many things," General Douglas MacArthur said back in 1935, "but you cannot blame us for not asking for money. That is one fault to which we plead not guilty."[16]

Slow to Change

Any large governmental organization has standard procedures through which it makes its decisions. And most standard procedures are essential if large numbers of people are to coordinate their work toward some common end. If rules were not clearly defined, those working within the bureaucracy would be so confused that they would soon be unable to do anything.

Standard procedures nonetheless make bureaucracies sluggish and slow to adjust to new circumstances.[17] Schools still provide long summer holidays that were originally allowed so that children could help harvest crops on family farms. Despite massive increases in the use of energy in the United States, the Federal Energy Regulatory Commission has changed its approach to regulation of the electricity grid very little over the course of four decades.[18] After a massive blackout in the northeastern part of the country in August 2003, former Energy Secretary Bill Richardson said, "We're a superpower with a third-world grid."[19] As one humorist observed, "Bureaucracy defends the status quo long past the time when the quo has lost its status."[20]

When events take unpredictable and catastrophic turns, existing guidelines can even lead to disaster. After New York's World Trade Center collapsed in 2001, killing hundreds of fire and emergency workers along with more than two thousand others, some experts questioned standard procedures that called for fighting skyscraper fires from the inside. "We're going to rewrite the book as far as how we're going to handle incidents like that," said one firefighting authority.[21]

Red Tape

Everyone complains about governmental red tape, but as one analyst has observed, "One person's red tape may be another's treasured procedural safeguard."[22] People often complain, for example, that it takes forever to get a bridge repaired. But bridge repair can be politically complicated. The design of any alterations must be acceptable to

Standard Operating Procedures

One of the drawbacks of standard procedures is that they may not work well in unprecedented circumstances, such as the 2001 terrorist attacks.

• *Will reorganization of the executive branch successfully adapt standard procedures to new terrorist threats?*

neighbors. If the bridge is regarded as a historical landmark—and a surprising number of bridges are so designated—a historical commission must approve of the project. After the design is accepted, the agency, when letting contracts, must advertise the job and allow time for companies to submit bids. To avoid accusations of political favoritism, the choice of contractors must be made according to published criteria. And the repairs themselves must be carefully inspected to make sure the bridge does not collapse upon completion. Once again, a common bureaucratic problem is caused not by malice or ignorance but by important considerations of politics and safety.

At times, bureaucratic agencies can make exceptions. After the terrorist attacks of 2001, the Internal Revenue Service made a dramatic effort to speed up its approval of tax-exempt status for new disaster-relief charities. During this period, reviews of applications that normally would have taken 8 to 12 weeks were sometimes finished within 3 days.[23] Similarly, after Hurricane Katrina hit the Gulf Coast region in 2005, the Securities and Exchange Commission, which regulates businesses with public stock, extended filing deadlines and reduced the amount of required paperwork for companies in the affected area. As SEC Chairman Chris Cox put it, "No one in the region should have to worry about attempting to file government documents in nearly impossible circumstances."[24] But red tape was eliminated in these cases only because the public insisted that disaster relief should override procedural formalities.

VIDEO ROUNDTABLE

Hurricane Katrina and New Orleans

American Bureaucracies: Particularly Political

The bureaucracy problem exists in all countries, but American bureaucracies have special problems that are rooted in the country's unusual political history. As we discuss in this section, U.S. bureaucracies had a difficult beginning, were built with patronage, and were only slowly modernized by a "bottom-up" civil-service reform. Government workers today fall into two categories: career civil servants who are hired according to educational qualifications and who have job security, and political appointees at the highest level who can be dismissed at any time. Though the policy of reserving the top spots for political appointees makes the government more responsive to elections, it makes civil service jobs less attractive to bright young people.

Difficult Beginnings

Evolution of the
Federal Bureaucracy

American bureaucrats lack the noble heritage of their counterparts in Europe and Japan, where government departments evolved out of the household of the king, queen, or emperor. In the late 1600s, King Louis XIV constructed a great French administration within the Palace of Versailles. The extraordinarily efficient German administration, which became a model for the world, descended from the household of the King of Prussia. Japan's powerful bureaucracy owes its prestige to a time-honored relationship with the emperor. The lineage of federal bureaucrats in the United States is less distinguished. As one scholar has pointed out, "In England, France and Germany, . . . it is considered an honor simply to serve the state . . . . In the United States civil servants, instead of being regarded with honor, are often considered tax eaters, drones, grafters, and bureaucrats."[25]

The American Revolution was fought against King George's bureaucrats, who had been appointed to oversee the governments of the colonies. The resulting suspicion of appointed officials carried over to the time that the Constitution was written, when the framers could not even agree on a site for the people who were to run the new national government. Finally, as part of a compromise, they agreed to locate the District of Columbia, the new home of the federal government, on the Maryland–Virginia border near the small city of Georgetown.

Thomas Jefferson believed that the location would attract virtuous Virginians to federal jobs, leading to "a favourable bias in the Executive officers."[26] In fact, the land Congress had chosen was swampy and miserable. Visitors complained that it was thick with "contaminated vapour" and that its mud-spattered, ramshackle buildings gave it "the appearance of a considerable town, which had been destroyed by some unusual calamity."[27] If the government were to attract quality workers, its location would not be its main selling point.

Mountains of Patronage

patronage
Jobs, contracts, or favors given to political friends and allies.

spoils system
A system of government employment in which workers are hired on the basis of party loyalty.

Not only did the disreputable living conditions in the District of Columbia diminish the prestige of the federal government, but bureaucrats were dealt a second blow after the election of 1828, when President Andrew Jackson handed out political **patronage**—government jobs, contracts, and other favors—to his supporters. Jackson reasoned that this practice made government more democratic, because it ensured that those who won elections were fully in control of the government. Furthermore, the quality of work would not suffer from political appointees, said Jackson, because "[t]he duties of all public officers are . . . so plain and simple that men of intelligence may readily qualify themselves for their performance."[28] The practice of hiring workers on the basis of party loyalty became known as the **spoils system** when New York Senator William Marcy attacked President Jackson for seeing "nothing wrong in the rule that to the victor belong the spoils."[29]

Family Ties
The Mayors Richard Daley, father and son, in a moment of family resemblance.

• *When it comes to getting elected, what advantages do children of politicians have over other candidates?*

Politicians in both political parties quickly discovered that the spoils system suited their needs.[30] As barriers to participation fell in the mid-1800s, more and more Americans went to the polls to cast ballots (see Chapter 6). Because local, state, and national elections occurred frequently, mobilizing this growing electorate became a complicated and time-consuming task. Party politicians could use promises of government posts to enlist campaign workers to take on such thankless jobs as passing out pamphlets, organizing rallies, and transporting voters to the polls. The New York machine-politician George Washington Plunkitt explained the logic of patronage this way: "You can't keep an organization together without patronage. Men ain't in politics for nothin'. They want to get somethin' out of it."[31]

Patronage also made it easier for parties to raise large amounts of cash to fund their frequent election campaigns. Every Pennsylvania state employee during this period received the following letter from the Republican State Committee: "Two percent of your salary is—. Please remit promptly. At the close of the campaign we shall place a list of those who have not paid in the hands of the head of the department you are in."[32] These practices were not conducted in secret; politicians felt they were a natural and legitimate part of politics.

Plunkitt defended patronage, or graft, by making the fine distinction between its dishonest and honest varieties. Dishonest graft wasted the taxpayers' money or engaged in "blackmailin' gamblers, saloonkeepers, [and] disorderly people."[33] Honest graft simply paid a friend to build a bridge or roadway that needed to be constructed anyway. Or, as the patronage-prone Chicago Mayor Richard J. Daley once said when asked to explain why he had given the city's insurance business to one of his sons, "If a man can't put his arms around his sons, then what kind of a world are we living in? . . . I make no apologies to anyone. There are many men in this room whose fathers helped them, and they went on to become fine public officials."[34] Mayor Daley's sons did well for themselves. Richard M. Daley was elected to a fifth term as Chicago mayor in 2003, and William Daley served as Secretary of Commerce under President Clinton.

FIGURE 14.3

Black Representation
in State and Local
Government Workforce
Is Higher Than in
Private Sector

• *Why are there different
patterns of employment success for
African Americans and Hispanics?
(See Figure 14.4.)*

Note: Government figures are
from 2003; private-sector figures
are from 2004.

*Source: Statistical Abstract of the United States
2006*, Table 454 (government workers),
Table 604 (private sector).

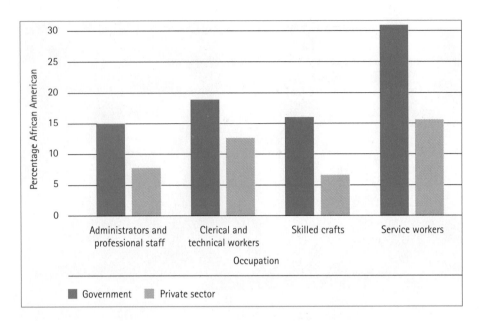

Advantages of the Spoils System

Looking back on American political history, many scholars have found much to praise in the old spoils system.[35] For one thing, it helped immigrants adjust to the realities of urban life in the United States. "I think there's got to be in every ward somebody that any bloke can come to—no matter what he's done—and get help," said one Boston politician. "Help, you understand; none of your law and your justice, but help."[36] Some of the help took the form of jobs in city government. Irish immigrants were particularly good at using politics as a way of getting ahead. In Chicago, the percentage of public-school principals of Irish background rose from 3 percent in the 1860s to 25 percent in 1914. In San Francisco, it climbed from 4 percent to 34 percent over a similar period.[37]

Some scholars have argued that contemporary affirmative-action programs have many of the same pluses and minuses as the old-fashioned spoils system. When African Americans became part of urban governing coalitions, they gained better access to government jobs by invoking the principle of affirmative action.[38] Nationwide, African Americans are more likely to get a job in government than in the private sector (see Figure 14.3), a sign that politics still seems to help some disadvantaged groups get a toehold on the ladder to success. However, government employment for Hispanics still lags behind their positions in the private sector (see Figure 14.4), probably because the percentage of Hispanics who vote and otherwise participate in politics remains comparatively low.

Disadvantages of the Spoils System

Even though the spoils system helped incorporate immigrants into American politics and society, it nonetheless contributed to the negative image of American bureaucracies. Education, training, and experience counted for little, and jobholders changed each time a new party came to power. As one Democratic leader joked after his party had been in power for years, a bureaucrat was "a Democrat who holds some office that a Republican wants."[39]

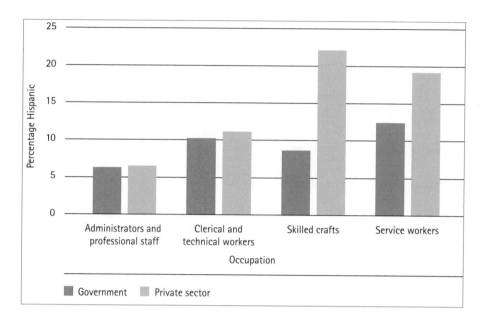

FIGURE 14.4

Hispanic Representation in State and Local Government Workforce Is Lower Than in Private Sector

Note: Government figures are from 2003; private-sector figures are from 2004.

Source: Statistical Abstract of the United States 2006, Table 454 (government workers), Table 604 (private sector).

The many decades of patronage politics produced an anti-bureaucratic sentiment among members of the public that continues to the present day. More than 60 percent of Americans think "people in the government waste a lot of money we pay in taxes."[40] When Americans were asked how they would rate the honesty and ethical standards of federal government workers, only 28 percent found them "very high" or "high."[41]

Merit System

Erosion of the Spoils System

The mountains of patronage created by the spoils system were gradually eroded by **civil service** reformers who, in the 1880s, were called **mugwumps**. A group of professors, journalists, clerics, and business leaders, mugwumps insisted that government officials should be chosen on the basis of merit, not for their political connections. Originally a sarcastic term of abuse, the name is a modification of a Native American word meaning "great man" or "chief." Mugwumps were also scorned for refusing to back either party. It was said that their "mugs" peered over one side of the fence while their "wumps" stuck out over the other. Mugwumps, in turn, accused politicians of appointing political hacks to crucial positions of public trust. One clergyman accused the mayor of Boston of appointing saloon keepers and bartenders to public office.

Even though the mountains of patronage did not erode easily, mugwumps won a succession of victories that gradually changed the system. Their first major breakthrough came in 1881 when President James Garfield was assassinated by a mentally disturbed man said to be a disappointed office seeker. Public scrutiny focused on the new president, Chester A. Arthur, who had once served as the New York customs collector and seemed the very personification of the spoils system. In 1883, as the demand for reform swept the country, Congress passed—and Arthur signed—the **Pendleton Act**, which created a Civil Service Commission to set up qualifications, examinations, and procedures for filling many government jobs.

Civil service reform occurred from the bottom up. In the first few years after the Pendleton Act, civil service requirements applied mainly to the lower-level, less skilled

civil service

A system in which government employees are chosen according to their educational qualifications, performance on examinations, and work experience.

mugwumps

A group of civil-service reformers, organized in the 1880s, who maintained that government officials should be chosen on a merit basis.

Pendleton Act

Legislation passed in 1883 creating the Civil Service Commission.

jobs performed by those who swept the floors and typed government forms. Gradually, higher-level positions were included in the civil service; such additions were especially plentiful when the party in power expected defeat in the next election. By making a job part of the civil service, soon-to-be-ousted presidents "blanketed in" their supporters, making it impossible for their successors to replace them with patronage workers from the other party. Civil service reform became nearly complete when, in 1939, Congress passed the **Hatch Act**, which barred federal employees from political campaigning and solicitation. The mountains of patronage were all but worn away.

Hatch Act

A 1939 law prohibiting federal employees from engaging in political campaigning and solicitation.

Political Appointees Today

In the arid expanses of Arizona and New Mexico stand mesas—often called islands in the desert—that tower over surrounding flatland. All that remain of ancient plateaus, long eroded by wind and water, mesas are ecologically distinct from the surrounding desert.

Just as one finds geological mesas in the deserts of the West, one can locate patronage mesas that have survived decades of civil-service reform. One of the most heavily populated patronage mesas is also the most prestigious, for it includes thousands of policy makers at the top levels of the federal government. It consists of most members of the White House staff, the heads of most departments and agencies, and the members of most government boards and commissions. Political appointees also predominate in the upper levels of individual agencies and departments, inhabiting offices that bear such titles as deputy secretary, undersecretary, deputy undersecretary, assistant secretary, deputy assistant secretary, and special assistant.

This high-level patronage mesa is becoming increasingly crowded. The estimated number of top-level agency appointees grew from less than 500 in 1960 to nearly 3,400 by the George W. Bush administration.[42] No other industrialized democracy gives its leader as much patronage power. (See *International Comparison*, page 401.)

The president's ability to recruit political allies for the top echelon of government has both advantages and disadvantages. On the positive side, it allows newly elected presidents to enlist many new people with innovative ideas. For example, President Clinton drew on think-tank experts and leaders from interest groups to design his economic stimulus and health care reform proposals after taking office in 1993. The wholesale changeover in personnel also helps presidents introduce their political agendas with minimal resistance from an entrenched executive branch. President George W. Bush's tax-cut plan and education policies were developed without the aid or obstruction of leftover Clinton advisers. Indeed, it is the power of appointment that makes presidents the most dynamic element in the American political system.

Yet the prevalence of political appointees at the highest levels may result in administrators who have little knowledge of their own organizations. European and Japanese governments are marked by close, informal, long-time associations among leading administrators. In the United States, the average presidential appointee leaves office after only a little more than two years; almost a third leave in less than 18 months.[43] Experienced career bureaucrats, on the other hand, often lack the political authority to make policy changes. In 2003, a bipartisan commission on reforming the government workforce found that, as a result, "Leadership responsibilities often fall into the awkward gap between inexperienced political appointees and unsupported career managers."[44]

Comparing
Bureaucracies

INTERNATIONAL COMPARISON

Political Versus Professional Bureaucrats

Most high-level administrative positions in Europe and Japan are occupied by well-educated, highly experienced, professional civil servants who refrain from participating actively in politics. Most achieve their positions by studying in prestigious training programs. In France, for example, bureaucracies recruit new employees from the prestigious and highly selective Ecole Nationale D'Administration, which graduates only 150 students per year, and in Japan, about 80 percent of the nation's high-level bureaucrats attended Tokyo University. In these countries, high-level administrators have spent years—even decades—in dedicated government service.

In the United States, high government officials often get their jobs only after gaining prominence outside government in business, law, medicine, education, or a policy institute. Usually, they have worked in a presidential campaign, made financial contributions, or given other evidence of party loyalty. For example, President Clinton's secretaries of commerce were not long-time government experts on trade policy, but Ron Brown, Mickey Kantor, and William Daley, each of whom played key roles in the Clinton and Gore campaigns. Similarly, President George W. Bush, when selecting his first secretary of energy, turned not to a long-time government servant who had worked on nuclear power or energy efficiency but to Spencer Abraham, a political supporter and former Michigan senator who had co-sponsored legislation to eliminate the department outright. Although some believed Abraham's management skills would be welcome at the Energy Department, others questioned his

qualifications. "I don't see where he has much expertise in energy," said one activist. Another critic was more blunt: "The cabinet is a pension system for political allies."

More professionalized bureaucracies are not necessarily more popular with the general public. In 2002, for example, French Prime Minister Jean-Pierre Raffarin won popularity with proposals to streamline what he said was an inefficient and stagnant government workforce. But there is evidence that bureaucrats in other countries are less frustrated by political interference than are bureaucrats in the United States. According to one study, American civil servants have more negative views of political parties and are more likely to resent the interference of politicians than are Japanese civil servants.

This difference in attitude probably occurs because in the United States the bureaucracy must respond to both the president and Congress. In most other industrial democracies, the legislative branch has less direct influence over the bureaucracy. Where the bureaucracy has only one master, bureaucrats can be professionals instead of politicians.

- *Should the bureaucracy be reformed so that it has only one master?*

- *What are the advantages and disadvantages of the tug of war between Congress and the president over the bureaucracy?*

SOURCES: "Toward the Multiversity," *The Economist*, July 11, 1987; Joel D. Aberbach, Ellis S. Krauss, Michio Muramatsu, and Bert A. Rockman, "Comparing Japanese and American Administrative Elites," *British Journal of Political Science*, 20:4 (October 1990), 461–488; Harry Eckstein, "The British Political System," in *Patterns of Government: The Major Political Systems of Europe*, ed. Samuel Beer and Adam Ulam (New York: Random House, 1962), 158–168; Hugh Heclo, *Modern Social Politics in Britain and Sweden: From Relief to Income Maintenance* (New Haven, CT: Yale University Press, 1974); Paul Pierson, *Dismantling the Welfare State* (New York: Cambridge University Press, 1994); and David Lazarus and John Wildermuth, "California Wants Abraham's Ear, But It's Unknown If He Can Ease Power Woes," *San Francisco Chronicle*, January 3, 2001, A11; "Profligate France," *The Times* (London), October 9, 1992, 21.

The rapid turnover in high-level governmental personnel is so pervasive that it has been called a government of **in-and-outers**—people who come in, go out, and come back in again with each change in administration.[45] Because they cannot count on long-term employment with the government, most political appointees begin planning a way of making a satisfactory departure shortly after they arrive. For some people, this will mean returning to their old positions in the business, legal, or academic world. For others, it will be a matter of using connections inside the beltway to win new financial opportunities in the private or nonprofit sectors. When the new Bush administration came to Washington in 2001, a number of "outers" reentered government, including Vice President Dick Cheney, who had become CEO of an energy company after serving as secretary of defense in the first Bush administration. President Bush's press secretary, Tony Snow, is another in-and-outer. He served as a speechwriter for President George H. W. Bush before embarking on a career as a television journalist. In April 2006, George W. Bush invited him back to the White House.

in-and-outers

Political appointees who come in, go out, and come back in again with each change in administration.

These rapid changes in personnel create a government that lacks the continuity necessary for sustained policy focus. The newcomers bring energy and ideas, but by the time their ideas are turned into plans that can be brought to fruition, they are gone, succeeded by another energetic group with an altogether different set of priorities. The newcomers also run the risk of trying to make too many changes at once. Clinton's inexperienced health-policy experts tried to introduce such massive changes that their efforts collapsed under the weight of their own ambitions.[46] Similarly, George W. Bush's inexperienced education advisers initially had difficulty designing an education policy that could withstand close scrutiny by experts in the field. New legislation was eventually passed, but the process was longer and more tortuous than originally anticipated.

With rapid change in personnel, governmental memory becomes as limited as that of an antiquated computer. One Japanese trade specialist who negotiated with the United States observed that the Japanese "look at politics in their historical perspective . . . . However, in the case of the U.S., almost all of their negotiators seem like they came in just yesterday."[47]

Worst of all, the denial of most top-level positions to nonpolitical civil servants makes the civil service a less attractive career for intelligent, ambitious young people. In Japan, many of the top students graduating from the country's most prestigious law schools go directly into government service, and the most gifted reach the highest levels of government. But the peak of the U.S. government is not part of a large mountain that employees can gradually ascend over a lifetime career. Instead, the top-level mesa positions are ordinarily cut off from the surrounding civil-service desert, at elevations scaled only by a patronage-filled presidential helicopter. It should not come as much of a surprise, then, that when asked what kinds of careers they are contemplating, less than a quarter of young people say they are "very" or "fairly" likely to consider working for the federal government.[48]

If young people knew that years of work in the civil service could eventually be rewarded by promotion to high-level policy positions, many more might consider this an attractive career option. But the best advice that can be given to a young person who wants to achieve a high policy-making position in government is to do an internship with a member of Congress, build connections with a political party, achieve distinction outside the government, and wait for the right moment to make Washington a temporary home.

The President and the Bureaucracy

CONSTITUTION, ARTICLE II, SECTION 3: *The President "shall take Care that the Laws be faithfully executed."*

The Constitution charges the president with enforcement of the laws. Presidents fulfill this obligation by overseeing the federal bureaucracy, which is formally responsible to the chief executive. The president's cabinet is the most visible and long-standing connection between the president and the bureaucracy. However, the president also exercises power through appointments to independent agencies and through the powerful Office of Management and Budget.

Despite these means of control, even presidents can be frustrated by the bureaucracy problem. As an exasperated President Harry Truman once said, "I thought I was the president, but when it comes to these bureaucrats I can't do a d—ed thing."[49]

PARTICIPATION

Who Wants to Be
a Bureaucrat?

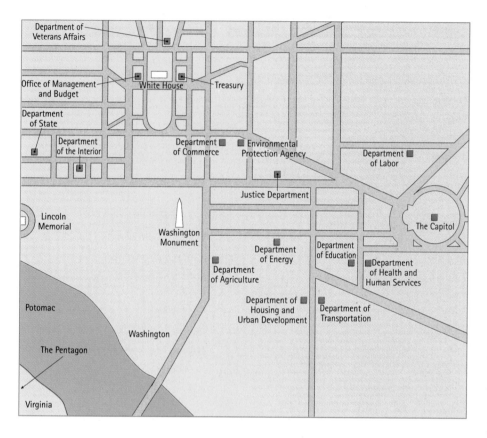

Figure 14.5

Where Are the Key Buildings in Washington?

The physical location of the headquarters of the inner cabinet suggests the comparatively close ties these departments have to the president. Treasury is located next door to the White House. The walks from State and Justice to the White House are also shorter than to Capitol Hill. Defense, almost a world unto itself, is headquartered in the Pentagon in nearby Virginia. Many of the departments of the outer cabinet, such as Transportation, Education, Agriculture, Labor, and Housing and Urban Development are located at the foot of Capitol Hill. There they hunker, almost on bended knee, faceless and humorless, in the shadow of the magnificent Capitol building. The Office of Management and Budget (OMB), the nerve center of the executive branch, stands at the president's side, physically as well as metaphorically.

• *When purchasing a home, buyers are warned to think first about location. Why might this also be true in politics?*

The Cabinet

Most federal agencies are located in one of the major departments. The president appoints secretaries to head these departments. The secretaries, along with a few other top-ranking officials, form the president's cabinet (see Chapter 13). The four original departments are known as the **inner cabinet**, because their secretaries typically have ready access to the president.[50] Even the locations of their offices are close to the White House, as you can see from Figure 14.5. These departments are:

inner cabinet

The four original departments (State, Defense, Treasury, and Justice) whose secretaries typically have the closest ties to the president.

- State, responsible for foreign policy;
- Defense, originally called War, responsible for the military;
- Treasury, responsible for tax collections, payments, and debt service;
- Justice, headed by the attorney general, who is responsible for law enforcement.

The remaining departments of the cabinet, which are known as the **outer cabinet**, have evolved in such a way as to provide interest-group access to the executive branch of government.[51] The Interior Department's job was originally to regulate the use of federal land, particularly in the West. Today, it maintains close ties to ranchers, timber companies, mining interests, and others who depend on federal lands for their livelihood. The Agriculture Department serves farmers; the Commerce Department helps business and industry, especially firms with overseas contracts; Labor works closely with unions; Health and Human Services heeds the American Association for Retired Persons; and Education pays attention to teacher organizations (see Table 14.1).

outer cabinet

Newer departments that have fewer ties to the president and are more influenced by interest-group pressures.

TABLE 14.1

ESTABLISHMENT YEAR AND INTEREST-GROUP ALLIES OF EACH CABINET DEPARTMENT

• *Why have outer-cabinet departments formed alliances with outside groups?*

Department	Year	Interest-Group Allies
Inner Cabinet		
State	1789	
Treasury	1789	
Justice (attorney general)	1789	
Defense	1789 (as War)	
Outer Cabinet		
Interior	1849	Timber, miners, ranchers
Agriculture	1889	Farm bureau, other farm groups
Commerce	1913	U.S. Chamber of Commerce, other business groups
Labor	1913	Labor unions
Health and Human Services	1953	American Association of Retired Persons
Housing and Urban Development	1965	National League of Cities, Urban League
Transportation	1966	Auto manufacturers, truckers, airlines
Energy	1977	Gas, oil, nuclear power interests
Education	1979	Teachers' unions
Veterans Affairs	1987	American Legion, Veterans of Foreign Wars
Department of Homeland Security	2003	Airlines, state and local governments
Environmental Protection Agency	Not an official department	Sierra Club, other environmental groups

The connections between departments and interest groups can change overnight, however, if an event activates the public spotlight. Nowhere was this more evident than in the case of the corporate accounting scandals that arose in 2002. Companies such as energy conglomerate Enron and telecommunications giants Global Crossing and WorldCom had engaged in bookkeeping trickery to hide losses and inflate apparent earnings. The CEOs of these companies had traveled on Commerce Department-sponsored trade missions and enjoyed access to high-level policy makers.[52] When the scandals broke, however, Commerce Department officials distanced themselves from the now-bankrupt firms and took the lead in crafting President Bush's proposed corporate policy reforms. "Business leaders need to understand that they have responsibilities," said one Commerce official, "not just to shareholders, [but also] to creditors, to employees, to pensioners, and [to] government agencies."[53]

Presidents exercise their control over the cabinet departments primarily by appointing political allies to top positions. But once they become agency heads, allies often more closely identify with their turf than with the president's program. As FDR's top budget adviser put it, "Cabinet members are vice presidents in charge of spending, and as such they are the natural enemies of the President."[54] The bureaucracy problem,

TABLE 14.2

INDEPENDENT AGENCIES AND THEIR INTEREST-GROUP ALLIES

• *Do the alliances many agencies form with interest groups undermine their initial goals?*

Independent Agency	Board Size	Length of Term (years)	Interest-Group Allies
National Credit Union Administration	3	6	Credit unions
Federal Reserve Board	7	14	Banks
Consumer Product Safety Commission	5	5	Consumers Union
Equal Employment Opportunity Commission	5	5	Civil rights groups
Federal Deposit Insurance Corporation	5	3[a]	Banks
Federal Energy Regulatory Commission	4	4	Oil/gas interests
Federal Maritime Commission	5	5	Fisheries
Federal Trade Commission	5	7	Business groups
National Labor Relations Board	5	5	Unions
Securities and Exchange Commission	5	5	Wall Street
Tennessee Valley Authority	3	9	Regional farmers and utilities

[a] One member, the comptroller of the currency, serves a 5-year term.

which tends to encourage sluggishness, red tape, and budgetary expansion, can be particularly frustrating for presidents, who are often interested in speed and efficiency.

Independent Regulatory Agencies

Not all agencies are members of cabinet departments. Some of the most important of these, the **independent regulatory agencies**, have quasi-judicial regulatory responsibilities, which are meant to be carried out in a manner free of presidential interference. These agencies are generally headed by a several-member board or commission appointed by the president and confirmed by the Senate. Independence from the president, which is considered desirable to insulate such agencies from partisan politics, is achieved by giving board members appointments that last for several years (see Table 14.2). In a number of cases, presidents may not be able to appoint a majority of board members until well into their second term in office.

Most independent regulatory agencies were established by Congress in response to widespread public pressure to protect workers and consumers from negligent or abusive business practices. For example, Congress created the Federal Trade Commission (FTC) in 1914 in response to the discovery of misbranding and adulteration in the meatpacking industry. The FTC was given the power to prevent price discrimination, unfair competition, false advertising, and other unfair business practices. Congress also created the Mine Safety and Health Review Commission in 1977 to preside over disputes about mine safety, and formed the Chemical Safety and Hazard Investigation Board in 1990 to investigate industrial chemical accidents.

When originally formed, most regulatory agencies aggressively pursued their reform mandates. But as the public's enthusiasm for reform fades, many agencies find their most interested constituents to be members of the very community they are

independent regulatory agencies
Agencies that have quasi-judicial responsibilities.

Bureaucratic Reform

expected to regulate. Thus the independent commissions, too, have tended to become connected to organized interest groups.[55] To protect against misleading business practices such as those undertaken by Enron, WorldCom, and Global Crossing, the Securities and Exchange Commission (SEC) has the responsibility for ensuring that publicly traded companies provide stockholders with continually updated information about their true financial condition. Yet Enron was exempted from a key regulation in 1997 when its lobbyist, Joel Goldberg, a former high-level SEC staff member, convinced a current SEC official, Barry Barback (who previously had served under Goldberg), that an exemption from the usual rule was warranted. The close connection between SEC officials and those who lobby them, an all too common phenomenon, can have serious consequences for stockholders.[56]

Office of Management and Budget

Before 1921, every federal agency sent its own budget to Congress to be examined by an appropriations subcommittee. Without a single overseer to review all the requests at once, no one—not even the president—knew whether agency requests exceeded government revenues. When President Woodrow Wilson asked for a bureau to coordinate these requests, Congress at first refused to create one, saying such a bureau encroached on congressional authority. However, when federal deficits ballooned during World War I, Congress, under pressure to make government more efficient, relented and gave the president the needed help.

Office of Management and Budget (OMB)

Agency responsible for coordinating the work of departments and agencies of the executive branch.

Originally known as the Bureau of the Budget, the agency is now called the **Office of Management and Budget (OMB)**, a name that reflects its enlarged set of responsibilities. Although development of the president's budget is still its most important job, OMB also sets personnel policy and reviews every piece of proposed legislation that the executive branch submits to Congress to ensure that it is consistent with the president's agenda. Agency regulations, too, must now get OMB approval. Even preliminary drafts have to be reviewed by OMB before they are unveiled to the public. One bureau chief claimed that OMB has "more control over individual agencies than . . . [the departmental] secretary or any of his assistants [do]."[57]

OMB was once considered a professional group of technicians whose only goals concerned efficiency and frugality in budgeting. But OMB became more political during the 1980s and 1990s, when budgetary priorities starkly defined the differences between Democrats and Republicans.[58] Clinton's first OMB director, Leon Panetta, had been a Democratic member of Congress and later became the White House chief of staff, an admittedly political office. George W. Bush's first OMB Director, Mitchell Daniels, drew criticism for his advocacy of big tax cuts, and his second OMB director, Josh Bolton, helped to negotiate congressional approval of a controversial $87 billion reconstruction aid package for Iraq.[59] Both Daniels and Bolton later took jobs that placed a high premium on political savvy—Daniels as Governor of Indiana and Bolton as George W. Bush's chief of staff.

end run

Effort by agencies to avoid OMB controls by appealing to allies in Congress.

Although OMB has given presidents greater control over agencies, agency officials can still make **end runs** around OMB by appealing to their allies on Capitol Hill. In 2001, for example, Democrats on congressional committees relied upon unapproved agency requests submitted to OMB to write legislation that increased funding to these agencies. The Coast Guard, the Customs Service, and the Department of Health and

Human Services all stood to gain millions of dollars. Although Senate Republican leader Trent Lott denounced the proposal as a "political scheme," the legislation nearly won passage as part of a defense spending bill.[60]

To check OMB's growing power, Congress in 1974 created the **Congressional Budget Office (CBO)**, an organization under the control of Congress that evaluates the president's budget as well as the budgetary implications of other legislation. CBO's sophisticated analyses of budget and economic trends have enhanced its influence in Washington to the point where it now stands as a strong rival to OMB. In the health care reform debate of 1994, for example, it proved to be a "critical player in the game" whose estimates of the costs of health care reform doomed both presidential and congressional proposals.[61] In 2003, CBO estimates of the cost of President Bush's Medicare reform legislation occasioned much debate in Congress over the affordability of the measure.[62]

Congressional Budget Office (CBO)
Congressional agency that evaluates the president's budget as well as the budgetary implications of all other legislation.

Congress and the Bureaucracy

It is a truism that no one should have more than one "boss." When two or more people can tell someone what to do, signals get crossed, delays ensue, and accountability is undermined. Government bureaucrats in Japan and in most European countries generally abide by this rule. Members of the civil service report to the heads of their departments, who report to the head of the government. Members of parliament have little to say about administrative matters.

Officially, federal bureaucrats in the United States have only one boss—the president, who according to the Constitution is the head of the executive branch. But they also have many bosses in Congress. One House-subcommittee chair declared, quite frankly, "I've been running the Medicare system, or our committee has, for the past nine years. We're its board of directors."[63] With Congress divided into House and Senate, and with each chamber divided into many committees, bureaucrats often find themselves reporting to multiple committees, each of which considers itself a "board of directors." Further, the pressures on bureaucracies have intensified in an era of high exposure and perpetual campaigns. As Martha Derthick has observed, "[Although] the U.S. Constitution has not changed . . . the presidency ha[s] become much more vigilant and intrusive . . . [while] Congress has become more critical."[64]

Senate Confirmations

Congressional influence begins with the very selection of executive-department officers. The Senate's confirmation power has long given senators a voice in administrative matters, traditionally via the practice of **senatorial courtesy**. This custom consists of an informal rule that the Senate will not confirm nominees for positions within a state unless they have the approval of the senior senator of the state from the president's party. For example, there are 93 U.S. attorneys in the Department of Justice, appointed by the president to positions throughout the United States. A senator could block the approval of a U.S. attorney in his or her home state if for some reason the senator found the nominee unsatisfactory. Through the practice of senatorial courtesy, senators can protect their political bases by controlling patronage and shaping administrative practices within their states.

senatorial courtesy
An informal rule that the Senate will not confirm nominees within or from a state unless they have the approval of the senior senator of the state from the president's party.

In recent years, the mass media have linked senatorial confirmations and election strategies even more closely. In an age when strong visual images are needed for the television screen, confirmation processes make for good political theater. Nominees have private lives to be examined. They can be asked embarrassing questions during their confirmation hearings. Conflicts between nominees and senators can elevate a little-known senator to the national stage.

Because the confirmation process has greater potential to affect elections than ever before, senators want more than just the usual "courtesy" traditionally extended to senators from the nominee's home state. They now want to be assured that presidential nominees take acceptable policy positions, do not have private investments that conflict with their public duties, have not violated any laws, and have not acted contrary to conventional moral norms. In 2001, George W. Bush encountered difficulties when he submitted John Ashcroft's name for confirmation as attorney general. As a former Missouri senator, Ashcroft anticipated an easy confirmation process—mainly because senators seldom are critical of their colleagues, present or past. However, Ashcroft had a conservative record on abortion and civil rights issues, and as a senator he had blocked Clinton's nomination of Ronnie White, an African American, to a judgeship. Although some Democrats alleged racial prejudice, Republican ranks held firm and Ashcroft was confirmed.

Senate rejections of presidential nominees are still the exception, not the rule. Yet because presidents know that nomination fights damage their standing with Congress and the public, the confirmation process has become more complicated and time-consuming. To decrease the likelihood that the Senate will reject a nominee, the prospective appointee must first survive ethics inquiries by the FBI, the IRS, the Office of Government Ethics (an independent agency), and the ethics official from the agency to which the nominee will be appointed.[65] The White House must then defend the nominee against exhaustive senatorial scrutiny. When John Kennedy was president, the average nominee was confirmed in less than two and a half months. The confirmation of George W. Bush's average nominee required nearly eight months (see Figure 14.6). Prolonging the confirmation process strengthens congressional control over administrative matters. As long as agency heads await confirmation, they hesitate before taking actions that might offend members of Congress. Bill Clinton was without half his administrative team throughout much of his first year as president, the very year in which he was expected to set the country on a new course.

recess appointment
An appointment made when the Senate is in recess.

Under Article II of the Constitution, presidents may make **recess appointments** without Senate confirmation "during the Recess of the Senate." Recess appointees may serve until the end of the next session of Congress, at which point they must resign if they have not been confirmed. Nothing in the Constitution precludes presidents from using the recess appointment repeatedly for the same person, even if that person is never confirmed. When Theodore Roosevelt could not secure confirmation of an African American as a customs collector in Charleston, South Carolina, the president reappointed him to the office during Senate recesses. Congress has since placed a check on the recess-appointment power by passing legislation prohibiting payment of salary to appointees who serve more than a year without Senate confirmation. As a result, presidents today seldom exercise this power over congressional objections.[66] One exception occurred in 2005 when President Bush used a recess appointment to install John Bolton as the United States ambassador to the United Nations. Democrats had

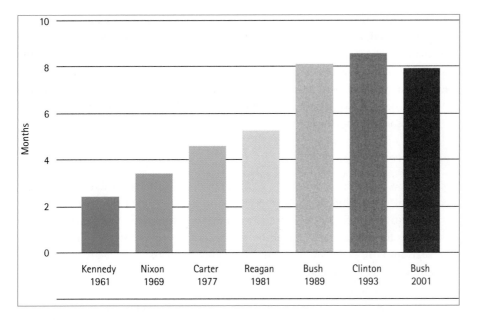

FIGURE 14.6

Average Time It Takes
Presidential Appointees to
Be Confirmed

• *Why has it taken longer in
recent years for presidential
appointees to be confirmed? What
role might elections have played in
this trend?*

Note: Columns show the mean
number of months from inauguration to confirmation of each
administration's executive
appointments at the level of
secretary, deputy secretary, undersecretary, and assistant secretary.

Sources: Paul Light, *Thickening Government*
(Washington, DC: Brookings, 1995), 68;
and Brookings Institution Presidential
Appointee Initiative Press Release,
"Critical Posts in the Bush Administration
Remain Vacant as Congressional Session
Nears End," December 18, 2001.

delayed Bolton's nomination because of his role as an advocate of the Iraq War, as well
as reports about his brash style as an undersecretary of state. The president said that the
unusual recess appointment was necessary because of the pressing nature of the situation. "This post is too important to leave vacant any longer," he said, "especially during
a war and a vital debate about U.N. reform."[67]

Agency Reorganization

Not only do presidents and Congress struggle over the appointment of agency officials,
but Congress often opposes presidential proposals to reorganize executive agencies.
Congress resists change because each agency reports to a specific congressional
committee, and these committees are frequently protective of their power. They therefore typically resist governmental reorganization, no matter how duplicative or antiquated existing organizational structures might be.[68] For example, in the first Clinton
administration, Vice President Gore proposed shifting the law-enforcement functions
of the Drug Enforcement Administration (in the Department of Justice) and the
Bureau of Alcohol, Tobacco and Firearms (in the Department of the Treasury) to the
Federal Bureau of Investigation. Although the idea seemed logical in principle, because
the agencies had similar functions, opposition from Congress and the agencies themselves killed the proposals.[69]

The Bush administration had to navigate similar opposition from some members
of Congress and executive agencies when it proposed the creation of a cabinet-level
Department of Homeland Security. Members of the House Transportation and
Infrastructure Committee, for example, argued that the Coast Guard should remain in
the Department of Transportation, which the committee supervises. Members of the
Senate Agriculture Committee objected to moving the Animal and Plant Health
Inspection Service from the Agriculture Department to Homeland Security.[70]

The creation of a new department appeared so difficult that one expert likened the reorganization effort to a hypothetical attempt to merge the (baseball) Texas Rangers with the (hockey) New York Rangers.[71] (See *Election Voices*, p. 421.) Even after the Department of Homeland Security was created, many of the old divisions were still in place. Although the House chose to create a new Select Committee on Homeland Security to handle most issues concerning the new department, the Senate divided oversight responsibilities among existing committees.

Legislative Detail

Congress also exercises its powers by writing detailed legislation outlining an agency's specific legal responsibilities. In European countries, most legislation is enacted in a form close to the draft prepared by the executive departments.[72] In Japan, 90 percent of all successful legislation is drafted by an executive agency.[73] In the United States, most legislation proposed by presidents is extensively revised by Congress, mainly by the committee with jurisdictional responsibility for the agency.[74] This route has been especially common in recent decades, when Congress and the presidency have more often been controlled by different parties. One study suggests that the average level of discretion that Congress grants the agencies fell by as much as 25 percent in the last half of the twentieth century.[75]

You Are a Federal Administrator

Sometimes detailed but conflicting laws can have nonsensical results. For more than a decade, critics have ridiculed laws that give the Agriculture Department the authority to regulate sausage pizzas but the Food and Drug Administration the authority to regulate cheese pizzas. The FDA operates under legislation authored by the House Commerce Committee and the Senate Human Resources Committee, whereas the Agriculture Department receives its mandates from the House and Senate Agriculture committees. Neither set of committees wishes to relax its control over its agency, so the peculiar division of responsibilities persists. The result, according to one report, "hinders the government's efforts to efficiently and effectively protect consumers from unsafe food."[76]

Even if the statute itself does not dwell on administrative issues, agency operations can be influenced by committee reports accompanying the legislation. These reports are considered by the courts to be evidence of congressional intent and have frequently been given the force of law. Even in the absence of court action, agencies pay attention to committee reports. In the words of one observer, "That language [in the reports] isn't legally binding, but the agencies understand very well what happens if they ignore it."[77]

The issue of legislative detail can be seen as a balancing act between administrative discretion, on the one hand, and congressional control, on the other. If the agency is mindful of congressional intent, Congress may allow it more freedom to act on its own. If an agency neglects a committee's wishes, Congress may enact legal restrictions or even use more forceful methods, such as its control over the agency's budget, to get its way.

Budgetary Control

Every year, each agency prepares a budget for the president to submit to Congress. Each agency must defend its budget before an appropriations subcommittee in both the House and the Senate, and those who offend committee members jeopardize their funding.

Congress and the Bureaucracy

ELECTION CONNECTION

Congressional Legislation: A Matter of Detail

To help get reelected, members of Congress try to get what they want out of bureaucracies through the practice of *earmarking*—that is, designating specific ways in which money is to be spent. The Stand Up For Animals animal shelter in Westerly, Rhode Island, was one of the hundreds of small projects funded in the 2005 transportation bill. Some members of Congress deride such projects as unnecessary "pork barrel" spending, while others see it as a fundamental part of the job of representing their constituents.

• *If you were an agency official, would you prefer more or less earmarking? What kinds of agencies might prefer more or less earmarking?*

• *Why do members of Congress care whether the money is spent for the animal shelter or for a highway?*

To ensure that agencies spend monies in ways consistent with congressional preferences, significant portions of many agency budgets are subject to an **earmark**—a very specific designation of the way money is to be spent, sometimes even specifying particular congressional districts. (See accompanying *Election Connection*.)

Earmarking seems to be on the increase. At one time, for example, Congress let the scientific-research community decide national research priorities, but between 1980 and 2001 the amount of research dollars earmarked for specific projects skyrocketed from $11 million to $1.7 billion,[78] often for pet projects at a representative's home university.

In 2005, Congress drew criticism for enacting about $24 billion in earmarks in a major transportation bill.[79] Among the most controversial was money for two bridges in Alaska to areas with such small populations that critics called them "bridges to nowhere."[80] When Senator Tom Coburn (R-OK) tried (unsuccessfully) to eliminate these and other projects, he earned the enmity of his colleagues. Alaska Senator Ted Stevens took to the Senate floor, shouting, "This amendment is offensive to me. It's not only an offense to me, it's a threat to every person in my state."[81]

The greatest "earmarker" of all time may be the former chair of the Senate Appropriations Committee, Robert Byrd, beloved by his constituents for earmarks requiring numerous agencies to locate their operations in his home state of West Virginia. For example, he once slipped into an emergency bill a provision that shifted the 2,600-employee FBI fingerprinting center from downtown Washington to Clarksburg, West Virginia.[82] After the 9/11 attack in 2001, he tried to slip funding for an "aquaculture center"—that is, a swimming pool—into a homeland security bill, despite the apparent lack of relationship between swimming and security. When opposition developed, Byrd instead found room in the bill for $2 million to fund a virtual medical campus at West Virginia University, which, in the senator's words, "will link local doctors and emergency personnel . . . with specialists . . . in the event of a terrorist attack."[83]

earmark
A specific congressional designation of the way money is to be spent.

Legislative Oversight

In addition to earmarking, committees hold hearings to ensure that agencies are not straying from their congressional mandates. The increase in such oversight hearings in recent decades has expanded committee control over administrative practice. The number of days each year that committees hold oversight hearings nearly quadrupled between the 1960s and the 1990s.[84] Although the number of oversight hearings has fallen as a result of reforms instituted in 1995, they still far outnumber hearings called to consider specific legislation.[85]

At oversight hearings, members of the administration are often asked to testify about agency experiences and problems. Witnesses representing outside groups are given opportunities to praise or criticize the bureaucrats. Through the oversight process, committees obtain information that can be used to revise existing legislation or modify agency budgets, sometimes to the consternation of bureaucrats. Even when committees do not hold hearings, the threat of doing so is sometimes enough to cow agency officials into following congressional wishes.[86] According to one survey, nearly half of high-level agency officials complain of "a great deal" of congressional "micro-management" of their jobs.[87]

Iron Triangles and Issue Networks

Congress has such power over bureaucracies that many agencies seek to build coalitions of allies among congressional committees and interest groups in order to survive. These connections have become so intimate that some political scientists have said that most federal government programs are run by **iron triangles**.[88] Interest groups form the base of the triangle, because they have the membership and money that can influence the outcome of congressional elections, and agencies listen to interest-group demands to obtain committee backing (see Figure 14.7a).

The relationship is said to be an iron triangle because the connections among the threesome remain a lot more stable than in the proverbial love triangle. In the case of the iron triangle, each of the three parties can deliver something the other needs. Compromises are readily arranged because interests are similar. Most oversight hearings are, in fact, three-way love fests. Interest-group representatives offer gracious testimony about agency work, and members of Congress chime in with words of endearment. When a congressional scholar asked congressional-committee staff whether they considered their committee to be agency advocates, nearly two-thirds said "yes." In response to this question, one staff person replied,

> I think any subcommittee . . . whatever its subject is, they're advocates. I mean the Aging Subcommittee is advocating for aging programs, the Arts for arts, you know, Education for education, Health for health. They wouldn't be doing their work if they weren't interested.

Added another,

> The trouble of it is we get in bed with agency people in some respects. We're hoping that they'll distribute good projects in our state, you know, and it's a kind of a working with them so that, you know, there'll be more, more and better of everything for everybody.[89]

These relationships often transcend partisan divisions. With the Republican takeover in 1995, the House leadership initially placed tight restrictions on committees in order to weaken the committee–agency relationship. Infuriated at the loss of committee power,

---

iron triangle

Close, stable connection among agencies, interest groups, and congressional committees.

(a) An iron triangle that existed during the 1950s–1960s

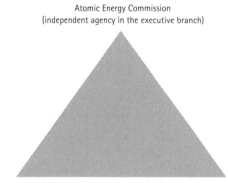

Atomic Energy Commission
(independent agency in the executive branch)

Joint Committee on Atomic Energy
(Congress)

"Big Four" of the nuclear-power industry
(General Electric, Westinghouse, Combustion Engineering, Babcock and Wilcox)

(b) A more modern issue network

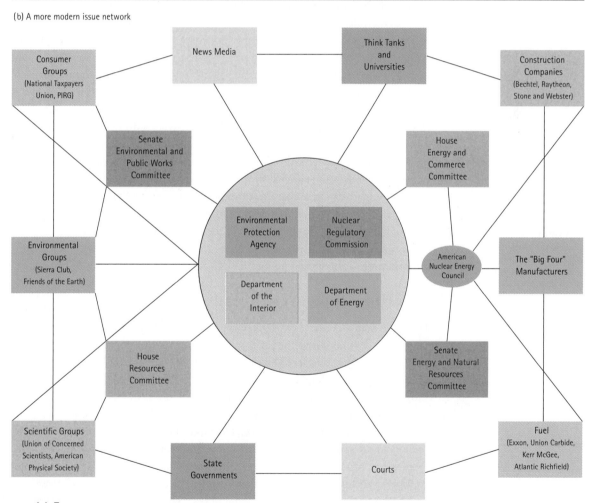

FIGURE 14.7
Change of Nuclear Energy Policy Arena from Iron Triangle to Issue Network
• *Why has the policy-making environment changed from a triangle to a web?*

Sources: Based on information in Seong-Ho Lim, "Changing Jurisdictional Boundaries in Congressional Oversight of Nuclear Energy Regulation: Impact of Public Salience," paper presented before the Annual Meeting of the American Political Science Association, 1992; and Frank R. Baumgartner and Bryan D. Jones, "Agency Dynamics and Policy Subsystems," *Journal of Politics* 53 (November 1991): 1044–1074.

Democrats on one committee complained that "the Republican leadership has decided that the considered judgment of expert committees no longer matters."[90] But within a year, the Republican leadership found it necessary to loosen its controls, and the natural tendency for committees to support "their" agencies reasserted itself. For example, in 1995 House Republican leaders proposed elimination of all funding for the Public Broadcasting Corporation. "We were read our last rites," said the corporation's president. But after Republican members of the key congressional subcommittee were besieged by letters and faxes from constituents, who feared the demise of *Sesame Street* and *Mister Rogers' Neighborhood*, they voted to keep the agency alive, though at a reduced level of funding.[91]

Some iron triangles are no longer as rigid as they once were. As the number of interest groups and policy experts has expanded, congressional committees and government agencies have been bombarded with competing demands from multiple sides, which together form issue networks (see Figure 14.7b).[92] For example, nuclear energy policy was, at one time, of interest mainly to just four companies that built nuclear reactors and to the utility companies that used the electricity. After an accident at the Three Mile Island reactor in Pennsylvania, however, the subject attracted the attention of environmental, safety, and antinuclear groups, all of whom pressed for tighter regulation of nuclear reactors. With the interests of the groups divided, the media took greater notice of the issue, and conflict between congressional committees and the Department of Energy intensified.[93] By 2006, when Congress considered President Bush's proposal to reinvest in nuclear energy, a wider variety of interest groups, companies, and even several U.S. states had become involved in the policy debate.[94] As this example illustrates, issue networks include more conflict, more players, and more publicity than iron triangles.

Many scholars argue that the concept of **issue networks** presents a more realistic picture of the way Washington works today than does the older concept of iron triangles. In past decades, the three points of the triangle provided a good image of the way many agencies, Congress, and interest groups did business, but increasingly, our current, more complicated politics looks less like a triangle and more like a web.

issue networks

Loose, competitive relationships among policy experts, interest groups, congressional committees, and government agencies.

Elections and the Bureaucracy

For more than a century, reformers have tried to separate politics from administration. Government should serve the people, they argue, not the special interests. Departments should make decisions according to laws and regulations, not in response to political pressure. Agencies should treat every applicant alike, not respond more favorably to those who contribute to political parties.

These reform principles are worthy of respect. When politics interferes, bureaucracies can be inefficient and ineffective. The Customs Service, its name once synonymous with political spoils, is still slow to report international economic transactions. The Department of Housing and Urban Development, always a political thicket, has at times so badly mismanaged its property that it has had to blow up buildings it constructed.[95]

Many of the more effective federal bureaucracies are less politically charged. The National Science Foundation, protected from political pressures by an independent board, is known for the integrity with which it allocates dollars among competing scientific projects. The Federal Bureau of Prisons does a better job than many state prisons of maintaining security without depriving prisoners of rights; it has succeeded in part because members of Congress, respectful of prison leadership, have left the agency alone.[96]

Even though agency autonomy has worked in some instances, electoral pressures have also played a positive role and in any case are an essential feature of modern bureaucracies.[97] Public pressure exerted through elections has affected the way bureaucracies keep secrets, enforce the law, manage their budgets, and make decisions. In the end, elections create pressures that force many agencies to balance competing interests by striking compromises.

Bureaucratic Secrecy

Bureaucracies like to protect their secrets. "Inside knowledge" is power. Secrecy can cover mistakes. In Europe, where administrators are less exposed to electoral pressure, they work hard to guard their private information. In Britain, it is a crime for civil servants to divulge official information, and political appointees swear themselves to secrecy upon taking office.

Electoral pressures have sharply curtailed the amount of secrecy in American government. In the view of one specialist, "secrecy has less legitimacy as a governmental practice in the United States than in any other advanced industrial society with the possible exception of Sweden," in large part because "Congress has done a great deal to open up the affairs of bureaucracy to greater outside scrutiny."[98] The **sunshine law**, passed in 1976, required that federal government meetings be held in public, unless military plans, trade secrets, or personnel questions are being discussed. Under the Freedom of Information Act of 1967, citizens have the right to inspect unprotected government documents. If the government believes the requested information needs to be kept secret, it must bear the burden of proof when arguing its case before a judge.

sunshine law
A 1976 law requiring that federal government meetings be held in public.

Even in the absence of new laws, the legislative and judicial branches can limit the degree to which executive agencies operate in secret. President Bush was furious when, in the aftermath of the terrorist attacks of 2001, members of Congress leaked classified information to the press.[99] And the president's executive order authorizing the trial of suspected terrorists by military tribunals was issued, in part, because of concern that secret intelligence information gathered by the FBI and CIA would be revealed during an ordinary trial. "We need to find some system of justice that allows us to punish guilty people without destroying our antiterrorism infrastructure around the world," said one law professor.[100]

Secrecy can sometimes be essential in pursuing national-security objectives. The Department of Homeland Security has often had to walk a delicate line between publicity, so as to keep the public adequately informed of threats, and secrecy, so as to more effectively detect or disrupt specific terrorist plotting. During the 2003 holiday season, Homeland Security secretary Tom Ridge publicly announced a heightened terrorism alert status, advising travelers and law-enforcement officials to be on the lookout for suspicious behavior. Meanwhile, radiation experts from the Department of Energy were secretly placed on duty in five major cities across the United States, as a contingency in case a radioactive device was detonated.[101]

Despite the acknowledged benefits of some kinds of secrecy, many elected officials feel public pressure to force executive agencies to disclose as much information as possible. One survey found that, by a 3 to 1 margin, Americans believe that "too many" government documents are classified.[102] Voters seem to believe that, as one observer put it, "In order for people to direct their own government, they must have information about governance and be able to examine the performance of elected leaders and bureaucrats."[103]

Bureaucratic Coercion

Bureaucracies are often accused of using their coercive powers harshly and unfairly. Police officers stop young drivers for traffic violations that are often ignored when committed by older drivers. Bureaucratic zealots trap sales clerks into selling cigarettes to heavily bearded 17-year-olds. Disabled people are refused benefits because they do not fill out their applications correctly.

Although such abuses occur, they happen less frequently because agencies are held accountable to the electorate. In 1998, for example, Republican senators sensed popular discontent with the Internal Revenue Service (IRS), the government's tax collection agency. The agency's approval rating was an embarrassingly low 38 percent.[104] The Senate Finance Committee held a series of hearings that brought to light a litany of agency failings. The IRS had lost $150 billion in 1995 because of mistakes, unreported income, or improper deductions. Taxpayers were overbilled an average of $5 billion per year.[105] The technology the agency used was so outdated that IRS commissioner Charles Rossotti himself admitted, "I have never seen a worse situation in a large organization."[106] And one rogue agent even tried to frame an ex-senator on money-laundering and bribery charges.[107] As a result of the hearings, Congress enacted a law restructuring the agency, making it harder for the IRS to accuse taxpayers of wrongdoing and bringing its tax collection systems up to date.[108] In the succeeding years, the IRS focused so much on customer service that some members of Congress ironically began to fear that the agency was not being tough enough in its enforcement actions.[109]

The example of the IRS illustrates a broader pattern in U.S. politics: if bureaucratic agencies make life difficult for the voting public, these agencies are more likely to be taken to task by elected officials.[110] Most agencies would prefer to avoid this painful scrutiny.

Agency Expansion

Agencies generally try to increase their budgets, but elections apply the brake to such tendencies, if only because politicians get blamed for raising taxes. "As a general rule," says analyst Martha Derthick, "Congress likes to keep bureaucracy lean and cheap."[111] The number of people working for the federal government, as a percentage of the workforce, has declined since the 1980s, in large part because elected officials are under public pressure to cut bureaucracy. The overall size of government grew during the George W. Bush administration for the first time in years, as agencies added half-a-million new anti-terrorism jobs.[112] But President Bush also worked to shrink the bureaucracy by forcing some bureaucrats to compete with private companies for their jobs. This "competitive sourcing" initiative rankled some federal employees, who staged a protest outside the White House and called upon their allies in Congress to defend them.[113] "The long-term [government] employee is feeling

Homeland Security Radiation Detection

This handheld cellular phone, of the sort used by the Department of Energy to secretly monitor threatened areas, combines a cellular phone, radiation sensors, and PDA and GPS interfaces to detect radiation and communicate the data quickly.

devalued," said an anonymous U.S. Park Service worker.[114] In one survey, 59 percent of federal workers said their agencies only "sometimes" or "rarely" have "enough employees to do their jobs well."[115]

Administrator Caution

Federal agencies are sometimes accused of going beyond their legislative mandates. But most federal agencies are more likely to err on the side of caution. The worst thing any agency can do is make a major mistake that captures national attention. As one official explained, "The public servant soon learns that successes rarely rate a headline, but government blunders are front-page news. This recognition encourages the development of procedures designed less to achieve successes than to avoid blunders."[116]

In 1962 it was discovered, to widespread horror, that thalidomide, a sedative available in Europe, increased the probability that babies would be born with serious physical deformities. Congress immediately passed a law toughening the procedures the Food and Drug Administration (FDA) was to follow before approving prescription drugs for distribution.[117] Decades later, in keeping with this policy, the FDA refused to approve the sale of several experimental drugs to terminally ill people suffering from AIDS. Patients desperate to try anything that might help them did not share the FDA's concern for ascertaining proven effectiveness. When the FDA's refusal to allow experimentation became a public issue, the agency began to allow AIDS patients to try the untested drugs, once again responding to pressure from the voting public.

You Are the President of MEDICORP

Compromised Capacity

Agency effectiveness is often undermined by the very terms of the legislation that created it. For legislation to pass Congress, a broad coalition of support is necessary. To build this support, proponents must strike deals with those who are at best lukewarm to the idea. Such compromise can cripple a program at birth.[118]

The politics of charter schools illustrates the restraint that compromises can place on organizational effectiveness. In the 1990s, school reform advocates began to establish charter schools—new schools free of most state regulations. Reformers expect charter schools to provide alternatives to, and competition for, traditional public schools. School boards and teacher organizations oppose the establishment of these schools, claiming they will attract students away from their local schools. Many state legislatures, under pressure from both sides, have compromised on the issue by passing legislation allowing charter schools but restricting their number, funding, and autonomy. Evidence on the effects of charter schools on student education has been mixed so far, and it remains to be seen whether charter schools can prosper within the constraints imposed by these legislative compromises.[119]

Muddling Through

American bureaucracies do not perform as badly as most Americans think. One survey examines the actual experiences of clients encountering government bureaucracies and then compares their reactions to these experiences with the impressions that these same people have of government bureaucracies in general. The differences between actual experiences and general impressions are striking:

> Seventy-one percent of all the clients said that their [own] problems were taken care of, but only 30 percent think that government agencies [generally] do well at taking care of problems. Eighty percent said that they were treated fairly, but only 42 percent think that government agencies treat most people fairly.
>
> In other words, most Americans . . . decide that their [good] experiences represent an exception to the rule. People who have had bad experiences, however, are likely . . . to think that everyone else is getting unfair treatment too.[120]

The advent of the Internet has provided an opportunity for bureaucracies to communicate even more effectively with citizens. According to one study, more than two-thirds of visitors to government Web sites found them to be useful and easy to navigate.[121]

When all the pluses and minuses are added up, the average government bureaucracy probably deserves something like a B-minus grade. A few agencies, such as NASA during the race to the moon, merited an A-plus, although its reputation has since slipped. A few others, such as the U.S. Customs and Border Protection Service, don't deserve a passing grade. But the general tendency is toward a bland, risk-free mediocrity. Too much imagination generates too much controversy, which invites political retribution. One bureaucrat offered the following guidelines for his colleagues: "1) When in charge, ponder; 2) When in trouble, delegate; 3) When in doubt, mumble."[122] The best way to survive politically is to try to muddle through, making only gradual changes in policy and striving to satisfy everyone.[123]

The Forest Service, which is responsible for managing most of the millions of acres owned by the federal government, does a pretty good job of muddling through. Although its rangers are professionally trained, talented individuals, its political problems are vexing. Ranchers, miners, and timber companies want to exploit the land's natural resources. Others want to use the land for hiking, camping, and fishing. Environmentalists want to convert as much of the land as they can into wilderness areas for the benefit of future generations.

To balance these pressures, the Forest Service came up with the doctrine of multiple use. It proposed to manage the land in such a way that its multiple uses could be blended together and harmonized. Timber harvests should be accompanied by reforestation. Especially scenic areas should be preserved for recreational activities. Mining should be as inconspicuous as possible.

But the doctrine of multiple use did not so much resolve conflicts as institutionalize them. As a result, the Forest Service is under constant pressure. Ranching, timber, and mining interests have clout at the local level, where local political leaders make the potent claim that the local economy will suffer unless these interests are protected. Environmentalists, however, have the greatest influence on those chosen in elections affected by the national media, which dramatically depict the desecration of the American landscape.

Any attempt to balance these interests antagonizes one or more sides of the dispute. Only by muddling through can the Forest Service survive politically and manage the federal lands as well as it does.[124]

Chapter Summary

Government bureaucracies are essential, and bureaucratic problems are inevitable. But American bureaucracies have specific troubles that can be attributed to the electoral climate in which they have evolved. With the creation of the spoils system, bureaucrats were often regarded as slow, inefficient, corrupt political hacks. Gradually, civil-service reforms eliminated the worst of the abuses. But the reforms occurred in a bottom-up, not top-down fashion. The highest levels of government continue to be filled with political appointees—generally capable but not always experienced government administrators.

As chief executive, the president is nominally in charge of the bureaucracy, appointing key officials and exerting control through the Office of Management and Budget. But

Congress also influences federal agencies via its confirmation of presidential nominees, detailed legislative enactments, the budget process, and legislative oversight. To survive, agencies build ties to key interest groups, who form the base of what are known as iron triangles. Today, some of these iron triangles are being transformed into more complex, unstable, and conflictual issue networks.

Elections influence agencies in diverse ways. On the one hand, they keep agencies from becoming too secretive and coercive. On the other hand, they can also make agencies too cautious or force them to operate under compromise-crafted laws that undermine their effectiveness. Most of the time, agencies respond to politics by muddling through, for which they deserve more credit than they usually get.

Key Terms

administrative discretion, p. 392

agency, p. 391

bureaucracy, p. 391

civil service, p. 399

Congressional Budget Office (CBO), p. 407

department, p. 391

earmark, p. 411

end run, p. 406

government corporation, p. 391

Hatch Act, p. 400

in-and-outers, p. 401

independent regulatory agencies, p. 405

inner cabinet, p. 403

iron triangle, p. 412

issue networks, p. 414

mugwumps, p. 399

Office of Management and Budget (OMB), p. 406

outer cabinet, p. 403

patronage, p. 396

Pendleton Act, p. 399

recess appointment, p. 408

senatorial courtesy, p. 407

spoils system, p. 396

sunshine law, p. 415

Suggested Readings

Of General Interest

Aberbach, Joel D., and Bert A. Rockman. *In the Web of Politics: Three Decades of the U.S. Federal Executive*. Washington, DC: The Brookings Institution, 2000. Traces controversies over the federal bureaucracy since the 1970s, including recent attempts to "reinvent" government.

Heclo, Hugh. "Issue Networks and the Executive Establishment." In *The New American Political System*, ed. Anthony King. Washington, DC: American Enterprise Institute, 1978. Describes the shift from iron triangles to issue networks.

Kettl, Donald F. *The Transformation of Governance: Public Administration for Twenty-First Century America*. Baltimore, MD: Johns Hopkins University Press, 2002. Discussion of the challenges facing modern bureaucracies.

Light, Paul. *Thickening Government: Federal Hierarchy and the Diffusion of Accountability*. Washington, DC: The Brookings Institution, 1995. Identifies and explains the growth in higher-level governmental positions.

Morone, James A. *The Democratic Wish: Popular Participation and the Limits of American Government*. New York: Basic Books, 1990. Account of the ways in which democratic movements have shaped the development of public administration in U.S. history.

Niskanen, William A. *Bureaucracy and Representative Government*. Chicago: Aldine-Atherton, 1971. Develops the argument that government bureaucracies seek to maximize their budgets.

Wilson, James Q. *Bureaucracy: What Government Agencies Do and Why They Do It*. New York: Basic Books, 1989. Comprehensive treatment of public bureaucracies.

Focused Studies

Chubb, John, and Terry Moe. *Politics, Markets and America's Schools*. Washington, DC: The Brookings Institution, 1990. Brilliant, controversial account of the way in which politics interferes with effective management of public schools.

Kaufman, Herbert. *The Forest Ranger*. Baltimore, MD: Johns Hopkins University Press, 1981. Classic study of a government agency.

Stanton, Thomas H. and Benjamin Ginsberg. *Making Government Manageable: Executive Organization and Management in the Twenty-First Century*. Baltimore, MD: Johns Hopkins University Press, 2004. A series of scholarly essays on various aspects of executive branch organization.

Young, James. *The Washington Community 1800–1828*. New York: Harcourt, 1966. Engaging, insightful account of political and administrative life in Washington during the first decades of the nineteenth century.

On the Web

www.firstgov.gov

Most U.S. government agencies and departments have informative Web sites that can be reached through the federal government's central site, FirstGov.

www.whitehouse.gov/omb

The Office of Management and Budget, the president's main resource in controlling and organizing the federal bureaucracy, offers Web-accessible copies of budget documentation, testimony before Congress, and regulatory information.

www.opm.gov

The Office of Personnel Management calls itself "the federal government's human resources agency." It organizes the federal civil-service system, and its Web site provides information on federal pay scales, worker performance, and job opportunities.

www.gsa.gov

The General Services Administration sets acquisitions and management policies for much of the federal bureaucracy.

www.cbo.gov

The Congressional Budget Office, created in 1974 as Congress's counterpart to the Office of Management and Budget, produces reports on the economy, the budget, and the impact of current proposed legislation.

www.gao.gov

The General Accounting Office is the investigative arm of Congress and assists Congress in its oversight of the executive branch. It produces reports that evaluate the effectiveness of various federal agencies.

www.gpo.gov

The Government Printing Office provides the text of the Federal Register, where all new and proposed regulations are published.

Election Voices

The Politics of the New Department of Homeland Security

THE ISSUE

Is government reorganization an effective way to tackle policy problems? Or do bureaucratic battles, congressional turf wars, and other disruptions make such efforts more trouble than they are worth?

Background

After the 9/11 tragedy, President George W. Bush created the office of White House homeland security adviser, and appointed former Pennsylvania governor Tom Ridge to the position. But Ridge had difficulty building a coordinated system to combat potential terrorist attacks because he was only a member of the president's staff and did not run any department of the government.

After nine months of struggling to manage a coordinated homeland security effort from the White House, Bush and Ridge concluded that a new cabinet department had to be created (see the section "Organizing for Homeland Security" in Chapter 14). The administration realized that creating the department would be a challenge. The last time the United States had undergone significant national security reorganization was in the late 1940s, after what President Truman called a "long hard battle" that lasted at least four years.[1]

Some present-day political scientists believe that in the United States, this kind of major governmental change is prohibitively difficult. Entrenched bureaucracies, allied with interest groups and key congressional committee members, have made it all but impossible to enact beneficial changes.[2]

The battle over creating a new department of homeland security in 2002 provides proof that major change in the structure of government can occur, at least under certain circumstances. But policy experts are still debating whether the reorganization has changed the government for the better.

A Secret Process, a Realistic Approach

Drawing a lesson from previous aborted attempts at reform, in late April 2002 Bush directed four trusted aides to begin work on a proposal for a new department. Meeting secretly in an underground White House office, these four officials—Ridge, Chief of Staff Andrew Card, Office of Management and Budget Director Mitchell Daniels, and White House Counsel Alberto Gonzales—worked for six weeks to draft a plan. No one in Congress knew about the pending administration proposal and even Bush's cabinet was in the dark.[3]

As a result of this secrecy, instead of being nibbled to death by agency and interest-group complaints, Bush's proposal garnered immediate acclaim. Those in Congress who had been drafting less ambitious legislation to streamline homeland security agencies swiftly embraced the Bush plan. "All of us agree the president's plan is better than what we have been working on," said one House member.[4]

Bush and his aides also chose a modest and realistic path to reorganization. This may seem an odd statement, considering the fact that the Bush plan led to the creation of a huge new agency, with 169,000 employees and a budget of $37.5 billion (see Figure 1). But Bush's team selected the agencies to incorporate into the department very carefully. Those that were easier to shift became part of the final proposal; others were left alone.

The administration chose to place in the new department the Federal Emergency Management Agency (FEMA), the

White House Homeland Security Secretary Michael Chertoff with President Bush

421

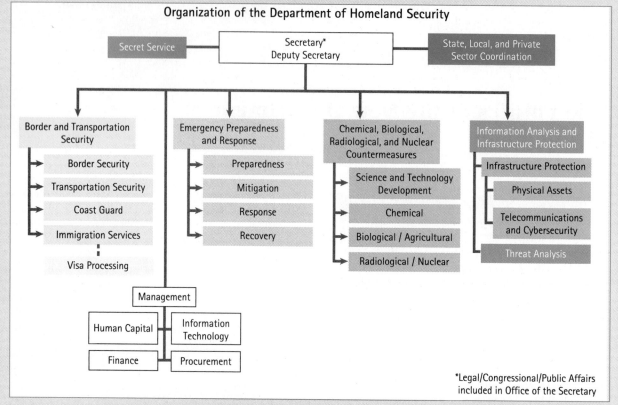

Organization of the Department of Homeland Security

Secret Service

Secretary*
Deputy Secretary

State, Local, and Private
Sector Coordination

Border and Transportation Security
- Border Security
- Transportation Security
- Coast Guard
- Immigration Services
  - Visa Processing

Emergency Preparedness and Response
- Preparedness
- Mitigation
- Response
- Recovery

Chemical, Biological, Radiological, and Nuclear Countermeasures
- Science and Technology Development
- Chemical
- Biological / Agricultural
- Radiological / Nuclear

Information Analysis and Infrastructure Protection
- Infrastructure Protection
  - Physical Assets
  - Telecommunications and Cybersecurity
- Threat Analysis

Management
- Human Capital
- Information Technology
- Finance
- Procurement

*Legal/Congressional/Public Affairs
included in Office of the Secretary

FIGURE 1

The Department of Homeland Security This organizational chart depicts the Department of Homeland Security, as originally proposed by President Bush.

• *Why isn't the FBI part of the new department?*

Coast Guard, and the Transportation Security Administration—in part because these bureaucracies had less clout. FEMA, an independent entity, had only 2,500 employees, many of whom were assigned to the agency's 10 regional offices, far from Washington power centers. The Coast Guard was bigger, with 35,000 active duty personnel, but it had been moved among cabinet departments before. The Transportation Security Administration, although large, was brand new—it had been created in November 2001 to restructure airport security systems—and it had had little time to sink deep roots within the Department of Transportation.

Contrast these agencies with one other organization that many critics thought should have been included in the Bush proposal but was not: the Federal Bureau of Investigation (FBI). With a workforce of 27,000, a distinctive agency culture, and a history in the Justice Department that stretches back to 1908, the FBI would have been hard to change. According to one aide, if they were threatened Bureau officials would "throw a major fit and their friends in Congress would run us out of town for even proposing it."[5] Accordingly, despite its key role in investigating terrorists in the United States, the Bush team decided that "the organizational integrity of the FBI needs to be maintained."[6]

Obstacles to the Administration Plan

Once the plan was announced, the entrenched congressional committee system, as well as the power of public employee unions, threatened to derail the proposal. The prospect of a brand new department raised the possibility that Congress would have to restructure its oversight committees—and the Bush administration urged legislators to do just that.[7] But existing committees resisted any organizational changes that would take power away from them (see the section "The Committee System" in Chapter 12). "Hell hath no fury like a committee chairman whose jurisdiction has been taken away," warned Republican senator Robert Bennett.[8]

To avoid facing such fury, the new department's proponents postponed questions of committee jurisdiction until after Congress passed legislation creating the new department. The Senate chose to debate the Bush proposal on the chamber floor rather than letting committees get their hooks into the plan, and House leaders created a temporary special committee, composed of House leaders, to consider the matter.

After the creation of the new department, the House gave jurisdiction over most homeland security matters to a select committee on homeland security, while the Senate chose to divide jurisdiction among existing committees. Still, in 2004 the report of the special commission appointed to investigate 9/11 called the congressional committee system "dysfunctional" and recommended major changes.[9]

The White House plan included a seemingly obscure provision that would allow the department to bypass ordinary civil service rules and use a merit-based management and promotion system. Homeland Security Adviser Tom Ridge argued that this policy was necessary to create a "motivated, high-performance, and accountable workforce."[10] But many of the 169,000 government workers who stood to be transferred into the new agency disagreed, and their allies in Congress protested. "We all want this process to succeed," said Democratic representative Martin Frost of Texas, "But we should not begin the process by asking federal workers to be treated less well than they are now."[11]

The conflict over civil service rules turned out to be the most difficult and partisan controversy in the debate over a new department. But Republicans won the day, and the final bill contained relaxed civil service provisions that largely mirrored those in the president's initial proposal.

The Department of Homeland Security and Elections

The successful plan for the new department received a critical boost from the high public regard for the proposal's sponsor. At the time, President Bush was enjoying a nearly unprecedented period of lofty approval ratings that outlasted the initial so-called "rally 'round the flag" boost after September 11. But over the next few years, critics charged that the new department had little to show for itself, and public opinion began to become more negative. Complaints about the agency's color-coded terror warning system prompted an internal review.[12] The department's isolation from the FBI and other intelligence agencies led one former homeland security official to admit that DHS had too often "been on the outside of the intelligence community with its nose pressed against the glass."[13] Worst of all, after the disastrous intergovernmental response to Hurricane Katrina in 2005, many experts argued that FEMA should never have been absorbed into a department that was primarily concerned with terrorist threats. "As long as you require the FEMA director to go through two and three layers of bureaucracy to get a decision from the president, you're going to have a major problem," argued one former FEMA director.[14] By 2006, as Figure 2 shows, most Americans thought the homeland security system needed major changes.

Opposing Viewpoints on the Department of Homeland Security

The homeland security bill passed Congress after the 2002 elections, and the new Department of Homeland Security (DHS) began operations shortly thereafter.

The Optimists

Optimists argue that the case of the Homeland Security Department shows that government can adapt to changing

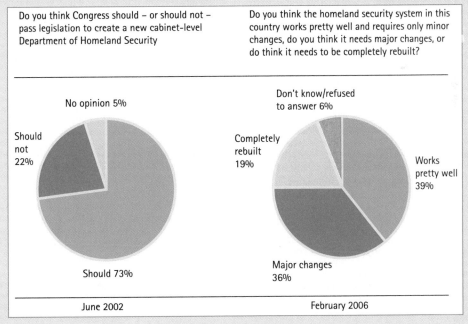

FIGURE 2

Americans Supported the Bush Plan, but Later Had Doubts

• *Did voters' opinions about the effectiveness of the Department of Homeland Security affect the 2006 congressional elections, in your view?*

Source: Gallup Poll, June 21–23, 2002; Pew Research Center survey, February 1–5, 2006.

circumstances and, in so doing, act in the public interest. Problems exist, but they are the growing pains of a new organization, not fundamental weaknesses:

> There are people who quibble and quarrel because we've now merged together and we're integrating the intelligence community, because there's always the cultural resistance. Understandably, each agency is proud of its heritage, and we don't want to obliterate that legacy. But . . . it is always better to be integrated and joint than to be separated.
>
> —Michael Chertoff, Secretary of Homeland Security, Remarks at the National Newspaper Association's Annual Government Affairs Conference, Washington, D.C., March 9, 2006

The Pessimists

Others argue that the new department represents more of the same: Bureaucratic squabbling limited the department's initial scope, the agency was slow to improve communications with state and local governments, and has even had trouble coordinating its message on terrorism with that of other departments and agencies.[15]

> Far from being greater than the sum of its parts, DHS is a bureaucratic Frankenstein, with clumsily stitched-together limbs and an inadequate, misfiring brain . . . . [E]ven allowing for inevitable transition problems, DHS has been a disaster: underfunded, undermanned, disorganized, and unforgivably slow-moving.
>
> —Michael Crowley, "Playing Defense," The New Republic, March 15, 2004

What Do Americans Believe?

As Figure 2 shows, Americans supported President Bush's plan to create the Department of Homeland Security, but had doubts about its performance years later. These doubts seem closely related to the department's botched response to Hurricane Katrina. When asked in 2006 whether Katrina was an "important reason" that their opinion of the Bush administration had worsened, 80 percent of voters said "yes."[16]

What Do You Think?

1. Was the creation of the new Homeland Security Department a substantive change or just a superficial one?
2. Does this case study show that the politics of elections do not interfere with effective government? Or does it illustrate the reverse?

Web Sites on the Homeland Security Department

www.dhs.gov

www.ready.gov

The Department of Homeland Security operates an official Web site with information about the department's current programs and activities, as well as Ready.gov, a practical Web guide that informs citizens about how to prepare for possible terrorist attacks.

http://hsc.house.gov/

http://hsgac.senate.gov/

The House of Representatives created a new committee to handle most homeland security matters, while the Senate divided oversight responsibilities among existing committees. These two links lead to the House Select Committee on Homeland Security and to the Senate Homeland Security and Government Affairs Committee, respectively, the latter of which has jurisdiction over many—but by no means all—homeland security programs.

[1]Harry Truman, *Memoirs, Vol. 2: Years of Trial and Hope* (Garden City, NY: Doubleday, 1956), 51.

[2]See, for example, Theodore Lowi, *The End of Liberalism: Ideology, Policy and the Crisis of Public Authority* (New York: Norton, 1969); Mancur Olson, *The Rise and Decline of Nations: Economic Growth, Stagflation, and Social Rigidities* (New Haven: Yale University Press, 1982); Jonathan Rauch, *Demosclerosis: The Silent Killer of American Government* (New York: Times Books, 1994); and Haynes Johnson and David Broder, *The System: The American Way of Politics at the Breaking Point* (Boston: Little, Brown, 1996).

[3]Ibid.

[4]William M. Thornberry (R-TX), quoted in Adriel Bettelheim and Jim Barshay, "White House Proposal for Security Department Goes Beyond Lawmakers' Request; Bush's Swift Sweeping Plan Is Battle Order for Congress," *CQWeekly*, June 8, 2002, 1498.

[5]Michael Kramer, "No Place Like Homeland for FBI, CIA," *New York Daily News*, June 14, 2002: 26.

[6]Bill Miller and Mike Allen, "Homeland Security Dept. Could Receive Raw FBI, CIA Data; Bush Still Opposes Merging FBI," *Washington Post*, June 19, 2002: A8.

[7]Bettelheim and Barshay.

[8]Ibid.

[9]*Final Report of the National Commission on Terrorist Attacks Upon the United States* (New York: W. W. Norton, 2004), 420.

[10]Nick Anderson and Richard Simon, "Democrats Attack Item in Bush's Security Plan," *Los Angeles Times*, June 21, 2002: A26.

[11]David Firestone, "In Party-Line Vote, House Panel Approves Security Department," *New York Times*, July 20, 2002: A8.

[12]Jennifer A. Dlouhy, "U.S. Terror Alert System to Be Revamped," *Houston Chronicle*, May 15, 2005: A18.

[13]Clark Kent Ervin, "Homeland Security's Intelligence Gap," *New York Times*, July 17, 2005: Section 4, 12.

[14]Seth Borenstein, "Disaster Response Fixes Pushed; Homeland Security Chief Set to Face Critics," *Pittsburgh Post-Gazette*, February 14, 2006: A8.

[15]Thomas Frank, "Terror Warnings not Coordinated," *Newsday*, May 28, 2004, A4.

[16]Newsweek/Princeton Survey Research Associates poll, May 11–12, 2006.

CHAPTER 15

★ ★ ★ ★ ★ ★ ★ ★ ★ ★ ★

The Courts

CHAPTER OUTLINE

Judge John Roberts

The Battle That Wasn't:
John Roberts' Appointment to the Supreme Court

"The Supreme Court of the United States is at stake in this race, ladies and gentlemen."[1] Whatever their political convictions, activists agreed with this statement by presidential candidate John Kerry in 2004. By the following June, the nation had gone for more than a decade without a Supreme Court retirement. Because of the Court's role in deciding controversial issues such as affirmative action, gay marriage, and abortion, activist groups on the left and the right saw the Court as critically important. As summer began in the nation's capital, these groups sensed that they would not have to wait much longer for a new nomination.

Indeed, when Justice Sandra Day O'Connor, the first woman to serve on the Court, sent a letter of resignation to the president on the first of July in 2005, two sets of groups sprang into action. Those affiliated with the Democratic Party, fearing that the president would name a conservative nominee, readied television advertisements, grassroots letter-writing efforts, and lobbying campaigns to oppose the new nominee. The National Abortion and Reproductive Rights Action League e-mailed a network of 800,000 activists within 15 minutes of hearing about O'Connor's retirement.[2] A conservative organization, Progress for America, announced within hours that it would spend $18 million to counter the efforts of liberals.[3] It looked like the fight over the next justice would be vicious and partisan. As one former Justice Department official put it, the nomination process could be the most "bitter and depressing" in history.[4]

But that was before anyone knew who the nominee would be. On July 19, President Bush nominated Appeals Court judge John G. Roberts for the position. Amiable and well-spoken, Roberts accepted the honor in the White House as his tow-headed four-year-old son, clad in a suit and short pants, danced near the podium, seemingly oblivious to the momentous event.

While Roberts was certainly on the conservative side of the spectrum (he had worked in the Reagan and George H. W. Bush administrations), he seemed squarely in the mainstream to most Americans, and not just because of his charming family. His court **opinions** were mild and measured, and his professional record—

John Roberts Accepts President Bush's Nomination as Son Jack Dances

among other things, he had argued no less than 339 cases before the Supreme Court—gave his opponents little ammunition.

When Chief Justice William Rehnquist succumbed to cancer in early fall, Bush proposed to have Roberts replace him at the head of the Court. Even though the change raised the significance of the Roberts appointment to the highest level, few questioned his qualifications. In Senate hearings he projected encyclopedic competence without revealing his opinions on the most controversial issues. Democrats at times seemed frustrated by his refusal to let senators pin him down to specific positions on hot-button issues. Senator Charles Schumer likened his reticence to a confusing discussion of movies:

> It's as if I asked you, "What kind of movies do you like? Tell me two or three good movies." And you say, "I like movies with good acting. I like movies with good directing. I like movies with good cinematography." And I ask you, "No, give me an example of a good movie." You don't name one . . . . Then I ask you if you like *Casablanca*, and you respond by saying, "Lots of people like *Casablanca*." You tell me it's widely settled that *Casablanca* is one of the great movies.[5]

Frustrations aside, Roberts' impressive performance in the hearings and his sterling professional record took the wind out of liberal activists' sails. Pollsters found that solid majorities of the public favored Roberts' confirmation.[6] Bush's opponents all but conceded defeat. Even Patrick Leahy, the senior Democrat on the Senate Judiciary Committee, announced that he would support the nominee. "Justice Roberts," said Leahy, "is a man of integrity."[7] The Senate confirmed Roberts by a vote of 78 to 22.

The Roberts nomination succeeded precisely because the president picked a candidate that Americans could support. Roberts' experience, his calm expertise on judicial matters, and even his photogenic smile won the backing of voters. In the absence of controversial statements or a record of incompetence, activists on the left found few senators willing and ready to fight a losing battle. "I think history will say that George W. Bush knocked it out of the park when he selected John Roberts to be chief justice of the United States," said Republican senator Lindsey Graham.[8]

MAKING THE CONNECTION

In recent years, the courts have been increasingly influenced by electoral politics, even though the founders meant the courts to be more isolated from public pressures than other institutions. This chapter describes the U.S. judicial system, which is headed by the Supreme Court and also includes other federal and state courts. Later in this chapter we look in more detail at the way in which the justices of the Supreme Court are selected and how they make their decisions, once appointed and confirmed. But first we shall place the Supreme Court in a larger context that discusses the role courts play in affecting public policy.

State Courts

The first American courts were state courts. Under the Articles of Confederation, there was no national judiciary, and virtually all disputes were handled by the various state legal systems. The Constitution created a national judicial branch, but most legal cases continued to be handled in the states, a practice that remains true today. The vast majority of judicial activity takes place within state trial courts under the control of state and local governments. In fact, 99 percent of all legal cases in the U.S. originate in these courts.[9]

opinion
In legal parlance, a court's written explanation of its decision.

Every state has its own way of organizing its court system, but in most the basic structure has three tiers: trial courts, courts of appeals, and a court of last resort, usually called the state supreme court. Parties to a case may appeal from a trial court to a higher court if they believe the trial court has made an error in judgment. Decisions of state supreme courts may be appealed to the federal Supreme Court if the case involves a federal statute or the interpretation of the federal Constitution. For example, the famous *Bush v. Gore* case was first decided in favor of Bush in a state trial court, then decided in favor of Gore by the state supreme court (after bypassing the state court of appeals), and finally decided in favor of Bush by the U.S. Supreme Court. But in very few instances does a case travel all this distance through the legal system.

State Trial Courts: The Judicial Workhorses

Most cases are decided at the very first tier, the trial court, where, as the name suggests, all trials in the state courts are held. In trials, there are two sides: the **plaintiff**, the person bringing the suit, and the **defendant**, the person against whom the complaint is made.

plaintiff
One who brings legal charges against another.

defendant
One accused of violating the civil or criminal code.

TABLE 15.1

DIFFERENCES BETWEEN CIVIL AND CRIMINAL TRIALS

• *Why can a defendant be forced to testify in a civil case, but not in a criminal case?*

	Criminal Trial	Civil Trial
Plaintiff	The government	Private person or group
At issue	Duty of citizens to obey the law	Legal rights and obligations of citizens to one another
Type of wrongdoing	Transgression against society	Harm to private person or group
Remedy	Punishment (fine, imprisonment, etc.)	Compensation for damages
Standard of proof	Beyond a reasonable doubt	Preponderance of the evidence
Can defendant be forced to testify?	No	Yes

civil code

Laws regulating relations among individuals. Alleged violators are sued by presumed victims, who ask courts to award damages and otherwise offer relief.

Trials settle alleged violations of the civil and criminal codes. The **civil code** regulates the legal rights and obligations of citizens with regard to one another. Alleged violations of the civil code are stated by individuals, who ask the court to award damages and otherwise offer relief for injuries they claim to have suffered. For example, if your landlord violates your lease by failing to heat your apartment, you can act as plaintiff and sue, asking for monetary damages and a guarantee that this will not happen in the future. People cannot be imprisoned for violating the civil code (although they can be jailed if they ignore a court order issued in conjunction with a civil suit).

Violations of the **criminal code**, offenses against society as a whole, are enforced by the government itself, which acts as plaintiff and initiates charges against suspects. If convicted, the criminal owes a debt to society, not just to the injured party. The debt may be paid by fine, imprisonment, or (in the case of capital crimes) execution. Table 15.1 summarizes the differences between civil and criminal cases.

criminal code

Laws regulating relations between individuals and society. Alleged violators are prosecuted by government.

The same action can simultaneously be a violation of both the criminal and the civil code. After a jury found former football star O. J. Simpson not guilty of criminal charges in conjunction with the murder of his ex-wife, Nicole Brown Simpson, her relatives filed civil charges, alleging that the family should be compensated for pain and suffering caused by her wrongful death. The plaintiffs were able to secure a guilty verdict in the civil suit and a monetary award, despite the finding of not guilty in the criminal prosecution, because in civil suits the accused can be forced to testify and the standards of proof are less stringent.

State courts are in a position to be significantly influenced by politics because of the way judges are selected. In 39 of the 50 states, at least some judges are chosen by elections. In the remaining states, judges are appointed by the state legislature, the governor, or a governmental agency. Exactly which judges are elected varies from state to state. In New York, trial court judges are elected but appellate judges are appointed.[10] In Georgia the process is the reverse.[11] In Texas, municipal judges are appointed by city governments, but all other judges are elected in partisan races.[12] Studies show that, at least on a few issues, elected state judges are more likely to

VIDEO DEBATE

Popular Election of Judges

follow closely the opinions of their constituents.[13] Although many state judges are subject to election, most judicial campaigns "are sedate and cordial," and voter turnout is low.[14]

As a result, in many cases judges attain office by appointment when another judge retires, and routinely win uncontested elections thereafter.[15] Political parties and elected officials can use these appointments to reward their allies. "It's a huge patronage scam," complains one observer.[16] A Florida lawyer puts it more colorfully: "Any idiot who's practiced [law] for five years can become a judge and, believe me, we've had some idiots."[17] Despite such complaints, party politics does not seem to have significant effects on judicial decisions; most studies find few differences between the decisions of Democratic and Republican state judges.[18]

Interest groups have also had a growing influence on judicial elections, especially as the cost of running campaigns for judgeships has increased. In Illinois in 2004, for example, the two candidates for a state supreme court seat raised and spent a total of $9.3 million.[19] Much of the money to fund judicial races is donated by single-issue groups—pro- or anti-abortion groups, for example—that may be especially concerned about the way certain cases are decided. According to one observer, "The involvement of such groups has . . . intensified the battles . . . and the viciousness of judicial campaigns has clearly increased."[20]

Prosecuting State Cases

After they receive information from the police about criminal wrongdoing, prosecutors in the office of the local **district attorney** determine whether the evidence is strong enough to justify asking a grand jury (usually consisting of about two dozen citizens) to indict, or bring charges against, the suspect. Because accused people cannot defend themselves before a grand jury, the prosecutor's advice usually determines the outcome. As one skeptic observed, "Under the right prosecutor, a grand jury would indict a ham sandwich."[21] After the indictment, government prosecutors may find it more difficult to convince the trial jury to convict the defendant, however.

In large cities the district attorney has enormous responsibilities. In Los Angeles, for example, the district attorney's office prosecutes close to 300,000 cases a year.[22] Because they are responsible for the prosecution of all criminal cases, some of which have high visibility in local news media, many prosecutors earn recognition that wins them election or appointment to the judiciary. About one-third of state supreme court judges were once prosecutors.[23] Many local district attorneys are interested in moving to other elected offices as well.

In 2000 Paul Howard, a Georgia district attorney, was up for reelection. He pressed for the arrest and trial of Baltimore Ravens football star Ray Lewis for two murders outside a suburban Atlanta bar. But prosecutors could find no evidence linking Lewis to the crime, and Lewis's attorney criticized them for "indicting before investigating."[24] After prosecutors dropped the charges and released Lewis, some observers blamed the botched investigation on the district attorney's desire for notoriety. "Because Howard tried to ride to fame on the back of Ray Lewis," one critic wrote, "he has damaged—not enhanced—his chances for reelection."[25]

district attorney
Person responsible for prosecuting criminal cases.

Case Overload

An Independent and Powerful Federal Judiciary

As the case of the John Roberts nomination to the Supreme Court shows, interest groups and politicians place great weight on each new appointee to the nation's highest court. They do this because of two fundamental characteristics of the federal judiciary: its independence from other political institutions, and its singular and long-established power to say what the Constitution means. The federal courts are independent from Congress and the presidency because of constitutional guarantees of life tenure and stable salaries. This independence does not set the courts apart from politics, however. On the contrary, the power to interpret the Constitution and laws passed by Congress has placed the judicial branch at the center of key political controversies throughout the country's history.

Tenure and Salary

CONSTITUTION, ARTICLE III: *"The Judges . . . shall hold their Offices during good behaviour and shall . . . receive for their Services a Compensation, which shall not be diminished during their Continuance in Office."*

The original advocates of the Constitution believed the appointment of federal judges for life tenure (or "good behaviour") was essential to the system of separation of powers. As Alexander Hamilton expressed it, life tenure was an "excellent barrier to the encroachments and oppressions of the representative body."[26] The only way Congress may remove federal judges is through the impeachment process (see Chapter 13). Standards for impeachment are so high, however, that only 13 federal judges have been impeached in U.S. history, and of these, only seven were removed from office.[27] The offenses in which these seven judges were found to have engaged included accepting bribes, committing perjury, and, in one case, applying for a job as a Confederate judge during the Civil War.[28] If judges avoid such extreme behavior, they are virtually assured their positions for as long as they wish to hold them.

The Constitution further protects judicial independence through its provision that fixes judicial salaries. Although Congress is permitted to increase the salaries of judges, it may not lower them for any judge, once that judge has taken office. Some legal scholars have argued that Congress has been less than diligent in raising judges' salaries to keep pace with inflation as well as with private sector salaries, and that the quality of the judiciary has suffered as a result. Chief Justice William Rehnquist even went so far as to argue that "Inadequate compensation seriously compromises the judicial independence fostered by life tenure."[29] Others point out, however, that, although pay is lower for judges than for many lawyers, the shorter work hours and job security are adequate to lure well-qualified people to the bench.[30]

Judicial Review

CONSTITUTION, ARTICLE VI: *"This Constitution, and the Laws of the United States which shall be made in Pursuance thereof . . . shall be the supreme Law of the Land."*

judicial review

Power of the courts to declare null and void laws of Congress and of state legislatures that they find unconstitutional.

The federal courts often find themselves at the center of major political controversies because their great political authority includes the power of **judicial review**—the power of the courts to declare null and void laws of Congress and of state legislatures that they find unconstitutional. This power can be exercised by any court, federal or state, but all lower-court decisions are subject to review by the Supreme Court, if it chooses to do so. The significance of the courts' power of judicial review can hardly be overestimated. Judicial review gives judges who are appointed for life the power to negate laws passed by the elected representatives of the people. As Senator George W. Norris complained, "The people can change Congress but only God can change the Supreme Court."[31]

While the Constitution affirms that it is the "supreme law of the land," it says nothing explicit about judicial review. The founders provided for a Supreme Court but offered few details about its powers (see Chapter 2, page 38). As political scientist Robert McCloskey observed, "The United States began its history . . . with a Supreme Court whose birthright was most uncertain."[32]

Despite its uncertain status during the first years of the new republic, in 1803 the Supreme Court successfully asserted the power of judicial review for the first time in the most important of all its decisions, *Marbury v. Madison*. In this complex case, Supreme Court Chief Justice John Marshall used a dispute over patronage as an occasion to assert the Court's power to declare the acts of Congress null and void.

In 1801, before John Adams and the Federalists relinquished control of the White House and Congress to Thomas Jefferson's Democratic-Republicans, they appointed and confirmed 42 new justices of the peace for Washington, D.C. The appointments had been so hastily arranged, however, that no one in the outgoing administration had time to deliver the official commissions to the appointees. Upon their arrival, Jefferson and his secretary of state, James Madison, declined to do so, making it impossible for the appointees to take office.

According to the Judiciary Act of 1789, the jilted appointees could request a court order to force the Jeffersonians to grant the appointments. Furthermore, said the act, the Supreme Court would have original jurisdiction in such cases—that is, it would be the first and only court to which such cases would be brought. On the basis of this law, one appointee, William Marbury, sued Madison for his job before the Supreme Court.

The case offered the Court no easy solution. The justices were sure that if they issued the order, the Jefferson administration would successfully ignore it, making the Court seem weak and ineffectual. On the other hand, if they declined to issue the order, they would appear to be caving in to pressure from the Jeffersonians.

Marshall solved this problem by asking an unexpected question: Was the Supreme Court the proper place to address Marbury's complaint? His stunning conclusion was that it was not—because the Constitution granted the Supreme Court original jurisdiction only in "all Cases affecting Ambassadors, other public Ministers and Consuls, and those in which a State shall be Party."[33] By giving the Court original jurisdiction in the case of the secretary of state (who did not qualify as a "public minister" in the accepted sense of the term), Section 13 of the Judiciary Act of 1789 had violated the Constitution and was therefore void.

Marshall's brilliant decision had transformed a situation that looked sure to sap the power of the federal courts into one that strengthened this power tremendously. By denying the Supreme Court's jurisdiction in the case, he invoked the power of judicial review for the first time. This authority has been acknowledged and accepted ever since.

In asserting the power of judicial review, Marshall's reasoning was simple and straightforward. Any new law overrides older laws on the same subject, except when the older law has been issued by a higher governmental entity. If a city passes a law

VIDEO ROUNDTABLE

Judicial Review

Marbury v. Madison
Supreme Court decision (1803) in which the court first exercised the power of judicial review.

John Marshall

Appointed by John Adams to serve as chief justice (1801–1835), John Marshall was also a Revolutionary War soldier, a supporter of the Constitution at the Virginia ratifying convention, a Federalist member of Congress, and secretary of state.

• *Aside from* Marbury v. Madison, *can you name another key court decision that Marshall wrote?*

original-intent theory

A theory of constitutional interpretation that determines the constitutionality of a law by ascertaining the intentions of those who wrote and ratified the Constitution.

declaring its speed limit to be 30 miles an hour, an older law that sets a speed limit of 40 miles an hour is automatically void, unless the old law was passed by a higher level of government, such as the state. In that case the state law, even if it is from an earlier date, takes precedence. The highest law of the land, according to Marshall, is the Constitution. It was established by the people, and no entity subject to the Constitution—not even Congress itself—can enact legislation that contravenes the will of the people, as expressed in the Constitution.

Three Theories of Constitutional Interpretation

The reasoning behind judicial review is impeccable as long as one assumes that judges only examine a law of Congress, compare it to the Constitution, and determine whether the law runs counter to clear constitutional language. The simplest case, perhaps, would be a law that postponed a constitutionally mandated Election Day. But very few issues of constitutionality are that simple. To help decide which laws are unconstitutional, judges and legal scholars have developed three distinct theories of constitutional interpretation: original intent, living constitution, and plain meaning of the text. Each of these theories reflects a different conception of what the role of the courts ought to be in key political controversies.

The theory of **original intent** determines whether a law is constitutional by ascertaining the intentions of those who wrote and ratified the Constitution. To establish the intentions of the founders, judges examine such documents as the notes that James Madison wrote down at the Constitutional Convention, the *Federalist Papers*, and the speeches made during the ratifying campaign in 1787 and 1788. Among today's sitting Supreme Court justices, Justice Clarence Thomas relies most frequently on the theory of original intent. For example, he favors overturning the 1973 *Roe v. Wade* decision legalizing abortion because he finds nothing in the Constitution that gives women the right to choose an abortion. On the contrary, he says that at the time the Constitution was ratified, many states outlawed abortion, making it clear that the framers had no intention of denying the states this authority.

Those who favor original-intent theory tend to believe that the courts should play a very limited role in politics. As Justice Thomas puts it, "When struggling to find the right answer to a case, judges should adopt principles of interpretation and methods of analysis that reduce judicial discretion."[34] By refusing to go beyond what the founders had in mind, argues Thomas, original intent theory "places the authority for creating the legal rules in the hands of the people and their representatives, rather than in the hands of the judiciary."[35]

Critics of original-intent theory say that many issues upon which the courts must render decisions were never contemplated by those who wrote the Constitution. Additionally, constitutional language may be the result of compromises between those who held contradictory beliefs. And, even if the founders were united in their opinions, should the perspectives of 55 men gathered together in Philadelphia in the summer of 1787 constrain the actions of the U.S. government more than 200 years later?

Those who criticize original-intent theory offer instead a **living-constitution theory** of judicial review, which says that a law's constitutionality ought to be judged in light of the entire history of the United States as a nation. The determining factors should include not only the opinions expressed at the time the Constitution was writ-

living-constitution theory

A theory of constitutional interpretation that places the meaning of the Constitution in light of the total history of the United States.

ten but also ideas and judgments shaped by American experience since then. In the words of Justice Oliver Wendell Holmes Jr., constitutional questions must be "considered in the light of our whole experience and not merely in that of what was said a hundred years ago."[36]

Those who support living-constitution theory see a broader role for the courts to play in contemporary political controversies, especially when fundamental principles are at stake. "Our constitution," argued Justice William Brennan, "was not intended to preserve a preexisting society, but to make a new one, to put in place principles that the prior community had not sufficiently recognized."[37] Consequently, there may be public policy issues on which the other branches of government and the public feel one way, but on which justices are "bound, by a larger constitutional duty to the community . . . to point toward a different path."[38] For example, Brennan believed that the death penalty violates the Eighth Amendment's prohibition of "cruel and unusual punishment," despite evidence that the founders did not oppose capital punishment.

The living-constitution theory is practical and helps the Constitution adapt to modern circumstances; however, it may reduce constitutional interpretation to the judge's personal understanding of the meaning of American history. And because no two judges' interpretations of the country's history are likely to be the same, constitutional interpretation may become highly subjective.

These difficulties have given rise to what has been called the **plain-meaning-of-the-text theory** of constitutional interpretation, which determines the constitutionality of a law in light of what the words of the Constitution obviously seem to say. Justice William Douglas pointed out that the First Amendment requires that, "Congress shall make no law . . . abridging freedom of speech," adding, "The First Amendment is couched in absolute terms—freedom of speech shall not be abridged . . . . No leeway is granted."[39]

plain-meaning-of-the-text theory
A theory of constitutional interpretation that determines the constitutionality of a law in light of what the words of the Constitution obviously seem to say.

Plain meaning has several clear advantages. Like original intent theory, it suggests that the courts should be cautious in the scope of their decisions, and should not go beyond the printed word. But, unlike original-intent theory, it does not require extensive inquiry into debates undertaken in the distant past. The constitutional text itself is taken as a guide to action. Nor does this approach require that judges evaluate the meaning of the totality of the American experience.

But plain-meaning theory has its own limitations. The Constitution is a short document that left many issues undecided and used ambiguous language in order to win ratification. Words that appear plain do not always have a clear meaning. Even Justice Douglas agreed to some limitations on free speech—for example, he agreed that one private person cannot libel another with impunity (see Chapter 16).

Justice John Stevens relied on plain-meaning theory to rule in the 2005 case of *Kelo v. City of New London* that New London, Connecticut, was within its constitutional rights when it took private property for use in a development plan that the city government deemed beneficial. The Constitution's Fifth Amendment stipulates that governments may only seize private property "for public use" and must provide "just compensation" when doing so. While New London adequately compensated property owners for their loss, a dispute arose over whether a development project owned and operated by private firms could qualify as "public use." Stevens answered "yes." Because city officials had determined that increased development would benefit the local economy, the land seizure "unquestionably serves a public purpose," he said.[40] Justice Sandra Day O'Connor,

Dred Scott

This painting depicts Dred Scott, a slave whose master had brought him outside slave-owning states. Scott sued for his freedom, arguing that when he set foot in a free state, he became free. In an infamous decision, the Supreme Court ruled that Scott had no right to sue and that Congress had no right to prohibit slavery in the territories.

• *How has the Dred Scott decision contributed to contemporary arguments against judicial review?*

however, saw Stevens' view as antithetical to a plain reading of the Constitution. His ruling, she argued, was so broad as to "effectively delete the words 'for public use' " from the Fifth Amendment.[41] If two noted jurists, Stevens and O'Connor, do not agree on the content of the Fifth Amendment, its meaning can hardly be plain and clear.

Judicial Review in Practice

The manner in which the courts interpret the Constitution can have serious consequences for the nation. In three celebrated instances, the Supreme Court created constitutional crises by declaring laws unconstitutional, thereby defying the declared will of Congress and the president. Because of its experience in cases such as these, the Supreme Court tends to be very cautious in exercising judicial review, using this power only when it feels that it is absolutely necessary.

The first case, *Dred Scott v. Sandford* (1857), declared unconstitutional the Missouri Compromise law passed in 1820.[42] The law drew a line coinciding with the Arkansas–Missouri border, north of which there could never be slavery (see Figure 15.1). Missouri, the exception, was allowed to legalize slavery. The Missouri Compromise had been so successful at preventing a breakup of the union that few politicians of the day even considered the possibility that the Supreme Court would dare call it unconstitutional. But, instead of respecting Congress's capacity to find satisfactory compromises, the Supreme Court denied the power of Congress to prohibit slavery in the territories, claiming it was an unconstitutional restriction on property rights. Few, if any, court decisions have been more disastrous. The Dred Scott decision alarmed many northerners, who feared that slavery would, in practice, be extended throughout the Union.[43] And, for southerners, the Court's arguments helped justify armed resistance.

In the late nineteenth century, the Supreme Court once again unwisely used its power of judicial review to declare a law unconstitutional, this time to block legislation designed to curb the abuses of industrial capitalism. In *Lochner v. New York* (1905), the Court said the state of New York could not regulate the number of hours that bakers worked, because to do so deprived them of the "right" to work as long and as hard as they pleased. The New York legislature had passed the law at issue, limiting the work week to 60 hours to protect workers from unscrupulous employers. In his dissent from the Court's decision, Oliver Wendell Holmes insisted that the Constitution be interpreted as a living document:

> This case is decided upon an economic theory which a large part of the country does not
> entertain. A Constitution is not intended to embody a particular economic theory. It is made
> for people of fundamentally differing views.[44]

Holmes's dissent in *Lochner* eventually became the view of the Supreme Court. Today, it is accepted that government can regulate working conditions.

A third unfortunate use of the power of judicial review occurred after Franklin Delano Roosevelt became president in 1933. Coming to power in the midst of a depression, Roosevelt and his Democratic Party allies in Congress passed a host of new legislation, known as the New Deal, designed to stimulate economic recovery.

The Supreme Court, which included a majority of justices appointed by Republican presidents, declared many of the New Deal laws unconstitutional. In

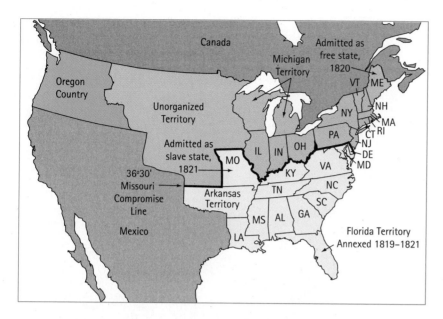

FIGURE 15.1

The Missouri Compromise

The Dred Scott decision invalidated the Missouri Compromise, an 1820 agreement that averted a sectional crisis by fixing a line (pictured) south of which slavery would be permitted. Areas north of the line would be free.

• *Why was the Supreme Court's invalidation of the compromise so destructive?*

Schechter Poultry Corp. v. United States (1935), the Supreme Court found the National Industrial Recovery Act, which addressed labor and competition in the private sector, an unconstitutional intrusion on the power of the states to regulate commerce inside their own borders.[45] In what was known as the "sick chicken" case, the Court said the law regulated the sale of poultry after it arrived within the state of New York, not while the chicks were being transported across a state line. Because Congress could regulate only commerce between states, not commerce within a state, the Court declared the law unconstitutional (see Chapter 3, page 68). The decision placed the Supreme Court at odds with the president and Congress, creating a constitutional crisis that was not resolved until several justices switched their votes on such cases in the wake of Roosevelt's overwhelming reelection.

Cases such as *Dred Scott*, *Lochner*, and *Schechter Poultry* have led some legal theorists to argue that judicial review should be abandoned because it is anti-democratic. "If judicial review is a means to check encroachments," asks John Agresto, "what means exist to check the encroachments of the judiciary[?]"[46] But others see judicial review as a valuable protection against majority infringement on minority civil rights and civil liberties. Despite the controversy, judicial review has become a well-established practice in American government. It survives in part because justices use this power sparingly, seldom defying the strongly held views of the president and Congress. On only 159 occasions between 1803 and 2004 did the Supreme Court decide that a federal law was unconstitutional.[47] Most of these decisions affected old laws no longer supported either by a majority of Congress or by the president.

Political scientist Robert Dahl has gone so far as to claim that "The Supreme Court is inevitably a part of the dominant political leadership. The main task of the Court is to confer legitimacy on [the government's] fundamental policies."[48] Although some scholars think the Court is less sensitive to political pressure than Dahl claims, a recent study has identified changes in Supreme Court policy that parallel swings in public opinion. These policy shifts are not so pronounced as those in Congress, the study finds, but justices still

A Federal District Court's Responsibility

In 2004, magazine publisher and television personality Martha Stewart appeared in federal district court to defend herself against allegations of insider stock trading.

• *How do federal district court responsibilities differ from those of a circuit court of appeals?*

seem to pay "attention to what the public wants."[49] Indeed, some have argued that political leaders might prefer an active Supreme Court because court decisions tend to add force to the majority's policy priorities.[50] The *Dred Scott* and *Schechter Poultry* cases are the exception, not the rule. Bartender Mr. Dooley, the Irish cartoon figure, was not wide of the mark when he observed years ago that "th' supreme court follows th' illiction returns."

Statutory Interpretation

statutory interpretation
The judicial act of interpreting and applying ordinary laws, rather than the Constitution, to specific cases.

Comparing Judiciaries

Judicial review is only the most sweeping and controversial of judicial powers. The courts also engage in **statutory interpretation**, the application of the laws of Congress and of the states to particular cases. American courts have great discretion in exercising this power, much more than their counterparts in Great Britain. (See the accompanying *International Comparison*.) For example, in 1973 Congress passed a vague and general law protecting endangered species. The Supreme Court gave teeth to this law by saying that Congress intended to protect all species, the tiny snail darter as well as the eagle. In reaching this decision, Chief Justice Warren Burger wrote that "it may seem curious to some that the survival of a relatively small number of three-inch fish among all the countless millions of species extant would require the permanent halting of a virtually completed dam for which Congress has expended more than $100 million." But the law, Burger said, required "precisely that result."[51] Although dissenting Justice Powell thought it was "absurd" to assume Congress had any such intention, the Court majority argued that all it was doing in this instance was interpreting and applying an act of Congress.

The Federal Court System in Practice

CONSTITUTION, ARTICLE III, SECTION 1: *"The judicial power . . . shall be vested in one supreme Court, and in such inferior Courts as the Congress may from time to time ordain and establish."*

INTERNATIONAL
COMPARISON

Statutory Interpretation in the United States and Britain

When interpreting statutes, British judges have less leeway than American judges because they operate within a less fragmented governmental system. In Britain, the party of the prime minister exerts effective control over Parliament. Every piece of legislation passed by the party in power is carefully examined by specialists, who ensure that new legislation is internally coherent and consistent with existing laws. If a judge says government administrators have misinterpreted the law, the party in power can also, if it chooses, quickly pass new legislation. Political scientist Shep Melnick points out that as a result, "it is not surprising that British judges seldom question the interpretive authority of administrators."[a]

American judges work within a more decentralized governmental context. To get a majority when writing legislation, members of Congress are tempted to use ambiguous language that may include phrases that come close to contradicting one another. In Melnick's words, "The openness and messiness of the legislative process in the United States ensures that when judges scrutinize a statute and its history, they will seldom discover a single, coherent purpose or intent."[b] In the voting-rights legislation of 1982, for example,

Congress forbade electoral arrangements that gave minorities "less opportunity than other members of the electorate to elect representatives of their choice" but, a few sentences later, said that nothing in the legislation required minorities to be elected "in numbers equal to their proportion in the population." The "less opportunity" forbidden in the first phrase seemed permitted by the second phrase, which indicated that "equal numbers" need not be elected.[c]

When courts are asked to sort out the meaning of this kind of vague and potentially contradictory language, the office of the solicitor general may express the opinion of the presidential administration. But, if the courts ignore the solicitor general, the administration must try to persuade Congress to enact a new law—a far more difficult task for American presidents than for British prime ministers. Knowing this, U.S. courts feel free to interpret laws in any way that is not plainly contrary to the intent of Congress. As Supreme Court Justice William Brennan once said, "the Court can virtually remake congressional enactments."[d]

- *The U.S. system is certainly more complex than the British one. Is it better?*

[a] R. Shep Melnick, *Between the Lines: Interpreting Welfare Rights* (Washington, DC: The Brookings Institution, 1994), 13.
[b] Melnick, *Between the Lines,* 13.
[c] As quoted in Bernard Grofman, Lisa Handley, and Richard G. Niemi, *Minority Representation and the Quest for Voting Equality* (New York: Cambridge University Press, 1992), 39.
[d] Melnick, *Between the Lines,* 13.

Although the Supreme Court provides the linchpin for the nation's system of courts, resolving difficult questions of constitutional or statutory interpretation, most of the day-to-day work of the federal judicial branch is carried out at lower tiers. These lower courts are less visible institutions, but they are no less affected by political and electoral forces. In this section we describe the federal court system.

District Courts

The Constitution established a Supreme Court, leaving it to Congress to decide what lower federal courts were needed. The first Congress enacted the Judiciary Act of 1789, which, though it has been updated in many ways, still provides the basic framework for the modern federal court system.

Most federal cases are initially filed in one of the 94 **federal district courts**, the lowest tier of the federal court system. These courts are the trial courts of the federal system, and are similar to the trial courts that exist in each state. As a consequence, many high-profile cases pass through the federal district courts. In 2006, for example, Vice President Dick Cheney's former chief of staff, I. Lewis Libby, was tried in district court for charges related to the leak of the name of a covert CIA officer. In another highly publicized 2004 case, magazine publisher and television personality Martha

federal district courts
The lowest level of the federal court system and the courts in which most federal trials are held.

FIGURE 15.2

Federal and State
Court Systems

• *Why does the Supreme Court
handle so few cases each year?*

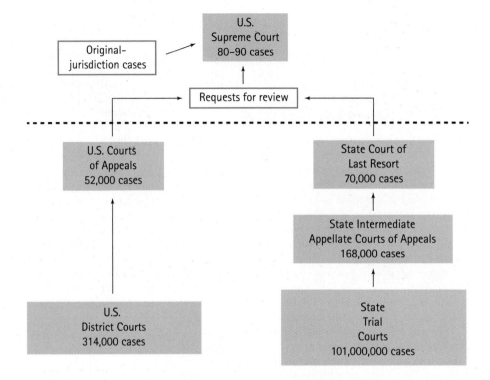

Stewart was convicted in a federal district court for offenses connected to insider stock trading. As Figure 15.2 shows, the vast majority of federal legal proceedings begin and end in these district courts.

Appeals Courts

The federal district courts are organized into 13 circuits (including 11 numbered regional circuits, a D.C. circuit, and a federal circuit), each of which has a **circuit court of appeals**, the court to which all district court decisions may be appealed (see Figure 15.3). The name circuit, which means "a regularly traveled route around a given territory," recalls the early history of the courts, in which judges journeyed by stage-coach from district to district, listening to cases. Because of the deplorable state of roads in the early republic, riding the circuit could be a perilous duty. Judges complained of "heat and exposure to the sun, lack of drinking water in many areas, deep ruts, high water, and indifferent accommodations."[52]

Nearly all cases today are heard in the same building, usually by 3 of the 6 to 28 judges who serve on the court of appeals. The senior appeals-court judge assigns the three judges to each case. In most courts of appeals, they are chosen by lot. In exceptionally important cases, a session may be held in which all of the appeals judges in the circuit participate. Courts of appeals confine their review to points of law under dispute; they ordinarily take as given the facts of the case, as stated in the trial record and decided by district judges. They do not accept new evidence or hear additional witnesses. Although decisions by the appeals court may be taken up by the Supreme Court, most appeals-court decisions are final.

circuit court of appeals

Court to which decisions by federal district courts are appealed.

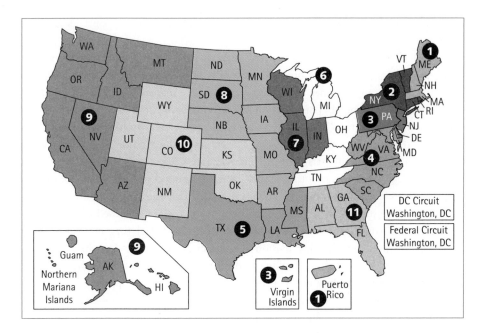

FIGURE 15.3

Courts of Appeals
Circuit Boundaries
What is the role of the federal appeals court?

Source: Robert A. Carp and Ronald Stidham, *The Federal Courts*, 2nd ed. (Washington, DC: CQ Press, 1991), 18.

Specialized Courts

Two trial courts have nationwide jurisdiction over specialized issues that do not fall within the purview of the district courts. The Court of International Trade handles cases concerning trade and customs. And the U.S. Court of Federal Claims hears suits concerning federal contracts, money damages against the United States, and other issues that involve the federal government. Cases originating in either of these courts may be appealed to the court of appeals for the federal circuit.

Selection of Federal Judges

All federal judges hold lifetime positions after their nomination by the president and confirmation by the Senate. Because of long-standing agreements among senators, known as **senatorial courtesy**, any presidential nominee must be acceptable to the senior senator of the state involved who is of the same political party as the president. Political influences play a major role in the selection of federal judges. Most share the same partisan identification as the president who nominates them; 87 percent of Bill Clinton's nominees were Democrats, and 90 percent of George W. Bush's nominees have been Republicans.[53] Most judges would not acknowledge it publicly, but political loyalty is often the key to appointment. Senator Herb Kohl (D-WI) probably expressed the opinions of politicians on both sides of the aisle when he said, "Ideology is important. You want to know where [judicial appointees] are on some of the major issues. If you can, you want to have some sense of what to expect."[54]

Although most lower-court nominees are confirmed, rejections do occur. Rejection is usually a result of some financial or personal problem uncovered during the confirmation process. Ideological and partisan considerations play a minor role. Conservative lawyer Robert Bork, for example, was easily confirmed as an appeals-court judge, even though he was later rejected as a nominee to the Supreme Court

senatorial courtesy
An informal rule that the Senate will not confirm nominees within or from a state unless they have the approval of the senior senator of that state from the president's party.

Selecting
Federal Judges

because of his right-wing views. But ideological battles over lower-court judges have become increasingly important.

Short of rejection, opposition-party senators may exert their power by simply refusing to bring a nomination to a vote. In the late 1990s, President Clinton complained of congressional foot-dragging and Republicans criticized his judicial nominations as too liberal. This situation failed to improve after the election of George W. Bush: the Democratic Senate acted on only 43 percent of Bush's judicial nominees in 2001, delaying action on the rest.[55] Even after the Senate changed back to Republican hands, Democrats used the filibuster (see Chapter 12) to block floor votes on a handful of nominees that they argued were "extreme conservatives."[56] This led to a heated dispute in 2005 when Republicans argued that the filibuster should not be used in the case of judicial nominations—only in the case of proposed bills and resolutions. A bipartisan group of 14 moderates brokered a deal that avoided a direct confrontation over the issue, but tension over judicial nominations remained.

One reason why parties are willing to do battle over nominations is that there are important ideological differences between potential judicial appointees. Overall, district judges' decisions reflect the political orientation of the president who nominated the particular judge—judges appointed by Democratic presidents are more likely than those appointed by Republican presidents to hand down liberal decisions.[57]

Deciding to Prosecute

U.S. attorney
Person responsible for prosecuting violations of the federal criminal code.

Suspected violations of the federal criminal code are usually investigated by the Federal Bureau of Investigation, although other federal agencies, such as the Secret Service and the Bureau of Alcohol, Tobacco and Firearms, also exercise investigative powers. The evidence collected is given to prosecutors in the office of a **U.S. attorney**, who is responsible for prosecuting violations of the federal criminal code. Appointed by the president and confirmed by the Senate, the 93 U.S. attorneys act as the government's chief litigators. If persuaded that a prosecution is warranted, a U.S. attorney asks a grand jury to indict the suspect.

You Are a
Young Lawyer

U.S. attorneys have a particularly high political profile. They usually share the president's party affiliation and, although they are expected to be incorruptible, they often are sensitive to the political needs of their superiors in Washington. Because routine law enforcement is left in the hands of state officials, U.S. attorneys concentrate on high-visibility, attention-grabbing federal crimes. If they are particularly successful, they may become candidates for higher office. For example, former New York mayor Rudolph Giuliani achieved prominence as a federal attorney who successfully prosecuted Wall Street inside-trader Ivan Boesky and tax-evading hotel magnate Leona Helmsley, as well as several high-profile organized crime figures. Supreme Court justice Samuel Alito also served as a U.S. attorney in New Jersey in the late 1980s, where he earned a reputation as a confident, if low-key, leader.[58]

Relations Between State and Federal Courts

For the first few decades under the Constitution, the relationship between state and federal legal and judicial systems remained vague. Then, in an important early decision, *Martin v. Hunter's Lessee* (1816), the Supreme Court ruled that it had the power to review and, if necessary, to overturn the decisions of state courts. In that case, a Virginia court had argued that the decisions of state courts were final and could not be appealed to the national level.

The Supreme Court disagreed, saying that "the importance, and even necessity of uniformity of decisions throughout the whole United States" made the Virginia court's argument untenable.[59] Three years later, in **McCulloch v. Maryland** (1819), the Supreme Court made it clear that the power of judicial review applied to state as well as federal laws (see Chapter 3, page 70). Maryland had imposed a tax on the congressionally chartered Bank of the United States. When a bank cashier, James McCulloch, refused to pay the tax, he was convicted of violating the law. But the Supreme Court overturned the conviction. Chief Justice Marshall argued that "the power to tax involves the power to destroy" and that no state had the power "to retard, impede, burden or in any manner control, the operations of the constitutional laws enacted by Congress."[60]

The Supreme Court's power to review state laws and the decisions of state courts is essential for maintaining basic uniformity in the laws of the United States. Over the decades, the Supreme Court has found nearly 1,100 state and local statutes and constitutional provisions contrary to the federal Constitution.[61] The judicial power to declare state laws unconstitutional is much less controversial than the power to declare laws of Congress unconstitutional. As Justice Holmes once said,

> I do not think the United States would come to an end if we lost our power to declare an act of Congress void. I do think the Union would be imperiled if we could not make that declaration as to the laws of the several states. For one in my place sees how often a local policy prevails with those who are not trained to national views.[62]

Most cases are heard in state courts, but any case can be shifted to a federal court if it can be shown that a federal law or constitutional principle is involved. The federal courts have higher prestige than state courts; to become a federal judge is to hold a position of great honor. But as Justice Sandra Day O'Connor, a former state judge, acutely observed, "When the state court judge puts on his or her federal court robe, he or she does not become immediately better equipped intellectually to do the job."[63]

The same act can simultaneously be a violation of both state and federal laws. Although the Fifth Amendment to the Constitution forbids **double jeopardy**—one person being tried twice for the same crime—something very close to double jeopardy can occur if a person is tried in both federal and state courts. In such cases, multiple trials are allowed if the same actions gave rise to distinct crimes. In 1897 the Supreme Court permitted dual prosecutions, saying that "an act denounced as a crime by both national and state sovereignties is an offense against the peace and dignity of both."[64]

Dual state and federal prosecutions remain unusual, however. Most of the time, federal and state officials reach an agreement allowing one or the other to take responsibility. Generally speaking, the federal government takes over the prosecution only when the case has national implications. For example, the 1995 bombing of a federal building in Oklahoma, in which 168 people lost their lives, constituted a violation of both state laws against murder and federal laws against conspiracy and manslaughter. Although state officials began the investigation, federal investigators quickly took charge and the accused, Timothy McVeigh and Terry Nichols, were convicted in a federal courtroom. Later, when Nichols failed to receive the federal death penalty for his role in the crime, state prosecutors brought state murder charges against him. (The jury in the state case also declined to give him the death penalty, however.)

If the state prosecution fails to result in a conviction in a sensational case where a federal law has been broken, the federal U.S. attorney may also bring charges. In 1992 the state of California was unable to win a conviction in the trial of four police officers charged with beating African American motorist Rodney King, an event that had been

McCulloch v. Maryland
Decision (1819) in which the Supreme Court first declared a state law unconstitutional.

double jeopardy
Placing someone on trial for the same crime twice.

A State Supreme Court

The Supreme Judicial Court of Massachusetts caused controversy in 2004 when it ruled that the Massachusetts constitution protected the right of gays and lesbians to marry.

• *Unlike many state supreme courts, the Massachusetts high court is appointed rather than elected. What difference do you think elections would make in this or other controversial cases?*

videotaped. The failure to convict officers for what seemed to be a well-documented offense provoked three days of civil disorder in Los Angeles minority communities.

To help calm the city, the U.S. attorney decided to bring federal civil rights violation charges against the officers, despite the fact that the state had already tried them once for assault. After hearing all the evidence, the jury in the federal trial convicted two officers and acquitted the other two. The decision to hold a second trial was almost certainly affected by public and media pressure.

The Supreme Court

The Supreme Court sits atop a massive pyramid of judicial activity. Each year prosecutors and private citizens bring more than 27 million criminal trials and civil suits before the state and federal courts.[65] Yet in the 2005–2006 term, the nation's high court decided only 74 cases.[66] In this section, we explain how the Court exerts its substantial influence through such a small number of cases and describe the practical process of how justices make decisions and write each opinion, the Court's written justification of its decision. First, we discuss Supreme Court appointments. Next, we consider two important rules of court procedure as well as the important players involved in the Court's activity. Finally, we consider the process of Supreme Court decision making itself.

The Politics of Supreme Court Appointments

CONSTITUTION, ARTICLE II: *"The President shall nominate . . . and by and with the Advice and Consent of the Senate, shall appoint . . . Judges of the Supreme Court."*

The judicial system is supposed to be politically blind. Justice is expected to fall equally, like the rain, on rich and poor, Democrat and Republican, black, white, Latino, Asian, and Native American. Judges are appointed for life because they are expected to decide each case without any concern for the political consequences. Chief Justice Warren E.

The Supreme Court
Originally conceived by President and Chief Justice William Howard Taft to instill public respect for the judicial branch, the Supreme Court building resembles a Greek temple built to house ancient gods.
• *Do you think the Supreme Court building succeeds in elevating public respect for the Court? Why or why not?*

Burger went so far as to claim that "Judges . . . rule on the basis of law, not public opinion, and they should be totally indifferent to pressures of the times."[67]

Despite this ideal, however, the process by which justices are selected is a political one, and it has become more so in recent decades. Justices are nominated by the president, evaluated by the Senate Judiciary Committee, and confirmed by a vote of the full Senate. The Court's chief justice must also be nominated and confirmed in this manner, even if he or she is already a member of the Court. Because of this procedure, elected officials, as well as interest groups and the media, have a voice in choosing members of the Court. These players pay close attention to the electoral consequences of their actions, so elections inevitably affect nominations to the Court, and confirmation battles affect elections.

For at least the first half of the twentieth century, presidential nominations to the Supreme Court were confirmed by the Senate as a matter of course. Most nominees were approved quietly without even testifying before the Judiciary Committee. One of Harry Truman's nominees declined an explicit invitation to testify but was confirmed anyway.[68] Earl Warren, the Eisenhower appointee who would write the opinion in the landmark 1954 school desegregation decision, *Brown v. Board of Education* (see Chapter 17), was also confirmed without giving testimony.[69]

This long-time separation of Supreme Court nominations from political disputes owed a great deal to the efforts of William Howard Taft, the only person ever to serve both as president (1909–1913) and as chief justice of the Supreme Court (1921–1930). Before Taft, political disputes openly affected confirmation decisions. In the nineteenth century, the Senate rejected a third of the presidents' nominees.[70] But Taft worked hard both as president and as chief justice to enhance the quality of nominees, minimize the significance of confirmation procedures, and elevate the prestige of the Court. He also made sure that the new Supreme Court building, eventually completed in 1935, was

TABLE 15.2
PRESIDENTIAL NOMINEES TO THE SUPREME COURT NOT CONFIRMED BY THE SENATE, 1900–2005

• *Why have nominees faced more difficulties in the Senate in recent years?*

Nominee	Year	President	Main Reason for Rejection/Withdrawal
John Parker	1930	Hoover	Anti-labor
Abraham Fortas (sitting justice nominated to be chief justice)	1968	Johnson	Too liberal; resigned from Court in 1969 over alleged financial abuses
Homer Thornberry	1968	Johnson	No vacancy when Fortas not confirmed for chief justice
Clement Haynesworth	1970	Nixon	Alleged financial abuses
G. Harrold Carswell	1970	Nixon	Racially conservative
Robert Bork	1987	Reagan	Controversial conservative record
Douglas Ginsburg	1987	Reagan	Smoked marijuana with students
Harriet Miers	2005	Bush	Controversy over qualifications

designed to resemble a Greek temple, so that Americans would respect their laws with the same reverence with which the ancient Greeks venerated their gods.

Taft was so successful that for nearly four decades, the Senate confirmed every nominee but one, most without significant dissent. But in recent years, the Senate has been more willing to exert its power to review nominations. Since 1955 every Supreme Court nominee has appeared before the judiciary committee, and since 1968 the Senate's propensity to reject presidential nominees has increased, as Table 15.2 indicates. One of the most celebrated cases involved Robert Bork, a Reagan nominee rejected by the Senate in 1987. A staunch conservative, Bork had produced a great many journal articles and speeches, which interest groups and Senate opponents used to attack him in a concerted national campaign.

borking

Politicizing the nomination process through an organized public campaign that portrays the nominee as a dangerous extremist.

Bork's rejection has, in fact, given American politics a new word, **borking**, which means politicizing the nomination process through an organized public campaign portraying the nominee as a dangerous extremist. Both Congress and the media now subject each nomination to scrutiny.

As the case of John Roberts shows, not every Supreme Court nomination is subject to borking. If the same party controls both Congress and the presidency, borking becomes less likely. Thus, for example, Bill Clinton was able to appoint both Ruth Bader Ginsburg and Stephen Breyer in the mid-1990s without significant controversy. Similarly, since Bush nominee Samuel Alito had a conservative record, he did not meet with major resistance from the Republican Senate. Even so, presidents must walk a careful line to avoid opposition from conservative and liberal interest groups alike. Clinton's picks were moderates rather than well-known liberals, and they thus escaped borking at the hands of Republicans. Bush's successful appointment of Alito came only after he had to withdraw the nomination of Harriet Miers in the face of a growing campaign against her from conservative groups (see the accompanying Election Connection).

Judges and Politics

The Harriet Miers Nomination to the Supreme Court

CNN legal analyst Jeffrey Toobin looked puzzled. As President George W. Bush stepped away from the podium after announcing his second nominee to the Supreme Court, Toobin struggled to explain the choice to the viewing audience and couldn't come up with much. Miers "has a very blank slate as far as a record," he said. "By the standards that we usually apply to Supreme Court justice nominees, she does not appear very distinguished."

After his triumph with the nomination of Chief Justice John Roberts (see chapter opening), Bush had chosen to nominate Miers, a long-time Bush loyalist, White House staffer, and former head of the Texas State Bar, to fill the Court's second vacancy. Whereas his first nominee had come with unquestionable qualifications, Miers was a relative unknown.

The absence of a long record did not have to be a bad thing. After all, the lack of a record is the telltale characteristic of a "stealth nominee," such as David Souter had been when George H. W. Bush had named him to the court in 1990 (see p. 446). Souter had no controversial decisions or law review articles to defend, and was therefore confirmed without controversy. But many conservatives saw the Souter nomination differently. Souter had turned out to be more liberal than expected. If Miers was this kind of "stealth nominee," conservative activists would not be supportive.

Conservatives strongly believed that this second Supreme Court nomination was crucial. For decades, Republicans had been laboring to elect like-minded people to office, and now control of the Supreme Court was within reach. Because conservative activists were a strong part of President Bush's party constituency (see Chapter 13, p. 360), many conservative leaders felt the president owed them the nomination of a proven conservative legal theorist. Miers was unknown and unproven. As one partisan put it, "President Bush is asking us to have faith in things unseen. We only have that kind of faith in God."

This dynamic created an unusual spectacle. While Democrats such as Senate minority leader Harry Reid said generally positive things about Miers, many prominent erstwhile allies of the president raised concerns. Less than a week after the president's announcement, David Frum, a writer for *National Review*, declared in his blog that "there is scarcely a single knowledgeable legal conservative in Washington who supports this nomination." Perhaps most ironically, a pro-Republican Web site established months earlier to build support for Bush court nominees, "confirmthem.com," began urging the Senate to reject the president's choice.

Harriet Miers
The nominee arrives at a Senate office as President Bush appears on television.

As conservative support for Miers dissolved, several embarrassing episodes complicated her situation. She admitted that her license to practice law had been briefly suspended because she had forgotten to pay her dues. In an interview with a prominent senator, she was rumored to have confused Chief Justice Warren Burger with Chief Justice Earl Warren. The Senate Judiciary Committee asked her to clarify and resubmit a questionnaire that seemed incomplete. Finally, within a month of being nominated, Miers withdrew her name from consideration.

Days later, Bush nominated Samuel Alito to take her place. An appeals court judge, Alito may not have had the charm of Justice Roberts, Bush's first nominee, but he had conservative credentials and a solid legal record. Conservatives rallied around Alito, and despite intense opposition from liberal organizations and the Democratic leadership that Republicans claimed was another attempt at borking, the Senate confirmed Alito by a vote of 58–42.

• *Why do you think conservative activists were willing to break with the President over the Miers nomination?*

• *Can you envision a similar situation with a Democratic president and liberal activists? Which activist groups would be most likely to confront a Democratic president about a nominee? Which issues would be most important?*

SOURCES: Toobin quote, "Bush Picks White House Counsel for Supreme Court," CNN Transcript, October 3, 2005, 8:07 am EST; Bush quote, Peter Baker and Shailagh Murray, "Bush Defends Supreme Court Pick," *Washington Post*, October 5, 2005, A1; activist quote, Michael Grunwald, Jo Becker, and John Pomfret, "Strong Grounding in Church Could be a Clue to Miers' Priorities," *Washington Post*, October 5, 2005, A1; Frum quote, Dana Milbank, "The State of the Union Between the Right and the White House Turns Frosty," *Washington Post*, October 7, 2005, A6; Warren confusion, Peter Baker and Dan Balz, "Miers to Face Tougher Time than Roberts in Hearings," *Washington Post*, October 9, 2005, A1.

Even if the Senate is controlled by the opposition, presidents may avoid borking by choosing a nominee whose views are unknown, a "stealth" strategy named after the bomber that cannot easily be detected by radar.[71] In 1990 President George H. W. Bush nominated stealth candidate David Souter, a New Hampshire state supreme court justice who had never written an opinion or treatise on any major constitutional question. Some legal scholars lamented such conflict avoidance, saying it made some brilliant intellects ineligible for consideration. But the bigger worry for presidents is that stealth candidates, however easy to appoint, can backfire upon taking office. Bush thought Souter would strengthen the conservative side of the Supreme Court, but the justice has proved to be one of the Court's most articulate liberals.

Although many critics think the politicization of judicial appointments destroys "the public's belief in the fairness of those on the bench and . . . undermine[s] confidence in the Court,"[72] future trends seem clear. The United States is unlikely to go back to the older way of selecting Supreme Court justices. Modern technology and the media ensure that presidents will choose justices with an eye to avoiding potential public controversies.

Stare Decisis

stare decisis

In court rulings, reliance on consistency with precedents. See also "precedent."

precedent

Previous court decision or ruling applicable to a particular case.

A small number of Supreme Court decisions can have a far-ranging impact because lower federal and state courts are expected to follow the principle of **stare decisis**. The phrase is Latin for "let the decision stand." This is to say that in deciding cases, judges should adhere to **precedents**, or prior decisions, as well as to the logic of their written opinions. Jonathan Swift used his biting satire to define *stare decisis* somewhat differently:

> Whatever has been done before may legally be done again; and therefore [judges] take special care to record all the decisions formerly made against common justice and the general reason of mankind. These, under the name of precedents, they produce as authorities, to justify the most iniquitous of opinions.[73]

Despite Swift's lampoon, *stare decisis* is a powerful judicial principle that can be ignored only at risk to the stability of the legal system. Only if court decisions are consistent with one another over time can a country live under a rule of law, where citizens know what it is that they are expected to obey. In the words of one judge, "We cannot meddle with a prior decision [unless it] strikes us as wrong with the force of a five-week-old unrefrigerated dead fish."[74]

legal distinction

The legal difference between a case at hand and previous cases decided by the courts.

When reaching a decision that seems contrary to a prior decision, courts try to find a **legal distinction** between the case at hand and earlier court decisions, usually by emphasizing that the facts of the current case differ. The process of drawing a legal distinction can sometimes become the refined art of perceiving a distinction when others can see no difference. As an attorney once bragged, "Law school taught me one thing: how to take two situations that are exactly the same and show how they are different."[75] If the legal distinctions drawn by a lower court seem unconvincing to the losing side, it may **appeal** the decision to the next-higher court. If the higher court thinks the lower court has strayed too far from legal precedents, it may decide on a **reversal**, or overturning, of the lower court's decision.

appeal

The procedure whereby the losing side asks a higher court to overturn a lower-court decision.

reversal

The overturning of a lower-court decision by an appeals court or the Supreme Court.

Certs

At one time the Supreme Court was required by law to review many appeals, but the workload became so excessive that in 1925 Congress gave the Court the power to refuse to review almost any case it did not want to consider. Today nearly all cases argued before the Court arrive upon the grant of what is known as a **cert** by court insiders. Cert is an abbreviation of the Latin term in **writ of *certiorari***, which means "to be informed of." The granting of a cert means the Court has agreed to consider the case.[76] The Court rejects most cert petitions because it is only practical to consider a fraction of the 8000 to 9000 cases appealed to it each year.[77] As one clerk for a Supreme Court justice put it, "You almost get to hate the guy who brings the cert petitions around. He is really a nice guy, but he gets abuse all the time."[78]

The number of certs granted by the Supreme Court has fallen markedly in recent decades. In the 1970s the Supreme Court decided as many as 400 cases annually.[79] But, as we have noted, only 74 cases were decided in the 2005–2006 term. Certs are granted only for those cases that raise the most important legal or constitutional issues. As the old saying goes, the Supreme Court cares less about justice than about the law. In the words of one chief justice,

> The Supreme Court is not, and never has been, primarily concerned with the correction of errors in lower court decisions . . . . To remain effective the Supreme Court must continue to decide only those cases which present questions whose resolution will have immediate importance far beyond the particular facts and parties involved."[80]

To issue a cert requires the vote of four justices. The mere fact that an issue is controversial does not necessarily mean the Court will grant a cert. The justices may decide to let the issue percolate in the lower courts for a few years until the matter is ripe for decision.

The case for cert is strongest if two lower courts have reached opposite conclusions on cases in which the facts seem virtually identical. In such cases, the Supreme Court feels a responsibility to clarify the law so that its effect is uniform throughout the United States. In 1998, for example, the Wisconsin Supreme Court upheld a state law establishing a school voucher program in Milwaukee. Low-income families could receive state money and use it to attend a private school of their choice. Although many religious schools participated in the program, the Wisconsin court ruled that the law did not violate the constitutional clause prohibiting the establishment of religion (see Chapter 16). When a similar law was passed by the Ohio legislature for low-income families in Cleveland, a federal appeals court ruled that it unconstitutionally established religion. Because two lower courts had decided the same issue in contrary ways, the Supreme Court granted a cert and heard the Ohio case in early 2002. That summer, the Court finally decided the issue. In a landmark ruling, a slim majority found that vouchers did not violate the establishment clause because parents could decide whether the money went to religious institutions. Such a program of "true private choice," said Chief Justice Rehnquist, passed the constitutional test.[81] (For more on the vouchers issue, see Election Voices, p. 487.)

The Role of the Chief Justice

The Supreme Court consists of eight **associate justices** and the **chief justice**, who heads the Court and is responsible for organizing its work. Although the chief justice has only one vote and many of the chief's tasks are of a ceremonial or housekeeping nature, certain responsibilities give the office added influence. For one thing, the chief justice, if voting with the majority, assigns the responsibility for writing the majority

cert
See "writ of *certiorari*."

writ of *certiorari* (cert)
A document issued by the Supreme Court indicating that the Court will review a decision made by a lower court.

associate justice
One of the eight justices of the Supreme Court who are not the chief justice.

chief justice
Head of the Supreme Court.

opinion. Because the Court's opinion is often as important as the actual decision, this assignment power can have far-reaching consequences; some cases are "destined for the history books, whereas others are, in [former Justice Lewis] Powell's term, 'dogs.' " Powell's biographer tells us that Warren Burger, not the most popular of chief justices, was suspected by his colleagues of voting with the majority, even when privately opposed, simply in order to exercise his assignment power.[82]

Some chief justices have used their position to facilitate compromise and achieve consensus. In the case of *Brown v. Board of Education of Topeka, Kansas* (1954), the landmark decision desegregating schools, Chief Justice Earl Warren was able to win the support of two judges who were initially inclined to dissent. To achieve the unanimity he thought crucial, Warren agreed to write a less-than-sweeping opinion. *Brown* banned segregation in schools but not in other public places, and it specified delay in the implementation of the ruling. Warren was willing to make these compromises because he thought that only a unanimous Court could order such a major social change—which at the time ran contrary to strongly held opinions of many southern whites.[83]

The Role of the Solicitor General

A powerful figure who regularly appears before the Supreme Court is the **solicitor general**, the government official responsible for presenting before the Court the position of the presidential administration. Involvement of the solicitor general is a signal that the president and the attorney general have strong views on the subject, which enhances its visibility and political significance. Because the Court pays close attention to the position of the solicitor general, the person who holds this office is sometimes referred to as "the tenth justice." About 60 percent of the solicitor general's cert petitions are accepted by the Court.[84]

Solicitors general are employees of the Justice Department and as such report to the attorney general. However, they are always carefully selected by the president for their legal skills and are "in fact what the Attorney General is in name—the chief legal officer of the United States government as far as the courts are concerned."[85] The solicitor general presents the case for the government whenever it is party to a suit. In other important cases, the solicitor general may submit an *amicus curiae* brief—literally, a brief submitted by a "friend of the court." (*Amicus curiae* briefs can also be submitted by others who wish to inform the court of a legal issue presented by a particular case.) When the office of the solicitor general files an *amicus curiae* brief, it finds itself on the winning side approximately three-quarters of the time, a batting average envied by even the most successful private attorneys.[86] Several solicitors general, including William Howard Taft and Thurgood Marshall, have gone on to become Supreme Court justices themselves.[87]

The Role of Clerks

Much of the day-to-day work within the Supreme Court building is performed by **law clerks**—young, influential aides hired by each of the justices. Recently out of law school, most will have spent a year as a clerk with a lower court before being asked to help a Supreme Court justice. Each justice has between two and four law clerks.[88] Not only do clerks initially review certs, but they also draft many opinions. After one year of service to the Court at comparatively low salaries, law clerks move on to illustrious

The Chief Justice
of the Supreme Court

solicitor general
Government official responsible for presenting before the courts the position of the presidential administration.

Solicitor General
Paul Clement

The solicitor general serves as the federal government's voice in many Supreme Court proceedings.
• *Why is the solicitor general known as the "tenth justice"?*

law clerk
Young, influential aide to a Supreme Court justice.

careers in the private sector, in legal academia, or perhaps on the bench. Three current justices (Roberts, Stevens, and Breyer) once served as Supreme Court clerks.

Law clerks have become so important to the Court's routine that some observers claim that a junior Supreme Court of bright but unseasoned attorneys, unconfirmed by the Senate or anybody else, is the true "Supreme Court" of today. Others reply that well-trained graduates of the country's most prestigious law schools may be better judges than aging titans who refuse to leave office well beyond the age of normal retirement. The truth probably lies between these two extremes: The brilliance of the young clerks and the political and legal experience of the justices are probably better in combination than either would be without the other.[89] As Chief Justice Rehnquist once said of the clerk system, "The Justice may retain for himself control not merely of the outcome of the case, but the explanation for the outcome, and I do not believe this practice sacrifices either."[90]

Supreme Court Decision Making

Before reaching its decisions, the Supreme Court considers **briefs**, written legal arguments submitted by the opposing sides. (Unfortunately for judges, briefs are often anything but brief.) The justices then listen to oral arguments from attorneys on both sides in a **plenary session**—one attended by all justices—the chief justice presiding. During the half-hour allotted to each side to present its case, attorneys often find themselves interrupted by searching questions from the bench. Former law professor Antonin Scalia is especially well known for his willingness to turn the plenary session into a classroom seminar. Yet it is not always clear how closely the justices attend to the responses. As Chief Justice John Marshall said many years ago, "The acme of judicial distinction means the ability to look a lawyer straight in the eye for two hours and not hear a damned word he says."[91]

After hearing the oral argument, the justices usually reach a preliminary decision the same week in a private conference presided over by the chief justice. There are "three levels of elbow room about the conference table." The most ample is that for the chief justice and the senior associate justice, who sit at opposite ends. The next best is grabbed by the three most senior justices sitting on one side, leaving the four most junior crowded together across from them. No outsiders, not even a secretary, are permitted to attend. The only record consists of handwritten notes taken by individual justices.

From the outside, it may appear that the private conferences are opportunities for great minds to gather and discuss fundamental legal questions. But in most instances, the justices have already discussed the case with their law clerks and enter the conference room with their intentions fixed. The justices express their views and preliminary votes in order of seniority, beginning with the chief justice.[92] If the chief justice is in the minority, the writing of the opinion is assigned by the senior associate justice in the majority.[93]

The justice assigned the responsibility for preparing the court opinion circulates a draft version among the other eight. The author may then revise the opinion in light of comments and criticisms from the other justices. On rare occasions, the justice writing the opinion has "lost a court"—that is, one or more justices who voted with the majority at the first conference have changed their minds. To keep a majority, the justice writing the opinion may produce a bland opinion that gives little guidance to lower-court judges. In the 1993 sexual harassment case *Harris v. Forklift Systems*, for

You Are a Clerk to Supreme Court Justice Judith Gray

brief
Written arguments presented to a court by lawyers on behalf of clients.

plenary session
Activities of a court in which all judges participate.

The Roberts Court

In this composite, the justices of the Supreme Court as of 2006 are pictured from left to right according to their judicial philosophies. On the left are John Paul Stevens, Ruth Bader Ginsburg, Stephen Breyer, and David Souter. In the middle, is moderate Justice Anthony Kennedy. On the right are Chief Justice John Roberts, Samuel Alito, Antonin Scalia, and Clarence Thomas.

• *When the next justice is appointed, where do you think the new justice's picture will be positioned?*

dissenting opinion

Written opinion presenting the reasoning of judges who vote against the majority.

concurring opinion

A written opinion prepared by judges who vote with the majority but who wish either to disagree with or to elaborate on some aspect of the majority opinion.

example, the majority hardly created any precedent at all, saying only that courts should look at the "totality of the circumstances" in order to decide whether harassment in the workplace had occurred.[94]

Justices who vote against the majority may prepare a **dissenting opinion** that explains their disagreement. **Concurring opinions** may be written by those members of the majority who agree with the basic decision but disagree with some aspect of the reasoning included in the majority opinion or who wish to elaborate by raising further considerations. Two hundred years ago, when John Marshall was chief justice, the court was nearly always unanimous, and the chief justice wrote most opinions. Today, the Court is unanimous in its judgments in only about half its cases,[95] and quite apart from the dissenting opinions, concurring opinions are filed often enough that it is sometimes difficult to ascertain exactly what the majority has decided.

In the historic case of *Bush v. Gore* in which the Court ended the disputed 2000 presidential election by calling a halt to recounts in Florida, the Court issued an unsigned "majority" opinion, a concurring opinion signed by three justices, and four separate dissenting opinions, each signed by a single justice. Many observers found both the concurring opinion and some of the dissenting opinions more persuasive than the unsigned majority opinion. Apparently it was difficult to write a cogent opinion when the time available was extremely limited, divisions within the Court were deep, and compromises had to be reached to obtain the signatures of a majority.

Although the proliferation of dissenting and concurring opinions has caused considerable confusion about overall Supreme Court rulings, these opinions themselves often have a clearer and more convincing style than majority opinions—in part because they are signed by only one or two justices, making compromise language unnecessary. In *Harris v. Forklift Systems*, the sexual harassment case mentioned above, Justice Ginsburg, although agreeing with the decision, wrote a crisp concurring opinion that proposed a simple, straightforward standard for ascertaining whether harassment had occurred: Harassment, she wrote, exists whenever discriminatory conduct makes it more difficult for a person to perform well at a job. Convincingly written concurring and dissenting opinions, such as Ginsburg's, sometimes become even more influential than majority opinions.

Once the Court reaches a decision, it usually sends, or **remands**, the case to a lower court for implementation. Because the Supreme Court regards itself as responsible for establishing general principles and an overall framework, it seldom becomes involved in the detailed resolution of particular cases. This practice leaves a great deal of legal responsibility in the hands of lower courts.

Voting on the Supreme Court

Justices of the Court fall into quite predictable voting blocs. While Chief Justice John Roberts and associate justice Samuel Alito are still establishing their place on the Court, the remainder of the current justices can be divided into three fairly well-defined blocs.

The more liberal justices, consisting of Souter, the two Clinton appointees, Ruth Bader Ginsburg and Stephen Breyer, and in most cases senior associate justice John Stevens, favor a certain amount of **judicial activism**—a doctrine that says that the principle of *stare decisis* should sometimes be sacrificed in order to adapt the Constitution to changing conditions. Ginsburg and Breyer contend that too rigid an application of the principle of *stare decisis* would place the country in a straitjacket and render it unable to adapt. Judicial activists also see the Court as a mechanism for preserving minority rights and fundamental freedoms that may be trampled upon by electoral majorities.

A second bloc of conservative **restorationists**, including Thomas and Scalia, believe in overturning earlier liberal decisions. They think the only way the original meaning of the Constitution can be restored is by ignoring the doctrine of *stare decisis* until earlier liberal decisions have been reversed. For example, they favor reversing *Roe v. Wade*, the decision that declared laws forbidding abortion unconstitutional.

A crucial swing vote on the Court belongs to Justice Anthony Kennedy, who tends to favor **judicial restraint**, a doctrine that says that courts should, if at all possible, avoid overturning prior court decisions. If the law is to be changed, it should be changed not by the courts but by the people's elected representatives. Kennedy is willing to uphold prior decisions even when he does not necessarily agree with them. Although he may not agree that *Roe v. Wade* was a correct decision, he has expressed a reluctance to reverse it.

Most of the time, justices vote along lines anticipated by those who nominated and confirmed them. Both statements made in testimony before Congress and other information available at the time the justice was confirmed generally provide a clear indication of the justice's future voting pattern. According to one study, information about the political views of Supreme Court justices at the time they were being confirmed by the Senate allows one to predict correctly the justices' decisions in civil liberties cases more than 60 percent of the time.[96] That the future behavior of the typical justice is predictable may seem to suggest that the justices do not decide each case on its facts and merits. But this may simply reflect the fact that certain types of judges are likely to give greater weight to certain types of evidence and arguments in their decisions. Predictability also allows elected officials—both presidents and senators—to influence the future direction of the Supreme Court, thereby maintaining some degree of popular control of the courts.

remand
To send a case to a lower court to determine the best way of implementing the higher court's decision.

Chief Justice John Roberts

judicial activism
Doctrine that says the principle of *stare decisis* should sometimes be sacrificed in order to adapt the Constitution to changing conditions.

restorationist
Judge who thinks that the only way the original meaning of the Constitution can be restored is by ignoring the doctrine of *stare decisis* until liberal decisions have been reversed.

judicial restraint
Doctrine that says courts should, if at all possible, avoid overturning a prior court decision.

Not every prediction of future behavior is correct, however. The justice who most surprised those who favored his selection was Harry Blackmun, thought to be a judicial conservative when President Nixon appointed him in 1970. Yet just three years later Blackmun wrote the famous opinion in *Roe v. Wade* declaring state laws forbidding abortion unconstitutional. Blackmun himself once said, "Having been appointed by a Republican president and being accused now of being a flaming liberal on the court, the Republicans think I'm a traitor, I guess, and the Democrats don't trust me. And so I twist in the wind . . . beholden to no one, and that's just exactly where I want to be."[97]

Checks on Court Power

Although the judicial system is more independent and powerful in the United States than in many countries, the consequences of court decisions can be limited by other political actors. As political scientist Jack Peltason has put it, "Judicial decision making is one stage, not the only nor necessarily the final one.[98] Alexander Hamilton, writing in the *Federalist Papers,* explained why this was to be expected under the Constitution:

> The judiciary will always be the least dangerous to the political rights of the Constitution. The executive not only dispenses honors but holds the sword of the community. The legislature not only commands the purse, but prescribes the rules. The judiciary, on the contrary, has no influence over either the sword or the purse. It may truly be said to have neither force nor will, but merely judgment.[99]

Other branches of government can alter or circumscribe court decisions in three important ways: by constitutional amendment, by statutory revision, and by nonimplementation.

Constitutional Amendment

The power to amend the Constitution is the formal constitutional check on the Supreme Court's power of judicial review. But this constitutional check has been used on only a few occasions. The Eleventh Amendment overturned an early Court decision that gave citizens of one state the ability to sue another state. The Sixteenth Amendment allowing an income tax was prompted by a Court decision that seemed to prohibit one. Many amendments under consideration by Congress today have been generated by court decisions, including proposed amendments to ban abortions, allow school prayer, and prohibit gay marriages. For amendments to pass, supporters must ordinarily win a two-thirds vote in Congress and the backing of three-quarters of the states. In practice, the complexities of the amendment process make it the weakest check on court power.

Statutory Revision

Congress can reverse court decisions without resorting to a constitutional amendment if the court decision involves only statutory interpretation. In such cases, Congress can simply pass a clarifying law that reverses a court interpretation of earlier legislation. In the case of *Wards Cove Packing Co. v. Atonio*, for example, the Supreme Court gave a narrow interpretation to a congressional law banning race and gender discrimination.

The Court said that Congress intended that women and minorities bringing a discrimination complaint bear the burden of proof, a difficult assignment in these kinds of cases. Under pressure from women's groups and civil rights organizations, Congress responded in 1991 by passing a law that said the burden of proof had to be borne by the business, thereby reversing the Supreme Court decision.

Although passing new legislation is much easier than amending the Constitution, it may still be difficult and is ineffective if the Court decision involves constitutional interpretation.

Nonimplementation

Court decisions can also be checked simply by being ignored. When told of a Supreme Court decision he did not like, President Andrew Jackson reportedly replied, "Justice Marshall has made his decision, now let him enforce it."[100] Since Jackson's day, the prestige and authority of the Supreme Court has become deeply entrenched in American life. Outright refusal to obey a Supreme Court decision is now most unlikely. Even in the extraordinary *Bush v. Gore* controversy, the parties to the case readily obeyed the Court's decisions. When the Court ordered vote counters in Florida to stop counting ballots, it took less than an hour for ballot counting to come to a halt—despite the emotional intensity that had been aroused by the dispute. By contrast, earlier in the dispute, ballot counting in one Democratic-controlled county had continued for several hours after a deadline had been imposed by Florida's Republican secretary of state, even though her authority to set deadlines was written into state law.

Still, the power of courts to implement their decisions is not unlimited. State and local governments may mount strong resistance to lower-court decisions. After the Supreme Court declared Bible reading in public schools unconstitutional, the practice in most Tennessee school districts continued unchanged. As one school board attorney explained, "My personal conviction is that the Supreme Court decisions are correct, and I so told the Board and Superintendent, but I saw no reason to create controversy. If the Board had made public a decision abolishing devotional exercises, there would have been public outcry."[101]

To ensure implementation of judicial orders, courts sometimes appoint a **receiver**, an official who has the authority to see that judicial orders are carried out. For example, in 2005 a federal district court judge in San Francisco ordered a receiver to take charge of the health care system in California state prisons. The judge described the conditions there as so "horrifying" and "abysmal" that they violated constitutional guarantees against cruel and unusual punishment.[102]

But even the monitoring power of the courts can be checked by elected officials. For two decades, the Correction Department of the city of New York had been overseen by a court monitor who enforced judicial orders ensuring respect for the civil rights of prisoners. Judge Harold Baer, Jr., reluctantly withdrew the monitor in 1995 after Congress and the president, concerned that the rights of the guilty were taking precedence over the rights of victims, enacted a law limiting court authority in such matters. "Although the court's concerns with this new legislation are myriad," Judge Baer wrote, "I am constrained under the law to uphold it."[103]

receiver
Court official who has the authority to see that judicial orders are carried out.

Litigation as a Political Strategy

Interest groups have increasingly used the courts to place issues on the political agenda, particularly when elected officials have not responded to group demands. This strategy was first used successfully by civil rights groups, a topic discussed in detail in Chapter 17. But the technique has since spread and become a common political phenomenon.[104] This development is fully consistent with Alexis de Tocqueville's observation more than a century and a half ago that "there is hardly a political question in the United States which does not sooner or later turn into a judicial one."[105]

PARTICIPATION

The Courts and School Vouchers

Disabled Americans owe many of their current legal rights in the United States to an extraordinarily successful use of litigation as a political strategy. As late as 1970, school officials told many parents of disabled children that their sons and daughters were not qualified to attend public school. Challenging such denial of equal educational opportunity, advocacy groups won, in 1972, two federal court rulings that gave the disabled a right to an "appropriate education." Anticipating further litigation, many school officials felt that a federal law might clarify the situation. In response, Congress within two years passed a law said to be the "most significant child welfare legislation" of the decade.[106]

class action suit

Suit brought on behalf of all individuals in a particular category, whether or not they are actually participating in the suit.

To advance an issue, advocacy groups often file a **class action suit** on behalf of all individuals in a particular category, whether or not they are actually participating in the suit. For example, in the late 1990s, groups of former smokers in several states filed class action suits against the major tobacco companies for lying to consumers about the harms caused by smoking. In the first such case to reach a verdict favorable to plaintiffs, a jury ordered the five major tobacco companies to pay millions of dollars in damages to up to 500,000 ill Florida smokers.[107] In 2002, investors and former employees sued the collapsed energy conglomerate Enron, claiming that the company had bilked them out of billions of dollars in stock and pensions.[108]

Attorneys have been accused of abusing their power to file class action suits by filing problematic claims and then reaching settlements that mainly benefit lawyers, not clients. A class action suit filed against the city of Chicago in 2001 on behalf of 5,000 homeless people who claimed to have been harmed by the city's anti-begging law resulted in an average payment of less than $20 per plaintiff, and $375,000 for the lawyers.[109] But proponents justify class action suits on the grounds that often a legal issue affects many people in essentially the same way, and it would be costly and complicated for each member of the class to bring a separate individual suit in order to secure relief.

Chapter Summary

The courts are the branch of government most removed from political influences. Federal judges are appointed for life. They are expected only to apply the law, not to revise it. Constrained by the principle of *stare decisis*, they are expected to rely on legal precedents when reaching their decisions. They have been accused of sometimes using the power of judicial review to frustrate the popular will. In

the famous *Dred Scott* and *Schechter Poultry* cases, the Supreme Court may well have done so.

Yet the courts are not immune to electoral pressures. Although many important political issues eventually reach the Supreme Court, the day-to-day work of the judiciary is carried out by state and lower federal court judges, who interpret the civil and criminal code. Many state judges and district attorneys are elected officials, and political factors also influence the operation of the lower courts in many other ways.

When justices are selected for the Supreme Court, their political and judicial philosophies are closely evaluated by both the president and Congress. Once appointed, most Supreme Court justices decide cases in ways that are consistent with views they were known to have at the time of their selection. Most of the time, court decisions are broadly responsive to contemporary political currents. If court deci-sions challenge deep-seated political views, they may be modified by new legislation, frustrated by nonimplementa-tion, or even reversed by constitutional amendment.

The judicial system may not work perfectly, but it is probably better than most alternatives. If the law were more removed from politics, the law would control people instead of the reverse. But if federal judges did not have the distance from politics that lifetime appointment gives many of them, they could easily come into great pressure to pervert justice toward narrow, partisan ends.

Key Terms

appeal, p. 446

associate justice, p. 447

borking, p. 444

brief, p. 449

cert, p. 447

chief justice, p. 447

circuit court of appeals, p. 438

civil code, p. 428

class action suit, p. 454

concurring opinion, p. 450

criminal code, p. 428

defendant, p. 427

dissenting opinion, p. 450

district attorney, p. 429

double jeopardy, p. 441

federal district courts, p. 437

judicial activism, p. 451

judicial restraint, p. 451

judicial review, p. 430

law clerk, p. 448

legal distinction, p. 446

living-constitution theory, p. 432

Marbury v. Madison, p. 431

McCulloch v. Maryland, p. 441

opinion, p. 427

original-intent theory, p. 432

plain-meaning-of-the-text theory, p. 433

plaintiff, p. 427

plenary session, p. 449

precedent, p. 446

receiver, p. 453

remand, p. 451

restorationist, p. 451

reversal, p. 446

senatorial courtesy, p. 438

solicitor general, p. 448

stare decisis, p. 446

statutory interpretation, p. 436

U.S. attorney, p. 440

writ of *certiorari* (cert), p. 447

Suggested Readings

Of General Interest

Breyer, Stephen. *Active Liberty: Interpreting Our Democratic Constitution.* New York: Knopf, 2005. A sitting justice explains his approach to constitutional interpretation.

Carp, Robert A., and Ronald Stidham, *The Federal Courts.* 4th ed. Washington, DC: CQ Press, 2001. Lucid description of the federal court system and its political context.

McCloskey, Robert G. *The American Supreme Court.* 3rd ed. Revised by Sanford Levison. Chicago: University of Chicago Press, 2000. Excellent analysis that shows the close connection between public opinion and court decisions.

Pritchett, C. Herman. *The American Constitution.* New York: McGraw-Hill, 1959. Dated, but still authoritative, account of constitutional issues.

Scalia, Antonin. *A Matter of Interpretation: Federal Courts and the Law.* Princeton, NJ: Princeton University Press, 1997. A sitting justice explains his approach to constitutional interpretation.

Focused Studies

Agresto, John. *The Supreme Court and Constitutional Democracy.* Ithaca, NY: Cornell University Press, 1984. Makes a powerful case against judicial review.

Bronner, Ethan. *Battle for Justice: How the Bork Nomination Shook America.* New York: Norton, 1989. Fascinating case study of the Senate refusal to confirm Robert Bork's nomination to the Supreme Court.

Epstein, Lee, and Jeffrey A. Segal. *Advice and Consent: The Politics of Judicial Appointments.* New York: Oxford University Press, 2005. Timely and comprehensive study of federal judicial appointments.

Melnick, R. Shep. *Between the Lines: Interpreting Welfare Rights*. Washington, DC: The Brookings Institution, 1994. Insightful analysis of the Court's role in the interpretation and elaboration of statutory law.

O'Brien, David M., Editor. *Judges on Judging: Views from the Bench*. 2nd ed. Washington, DC: CQ Press, 2004. A fine selection of writings from Supreme Court justices and other judges.

Perry, H. W., Jr. *Deciding to Decide: Agenda Setting in the United States Supreme Court*. Cambridge, MA: Harvard University Press, 1991. Comprehensive explanation of the process by which the Supreme Court decides whether to review a case.

Simon, James F. *The Center Holds: The Power Struggle Inside the Rehnquist Court*. New York: Simon & Schuster, 1995. Describes the split between conservative and moderate justices.

On the Web

www.supremecourtus.gov

The official Web site of the U.S. Supreme Court contains information on the Court's docket, the text of recent opinions, the rules of the Court, and links to related Web sites. It also posts copies of Chief Justice Rehnquist's annual report on the federal judiciary.

www.usdoj.gov/osg/

Sometimes called "the tenth justice," the solicitor general participates in about two-thirds of Supreme Court cases. The Solicitor General's Office in the U.S. Department of Justice offers copies of briefs it has filed in federal court.

www.fjc.gov

In 1967 Congress created the Federal Judicial Center to produce research aimed at improving the administration of the judicial branch. Its reports, which are available online, cover general legal topics, such as antitrust law, as well as practical and institutional questions, such as media in the courtroom, caseloads, and the relationship between state and federal courts.

www.law.cornell.edu

The Legal Information Institute at Cornell Law School archives information on federal and state laws, and rules of civil and criminal procedure, and also provides a searchable database of Supreme Court decisions.

www.uscourts.gov

There is more to the federal court system than the Supreme Court. The Federal Judiciary homepage provides a concise guide to the federal court system, a regular newsletter, and annual reports on the state of the judiciary written by Chief Justice William Rehnquist.

www.ncsconline.org/

The National Center for State Courts showcases statistical information on the caseload of state court systems, as well as links to state-level legal associations.

CHAPTER 16

★ ★ ★ ★ ★ ★ ★ ★ ★ ★

Civil Liberties

CHAPTER OUTLINE

Privacy in the Age of Terrorism

When most people think of government surveillance and spying, they think of the Central Intelligence Agency (CIA), based in Langley, Virginia, on the outskirts of Washington, D.C. But the largest U.S. spy agency is actually a 45-minute drive northeast, in a boxy, obsidian building in Fort Meade, Maryland: the National Security Agency (NSA).

Created in 1952, the NSA is charged with breaking enemy codes and eavesdropping on suspicious communications around the world. Its 30,000 employees are more likely to be experts on mathematics and cryptography than they are to be adept at disguise or misdirection.[1] They use these skills to sift through a mind-boggling 650 million intercepted communications per day, searching for patterns, contacts with suspicious persons, and other "red flags" that would signal terrorist plotting, espionage, and other threats against the United States.[2]

While Americans have always accepted the need to spy on those who might be threats to the country, they have also been reluctant to allow espionage agencies to operate unchecked. A zeal to catch foreign plotters can easily evolve into a determination to apprehend American criminals, and in turn lead to surveillance of innocent Americans. A cautionary tale on this note occurred in the 1960s and early 1970s, when the NSA and other agencies spied on such "subversives" as folk singer Joan Baez and civil rights activist Martin Luther King, Jr.[3] Since that time, spy agencies have been prohibited by law from monitoring Americans without obtaining a warrant from a secret federal court, established exclusively to handle such sensitive cases.

But in the age of terrorism, things may be changing. In late 2005, the *New York Times* revealed that, pursuant to an executive order from the Bush White House (see executive orders, Chapter 13), the NSA had been wiretapping many (perhaps millions of) communications between American citizens and foreigners abroad without obtaining a warrant.[4] Grounding his justifications on congressional enactments that authorized steps to be taken against Al Qaeda terrorists, President Bush argued that the wiretaps were a crucial part of the war on terror, and said "there's no doubt in my mind it is legal."[5] Months later, more press reports claimed that, in a second program, the NSA had worked with major telephone companies such as Verizon, AT&T, and BellSouth to compile a massive database of billions of domestic telephone records. These records were then used in so-called "network analysis" that might reveal patterns that could lead to the uncovering of terrorist plots.[6] The spy agency did not listen to the content of phone conversations in this second program, but scanned only the numbers called and the times calls were made.

Is this kind of monitoring acceptable? Some experts argued that it was essential in the new terror war, and did not unduly intrude into Americans' lives.[7] "The architect of [the telephone records] program deserves our thanks and probably a medal," wrote one authority on terrorism, stressing that the phone records the NSA used were stripped of information that could easily identify individuals.[8] President Bush insisted that "the privacy of ordinary Americans is fiercely protected in all our activities."[9] Others argued that the White House and the NSA had gone too far. The telecommunications company Qwest said it had refused to hand over its records to the government because of privacy concerns.[10] Senator Hillary Clinton (D-NY) said she was "deeply disturbed" by news of the program.[11]

Surveys revealed cautious public support of the NSA intelligence gathering initiatives—a slim majority in several national polls voiced approval of the president's policies.[12] But many Americans—voters and government officials alike—seemed to need more time to absorb the news about the NSA programs and consider whether they violated privacy guarantees. As Senator Arlen Specter put it, "We're really flying blind on the subject [right now] and that's not a good way to approach . . . the constitutional issues involving privacy."[13]

MAKING THE CONNECTION

For some, NSA eavesdropping is an essential and appropriate response to a significant threat. To others, the new measures represented an infringement of the rights of individuals driven by a desire to respond to public demands for security. In this chapter we place such debates in a larger constitutional context by describing the evolution of civil liberties under the U.S. Constitution. The concept of **civil liberties**, the fundamental freedoms that together preserve the rights of a free people, is never mentioned in the Constitution, nor has it ever been explicitly defined by the Supreme Court. But specific rights that together make up the civil liberties of U.S. citizens are to be found in the Bill of Rights—the first 10 amendments to the Constitution—and again in amendments added to the Constitution after the Civil War. These rights include the right to free speech, free association, and free exercise of religion.

Civil liberties should be distinguished from civil rights (considered in Chapter 17), which concern the rights of citizens to equal treatment under the law. This distinction may seem confusing, because at times both categories of protection may be referred to as "rights." But civil liberties are fundamental freedoms from government interference, whereas civil rights are fundamental guarantees of equal treatment by the government. In this chapter we focus on civil liberties.

First, we discuss the origins and evolution of civil liberties in the United States. Next, we consider the practical meaning of the freedoms of speech, press, and assembly. We then describe the two components of the Constitution's guarantee of freedom of religion, and discuss how these two components may at times conflict with one another. Finally, we examine the rights that accused criminals have under the law, and explain how conflicting views of citizens' right to privacy shape modern court decisions and policy disputes.

Origins of Civil Liberties in the United States

The evolution of civil liberties in the United States has been shaped by Supreme Court rulings. But these liberties have also been affected by political debates, interest group activism, and election outcomes. Civil liberties have not been created simply through the decisions of a small number of justices; rather, they reflect basic values shared by most citizens (see Chapter 4). In this section we discuss the constitutional beginnings of civil liberties and how Americans' understanding of these liberties has evolved since then.

civil liberties
Fundamental freedoms that together preserve the rights of a free people.

Balancing Liberty and Security at a Time of War

Origins of the Bill of Rights

America's revolutionary leaders rallied supporters to their side by invoking the liberties of Americans. Not only did the Declaration of Independence assert fundamental rights to "Life, Liberty and the pursuit of Happiness," but many states incorporated similar principles into their constitutions and statutes. For example, the Virginia Assembly passed a bill of rights a month before the Continental Congress approved the

Declaration of Independence. Among its provisions was the pronouncement that "freedom of the press" was "one of the great bulwarks of liberty."[14]

Despite their expressed commitment to basic freedoms, the colonial revolutionaries had little regard for the liberties of the Tories, who opposed the revolution. They closed Tory newspapers, threatened well-known Tory editors, confiscated their property, and so intimidated the royalists that some 80,000 to 100,000 people fled to Canada, England, and the West Indies.[15] Even John Adams, a future president of the United States, vowed that "the [Tory] presses will produce no more seditious or traitorous speculations."[16]

Nor did those who drafted the Constitution include explicit protection for individual civil liberties. When anti-Federalist Charles Pinckney offered a motion at the Constitutional Convention to guarantee freedom of the press, the Federalist majority voted the measure down—on the grounds that states, not the central government, should be responsible for regulating speech and the press.[17] Only when ratification of the Constitution seemed in danger did Federalists agree to add a bill of rights in the form of a series of amendments to the Constitution (see Chapter 2). The first Congress approved the 10 amendments that make up the Bill of Rights in 1790 only at James Madison's insistence. Madison, then a member of the House of Representatives, felt significant pressure from his Virginia constituents to press for the amendments. Most others in Congress voted for the amendments, it seems, because they thought the provisions would have little practical effect.

Few Liberties Before the Civil War

At first, the Bill of Rights applied only to the national government, not to the states. The First Amendment, for example, focused solely on the national legislature, saying that "Congress shall make no law" abridging speech or religious practice. As a result, for example, Massachusetts, Connecticut, and New Hampshire continued to support Congregationalist ministers with tax money for several decades.[18]

Other provisions in the Bill of Rights did not specifically mention either the national or the state governments, leaving open the possibility that they applied to both. For example, the Fifth Amendment said that "no person shall . . . be deprived of life, liberty, or property, without due process of law." But when the owner of Barron's Wharf complained that the City of Baltimore had deprived his company of property without "due process of law," the Supreme Court, in 1833, said the Fifth Amendment limited the powers of the federal government but not those of the states. The Bill of Rights, wrote Chief Justice John Marshall in *Barron v. Baltimore*, "contain[s] no expression indicating an intention to apply them to the state governments. This court cannot so apply them."[19]

It would have been difficult for Marshall to apply the Bill of Rights to the states prior to the Civil War, because doing so would have forced the country to confront the slavery issue head-on. Were slaves people who had liberties granted to them by the First Amendment, or were they property that belonged to their masters, according to the Fifth Amendment? For decades, this was a question too controversial to consider.

When the Supreme Court finally did consider the issue in 1857, coming down on the side of slave owners, the decision damaged the authority of the Court and helped accelerate a national crisis. In the extraordinary *Dred Scott v. Sandford* case, Chief Justice

Not Much Free Speech

Many a Tory editor was hanged in effigy before and during the American Revolution.

• *Why was free speech limited at the time of the American Revolution?*

Roger Taney reached the conclusion that the Fifth Amendment precluded Congress from denying Dred Scott's master his right of property. As for Dred Scott, the slave, Taney ruled that he did not qualify as a "person" and therefore was entitled to no protections under the Fifth Amendment (see Chapter 15, p. 434).

Applying the Bill of Rights to State Governments

CONSTITUTION, FOURTEENTH AMENDMENT: *"No State shall . . . deprive any person of life, liberty, or property, without due process of law."*

The Civil War transformed the spirit, meaning, and application of the Bill of Rights. Once slavery had been abolished, the words in the first 10 amendments could begin to be applied to all Americans. To give the Bill of Rights new meaning, Congress and the states enacted three **civil rights amendments**, the Thirteenth, Fourteenth, and Fifteenth Amendments, which abolished slavery, redefined civil rights and liberties, and guaranteed the right to vote to all adult male citizens, respectively.

Of all the provisions in the civil rights amendments, the one that has had the greatest significance for civil liberty is the **due process clause** of the Fourteenth Amendment, which says that a person cannot be "deprive[d] . . . of life, liberty, or property without due process of law." As we have noted, a nearly identical phrase had already appeared in the Fifth Amendment, but the Fourteenth Amendment, by specifying that "no *state* shall" infringe upon these liberties, greatly expanded individual freedoms. Now neither the national government nor the states were permitted to arbitrarily interfere with personal freedoms.

This expansion did not occur all at once, however. Despite the language in the Fourteenth Amendment, the Supreme Court did not immediately conclude that the states must abide by the entire Bill of Rights. The Fourteenth Amendment does not refer to the Bill of Rights, and the Court appeared to conclude that a sweeping decision applying the entire Bill of Rights to the states would be impractical, creating a "vast and perhaps unmanageable problem" of enforcement.[20] Instead, the Court has

civil rights amendments
The Thirteenth, Fourteenth, and Fifteenth Amendments, which abolished slavery, redefined civil rights and liberties, and guaranteed the right to vote to all adult male citizens.

due process clause
Found in the Fifth and Fourteenth Amendments to the Constitution; forbids deprivation of life, liberty, or property without due process of law.

selective incorporation

The case-by-case process through which the courts apply the Bill of Rights to the states by invoking the due process clause of the Fourteenth Amendment.

taken a gradual approach known as **selective incorporation**, a process by which it considers provisions of the Bill of Rights on a case-by-case basis, deciding over time whether or not the Fourteenth Amendment's due process clause applies sections of the Bill of Rights to the states.

In the 1930s, Justice Benjamin Cardozo justified the Court's method of selective incorporation by arguing that there are some rights that are more important than others. Rights such as freedom of speech, for example, are so essential that "neither liberty nor justice would exist if they were sacrificed."[21] These rights may naturally fall under Fourteenth Amendment protection, while other less essential rights may not. Over the course of many decades, nearly all of the provisions in the Bill of Rights have been incorporated. But a few exceptions remain, such as the Second Amendment, which says that inasmuch as "a well-regulated militia" is necessary to "the security of a free state, the right of the people to keep and bear arms shall not be abridged." Although the National Rifle Association (NRA) has argued that state laws banning or restricting the use of guns are contrary to the Constitution, the Supreme Court has maintained that this amendment guarantees only the state governments' right to have a militia.[22]

Freedom of Speech, Assembly, and Press

What Speech Is Protected by the Constitution?

CONSTITUTION, FIRST AMENDMENT: *"Congress shall make no law . . . abridging the freedom of speech, or of the press; or the right of the people peaceably to assemble, . . . "*

Of the liberties listed in the Bill of Rights, one trio is paramount: freedom of speech, press, and assembly. The three are closely intertwined. If free speech is to be effective, it must be communicated through a free press. Unless an audience can be assembled to listen, speakers might as well keep silent.

Even though the beginnings of these freedoms date back to the colonial period, the doctrine of free expression, as we know it today, is not so deeply entrenched in the American tradition as Fourth of July speakers often proclaim. Despite the First Amendment, people have been jailed for expressing controversial thoughts as long ago as 1798 and as recently as 1968. As activists have challenged state and federal laws restricting freedoms, the Supreme Court has developed a set of standards for interpreting the First Amendment that has been as much a reaction to the climate of public sentiment as it has been a reading of clear legal precedents. We spend the bulk of this section considering free speech, and then illustrate how the Supreme Court has applied constitutional doctrines developed in free-speech cases to cases involving freedom of the press and free assembly. Finally, we point out key limitations of free expression in such areas as commercial speech, obscenity, and libel, areas that the public—and the courts—are more willing to regulate.

Free Speech and Majoritarian Democracy

Free speech is vital to the workings of free elections in a democratic society. In the absence of free speech, government officials could manipulate public opinion without fear of contradiction. Elections have little meaning when candidates cannot express their opinions without fear of punishment.

Even so, elections are won by candidates who are backed by a majority of the voters, and majorities can at times be as tyrannical as single-minded despots. The greatest threat to the rights of the people, said James Madison, is the **tyranny of the majority**—the suppression of minority opinions by those voted into power by a majority.[23] The larger a majority gets, the more sure it is that its views are correct, and the more capable it is of punishing dissenters. As British historian Lord Acton said in 1878, "The one pervading evil of democracy is the tyranny of the majority, or rather of that party, not always the majority, that succeeds, by force or fraud, in carrying elections."[24]

tyranny of the majority
Stifling of dissent by those voted into power by the majority.

Because of such fears about unscrupulous political coalitions, Madison believed that free speech should be placed outside the reach of even very powerful majorities. Accordingly, the Constitution's First Amendment specifically protects speech from regulation by Congress. Enshrining free-speech rights in the Constitution meant that majorities would have to tolerate dissent—at least until they could muster the strength to change the Bill of Rights.

The classic defense of free speech was provided by the English civil libertarian John Stuart Mill, who insisted that in the free exchange of ideas, truth would eventually triumph over error. This argument, said Mill, applied not just to politics, but to many aspects of life. Galileo's declaration that the Earth was not at the center of the universe eventually became accepted as true, although informed opinion initially regarded his claims as preposterous. Modern events seem to bear out Mill's argument. Sixty years ago, geologists laughed at Alfred Wegener's suggestion that the world's continents gradually drifted over long distances. We now know that they do.

These examples illustrate the value of free speech in scientific debates, but must we tolerate even offensive and vicious error? It is not easy to accept the idea of people enjoying the freedom to spread doctrines of racial hatred. Are their beliefs not founded on false premises that could never be shown to be true? To such contentions, Mill replied that "he who knows only his own side of the case, knows little of that."[25] Mill argued further that error suppressed becomes more powerful by virtue of its suppression. Only if error is allowed to express itself can its proponents be denied the privilege of a false martyrdom.

From "Bad Tendency" to "Clear and Present Danger"

In colonial days, punishment for supposedly harmful speech was allowed under an English judicial standard known as the **bad tendency test**, a rule that held that expression could be punished if it could ultimately lead to illegal behavior. British courts developed the bad tendency standard to protect the monarchy from criticism, and also used it broadly to punish speech that was harmful to public morals and to the official church.[26] After the ratification of the Constitution, many Americans disagreed about whether the First Amendment simply restated the bad tendency test, or instead provided a much broader range of protection from government interference.

bad tendency test
Rule from English law saying that expression could be punished if it could ultimately lead to illegal behavior.

Unfortunately, an answer to this question would have to wait for many years. The courts did not enforce the Bill of Rights immediately, in part because until the ratification of the Fourteenth Amendment, it protected the right of free speech only against actions by Congress, not against those by state governments.

Even in more recent times, the Supreme Court has not been a leader in protecting those with unpopular opinions from the tyranny of the majority. Instead, the Supreme Court's view of what free speech entails has moved along at about the same speed as—or perhaps a little slower than—that of the rest of the country. In the words of one scholar, "the Court has seldom lagged far behind or forged far ahead of America."[27] Nonetheless, progress toward free speech in the United States can best be traced by noting the evolution in Court doctrine.

The first major Supreme Court decision affecting freedom of speech arose out of the conscription of young men into the army during World War I. Wartime creates conditions that test the boundaries of civil liberties. As the country mobilizes to fight a common foe, elected officials are often under public pressure to identify pacifists or other dissenters as being in league with the enemy. As Alexis de Tocqueville wrote, "All those who seek to destroy the liberties of a democratic nation ought to know that war is the surest and shortest means to accomplish it."[28]

The occasion for the ruling was the conviction of Charles Schenck, a socialist who had mailed anti-conscription materials to draft-age men during the war. The jury decided that Schenck had violated the 1917 Espionage Act, which made it illegal to obstruct armed forces recruitment.

When asked to review Schenck's conviction, the Supreme Court, in *Schenck v. United States* (1919), enunciated the **clear and present danger doctrine**—the principle that people should have complete freedom of speech unless there is a "clear and present danger" that their language will provoke "evils that Congress has a right to prevent." The Supreme Court, which was no more sympathetic to socialists than Congress had been when it passed the Espionage Act, upheld Schenck's conviction. The Schenck case nevertheless marked the first time the Court moved to limit the regulation of speech by proposing a definite standard. Justice Oliver Wendell Holmes, author of the Court's opinion in the case, made the common-sense observation that no person has the right falsely to cry "Fire" in a crowded theater: Such a cry creates a clear and present danger to the public safety. In the same way, he argued, Congress could regulate speech only when there was a clear and present danger that the speech would provoke serious evils. His example seemed to capture succinctly the appropriate balance between the right of free speech and the need to maintain social order.

The meaning of clear and present danger, however, is open to different interpretations. A critical question is whether this standard simply restates the old bad tendency test (which allows limitations if speech *could* lead to illegal activities), or whether it instead defines a much narrower set of circumstances under which the government could legitimately limit speech (involving a determination about whether speech is *very likely* to lead to illegal activities). For example, many college campuses have sought to limit the use of so-called hate speech. (See the accompanying *Democratic Dilemma.*) Critics of such regulations might argue that in no sense does hate speech pose the kind of immediate peril that crying "Fire" in a crowded theater does. Others might reply that if racial and ethnic slurs came to be widely used, they would indeed constitute a clear and present danger to the safety of individuals, to the public order, and to the climate of intellectual growth; to keep that from happening, speech should be restricted before the danger becomes too present. Under this second interpretation, the clear and present danger standard seems to be equivalent to the bad tendency test.

Holmes himself took this second point of view in the Schenck case, appearing to argue that the clear and present danger test was the same as the bad tendency test. He said that Schenck's actions constituted a clear and present danger to the successful prosecution of the war because, if it achieved its ends, the mailing of anti-draft pamphlets

clear and present danger doctrine

The principle that people should have complete freedom of speech unless their language endangers the nation.

DEMOCRATIC DILEMMA

Do Campus Speech Codes Unduly Restrict Free Speech?

College campuses are supposed to foster creativity and intellectual growth. But since the 1980s, a majority of the nation's colleges and universities have attempted to adopt speech codes that proscribe faculty members and students' uttering offensive words or promoting unacceptable ideas.

Some proponents argue that such codes are essential for intellectual activity to thrive on campus. Racist or sexist language, say proponents of speech codes, only serves to stifle discussion and put many students on edge. Take, for example, the true story of a farm-science professor who used a *Playboy* centerfold to illustrate different cuts of meat. Is this a legitimate exercise of freedom of expression, or is it offensive and punishable behavior?

Or take another example provided by Sharon Gwyn of Stanford University, who speaks from personal experience:

> When I was in sixth grade, my teacher gave us the word "slavery" in a spelling test. He recited a sentence to clarify its meaning: "Sharon is lucky she is not in slavery." As my stomach began to lurch, my hands held tighter to my pencil . . . . My teacher merely smiled; he never apologized . . . . If I was hurt in a situation of that level, think of how the person who is the target of a racial epithet must feel.

Others maintain that offensive language and behavior, though sometimes painful, are part of intellectual growth. Says Jason Shepard, an openly gay student at the University of Wisconsin, "Racism, sexism, homophobia are all parts of our society, whether we like it or not. We can't erect a wall around our university and pretend those things don't exist." Philosophy professor Lester Hunt agrees:

> Some people, like me, teach subjects that concern all the hot-button areas—race, gender, you name it—and what the [speech] code does is threaten you with punishment if you say the wrong thing. That makes it difficult or impossible to teach these subjects effectively.

• *Should colleges and universities restrict certain types of speech on campus?*

• *In early 2006, professors and student groups at several colleges and universities generated controversy by displaying Danish cartoons of the Muslim prophet Muhammad that had sparked riots in the Middle East. Muslim students found the images grossly offensive, but one professor justified her display of the cartoons as creating "a teaching moment." With whom do you agree?*

SOURCES: Gwyn's remarks are quoted from the *New York Times*, May 12, 1989: B12; Danish cartoon case from Nat Hentoff, "'Free Speech' Cries Ring Hollow on College Campuses and Beyond," *USA Today*, April 19, 2006, 11A. Other material is from Mitchell Zuckoff, "A New Word on Speech Codes; One School That Led Way Is Rethinking Its Rules," *Boston Globe*, October 21, 1998: A1; and Tom Mashberg, "Debates Rage on Campus Over Free-Speech Rules," *Boston Herald*, October 31, 1999: 1.

to draft-age men could endanger the war effort.[29] Holmes ignored the fact that few prospective servicemen paid much attention to Schenck and his associates. In a very similar case, however, Holmes tried to separate his clear and present danger test from the bad tendency standard. In *Abrams v. United States* (1919), several activists were charged with violating the Espionage Act when they printed and distributed leaflets advocating socialism. Although the majority of the Court felt that the pamphlets had a tendency harmful enough for the government to jail the activists, Holmes dissented, arguing that the "publishing of a silly leaflet by an unknown man" posed no grave danger to the war effort.[30]

In cases after *Abrams*, Holmes continued to argue for a clear and present danger test that allowed for fewer restrictions on speech than the bad tendency test did. Although the rest of the Court was at first reluctant to follow him, the doctrine became the foundation upon which a free-speech tradition was gradually built. During the 1930s, when the public was more tolerant of dissenting opinion, the Supreme Court, reflecting the changing political climate, explicitly defended the civil liberties of minorities. One case decided in 1931, *Stromberg v. California*, was particularly important, because for the first time it gave First Amendment protection to extremely unpopular opinions. Yetta Stromberg had encouraged children attending a camp operated by the Young Communist League to pledge allegiance to the flag of the Soviet Union, a violation of California's "red-flag" law.[31] The Supreme Court overturned her conviction, saying that the California law limited "free political discussion." Because Stromberg did not constitute a clear and present danger, said the Court, her civil liberties should not be curtailed.

Fighting Words Doctrine

The toleration that emerged during the 1930s did not survive the onset of World War II. In 1940 Congress responded to public outrage against fascism by enacting the Smith Act, which forbade advocating the overthrow of the government by force. Even some university administrators prohibited demonstrations against the draft, arguing that such demonstrations would reflect poorly on their schools. Columbia University president Nicholas Butler justified the ban in these words: "Before academic freedom comes university freedom to pursue its high ideals, unembarrassed by conduct which tends to damage its reputation."[32]

Instead of acting as a bulwark against majority tyranny during World War II, the Supreme Court endorsed limitations on free speech. In the 1942 case of *Chaplinsky v. New Hampshire*, the Court enunciated the **fighting words doctrine** that some words constitute violent acts and are therefore not protected under the First Amendment. Walter Chaplinsky, a member of the Jehovah's Witnesses religious group, had asked a policeman to guard him from a threatening crowd objecting to his pacifist address. When the policeman gave him no protection but instead cursed him and asked him to "come along," Chaplinsky called the policeman "a God damned racketeer" and "a damned Fascist." Enunciating the fighting words doctrine, the Supreme Court upheld Chaplinsky's conviction on the grounds that he had used threatening words that "are no essential part of any exposition of ideas" and that "by their very utterance inflict injury or intend to incite an immediate breach of the peace."[33] This new fighting words doctrine seriously qualified the Court's earlier inclination to protect most speech under the clear and present danger doctrine.

fighting words doctrine
The principle, endorsed by the Supreme Court in *Chaplinsky v. New Hampshire* (1942), that some words constitute violent acts and are therefore not protected under the First Amendment.

Balancing Doctrine

The end of World War II did not automatically restore civil liberties to dissident groups. Instead, those who were regarded as Communist sympathizers suffered harassment by government officials responding to public concern about the growing conflict between the United States and the Soviet Union. Republican senator Joseph McCarthy of Wisconsin gained political popularity by accusing artists, teachers, and government officials of having ties to the Communist Party. As part of the anti-Communist crusade, Congress voted to require that all employees of the federal government take an oath swearing loyalty to the United States. Students also had to take this oath when applying for student loans.

Once again, it was up to the courts to protect the free speech of minority dissidents. But, instead of taking special care to protect free speech, the Supreme Court enunciated the **balancing doctrine**—the principle that freedom of speech had to be balanced against other competing public interests at stake in particular circumstances. The Court developed this doctrine when considering a case in which 11 leaders of the Communist Party had been convicted under the Smith Act for espousing the revolu-

balancing doctrine
The principle enunciated by the courts that freedom of speech must be balanced against other competing public interests at stake in particular circumstances.

tionary overthrow of the government. In *Dennis v. United States* (1951), the Court said the convictions had been constitutional, arguing that the "balance . . . must be struck in favor" of the governmental interest in resisting subversion.[34] The balancing doctrine was used to reinterpret and place limits on the clear and present danger doctrine.

It was elected political leaders, not judges, who resisted the threat that McCarthyism posed to the country's civil liberties. A disgusted President Eisenhower refused to act on McCarthy's most outrageous accusations, and McCarthy's Senate colleagues finally inquired into the senator's methods of operation, later censuring him for his inappropriate conduct.

Fundamental Freedoms Doctrine

After an elected president and Congress had exposed and discredited McCarthy, public opinion became increasingly supportive of protecting the free-speech rights of all Americans, even radicals and Communists. Although 70 percent of people surveyed in the 1950s said they would oppose allowing a Communist to speak in their community, this number fell to about 40 percent by 1975, and to 29 percent by 2004.[35] Reflecting these changes in public opinion, the Supreme Court gradually became committed to the **fundamental freedoms doctrine**—the principle that some constitutional provisions ought to be given special preference because they are basic to the functioning of a democratic society. The doctrine has its origins in a Supreme Court opinion written in 1938 by Justice Harlan Stone, who said that some freedoms, such as freedom of speech, have a "preferred position" in the Constitution; any law threatening these freedoms must be subject to strict scrutiny by the Supreme Court.[36]

Although no single court case specifically set forth the fundamental freedoms doctrine, it became the Supreme Court's governing principle during the 1960s in the midst of the Vietnam War. Under its guidance, the Court was more effective at defending dissenters against government repression than in any previous war. As one civil libertarian wrote in 1973, "The truly significant thing in recent years has not been the attempt of the current administration to suppress criticism, but rather the marked inability of the administration to do so effectively."[37] In virtually every case that came before it, the Court ruled against efforts to suppress free speech. For example, it overturned the expulsion from the University of Missouri of a student who had distributed a newspaper containing a picture of a policeman raping the Statue of Liberty. Said the Court, "The mere dissemination of ideas—no matter how offensive to good taste—on a state university campus may not be shut off" in the name of decency.[38]

The fundamental freedoms doctrine has now become firmly established. Nothing better illustrates the contemporary Supreme Court's strong commitment to this principle than its rulings with respect to flag burning.[39] During the 1984 Republican National Convention in Dallas, Gregory Johnson was arrested for burning an American flag to protest the policies of the Reagan administration. Five years later, Johnson's case came before the Supreme Court. The Court, in *Texas v. Johnson* (1989), overturned his conviction, saying the principal purpose of free speech is to invite dispute and the mere burning of the flag was "expressive conduct" that did not breach the peace.[40]

Unlike earlier court decisions on the matter, the Supreme Court in the flag-burning case went well beyond popular opinion of the day. In a spirited dissent to the case,

Senator Joseph McCarthy
Senator Joseph McCarthy, built a career in the 1950s on investigating alleged Communist sympathizers.
• *His methods outraged many, but should civil liberties be balanced against other important governmental interests, such as national security?*

fundamental freedoms doctrine
Court doctrine stating that laws impinging on the freedoms that are fundamental to the preservation of democratic practice—the freedoms of speech, press, assembly, and religion—are to be scrutinized by the courts more closely than other legislation. These are also termed the preferred freedoms.

Gregory Johnson and the Flag

Gregory Johnson's conviction for torching the American flag in 1984 was overturned by the Supreme Court.

• *Is flag burning protected free expression, as the Court argued, or is the flag a unique national symbol that is worthy of special treatment?*

prior restraint doctrine

Legal doctrine that gives individuals the right to publish without prior restraint—that is, without first submitting material to a government censor.

Political Correctness

Chief Justice Rehnquist quoted Ralph Waldo Emerson and the national anthem, arguing that "For more than 200 years, the American flag has occupied a unique position as the symbol of our Nation, a uniqueness that justifies a governmental prohibition against flag burning."[41] President George H. W. Bush called for a constitutional amendment that would prohibit flag desecration, and more than 70 percent of the public supported him. Almost immediately, Congress passed a law making it a federal offense to burn the flag. The very day the law was passed, activists set fire to flags in Seattle and Washington, D.C., preparing the ground for another court decision. The next year the Supreme Court, in *United States v. Eichman* (1990), declared the new law unconstitutional.[42] Many thought it an indication that the commitment to free speech was now very broadly based when Antonin Scalia, one of the Court's most conservative justices, voted with the majority.

If anything, Supreme Court conservatives have become champions of free speech. In *R.A.V. v. City of St. Paul* (1990), Scalia wrote a majority opinion that gave protection to speech criticizing particular ethnic groups. The City of St. Paul had passed an ordinance forbidding the placement on public or private property of a symbol that "arouses anger, alarm or resentment in others on the basis of race, color, creed, religion or gender." When a group of teenagers was caught placing a "crudely made cross" made of "broken chair legs" inside the fence of the yard of a black neighbor and setting fire to it, the City of St. Paul charged them with violating the city ordinance. The Supreme Court unanimously ruled that the ordinance violated their right of free speech, saying that ordinary trespassing laws were adequate to deal with the alleged intrusion on a person's property.[43]

Freedom of the Press

Freedom of the press during the early colonial period was governed by the **prior restraint doctrine**, which said the government could not censor an article before it was published. However, the prior restraint doctrine did not prevent prosecution after the fact. Instead, the publisher could be convicted under the bad tendency test for bringing the government's "dignity into contempt," even if what he said were true. Thus in 1734, when John Peter Zenger published an accurate critique of an incompetent, unprincipled New York governor, the governor put Zenger in jail at excessive bail for 10 months while he was awaiting trial. In one of the great early victories for freedom of the press, the jury found Zenger innocent after his attorney argued that the issue at stake was "the Liberty—both of exposing and opposing arbitrary Power . . . by speaking and writing Truth."[44]

Although the Zenger case was an important event in the history of press freedom, it was nearly two centuries later before the Supreme Court ruled that a publisher could not be punished for promoting a particular point of view. In 1931 the Supreme Court, in *Near v. Minnesota*, overruled a Minnesota law that prohibited newspapers from publishing "malicious, scandalous and defamatory" material. Even though a publication banned under the law had printed vicious anti-Semitic and racist harangues, the Court regarded the law as "the essence of censorship."[45]

In one of its most significant decisions, *New York Times v. United States* (1971), the Supreme Court rejected an attempt by the Nixon administration to prevent, on grounds of national security, the *New York Times* from publishing the "Pentagon Papers," a lengthy and detailed Defense Department document revealing many mistakes made by government officials in their conduct of the Vietnam War. Although the Court suggested that prior restraint might be permitted under particularly extreme circumstances if national security were endangered, it ruled in the newspaper's favor on the grounds that the "Pentagon Papers" did not, in fact, include highly sensitive material.

The Supreme Court has often treated freedom of the press as synonymous with freedom of speech. If speech is permitted in a certain case, a publication containing the same message is also permitted under the Constitution. On the one hand, newspapers, pamphlets, and the Internet enjoy the broadest First Amendment protections because they are, in theory, accessible to all. On the other, the Court has ruled that radio and television may be regulated by the government, since technically the airwaves are public property and comparatively few people have access to them (see Chapter 9). While prior restraint of radio and television programs is not permitted, the Federal Communications Commission may levy fines or refuse to renew a station's broadcast license if it fails to meet particular standards. After Janet Jackson bared a breast during the 2004 Superbowl halftime show, many in Congress and the general public called for increased penalties for broadcasters who aired offensive material.[46] In 2006, Congress increased maximum fines for indecency from $32,500 per violation to $325,000.[47]

Freedom of Association

The freedom of association has long been considered to be inseparable from the freedoms of speech and of the press. Without the ability to assemble, the free exchange of ideas that John Stuart Mill advocated would be difficult if not impossible. Although the Court was willing to limit the activities of some fringe groups in the 1950s, as the *Dennis v. United States* case discussed above shows, the justices gradually broadened their interpretation of the rights of popular assembly in succeeding years. In the case of *NAACP v. Alabama* (1958), for example, the Court ruled that Alabama could not compel the National Association for the Advancement of Colored People to turn over its membership lists to the state. In this case, said Justice Harlan, a requirement of membership disclosure would be "as effective a restraint on freedom of association" as the direct governmental punishment in cases such as *Near v. Minnesota*.[48]

Several recent rulings on freedom of association have been controversial because they concern the ability of private organizations to exclude particular members. In *Boy Scouts of America v. Dale* (2000), for example, the Court ruled that the Scouts could refuse to accept a prospective scoutmaster who was gay. Accepting gay scoutmasters, argued the Court, would infringe upon the Scouts' ability to convey their system of values to youth, one of the tenets of which is that "homosexual conduct is not morally straight."[49]

Limitations on Free Expression

Although free expression has now been firmly established as one of the country's fundamental freedoms, not all expression is free of government control. In particular, three types of speech are subject to regulation: commercial speech, obscenity, and libel.

Commercial speech—advertising or other speech made for business purposes—may be regulated. According to the Court, regulation of commercial speech is needed

commercial speech
Advertising or other speech made for business purposes; may be regulated.

so that companies will not take advantage of consumers by providing false or misleading information. Also, commercial speech can be controlled to discourage the consumption of substances the government regards as harmful. For example, cigarette advertising on television and radio is forbidden, despite the complaints by tobacco companies that this prohibition interferes with their right to free speech.

obscenity
Publicly offensive language or portrayals with no redeeming social value.

Obscenity—publicly offensive language or portrayals with no redeeming social value—is not protected under the First Amendment. Whether explicit sexual material is obscene depends on whether it has some social or cultural purpose. The Court, in *Redrup v. New York* (1967), came close to saying that it would not uphold any obscenity conviction unless the obscenity involved a juvenile, was forced upon unwilling adults, or "pandered" to the most disgusting of prurient interests. But just a few years later, in *Miller v. California* (1973), a more conservative Court said that obscenity is a matter to be settled according to local community standards.[50] Overall, the Court seems to have said that local communities may ban hard-core pornography if they wish to do so. Less explicit sexual material may not be outlawed, particularly if presented within an artistic or literary context.

Hate Speech

With the growth of the Internet, the distinction between national and local standards is rapidly disappearing, and sexually explicit material has become generally available. In 1996 Congress passed the Communications Decency Act, which prohibited posting or sending on the Internet obscene material that might be viewed by minors. The following year the Supreme Court struck down this law as unconstitutional, arguing that its restrictions were too broad.[51] But Congress responded by writing a narrower law targeting commercial pornographers. In 2002, a divided Court suggested that even this narrower statute might not meet constitutional standards, but it reserved final judgment until lower courts devoted more attention to the issue.[52]

libel
False statement defaming another.

Libel—a false statement defaming another—is not constitutionally protected if made by one private person about another. But what if press reports about public figures are erroneous? Can a newspaper then be successfully sued? This issue was raised by a fund-raising advertisement placed in the *New York Times* on March 29, 1960, by a civil rights group. The advertisement reported on student demonstrations against segregation in Montgomery, Alabama. In addition to containing several relatively innocuous errors (student demonstrators sang the national anthem, not "My Country 'Tis of Thee," as claimed), the advertisement implied that the local police were part of a "wave of terror" directed at protesters. "When the entire student body protested to state authorities by refusing to reregister," read the advertisement, "their dining hall was padlocked in an attempt to starve them into submission."

Pointing out that the police had never padlocked the dining hall, the local official charged with supervising the police department, Montgomery County Commissioner J. L. Sullivan, sued for libel. An all-white Alabama jury found the *New York Times* and those who placed the ad guilty to the tune of half a million dollars per allegation.[53]

The Supreme Court's decision in this case reflected national public opinion, which at the time was supportive of the civil rights movement. In *New York Times v. Sullivan* (1964), the Court reversed the libel conviction, holding that untruthful statements made about public figures were not actionable for libel unless the errors were made knowingly or with reckless disregard for the truth. In the Court's view, the errors in the advertisement were reasonable mistakes.

Some critics wonder whether the *Sullivan* decision, by freeing the media from legal responsibility for "accidental" errors and falsehoods, granted them too much power. Certainly, the news media have adopted an aggressive, investigative style that at times has led them to make erroneous accusations. In 1992, ABC's *Primetime Live* had an employee with a hidden camera submit a fake résumé to get a job in the meat section of a grocery store that it accused of selling doctored and outdated fish. A federal jury found ABC liable for $5.5 million in damages due to fraud, but an appeals court threw out the award in late 1999, granting the grocery store only a symbolic $2 for trespassing and encouraging employee disloyalty.[54] Although these cases prompted some editorial writers to question journalistic ethics, legal efforts to restrain the media must still clear very high hurdles.

Freedom of Religion

CONSTITUTION, FIRST AMENDMENT: *"Congress shall make no law respecting an establishment of religion, or prohibiting the free exercise thereof."*

Freedom of religion is guaranteed by two clauses in the First Amendment. The **establishment of religion clause** denies the government the power to establish any single religious practice as superior. The **free exercise of religion clause** protects the right of individuals to practice their religion without government interference. When interpreting these clauses, the Supreme Court, as we shall see, has often been influenced by the political and electoral context in which its decisions have been made.

establishment of religion clause
Denies the government the power to establish any single religious practice as superior.

free exercise of religion clause
Protects the right of individuals to practice their religion without government interference.

Establishment of Religion Clause

The constitutional prohibition against government establishment of religion may seem stark, but one can point out many gray areas and seeming contradictions in the way it has been enforced. The motto "In God We Trust" appears on U.S. currency, yet courts have ruled against nativity scenes in village squares. Each session of Congress opens with a prayer, but public schools cannot begin their day in a similar fashion.

Religious issues often arise in conjunction with the provision of public education, in large part because many parents and policy makers think schools need to teach not only reading and arithmetic but morals and values as well. The issue is one of the oldest in American politics. Massachusetts passed the nation's first compulsory-schooling law in 1852, because many Protestants felt something had to be done about the waves of Catholic immigrants arriving in Boston from Ireland and Germany. Distressed by the changing composition of the city's population, the Boston School Committee urged,

> We must open the doors of our school houses and invite and compel them to come in. There is no other hope for them or for us . . . . In our schools they must receive moral and religious teaching, powerful enough if possible to keep them in the right path amid the moral darkness which is their daily and domestic walk.[55]

Catholic parents did not think they were allowing their sons and daughters to live in "moral darkness" and saw little reason why their children should acquire their moral and religious training in public schools run by Protestants, so they requested instead public monies to help fund Catholic schools. But Catholic demands for government financing only heightened Protestant fears of immigrants and "the power of the

Catholic pope." The anti-Catholic forces were so strong that in 1875 they nearly succeeded in passing a constitutional amendment that explicitly forbade state aid to religious schools.[56]

Although the proposed amendment failed to pass, Supreme Court decisions interpreting the establishment of religion clause reflected the views of the Protestant majority, which opposed aid to religious schools. As a result, the Court has for the most part followed Thomas Jefferson's **separation of church and state doctrine**, which says that a wall should separate the government from religious activity. For example, in *Meek v. Pittenger* (1975), the Court struck down most forms of aid that Pennsylvania provided to religious schools as part of its federally funded compensatory education program.[57] The Court said public monies cannot be used for payment to religious-school teachers, for curricular materials, or for any other expense at such schools, except for textbooks and the cost of transporting students to school.

During the 1960s and 1970s, as the Court was reinforcing its commitment to broad interpretations of other parts of the Bill of Rights, the doctrine was applied quite rigorously to most forms of state-supported religious activity. School prayer, a sacred moment of silence, reading from the Bible as a sacred text, and the celebration of religious holidays in schools—all once widely practiced—were banned.[58] After evangelical religious groups protested these decisions in the 1980s and 1990s, however, a more conservative Supreme Court relaxed the ban on prayer in school somewhat, saying students may form Bible-reading or school prayer clubs as long as other clubs are allowed to use school property.[59]

Other recent decisions have also opened up windows in the wall of separation between church and state. In 2000 the Supreme Court ruled that states could provide private religious schools with computer equipment.[60] More important, in *Agostini v. Felton* (1997) the Supreme Court ruled that public school teachers can provide specialized remedial instruction in religious schools, so long as this instruction does not discriminate against students on the basis of religion, and any aid to religious institutions occurs "only as a result of the genuinely independent and private choices of individuals."[61] By justifying its decision in terms of the "private choices of individuals," the Court showed a concern for the right to the free exercise of religion, the subject to which we now turn.

separation of church and state doctrine

The principle that a wall should separate the government from religious activity.

Free Exercise of Religion Clause

If the establishment of religion clause seems to bar state involvement in religion, the free exercise of religion clause seems to instruct states not to interfere with religious practices. Once again, this issue frequently arises in the context of education policy. The Supreme Court has often protected private religious schools from hostile action by state legislatures. For example, during the 1920s, anti-immigrant sentiments were so strong in Nebraska that the legislature tried to close private religious schools that provided instruction in foreign languages. In 1923 the Supreme Court ruled that the law violated the free exercise clause of the First Amendment, because it prevented parents from exercising "the right of the individual to . . . establish a home and bring up children [and] to worship God according to the dictates of his own conscience."[62] Extending this line of reasoning, the Court in *Wisconsin v. Yoder* (1972) disallowed the application of a compulsory public school attendance law to two Amish children, whose parents opposed their attendance on religious grounds.[63]

The guarantee of free exercise of religion has often forced the Court to draw fine distinctions about how the government can make its rules. In a 1993 case, the Court invalidated a Hialeah, Florida, city ordinance that banned animal sacrifices because it unduly infringed on the practices of the Santeria religion.[64] On the other hand, in *Oregon v. Smith* (1990) the Court ruled that members of a Native American church could be denied unemployment compensation under Oregon law after getting fired from their jobs as drug rehabilitation counselors because of their peyote use. Although the peyote was used as a sacrament, Justice Antonin Scalia wrote in his majority opinion that the state could enforce its ban on the drug in this case because the law was "not specifically directed at [Native American] religious practice."[65]

Establishment of Religion or Free Exercise?

The *Wisconsin v. Yoder* case involving the Amish children raises the issue of what the courts ought to do when the establishment clause and the free exercise clause come into conflict with one another. Some critics might argue that by allowing the Amish to be exempt from certain laws to ensure that they could exercise their religion freely, the Court was violating the establishment clause by giving the Amish preferential treatment. A similar quandary arises when we consider considers the case of overseas members of the armed services. Should the army hire chaplains to ensure soldiers' right of free religious exercise? Or does the army violate the establishment clause by employing religious leaders?[66]

The debate over school choice raises the question of whether the establishment clause is violated if families and students are given a choice of school, whether religious or secular. Many Republicans, including President George W. Bush, favor giving families vouchers that allow parents to choose among public schools and private schools, whether religious or secular. In their view, school vouchers do not violate the establishment clause because it is the parent, not the government, that decides whether the child attends a religious school. But many Democrats say that the inclusion of private religious schools in any choice program is unconstitutional because the federal dollars flowing to religious schools could be used for any aspects of the school's program, even those aspects that are clearly religious in nature.

The issue was addressed by the Supreme Court in 2002 in *Zelman v. Simmons-Harris*, which found constitutional a small voucher program serving low-income families in Cleveland, despite the fact that most of the students using the program were attending religious schools. The Court reasoned that students had the option of either attending secular public schools or making use of the voucher opportunity. (For more on the voucher issue, see *Election Voices*, p. 487.)

Law, Order, and the Rights of Suspects

Elections also affect court interpretations of the procedural rights of the accused. These procedural rights are often thought to conflict with the need for government to maintain social order. Many public officials believe procedural obstacles protecting the rights of suspects unduly handicap the efforts of the police to find and prosecute criminals. They seem to share the view of the ancient jurist who said, "The judge is condemned when the criminal is absolved."[67] But others think that unless procedural safeguards are

Civil Liberties
in Today's World:
Privacy and the
Rights of the Accused

carefully observed, innocent people will be unjustly convicted. "I think it a less evil," said Justice Oliver Wendell Holmes, "that some criminals should escape than that the government should play an ignoble part."[68] In this section we first summarize the role that elections play in this debate and then review the rights of the accused, including the rights of suspects against unreasonable police intrusion, as well as their rights at and after criminal trials.

Election Politics and Criminal Justice

Comparing
Civil Liberties

Politics affects criminal justice routines, because almost everyone worries about being a victim of a crime. According to the Department of Justice, around a quarter of a million violent and property crimes occur each year.[69] Most of these crimes—thefts, burglaries, and robberies—take place at more or less the same rate in the United States as in other major industrial countries. But many people in the United States today are especially afraid of personal injury and violent death, and their fears are not unfounded. (See *International Comparison*, p. 475.) After 2001, fears of further terrorist attacks on the United States were also widespread.

In response to public demands to solve these problems, politicians often feel they must "do something." As one senator remarked, "There is a mood here that if someone came to the floor and said we should barbwire the ankles of anyone who jaywalks, I suspect it would pass."[70]

The ways in which the police and the courts treat suspects were severely scrutinized during the 1960s, when civil liberties and civil rights groups focused public attention on the rights of the disadvantaged. Influenced by political currents at the time, the Supreme Court, under the leadership of Chief Justice Earl Warren, issued a series of decisions (discussed below) that interpreted the Bill of Rights as providing significant protections of the rights of the accused. Warren was a former governor of California who one of his colleagues described as holding "a simple belief in the things we now laugh at: motherhood, marriage, family, flag, and the like."[71] He also believed that the Court had a duty to actively adapt constitutional principles to modern circumstances, as the living-constitution theory says (see Chapter 15). Warren guided the Court through what one historian calls one of the "great creative periods in American public law."[72]

As the rights of the accused were being extended by these Warren Court decisions, many law-enforcement officials claimed that the courts had forgotten about the rights of victims. An increasing number of voters agreed, favoring rigorous enforcement of laws and harsh punishments for criminals, including the death penalty. Court procedures soon became a campaign issue, and many who sought office called for tougher law enforcement. Richard Nixon's successful 1968 campaign was the first to become known as the "law and order" election. After that, the issue arose frequently in national and local campaigns.

After Warren's retirement in 1969, the Supreme Court, responding to changing political circumstances, began to temper its decisions on the rights of those accused of a crime. Yet, as we shall see in the remainder of this section, the post-Warren Court did not reverse but only qualified the major Warren Court decisions (see Table 16.1). Most debate over the rights of those suspected of criminal activity has focused on five constitutional provisions: (1) search and seizure, (2) immunity against self-incrimina-

INTERNATIONAL COMPARISON

United States Has Much Higher Murder, but Not Burglary, Rates Than Most Other Countries

Many Americans fear being the victim of a violent crime.

- *Why do you think the murder rate is so much higher in the United States than in other countries, while the rate of burglaries is about average?*

NOTE: Comparisons among nations should be interpreted with caution because of different definitions of crimes and methods of calculation.

SOURCES: Gordon Barclay and Cynthia Tavares, *International Comparisons of Criminal Justice Statistics*, 2001 (London: Research, Development, and Statistics Directorate, Home Office, October 24, 2003), Table 1.1, Table 2.

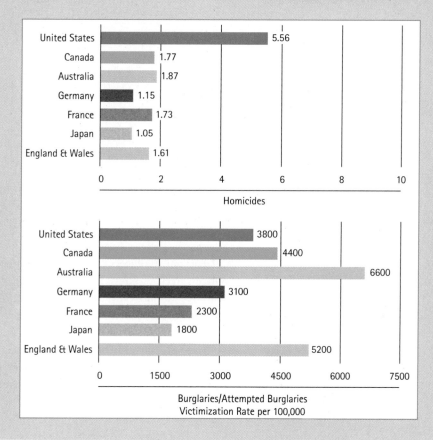

tion, (3) impartial jury, (4) legal counsel, and (5) double jeopardy. These are the topics of the remainder of this section.

Search and Seizure

CONSTITUTION, FOURTH AMENDMENT: *"The right of the people to be secure in their persons, houses, papers, and effects, against unreasonable searches and seizures, shall not be violated, and no Warrants shall issue, but upon probable cause."*

Your house cannot be searched without your permission unless a search warrant, based on evidence that a crime has probably been committed, is properly issued by a court.

TABLE 16.1			
KEY CHANGES IN THE RIGHTS OF THE ACCUSED			

• *How did voter concerns affect court decisions on the rights of the accused from the 1960s to the 1980s?*

Constitutional Post-Provision	Amendment	Extensions by Warren Court	Limitations by Warren Court
Search and seizure	4	*Mapp v. Ohio*, 1961 Improperly collected evidence cannot be introduced in court.	*United States v. Leon*, 1984 But such evidence can be used if officers collected it in "good faith" belief that search was legal.
No self-incrimination	5	*Miranda v. Arizona*, 1966 Officers must tell suspects their rights before questioning.	*Harris v. New York*, 1971 But if suspects testify, evidence obtained without their "rights" can be introduced.
		Dickerson v. U.S., 2000 *Miranda* reaffirmed.	
Impartial jury	6	*Sheppard v. Maxwell*, 1966 Establishes guidelines to protect jurors from biased news coverage.	*Nebraska Press Association v. Stuart*, 1976 But pretrial publicity does not necessarily preclude a fair trial.
Legal counsel	6	*Gideon v. Wainwright*, 1963 Poor defendants are guaranteed legal counsel.	No limitation
No double jeopardy	5	*Benton v. Maryland*, 1969 Applies to state as well as federal trials.	No limitation

You Are a
Police Officer

exclusionary rule

Legal standard that says that illegally obtained evidence cannot be admitted in court.

Mapp v. Ohio

Supreme Court decision saying that any evidence obtained without a proper search warrant may not be introduced in a trial.

Prior to the Warren Court era, police officers could conduct thorough searches of a suspect's property based only on arrest warrants. In 1969, however, the Court ruled, in *Chimel v. California*, that arrest warrants only allowed officers to search a suspect's person and his or her close proximity (to prevent the suspect from retrieving a weapon, for example).[73]

If law enforcement officers illegally search a suspect's belongings and discover incriminating evidence, a legal standard known as the **exclusionary rule** prohibits that evidence from being admitted in a court of law. First enunciated for federal trial proceedings in 1914, the exclusionary rule was firmly established as constitutional law and applied to the states in the case of ***Mapp v. Ohio*** (1961). In that case, Cleveland police officers had searched Dollree Mapp's property without a proper warrant and had arrested her for possession of "certain lewd and lascivious books, pictures, and photographs" that they found there.[74] Saying that "[t]here is no war between the Constitution and common sense," the Court ruled that Mapp could not be convicted on the basis of such illegally obtained evidence.[75]

In the post-Warren Court years, there have been several significant conservative modifications of the principle enunciated in *Mapp*. In 1984 the Court heard a case in which a California police officer seized evidence based on a search warrant that was later discovered to be invalid. This evidence was admissible, said the Court majority, because the officer had acted in "good faith," believing the search was proper.[76] In 2000 a unanimous Court ruled that officers may sometimes stop and search people simply because they turn and run when they see police approaching. Running away, argued the Court, is cause for "reasonable suspicion," which can justify such a search. "Headlong flight—whenever it occurs—is the consummate act of evasion," Chief Justice William Rehnquist wrote in his opinion. "It is not necessarily indicative of wrongdoing, but it is certainly suggestive of such."[77]

Immunity Against Self-Incrimination

CONSTITUTION, FIFTH AMENDMENT: *"Nor shall [any person] be compelled in any criminal case to be a witness against himself."*

The Fifth Amendment protects individuals from torture and coerced confessions by saying that persons cannot be forced to testify against themselves. In ***Miranda v. Arizona*** (1966), the Warren Court gave teeth to this constitutional provision by requiring police officers to tell suspects, before questioning them, that they have the right to remain silent and that they may request the presence of an attorney. If suspects are not so "Mirandized," then any information obtained may not be presented in court. After Richard Nixon made the Miranda decision an issue in his 1968 presidential campaign, the Supreme Court softened the ruling when it decided, in *Harris v. New York* (1971), that information gathered in violation of the Miranda decision may be introduced in evidence if defendants testify in their own defense.

In 2000 the Supreme Court finally ruled on a 1968 law passed by Congress that some observers believed overturned the *Miranda* decision. In a 7 to 2 decision, the Court affirmed the *Miranda* ruling. Chief Justice Rehnquist, writing for the majority, pointed out that "*Miranda* has become embedded in routine police procedure to the point where the warnings have become part of our national culture." Reluctant to reverse earlier Supreme Court decisions and modern police practices, the majority chose judicial restraint in the case. Many commentators found it particularly interesting that Rehnquist, usually a judicial restorationist who had in the past specifically questioned the *Miranda* decision, joined the moderates on the Court in showing a reluctance to overturn prior decisions. In a heated dissent, Justice Antonin Scalia, who remained a judicial restorationist in this case as in others, objected that the *Miranda* requirements had no basis in the Constitution. He argued that according constitutional force to the original *Miranda* decision simply on the grounds that an earlier court had (in his view, wrongly) so decided would give the courts an "immense and frightening antidemocratic power." Priority was being given not to the Constitution but, instead, to a prior court decision.[78] (See the discussion of judicial restraint and restorationists in Chapter 15, p 451.)

Impartial Jury

CONSTITUTION, SIXTH AMENDMENT: *"The accused shall enjoy the right to a speedy and public trial, by an impartial jury."*

The requirement that a jury be impartial is difficult to meet when a crime becomes newsworthy, because jurors may be biased by media accounts of the alleged crime both before and during the trial. The Warren Court considered these issues in *Sheppard v. Maxwell* (1966), a case that grew out of the trial of medical doctor Sam Sheppard, who was accused of murdering his wife. (The case became the basis for the television show and movie *The Fugitive*.) Sheppard complained about the excessive news coverage to

Ernesto Miranda

Ernesto Miranda, the namesake of the "Miranda rights" that are read to all suspects before questioning. The Supreme Court ruled that Miranda's confession was inadmissible in court because he had not been advised of his right not to answer questions.

• *Are Miranda rights now part of American culture?*

Miranda v. Arizona

Supreme Court decision stating that accused persons must be told by police that they need not testify against themselves.

Rights of the Accused

which jurors were exposed, including the fact that the media were positioned in the courtroom in such a way that they could listen in on his conversations with his attorneys.[79] This complaint has been echoed in later years by such high-profile suspects as Oklahoma City bomber Timothy McVeigh and Washington, D.C.-area snipers John Muhammad and Lee Boyd Malvo. The Supreme Court overturned Sheppard's conviction and set forth the following guidelines in an effort to ensure impartial juries in the future:

1. Trials should be postponed until public attention has subsided.
2. Jurors should be questioned to screen out those with detailed knowledge or fixed opinions.
3. Judges should emphatically instruct jurors to consider only the evidence presented in the courtroom, not any evidence obtained from an external source.
4. A court may **sequester** jurors during a trial—that is, keep them away from all sources of information about the crime other than information presented in the courtroom.
5. Courts should consider changing the **trial venue**—the place where the trial is held—in order for the case to be heard by a jury less exposed to pre-trial publicity.[80]

Although these constitutional safeguards designed to prevent the jury from becoming biased have never been reversed, the post-Warren Court, in *Nebraska Press Association v. Stuart* (1976), handed down a decision reflecting the country's more conservative political mood. It said that "pre-trial publicity—even pervasive, adverse publicity—does not inevitably lead to an unfair trial."[81]

Legal Counsel

CONSTITUTION, SIXTH AMENDMENT: *" . . . and to have Assistance of Counsel for his defense."*

The Warren Supreme Court ruled in **Gideon v. Wainwright** (1963) that all citizens accused of serious crimes, even the indigent, are constitutionally entitled to legal representation. If the accused is too poor to hire an attorney, then the court must assign one.

As a result, most states have created the office of **public defender**, an attorney whose full-time responsibility is to provide for the legal defense of indigent criminal suspects. But this solution has had its problems. For one thing, the job of a public defender is thankless, pay is low, and defenders are forced to deal with "rotten case after rotten case."[82]

For another, public defender systems and standards vary widely from state to state and, in some cases, from county to county.[83] One felon, when asked by a judge whether he had had an attorney, replied, "No, I had a public defender."[84] Public prosecutors probably appreciate the work of the public defender more than anyone else. As fellow attorneys, they know that those working on the other side are just doing their job.

Double Jeopardy

CONSTITUTION, FIFTH AMENDMENT: *"Nor shall any person be subject for the same offence to be twice put in jeopardy of life or limb."*

sequester
To house jurors privately, away from any information other than that presented in the courtroom.

trial venue
Place where a trial is held.

Gideon v. Wainwright
Supreme Court decision in 1963 giving indigent people accused of crimes the right to court-appointed counsel.

public defender
Attorney whose full-time responsibilities are to provide for the legal defense of indigent criminal suspects.

double jeopardy
Fifth Amendment provision that prohibits prosecution for the same offense twice.

The Warren Court ruled in *Benton v. Maryland* (1969) that states cannot try a person twice for the same offense, thereby placing the defendant in **double jeopardy**. Despite this rule, the Supreme Court, in an old decision that has never been overturned, has said that a person can be tried in federal courts, even if acquitted in a state court. "An act denounced as a crime by both national and state sovereignties is an offense against the peace and dignity of both."[85] As noted in Chapter 15, the same conduct may constitute a violation of both state and federal criminal statutes, and both levels of government can prosecute without technically placing the defendant in double jeopardy.

Prosecution by both federal and state governments is most likely in high-visibility cases. For example, in 1992 when the state of California was unable to win a conviction in the trial of the four police officers charged with beating Rodney King, the officers were tried again under a federal law for violating King's civil rights.

Rights in Practice: Habeas Corpus

CONSTITUTION, ARTICLE ONE: *"The privilege of the Writ of Habeas Corpus shall not be suspended, unless when in Cases of Rebellion or Invasion the public Safety may require it."*

If a prisoner believes his or her constitutional rights have been violated, he or she may file for a **writ of habeas corpus**, a judicial order that a prisoner be brought before a judge to determine the legality of his or her imprisonment. A prisoner may petition for such a hearing for a variety of reasons, usually having to do with violation of procedural rights, and may do so before trial, during a trial, or after conviction.

writ of habeas corpus
A judicial order that a prisoner be brought before a judge to determine the legality of his or her imprisonment.

Legal scholars have called the writ of habeas corpus "the Great Writ" because it preserves the right of the accused to due process of law. Even after having been convicted of a crime and after having exhausted all normal appeals, a prisoner may still file for a writ of habeas corpus. Similarly, if a person is detained indefinitely without trial, he or she may file for a writ of habeas corpus, arguing that his or her right to a speedy trial has been violated.

After the 9/11 terrorist attacks, civil libertarians used writs of habeas corpus on a variety of occasions to challenge the Bush administration's detention of suspects. In 2004, in the most famous such case, the Supreme Court ruled that Yasser Hamdi, a United States citizen who had been imprisoned indefinitely as a so-called "enemy combatant," had the right to appear before a judge despite alleged ties to the Al Qaeda terrorist organization. In a similar case, the Court also said that noncitizens detained at the Guantanamo Bay naval base in Cuba must be granted an opportunity to legally contest their detention.[86]

The Patriot Act

Rights in Practice: The Plea Bargain

If a case is newsworthy, constitutional procedures are generally observed: The public is looking on, and those participating in the trial must take political pressures into account. But the reality of justice in most criminal cases is very different from that in the most high-profile cases. Hardly anyone accused of a crime is actually tried by a jury, and nearly all those convicted of a crime testify against themselves. The accused have their rights, to be sure, but very few of the accused actually choose to exercise them. Most of the time, it is to their advantage not to do so.[87]

Trial court judges depend on the willingness of prosecutors and defenders to settle cases before going to trial. The number of people accused of crimes is high, the list of cases on the court docket is seemingly endless, court personnel resources are limited, and court time is precious. To speed the criminal justice process, defenders and prosecutors are usually expected to try to arrange a **plea bargain**—an agreement between prosecution and defense that the accused will admit to having committed a crime, provided that other charges are dropped and a reduced sentence is recommended. The Supreme Court has approved of this transformation of the rights of the accused into bargaining chips that can be used "to cop a plea." In the words of Justice Burger, plea bargaining is "an essential component of the administration of justice. Properly administered, it is to be encouraged."[88]

Extensive use of the plea bargain has become an issue in electoral politics, and many candidates insist that those convicted should serve longer sentences. One popular proposal, enacted in a number of states, is known as "three strikes and you're out." After having been convicted of three felonies, a convict must receive life imprisonment, whether or not a plea bargain is struck. As a result of these tough new laws, incarceration rates are rising and prison costs are becoming one of the fastest-growing items in state budgets.

Whether a higher incarceration rate is the best way to reduce crime has become a subject of considerable debate. Even some judges now argue that the laws are too severe. In 2000 a Michigan judge rejected prosecutors' pleas to imprison, with adults, a boy who had killed at age 11. Handing down a seven-year sentence to be served in a juvenile facility, Judge Eugene Moore chastised the legislature for writing laws that were not "helping to prevent [crimes] and rehabilitate" criminals. The Speaker of the Michigan House of Representatives told the judge, in effect, to mind his own business: "We don't need judges on a soapbox; we need judges who will uphold the law."[89]

The Right of Privacy

CONSTITUTION, NINTH AMENDMENT: *"The enumeration in the Constitution, of certain rights, shall not be construed to deny or disparage others retained by the people."*

The civil liberties discussed thus far are explicitly mentioned in the Bill of Rights. In addition, the Supreme Court has enunciated another liberty, the **right of privacy**— the right to be free of government interference in those aspects of one's personal life that do not affect others. Although the right of privacy is not explicitly mentioned in the Constitution, the Ninth Amendment says that some rights may be retained by the people even though they are not explicitly mentioned in the Constitution.

Some constitutional scholars believe that the judicial power to identify any right not explicitly mentioned in the Constitution should be exercised with great caution, because abuse of this power would give an unelected judiciary the authority to overrule the will of elected public officials. "Where constitutional materials do not clearly specify [a right]," judicial scholar Robert Bork has said, "the judge must stick close to the text and history, and their fair implications, and not construct any new rights."[90]

Nevertheless, in the 1960s and 1970s the Court went a long way toward recognizing a right to privacy. In this section we first consider the Court's rulings on this

plea bargain
Agreement between prosecution and defense that the accused will admit having committed a crime, provided that other charges are dropped and the recommended sentence is shortened.

right of privacy
Right to be free of government interference in those aspects of one's personal life that do not affect others.

issue with regard to private sexual behavior and abortion. Finally, we consider the growing concerns about personal privacy in the information age.

Regulation of Sexual Behavior

The modern right to privacy owes its existence to the Supreme Court's ruling in *Griswold v. Connecticut* (1965).[91] Estelle Griswold, executive director of Planned Parenthood, was fined $100 for violating a Connecticut law prohibiting the use of any instrument for the purpose of contraception. Declaring the law unconstitutional, Justice William Douglas discerned "a right of privacy older than the Bill of Rights." "Would we allow the police to search the sacred precincts of marital bedrooms for telltale signs of the use of contraceptives?" asked Douglas. "The very idea is repulsive to the notions of privacy surrounding the marriage relationship." In a dissent, Justice Potter Stewart declared the Ninth Amendment "but a truism" that could hardly be used to "annul a law passed by the elected representatives of the people."[92]

Celebrating a Landmark Ruling

Activists celebrate the Supreme Court's 2003 ruling in *Lawrence v. Texas*, which declared anti-sodomy laws unconstitutional.

• *Which provisions in the Constitution provide the basis for a right to privacy?*

Despite Stewart's objection, there is little doubt that a national majority agreed with the Supreme Court that a married couple should have the right to use contraceptives. But would the Supreme Court be equally protective of the right of privacy when the actions in question were not approved by a majority of the public? This question arose in 1986 in *Bowers v. Hardwick*, when the Court was asked to declare unconstitutional a Georgia law prohibiting sodomy under which two homosexuals had been convicted. Noting that laws against sodomy existed at the time the Constitution was written, the Court majority found no reason to think that its authors intended to exempt homosexual behavior from state regulation. In the 2003 case of *Lawrence v. Texas*, however, the Court revisited this issue and made an almost complete reversal. In a very unusual repudiation of a case so recently decided, Justice Kennedy wrote in the majority opinion that "Bowers was not correct when it was decided, and it is not correct today. It ought not to remain binding precedent."[93]

Although these rulings are clearly at odds with one another, they are consistent with one measure: public opinion. In 1986, when *Bowers* was decided, a majority of those surveyed believed that homosexual relations should be outlawed. But by 2001, polls found that Americans favored legalizing homosexual behavior by a margin of 54 to 42 percent. Similarly, 85 percent of people thought gays and lesbians should have equal rights in the workplace—a figure up more than 25 percentage points from the early 1980s. In deciding the *Lawrence* case in favor of privacy rights, the Supreme Court once again has shifted with changing public sentiment.[94]

Abortion: Right to Life or Right to Choose?

Although the Court has left uncertain the range of sexual acts to which the right of privacy extends, it ruled, in *Roe v. Wade* (1973), that the right of privacy was broad enough to include at least a partial right of abortion. The case arose out of a request from Norma McCorvey, using the pseudonym Jane Roe. Roe, seeking to terminate a pregnancy, asked for a judgment declaring unconstitutional the Texas law prohibiting abortion. Writing for the Court majority, Justice Harry Blackmun said that the woman's right of privacy was so fundamental that it could be abridged only when the state interest in doing so was compelling. Dissenting justices objected to judicial interference with a state legislature's right to balance a woman's rights against the welfare of her unborn child.

Roe v. Wade launched two powerful political movements that have helped to shape American politics in the three decades since the Court's decision. The "right-to-life" crusade was organized by Catholic and other religious groups opposed to abortion on the grounds that inasmuch as human life begins at conception, abortion cannot be distinguished from infanticide.

These "right-to-life" supporters became actively engaged in state and national politics, lobbying legislatures to impose as many restraints on abortion as the courts would allow. Responding to "right-to-life groups," Congress in 1976 enacted legislation preventing coverage of abortion costs under government health insurance programs, such as Medicaid. In 1980 the Republican Party promised to restore the "right to life," and in subsequent years, Republican presidents began appointing to the Supreme Court justices who were expected either to reverse *Roe v. Wade* or to limit its scope.

In response to these political pressures and to the change in its membership, the Supreme Court began to allow certain restrictions on abortion. The Court ruled in 1980 that the law Congress had enacted prohibiting the public funding of abortions was constitutional.[95] In 1989 it said that states could require a doctor to ascertain the viability of a fetus before permitting an abortion, if the woman was 20 or more weeks pregnant.[96]

VIDEO DEBATE

Abortion

Opposition to "right-to-life" groups was at first weak and uncertain, mainly because many of those who supported a woman's constitutional "right of choice" thought it had been permanently protected by the Supreme Court decision. But as the "right-to-life" movement gained momentum and it appeared more likely that *Roe v. Wade* would be overturned, the "right-to-choose" movement gained in strength and aggressiveness. Abortion-rights activists became an important force in Democratic Party politics.

Both sides of the controversy waited anxiously for the 1992 court decision in *Planned Parenthood v. Casey*.[97] The organization challenged a Pennsylvania law that placed a number of restrictions on the right to an abortion that went well beyond what seemed permissible under *Roe v. Wade*. The Court majority satisfied neither side entirely, finding a compromise that upheld some of the Pennsylvania restrictions on abortion but left intact the principle that states cannot simply outlaw all abortions.

The majority based its decision on nothing other than the principle of *stare decisis*, the rule stating that court decisions, once made, should be followed by subsequent judges if at all possible (see Chapter 15, p. 446). To do otherwise, argued the Court, is to make a mockery of the law. In the words of Justice Sandra Day O'Connor, "Where . . . the Court decides a case in such a way as to resolve the sort of intensely divisive controversy reflected in Roe . . . the promise of constancy, once given, binds its maker for as long as . . . the understanding of the issue has not changed so fundamentally as to render the commitment obsolete."[98] In other words, the Court said it was not changing its mind.

In *Casey*, the Court majority once again adopted a position very close to that of the average American voter. It permitted restrictions (such as a requirement that teenagers obtain parental consent) endorsed by a majority of voters but rejected those most people think are not warranted (such as a requirement that a married woman obtain the consent of her husband). Even in matters as sensitive as the right of privacy, the Court seems to be influenced by majority opinion, as expressed in the outcome of recent elections.

Privacy in the Information Age

The Internet and related technologies have sparked an information revolution, but technology also reduces the privacy of individuals. A number of free or low-cost Web sites, for example, allow researchers to uncover all publicly available data about a person, from criminal records to property holdings to professional licensing information. Armed with such details, businesses can target consumers for nuisance appeals, or—much worse—unscrupulous outlaws can commit the growing crime of so-called "identity theft." Credit-card records and other financial data are protected by 1970s-era laws that allow customers to review their files and demand corrections, but some lawmakers and experts have called for strict new laws that would guarantee consumer privacy.

Private firms are, of course, not the only ones in the information business. Whereas some advocates urge the government to protect personal privacy with new legislation, others fear that the government itself will be the biggest intruder into the private lives of average Americans. The case of the National Security Agency's surveillance programs, discussed at the beginning of this chapter, shows only one way that the government can monitor citizens. Passengers boarding planes at some airports now have their faces electronically scanned and checked against databases of known criminals.[99] The federal government and state agencies began work in 2002 to encode driver's licenses with data—such as fingerprints—that could create a de facto "national identity card" system.[100] And there are already more than 2 million video cameras stationed in public places in the United States, from street corners to subway tunnels, which may soon be used to search for and apprehend dangerous suspects.[101]

Many supporters of these efforts argue that keeping track of outlaws in this way achieves the goal of protecting Americans from criminals and terrorists without compromising citizens' fundamental freedoms. As one expert put it, "We as a people are willing to trade a little less privacy for a little more security . . . . If using more intrusive technology is the only way to prevent horrible crimes, chances are that we'll decide to use the technology, then adjust our sense of what is private and what is not."[102] But critics fear that such technological innovations will lead to increased government suppression of dissent. One authority cautioned that "law enforcement has a history of snooping on 'enemies' that are a far cry from terrorists, such as Martin Luther King, Jr. and John Lennon."[103]

Because technology has advanced so quickly, the Supreme Court has not yet had time to establish a clear set of rules with which it will interpret the Constitution in cases involving information-age privacy. But, unless the newfound concern with terrorism alters Supreme Court thinking, a 2001 ruling suggests that the Court remains concerned with protecting the privacy of individuals. In the case of *Kyllo v. United States*, the Court considered whether police departments could make use of thermal imaging equipment to examine a suspect's home without a search warrant. Officers suspected that the defendant, Danny Kyllo, was illegally growing marijuana in his

Surveillance in Law Enforcement

The cameras of the Chicago's Citizen Law Enforcement Analysis and Reporting System allow crews to watch over crime behavior and let them figure out where to send in the police on patrol.

• *Do such measures violate privacy, or are they essential to controlling criminal activity?*

Civil Liberties and National Security

home, and they used the thermal equipment to check for the hot halide lamps necessary to grow the plants indoors. Police argued that no violation of the Fourth Amendment's ban on "search and seizure" had occurred, because officers did not actually enter the suspect's home, but Kyllo argued that his home had for all practical purposes been unconstitutionally searched without a warrant. In a 5 to 4 opinion that surprised many observers, the Court sided with Kyllo. Justice Scalia, writing for the majority, argued that, although "It would be foolish to contend that the degree of privacy secured to citizens by the Fourth Amendment has been entirely unaffected by the advance of technology"; nevertheless, "we must take the long view, from the original meaning of the Fourth Amendment forward."[104]

Chapter Summary

The Bill of Rights remained pretty much a dead letter until the Civil War ended slavery. Only as key provisions of the Bill of Rights were gradually and selectively incorporated into the due process clause of the Fourteenth Amendment did they become effective components of the country's constitutional makeup.

Although the courts are expected to protect civil liberties against majority tyranny, most of the time the Supreme Court has followed, not led, public opinion. In 1919 the Supreme Court said speech could not be prohibited unless it created a clear and present danger to a peaceful society, but it initially applied the doctrine in a way consistent with the common law bad tendency test, convicting a socialist for his political speech. Although it protected minority dissent during the 1930s, it later elaborated the fighting words doctrine, which declared certain phrases to be the equivalent of violent acts. Not until McCarthyism had been rejected by elected officials did a Court majority say free speech was a fundamental freedom that required special protection.

Freedom of religion is protected by two separate clauses in the First Amendment. The establishment of religion clause prohibits the propagation of religious beliefs by public institutions and direct aid to churches, religious schools, and other religious institutions. The free exercise

of religion clause prevents the government from interfering with the religious activities of citizens. At times the two clauses come into conflict, as the issue of school vouchers has shown.

When balancing the rights of the accused against the need to maintain social order, Supreme Court decisions have fluctuated with changes in public opinion. During the 1960s the Warren Court expanded the rights of the accused by tightening the rules under which police and prosecutors could obtain evidence, question suspects, and hold trials. After "law and order" became a campaign issue, the Supreme Court modified, though it did not reverse, many of these decisions.

The Court has also discerned a right of privacy, despite the fact that no such right is mentioned explicitly in the Bill of Rights. This right of privacy is broad enough to cover private consensual sexual behavior as well as to include a woman's right to terminate a pregnancy. But it is not absolute. As interpreted by the Court, the right of privacy does not preclude regulation of abortions, especially among children and after the first trimester of pregnancy. The right of privacy discerned by the Court comes very close to the viewpoint held by most Americans. The country's definition of civil liberties seems to depend as much on the thinking of its citizens as on its judicial system.

Key Terms

balancing doctrine, p. 466

bad tendency test, p. 463

civil liberties, p. 459

civil rights amendments, p. 461

clear and present danger doctrine, p. 464

commercial speech, p. 469

double jeopardy, p. 478

due process clause, p. 461

establishment of religion clause, p. 471

exclusionary rule, p. 476

fighting words doctrine, p. 466

free exercise of religion clause, p. 471

fundamental freedoms doctrine, p. 467

Gideon v. Wainwright, p. 478

libel, p. 470

Mapp v. Ohio, p. 476

Miranda v. Arizona, p. 477

obscenity, p. 470

plea bargain, p. 480

prior restraint doctrine, p. 468

public defender, p. 478

right of privacy, p. 480

selective incorporation, p. 462

separation of church and state doctrine, p. 472

sequester, p. 478

trial venue, p. 478

tyranny of the majority, p. 463

writ of habeas corpus, p. 479

Suggested Readings

Of General Interest

Abraham, Henry J. and Barbara A. Perry. *Freedom and the Court: Civil Rights and Liberties in the United States.* 8th Edition. Lawrence, KS: University Press of Kansas, 2003. Comprehensive discussion of the Constitution's protections of civil rights and civil liberties.

Casper, Jonathan D. *American Criminal Justice: The Defendant's Perspective.* Englewood Cliffs, NJ: Prentice-Hall, 1972. Discusses the day-to-day realities of the criminal justice system.

Friedman, Lawrence M. *Crime and Punishment in American History.* New York: Basic Books, 1993. Readable overview of the changing nature of the American system of criminal justice.

Rehnquist, William H. *All the Laws but One: Civil Liberties in Wartime.* New York: Knopf, 1998. The late chief justice of the Supreme Court considers instances in which civil liberties have been sacrificed for the sake of security, focusing on cases from the Civil War and World War II.

Walsh, James. *Liberty in Troubled Times: A Libertarian Guide to Laws, Politics, and Society in a Terrorized World.* Lansdowne, PA: Silver Lake Publishing, 2004. A committed libertarian argues for the protection of all liberties from government interference.

Focused Studies

Garrow, David J. *Liberty and Sexuality, Updated Edition.* New York: Macmillan, 1998. Comprehensive account of the legal debate over abortion before and after Roe.

Goldstein, Robert. *Saving "Old Glory": The History of the Desecration Controversy.* Boulder, CO: Westview, 1995. Authoritative political and constitutional history of the flag-burning controversy.

Lessig, Lawrence. *The Future of Ideas: The Fate of the Commons in a Connected World.* New York: Random House, 2001. A law professor's view of the potential for, and dangers to, free expression on the Internet.

Lewis, Anthony. *Make No Law: The Sullivan Case and the First Amendment.* New York: Random House, 1992. Excellent, readable case study of the politics of the Sullivan decision and the evolution of the free-speech doctrine.

Meiklejohn, Alexander. *Free Speech and Its Relation to Self-Government.* New York: Harper, 1948. Influential, early statement of the absolutist, fundamental freedoms position.

Skolnick, Jerome. *Justice Without Trial.* New York: Wiley, 1966. Classic study of the way in which police and courts resolve low-visibility criminal cases.

Wice, Paul B. *Public Defenders and the American Justice System.* Westport, CT: Praeger, 2005. A detailed case study of public defenders in Newark, NJ, shows the role that public defenders play in the modern justice system.

Wilson, James Q. *Thinking About Crime.* New York: Basic Books, 1975. Makes a persuasive, realistic, and conservative case for ways of controlling crime.

On the Web

www.aclu.org

The American Civil Liberties Union provides legal assistance to many who feel that their civil liberties have been violated. The sometimes-controversial organization has a detailed Web site outlining its agenda for promoting civil liberties, as well as describing the history and present status of civil-liberties law.

www.freedomforum.org

The First Amendment freedoms of speech and of religion may seem clear-cut, but some First Amendment issues remain controversial, as we have seen in this chapter. The Freedom Forum is a nonpartisan foundation that publicizes and analyzes current issues involving First Amendment freedoms.

http://religiousfreedom.lib.virginia.edu/

Thomas Jefferson, founder of the University of Virginia, argued for a "wall of separation" between government and religion. The University of Virginia's Religious Freedom Page carries on the Jeffersonian tradi-

tion by providing analysis of many key Supreme Court decisions concerning religious freedom and by including links to other key religious freedom organizations.

www.naral.org
www.nrlc.org

Does a constitutional right of privacy protect a woman's right to have an abortion? The National Abortion and Reproductive Rights Action League (NARAL) says yes, whereas the National Right to Life Committee (NRLC) disagrees.

www.eff.org
www.cdt.org

As we have seen in this chapter, a growing area of controversy regarding civil liberties concerns issues of information technology and privacy on the Internet. The Electronic Frontier Foundation (EFF) and the Center for Democracy and Technology (CDT) follow issues and provide information about free speech and privacy in the information age.

Election Voices

School Choice:
Vouchers and Charter Schools

THE ISSUE

Should parents be given a choice of the school their child attends? Would competition among schools prompt them to improve their performance?

Background

Although per pupil expenditures in constant dollars have more than doubled since the early 1970s, American students have only made modest—if any—academic advancements.[1] Based on the National Assessment of Educational Progress (NAEP), which is periodically administered to nationally representative samples of students, the math, reading, and science performance of nine-year-olds has improved over the last three decades, but these gains do not hold as the students become older. Seventeen-year-olds are currently scoring at the same level in math, reading, and science as their peers did more than a generation ago.[2]

Critics of the American educational system have proposed to induce reform by generating competition for the traditional public schools. School choice programs allow parents to send their children to a school other than the one assigned to them by the local school district. The most controversial forms of school choice are vouchers and charter schools.

Vouchers are scholarships that allow students to attend a private school. Vouchers are typically offered to students from low-income families or to students attending chronically underperforming schools.[3] Participating private schools are usually asked to accept all eligible students that choose to attend them, regardless of academic aptitude, behavioral history, and religious background. When applicants surpass available seats, scholarships are awarded via lottery.

Charters are privately managed schools that operate under a performance contract. Although they are publicly funded and are generally open to all students within the district, charters operate free from most regulations to which traditional public schools must conform; for example, only a few find their policies subject to collective bargaining agreements with teachers' unions. Consequently, charters have more flexibility to innovate and provide alternative curricula. In exchange for this freedom, charter schools are held to a higher degree of accountability. Unlike traditional public schools, charters can be closed for poor academic performance or financial misman-agement, or inadequate enrollments.

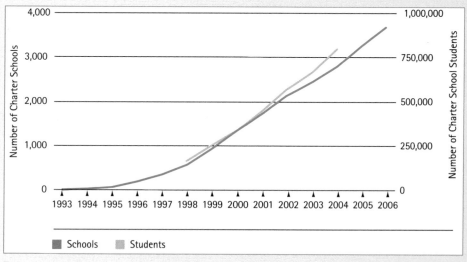

FIGURE 1

Charter Schools and Charter Enrollment

SOURCE: U.S. Department of Education, Common Core of Data; and Center for Education Reform.

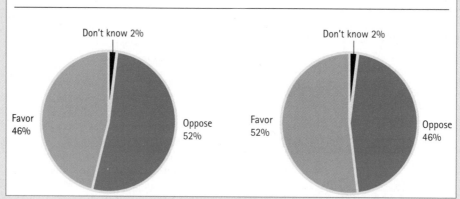

Do you favor or oppose allowing students and parents to choose a private school to attend at public expense?

A proposal has been made that would allow parents to send their school-age children to any public, private, or church-related school they choose. For those parents choosing nonpublic schools, the government would pay all or part of the tuition. Would you favor or oppose this proposal in your state.

Don't know 2%

Favor 46%

Oppose 52%

Don't know 2%

Favor 52%

Oppose 46%

FIGURE 2

Public Support of School Vouchers, 2002

Proponents of school choice state that it is only fair to provide alternative educational opportunities to the children of impoverished families who can not afford to change residential areas or to pay private school tuition in order to exercise school choice on their own. It is, they argue, a matter of social justice. In addition, by making traditional public schools compete to retain students—and the corresponding per pupil funds—public schools are given incentives to improve. Opponents contend that school choice programs drain public schools of financial resources and talent. Moreover, critics maintain that voucher programs, in which sectarian private schools are allowed to participate, violate the separation of church and state.

Charter schools and, especially, voucher programs have faced strong opposition from the teachers' unions and other staunch supporters of traditional forms of public education. Unions and other pro-public-school groups have fought numerous legislative battles and spurred multiple lawsuits in state and federal courts that have slowed expansion of school choice. Since 1990, voucher programs have been implemented in Milwaukee, Cleveland, and the nation's capital.[4] In the 2005–2006 school year, no more than 22,000 children were enrolled in private schools via these programs.[5]

Charter schools have spread more rapidly, however. Since 1991, 40 states and the District of Columbia have enacted charter school laws allowing this type of public school to be created, with various degrees of flexibility. In spite of a steady increase of charter school enrollment (see Figure 1), the more than one million students attending one of the 3,617 charter schools in 2006 represent less than 2.3 percent of all public school students.[6]

The Politics of School Choice

Generally speaking, most Republicans find school choice consistent with their political philosophy that supports free markets and

small government. George Bush, for example, succeeded in 2004 in winning congressional support for a pilot voucher program for the District of Columbia. Meanwhile, most Democrats, who have close ties to the union movement and a history of support for public institutions, are skeptical of many forms of choice, especially vouchers, as is indicated by the opposition by a majority of Democrats in Congress to the District of Columbia pilot plan.

But positions do not always break out along partisan lines. Both Bill and Hillary Clinton supported charter schools, and some suburban Republicans think vouchers are just another form of charity for inner-city families. Indeed, some school choice initiatives, with their focus on helping inner-city, low-income children, have created unusual alliances between small government proponents and civil right advocates. The bipartisan support of charter schools led even the teachers' unions to start some charters of their own.

Opposing Viewpoints on School Choice
For School Choice

The origin of the modern voucher movement can be traced to Nobel laureate Milton Friedman's 1955 defense of parental school choice as a way to "create effective competition and improve performance in education, all to the eventual benefit of children, parents, educators, taxpayers and the society at large":

> [T]he denationalization of education would widen the range of choice available to parents . . . . Let the [government] subsidy be made available to parents regardless where they send their children—provided only that it be to schools that satisfy specified minimum standards—and a wide variety of schools will spring up to meet the demand. Parents could express their views about schools directly, by with-

drawing their children from one school and sending them to another, to a much greater extent than is now possible. . . . The interjection of competition would do much to promote a healthy variety of schools. It would do much, also, to introduce flexibility into school systems.

—Milton Friedman, "The Role of Government in Education," *Economics and the Public Interest*, ed. Robert A. Solo (Rutgers University, N.J.)

Among the arguments supporting school choice, besides the free-market justifications, stand claims pronouncing school choice to be the civil rights movement of our time:

U.S. citizenship guarantees all parents an education for their children. This is a true civil right. Yet some children receive a better education than others due to their parents' abilities to pay for benefits that are often missing in public schools. This inequity is a violation of the civil rights of the parents and children who are so afflicted by lack of income and by the mismanagement endemic to so many of the country's public school systems.

—Alveda C. King, niece of Dr. Martin Luther King, in "Fighting for School Choice: It's a Civil Right" op-ed published by the *Wall Street Journal*, September 11, 1997

School choice is widespread in America—unless you are poor. Affluent families have choice because they can move to different neighborhoods or communities, send their children to private schools or supplement schooling with tutors and enrichment programs. Lower-income and working-class families, meanwhile, are typically trapped with one option—a school in need of improvement.

—Black Alliance for Educational Options

Against School Choice

Opponents argue that school choice programs in general, and vouchers in particular, are damaging the education system by taking resources away from traditional public schools and reducing the public control over the instruction financed with public funds:

The AFT supports parents' right to send their children to private or religious schools but opposes the use of public funds to do so. The main reason for this opposition is because public funding of private or religious education transfers precious tax dollars from public schools, which are free and open to all children, accountable to parents and taxpayers alike, and essential to our democracy, to private and religious schools that charge for their services, select their students on the basis of religious or academic or family or personal characteristics, and are accountable only to their boards and clients.

—American Federation of Teachers

In direct opposition to the advocates' arguments, opponents contend that vouchers would worsen the racial, ethnic, and economic injustices already present in our social fabric:

A pure voucher system would only encourage economic, racial, ethnic, and religious stratification in our society. . . . Despite desperate efforts to make the voucher debate about "school choice" and improving opportunities for low-income students, vouchers remain an elitist strategy . . . . [P]rivatization strategies are about subsidizing tuition for students in private schools, not expanding opportunities for low-income children.

—National Education Association

Finally, opponents accuse voucher programs that allow sectarian schools to participate of violating the separation of church and state:

Americans must be free to contribute only to the religious groups of their choosing. Voucher programs violate this principle by forcing all taxpayers to underwrite religious education. . . . Taxpayers should not be required to subsidize the spread of religious/moral opinions they may strongly disagree with.

—Americans United for Separation of Church and State

What Do Americans Believe?

Support for vouchers depends in part on the way the question is worded. (See Figure 2.) Why do you think some Americans responded differently to questions that seem to ask about the same thing? Which way of wording the question do you think is superior?

The same poll has reported a modest rise in support for charter schools over the last few years. Whereas in 2000 42 percent of respondents were in favor of charter schools, by 2005 support had increased to 49 percent.

Is School Choice Constitutional?

In 2002 the Supreme Court ruled 5–4 in favor of the constitutionality of the Cleveland voucher program in *Zelman v. Simmons-Harris*, denying that allowing parents to use public funds to send their children to a religious school violated the Establishment Clause of the First Amendment (see Chapter 16). The Court deemed the program to be neutral with respect to religion because it simply permitted parents "to exercise genuine choice among options."[7]

The Supreme Court decision aside, challenges against voucher programs continue to be fought in state courts on the basis that they violated state constitutions. A pilot voucher program in Colorado never saw the light of the day as it was ruled to violate the local control requirement of the Colorado state constitution before it went into effect. The program was determined to strip districts of control over locally raised funds and of "any discretion over the character of instruction participating students will receive at district expense"[8] In early 2006, school choice opponents had another major victory when the Florida Supreme Court struck down the state's voucher program in the name of educational "uniformity."[9]

What Do You Think?

1. Should the government increase the educational options provided to low-income children? What about options for those students trapped in underperforming schools?

2. Should those options include vouchers to attend religious schools?

3. Do you think that competition among schools would spur higher performance? Or do you think public schools would suffer needlessly?

Web Sites on School Choice

School choice is a subject of heated national debate. To conscientiously investigate this controversial issue and the arguments pro and con, be sure to go to the Web sites of both those groups that are in favor of voucher programs and charter schools and those groups that are opposed. In your opinion, which Web site(s) presents the most convincing argument?

PRO
The Center for Education Reform:
www.edreform.com/
Alliance for School Choice:
www.allianceforschoolchoice.org/
Cato Institute:
www.cato.org/
Institute for Justice:
www.ij.org/
The Heritage Foundation:
www.heritage.org/
Milton and Rose D. Friedman Foundation:
www.friedmanfoundation.org/
School Choice Info:
www.schoolchoiceinfo.org/
Parents for Choice in Education:
http://choiceineducationpac.com/

National Alliance for Public Charter Schools:
www.publiccharters.org/
U.S. Charter Schools:
www.uscharterschools.org/
Black Alliance for Educational Options:
www.baeo.org/

CON
American Federation of Teachers:
www.aft.org/
National Education Association:
www.nea.org/
Americans United for Separation of Church and State:
www.au.org/
National School Board Association:
www.nsba.org/
Economic Policy Institute:
www.epinet.org/

---

[1]For the 1970-1971 school year, an average of $4,682 (in constant 2004–2005 dollars) was spent per pupil in public elementary and secondary schools. For the 2002–2003 school year, the average per pupil expenditure had raised to $9,788 (also in constant 2004–2005 dollars). U.S. Department of Education, Institute of Education Sciences, National Center for Education Statistics, *Digest of Education Statistics,* 2005, Table 162: Total and current expenditure per pupil in public elementary and secondary schools: Selected years, 1919–1920 through 2002–2003.

[2]U.S. Department of Education, Institute of Education Sciences, National Center for Education Statistics, *NAEP 2004 Trends in Academic Progress Three Decades of Student Performance in Reading and Mathematics,* July 2005; and U.S. Department of Education, Institute of Education Sciences, National Center for Education Statistics, *NAEP 1999 Trends in Academic Progress: Three Decades of Student Performance,* August 2000.

[3]Voucher programs only offered to students with disabilities are excluded from this discussion because they are not justified on the same grounds.

[4]In addition, Ohio has enacted a pilot voucher program that will begin its operations in 2006–2007; and Vermont and Maine have voucher-like tuitioning programs, which provide scholarships to children residing in districts without public schools to attend either a secular private school or a public school in another district.

[5]About 14,200 students made use of the voucher program in Milwaukee, 5,700 in Cleveland, 733 in Florida, and 1,090 in Washington, D.C. These calculations do not include enrollment in vouchers offered only to students with disabilities or the recently enacted pilot program in Ohio.

[6]According to the Center for Education Reform, in 2005–2006 there were 3,617 charter schools serving 1,074,809 students. The National Center for Education Statistics projected that in the fall of 2005 48.4 millions of students would enroll in one of the public elementary and secondary schools in the country. Sources: Center for Education Reform, "National Charter School Data At-a-Glance," and U.S. Department of Education, "Digest of Education Statistics, 2005," Table 1.

[7]*Zelman v. Simmons-Harris,* 536 U.S. 662 (2002).

[8]*Owens v. Colorado Congress of Parents,* No. 03-0364 (Colo. June 28, 2004).

[9]*Holmes v. Bush,* No. 04-2323 (Fla. Jan. 5, 2006).

CHAPTER 17

★ ★ ★ ★ ★ ★ ★ ★ ★ ★ ★

Civil Rights

CHAPTER OUTLINE

Racial Profiling in the Terror War

On October 23, 2001, Arshad Chowdhury walked into the San Francisco airport to board a flight back to the northeast. A graduate student in business at Carnegie Mellon University in Pittsburgh, Chowdhury had been visiting friends in Berkeley over mid-semester break. Little more than a month after the 9/11 attacks, airports across the country were on edge, and Chowdhury was resigned to a bit of extra scrutiny. Although he was an American citizen, his parents had immigrated to the United States in 1967 from Bangladesh, and Chowdhury's dark skin automatically made him suspicious to some people. Still, he could not have anticipated what happened next.

While Chowdhury was in line to board, FBI agents, police, and airport security asked him to step aside for additional checks. After satisfying the authorities, he got back in line, only to be told that the Northwest Airlines pilot had decided that he would not be allowed onto the aircraft. "People were looking at me, pointing at me, whispering," he said. "I've never felt that way before."[1] As someone who had once worked in the World Trade Center as an investment banker, Chowdhury said he understood that a certain degree of added security was necessary: "The attack on the World Trade Center was an attack on my colleagues, my livelihood, and me. So I endorse increased security at airports."[2] But, he added, he felt unfairly scrutinized. "I don't want this to happen to anybody else."[3] Chowdhury missed his plane, and had to take a later flight escorted by an airline official.[4]

Chowdhury's experience appears to be one example of so-called **racial profiling**, the singling out of certain people for suspicion based on their race or ethnicity. Long a concern regarding police stops of African American motorists, the issue of racial profiling has taken on new meaning in the age of terror. The practice has few outright advocates—indeed, the

Constitution and congressional enactments prohibit governments and private companies from drawing distinctions on the basis of race and ethnicity unless business necessity requires it. Some experts argue that this is one of the few cases where business necessity requires drawing a distinction that would otherwise be prohibited. "Suspecting people because of who they are rather than what they do is unacceptable," says one commentator. "But ignoring who they are in the course of scrutinizing what they do is equally unacceptable if—as with militant Islam, Italian mafia groups, Russian organized crime, Chinese tongs, etc.—who they are is relevant to the determination of whether they are likely to pose a threat."[5] The public appears to be split about evenly on the issue: in a 2004 poll, 45 percent said it was sometimes justified to use "racial or ethnic profiling" at airport checkpoints, while 53 percent said it was never justified.[6]

One complicating factor is that security officials often cannot use precise criteria when identifying suspects. In 2005, the Transportation Security Administration (TSA), the government agency that handles airport security, announced a program that trains officers to identify potential suspects based on nervousness, facial tics, and perceived deception.[7] Critics argued that this would lead to discrimination. As one American Civil Liberties Union (ACLU) official put it, "It's completely subjective . . . . You just told officers you can interrogate anyone you want."[8]

After being bumped from his flight, Arshad Chowdhury joined an ACLU lawsuit against four airlines accused of unjustly discriminating on the basis of race or ethnicity. As his case made its way through the court system, Chowdhury graduated from business school and started his own company: a firm that manufactures small "pods" in which weary travelers can take quick naps if, for some reason, they are delayed at the airport.[9]

MAKING THE CONNECTION

The debate over racial profiling raises broader questions. What does it mean to say the Constitution is colorblind? When may people be legally classified by race, ethnicity, or gender? Do the courts define the issues, and then voters and elected officials follow? Or is it the other way around? In this chapter we shall discuss the struggle for civil rights for African Americans, other minority groups, women, and the disabled. These struggles shaped the context in which modern debates over civil rights occur.

In most cases we shall find that in characterizing the legal meaning of civil rights, the Supreme Court followed trends initiated by the public debates and coalition building that make up electoral politics. As Justice Ruth Bader Ginsburg once observed, "With prestige to persuade, but not physical power to enforce, and with a will for self-preservation, the Court generally follows, it does not lead, changes taking place elsewhere in society."[10] Nonetheless, the Court has played a major role by codifying civil rights policy into constitutional doctrine. We explore these issues by first discussing the beginnings of the struggle for the civil rights of African Americans, moving on to examine how civil rights activists persuaded the Supreme Court to become involved. Next, we discuss how the Supreme Court's interpretation of the Fourteenth Amendment's equal protection clause shaped the development of civil rights. Finally, we detail the steps that other groups, such as women, the disabled, gays, and others, have taken to ensure their civil rights, and we note how the courts and elected officials have responded.

Origins of Civil Rights

CONSTITUTION, FOURTEENTH AMENDMENT: *"No state shall . . . deny to any person within its jurisdiction the equal protection of the laws."*

Although the terms civil liberties and civil rights are often used interchangeably, there is an important distinction between them. Civil liberties are the freedoms that together preserve the rights of a free people (see page 459). **Civil rights** embody the right to equal treatment under the law. In Chapter 16 we emphasized how important the due process clause of the Fourteenth Amendment has been to the protection of civil liberties in the United States. The civil rights of Americans are guarded by a no less important provision in the Fourteenth Amendment, **the equal protection clause**, which says that no state can deny any of its people equal protection under the law.

Although the equal protection clause has been a part of the Constitution since 1868, its legal and cultural meaning has changed over the years. These changes have most often been the result of one of two phenomena. First, minority groups with grievances have mobilized in electoral politics and other venues, such as protests or

racial profiling
The singling out of certain people for suspicion based on their race or ethnicity.

civil rights
Specific rights that embody the general right to equal treatment under the law.

equal protection clause
Fourteenth Amendment clause specifying that no state can deny any of its people equal protection under the law.

boycotts. By undertaking such activities, they unify their numbers so as to influence elections more effectively, and they win popular opinion to their side, broadening their impact on elected officials. "One of the difficult lessons we have learned," wrote Martin Luther King Jr., "is that you cannot depend on American institutions to function without pressure. Any real change in the status quo depends on continued creative action to sharpen the conscience of the nation."[11]

Second, because minorities are seldom able to control the outcome of elections directly, and because at times in American history they have been prevented from freely exercising their right to vote, they have often pursued a legal strategy, bringing apparent violations of civil rights to the attention of the courts. But legal strategies do not always work. Judges, too, are concerned about preserving credibility with majorities. If judges defy public opinion regularly, they might undermine confidence in the courts. Also, if judges persist in deviating from the majority view, elected officials will eventually appoint judges willing to reverse direction. As a result, the Supreme Court has not provided steady leadership on civil rights questions. As one legal scholar has noted, "For every case destructive of racial segregation, other cases can be cited with greater force to support the view of judicial power as fundamentally unfriendly to civil rights, unnecessarily illiberal in its judgment, and oppressive in its results."[12]

Because most people have personal experience with the relationships among races, genders, and ethnic groups, differing interpretations of the meaning of the equal protection clause have generated intense political controversy.[13] In this section, we first describe actions taken in the years following the Civil War that affected the civil rights of African Americans, then review the Supreme Court's early rulings on these efforts, and finally examine the changes in political power that led up to the Court's major rulings on civil rights in the mid-twentieth century.

Conflict Over Civil Rights After the Civil War

black codes

Restrictive laws that applied to newly freed slaves but not to whites.

The Struggle for Equal Protection

Reconstruction

Period after the Civil War when southern states were subject to a federal military presence.

At the end of the Civil War, some southern states passed **black codes**, restrictive laws that applied to newly freed slaves but not to whites. "Persons of color . . . must make annual written contracts for their labor," one of the codes read, adding that if blacks ran away from their employers, they had to forgo a year's wages.[14] Other black codes denied African Americans access to the courts or the right to hold property, except under special circumstances. Northern abolitionists, who thought the fight against slavery had been won, urged Congress to override these black codes. Congress responded by passing the Civil Rights Act of 1866, which gave citizens "of every race and color . . . the same right . . . to full and equal benefit of all laws." Almost the same words were incorporated into the equal protection clause of the Fourteenth Amendment, which won final ratification two years later.

The federal government's civil rights stance was imposed on southern whites during **Reconstruction**, a period after the Civil War when southern states were subject to a federal military presence. During this period, blacks exercised their right to vote, while that right was denied to many whites who had served in the Confederate army. In addition, Congress established a Freedman's Bureau, which was designed to provide blacks with education, immediate food relief, and inexpensive land from former plantations.[15]

Many southern whites bitterly resented the federal Reconstruction policies, and some took violent action to resist them. The Ku Klux Klan, a fraternal organization founded in Tennessee, terrorized blacks and Republicans throughout the South from 1866 to the early 1870s. Hooded Klansmen burned black churches and schoolhouses, drove black elected officials from their homes, and lynched those who seemed to threaten white supremacy.[16] Whites became targets if they aided Republicans or blacks; blacks could fall under suspicion just by becoming educated. The Klan murdered one former slave in Georgia because "he can write and read and put it down himself."[17] In 1871 Congress passed the Force Act, which temporarily succeeded in disbanding the Klan, but similar organizations continued to terrorize African Americans for many years.

Reconstruction was motivated both by moral outrage at racial injustice and by northern postwar bitterness toward the Confederacy. But as the years passed, moral commitment evaporated and war memories faded. The programs of the Freedman's Bureau ultimately proved to be a disappointment to many blacks and abolitionists. Northerners were thrown on the defensive by charges of fraud, corruption, and mismanagement in the new southern state governments. Though not always justified, complaints were effectively leveled against both black elected officials and new arrivals from the North, who were derisively called carpetbaggers, after the luggage in which they kept their clothing.

The close election of 1876 brought Reconstruction to an end. Republican presidential candidate Rutherford B. Hayes claimed victory, but the outcome depended on allegedly fraudulent vote counts reported by several southern states. The compromise resolving the dispute gave each side what it most wanted. Republicans were given the presidency, but Democrats won removal of the federal army from the South and control of future southern elections.

With the end of Reconstruction, whites gradually restored many of the old racial patterns.[18] State legislatures enacted laws requiring voters to pass a literacy test, meet strict residency requirements, and pay a **poll tax**, a fee that allowed one to vote. Although the laws themselves avoided specific mention of African Americans, blacks were in fact the target. As the chair of the suffrage committee in Virginia bluntly admitted, "I expect the [literacy] examination with which the black men will be confronted to be inspired by the same spirit that inspires every man in this convention. I do not expect an impartial administration of this clause."[19] States also enacted what was to become known as a **grandfather clause**, a law that exempted men from voting restrictions if their fathers and grandfathers were eligible to vote before the Civil War. Of course, only whites benefited from this exemption.

The most successful restriction on the right to vote was the **white primary**, elections held by the Democratic Party that excluded nonwhites from participation. Southerners saw Republicans as the hated instigators of Reconstruction, so Democrats won nearly all southern elections at that time. As a result, the winner of the white primary nearly always won the general election.[20] Because blacks were denied a meaningful vote, in 1910 only 10 percent of adult African American males were registered to vote in most of the states of the old Confederacy.[21] African Americans were also subject to **Jim Crow laws**, state laws that segregated the races from each other. (The name comes from a stereotypical, belittling characterization of African Americans used in minstrel shows popular at the time.) Jim Crow laws required African Americans to attend segregated schools, sit in separate areas on public trains and buses, eat in separate restaurants, and use separate public facilities. The reason for these regulations was clear. As one (white-owned) New Orleans

poll tax
Fee that one must pay in order to be allowed to vote.

grandfather clause
Racially restrictive provision of certain southern laws after Reconstruction, permitting a man to vote if his father or grandfather could have voted before the Civil War.

white primary
Primary elections, held by the Democratic Party after Reconstruction, that excluded nonwhites from participation in many southern states.

Jim Crow laws
Laws, passed by southern states after Reconstruction, enforcing segregation.

newspaper put it, "The quarter-century that has passed since the war has not diminished in the slightest degree the determination of the whites to prevent such dangerous doctrine as social equality, even in the mildest form."[22]

Early Court Interpretations of Civil Rights

With little public support for civil rights, the Supreme Court of the day took a very restrictive view of the Fourteenth Amendment's equal protection clause. Two Court decisions were of particular significance. In a decision that was given the ironic title the *Civil Rights Cases* (1883), the Court declared the Civil Rights Act of 1875 unconstitutional.[23] This law, written just before Reconstruction came to an end, had abolished segregation in restaurants, train stations, and other public places. In declaring the law unconstitutional, the Supreme Court invoked the **state action doctrine**—the principle that only the actions of state and local governments, not those of private individuals, must conform to the equal protection clause. The Court said that Congress could prevent state and local governments from discriminating against blacks but that it had no constitutional authority to tell private individuals whom to serve in their restaurants, railroads, and hotels.[24]

A second major decision by the Supreme Court, **Plessy v. Ferguson** (1896), had even more sweeping consequences. It developed the **separate but equal doctrine**, the principle that laws mandating segregated facilities were constitutional as long as the facilities were equivalent. Homer Plessy had challenged a Louisiana law that required "equal but separate accommodations" for white and black railroad passengers.[25] Plessy argued that his inability to use white facilities denied him equal protection before the law. But, by a majority of 8 to 1, the Supreme Court said the Louisiana statute was constitutional, because the mere fact that the racial groups were being separated did not stamp African Americans with a "badge of inferiority." In a famous dissent, Justice Harlan protested that "Our Constitution is color-blind, and neither knows nor tolerates classes among citizens." Laws enforcing segregation, argued Harlan, violated this constitutional principle.[26]

Blacks Get Electoral Power

Because of the court decisions in the *Civil Rights Cases* and *Plessy v. Ferguson*, legally sanctioned segregation remained intact until well into the middle of the twentieth century. Black civil rights activists were by no means quiescent during this period. Between 1900 and 1910, for example, African Americans in more than two dozen cities took part in organized boycotts of segregated streetcars.[27] But significant gains in dismantling the old system of segregation took place only after African Americans gained electoral clout by moving in large numbers from southern states, where they could not vote, to northern states, where they could. During World War I, industrial northern cities faced a labor shortage, and many African Americans gave up sharecropping in Mississippi and Alabama for factory work in the sweatshops of New York, Chicago, and Detroit. When World War II created another shortage of factory workers, blacks left southern farms for northern big-city tenements in even larger numbers.

Northerners were not much more tolerant of blacks than were southerners. Most northern blacks attended segregated schools, ate in segregated restaurants, and shopped

state action doctrine
Rule stating that only the actions of state and local governments, not those of private individuals, must conform to the equal protection clause.

Plessy v. Ferguson
Court decision declaring separate but equal public facilities constitutional.

separate but equal doctrine
Rule stating that the equal protection clause was not violated by the fact of state mandated racial segregation alone, provided that the separated facilities were equal.

VIDEO
ROUNDTABLE

Equality

Rosa Parks
• *Why did acts of civil disobedience prove so effective during the civil rights movement?*

in segregated stores. Housing was even more segregated than in the South. But at least African Americans in the North could vote.

Unlike those who governed the South, northern machine politicians who dominated big-city politics were not fussy about the color or religion of the voters they organized. The tough, shrewd, urban political organizer knew that black votes counted as much as the vote of any other resident of the city.[28] One Chicago newspaper assessed the situation in 1927: "Their solid vote is the Negroes' greatest weapon. They have a total vote in Chicago of about 40,000. This total vote is cast for the candidate who makes the best bargain with them."[29]

By the 1930s, African Americans used their votes to win a small place in the politics of a few big cities. African American politicians won election to city councils and became neighborhood leaders in party organizations, obtaining jobs and other benefits for their constituents.[30] By 1945, two African Americans, William Dawson of Chicago and Adam Clayton Powell of New York, held seats in the House of Representatives.[31] But the biggest political breakthrough for African Americans occurred in 1948, when many observers gave them credit for casting the decisive votes electing Harry Truman president. Recognizing the power of black voters in key states such as Ohio, Illinois, and Michigan early in the campaign, Truman delivered the strongest civil rights message that any president had ever presented. He called for the abolition of poll taxes, more effective protection of voting rights, the creation of a Fair Employment Practices Commission with authority to stop racial discrimination, and an end to racial segregation within the armed forces. Some scholars have argued that the president's slim margins of victory in several crucial states were due to his two-thirds support among

African Americans.[32] This growing electoral clout, and the increasing rhetorical support President Truman gave to the cause of civil rights, lent added force to civil rights lawsuits that activists began to bring before the Supreme Court.

Awakening the Supreme Court to Civil Rights

National Association for the Advancement of Colored People (NAACP)

Civil rights organization, dating from 1909, that relied heavily on a legal strategy to pursue its objectives.

The legal case against segregation was gradually developed by the **National Association for the Advancement of Colored People (NAACP)**, a civil rights organization that relied heavily on a legal strategy to pursue its objectives. Founded in 1909 by a group of African American intellectuals and activists, the NAACP bears a name that strikes readers today as odd but is rooted in the historical moment when it was established. After several failed attempts to persuade Congress to pass a law against lynching, the NAACP chose the courtroom strategy because its leaders concluded that the electoral strength of African Americans was too small to effect dramatic change.

But a legal strategy carried out without the support of black votes was not very effective. Despite the care with which cases were prepared by the NAACP's lead attorney, Thurgood Marshall (who later became the first black Supreme Court justice), the organization initially had few successes in the courtroom. It could get outlawed neither the poll tax nor education requirements. For all of the legal efforts of the NAACP, only 12 percent of the southern black adult population was registered to vote in 1947.[33]

The NAACP's legal strategy gained strength as northern blacks became more politically potent. President Roosevelt took minor symbolic steps to court the black vote in the 1940 presidential race, and in 1941 the threat of a summer march on Washington by up to 100,000 African Americans drew a promise from the president to eliminate discriminatory employment practices in the defense industry.[34] Around this time, FDR appointed to the Supreme Court five justices who were known to be friendly to the NAACP's point of view.[35] Finally, this substantially new Court outlawed the white primary in the 1944 case *Smith v. Allwright*, saying that political parties were not private organizations but integral parts of a state electoral system.[36] After this decision, black voting in the South gradually began to increase.

restrictive housing covenant

Legal promise by home buyers that they would not resell to an African American; enforcement declared unconstitutional by Supreme Court.

In 1948, the very year blacks helped elect Harry Truman, the Court outlawed **restrictive housing covenants**, legal promises by those buying houses that they would not resell to an African American. Under the state action doctrine enunciated by the Court in the *Civil Rights Cases*, the contract seemed a private matter, not subject to constitutional scrutiny. But, in its 1948 ruling in *Shelly v. Kramer*, the Court held that although the contracts themselves were indeed private, any state enforcement of such covenants was a public act that violated the equal protection clause.[37] By making this decision, the Court greatly narrowed the range of activities in which segregation could be legally practiced, laying the groundwork for a redefinition of the equal protection clause.

Redefining the Equal Protection Clause

Although Harry Truman's election and the Court's decisions in *Smith v. Allwright* and *Shelly v. Kramer* offered some hope, the legal rights of African Americans in the United States had changed little from the 1890s to the 1940s. Most blacks lived in segregated neighborhoods, many could not vote, and violence and intimidation directed against blacks continued.

From the mid-1950s to the early 1970s, however, the status of African Americans changed dramatically, through both legal victories and popular mobilization. By no means were all problems solved in this period, but blacks made great advances in redefining and strengthening the constitutional guarantee of "equal protection of the laws." In this section, we review the history of the civil rights movement that began in the 1950s, consider the debate over affirmative action, and assess the current state of civil rights for African Americans.

Brown v. Board of Education of Topeka, Kansas

Civil rights groups tried hard to reverse the separate but equal doctrine set forth in *Plessy v. Ferguson*, but for decades the Supreme Court resisted. In one extraordinary case, the Court allowed a school district to operate with a white high school, but no black high school, saying that blacks would gain little from a decision to shut down the white school, and ignoring the possibility that blacks and whites might share the same facility.[38]

The NAACP seemed more successful in 1938 when it won a suit on behalf of a black law student denied access to Missouri's all-white law school.[39] Missouri had no black law school but offered to pay students' tuition to attend a law school in an adjacent state. When the Court ruled that this policy was unconstitutional, Missouri and other southern states responded by creating all-black law schools of inferior quality, leaving blacks worse off than they were before the decision.

After blacks demonstrated their electoral influence in 1948, the NAACP proved more effective in the courtroom, as the Supreme Court began to reconsider the separate but equal doctrine enunciated in *Plessy*. First, in 1950, the Court unanimously declared that requiring black law students to attend an all-black school was inherently unconstitutional because such a school could not be an effective "proving ground for legal learning and practice."[40] By focusing on law schools, the NAACP had shrewdly aimed at the weakest point in the separate but equal doctrine. Most Supreme Court justices were attorneys, and they knew from personal experience the importance of a law school's reputation for a lawyer's subsequent career.

Once the law-school decision provided an opening wedge, the NAACP attacked the separate but equal doctrine directly by encouraging Oliver Brown to file suit saying his daughter, Linda, was being denied equal protection by Topeka, Kansas, by being forced to attend an all-black school. The fact that the black schools in Topeka seemed to be just as good as the white schools was irrelevant, argued the NAACP. This suit led to the Supreme Court's **Brown v. Board of Education of Topeka, Kansas** decision in 1954 that finally declared racial segregation unconstitutional.[41]

Newly appointed Chief Justice Earl Warren, a former California governor, was keenly aware of the political significance of the Brown case, so he worked hard to convince the rest of the Court to issue a unanimous decision. At first it seemed that Warren would fail in this effort, because two members of the Court thought a decision to reverse *Plessy v. Ferguson* would violate the principle of *stare decisis*, a rule that says courts should adhere to the doctrines set forth in prior decisions (see Chapter 15, page 446). But Warren argued that the *Brown* decision could be distinguished from *Plessy* because the *Plessy* case had involved trains, not schools.

To distinguish segregation in school from segregation in transportation, Warren cited psychological studies provided by the NAACP to show that racial separation

Brown v. Board of Education of Topeka, Kansas
1954 Supreme Court decision declaring racial segregation in schools unconstitutional.

created a sense of inferiority among black children. One study showed, for example, that black children favored white dolls over black ones.[42] Focusing on the particularly harmful effects of segregation on children allowed Warren to limit his opinion to schools, thereby avoiding a direct repeal of *Plessy*. By so limiting the effect of the decision, Warren was able to obtain a unanimous vote from the justices, but in pursuing a legal doctrine Warren might have done better to have followed Harlan's dissent in *Plessy* that simply said, "the Constitution is color-blind." Since the *Brown* decision, many have argued that the constitutionality of racial segregation should depend not on its psychological effects, which may vary from person to person, but on whether racial criteria are valid grounds for classifying individuals.

Years later, the Supreme Court did provide this very rationale for its finding that segregation was unconstitutional. In 1973 it said that any legal distinction based on race or on membership in any other ethnic group that had been discriminated against in the past was a **suspect classification**, which required strict scrutiny by the courts to make sure that its use did not violate the Fourteenth Amendment's equal protection clause. This concept, which is now the standard tool with which the courts adjudicate civil rights cases, soon became crucial for ensuring that racial and ethnic minorities received equal protection before the law.[43]

In 1954, however, Chief Justice Warren realized he could not get a unanimous Court to back such a sweeping statement outlawing all forms of segregation, so, in *Brown*, he settled for less by focusing on segregation's psychological effects on young children. Also to preserve court unanimity, Warren postponed consideration of the exact way in which school boards were to rectify their segregated practices. The following year, the Court handed down a separate ruling on this enforcement issue, calling for school desegregation "with all deliberate speed," a phrase that appeared to have contradictory meanings. "Deliberate" implied a slow, methodical pace, whereas "speed" suggested a need for prompt compliance. Most southern school boards focused on deliberation, enacting as little desegregation as possible.

In spite of its defects, scholars believe *Brown* to be among the most important decisions the Supreme Court has ever made.[44] In this decision, the Supreme Court declared unconstitutional a system of racial segregation that from the earliest colonial settlements had organized social life in a large part of the United States. Within two years, the border states of Maryland, Kentucky, and Missouri, as well as Kansas and the District of Columbia, eliminated formal segregation in their schools.

Civil Rights After *Brown*

Brown also energized civil rights activists around the country. The impact on young people and church leaders was particularly noticeable. Immediately after the decision, three new civil rights organizations—the Congress of Racial Equality (CORE), the Student Nonviolent Coordinating Committee (SNCC), and the Southern Christian Leadership Conference (SCLC)—rose to prominence. Consisting mainly of college students and ministers, these groups held demonstrations, led boycotts, undertook voter registration drives, and appealed to the federal government for intervention into southern racial practices.[45]

One year after *Brown*, a more activist phase of the civil rights movement erupted. In December 1955, Rosa Parks of Montgomery, Alabama, engaged in an extraordi-

suspect classification
Categorization of a particular group that will be closely scrutinized by the courts to see whether its use is unconstitutional.

Suspect Classification and Gay Marriage

Civil Rights Activist
• *Did these activists or the courts contribute more to the end of formal segregation?*

narily successful act of **civil disobedience**—a peaceful, well-publicized violation of a law designed to dramatize that law's injustice. Her arrest for refusing to vacate her seat in the white section of a segregated bus prompted a bus boycott led by a young Baptist minister, Martin Luther King, Jr., who had just earned his Ph.D. in theology. He was only 27 years old at the time, but he had the resourcefulness and rhetorical capacity to give the event national significance.[46] "If there is a victory [over segregation]," King wrote, "the victory will not be merely for the Negro citizens and a defeat of the white citizens, but it will be a victory for justice and a defeat of injustice. It will be a victory for goodness in its long struggle with the forces of evil."[47]

Using boycotts, protests, and acts of civil disobedience, the southern civil rights movement gained strength by winning sympathetic coverage in the northern press.[48] But activists met intense opposition from government officials at home. In March 1956, nearly every southern member of Congress signed the Southern Manifesto, committing themselves to resist the enforcement of the *Brown* decision by "all lawful means."[49] Southern resistance to court-ordered integration was so consistent and complete that in the states of the old Confederacy, hardly any school desegregation actually occurred. When school began in the fall of 1964, 10 years after the *Brown* decision, only 2.3 percent of black students in the states of the old Confederacy attended integrated schools.[50]

Yet the protests and demonstrations gradually had their effect. For one thing, southern African Americans were registering to vote. The percentage that was registered more than doubled from 12 percent in 1947 to 28 percent in 1960. At the same time, African Americans were becoming a more powerful political force in the large

civil disobedience

A peaceful, well-publicized violation of a law designed to dramatize that law's injustice.

I Have a Dream

Martin Luther King, Jr., delivers his "I Have a Dream" speech at the March on Washington in August 1963.

• *Why did the civil rights movement lose support just a few years later?*

Civil Rights
Movement

industrial states of the North. With civil rights demonstrators focusing national attention on racial issues, presidential candidates had to balance southern resistance against the need to get black votes in big northern states.

John Kennedy's victory over Richard Nixon in the breathtakingly close election of 1960 owed much to his success in attracting the black vote. When the 1960 campaign began, Kennedy realized that he needed to improve his civil rights credentials, especially because he had won the Democratic nomination by defeating two candidates with stronger civil rights records: Hubert Humphrey and Adlai Stevenson. To strengthen his support in the black community, Kennedy placed a well-publicized phone call to Coretta Scott King expressing sympathy for the plight of her husband, Martin Luther King, who had been jailed in Birmingham after participating in a student sit-in. That phone call took on great symbolic significance and helped generate support for Kennedy in the black community. Kennedy, who had begun the campaign with little support among African Americans,[51] captured enough black votes to win such crucial states as Ohio, Michigan, and Illinois.

Once in office, Kennedy introduced civil rights legislation that received vigorous support from civil rights demonstrators. In the largest of these demonstrations, more than 200,000 black and white demonstrators marched on the Washington Mall in the summer of 1963, calling for congressional passage of the proposed legislation and other reforms. From the steps of the Lincoln Memorial, King delivered his powerful and moving "I Have a Dream" oration, in which he firmly connected the struggle for civil rights to mainstream American values. The dream of African Americans, he said, was "deeply rooted in the American dream that one day this nation will rise up and live out the true meaning of its creed . . . that all men are created equal."[52] These appeals persuaded many ordinary voters. In the wake of the march, for the first time a plurality of Americans that were polled said they viewed civil rights as the country's most important problem.[53] Just a few months later, Kennedy's assassination generated an unprecedented outpouring of moral commitment to racial justice.

Elected political leaders responded quickly to this transformation in the public mood. The new president, Lyndon Johnson, though himself a southerner, called upon Congress to memorialize the dead president by enacting his civil rights legislation. After intense debate, majorities of both Republican and Democratic members of Congress voted in favor of the Civil Rights Act of 1964, the most sweeping civil rights legislation passed since Reconstruction. This act banned segregation in all places of public accommodation, prohibited federal money from being used to support segregated programs, and created the Equal Employment Opportunity Commission (EEOC) to guard against employment discrimination. The law brought about major changes in race relations throughout the South. Enticed by new federal funds facilitating desegregation, and intimidated by the new enforcement powers of federal officials, many southern schools desegregated. The percentage of black students in southern schools that included whites increased dramatically from 2.3 percent in 1964 to 91.3 percent in 1972.[54]

Buoyed by economic prosperity and his civil rights achievements, Lyndon Johnson won a sweeping election victory in the fall of 1964. Not one to rest on his accomplishments, Johnson soon engineered congressional passage of the Voting Rights Act of 1965, which guaranteed black voting rights by stationing federal examiners in southern registration halls and polling places.[55] As a result, the percentage of voters among southern black adults jumped upward after 1964, as shown in Figure 17.1.[56] The number of elected officials of African American descent rose from less than 500 in 1965, to 6,056 in 1985, to more than 9,100 in 2001.[57] In 2006, Massachusetts elected Deval Patrick governor—the second African American governor since Reconstruction.

Decline in Strength of the Civil Rights Movement

Segregation and discrimination were not limited to the South. Most northern blacks lived in racially isolated neighborhoods, sent their children to predominantly black schools, and found it hard to get good jobs. Even as Congress was passing the Voting Rights Act of 1965, Martin Luther King shifted the focus of the civil rights movement by mounting a series of civil rights demonstrations in Chicago.[58] This shift changed the way the public viewed the civil rights movement. As school busing and job discrimination became a northern issue as well, support for civil rights protests among many northern whites dwindled.[59] At the same time, new black leaders, such as black nationalist Malcolm X, took a more militant position, affirming black culture, denying the value of integration, and suggesting that violent "self defense" might be needed. "If Negroes can get freedom nonviolently, good," said Malcolm X. "But that's a dream. Even King calls it a dream."[60]

Civil violence began to break out in black neighborhoods, beginning in Los Angeles in 1964 and spreading to other cities over the next three years. When King was assassinated by a white man in Memphis, Tennessee, in April 1968, violent racial disturbances broke out simultaneously in dozens of cities throughout the country.

After these events, the white majority began to view the problem of civil rights as less important. As long as civil rights issues were being addressed by nonviolent demonstrations in the South, African Americans appealed successfully to the moral instincts

FIGURE 17.1

Changes in Black and White Participation in Presidential Elections, by Region

• *Why do you think blacks still vote at lower rates than whites? Why do southern and northern blacks now vote at similar rates?*

Source: U.S. Bureau of the Census, *Current Population Survey Reports.* (South is defined as the states that formed the Confederacy.)

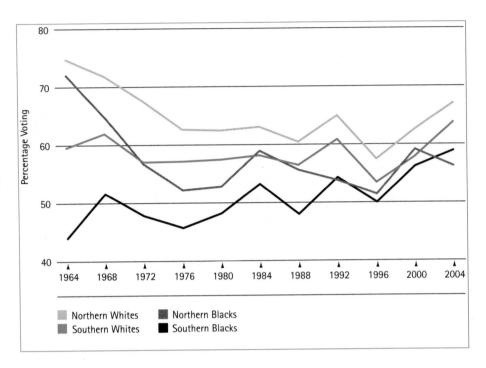

of northern whites. But once whites realized that the problem was national in scope, and that civil disobedience could turn violent, many had second thoughts. Opposition to busing, affirmative action, and other programs of racial integration split the biracial political coalition that had elected Harry Truman and John Kennedy.

Race issues then began to divide the two political parties further. When Senator Barry Goldwater voted against the Civil Rights Act of 1964, he was among a minority of Republicans to do so. But by 1968, Republicans were pursuing what was known as a "southern strategy," an appeal to those who thought the civil rights movement had gone too far. Meanwhile, blacks solidified their allegiance to the Democratic Party.[61] The percentage of delegates attending the Democratic convention who were black grew from 6.7 to 14.6 percent between 1968 and 1972.

Supreme Court No Longer Forges Ahead

Race and the Death Penalty

de jure segregation
Racial segregation that is legally sanctioned.

de facto segregation
Segregation that occurs as the result of decisions by private individuals.

Encountering increasing popular resistance to further legislative initiatives, civil rights groups once again turned to the courts for assistance. But the courts, following the direction in which public opinion was moving, also adopted a more conservative attitude. For example, the Supreme Court drew a distinction between two types of segregation. **De jure segregation**, the legal separation of the races practiced in the South, was said by the Court to violate the equal protection clause of the Constitution. But segregation in the North was said to be **de facto segregation**, occurring as the result of private decisions made by individuals, such as their choice of residence.

In *Milliken v. Bradley* (1974), the Supreme Court considered the constitutionality of the most pervasive form of *de facto* segregation.[62] Bradley argued that the state of Michigan (under Governor William Milliken) tolerated racial segregation by allowing virtually all-white suburban school districts to surround the city of Detroit, whose schools were predominantly black. In rejecting Bradley's argument that the whole metropolitan

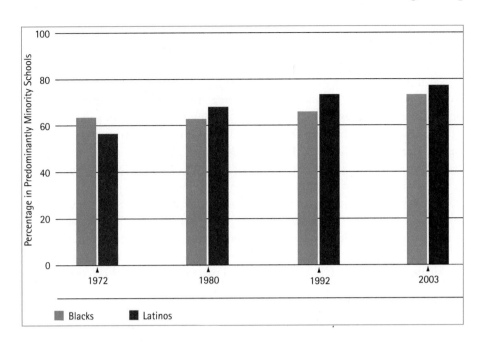

FIGURE 17.2

Percentage of African American and Latino Students in Segregated Schools, 1972–2003

• *In your opinion, why has segregation increased since the 1980s?*

Source: Gary Orfield, *Schools More Separate: Consequences of a Decade of Resegregation* (Cambridge, MA: The Civil Rights Project, Harvard University, July 2001), Table 9; Gary Orfield and Chungmei Lee, *Racial Transformation and the Changing Nature of Segregation* (Cambridge, MA: The Civil Rights Project, Harvard University, January 2006), Table 3, 10, Table 4, 11.

area ought to be desegregated, the Court ruled that suburban school districts in the North had never practiced *de jure* racial segregation. The segregation that had occurred was *de facto*—simply the result of private decisions to live in Detroit or in its suburbs.

Writing for the majority, Warren Burger, who had replaced Earl Warren as chief justice, said that the lower courts, in siding with Bradley, were trying to produce "the racial balance which they perceived as desirable." But the Constitution only forbids segregation; it "does not require any particular racial balance." Dissenting from the decision, Justice Thurgood Marshall, the former NAACP attorney, responded, "Negro students will continue to perceive their schools as segregated educational facilities and this perception will only be increased when whites flee . . . to the suburbs to avoid integration." After the Milliken decision, little additional school desegregation took place in either the North or the South. In recent years, school segregation among African Americans and Latinos has actually increased, as Figure 17.2 illustrates.

Affirmative Action

Civil rights groups also called upon government agencies, universities, and businesses to rectify past discrimination by taking affirmative steps to provide increased educational and job opportunities for African Americans. In response to these demands, many organizations have instituted policies of **affirmative action**, programs designed to enhance opportunities for race- or gender-based groups that have suffered discrimination in the past. In some cases, these programs may consist of nothing more than special advertising, recruitment, and counseling initiatives designed to help members of disadvantaged groups learn about available opportunities. In other cases, universities and employers may also take note of a person's membership in a disadvantaged group as one factor among many to be considered in admissions or hiring decisions. The strongest form of affirmative action involves setting aside a **quota**, or a specific number of positions, for members of disadvantaged groups.

VIDEO DEBATE

Affirmative Action

affirmative action

Programs designed to enhance opportunities for groups that have suffered discrimination in the past.

quota

Specific number of positions set aside for a specific group; said by the Supreme Court to be unconstitutional.

Jennifer Gratz

Jennifer Gratz sued to challenge the University of Michigan's undergraduate admissions system, which assigned a set number of "points" based on race or ethnicity.

• *Do you believe it is appropriate to consider race in university admissions? Is a desire for a diverse student body a good enough reason to do so?*

The Supreme Court first considered the constitutionality of affirmative action programs in a 1978 case that involved Allen Bakke, a Norwegian American, who sued for admission to the medical school of the University of California at Davis.[63] Bakke argued that he had been denied admission because of the school's affirmative action policy, which set aside 16 spots in each entering class of 100 for minority applicants. In an unusually complex ruling, a divided Court found that strict quotas such as Davis's were unconstitutional, but that affirmative action programs that used race as one among many factors were permissible. Justice Lewis Powell, the deciding vote in the case, argued that some kinds of affirmative action were justified if the goal was to create a diverse community that would benefit all.

During the 1990s, all forms of affirmative action came under increasing criticism. In 1995 the University of California's Board of Regents voted to end the use of race as a factor in its admissions policies, a decision that took on broader significance when the state later passed an initiative banning affirmative action. That same year, voters in Washington State passed a similar measure, and two years later, a federal court ordered Texas to eliminate race-based preferences from its state university admissions system.

In 2003, the Supreme Court heard two affirmative action cases that prompted the justices to reexamine the *Bakke* decision. Both cases began at the University of Michigan. In the first, *Grutter v. Bollinger*, Barbara Grutter argued that she had been denied admission to the University of Michigan's law school because of an affirmative action system that considered race as one of a number of criteria in a process that placed great importance on creating a diverse student body.[64] In the second, *Gratz v. Bollinger*, Jennifer Gratz similarly argued that she had been refused a spot in Michigan's undergraduate program because of the school's affirmative action policy. Both Grutter and Gratz alleged that they had been denied equal protection under the law, and that Michigan's affirmative action programs should be struck down as a violation of the Fourteenth Amendment.

The undergraduate admission system differed from the law school system, however. Law school admissions officers considered race as one "plus" factor in a "highly individualized, holistic review" of each candidate.[65] The undergraduate process operated under a "points" system, in which academic record, standardized test scores, high school quality, and other factors each garnered an applicant a set number of points. Prospective students needed 100 points or more to be admitted, and membership in an "underrepresented minority group" automatically secured an applicant 20 points.[66] The Court invalidated this points system because it was too blunt an instrument. Even though the Court admitted that diversity was a valid goal, the undergraduate system was not "narrowly tailored" to avoid undue discrimination.

The law school system, on the other hand, was acceptable, wrote Justice Sandra Day O'Connor for the majority in *Grutter*. O'Connor reaffirmed Powell's argument in *Bakke* that "diversity will, in fact, yield educational benefits," and argued further that affirmative action would help educational institutions train "a set of leaders with legitimacy in the eyes of the citizenry."[67]

In rejecting a rigid points system while allowing some forms of affirmative action, the Court again struck a compromise that placed it in the mainstream of public opinion. Perhaps recognizing this fact, George W. Bush, whose administration had urged the Court to ban all types of affirmative action, praised the Court "for recognizing the value of diversity on our nation's campuses." Still, Bush added, "I look forward to the day when America will truly be a color-blind society."[68]

Comparing
Civil Rights

Elections, Courts, and Civil Rights: An Appraisal

Significant problems still beset African Americans in the United States as well as else-where. Chief among them is the persistence of poverty in the black community. Poverty rates among blacks remain nearly two and one half times those of whites.[69] Black unemployment is nearly double the national average.[70] And teen pregnancy and infant mortality rates are far higher among African Americans than among others.[71] Critics argue that although middle- and upper-class blacks have made progress, these successes have not translated into wide-reaching economic gains for all African Americans.[72]

But there is increasing reason for optimism about the status of African Americans in the United States. The victories of the civil rights movement have promoted advancement in almost every sector. The percentage of black men and women in professional and managerial positions increased markedly in the decades following the passage of the Civil Rights and Voting Rights Acts.[73] Blacks have also made political gains, winning an increasing number of mayoral elections, state legislative races, and seats in Congress, and they have made noticeable educational advances. Whereas in 1960, only 20 percent of African Americans were high school graduates, by 2004, 80 percent were.[74] And between 1971 and 2004 the math test scores of black high school seniors improved by 5.3 percent, while the scores of white students improved only 1 percent over the same period.[75] African American poverty rates, while still high, shrank from more than 32 percent to less than 25 percent from 1980 to 2004.[76]

Civil Rights of Other Minorities

Most of the civil rights issues and rulings discussed thus far apply as much to other racial and ethnic groups as they do to African Americans. The civil rights of other ethnic groups nonetheless assume distinctive legal and political significance under two circumstances: (1) when groups eligible for affirmative action need to be defined, and (2) when language or other group-specific issues arise.

The Supreme Court has never specifically delineated the groups in American society whose treatment over the course of U.S. history makes them eligible for affirmative action. Neither the 1964 nor the 1965 civil rights legislation identified any groups other than blacks as deserving affirmative action to redress historical grievances. But, after the civil rights movement defined many issues in terms of equal protection under the Constitution, groups representing other ethnic minorities began to make similar civil rights claims, and Congress, through voting rights legislation, has given them recognition.

The pace of this process and the degree to which each group receives recognition in law have in large part depended on how effectively each group has been able to mobilize its members in elections. Latinos, Asian Americans, and gays and lesbians have recently begun to exert their influence on national electoral politics. But until very recently Native Americans remained a small, politically inactive voting bloc.

Latinos

Latinos are now the largest minority group in the United States. In 1980 they made up only 6.4 percent of the U.S. population, but by 2005 they had grown to 14.4 percent, surpassing the 13.4 percent that are African American.[77] In contrast to African

Courting the Latino Vote

New York City Mayor Michael Bloomberg speaks entirely in Spanish during one of his many 2005 campaign spots aimed at wooing Hispanics.

• *Why are parties paying closer attention to Latino voters?*

Americans, who have been politically assertive for nearly 50 years, Latinos are only beginning to exercise their influence regularly in elections. There are several reasons for this difference. A sizeable percentage of the Latino population lacks citizenship, and even among Latino citizens voting rates are much lower than among African Americans, partly because most Latinos have not experienced a prolonged—and unifying—civil rights struggle.[78]

Building a broad-based political coalition is further complicated by the fact that Latinos come from many different countries and differ from one another in important cultural and political respects. For example, Mexican Americans in California and Texas who are concerned about job discrimination and working conditions may have a hard time identifying with Cuban Americans in Florida who are primarily concerned with the restoration of democracy in their home country. Latino voters are also much less likely than African Americans to vote as a bloc. Whereas 81 percent of blacks consider themselves Democrats, only 55 percent of Latinos do.[79]

Like African Americans, Latinos have mobilized through both social protest and legal activism. In the late 1960s and early 1970s, Mexican Americans in the Southwest founded the Chicano movement, which argued for cultural and social separatism from white America. But it was the United Farm Workers Union, under the leadership of César Chávez, that drew mainstream public attention to Latino concerns. In the late 1960s, Chávez organized a five-year national boycott of grapes to protest working conditions for migrant farm workers. The boycott, along with marches, strikes, and other nonviolent protest tactics, led to California legislation that guaranteed farm workers rights. In addition, Chávez's principled appeals drew respect from large numbers of Americans, just as the African American civil rights movement had. Reflecting on his uncle's legacy, Federico Chávez said, "He taught us to persevere in a nonviolent way so when you won, it would be a moral victory as well as an organizing victory . . . . In that way, I think, he was able to gain the support of the American people."[80]

In 1968, while Chávez was organizing California farm workers, Latinos in Texas founded the Mexican American Legal Defense and Education Fund (MALDEF), a legal advocacy organization that has focused on voting, education, and immigration issues (see Chapter 4 for discussion of immigration). In 1974, in response to MALDEF complaints, the Supreme Court interpreted the 1964 Civil Rights Act to mean that schools must provide special educational programs for those not proficient in the English language.[81] MALDEF and other groups also argued that Latinos and other language minorities were discriminated against because ballots and other voter registration materials were published only in English. Congress responded to these concerns in 1982 by requiring that ballots be printed in the language of any protected minority that constitutes more than 5 percent of a county's population, thereby extending protection not only to Latinos but also to Asian Americans and American Indians.[82]

Latinos have also begun to make their influence felt in elections—first in state and local politics, later in national campaigns—although their voter turnout remains low relative to other groups.[83] A key turning point came in 1994 when California voters passed Proposition 187, which would have denied state and local public services to illegal aliens. Although courts blocked the measure before it could be implemented, the bitter campaign over its passage energized the California Latino community and caused many Latinos to support the Democratic Party, which had opposed the measure.[84]

Both national parties, anticipating that Latinos would make up nearly a tenth of the voting population in 2004, actively courted the Latino vote as the election approached.[85] George W. Bush stressed his support for some bilingual education programs and his opposition to English-only mandates. He also presided over aggressive efforts to appoint Latinos to many top government positions, including Alberto Gonzales as Attorney General and Mel Martinez as Secretary of Housing and Urban Development.[86] Finally, he suggested a new guest-worker program for immigrants that would allow noncitizens to work legally in the United States for up to six years.[87]

In 2006 Bush pushed similar legislation, as Democrats argued that the measures were too harsh on new immigrants, and some conservative Republicans complained that the bill did not go far enough. Meanwhile, Latinos rallied around the country in support of immigrants' rights. (See *Election Voices*, p. 117.) Some observers predicted that the 2006 immigration debate would galvanize Latinos nationwide the same way the Proposition 187 issue energized Hispanic activists in California in the mid-1990s. (See Chapter 4.)

Asian Americans

Like Latinos, Asian Americans have only recently begun to make their voices heard in national electoral politics. They constitute 5 percent of the population, and more than 60 percent are foreign-born.[88] Like Latinos, they represent many different nationalities and have differing—even conflicting—policy concerns. Asian Americans are also less likely to support affirmative action programs and more likely to vote Republican than other ethnic minorities.[89]

In 1996 activists in the Asian American community flexed their political muscle by mounting a coordinated national fund-raising and voter-registration drive.[90] That year, Gary Locke of Washington State was elected the first Asian American governor of a state other than Hawaii. But fund-raising scandals in the Clinton campaign, in which several Asians and Asian Americans were involved, caused many to worry about a backlash against the Asian American community. Since the 1990s, Asian Americans have become increasingly active at the state and local levels, organizing cultural celebrations, urging quick responses to anti–Asian slurs and ethnically motivated violence, and lobbying for official recognition of the Chinese New Year holiday.[91]

The major civil rights victory for Asian Americans has been the compensation paid to Japanese Americans for their internment in relocation camps during World War II. Responding to public concern that Japanese Americans on the West Coast might act as spies or saboteurs for Japan, President Franklin Roosevelt ordered 70,000 Japanese American citizens and another 40,000 resident Japanese—men, women, and children—to leave their homes and live in "relocation centers" for the duration of the war. Those adults who swore loyalty to the United States were released, but if they lived close to either coast, they were told they could not return home. Earl Warren, the California attorney general and later chief justice of the Supreme Court, gave a race-based rationale for these actions: "When we are dealing with the Caucasian race we have methods that will test the loyalty of them . . . . But when we deal with the Japanese . . . we cannot form any opinion that we believe to be sound."[92]

In *Korematsu v. United States* (1944), the Supreme Court went along with ferociously anti-Japanese public opinion and found the relocation centers constitutional. But in his dissent from the Court's decision, Justice Frank Murphy condemned the relocation as "one of the most sweeping and complete deprivations of constitutional rights in the history of this nation."[93] At the instigation of Japanese American activists organized as the National Coalition for Redress and Reparations, Congress agreed in 1988 to apologize for the incident and pay each internee (or the internee's heirs) $20,000.[94]

Because of the diversity of the Asian American community, a unified political agenda for the future has yet to take shape. Some Asian American activists and political organizations are concerned with issues such as immigrant rights and expanding the Supreme Court's definition of a suspect classification to include Asian language speakers.[95] However, other Asian Americans favor the elimination of quotas and affirmative action programs from which they are excluded.

Gays and Lesbians

Some of the most contentious political debates in the early twenty-first century surrounded the rights of gays and lesbians. It is no accident that at the same time, homosexuals were more engaged in electoral politics than ever before. Although the first local law protecting individuals against discrimination on the basis of sexual orientation was passed in 1973, and the first such state law in 1982, it has only been since the early 1990s that the gay and lesbian community has exerted significant influence in national elections.[96] In 1992, gay and lesbian donors gave an estimated $3.5 million to the Clinton campaign, persuading Clinton to promise, among other things, an end to the ban on gays in the military.[97] Congressional and media attention paid to gay and lesbian issues also rose around the same time, in part as a result of pressure from organized gay and lesbian interest groups.[98] Since the early 1990s the number of openly gay government officials has jumped from 49 to more than 300.[99]

In the last decade a majority of the American public grew to believe that gays deserve equal job opportunities, as Figure 17.3 shows. Laws barring employment discrimination on the basis of sexual orientation have been passed in 16 states and have bipartisan support in Congress.[100] In 2000 Vermont became the first state legally to

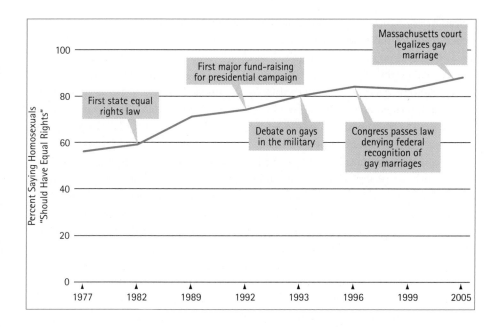

FIGURE 17.3

Public Opinion on Gay
Rights Has Changed
as Gay and Lesbian
Political Activism
Has Increased

• *Why do you think support
for gay rights declined slightly
in the late 1990s after rising
steadily for so long?*

Source: The Gallup Poll.

recognize same-sex civil unions. Three years later, the Massachusetts Supreme Judicial Court ruled that the state's constitution protected the right of gays to marry, and the first legal gay weddings began occurring there in May 2004. That same year, local officials in San Francisco, New Mexico, and upstate New York began marrying gay couples in the absence of a specific legal mandate to do so. Although the actions of these localities were later overturned by states, Newsom was unrepentant: "Most politicians don't get away with doing the right thing at a time when society is not necessarily unanimously ready for that."[101]

Newsom is correct in his assessment that public opinion remains conservative on many issues regarding homosexuality. Large majorities disapprove of gay marriage and have serious reservations when asked whether gays should be allowed to serve as teachers or youth leaders.[102] Forty-five states have passed laws or state constitutional amendments banning same-sex marriages.[103] Many in Massachusetts and around the country reacted negatively to that state's supreme court ruling, and the legislature moved to place a state constitutional amendment on the 2008 ballot that would restrict same-sex unions.[104] At the national level, President Bush and Republicans in Congress urged the passage of a federal marriage amendment, while some Democrats said that such a move was unnecessary and divisive.

**Civil Rights and
Gay Adoption**

Native Americans

The rights and liberties of descendants of indigenous tribes are not protected by the Bill of Rights, because at the time of the writing of the Constitution, these peoples were considered members of a foreign nation. As one authority on Indian rights has put it, "No constitutional protections exist for Indians in either a tribal or an individual sense."[105]

The relations between Native Americans and the government are instead governed by laws of Congress and by the many treaties that have been signed by the United States and American Indian tribes. Over the long course of American history, the United

States government, under political pressure from those migrating westward, ignored or broke many of the treaties it made with indigenous tribes. Still, the Supreme Court today interprets some of these treaties as binding.[106] As a result, members of these tribes have certain rights and privileges not available to other groups. For example, Court interpretations of treaties have given tribes in the Pacific Northwest special rights to fish for salmon—rights that tribes view as vital in preserving their cultural and religious traditions. These exemptions can also be economically important for Native Americans, who suffer from the highest poverty rates of all U.S. racial and ethnic groups.[107]

Another economically significant tribal right recognized in recent years has been the authority to provide commercial gambling on tribal property. In several cases, tribes have used resources from these gambling operations to increase their political clout. For example, the Choctaw Native American tribe in Mississippi spends $3 million annually on Washington, D.C., lobbyists. According to Choctaw chief Philip Martin, "If you don't have some political influence in this country, you don't have anything."[108]

Most of the rights contained in the Bill of Rights have been applied to members of tribes through congressional legislation. To protect tribal religious freedom, Congress in 1978 passed the American Indian Religious Freedom Resolution. Tribal leaders have argued that the resolution gives them special access to traditional religious sites in national parks and other government-owned lands. But the federal courts have interpreted the resolution narrowly, saying it does not make indigenous Americans "supercitizens." Rather, it gives them religious freedoms comparable to those granted to other citizens.[109]

Women's Rights

Although gender is not mentioned in the equal protection clause of the Fourteenth Amendment, the meaning of the clause has been gradually redefined to refer to equal rights for women as well as for racial and ethnic groups. As one constitutional scholar has written, "It is in the very nature of ideas to grow in self-awareness, to work out all their implications over time . . . ."[110] Changes in the meaning of the equal protection clause were won as a result of a broad struggle for women's rights played out as much among the electorate as in the legal arena.

The first struggle for women's rights focused on the right to vote (see Chapter 6). Once the Nineteenth Amendment was passed in 1920, the women's movement became dormant for nearly 50 years, finally to be awakened in the late sixties by the civil rights movement.[111] Since then, women's groups have achieved four civil rights objectives: the right to equal treatment before the law, tough enforcement of this right, the right not to be sexually harassed in the workplace, and access to state-funded military academies. Achievement of these objectives required both electoral involvement and courtroom presentations.

The Right to Equality Before the Law

As unlikely as it may seem, it was a conservative southerner, Representative Howard Smith of Virginia, who proposed an amendment to Title VII of the Civil Rights Act of 1964 that would prohibit discrimination on the basis of sex as well as race, religion, or national origin. Although the amendment passed overwhelmingly, activist women

Women's Rights Across the Century

(left) Women's rights issues in the United States at first focused on women's right to vote. (right) In August 1970, 50 years after women had won the franchise, 10,000 women's liberationists marched to a "Women's Strike for Equality" rally at New York City's Bryant Park.
• *Why did the women's rights movement begin in the 1970s, when women had voting rights as early as 1920?*

formed the National Organization for Women (NOW) in 1966 because they became concerned that the gender provision in Title VII would not be enforced. To guarantee enforcement of women's civil rights, NOW, together with other women's organizations, backed the **Equal Rights Amendment**, a proposed amendment to the Constitution that banned gender discrimination. Proponents expected this amendment to give the courts the tools necessary to strike down gender inequities.

At first it seemed that women's groups would succeed in winning passage of this constitutional amendment. Responding to polls that showed overwhelming public approval for the measure,[112] Congress passed the ERA by large majorities by the spring of 1972. Within a year most states had voted to ratify it.[113] But at the very moment when the ERA was about to become a part of the U.S. Constitution, it encountered increasing resistance led by groups of conservative women who were concerned, among other things, that the amendment would require government funding of abortions and the application of the military draft to women.[114] Upon hearing these arguments, the public began to have second thoughts. In the end, 35 states approved the ERA—three states short of the three-fourths majority necessary to enact a constitutional amendment (see Chapter 2).

As discouraging as the ERA defeat was for its supporters, in retrospect it seems that they won the war by losing the battle. Fifty years earlier, the women's movement had collapsed immediately following passage of the Nineteenth Amendment. This time, the women's movement continued to forge on, perhaps partly because the Equal Rights Amendment did not pass. In the 25 years after the ERA campaign began in earnest, women's place in politics changed more dramatically than in any previous quarter-century. More women were elected to public office in the 1990s than ever before.[115] In 2007 the House of Representatives included 73 women, the Senate had 16, 2 of the 9 Supreme Court justices were female, and women held 3 of 15 positions in President Bush's cabinet.

Equal Rights Amendment (ERA)

Proposed amendment to the Constitution that banned gender discrimination.

Women in the Military

Classifications by gender still exist in the military. Although women can serve as combat pilots, they may not serve in front line Army infantry units, for example.

• *Are these gender distinctions justified?*

Initial Court Response to Women's Rights

The ERA also had an impact on Supreme Court decisions. Before the ERA campaign, the Court had done little for women's rights. As late as 1961, in an opinion ironically signed by the same chief justice who wrote the *Brown* decision, Earl Warren, the Court unanimously upheld a Florida law that made a clear gender distinction. It said that men were required to serve on juries but that women could serve on a jury only if they volunteered for duty.[116]

Court opinions changed after the House of Representatives voted overwhelmingly in favor of the ERA. The Supreme Court, in *Craig v. Boren* (1976), declared unconstitutional an Oklahoma law that allowed women to drink at age 18 but denied that privilege to men until the age of 21. Oklahoma defended the law on the grounds that young men were more likely than young women to drive when drunk and were therefore more likely to have accidents. But the Supreme Court rejected this argument as irrelevant on the grounds that the law constituted "invidious gender-based discrimination" that constituted "a denial [to males] of equal protection of the laws in violation of the Fourteenth Amendment."[117] (Oklahoma subsequently made 21 the legal drinking age for both men and women.)

Although the Supreme Court said that gender discrimination violates the equal protection clause, it has never said that gender, like race, is a suspect classification that will be strictly scrutinized by the courts to see whether its use is constitutional. Instead, the Court has said only that it will rule against a law that includes gender distinctions unless those distinctions have "a substantial relationship to an important objective."[118]

National defense remains the most important arena in which classifications by gender remain intact. According to federal law, men must register for the draft but women need not, and men carry out combat assignments whereas women are not allowed to do so—although many "noncombat" positions now assigned to women may actually place women in danger of enemy fire. In Iraq, where insurgents could attack anywhere at any time, many women in so-called "support units" felt as if they were on the front lines.[119] The

Supreme Court ruled gender distinctions within the military constitutional in *Rostker v. Goldberg* (1981) on the grounds that on military matters, "Congress' constitutional power" is broad and "the lack of competence on the part of the courts is marked."[120] The ruling was consistent with the view of a majority of the voters, who favored—and continue to favor—certain restrictions on female participation in military combat.[121]

Discrimination in the Workplace

Employers sometimes argue that they have legitimate reasons for not hiring representative numbers of women and members of disadvantaged groups. Certain jobs might be performed effectively only by people of a particular gender. (The position of prison guard could be one example.) Qualified job applicants from disadvantaged groups may also be in short supply. In such cases of "business necessity," the Supreme Court has allowed employers to maintain unrepresentative workforces.[122] In the 1989 case of *Ward's Cove Packing Co. v. Antonio*, the Court also said that, under Title VII of the Civil Rights Act of 1964, workers who bring discrimination suits have a responsibility to prove that business necessity is not at issue in their cases.[123] This ruling prompted quick action from Congress, which overruled the Court by passing a new Civil Rights Act in 1991 to place the burden of proof back on businesses rather than on employees. As in past cases, elected officials, not the Court, took the lead on this gender discrimination issue.

Sexual Harassment

The Supreme Court did not rule on the meaning of sexual harassment in the workplace until *Meritor Savings Bank v. Vinson*, a case decided in 1986.[124] In this case, Michelle Vinson said that she had been psychologically damaged as a result of sexually abusive language used in her presence. In deciding in Vinson's favor, Justice Rehnquist wrote a narrow opinion that strongly implied that sexual harassment would be considered illegal only if it caused psychological damage to the victim. In other words, the Court said sexual harassment had to be experienced as personally devastating before it constituted a violation of Title VII.

Sexual harassment became a major political issue in 1991, when Clarence Thomas was nominated to serve on the Supreme Court, and a former aide publicly accused him of sexual harassment. The issue so energized the women's movement that 1992, the election year that followed, became known as the "year of the woman." NOW reported a dramatic jump in membership that year and presided over a 750,000-person march in Washington, D.C.[125] The number of women elected to the House of Representatives increased by 19, and 4 more women were elected to the Senate. Responding to the change in the political atmosphere, the Supreme Court, in the unanimous 1993 decision *Harris v. Forklift Systems*, expanded its definition of sexual harassment.[126] Teresa Harris resigned her position at Forklift Systems Inc., a heavy equipment rental firm, because her employer called her "a dumb-ass woman" and made other derogatory remarks. Lower courts denied her compensation, because no psychological damage could be shown. But Justice Sandra Day O'Connor wrote, in the majority opinion, that Title VII "comes into play before harassing conduct leads to a nervous breakdown." Once again, the Supreme Court moved forward in the wake of public pressure and political events.

Single-Sex Schools and Colleges

Single-sex schools have long been a significant part of American education. As late as the 1950s, well-known private colleges, such as Princeton and Yale, limited their admissions to men. Although these colleges now admit approximately equal numbers of men and women, single-sex education survives at some private women's colleges. These colleges assert that women learn more in an environment where many can assume leadership roles. Hillary Rodham Clinton, who graduated from Wellesley, a Massachusetts women's college, said it "was very, very important to me and I am so grateful that I had the chance to go to college at a place where women were valued and nurtured and encouraged."[127] Arguments have recently been made for all-male education as well. In 1989 the Dade County, Florida, school system established an all-male elementary school serving African American boys.[128] The school system claims that the school has succeeded in increasing student attendance and test scores, while reducing hostility among the students. In 2004, in response to such claims, the Bush administration drafted new regulations designed to make it easier to establish single-sex public schools.[129]

Although policy makers continue to debate the pros and cons of single-sex education, the Supreme Court in 1996 cast doubt on its constitutionality. In *United States v. Virginia*, the Court ruled that women must be admitted to Virginia Military Institute (VMI), even though the state had recently established a separate military education program for women.[130] The Court said the newly established military training program for women did not match the history, reputation, and quality of VMI. It remains unclear, however, whether the Court will extend its decision to private schools or to state programs beyond those that prepare young people for military careers.

The Future of Women's Rights

Despite many gains, the women's movement has not yet realized all of its civil rights agenda. Sexual harassment remains a burning issue within the military and in many business firms. Women still face difficulties breaking through what is known as the **glass ceiling**—the invisible barrier that has limited their opportunities for advancement to the highest ranks of politics, business, and the professions.[131] Few women are chosen as college presidents, as heads of major corporations, or as partners in major law firms. And no woman has yet been nominated for president by either major political party.

The changing American family has also left many women in difficult circumstances. The percentage of children raised in single-parent families headed by a woman has increased sharply in the past quarter-century, and these households are much more likely to be poor than households headed by males or couples. In 2002 the Bush administration announced plans to address this problem by promoting marriage through educational campaigns and counseling programs for poor women. But some women's advocates argued that federal money would be better spent on financial assistance. "To say that the path to economic stability for poor women is marriage is an outrage," argued NOW's president, Kim Gandy.[132] This and other debates suggest that women's issues are likely to remain an important feature in American politics in the twenty-first century.

Americans with Disabilities

According to the U.S. Census Bureau, disabled people constitute 20 percent of the working-age population.[133] Ironically, they have one political advantage that both women and minorities lack: Every person runs the risk of someday becoming disabled. The rights of disabled people thus have broad appeal. Yet this advantage is offset by a number of factors that make coordinated political efforts more difficult: disabilities

glass ceiling
The invisible barrier that has limited women's opportunities for advancement to the highest ranks of politics, business, and the professions.

Disability Rights Rally in Washington, D.C.
Some 300 wheelchair-bound people protest in front of the White House.

• *Are the rights of the disabled more effectively protected by the courts or by elected officials? Why?*

differ in kind and severity, the disabled are more scattered geographically and less visible than ethnic minorities, and the more severely mentally disabled neither vote nor engage directly in politics. The cost of helping people with disabilities is another drawback. It is estimated that the annual cost of disability payments and health care services for this group exceeds $300 billion.[134] Although many people are, in principle, sympathetic to the needs of the disabled, they do not necessarily like to pay the taxes needed to fund appropriate services.

The needs of the disabled were first successfully cast in terms of civil rights not by an interest group but by one individual, Hugh Gallagher, a wheelchair-bound polio victim who in the mid-sixties served as a legislative aide to Alaska senator E. L. Bartlett. Gallagher constantly faced great difficulty using public toilets and gaining access to such buildings as the Library of Congress. At his prodding, Congress in 1968—just four years after the 1964 Civil Rights Act—enacted a law requiring that all future public buildings constructed with federal monies provide access for the disabled. Similar language was subsequently inserted into transportation legislation in 1970.[135]

Once elected officials had responded to the demands of the disabled, the courts, too, became more sensitive. Previously, many developmentally disabled children were denied access to public education on the grounds that they were not mentally competent. But in the early seventies, federal courts required that states provide disabled children with equal educational opportunity.[136] These decisions generated a nationwide movement for disabled children, culminating in the passage in 1975 of the Education for All Handicapped Children Act. Reauthorized as the Individuals with Disabilities Education Act in 2004, this legislation guarantees children with special needs the right to an appropriate education.[137]

Encouraged by both judicial and legislative victories, disability rights groups became increasingly energetic and assertive. Legislative victories in education, transportation, and construction of public buildings finally culminated in the Americans with Disabilities Act of 1991, signed by President George H. W. Bush. This act made it illegal to deny employment to individuals on the grounds that they are disabled,

SIMULATION

You Are the Mayor

unless the person's disability "pose[s] a direct threat to the health or safety of other individuals in the workplace."[138] In addition, workplaces and public accommodations must be adapted to the capacities of disabled persons, whenever feasible.

Because of these legislative changes, opportunities for the disabled have greatly increased. Twenty years ago, public toilets for the disabled hardly existed; sidewalks and staircases had no ramps; buses and trains were inaccessible to those in wheelchairs; colleges and universities were designed in ways that all but precluded attendance by the physically challenged; and developmentally disabled children were denied a public education. Unlike President Franklin Roosevelt, who 50 years ago felt it necessary to avoid being photographed in the wheelchair to which he was confined, Robert Dole referred constantly to his disabled arm during his 1996 campaign for the presidency.

The courts themselves have shown considerable reluctance to interpret the rights of the disabled in sweeping terms. For example, in 2001 the Supreme Court ruled against an Alabama state employee who was punished for taking time off from her job to be treated for breast cancer. The employee, Patricia Garrett, argued that the Americans with Disabilities Act protected her from discrimination. But the Court said that state governments were not covered by the act because of their rights under federalism (see Chapter 3).[139] In 2002, a unanimous Court ruled that to qualify for protection under the ADA, a person must have a condition that impairs activities "central to daily life"—not just workplace activities.[140] In these and other cases, the disabled have found that legislators have been friendlier to their cause than judges.

Yet the disabled, too, have begun to encounter increasing political resistance. Educators complain that too many school dollars are set aside for special-education programs. Architectural changes in public buildings and adaptations in transportation are said to be far too expensive to justify the limited amount of usage they receive. One example of the controversy that accommodations for the disabled can stir occurred in 2001, when the Supreme Court ruled that disabled golfer Casey Martin should be allowed to use a golf cart in competition. Many golfers had argued that walking from hole to hole was fundamental to the game. "I don't think the Supreme Court is in a position to tell me what is or is not important to the game of golf," argued one golf pro who was upset with the decision. "They're not players."[141] It remains to be seen whether such complaints are a sign that the rights of the disabled are soon to be subjected to more limits or whether the extensions enacted in recent years will continue.

Chapter Summary

Civil rights groups have achieved many of their advances by persuading majority populations of the justice of their causes through participation in political demonstrations and electoral politics.[142] The 1954 *Brown* decision, to be sure, had an impact of its own, but even this decision came only after blacks had demonstrated political clout in the 1948 presidential election. Otherwise, the Supreme Court has usually followed the moods and trends of the rest of the country. When the country abandoned

Reconstruction in the latter part of the nineteenth century, the Supreme Court, in the *Civil Rights Cases* and *Plessy v. Ferguson*, ruled against civil rights demands. When blacks moved north and thereby acquired the right to vote, the Supreme Court reversed these decisions and redefined the equal protection clause, banning discrimination against African Americans, Latinos, Asians, and members of other minority groups. Yet the most notable progress toward racial desegregation occurred as the result of legislation passed by bipartisan majorities in Congress in 1964 and 1965.

When civil rights groups called for desegregation and affirmative action programs in the North, many northern whites, no less than southern whites, felt threatened by racial change. Supreme Court decisions in the 1970s reflected this new mood. The Court said de facto segregation was not contrary to the Constitution, and the Court also forbade quotas as part of affirmative action programs.

Latinos, Asian Americans, gays and lesbians, and American Indians have achieved varying degrees of legal rights, and the differences have largely reflected their electoral clout. In general, these groups have only begun to exert their strength in national elections, although they were influential in some states and localities much earlier.

The modern women's rights movement grew out of the civil rights movement. Once women's groups became active, they achieved striking changes in legal doctrine, even though they did not succeed in securing passage of the ERA. The Supreme Court has outlawed most forms of gender discrimination, but women are not allowed in combat positions within the military. The Court has declared gender discrimination and sexual harassment in the workplace contrary to the Civil Rights Act of 1964 and has ruled state-funded, single-sex military training unconstitutional.

The civil rights movement also helped focus attention on the rights of the disabled. Once again, the most important steps forward were taken not by the courts but by Congress, which acted in response to electoral-based political pressure.

Key Terms

affirmative action, p. 505
black codes, p. 494
Brown v. Board of Education of Topeka, Kansas, p. 499
civil disobedience, p. 501
civil rights, p. 493
de facto segregation, p. 504
de jure segregation, p. 504
equal protection clause, p. 493

Equal Rights Amendment (ERA), p. 513
glass ceiling, p. 516
grandfather clause, p. 495
Jim Crow laws, p. 495
National Association for the Advancement of Colored People (NAACP), p. 498
Plessy v. Ferguson, p. 496

poll tax, p. 495
quota, p. 505
racial profiling, p. 493
Reconstruction, p. 494
restrictive housing covenant, p. 498
separate but equal doctrine, p. 496
state action doctrine, p. 496
suspect classification, p. 500
white primary, p. 495

Suggested Readings

Of General Interest

Browning, Rufus, Dale Rogers Marshall, and David H. Tabb. *Protest Is Not Enough: The Struggle of Blacks and Hispanics for Equality in Urban Politics.* Berkeley: University of California Press, 1984. Excellent analysis of the importance of electoral politics for black advances.

Lipsky, Michael. "Protest as a Political Resource." *American Political Science Review* LXII (December 1968): 1144–1158. Shows the limits of protest as a political bargaining tool.

Rosenberg, Gerald N. *The Hollow Hope: Can Courts Bring About Social Change?* Chicago: University of Chicago Press, 1991. Argues that courts are generally unable to act contrary to majority opinion.

Skocpol, Theda. *Protecting Soldiers and Mothers: The Political Origins of Social Policy in the United States.* Cambridge, MA: Harvard University Press, 1992. Analyzes the way women's groups have influenced U.S. social policy.

Wolbrecht, Christina. *The Politics of Women's Rights: Parties, Positions, and Change.* Princeton, NJ: Princeton University Press, 2000. Shows how divisions between Democrats and Republicans have been affected by debates over women's rights.

Focused Studies

Chang, Gordon H. *Asian Americans and Politics: Perspectives, Experiences, Prospects.* Stanford, CA: Stanford University Press, 2001. A series of articles detailing Asian Americans' engagement in U.S. politics.

Deloria, Vine, Jr., and David E. Wilkins. *Tribes, Treaties, and Constitutional Tribulations.* Austin: University of Texas Press, 1999. Discusses the constitutional status of the rights of indigenous peoples.

Garcia, F. Chris, ed. *Pursuing Power: Latinos and the Political System.* Notre Dame, Indiana: University of Notre Dame Press, 1997. A comprehensive series of essays concerning Latino politics.

Cushman, Clare, ed. *Supreme Court Decisions and Women's Rights.* Washington DC: CQ Press and the Supreme Court Historical Society, 2000. With a foreword by Supreme Court Justice Ruth Bader Ginsburg, this volume provides a comprehensive resource on court decisions affecting women's rights.

Higginbotham, A. Leon, Jr. *Shades of Freedom: Racial Politics and Presumptions of the American Legal Process.* New York: Oxford University Press, 1996. A former jurist's sharp critique of the racial bias in American legal practice.

Hochschild, Jennifer L. *Facing Up to The American Dream: Race, Class and the Soul of the Nation.* Princeton, NJ: Princeton University Press, 1995. Discusses how whites and blacks think about one another and argues that racial divisions pose a threat to the American dream.

Key, V. O., Jr. *Southern Politics.* New York: Random House, 1949. Classic study of the effects of racial conflict on southern politics.

Lublin, David. *The Paradox of Representation: Racial Gerrymandering and Minority Interests in Congress.* Princeton, NJ: Princeton University Press, 1997. Discusses dilemmas of affirmative action in redistricting.

Mansbridge, Jane J. *Why We Lost the ERA.* Chicago: University of Chicago Press, 1986. Insightful, readable case study.

Riggle, Ellen D. B., and Barry L. Tadlock, eds., *Gays and Lesbians in the Democratic Process: Public Policy, Public Opinion, and Political Representation.* New York: Columbia University Press: 1999. A series of sophisticated essays on gay and lesbian participation in politics.

Switzer, Jacqueline Vaughn. *Disabled Rights: American Disability Policy and the Fight for Equality.* Washington, DC: Georgetown University Press, 2003. A political scientist examines the evolution of disability policy and the disability rights movement.

Tate, Kathryn. *From Protest to Politics.* Cambridge, MA: Harvard University Press, 1993. Explains black political choices in the 1980s.

On the Web

www.usdoj.gov

In this chapter, we discussed several important pieces of civil rights legislation, such as the Voting Rights Act and the Americans with Disabilities Act. The U.S. Department of Justice's Civil Rights Division provides information on its enforcement of these and other civil rights laws.

www.usccr.gov

In 1957, one year after the Montgomery bus boycott, Congress created the U.S. Commission on Civil Rights. The commission remains active today, investigating complaints of discrimination in many sectors of American society.

www.stanford.edu/group/King/

Martin Luther King, Jr., effectively used nonviolent protest tactics to persuade the majority of Americans of the importance of civil rights. The Martin Luther King, Jr. Papers Project at Stanford University maintains a Web site with many of King's speeches and sermons, as well as several scholarly articles and book chapters.

www.naacp.org

The NAACP, the nation's oldest civil rights organization, successfully pursued the legal strategy that led to the *Brown v. Board of Education* decision.

www.now.org

Created to promote the Equal Rights Amendment, the National Organization for Women is the country's largest feminist organization, with more than 500,000 members.

www.nclr.org

In the 2000 census, Latinos surpassed African Americans in population for the first time. This and other factors have convinced Democrats and Republicans that future victories may depend on the Latino vote. The National Council of La Raza monitors issues of concern to Hispanic Americans.

www.hrc.org

Gay and lesbian activists have achieved important goals, but public opinion on this group remains divided. Human Rights Campaign, a leading gay rights organization, monitors changes in public policy toward gays and lesbians at the local, state, and federal levels.

www.leap.org

Leadership Education for Asian Pacifics, Inc. (LEAP), houses the Asian Pacific American Public Policy Institute, which authors numerous reports on Asian Americans.

www.ncd.gov

The National Council on Disability is an independent federal agency that makes recommendations to the president and Congress regarding policy on Americans with disabilities. The agency's site provides links to other relevant federal agencies, press releases, and in-depth reports.

Domestic Policy

CHAPTER OUTLINE

Medicare Reform and U.S. Domestic Policy

In January 2003, congressional analysts and administration officials predicted that the government would spend significantly more money over the next year than it collected in taxes. Despite record-setting surpluses in 1999 and 2000, an economic downturn, terrorist attacks, and tax cuts had sent federal budget figures plunging back into the red. The Iraq War promised to deplete government resources even further. Meanwhile, the so-called "baby boom" generation, born from 1945 to the early 1960s, grew ever closer to retirement. When this large generation begins to leave the workforce and rely on social programs for the elderly sometime around 2010, policy experts warn of an unprecedented strain on the federal budget. "The collision course is pretty easy to see," said one economist.[1]

In light of these budget pressures, it might have seemed that politicians in Washington would work to raise taxes or reduce spending on programs for the elderly in order to place the budget back on an even footing. In fact, the opposite occurred. In addition to enacting a significant tax cut in spring 2003, the president and nearly all of Congress supported increased spending on **Medicare**, the government health insurance program for Americans over the age of 65. In his January State of the Union address, President George W. Bush promised to "commit an additional $400 billion over the next decade to reform and strengthen Medicare."[2]

Democrats opposed Bush only insofar as they preferred more generous new benefits, as well as limitations on the profits of drug companies. While Bush proposed to cover the cost of prescription drugs only for those Medicare recipients who chose to receive coverage through private insurance providers, Democrats pressed for drug coverage for all Medicare enrollees. Said Democratic Senate leader Tom Daschle, "America's seniors should never be forced to choose between the doctor they trust and the prescriptions they need."[3]

By the end of the year, Republicans and some Democrats agreed on a compromise plan that would provide limited prescription drug coverage for all elderly Medicare recipients. Supported by the American Association of Retired Persons (AARP), this bill was criticized as incomplete by Democratic leaders, but many others saw it as a major victory. As California Democratic senator Dianne Feinstein put it, "I knew in my heart of hearts that the seniors in my great state are going to be better served by this bill than they are today."[4]

When the new benefit went into effect in 2006, many seniors, doctors, and pharmacists found the program to be confusing and bureaucratic. Responding to these concerns, members of Congress on both sides of the aisle proposed relaxing deadlines for enrollment and giving money to states to help smooth the transition.[5] Ten-year cost estimates for the program grew from $400 billion to as much as $700 billion, but even in a time of budget deficits, benefits for senior citizens remained secure.[6]

MAKING THE CONNECTION

Why did Congress and the president rush to add benefits to Medicare even in the face of a growing budget shortfall? Are the needs of the elderly great enough to override concerns about fiscal discipline? Do older Americans have more urgent needs than other groups, such as low income families with children? Or are senior citizens and the middle class better organized and do they exercise more voting power?

To provide a way of thinking about these questions, this chapter examines the electoral and political forces that shape domestic policy. We discuss the various stages through which all domestic policies proceed and then consider three major types of domestic policy: social policy, education policy, and regulatory policy. For each, we examine the political factors that help shape policy outcomes.

Types of Public Policy

Public policy is a term applied to all government programs and regulations. Often policies are classified as foreign or domestic. Foreign policy involves relations with other nations (see Chapter 20). **Domestic policy** consists of all government programs and regulations that directly affect those living within a country. It includes everything from education and health care to transportation and garbage collection—hundreds of different kinds of governmental activity. However, the distinction between domestic and foreign policy is not always sharp and clear. Some domestic policies, such as immigration policy or homeland security, affect relations with other countries. Some foreign policies, such as foreign trade regulations, have major domestic consequences. Of all the domestic policies, economic ones are among the most complex and important, and Chapter 19 is devoted to a discussion of economic policy. In this chapter we look at a variety of other domestic policies.

Stages of Policy Making

The making of policy is a complex, never-ending series of events. To clarify what is often a very messy process, political scientists have described it in terms of six stages that are together known as the policy-making round, shown in Figure 18.1. At each stage, policy makers pay close attention to public opinion and try to estimate the consequences of their choices for the next election.

The first stage is **agenda setting**, making an issue visible enough that important political leaders take it seriously.[7] When elected officials think a problem is serious and might even affect an election, the issue has reached the agenda stage. The second stage consists of **policy deliberation**, the debate and discussion over issues placed on the policy agenda.[8] At this stage, groups and policy experts try to convince leaders not only that their proposals are a good way to deal with the problem, but also that these proposals are popular with the electorate. Next comes **policy enactment**, the passage of a law by public officials. Enactment may involve passage by Congress, a state legislature, or a city council and signing into law by a president, governor, or mayor. Elected officials who vote for the law usually expect that its passage will enhance their popularity, although there have been a few celebrated instances in which political leaders have sacrificed their careers for what they saw as the good of the country. The fourth stage is **policy implementation**, translation of the legislation into an actual set of government programs or regulations.[9] When fashioning the details, bureaucrats are expected to carry out the intentions of the legislative branch and not to stray too far from what is politically acceptable. At the fifth stage, government produces **policy outputs**, the provision of services to citizens or the regulation of their conduct. Beneficiaries usually think well of those who established the program; those who are hurt by the policy outputs probably feel otherwise. Finally, **policy outcomes** are the effects of policy outputs on individuals and businesses.[10] These outcomes often give rise to new issues, which are then placed on the policy agenda, completing the policy-making round.

The history of the 1996 welfare reform law, **Temporary Assistance for Needy Families (TANF)**, illustrates the way politics affects the various stages of the policy round. The first stage, placing the issue on the policy agenda, occurred when Bill Clinton scored points in his 1992 campaign for president by promising to "end welfare as we

Medicare
Program that provides social security recipients a broad range of medical benefits.

domestic policy
Government programs and regulations that directly affect those living within a country.

agenda setting
Making an issue so visible that important political leaders take it seriously.

policy deliberation
Debate and discussion by groups and political leaders over issues placed on the policy agenda.

policy enactment
Passage of a law by public officials.

policy implementation
Translation of legislation into a set of government programs or regulations.

policy output
Provision of services to citizens or regulation of their conduct.

policy outcome
Effect of policy outputs on individuals and businesses.

Temporary Assistance for Needy Families (TANF)
Welfare reform law passed by Congress in 1996.

FIGURE 18.1

Policy-Making Stages

• *Can you match each stage with events in the development of welfare policy?*

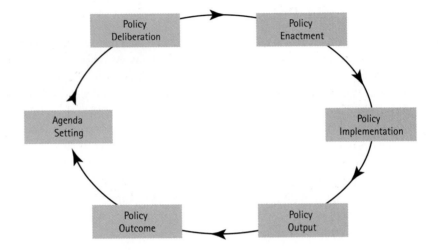

know it." The second stage, policy deliberation, occurred when interest groups, policy experts, members of Congress, and the media debated many different ways of redesigning welfare policy. Throughout the debate, polls revealed that a majority of the public supported changing the existing welfare program, increasing the likelihood that something would be approved. The third stage, policy enactment, saw Congress enact a new law that shifted responsibility for much welfare policy from the federal to state governments via block grants (see Chapter 3), created a work requirement for beneficiaries, and imposed an overall time limit on receipt of benefits. President Clinton signed the bill into law in part because voters supported the idea, even though he had expressed strong reservations about many of the bill's provisions. The fourth stage, policy implementation, began in early 1997 when many state governments started revising their welfare plans, often in response to electoral pressures at the state level. The fifth stage, policy outputs, took place when many families left or were removed from the welfare rolls.

After 10 years under the new law, analysts took stock of policy outcomes. Welfare rolls had declined dramatically; only one-third as many people received assistance in 2005 as in 1995.[11] Supporters of the reform argued that this proved the policy was a long-term success. But critics charged that this decline was a sign that welfare was not reaching those it was designed to help. "Falling caseloads amid rising poverty should be a cause for concern," argued one expert.[12] In 2006, after considering the outcomes, Congress renewed TANF for five more years, and further strengthened work requirements for recipients.[13] Another policy-making round had begun.

The political forces that shape public policies differ from one policy to the next. In the remainder of this chapter we describe the political factors shaping three major types of public policy: social policy, education policy, and regulatory policy.

Social Policy

social policy

Domestic policy programs designed to help those thought to be in need of government assistance.

Social policy is a type of domestic policy that consists of programs designed to help those thought to be in need of government assistance. People may be regarded as needy because they are old, infirm, young, disabled, unemployed, poor, or some combination of these. One of the central issues in the making of social policy is finding an appropriate balance between government assistance to the elderly and to the young. As the

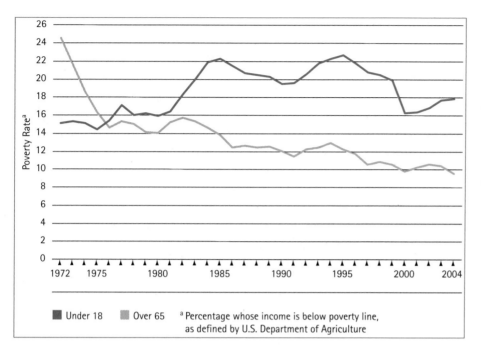

FIGURE 18.2

U.S. Poverty Rates for
Senior Citizens and
Children, 1970–2004

• *Why are poverty rates higher
for children than for seniors?*

Source: U.S. Census Bureau, *Historical
Poverty Tables—People*, Table 3: Poverty
Status by Age, Race, and Hispanic Origin,
1959–2004, www.census.gov/hhes/www/
poverty/histpov/hstpov3.html, accessed
June 10, 2006.

case of the Medicare prescription drug benefit emphasizes, the elderly have done particularly well in securing government help.

We can observe the different effects of social policy on the young and the old by comparing some basic statistics concerning changes in the nation's poverty rate. As Figure 18.2 illustrates, poverty among senior citizens fell from 25 percent in 1970 to about 10 percent in 2004, but child poverty did not decline over this same period of time. The poverty rate among families with children in the United States is twice as high as in most other advanced industrial societies;[14] however, the poverty rate among senior citizens is about the same in the United States as in these societies.[15]

Poverty is not just a matter of money; it pervades many aspects of life. For example, the chances of being in good health are different for senior citizens and children. Of the seven developed countries with the largest economies, the United States has the highest infant mortality rate.[16] But if one reaches old age, one has a better chance of living longer in the United States than in any of the other six countries. As one analyst put it, the United States is perhaps the "healthiest place to grow old but the riskiest [in which] to be born."[17]

In the next two sections, we explain how this phenomenon came to be. First we describe the development of social programs for senior citizens and the powerful political support that sustains them. Then we examine the development of social programs for children and the more limited support that they enjoy.

Comparing Social
Welfare Policy

Social Insurance for Senior Citizens

The improvement in the well-being of senior citizens today is due in large part to the country's social policy. As the population has aged, the government has expanded programs to meet the retirement income and medical needs of the elderly. The amount spent on social programs for senior citizens grew from $10,030 per senior citizen in

1971 to more than $20,000 in 2005.[18] (Unless otherwise indicated, all dollar figures in this chapter are expressed in constant 2005 dollars so as to adjust for inflation.) In this section we describe the conditions that led to this dramatic increase in social insurance.

Origins and Development of Social Insurance Programs   Public demands for aid to senior citizens escalated during the Great Depression of the 1930s, when poverty among the elderly was particularly acute. Approximately five million senior citizens rallied behind the proposals of Dr. Francis E. Townsend, a 67-year-old Californian who promised to end the depression by giving everyone over the age of 60 the equivalent in today's dollars of $2,900 a month, provided that they spent it immediately.[19] Always quick to recognize potential electoral threats, President Franklin Roosevelt checked Townsend's soaring popularity by appointing an advisory committee to recommend better ways of meeting the needs of the elderly. The committee recommended a policy of **social insurance**, a program that provides benefits in return for contributions made by workers. In a response consistent with the committee's recommendations, in 1935 Congress enacted the landmark Social Security Act, which created a broad range of social programs, including a social insurance program for senior citizens generally known as **social security**.[20]

The social security program initially cost the government little. Most of those who first retired under the program received minimal benefits because they had paid into the program for only a brief time. Also, retirement costs were low because, in 1935, average life expectancy for those reaching the age of 65 was only an additional 13 to 15 years. In contrast, a worker retiring at 65 today is expected to live more than 18 more years.[21]

Gradually, the program expanded. The number of people covered went up; so did the length of their retirement. Benefits increased in size and cost. Two major changes deserve particular attention. In 1965, the year after Democrats won an overwhelming election victory, Congress enacted Medicare, which provides a broad range of medical benefits to social security recipients. In 1972, an election year, Congress gave senior citizens a large increase in their monthly social security checks and linked, or indexed, this amount to the cost of living. If inflation goes up 10 percent, so does the paycheck.[22] Passed at a time when prices were rising, this new benefit soon became very popular.

The popularity of both social security and Medicare is due in part to the fact that they are based on the insurance principle—that is, the principle that people receive benefits in return for contributions they have made. In the case of social security, the insurance principle works in the following way: People become eligible for benefits by paying a portion of their regular salary—a payroll tax—to social security during their working years. To get social security benefits, beneficiaries need only prove that they are over the age of 65. (This eligibility age will gradually increase to 67 for those born after 1959.) Because of the insurance principle, a retiree does not have to show a need. Upon reaching the age of 65, even billionaire Microsoft founder Bill Gates will be eligible to receive a social security check.

Although social security is called an insurance program, it differs from a true insurance program in one fundamental respect: It operates at a loss. In private insurance programs, most people pay more in initial payments and forgone interest than they receive in benefits; if this were not the case, the insurance company could not make a profit. From the beginning, however, social security has given most people more in benefits than they contributed in their social security tax. For example, a couple with a single average wage earner retiring in 2008 can expect to receive 4.4 percent more in benefits than the worker in the family paid in, even after taking inflation into account.[23]

The Evolution of
Social Welfare Policy

social insurance

Program that provides benefits in return for contributions made by workers.

social security

Social insurance program for senior citizens.

How is this magic possible? How can benefits exceed contributions? Why have social security and Medicare not gone broke? Up until now, there have been three reasons:

1. Workers have grown in number, as women and "baby boomers" have entered the workforce and unemployment rates have fallen. Thus, more people are contributing to the social security program.
2. Workers today produce more and earn more than their predecessors did. As result, more money is available to distribute to retirees.
3. Workers today pay a higher percentage of their earnings in social security taxes than their predecessors did. Essentially, younger generations have been asked to pay more to cover the expenses of older ones. As economist Lester Thurow has pointed out, "the current generation of retirees . . . did not have to pay [much] into the system but gets benefits financed by those behind them."[24] The practice is not new. Jonathan Swift saw the same thing happening in England three centuries ago. "'Tis pleasant to observe," he said, "how free the present Age is in laying taxes on the next."[25]

Unfortunately, some of these circumstances may be changing:

1. Experts do not expect the number of workers to increase much in the next couple of decades. The massive baby boom generation will reach retirement age from 2010 to 2030. As they leave the workforce, the number of retirees will grow faster than the number of workers. As a result, the cost of retirement programs will increase, as Figure 18.3 shows.
2. Rates of growth in economic productivity may not always be as high as they have been in recent decades. In 2001, experts were reminded that a serious economic recession could quickly change the picture. Then workers in the future would not be producing enough to cover the higher cost of social security caused by the retirement of the baby boomers.
3. Workers may be less willing to pay higher taxes. It will be difficult to increase taxes to cover the retirement costs of the baby boomers.

FIGURE 18.3

Projected Cost of Social
Insurance for
Senior Citizens

• *Why will costs of programs for
senior citizens rise rapidly in the
coming years?*

Note: Figures after 2005 are estimates; projections are for an
'intermediate cost' scenario.

Source: U.S. Department of Health and
Human Services, Social Security
Administration, "Status of the Social
Security and Medicare Programs," A
Summary of the 2006 Annual Reports,
www.ssa.gov/OACT/TRSUM/trsummar
y.html, accessed May 25, 2006.

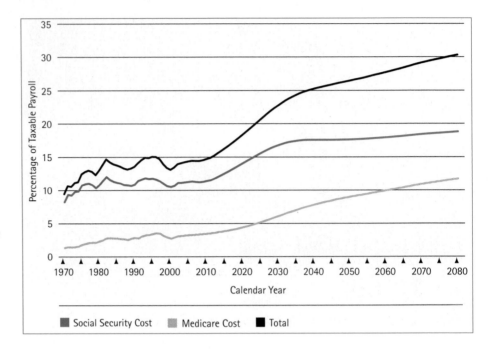

For these reasons, a presidential panel declared in December 2001 that "the system is not sustainable as currently structured."[26] Politicians agreed on the problems with the program but disagreed over the varied proposals for reform. More than most other issues, changes in social security are politically excruciating to make, as we explain in the next section.

Politics of Social Insurance   Many subway systems use dangerous middle rails, or third rails, that provide the electricity that drives the trains. Social security and Medicare are said to be the "third rail" of American politics—"touch it and you die." Richard Morin put it another way: "The bottom line on the public's attitude is: Spend whatever is needed—particularly on me—just don't bill us for it."[27]

The Risks of Change to Social Security—Because most public officials know they will be punished by the voters if they are perceived as threatening social security programs, only rarely do they suggest changes. In 2005, however, President George W. Bush advocated major alterations to social security in order to avert a predicted shortfall in the budget for the program resulting from the factors outlined above. Bush's plan included two main components. First, younger workers would have the option of diverting a portion of their payroll taxes into private, market-based, accounts that, the president argued, would earn higher rates of return than these young workers could expect from social security. Second, the president proposed slowing the expansion of benefits for all but the poorest social security recipients. Although Bush and members of his cabinet traveled around the country promoting the plan, Democrats attacked it as an attempt to undermine the insurance principle. For their part, congressional Republicans offered what one analyst described as a "din of silence."[28] Outside Washington, the AARP led a campaign of television ads and letter-writing against the Bush proposal. By the time Hurricane Katrina's impact on New Orleans diverted the nation's attention, social security changes were all but dead. The "third rail of American politics" remained intact.

Understandable Confusion?

Senior citizens express their frustration at the new Medicare-approved discount card plan to House Speaker Dennis Hastert during a meeting to answer questions about the plan.

• *Why is there less activism about programs for the poor?*

Complexities of Medicare—The politics of Medicare are much the same, making it difficult to keep the program from growing rapidly. The cost of the program grew from less than $36 billion in 1970 to over $330 billion by 2005.[29] Numerous factors contribute to the rapidly rising cost of Medicare. Although some critics accuse doctors and hospitals of profiteering, other factors play a more important role. The number of elderly is growing rapidly, increasing the demand for medical services. Doctors can use better (and more expensive) technology to diagnose and treat more crippling injuries and life-threatening diseases. Finally, patients expect error-free medicine; when mistakes are made, lawsuits drive up doctors' insurance costs (and the fees doctors must charge to cover them).

Analysts expect Medicare costs to rise even faster when the baby boom generation retires and needs more medical services. Meanwhile, politicians have been reluctant to engage in such cost-saving proposals as raising medical premiums and requiring patients to pay a larger share of the costs, and instead have more often moved in the opposite direction. As we discussed at the beginning of this chapter, new prescription drug benefits that President Bush and Congress enacted in 2003 will result in up to an additional $700 billion in Medicare expenses from 2005 to 2015.

The Influence of Senior Citizens—The electoral impact of the social security issue is likely to remain central to American politics. At a time when overall voter turnout has been declining, senior citizen turnout rates are high and have been climbing. Between 1972 and 2004, turnout among voters aged 18 to 24 dropped by 3 percent, while turnout among voters over 65 climbed by more than 8 percent.[30] Around 72 percent of voters over the age of 65 said they voted in the 2004 presidential election, but only 47 percent of those between the ages of 18 and 24 reported voting.[31]

Senior citizens are also much more likely than young people to back up their votes with other political actions, such as writing letters to elected officials and contributing money to political campaigns.[32] More than 35 million people have joined the American Association of Retired Persons (AARP), the largest interest group in the United States.[33]

AARP is a large and influential organization. Upon reaching the age of 50, any person can become a member of AARP for $12.50 per year. Members are eligible for a

PARTICIPATION

Making a Difference: Welfare Reform

FIGURE 18.4

Federal Government
Spending

• *Why is social security the most
costly social program?*

Note: Percentages based on 2005
federal budget.

Source: Congressional Budget Office, *The
Budget and Economic Outlook: Fiscal Years
2007 to 2016,* Washington, DC:
Congressional Budget Office, 2006,
Tables 3-1, 3-3, and 3-9.

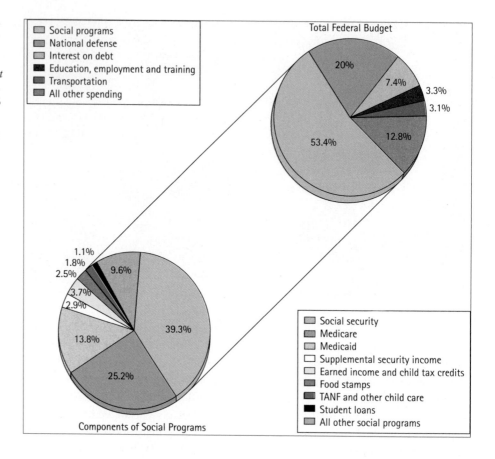

Components of Social Programs

wide range of travel and other discounts worth much more than their annual dues. They
also receive a magazine that keeps them up to date on policy proposals that might affect
their social security and Medicare benefits. AARP employs more than 1,800 people,
works with more than 160,000 volunteers, and has an annual budget of $800 million.[34]

Broad Support—AARP has the advantage of promoting a cause that few voters
strongly oppose. In fact, young people are just about as likely to support benefits for
senior citizens as those over the age of 65. When asked during the debate over expanding Medicare whether they would be willing to pay higher taxes to fund a prescription
drug program for seniors, overwhelming majorities of both young and elderly voters
say they would do so (see Figure 18.4).

There are three main reasons for the broad support that social security and Medicare
enjoy. First, most people hope to benefit from these programs someday themselves. In
addition, many have parents who currently receive these benefits, relieving their children of financial responsibility. Finally, most people think that because senior citizens
contributed to social security, they now deserve the benefits they were promised, and
few are aware that these benefits are usually in excess of the contributions.

Public Assistance to Poor Families

The interests of the elderly may be well protected by AARP and both political parties,
but the same cannot be said for the interests of poor families with children. Programs

designed for poor families are neither as lavish nor as user-friendly as those designed for the elderly. Neither political party is strongly committed to expanding them, and no association comparable to AARP defends the interests of Americans with low incomes.

Origins and Development of Public Assistance Programs   **Public assistance** consists of programs that provide low-income households with income subsidies and access to essential goods and services. Together, the programs make up what is often known as the "safety net" that catches those who fall into financial difficulty. The sheer number of major public assistance programs actually exceeds the number of major programs for the elderly. Public assistance programs include Temporary Assistance for Needy Families, food stamps, the Earned Income Tax Credit, rent subsidies, and Medicaid.

Temporary Assistance for Needy Families (TANF)—As we noted earlier in this chapter, this program, enacted by Congress in 1996, gave the states the responsibility for designing income-maintenance programs for poor families. However, state programs are subject to certain limitations. For example, no family may receive more than two consecutive years of assistance, and no family may receive more than five years of assistance altogether.

TANF replaced the long-standing public assistance program known as Aid to Families with Dependent Children (AFDC), which was established in 1935 as part of the Social Security Act. AFDC was designed to serve widows, but as the number of unmarried women increased, the size of the program grew sharply and the social composition of beneficiaries changed markedly. Branded "the welfare program," AFDC was criticized by liberals and conservatives alike. Conservatives claimed that it discouraged recipients from working, an argument that became increasingly potent as the percentage of working women increased.[35] Liberals believed that the benefits were too low and that program eligibility and administrative restrictions were too harsh.[36] TANF has proved to be a more popular program, because welfare rolls have fallen and poverty rates have not increased dramatically, as some critics predicted.

Food Stamps—This public assistance program provides recipients with coupons that can be used to purchase food. Enacted by Congress on an experimental basis in the early 1970s, it has been gradually expanded, and today it is larger than TANF. Benefits depend on the recipient's income and household size, but the average is about $89 per person per month.[37] The **food stamps** program has been more popular than AFDC was, because most Americans believe everyone should be provided with enough food to avoid going hungry—especially when agricultural surpluses exist.

Earned Income Tax Credit (EITC)—This program uses the tax structure to benefit those who have little income. Initially proposed by Republicans in the early 1970s as a way of simultaneously helping the poor and rewarding work, the **Earned Income Tax Credit** program was greatly expanded in 1993. Only those in the labor force qualify for this benefit, a provision designed to make even low-paying jobs worthwhile. An eligible person who fills out a tax return can receive an EITC reimbursement even if he or she has paid no taxes. In 2005, an eligible family of four could receive a credit of as much as $4,400 a year.[38]

Supplemental Security Income (SSI)—**Supplemental Security Income** provides disabled people of low income with income assistance. Created in 1972, SSI succeeds programs of aid to the blind and the deaf established by the Social Security Act of

public assistance
Programs that provide to low-income households a limited income and access to essential goods and services.

Where the Money Goes...

food stamps
Public assistance program that provides recipients with stamps that can be used to purchase food.

Earned Income Tax Credit (EITC)
Provision that gives back tax payments to those who have little income.

Supplemental Security Income (SSI)
Program that provides disabled people of low income with income assistance.

Food Assistance

Using his California State Advantage EBT card, which is akin to food stamps, this home-less man is able to buy meals at specific restaurants in the San Francisco area.

• *Why do you think food stamps are more popular than other "welfare" programs?*

1935. As of December 2004, the average monthly benefit for SSI's 7 million recipients was $428.[39]

Rent Subsidies—This policy provides low-income families with government vouchers to help pay their rent, provided that they select designated housing. Congress created the **rent subsidies** program in the early 1970s to replace public housing programs, which had been criticized for encouraging racial segregation and creating large concentrations of poverty.[40]

rent subsidies

Help in paying rent for low-income families, provided that they select designated housing.

Medicaid—This program pays for medical services for the poor. A person becomes eligible only if he or she has no more than a minimal income and few assets other than a home. Congress created **Medicaid** in 1965, at the same time as Medicare, in response to Republican objections to Medicare on the grounds that it was designed to serve the middle class but not the poor. The cost of Medicaid benefits has risen rapidly—from around $13.6 billion in 1970 to $182 billion in 2005.[41]

Medicaid

Program that provides medical care to those of low income.

Although Medicaid serves poor families regardless of age, over one-quarter of all Medicaid costs cover the medical expenditures of low-income senior citizens.[42] Thus, Medicaid is an important supplement to the better-known Medicare program discussed earlier.

Limitations on Public Assistance Programs   This list of public assistance programs that help poor families with children seems impressive, but the government spends more than twice as much on social security and Medicare as it spends on all these programs combined, as Figure 18.4 illustrates. In addition, programs for families with children are more restrictive than programs for senior citizens. Five factors make programs for families with children less user-friendly.[43]

Fewer Cash Benefits—The elderly receive about 64 percent of their benefits in cash,[44] whereas only 32 percent of the benefits received by poor families with children are cash benefits.[45] Because most people prefer cash income to benefits in the form of goods and services, senior citizens have the better arrangement. Cash income enables one to purchase what one wants and to purchase it when, where, and from whom one wishes.

Less Indexation—Nearly all benefits to the elderly, including social security and other retirement pensions, are indexed to changes in the cost of living. Although some programs for families with children are also indexed, the main welfare program, TANF, is not. Instead of keeping pace with increases in the cost of living, average monthly benefits under this program fell nearly 60 percent between 1977 and 2003.[46]

Assistance, Not Insurance—Unlike social security, which distributes benefits automatically according to age and contributions made to an insurance fund, programs for families with children are paid out only after family income has been carefully scrutinized. To become eligible for benefits, a low-income family must demonstrate that it has virtually no other means of livelihood. To receive cash benefits, the potential recipient must document that the family does not own a home of any significant value, has virtually no savings, and has hardly any income. According to one survey, more than 20 percent of charity food bank users had not even applied for food stamps because it was "too much hassle."[47]

State, Not National, Programs—Families with children receive benefits that vary from one state to another. Only EITC benefits are uniform throughout the country. For the other major programs—TANF, food stamps, SSI, housing assistance, and Medicaid—eligibility rules and benefit levels vary from state to state. In the case of TANF, the benefits can be five times as much in one state as in another.[48]

Because public assistance programs are state-operated, families who have children and who move from one state to another must reconnect to public assistance programs. In a recent extreme example of this problem, tens of thousands of evacuees from New Orleans after Hurricane Katrina had to re-enroll in public assistance programs in Texas and other states. In this case, Congress enacted special legislation to make the transition easier, but in normal circumstances, such help is not available.[49] As a result, poor families may not be able to respond quickly to job opportunities or changing family circumstances.[50]

These restrictions do not apply to senior citizens because social security is a national program. Senior citizens can move from New Jersey to Florida (or even overseas) without jeopardizing the amount or delivery of their social security check.

Benefits Cannot Supplement Income—The benefits that poor families with children receive are usually a substitute for other income; they do not supplement it. In many states, families are not eligible for income assistance if they have savings of more than $2,000, a car worth more than $5,000, or anything other than a very modest home (the exact value varies from state to state).[51] Under the old AFDC program, families lost a dollar in benefits for every dollar they earned. Under TANF, states have the flexibility to continue benefits for some working recipients,[52] but these benefits count toward a federal lifetime limit of five years of TANF participation.[53]

By comparison, senior citizen benefits supplement the recipient's own resources. Senior citizens may receive their Medicare and social security benefits even if they are working full-time, have savings, earn dividends and interest on their investments, and are homeowners. Before 2000, social security recipients between 65 and 69 years old lost $1 in benefits for every $3 they earned in wages above $17,000 per year. But Republicans and Democrats in Congress, eager to please elderly voters in an election year, repealed this "earnings penalty" unanimously.[54]

Politics of Public Assistance   Programs for poor families with children are poorly funded and restrictively designed because, unlike the elderly, children and the poor do not exercise direct political power. Instead, they are dependent on others who provide only limited help: policy analysts who offer competing explanations for the persistence of poverty, a weak network of interest groups that fight among themselves, a divided public, and opportunistic political parties.

Policy Debate—Before the government can design solutions, it has to decide what the problem is. But policy experts disagree about the causes of poverty among families with children. Three different theories have influenced the welfare debate.

Liberal theory argues that poverty rates among children have risen because the government has not maintained an adequate level of governmental assistance. Sociologist Theda Skocpol points out that lower poverty rates in European countries are due in part to government programs that aid low-income families.[55] She advocates the establishment of a similar family allowance program that would guarantee all families with children a basic stipend not unlike the social security checks that the elderly receive.

Conservative theory finds the explanation for rising poverty rates in what is identified as a "culture of poverty," in which young people are encouraged to place short-term pleasures ahead of long-term goals. Beliefs that opportunities for advancement do not exist become self-fulfilling prophecies as the poor do not seek the jobs they assume they cannot find. Furthermore, public assistance programs can perpetuate this cycle. "Until recently," says policy analyst Lawrence Mead, "a defeatist culture was abetted by permissive public policies. Programs [such as AFDC] gave benefits to people . . . without expecting constructive behavior from them."[56]

Conservatives also point out that between 1970 and 2004, the percentage of women with children who were living without a mate more than doubled—from 11 percent to 24 percent.[5] These female-headed families are particularly at risk of living in poverty. Many women find it difficult to both work and raise children. Mothers who do work find it hard to get full-time jobs at good wages. Poverty rates among single female-headed households are over five times greater than poverty rates among households headed by a married couple.[58] Liberals respond by noting that poverty rates among families with children are much lower in other countries such as Great Britain, France, and Sweden, despite the fact that the frequency of out-of-wedlock births is higher than that of the U.S.[59]

Offering a third explanation, sociologist William J. Wilson attributes a growing culture of poverty to changes in the postindustrial economy. Physically demanding blue-collar jobs, which can be performed by unskilled workers with minimal education, are declining in number. These jobs have been lost to technology or have moved overseas.[60] As a result, from 1975 to 2004, annual salaries for men without a high school degree plunged from 92 percent to less than 60 percent of the national average.[61] According to Wilson, when young men cannot find work, they refuse to take on the responsibilities of marriage and child rearing. Young women don't want to marry men with few prospects.

Group Organization—No group speaking on behalf of children has a mass membership of a size remotely comparable to that of AARP. Instead, many small, competing groups take stances as varied as the alternative explanations for rising poverty rates. The most significant pro-welfare group, the Children's Defense Fund, headed by Marion Wright Edelman, fought welfare reform to no avail. Although the group has an annual budget of $19 million and a staff of 178, it lacks a large membership that can effectively lobby Congress.[62]

On the conservative side, Gary L. Bauer, a Republican candidate for president in 2000, built the Family Research Council into a 450,000-member organization committed to the protection of family values.[63] The group favored the welfare reform bill, a stance reflecting its conviction that welfare programs, by helping unwed mothers make ends meet, discourage family formation and allow fathers to neglect family responsibilities.

Other groups adopt positions on issues that affect children's welfare, but these groups typically have other objectives more central to their mission. For example, the Urban League has long emphasized the importance of youth programs, but its fundamental objective remains protection of the civil rights of African Americans. Major labor unions such as the AFL-CIO support most legislation intended to promote child welfare, but their main concern is protection of the interests of workers. Although many women's groups care about children's issues, they tend to remain focused on issues of gender discrimination and sexual harassment. In short, the interest-group chorus on children's issues sings separate songs in different keys. They are unable to focus on a common cause in the way AARP does.

Public Opinion—The general public wavers between liberal and conservative beliefs about rising poverty rates. In 2005, during a period of economic uncertainty, the population was evenly divided on the question of whether poverty was due mainly to circumstances beyond a person's control or whether it was due mainly to a lack of effort. But 10 years earlier, when the economy was booming, twice as many people thought poverty was due to a lack of effort than thought it was due to circumstances beyond a person's control.[64] This public variability makes it difficult for policy makers to generate enthusiasm for public-assistance programs.

Political Parties—Because public opinion on welfare policy fluctuates, so do the positions of the political parties. Most of the time, the Democratic Party takes a more liberal position, the Republicans a more conservative one. Senator Hillary Clinton, for example, was once a member of the liberal Children's Defense Fund's board of directors. Tony Perkins, the current director of the Family Research Council, is a former Republican state legislator and candidate for U.S. Senate.[65] Despite these underlying partisan differences, party leaders often search for the middle ground. As a result, their positions shift over time, and they do not always disagree.

When the country was building the Great Society in the 1960s and 1970s (see Chapter 3), Democrats took the lead, but Republicans were not far behind. Republican presidents signed into law several welfare programs for children. President Nixon proposed the food stamp and SSI programs. Republicans proposed, and President Ford signed, the law creating the Earned Income Tax Credit. Republicans in Congress initiated the Medicaid program.

As the public mood shifted in a conservative direction, the positions of both parties changed accordingly. In 1995 it was the Republicans who took the lead, proposing cuts in many of the programs they had once sponsored.[66] Although some Democrats opposed the cuts, a majority voted in favor of welfare reform, and President Clinton signed the bill into law. Today, both parties take credit for the passage of TANF.

Spokeswoman for Children

Marian Wright Edelman, founder of the Children's Defense Fund.

• *Why does Edelman have less clout in Washington than the head of AARP?*

Education Policy

Although social policy has long been one of the domestic policies of great interest to voters, education policy has recently become almost as significant in the public debate.

Historically, Americans have supported a large, well-financed education system. Equal opportuniy meant equal access to good schools. But the commitment to public schools, though still strong, has been modified by increasing concern about the quality of education provided in traditional public schools. In this section we discuss the history of locally controlled public education in the United States, current policy on education, and the groups that shape this increasingly visible policy debate.

Local Control

Responsibility for education is divided among local school boards, state departments of education, and the federal Department of Education, but the bulk of control over education policy remains at the state and local levels. Keeping control of public schools in the hands of local communities is an important issue for many parents and educators who do not want distant politicians making decisions about their children's lives.

Today, 93 percent of the cost of public education is paid for out of state and local budgets, each contributing approximately half the cost (although the exact percentage paid varies widely from one state to another). The 7 percent contribution by the federal government is spent mainly on programs enhancing equal opportunity, such as special education for the disabled and compensatory programs for disadvantaged children.[67] Core education programs are generally paid for with state and local dollars.

Development of Public Education

The public's commitment to its schools is deeply rooted. As early as 1785, Congress set aside the revenue from the sale of one-sixteenth of the land west of the Appalachian Mountains to help pay for "the maintenance of public schools."[68] Support for public schools intensified with the flood of immigrants that arrived in the nineteenth century. As immigrants gained the right to vote, they won access to public education. In Chicago and San Francisco, for example, children from immigrant backgrounds were no more likely to suffer from crowded classrooms than were children from native-born families. On the other hand, where racial minorities lacked adequate political representation, they were given second-class schools. Before gaining the right to vote, African Americans in the South and Chinese Americans in California were segregated into badly maintained, inferior schools.[69]

Despite the discriminatory treatment of racial minorities, public schools did much to build American democracy. The percentages of young people enrolled in American schools far surpassed those in European countries. Public schools helped foster a common language among people from disparate parts of the world. Open to most, if not all, citizens, they reinforced a distinctive American identity built around the concepts of liberty and equality. They also educated the workforce that operated the new machines that were to make the country the world's greatest industrial power.

Contemporary Issues in Education Policy

Despite the strength of the American educational tradition, Americans seem to be increasingly dissatisfied with traditional public schools. The per pupil cost of schooling has increased by 60 percent since 1980, even after adjusting for inflation.[70] But because salaries for other professionals have also risen rapidly during this same period of time, teacher salaries, relative to that of other college-educated workers, have slipped considerably.[71]

Other nations, once far behind in school spending, have now nearly caught up. Governments in the United States spend 3.8 percent of the U.S. GDP on primary and secondary education. Although Japan and Germany still spend less than the United States, countries such as Canada, Sweden, and France spend more. (See *International Comparison*, p. 538.)

American schools also seem to be doing an inferior job at converting dollars into schools that help students learn.[72] Students in American schools are learning less in reading, science, math, and geography than are students in most other industrial countries (see *International Comparison*). Not surprisingly, the public's assessment of the quality of its schools has slipped. The percentage of Americans who expressed "a good deal" or "quite a lot" of confidence in the public schools dropped from 58 percent in 1973 to 40 percent in 2003.[73]

As in other areas, different policy makers diagnose the problem differently and offer competing solutions. There are at least three major sets of proposals that seek to improve the system of education in the U.S.

First, some policy makers recommend redesigning the educational system so that students and parents have their choice of schools, just as senior citizens, under Medicare, have their choice of doctors and hospitals.[74] Proponents say the resulting competition among schools would prompt poorly performing schools to improve. Opponents argue that giving parents choice would increase disparities between schools, thereby broadening racial, religious, and ethnic divisions.[75] For more on this conversation, see *Election Voices: School Vouchers and Charter Schools* on p. 487.

A second set of policy makers suggests that the problem with public schools is that their educational goals are seldom well defined, and that they are often unable to tell whether students are really learning. Accordingly, these policy makers recommend a set of national standards, as well as a national curriculum.[76] Critics worry that rigid nationwide standards would rob states and school districts of flexibility and prevent adaptation to new conditions. In 2002 President George W. Bush signed the "No Child Left Behind Act," a new law that compromised on the issue. Under the new system, states must establish clear goals in math and reading, testing children in grades 3 through 8 to make sure that students meet these expectations. However, states may set their own standards and design their own tests and procedures for meeting them. At the same time, new federal funds assist students at poorly performing schools.

Critics of the bill argued that, while it was well intentioned, it was underfunded and thus did not give schools the resources necessary to improve themselves. Calling the act a "bait-and-switch," 2004 Democratic presidential candidate John Kerry proposed a national education trust fund that would "guarantee we fully fund our schools."[77]

This criticism of the No Child Left Behind Act leads to a third set of proposals for improving public education. Many liberals argue that schools could be more effective if they were given more resources.[78] These analysts point out that between 1985 and 2000, government spending on health care jumped over 40 percent—from 4.2 to nearly 6 percent of GDP.[79] But spending on elementary and secondary education has inched up from only 3.2 percent to 3.8 percent of GDP (see *International Comparison, next page*).[80] In other words, government has committed itself to helping to pay more of the costs of medical care in order to extend the last years of life, while doing little more to enhance the capacities of those in the first years of life.

On the other hand, there are those who argue that money is neither the problem nor the solution. Replying to the critics of the No Child Left Behind Act, some scholars have

INTERNATIONAL COMPARISON

Student Learning and School Expenditures

Student math literacy is lower in the United States than in other industrial countries, yet Americans pay more for schools than many other countries.

• *Do you believe that test scores would improve if the United States spent more on education? Why or why not?*

SOURCE: U.S. Department of Education, National Center for Education Statistics, *Digest of Education Statistics, 2005*, http://nces.ed.gov/programs/digest/d05_tf.asp, accessed June 10, 2006, Table 391 and Table 407. Mathematics figures from 2003; expenditures figures from 2002 except for Canada, figures for 2001.

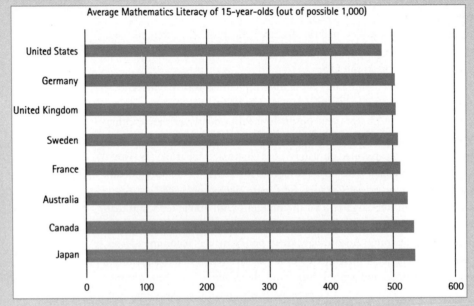

Average Mathematics Literacy of 15-year-olds (out of possible 1,000)

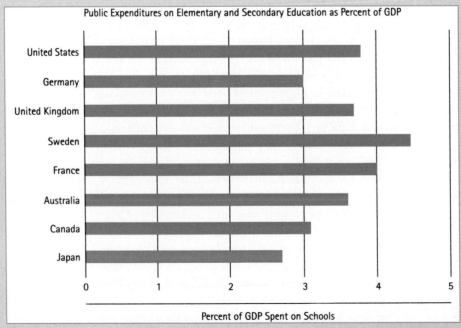

Public Expenditures on Elementary and Secondary Education as Percent of GDP

Percent of GDP Spent on Schools

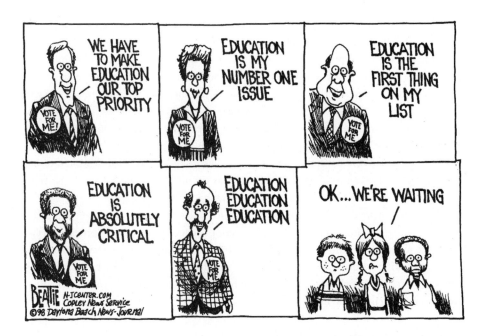

Campaigning on
Education
• *Can presidential decisions have
a significant effect on school policies? Why or why not?*

pointed out that federal aid to schools increased by $300 per student between 2000 and
2004, while the cost of new testing that the bill required was only $20 per student.[81] These
skeptics also cite numerous independent studies showing that the amount that young
people learn in school is seldom affected much by the amount of money a school has.[82]

Politics of Education

In the past, public schools were, like baseball and apple pie, beyond partisan dispute. But
in recent years, the two political parties have begun to disagree over a broad range of
educational issues. Republicans have increasingly supported holding schools to high
standards by testing students annually and giving parents greater choice through vouchers and charter schools, whereas Democrats have won strong support from the two
largest teacher groups, the National Education Association and the American Federation
of Teachers, by proposing higher levels of funding for traditional public schools.

Despite the partisan controversy, both parties remain strongly committed to public
education. No Child Left Behind was passed by overwhelming majorities in both houses
of Congress, and both have remained committed to its essentials. For all the current
discontent, Americans still think schools are crucial for achieving the American dream.
As long as the electorate feels this way, schools will continue to have bipartisan support.

Regulation

On December 23, 2003, as many American families headed home for the holiday
season, the United States Department of Agriculture (USDA) announced that a case of
bovine spongiform encephalopathy, otherwise known as "mad cow disease" had been
discovered in one Washington State cow. The fatal disease, which rapidly destroys brain
tissue, can spread from cattle to humans and is exceedingly difficult to eradicate from
the environment.

This was the first case of the disorder in the United States, but it had not come
without warning. Dr. Stanley Prusiner, a Nobel Prize-winning biologist who had

studied the disorder, said he had recently warned Secretary of Agriculture Ann Veneman that her department's animal inspection procedures were too lax to determine even the extent of the problem.[83] In fact, many so-called "downer cows," animals that are too sick to walk, had been slaughtered and added to the country's meat supply.

The USDA acted swiftly to calm public fears and shore up the international market for American beef, banning the use of downer cows for food, stepping up inspections, and implementing several other safeguards. Between 2004 and 2006, USDA tested 700,000 cows and found two more infected animals.[84] "The downer decision is a huge leap forward," said one consumer advocate "but it's really too bad USDA waited to take this step and others until after the first case was found. These are changes that many scientists and consumer advocates have been calling for for years."[85]

The case of mad cow disease raises questions about the government's regulatory policy making, an important and often overlooked component of domestic policy. Does the federal government have a responsibility to ensure public safety? What other kinds of activities should be regulated? How should this responsibility be exercised? In the remainder of this chapter, we discuss why and how the federal government regulates many aspects of our lives.

The Rise of Federal Regulation

regulation
Rules and standards that control economic, social, and political activities.

Government **regulation** consists of rules and standards that control economic, social, and political activities. Although Congress can itself pass regulations, usually it gives the responsibility to agencies within the executive branch, which issue rules within general congressional guidelines. Such rules affect the lives of average Americans at nearly every turn. For example, the Food and Drug Administration sets safety standards for medical devices, agricultural products, and nutrition; the Securities and Exchange Commission protects small investors by requiring companies to disclose standardized financial information; and the Consumer Products Safety Commission organizes the recall of products deemed to be hazardous.

Regulation dates back to feudal times. For example, businesses in sixteenth-century England "were required to set prices and render service in a socially responsible manner."[86] In the United States, the basis for federal regulation is found in the Constitution, which gives Congress the power "to regulate Commerce." Regulations under the authority of the commerce clause were originally applied to the railroad industry, with the passage of the Interstate Commerce Act of 1887. They have since been applied by Congress to regulate everything from civil rights to national insurance standards. Since the New Deal, the Supreme Court has generally found regulatory policies constitutional (see Chapter 3).[87]

Government regulations increased in number and significance at three distinct periods in the country's history: the Progressive Era, the New Deal era, and the 1960s and 1970s. Each period is marked by a strong political movement that identified major abuses in certain sectors of society, and each produced legislation that created a host of new government agencies with new regulatory powers.

During the Progressive Era of the 1890s and early 1900s, writers and journalists known as muckrakers exposed the worst abuses of industrialization. Initially, they focused attention on the power of large corporations, such as Standard Oil Company, which exercised almost complete control over the oil industry. When the public demanded antitrust legislation, Congress enacted the Sherman Act (1890), which made it a crime to "restrain" or "monopolize" trade. This law still plays a major role in government–industry relations. Under this statute, for example, Microsoft, producer of computer operating systems and software, was found guilty of creating a monopoly and restraining trade. While the company was not required to break itself into pieces, as some had hoped, Microsoft did have to abide by an agreement with the Justice Department aimed at halting unfair business practices, and also had to submit to close government supervision through at least 2009.[88]

The muckrakers also publicized other abuses, leading to the creation of additional regulatory agencies. For example, Upton Sinclair's best-selling novel *The Jungle* detailed horrible sanitation conditions in the meat-packing industry and resulted in the passage of the Meat Inspection Act of 1906.

The second regulatory wave occurred during the 1930s, when the government tried to prevent practices that were thought to have caused the Great Depression. The eight major regulatory agencies created at that time, including the Federal Deposit Insurance Corporation (FDIC), the Federal Communications Commission (FCC), and the Civil Aeronautics Board (predecessor to the modern Federal Aviation Administration), formed an important component of Franklin Roosevelt's New Deal.

A third wave of regulatory innovation took place in the 1960s and 1970s. During this period, the issues were consumer safety, occupational safety, and environmental protection. In 1965 Ralph Nader, an enterprising young lawyer, published a best-selling book, *Unsafe at Any Speed*, that revealed serious safety problems with a popular sports car, the Corvair. His efforts were so effective that General Motors halted production and new government regulations required manufacturers to install seat belts in all cars. Nader founded several consumer advocacy organizations, hiring young people who came to be known as "Nader's Raiders." In time, they found safety problems in many domains, including other consumer products, occupational environments, and industrial pollutants. In the ensuing years, Congress passed 61 significant pieces of new regulatory legislation and established or substantially enhanced the role of 9 regulatory agencies. Nader has remained politically active, running for president in 2000 and 2004.

The most important of the new agencies formed in this period was the **Environmental Protection Agency (EPA)**, which has the main responsibility for issuing regulations designed to protect the environment from unwanted pollutants. Its controls on air and water pollution have done much to improve air and water quality throughout the United States. As one analyst has pointed out,

> Air pollution from lead, by far the worst atmospheric poison, declined 89 percent during the 1980s; pollution from carbon monoxide, also poisonous, went down 31 percent. In 1992, the number of Americans living in counties that failed some aspect of air-quality standards was only half [those] who lived in dirty air in 1982.[89]

Environmental Protection Agency (EPA)
Agency responsible for issuing regulations designed to protect the environment from unwanted pollutants.

Energy Policy

Justifications for Regulation

As a result of these waves of regulatory expansion, the government now regulates many business and social activities. According to Murray Weidenbaum, a former chairman of the Council of Economic Advisers,

> No business, large or small, can operate without obeying a myriad of government rules and restrictions. Costs and profits can be affected as much by a directive written by a government official as by a management decision in the front office or a customer's decision at the checkout counter.[90]

Why have the regulatory responsibilities of government expanded so dramatically during the past century? Scholars have identified three broad types of circumstances in

Snowmobiling in Yellowstone

• *Do snowmobilers in U.S. national parks represent an externality-producing nuisance that must be regulated?*

which they find government regulation most easily justified: natural monopoly, externalities, and protection of the uninformed.

natural monopoly
A situation in which a public service is best provided by a single company.

Natural Monopoly   In a **natural monopoly** a public service is best provided by a single company. To make sure that the company does not take advantage of its monopoly power and charge consumers unnecessarily high prices, natural monopolies are usually subject to regulation. For example, regulations control the charges set by telephone companies that until recently have had exclusive rights in a particular region. Regulations also control the prices of gas, electricity, cable television, and other utilities that have exclusive rights in a particular state or locality. Otherwise, it is likely that these companies would charge excessively high rates.

externalities
Consequences affecting people who are not directly engaged in the activities that bring those consequences about.

Negative Externalities—An **externality** is any consequence of an activity that has an impact on those not responsible for the action. An externality may be positive or negative. If neighbors plant beautiful flowers in their front yard, then they provide those nearby with a positive externality. But if the same neighbors pile unsightly, reeking junk on their front lawn, then those nearby suffer a negative externality. Because neighbors—and corporations—may not care about the consequences of their actions for others, the government may regulate to prevent or adjust for externalities.

One of the best examples of an externality is air pollution. A company may try to keep its costs low by using cheap fuel, even though burning that fuel emits black soot into the air. The black soot does not seriously affect the company, although it both threatens the health of those living nearby and creates a nuisance for them. To prevent companies from imposing this externality on others by polluting their environments, the EPA has imposed numerous regulations on industry to control the emission of pollutants.

A recent controversy over government regulation of externalities took place over the use of U.S. national park land. Until 2000, more than 180,000 snowmobile aficionados used the national parks each winter, sometimes racing through the woods at speeds in excess of 60 miles per hour. Environmentalists protested this use of public property, arguing that "the national parks should be places where the public can go to escape traffic . . . . And clearly these snow machines are loud, they're polluting, and they cause conflict with other visitors." In 2000 the National Park Service sided with the environmentalists, announcing a sweeping ban on snowmobile use in the national parks, with only minor exceptions. As in many other cases of regulation, those being regulated became very upset. Fumed one angry rider, "It's part of a planned campaign by this administration to limit access to public lands."[91] The Bush administration reversed most of these restrictive rules in 2001, but a federal judge blocked this move in 2003, denouncing it as "completely politically driven."[92] An exasperated pro-snowmobile spokesman admitted "We're totally confused."[93] A new environmental study will lead to a revised set of rules, expected to go into effect in early 2007.[94]

Protecting the Uninformed   Regulations are also used to protect those who cannot be expected to be well informed, most notably consumers. For example, many government rules forbid the marketing of unsafe products or the use of deceptive advertising and labeling.

The need for regulation is especially great in the case of medications. When citizens catch the flu, they cannot be expected to research the side effects of every cold medication on the market. Thus, government regulation is necessary to ensure that drugs sold over the counter meet specified safety standards.

Regulation of drugs began during the Progressive Era. In 1906 Congress created the Food and Drug Administration (FDA), granting it the power to regulate the production and labeling of goods sold in interstate commerce. The initial legislation gave the FDA only limited powers. To garner public support for stronger regulatory authority, in the 1920s the FDA established a museum known as the Chamber of Horrors that contained such atrocities as

> Samples seized from goods on public sale—samples of patent medicines to cure every known disease, with testimonials from their users, accompanied by copies of their death certificates; and samples of cosmetics—eye-lash beautifiers containing poisonous aniline dyes, hair removers containing thallium acetate, and hair tonics, freckle removers, ointments, and salves containing mercury or other dangerous ingredients—together with photographs of women who had been blinded, paralyzed, or permanently disfigured by their use.[95]

The museum effectively aroused public concern. The FDA now monitors the production of everything from drugs to cosmetics to therapeutic devices such as muscle developers and sun lamps.

Politics of Regulation

When and how regulations are imposed are political decisions. Regulations are thus shaped by election pressures on Congress, government agencies, and even the courts.

You Are a
State Legislator

Congress   Members of Congress often create regulatory agencies in order to escape criticism when things go wrong. Laws frequently win passage in response to a well-publicized incident or disaster. After a series of accounting scandals at companies such as Enron and WorldCom, for example, Congress passed the Corporate Accountability Act of 2002, which more strictly regulated corporations and corporate auditing firms.

With each disaster or scandal, congressional representatives demonstrate their responsiveness to public concerns by passing another regulatory act. The end result is that regulations often duplicate and overlap one another.

Although regulation may help reassure the public after a crisis has occurred, it is inherently unpopular with at least some voters. Regulations require some people to follow restrictive procedures in order to avoid injuring others. For example, the regulations that prohibit snowmobiles in national parks may win the approval of environmentalists, but they almost certainly alienate devotees of the sport. Because compelling people to do something is likely to make them upset or angry, members of Congress usually employ a strategy known as **blame avoidance**, a set of political techniques designed to disguise their actions and shift the blame to others. In the case of regulatory policy, Congress avoids blame by not directly imposing the regulations but handing that job off to a regulatory agency.

When creating a regulatory agency, Congress often defines its task in general terms. As one group of policy analysts has said about the EPA, its "discretion [is] truly enormous. It produce[s] hundreds of pages of regulations, embodying dozens of significant policy choices, all on the basis of the most elliptical statutory language and the sparsest of legislative records."[96] Congress justifies leaving the terms of reference vague on the grounds that the authors of the legislation cannot anticipate every circumstance requiring regulatory action. Legislators can correctly claim that only those who know the facts in detail can come up with the appropriate regulation. But Congress has also discovered that it can avoid "unpleasant truths" by keeping regulatory legislation broad and general.[97] Different members of Congress may then interpret the law in contrasting ways. Some may claim they have satisfied the concerns of environmentalists and consumers; others will insist they have not imposed undue burdens on business and industry.

In rare cases where the public has become upset at the vagueness of congressional legislation, Congress has taken further (though still less than specific) steps. One such measure is to set specific goals and then to include a **hammer**—a harsh penalty—to be imposed if these goals are not met somehow. For example, the Clean Air Act of 1990 says that if certain goals are not met in particular metropolitan areas by a specific deadline, then the "sale of all gasoline in the designated area must cease."[98] Such draconian penalties make Congress appear tough, but in fact they are typically so impractical that they would never be imposed, and the legislation still usually includes no guidelines regarding how the goals should be met.

Agency Discretion   Because of the very ambiguity of much congressional legislation, agencies often enjoy considerable freedom in deciding how to execute their mandates. When Congress charged the EPA with improving air quality in metropolitan areas, the agency had to decide the following kinds of questions: Should automobile manufacturers be required to build and sell some electric cars within 10 years? Should every vehicle be checked at a state-run inspection station? Should inner-city highways be subject to a toll during rush hour? Should states be told they cannot build new roads? Although EPA officials have considered each of these difficult questions, nothing in the Clean Air Act of 1990 provides precise answers.

The autonomy afforded to regulatory agencies is not limitless. There exists a **zone of acceptance**—a range within which Congress will accept whatever an agency

blame avoidance
Set of political techniques employed by political leaders to disguise their actions and shift blame to others.

hammer
Harsh penalty set by Congress to be imposed if a regulatory agency does not achieve a statutory objective.

zone of acceptance
Range within which Congress allows agencies to interpret and apply statutes.

decides is the correct interpretation of the statutes.[99] When an agency goes beyond this informal and ambiguous zone, political opposition arises and the agency backtracks. For example, all of the clean-air options mentioned here provoked controversy and, as a result, the EPA has been slow to implement them.

Courts   Although regulatory policies are enacted by Congress and executed by agencies, courts interpret the meaning of congressional statutes and decide whether their application in specific cases conforms to congressional intent. Courts exercise considerable discretion when performing this role, because they are often asked to interpret vague, and even contradictory, laws passed by Congress.

Court interpretations of the 1973 Endangered Species Act illustrate how federal judges influence public policy. The law protects any species on federal lands that is found by the U.S. Fish and Wildlife Service to be threatened with extinction. Such a species' natural habitat is to be safeguarded from human activity that threatens it, no matter what the economic consequences of such protection. In voting for this legislation, most members of Congress probably thought they were protecting large mammals and birds, such as wolves, whooping cranes, and eagles. And, indeed, the Endangered Species Act has been successful in protecting the American bald eagle. In 1963 there were only 417 nesting pairs; by 2006, the numbers had increased to 7,066, and the Department of Interior announced that it was prepared to remove the animal from the endangered species list.[100] However, the Fish and Wildlife Service greatly expanded the scope of the legislation when it found nearly 1,000 species to be in danger of extinction. And the federal courts have interpreted the law as applicable even to little-known species. Judges have halted the growth of suburbs in order to protect desert kangaroo rats; they have prevented the construction of a billion-dollar dam in order to save a tiny snail darter; and they have halted logging operations in order to safeguard the spotted owl.

Deregulation

Although regulation is an inevitable part of modern society, it can be carried to excess, and regulations intended to protect consumers may have the opposite effect. For example, regulating drugs may prevent some patients from getting the treatment they need. Furthermore, regulation is expensive. Salaries for bureaucrats, lawyers, and investigators generate an annual price tag that runs to billions of dollars. Regulatory policies may also limit the ability of businesses to compete effectively. The additional paperwork, inspections, procedures, and mandates imposed by regulatory agencies can spell the difference between a business that thrives and provides good jobs to Americans and one that cannot remain solvent and has to reduce its workforce.

To address these concerns, Congress has introduced in many areas policies of **deregulation**, the removal of government rules that once controlled an industry. It has systematically authorized the partial deregulation of the trucking, banking, and communications industries.[101] Banks may now provide customers with insurance and handle the purchase and sale of stocks. Regional telephone companies may now offer long-distance and cellular service.

Perhaps the most celebrated deregulation occurred within the airline industry. At one time, a government agency approved the airfare set for every route a plane flew.

deregulation
Removal of government rules that once controlled an industry.

Though it was originally enacted to prevent price gouging by airlines that had a monopoly in a particular city, many policy analysts claimed that the effect of the law was precisely the opposite of its intent: Regulators were letting airlines charge excessively high prices.

To address this and other problems, Congress enacted the Airline Deregulation Act of 1978. Most policy outcomes were favorable. Airline competition increased, companies became more efficient, service to remote areas increased, and air fares fell with the emergence of low-cost carriers such as JetBlue and Southwest.[102] Although some worried about the effect on safety,[103] the number of deaths per passenger mile also declined. Yet many experts argue that some regulation must remain in place to ensure that airline companies, in their eagerness for profit, do not cut corners too closely.[104] Furthermore, even the most committed deregulators backed government assistance to the airline industry after the 9/11 attacks.[105] In this, as in many industries, complete deregulation is unlikely, because the public will always expect government to act in the wake of disasters or to prevent costly externalities.

Chapter Summary

Domestic policy involves government spending on social policies, education, and other policies, as well as government regulation of these activities. The two political parties are divided on many domestic policies. Democrats typically want to spend more on social and education policy, and they usually favor more regulation. Republicans usually favor less spending and less regulation.

Beyond these partisan differences, however, there are also differences in the way these policies affect different interest groups and portions of the electorate. These cause the policy-making process to vary from one policy to another and result in policy outcomes that

at times seem self-contradictory. Social policies designed to aid the elderly are far more popular and more extensive than similar policies designed to aid poor children. The public wants national candidates to address education policy but does not want to relinquish local control over public schools. And Congress is quick to pass regulatory legislation in the wake of disasters, but otherwise tends to write vague legislation, leaving interpretation to the agencies and the courts. Only through a clear understanding of how elections affect the policy process can one understand these complex, even contradictory outcomes.

Key Terms

agenda setting, p. 523
blame avoidance, p. 544
deregulation, p. 545
domestic policy, p. 523
Earned Income Tax Credit (EITC), p. 531
Environmental Protection Agency (EPA), p. 541
externalities, p. 542
food stamps, p. 531

hammer, p. 544
Medicaid, p. 532
Medicare, p. 523
natural monopoly, p. 542
policy deliberation, p. 523
policy enactment, p. 523
policy implementation, p. 523
policy outcome, p. 523
policy output, p. 523
public assistance, p. 531

regulation, p. 540
rent subsidies, p. 532
social insurance, p. 526
social policy, p. 524
social security, p. 526
Supplemental Security Income (SSI), p. 531
Temporary Assistance for Needy Families (TANF), p. 523
zone of acceptance, p. 544

Suggested Readings

Of General Interest

Bane, Mary Jo, and Lawrence M. Mead. *Lifting Up the Poor: A Dialogue on Religion, Poverty, and Welfare Reform.* Washington, DC: Brookings Institution Press, 2003. A liberal and a conservative debate U.S. policy on poverty.

Kingdon, John. *Agendas, Alternatives and Public Policies.* Boston: Little, Brown, 1984. Discusses the policy-making process, paying special attention to how problems become issues on the political agenda.

Pierson, Paul. *Dismantling the Welfare State? Reagan, Thatcher and the Politics of Retrenchment.* New York: Cambridge University Press, 1994. Insightful analysis of political battles over cuts in welfare expenditure.

Skocpol, Theda. *Protecting Soldiers and Mothers: The Politics of Social Provision in the United States.* Cambridge, MA: Harvard University Press, 1993. Fascinating, comprehensive historical analysis of the evolution of the U.S. welfare state.

Focused Studies

Burtless, Gary, ed. *Does Money Matter? The Effect of School Resources on Student Achievement and Adult Success.* Washington, DC: The Brookings Institution, 1996. Excellent collection of essays that debate the current state of public education.

Derthick, Martha, and Paul Quirk. *The Politics of Deregulation.* Washington, DC: The Brookings Institution, 1985. Engaging accounts of the political circumstances that enable the federal government to eliminate existing regulations.

Howell, William, and Paul E. Peterson, with Patrick Wolf and David Campbell. *The Education Gap: Vouchers and Urban Public Schools.* Washington, DC: The Brookings Institution, 2002. Analysis of school choice initiatives by scholars sympathetic to vouchers.

Landy, Marc K., Marc J. Roberts, and Stephen R. Thomas. *The Environmental Protection Agency: Asking the Wrong Questions from Nixon to Clinton.* Expanded edition. New York: Oxford University Press, 1994. Thorough, critical analysis of EPA policy making.

Vig, Norman J., and Michael E. Kraft, Eds. *Environmental Policy: New Directions for the Twenty-First Century.* 6th ed. Washington, DC: CQ Press, 2005. Excellent essays on modern U.S. environmental policy.

Wilson, James Q. *The Politics of Regulation.* New York: Basic Books, 1980. Comprehensive text on regulatory politics and policy.

Wilson, William J. *The Truly Disadvantaged: The Inner City, the Underclass, and Public Policy.* Chicago: University of Chicago Press, 1987. Argues that poverty has been caused by the internationalization of the economy and the disappearance of blue-collar jobs. Maintains that government should provide jobs.

On the Web

In this chapter, we discussed a variety of government programs and regulations. Many programs and regulatory agencies have Web sites that provide information to the public. They including the following:

www.medicare.gov

The official government information site for Medicare, the health insurance program for the elderly.

www.ssa.gov

The Social Security Administration (SSA), which administers the social insurance program that makes up a quarter of the federal budget.

www.acf.dhhs.gov

The Administration for Children and Families, which runs the federal side of the Temporary Assistance for Needy Families (TANF) program.

www.ed.gov

The U.S. Department of Education, which provides statistical information on the state of education in the United States and describes national education programs.

www.fda.gov

www.epa.gov

www.sec.gov

www.osha.gov

www.cpsc.gov

The Food and Drug Administration, the Environmental Protection Agency, the Securities and Exchange Commission, the Occupational Safety and Health Administration, and the Consumer Product Safety Commission, five major regulatory agencies.

In this chapter we also discussed a number of interest groups and organizations that affect the design and implementation of domestic policy in the United States. They include:

www.aarp.org

The American Association of Retired Persons (AARP), the large and influential lobby for senior citizens.

www.childrensdefense.org

The Children's Defense Fund, which works to provide "a voice for all the children of America who cannot vote, lobby or speak for themselves."

www.frc.org

The Family Research Council, a conservative foundation that "champions marriage and family."

www.educationnext.org

Education Next is a journal that discusses contemporary education policy issues.

www.aft.org

The American Federation of Teachers (AFT), one of the most powerful lobbying organizations on education issues.

www.publiccitizen.org

Ralph Nader's Public Citizen, which lobbies for consumer protection regulations.

www.heritage.org/Research/Regulation/

The conservative Heritage Foundation's regulation project advocating deregulation.

CHAPTER 19

★ ★ ★ ★ ★ ★ ★ ★ ★ ☆

Economic Policy

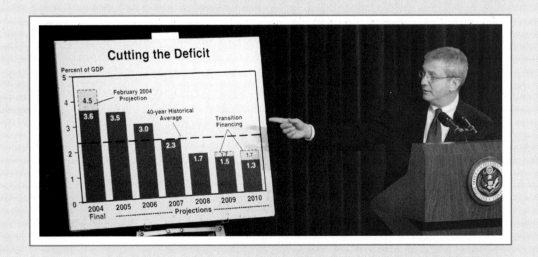

The Bush Tax Cuts

When George W. Bush took office in 2001, the economy was entering a downturn after the longest economic expansion in American history. During the administration of his predecessor, Bill Clinton, the **gross domestic product (GDP)**, the official measure of the total value of economic activity in the United States, had grown by a yearly average of 5.8 percent, an unusually robust figure.[1] Unemployment dropped to its lowest level in 30 years,[2] and the value of stocks on Wall Street tripled.[3] The healthy economy had helped Clinton maintain positive public approval ratings despite a damaging sex scandal and even his impeachment by a Republican Congress.

Bush's aides worried that just as Clinton got credit for the booming 1990s, Bush would be blamed for the stagnating stock market, escalating unemployment, and slow GDP growth that began in 2001. Regardless of whether presidents are capable of doing much to affect the economy, most scholars and politicians agree that voters consider the state of the economy when they go to the polls. Indeed, in the first half of 2001, polls showed voters losing confidence in Bush on economic matters.[4] Accordingly, Bush and his advisers made tax cuts central to the early months of the administration. Americans "need tax relief fast," the president said. "In fact, they need it yesterday."[5]

The tax cut the Bush administration proposed and shepherded through Congress became one of the three largest in American history, reducing taxes on income for nearly all taxpayers. Furthermore, in a novel measure, taxpayers would get a one-time tax rebate of up to $600 to spend as they pleased. In theory, people would spend this unexpected cash on consumer goods, thus boosting the nation's flagging economy. After the bill passed and rebate checks were mailed out, the White House anticipated immediate political gains. As one presidential aide put it, "People will open the mail and say, 'Holy cow, he really did do something!' "[6]

Buoyed by the political success of the 2001 tax bill, Bush and congressional Republicans passed further tax cuts in 2002, 2003, and 2004. Although Democrats argued that these policies disproportionately favored the rich, the American public gave the president significant credit for the cuts.[7] But, if the political benefits of the plans were clear, their effect on the economy was widely debated.[8] Some experts said the tax cuts gave the economy a boost just when it was needed, and indeed the economy began to recover within a year of the 2001 rebates. Others said that the recovery was more influenced by the Federal Reserve Board, an agency of the government over which President Bush had only limited indirect influence. Bush's narrow reelection in 2004 appeared to show that at the very least, he had escaped blame for the economic downturn early in his administration.

MAKING THE CONNECTION

Elected officials place great emphasis on formulating and implementing the policies that affect economic conditions. And elections are often decided on the basis of economic factors. But were the voters correct to base their assessments of Presidents Clinton and George W. Bush on the state of the economy? How much control do the president and Congress have over economic trends? What other governmental institutions besides the president are able to make economic policy and what powers do they have? In this chapter, we address these and related questions by considering the policies that the government may use to affect the economy, and the effects of these policies on elections.

Economic Growth and the Business Cycle

Economies grow as the result of technological innovations, investments in physical capital (factories, agricultural production, communication systems, and so on), and investments in human capital (education, worker training, and the like). As a result of technological change and investments in physical and human capital, the U.S. economy has grown enormously, and many of those who have invested in American industry have reaped huge rewards. For example, if you had purchased $25 worth of stock in a cross section of American companies in the late 1920s, that stock would be worth about $1,200 today.[9]

In any given year, however, short-term fluctuations in the economy can adversely affect stock values. For example, that $25 investment would have lost more than two-thirds of its value from 1929 to 1933, the early years of the Great Depression, and would not have regained its original value until the mid-1950s.

Few economic downturns are as severe as was the Great Depression. But **recessions**—slowdowns in economic activity—occur relatively often, if unpredictably. Economists refer to these periodic episodes of economic slowdown, followed by recovery, renewed expansion, and rising prices, as the **business cycle**. Figure 19.1 provides an illustration of this phenomenon.

Governments try to set economic policies in such a way as to minimize the disruptions caused by the business cycle so that most people keep their jobs and prices remain stable. In other words, they try to avoid two major problems: inflation and unemployment. **Inflation**—a rise in the price level—makes consumers pay more money for an equal amount of goods and services. For example, in 1995, the average ticket for a movie cost $4.35, a price that seems a bargain by today's standards.[10] If inflation rates become too high, the cost of necessities such as food, clothing, and transportation consume a larger and larger portion of people's income, making the general public unhappy. **Unemployment**—which occurs when people willing to work at prevailing wages cannot find jobs—harms a smaller number of people but harms them in ways that are marked and visible. When General Motors announced in 2006 that it would reduce its workforce by 30,000 over the next few years, auto workers across the United States felt, as one put it, "furious and terrified."[11] Unemployment also makes it difficult for many people who have jobs to change jobs or win wage increases.

Political leaders try to avoid both misfortunes, but they are not always successful. For a long time, the two conditions were thought to be closely related: Lower unemployment was assumed to mean higher inflation, and vice versa.[12] But economists no longer believe the relationship is so close. In fact, President Jimmy Carter had the misfortune to run for reelection at a time of "stagflation," when both inflation and unemployment were high. He suffered a humiliating defeat. For the next three elections, Republicans reminded the public of the economic chaos of the Carter years.

gross domestic product (GDP)
The measure of the total value of economic activity in a nation in one year.

recession
A slowdown in economic activity, officially defined as a decline that persists for two quarters (six months).

business cycle
The alternation of periods of economic growth with periods of economic slowdown.

inflation
A sustained rise in the price level such that people need more money to purchase the same amount of goods and services.

unemployment
The circumstance that exists when people who are willing to work at the prevailing wage cannot get jobs.

FIGURE 19.1

Long-Term Growth and
the Business Cycle in the
United States

Although the general economic
trend may be upward over the
long run, expansions and recessions that characterize the business cycle can—in the short
term—harm both citizens and
elected officials.

• *Can you name the president in
office during each economic downturn labeled in the figure?*

Sources: Statistical Abstract of the United
States, 1999, 881, Table 1434 and U.S.
Department of Commerce, Bureau of
Economic Analysis, "National Income and
Product Accounts,"
www.bea.gov/bea/dn1.htm, accessed June
12, 2006.

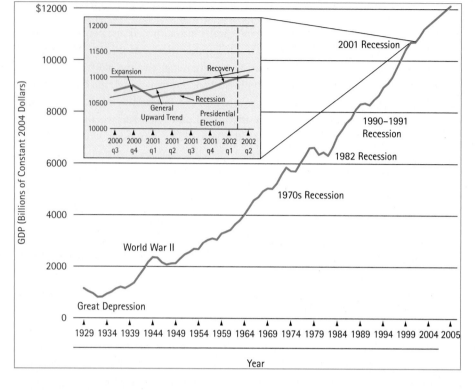

Economic Conditions and Political Fortunes

As Carter's experience shows, people tend to blame those in charge when times are
hard. George W. Bush weathered criticism of his lax regulation of business in the wake
of malfeasance at major corporations such as Enron, Global Crossing, and WorldCom.
And during the 2004 campaign, Democratic presidential candidate John Kerry blamed
Bush for disappointing employment figures, as well as for allowing corporations to
"outsource" jobs to locations in other countries.

Bush and Carter have not been the only presidents to have lost popularity when the
economy faltered. President George H. W. Bush also suffered from economic adversity
in 1992. His popularity ratings fell 40 percentage points during a recession in the second
half of his administration—from 78 percent in July 1990, when the rate of unemployment first began to rise, to 38 percent two years later, when unemployment peaked.
Presidents Eisenhower and Nixon suffered similar fates, losing significant public support
when recessions hit. Some critics called Ronald Reagan the "Teflon president" because
they believed that none of the usual political dirt and grease stuck to him; but even
Ronald Reagan's popularity dropped precipitously during the 1981–1982 recession.[13]

Terrible economic times in American history are associated with massive election
losses for the party of the president. The depression of the 1890s ushered in an era of
Republican dominance, and the Great Depression of the 1930s did the same for the
Democrats. Indeed, Republican president Herbert Hoover (1929–1933) became one
of history's most unpopular presidents simply because he was in office when the Great
Depression began. For decades afterward, Democrats ran against the party of Hoover,
using the Depression issue to help them win the next five elections.

Prosperity, in contrast, strengthens a president's position in a bid for reelection, as
Figure 19.2 illustrates. Riding booming economies, Lyndon Johnson trampled Barry

Herbert Hoover

Herbert Hoover, a Republican,
was president when the United
States plunged into the Great
Depression.

• *How did this event affect
Republican Party fortunes? Why?*

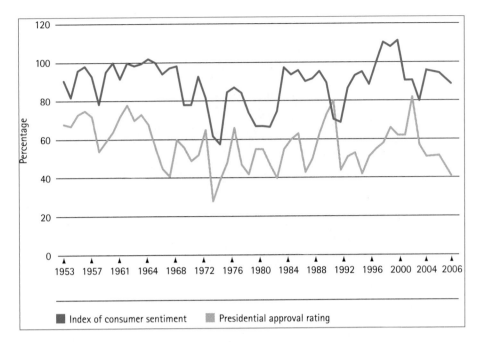

FIGURE 19.2

When Americans Feel Positively About the Economy, They Also Approve of the President

• *Under what circumstances would the economy be least likely to have a major impact on the public's view of the president?*

Note: The figure displays data for the first quarter of each year.

Sources: Index of Consumer Sentiment, Surveys of Consumers, University of Michigan; and Gallup polls, various years.

Goldwater in 1964, Richard Nixon crushed George McGovern in 1972, Ronald Reagan trounced Walter Mondale in 1984, and Bill Clinton overwhelmed Bob Dole in 1996. Of course, a healthy economy does not guarantee presidential popularity. For example, prosperity did not keep Johnson's popularity from falling sharply in response to the rising casualty rate in Vietnam.[14] Nonetheless, presidents usually do better in elections when the economy is strong.

National economic conditions may influence congressional elections as well.[15] In 1930 Democrats captured control of Congress when voters blamed Republicans for the onset of the Great Depression. The Eisenhower recession of 1958 inflated the narrow Democratic majorities in the House and Senate. The huge Democratic majorities of 1974 were due both to the Watergate scandal and to an economic downturn.[16] When the economy dragged Carter under in 1980, the Republicans took control of the Senate and made large gains in the House. To be sure, economics is not the only force at work in congressional elections. The Democrats suffered serious congressional losses in 1966, even though the economy was fine. That election turned on Vietnam and racial tensions. Similarly, the Republicans lost control of Congress in 2006 even though unemployment had remained low throughout the preceding two years.

But the economy is most critical for presidential elections, so it is the president who pays the closest attention to economic policy. Presidents may make narrow economic policies with an eye toward key groups of voters, as George W. Bush did with steel import policy in 2002. Presidents may also try to shape overall economic conditions by using two major policy tools, fiscal policy and monetary policy. We discuss these policy tools in the next two sections.

Fiscal Policy

A government's **fiscal policy**, the sum total of government taxation and spending, determines whether government revenues exceed expenditures. When yearly spending exceeds tax receipts, the government runs a **deficit**. When the amount collected

fiscal policy
The sum total of government taxing and spending decisions, which determines the level of the deficit or surplus.

deficit
The amount by which annual spending exceeds revenue.

FIGURE 19.3

Federal Revenues by
Source

• *Do these revenue figures
surprise you? Can you think of
programs that deserve less taxation? More taxation?*

Note: Excise taxes include taxes
on alcohol, cigarettes, and gasoline. See Chapter 18 for details
on social insurance taxes.

Source: Historical Budget Data,
Washington, DC: Congressional Budget
Office, January 26, 2006, Table 3.

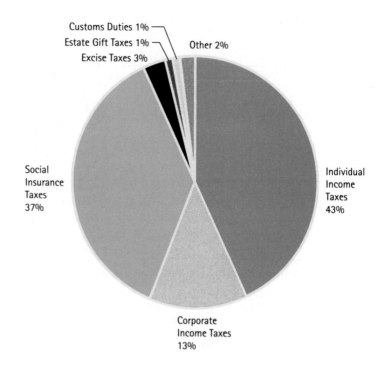

surplus

The amount by which annual
revenue exceeds spending.

budget

The government's annual plan for
taxing and spending.

Deficit Spending

Keynesianism

Economic policy based on the belief
that governments can control the
economy by manipulating demand,
running deficits to expand it, and
surpluses to contract it.

in taxes exceeds spending, the government enjoys a **surplus**. When the two are
exactly the same, the budget is said to be balanced. The nation's fiscal policy is
formulated in a **budget**, the government's annual plan for taxing and spending. The
government collects taxes from a variety of sources, as Figure 19.3 indicates, and uses
these funds in addition to some borrowed ones to finance all government programs.
In 2006 the federal budget amounted to about $2.7 trillion, or about 21 percent of
the nation's GDP.[17] Since the 1970s the president has proposed a budget to Congress
each year, but Congress usually makes major changes to the president's plan before
passing it. The largest portion of federal budget expenditures—just over 20
percent—goes to the social security program. National defense claims another 20
percent and Medicare and Medicaid account for 19 percent of the nation's spending
(for more on social security, Medicare, and Medicaid, see Chapter 18). Interest paid
on the sizable national debt consumes an additional 8 percent. Everything else the
government spends money on—from highway funds and education programs to
child nutrition, housing subsidies, and foreign aid—constitutes the remaining 33
percent of the budget.[18]

Use of the Budget Deficit

According to an influential English economist of the 1920s and 1930s, John Maynard
Keynes, there is nothing sacred about a balanced government budget; on the contrary,
he said, budget deficits can lift an economy out of a recession. If government spends
money when no one else does, it can jump-start the economy, which then can begin
to grow on its own. Following this line of reasoning, which came to be called
Keynesianism, Franklin Roosevelt broke with the traditional belief in a balanced

budget (a belief held by his predecessor Herbert Hoover) and ran large deficits during the 1930s in an attempt to get the country moving again.

After World War II, Keynesian thinking became widely accepted. In 1946 Congress established a **Council of Economic Advisers (CEA)** composed of three prominent economists who would advise the president about the state of the national and international economy, present economic forecasts, and make recommendations about the budget. Because deficits were thought to create jobs, whereas surpluses held prices down, these expert economists tried to help presidents "fine-tune" the economy to ensure steady prosperity. On the recommendation of the CEA to stimulate a sluggish economy, John Kennedy urged Congress to pass a deficit-creating tax cut. Some credit the cut, passed in 1964, with stimulating the mid-1960s economic boom.[19] Conversely, to slow down the inflation rate, Lyndon Johnson followed CEA advice and persuaded Congress to pass a tax increase in 1968. Despite the tax, inflation continued. Some said that the tax increase failed to have the desired effect because the it was not big enough.[20] Others said that the failure of the tax increase to stop inflation proved Keynes's theory wrong.

The CEA declined in importance in the 1980s and 1990s, as presidents relied more on White House staffers, treasury secretaries, and other political aides for advice on economic policy. Under George W. Bush, the CEA reclaimed some of the prestige and policy influence of years past, exerting influence over trade initiatives, tax policy, and even some aspects of homeland security.[21]

John Maynard Keynes
John Maynard Keynes, the economic theorist responsible for the school of macroeconomics that came to be called "Keynesianism."
• *Why is Keynesian thinking on fiscal policy less influential today?*

Decline of Fiscal Policy

Administrations today are much less likely to use fiscal policy as a tool for managing the economy than they were during the Kennedy-Johnson era. Several factors have contributed to the decline in the economic significance of fiscal policy. These factors include divided government, monetarism, budget deficits, and internationalization.

Divided Government   Fiscal policy and divided government do not mix well together. An economic policy must be implemented quickly if it is to alleviate the economic conditions it is aimed at. But when government is divided between the two parties, it is difficult to enact fiscal policy quickly in response to changing economic conditions.

Fiscal policy is a product of the taxing and spending decisions recommended by presidents and passed by Congress. Even under the most favorable conditions, it takes considerable time for the two institutions to iron out their differences and adopt a budget. When George W. Bush proposed a tax cut in 2001, he justified the cut according to Keynesian principles, arguing that the cut was needed to stimulate a slowing economy. Responding to the president's urgent request, Congress moved quickly to pass a long-term tax cut and an immediate tax rebate for Americans. However, the bulk of the tax cuts took effect only several years later, too late to jump-start the faltering economy, and experts differed on whether 2001's one-time tax rebate provided much stimulus.

Similarly, in 2003, Bush pressed for the elimination of taxes on stock dividends, saying that "[l]ower taxes and greater investment will help this economy expand."[22] Although Congress enacted the bulk of his proposals, and the Bush administration

Council of Economic Advisers (CEA)

Three economists who head up a professional staff that advises the president on economic policy.

Evaluating Federal Spending and Economic Policy

claimed that his tax cuts had revived the economy, many economists remained skeptical of this claim.

Monetarism   The second factor that has reduced the significance of fiscal policy is the increased influence of **monetarism**, a school of economic thinking that says that the money supply, not the pattern of government taxing and spending, is the most important influence on the economy. Monetarists argue that the deficits that Keynesians favor in times of economic distress are paid for by borrowing money from investors. Thus, every dollar the government spends is one less dollar to be invested in other productive activities. According to this point of view, budget deficits do not add any extra stimulus—they just transfer available dollars from the private sector to the government. In the next section, we outline what steps monetarists favor in lieu of deficits.

Even Keynesians favor only temporary deficits; they do not believe that a government budget can be continuously in deficit. Over the long run, a nation's economy can grow only if people save money and invest it in productive enterprises. The problem is that when a government borrows money, it soaks up some of the country's savings, and with less savings-to-finance investment, economic growth slows. Thus, most economists today agree that persistent deficits result in lower long-term economic growth.

Growing Budget Deficits   Fiscal policy has also been undermined by the large budget deficits of recent decades. In the 1960s, when regulation of the economy by means of fiscal policy was a popular idea, the federal **debt**—the accumulation of annual deficits—was still declining from the peak to which it had climbed during World War II. Thus, modest adjustments in fiscal policy could be made from one year to the next without creating long-term problems. But in the 1970s, large defense expenditures, coupled with growing spending on social programs, began to regularly produce unbalanced budgets in which total expenditures exceeded tax revenues by significant amounts.

During the 1980s and most of the 1990s, the budget deficit gradually but inexorably became a major issue in American politics. In the 1980s, supply-side economics, implemented by the Reagan administration, further exacerbated the large deficits of the 1970s.[23] The central tenet of **supply-side economics** (called "Reaganomics" by its critics) held that lowering tax rates would stimulate so much additional productive economic activity that the government would raise more in revenues even if tax rates were lower. The theory proved incorrect. Large tax cuts enacted during the 1980s, coupled with increases in defense spending and continued high spending for social programs, led to sustained deficits unprecedented in American history (see Figure 19.4). Nevertheless, some experts argued that deficits were neither a substantive nor a political problem. "You just don't have people running through the streets to have the deficit cut," pointed out one Reagan administration official.[24]

But, by the 1990s, sustained voter concern about the deficit, coupled with the independent presidential candidacy of Ross Perot, provoked action on the issue. Perot made deficit reduction the centerpiece of his campaign for the presidency in 1992, and the 19 percent of the vote that he received convinced Bill Clinton that budgetary reform had popular backing. Still, elected officials struggled to find a way to satisfy public demands for a reduced deficit without angering voters by raising taxes or cutting spending.

In 1997 Clinton and a Republican Congress finally agreed on a balanced budget. But this achievement was due almost entirely to unexpected economic growth that by

monetarism
An economic school of thought that rejects Keynesianism, arguing that the money supply is the most important influence on the economy.

debt
The accumulation of yearly deficits.

supply-side economics
Economic policy based on the belief that governments can keep the economy healthy by supplying the conditions (especially low taxes and minimal regulation) that encourage private economic activity.

Growth of the Budget
and Federal Spending

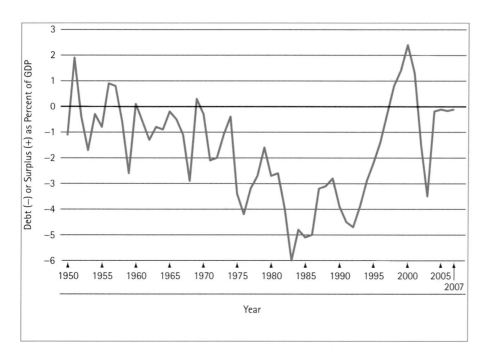

FIGURE 19.4

The Federal Deficit or Surplus, 1950–2007

• *What accounts for the large deficits of the 1980s and the sudden surpluses of the late 1990s?*

Note: Figures for 2006–2007 are estimates.

Source: Office of Management and Budget, *The Budget of Fiscal Year 2007, Historical Tables*, 23–4, Table 1.2.

itself dramatically cut budget deficits. Suddenly it became easy to balance the budget while at the same time increasing social spending.

Predictably, when economic growth slowed, deficits moved back into the picture. Beginning in 2002, the federal government began running deficits again, and the budget shortfall in 2006 was expected to be more than $400 billion.[25] The Bush tax cuts, as well as increased spending on the war in Iraq, homeland security, and Medicare, seemed likely to result in deficit spending for the foreseeable future. Although Americans no longer view the deficit as the most important problem facing the country, many policy analysts continue to view it as an important issue.[26] High deficits, coupled with public concern about their size, make it difficult for the president and Congress to consciously use deficit spending to affect the economy.

Internationalization   Fiscal policy has been further limited by the internationalization of the economy. Economic activity has become increasingly linked to overseas markets, so the reactions of economic actors to government policies are no longer limited to conditions in their own countries. If American investors think the government is spending too much, they can move billions of dollars to markets in Europe or Asia. Investors in other countries can do the same. Thus advances in communications have enabled investors in stocks and bonds to penalize governments for poor economic policies.

Many foreign investors in Japan, China, India, Europe, and the oil-holding countries of the Middle East have extremely large investments in U.S. bonds, because they see America's economic and political institutions as very strong and enduring, which ensures that their investments will be safe over long periods of time. But, if these investors should come to believe that the United States is no longer a safe place to invest their monies, perhaps because the government's tax and spending politics are unwise, then they may decide to move a significant share of their investments to another country. If that happens, the price of bonds will fall, and presidents could get the blame for what is happening. Political commentator James Carville, President Clinton's 1992 campaign manager, made a humorous remark recognizing the power of investors in the stock and bond markets: "I used to think if there was reincarnation, I wanted to come back as the president or the Pope . . . but now I would like to come back as the bond market. You can intimidate everybody."[27]

These changes in the international economy gave rise to another school of economic thinking called "rational expectations." According to this theory, firms, investors, and other private economic actors rationally anticipate what government plans to do and then act in ways that offset what the government subsequently does.[28] For example, if the government plans to run a budget deficit in order to stimulate the economy, rational investors anticipate inflation and, to protect their investments, demand a higher interest rate on government bonds and other investments. But higher interest rates dampen economic growth, which offsets the intended stimulus effect of the budget deficit. In other words, government objectives are undermined by investors in the bond market.

Of course, people are not perfectly informed and even professional economic forecasters cannot predict economic developments very well, but rational-expectations arguments are sensible enough to raise doubts about the ability of government to manage the economy, especially when government plans become widely known during the lengthy public process of setting fiscal policy. By the beginning of the twenty-first century, governments appeared especially sluggish at a time when the communications revolution was making it possible for investors to react very quickly to changes in government policy.

Monetary Policy: The Federal Reserve System

monetary policy
The actions taken by government to vary the supply of money in an effort to stabilize the business cycle.

Although fiscal policy was once a significant method of regulating the economy, today **monetary policy**, varying the supply of money to stabilize the business cycle, is the government's most important tool in this regard. When the supply of money is increased, it becomes cheaper for private citizens and investors to borrow and spend more of it (interest rates—the cost of borrowing money—go down). This increase in borrowing and spending in turn leads to economic growth and lower unemployment. If the supply of money increases too fast, however, inflation may result. Conversely, when the supply of money goes down, it becomes more costly to borrow and spend (interest rates go up). With less to spend and invest, the economy slows and inflationary pressures ease. If the economy contracts too rapidly, of course, unemployment may increase.

Federal Reserve Board
The governing board of the country's central bank, which executes monetary policy by manipulating the supply of funds that member banks can lend.

Many economists believe that monetary policy is an effective tool for managing the economy because, unlike fiscal policy, it can be altered quickly in response to changing economic circumstances. A rapid reaction is possible because decisions affecting the money supply are made not by Congress or even by the president, but by the **Federal Reserve Board**, a government authority that manages U.S. monetary policy through the Federal Research System. Created in 1913, the Federal Reserve System (commonly known as the Fed) is headed by a board consisting of seven governors appointed by the president and confirmed by the Senate, each Fed governor holding office for 14 years. The Fed acts on the economy through the operations of its 12 regional banks, each of which oversees member banks in its part of the country. Figure 19.5 illustrates the structure of the Fed and its relationship to the federal government.

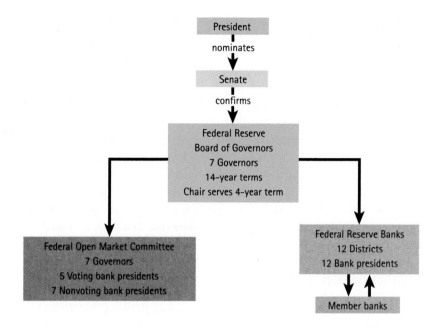

FIGURE 19.5

The Structure of the
Federal Reserve System
• Do banks have too much say?

The most important decisions affecting the day-to-day workings of the economy are made by the Fed's Open Market Committee. This committee considers whether interest rates are too high or too low and what adjustments it should make. The committee consists of the 7 governors, all of whom vote, and the 12 regional bank presidents, only 5 of whom have a vote (the New York bank president always has a vote; the remaining 4 votes rotate among the other 11 banks). The Open Market Committee has three primary tools with which to affect the supply of money: it may buy and sell federal securities (treasury bills, notes, and bonds); it may change the interest rate it charges other banks; and it may change the percentage of deposits that banks are required to hold in reserve. In practice, the Fed usually makes policy through the first two methods.

Often the Fed is said to be the most powerful agency in the government after the Executive Office of the President. Its decisions affect interest rates, employment levels, and economic growth rates. The great American humorist Will Rogers once remarked that "two things can disrupt business in this country. One is a war and the other is a meeting of the Federal Reserve Board."[29] Surprisingly (given its importance), the Fed's activities are relatively unknown to many Americans.

The Fed Chair

If the Fed is the second most powerful agency in Washington, the chair of the Federal Reserve Board, currently Benjamin Bernanke (an economist and former chair of President Bush's Council of Economic Advisers), ranks among the most powerful persons in government. The chair's great power derives from close ties to the president, direct access to up-to-date economic information supplied by the Fed staff, and the power to approve the appointment of the 12 presidents of the Federal Reserve Banks (upon the recommendation of the member banks in each region). In addition, the chair inherits a job held in the past by powerful, prestigious people. Martin Eccles, head of the Fed during the 1930s, is acclaimed for taking actions to get the country out of the Great

Benjamin Bernanke, Chairman of the Fed

Ben S. Bernanke, chairman of the Fed, testifies on the state of the U.S. economy.

• *Why is congressional influence over the Fed less than its influence over other agencies?*

Depression, Paul Volcker is remembered for bringing the double-digit inflation of the late 1970s to an end, and Alan Greenspan added to this tradition by managing the sustained economic growth of the 1990s. Greenspan also received plaudits for swiftly slashing interest rates less than a week after the September 11 terrorist attacks to shore up confidence in the financial system.

The Fed chair's influence is so great that those involved in financial markets pay close attention to every word he says, seeking any hint of whether the Federal Reserve might raise or lower interest rates. Current Fed chair Benjamin Bernanke was reminded of this fact when, in 2006, a reporter to whom he had spoken at a private gathering said on CNBC that Bernanke thought interest rates were too low. After he made these comments, financial experts became concerned that the new Fed chair might not appreciate the effect that even his casual musings could have on the financial system. The stock market plunged on the news, and Bernanke later said his remarks to the reporter were "a lapse in judgment on my part."[30]

Who Controls the Fed?

Surprisingly, in an elections-dominated political system, this key government agency is relatively insulated from electoral pressures. The Fed's power, independence, and objectivity are symbolized by its Washington home, a magnificent quasi-palace fronted by a remote—almost forbidding—facade and located two miles from Capitol Hill, adjacent to the National Academy of Sciences. Of course, the Fed is not immune to political pressure, but it is more insulated than most government agencies.

Congressional Influence   Like all other government agencies, the Fed was created and its powers were defined by congressional statutes. Nominees to the Federal Reserve Board must be approved by the Senate, and the Fed must make quarterly reports to the banking committees of the House and Senate.

Despite these legal obligations to Congress, the Fed is remarkably free of congressional influence. For one thing, the Fed's budget is not congressionally determined. Instead, the Fed raises its own revenue by creating money (almost literally) and using this money to buy U.S. Treasury bonds, from which it earns interest. Creating money and buying Treasury bonds are a necessary part of the Fed's job—they are among the ways the Fed puts money into and takes money out of the economy. But Fed investments have a side benefit for the agency. Every year Fed investments earn billions of dollars (about $29 billion in 2005).[31] Most of this money is turned over to the federal treasury, but the Fed keeps about a tenth for its own operations.[32] As a result, the Fed does not need to ask Congress for an appropriation in the way most agencies must. The Fed owns squash courts in its building near the Washington Monument and bowling alleys on Wall Street, the most expensive real estate in the world—a reflection of the fact that it can almost literally manufacture its own money.

The Fed is also relatively free of congressionally determined salary schedules and personnel controls. Consequently, it is able to hire a better-trained, more professional, more prestigious staff than are other government agencies. In fact, the Fed is the one agency of the United States government that has a civil service that resembles the type found in Europe and Japan (see *International Comparison*, Chapter 14). Instead of political appointees who rotate in and out of office, the Fed staff consists of expert, career appointees.

In general, congressional influence on the Fed is exerted indirectly. Congress "jawbones" the Fed when it feels that monetary policy is not appropriate for prevailing conditions. Individual members make critical speeches and committees hold hearings at which the Fed chair is asked to testify. In these ways, some members make known their belief that monetary policy is too restrictive, and others announce their conviction that monetary policy is too loose. In these pronouncements there is an implied warning that if the Fed is not responsive, more serious attempts to influence it may be forthcoming. But members of Congress usually cannot agree on any specific course of action.

Although observers usually agree that Congress does not exert significant control over the Fed, there is less consensus on the influence of other groups and institutions. Three distinct interpretations of the source of influence over Fed operations have been offered: banker dominance, presidential control, and Fed independence.

Banker Dominance   The first interpretation, held by many liberal critics of the Fed, is that the banks control the Fed.[33] Just as interest groups underpin other iron triangles (see Chapter 14), so the banking industry, which has a huge stake in Fed decisions, forms the primary base of support for the Fed. Bankers influence the appointment of the Board of Governors, and they nominate the Federal Reserve Bank presidents, who cast five votes on the Open Market Committee.

As evidence of banker dominance, proponents point to the apparent policy bias of the Fed, which is generally viewed as being less concerned about reducing unemployment than about lowering inflation rates. To put it another way, the Fed seems to be more worried about avoiding rising prices than about staving off recessions. The Fed "can't stand prosperity." When jobs are plentiful and people are spending freely, the Fed typically responds by raising interest rates and slowing down the economy: "Just when the party gets going, the Fed takes away the beer."[34]

The Fed defends itself against such accusations of policy bias by saying that unless inflation is checked quickly, much stronger action will eventually have to be taken, creating more hardship in the long run. The Fed offers as evidence its policy in the late 1970s, when it mistakenly let inflation get out of control. Only after the deep and painful recession of 1981–1982 did it bring inflation and interest rates down to acceptable levels.

Presidential Dominance   A second interpretation emphasizes not the bankers, but the president, as the main source of influence on the Fed. And, indeed, most observers believe that the president, who appoints its members and chairs, has a great deal more influence than Congress.[35] But how much influence do presidents have, and to what ends do they use it?

Some political scientists suggest that presidents try to manipulate Fed policy for their own political purposes. These scholars note that the chair of the Federal Reserve Board, in order to win reappointment, must be sensitive to signals from the White House. Even more important, the Fed's very desire to appear nonpolitical creates a dependence on the president. If the president publicly criticizes the Fed, it becomes the subject matter of news commentaries and talk shows because the Fed's actions have become matters of partisan controversy. The best way for the Fed to appear independent is for its chair to listen carefully to suggestions coming from presidents and their advisers and to avoid acting in such a way as to provoke controversy.

partisan interpretation

The argument that Democratic administrations set economic policy to benefit lower-income, wage-earning groups and that Republican administrations set economic policy to benefit higher-income, business, and professional groups.

There are two versions of the presidential-control interpretation—the partisan and the election-cycle interpretations.[36] The **partisan interpretation** distinguishes between the constituencies of Republican and Democratic presidents.[37] The Republican constituency includes more upper-income business and professional people, who traditionally are less worried about unemployment (which strikes them less frequently) than about inflation. The Democratic constituency includes more lower-income, blue-collar workers, who traditionally are more concerned about rising unemployment (which hits them hardest normally). Indeed, studies show that inflation rates tend to rise under Democratic presidents and fall under Republican presidents, and that stocks and bonds earn higher returns under Republican administrations.[38]

But there are reasons to doubt the more extreme version of the partisan interpretation. Most citizens, regardless of income, occupation, or partisan affiliation, dislike both rising unemployment and rising prices; they do not want to lose their jobs, but neither do they want to see the purchasing power of their wages eroded by inflation. Similarly, investors dislike inflation, but if growth slows and unemployment rises, their investments will earn lower returns. Thus, whatever their party, presidents are better off striking a balance between the two goals rather than focusing on either one and neglecting the other. Nevertheless, Democrats and Republicans strike different balances, reflecting their different constituencies. Republican administrations seem more willing to accept a little more unemployment in order to avoid inflation. Democrats strike the opposite balance. They appear more likely to accept somewhat higher inflation in order to avoid unemployment. To keep from provoking presidents, the Fed probably tends to slant its decisions in the direction of these well-known partisan preferences. But the effect is too small to call it presidential control.

election-cycle interpretation

The argument that, whatever their party, presidents attempt to slow the economy early in their terms and then to expand it as their opportunity for reelection approaches.

The second version of the presidential dominance view, the **election-cycle interpretation**, says that presidents deliberately manipulate the economy to engineer their reelection. They tolerate slow growth, even a recession, early in their term of office so they can step on the gas and "rev up" the economic engine when the election payoff is greatest.

Richard Nixon's first term is a clear example of presidential manipulation. The Nixon administration pulled out all the stops and achieved a huge increase in household income during the election year 1972.[39] Nixon was reelected overwhelmingly.

If Nixon's first term fit the election-cycle interpretation, George H.W. Bush's single term directly contradicts it. The first President Bush also seems to have done things exactly backward. In the beginning of his term the country enjoyed steady growth, but later the economy reversed, and Bush's fortunes shifted with it. Bush's timing could not have been worse. Bush's son, George W. Bush, appears to fall somewhere in between. The slowdown of 2001 occurred very early in the younger Bush's presidency, allowing plenty of time for recovery in advance of the 2004 elections. However, the effects of the economic slowdown were still evident in 2004, giving Bush's advisers cause to worry. According to one pollster, "The economy and jobs are the number one issue, in my polling and everyone else's polling that I have seen."[40]

Not surprisingly, Bush won 80 percent of the votes of those who said their economic situation had improved over the previous four years, and his opponent, John Kerry, won nearly 80 percent of the votes of those who said their situation had worsened. Bush's win might be attributed to the fact that slightly more Americans felt they had done well than felt they had done poorly.[41] Of course, voters also had many other issues to consider when making their decisions, not least of which were Iraq and the war on terrorism.

Combining information for all years since World War II yields some evidence, but not a lot, that presidents manipulate the economy to their political advantage. In years when presidents themselves are running for reelection, growth rates are, on average, somewhat higher, but not a lot higher, than in other years.[42]

An Independent Fed   Fed supporters say the agency is independent of both politics and external pressure groups.[43] The independence of the Fed is guaranteed by the fact that board members are appointed for 14-year terms. They can be removed only through the impeachment process. Because board members serve such long terms, presidents may not be able to appoint a majority of the board until they themselves have been in office six years. And because the chair of the Fed serves a four-year term, in the worst case a president may not be able to appoint a new chair until the fourth year of an administration.

There are other reasons for the Fed's independence. Business confidence in government economic policy is strengthened by the belief that Fed decisions are above politics. The board acts on the advice of a strong, independent staff. The chair is usually more knowledgeable about economic policy than any other presidential appointee. Monetary policy is too arcane to engage the general public; consequently, Fed-bashing is not a very effective campaign tactic.

Further, those who say the Fed is independent usually believe this is a good idea. They say that an independent Fed has improved the management of the economy. In particular, they emphasize that the country has had fewer and shorter recessions since the Fed was established than it had earlier in its history.

Perhaps it is impossible to conclude that anyone tightly controls the Fed. The Fed operates with a considerable amount of independence, mainly because it tries to achieve not only what presidents want but also what nearly everyone desires: steady, stable economic growth. Presidents need good economic news their first year, because that is when they are getting their political agenda off the ground. They need good economic news their second year to help the congressional candidates of their party. It is dangerous for a president to encourage a recession in the third year because it could spill over into the election campaign and, of course, no president wants a recession in the election year.

The Fed's emphasis on steady, moderate growth is pretty much what the president wants, so the president can usually leave the Fed alone. A case in point is the relationship President Clinton had with Fed chair Alan Greenspan. Ronald Reagan first appointed Greenspan as Fed chair, and Clinton sought to reassure financial markets in the election year of 1996 by renominating him.[44] Because both Greenspan and Clinton were interested in stable growth, each felt it was in his interest to leave the other alone. Perhaps the Fed is an example of the proposition that good public policy in a democracy is not necessarily produced by the most democratic processes.

The "T" Word: Taxes

Hardly anyone likes to pay taxes. As Figure 19.6 shows, most people think that their tax bill is too high. As a result, tax policy is a major topic of public concern, and various aspects of the American tax system are subject to heated debate.[45] In this section

FIGURE 19.6

Public Opinion About Taxes

• *Do you think taxes are too low or too high? Why?*

Source: National Opinion Research Center, *General Social Survey;* 2003 and 2004 figures from identical question asked by Gallup, April 6–8, 2001, question ID USGALLUP.01APL06, R21.

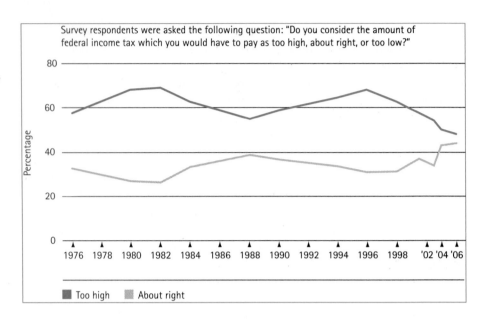

Survey respondents were asked the following question: "Do you consider the amount of federal income tax which you would have to pay as too high, about right, or too low?"

■ Too high   ■ About right

we discuss the three most important issues in this debate: the tax burden, the breadth of the tax base, and the progressivity of the tax structure.

The Tax Burden

tax burden

The total amount of tax that a household pays.

Protesting the Tax Burden

• *Why are antitax sentiments widespread in the United States, despite the fact that the country's taxes are lower than in many comparable nations?*

In considering changes in tax policy, officials must take into account the **tax burden**— the total level at which Americans are taxed. Federal individual income tax receipts, as a percentage of the nation's GDP, rose by more than 60 percent between 1950 and 1970.[46] Although they stabilized after 1970, the steep increase in the earlier period put the tax burden issue high on the country's political agenda. Some advocates of higher government spending argue that Americans have become selfish over the course of the past generation and are increasingly unwilling to tax themselves for good purposes. Others, writing in defense of taxpayers, point to the stagnation of personal incomes that began in the early 1970s. As long as standards of living were rising, people were willing to absorb higher taxes, but once living standards stagnated, frustrated citizens increasingly vented their unhappiness on the tax system. At any rate, many Americans came to feel that the tax burden was too high, and elected officials responded—from Reagan's tax cuts to President George H. W. Bush's 1988 campaign pledge of "no new taxes" to George W. Bush's two successful tax cut proposals.

The budget surpluses that emerged in the late 1990s encouraged politicians to propose tax reductions. Almost immediately after taking office, George W. Bush guided the most extensive tax reduction in several decades through both houses of Congress. The bill, which included the one-time refund provision discussed at the beginning of the chapter, also cut tax rates gradually from 2002 to 2010, at an overall cost of nearly $1.4 trillion. Critics charged the president with "accounting gimmickry" and with allowing the cost of the tax cut to fall on future generations of Americans. "Our kids and grandkids are the real losers . . . ," said one member of Congress; "they will have to dig out of the hole that this tax bill causes."[47] But others saw the bill as a reasonable use of the budget surplus and as fulfilling Bush's promise to give the excess money "back to the people who earned it, the taxpayers."[48] Republicans praised Bush for making tax cuts central to his campaign and his presidency.

In 2003 Bush again proposed tax cuts, this time arguing for an elimination of the tax on stock dividends. The president claimed the measure would increase investment and would make the tax structure fairer, because taxing corporate profits as well as the dividends companies paid to shareholders constituted a type of "double taxation." Although the president did not get everything he wanted, Congress did pass a significant reduction in the dividend tax as part of a 10-year, $350 billion tax cut package.

In 2004 Democratic presidential candidate John Kerry responded to the Bush tax cuts by arguing that Bush had done too little to shift the tax burden off of average Americans. As part of what he called a focus on "middle class families who are working hard to cover the mortgage, pay the high cost of health care, child care and tuition, or just trying to get ahead," Kerry proposed new tax breaks for health care expenses and college tuition costs.[49]

The Tax Base

Even though the tax burden is the most frequently discussed tax-related topic, it is not necessarily the most important. At least as critical is the breadth of the **tax base**: the income, property, wealth, or economic activity that is taxed. Many economists argue that taxes are less intrusive if they are broad-based—that is, imposed on all economic activity at the same rate. Thus, the amount you pay in taxes should depend only on the amount you make, not on how you make it. Whether you make your money growing crops, making movies, writing wills, or running a charity should not matter. Nor should the amount you pay in taxes depend on whether you spend money on groceries, cars, beer, or medical insurance. If everything is taxed alike, then tax policy will not distort the economy. That is, it will not influence the choices people make.

Broad-based taxes are more easily recommended than enacted into law, however. Frequently, good reasons can be given for not taxing some particular activity, and there are numerous organized groups that offer good (and often not-so-good) reasons to persuade elected officials to give favorable treatment to the activities of their members. In response to these pressures, national and state legislators have enacted thousands of **tax preferences** that exempt particular types of economic activity from taxation. Critics say these tax preferences distort economic activity and cost the government billions of dollars in forgone revenues. Here are some major examples of tax preferences and the economic distortions that critics say they foster:

- *Tax credits for college tuition* ($10.7 billion).[50] In 1997 Congress allowed a tax credit for college tuition, a tax break popular with college students. Critics say colleges, realizing that students have more tuition dollars, will simply boost tuition.
- *Deductions for mortgage interest on owner-occupied homes* ($62.2 billion). Developers and brokers claim that this tax preference encourages home ownership, which is said to be good for families and to boost community stability. Critics say the preference primarily benefits higher-income people who can afford huge mortgages and subsidizes their over-investment in big houses and vacation homes.
- *Deductions for charitable contributions* ($36.4 billion). Defenders of this tax preference claim that it encourages public support for the arts, education, and the needy. But critics say many charities are actually businesses that provide services to those who "give" them money.

tax base
Types of activities, types of property, or kinds of investments that are subject to taxation.

tax preferences
Special tax treatment received by certain activities, property, or investments.

Farm Subsidies
and Domestic Policy

Tax preferences are the classic "slippery slope." Once government grants them to any group, it abandons the principle of neutral taxation and encourages other groups to lobby for their own preferences. Tax preferences distort the economy by encouraging people to make economic decisions on the basis of tax considerations. Moreover, granting preferences to some activities requires that taxes be higher on other activities that lack defenders strong enough to get their own tax break. Some economists argue that the only solution to this dilemma is somehow to restrict the government's ability to grant tax breaks to any activity or group.[51] Yet it is unlikely that all tax preferences will be eliminated. Some activities—home ownership, education, charities—are so popular that most people think they should get a tax break.

Not all special treatment is favorable. The government also sometimes imposes **sin taxes**, taxes intended to discourage unwanted behavior. The most prominent examples of sin taxes are the taxes on the consumption of cigarettes and alcohol. Critics of such measures argue that they fall primarily on the poorest segments of the population and fail to have a significant impact on the consumption of addictive products.

Tax Progressivity

If some economists think the breadth of the tax base is the most important tax issue, others think tax progressivity is. Taxes are said to be **progressive taxes** if people with higher income pay a higher tax rate. The most important progressive tax is the federal income tax. In 2005, individual taxable incomes up to $7,300 were taxed at a 10 percent rate, while additional income between $7,300 and $29,700 was taxed at a 15 percent rate. For example, if your annual income was $20,000, you paid 10 percent, or $730, in taxes on the first $7,300, and then 15 percent, or $1,905 on the remaining $13,000. Tax rates on additional income (called "marginal rates") increased up to a maximum rate of 35 percent for income more than about $326,000.

Taxes that require low-income people to pay a higher rate are called **regressive taxes**. The payroll or social security tax is a regressive tax, because as of 2006 it was levied only on the first $94,200 that a person earns. Because all earnings in excess of that figure are exempt from the tax, higher-income people pay a smaller share of their income for social security than do lower-income people.

For example, if you made $40,000 per year, you would pay 6.2 percent of your income, or $2,480, in social security taxes. If you made $1 million, you would pay 6.2 percent in taxes on the first $94,200 you made, or $5,840. In the second case, the amount paid is larger, but note that it makes up only half a percent of total income, whereas in the first case, 6.2 percent of total income goes for the tax.

Numerous taxes are levied in the United States. The federal personal income tax and some state personal income taxes are progressive. Social security and state sales taxes are regressive. Property taxes vary a great deal, but generally fall in between. When all taxes levied by federal, state, and local governments are taken into account, it is difficult to say whether the tax structure in the United States is progressive or not.[52]

Progressive taxes traditionally have been defended by liberals, who claim that progressive rates reduce income inequality in the society. Thus, Bill Clinton and congressional Democrats pushed through an increase in the taxes paid by high-income

sin tax
A tax intended to discourage unwanted behavior.

progressive tax
A tax structured so that higher-income people pay a larger proportion of their income in taxes than do lower-income people.

regressive tax
A tax structured so that higher-income people pay a smaller proportion of their income in taxes than do lower-income people.

taxpayers over united Republican opposition in 1993. Progressive taxes traditionally have been opposed by conservatives, who claim that progressive rates discourage investment and hard work by the most productive members of society. Thus, the Bush tax cut of 2001 made the tax system less progressive because the largest cuts in tax rates went to those with the highest incomes. In 2004 and 2006, Democrats argued that the tax system ought to be made more progressive again, and that Republican tax policy "mostly benefits the wealthy and Wall Street"; Republicans countered that most Americans had benefited from the tax cuts.[53] Evidence from public opinion surveys seems to show that Americans are sensitive to their own individual tax burdens, but place less weight on the overall progressivity of the tax system when deciding on how to vote.[54]

You Are Trying
to Get a Tax Cut

Tax Reform

Debates over tax reform traditionally focus on the breadth and progressivity of the tax system. In 1986 Congress passed a widely acclaimed reform that lowered individual income tax rates, raised corporate rates, and broadened the tax base by eliminating many tax preferences. The federal income tax burden for a typical family of four dropped from 10.5 to 8.9 percent of total income without reducing government revenue.[55]

In recent years, many members of Congress have proposed even more sweeping tax reforms. The best known is the **flat tax**, a proposal that would eliminate progressive income tax rates and would tax all income groups above a certain minimum at the same rate.[56] Advocates argue that it is unfair to require some people to pay a higher percentage of their income in taxes than others. Supporters of a flat tax also defend it on the grounds of efficiency—the more progressive taxes are, the greater the incentive for the wealthy to hire accountants, lawyers, and lobbyists to help them avoid taxes. Indeed, the wealthy are not the only ones who pay: As of 2003, 59 percent of Americans used professional tax preparers,[57] and taxpayers spent more than $240 billion a year on record keeping, filling out forms, complying with audits, and paying for accountants and lawyers.[58]

flat tax
A tax that is neither progressive nor regressive; everyone pays at the same rate.

The debate over tax reform is likely to remain fractious and many-sided because people want to use the tax system to achieve different—often conflicting—goals. They want to raise revenue, to reduce income inequality, to discourage some kinds of behavior, and to give breaks so as to promote other kinds of activity, such as education and home ownership.

The U.S. Economy: An International Comparison

Even though we have focused on government and the economy, the truth is that the extent to which the economy can be controlled by government is limited—and has become much more so in recent years. When the Fed loosens or tightens the money supply, it is reacting to national and global economic forces that may overcome its best efforts. Indeed, all over the world, countries with very different political systems are struggling to meet economic challenges similar to those in the United States. Relative to other advanced democracies, the United States is dealing reasonably well with its economic challenges and difficulties. In this section we shall place U.S. taxes, national debt, and employment opportunities in comparative perspective.

FIGURE 19.7

U.S. Tax Burden Is Less Than That in Many Other Democracies

• *Why are U.S. taxes lower than taxes in other countries?*

Source: U.S. Bureau of the Census, *Statistical Abstract of the United States, 2006,* Table 1335.

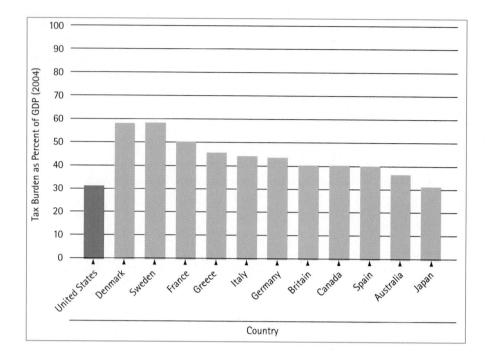

Comparing Economic Policy

Taxes

The tax burden in the United States compares very favorably with that in the world's other developed countries. As of 2004, the tax burden in the United States was among the lowest of 13 major industrialized countries: about 32 percent of GDP. At the other extreme, the public sector in Denmark taxes away more than 58 percent of the country's GDP. Taxes in Sweden, France, Greece, and Italy all exceed 45 percent of GDP (see Figure 19.7).

To be sure, other countries provide more services in exchange for the money they extract in taxes. The most important example is health care; about half of it is paid for by the private sector in the United States, whereas it is almost entirely government-provided in other countries.

If their tax rates and the overall tax burden are the lowest in the developed world and are continuing to fall, why have Americans traditionally been so unhappy with taxes, and why did George W. Bush win so much praise for lowering taxes further in 2001 and 2003?

We doubt that there is any single explanation for the American aversion to taxes. Part of the answer may lie in the nature of the American tax system. The United States relies more heavily than most other countries on income and payroll taxes to raise revenues; nearly two-thirds of total tax revenues come from such sources, a figure exceeded only by Switzerland and Belgium. Other countries rely more heavily on consumption taxes, such as a sales tax known as the value-added tax (VAT), which is hidden in the prices of goods and services. Thus, their voters may not realize the full tax cost of the services they receive, despite the fact that the VAT affects low-income families the most. Ironically, Sweden, Germany, and Italy—with their large welfare states—rely heavily on the VAT, a tax that American liberals view as regressive. Only Japan, with its minimal provision of social services, relies less on sales taxes than the United States.

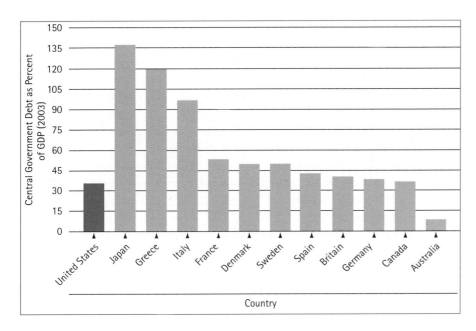

FIGURE 19.8

U.S. Debt Is Smaller Than the Debt of Other Countries

• *Are budget deficits and the national debt important problems in the U.S.? Why or why not?*

Source: *Central Government Debt: Statistical Yearbook 1994–2003, 2005 Edition*, Paris, France: Organisation for Economic Cooperation and Development, 2005.

U.S. historical experience is probably more important for explaining the views of Americans than the type of tax levied, however. In Chapter 4 we saw that, more than the citizens in other countries, Americans are economic individualists who wish to keep the role of government limited. They expect less from government, and they wish to keep more of their money for their own use.

National Debt

Eight and one-half trillion dollars, the size of the national debt in 2006, is an almost unimaginable number. But such numbers are meaningful only relative to baselines, and the natural baseline—the size of the American economy—was more than $12 trillion. Relative to the size of the economy, the public debt in the United States is moderate. For example, as a proportion of GDP, France, Germany, and Canada all have larger national debts than the United States—and Japan and Italy have debts that are more than twice as large (see Figure 19.8).

Certainly, this is not to say that historical and continuing concern about the debt was and is unwarranted. That so much debt has accumulated is worrisome, but the debt in other democracies has increased more rapidly than in the U.S. For example, between 1990 and 2003, the total U.S. debt declined as a percentage of GDP, while France's debt increased by about 32 percent.[59]

Immigration

Employment Opportunities

The United States has done a better job than most countries of incorporating new workers into the economy. In 2005, for example, the unemployment rate in Germany and France was between 9 and 10 percent—significantly higher than the 5.1 percent rate in the United States.

The situation in 2005 is the result of changes that date back to the 1980s. At that time, the workforce in the Western world expanded rapidly as the baby boom generation reached working age and as women moved into the workforce in greater numbers. The American economy absorbed these new workers far more successfully than did European economies, creating three times more new jobs per 1,000 people than did France and Germany. Moreover, European countries were able to keep their unemployment rates as low as they did only by introducing policies that would be unacceptable in the United States. For example, policies in Germany and Switzerland induced so-called guest workers to return to their countries of origin. The United States, in contrast, allowed immigration to increase during the 1980s. Some countries absorbed new workers by expanding their public sectors. Sweden, for example, dealt with the surge of women into the labor force by doubling public-sector employment.[61] In the United States, public-sector employment grew very slowly.

Some critics object that many of the jobs that have been created in the United States are low-skill, low-paying "McJobs," and that many good jobs have been exported abroad by U.S. companies, but the evidence suggests that such claims are at least somewhat exaggerated. According to several studies, much of the job growth in recent years has been in higher-paying occupations and industries—again, a performance far superior to Western European democracies.[62]

Compared to most other countries, the American economy is less restricted by government policies and regulations. This lack of restriction gives it a greater capacity to adapt to changing economic conditions. For example, changes in the world economy have had an adverse effect on workers in the manufacturing sector. In 1950 these industries accounted for 34 percent of U.S. jobs, and by 2004 this figure had shrunk to 12 percent.[63] Amazingly, the United States produces no more steel today than it did in the early 1960s.[64]

But these adverse consequences have been offset by gains in the service, communications, and technology industries. In the late 1990s, the U.S. information technology sector grew at stunning rates, and officials estimated that employment in such occupations as software engineers, network analysts, and database administrators would increase by at least 40 percent between 2002 and 2012.[65] The United States is better equipped than most of its European peers to handle this rapid transition to a high-technology economy. For example, the proportion of people with access to the Internet is about 50 percent higher in the United States than in the European Union.[66]

Inequality

The price of limited government seems to be greater social inequality. Compared to other advanced democracies, income inequality in the United States is higher (see Figure 19.9). Moreover, after declining between 1930 and 1970, inequality rose until, by 2001, it was higher than at any time since the 1930s.[67] Some social critics see in such trends a "class war" of the rich against the poor,[68] but there seems to be no great popular demand for government to intervene directly to reverse the trend toward inequality. Candidates who advocate a greater role for government and a greater degree of income redistribution regularly run for office, but the American people have usually not elected them. Nor have they demanded such policies from their representatives in Congress and the state legislatures.

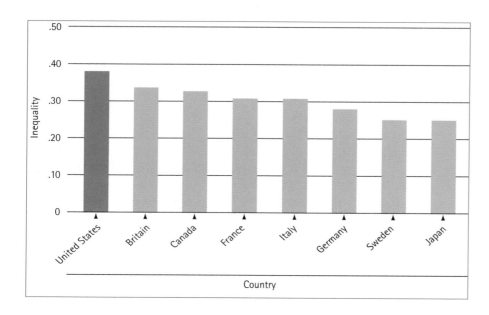

FIGURE 19.9

Income Inequality Greater in United States Than in Many Other Countries

• *Why is inequality greater in a wealthy country such as the United States?*

Note: The bars represent the value of the Gini index for each country. A Gini index value of zero represents complete equality; a value of 1 represents complete inequality.

Source: *World Development Report 2006: Equity and Development* (Washington, DC: World Bank, 2005), Table A2, 279–280.

Chapter Summary

People care a lot about whether they can find a job and what they have to pay for the things they buy. When times are bad, the president takes the blame. When times are good, the president usually—but not always—gets the credit. Presidents' popular standing and their odds of reelection are significantly influenced by national economic conditions. To a somewhat lesser extent, these also have an effect on members of Congress and even on state-level elected officials.

Given these political facts of life, presidents assign economic policy top priority. To achieve this objective, they grant the agency responsible for monetary policy, the Federal Reserve, a good deal of independence. Although they may try to shape policy on occasion, presidents generally realize that the Fed needs independence to do its job well. And when the Fed does a good job by keeping economic growth steady, the president usually gets the credit.

For half a century, presidents tried to use fiscal policy—the management of budget deficits and surpluses—to manage the economy. But the importance of fiscal policy for managing the economy has been reduced by a combination of factors, including divided government, declining faith in Keynesian theory, a rising public debt, and the globalization of economic activity.

Debates over tax reform typically involve discussion of the tax burden, whether tax preferences should be eliminated in order to broaden the tax base, and whether the progressivity of the tax system needs to be raised or lowered. Although the two parties fought for much of the 1980s and 1990s over whether to increase taxes to eliminate the deficit, in 2001 and 2003 President Bush pushed major tax cuts through Congress, arguing that the cuts would stimulate economic growth and propel the nation out of an economic slowdown.

The United States has a lower tax burden, a smaller national debt, and lower unemployment rates than many other countries have. But Americans also seem more willing to tolerate economic inequality than people in other nations are.

Key Terms

budget, p. 554

business cycle, p. 551

Council of Economic Advisers (CEA), p. 555

debt, p. 556

deficit, p. 553

election-cycle interpretation, p. 562

Federal Reserve Board, p. 558

fiscal policy, p. 553

flat tax, p. 567

gross domestic product (GDP), p. 551

inflation, p. 551

Suggested Readings

Of General Interest

Krugman, Paul. *Peddling Prosperity*. New York: Norton, 1994. Written for the noneconomist, this critique of many of those who have influenced economic policy provides a comprehensible discussion of schools of economic thought and an overview of economic trends of the past several decades.

Stiglitz, Joseph. *The Roaring Nineties: A New History of the World's Most Prosperous Decade*. New York: W. W. Norton & Co., 2003. A Nobel Prize-winning economist critiques recent U.S. economic policy.

Weir, Margaret. *Politics and Jobs: The Boundaries of Employment Policies in the United States*. Princeton, NJ: Princeton University Press, 1992. Broad historical and political analysis of government efforts to guarantee full employment.

Woodward, Bob. *Maestro: Greenspan's Fed and the American Boom*. New York: Simon & Schuster, 2000. A diverting account of how Fed Chair Alan Greenspan managed monetary policy in the 1990s.

Yergin, Daniel, and Joseph Stanislaw. *The Commanding Heights: The Battle Between Government and the Marketplace That is Remaking the Modern World, Revised and Updated Edition*. New York: Free Press, 2002. A Pulitzer Prize-winning writer and a business consultant examine the implications of globalization for the United States and other nations.

Focused Studies

Birnbaum, Jeffrey H., and Alan S. Murray. *Showdown at Gucci Gulch*. New York: Random House, 1987. Fast-paced case study of the passage of the 1986 tax reforms.

Hibbs, Douglas A., Jr. *The American Political Economy*. Cambridge, MA: Harvard University Press, 1987. Provides detailed statistical evaluations of partisan and election-cycle interpretations of presidential management of the economy.

Kettl, Donald. *Deficit Politics, Second Edition*. New York: Longman, 2002. Short, readable book on budget deficits.

Weaver, R. Kent. *Automatic Government: The Politics of Indexation*. Washington, DC: The Brookings Institution, 1988. Explains how government benefits came to be indexed.

On the Web

www.federalreserve.gov

Some claim that the Federal Reserve holds power second only to the president of the United States. The Federal Reserve System maintains an informative Web site, complete with publications, congressional testimony, and economic data.

www.commerce.gov

The Department of Commerce houses the Economics and Statistics Administration and the Bureau of Economic Analysis, which provide regular data and analysis on the U.S. economy.

www.nber.org

The National Bureau of Economic Research is considered the unofficial arbiter of many economic issues, such as when recessions begin and end. It publishes an excellent series of working papers by eminent economists.

www.publicdebt.treas.gov

Debate over the budget deficit defined economic policy debates in the 1970s and 1980s and continues to affect discussions of new taxing and spending. The Bureau of the Public Debt, located in the Department of the Treasury, provides precise daily updates of how much the government owes. While there, you may peruse information on how to buy federal securities, thus helping to finance the national debt.

www.ctj.org

www.taxfoundation.org

The contentious debates over taxation in Washington have been enough to inspire a number of interest groups to people the barricades on both sides. Citizens for Tax Justice (CTJ) argues for progressive taxation, whereas the Tax Foundation promotes the idea of a flat tax.

CHAPTER 20

✩ ✩ ✩ ✩ ✩ ✩ ✩ ✩ ✩ ✩

Foreign and Defense Policy

CHAPTER OUTLINE

The Resurgent Importance of Foreign Affairs

In 2000, the Council on Foreign Relations, a prestigious research and policy organization, decided to arrange a series of public debates between prominent government officials and experts on foreign policy topics. Timed to coincide with the presidential race that year between Vice President Al Gore and Texas governor George W. Bush, these forums were to be held on university campuses and were to draw attention to some of the most important issues that the United States would have to confront in its role as a world power over the coming four years.

But organizers quickly discovered that they faced an almost complete lack of interest on the part of the public. After decades of global competition with the monolithic communist Soviet Union, the United States was now enjoying what many voters saw as the fruits of victory. Since 1991, when the Soviet empire had finally collapsed, there had been few wars to speak of, little international conflict, and a booming economy. As one former policy-maker put it, "The American public is not engaged in foreign affairs because they say 'Look, we're secure.' They're not making . . . demands on either candidate to spell out details in foreign affairs."[1] Another expert put it more bluntly. Americans, he said, are "fat and happy."[2] "I've been here [in Washington] for six presidents," said Senator Joe Biden (D-DE), "and I can't think of a time when foreign and defense policy was less of an issue in a presidential campaign."[3] Bowing to this lack of interest, the Council on Foreign Relations cancelled most of its planned debates.

It may have seemed natural at the time, but the 2000 campaign's lack of attention to foreign policy is remark-able in light of the dramatic changes in U.S. foreign policy that were to occur over the next four years and beyond. In September 2001, the United States suffered the most devastating terrorist attack in its history. Within a month, U.S. forces began a retaliatory invasion of Afghanistan. In 2002, President Bush signed into law an act creating the Department of Homeland Security, the largest reorganization of government in nearly a half-century. That same year, the White House announced its strategy of preemption, a doctrine that advocates striking terrorists and hostile nations before they strike the U.S. "We recognize," wrote the president and his advisers, "that our best defense is a good offense."[4] Finally, in the first test of this doctrine, U.S. forces invaded Iraq in 2003, deposing the dictator Saddam Hussein.

The 2004 presidential campaign and the 2006 congressional races took place in an atmosphere that seemed worlds apart from the placid, inwardly focused environment of 2000. In 2004, even the televised "domestic policy" debate between President Bush and challenger John Kerry concerned issues of national security. In 2006, congressional candidates wrangled over whether to bring troops home from Iraq immediately, or to stay longer in an effort to quell the ongoing insurgency and help stabilize the nascent democracy there. Many experts argued that the Iraq War issue was a key reason for Democrats' congressional victories that year. The changes in foreign policy that two expert observers called a "revolution" had made foreign affairs central to elections once again.[5]

MAKING THE CONNECTION

Democracies are slow to respond to problems until they become full-blown crises, because the public pays little attention to these issues if outward appearances suggest no imminent danger. This is why between the early 1990s and 9/11, elected officials generally paid less attention to foreign affairs than they did thereafter. While presidents are uniquely positioned to make a difference in world politics, even they may not be able to mobilize public support for strong action until a foreign policy problem becomes urgent. Still, once major dangers appear, voters can make rapid adjustments in their priorities, and can rally behind presidents, generating momentum in favor of policy changes even if elections are years away. Presidents and members of Congress may be rewarded or punished in the long run for successes and failures in foreign affairs, and therefore officials pay close attention to what the public thinks. In this chapter, we explore how America conducts foreign policy and examine the connections between foreign policy and electoral politics. In doing so, we pay close attention to the transitions that the major foreign policy-making institutions have made in light of the campaign against terrorism and the Iraq War.

Elections, Presidents, and Foreign Policy

Foreign policy is the conduct of relations among nation-states. The most important foreign policy issues involve war and peace. Of all foreign policy objectives, the most critical is to prevent the country from being attacked or invaded by a foreign power. But foreign policy also involves economic trade among nations, as well as such mundane matters as issuing passports to citizens who wish to travel abroad.

foreign policy
Conduct of relations among nation-states.

Whereas many scholars see the domestic policy-making process as a complex, messy process with numerous groups and elected officials competing for attention (see Chapter 18), in the foreign policy arena, one person stands above all others: the president. In a classic essay, political scientist Aaron Wildavksy developed the **two-presidency theory**, which explains why presidents exercise greater power over foreign affairs than over domestic policy.[6] On domestic matters, presidents are usually subject to interest group politics and congressional checks. On foreign policy questions, however, presidents have a degree of autonomy that enables them to manage the external relations of the country in relative freedom from short-term interference. In this section we describe four reasons why foreign policy differs from domestic policy: (1) the need for fast action, (2) the voters' focus on presidents, (3) the limited role of interest groups, and (4) the comparatively minor role of Congress.

two-presidency theory
Theory that explains why presidents exercise greater power over foreign affairs than over domestic policy.

Need for Fast Action

On domestic issues, the president may negotiate with Congress over the course of several years, but foreign policy questions often require rapid, decisive action. As Alexander Hamilton observed, governments require a single executive leader in order to achieve "decision, activity, secrecy, and dispatch."[7] Or, in the words of nineteenth-century humorist Artemus Ward, "Thrice is he armed that has his quarrel just—And four times he who gets his fist in first."[8] Following this principle, President Bush sent marines to Haiti in 2004 to guard U.S. interests as the government of Haitian president Jean Bertrand Aristide crumbled. Secretary of State Colin Powell briefed Congress on the operation, but Bush did not seek lawmakers' approval for it.

Voters' Focus on Presidents

On key domestic issues, members of Congress know that voters hold them to account, but on foreign affairs, Wildavksy points out, voters "expect the president to act."[9] In the

Patriotic Fervor
Three spectators watch on a rooftop as an American flag is carried in the "Maine Heroes Parade," billed as the largest ever ticker-tape parade in Maine.

• *Why does the rally 'round the flag effect dissipate over time?*

"rally 'round the flag" effect
The tendency for the public to back presidents in moments of crisis.

SIMULATION

You Are President
John F. Kennedy

early days of a crisis, voters often ignore those who criticize presidential actions. After the 9/11 terrorist attacks, for example, President George W. Bush's popularity, which had been hovering around the 50 percent level, skyrocketed to above 90 percent.

The tendency among the public to back presidents in foreign crises, which is often called the **"rally 'round the flag" effect**, shows up in opinion polls in almost every instance in which the United States becomes involved in a foreign policy emergency.[10] Support for the president nearly always goes up in the first days of a conflict with another nation. Figure 20.1 shows the crises that presidents from Truman to Bush have faced and the changes in opinion polls that have occurred after those crises broke. Between 1950 and 2006, public support for presidents increased by an average of 7 percentage points in the month after a foreign policy crisis occurred.

Although voters support presidents initially, they nonetheless demand quick results. When Iranian radicals took dozens of American embassy workers hostage in 1979, President Jimmy Carter's approval rating initially rose by nearly 20 points. But as the Tehran hostage crisis dragged on—eventually lasting more than a year—Carter's support evaporated and he was defeated in the 1980 election.

The public seems especially ready to hold presidents accountable when war breaks out and American casualties mount. The public supported U.S. entry into both the Korean War and the Vietnam War. But when the conflicts dragged on, both Harry Truman, in the case of the Korean War, and Lyndon Johnson, in the case of Vietnam, lost so much public support that they announced they would not run for reelection. The opposition party won the next election in each instance.[11] More than two-thirds of the public approved of President George W. Bush's presidency during the initial phase of the Iraq War in 2003, but as casualties mounted and occupation forces failed to prevent repeated attacks by insurgents, the president's popularity suffered. By early 2006, Bush's approval rating had fallen to around 35 percent, and some Republican congressional candidates began distancing themselves from the president on the Iraq issue.[12]

Not only do voters demand quick results, but they also soon forget foreign policy victories. If the economy steadily improves, presidents receive credit for the progress year after year. But, unless a foreign policy accomplishment immediately precedes an

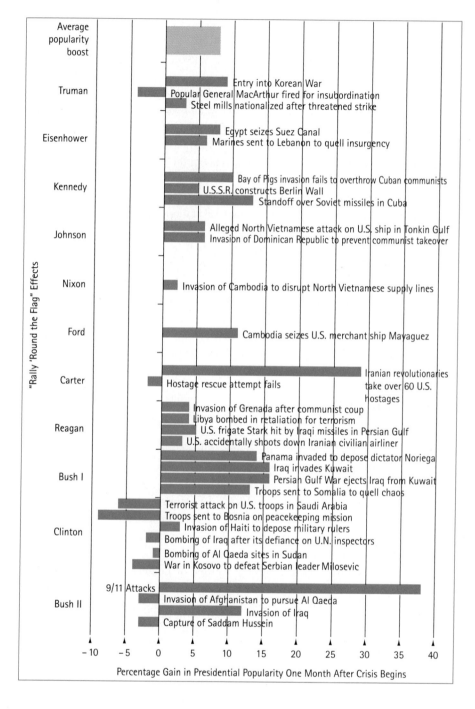

FIGURE 20.1

"Rally 'Round the Flag" Effect

Presidents' gains in popularity average 7 percentage points in the months following a crisis.

• *Why do you think President Clinton did not experience as large a boost in public support after foreign policy crises as his predecessors?*

election, there are few electoral dividends. Before too long, voters forget and turn to domestic concerns. For example, during the first three years of the George H. W. Bush presidency, the Soviet Union collapsed and the United States won the Persian Gulf War. Yet one year later, the voters, deciding that domestic issues were more important, voted Bush out of office.

As media coverage has become more intense and technologically more sophisticated, pressure on presidents has increased. During the Iraq War, many journalists traveled into combat zones with troops, and news networks aired live video and audio feeds of battles taking place at remote desert outposts. Although in the early phases of the conflict the effect of this unprecedented access was to improve the president's stature by highlighting the armed forces' rapid progress, later events made journalistic scrutiny more problematic. When media outlets published graphic photographs of prisoner abuse at Iraq's Abu Ghraib prison, President Bush was placed on the defensive, and repeatedly denied that he or other top administration officials had condoned the abuse. "We do not condone torture. I have never ordered torture. I will never order torture," the president said.[13]

As media pressures on presidents have increased, the political benefits of foreign policy action have become less predictable. President Clinton, for example, did not get the same "rally 'round the flag" boost enjoyed by his predecessors. During the major foreign policy crises of the Clinton administration, the president's popularity underwent a downward shift of an average of 3 points, rather than the boost that previous presidents had enjoyed. President Bush received an overwhelming and sustained popularity boost after 9/11, but the capture of Saddam Hussein two years later generated only a minor surge in approval, lasting less than a month. Perhaps because of the uncertain nature of public support, presidents have sought to dampen high expectations in the foreign policy arena. For example, after U.S. bombs killed a leading Iraqi terrorist, Abu Musab al Zarqawi, in 2006, President Bush refrained from celebration. "Zarqawi is dead," he said, "but the difficult and necessary mission in Iraq continues."[14]

Limited Role of Interest Groups

On domestic issues, many groups with large constituencies constantly mobilize voters and urge members of Congress to take action. But on foreign policy questions, "the interest group structure is weak, unstable, and thin."[15] The most important national membership organization influencing foreign affairs is the Council on Foreign Relations, a prestigious group that includes former secretaries of state, former ambassadors, foreign policy experts, and prominent business leaders. But the organization influences government action by the quality of its advice, not by its ability to mobilize votes, as the chapter opening shows.

Economic Sanctions and Cuba

On some occasions, organized groups capable of mobilizing large numbers of voters play a role in foreign policy issues. For example, the hundreds of thousands of people living in Florida whose families fled Cuba in the 1950s when communist leader Fidel Castro came to power have persuaded the U.S. government not to recognize the legitimacy of the Castro regime, despite the fact that nearly every other country now does.

Middle East policies are also shaped by group pressures. Former Secretary of State James Baker has observed that the conflict between Israel and the Palestinians is "a perpetual fixture of domestic politics" as a result of "the political power of the American Jewish community."[16] Because a strong domestic constituency is vitally interested, Congress regularly becomes actively engaged.

The examples of Cuba and Israel are "exceptions that prove the rule," however. Most nationality groups are not large enough, or concentrated enough, or sufficiently attentive to events overseas to have influence over election outcomes and, thereby, a decisive effect on U.S. foreign policy.

Congressional Role

Although Congress plays a central role in the formation of domestic policy, when it comes to foreign affairs, members of Congress follow a "self-denying ordinance." They do not think it is their job to determine the nation's defense policies."[17] This self-denial position was particularly true in the years immediately after World War II. During these years, Congress's prestige with respect to foreign policy was seriously damaged because it had left the country unprepared for the war. Just four months before the Japanese attacked Hawaii's Pearl Harbor, the incident that provoked U.S. involvement in the war, a bill requiring young men to register for service in the armed forces passed the House of Representatives by only a single vote. In the period after World War II, Congress, embarrassed by its earlier mistakes, let the president make most major foreign policy decisions.

Later, after the Vietnam War, Congress played a more assertive foreign policy role, and conflict between Congress and the president intensified.[18] But the victory in the Persian Gulf War in 1991 erased some of the bad memories from the Vietnam War and helped boost the prestige of the executive. For example, after 9/11 Congress for the most part allowed the Bush administration to develop antiterrorist policy on its own and overwhelmingly approved military action in Afghanistan and Iraq.

Foreign Policy Responsibilities of the President and Congress

> CONSTITUTION, ARTICLE I, SECTION 8: *"The Congress shall have power to . . . declare war, . . . raise and support armies, . . . provide and maintain a navy, . . . [and] make rules for the government and regulation of the land and naval forces."*
>
> CONSTITUTION, ARTICLE II, SECTION 2: *"The President shall be commander in chief of the army and navy."*
>
> CONSTITUTION, ARTICLE II, SECTION 1: *"The executive power shall be vested in a President of the United States."*

Although the president plays the dominant role in the making of foreign policy, the Constitution gives clear responsibilities to Congress as well. As a consequence, a constitutional debate over the power of Congress and of the presidency has continued from the early years of the republic down to the present day. In this section we review how the power to wage war has evolved through history, describe congressional attempts to limit presidential war powers, and consider the treaty-making power, which the Constitution divides between the president and the Senate.

From Stand-Alone to Superpower: The Evolution of Foreign Policy

War Power

The debate over which institution ought to control the nation's war power predates even the ratification of the Constitution. Writing in support of the new form of government, Alexander Hamilton argued that "Of all the concerns of government, the direction of war most peculiarly demands the exercise of power by a single hand."[19] Yet the Constitution gives Congress the authority to declare war and to raise and maintain the armed forces. The president's constitutional powers are less clearly defined; the Constitution says only that the president is commander in chief and exercises executive power. Chief Justice John Marshall interpreted these powers broadly: "The President is the sole organ of the nation in its external relations, and its sole representative with foreign nations."[20] But nineteenth-century representative Thaddeus Stevens, a great defender of congressional prerogatives, proclaimed that "though the president is commander-in-chief, Congress is his commander, and God willing, he shall obey."[21] The issue has been debated ever since.

Prior to the Civil War, presidents seldom acted on their own on military matters. President James Madison refused to attack Great Britain in 1812 until Congress had declared war. And in 1846, President James K. Polk, although he provoked war by placing troops in disputed territory, did not actually order troops into battle against Mexico until Congress passed a war declaration.

Faced with a national emergency, Abraham Lincoln was the first president to take action based on an expanded interpretation of the role of commander in chief. When the southern states seceded from the Union, Lincoln proclaimed a blockade of southern ports and enlisted 300,000 volunteers before Congress had a chance to convene. A few decades later, Theodore Roosevelt further broadened the role of commander in chief by exercising executive powers in a much less urgent situation. He sent naval ships to Japan even when Congress refused to appropriate enough money for the trip. He said that the president, in his role as commander in chief, would send the ships. Congress, if it wished, could appropriate enough funds to get them back. Congress did.

Following Lincoln and Roosevelt's lead, modern presidents have felt free to initiate military action even in the absence of congressional approval. Not since World War II has Congress officially declared war, and many presidential uses of force have never received even nonbinding resolutions of support from Congress. President Truman fought the Korean War without any congressional declaration whatsoever. More recently, President Clinton ordered the bombing of Kosovo without securing congressional approval.

Two major Supreme Court decisions have set the boundaries within which presidents exercise their authority as commander in chief. In 1936 the Court was asked, in *U.S. v. Curtiss-Wright*, whether Congress could delegate to the president the power to determine whether arms could be sold to Bolivia and Paraguay, countries engaged in a border dispute. In his decision in favor of presidential power, Justice George Sutherland wrote that the authority of presidents on foreign affairs was greater than their discretion over domestic policy. Echoing Justice Marshall's statement of many years before, Sutherland referred to "the very delicate, plenary and exclusive power of the president as the sole organ of the federal government in the field of international relations." He went on to say that the president had "a degree of discretion and freedom . . . which would not be admissible were domestic affairs alone involved."[22]

Curtiss-Wright was qualified by the 1952 **Youngstown Sheet and Tube Co. v. Sawyer** case, in which the Supreme Court placed limits on the executive power of the president. At the height of the Korean War, trade unions in the steel industry announced that they would go on strike. Claiming that the steel industry was crucial for national defense, President Truman ordered the federal government to seize control of the steel mills and commanded union members to continue to work. In doing so, Truman ignored alternative procedures for handling labor disputes that had recently been enacted by Congress. When the steel companies challenged Truman's claim of executive power in this case, the Supreme Court ruled against the president, saying he should

U.S. v. Curtiss-Wright
Supreme Court decision in which Congress is given the authority to delegate foreign policy responsibilities to the president.

Youngstown Sheet and Tube Co. v. Sawyer
Case in which the Supreme Court placed limits on the executive power of the president.

have instead observed the congressionally defined procedures. Justice Robert Jackson wrote that when a president "takes measures incompatible with the expressed or implied will of Congress, his power is at its lowest ebb."[23]

When the *Curtiss-Wright* and *Youngstown* cases are considered together, the Court seems to have said that presidents have more constitutional discretion with respect to foreign than to domestic questions. However, presidents may not act contrary to the clearly expressed will of Congress.[24]

War Powers Resolution

The issue of executive authority arose again during the Vietnam War. Presidents Eisenhower and Kennedy had sent soldiers to Vietnam to serve as "advisers" to the South Vietnamese army, which was engaged in a war against communist guerrillas trained in North Vietnam. Neither Eisenhower nor Kennedy had received congressional authorization to send these advisers and, as the war intensified, U.S. military personnel became ever more directly involved. Then, in the summer of 1964, North Vietnamese torpedo boats apparently fired on several U.S. destroyers stationed in Tonkin Bay off the coast of Haiphong, Vietnam's second-largest city. President Lyndon Johnson denounced the action as an unlawful attack on U.S. ships that, he said, were sailing in international waters. He asked Congress for a resolution authorizing him to respond with armed force. By a nearly unanimous vote, Congress passed the **Tonkin Gulf Resolution**, which gave the president the authority to "take all necessary measures" to repel any attacks and to "prevent further aggression."[25] The resolution became the legal basis for a war that would last for eight more years. Only much later was it revealed that Johnson had misled Congress by inaccurately claiming that the United States had not invaded North Vietnam's territorial waters.

The experience of a long and discouraging war in Vietnam prompted Congress to rethink its broad approval of the president's authority over military action. In 1970 it repealed the Tonkin Gulf Resolution. As a further precaution against presidential usurpation of congressional prerogatives, Congress in 1973 passed, over President Nixon's veto, the **War Powers Resolution**, which required that the president formally notify Congress any time he orders U.S. troops into military action. The resolution further specifies that troops must be withdrawn unless Congress approves the presidential decision within 60 days after notice of the military action has been received.

In many cases, presidents have simply ignored the War Powers Resolution. President Reagan invaded Grenada, bombed Libya, and placed military troops in Lebanon without notifying Congress. President Clinton bombed Iraq, deployed troops in Bosnia, bombarded Serb positions in Kosovo, and struck at terrorist sites in Sudan and Afghanistan without notifying Congress as called for by the War Powers Resolution. On five separate occasions, individual members of Congress sued in federal courts, attempting to force the president to abide by that resolution. In each case, however, judges dismissed the suits.[26]

Some analysts believe that these failed legal efforts, coupled with presidential refusal to notify Congress of military engagements, have made the War Powers Resolution a dead letter without any legal significance. But other analysts have pointed out that Congress can, by majority vote, pass a resolution that takes formal notice of any

You Are the
President

Tonkin Gulf Resolution
Congressional resolution giving the president the authority to send troops to Vietnam.

War Powers Resolution
1973 congressional resolution requiring the president to notify Congress formally upon ordering U.S. troops into military action.

U.S. Troops in Iraq

A large majority of Congress voted for the resolution granting President Bush the authority to attack Iraq.

• *Why did President Bush seek congressional approval of this military operation?*

SECURE ALL CHAINS

VIDEO DEBATE

Americans
in Iraq

military engagement. Once it has done so, the 60-day clock begins to tick, and after those 60 days, troops must be withdrawn. Although lawsuits have been filed by individual representatives, Congress as a whole has never been willing to challenge presidential refusal to observe the War Powers Resolution by passing this type of measure.

Although they did not accept the validity of the War Powers Resolution, both Presidents Bush sought Congressional approval for their military actions. In doing so, they turned a potential weakness into a strength by rallying congressional support around their policies. President George H. W. Bush asked for and received congressional authorization to use force against Iraq before the Gulf War of 1991. George W. Bush went even further: after 9/11, at the administration's request, Congress passed, with but one dissenting vote in the House of Representatives, a sweeping resolution that gave President Bush all the discretion he needed to carry out the war on terrorism. Congress authorized the president to "use all necessary and appropriate force against those nations, organizations, or persons he determines planned, authorized, committed, or aided the terrorist attacks that occurred on September 11, or harbored such organizations or persons, in order to prevent any future acts of international terrorism." Although the resolution limits the president to taking action against those involved in the 9/11 attacks, its definition of such individuals and entities is extraordinarily wide-ranging. The president alone is to determine who was involved, and action can be taken not only against those who committed the acts but also against those who "aided" or "harbored" the terrorists. No limit is placed on the time period in which the president may act.[27]

A second resolution, authorizing the use of force to "defend the national security of the United States against the continuing threat posed by Iraq" passed Congress overwhelmingly in late 2002. The resolution gave President Bush crucial backing for the subsequent Iraq War, but also offered political cover for those members of Congress who were wary of military involvement: It required Bush to exhaust "diplomatic or other peaceful means" of resolving the conflict prior to resorting to force.[28] Despite the caveat, this congressional statement of support became a liability for Democrats who, in the campaigns of 2004 and 2006, had to explain to voters their criticisms of the Bush administration's handling of the war in light of their own votes in favor of the resolution.

Treaty Power

CONSTITUTION, ARTICLE II, SECTION 2: *"[The President] shall have power, by and with the advice and consent of the Senate, to make Treaties, provided two-thirds of the Senators present concur."*

The power of the president to negotiate **treaties**—official agreements with foreign countries that are ratified by the Senate—is the most circumscribed of all presidential powers. A treaty does not take effect until it wins approval by a two-thirds vote in the Senate. Because this super-majority can be difficult to achieve unless a treaty has overwhelming public support, presidents have often felt constrained by senatorial pressures when negotiating with foreign countries. Although the Senate has approved about 90 percent of the treaties that presidents have submitted to it from the 1780s to the present, this fact may simply indicate that presidents decline to negotiate or submit treaties that they feel have no chance of passage.[29]

No president was more frustrated than Woodrow Wilson by this constitutional check on presidential power. When negotiating the Versailles Treaty that ended World War I, President Wilson pursued one objective above all others: the establishment of a **League of Nations**, an international organization created to settle international disputes, which became the precursor to the United Nations. Wilson felt that such an organization was essential if future world wars were to be avoided. The other nations at the Versailles conference and a considerable portion of the American public supported Wilson's ideas. But the Senate voted down the treaty, primarily because many members believed the League of Nations would undermine U.S. sovereignty.

Eighty years later, President Clinton faced similar difficulties with Congress. In October 1999 the Senate considered the Comprehensive Nuclear Test Ban Treaty, which was negotiated in 1996. The multinational agreement would have prohibited the testing of nuclear weapons and would have enacted more stringent monitoring systems to ensure compliance. Proponents of the treaty argued that it was essential to slowing the spread of nuclear weapons around the world. But critics, including many Senate Republicans, were skeptical of its effectiveness and worried that it would hamper the nation's ability to modernize its armed forces. After negotiations broke down between Republican leaders and the Clinton administration, the Senate voted against ratification, 51 to 48.

Because one-third-plus-one of the Senate can block passage of a treaty, presidents often negotiate **executive agreements**, legal contracts with foreign countries that require only a presidential signature. Nothing in the Constitution explicitly gives the president the power to make executive agreements, but the practice has long been established. The first executive agreement—limiting the size of the U.S. and Great Britain's naval forces on the Great Lakes—was signed by President James Monroe in 1817. In 1937 the Supreme Court affirmed the constitutionality of executive agreements.[30] Since that decision, presidents have increasingly relied on this method as a vehicle for negotiating with other nations. Most executive agreements either are extensions of treaties ratified by

treaties
Official agreements with foreign countries that are ratified by the Senate.

League of Nations
International organization created after World War I to settle international disputes; precursor of the United Nations.

Unilateralism and Multilateralism

executive agreement
Agreement with foreign countries that requires only a presidential signature.

FIGURE 20.2

Growing Presidential
Power: Executive
Agreements Are Replacing
Treaties

• *Why have presidents increasingly turned to executive agreements? Does this behavior deny the Senate its constitutional role in foreign policy?*

Note: Data for George W. Bush are for 2001–2005.

Sources: Gary King and Lynn Ragsdale, *The Elusive Executive: Discovering Patterns in the Presidency* (Washington, DC: CQ Press, 1988), 131–140; Harold Stanley and Richard Niemi, *Vital Statistics on American Politics, 2001–2002* (Washington, DC: CQ Press, 2001), 334; Data for George W. Bush calculated by authors from data on treaty actions available at Department of State, Office of the Legal Adviser, www.state.gov/s/l/index.htm, accessed June 19, 2006.

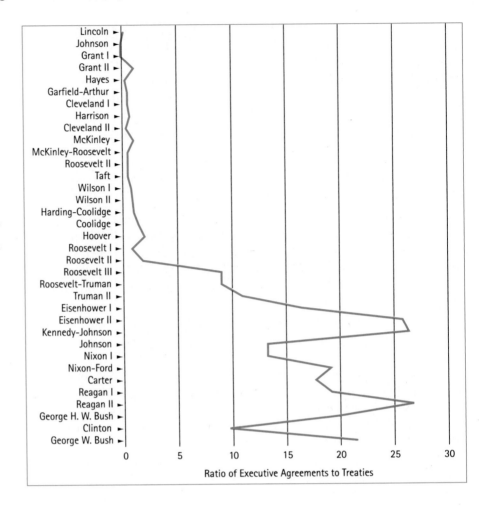

the Senate or involve routine presidential actions that have otherwise been authorized by Congress. But presidents sometimes use executive agreements to implement major foreign policy decisions. For example, President Clinton relied on an executive agreement to coax newly independent Ukraine into giving up its nuclear arsenal in exchange for economic aid.[31] In recent years about 20 executive agreements have been signed for every treaty submitted to the Senate for its approval (see Figure 20.2).

Foreign Policy Institutions: From Cold War to Homeland Defense

World politics changed quickly in the last decade of the twentieth century and the first decade of the twenty-first, but most critical institutions that are responsible for U.S. foreign policy today were designed to address a far different global situation. These cabinet posts, agencies, and advisory structures took shape in the early years of the **Cold War**, the 43-year conflict (1946–1989) between the United States and the Soviet Union. The modern Department of State, the Department of Defense, the Central Intelligence Agency, and the office of the National Security Adviser were all designed to meet the Cold War threat posed by the Soviet Union. The relationships of each to one another and to the president are shown in Figure 20.3. In the wake of 9/11, poli-

Cold War
The 43-year period (1946–1989) during which the United States and the Soviet Union threatened one another with mutual destruction by nuclear warfare.

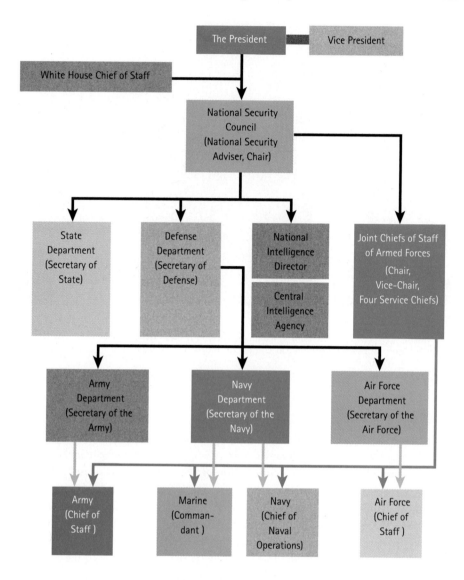

FIGURE 20.3

The Foreign Policy Institutions

• *Why does the Army Chief of Staff report both to the Joint Chiefs and to the Secretary of the Army?*

cymakers reevaluated their design and capacities in light of the new threat posed from terrorist organizations, in some cases making significant changes. In this section we begin with a comparison of the Cold War world to the post-Cold War era, discuss the emergence of each of the foreign policy institutions, and consider their new role in an era of potential terrorist attacks.

The Cold War and the Post-Cold War World

At the outset of the Cold War, U.S. officials recognized that it represented the greatest foreign policy challenge the country had yet faced. In the months following World War II, Germany was divided into eastern and western parts, and Korea was split into a North and South, one-half of each country under Western influence, the other within the communist domain. In short order, the Soviet Union consolidated its control over much of Eastern Europe, establishing communist governments in Poland, Hungary, Bulgaria, Romania, and Czechoslovakia. In 1961, pursuant to Soviet directives, East

The Berlin Wall
Built during the presidency of John F. Kennedy, the Berlin Wall (left) symbolized what British Prime Minister Winston Churchill called the Iron Curtain. The wall, and the curtain, crumbled in 1989 (right).

• *How has American foreign policymaking changed since the end of the Cold War?*

Germany constructed a huge concrete wall through the middle of Berlin, dramatically symbolizing the division of the world into communist and Western parts.

The Cold War began at a time when the prestige of the executive branch had been greatly enhanced by its successful prosecution of World War II. As a result, President Truman was able to mobilize bipartisan support for his foreign policy and recruit to key positions the most talented group of foreign policy advisers the country had ever assembled. These advisers saw the world as **bipolar**, divided between two major centers of power: the U.S. and its allies, and the Soviet Union and its allies. "The assault on free institutions is worldwide now," they wrote in a 1950 memo to the president, "and in the context of the present polarization of power a defeat of free institutions anywhere is a defeat everywhere."[32] Accordingly, they decided that the U.S. should use its military might to deter a direct attack from the Soviet Union, while at the same time countering aggression by the Soviets in other countries, when it occurred.[33] This overall strategy was called **containment**, a policy that attempted to stop the spread of communism in the expectation that this system of government would eventually collapse on its own. The policy, originally proposed by George Kennan, a brilliant State Department specialist, won bipartisan support.[34]

Although it took nearly 50 years, containment proved successful. Unrest began in the communist-dominated countries of Eastern Europe during the 1980s and spread to the Soviet Union by the end of the decade. When East Germany allowed demonstrators to tear down the Berlin Wall in 1989, the Cold War finally came to an end. Two years later, the Soviet Union officially dissolved itself.

At the end of the Cold War, some observers predicted an era of peace and security. But more astute experts cautioned that new and unpredictable conflicts might

bipolar
Cold War view of the world as divided into two centers of power, the United States and its allies, and the Soviet Union and its allies.

containment
U.S. policy that attempted to stop the spread of communism in the expectation that this system of government would eventually collapse on its own.

surface, leading to dangerous instability in key areas of the world. During the 1990s, Presidents George H.W. Bush and Bill Clinton sought to lessen regional instability by intervening in important local conflicts. The first President Bush, for example, fought the 1991 Persian Gulf War in response to an Iraqi invasion of Kuwait, and sent troops to Somalia when it seemed that chaos in that country was creating a humanitarian and political crisis. For his part, Clinton led an international effort to defeat Serbian leader Slobodan Milosevic, who had engaged in years of destructive wars in the former Yugoslavia.

After 9/11, however, the George W. Bush administration reevaluated the nature of threats to the United States. Rather than the clear threat of a competing nation, as in the Cold War, or indirect political and economic threats resulting from regional instability, as in the 1990s, foreign policy-making officials now saw direct peril from secretive terrorist organizations that might not even be linked to specific countries. "Enemies in the past needed great armies and great industrial capabilities to endanger America," wrote the White House national security staff in 2002, "Now, shadowy networks of individuals can bring great chaos and suffering to our shores for less than it costs to purchase a single tank."[35]

Leaders in both political parties agreed that the U.S. should dedicate itself to addressing this new environment. Because the major foreign policy-making institutions in the United States were developed to address the Cold War, however, the new threat required policy makers to critically examine the role that each of these institutions plays. Large organizations develop routines and standard operating procedures that are often difficult to alter, and are not always suited for unexpected circumstances, as we discuss in Chapter 14. On 9/11, for example, the pilot of a military jet that was ordered to Washington to defend U.S. airspace later told investigators, "I reverted to the Russian threat . . . I'm thinking cruise missile threat from the sea."[36] In the sections that follow, we examine each of the major U.S. foreign policy-making institutions, and discuss the challenges that each institution faces in the post-Cold War world.

State Department

It was during the Cold War that the modern professional State Department emerged out of the patronage-ridden entity that preceded it. However, the State Department itself—the agency responsible for conducting diplomatic relations—dates back to the administration of George Washington and his secretary of state, Thomas Jefferson.

Ever since that time, the **secretary of state** has been the president's official foreign policy adviser. In most administrations, the secretary of state is also the nation's chief diplomat. For example, Condoleezza Rice, George W. Bush's secretary of state, played a major role in international crisis negotiations during Israel's 2006 war with the militant group Hezbollah in southern Lebanon. The job of chief diplomat is extremely challenging. As former Secretary of State George Marshall once commented, "In diplomacy, you never can tell what a man is thinking. He smiles at you and kicks you in the stomach at the same time."[37] Or, as one pundit put it, "Diplomacy is the art of saying 'nice doggie' until you can find a rock."[38]

Reporting to the secretary of state are **ambassadors**, who head the diplomatic delegations to major foreign countries. Ambassadors are responsible for the management of major U.S. **embassies** abroad, which house diplomatic delegations in the

secretary of state
Officially, the president's chief foreign policy adviser and head of the Department of State, the agency responsible for conducting diplomatic relations.

ambassador
The head of a diplomatic delegation to a major foreign country.

embassy
The structure that houses ambassadors and their diplomatic aides in the capital cities of foreign countries.

**Secretary of State
Condoleezza Rice**

• *How does a modern secretary
of state use the resources of the
State Department to influence
U.S. foreign policy?*

foreign service

Diplomats who staff U.S. embassies
and consulates.

capital cities of foreign countries. Consulates are maintained in important cities that are
not foreign capitals. If you wish to travel abroad, you must first obtain a passport from
the State Department. If you encounter difficulty while traveling in a foreign country,
your first phone call might well be made to the closest embassy or consulate.

Although embassies and consulates help American tourists and businesses, their
most important political responsibility is to provide the State Department with detailed
information on the government and politics, as well as on the economic and social
conditions, of the host country. The ambassador also conveys to the host country the
views of the U.S. government, as instructed by the State Department. An ambassador
must be able to listen to others carefully and communicate no more than what the president wants to convey. As the British diplomat Sir Henry Wotton put it, "an ambassador is an honest man sent to lie abroad" for his country.[39]

Before the Cold War, U.S. ambassadorial appointments were as important for
rewarding those who helped presidents win elections as for the diplomacy they carried
out. The most prestigious ambassadorships were given to long-time political supporters who had raised large sums of money for the president's election. As one historian
put it, "Most diplomats earned their appointments through party affiliation, personal
wealth, or social position, seldom through training. Many lacked knowledge; some
lacked dignity, although few were as tactless as John Randolph, who allegedly
commented, when presented to the czar in 1830, "Howaya Emperor? And how's the
madam?"[40] Even today, some ambassadorial positions remain frankly political. For
example, when President Bush entered office, he appointed 19 of his top fund-raisers
as ambassadors, including those appointed to France, the Netherlands, New Zealand,
Norway, Portugal, Spain, and Switzerland.[41]

But patronage today is more the exception than the rule. Those appointed to less
prestigious diplomatic positions are nearly always trained career officers who are familiar with the language and customs of the host country.

Ever since the 1920s these officers have been organized into a **foreign service**,
which consists of the diplomats who staff U.S. embassies and consulates. After World
War II, the foreign service was strengthened as part of the effort to fight the Cold War.
In particular, Dean Acheson, President Truman's secretary of state, did much to
improve the professional caliber of the foreign service. A reporter at the time declared,
"For the first time in the memory of living man, the American foreign office comes
somewhere near being adequate to the needs of the country."[42]

Today, the State Department is responsible for holding together a worldwide
coalition in the war against terrorism. Even the definition of terrorism poses diplomatic problems. Does the concept include any explicit attack on civilians and civilian property, regardless of circumstance? Or are there conditions under which
civilians are appropriately treated as military targets? These questions pose problems
for U.S. diplomats seeking to resolve the conflict between Israel and the Palestinians.
In support of Israel, the United States has denounced as terrorism the attacks on
civilians by Palestinian suicide bombers. But Arab leaders, in support of the
Palestinians, contend that Israel illegally occupies Palestinian territory. They say the
attacks against the occupying nation are simply military operations being carried out
against an occupying power that has killed thousands of Palestinians. Inasmuch as the
United States, while supporting Israel, still needs to maintain good relations with

Arab governments in order to further its search for Al Qaeda terrorists, the State Department is constantly challenged to find new diplomatic ways to resolve these alternative definitions of terrorism.

Defense Department

Ever since the first decades of the country's independence, Americans have been concerned about the ill effects of a large military. The nation has sometimes looked to popular generals, such as George Washington, Andrew Jackson, Ulysses S. Grant, and Dwight Eisenhower, for political leadership. But generals must give up their military appointment when running for president. In general, Congress and the president have always made certain that the military was controlled by civilian appointees. As one analyst puts it, freedom "demands that people without guns be able to tell people with guns what to do."[43] The Cold War posed new challenges for this ideal of civilian control. To ensure the country's continued international leadership and to carry out the policy of containment, Congress provided for the largest military establishment in the nation's history. In an effort to better handle this large peacetime standing army, the military went through several major organizational changes.

Organization of the Defense Department   At the close of World War II, the army and navy were two separate departments, each with its own air force and each with its own seat in the president's cabinet. With the onset of the Cold War, to coordinate civilian control of the armed forces better, the 1947 National Security Act created a single **Department of Defense** that contained within it the Departments of the Army, Navy, and Air Force, each with its own civilian secretary appointed by the president. The secretaries for the army and the air force are responsible for their respective branches of the armed services. The secretary of the navy is responsible for both the naval forces and the marines. All three secretaries report to the **secretary of defense**, the president's chief civilian adviser on defense matters and the overall head of all three departments.

Subordinate to the civilian leadership of the secretary of defense and the other three appointed secretaries, military professionals direct the armed forces. At one time, each armed force had its own military leadership, and they acted more or less independently of each other. To achieve better coordination, Congress formally created the **Joint Chiefs of Staff** in 1947. The Joint Chiefs consist of the heads of all the military services—the army, navy, air force, and Marine Corps—together with a chair and vice-chair nominated by the president and confirmed by the Senate. Omar Bradley, the first chairman of the Joint Chiefs of Staff, suggested that the organization was essential if the country were to achieve a unified, effective military force: "Our military forces are one team—in the game to win regardless of who carries the ball. This is no time for 'fancy dans' who won't hit the line with all they have on every play unless they can call the signals."[44] (See the *International Comparison* on the next page)

Rivalries among the armed services have been so intense that it took decades to achieve what Bradley promised in 1949, but eventually a unified command structure was created in each of the regions of the world. This unified structure proved extraordinarily effective during the 1991 Persian Gulf War when General Norman Schwarzkopf, an army general, directly controlled not only the actions of the army but

Department of Defense
Cabinet department responsible for managing the U.S. armed forces.

secretary of defense
The president's chief civilian adviser on defense matters and overall head of the army, navy, and air force.

Joint Chiefs of Staff
The heads of all the military services, together with a chair and vice-chair nominated by the president and confirmed by the Senate.

INTERNATIONAL
COMPARISON

United States—Lucky in War

Isolationist sentiments have been fed by the country's wartime successes, which have fostered the belief that the United States is invincible. After the War of 1812 and until the Vietnam War, the United States had an impressive military record. The Mexican War, the Spanish–American War, and World Wars I and II all ended in overwhelming victories. Few, if any, other world powers have achieved such an unbroken string of successes. Japan and Germany can never forget their humiliating defeats in World War II. The French cannot forget the ease with which German troops captured Paris in both 1870 and 1940. The Russians cannot readily dislodge the memory of their defeat by Japan in 1905 or the collapse of their army in 1917. Only the British have nearly as enviable a historical record as the Americans, and even Britain suffered more than one defeat at the hands of the French.

Not only has the United States won its wars, but it has done so quickly. The Mexican War, though spread over three years, consisted of three short and decisive campaigns. The Spanish-American War was over in eight months. Even U.S. involvement in the two world wars was of relatively short duration. Within six months of the arrival of U.S. troops in Europe, an armistice brought World War I to an end. The pattern was not altogether different in World War II. Little more than a

year after U.S. troops landed in Normandy, Germany was defeated. Japan struggled for an additional two months until nuclear bombs dropped by the United States over Hiroshima and Nagasaki forced surrender. Before 9/11, American civilians rarely suffered significantly from foreign attack. Not since the British burning of Washington, D.C., in 1814 has the mainland of the United States been invaded by foreign troops. Apart from the 9/11 attack and the bombing of Pearl Harbor, the United States has been free of aerial raids. During World War II, German tanks overran Europe and Russia, German airplanes bombed Britain, and U.S. airplanes all but destroyed German and Japanese cities. As the graph here shows, even U.S. troop casualties have been small.

• *What effects did the loss in Vietnam and the victory in the Persian Gulf have on U.S. strategy in Iraq and Afghanistan?*

• *Do you think that this history of success has made the U.S. public more likely or less likely to support wars? More likely or less likely to become impatient with lengthy conflicts?*

SOURCES: R. Ernest Dupuy and Trevor N. Dupuy, *The Harper Encyclopedia of Military History: From 3500 b.c. to the Present* (New York: HarperCollins, 1993); Y. Takenob, *The Japan Year Book: 1919–1920* (Tokyo: Japan Year Book Office, 1921); B. R. Mitchell, *International Historical Statistics: Europe 1750–1988* (New York: Stockton Press, 1992); B. R. Mitchell, *International Historical Statistics of the Americas: 1750–1988* (New York: Stockton Press, 1993); B. R. Mitchell, *International Historical Statistics: Africa and Asia* (New York: New York University Press, 1982); and Raymond E. Zickel, ed., *Soviet Union: A Country Study* (Washington, DC: U.S. Government Printing Office, 1991).

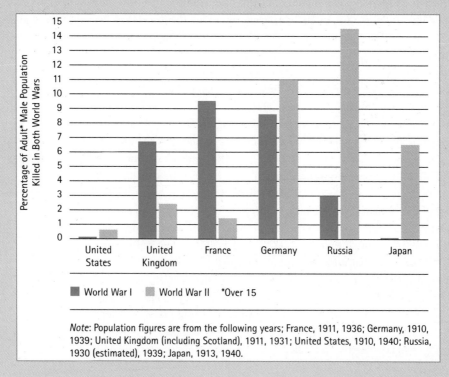

Note: Population figures are from the following years; France, 1911, 1936; Germany, 1910, 1939; United Kingdom (including Scotland), 1911, 1931; United States, 1910, 1940; Russia, 1930 (estimated), 1939; Japan, 1913, 1940.

also those of the navy, air force, and marines, achieving one of the best-coordinated military attacks the United States has ever mounted.

Military Response to Terrorism The military was given the central role in responding to the 9/11 terrorist attack in part because the Bush administration redefined U.S. counterterrorism policy in two important respects.[45] First, the president called upon government agencies to treat terrorist actions as acts of war that need to be anticipated and prevented, not criminal activities to be investigated and prosecuted. Second, the problem was defined not simply as consisting of private individuals or groups engaged in terrorist activities but, rather, as also including governments and states that allowed such activities within their borders. These governments and states had to be held accountable, just as much as the terrorists themselves.

The initial military actions in Afghanistan and Iraq were surprisingly effective—so effective that they surpassed the expectations of many commentators. The explanation for this fact illustrates some of the changes that have been underway in the armed forces since the end of the Cold War. Whereas Cold War planners anticipated large-scale land attacks that placed a premium on heavy equipment and brute force, modern strategists are more likely to value lightweight, high-technology weapons. As a result, military campaigns can be executed with greater precision than ever before. In Iraq and Afghanistan, pilotless drones dropped bombs without risking the lives of American pilots. Heat sensors could detect movement within buildings and caves. Communication detection devices could pinpoint signs of enemy activity. Precision bombing reduced the amount of civilian damage. All in all, technology had advanced far beyond that employed at the height of the Vietnam War.

But technology is only part of the story. Just as important are the new governance structures that have been created within the U.S. armed forces. In conflicts prior to the first Gulf War, presidents and secretaries of defense found that the chain of command from the White House to military field commanders was layered and cumbersome, and rivalries between different branches of the armed forces hampered the military's effectiveness. A reorganization in the late 1980s placed unified command over each particular conflict in the hands of one officer, who then reported directly to the secretary of defense and to the president.[46] This system worked smoothly in the first Gulf War, as well as the Iraq and Afghanistan conflicts.

Technological advances and a unified command structure also made it possible to rethink basic war planning, which since Vietnam had been characterized by large-scale attacks with hundreds of thousands of ground troops. Defense Secretary Donald Rumsfeld sought to reduce the use of such overwhelming attacks, and instead favored elite specialized technical forces, where possible—Army Green Berets, Navy Seals, CIA operatives, the British Royal Marine Special Boat Service, and other highly trained personnel. He also called for "flexible, light, and agile" deployments from the regular armed forces.[47] Although in the late 1990s, the Pentagon estimated that an attack on Iraq would require up to half a million troops,[48] in 2003 the U.S. invaded with about 130,000, plus 30,000 British allied forces.[49] These troops quickly swept north through the desert, subduing the enemy forces with apparent ease.

But Al Qaeda terrorists remain scattered all over the globe, and a swift and successful war to depose dictator Saddam Hussein gave way to a costly occupation in Iraq, during which congressional critics complained that technology and agility were no substitutes for the larger numbers of troops needed to keep the peace.

Afghanistan, too, remained dangerous and unstable years after the 2001 U.S. invasion. While the Bush administration pointed to encouraging signs, such as the successful free elections in both countries, skeptics argued that the new approach to fighting wars had failed to take into account the need to maintain control of occupied territories. New technologies are not much different from ancient bayonets. As one witticism has put it: "You can do almost anything but sit on them." And "sitting" is precisely the challenge that comes with occupying and holding territories one has invaded.

The correct approach to military conflict may be disputed for some time, but what is clear is that the national defense has become more expensive in recent years. To pursue the campaign against terrorism and the Iraq War, the Bush administration has sought and received more congressional funding for national defense. This reversed a decline in military spending that had been underway since the end of the Cold War. In the 1950s, during the height of the Cold War, the United States spent 10 percent of its total gross domestic product (GDP) on defense. Although the expenditure rate declined after the Vietnam War, it was still 6 percent as recently as the mid-1980s. But with the end of the Cold War, Congress began to cut the defense budget, responding to the decline in public concern about the communist threat. By 1999, as Figure 20.4 shows, defense expenditures had dropped to 3 percent of GDP—the lowest level since before World War II. The campaign against terrorism brought this downward trend to a halt.

Evaluating
Defense Spending

Central Intelligence Agency

"I only regret that I have but one life to lose for my country," said the Revolutionary War hero Nathan Hale, after he had been caught spying and was about to be hanged by the British. A statue erected in Hale's memory stands at the entrance to the main offices of the **Central Intelligence Agency (CIA)**, the agency primarily responsible for gathering and analyzing information about the political and military activities of other nations. The subject of many a spy novel, it is lovingly referred to as "the Company" or "the Pickle Factory" by members of the intelligence community.[50]

Central Intelligence Agency (CIA)

Agency primarily responsible for gathering and analyzing information about the political and military activities of other nations.

Formation of CIA   If spying is an ancient and honorable practice, its organization into an independent agency is of fairly recent vintage. The need for better-organized intelligence became clear during World War II, especially at Hawaii's Pearl Harbor on December 7, 1941, called a "day of infamy" by President Roosevelt. It was a day of particular disrepute for the intelligence community, inasmuch as naval officers at Pearl Harbor were completely unaware that Japan had both the capability and the intention of destroying half the U.S. naval force. (The chief naval official in Hawaii had an appointment with the Japanese envoy on that infamous day.)

The U.S. government made haphazard efforts to improve intelligence capabilities in the wake of the Pearl Harbor attack, but it was not until the Cold War began that Congress established a systematic, centralized system of intelligence gathering. The National Security Act of 1947 created the CIA as a separate agency independent of both the Department of State and the Department of Defense. Although State and Defense (as well as other departments) continue to have their own sources of intelligence, the 1947 law made the CIA the main intelligence-collection agency. It also gave the CIA the authority to conduct secret operations abroad at the request of the president.

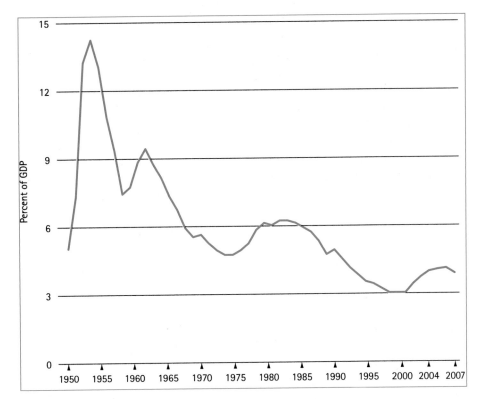

FIGURE 20.4

Defense Expenditures as a Percentage of GDP, 1950–2007

• *What accounts for the increases in defense expenditures in the early 1950s, the late 1960s, and the mid-1980s?*

Note: Figures for 2006 and 2007 are estimates.

Sources: Office of Management and Budget, "Budget of the United States Government, Fiscal Year 2007," Historical Tables, Table 3.1, 46–54.

Covert Operations   It is the CIA's authority to conduct clandestine, or covert, operations that has been most controversial, because critics argue that only the armed forces ought to conduct secret military activities. The CIA's most notorious covert operation was the ill-fated attempt in 1961 to dislodge communist leader Fidel Castro from Cuba.[51] In an effort to overthrow Castro, the CIA helped Cuban exiles plan an invasion on the shores of Cuba's **Bay of Pigs** that was expected to foment a popular insurrection. President Kennedy approved the invasion attempt but decided against giving it naval or air support. The effort failed, leaving in doubt the CIA's ability to conduct large-scale military operations. Although the Bay of Pigs has been the CIA's most visible covert operation, the agency drew criticism for covert activities in Chile in the early 1970s, in Nicaragua and Afghanistan in the 1980s, and in other nations.

Bay of Pigs
Location of CIA-supported effort by Cuban exiles in 1961 to invade Cuba and overthrow Fidel Castro.

Response to Terrorism   To avoid such criticism, the CIA limited the scale of its covert operations, reducing the number of agents. In the period leading up to the 9/11 terrorist attack, it actually had "fewer Arabic-speaking case officers than in the Cold War," making it difficult for the agency to interpret conversations that were intercepted. Agents who can penetrate terrorist groups have proved extremely difficult to recruit. Perhaps, as one former CIA official observed, it is not easy to find talented individuals willing to participate in "operations that include diarrhoea as a way of life."[52]

Just as important, the CIA in recent decades has not found it easy to work closely with the Federal Bureau of Investigation (FBI). Cooperation between the two agencies was curtailed because both had been criticized for illegal spying on U.S. citizens during the Vietnam War. (The secretive National Security Agency also participated in this spying, as we point out in Chapter 16.) As a result, intelligence operations within the United States were left solely to the FBI, which lacked information on the presence of foreign terrorists within the United States and could wiretap suspects only after obtaining a court order. Although these procedures helped safeguard the civil liberties of American citizens, they also contributed to a major intelligence failure on September 11. As one analyst pointed out, "At least 19 people worked for as long as five years, mostly in the United States, on a complex operation to crash multiple airliners into several targets. And America's $30-billion-a-year intelligence services hardly got a whiff of them."[53]

In response to such failures, the special commission appointed to investigate the 9/11 attacks proposed creating the position of **national intelligence director** to coordinate intelligence gathering among the CIA, the FBI, and a dozen other intelligence agencies. Congress created this position in 2004. While some observers worried that the CIA would be discontented with the arrangement because of its loss in rank (the CIA director now reports to the national intelligence director rather than directly to the president), others argued that a discontented CIA was less of a concern than the need for a better coordinated intelligence.

National Security Council

Because so many departments and agencies needed to work together to formulate U.S. Cold War policy, Congress created the **National Security Council (NSC)** in 1947. This organization, located inside the White House Executive Office of the President, is responsible for coordinating U.S. foreign policy. Meetings of the NSC are generally attended by the president, the vice president, the secretary of state, the secretary of defense, the national intelligence director, the chair of the military Joint Chiefs of Staff, the president's chief of staff, and such other individuals as the president designates.[54] The council is assisted by a staff located in the White House under the direction of the national security adviser (NSA). The NSA has often played simply a coordinating role by reconciling interagency disagreements or, if that proved impossible, by reporting them to the president. Because it has no budget authority over other departments and agencies, its ability to control ongoing policy operations is limited. But inasmuch as the NSA has more access to the president than does any member of the foreign policy team, the adviser can wield great influence in crises. During the Nixon administration, National Security Adviser Henry Kissinger became the president's most influential aide, overshadowing the secretary of state. In the George W. Bush administration, NSA Condoleezza Rice won the trust of the president and, as a result, emerged as one of his most influential advisers. After President Bush appointed Rice secretary of state in 2005, her replacement, longtime White House aide Stephen Hadley, played a key role in publicly defending U.S. antiterrorism policies.

The office of the NSA has not escaped controversy. The most notorious event in which it played a major part has become known as the **Iran-Contra affair**, an allegedly illegal diversion of funds from an Iranian arms sale to anticommunist rebels in Nicaragua known as the Contras. In this case, President Ronald Reagan's NSA office, which was officially responsible only for policy coordination, actually attempted to conduct a covert operation of the type ordinarily conducted by the CIA. In a clear violation of U.S. antiterrorist policy, National Security Adviser Robert McFarlane helped orchestrate a secret arms sale to Iran in an effort to secure the release of several American hostages in the Middle East. Profits from this sale were then diverted to the Contras, to whom Congress had cut off U.S. aid several years before.

national intelligence director
An office that coordinates intelligence gathering among the CIA, the FBI, and other intelligence agencies.

National Security Council (NSC)
White House agency responsible for coordinating U.S. foreign policy.

National Security Adviser
George W. Bush, Secretary of State Condoleezza Rice, and National Security Adviser Stephen Hadley
• *What role does the NSA play in foreign policy formulation?*

Iran-Contra affair
An allegedly illegal diversion of funds, derived from the sale of arms to Iran, to a guerrilla group in Nicaragua during the Reagan administration.

In the Iran–Contra episode, the NSC staff appeared to have ignored both administration antiterrorist policy and clear congressional directives. Congress held hearings on the scandal, and an independent prosecutor conducted a thorough investigation, although the most significant convictions were overturned in courts of appeals. A specially appointed presidential commission recommended that, in the future, the office of the NSA limit itself to a coordinating role and not involve itself in covert operations. By following these guidelines, the NSA has since then avoided political controversy.

The National Security Council initially served as an organizational model for the George W. Bush administration's homeland security efforts. Bush appointed Tom Ridge to serve as a "homeland security adviser" analogous to the NSA. Ridge was then expected to coordinate the activities of dozens of agencies from his White House office. As we discuss in Chapter 14, however, this proved to be an impossible task. President Bush finally proposed, and Congress created, the cabinet-level Department of Homeland Security to give Ridge the budgetary authority and political clout necessary to manage homeland defense (see *Election Voices*, p. 421).

Ideals, Interests, and the Worldwide Campaign Against Terror

The way in which the president and his advisers resolve foreign policy questions is shaped by a long-standing tension that exists between American philosophical ideals and the country's practical need to defend itself against foreign aggression. Alexander Hamilton, in the *Federalist Papers*, made the best case for placing the highest priority on the country's practical interests: "No Government [can] give us tranquility and happiness at home, which [does] not possess sufficient stability and strength to make us respectable abroad."[55] The idealist point of view was best expressed by Abraham Lincoln, who reminded his fellow citizens that one purpose of the American experiment was to spread liberty throughout the world. "The Declaration of Independence . . . [gave] liberty, not alone to the people of this country, but hope to the world for all future time."[56]

The tension between ideals and interests that has long been part of the American foreign policy tradition continues to shape policy debates today. On the one side, **idealists** say that U.S. foreign policy should be guided primarily by democratic principles—the spread of liberty, equality, human rights, and respect for international law throughout the world. On the other side, **realists** say that U.S. foreign policy best protects democracy when it guards its own economic and military strength.

One can find both idealists and realists in each political party and in all government agencies, and some people are idealistic on one issue yet realistic on another. In fact, many foreign policy makers use both idealist and realist arguments to make their points.

The events of 9/11 have changed the nature of the debate between idealists and realists in many ways, including their consideration of strategies for nation building, the role of international organizations, and the role of human rights in relations with Russia and China.

Strategies for Nation Building

Interventions designed to enhance democratic practices in other countries—actions known as **nation building**—have long been a point of contention between idealists and realists. According to realists, the United States should avoid getting involved in

idealists
Those who say that U.S. foreign policy should be guided primarily by democratic principles—the spread of liberty, equality, human rights, and respect for international law throughout the world.

realists
Those who say that U.S. foreign policy best protects democracy when it safeguards its own economic and military strength.

nation building
Interventions designed to enhance democratic practices in another country.

nation building unless U.S. interests are directly at stake. Realists opposed the first President Bush's decision to send troops into Somalia and Clinton's decision to send them to Bosnia and Kosovo. If the United States continues to involve itself in the internal political life of foreign countries, they argue, it will eventually find itself unprepared or unable to defend its true interests when they are threatened.

Nation building can at times be fraught with peril. For one thing, actions taken can have unanticipated consequences. Unjustified intervention in the internal affairs of other countries, moreover, runs contrary to international law, which regards each legitimate government as sovereign over its own citizens. Idealists nonetheless suggest that Americans should intervene to enhance democratic practices and safeguard human rights, especially if governments seek to deport or eliminate entire ethnic groups, a practice known as **ethnic cleansing**.

Differences between idealists and realists were evident after the collapse of Yugoslavia in Eastern Europe at the end of the Cold War. When the country split into pieces, armed struggle broke out among Bosnians, Serbs, and Croats. Idealists supported the Clinton administration's decision to send troops to separate the warring parties in Bosnia, and to conduct aerial bombing to end the Serbian invasion of Kosovo. By such actions, the United States tries to prevent violation of human rights by punishing governments that engaged in ethnic cleansing and by capturing war criminals and referring them to international tribunals.

When George W. Bush campaigned for president in 2000, he questioned the U.S. efforts to secure human rights and other efforts to enhance democratic practices in other countries. He doubted whether the United States should become engaged in the business of nation building. In the words of Condoleezza Rice, "Carrying out civil administration policy functions is simply going to degrade the American capability to do the things America has to do. We don't need to have the 82nd Airborne escorting kids to kindergarten."[57]

But after the terrorist attack on 9/11, Bush administration policies changed sharply. If nation building had at one time seemed little other than dreamy-eyed idealism, it suddenly emerged as an important realist objective as well. Where foreign governments were weak and illegitimate, terrorists could roam unchecked. From Bush's perspective, the clearest examples of such weak governments were Afghanistan and Iraq. In Afghanistan, the Al Qaeda terrorist organization formed an alliance with the Taliban government and operated for years without hindrance. In Saddam Hussein's Iraq, the Bush administration argued, terrorists had also been granted safe haven and might have had access to dangerous weapons. The president stated the case for involvement in Iraq in both realist and idealist terms: "Our actions . . . are guided by a vision. We believe that freedom can advance and change lives in the greater Middle East, as it has advanced and changed lives in Asia, and Latin America, and Eastern Europe, and Africa . . . . And when that day comes, the bitterness and burning hatreds that feed terrorism will fade and die away. America and all the world will be safer when hope has returned to the Middle East."[58]

But Bush's critics, who had in many cases defended President Clinton's involvement in the former Yugoslavia, made the realist argument that the Iraq operation was contrary to our national interest. From this perspective, the war in Afghanistan was justifiable as retaliation for specific attacks on U.S. soil, but the war in Iraq was an

ethnic cleansing
Seeking to deport or eliminate entire ethnic groups from a country or region.

Comparing Foreign and Security Policies

unnecessary distraction. As former vice president Al Gore put it, "As the main body of our troops were deployed for the new invasion [in Iraq], those who had organized the attack against us escaped, and many are still at large."[59]

Role of International Organizations

Foreign policy analysts Ivo Daalder and James Lindsay argue that much of the history of American foreign policy can be viewed as a debate among leaders over whether to enter into cooperative alliances with other nations or whether to resist such arrangements. From George Washington, who warned against "permanent alliances," to Woodrow Wilson's effort to establish the League of Nations, leaders have taken different attitudes towards international cooperation, based on historical circumstances and leaders' interpretations of U.S. ideals and interests.[60]

Critics of the Bush administration argue that its foreign policy initiatives have been too frequently unilateralist, that is, unwilling to cooperate with other nations. Defenders of the Bush approach argue that many of the policies needed to fight the modern war on terror, such as preemption, are too important to subject to compromise or delay.[61] Regardless of whether cooperation occurs in any specific instance, two major types of international organizations are of abiding concern to policy makers: the United Nations and free trade agreements.

The United Nations   At the end of World War II, the victorious nations agreed to establish the **United Nations**, an international organization whose purpose is to preserve world peace and foster economic and social development throughout the world. Although the United Nations has been more successful than its predecessor, the ill-starred League of Nations, idealists and realists within the United States often find themselves at odds concerning the usefulness of the United Nations and other international organizations as vehicles for the conduct of U.S. foreign policy.

Idealists recommend that the United States work through the United Nations and other international organizations to achieve closer international cooperation. Idealists argue not only that these goals place American foreign policy on a high ethical plane, but also that they are an important tool for promoting peace and stability. If countries work together in international organizations, they are less likely to engage in warfare.[62]

Realists are reluctant to give the United Nations or other international organizations responsibility for the conduct of U.S. policy. They insist that decisions to intervene in world affairs must be predicated not on some vague ideal but on a calculation of the extent to which the United States has a substantial and visible interest at stake.[63] These decisions must be made on a case-by-case basis by the United States alone. Realists point out, for example, that the United Nations has condemned Israel, a U.S. ally, for its treatment of Arab Palestinians. They also criticize U.N. officials for wasteful and inefficient administration of the organization.

President Bush turned to the U.N. at key moments in the war against terrorism: the international body coordinated relief efforts in Afghanistan and helped set up an interim government in Iraq after the U.S. relinquished administrative control in July 2004. But Bush conducted the war in Iraq without U.N. approval, an action that drew criticism from Democrats. He also appointed John Bolton, an acerbic critic of U.N. policies, as the United States ambassador to the U.N.

United Nations
Organization of all nation-states, whose purpose is to preserve world peace and foster economic and social development throughout the world.

VIDEO DEBATE

Exporting American Democracy

The United Nations

The United States has worked with countries around the world to combat terrorism, but was criticized for going to war in Iraq without a broad coalition.

• *Are international coalitions more important or less important now than during the Cold War?*

Free Trade Agreements   When the Cold War began, the Truman administration took the position that the growth of free markets would aid in the effort to contain communism. International banks were created to lend money to needy countries, United Nations organizations handled world health and refugee problems, and an international trade agreement reduced tariffs around the world. In late 1947, for example, 23 countries founded the General Agreement on Tariffs and Trade (GATT) in Geneva, Switzerland.

Believing that it might be difficult to persuade Congress to approve GATT, Truman signed on to the measure anyway, proclaiming that it was an executive agreement that did not need Senate approval. This action set the pattern for the conduct of trade policy ever since. The executive branch takes the lead in formulating trade policy, although Congress must approve the overall framework within which policies are determined.[64]

In recent years, trade policy has grown increasingly contentious, as labor and environmental groups have become concerned that firms in other countries need not follow the labor and environmental regulations to which U.S. firms are subject. First came the 1993 battle over the North American Free Trade Agreement (NAFTA), which eliminated trade barriers among the United States, Canada, and Mexico. Negotiated by President George H. W. Bush and promoted by President Clinton, NAFTA won only a narrow majority in Congress after fierce lobbying by all sides.

More significant than the publicity surrounding NAFTA was the unusual profile of the coalitions on both sides of the debate. Although it was promoted by a Democratic president, only 40 percent of Democratic members of Congress supported the measure.[65] Opponents included not only some business interests but also labor unions, environmental groups, consumer groups, and isolationist politicians. They worried that trade agreements would cost jobs, harm the environment, and lead to the nullification of U.S. laws and standards. Proponents included business groups and those who favored greater ties with other nations.

The battle over NAFTA proved to be only the beginning of a very public debate over the status of world trade. In 1994, negotiators from 104 nations officially transformed GATT into the World Trade Organization (WTO), a trade body much more powerful than GATT, with enforcement and dispute resolution mechanisms. Opposition to the organization was significant and vocal and was led by the same groups that opposed NAFTA. Tens of thousands of protesters disrupted a meeting of WTO trade ministers in Seattle in 1999, blocking streets and preventing delegates from attending the meetings. World trade became the subject of public controversy as never before. As California state senator Tom Hayden said, "the WTO, which was unknown in this country yesterday, is going to be a household word now . . . . This is a great turning point."[66]

In 2001 President Bush called for the expansion of NAFTA to include other Latin American countries, thereby greatly increasing its size and scope. He also asked for congressional backing for another round of world trade talks. But Congress has balked at these proposed relaxations of trade restrictions.

Election pressures limit congressional enthusiasm for increased free trade. Even the president is not free of them. In 2002 such pressures proved particularly significant for tariffs on steel. This industry has been subject to growing competition from steel companies in Japan, South Korea, and Europe. Because the U.S. steel industry is concentrated in Pennsylvania, Ohio, and Michigan, states that President Bush hoped to win in 2004, the president proved particularly sensitive to industry complaints of unfair competition by steel companies abroad. In response to these complaints, Bush briefly raised tariffs by as much as 30 percent on some steel products—a policy markedly at odds with his overall goal of increasing worldwide trade.

The pressures on members of Congress from these states are even greater. Many observers thought that unless the president raised steel tariffs, he would lose all hope of getting congressional support for NAFTA expansion and further world trade negotiations. Said one analyst, "This is the necessary step backward so the president can make two steps forward on what really matters."[67] However these issues are resolved, the Bush administration will need to balance its commitment to international free trade with strong political pressures from vulnerable domestic industries.

Chapter Summary

Electoral considerations help account for the fact that presidents dominate policy making on foreign policy questions more than on domestic ones. Voters expect presidents to take the lead. In the short run, they tend to support presidents in crises no matter what action is taken. Only later, if things do not turn out well, do voters penalize presidents for choosing the wrong policy.

Other factors reinforce the president's dominant role in foreign policy. Fast action is often needed; interest-group pressures are less intense than on domestic issues; the Supreme Court has interpreted the powers of the president broadly; and Congress tends to defer to the executive. In the campaign against terrorism, Congress, acting under procedures set forth in the War Powers Resolution, authorized the president to take all military action necessary to find and punish those who aided or harbored the 9/11 terrorists, as well as to conduct action against Iraq as a last resort.

The Department of State, the Department of Defense, and the national intelligence director (who oversees the Central Intelligence Agency as well as other agencies), together with the head of the Joint Chiefs of Staff, all sit on the National Security Council, which is managed by a national security adviser responsible to the president for overall coordination of foreign policy. These institutions took their modern shape during the early years of the Cold War, and are all seeking to adapt to the post–Cold War world of terrorist threats.

Both idealistic and realistic factors help shape American foreign policy. On the one hand, the United

States feels responsible for promoting the democratic experiment abroad. On the other hand, the United States, like any other country, has its own interests to protect. Idealist and realist considerations both play a role in current debates over international organizations and nation building. But in the aftermath of 9/11, both realists and idealists believe it is important to help establish strong, legitimate governments throughout the world.

Key Terms

ambassador, p. 587
Bay of Pigs, p. 593
bipolar, p. 586
Central Intelligence Agency (CIA), p. 592
Cold War, p. 584
containment, p. 586
Department of Defense, p. 589
embassy, p. 587
ethnic cleansing, p. 596
executive agreement, p. 583

foreign policy, p. 575
foreign service, p. 588
idealists, p. 595
Iran-Contra affair, p. 594
Joint Chiefs of Staff, p. 589
League of Nations, p. 583
nation building, p. 595
national intelligence director, p. 594
National Security Council (NSC), p. 594
"rally 'round the flag" effect, p. 576

realists, p. 595
secretary of defense, p. 589
secretary of state, p. 587
Tonkin Gulf Resolution, p. 581
treaties, p. 583
two-presidency theory, p. 575
United Nations (U.N.), p. 597
U.S. v. Curtiss-Wright, p. 580
War Powers Resolution, p. 581
Youngstown Sheet and Tube Co. v. Sawyer, p. 580

Suggested Readings

Of General Interest

Corwin, Edward S. *Total War and the Constitution*. New York: Knopf, 1947. Classic, if dated, discussion of constitutional arrangements as they affect foreign policy.

Daalder, Ivo, and James Lindsay. *America Unbound: The Bush Revolution in Foreign Policy*. Washington, DC: Brookings Institution Press, 2003. Two foreign policy scholars argue that George W. Bush has made dramatic changes in U.S. foreign policy.

Jervis, Robert. *American Foreign Policy in a New Era*. New York: Routledge, 2005. A scholar of international relations examines the recent changes in U.S. foreign policy.

Peterson, Paul E., ed. *The President, the Congress, and the Making of Foreign Policy*. Norman, OK: Oklahoma University Press, 1994. Essays describing changes in presidential and congressional policy-making roles.

Pillar, Paul. *Terrorism and U.S. Foreign Policy*. Washington, D.C.: Brookings Institution Press, 2001. An assessment of U.S. policy, by a former CIA official, just prior to 9/11.

Wildavsky, Aaron. "The Two Presidencies." In Steven A. Shull, ed., *The Two Presidencies: A Quarter Century Assessment*. Chicago: Nelson-Hall, 1991, 11–25. Explains how politics differs between foreign and domestic issues.

Focused Studies

Allison, Graham. *Essence of Decision*. Boston: Little, Brown, 1971. Fascinating account of the Cuban missile crisis, the closest the United States and the Soviet Union ever came to nuclear confrontation.

Gordon, Michael R., and Bernard E. Trainor. *Cobra II: The Inside Story of the Invasion and Occupation of Iraq*. New York: Random House, 2006. A journalist and a general conduct a detailed study of the early stages of the Iraq War.

Huntington, Samuel. *The Clash of Civilizations*. New York: Simon & Schuster, 1996. Argues that future world conflicts will occur between clusters of nations that share a common cultural heritage.

Jeffreys-Johnes, Rhodri. *The CIA and American Democracy*. New Haven, CT: Yale University Press, 1989. A solid history of the Cold War CIA.

Johnson, Loch K. *America's Secret Power: The CIA in a Democratic Society*. New York: Oxford University Press, 1989. Informed critique of CIA power and tactics.

Leffler, Melvyn P. *A Preponderance of Power: National Security, the Truman Administration, and the Cold War*. Stanford, CA: Stanford University Press, 1992. Historical account of the establishment of U.S. Cold War strategy under Truman.

Silverstein, Gordon. *Imbalance of Powers: Constitutional Interpretation and the Making of American Foreign Policy*. New York: Oxford University Press, 1996. Argues that the president's constitutional authority over foreign policy has not been ceded to Congress.

Weissman, Stephen R. *A Culture of Deference: Congress's Failure of Leadership in Foreign Policy*. New York: Basic Books, 1995. Argues that Congress defers too much to presidential authority in foreign affairs.

On the Web

www.state.gov

www.defenselink.mil

The Department of State and the Department of Defense are the oldest and most important cabinet agencies with responsibility for conducting American foreign policy.

www.dni.gov

www.odci.gov (Central Intelligence Agency)

www.whitehouse.gov/nsc/

www.jcs.mil

In this chapter we discussed the changes to the U.S. foreign policy-making agencies that occurred at the beginning of the Cold War. The Central Intelligence Agency, the National Security Council, and the Joint Chiefs of Staff all were created after World War II to conduct foreign affairs more effectively. The director of national intelligence (DNI) is a new office, designed to address intelligence failings prior to 9/11.

www.ustr.gov

The U.S. trade representative, located in the Executive Office of the President, is the U.S. government's chief trade negotiator.

www.un.org

www.wto.org

The United Nations and the World Trade Organization are two key international organizations that have at times weathered criticism from both realists and idealists in the United States.

www.cfr.org

www.aipac.org

www.canf.org

One of the reasons why the president has more authority over foreign affairs than over domestic affairs is the comparative lack of interest groups with a foreign policy focus. Nevertheless, there are at least several interest groups that pay close attention to foreign policy, including the Council on Foreign Relations (CFR), the American Israel Public Affairs Committee (AIPAC), and the Cuban American National Foundation (CANF).

www.senate.gov/~foreign/

Although Congress plays a smaller role in foreign affairs than in domestic politics, the U.S. Senate has the constitutional responsibility to approve or reject foreign treaties and confirm nominees for key posts. Such issues are handled by the Senate's Committee on Foreign Relations.

Election Voices

The U.S. Politics of the Arab-Israeli Conflict

I have about come to the conclusion that the Palestine problem is insoluble, but I suppose we will have to keep working on it.

—President Harry S. Truman, letter to Senator Elbert Thomas, November 9, 1947[1]

THE ISSUE

Israel and Palestinian Arabs are unable to resolve their differences over their competing territorial claims. Should the U.S. back Israel, back the Palestinians, back neither, or impose a settlement?

Background

When Israel became a nation in 1948, the United States was the first country to recognize it. Arab states in the region, however, were upset by the creation of a Jewish nation on land that until the twentieth century had been occupied mainly by Arabs. As Jewish migration to the area increased during the 1930s, guerrilla skirmishes between Jews and Arabs intensified. In 1947 a United Nations partition proposal called for the creation of separate Jewish and Arab states. But, when a provisional Israeli government declared itself to be a sovereign state, six Arab nations invaded Israel. Israel won that war, gained more territory than it lost, and then greatly expanded the territory under its control in successive wars with its Arab neighbors in 1956, 1967, and 1973. As a result, many Palestinians left Israel to live in refugee camps in neighboring countries.

Egypt and Jordan sought to make peace with Israel beginning in the late 1970s. But many Palestinian Arabs, especially those in refugee camps who longed to return to the land where they had once lived, resented their status and condemned the atrocities the Israelis were alleged to have committed. They especially resented the establishment of a large number of Jewish settlements within areas that had historically been settled by Arabs, but that Israeli armies occupied at the conclusion of the series of Arab-Israeli wars.

Control of the ancient, religiously significant city of Jerusalem was still another point of great controversy between the two sides. Many Palestinians engaged in strikes, civil disorder, and even suicide bombings and other terrorist attacks to advance their cause. Meanwhile, Israel continued to occupy Palestinian regions captured in the wars, such as the West Bank and Gaza Strip areas (see Figure 1) and refused to allow millions of displaced Palestinians to return to their ancestral lands.

In recent years, there have been brief periods in which peace has appeared to be within reach, but resurgent hostility has inevitably followed. In 1993, then-prime minister Yitzhak Rabin signed a landmark U.S.-sponsored peace accord with Yasir Arafat, leader of the Palestinian Liberation Organization (PLO). This agreement paved the way for the West Bank and the Gaza Strip to enjoy limited self-government under a so-called Palestinian Authority. But Rabin was assassinated by a Jewish extremist in 1995. Even more disconcerting, new Palestinian terrorists (said by the PLO to be operating illegally and beyond the control of the weak Palestinian Authority) stepped up their suicide bombings and other attacks. After Arafat's death in 2004, further progress seemed possible, and Israel voluntarily vacated the occupied Gaza Strip region. But then, in 2006, the militant group Hamas, an organization that experts believe is responsible for at least 350 terrorist attacks,[2] won parliamentary elections in the Palestinian Authority. Later that year, the kidnappings of several Israeli soldiers by Hamas and another militant group, Hezbollah, provoked widespread fighting in the Gaza Strip and in Lebanon (where Hezbollah was based).

Options for U.S. policy include the following alternatives, each with its own drawbacks:

1. Support Israel's crackdowns on Palestinians and militant groups. But would this position alienate Arab allies of the United States, such as Saudi Arabia, and complicate the war on terrorism?

2. Support the rapid creation of a Palestinian state. But would this position send the message that terrorist bombings are effective?

3. Force the two parties to the bargaining table, taking a hands-on role in negotiations and in the implementation of whatever peace plan might result. But would such an effort waste U.S. diplomatic energy, taking attention away from the nation's other international responsibilities?

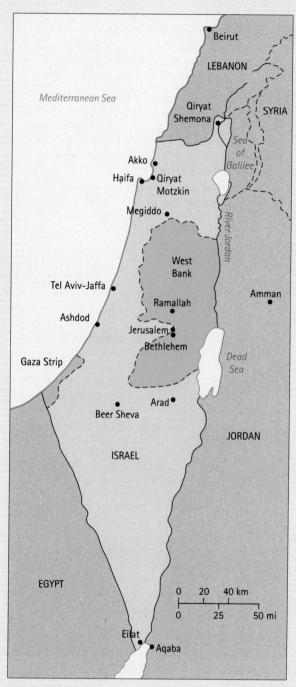

FIGURE 1

Israel This map shows Israel, as well as the Palestinian regions of the West Bank and Gaza Strip.

• *Why is a permanent settlement so difficult to achieve?*

Elections and U.S. Policy Toward Israel

The United States has always been a key ally of Israel. In the aftermath of the Holocaust, Americans felt sympathy for the

Zionists, advocates of a Jewish state in Palestine, many of whom had escaped from Europe and had endured great hardships under the Nazi regime. The case for a Jewish homeland, wrote one senator at the time, had been "written in blood and suffering."[3] During the Cold War, foreign policy experts saw Israel as strategically important because of its status as the only democracy in a region rich with oil. In the aftermath of the September 11 terrorist attacks, many people in the United States felt renewed kinship with Israeli citizens, who had long lived their daily lives under the threat of terrorism.

Since 1976, Israel has been the number-one recipient of U.S. foreign aid. American presidents have also often backed Israel in the United Nations, where it otherwise might have been outvoted by Arab states.

In recent decades, however, the U.S. alliance with Israel has become an uneasy one. Many critics in the United States and abroad have objected to the Israeli government's "aggressive behavior" in its responses to the suicide bombers. These responses have included such tactics as assassinating terrorist leaders, bulldozing the homes of terrorists' families, constructing a 450-mile "security fence" that would restrict travel between the West Bank and the rest of Israel, and engaging in retaliatory military incursions into Palestinian cities.[4] More than 1,000 Israeli citizens were killed in the spate of conflict from 2000 to mid-2006, but nearly four times as many Palestinians died during the same period.[5] Accordingly, the U.S. government has officially stated that, in George W. Bush's words, "A stable, peaceful [independent] Palestinian state is necessary to achieve the security that Israel longs for."[6]

Some members of Congress have criticized Bush for doing too little to resolve the conflict. Whatever the merits of the issue, it can be perilous for U.S. elected officials to appear to be anti-Israel. Although Jewish Americans make up only 2 percent of the population,[7] several key interest groups are extremely well-organized advocates for Israel. In particular, the American Israel Public Affairs Committee (AIPAC) has more than 100,000 members, meets with members of Congress more than 2,000 times a year, and is active on many college campuses.[8] In addition to lobbying, political fund-raising by pro-Jewish groups exceeds fund-raising by pro-Arab groups by a factor of about 140 to 1.[9] Two prominent foreign policy scholars have gone so far as to argue that "the overall thrust of U.S. policy in the region is due almost entirely to U.S. domestic politics, and especially to the activities of the 'Israel Lobby.'"[10] Other academics dismiss this perspective as "paranoid and conspiratorial."[11]

Opposing Viewpoints on a Palestinian State

For a Palestinian State

Advocates of a Palestinian state argue that the United States should act quickly to force Israel to accept a new nation of Palestine within the territories of the West Bank and Gaza Strip:

> As President Bush has stated, the future of humanity lies with freedom and democracy. The

Palestinian people have created their democracy. Now, they must have their freedom. There are no other people on earth who need freedom more than the Palestinians, who have lived under the longest military occupation of modern times . . . . The urgency of timely intervention cannot be overstated.

—Ziad Asali, president, American Task Force on Palestine, "The Way Forward in the Middle East Peace Process," Testimony before the House Committee on International Relations, February 10, 2005

Some who favor an independent Palestine also argue that to build a lasting solution, the United States should use its clout to help mend some of the destruction that the Middle East conflict has created:

Provocation from the Israeli side will continue . . . until the U.S. moves to publicly challenge the government's use of aggressive military force against the Palestinians . . . . To break this cycle of despair and violence that has gripped the Palestinians, the U.S., the European Union, and the Arab states should lead an international effort to help radically transform the West Bank and Gaza . . . . New roads and infrastructure, repaired buildings and restored services will create hope and invest people in the promise of peace.

—John Zogby, president, Arab American Institute, "The Steps We Must Now Take," May 20, 2002, www.aaiusa.org

Against a Palestinian State

Advocates of the Israeli position argue that the Palestinian Authority either has allowed terrorism to continue or even has encouraged it. According to this perspective, the Hamas victory in the 2006 elections makes it even more likely that a Palestinian state would constitute a terrorist state:

A government dominated by a terrorist organization undermines the effort to establish a democratic, non-violent society and jeopardizes efforts to achieve a lasting peace . . . . The United States must not recognize Hamas as a legitimate party in the democratic process until it agrees to renounce and end violence, dismantle the terrorist infrastruc-

ture, recognize Israel's right to exist, and agree to conduct direct negotiations with Israel.

—AIPAC, press release, January 26, 2006. www.aipac.org/PDFdocs/Press_PLC_Election s012606.pdf, accessed June 15, 2006

This rewarding of terrorism is not just a moral scandal. It is disastrous diplomacy. What does [an offer of a] provisional state say to the Palestinians? If . . . years of blood-letting gives the Palestinians an interim state . . . what possible disincentive do they have to continue the violence?

—Charles Krauthammer, "Offering Statehood for Palestinians in the Absence of Peace is Utter Folly," *Pittsburgh Post–Gazette*, June 22, 2002: p. A10

What Do Americans Believe?

Americans have consistently expressed support for Israel (see Figure 2). Nevertheless, they also feel that a Palestinian state is justified—especially if terrorist groups pledge to end the suicide bombings.[12]

Public sympathy for Israel, coupled with the active organization and fund-raising skills of pro-Israel organizations such as AIPAC, has convinced many elected officials that they oppose Israel at their peril. Members of Congress are reluctant to be seen as opposing the only democracy in the Middle East and, especially since 9/11, members who support the Palestinians risk appearing to be soft on terrorism. As one Arab American expert lamented, "You see more criticism of Israel in Israeli newspapers than you do in Congress. I guess the newspaper editors aren't trying to get reelected."[13]

The following list of Web sites includes some that represent each side of this complex issue.

What Do You Think?

1. Should Americans become deeply involved in bringing the two parties to agreement, or would this waste energy that could be better expended elsewhere?

2. Should the fact that Israel is a democracy affect our foreign policy decisions related to the country? Why or why not?

3. Should elected officials pay much attention to public opinion on this issue, or are Americans' views on foreign policy too vague and ill-informed to be meaningful?

[1]Available at the Truman Presidential Museum and Library, Recognition of Israel Study Collection, www.trumanlibrary.org, accessed July 18, 2002.
[2]Council on Foreign Relations, "Backgrounder: Hamas," Updated June 14, 2006, www.cfr.org/publication/8968/, accessed June 15, 2006.
[3]Letter from Senator Robert F. Wagner (D-NY) to President Harry S. Truman, June 20, 1946, Truman Presidential Museum and Library, Recognition of Israel Study Collection, www.trumanlibrary.org, accessed July 19, 2002.

[4]Laura King and Fayed abu Shammalah, "Israel Kills New Leader of Hamas," *Los Angeles Times*, April 18, 2004: A1; Patrick McMahon, "Terrorism Stirs Jews in USA to Activism," *USAToday*, June 25, 2002: 13A.
[5]"Conflict Statistics," Middle East Policy Council, www.mepc.org/resources/mrates.asp, accessed June 14, 2006.
[6]Robin Wright, "A Palestinian State Requires New Leadership, Bush Says," *Los Angeles Times*, June 25, 2002: A1.
[7]U. S. Bureau of the Census, *Statistical Abstract of the United States: 2006*, Table 71.

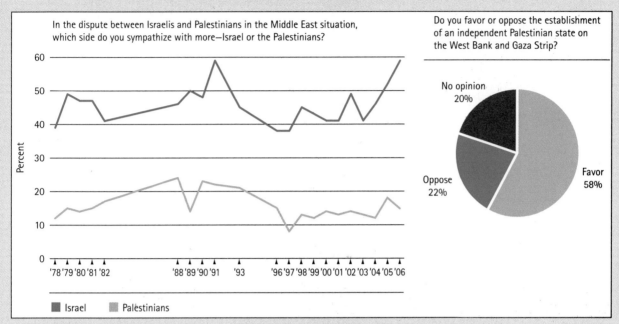

In the dispute between Israelis and Palestinians in the Middle East situation, which side do you sympathize with more—Israel or the Palestinians?

Do you favor or oppose the establishment of an independent Palestinian state on the West Bank and Gaza Strip?

No opinion 20%

Oppose 22%

Favor 58%

■ Israel ■ Palestinians

FIGURE 2

Americans Express More Sympathy with Israel in the Arab–Israeli Conflict But Also Support Creation of a Palestinian State

• *Do you think Americans express support for Israel because of cultural affinities between the two countries, because Israel is a democracy, or for reasons of strategic national interest?*

SOURCES: Gallup, Harris, Pew Research Center polls, various years; and Gallup poll, May 30–June 1, 2003.

PRO-ISRAEL

The American Israel Public Affairs Committee (AIPAC) is the largest pro-Israel lobby in Washington, and conducts many outreach activities in the rest of the country as well. Browse its issue papers for a detailed defense of the Israeli perspective.

www.aipac.org

The American Jewish Committee publishes a variety of briefings and issue papers on the Arab-Israeli conflict and other issues.

www.ajc.org

The Israeli government, through its ministry of foreign affairs, sponsors an official website with the latest details on Israel's policies and actions in the conflict.

www.israel.org

PRO-PALESTINIAN

The Arab American Institute is a lobbying and outreach organization concerned with the Middle East conflict and with other issues of concern to Arab Americans.

www.aaiusa.org

The Palestine Solidarity Campaign is an activist organization dedicated to an independent Palestinian state.

www.palestinecampaign.org

The official Web site of the Palestinian Authority offers the Palestinian perspective on the conflict.

www.pna.gov.ps/

[8]American Israel Public Affairs Committee, www.aipac.org, accessed June 14, 2006.

[9]David Lightman, "Arab Lobby Gains Clout; Fighting Image, History; Small Victories Add Up," *Hartford Courant*, May 26, 2002: A1.

[10]John J. Mearsheimer and Stephen M. Walt, "The Israel Lobby and U.S. Foreign Policy," Harvard University, John F. Kennedy School of Government, Faculty Working Paper RWP06-011, March 2006, 1.

[11]Harvard University Law Professor Alan Dershowitz, quoted in Michael Powell, "Academic Paper Stirs Debate," *Washington Post*, April 3, 2006: A3.

[12]This is especially true if the establishment of such a state would lead to an end to terrorism. Fully 74 percent say "favor" when asked the question "Do you favor or oppose the establishment of an independent Palestinian state on the West Bank if the Palestinian government demonstrates that it can end the suicide bombings in Israel?" Gallup Poll, June 21–23, 2002.

[13]Abraham Hooper, spokesman for the Council on American-Islamic Relations, quoted in Deirdre Shegreen, "Gephardt Says Bush's Proposal for Palestinian State is 'Problematic,'" *St. Louis Post-Dispatch*, June 21, 2002: A7.

APPENDIX I

The Declaration of Independence

In Congress, July 4, 1776

The Unanimous Declaration of the Thirteen United States of America

WHEN IN THE COURSE of human events it becomes necessary for one people to dissolve the political bands which have connected them with another, and to assume, among the powers of the earth, the separate and equal station to which the Laws of Nature and of Nature's God entitle them, a decent respect to the opinions of mankind requires that they should declare the causes which impel them to the separation.

We hold these truths to be self-evident, that all men are created equal, that they are endowed by their Creator with certain unalienable Rights, that among these are Life, Liberty and the pursuit of Happiness. That to secure these rights, Governments are instituted among Men, deriving their just powers from the consent of the governed. That whenever any Form of Government becomes destructive of these ends, it is the Right of the People to alter or to abolish it, and to institute new Government, laying its foundation on such principles and organizing its powers in such form, as to them shall seem most likely to effect their Safety and Happiness. Prudence, indeed, will dictate that Governments long established should not be changed for light and transient causes; and accordingly all experience hath shewn that mankind are more disposed to suffer, while evils are sufferable, than to right themselves by abolishing the forms to which they are accustomed. But when a long train of abuses and usurpations, pursuing invariably the same Object evinces a design to reduce them under absolute Despotism, it is their right, it is their duty, to throw off such Government, and to provide new Guards for their future security.—Such has been the patient sufferance of these Colonies; and such is now the necessity which constrains them to alter their former Systems of Government. The history of the present King of Great Britain is a history of repeated injuries and usurpations, all having in direct object the establishment of an absolute Tyranny over these States. To prove this, let Facts be submitted to a candid world.

He has refused his Assent to Laws, the most wholesome and necessary for the public good.

He has forbidden his Governors to pass Laws of immediate and pressing importance, unless suspended in their operation till his Assent should be obtained; and when so suspended, he has utterly neglected to attend to them.

He has refused to pass other Laws for the accommodation of large districts of people, unless those people would relinquish the right of Representation in the Legislature, a right inestimable to them and formidable to tyrants only.

He has called together legislative bodies at places unusual, uncomfortable, and distant from the depository of their Public Records, for the sole purpose of fatiguing them into compliance with his measures.

He has dissolved Representative Houses repeatedly, for opposing with manly firmness his invasions on the rights of the people.

He has refused for a long time, after such dissolutions, to cause others to be elected; whereby the Legislative Powers, incapable of Annihilation, have returned to the People at large for their exercise, the State remaining in the mean time exposed to all the dangers of invasion from without, and convulsions within.

He has endeavored to prevent the population of these States; for that purpose obstructing the Laws of Naturalization of Foreigners; refusing to pass others to encourage their migration hither, and raising the conditions of new Appropriations of Lands.

He has obstructed the Administration of Justice, by refusing his Assent to Laws for establishing Judiciary powers.

He has made Judges dependent on his Will alone, for the tenure of their offices, and the amount and payment of their salaries.

He has erected a multitude of New Offices, and sent hither swarms of Officers to harass our people, and eat out their substance.

He has kept among us, in times of peace, Standing Armies without the Consent of our legislatures.

He has affected to render the Military independent of and superior to the Civil power.

He has combined with others to subject us to a jurisdiction foreign to our constitution, and unacknowledged by our laws, giving his Assent to their Acts of pretended Legislation:

For quartering large bodies of armed troops among us:

For protecting them, by a mock Trial, from punishment for any Murders which they should commit on the Inhabitants of these States:

For cutting off our Trade with all parts of the world:

For imposing Taxes on us without our Consent:

For depriving us in many cases, of the benefits of Trial by Jury:

For transporting us beyond Seas to be tried for pretended offences:

For abolishing the free System of English Laws in a neighboring Province, establishing therein an Arbitrary government, and enlarging its Boundaries so as to render it at once an example and fit instrument for introducing the same absolute rule into these Colonies:

For taking away our Charters, abolishing our most valuable Laws, and altering fundamentally the Forms of our Governments:

For suspending our own Legislatures, and declaring themselves invested with power to legislate for us in all cases whatsoever.

He has abdicated Government here, by declaring us out of his Protection and waging War against us.

He has plundered our seas, ravaged our Coasts, burnt our towns, and destroyed the lives of our people.

He is at this time transporting large Armies of foreign Mercenaries to compleat the works of death, desolation and tyranny, already begun with circumstances of Cruelty and perfidy scarcely paralleled in the most barbarous ages, and totally unworthy the Head of a civilized nation.

He has constrained our fellow Citizens taken Captive on the high Seas to bear Arms against their Country, to become the executioners of their friends and Brethren, or to fall themselves by their Hands.

He has excited domestic insurrections amongst us, and has endeavored to bring on the inhabitants of our frontiers, the merciless Indian Savages, whose known rule of warfare, is an undistinguished destruction of all ages, sexes and conditions.

In every stage of these Oppressions We have Petitioned for Redress in the most humble terms: Our repeated Petitions have been answered only by repeated injury: A Prince, whose character is thus marked by every act which may define a Tyrant, is unfit to be the ruler of a free people.

Nor have We been wanting in attention to our British brethren. We have warned them from time to time of attempts by their legislature to extend an unwarrantable jurisdiction over us. We have reminded them of the circumstances of our emigration and settlement here. We have appealed to their native justice and magnanimity; and we have conjured them by the ties of our common kindred to disavow these usurpations, which would inevitably interrupt our connections and correspondence. They too have been deaf to the voice of justice and consanguinity. We must, therefore, acquiesce in the necessity, which denounces our Separation, and hold them, as we hold the rest of mankind, Enemies in War, in Peace Friends.

We, therefore, the Representatives of the United States of America, in General Congress, Assembled, appealing to the Supreme Judge of the world for the rectitude of our intentions, do, in the Name, and by Authority of the good People of these Colonies, solemnly publish and declare, That these United Colonies are, and of Right ought to be Free and Independent States; that they are Absolved from all Allegiance to the British Crown, and that all political connection between them and the State of Great Britain, is and ought to be totally dissolved: and that as Free and Independent States, they have full power to levy War, conclude Peace, contract Alliances, establish Commerce, and to do all other Acts and Things which Independent States may of right do. And for the support of this Declaration, with a firm reliance on the protection of divine Providence, we mutually pledge to each other our Lives, our Fortunes and our sacred Honor.

JOHN HANCOCK

NEW HAMPSHIRE
Josiah Bartlett,
Wm. Whipple,
Matthew Thornton.

MASSACHUSETTS BAY
Saml. Adams,
John Adams,
Robt. Treat Paine,
Elbridge Gerry.

RHODE ISLAND
Step. Hopkins,
William Ellery.

CONNECTICUT
Roger Sherman,
Samuel Huntington,
Wm. Williams,
Oliver Wolcott.

NEW YORK
Wm. Floyd,
Phil. Livingston,
Frans. Lewis,
Lewis Morris

NEW JERSEY
Richd. Stockton,
In. Witherspoon,
Fras. Hopkinson,
John Hart,
Abra. Clark.

PENNSYLVANIA
Robt. Morris,
Benjamin Rush,
Benjamin Franklin,
John Morton,
Geo. Clymer,
Jas. Smith,
Geo. Taylor,
James Wilson,
Geo. Ross.

DELAWARE
Caesar Rodney,
Geo. Read,
Tho. M'kean.

MARYLAND
Samuel Chase,
Wm. Paca,

Thos. Stone,
Charles Caroll of Carollton.

VIRGINIA
George Wythe,
Richard Henry Lee,
Th. Jefferson,
Benjamin Harrison,
Thos. Nelson, jr.,
Francis Lightfoot Lee,
Carter Braxton.

NORTH CAROLINA
Wm. Hooper,
Joseph Hewes,
John Penn.

SOUTH CAROLINA
Edward Rutledge,
Thos. Heyward, Junr.,
Thomas Lynch, jnr.,
Arthur Middleton.

APPENDIX II

The Constitution of the United States of America

WE THE PEOPLE of the United States, in Order to form a more perfect Union, establish Justice, insure domestic Tranquility, provide for the common defence, promote the general Welfare, and secure the Blessings of Liberty to ourselves and our Posterity, do ordain and establish this Constitution for the United States of America.

ARTICLE I

SECTION 1. All legislative Powers herein granted shall be vested in a Congress of the United States, which shall consist of a Senate and House of Representatives.

SECTION 2. The House of Representatives shall be composed of Members chosen every second Year by the People of the several States, and the Electors in each State shall have the Qualifications requisite for Electors of the most numerous Branch of the State Legislature.

No person shall be a Representative who shall not have attained to the Age of twenty five Years, and been seven Years a Citizen of the United States, and who shall not, when elected, be an Inhabitant of that State in which he shall be chosen.

Representatives and direct Taxes shall be apportioned among the several States which may be included within this Union, according to their respective Numbers which shall be determined by adding to the whole Number of free Persons, including those bound to Service for a Term of Years, and excluding Indians not taxed, three fifths of all other Persons. The actual Enumeration shall be made within three Years after the first Meeting of the Congress of the United States, and within every subsequent Term ten Years, in such Manner as they shall by Law direct. The Number of Representatives shall not exceed one for every thirty Thousand, but each State shall have at Least one Representative; and until such enumeration shall be made, the State of New Hampshire shall be entitled to chuse three, Massachusetts eight, Rhode-Island and Providence Plantations one, Connecticut five, New-York six, New Jersey four, Pennsylvania eight, Delaware one, Maryland six, Virginia ten, North Carolina five, South Carolina five, and Georgia three.

When vacancies happen in the Representation from any State, the Executive Authority thereof shall issue Writs of Election to fill such Vacancies.

The House of Representatives shall chuse their speaker and other Officers; and shall have the sole Power of Impeachment.

SECTION 3. The Senate of the United States shall be composed of two Senators from each State chosen by the Legislature thereof, for six Years; and each Senator shall have one Vote.

Immediately after they shall be assembled in Consequence of the first Election, they shall be divided as equally as may be into three Classes. The Seats of the Senators of the first Class shall be vacated at the Expiration of the second year, of the second Class at the Expiration of the fourth Year, and of the third Class at the Expiration of the sixth Year, so that one third may be chosen every second Year and if Vacancies happen by Resignation, or otherwise, during the Recess of the Legislature of any State, the Executive thereof may make temporary Appointments until the next Meeting of the Legislature, which shall then fill such Vacancies.

No Person shall be a Senator who shall not have attained to the Age of thirty Years, and been nine Years a Citizen of the United States, and who shall not, when elected, be an Inhabitant of that State for which he shall be chosen.

The Vice President of the United States shall be President of the Senate, but shall have no Vote, unless they be equally divided.

The Senate shall chuse their other Officers, and also a President pro tempore, in the Absence of the Vice President, or when he shall exercise the Office of President of the United States.

The Senate shall have the sole Power to try all Impeachments. When sitting for that Purpose, they shall be on Oath or Affirmation. When the President of the United States is tried, the Chief Justice shall preside: And no Person shall be convicted without the Concurrence of two thirds of the Members present.

Judgment in Cases of Impeachment shall not extend further than to removal from Office, and disqualification to hold and enjoy any Office of honor, Trust or Profit under the United States; but the Party convicted shall nevertheless be liable and subject to Indictment, Trial, Judgment and Punishment, according to Law.

SECTION 4. The Times, Places and Manner of holding Elections for Senators and Representatives, shall be prescribed in each State by the Legislature thereof; but the Congress may at any time by law make or alter such Regulations, except as to the Places of chusing Senators.

The Congress shall assemble at least once in every Year, and such Meeting shall be on the first Monday in December, unless they shall by Law appoint a different Day.

SECTION 5. Each House shall be the Judge of the Elections, Returns and Qualifications of its own Members, and a Majority of each shall constitute a Quorum to do Business; but a smaller Number may adjourn from day to day, and may be authorized to compel the Attendance of absent Members, in such Manner, and under such Penalties as each House may provide.

Each House may determine the Rules of its Proceedings, punish its Members for disorderly Behaviour, and with the Concurrence of two thirds, expel a Member.

Each House shall keep a journal of its Proceedings, and from time to time publish the same, excepting such Parts as may in their judgment require Secrecy; and the Yeas and Nays of the Members of either House on any question shall, at the Desire of one fifth of those present, be entered on the Journal.

Neither House, during the Session of Congress, shall, without the Consent of the other, adjourn for more than three days, nor to any other Place than that in which the two Houses shall be sitting.

SECTION 6. The Senators and Representatives shall receive a Compensation for their Services, to be ascertained by Law, and paid out of the Treasury of the United States. They shall in all Cases, except Treason, Felony and Breach of the Peace, be privileged from Arrest during their Attendance at the Session of their respective Houses, and in going to and returning from the same; and for any Speech or Debate in either House, they shall not be questioned in any other Place.

No Senator or Representative shall, during the Time for which he was elected, be appointed to any civil Office under the Authority of the United States, which shall have been created, or the Emoluments whereof shall have been encreased during such time; and no Person holding any Office under the United States, shall be a Member of either House during his Continuance in Office.

SECTION 7. All Bills for raising Revenue shall originate in the House of Representatives; but the Senate may propose or concur with Amendments as on other Bills.

Every Bill which shall have passed the House of Representatives and the Senate, shall, before it become a Law, be presented to the President of the United States; If he approves he shall sign it, but if not he shall return it, with his Objections to that House in which it shall have originated, who shall enter the Objections at large on their journal, and proceed to reconsider it. If after such Reconsideration two thirds of that House shall agree to pass the Bill, it shall be sent, together with the Objections, to the other House, by which it shall likewise be reconsidered, and if approved by two thirds of that House, it shall become a Law. But in all such Cases the Votes of both Houses shall be determined by Yeas and Nays, and the Names of the Persons voting for and against the Bill shall be entered on the Journal of each House respectively. If any Bill shall not be returned by the President within ten Days (Sundays excepted) after it shall have been presented to him, the Same shall be a Law, in like Manner as if he had signed it, unless the Congress by their Adjournment prevent its Return, in which Case it shall not be a Law.

Every Order, Resolution, or Vote to which the Concurrence of the Senate and House of Representatives may be necessary (except on a question of Adjournment) shall be presented to the President of the United States; and before the Same shall take Effect, shall be approved by him, or being disapproved by him, shall be repassed by two thirds of the Senate and House of Representatives, according to the Rules and Limitations prescribed in the Case of a Bill.

SECTION 8. The Congress shall have Power To lay and collect Taxes, Duties, Imposts and Excises, to pay the Debts and provide for the common Defence and general Welfare of the United States; but all Duties, Imposts and Excises shall be uniform throughout the United States;

To borrow Money on the credit of the United States;

To regulate Commerce with foreign Nations, and among the several States, and with the Indian Tribes;

To establish a uniform Rule of Naturalization, and uniform Laws on the subject of Bankruptcies throughout the United States;

To coin Money, regulate the Value thereof, and of foreign Coin, and fix the Standard of Weights and Measures;

To provide for the Punishment of counterfeiting the Securities and current Coin of the United States;

To establish Post Offices and post Roads;

To promote the Progress of Science and useful Arts, by securing for limited Times to Authors and Inventors the exclusive Right to their respective Writings and Discoveries;

To constitute Tribunals inferior to the supreme Court;

To define and punish Piracies and Felonies committed on the high Seas, and Offences against the Law of Nations;

To declare War, grant Letters of Marque and Reprisal, and make Rules concerning Captures on Land and Water;

To raise and support Armies, but no Appropriation of Money to that Use shall be for a longer Term than two Years;

To provide and maintain a Navy;

To make Rules for the Government and Regulation of the land and naval Forces;

To provide for calling forth the Militia to execute the Laws of the Union, suppress Insurrections and repel Invasions;

To provide for organizing, arming, and disciplining, the Militia, and for governing such Part of them as may be employed in the Service of the United States, reserving to the States respectively, the Appointment of the Officers, and the Authority of training the Militia according to the discipline prescribed by Congress;

To exercise exclusive Legislation in all Cases whatsoever, over such District (not exceeding ten Miles square) as may, by Cession of particular States, and the Acceptance of Congress, become the Seat of the Government of the United States, and to exercise like Authority over all

Places purchased by the Consent of the Legislature of the State in which the Same shall be for the Erection of Forts, Magazines, Arsenals, dock-Yards, and other needful Buildings;—And

To make all Laws which shall be necessary and proper for carrying into Execution the foregoing Powers, and all other Powers vested by this Constitution in the Government of the United States, or in any Department or Officer thereof.

SECTION 9. The Migration or Importation of such Persons as any of the States now existing shall think proper to admit, shall not be prohibited by the Congress prior to the Year one thousand eight hundred and eight, but a Tax or duty may be imposed on such Importation, not exceeding ten dollars for each Person.

The Privilege of the Writ of Habeas Corpus shall not be suspended, unless when in Cases of Rebellion or Invasion the public Safety may require it.

No Bill of Attainder or ex post facto Law shall be passed.

No Capitation, or other direct, Tax shall be laid, unless in Proportion to the Census or Enumeration herein before directed to be taken.

No Tax or Duty shall be laid on Articles exported from any State.

No Preference shall be given by any Regulation of Commerce or Revenue to the Ports of one State over those of another; nor shall Vessels bound to, or from, one State, be obliged to enter, clear, or pay Duties in another.

No Money shall be drawn from the Treasury, but in Consequence of Appropriations made by Law; and a regular Statement and Account of the Receipts and Expenditures of all public Money shall be published from time to time.

No Title of Nobility shall be granted by the United States: And no Person holding any Office of Profit or Trust under them, shall, without the Consent of the Congress, accept of any present, Emolument, Office, or Title, of any kind whatever, from any King, Prince, or foreign State.

SECTION 10. No state shall enter into any Treaty, Alliance, or Confederation; grant Letters of Marque and Reprisal; coin Money; emit Bills of Credit; make any Thing but gold and silver Coin a Tender in Payment of Debts; pass any Bill of Attainder, ex post facto Law, or Law impairing the Obligation of Contracts, or grant any Title of Nobility.

No State shall, without the Consent of the Congress, lay any Imposts or Duties on Imports or Exports, except what may be absolutely necessary for executing its inspection Laws: and the net Produce of all Duties and Imposts, laid by any State on Imports or Exports, shall be for the Use of the Treasury of the United States, and all such Laws shall be subject to the Revision and Controul of the Congress.

No State shall, without the Consent of Congress, lay any Duty of Tonnage, keep Troops, or Ships of War in time of Peace, enter into any Agreement or Compact with another State, or with a foreign Power, or engage in War, unless actually invaded, or in such imminent Danger as will not admit of delay.

ARTICLE II

SECTION 1. The executive Power shall be vested in a President of the United States of America. He shall hold his Office during the Term of four Years, and, together with the Vice President, chosen for the same Term, be elected as follows.

Each State shall appoint, in such Manner as the Legislature thereof may direct, a Number of Electors, equal to the whole Number of Senators and Representatives to which the State may be entitled in the Congress; but no Senator or Representative, or Person holding an Office of Trust of Profit under the United States, shall be appointed an Elector.

The Electors shall meet in their respective States, and vote by Ballot for two Persons, of whom one at least shall not be an Inhabitant of the same State with themselves. And they shall make a List of all the Persons voted for, and, of the Number of Votes for each; which List they shall sign and certify, and transmit sealed to the Seat of the Government of the United States, directed to the President of the Senate. The President of the Senate shall, in the Presence of the Senate and House of Representatives, open all the Certificates, and the Votes shall then be counted. The Person having the greatest Number of Votes shall be the President, if such Number be a Majority of the whole Number of Electors appointed; and if there be more than one who have such Majority, and have an equal Number of Votes, then the House of Representatives shall immediately chuse by Ballot one of them for President; and if no Person have a Majority, then from the five highest on the List the said House shall in like Manner chuse the President. But in chusing the President, the Votes shall be taken by States, the Representation from each State having one Vote; A quorum for this Purpose shall consist of a Member or Members from two thirds of the States, and a Majority of all the States shall be necessary to a Choice. In every Case, after the Choice of the President, the Person having the greatest Number of Votes of the Electors shall be the Vice President. But if there should remain two or more who have equal Votes, the Senate shall chuse from them by Ballot the Vice President.

The Congress may determine the Time of chusing the Electors, and the Day on which they shall give their Votes; which Day shall be the same throughout the United States.

No Person except a natural born Citizen, or a Citizen of the United States, at the time of the Adoption of this Constitution, shall be eligible to the Office of President; neither shall any Person be eligible to that Office who shall not have attained to the Age of thirty five Years, and been fourteen Years a Resident within the United States.

In Case of the Removal of the President from Office, or of his Death, Resignation, or Inability to discharge the Powers and Duties of the said Office, the Same shall devolve on the Vice President, and the Congress may by Law provide for the Case of Removal, Death, Resignation or Inability, both of the President and Vice President, declaring what Officer shall then act as President, and such Officer shall act accordingly, until the Disability be removed, or a President shall be elected.

The President shall, at stated Times, receive for his Services, a Compensation, which shall neither be encreased nor diminished during the Period for which he shall have been elected, and he shall not receive within that Period any other Emolument from the United States, or any of them.

Before he enter on the Execution of his Office, he shall take the following Oath or Affirmation—"I do solemnly swear (or affirm) that I will faithfully execute the Office of President of the United States, and will to the best of my Ability, preserve, protect and defend the Constitution of the United States."

SECTION 2. The President shall be Commander in Chief of the Army, and Navy of the United States, and of the Militia of the several States, when called into the actual Service of the United States; he may require the Opinion, in writing, of the principal Officer in each of the executive Departments, upon any Subject relating to the Duties of their respective Offices, and he shall have Power to grant Reprieves and Pardons for Offences against the United States, except in Cases of Impeachment.

He shall have Power, by and with the Advice and Consent of the Senate, to make Treaties, provided two thirds of the Senators present concur; and he shall nominate, and by and with the Advice and Consent of the Senate, shall appoint Ambassadors, other public Ministers and Consuls, Judges of the supreme Court, and all other Officers of the United States, whose Appointments are not herein otherwise provided for, and which shall be established by Law: but the Congress may by Law vest the Appointment of such inferior Officers, as they think proper, in the President alone, in the Courts of Law, or in the Heads of Departments.

The President shall have Power to fill up all Vacancies that may happen during the Recess of the Senate, by granting Commissions which shall expire at the end of their next Session.

SECTION 3. He shall from time to time give to the Congress Information of the State of the Union, and recommend to their Consideration such Measures as he shall judge necessary and expedient; he may, on extraordinary Occasions, convene both Houses, or either of them, and in Case of Disagreement between them, with Respect to the Time of Adjournment, he may adjourn them to such Time as he shall think proper; he shall receive Ambassadors and other public Ministers; he shall take Care that the Laws be faithfully executed, and shall Commission all the Officers of the United States.

SECTION 4. The President, Vice President and all civil Officers of the United States, shall be removed from Office on Impeachment for, and Conviction of, Treason, Bribery, or other high Crimes and Misdemeanors.

ARTICLE III

SECTION 1. The judicial Power of the United States, shall be vested in one supreme Court, and in such inferior Courts as the Congress may from time to time ordain and establish. The Judges, both of the supreme and inferior Courts, shall hold their Offices during good Behaviour, and shall, at stated Times, receive for their Services, a Compensation, which shall not be diminished during their Continuance in Office.

SECTION 2. The judicial Power shall extend to all Cases, in Law and Equity, arising under this Constitution, the Laws of the United States, and Treaties made, or which shall be made, under their Authority;—to all Cases affecting Ambassadors, other public Ministers and Consuls;—to all Cases of admiralty and maritime Jurisdiction;—to Controversies to which the United States shall be a Party;—to Controversies between two or more States;—between a State and Citizens of another State;—between Citizens of different States,—between Citizens of the same State claiming Lands under Grants of different States,—and between a State, or the Citizens thereof, and foreign States, Citizens of Subjects.

In all Cases affecting Ambassadors, other public Ministers and Consuls, and those in which a State shall be Party, the supreme Court shall have original Jurisdiction. In all the other Cases before mentioned, the supreme Court shall have appellate Jurisdiction, both as to Law and Fact, with such Exceptions, and under such Regulations as the Congress shall make.

The Trial of all Crimes, except in Cases of Impeachment, shall be by Jury; and such Trial shall be held in the State where the said Crimes shall have been committed; but when not committed within any State, the Trial shall be at such Place or Places as the Congress may by Law have directed.

SECTION 3. Treason against the United States, shall consist only in levying War against them, or in adhering to their Enemies, giving them Aid and Comfort. No Person shall be convicted of Treason unless on the Testimony of two Witnesses to the same overt Act, or on Confession in open Court.

The Congress shall have Power to declare the Punishment of Treason, but no Attainder of Treason shall work Corruption of Blood, or Forfeiture except during the Life of the Person attainted.

ARTICLE IV

SECTION 1. Full Faith and Credit shall be given in each State to the public Acts, Records, and judicial Proceedings of every other State. And the Congress may by general Laws prescribe the Manner in which such Acts, Records and Proceedings shall be proved, and the Effect thereof.

SECTION 2. The Citizens of each State shall be entitled to all Privileges and Immunities of Citizens in the several States.

A Person charged in any State with Treason, Felony, or other Crime, who shall flee from Justice, and be found in another State, shall on Demand of the executive Authority of the State from which he fled, be delivered up, to be removed to the State having Jurisdiction of the Crime.

No Person held to Service or Labour in one State under the Laws thereof, escaping into another, shall, in Consequence of any Law or Regulation therein, be discharged from such Service or Labour, but shall be delivered up on Claim of the Party to whom such Service or Labour may be due.

SECTION 3. New States may be admitted by the Congress into this Union; but no new State shall be formed or erected within the Jurisdiction of any other State; nor any State be formed by the Junction of two or more States, or Parts of States, without the Consent of the Legislatures of the States concerned as well as of the Congress.

The Congress shall have Power to dispose of and make all needful Rules and Regulations respecting the Territory or other Property belonging to the United States; and nothing in this Constitution shall be so construed as to Prejudice any Claims of the United States, or of any particular State.

SECTION 4. The United States shall guarantee to every State in this Union a Republican Form of Government, and shall protect each of them against Invasion, and on Application of the Legislature, or of the Executive (when the Legislature cannot be convened) against domestic Violence.

ARTICLE V

The Congress, whenever two thirds of both Houses shall deem it necessary, shall propose Amendments to this Constitution, or, on the Application of the Legislatures of two thirds of the several States, shall call a Convention for proposing Amendments, which, in either Case, shall be valid to all Intents and Purposes, as Part of this Constitution, when ratified by the Legislatures of three fourths of the several States, or by Conventions in three fourths thereof, as the one or the other Mode of Ratification may be proposed by the Congress; Provided that no Amendment which may be made prior to the Year One thousand eight hundred and eight shall in any Manner affect the first and fourth Clauses in the Ninth Section of the first Article; and that no State, without its Consent, shall be deprived of its equal Suffrage in the Senate.

ARTICLE VI

All Debts contracted and Engagements entered into, before the Adoption of this Constitution, shall be as valid against the United States under this Constitution, as under the Confederation.

This Constitution, and the laws of the United States which shall be made in Pursuance thereof; and all Treaties made, or which shall be made, under the Authority of the United States, shall be the supreme Law of the Land; and the Judges in every State shall be bound thereby, any Thing in the Constitution or Laws of any State to the Contrary notwithstanding.

The Senators and Representatives before mentioned, and the Members of the several State Legislatures, and all executive and judicial Officers, both of the United States and of the several States, shall be bound by Oath or Affirmation, to support this Constitution; but no religious Test shall ever be required as a Qualification to any Office or public Trust under the United States.

ARTICLE VII

The Ratification of the Conventions of nine States, shall be sufficient for the Establishment of this Constitution between the States so ratifying the Same.

Done in Convention by the Unanimous Consent of the States present the Seventeenth Day of September in the Year of our Lord one thousand seven hundred and Eighty seven and of the Independence of the United States of America the Twelfth. In witness whereof we have hereunto subscribed our Names,

GO. WASHINGTON
Presid't. and deputy from Virginia

Attest
WILLIAM JACKSON
Secretary

Articles in addition to, and amendment of the Constitution of the United States of America, proposed by Congress and ratified by the Legislatures of the several states, pursuant to the Fifth Article of the original Constitution.

(The first ten amendments were passed by Congress on September 25, 1789, and were ratified on December 15, 1791.)

AMENDMENT I

Congress shall make no law respecting an establishment of religion, or prohibiting the free exercise thereof; or abridging the freedom of speech, or of the press; or the right of the people peaceably to assemble, and to petition the Government for a redress of grievances.

AMENDMENT II

A well regulated Militia, being necessary to the security of a free State, the right of the people to keep and bear Arms, shall not be infringed.

AMENDMENT III

No Soldier shall, in time of peace be quartered in any house, without the consent of the Owner, nor in time of war, but in a manner to be prescribed by law.

AMENDMENT IV

The right of the people to be secure in their persons, houses, papers, and effects, against unreasonable searches and seizures, shall not be violated, and no warrants shall issue, but upon probable cause, supported by Oath or affirmation, and particularly describing the place to be searched, and the persons or things to be seized.

AMENDMENT V

No person shall be held to answer for a capital, or otherwise infamous crime, unless on a presentment or indictment of a Grand Jury, except in cases arising in the land or naval forces, or in the Militia, when in actual service in time of War or public danger; nor shall any person be subject for the same offence to be twice put in jeopardy of life or limb; nor shall be compelled in any criminal case to be a witness against himself, nor be deprived of life, liberty, or property, without due process of law; nor shall private property be taken for public use, without just compensation.

AMENDMENT VI

In all criminal prosecutions, the accused shall enjoy the right to a speedy and public trial, by an impartial jury of the State and district wherein the crime shall have been committed, which district shall have been previously ascertained by law, and to be informed of the nature and cause of the accusation; to be confronted with the witnesses against him; to have compulsory process for obtaining witnesses in his favor, and to have the assistance of counsel for his defence.

AMENDMENT VII

In Suits at common law, where the value in controversy shall exceed twenty dollars, the right of trial by jury shall be preserved, and no fact tried by a jury, shall be otherwise re-examined in any Court of the United States, than according to the rules of the common law.

AMENDMENT VIII

Excessive bail shall not be required, nor excessive fines imposed, nor cruel and unusual punishments inflicted.

AMENDMENT IX

The enumeration in the Constitution, of certain rights, shall not be construed to deny or disparage others retained by the people.

AMENDMENT X

The powers not delegated to the United States by the Constitution, nor prohibited by it to the States, are reserved to the States respectively, or to the people.

AMENDMENT XI
(Ratified on February 7, 1795)

The Judicial power of the United States shall not be construed to extend to any suit in law or equity, commenced or prosecuted against one of the United States by Citizens of another State, or by Citizens or Subjects of any Foreign State.

AMENDMENT XII
(Ratified on June 15, 1804)

The Electors shall meet in their respective states, and vote by ballot for President and Vice-President, one of whom, at least, shall not be an inhabitant of the same state with themselves; they shall name in their ballots the person voted for as President, and in distinct ballots the person voted for as Vice-President, and they shall make distinct lists of all persons voted for as President, and of all persons voted for as Vice-President, and of the number of votes for each, which lists they shall sign and certify, and transmit sealed to the seat of the government of the United States, directed to the President of the Senate;—The President of the Senate shall, in the presence of the Senate and House of Representatives, open all the certificates and the votes shall then be counted;—The person having the greatest number of votes for President, shall be the President, if such number be a majority of the whole number of Electors appointed; and if no person have such majority; then from the persons having the highest numbers not exceeding three on the list of those voted for as President, the House of Representatives shall choose immediately, by ballot, the President. But in choosing the President, the votes shall be taken by states, the representation from each state having one vote; a quorum for this purpose shall consist of a member or members from two-thirds of the states, and a majority of all the states shall be necessary to a choice. And if the House of Representatives shall not choose a President whenever the right of choice shall devolve upon them, before the fourth day of March next following, then the Vice-President shall act as President, as in the case of the death or other constitutional disability of the President.—The person having the greatest number of votes as Vice-President, shall be the Vice-President, if such number be a majority of the whole number of Electors appointed, and if no person have a majority, then from the two highest numbers on the list, the Senate shall choose the Vice-President; a quorum for the purpose shall consist of two-thirds of the whole number of

Senators, and a majority of the whole number shall be necessary to a choice. But no person constitutionally ineligible to the office of President shall be eligible to that of Vice-President of the United States.

AMENDMENT XIII
(Ratified on December 6, 1865)

SECTION 1. Neither slavery nor involuntary servitude, except as a punishment for crime whereof the party shall have been duly convicted, shall exist within the United States, or any place subject to their jurisdiction.

SECTION 2. Congress shall have power to enforce this article by appropriate legislation.

AMENDMENT XIV
(Ratified on July 9, 1868)

SECTION 1. All persons born or naturalized in the United States, and subject to the jurisdiction thereof, are citizens of the United States and of the State wherein they reside. No State shall make or enforce any law which shall abridge the privileges or immunities of citizens of the United States; nor shall any State deprive any person of life, liberty, or property, without due process of law; nor deny to any person within its jurisdiction the equal protection of the laws.

SECTION 2. Representatives shall be apportioned among the several States according to their respective numbers, counting the whole number of persons in each State, excluding Indians not taxed. But when the right to vote at any election for the choice of electors for President and Vice President of the United States, Representatives in Congress, the Executive and Judicial officers of a State, or the members of the Legislature thereof, is denied to any of the male inhabitants of such State, being twenty-one years of age, and citizens of the United States, or in any way abridged, except for participation in rebellion, or other crime, the basis of representation therein shall be reduced in the proportion which the number of such male citizens shall bear to the whole number of male citizens twenty-one years of age in such State.

SECTION 3. No person shall be a Senator or Representative in Congress, or elector of President and Vice President, or hold any office, civil or military, under the United States, or under any State, who, having previously taken an oath, as a member of Congress, or as an officer of the United States, or as a member of any State legislature, or as an executive or judicial officer of any State, to support the Constitution of the United States, shall have engaged in insurrection or rebellion against the same, or given aid or comfort to the enemies thereof. But Congress may by a vote of two-thirds of each House, remove such disability.

SECTION 4. The validity of the public debt of the United States, authorized by law, including debts incurred for payment of pensions and bounties for services in suppressing insurrection or rebellion, shall not be questioned. But neither the United States nor any State shall assume or pay any debt or obligation incurred in aid of insurrection or rebellion against the United States, or any claim for the loss or emancipation of any slave, but all such debts, obligations and claims shall be held illegal and void.

SECTION 5. The Congress shall have power to enforce, by appropriate legislation, the provisions of this article.

AMENDMENT XV
(Ratified on February 3, 1870)

SECTION 1. The right of citizens of the United States to vote shall not be denied or abridged by the United States or by any State on account of race, color, or previous condition of servitude.

SECTION 2. The Congress shall have power to enforce this article by appropriate legislation.

AMENDMENT XVI
(Ratified on February 3, 1913)

The Congress shall have power to lay and collect taxes on incomes, from whatever source derived, without apportionment among the several States, and without regard to any census or enumeration.

AMENDMENT XVII
(Ratified on April 8, 1913)

The Senate of the United States shall be composed of two Senators from each State, elected by the people thereof, for six years; and each Senator shall have one vote. The electors in each State shall have the qualifications requisite for electors of the most numerous branch of the State legislatures.

When vacancies happen in the representation of any State in the Senate, the executive authority of such State shall issue writs of election to fill such vacancies: Provided, That the legislature of any State may empower the executive thereof to make temporary appointments until the people fill the vacancies by election as the legislature may direct.

This amendment shall not be so construed as to affect the election or term of any Senator chosen before it becomes valid as part of the Constitution.

AMENDMENT XVIII
(Ratified on January 16, 1919)

SECTION 1. After one year from the ratification of this article the manufacture, sale, or transportation of intoxicating liquors within, the importation thereof into, or the exportation thereof from the United States and all territory subject to the jurisdiction thereof for beverage purposes is hereby prohibited.

SECTION 2. The Congress and the several States shall have concurrent power to enforce this article by appropriate legislation.

SECTION 3. This article shall be inoperative unless it shall have been ratified as an amendment to the Constitution by the legislatures of the several States, as provided in the Constitution, within seven years from the date of the submission hereof to the States by the Congress.

AMENDMENT XIX
(Ratified on August 18, 1920)

The right of citizens of the United States to vote shall not be denied or abridged by the United States or by any State on account of sex.

Congress shall have power to enforce this article by appropriate legislation.

AMENDMENT XX
(Ratified on February 6, 1933)

SECTION 1. The terms of the President and Vice President shall end at noon on the 20th day of January, and the terms of Senators and Representatives at noon on the 3d day of January, of the years in which such terms would have ended if this article had not been ratified; and the terms of their successors shall then begin.

SECTION 2. The Congress shall assemble at least once in every year, and such meeting shall begin at noon on the 3d day of January, unless they shall by law appoint a different day.

SECTION 3. If, at the time fixed for the beginning of the term of the President, the President elect shall have died, the Vice President elect shall become President. If a President shall not have been chosen before the time fixed for the beginning of his term, or if the President elect shall have failed to qualify, then the Vice President elect shall act as President until a President shall have qualified; and the Congress may by law provide for the case wherein neither a President elect nor a Vice President elect shall have qualified, declaring who shall then act as President, or the manner in which one who is to act shall be selected, and such person shall act accordingly until a President or Vice President shall have qualified.

SECTION 4. The Congress may by law provide for the case of the death of any of the persons from whom the House of Representatives may choose a President whenever the rights of choice shall have devolved upon them, and for the case of the death of any of the persons from whom the Senate may choose a Vice President whenever the right of choice shall have devolved upon them.

SECTION 5. Sections 1 and 2 shall take effect on the 15th day of October following the ratification of this article.

SECTION 6. This article shall be inoperative unless it shall have been ratified as an amendment to the Constitution by the legislatures of three-fourths of the several States within seven years from the date of its submission.

AMENDMENT XXI
(Ratified on December 5, 1933)

SECTION 1. The eighteenth article of amendment to the Constitution of the United States is hereby repealed.

SECTION 2. The transportation or importation into any State, Territory, or possession of the United States for delivery or use therein of intoxicating liquors, in violation of the laws thereof, is hereby prohibited.

SECTION 3. This article shall be inoperative unless it shall have been ratified as an amendment to the Constitution by conventions in the several States, as provided in the Constitution, within seven years from the date of the submission hereof to the States by the Congress.

AMENDMENT XXII
(Ratified on February 27, 1951)

No person shall be elected to the office of the President more than twice, and no person who has held the office of President, or acted as President, for more than two years of a term to which some other person was elected President shall be elected to the office of the President more than once. But this Article shall not apply to any person holding the office of President when this Article was proposed by the Congress, and shall not prevent any person who may be holding the office of President, or acting as President, during the term within which this Article becomes operative from holding the office of President or acting as President during the remainder of such term.

AMENDMENT XXIII
(Ratified on March 29, 1961)

SECTION 1. The District constituting the seat of Government of the United States shall appoint in such manner as the Congress may direct:

A number of electors of President and Vice President equal to the whole number of Senators and Representatives in Congress to which the District would be entitled if it were a State, but in no event more than the least populous State; they shall be in addition to those appointed by the States, but they shall be considered, for the purposes of the election of President and Vice President, to be electors appointed by a State; and they shall meet in the District and perform such duties as provided by the twelfth article of amendment.

SECTION 2. The Congress shall have power to enforce this article by appropriate legislation.

AMENDMENT XXIV
(Ratified on January 23, 1964)

SECTION 1. The right of citizens of the United States to vote in any primary or other election for President or Vice President, for electors for President or Vice President, or for Senator or Representative in Congress, shall not be denied or abridged by the United States or any State by reason of failure to pay any poll tax or other tax.

SECTION 2. The Congress shall have power to enforce this article by appropriate legislation.

AMENDMENT XXV
(Ratified on February 10, 1967)

SECTION 1. In case of the removal of the President from office or of his death or resignation, the Vice President shall become President.

SECTION 2. Whenever there is a vacancy in the office of the Vice President, the President shall nominate a Vice President who shall take office upon confirmation by a majority vote of both Houses of Congress.

SECTION 3. Whenever the President transmits to the President pro tempore of the Senate and the Speaker of the House of Representatives his written declaration that he is unable to discharge the powers and duties of his office, and until he transmits to them a written declaration to the contrary, such powers and duties shall be discharged by the Vice President as Acting President.

SECTION 4. Whenever the Vice President and a majority of either the principal officers of the executive departments or of such other body as Congress may by law provide, transmit to the President pro tempore of the Senate and the Speaker of the House of Representatives their written declaration that the President is unable to discharge the powers and duties of his office, the Vice President shall immediately assume the powers and duties of the office as Acting President.

Thereafter, when the President transmits to the President pro tempore of the Senate and the Speaker of the House of Representatives his written declaration that no inability exists, he shall resume the powers and duties of his office unless the Vice President and a majority of either the principal officers of the executive department or of such other body as Congress may by law provide, transmit within four days to the President pro tempore of the Senate and the Speaker of the House of Representatives their written declaration that the President is unable to discharge the powers and duties of his office. Thereupon Congress shall decide the issue, assembling within forty-eight hours for that purpose if not in session. If the Congress, within twenty-one days after receipt of the latter written declaration, or, if Congress is not in session, within twenty-one days after Congress is required to assemble, determines by two-thirds vote of both Houses that the President is unable to discharge the powers and duties of his office, the Vice President shall continue to discharge the same as Acting President; otherwise, the President shall resume the powers and duties of his office.

AMENDMENT XXVI
(Ratified on July 1, 1971)

SECTION 1. The right of citizens of the United States, who are eighteen years of age or older, to vote shall not be denied or abridged by the United States or by any State on account of age.

SECTION 2. The Congress shall have power to enforce this article by appropriate legislation.

AMENDMENT XXVII
(Ratified on May 7, 1992)

No law varying the compensation for the services of Senators and Representatives shall take effect until an election of Representatives shall have intervened.

APPENDIX III

The Federalist No. 10

November 22, 1787

James Madison

TO THE PEOPLE OF THE STATE OF NEW YORK.

Among the numerous advantages promised by a well constructed Union, none deserves to be more accurately developed than its tendency to break and control the violence of faction. The friend of popular governments, never finds himself so much alarmed for their character and fate, as when he contemplates their propensity to this dangerous vice. He will not fail therefore to set a due value on any plan which, without violating the principles to which he is attached, provides a proper cure for it. The instability, injustice and confusion introduced into the public councils, have in truth been the mortal diseases under which popular governments have every where perished; as they continue to be the favorite and fruitful topics from which the adversaries to liberty derive their most specious declamations. The valuable improvements made by the American Constitutions on the popular models, both ancient and modern, cannot certainly be too much admired; but it would be an unwarrantable partiality, to contend that they have as effectually obviated the danger on this side as was wished and expected. Complaints are every where heard from our most considerate and virtuous citizens, equally the friends of public and private faith, and of public and personal liberty; that our governments are too unstable; that the public good is disregarded in the conflicts of rival parties; and that measures are too often decided, not according to the rules of justice, and the rights of the minor party; but by the superior force of an interested and over-bearing majority. However anxiously we may wish that these complaints had no foundation, the evidence of known facts will not permit us to deny that they are in some degree true. It will be found indeed, on a candid review of our situation, that some of the distresses under which we labor, have been erroneously charged on the operation of our governments; but it will be found, at the same time, that other causes will not alone account for many of our heaviest misfortunes; and particularly, for that prevailing and increasing distrust of public engagements, and alarm for private rights, which are echoed from one end of the continent to the other. These must be chiefly, if not wholly, effects of the unsteadiness and injustice, with which a factious spirit has tainted our public administrations.

By a faction I understand a number of citizens, whether amounting to a majority or minority of the whole, who are united and actuated by some common impulse of passion, or of interest, adverse to the rights of other citizens, or to the permanent and aggregate interests of the community.

There are two methods of curing the mischiefs of faction: the one, by removing its causes; the other, by controlling its effects.

There are again two methods of removing the causes of faction: the one by destroying the liberty which is essential to its existence; the other, by giving to every citizen the same opinions, the same passions, and the same interests.

It could never be more truly said than of the first remedy, that it is worse than the disease. Liberty is to faction, what air is to fire, an aliment without which it instantly expires. But it could not be a less folly to abolish liberty, which is essential to political life, because it nourishes faction, than it would be to wish the annihilation of air, which is essential to animal life, because it imparts to fire its destructive agency.

The second expedient is as impracticable, as the first would be unwise. As long as the reason of man continues fallible, and he is at liberty to exercise it, different opinions will be formed. As long as the connection subsists between his reason and his self-love, his opinions and his passions will have a reciprocal influence on each other; and the former will be objects to which the latter will attach themselves. The diversity in the faculties of men from which the rights of property originate, is not less an insuperable obstacle to a uniformity of interests. The protection of these faculties is the first object of Government. From the protection of different and unequal faculties of acquiring property, the possession of different degrees and kinds of property immediately results: and from the influence of these on the sentiments and views of the respective proprietors, ensues a division of the society into different interests and parties.

The latent causes of faction are thus sown in the nature of man; and we see them every where brought into different degrees of activity, according to the different circumstances of civil society. A zeal for different opinions concerning religion, concerning Government and many other points, as well of speculation as of practice; an attachment to different leaders ambitiously contending for pre-eminence and power; or to persons of other descriptions whose fortunes have been interesting to the human passions, have in turn divided mankind into parties, inflamed them with mutual animosity, and rendered them much more disposed to vex and oppress each other, than to cooperate for their common good. So strong is this propensity of mankind to fall into mutual animosities, that where no substantial occasion presents itself, the most frivolous and fanciful distinctions have been sufficient to kindle their unfriendly passions, and excite their most violent conflicts. But the most common and durable source of factions, has been the various and unequal distribution of property. Those who hold, and those who are without property, have ever formed distinct interests in society. Those who are creditors, and those who are debtors, fall under a like discrimination. A landed interest, a manufacturing interest, a mercantile interest, a monied interest, with many lesser interests, grow up of necessity in civilized nations, and divide them into different classes, actuated by different sentiments and views. The regulation of these various and interfering interests forms the principal task of modern Legislation, and involves the spirit of party and faction in the necessary and ordinary operations of Government.

No man is allowed to be a judge in his own cause; because his interest would certainly bias his judgment, and, not improbably, corrupt his integrity. With equal, nay with greater reason, a body of men, are unfit to be both judges and parties, at the same time; yet, what are many of the most important acts of legislation, but so many judicial determinations, not indeed concerning the rights of single persons, but concerning the rights of large bodies of citizens, and what are the different classes of legislators, but advocates and parties to the causes which they determine? Is a law proposed concerning private debts? It is a question to which the creditors are parties on one side, and the debtors on the other. Justice ought to hold the balance between them. Yet the parties are and must be themselves the judges; and the most numerous party, or, in other words, the most powerful faction must be expected to prevail. Shall domestic manufactures be encouraged, and in what degree, by restrictions on foreign manufactures? are questions which would be differently decided by the landed and the manufacturing classes; and probably by neither, with a sole regard to justice and the public good. The apportionment of taxes on the various descriptions of property, is an act which seems to require the most exact impartiality; yet, there is perhaps no legislative act in which greater opportunity and temptation are given to a predominant party, to trample on the rules of justice. Every shilling with which they over-burden the inferior number, is a shilling saved to their own pockets.

It is in vain to say, that enlightened statesmen will be able to adjust these clashing interests, and render them all subservient to the public good. Enlightened statesmen will not always be at the helm: Nor, in many cases, can such an adjustment be made at all, without taking into view indirect and remote considerations, which will rarely prevail over the immediate interest which one party may find in disregarding the rights of another, or the good of the whole.

The inference to which we are brought, is, that the causes of faction cannot be removed; and that relief is only to be sought in the means of controlling its effects.

If a faction consists of less than a majority, relief is supplied by the republican principle, which enables the majority to defeat its sinister views by regular vote: It may clog the administration, it may convulse the society; but it will be unable to execute and mask its violence under the forms of the Constitution. When a majority is included in a faction, the form of popular government on the other hand enables it to sacrifice to its ruling passion or interest, both the public good and the rights of other citizens. To secure the public good, and private rights, against the danger of such a faction, and at the same time to preserve the spirit and the form of popular government, is then the great object to which our enquiries are directed: Let me add that it is the great desideratum, by which alone this form of government can be rescued from the opprobrium under which it has so long labored, and be recommended to the esteem and adoption of mankind.

By what means is this object attainable? Evidently by one of two only. Either the existence of the same passion or interest in a majority at the same time, must be prevented; or the majority, having such co-existent passion or interest, must be rendered, by their number and local situation, unable to concert and carry into effect schemes of oppression. If the impulse and the opportunity be suffered to coincide, we well know that neither moral nor religious motives can be relied on as an adequate control. They are not found to be such on the injustice and violence of individuals, and lose their efficacy in proportion to the number combined together; that is, in proportion as their efficacy becomes needful.

From this view of the subject, it may be concluded, that a pure Democracy, by which I mean, a Society, consisting of a small number of citizens, who assemble and administer the Government in person, can admit of no cure for the mischiefs of faction. A common passion or interest will, in almost every case, be felt by a majority of the whole; a communication and concert results from the form of Government itself; and there is nothing to check the inducements to sacrifice the weaker party, or an obnoxious individual. Hence it is, that such Democracies have ever been spectacles of turbulence and contention; have ever been found incompatible with personal security, or the rights of property; and have in general been as short in their lives, as they have been violent in their deaths. Theoretic politicians, who have patronized this species of Government, have erroneously supposed, that by reducing mankind to a perfect equality in their political rights, they would, at the same time, be perfectly equalized and assimilated in their possessions, their opinions, and their passions.

A republic, by which I mean a government in which the scheme of representation takes place, opens a different prospect, and promises the cure for which we are seeking. Let us examine the points in which it varies from pure democracy, and we shall comprehend both the nature of the cure and the efficacy which it must derive from the union.

The two great points of difference, between a democracy and a republic, are, first, the delegation of the government, in the latter, to a small number of citizens, elected by the rest; secondly, the greater number of citizens, and greater sphere of country, over which the latter may be extended.

The effect of the first difference is, on the one hand, to refine and enlarge the public views, by passing them through the medium of a chosen body of citizens, whose wisdom may best discern the true interest of their country, and whose patriotism and love of justice, will be least likely to sacrifice it to temporary or partial considerations. Under such a regulation, it may well happen, that the public voice, pronounced by the representatives of the people, will be more consonant to the public good, than if pronounced by the people themselves, convened for the purpose. On the other hand the effect may be inverted. Men of factious tempers, of local prejudices, or of sinister designs, may by intrigue, by corruption, or by other means, first obtain the suffrages, and then betray the interest of the people. The question resulting is, whether small or extensive republics are most favorable to the election of proper guardians of the public weal, and it is clearly decided in favor of the latter by two obvious considerations.

In the first place, it is to be remarked that, however small the republic may be, the representatives must be raised to a certain number, in order to guard against the cabals of a few; and that however large it may be, they must be limited to a certain number, in order to guard against the confusion of a multitude. Hence, the number of representatives in the two cases not being in proportion to that of the constituents, and being proportionally greatest in the small republic, it follows, that if the proportion of fit characters be not less in the large than in the small republic, the former will present a greater option, and consequently a greater probability of a fit choice.

In the next place, as each Representative will be chosen by a greater number of citizens in the large than in the small Republic, it will be more difficult for unworthy candidates to practise with success the vicious arts, by which elections are too often carried; and the suffrages of the people being more free, will be more likely to center on men who possess the most attractive merit, and the most diffusive and established characters.

It must be confessed, that in this, as in most other cases, there is a mean, on both sides of which inconveniences will be found to lie. By enlarging too much the number of electors, you render the representatives too little acquainted with all their local circumstances and lesser interests; as by reducing it too much, you render him unduly attached to these, and too little fit to comprehend and pursue great and national objects. The Federal Constitution forms a happy combination in this respect; the great and aggregate interests being referred to the national, the local and particular, to the state legislatures.

The other point of difference is, the greater number of citizens and extent of territory which may be brought within the compass of Republican, than of Democratic Government; and it is this circumstance principally which renders factious combinations less to be dreaded in the former, than in the latter. The smaller the society, the fewer probably will be the distinct parties and interests composing it; the fewer the distinct parties and interests, the more frequently will a majority be found of the same party; and the smaller the number of individuals composing a majority, and the smaller the compass within which they are placed, the more easily will they concert and execute their plans of oppression. Extend the sphere, and you take in a greater variety of parties and interests; you make it less probable that a majority of the whole will have a common motive to invade the rights of other citizens; or if such a common motive exists, it will be more difficult for all who feel it to discover their own strength, and to act in unison with each other. Besides other impediments, it may be remarked, that where there is a consciousness of unjust or dishonorable purposes, communication is always checked by distrust, in proportion to the number whose concurrence is necessary.

Hence it clearly appears, that the same advantage, which a Republic has over a Democracy, in controlling the effects of faction, is enjoyed by a large over a small Republic—is enjoyed by the Union over the States composing it. Does this advantage consist in the substitution of Representatives, whose enlightened views and virtuous sentiments render them superior to local prejudices, and to schemes of injustice? It will not be denied, that the Representation of the Union will be most likely to possess these requisite endowments. Does it consist in the greater security afforded by a greater variety of parties, against the event of any one party being able to outnumber and oppress the rest? In an equal degree does the increased variety of parties, comprised within the Union, increase this security? Does it, in fine, consist in the greater obstacles opposed to the concert and accomplishment of the secret wishes of an unjust and interested majority? Here, again, the extent of the Union gives it the most palpable advantage.

The influence of factious leaders may kindle a flame within their particular States, but will be unable to spread a general conflagration through the other States: a religious sect, may degenerate into a political faction in a part of the Confederacy but the variety of sects dispersed over the entire face of it, must secure the national Councils against any danger from that source: a rage for paper money, for an abolition of debts, for an equal division of property, or for any other improper or wicked project, will be less apt to pervade the whole body of the Union, than a particular member of it; in the same proportion as such a malady is more likely to taint a particular county or district, than an entire State.

In the extent and proper structure of the Union, therefore, we behold a Republican remedy for the diseases most incident to Republican Government. And according to the degree of pleasure and pride, we feel in being Republicans, ought to be our zeal in cherishing the spirit, and supporting the character of Federalists.

PUBLIUS

APPENDIX IV

The Federalist No. 51

February 6, 1788
James Madison

TO THE PEOPLE OF THE STATE OF NEW YORK.

To what expedient then shall we finally resort for maintaining in practice the necessary partition of power among the several departments, as laid down in the constitution? The only answer that can be given is, that as all these exterior provisions are found to be inadequate, the defect must be supplied, by so contriving the interior structure of the government, as that its several constituent parts may, by their mutual relations, be the means of keeping each other in their proper places. Without presuming to undertake a full development of this important idea, I will hazard a few general observations, which may perhaps place it in a clearer light, and enable us to form a more correct judgment of the principles and structure of the government planned by the convention.

In order to lay a due foundation for that separate and distinct exercise of the different powers of government, which to a certain extent, is admitted on all hands to be essential to the preservation of liberty, it is evident that each department should have a will of its own; and consequently should be so constituted, that the members of each should have as little agency as possible in the appointment of the members of the others. Were this principle rigorously adhered to, it would require that all the appointments for the supreme executive, legislative, and judiciary magistracies, should be drawn from the same fountain of authority, the people, through channels, having no communication whatever with one another. Perhaps such a plan of constructing the several departments would be less difficult in practice than it may in contemplation appear. Some difficulties however, and some additional expense, would attend the execution of it. Some deviations therefore from the principle must be admitted. In the constitution of the judiciary department in particular, it might be inexpedient to insist rigorously on the principle; first, because peculiar qualifications being essential in the members, the primary consideration ought to be to select that mode of choice, which best secures these qualifications; secondly, because the permanent tenure by which the appointments are held in that department, must soon destroy all sense of dependence on the authority conferring them.

It is equally evident that the members of each department should be as little dependent as possible on those of the others, for the emoluments annexed to their offices. Were the executive magistrate, or the judges, not independent of the legislature in this particular, their independence in every other would be merely nominal.

But the great security against a gradual concentration of the several powers in the same department, consists in giving to those who administer each department, the necessary constitutional means, and personal motives, to resist encroachments of the others. The provision for defense must in this, as in all other cases, be made commensurate to the danger of attack. Ambition must be made to counteract ambition. The interest of the man must be connected with the constitutional right of the place. It may be a reflection on human nature, that such devices should be necessary to control the abuses of government. But what is government itself but the greatest of all reflections on human nature? If men were angels, no government would be necessary. If angels were to govern men, neither external nor internal controls on government would be necessary. In framing a government which is to be administered by men over men, the great difficulty lies in this: You must first enable the government to control the governed; and in the next place, oblige it to control itself. A dependence on the people is no doubt the primary control on the government; but experience has taught mankind the necessity of auxiliary precautions.

This policy of supplying by opposite and rival interests, the defect of better motives, might be traced through the whole system of human affairs, private as well as public. We see it particularly displayed in all the subordinate distributions of power; where the constant aim is to divide and arrange the several offices in such a manner as that each may be a check on the other; that the private interest of every individual, may be a sentinel over the public rights. These inventions of prudence cannot be less requisite in the distribution of the supreme powers of the state.

But it is not possible to give to each department an equal power of self defense. In republican government the legislative authority, necessarily, predominates. The remedy for this inconveniency is, to divide the legislature into different branches; and to render them by different modes of election, and different principles of action, as little connected with each other, as the nature of their common functions, and their common dependence on the society, will admit. It may even be necessary to guard against dangerous encroachments by still further precautions. As the weight of the legislative authority requires that it should be thus divided, the weakness of the executive may require, on the other hand, that it should be fortified. An absolute negative, on the legislature, appears at first view to be the natural defense with which the executive magistrate should be armed. But perhaps it would be neither altogether safe, nor alone sufficient. On ordinary occasions, it might not be exerted with the requisite firmness; and on extraordinary occasions, it might be perfidiously abused. May not this defect of an absolute negative be supplied, by some qualified connection between this weaker department, and the weaker branch of the stronger department, by which the latter may be led to support the constitutional rights of the former, without being too much detached from the rights of its own department?

If the principles on which these observations are founded be just, as I persuade myself they are, and they be applied as a criterion, to the several state constitutions, and to the federal constitution, it will be found, that if the latter does not perfectly correspond with them, the former are infinitely less able to bear such a test.

There are moreover two considerations particularly applicable to the federal system of America, which place that system in a very interesting point of view.

First. In a single republic, all the power surrendered by the people, is submitted to the administration of a single government; and usurpations are guarded against by a division of the government into distinct and separate departments. In the compound republic of America, the power surrendered by the people, is first divided between two distinct governments, and then the portion allotted to each, subdivided among distinct and separate departments. Hence a double security arises to the rights of the people. The different governments will control each other; at the same time that each will be controlled by itself.

Second. It is of great importance in a republic, not only to guard the society against the oppression of its rulers; but to guard one part of the society against the injustice of the other part. Different interests necessarily exist in different classes of citizens. If a majority be united by a common interest, the rights of the minority will be insecure. There are but two methods of providing against this evil: The one by creating a will in the community independent of the majority, that is, of the society itself, the other by comprehending in the society so many separate descriptions of citizens, as will render an unjust combination of a majority of the whole, very improbable, if not impracticable. The first method prevails in all governments possessing an hereditary or self appointed authority. This at best is but a precarious security; because a power independent of the society may as well espouse the unjust views of the major, as the rightful interests, of the minor party, and may possibly be turned against both parties. The second method will be exemplified in the federal republic of the United States. While all authority in it will be derived from and dependent on the society, the society itself will be broken into so many parts, interests and classes of citizens, that the rights of individuals or of the minority, will be in little danger from interested combinations of the majority. In a free government, the security for civil rights must be the same as for religious rights. It consists in the one case in the multiplicity of interests, and in the other, in the multiplicity of sects. The degree of security in both cases will depend on the number of interests and sects; and this may be presumed to depend on the extent of country and number of people comprehended under the same government. This view of the subject must particularly recommend a proper federal system to all the sincere and considerate friends of republican government: Since it shows that in exact proportion as the territory of the union may be formed into more circumscribed confederacies or states, oppressive combinations of a majority will be facilitated, the best security under the republican form, for the rights of every class of citizens, will be diminished; and consequently, the stability and independence of some member of the government, the only other security, must be proportionally increased. Justice is the end of government. It is the end of civil society. It ever has been, and ever will be pursued, until it be obtained, or until liberty be lost in the pursuit. In a society under the forms of which the stronger faction can readily unite and oppress the weaker, anarchy may as truly be said to reign, as in a state of nature where the weaker individual is not secured against the violence of the stronger: And as in the latter state even the stronger individuals are prompted by the uncertainty of their condition, to submit to a government which may protect the weak as well as themselves: So in the former state, will the more powerful factions or parties be gradually induced by a like motive, to wish for a government which will protect all parties, the weaker as well as the more powerful. It can be little doubted, that if the state of Rhode Island was separated from the confederacy, and left to itself, the insecurity of rights under the popular form of government within such narrow limits, would be displayed by such reiterated oppressions of factious majorities, that some power altogether independent of the people would soon be called for by the voice of the very factions whose misrule had proved the necessity of it. In the extended republic of the United States, and among the great variety of interests, parties and sects which it embraces, a coalition of a majority of the whole society could seldom take place on any other principles than those of justice and the general good; and there being thus less danger to a minor from the will of the major party, there must be less pretext also, to provide for the security of the former, by introducing into the government a will not dependent on the latter; or in other words, a will independent of the society itself. It is no less certain than it is important, notwithstanding the contrary opinions which have been entertained, that the larger the society, provided it lie within a practicable sphere, the more duly capable it will be of self government. And happily for the republican cause, the practicable sphere may be carried to a very great extent, by a judicious modification and mixture of the federal principle.

PUBLIUS

APPENDIX V

Presidents of the United States

President	Year	Party	Most Noteworthy Event
George Washington	1789–1797	Federalist	Establishment of Federal Judiciary
John Adams	1797–1801	Federalist	Alien-Sedition Acts
Thomas Jefferson	1801–1809	Dem.-Republican	First President to Defeat Incumbent/Louisiana Purchase
James Madison	1809–1817	Dem.-Republican	War of 1812
James Monroe	1817–1825	Dem.-Republican	Monroe Doctrine/ Missouri Compromise
John Quincy Adams	1825–1829	Dem.-Republican	Elected by "King Caucus"
Andrew Jackson	1829–1837	Democratic	Set up Spoils System
Martin Van Buren	1837–1841	Democratic	Competitive Parties Established
William H. Harrison	1841	Whig	Universal White Male Suffrage
John Tyler	1841–1845	Whig	Texas Annexed
James K. Polk	1845–1849	Democratic	Mexican-American War
Zachary Taylor	1849–1850	Whig	California Gold Rush
Millard Fillmore	1850–1853	Whig	Compromise of 1850
Franklin Pierce	1853–1857	Democratic	Republican Party Formed
James Buchanan	1857–1861	Democratic	Dred Scott Decision
Abraham Lincoln	1861–1865	Republican	Civil War
Andrew Johnson	1865–1869	Republican	First Impeachment of President
Ulysses S. Grant	1869–1877	Republican	Reconstruction of South
Rutherford B. Hayes	1877–1881	Republican	End of Reconstruction
James A. Garfield	1881	Republican	Assassinated by Job-seeker
Chester A. Arthur	1881–1885	Republican	Civil Service Reform
Grover Cleveland	1885–1889	Democratic	Casts 102 Vetoes in One Year
Benjamin Harrison	1889–1893	Republican	McKinley Law Raises Tarrifs
Grover Cleveland	1893–1897	Democratic	Depression/Pullman Strike
William McKinley	1897–1901	Republican	Spanish-American War
Theodore Roosevelt	1901–1909	Republican	Conservation/Panama Canal
William H. Taft	1909–1913	Republican	Judicial Reform
Woodrow Wilson	1913–1921	Democratic	Progressive Reforms/ World War I
Warren G. Harding	1921–1923	Republican	Return to Normalcy
Calvin Coolidge	1923–1929	Republican	Cuts Taxes/Promotes Business
Herbert C. Hoover	1929–1933	Republican	Great Depression
Franklin D. Roosevelt	1933–1945	Democratic	New Deal/ World War II
Harry S Truman	1945–1953	Democratic	Beginning of Cold War
Dwight D. Eisenhower	1953–1961	Republican	End of Korean War
John F. Kennedy	1961–1963	Democratic	Cuban Missile Crisis
Lyndon B. Johnson	1963–1969	Democratic	Great Society/Vietnam War
Richard M. Nixon	1969–1974	Republican	Watergate Scandal
Gerald R. Ford	1974–1977	Republican	War Powers Resolution
James Earl Carter	1977–1981	Democratic	Iranian Hostage Crisis
Ronald Reagan	1981–1989	Republican	Tax Cut/ Expenditure Cuts
George Bush	1989–1993	Republican	End of Cold War/Persian Gulf War
William J. Clinton	1993–2001	Democratic	Deficit Reduction
George W. Bush	2001–	Republican	U.S. Response to Terrorism

Refer to www.ablongman.com.fiorina

GLOSSARY

administration The president and his political appointees responsible for directing the executive branch of government.

administrative discretion Power to interpret a legislative mandate.

advice and consent Support for a presidential action by a designated number of senators.

affirmative action Programs designed to enhance opportunities for groups that have suffered discrimination in the past.

affirmative action redistricting The process of drawing district lines to maximize the number of majority-minority districts.

agency Basic organizational unit of federal government. Also known as *office* or *bureau*.

agenda setting Making an issue so visible that important political leaders take it seriously; occurs when the media affect the issues and problems people think about, even if the media do not determine what positions people adopt.

ambassador The head of a diplomatic delegation to a major foreign country.

Annapolis Convention 1786 meeting to discuss constitutional reform.

Anti-Federalists Those who opposed ratification of the Constitution.

appeal The procedure whereby the losing side asks a higher court to overturn a lower-court decision.

appropriations process Process of providing funding for governmental activities and programs that have been authorized.

aristocracy Government by a few leaders made eligible by birthright.

Articles of Confederation The first (1781–1789) basic governing document of the United States and forerunner to the Constitution.

associate justice One of the eight justices of the Supreme Court who are not the chief justice.

authorization process Term applied to the entire process of providing statutory authority for a government program or activity.

bad tendency test Rule from English law saying that expression could be punished if it could ultimately lead to illegal behavior.

balancing doctrine The principle enunciated by the courts that freedom of speech must be balanced against other competing public interests at stake in particular circumstances.

Bay of Pigs Location of CIA-supported effort by Cuban exiles in 1961 to invade Cuba and overthrow Fidel Castro.

beltway insider Person living in the Washington metropolitan area who is engaged in, or well informed about, national politics and government.

bicameral Containing two chambers, as does a legislature such as the U.S. Congress.

Bill of Rights The first 10 amendments to the Constitution, which protect individual and state rights.

bipolar Cold War view of the world as divided into two centers of power, the United States and its allies, and the Soviet Union and its allies.

black codes Restrictive laws that applied to newly freed slaves but not to whites.

blame avoidance Set of political techniques employed by political leaders to disguise their actions and shift blame to others.

bloc voting Voting in which nearly all members of one group (such as African Americans) vote for a candidate of their race, whereas nearly all members of another group (such as whites) vote against that candidate.

block grant Federal grants to a state and/or local government that impose minimal restrictions on the use of funds.

borking Politicizing the nomination process through an organized public campaign that portrays the nominee as a dangerous extremist.

brief Written arguments presented to a court by lawyers on behalf of clients.

Brown v. Board of Education of Topeka, Kansas 1954 Supreme Court decision declaring racial segregation in schools unconstitutional.

budget The government's annual plan for taxing and spending.

bully pulpit The nature of presidential status as an ideal vehicle for persuading the public to support the president's policies.

bureaucracy Hierarchical organization designed to perform a particular set of tasks.

business cycle The alternation of periods of economic growth with periods of economic slowdown.

cabinet Top administration officials; mostly heads of departments in the executive branch.

casework Effort of members of Congress to help individuals and groups when they have difficulties with federal agencies.

categorical grant Federal grants to a state and/or local government that impose programmatic restrictions on the use of funds.

caucus Meeting of candidate supporters that chooses delegates to a state or national convention. All Democratic members of the House or Senate. Members in caucus elect the party leaders, ratify the choice of committee leaders, and debate party positions on issues.

Central Intelligence Agency (CIA) Agency primarily responsible for gathering and analyzing information about the political and military activities of other nations.

cert See *writ of certiorari.*

checks and balances Constitutional division of power into separate institutions, giving each institution the power to block the actions of the others.

chief justice Head of the Supreme Court.

chief of staff Head of White House staff. Has continuous, direct contact with the president.

circuit court of appeals Court to which decisions by federal district courts are appealed.

citizen duty The belief that it is a citizen's duty to be informed and to participate in politics.

citizenship Status held by someone entitled to all the rights and privileges of a full-fledged member of a political community.

civic republicanism A political philosophy that emphasizes the obligation of citizens to act virtuously in pursuit of the common good.

civil code Laws regulating relations among individuals. Alleged violators are sued by presumed victims, who ask courts to award damages and otherwise offer relief.

civil disobedience A peaceful, well-publicized violation of a law designed to dramatize that law's injustice.

civil liberties Fundamental freedoms that together preserve the rights of a free people.

civil rights Specific rights that embody the general right to equal treatment under the law.

civil rights amendments The Thirteenth, Fourteenth, and Fifteenth Amendments, which abolished slavery, redefined civil rights and liberties, and guaranteed the right to vote to all adult male citizens.

civil service A system in which government employees are chosen according to their educational qualifications, performance on examinations, and work experience.

class action suit Suit brought on behalf of all individuals in a particular category, whether or not they are actually participating in the suit.

clear and present danger doctrine The principle that people should have complete freedom of speech unless their language endangers the nation.

cloture Motion to end debate; requires 60 votes to pass.

CNN effect Purported ability of TV to raise a distant foreign affairs situation to national prominence by broadcasting vivid pictures.

coalition government Occurs when two or more minority parties must join together in order to elect a prime minister. Such governments are common in multi-party systems.

coattails Positive electoral effect of a popular presidential candidate on congressional candidates of the party.

Cold War The 43-year period (1946–1989) during which the United States and the Soviet Union threatened one another with mutual destruction by nuclear warfare.

colonial assembly Lower legislative chamber elected by male property owners in a colony.

colonial council Upper legislative chamber whose members were appointed by British officials on the recommendation of the governor.

commander in chief The president in his constitutional role as head of the armed forces.

commerce clause Constitutional provision that gives Congress power to regulate commerce "among the states."

commercial speech Advertising or other speech made for business purposes; may be regulated.

communism An extreme type of socialism based on the work of Karl Marx, who taught that history is a product of the struggle between those who exploit and those who are exploited.

compositional effect A change in the behavior of a group that arises from a change in the group's composition, not from a change in the behavior of individuals in the group.

concurring opinion A written opinion prepared by judges who vote with the majority but who wish either to disagree with or to elaborate on some aspect of the majority opinion.

conference committee Group of representatives from both the House and the Senate who iron out the differences between the two chambers' versions of a bill or resolution.

Congressional Budget Office (CBO) Congressional agency that evaluates the president's budget as well as the budgetary implications of all other legislation.

Connecticut Compromise Constitutional Convention proposal that created a House proportionate to population and a Senate in which all states were represented equally.

constituency Those legally entitled to vote for a public official.

constituency service The totality of Congress members' district service and constituent assistance work.

Constitution Basic governing document of the United States.

containment U.S. policy that attempted to stop the spread of communism in the expectation that this system of government would eventually collapse on its own.

cooperative federalism See *marble-cake federalism.*

corporatist The official representation of important interest groups in government decision-making bodies.

Council of Economic Advisors (CEA) Three economists who head up a professional staff that advises the president on economic policy.

criminal code Laws regulating relations between individuals and society. Alleged violators are prosecuted by government.

critical election Election that marks the emergence of a new, lasting alignment of partisan support within the electorate.

debt The accumulation of yearly deficits.

Declaration of Independence Document signed in 1776 declaring the United States to be a country independent of Great Britain.

de facto **segregation** Segregation that occurs as the result of decisions by private individuals.

defendant One accused of violating the civil or criminal code.

deficit The amount by which annual spending exceeds revenue.

de jure **segregation** Racial segregation that is legally sanctioned.

delegate Role a representative plays when following the wishes of those who have elected him or her.

democracy System in which governmental power is widely shared among the citizens, usually through free and open elections.

department Organizational unit into which many agencies of the federal government are grouped.

Department of Defense Cabinet department responsible for managing the U.S. armed forces.

deregulation Removal of government rules that once controlled an industry.

devolution Return of governmental responsibilities to state and local governments.

dignified aspect According to Walter Bagehot, the aspect of government, including royalty and ceremony, that generates citizen respect and loyalty.

Dillon's rule Legal doctrine that local governments are mere creatures of the state.

direct action Everything from peaceful sit-ins and demonstrations to riots and even rebellion.

direct democracy Type of democracy in which ordinary people are the government, making all the laws themselves.

direct mail Computer-generated letters, faxes, and other communications to people who might be sympathetic to an appeal for money or support.

direct primary A method of choosing party candidates by popular vote of all self-identified party members. This method of nominating candidates is virtually unknown outside the United States.

dissenting opinion Written opinion presenting the reasoning of judges who vote against the majority.

district attorney Person responsible for prosecuting criminal cases.

divided government Said to exist when a single party does not control the presidency and both houses of Congress.

divine right Doctrine that says God selects the sovereign for the people.

domestic policy Government programs and regulations that directly affect those living within a country.

double jeopardy Fifth Amendment provision that prohibits prosecution for the same offense twice.

dual sovereignty A theory of federalism saying that both the national and state governments have final authority over their own policy domains.

due process clause Found in the Fifth and Fourteenth Amendments to the Constitution; forbids deprivation of life, liberty, or property without due process of law.

earmark A specific congressional designation of the way money is to be spent.

Earned Income Tax Credit (EITC) Provision that gives back tax payments to those who have little income.

efficient aspect According to Walter Bagehot, the aspect of government that involves making policy, administering the laws, and settling disputes.

election-cycle interpretation The argument that, whatever their party, presidents attempt to slow the economy early in their terms and then to expand it as their opportunity for reelection approaches.

electoral college Those chosen to cast a direct vote for president by a process determined by each state.

electoral incentive Desire to obtain or retain elected office.

electoral system A means of translating popular votes into control of public offices.

electoral vote Cast by electors, with each state receiving one vote for each of its members of the House of Representatives and one vote for each of its senators.

embassy The structure that houses ambassadors and their diplomatic aides in the capital cities of foreign countries.

Environmental Protection Agency (EPA) Agency responsible for issuing regulations designed to protect the environment from unwanted pollutants.

equal protection clause Fourteenth Amendment clause specifying that no state can deny any of its people equal protection under the law.

Equal Rights Amendment (ERA) Proposed amendment to the Constitution that banned gender discrimination.

equality of opportunity The notion that individuals should have an equal chance to advance economically through individual talent and hard work.

equal-time rule Promulgated by the FCC, required any station selling time to a candidate to sell time to other candidates at comparable rates.

establishment of religion clause Denies the government the power to establish any single religious practice as superior.

ethnic cleansing Seeking to deport or eliminate entire ethnic groups within a country or region.

exclusionary rule Legal standard that says that illegally obtained evidence cannot be admitted in court.

executive agreement Agreement with foreign countries that requires only a presidential signature.

Executive Office of the President (EOP) Agency that houses both top coordinating offices and other operating agencies.

executive order A presidential directive that has the force of law, though it is not enacted by Congress.

executive privilege The right of members of the executive branch to have private communications among themselves that need not be shared with Congress.

externalities Consequences that affect people who are not directly engaged in the activities that bring those consequences about.

fascism Rule by a dictator supported by a strong party that permeates society; generally supports capital against labor and is associated with extreme nationalism.

federal district courts The lowest level of the federal court system and the courts in which most federal trials are held.

Federal Reserve System The country's central bank, which executes monetary policy by manipulating the supply of funds that lower banks can lend.

federalism Division of sovereignty between at least two different levels of government.

Federalist Papers Essays that were written in support of the Constitution's ratification and have become a classic argument for the American constitutional system.

Federalists Those who wrote and campaigned on behalf of ratification of the Constitution.

fiduciary Someone whose duty is to act in the best interest of someone else.

fighting words doctrine The principle, endorsed by the Supreme Court in *Chaplinsky v. New Hampshire* (1942), that some words constitute violent acts and are therefore not protected under the First Amendment.

filibuster Delaying tactic by which one or more senators refuse to allow a bill or resolution to be considered, either by speaking indefinitely or by offering dilatory motions and amendments.

filing deadline The latest date on which a candidate for office may file official papers or pay required fees to state election officials.

First Continental Congress The first quasi-governmental institution that spoke for nearly all the colonies (1774).

First Lady Traditional title of the president's wife.

fiscal policy The sum total of government taxing and spending decisions, which determines the level of the deficit or surplus.

flat tax A tax that is neither progressive nor regressive; everyone pays at the same rate.

focus groups Small groups used to explore how ordinary people think about issues and how they react to the language of political appeals.

food stamps Public assistance program that provides recipients with stamps that can be used to purchase food.

foreign policy Conduct of relations among nation-states.

foreign service Diplomats who staff U.S. embassies and consulates.

framing Stating an argument in such a way as to emphasize one set of considerations and deemphasize others.

franchise The right to vote.

frank Name given to representatives' and senators' free use of the U.S. mail for sending communications to constituents.

free exercise of religion clause Protects the right of individuals to practice their religion.

free-rider problem Problem that arises when people can enjoy the benefits of group activity without bearing any of the costs.

fundamental freedoms doctrine Court doctrine stating that laws impinging on the freedoms that are fundamental to the preservation of democratic practice—the freedoms of speech, press, assembly, and religion—are to be scrutinized by the courts more closely than other legislation. These are also termed the *preferred freedoms*.

general election Final election that selects the office holder.

general revenue sharing The most comprehensive of block grants, which gives money to state and local governments to be used for any purpose whatsoever.

gerrymandering Drawing boundary lines of congressional districts in order to confer an advantage on some partisan or political interest.

Gideon v. Wainwright Supreme Court decision in 1963 giving indigent people accused of crimes the right to court-appointed counsel.

glass ceiling The invisible barrier that has limited women's opportunities for advancement to the highest ranks of politics, business, and the professions.

government The institution in society that has a "monopoly of the legitimate use of physical force."

government corporation Independent organization created by Congress to fulfill functions related to business.

governor State chief executive whose responsibilities roughly parallel those of the president.

grandfather clause Racially restrictive provision of certain southern laws after Reconstruction, permitting a man to vote if his father or grandfather could have voted.

grassroots lobbying Efforts by groups and associations to influence elected officials indirectly, by arousing their constituents.

Great Society Series of programs enacted under President Lyndon Johnson, designed to address social ills in the nation's poor, elderly, and minority communities.

gross domestic product (GDP) The measure of the total value of economic activity in a nation in one year.

hammer Harsh penalty set by Congress to be imposed if a regulatory agency does not achieve a statutory objective.

Hatch Act 1939 law prohibiting federal employees from engaging in political campaigning and solicitation.

honeymoon Period early in a president's term when partisan conflict and media criticism are minimal.

idealists Those who say that U.S. foreign policy should be guided primarily by democratic principles——the spread of liberty, equality, human rights, and respect for international law throughout the world.

ideology System of beliefs in which one or more organizing principles connect the individual's views on a wide range of issues.

impeachment Recommendation by a majority of the House of Representatives that a president, other official in the executive branch, or judge of the federal courts be removed from office; removal depends on a two-thirds vote of the Senate.

implementation The way in which grant programs are administered at the local level.

incumbency advantage The electoral advantage a candidate enjoys by virtue of being an incumbent, over and above his or her other personal and political characteristics.

independent counsel (Originally called special prosecutor) Legal officer appointed by a court to investigate allegations of criminal activity on the part of high-ranking members of the executive branch. Law expired in 1999.

independent regulatory agencies Agencies that have quasi-judicial responsibilities.

individual motivations for voting The tangible and intangible benefits and costs of exercising one's right to vote.

inflation A sustained rise in the price level such that people need more money to purchase the same amount of goods and services.

information cost The time and mental effort required to absorb and store information, whether from conversations, personal experiences, or the media.

inherent executive power Presidential authority inherent in the executive branch of government, though not specifically mentioned in the Constitution.

initiative Proposed laws or state constitutional amendments placed on the ballot via citizen petition.

inner cabinet The four original departments (State, Defense, Treasury, and Justice) whose secretaries typically have the closest ties to the president.

interest group Organization or association of people with common interests that engages in politics on behalf of its members.

intergovernmental grant Grant from the national government to a state or local government.

Iran–Contra affair An allegedly illegal diversion of funds, derived from the sale of arms to Iran, to a guerrilla group in Nicaragua during the Reagan administration.

iron triangle Close, stable connection among agencies, interest groups, and congressional committees.

issue advocacy Advertising campaigns that attempt to influence public opinion on an issue.

issue network Loose, competitive relationship among policy experts, interest groups, congressional committees, and government agencies.

issue public Group of people particularly affected by or concerned with a specific issue.

Jim Crow laws Laws passed by southern states after Reconstruction, enforcing segregation.

Joint Chiefs of Staff The heads of all the military services, together with a chair and vice-chair nominated by the president and confirmed by the Senate.

judicial activism Doctrine that says the principle of *stare decisis* should sometimes be sacrificed in order to adapt the Constitution to changing conditions.

judicial restraint Doctrine that says courts should, if at all possible, avoid overturning a prior court decision.

judicial review Power of the courts to declare null and void laws of Congress and of state legislatures they find unconstitutional.

Keynesianism Economic policy based on the belief that governments can control the economy by manipulating demand, running deficits to expand it and surpluses to contract it.

laboratories of democracy Doctrine that state and local governments contribute to democracy by providing places where experiments are tried and new theories tested.

law clerk Young, influential aide to a Supreme Court justice.

League of Nations International organization created after World War I to settle international disputes; precursor of the United Nations.

legal distinction The legal difference between a case at hand and previous cases decided by the courts.

libel False statement defaming another.

liberalism A philosophy that elevates and empowers the individual as opposed to religious, hereditary, governmental, or other forms of authority.

line item veto Presidential authority to negate particular provisions of a law, granted by Congress in 1996 but struck down by the Supreme Court in 1998; power (enjoyed by most governors) to reject specific components of legislation rather than rejecting entire bills.

living-constitution theory A theory of constitutional interpretation that places the meaning of the Constitution in light of the total history of the United States.

lobbying Interest-group activities intended to influence directly the decisions that public officials make.

lobbyist One who engages in lobbying.

log-rolling Colloquial term given to politicians' trading of favors, votes, or generalized support for each other's proposals.

machine A highly organized party under the control of a boss, based on patronage and control of government activities. Machines were common in many cities in the late nineteenth and early twentieth centuries.

majority Fifty percent plus one.

majority leader Title used for the Speaker's chief lieutenant in the House and for the most important officer in the Senate. Each is responsible for managing the floor of his or her chamber.

majority-minority district District in which a minority group is the numerical majority.

Mapp v. Ohio Supreme Court decision saying that any evidence obtained without a proper search warrant may not be introduced in a trial.

marble-cake federalism The theory that all levels of government can work together to solve common problems. Also known as *cooperative federalism*.

Marbury v. Madison Supreme Court decision (1803) in which the court first exercised the power of judicial review.

markup Process in which a committee or subcommittee considers and revises a bill that has been introduced.

mass media Means of communication that are technologically capable of reaching most people and economically affordable to most.

mass public Ordinary people for whom politics is a peripheral concern.

matching funds Public moneys (from $3 check-offs on income tax returns) that the Federal Election Commission distributes to primary candidates according to a prespecified formula.

Mayflower Compact First document in colonial America in which the people gave their expressed consent to be governed.

McCulloch v. *Maryland* Decision of 1819 in which the Supreme Court declared unconstitutional the state's power to tax a federal government entity.

measurement error The error that arises from attempting to measure something as subjective as opinion.

Medicaid Program that provides medical care to those of low income.

Medicare Program that provides social security recipients a broad range of medical benefits.

minimal-effects thesis Theory that the mass media have little or no effect on public opinion.

minority leader Leader of the minority party, who speaks for the party in dealing with the majority.

Miranda v. *Arizona* Supreme Court decision stating that accused persons must be told by police that they need not testify against themselves.

monetarism An economic school of thought that rejects Keynesianism, arguing that the money supply is the most important influence on the economy.

monetary policy The actions taken by government to vary the supply of money in an effort to stabilize the business cycle.

Monroe Doctrine Policy that declared the Western Hemisphere to be free of European colonial influence (1819).

mugwumps A group of civil service reformers organized in the 1880s who maintained that government officials should be chosen on a merit basis.

multiculturalism The idea that ethnic and cultural groups should maintain their identity within the larger society and respect one another's differences.

multi-party system System in which more than two parties compete for control of government. Most of the world's democracies are multi-party systems.

multiple referrals Said to occur when party leaders give more than one committee responsibility for considering a bill.

nation building Interventions designed to enhance democratic practices in another country.

National Association for the Advancement of Colored People (NAACP) Civil rights organization, dating from 1909, that relied heavily on a legal strategy to pursue its objectives.

national convention Quadrennial gathering of party officials and delegates who select presidential and vice-presidential nominees and adopt party platforms. Extension of the direct primary to the presidential level after 1968 has greatly reduced the importance of the conventions.

national forces Electoral effects felt across most states and congressional districts, most often generated by especially strong or weak presidential performance, party performance, or the state of the economy.

National Security Council (NSC) White House agency responsible for coordinating U.S. foreign policy.

natural monopoly A situation in which a public service is best provided by a single company.

necessary and proper clause Constitutional clause that gives Congress the power to take all actions that are "necessary and proper" to the carrying out of its delegated powers. Also known as the *elastic clause*.

New Deal Programs created by the Franklin Roosevelt administration that expanded the power of the federal government for the purpose of stimulating economic recovery and establishing a national safety net.

New Jersey Plan Small-state proposal for constitutional reform.

new media Cable and satellite TV, fax, e-mail, and the Internet—the media that have grown out of the technological advances of the past few decades.

NIMBY problem Everyone wants the problem solved, but "Not In My Back Yard."

nullification A doctrine that says that states have the authority to declare acts of Congress unconstitutional.

obscenity Publicly offensive language or portrayals with no redeeming social value.

Office of Management and Budget (OMB) Agency responsible for coordinating the work of departments and agencies of the executive branch.

oligarchy Government by a few who gain office by means of wealth, military power, or membership in a single political party.

open seat A House or Senate race with no incumbent (because of death or retirement).

opinion In legal parlance, a court's written explanation of its decision.

original-intent theory A theory of constitutional interpretation that determines the constitutionality of a law by ascertaining the intentions of those who wrote the Constitution.

outer cabinet Newer departments that have fewer ties to the president and are more influenced by interest-group pressures.

override Congressional passage of a bill by a two-thirds vote over the president's veto.

overvotes Ballots that have more than one choice for an office (e.g., for president in 2000), whether because the voter voted for more than one candidate or wrote in a name as well as making a mark.

partisan interpretation The argument that Democratic administrations set economic policy to benefit lower-income, wage-earning groups and that Republican administrations set economic policy to benefit higher-income, business, and professional groups.

party alignment The existence of social and economic groups that consistently support each party.

party caucus All Democratic members of the House or Senate. Members in caucus elect the party leaders, ratify the choice of committee leaders, and debate party positions on issues.

party conference What Republicans call their caucus.

party identification A person's subjective feeling of affiliation with a party.

party image A set of widely held associations between a party and particular issues and values.

Patriots Political group defending colonial American liberties against British infringements.

patronage Appointment of individuals to public office in exchange for their political support. Widely practiced in the eighteenth and nineteenth centuries and continues to present day.

Pendleton Act Legislation in 1883 creating the Civil Service Commission.

permanent campaign Condition that prevails when the next election campaign begins as soon as the last has ended and the line between electioneering and governing has disappeared.

plain-meaning-of-the-text theory A theory of constitutional interpretation that determines the constitutionality of a law in light of what the words of the Constitution obviously seem to say.

plaintiff One who brings legal charges against another.

plea bargain Agreement between prosecution and defense that the accused will admit having committed a crime, provided that other charges are dropped and the recommended sentence is shortened.

plenary session Activities of a court in which all judges participate.

Plessy v. Ferguson Court decision declaring separate but equal public facilities constitutional.

pluralism A school of thought holding that politics is the clash of groups that represent all important interests in society and that check and balance each other.

pocket veto Presidential veto after congressional adjournment, executed merely by not signing a bill into law.

policy deliberation Debate and discussion by groups and political leaders over issues placed on the policy agenda.

policy enactment Passage of a law by public officials.

policy implementation Translation of legislation into a set of government programs or regulations.

policy outcome Effect of policy outputs on individuals and businesses.

policy output Provision of services to citizens or regulation of their conduct.

political action committee (PAC) Specialized organization for raising and contributing campaign funds.

political activists People who voluntarily participate in politics; they are more interested in and committed to particular issues and candidates than are ordinary citizens.

political culture Collection of beliefs and values about the justification and operation of a country's government.

political efficacy The belief that one can make a difference in politics by expressing an opinion or acting politically.

political elite Activists and office holders who are deeply interested in and knowledgeable about politics.

political entrepreneurs People willing to assume the costs of forming and maintaining an organization even when others may free-ride on them.

political parties Groups of like-minded people who band together in an attempt to win control of government.

political socialization The set of psychological and sociological processes by which families, schools, religious organizations, communities, and other societal units inculcate beliefs and values in their members.

poll tax Fee that one must pay in order to be allowed to vote.

popular model of democracy Type of representative democracy in which ordinary people participate actively and closely constrain the actions of public officials.

popular vote The total vote cast for a candidate across the nation.

pork barrel projects Special legislative benefits targeted toward the constituents of particular members of Congress.

precedent Previous court decision or ruling applicable to a particular case.

president pro tempore President of the Senate, who presides in the absence of the vice-president.

presidential popularity Evaluation of president by voters, usually as measured by a survey question asking the adult population how well they think the president is doing the job.

primary election Preliminary election that narrows the number of candidates by determining who will be the nominees in the general election.

priming Occurs when the media affect the standards people use to evaluate political figures or the severity of a problem.

prior restraint doctrine Legal doctrine that gives individuals the right to publish without prior restraint—that is, without first submitting material to a government censor.

professional legislature Legislature whose members serve full-time and for long periods.

progressive tax A tax structured so that higher-income people pay a larger proportion of their income in taxes than do lower-income people.

Progressives Middle-class reformers of the late nineteenth and early twentieth centuries who weakened the power of the machines and attempted to clean up elections and government.

proportional representation (PR) Electoral system in which parties receive a share of seats in parliament that is proportional to the popular vote they receive.

proposition A shorthand reference to an initiative or a referendum.

proprietary colony Colony governed either by a prominent English noble or by a company. See *royal colony*.

prospective voting Voting on the basis of the candidates' policy promises.

public assistance Programs that provide to low-income households a limited income and access to essential goods and services.

public defender Attorney whose full-time responsibilities are to provide for the legal defense of indigent criminal suspects.

public goods Goods enjoyed simultaneously by a group, as opposed to a private good that must be divided up to be shared.

public opinion The aggregation of people's views about issues, situations, and public figures.

quota Specific number of positions set aside for a specific group; said by the Supreme Court to be unconstitutional.

racial profiling The singling out of certain people for suspicious behavior based on their race or ethnicity.

"rally 'round the flag" effect The tendency for the public to back presidents in moments of crisis.

realigning election Another term for a critical election.

realignment Occurs when the pattern of group support for political parties shifts in a significant and lasting way.

realists Those who say that U.S. foreign policy best protects democracy when it safeguards its own economic and military strength.

reapportionment Redrawing of electoral district lines to reflect population changes; the allocation of House seats to the states after each decennial census.

recall election Attempt to remove an official from office before completion of the term.

receiver Court official who has the authority to see that judicial orders are carried out.

recess appointment An appointment made when the Senate is in recess.

recession A slowdown in economic activity, officially defined as a decline that persists for two quarters (six months).

Reconstruction Period after the Civil War when southern states were subject to a federal military presence.

redistricting Drawing new boundaries of congressional districts, usually after the decennial census.

referendum A law or state constitutional amendment that is proposed by a legislature or city council but does not go into effect unless the required majority of voters approve it.

registered voters Those legally eligible to vote who have registered in accordance with the requirements prevailing in their state and locality.

regressive tax A tax structured so that higher-income people pay a smaller proportion of their income in taxes than do lower-income people.

regulation Rules and standards that control economic, social, and political activities.

remand To send a case to a lower court to determine the best way of implementing the higher court's decision.

remedy Court-ordered action designed to compensate plaintiffs for wrongs they have suffered.

rent subsidies Help in paying rent for low-income families, provided that they select designated housing.

representative democracy An indirect form of democracy in which the people choose representatives who determine what government does.

responsible model of democracy Type of representative democracy in which public officials have considerable freedom of action but are held accountable by the people for the decisions they make.

restorationist Judge who thinks that the only way the original meaning of the Constitution can be restored is by ignoring the doctrine of *stare decisis* until liberal decisions have been reversed.

restrictive housing covenant Legal promise by home buyers that they would not resell to an African American; enforcement declared unconstitutional by Supreme Court.

retrospective voting Voting on the basis of the past performance of the incumbent administration.

reversal The overturning of a lower-court decision by an appeals court or the Supreme Court.

right of privacy Right to keep free of government interference those aspects of one's personal life that do not affect others.

rotation The practice whereby a member of Congress stepped down after a term or two so that someone else could have the office.

royal colony Colony governed by the king's representative with the advice of an elected assembly. See *proprietary colony*.

rule Specifies the terms and conditions under which a bill or resolution will be considered on the floor of the House—in particular, how long debate will last, how time will be allocated, and the number and type of amendments that will be in order.

safe seat A congressional district certain to vote for the candidate of one party.

sampling error The error that arises in public opinion surveys as a result of relying on a representative but small sample of the larger population.

Second Continental Congress Political authority that directed the struggle for independence beginning in 1775.

secretary Head of a department within the executive branch.

secretary of defense The president's chief civilian adviser on defense matters and overall head of the army, navy, and air force.

secretary of state Officially, the president's chief foreign policy advisor and head of the Department of State, the agency responsible for conducting diplomatic relations.

select committee Temporary committee appointed to deal with a specific issue or problem.

selection bias The error that occurs when a sample systematically includes or excludes people with certain attitudes.

selection principle Rule of thumb according to which stories with certain characteristics are chosen over stories without those characteristics.

selective benefits Side benefits of belonging to an organization that are limited to contributing members of the organization.

selective incorporation The case-by-case incorporation, by the courts, of the Bill of Rights into the due process clause of the Fourteenth Amendment.

selective perception Tendency to discount information that is inconsistent with one's prior predispositions in favor of information consistent with what one already believes.

senatorial courtesy An informal rule that the Senate will not confirm nominees within or from a state unless they have the approval of the senior senator of that state from the president's party.

seniority Practice by which the majority party member with the longest continuous service on a committee becomes the chair.

separate but equal doctrine Rule stating that the equal protection clause was not violated by the fact of racial segregation alone, provided that the separated facilities were equal.

separation of church and state doctrine The principle that a wall should separate the government from religious activity.

separation of powers A system of government in which different institutions exercise different components of governmental power.

sequester To house jurors privately, away from any information other than that presented in the courtroom.

Shays' Rebellion Uprising in western Massachusetts in 1786 led by Revolutionary War captain Daniel Shays.

sin tax A tax intended to discourage unwanted behavior.

single-issue group An interest group narrowly focused to influence policy on a single issue.

single-issue voter Voter who cares so deeply about some particular issue that a candidate's position on this one issue determines his or her vote.

single-member, simple-plurality (SMSP) system Electoral system in which the country is divided into geographic districts, and the candidates who win the most votes within their districts are elected.

social connectedness The degree to which individuals are integrated into society—families, churches, neighborhoods, groups, and so forth.

social insurance Program that provides benefits in return for contributions made by workers.

social issues Issues (such as abortion, obscenity, gay rights, capital punishment, gun control, and prayer in schools) that reflect personal values more than economic interests.

social movement Broad-based demand for government action on some problem or issue, such as civil rights for blacks and women or environmental protection.

social policy Domestic policy programs designed to help those thought to be in need of government assistance.

social security Social insurance program for senior citizens.

socialism A philosophy that supports government ownership and operation of the means of production, as well as government determination of the level of social and economic benefits that people receive.

socialization The end result of all the processes by which individuals form their beliefs and values in their homes, schools, churches, communities, and workplaces.

solicitor general Government official responsible for presenting before the courts the position of the presidential administration.

sovereignty Fundamental governmental authority.

Speaker The presiding officer of the House of Representatives; normally, the Speaker is the leader of the majority party.

spending clause Constitutional provision that gives Congress the power to collect taxes to provide for the general welfare.

spin The positive or negative slant that reporters or anchors put on their reports.

spoils system A system of government employment in which workers are hired on the basis of party loyalty.

sponsor Representative or senator who introduces a bill or resolution.

Stamp Act Congress A meeting in 1765 of delegates from nine colonies to oppose the Stamp Act; the first political organization that brought leaders from several colonies together for a common purpose.

stamp tax Passed by Parliament in 1765, it required people in the colonies to purchase a small stamp to be affixed to legal and other documents.

standing committee Committee with fixed membership and jurisdiction, continuing from Congress to Congress.

stare decisis In court rulings, reliance on consistency with precedents. See also *precedent*.

state action doctrine Rule stating that only the actions of state and local governments, not those of private individuals, must conform to the equal protection clause.

State of the Union address Annual speech delivered by the president in fulfillment of the constitutional obligation of reporting to Congress on the state of the Union.

state sovereign immunity Legal doctrine, based on the Eleventh Amendment, that says states cannot be sued under federal law.

statutory interpretation The judicial act of interpreting and applying the law to particular cases.

subgovernment Alliance of a congressional committee, a bureaucratic agency, and a small number of allied interest groups that combine to dominate policy making in some specified policy area.

suffrage Another term for the right to vote.

sunshine law A 1976 law requiring that federal government meetings be held in public.

Supplemental Security Income (SSI) Program that provides disabled people of low income with income assistance.

supply-side economics Economic policy based on the belief that governments can keep the economy healthy by supplying the conditions (especially low taxes and minimal regulation) that encourage private economic activity.

supremacy clause Constitutional provision that says the laws of the national government "shall be the supreme Law of the Land."

surplus The amount by which annual revenue exceeds spending.

suspect classification Categorization of a particular group that will be closely scrutinized by the courts to see whether its use is unconstitutional.

suspension of the rules Fast-track procedure for considering bills and resolutions in the House; debate is limited to 40 minutes, no amendments are in order, and a two-thirds majority is required for passage.

tax base Types of activities, types of property, or kinds of investments that are subject to taxation.

tax burden The total amount of tax that a household pays.

tax preferences Special tax treatment received by certain activities, property, or investments.

taxation without representation Levying of taxes by a government in which the people are not represented by their own elected officials.

Temporary Assistance for Needy Families (TANF) Welfare reform law passed by Congress in 1996.

three-fifths compromise Constitutional provision that counted each slave as three-fifths of a person when calculating representation in the House of Representatives; repealed by the Fourteenth Amendment.

ticket splitting Occurs when a voter does not vote a straight party ticket.

Tonkin Gulf Resolution Congressional resolution giving the president the authority to send troops to Vietnam.

Tories Those colonists who opposed independence from Great Britain.

transition The period after a presidential candidate has won the November election but before the candidate assumes office as president on January 20.

treaties Official agreements with foreign countries that are ratified by the Senate.

trial venue Place where a trial is held.

trustee Role a representative plays when acting in accordance with his or her own best judgment.

two-party system System in which only two significant parties compete for office. Such systems are in the minority among world democracies.

two-presidency theory Theory that explains why presidents exercise greater power over foreign affairs than over domestic policy.

two-thirds rule Rule governing Democratic national conventions from 1832 to 1936. It required that the presidential and vice-presidential nominees receive at least two-thirds of the delegates' votes.

tyranny of the majority Stifling of dissent by those voted into power by the majority.

unanimous-consent agreement Agreement that sets forth the terms and conditions according to which the Senate will consider a bill; these are individually negotiated by the leadership for each bill.

undervotes Ballots that indicate no choice for an office (e.g., for president in 2000), whether because the voter abstained or because the voter's intention could not be determined.

unemployment The circumstance that exists when people who are willing to work at the prevailing wage cannot get jobs.

unfunded mandates Federal regulations that impose burdens on state and local governments without appropriating enough money to cover costs.

unitary government System under which all authority is held by a single, national government.

United Nations Organization of all nation-states, whose purpose is to preserve world peace and foster economic and social development throughout the world.

U.S. attorney Person responsible for prosecuting violations of the federal criminal code.

U.S. v. Curtiss-Wright Supreme Court decision in which Congress is given the authority to delegate foreign policy responsibilities to the president.

veto power Presidential rejection of congressional legislation. May be overridden by a two-thirds vote in each congressional chamber. Most state governors also have veto power over their legislatures.

Virginia Plan Constitutional proposal supported by convention delegates from large states.

voter mobilization The efforts of parties, groups, and activists to encourage their supporters to turn out for elections.

voting-age population All people in the United States over the age of 18.

War on Poverty One of the most controversial of the Great Society programs, designed to enhance the economic opportunity of low-income citizens.

War Powers Resolution 1973 congressional resolution requiring the president to notify Congress formally upon ordering U.S. troops into military action.

Whigs Political opposition in eighteenth-century England that developed a theory of rights and representation.

whips Members of Congress who serve as informational channels between the leadership and the rank-and-file, conveying the leadership's views and intentions to the members, and vice versa.

White House Office Political appointees who work directly for the president, many of whom occupy offices in the White House.

white primary Primary elections, held by the Democratic party after Reconstruction, that in many southern states excluded nonwhites from participation.

winner-take-all voting Any voting procedure in which the side with the most votes gets all of the seats or delegates at stake.

writ of *certiorari* (cert) A document issued by the Supreme Court indicating that the Court will review a decision made by a lower court.

writ of habeas corpus A judicial order that a prisoner be brought before a judge to determine the legality of his or her imprisonment.

Youngstown Sheet and Tube Co. v. Sawyer Case in which the Supreme Court placed limits on the executive power of the president.

zone of acceptance Range within which Congress allows agencies to interpret and apply statutes.

ENDNOTES

PREFACE

1. *Pluralist Democracy in the United States: Conflict and Consent* (Chicago: Rand McNally, 1967).

2. Robert Dahl, *The New Political (Dis)Order* (Berkeley, CA: IGS Press, 1994): 1.

3. Ibid., 5.

4. "The Civic Culture: Prehistory, Retrospect, and Prospect," Center for the Study of Democracy Research Monograph No. 1, University of California, Irvine, 1996: 14.

5. James Stimson, "Opinion and Representation," *American Political Science Review* 89 (1995): 181.

6. James Barnes, "Clinton's Horse Race Presidency," *National Journal* (May 29, 1993): 1310.

7. Kenneth T. Walsh, "So, Why is This Man Laughing?" *U.S. News and World Report*, September 6, 2004, p. 30.

8. The Transition to Governing Project, directed by Norman Ornstein and Thomas Mann.

CHAPTER 1

1. John F. Harris, "Campaign Promises Aside, It's Politics As Usual," *Washington Post Weekly Edition*, July 2–8, 2001: 11.

2. On the importance of political consultant Karl Rove to George W. Bush's White House, see Dana Milbank, "The White House Lightning Rod: If Sparks are Flying, Karl Rove Is Probably at the Center," *Washington Post Weekly Edition*, July 23–29, 2001: 13–14; and Thomas B. Edsall, "Bush's Big Gamble: An Amnesty Proposal for Illegal Immigrants Angers GOP Conservatives," *Washington Post Weekly Edition*, July 23–29, 2001: 14.

3. Evelyn Nieves, "Heinz Kerry's Campaign Balancing Act," *Washington Post*, September 12, 2004: A1; *New York Times*, "Political Family Rules," August 1, 2004: Section 4, p. 10.

4. "Half a Million Voters' Choices," *Governing*, April 1995, 15.

5. *The Book of the States, 2002* (Lexington, KY: Council of State Governments, 2002), pp. 209–211.

6. Herbert Jacob and Kenneth Vines, "Courts," in *Politics in the American States: A Comparative Analysis,* 4th ed., ed. Virginia Gray, Herbert Jacob, and Kenneth Vines (Boston: Little, Brown, 1983), p. 238.

7. Thomas Cronin, *Direct Democracy* (Cambridge, MA: Harvard University Press, 1989); and David Magleby, *Direct Legislation* (Baltimore, MD: Johns Hopkins University Press, 1984).

8. Anthony King, *Running Scared: Why America's Politicians Campaign Too Much and Govern Too Little* (New York: Free Press, 1996), pp. 2–3.

9. Joseph S. Nye, Jr., Philip D. Zelikow, and David C. King, eds., *Why People Don't Trust Government* (Cambridge, MA: Harvard University Press, 1997).

10. H. H. Gerth and C. W. Mills, trans., *From Max Weber* (New York: Oxford University Press, 1946), p. 78.

11. Chuck Henning, *The Wit and Wisdom of Politics: Expanded Edition* (Golden, CO: Fulcrum, 1992), p. 91.

12. Todd Purdom, "Prep School Peers Found Kerry Talented, Ambitious, and Apart," *New York Times*, May 16, 2004: A1.

13. Jimmy Carter, *A Government as Good as Its People* (New York: Simon & Schuster, 1977), p. 102.

14. "Federalist No. 51," in James Madison, Alexander Hamilton, and John Jay, *The Federalist Papers* (New York: Penguin Books, 1987 [1788]), p. 319

15. Hobbes, *Leviathan* (New York: Dutton, 1973), 65.

16. Henning, *Wit and Wisdom*, p. 89.

17. "How to Run a Referendum," *The Economist*, November 23, 1996, 66.

18. Good surveys of democratic theory include J. Roland Pennock, *Democratic Political Theory* (Princeton, NJ: Princeton University Press, 1979); and Giovanni Sartori, *The Theory of Democracy Revisited* (Chatham, NJ: Chatham House, 1987).

19. James Morone, *Democratic Wish: Popular Participation and the Limits of American Government* (New York: Basic Books, 1990), p. 5. Morone is summarizing the claims of others; he himself is a critic of popular democracy.

20. Benjamin Barber, *Strong Democracy* (Berkeley, CA: University of California Press, 1984).

21. Alexis de Tocqueville, *Democracy in America*, 2nd ed., trans. Henry Reeve, 2 vols. (Cambridge, MA: Sever & Francis, 1863), I, pp. 318–319, as quoted in Morone, *Democratic Wish,* p. 86.

22. John Adams, *The Political Writings of John Adams*, ed. George Peek, Jr. (New York: Macmillan, 1985), p. 89.

23. Morone, *Democratic Wish*, pp. 5–6.

24. "Federalist No. 51."

25. Sidney Blumenthal, *The Permanent Campaign* (New York: Simon & Schuster, 1982).

26. Hugh Heclo, "The Permanent Campaign: A Conspectus," in *Campaigning to Govern or Governing to Campaign?*, eds. Thomas Mann and Norman Ornstein (Washington, DC: The Brookings Institution, 2000).

27. Woodrow Wilson, *Congressional Government* (Cleveland, OH: Meridian Books, 1956), p. 39.

28. Richard Boyd, "Decline of U.S. Voter Turnout: Structural Explanations," *American Politics Quarterly* 9 (1981), pp. 133–159.

29. Frank Sorauf, *Political Parties in the American System* (Boston: Little, Brown, 1964); and Martin Wattenberg, *The Decline of American Political Parties, 1952–1984* (Cambridge, MA: Harvard University Press, 1986).

30. Gary Jacobson finds that national swings in House elections are much more heterogeneous than at mid-century. See "The Marginals Never Vanished: Incumbency and Competition in Elections to the U.S. House of Representatives, 1952–1982," *American Journal of Political Science* 31 (1987): 126–141.

31. Susan Baer, "Candidates' Spouses Revisit Traditional Role," *Baltimore Sun*, January 23, 2004: 1A.

32. Carolyn Lochhead, "GOP Rebels Keep Bush's Tax Cut Bill on the Ropes," *San Francisco Chronicle*, May 14, 2003.

33. Joseph Cantor, *Congressional Campaign Spending, 1976–1996*, Congressional Research Service Report Number 97–793, (Washington, DC: Congressional Research Service, August 19, 1997), p. 2, Table 1; Center for Responsive Politics, www.crp.org, accessed May 16, 2004.

34. John Broder, "Governors Join Ranks of Full-Time Campaign Money-Raisers," *New York Times*, December 5, 1999: 22.

35. John Alford and John Hibbing, "Electoral Convergence of the Two Houses of Congress," paper presented at the Norman Thomas Conference on Senate Exceptionalism, Vanderbilt University, Nashville, TN, October 21–23, 1999.

36. Susan A. Macmanus, *Young v. Old: Generational Combat in the 21st Century* (Boulder, CO: Westview Press, 1996), chap. 2.

37. R. Douglas Arnold, *The Logic of Congressional Action* (New Haven, CT: Yale University Press, 1990).

38. Benjamin Ginsberg and Martin Shefter, *Politics by Other Means: The Declining Importance of Elections in America* (New York: Basic Books: 1990); and Terry Moe, "The Politics of Bureaucratic Structure," in *Can the Government Govern?*, eds. John Chubb and Paul Peterson (Washington, DC: The Brookings Institution, 1989), pp. 267–329.

39. John Dewey, as quoted in Morone, *Democratic Wish*, p. 322.

40. Morone, *Democratic Wish*.

41. Henning, *Wit and Wisdom*, p. 94.

42. "A League of Evil," *The Economist*, September 11, 1999, 7.

43. Henning, *Wit and Wisdom*, p. 58.

44. Charles Masters, "Riviera Tramps Run Risk of 'Tourist Cleansing' Round-Ups," *Daily Telegraph*, July 27, 1996, International Section: 15.

CHAPTER 2

1. Herbert Storing, ed., *The Complete Anti-Federalist: Maryland and Virginia and the South*, vol. 5 (Chicago: University of Chicago Press, 1981), pp. 210, 212; selections from two speeches.

2. Herbert Storing, ed., with the assistance of Murray Dry, *The Complete Anti-Federalist* (Chicago: University of Chicago Press, 1981).

3. Alexander Hamilton, "Federalist 7," *The Federalist Papers* (New York: Bantam Books, 1982), p. 31.

4. Owen S. Ireland, *Religion, Ethnicity and Politics: Ratifying the Constitution in Pennsylvania* (University Park, PA: Pennsylvania State University Press, 1995).

5. Quoted in Jack Rakove, *Original Meanings: Politics and Ideas in the Making of the Constitution* (New York: Vintage, 1997), p. 17.

6. Alan Brinkley, *The Unfinished Nation: A Concise History of the American People, Second Edition* (New York: Alfred A. Knopf, 1997), pp. 23-32.

7. Thomas A. Bailey, *The American Pageant: A History of the Republic* (Boston: D.C. Heath, 1956).

8. Gordon S. Wood, *The Radicalism of the American Revolution* (New York: Knopf, 1992), p. 80.

9. Jack P. Greene, "The Role of the Lower Houses of Assembly in Eighteenth-Century Politics," in *The Reinterpretation of the American Revolution 1763–1789*, ed. Jack P. Greene (New York: Harper & Row, 1968), pp. 86–109.

10. Merrill D. Peterson, *Thomas Jefferson and the New Nation* (New York: Oxford University Press, 1970), pp. 22–23.

11. Robert J. Dinkin, *Voting in Revolutionary America: A Study of Elections in the Original Thirteen States, 1776–1789* (Westport, CT: Greenwood Press, 1982) and Robert J. Dinkin, Voting in Provincial America: A Study of Elections in the Thirteen Colonies, 1689–1776 (Westport, CT: Greenwood Press, 1977).

12. Wood, *Radicalism*, p. 55.

13. J. Franklin Jameson, *The American Revolution Considered as a Social Movement* (Princeton, NJ: Princeton University Press, 1926).

14. Edmund S. Morgan and Helen M. Morgan, *The Stamp Act Crisis: Prologue to Revolution* (Chapel Hill: University of North Carolina Press, 1953), p. 106.

15. Morgan and Morgan, *Stamp Act Crisis*, p. 106.

16. Bernard Bailyn, *The Origins of American Politics* (New York: Knopf, 1968), p. 12.

17. Thomas Hobbes, *Leviathan* (New York: Oxford University Press, 1996). Originally published in 1651.

18. John Locke, *Two Treatises on Civil Government* (London: Dent, 1924). Originally published in 1690.

19. J. H. Plumb, *The Origins of Political Stability* (Boston: Houghton Mifflin, 1967).

20. For a discussion of the influence of James Harrington on colonial thought, see Samuel H. Beer, *To Make a Nation: The Rediscovery of American Federalism* (Cambridge, MA: Harvard University Press, 1993).

21. Thomas Paine, *Common Sense* (New York: Penguin, 1986). Originally published in 1776.

22. John Bartlett, *Familiar Quotations*, 15th ed. (Boston: Little, Brown, 1980), pp. 334, 342, 414.

23. C. L. Becker, *Freedom and Responsibility in the American Way of Life* (New York: Knopf, 1945), p. 16, as quoted by Louis Hartz, *Liberal Tradition in America* (New York: Harcourt, 1955), p. 61.

24. Dinkin, *Voting in Revolutionary America*; and Dinkin, *Voting in Provincial America*.

25. Willi Paul Adams, *The First American Constitutions: Republican Ideology and the Making of the State Constitutions in the Revolutionary Era* (Chapel Hill: University of North Carolina Press, 1980), pp. 245, 308–311.

26. Adams, *First American Constitution*, p. 207.

27. Bailey, *American Pageant*, p. 136.

28. Alexander Hamilton, James Madison, John Jay, *The Federalist Papers* (New York: Mentor Books, 1999 [1787]), p. 76 (Federalist 15).

29. James Madison, Letter to Thomas Jefferson, October 24, 1787, in James Madison, *Letters and Other Writings of James Madison* (Philadelphia: Lippincott, 1865).

30. "Report of Proceedings in Congress, February 21, 1787," The Avalon Project at Yale Law School, www.yale.edu/lawweb/avalon/const/const04.htm, accessed January 22, 2004.

31. Charles A. Beard, *An Economic Interpretation of the Constitution of the United States* (New York: Free Press, 1913).

32. Robert E. Brown, *Charles Beard and the Constitution* (Princeton, NJ: Princeton University Press, 1956); and Forrest McDonald, *We the People* (Chicago: University of Chicago Press, 1958).

33. John P. Roche, "The Founding Fathers: A Reform Caucus in Action," *American Political Science Review 55* (December 1961): 799–816.

34. Winton U. Solberg, ed., *The Federal Convention and the Formation of the Union of the American States* (New York: Bobbs-Merrill, 1958), p. 78.

35. Solberg, *Federal Convention*, p. 78.

36. Ibid., pp. 131–134.

37. Max Farrand, *The Framing of the Constitution of the United States* (New Haven: Yale University Press, 1913), p. 113.

38. Thornton Anderson, *Creating the Constitution: The Convention of 1787 and the First Congress* (University Park, PA: Pennsylvania State University Press, 1993).

39. Arthur M. Schlesinger, Jr., ed., *History of American Presidential Elections, 1789–1968*, vol.2 (New York: McGraw-Hill, 1971), p. 1244.

40. Anderson, *Creating the Constitution*, p. 148.

41. Anderson, *Creating the Constitution*, p. 148.

42. Henry Steele Commager, ed., *Documents of American History* (New York: Appleton-Century-Crofts, 1958), p. 104; and Willi Paul Adams, *The First American Constitutions: Republican Ideology and the Making of the State Constitutions in the Revolutionary Era* (Chapel Hill: University of North Carolina Press, 1980).

43. Arthur M. Schlesinger, *Prelude to Independence* (New York: Knopf, 1958), p. 299.

44. C. M. Kenyon, "Men of Little Faith: The Anti-Federalists on the Nature of Representative Government," in *The Reinterpretation of the American Revolution, 1763–1789*, ed. Jack P. Green (New York: Harper & Row, 1968), pp. 526–567; and

Herbert J. Storing, ed., *The Anti-Federalist* (Chicago: University of Chicago Press, 1986).

45. John Jay, Alexander Hamilton, and James Madison, writing under the pseudonym Publius, *The Federalist Papers* (New York: New American Library, 1961).

46. James Madison, "Federalist 10," in John Jay, Alexander Hamilton, and James Madison, writing under the pseudonym Publius, *The Federalist Papers* (New York: New American Library, 1961).

47. Jane Mansbridge, *Why We Lost the ERA* (Chicago: University of Chicago Press, 1986).

48. Beard, *An Economic Interpretation of the Constitution of the United States.*

49. Bernard Bailyn, *The Ideological Origins of Revolution* (Cambridge, MA: Harvard University Press, 1967); and Gordon S. Wood, *The Creation of the American Republic, 1776–1787* (Chapel Hill: University of North Carolina Press, 1969).

50. Frederick Douglass, "Is the Plan of the American Union Under the Constitution Anti-Slavery or Not?" *The Frederick Douglass Papers*, ed. John W, Blassingame (New Haven: Yale University Press, 1979), vol. 3, p. 157.

51. Beard, *Economic Interpretation*, chap. 9.

52. Second Inaugural Address, 1865, as quoted in John Bartlett, *Familiar Quotations*, 16th ed. (Boston: Little, Brown, 1992), p. 450.

CHAPTER 3

1. Evan Thomas, "The Lost City; What Went Wrong: Devastating a Swath of South, Katrina Plunged New Orleans into Agony," *Newsweek*, September 12, 2005, 42.

2. Robert Travis Scott, "Katrina's Death Toll is Anybody's Guess," *New Orleans Times Picayune*, November 2, 2005, available at www.nola.com/news/t-p/frontpage/index.ssf?/base/news-4/113091550371970.xml, accessed January 15, 2006.

3. For estimates of job losses and property damage, see Douglas Holtz-Eakin, Director, Congressional Budget Office, "CBO Testimony: Macroeconomic and Budgetary Effects of Hurricanes Katrina and Rita," testimony before the Committee on the Budget, U.S. House of Representatives, October 6, 2005, available at www.cbo.gov/ftpdocs/66xx/doc6684/10-06-Hurricanes.pdf, accessed January 15, 2006; and Congressional Budget Office, "The Macroeconomic and Budgetary Effects of Hurricanes Katrina and Rita: An Update," September 29, 2005, available at www.cbo.gov/ftpdocs/66xx/doc6669/09-29-EffectsOfHurricanes.pdf, accessed

January 15, 2006.

4. Mark Fischetti, "Drowning New Orleans," *Scientific American*, October 2001: 76–85.

5. Fischetti, p. 85.

6. Robert Block, Amy Schatz, Gary Fields, and Christopher Cooper, "Behind Poor Katrina Response, a Long Chain of Weak Links," *Wall Street Journal*, September 6, 2005: A1.

7. Eric Lipton, Christopher Drew, Scott Shane, and David Rohde, "Breakdowns Marked Path From Hurricane to Anarchy," *New York Times*, September 11, 2005: 1.

8. "A Failure of Initiative: Final Report of the Select Bipartisan Committee to Investigate the Preparation for and Response to Hurricane Katrina," United States House of Representatives, Washington, DC, February 15, 2006, pp. 3–5; 108.

9. See, for example: Office of Senator Trent Lott (R–MS), "Senator Lott Demands Help for Katrina Victims," press release, September 5, 2005, http://lott.senate.gov/index.cfm?FuseAction=PressReleases.Detail&PressRelease_id=187&Month=9&Year=2005, accessed September 6, 2005; Block, et al., "Behind Poor Katrina Response, a Long Chain of Weak Links,"; Spencer S. Hsu and Susan B. Glasser, "FEMA Director Singled Out by Response Critics," *Washington Post*, September 6, 2005: A1.

10. "A Failure of Initiative: Final Report of the Select Bipartisan Committee to Investigate the Preparation for and Response to Hurricane Katrina," United States House of Representatives, Washington, DC, February 15, 2006, p. 135.

11. Spencer S. Hsu, "Brown Defends FEMA's Efforts," *Washington Post*, September 28, 2005: A1.

12. Jere Longman and Sewell Chan, "Flooding Recedes in New Orleans; U.S. Inquiry is Set," *New York Times*, September 7, 2005: 1.

13. John Bartlett, *Familiar Quotations: Revised and Enlarged,* 15th ed. (Boston: Little, Brown, 1980), p. 452.

14. Alexis de Tocqueville, *Democracy in America*, vol. I, ed. Philips Bradley (New York: Knopf, 1945), p. 169.

15. Gordon S. Wood, *The Creation of the American Republic, 1776–1787* (New York: Norton, 1972), pp. 483–499.

16. Ibid.

17. Jean E. Smith, *John Marshall: Definer of a Nation* (New York: Henry Holt, 1996), pp. 440–446.

18. *McCulloch v. Maryland* (1819), 4 Wheaton 316, as reprinted in Henry Steele Commager, ed., *Documents of American History,*

6th ed. (New York: Appleton-Century-Crofts, 1949), p. 217.

19. *United States v. E. C. Knight Co.*, 156 U.S. 1 (1895).

20. *A. L. A. Schechter Poultry Corp. v. United States*, 295 U.S. 495 (1935).

21. James MacGregor Burns, *Roosevelt: The Lion and the Fox*, (New York: Harcourt Brace, 1956), p. 223.

22. Burns, p. 298.

23. *NLRB v. Jones & Laughlin Co.*, 301 U.S. 1 (1937).

24. *Wickard v. Filburn*, 317 U.S. 111 (1942).

25. *United States v. Lopez*, 514 U.S. 549 (1995).

26. *United States v. Morrison*, 99-5 (2000).

27. *Gonzales v. Raich*, No. 03-1454 (2005).

28. *McCulloch v. Maryland* (1819), as reprinted in Commager, p. 217.

29. Dan M. Berkovitz, "Waste Wars: Did Congress 'Nuke' State Sovereignty in the Low-Level Radioactive Waste Policy Amendments Act of 1985?" *Harvard Environmental Law Review 11,* (1987): 437–440.

30. *New York Times*, January 18, 1991.

31. *New York v. U.S.*, 488 U.S. 1041 (1992).

32. *Printz v. U.S.*, 521 U.S. 98 (1997).

33. *Seminole Tribe of Florida v. Florida et al.*, 517 U.S. 44 (1996).

34. *Board of Trustees of the University of Alabama v. Garrett*, 99-1240 (2001).

35. Federal Maritime Commission v. South Carolina State Ports Authority, 01-46 (2002).

36. *Helvering v. Davis*, 301 U.S. 548, 599 (1937).

37. *South Dakota v. Dole*, 483 U.S. 203 (1987).

38. Simon Lazarus, "The Federalist Society; Their Judicial Ideology Would Dismantle Accepted Social Policy," *Milwaukee Journal Sentinel*, July 1, 2001: 1J.

39. Morton Grodzins, *The American System: A New View of Government in the United States*, ed. Daniel J. Elazar (Chicago: Rand McNally, 1966).

40. Calculated from data in Ester Fuchs, *Mayors and Money* (Chicago: University of Chicago Press, 1992), p. 210.

41. Chuck Henning, comp., *The Wit and Wisdom of Politics: Expanded Edition* (Golden, CO: Fulcrum, 1992), p. 208.

42. Carl Hulse, "Spending Bill Is Approved, With Its Storehouse of Pork," *New York Times*, February 14, 2003: A24.

43. Shailagh Murray, "For a Senate Foe of Pork Barrel Spending, Two Bridges too

Far," *Washington Post*, October 21, 2005: A8; Shailagh Murray, "Some in GOP Regretting Pork-Stuffed Highway Bill," *Washington Post*, November 5, 2005: A1.

44. Shailagh Murray, "Funding for Alaskan Bridges Eliminated; Republicans Make Largely Symbolic Move in Reaction to Criticism of Transportation Spending," *Washington Post*, November 17, 2005: A18.

45. Jeffrey L. Pressman and Aaron Wildavsky, *Implementation*, 3rd ed. (Berkeley: University of California Press, 1984); Martha Derthick, *New Towns in Town: Why a Federal Program Failed* (Washington, DC: Urban Institute, 1972); and Eugene Bardach, *The Implementation Game*, 4th ed. (Cambridge, MA: MIT Press, 1982).

46. Jonathan Walters, "Good Deed, Punished," *Governing*, March 2005, 14.

47. Christopher Logan, "Politics and Promises: Rhetoric meets the reality of a slowdown in homeland security funding," in *Securing the Homeland: A Special Report from Governing Magazine and Congressional Quarterly*, October 2004, 10.

48. Logan, p. 12.

49. Paul E. Peterson, Barry Rabe, and Kenneth Wong, *When Federalism Works* (Washington, DC: The Brookings Institution, 1986).

50. Timothy Conlan, *New Federalism: Intergovernmental Reform from Nixon to Reagan* (Washington, DC: The Brookings Institution, 1988).

51. Executive Office of the President, Office of Management and Budget, *Budget for Fiscal Year 2006, Historical Tables*, Table 12.3.

52. David McKay, *Domestic Policy and Ideology: Presidents and the American State, 1964–1987* (New York: Cambridge University Press, 1989), chap. 4.

53. Paul E. Peterson and Mark Rom, *Welfare Magnets: A New Case for a National Standard* (Washington, DC: The Brookings Institution, 1990).

54. Calculated from *Temporary Assistance for Needy Families (TANF) Program: Sixth Annual Report to Congress* (Washington, DC: U.S. Department of Health and Human Services), November 2004, Chapter 1, Appendix Table 1-1; *Budget of the United States Government, Fiscal Year 2006, Historical Tables*, Table 12.3 (Washington DC: Office Of Management and Budget, February 2005).

55. Matthew C. Fellowes and Gretchen Rowe, "Politics and the New American Welfare States," *American Journal of Political Science* 48:2 (April 2004): 362–373. Quote from p. 370.

56. Peterson, *The Price of Federalism*.

57. William Fulton, "The Stimulator," *Governing*, June 2005, 64.

58. Timothy Conlan, "And the Beat Goes On: Intergovernmental Mandates and Preemption in an Era of Deregulation," *Publius* 21 (Summer 1991): 57.

59. On the costs of environmental mandates, see Richard C. Feiock, "Estimating Political, Fiscal and Economic Impacts of State Mandates: A Pooled Time Series Analysis of Local Planning and Growth Policy in Florida." Paper prepared for the annual meeting of the American Political Science Association, 1994.

60. Colleen M. Grogan, "The Influence of Federal Mandates on State Policy Decision-Making." Paper prepared for the annual meeting of the American Political Science Association, 1994; Teresa Coughlin, Leighton Ku, and John Holahan, *Medicaid Since 1980* (Washington, DC: Urban Institute, 1994); and John Holahan et al., "Explaining the Recent Growth in Medicaid Spending," *Health Affairs* 12 (Fall 1993): 177–193.

61. Jim VandeHei, "Education Law May Hurt Bush; No Child Left Behind's Funding Problems Could Be '04 Liability," *Washington Post*, October 13, 2003: A01.

62. Alan Greenblatt, "The Washington Offensive," *Governing*, January 2005, 26.

63. James Bryce, *Modern Democracies* (New York: Macmillan, 1921), vol. I, p. 132.

64. This figure excludes school districts. School districts have dramatically decreased in number, from over 108,000 in 1942 to about 14,000 today. This is, for the most part, the result of consolidation of rural school districts in the 1940s and 1950s. (See *Statistical Abstract of the United States, 2000*, Table 490.)

65. For more data on special districts, see *Finances of Special District Governments, 1997* (Washington, DC: U.S. Census of Governments, 2000). For a study of how and why special districts form, see Nancy Burns, *The Formation of American Local Governments: Private Values in Public Institutions* (New York: Oxford University Press, 1994).

66. Robert R. Alford and Eugene C. Lee, "Voting Turnout in American Cities," *American Political Science Review* 62 (September 1968): 796–813; and Albert Karnig and B. Oliver Walter, "Decline in Municipal Voter Turnout: A Function of Changing Structure," *American Politics Quarterly*, 11: 4 (October, 1983): 491–505.

67. Adam Nossiter, "For New Orleans, Election Could Bring a New Order," *New York Times*, February 3, 2006: A1.

68. Village politics are well described in A. J. Vidich and J. Bensman, *Small Town in Mass Society* (New York: Harper & Row, 1972). For descriptions of courthouse gangs in the county politics of the South, see V. O. Key, *Southern Politics* (New York: Random House, 1949).

69. Paul E. Peterson, *City Limits* (Chicago: University of Chicago Press, 1981).

70. Soloman Moore, "A Heavy Turnout for Apathy," *Los Angeles Times*, May 25, 2001: 12.

71. Edward Walsh, "Report Urges Expanding Federal Role in Elections; Task Force Recommends Guidance, Not Mandates," *Washington Post*, August 10, 2001: A02.

72. Daniel B. Wood, "As Election Season Nears, Efforts to Upgrade Voting Machines Bog Down," *Christian Science Monitor*, January 19, 2006: 3.

73. Gallup Poll, September 12–15, 2005.

74. *Statistical Abstract of the United States*, 2000, Table 28.

75. Greta Anand, "Circling of the Welcome Wagons: Selectman Candidates Rip Social Programs," *Boston Globe*, West Weekly Section, March 19, 1995: 1, 8.

76. Calculated from *Statistical Abstract of the United States, 2006*, Tables 440, 442, and 460. "Social programs" is defined for state and local governments as the U.S. census of government categories "public welfare" and "health and hospitals." For the federal government, "social programs" include Office of Management and Budget categories "health," "Medicare," "income security," "social security," and "veterans benefits and services."

77. "Money to Burn," *The Economist*, August 14, 1993: 23.

78. Steve Rushin, "The Heart of a City," *Sports Illustrated*, December 4, 1995.

79. Frances Stokes Berry and William D. Berry, "State Lottery Adoptions as Policy Innovations: An Event History Analysis," *American Political Science Review*, 84:2 (June, 1990): 395–415.

80. Daniel Elazar, *American Federalism: A View From the States* (New York: Harper & Row, 1984).

81. See, for example, John Kincaid, ed. *Political Culture, Public Policy, and the American States* (Philadelphia: Institute for the Study of Human Issues, 1982).

82. Morris Fiorina, *Divided Government* (New York: Macmillan, 1992).

83. Calculated from *Statistical Abstract of the United States, 2006*, Tables 437 and 654. Data are expressed in 2005 dollars and combine expenditures by state and local governments. Because the sharing of responsibilities by state and local governments varies widely from state to state, any interstate comparison that looks at state government expenditures alone can be quite misleading.

84. Peterson, *The Price of Federalism*, p. 105.

85. Jodi Wilgoren, "With Deadline Near, States Are in Budget Discord," *New York Times*, June 27, 2003: A14.

86. Jodi Wilgoren and David Rosenbaum, "Defying Labels Left or Right, Dean's '04 Run Is Making Gains," *New York Times*, July 30, 2003: A1.

87. *Baker v. Carr*, 369 U.S. 186 (1962); *Reynolds v. Sims*, 377 U.S. 533 (1964).

88. See Gordon E. Baker, *The Reapportionment Revolution* (New York: Random House, 1966); and Timothy G. O'Rourke, *The Impact of Reapportionment* (New Brunswick, NJ: Transaction Books, 1980).

89. John Sanko, "Boundary Map Favors Democrats," *Rocky Mountain News*, November 28, 2001: 23A.

90. Paul Bartels, "Plan to Redraw 11th District Opposed," *New Orleans Times-Picayune*, October 4, 2001: Metro 1.

91. Peggy Ficak, "Lights! Camera! Lawmakers!"*San Antonio Express News*, May 15, 2003: 9A.

92. Edward Walsh, "DeLay, Barton Subpoenaed in Texas Redistricting Case," *Washington Post*, November 22, 2003: p. A2; Warren Richey, "Supreme Court to Weigh Texas Redistricting," *Christian Science Monitor*, December 13, 2005, 1.

93. John Bull, "Redistricting Critics Unappeased; Panel Finalizes Boundaries, But Court Challenge Likely," *Pittsburgh Post-Gazette*, November 20, 2001: B-1.

94. The Council of State Governments, *The Book of the States: 2004 Edition* (Lexington, KY: Council of State Governments), Tables 3.2 and 3.9, pp. 78–80; 94–95; Peter Hecht, "Most Take Pay Hikes in Capitol," *Sacramento Bee*, December 6, 2005: p. A1.

95. Thad Kousser, quoted in Alan Greenblatt, "The Truth About Term Limits," *Governing*, January 2006, pp. 24–26.

96. Alan Greenblatt, "The Truth About Term Limits," *Governing*, January 2006, 24–26.

97. Matea Gold, "Gov-Elect Rolls Up His Sleeves on Budget," *Los Angeles Times*, October 22, 2003: 1.

98. Mark Niquette, "Trade Mission Led to 550 Jobs, Taft Says," *Columbus Dispatch*, December 7, 2005: 8E.

CHAPTER 4

1. Karen Breslau, "Hate Crime: He Wasn't Afraid," *Newsweek*, October 15, 2001, 8.

2. "Rights and the New Reality," *Los Angeles Times*, (September 21, 2002): part 2, p. 22.

3. Sam Howe Verhovek, "Americans Give in to Racial Profiling," *New York Times*, September 23, 2001: 1A; Sandra Tan, "Change of Heart," *The Buffalo News*, October 22, 2001: A1.

4. American Arab Anti-Discrimination Committee, press release, September 21, 2001.

5. Mary Jordan, "It's Harder to Cross the Mexican Border," *Washington Post Weekly Edition*, June 3–9, 2002: 17; Anne Hull, "A New Anxiety," *Washington Post Weekly Edition*, December 3–9, 2002: 9.

6. "Fewer Foreign Students," *Lexington* (KY) *Herald-Leader*, November 3, 2003: A3; David J. Jefferson, "Stopped at the Border," *Newsweek*, October 14, 2002, 59.

7. For background, go to www.oz.net/~cyu/internment/main.html.

8. Elizabeth Becker, "All White, All Christian, and Divided by Diversity," *New York Times*, June 10, 2001.

9. Some German children pricked their fingers "to let the German blood out." Recollection of Louise Bauer Ritschard, mother-in-law of Morris Fiorina.

10. Carl J. Friedrich, *Problems of the American Public Service* (New York: McGraw-Hill, 1935), p. 12.

11. See Alvin Rabushka and Kenneth Shepsle, *Politics in Plural Societies* (Columbus, OH: Merrill, 1972).

12. John A. Garrity and Peter Gay, eds., *The Columbia History of the World* (New York: Harper & Row, 1972), p. 673.

13. Quoted in Marc Shell, "Babel in America; or, The Politics of Language Diversity in the United States," *Critical Inquiry* 20 (1993): 109.

14. Richard McCormick, "Ethno-Cultural Interpretations of Nineteenth-Century American Voting Behavior," *Political Science Quarterly* 89 (1974): 351–377.

15. Richard Wayman, "Wisconsin Ethnic Groups and the Election of 1890," *Wisconsin Magazine of History 51* (1968): 273. More generally, see Paul Kleppner, *The Third Electoral System, 1853–1892: Parties, Voters, and Political Cultures* (Chapel Hill, NC: University of North Carolina Press, 1979).

16. On the multicultural character of California after it was annexed to the United States, see Ronald Takaki, *A Different Mirror* (Boston: Little, Brown, 1993), chap. 8.

17. John Miller, "Chinese Exclusion Act," *Congressional Record–Senate 1882* (13, Pt. 2): 1484–1485.

18. This is Oscar Handlin's sardonic characterization. See his *Race and Nationality in American Life* (Boston: Little, Brown, 1957), p. 95.

19. Madison Grant, *The Passing of the Great Race* (New York: Scribner's, 1916), pp. 80–81.

20. *Abstracts of Reports of the Immigration Commission* (Washington, DC: U.S. Government Printing Office, vol. 1, 1911). The quoted passages can be found on pp. 244, 251, 259, 261, 265, and 229. The characterization of southern Italians is based on work by an Italian (presumably a northern Italian) sociologist, but the Commission clearly agrees with the description.

21. Henry Cabot Lodge, "Immigration Restriction," *Congressional Record–Senate 1896* (28, Pt. 3): 2817.

22. "Emergency" immigration restrictions passed in 1921 were fine-tuned and formalized in the National Origins Act of 1924 and the National Origins Quota Act of 1929.

23. Seymour Martin Lipset and Earl Raab, *The Politics of Unreason* (New York: Harper & Row, 1970), p. 111.

24. Alan Lichtman, *Prejudice and the Old Politics: The Presidential Election of 1928* (Chapel Hill, NC: University of North Carolina Press, 1979).

25. Michael Fletcher and Darryl Fears, "Bush Pushes Guest-Worker Program," http://washingtonpost.com, November 29, 2005.

26. George Borhas, "Increasing the Supply of Labor Through Immigration," Washington, DC: Center for Immigration Studies, May 2004.

27. For example, a recent study by a pro-immigration economist estimated that an average immigrant family in Florida consumes $1800 per year more in state services than they pay in state and local taxes. David Denslow, "The Myth of No-Cost Immigrants," *Investor's Business Daily*, November 14, 2005.

28. McKay Ramah, "Family Reunification," Washington DC: Migration Policy Institute, May 1, 2003.

29. Samuel Huntington, *Who Are We? The Challenges to America's National Identity* (New York: Simon & Schuster, 2004.)

30. Arthur Schlesinger, Jr., *The Disuniting of America* (Knoxville, TN: Whittle, 1991).

31. Louis Hartz, *Liberal Tradition in America* (New York: Harcourt, 1955).

32. Bernard Bailyn, *The Ideological Origins of the American Revolution* (Cambridge, MA: Harvard University Press, 1967).

33. Gordon Wood. *The Creation of the American Republic* (New York: Norton, 1972); and J. G. A. Pocock, *The Machiavellian Moment* (Princeton, NJ: Princeton University Press, 1975).

34. Rogers Smith, "Beyond Tocqueville, Myrdal and Hartz: The Multiple Traditions in America," *American Political Science Review* 87 (1993): 549–566. These inconsistencies were not lost on earlier thinkers, to be sure. Recall

Jefferson's pessimistic predictions in his *Notes on the State of Virginia 1781–1785*. Also see Alexis de Tocqueville, *Democracy in America*, ed. J. P. Mayer (New York: Harper, 1969), pp. 340–363.

35. Samuel Huntington, *American Politics: The Promise of Disharmony* (Cambridge, MA: Harvard University Press, 1981).

36. Everett Carll Ladd, *American Ideology* (Storrs, CT: The Roper Center, 1994): 76.

37. I. A. Lewis and William Schneider, "Hard Times: The Public on Poverty," *Public Opinion*, June/July 1985, 2–8, 59–60.

38. "Income Tax Irritation." *Public Perspective* (July/August, 1990): 86.

39. Stanley Feldman, "Structure and Consistency in Public Opinion: The Role of Core Beliefs and Values," *American Journal of Political Science* 32 (1988): 416–440.

40. Ladd, *American Ideology*, pp. 56–57.

41. Sidney Verba and Gary Orren, *Equality in America* (Cambridge, MA: Harvard University Press, 1985).

42. Mariana Servin-Gonzalez and Oscar Torres-Reyna, "Trends: Religion and Politics," *Public Opinion Quarterly* 63 (1999): 613–614.

43. Robert Booth Fowler, *Religion and Politics in America* (Metuchen, NJ: American Theological Library Association, 1985), p. 27.

44. Huntington, *American Politics*.

45. Hartz, *Liberal Tradition*.

46. Frederick Jackson Turner, *The Frontier in American History* (New York: Holt, 1920).

47. For a discussion, see Seymour Martin Lipset, "Why No Socialism in the United States?" in *Sources of Contemporary Radicalism*, ed. Seweryn Bialer and Sophia Sluzar (New York: Westview Press, 1977).

48. Sven Steinmo, "American Exceptionalism Reconsidered," in *The Dynamics of American Politics*, ed. Larry C. Dodd and Calvin Jillson (Boulder, CO: Westwood, 1994), pp. 106–131.

49. For a sympathetic description of the trials and ordeals of the immigrants, see Oscar Handlin, *The Uprooted*, 2nd ed. (Boston: Little, Brown, 1973).

50. Hartz, *Liberal Tradition*, p. 18.

51. *Abstracts of Reports of the Immigration Commission*, p. 170.

52. Gregory Rodriguez, quoted in Patrick McDonnell, "Immigrants Quickly Becoming Assimilated, Report Concludes," *San Francisco Chronicle*, July 7, 1999: A4.

53. Philip Martin and Elizabeth Midgley, *Immigration to the United States* (Washington, DC: Population Reference Bureau, June 1999), p. 37.

54. James Smith, "Assimilation Across the Latino Generations," *American Economic Review* 93 (2003): 315–319.

55. Rodolfo de la Garza, "The Effects of Ethnicity on Political Culture," in *Classifying by Race*, ed. Paul Peterson (Princeton, NJ: Princeton University Press, 1995), pp. 351–352.

56. Rodolfo de la Garza, Angelo Falcon, and F. Chris Garcia, "Will the Real Americans Please Stand Up: Anglo and Mexican American Support of Core American Political Values," *American Journal of Political Science* 40 (1996): 335–351.

57. Lydia Saad, "Immigrants See United States as Land of Opportunity," *Gallup Poll Monthly*, July 1995, 19–33.

CHAPTER 5

1. John E. Mueller, *War, Presidents, and Public Opinion* (New York: Wiley, 1973), 59–63.

2. Paul Quirk and Joseph Hinchliffe, "The Rising Hegemony of Mass Opinion," *Journal of Policy History* 10 (1998): 19–50.

3. V. O. Key, *Public Opinion and American Democracy* (New York: Knopf, 1961).

4. Carl Friedrich, *Man and His Government* (New York: McGraw-Hill, 1963), pp. 199–215.

5. Elizabeth Cook, Ted Jelen, and Clyde Wilcox, *Between Two Absolutes: Public Opinion and the Politics of Abortion* (Boulder, CO: Westview Press, 1992).

6. David Leege, Kenneth Wald, and Lyman Kellstedt, "The Public Dimension of Private Devotionalism," in *Rediscovering the Religious Factor in American Politics*, ed. David Leege and Lyman Kellstedt (Armonk, NY: Sharpe, 1993), pp. 139–156; and Alan Hertzke and John Rausch, "The Religious Vote in American Politics: Value Conflict, Continuity, and Change," in *Broken Contract*, ed. Stephen Craig (Boulder, CO: Westview Press, 1996), p. 188.

7. The ANES Guide to Public Opinion and Electoral Behavior: www.umich.edu/~nes/nesguide/nesguide.htm.

8. Robert Hess and Judith Horney, *The Development of Political Attitudes in Children* (Garden City, NY: Doubleday, 1967).

9. Fred Greenstein, *Children and Politics* (New Haven, CT: Yale University Press, 1969), chap. 4.

10. M. Kent Jennings and Richard G. Niemi, *Generations and Politics* (Princeton, NJ: Princeton University Press, 1981), p. 51.

11. Arthur Lupia, "Shortcuts versus Encyclopedias: Information and Voting Behavior in California Insurance Reform Elections," *American Political Science Review* 88 (1994): 63–76.

12. For a survey of positive and negative findings, see Jack Citrin and Donald Green,

"The Self-Interest Motive in American Public Opinion," *Research in Micropolitics*, vol. 3 (Greenwich, CT: JAI Press, 1993), pp. 1–28.

13. David Sears and Leonie Huddy, "On the Origins of Political Disunity Among Women," in *Women, Politics, and Change*, ed. L. Tilly and P. Gurin (New York: Russell Sage, 1990), pp. 249–277.

14. Norman Nie, Jane Junn, and Kenneth Stehlik-Barry, *Education and Democratic Citizenship in America* (Chicago: University of Chicago Press, 1996).

15. Larry Bartels, "Messages Received: The Political Impact of Media Exposure," *American Political Science Review* 87 (1993): 267–285.

16. Details on how these polls are conducted appear in D. Stephen Voss, Andrew Gelman, and Gary King, "Preelection Survey Methodology: Details from Eight Polling Organizations, 1988 and 1992," *Public Opinion Quarterly* 59 (Spring): 98–132.

17. The figure for the 1950s and 1960s is based on the complete collection of Gallup results reported in George C. Edwards III and Alec M. Gallup, *Presidential Approval: A Sourcebook* (Baltimore, MD: Johns Hopkins University Press, 1990). Results for 2005 are based on the polls listed at www.realclearpolitics.com.

18. "Poll Leaves Democrats with Red Faces," Reuters, January 5, 2000.

19. Don Van Natta, Jr., "Polling's 'Dirty Little Secret': No Response," *New York Times*, November 21, 1999: sect. 4, pp. 1, 16.

20. John Brehm, *The Phantom Respondents* (Ann Arbor, MI: University of Michigan Press, 1993), chap. 2.

21. Everett Ladd, "The Pollsters' Waterloo," *Wall Street Journal*, November 19, 1996.

22. Jon Krosnick and Matthew Barent, "Comparisons of Party Identification and Policy Preferences: The Impact of Survey Question Format," *American Journal of Political Science* 37 (1993): 941–964.

23. On these topics, see Howard Schuman and Stanley Presser, *Questions and Answers in Attitude Surveys* (New York: Harcourt, Academic Press, 1981); and the essays in Thomas Mann and Gary Orren, eds., *Media Polls in American Politics* (Washington, DC: The Brookings Institution, 1992).

24. Adam Clymer, "The Unbearable Lightness of Public Opinion Polls," *New York Times*, July 22, 2001: 3.

25. For a full discussion, see David Moore and Frank Newport, "Misreading the Public: The Case of the Holocaust Poll," *Public Perspective*, March/April 1994, 28–30; and Tom Smith, "Review: The Holocaust Denial

Controversy," *Public Opinion Quarterly* 59 (1995): 269–295.

26. Tom Smith, "Public Support for Public Spending, 1973–1994," *The Public Perspective* 6, (April/May 1995), p. 2.

27. "Abortion: Overview of a Complex Opinion," *The Public Perspective*, November/December, 1989, 19, 20.

28. Morris Fiorina, Samuel Abrams, and Jeremy Pope, *Culture War? The Myth of a Polarized America* (New York: Longman, 2006), p. 81.

29. Greg Shaw, "Trends: Abortion," *Public Opinion Quarterly* 67 (2003): 408–409.

30. Ibid.: 409–411.

31. For a comprehensive breakdown of federal spending, see "Where the Money Goes," *Congressional Quarterly*, December 11, 1993.

32. Anthony King, "Names and Places Lost in the Mists of Time," *Daily Telegraph*, August 26, 1997: 4.

33. Anthony Downs, *An Economic Theory of Democracy* (New York: Harper & Row, 1957), chaps. 11–13.

34. Morris P. Fiorina, "Information and Rationality in Elections," in *Information and Democratic Processes*, ed. John Ferejohn and James Kuklinski (Urbana: University of Illinois Press, 1990), pp. 329–342.

35. John Krosnick, "Government Policy and Citizen Passion: A Study of Issue Publics in Contemporary America," *Political Behavior* 12 (1990): 59–92. The seminal study is Peter Natchez and Irvin Bupp, "Candidates, Issues, and Voters," *Public Policy* 1 (1968): 409–437.

36. Fiorina, "Information and Rationality in Elections."

37. George F. Bishop, Robert W. Oldendick, Alfred J. Tuchfarber, and Stephen E. Bennett, "Pseudo-Opinions on Public Affairs," *Public Opinion Quarterly* 44 (1980): 198–209.

38. For this and many similar results, see the classic study by Howard Schuman and Stanley Presser, *Questions and Answers in Attitude Surveys* (New York: Academic Press, 1981), chap. 4.

39. Philip Converse, "The Nature of Belief Systems in Mass Publics," in *Ideology and Discontent*, ed. David Apter (New York: Free Press, 1964), pp. 206–261.

40. M. Kent Jennings, "Ideological Thinking Among Mass Publics and Political Elites," *Public Opinion Quarterly* (1992): 419–441.

41. The ANES Guide.

42. Ibid.

43. Vernon Van Dyke, *Ideology and Political Choice* (Chatham, NJ: Chatham House, 1995), chaps. 3–5.

44. James A. Davis, "Changeable Weather in a Cooling Climate Atop the Liberal Plateau," *Public Opinion Quarterly* 56 (1992): 261–306; and Morris P. Fiorina, "The Reagan Years: Turning to the Right or Groping Toward the Middle?" in *The Resurgence of Conservatism in Anglo-American Democracies*, eds. Barry Cooper, Allan Kornberg, and William Mishler (Durham, NC: Duke University Press, 1988), pp. 430–459.

45. Morris P. Fiorina, *Divided Government*, 2nd ed. (Boston: Allyn & Bacon, 1995), pp. 173–177.

46. "Public Expects GOP Miracles," *Times-Mirror News Release*, December 8, 1994; CNN, "Gallup Poll: 50 Percent Americans Support, 33 Percent Oppose, Bush Tax Plan," February 27, 2001.

47. Classic studies include Samuel Stouffer, *Communism, Conformity, and Civil Liberties* (New York: Doubleday, 1955); and James Prothro and Charles Grigg, "Fundamental Principles of Democracy: Bases of Agreement and Disagreement," *Journal of Politics* 22 (1960): 176–194.

48. For evidence that people's opinions reflect a smaller number of "core beliefs" that may conflict with each other or situational characteristics, see Stanley Feldman, "Structure and Consistency in Public Opinion: The Role of Core Beliefs and Values," *American Journal of Public Opinion* 32 (1988): 416–440; and Stanley Feldman and John Zaller, "A Simple Theory of the Survey Response: Answering Questions Versus Revealing Preferences," *American Journal of Political Science* 36 (1992): 579–616.

49. R. Michael Alvarez and John Brehm, "American Ambivalence Toward Abortion Policy," *American Journal of Political Science* 39 (1995): 1055–1082.

50. On the effects of posing political conflicts as matters of conflicting rights, see Mary Anne Glendon, *Rights Talk: The Impoverishment of Political Discourse* (New York: Free Press, 1991).

51. "A Macro Theory of Information Flow," in *Information and Democratic Processes*, ed. John Ferejohn and James Kuklinski (Urbana: University of Illinois Press, 1990), pp. 345–368.

52. James Stimson, *Public Opinion in America: Moods, Cycles, and Swings* (Boulder, CO: Westview Press, 1991).

53. Christopher Wlezien, "The Public as Thermostat: Dynamics of Preferences for Spending," *American Journal of Political Science* 39 (1995): 981–1000.

54. Benjamin Page and Robert Shapiro, *The Rational Public* (Chicago: University of Chicago Press, 1992).

55. Dan Carney, "House GOP Embrace of Gun Curbs Not Yet Lock, Stock and Barrel," *CQ Weekly*, May 29, 1999, 1267.

56. Dan Carney, "Beyond Guns and Violence: A Battle for House Control," *CQ Weekly*, June 1999, 1426–1432.

57. Ibid.

58. Kathy Keily, "After Failed Gun Legislation, Political Finger Pointing Begins," *USA Today*, June 21, 1999: 14A.

59. ABC News/*Washington Post* poll of August 30–September 2, 1999.

60. Francis X. Clines, "In a Bitter Cultural War, an Ardent Call to Arms," *New York Times*, June 17, 1999.

61. "Increased Gun Control Not Necessarily a Cure-All," *The Public Perspective*, June/July 1999, 35.

CHAPTER 6

1. Darrel Rowland, "Campaigns Hope Personal Contacts Win Voters One by One," *Columbus Dispatch*, August 26, 2004: 1A.

2. Robert D. McFadden, "Record Turnout Forecast; Vote Drives Intensify," *New York Times*, November 2, 2004: A1.

3. All of the statistics in this paragraph are taken from the final report of the Committee for the Study of the American Electorate, available at http://election04.ssrc.org/research/csae_2004_final_report.pdf.

4. Benjamin Barber, *Strong Democracy: Participatory Politics for a New Age* (Berkeley and Los Angeles: University of California Press, 1984), p. xiii.

5. Chilton Williamson, *American Suffrage from Property to Democracy: 1760–1860* (Princeton, NJ: Princeton University Press, 1960); and Alexander Keyssar, *The Right to Vote* (New York: Basic Books, 2000), p. 29.

6. Ibid., p. 277.

7. Eleanor Flexner, *Century of Struggle*, rev. ed. (Cambridge, MA: Harvard University Press, 1975); and Anne Scott and Andrew Scott, *One Half the People* (Philadelphia: Lippincott, 1975).

8. For a history of the drive to enfranchise women, see Keyssar, *The Right to Vote*, chap. 6. On the strategies used by the suffrage movement, see Anna Harvey, "The Political Consequences of Suffrage Exclusion," *Social Science History* 20 (1996): 97–132.

9. "18-Year-Old Vote: Constitutional Amendment Cleared," *Congressional Quarterly Almanac* (Washington, DC: Congressional Quarterly, 1972), pp. 475–477.

10. Keyssar, *Right to Vote*, pp. xxi, 14–15.

11. "Felons and the Right to Vote, *nytimes.com*, July 11, 2004. "Can the Black Vote Hold Up?" *The Economist*, April 3, 1999: 24.

12. Paul Peterson, "An Immodest Proposal," *Daedalus* 121 (1992): 151–174.

13. Keyssar, *Right to Vote*.

14. For a comparative study of the American and Swiss suffrage movements, see Lee Ann Banaszak, *Why Movements Succeed or Fail* (Princeton, NJ: Princeton University Press, 1996).

15. Rosenstone and Hansen, *Mobilization, Participation, and Democracy*, chap. 2.

16. Jeffrey Jones, "Does Bringing Out the Candidate Bring Out the Votes?" *American Politics Quarterly* 26 (1998): 406.

17. John Ferejohn and Morris Fiorina, "The Paradox of Not Voting: A Decision Theoretic Analysis," *American Political Science Review* 68 (1974): 525–535.

18. John Milholland, "The Danger Point in American Politics," *North American Review* 164 (1897).

19. Raymond Wolfinger and Steven Rosenstone, *Who Votes?* (New Haven, CT: Yale University Press, 1980), p. 101.

20. A more sophisticated variant of this argument appears in Alexander A. Schuessler, *The Logic of Expressive Choice* (Princeton, NJ: Princeton University Press).

21. Howard Rosenthal and Subrata Sen, "Electoral Participation in the French Fifth Republic," *American Political Science Review* 67 (1973): 29–54.

22. Wolfinger and Rosenstone, *Who Votes?*, p. 116.

23. Ruy Teixeira, *The Disappearing American Voter* (Washington, DC: The Brookings Institution, 1992), p. 10.

24. Michael McDonald and Samuel Popkin, "The Myth of the Vanishing Voter," *American Political Science Review* 95 (2001): 963–974.

25. Wolfinger and Rosenstone, *Who Votes?*, p. 88.

26, Stephen Knack estimates that Election-Day registration boosts turnout by 3 to 6 percent on average. See his "Election Day Registration: The Second Wave," *American Politics Research* 29 (2001): 65–78.

27. Stephen Knack, "Drivers Wanted: Motor Voter and the Election of 1996," *PS: Political Science and Politics* 32 (1999): 237–243; and Michael Martinez and David Hill, "Did Motor Voter Work?" *American Politics Quarterly* 27 (1999): 296–315.

28. Mark Franklin, "Electoral Engineering and Cross-National Turnout Differences: What Role for Compulsory Voting? *British Journal of Political Science* 29 (1999): 205.

29. Richard Boyd, "Decline of U.S. Voter Turnout: Structural Explanations," *American Politics Quarterly* 9 (1981): 133–159.

30. Stephen Knack, "The Voter Participation Effects of Selecting Jurors from Registration Lists," Working Paper No. 91-10, University of Maryland, Department of Economics; and J. Eric Oliver and Raymond Wolfinger, "Jury Aversion and Voter Registration." paper presented at the 1997 Annual Meeting of the American Political Science Association, Washington, D.C.

31. Rosenstone and Hansen, *Mobilization, Participation, and Democracy*, p. 175.

32. Martin Wattenberg, *The Decline of American Political Parties, 1952–1996* (Cambridge, MA: Harvard University Press, 1998). Interestingly, the percentage of voters who reported being contacted by a party rose from 1956 to 1982 but declined thereafter. Party efforts would appear to have met with very limited success, inasmuch as turnout was falling throughout the period. See Rosenstone and Hansen, *Mobilization, Participation, and Democracy*, p. 163.

33. G. Bingham Powell, "American Voter Turnout in Comparative Perspective," *American Political Science Review* 80 (1986): 17–43; and Robert Jackman, "Political Institutions and Voter Turnout in the Industrial Democracies," *American Political Science Review* 81 (1987): 405–423.

34. Rosenstone and Hansen, *Mobilization, Participation, and Democracy*, pp. 63–70. There is some conflict between their figures and those reported by Verba, Schlozman, and Brady in *Voice and Equality*, pp. 69–74. Part of the explanation may be that the survey items relied on by Rosenstone and Hansen generally have more specific referents (such as this year's elections), whereas the items relied on by Verba, Schlozman, and Brady ask more generally about activity in the last year or two years. Thus, the Verba, Schlozman, and Brady figures may reflect the increasing number of opportunities.

35. Teixeira, *Disappearing American Voter*, p. 49.

36. Michael Delli Carpini and Scott Keeter, *What Americans Know About Politics and Why It Matters* (New Haven, CT: Yale University Press, 1996).

37. See the National Election Studies data archived at http://electionstudies.org/nesguide/gd-index.htm#6.

38. Rosenstone and Hansen, *Mobilization, Participation, and Democracy*, p. 183.

39. Marshall Ganz, "Motor Voter or Motivated Voter?" *The American Prospect*, September-October, 1996, 46–48; and

Marshall Ganz, "Voters in the Crosshairs," *The American Prospect*, Winter 1994, 100–109.

40. David S. Broder, "Shoe-Leather Politicking," *Washington Post Weekly Edition*, June 25–July 1, 2001: 4.

41. Warren Miller, "The Puzzle Transformed: Explaining Declining Turnout," *Political Behavior* 14 (1992): 1–43.

42. Martin Wattenberg, *Is Voting for Young People?* (New York: Longman, 2007).

43. Robert Putnam, *Bowling Alone* (New York: Simon & Schuster, 2000), chap. 14.

44. Stephen Knack, "Civic Norms, Social Sanctions, and Voter Turnout," *Rationality and Society* 4 (1992): 133–156.

45. Fareed Zakaria, "The Character of Our Campuses," *Newsweek*, May 28, 2001, 31.

46. Knack, "Civic Norms."

47. Rosenstone and Hansen, *Mobilization, Participation, and Democracy*, chap. 7; and Teixeira, *Disappearing American Voter*, chap. 2.

48. Eric Uslaner, "Faith, Hope, and Charity: Social Capital, Trust, and Collective Action" (College Park, MD: University of Maryland, unpublished manuscript).

49. For detailed analyses of the relationship between demographic characteristics and voting, see Wolfinger and Rosenstone, *Who Votes?*, and Rosenstone and Hansen, *Mobilization, Participation, and Democracy*, chap. 5.

50. Sidney Verba and Norman H. Nie, *Participation in America: Political Democracy and Social Equality* (New York: Harper & Row, 1972), pp. 170–171; and Wolfinger and Rosenstone, *Who Votes?*, p. 90.

51. See, for example, Rosenstone and Hansen, *Mobilization, Participation, and Democracy in America*, chap. 5.

52. On language and political participation, see Sidney Verba, Kay Schlozman, and Henry Brady, *Voice and Equality: Civic Volunteerism in American Politics* (Cambridge, MA: Harvard University Press, 1995).

53. Russell Dalton, *Citizen Politics in Western Democracies* (Chatham, NJ: Chatham House, 1988), pp. 51–52.

54. Herbert Tingsten, *Political Behavior: Studies in Election Statistics* (London: King & Son, 1937), pp. 225–226.

55. "Why Poor Turnout Points to a Healthy Democracy," *Gallup Poll Release*, May 23, 2001.

56. Quoted in Seymour Martin Lipset, *Political Man* (New York: Anchor, 1963), p. 228, note 90.

57. George Will, "In Defense of Nonvoting," in *The Morning After*, ed. George Will (New York: Free Press, 1986), p. 229.

58. A classic example is C. Wright Mills, *The Power Elite* (New York: Oxford University Press, 1956).

59. Stephen Bennett and David Resnick, "The Implications of Nonvoting for Democracy in the United States," *American Journal of Political Science* 34 (1990): 771–802.

60. Teixeira, *Disappearing American Voter*, p. 92.

61. Figures are based on the 2004 American National Election Study survey. Independent category includes only pure independents: i.e., independent leaners are classified as partisans.

62. Joseph Carroll and Frank Newport, "A Quarter of Americans Say Iraq Nation's Most Important Problem; But Americans Still More Likely to Name Economic Issues as Top Problem Facing Country," Gallup Poll News Service, April 15, 2004.

63. Political theorist Benjamin Barber refers to the former as an example of "strong democracy" and to the latter as an example of "thin democracy." See Barber, *Strong Democracy*.

64. Verba, Schlozman, and Brady, *Voice and Equality*, p. 50.

65. Ibid, p. 72.

66. David Nexon, "Asymmetry in the Political System: Occasional Activists in the Democratic and Republican Parties, 1956–1964," *American Political Science Review* 65 (1971): 716–730; and Warren Miller and M. Kent Jennings, *Parties in Transition* (New York: Russell Sage, 1986), chap. 2.

67. Fareed Zakaria, "The New Face of the Left," *Newsweek*, April 30, 2001, 32.

CHAPTER 7

1. The following account is based on Phil Kunz, "Home Schooling Movement Gives House a Lesson," *Congressional Quarterly Weekly Report*, February 26, 1994: 479–480.

2. There is some controversy about how to measure group membership and consequently about the exact figures. For differing viewpoints, see Frank Baumgartner and Jack Walker, "Survey Research and Membership in Voluntary Associations," *American Journal of Political Science* 32 (1988): 908–928; Tom Smith, "Trends in Voluntary Group Membership: Comments on Baumgartner and Walker," *American Journal of Political Science* 34 (1990): 646–661; and Baumgartner and Walker, "Response to Smith's 'Trends in Voluntary Group Membership,'" *American Journal of Political Science* 34 (1990): 662–670.

3. Alexis de Tocqueville, *Democracy in America*, ed. J. P. Mayer (New York: HarperPerennial, 1969), p. 513.

4. Theda Skocpol, *Diminished Democracy* (Norman, OK: Oklahoma University Press, 2003): chap. 2.

5. Kay Schlozman and John Tierney, *Organized Interests and American Democracy* (New York: Harper & Row, 1981), p. 75.

6. Robert Wiebe, *The Search for Order, 1877–1920* (New York: Hill and Wang, 1967).

7. Kristen Luker, *Abortion and the Politics of Motherhood* (Berkeley: University of California Press, 1984), chaps. 5–6.

8. Robert H. Salsbury, "Interest Representation: The Dominance of Institutions," *American Political Science Review* 78 (1984): 64–76.

9. Jeffrey Berry, *Lobbying for the People* (Princeton, NJ: Princeton University Press, 1977).

10. Jack L. Walker, *Mobilizing Interest Groups in America* (Ann Arbor: University of Michigan Press, 1991), p. 10.

11. An excellent source of basic information about groups and associations in the United States is the *Encyclopedia of Associations*, ed. Carol Schwartz and Rebecca Turner (Detroit, MI: Gale Research, annual).

12. These figures represent the combined membership of the Sierra Club, Environmental Defense Fund, Friends of the Earth, the Audubon Society, the National Wildlife Federation, the Natural Resources Defense Council, and the Wilderness Society. See *Encyclopedia of Associations*, 2000 ed.

13. Henry Brady, Sidney Verba, and Kay Schlozman, "Beyond SES: A Resource Model of Political Participation," *American Political Science Review* 89 (1995): 271–294.

14. James Q. Wilson, *Political Organizations* (New York: Basic Books, 1973), chap. 3.

15. Mancur Olson, *The Logic of Collective Action* (Cambridge, MA: Harvard University Press, 1965).

16. R. Cornes and T. Sandler, *The Theory of Externalities, Public Goods and Club Goods* (Cambridge, England: Cambridge University Press, 1986), chap. 6.

17. Documented in annual editions of U.S. Department of Labor, *Employment and Earnings* (Washington, DC: U.S. Government Printing Office, 1945–2005).

18. Jane Mansbridge, *Why We Lost the ERA* (Chicago: University of Chicago Press, 1986).

19. Kenneth Wald, *Religion and Politics in the United States*, 2nd ed. (Washington, DC: CQ Press, 1992), chap. 7.

20. See www.unicefusa.org, viewed May 19, 2006.

21. The organization referred to is Christian Foundation for Children and Aging. See www.cfcausa.org.

22. The term is from Richard Wagner, "Pressure Groups and Political Entrepreneurs," *Papers in Nonmarket Decision Making* 1 (1966): 161–170. For extended discussions, see Norman Frolich, Joe Oppenheimer, and Oran Young, *Political Leadership and Collective Goods* (Princeton, NJ: Princeton University Press, 1971); and Terry Moe, *The Organization of Interests* (Chicago: University of Chicago Press, 1980), chaps. 3–4.

23. "As Green Turns to Brown," *The Economist*, March 5, 1994, 28.

24. Walker, *Mobilizing Interest Groups in America*, pp. 98–99.

25. Jack Walker, "The Origins and Maintenance of Interest Groups in America," *American Political Science Review* 77 (1983): 390–406.

26. PoliticalMoneyLine, "Health Care and Tort Reform Push Lobbying Expenditures over $154 Million a Month," www.politicalmoneyline.com (2003); Frederick J. Frommer, "Miller Leads Beer Companies in Spending on Lobbying," Associated Press, October 5, 2003.

27. Carl Weiser, "Enforcement of Law Almost Non-existent," *USA Today*, November 16, 1999: 11A.

28. Center for Responsive Politics, various issues of *Influence, Inc.*, available at www.opensecrets.org.

29. Jack Wright, *Interest Groups and Congress* (New York: Longman, 2003).

30. Chuck Henning, *The Wit and Wisdom of Politics* (Golden, CO: Fulcrum Publishing, 1992), p. 137.

31. For figures see Mark Petracca, ed., *The Politics of Interests* (Boulder, CO: Westview Press, 1992), pp. 14–15; and Edward Laumann, John Heinz, Robert Nelson, and Robert Salisbury, "Washington Lawyers—and Others: The Structure of Washington Representation," *Stanford Law Review* 37 (1985): 465–502.

32. Lobbyist Michael Bromberg, quoted in Eleanor Clift and Tom Brazaitis, *War Without Bloodshed: The Art of Politics* (New York: Scribner, 1996), p. 100.

33. Jackie Koszczuk, "Hitting Them Where They Live," *Congressional Quarterly Weekly Report*, October 2, 1999, 2283–2286.

34. Peter H. Odegard, *Pressure Politics: The Story of the Anti-Saloon League* (New York: Columbia University Press, 1928), p. 76.

35. Frank Sorauf, *Inside Campaign Finance* (New Haven, CT: Yale University Press, 1992), chap. 4. A basic reference on PACs is *The PAC Directory* (Cambridge, MA: Ballinger, various editions).

36. Ross Baker, *The New Fat Cats: Members of Congress as Political Benefactors* (New York: Priority Press, 1989); and Eliza Carney, "PAC Men," *National Journal*, October 1, 1994: 2268–2273.

37. Figures are calculated from data in Marian Currinder, "Campaign Finance: Funding the Presidential and Congressional Elections," in *The Elections of 2004*, ed. Michael Nelson (Washington: CQ Press, 2005), Table 6-3, p. 125.

38. For a discussion, see Richard Hall and Frank Wayman, "Buying Time: Moneyed Interests and the Mobilization of Bias in Congressional Committees," *American Political Science Review* 84 (1990): 797–820.

39. See Edward Epstein, "Business and Labor Under the Federal Election Campaign Act of 1971," in *Parties, Interest Groups, and Campaign Finance Laws*, ed. Michael Malbin (Washington, DC: American Enterprise Institute, 1980), pp. 107–151.

40. Jim Drinkard, "Issue Ads Crowd Airwaves Before 2000 Election," *USA Today*, November 29, 1999: p. 11A; Center for Response Politics, 2005.

41. R. Kenneth Godwin, *One Billion Dollars of Influence* (Chatham, NJ: Chatham House, 1988).

42. Andrew McFarland, *Common Cause: Lobbying for the People* (Chatham, NJ: Chatham House, 1984), pp. 74–81.

43. Ed Henry, "It's the '90s: Old Dogs, New Tricks," *Roll Call Monthly*, November 1997, 13.

44. For details, see Hugh Graham and Ted Gurr, *The History of Violence in America* (New York: Bantam, 1969).

45. For an analysis of the expansion by the judiciary of federal programs for the handicapped and the poor, see R. Shep Melnick, *Between the Lines* (Washington, DC: The Brookings Institution, 1994).

46. Karen O'Connor and Bryan McFall, "Conservative Interest Group Litigation in the Reagan Era and Beyond," in *The Politics of Interests*, ed. Mark Petracca (Boulder, CO: Westview Press, 1992), pp. 263–281.

47. Jeffrey Milyo, David Primo, and Timothy Groseclose, "Corporate PAC Campaign Contributions in Perspective," *Business and Politics* 2 (2000): 75–88.

48. Jonathan Rauch, *Demosclerosis* (New York: Random House, 1994).

49. Philip Stern, *The Best Congress Money Can Buy* (New York: Pantheon, 1988).

50. John Heinz, Edward Laumann, Robert Nelson, and Robert Salisbury, *Representing Interests: Structure and Uncertainty in National Policy Making* (in press).

51. J. Leiper Freeman, *The Political Process*, rev. ed. (New York: Random House, 1965); Grant McConnell, *Private Power and American Democracy* (New York: Knopf, 1966); and Theodore Lowi, *The End of Liberalism* (New York: Norton, 1969).

52. David Hosansky, "House and Senate Assemble Conflicting Farm Bills," *Congressional Quarterly Weekly Report*, February 3, 1996, 298.

53. Hugh Heclo, "Issue Networks and the Executive Establishment, in *The New American Political System*, ed. Anthony King (Washington, DC: The Brookings Institution, 1978), pp. 87–124.

54. Robert Salisbury, John Heinz, Robert Nelson, and Edward Laumann, "Triangles, Networks, and Hollow Cores: The Complex Geometry of Washington Interest Representation," in *The Politics of Interests*, ed. Mark Petracca (Boulder, CO: Westview Press, 1992), pp. 130–149.

55. John Chubb, *Interest Groups and the Bureaucracy* (Stanford, CA: Stanford University Press, 1983), pp. 249–265; and Richard Harris, "Politicized Management: The Changing Face of Business in American Politics," in *Remaking American Politics*, ed. Richard Harris and Sidney Milkis (Boulder, CO: Westview Press, 1989), pp. 261–286.

56. Schlozman and Tierney, *Organized Interests and American Democracy*, pp. 314–317.

57. John Hibbing and Elizabeth Theiss-Morse, *Congress as Public Enemy* (New York: Cambridge University Press, 1995), pp. 63–65, 147.

58. Earl Latham, *The Group Basis of Politics* (New York: Cornell University Press, 1952); and David Truman, *The Governmental Process* (New York: Knopf, 1958).

59. E. E. Schattschneider, *The Semisovereign People* (New York: Holt, 1960), pp. 34–35.

60. ———. *Politics, Pressures, and the Tariff* (New York: Prentice-Hall, 1935).

61. E. E. Schattschneider, "The Gerontocrats," *The Economist*, May 13, 1995: 32.

62. Mansbridge, *Why We Lost the ERA*, p. 73.

63. Peter Aranson and Peter Ordeshook, "A Prolegomenon to a Theory of the Failure of Representative Democracy," in *American Re-evolution*, ed. Aranson and Ordeshooks (Tucson: University of Arizona, 1977), pp. 23–46.

CHAPTER 8

1. Terence Smith, "Media Notebook on the Republican National Convention," PBSOnline NewsHour, September 1, 2004; Shorenstein Center, "Election Interest Is Up Sharply but Convention Interest Is Not," Cambridge, MA: John F. Kennedy School of Government.

2. The first phrase comes from Richard Katz, "Party Government: A Rationalistic Conception," in *Visions and Realities of Party Government*, ed. F. Castles and R. Wildenmann (Berlin: deGruyter, 1986), p. 31. The second comes from Geoffrey Smith, "The Futures of Party Government," p. 206 of the same volume.

3. E. E. Schattschneider, *Party Government* (New York: Farrar and Rinehart, 1942), p. 1.

4. Martin Wattenberg, *The Decline of American Political Parties, 1952–1992* (Cambridge, MA: Harvard University Press, 1994).

5. John Aldrich, *Why Parties?* (Chicago: University of Chicago Press, 1995), chap. 2.

6. See, for example, James Campbell, *The Presidential Pulse of Congressional Elections* (Lexington: University Press of Kentucky, 1993).

7. V. O. Key, Jr., *Southern Politics* (New York: Knopf, 1949).

8. Richard Fenno, *Home Style* (Boston: Little, Brown, 1978), chap. 3.

9. Juliet Eilperin, "GOP, Trying to Expand, Aids Black Candidates," *Washington Post*, July 16, 2000: A6.

10. Anthony Downs, *An Economic Theory of Democracy* (New York: Harper & Row, 1957).

11. Gavin Wright, "The Political Economy of New Deal Spending: An Econometric Analysis," *Review of Economics and Statistics* 56 (1974): 30–38.

12. Morris Fiorina, *Divided Government*, 2nd ed. (Boston: Allyn & Bacon, 1996), pp. 107–110.

13. R. Michael Alvarez and Jonathan Nagler, "Economics, Issues, and the Perot Candidacy: Voter Choice in the 1992 Presidential Election," *American Journal of Political Science* 39 (1995): 714–744.

14. Discussed in James MacGregor Burns, *The Deadlock of Democracy* (Englewood Cliffs, NJ: Prentice-Hall, 1964), chap. 2.

15. Austin Ranney, *Curing the Mischiefs of Faction* (Berkeley: University of California Press, 1975); and Nelson Polsby, *Consequences of Party Reform* (New York: Oxford University Press, 1983).

16. James Bryce, *The American Commonwealth*, 4th ed. (London: Macmillan, 1910), vol. 2, p. 5.

17. See, for example, William Chambers and Walter Dean Burnham, eds., *The American Party Systems: Stages of Political Development* (New York: Oxford University Press, 1975).

18. The seminal contribution was V. O. Key, Jr., "A Theory of Critical Elections," *Journal of Politics* 17 (1955): 3–18. The most influential elaborations and extensions of the idea are Walter Dean Burnham, *Critical Elections and the Mainsprings of American Politics*

(New York: Norton, 1970) and James Sundquist, *Dynamics of the Party System*, rev. ed. (Washington, DC: The Brookings Institution, 1983).

19. David R. Mayhew, *Electoral Realignments: A Critique of an American Genre* (New Haven, CT: Yale, 2002).

20. For a good overview of the origin and development of America's first political parties, see William Nisbet Chambers, *Political Parties in a New Nation: The American Experience, 1776–1809* (New York: Oxford University Press, 1963).

21. Jack N. Rakove, *James Madison and the Creation of the American Republic*, 2nd ed. (New York: Longman, 2002), p. 149.

22. It is sometimes claimed that Lincoln was elected only because of a split in the Democratic Party. Actually, Lincoln won an absolute majority in enough northern states to achieve a majority in the electoral college.

23. For a recent history of the period, see Paul Kleppner, *The Third Electoral System, 1853–1892: Parties, Voters, and Political Cultures* (Chapel Hill: University of North Carolina Press, 1979).

24. Michael McGerr, *The Decline of Popular Politics* (New York: Oxford University Press, 1986).

25. Harold Gosnell provides a classic study of a machine. See his *Machine Politics: Chicago Model* (Chicago: University of Chicago Press, 1937). See also M. C. Brown and C. N. Halaby, "Machine Politics in America, 1870–1945," *Journal of Interdisciplinary History* 17 (1987): 587–612.

26. Richard Hofstadter, *The Age of Reform* (New York: Vintage, 1955); and Gabriel Kolko, *The Triumph of Conservatism* (New York: Free Press, 1963).

27. For a more detailed examination of the changes discussed in the next several paragraphs and the various schools of thought on realignment, see William G. Mayer, "Changes in Elections and the Party System: 1992 in Historical Perspective," in *The New American Politics: Reflections on Political Change and the Clinton Administration*, ed. Bryan D. Jones (Boulder, Colo.: Westview Press, 1995), pp. 19–50.

28. See, for example, Jerome M. Clubb, William H. Flanigan, and Nancy H. Zingale, *Partisan Realignment: Voters, Parties, and Government in American History* (Beverly Hills, Calif.: Sage, 1980); and Sundquist, *Dynamics of the Party System*, pp. 444–49.

29. For a good overview of the various theories about the electoral origins of divided government, see Gary W. Cox and Samuel Kernell, ed., *The Politics of Divided Government* (Boulder, CO: Westview Press, 1991).

30. See, for example, the essays by Everett Carll Ladd and Byron E. Shafer, in *The End of Realignment?: Interpreting American Electoral Eras*, ed. Byron E. Shafer (Madison, WI: University of Wisconsin Press, 1991).

31. Steven Rosenstone, Roy Behr, and Edward Lazarus, *Third Parties in America* (Princeton, NJ: Princeton University Press, 1981).

32. Maurice Duverger, *Political Parties: Their Organization and Activity in the Modern State* (New York: Wiley, 1963), book II, chap. 1.

33. Ibid. For elaboration, see Thomas Palfrey, "A Mathematical Proof of Duverger's Law," in *Models of Strategic Choice in Politics*, ed. Peter Ordeshook (Ann Arbor: University of Michigan Press, 1989), pp. 69–91.

34. For a good introductory discussion of how ballot access laws work, see Emmet T. Flood and William G. Mayer, "Third-Party and Independent Candidates: How They Get on the Ballot, How They Get Nominated," in *In Pursuit of the White House: How We Choose Our Presidential Nominees*, ed. William G. Mayer (Chatham, N.J.: Chatham House, 1996), pp. 285–306.

35. The books referred to are: David S. Broder, *The Party's Over: The Failure of Politics in America* (New York: Harper & Row, 1971); Xandra Kayden and Eddie Mahe, Jr., *The Party Goes On: The Persistence of the Two-Party System in the United States* (New York: Basic, 1985); and Larry Sabato, *The Party's Just Begun: Shaping Political Parties for America's Future* (Glenview, IL: Scott, Foresman, 1988).

36. The idea that the word "party" can be used to refer to "many types of groups and near-groups" is generally credited to V. O. Key, Jr. See *Politics, Parties, and Pressure Groups*, 4th ed. (New York: Thomas Y. Crowell, 1958), pp. 180–82. Our own discussion draws heavily on Paul Allen Beck and Frank Sorauf, *Party Politics in America*, 7th ed. (New York: HarperCollins, 1992), chap. 1.

37. Clinton Rossiter, *Parties and Politics in America* (Ithaca, N.Y.: Cornell University Press, 1960), pp. 11–12.

38. The seminal case here is *Elrod v. Burns*, 427 U.S. 347 (1976).

39. Writing in the 1970s, Hugh Heclo put the number at 3000. See his *A Government of Strangers* (Washington, DC: The Brookings Institution, 1977). By 1992 Thomas Weko put the number at about 3700. See *The Politicizing Presidency* (Lawrence: University of Kansas Press, 1995), p. 161.

40. Stephen Skowronek, *Building a New American State* (New York: Cambridge University Press, 1992), p. 69.

41. Stephen Frantzich, *Political Parties in the Technological Age* (New York: Longman, 1989).

42. "The Winner's Room," *U.S. News & World Report*, December 1, 2003, 8.

43. Cornelius Cotter, James Gibson, John Bibby, and Robert Huckshorn, *Party Organizations in American Politics* (New York: Praeger, 1984).

44. Ibid.

45. Dick Polman, "American Politics Circa 2003: Neither Kind nor Gentle," Knight-Ridder News Service, August 17, 2003; and David S. Broder, "Fighting Over the Economy," *Washington Post Weekly Edition*, November 5–11, 2001: 4.

46. John Coleman, "Resurgent or Just Busy? Party Organizations in Contemporary America," in *The State of the Parties*, 2nd ed., ed. John Green and Daniel Shea (Lanham, MD: Rowman & Littlefield, 1996), pp. 312–326.

47. Robert Dahl, *Dilemmas of Pluralist Democracy* (New Haven, CT: Yale University Press, 1982).

CHAPTER 9

1. Allen J. Matusow, *The Unraveling of America* (New York: Harper and Row, 1984), p. 413; Jules Witcover, *The Year the Dream Died* (New York: Warner Books, 1997), p. 321; and Todd Gitlin, *Sixties* (New York: Bantam, 1987), p. 322.

2. Ronald Radosh, *Divided They Fell* (New York: Free Press, 1996), p. 123; and Gitlin, *The Sixties*, p. 320.

3. Matusow, *Unraveling of America*, p. 413; and Gitlin, *Sixties*, p. 322.

4. Radosh, *Divided They Fell*, pp. 124–128; and Matusow, *Unraveling of America*, pp. 418–419.

5. Witcover, *Year the Dream Died*, p. 327; and Matusow, *Unraveling of America*, p. 418.

6. On the British reporters, see Lewis Chester, Godfrey Hodgson, and Bruce Page, *An American Melodrama* (New York: Viking, 1969), p. 582. For an attempt to interpret Daley's verbal abuse of Ribicoff, see Gitlin, *Sixties*, p. 334.

7. Chester, Hodgson, and Page, *American Melodrama*, p. 592.

8. John Robinson, "Public Reaction to Political Protest: Chicago 1968," *Public Opinion Quarterly* 34 (1970): 1–9.

9. Edwin Emery and Michael Emery, *The Press and America: An Interpretive of the Mass Media*, 5th ed. (Englewood Cliffs, N.J.: Prentice-Hall, 1984), chap. 2.

10. Daniel J. Boorstin, *The Americans: The Colonial Experience* (New York: Vintage Books, 1958), chap. 50.

11. Jeffrey B. Abramson, F. Christopher Arterton, and Gary R. Orren, *The Electronic*

Commonwealth: The Impact of New Media Technologies on Democratic Politics (New York: Basic Books, 1988), pp. 74–75.

12. Timothy E. Cook, Governing with the News: The News Media as a Political Institution (Chicago: University of Chicago Press, 1998), p. 26.

13. Our discussion of the penny press draws especially on Michael Schudson, Discovering the News: A Social History of American Newspapers (New York: Basic Books), chap. 1.

14. For a more detailed discussion of these events, see Emery and Emery, Press and America, chap. 17.

15. Our history of early radio draws especially on Emery and Emery, Press and America, chap. 20.

16. For more data on the early spread of television, see William G. Mayer, "Trends in Media Usage," Public Opinion Quarterly 57 (Winter 1993): 593–611.

17. Data are taken from Emery and Emery, Press and America, p. 676.

18. Editor & Publisher International Yearbook, 85th ed. (New York: Editor & Publisher, 2005), p. vi.

19. William G. Mayer, "Why Talk Radio Is Conservative," Public Interest, No. 156, (Summer 2004): 87.

20. Figures are from Magazine Publishers of America, as reprinted in Time Almanac 2006 (Boston: Pearson Education, 2005).

21. For a good discussion of the differences between the old and new media, see Abramson, Arterton, and Orren, Electronic Commonwealth, chap. 2.

22. See, for example, Michael J. Robinson, "Public Affairs Television and the Growth of Political Malaise: The Case of 'The Selling of the Pentagon,'" American Political Science Review 70 (June 1976): 426–27.

23. Michael Delli Carpini and Scott Keeter, What Americans Know About Politics and Why It Matters (New Haven, CT: Yale University Press, 1996).

24. William G. Mayer, "The Rise of the New Media," Public Opinion Quarterly 58 (Spring 1994): 128.

25. This incident is discussed in Edwin Diamond, The Tin Kazoo (Cambridge: MIT Press, 1975), p. 24.

26. For this and a number of related studies, see John P. Robinson and Mark Levy, The Main Source: Learning from Television News (Beverly Hills: Sage, 1986).

27. Data are reported in Mayer, "Trends in Media Usage," p. 610.

28. As quoted in Evans Witt, "Here, There, and Everywhere: Where Americans Get Their News," Public Opinion 6 (August/September 1983): 45–48.

29. The best study of the broadcast is Hadley Cantril, The Invasion from Mars: A Study in the Psychology of Panic (Princeton: Princeton University Press, 1940).

30. Paul F. Lazarsfeld, Bernard Berelson, and Hazel Gaudet, The People's Choice, 2nd ed. (New York: Columbia University Press, 1948).

31. The single best summary of this literature is Joseph Klapper, The Effects of Mass Communication (New York: Free Press, 1960).

32. It is worth noting, for example, that V. O. Key, Jr.'s celebrated textbook, Politics, Parties, and Pressure Groups, 4th ed. (New York: Thomas Y. Crowell, 1958), devotes just four of its 764 pages to the mass media.

33. Bernard Cohen, The Press and Foreign Policy (Princeton, NJ: Princeton University Press, 1963), p. 13.

34. Presentation by Steven Livingston at the John F. Kennedy School of Government, Harvard University, March 1996.

35. Robert Rotberg and Thomas Weiss, eds., From Massacres to Genocide (Washington, DC: The Brookings Institution, 1996).

36. M. McCombs and D. Shaw, "The Evolution of Agenda-Setting: Twenty-Five Years in the Marketplace of Ideas," Journal of Communications 43 (1993): 58–67.

37. Steven Livingston and Todd Eachus, "Humanitarian Crises and U.S. Foreign Policy: Somalia and the CNN Effect Reconsidered," Political Communication 12 (1995): 413–429.

38. Lawrence Jacobs and Robert Shapiro, Politicians Don't Pander (Chicago: University of Chicago Press, 2000).

39. Shanto Iyengar and Donald Kinder, News That Matters: Television and American Opinion (Chicago: University of Chicago Press, 1987).

40. Jon Krosnick and Laura Brannon, "The Impact of the Gulf War on the Ingredients of Presidential Evaluations," American Political Science Review 87 (1993): 963–975.

41. Marc Hetherington, "The Media's Role in Forming Voters' National Economic Evaluations in 1992," American Journal of Political Science 40 (1966): 372–395.

42. The most extensive study of framing is Shanto Iyengar's Is Anyone Responsible? (Chicago: University of Chicago Press, 1991).

43. Chicago Tribune, "TV Showing More Sex, More Safe-Sex Messages," published in the Lexington (KY) Herald-Leader, February 21, 2003: A17.

44. David Bauder, "Smash-Mouth Programming," Associated Press, December 10, 2003.

45. Robert D. Putnam, "Tuning In, Tuning Out: The Strange Disappearance of

Social Capital in America," PS: Political Science and Politics 27:4: 664–683.

46. Marc Peyser, "Family TV Goes Down the Tube," Newsweek, February 23, 2004, 52–54.

47. Allan McBride, "Television, Individualism, and Social Capital," PS: Political Science and Politics (September 1998): 542–552.

48. Robert M. Entman and Andrew Rojecki, The Black Image in the White Mind (Chicago: University of Chicago Press, 2000).

49. Michael Eric Dyson, quoted in "Guess Who's Coming to the Rescue," Newsweek, November 13, 2000, 14.

50. Iyengar and Kinder, News That Matters, chaps. 6, 10.

51. Bernard Cohen, Press and Foreign Policy. See also Lutz Erbring, Edie Goldenberg, and Arthur Miller, "Front-Page News and Real-World Clues: A New Look at Agenda-Setting by the Media," American Journal of Political Science 24 (1980): 16–49.

52. Don Oberdorfer, Tet! (New York: Doubleday, 1971); and Peter Braestrup, Big Story, Abridged Edition (New Haven, CT: Yale University Press, 1983).

53. William Schneider and I.A. Lewis, "Views on the News," Public Opinion 8 (August/September 1985): 6–11.

54. See, for example, the data in S. Robert Lichter, Stanley Rothman, and Linda S. Lichter, The Media Elite: America's New Powerbrokers (New York: Hastings House, 1986), pp. 29–30.

55. Charlie Cook, "It's More, Much More, Than Just a Kiss," National Journal (September 23, 2000): 2993.

56. Maura Clancy and Michael Robinson, "The Media in Campaign '84: General Election Coverage, Part I," Public Opinion (December/January 1985): 49–54, 59.

57. Daniel Amundson and S. Robert Lichter, "Heeeeeeree's Politics," Public Opinion (July/August 1988): 46.

58. Martha Moore, "Candidates Try to Reach Voters by Joking with Jay, Dueling with Dave," USA Today, March 1, 2000: p. 14A.

59. Schneider and Lewis note that in the Los Angeles Times study that they report on, one-quarter of the readership thought their papers were conservative, one-quarter thought liberal, one-quarter thought moderate, and one-quarter didn't know. See "Views on the News."

60. Jeff Leeds, "More Negative Coverage for Gore Than Bush This Fall," San Francisco Chronicle, November 1, 2000: A2.

61. Harold Stanley and Richard Niemi, Vital Statistics on American Politics, 2005–2006, (Washington, DC: CQ Press, 2006), p. 200.

62. Ben Bagdikian, *Double Vision* (Boston: Beacon Press, 1995), p. 48.

63. Harold Meyerson, "Misinformed? You May Be Getting Your News from Fox," *Washington Post*, printed in the *Lexington Herald-Leader*, October 17, 2003: A13.

64. John Leo, "A Surprising Jog to the Right," *U.S. News & World Report*, November 24, 2003, 64; Brian Anderson, *South Park Conservatives: The Revolt Against Liberal Media Bias* (Washington, DC: Regnery, 2005).

65. G. C. Stone and E. Grusin, "Network TV as Bad News Bearer," *Journalism Quarterly* 61 (1984): 517–523; R. H. Bohle, "Negativism as News Selection Predictor," *Journalism Quarterly* 63 (1986): 789–796; and D. E. Harrington, "Economic News on Television: The Determinants of Coverage," *Public Opinion Quarterly* 53 (1989): 17–40.

66. Larry Sabato, *Feeding Frenzy* (New York: Simon & Schuster, 1991).

67. Michael Robinson, "Public Affairs Television and the Growth of Political Malaise," *American Political Science Review* 70 (1976): 409–432. On TV making people more negative about human nature generally, see George Comstock, *The Evolution of American Television* (Newbury Park, CA: Sage, 1989), pp. 265–269.

68. *Newsweek*, September 28, 1998, 31.

69. A widely cited study of what constitutes news is provided by Herbert Gans, *Deciding What's News: A Case Study of CBS Evening News, NBC Nightly News, Newsweek and Time* (New York: Vintage, 1979).

70. The following account is based on Thomas Romer and Barry Weingast, "Political Foundations of the Thrift Debacle," in *Politics and Economics in the 1980s*, ed. Alberto Alesina and Geoffrey Carliner (Chicago: University of Chicago Press, 1981), pp. 175–214.

71. Ellen Hume, "Why the Press Blew the S & L Scandal," *New York Times*, May 24, 1990: A25.

72. Mark Rom, *Public Spirit in the Thrift Tragedy* (Pittsburgh: University of Pittsburgh Press, 1996).

73. Quoted in James Fallows, *Breaking the News* (New York: Pantheon, 1966), p. 137.

74. John David Rausch, Jr., "The Pathology of Politics: Government, Press, and Scandal," *Extensions: A Publication of the Carl Albert Congressional Research and Studies Center* (Norman, OK: Carl Albert Congressional Research and Studies Center, Fall 1990), pp. 11–12.

75. A Gallup survey of former Nieman Journalism Fellows found that more than three-quarters believe that traditional journalism is being replaced by tabloid journalism. See "The State of the Public Media Today" (Cambridge, MA: Nieman Foundation, April 1995).

76. Sabato, *Feeding Frenzy*.

77. Marc Peyser, "Red, White, and Funny," *Newsweek*, December 29, 2003, 77.

78. Fallows, *Breaking the News*, p. 132.

79. John Kramer, vice president for communication, Institute of Justice, personal communication, September 9, 1999.

80. Alison Carper, "Paint-by-Numbers Journalism: How Reader Surveys and Focus Groups Subvert a Democratic Press" (Barone Center on the Press, Politics and Public Policy, Harvard University Kennedy School of Government, Discussion Paper D-19, April 1995).

81. Peter Canellos, "Perot Ad Announcement is Also-Ran Against Reruns," *Boston Globe*, September 13, 1996: A24.

82. Thomas Patterson, *Out of Order* (New York: Knopf, 1993), chap. 2.

83. Kiku Adatto, *Picture Perfect* (New York: Basic, 1993).

84. Stephen J. Farnsworth and S. Robert Lichter, *The Nightly News Nightmare: Network Television's Coverage of U.S. Presidential Elections, 1988–2000* (Lanham, Md.: Rowman & Littlefield, 2003), p. 81.

85. Quoted in Craig Lambert, "Hertzberg of the *New Yorker*," *Harvard Magazine*, January-February 2003, 36.

86. Ibid.

87. Pippa Norris, "Editorial," *Press/Politics* 2 (1997): 1.

88. "Parties Take Their Conventions to the Web," *Washington Post*, July 14, 2000; Smith, "Media Notebook."

89. Elihu Katz and Jacob Feldman, "The Debates in the Light of Research: A Survey of Surveys," in *The Great Debates*, ed. Sidney Kraus (Bloomington: University of Indiana Press, 1962), pp. 173–223.

90. Thomas Holbrook, "Campaigns, National Conditions, and U.S. Presidential Elections," *American Journal of Political Science* 38 (1994): 973–998.

91. Michael Robinson and Margaret Sheehan, *Over the Wire and on TV* (New York: Russell Sage, 1983).

92. S. Robert Lichter and Daniel Amundson, "Less News Is Worse News: Television News Coverage of Congress, 1972–92," in *Congress, the Press, and the Public*, ed. Thomas Mann and Norman Ornstein (Washington, DC: American Enterprise Institute, 1994), pp. 131–140.

93. Shanto Iyengar, *Is Anyone Responsible?*.

94. David Ignatius, "Did You Say Change?" *Washington Post Weekly Edition*, September 10–16, 2001: 27.

95. Lichter and Amundson, "Less News Is Worse News."

96. Kenneth T. Walsh, "A White House Whodunit," *U.S. News & World Report*, October 13, 2003, 18–20; Evan Thomas and Michael Isikoff, "Secrets and Leaks," *Newsweek*, October 13, 2003, 26–32.

97. *Newsweek*, August 17, 1998, 21.

98. Ibid.

99. S. Robert Lichter, Linda S. Lichter, and Daniel Amundson, "Government Goes Down the Tube, Images of Government in TV Entertainment, 1955–1998," *Press/Politics* 5 (2) (2000): 96–103.

100. Quoted in Fallows, *Breaking the News*, pp. 187–188.

CHAPTER 10

1. Information on polls and journalistic commentary comes from: Dan Balz and David S. Broder, "Election Day Dawns With Unpredictability," *Washington Post*, November 2, 2004: A1; Jim Rutenberg, "Report Says Problems Led to Skewed Survey Data," *New York Times*, November 5, 2004: 23; David Andreatta, "Swervy Surveys," *New York Post*, November 4, 2004: 9; Martin Sieff, "October Surprises Rock Bush," United Press International, October 14, 2004; Agence France Presse, "British Bookmakers Report Flurry of Bets on Kerry Victory," November 2, 2004; The Frontrunner, "Bush Maintains Small Edge in National Polls," October 29, 2004; The Frontrunner, "GOP Defectors May Give Kerry Victory in Iowa," November 1, 2004; William Raspberry, "'Unwanted, Unpolled' Voters Could Spur Kerry Victory," *Deseret Morning News*, November 1, 2004; Anatole Kaletsky, "Opinion Poll Tie Suggests Kerry Is On Course to Win," *The Times* (London), October 26, 2004: 50.

2. Information on political science predictions appears in the October 2004 issue of *PS: Political Science and Politics* as well as *U.S. Newswire*, "Political Scientists Forecast Bush Victory in 2004," October 15, 2004.

3. For a good history of the early presidential nomination process, on which the following account draws, see Richard P. McCormick, *The Presidential Game: The Origins of American Presidential Politics* (New York: Oxford University Press, 1982).

4. The best account of the origins of presidential primaries and their use during the "mixed system" period is James W. Davis, *Springboard to the White House* (New York: Crowell, 1967).

5. The classic history of the Commission and its aftermath is Byron E. Shafer, *Quiet Revolution: The Struggle for the Democratic Party and the Shaping of Post-Reform Politics* (New York: Russell Sage, 1983).

6. For a more detailed discussion of the caucus process, see William G. Mayer, "Caucuses: How They Work, What Difference They Make," in *In Pursuit of the White House: How We Choose Our Presidential Nominees*, ed. William G. Mayer (Chatham, N.J.: Chatham House, 1996), pp. 105–57.

7. Then-Senate Majority Leader Howard Baker, as quoted in Jack W. Germond and Jules Witcover, *Blue Smoke and Mirrors: How Reagan Won and Why Carter Lost the Election of 1980* (New York: Viking, 1981), p. 96.

8. For announcements dates for all presidential candidates between 1952 and 1996, see Michael G. Hagen and William G. Mayer, "The Modern Politics of Presidential Selection: How Changing the Rules Really Did Change the Game," in *In Pursuit of the White House 2000: How We Choose Our Presidential Nominees*, ed. William G. Mayer (New York: Chatham House, 2000), pp. 22–25.

9. Emmett H. Buell, Jr., "The Invisible Primary," in *In Pursuit of the White House*, pp. 1–43.

10. Lamar Alexander, "Off with the Limits," *Campaigns & Elections*, October–November, 1996, 33.

11. For data on the dominance of these two states, see William G. Mayer and Andrew E. Busch, *The Front-Loading Problem in Presidential Nominations* (Washington: Brookings Institution, 2004), pp. 24–30.

12. For an extended account of front-loading and its effects, see Mayer and Busch, *The Front-Loading Problem*.

13. Not so long ago, one could say that the use of primary elections to select candidates for national leadership positions was a distinctively American institution. In recent years, however, a number of other countries have also started to use primaries for this purpose. See James A. McCann, "The Emerging International Trend toward Open Presidential Primaries: The American Presidential Nomination Process in Comparative Perspective," in *The Making of the Presidential Candidates 2004*, ed. William G. Mayer (Lanham, Md.: Rowman & Littlefield, 2004), pp. 265–293.

14. E. E. Schattschneider, *Party Government* (New York: Holt, Rinehart and Winston, 1942).

15. Thomas Patterson, *Out of Order* (New York: Vintage, 1994), p. 74.

16. Roll call participation figures are taken from *Congressional Quarterly Almanac* (Washington, D.C.: Congressional Quarterly, various years).

17. See William G. Mayer, "A Brief History of Vice Presidential Selection," in *In Pursuit of the White House 2000: How We Choose Our Presidential Nominees*, ed. William G. Mayer (New York: Chatham House, 2000), 313–374.

18. During the last two months of the presidential campaigns of 1976–1988, about 40 percent of the lead stories on the CBS evening news were about the election, as were 20 percent of all the stories reported. See Stephen J. Rosenstone and John Mark Hansen, *Mobilization, Participation, and Democracy in America* (New York: Macmillan, 1993), p. 178, n. 26.

19. For a good summary of the BCRA's provisions, see Anthony Corrado, "Money and Politics: A History of Federal Campaign Finance Law," in Anthony Corrado, Thomas E. Mann, Daniel R. Ortiz, and Trevor Potter, *The New Campaign Finance Sourcebook* (Washington, D.C.: Brookings Institution, 2006), pp. 35–43.

20. For a nice explanation of the law with regard to 527s, from which we quote here, see Trevor Potter, "The Current State of Campaign Finance Law," in Anthony Corrado, Thomas E. Mann, Daniel R. Ortiz, and Trevor Potter, *The New Campaign Finance Sourcebook* (Washington, D.C.: Brookings Institution, 2006), pp. 76–80.

21. See Stephen R. Weissman and Ruth Hassan, "BCRA and the 527 Groups," in *The Election after Reform: Money, Politics, and the Bipartisan Campaign Reform Act*, ed. Michael J. Malbin (Lanham, Md.: Rowman & Littlefield, 2006), pp. 79–111.

22. Thomas Patterson and Robert McClure, *The Unseeing Eye: The Myth of Television Power in National Elections* (New York: Putnam, 1976); and Stephen Ansolabehere and Shanto Iyengar, *Going Negative: How Attack Ads Shrink and Polarize the Electorate* (New York: Free Press, 1995).

23. Darrel West, *Air Wars: Television Advertising in Election Campaigns, 1952–1992* (Washington, DC: Congressional Quarterly, 1993).

24. Edwin Diamond and Stephen Bates, *The Spot*, 3rd ed. (Cambridge, MA: MIT Press, 1992).

25. William G. Mayer, "In Defense of Negative Campaigning," *Political Science Quarterly* 111 (1996): 437–455.

26. Craig Brians and Martin Wattenberg, "Campaign Issue Knowledge and Salience: Comparing Reception from TV Commercials, TV News, and Newspapers," *American Journal of Political Science* 40 (1996): 172–193.

27. Ibid. Not all scholars agree that negative ads are more effective than positive ones or that negative ads depress turnout. For a thorough airing of the issues, see the Forum in the December 1999 issue of the *American Political Science Review*.

28. Brian J. Gaines, "Popular Myths About Popular Vote-Electoral College Splits," *PS: Political Science and Politics* 34 (March, 2001): 71–75.

29. All figures come from the American National Election Studies, conducted by the Center for Political Studies at the University of Michigan.

30. Although the general notion of "partisanship" has been around for centuries, the social-psychological concept of party ID was advanced in the pioneering work of Angus Campbell, Philip Converse, Warren Miller, and Donald Stokes, *The American Voter* (New York: Wiley, 1960), chaps. 6–7.

31. This is the wording used in the American National Election Studies. The Gallup Poll, which actually invented the question, employs a slightly different wording.

32. Morris Fiorina, *Retrospective Voting in American National Elections* (New Haven, CT: Yale University Press, 1981); and Michael MacKuen, Robert Erikson, and James Stimson, "Macropartisanship," *American Political Science Review* 83 (1989): 1125–1142.

33. The classic demonstration appears in Chapter 8 of Campbell et al., *The American Voter*, although there is general agreement that the picture presented there is overstated. For balanced treatments of policy issues in recent campaigns, see the series of *Change and Continuity* volumes by Paul Abramson, John Aldrich, and David Rohde, published by CQ Press.

34. Benjamin Page and Richard Brody, "Policy Voting and the Electoral Process: The Vietnam War Issue," *American Political Science Review* 66 (1972): 979–995.

35. Edward Carmines and James Stimson, "The Two Faces of Issue Voting," *American Political Science Review* 74 (1980): 78–91.

36. Ibid. Also see R. Douglas Arnold, *The Logic of Congressional Action* (New Haven, CT: Yale University Press, 1990), chap. 2.

37. Richard Trilling, *Party Image and Electoral Behavior* (New York: Wiley, 1976).

38. Fiorina, *Retrospective Voting*.

39. Scott Teeter, "Public Opinion in 1984," and Gerald Pomper, "The Presidential Election," both in Gerald Pomper et al., *The Election of 1984* (Chatham, NJ: Chatham House, 1985).

40. Samuel Popkin, *The Reasoning Voter* (Chicago: University of Chicago Press, 1991), pp. 60–67.

41. Donald Stokes, "Some Dynamic Elements of Contests for the Presidency," *American Political Science Review* 60 (1966): 19–28.

42. Morris Fiorina, Samuel Abrams, and Jeremy Pope, "The 2000 US Presidential Election: Can Retrospective Voting Be Saved?" *British Journal of Political Science* 33 (2003): 163–187.

43. Stokes, "Some Dynamic Elements," p. 222.

44. Indeed, by some calculations, Kennedy ran worse than a "generic" Democrat for that time. See Angus Campbell, Philip Converse, Warren Miller, and Donald Stokes, "Stability and Change in 1960; A Reinstating Election," in *Elections and the Political Order* (New York: Wiley, 1966), pp. 78–95.

45. Fiorina, Abrams, and Pope, "The 2000 US Presidential Election," p. 180.

46. Frank Newport, Jeffrey Jones and Lydia Saad, "Ronald Reagan From the People's Perspective: A Gallup Poll Review," The Gallup Organization, June 15, 2004.

47. Thus, an important correlate of support for Bush in 1988 was what citizens thought of *Reagan's* performance as president. See Paul Abramson, John Aldrich, and David Rohde, *Change and Continuity in the 1988 Elections* (Washington, DC: CQ Press, 1990), chap. 7.

48. James Campbell, "When Have Presidential Campaigns Decided Election Outcomes?" *American Politics Research* 19 (2001): 437–460.

49. See Thomas Holbrook, *Do Campaigns Matter?* (Thousand Oaks, CA: Sage, 1996).

50. For a discussion, see Marjorie Hershey, "The Campaign and the Media," in Gerald Pomper et al., *The Election of 1988* (Chatham, NJ: Chatham House, 1989), chap. 3.

51. Donald Kinder and Lynn Sanders, *Divided by Color* (Chicago: University of Chicago Press, 1996).

52. Paul Sniderman and Thomas Piazza, *The Scar of Race* (Cambridge, MA: Harvard University Press, 1993).

53. Paul Abramson, John Aldrich, and David Rohde, *Change and Continuity in the 1992 Elections* (Washington, DC: Congressional Quarterly, 1994); and Herbert Weisberg and David Kimball, "Attitudinal Correlates of the 1992 Presidential Vote: Party Identification and Beyond," in *Democracy's Feast: Elections in America*, ed. Herbert Weisberg (Chatham, NJ: Chatham House, 1995), pp. 72–111.

54. Everett Ladd, "The Public's Views of National Performance," *The Public Perspective*, October/November 1996, 17–20.

55. Robert Merry, "A Rule for Presidents: Go Centrist or Perish," *Congressional Quarterly Weekly Report*, October 26, 1996, 3106.

56. Jane Mansbridge, "Myth and Reality: The ERA and the Gender Gap in the 1980 Election," *Public Opinion Quarterly* 49 (1985): 164–178.

57. Emily Stoper, "The Gender Gap Concealed and Revealed," *Journal of Political Science* 17 (1989): 50–62; and Tom Smith, "The Polls: Gender and Attitudes Toward Violence," *Public Opinion Quarterly* 48 (1984): 384–396.

58. Rhodes Cook, "Race of Muted Differences Has the Nation Yawning," *Congressional Quarterly Weekly Report*, October 19, 1996, 2950.

59. Peter Canellos, "New TV Ad Mentions a GOP Unmentionable," *Boston Globe*, October 29, 1996: A23.

60. For discussions, see Pamela Conover, "Feminists and the Gender Gap," *Journal of Politics* 50 (1988): 985–1010; and Elizabeth Cook and Clyde Wilcox, "Feminism and the Gender Gap—A Second Look," *Journal of Politics* 53 (1991): 1111–1122.

61. "Where the Parties Are," *The Public Perspective*, March/April 1994, 78–79; and "Which Party Is Better on Which Issues?" *The Public Perspective*, June/July 1996, 65.

62. This was first noted by Herbert Weisberg, "The Demographics of a New Voting Gap: Marital Differences in American Voting Behavior," *Public Opinion Quarterly* 51 (1987): 335–343.

63. Fiorina, Abrams, and Pope, "The 2000 U.S. Presidential Election."

64. Michael Kinsley, as quoted by Howard Kurtz, "The Premature Post-Mortems Are Starting," *Washington Post*, online extras, October 31, 2000.

CHAPTER 11

1. Isaiah Poole, "Votes Echo Electoral Themes," *CQ Weekly*, December 11, 2004, 2906–08.

2. Morris Fiorina, Samuel Abrams, and Jeremy Pope, *Culture War? The Myth of a Polarized America*, 2nd ed. (New York: Longman, 2006), chap. 8.

3. For a run-down of the President Bush's problems in Congress in 2005, see Jim VandeHei and Charles Babington, "Newly Emboldened Congress Has Dogged Bush This Year," *washingtonpost.com*, December 23, 2005: A05.

4. "Federalist 52," *The Federalist Papers*, ed. Clinton Rossiter (New York: Mentor, 1961), p. 327.

5. Max Farrand, ed., *The Records of the Federal Convention of 1787* (New Haven, CT: Yale University Press, 1966), vol. 1, p. 151.

6. Morris Fiorina, David Rohde, and Peter Wissel, "Historical Change in House Turnover," in *Congress in Change,* ed. Norman Ornstein (New York: Praeger, 1975), pp. 24–57; and Nelson Polsby, "The Institutionalization of the U.S. House of Representatives," *American Political Science Review* 62 (1968): 144–168.

7. James Young, *The Washington Community, 1800–1828* (New York: Harcourt, 1966), chap. 2.

8. The South was primarily agricultural and had fewer high-status career opportunities outside of politics. From the very beginning, southern members of Congress stayed longer than northerners. Fiorina, Rohde, and Wissel, "Historical Change in House Turnover," pp. 34–38.

9. Robert Struble, Jr., "House Turnover and the Principle of Rotation," *Political Science Quarterly* 94 (1979–1980): 660.

10. Douglas Price, "The Congressional Career—Then and Now," in *Congressional Behavior*, ed. Nelson Polsby (New York: Random House, 1971), pp. 14–27.

11. Rhodes Cook, "The Rhodes Cook Letter," May 2001, 14.

12. A good overview of the variety of rules governing congressional primaries is contained in Kristin Kanthak and Rebecca Morton, "The Effects of Electoral Rules on Congressional Primaries," in *Congressional Primaries and the Politics of Representation*, ed. Peter Galderisi, Marni Ezra, and Michael Lyons (Lanham, MD: Rowman and Littlefield, 2000).

13. For a list of 2006 Congressional filing and primary dates, see www.fec.gov/pubrec/ fe2006/2006pdates.pdf.

14. Norman Ornstein, Thomas Mann, and Michael Malbin, *Vital Statistics on Congress, 1999–2000* (Washington, DC: American Enterprise Institute, 2000), pp. 70–71.

15. Robert Erikson, "Malapportionment, Gerrymandering and Party Fortunes in Congressional Elections," *American Political Science Review* 66 (1972): 1234–1245; and Gary King and Andrew Gelman, "Systemic Consequences of Incumbency Advantage in U.S. House Elections," *American Journal of Political Science* 35 (1991): 110–138.

16. Burdett Loomis, "The Congressional Office as a Small Business: New Members Set Up Shop," *Publius* 9 (1979): 35–55.

17. Ornstein, Mann, and Malbin, *Vital Statistics*, p. 133.

18. Glenn Parker, *Homeward Bound* (Pittsburgh, PA: University of Pittsburgh Press, 1986).

19. Juliet Eilperin, "The House Member as Perpetual Commuter," *Washington Post Weekly Edition*, September 10–16, 2001: 29.

20. E. Scott Adler, Chariti Gent, and Cary Overmeyer, "The Home Style Homepage: Legislator Use of the World Wide Web for Constituency Contact," *Legislative Studies Quarterly* 23 (1998): 585–595.

21. Diana Owen, Richard Davis, and Vincent James Strickler, "Congress and the Internet," *Harvard International Journal of Press/Politics* 4 (1999): 10–29.

22. For classic discussions of the multiple roles of representatives, see Heinz Eulau, "Changing Views of Representation," in *The Politics of Representation,* ed. Heinz Eulau and John Wahlke (Beverly Hills, CA: Sage, 1978), pp. 31–53; and Richard F. Fenno, Jr., *Home Style* (New York: Longman Classics, 2003).

23. Morris Fiorina, *Congress—Keystone of the Washington Establishment,* 2nd ed. (New Haven, CT: Yale University Press, 1989).

24. Ibid., chap. 10. See also Bruce Cain, John Ferejohn, and Morris Fiorina, *The Personal Vote* (Cambridge, MA: Harvard University Press, 1987), chap. 2.

25. Morris Fiorina, "Congressmen and Their Constituents: 1958 and 1978," in *The United States Congress: Proceedings of the Thomas P. O'Neill, Jr. Symposium,* ed. Dennis Hale (Leominster, MA: Eusey Press, 1982), pp. 33–64.

26. The first to make this observation was Gary Jacobson, "Practical Consequences of Campaign Finance Reform: An Incumbent Protection Act?" *Public Policy* 42 (1976): 1–32.

27. Gary C. Jacobson, *Money in Congressional Elections* (New Haven, CT: Yale University Press, 1980).

28. "Different Races, Different Costs," from "The Big Picture" on www.opensecrets. org.

29. Gary C. Jacobson, *The Politics of Congressional Elections,* 6th ed. (New York: Pearson Longman, 2004), chap. 3.

30. Kenneth Bickers and Robert Stein, "The Electoral Dynamics of the Federal Pork Barrel," *American Journal of Political Science* 40 (1996): 1300–1326.

31. David Magleby and Kelly Patterson, "The Polls—Poll Trends: Congressional Reform," *Public Opinion Quarterly* 58 (1994): 420–421.

32. Amihi Glazer and Bernard Grofman, "Two Plus Two Equals Six: Tenure in Office of Senators and Representatives, 1953–1983," *Legislative Studies Quarterly* 12 (1987): 555–564.

33. Alan Abramowitz and Jeffrey Segal, *Senate Elections* (Ann Arbor, MI: University of Michigan Press, 1992), pp. 34–35.

34. Morris Fiorina, *Representatives, Roll Calls, and Constituencies* (Lexington, MA: D. C. Heath, 1974), pp. 90–100.

35. Joe Foote and David Weber, "Network Evening News Visibility of Congressmen and Senators," paper presented to the Association for Education in Journalism and Mass Communication, August 1984.

36. Glenn Parker, "Interpreting Candidate Awareness in U.S. Congressional Elections," *Legislative Studies Quarterly* 6 (1981): 219–233.

37. Abramowitz and Segal, *Senate Elections,* pp. 228–231; and Jonathan Krasno, *Challengers, Competition, and Reelection: Comparing Senate and House Elections* (New Haven, CT: Yale University Press, 1995).

38. Joseph Schlesinger, *Ambition in Politics* (Chicago: Rand McNally, 1966).

39. This charge was leveled at Senator Dick Clark of Iowa in his losing 1978 race.

40. David Brady and Morris Fiorina, "Ruptured Legacy: Presidential Congressional Relations in Historical Perspective," in *Looking Back on the Reagan Presidency,* ed. Larry Berman (Baltimore, MD: Johns Hopkins University Press, 1989), pp. 268–287.

41. Morris Fiorina, *Divided Government,* 2nd ed. (New York: Longman Classics, 2003), pp. 135–139.

42. Jon Healey, "Projects' Are His Project," *Congressional Quarterly Weekly Report,* September 21, 1996, 2672. Also see Jonathan Salant, "Some Republicans Turned Away from Leadership," *Congressional Quarterly Weekly Report,* December 7, 1996, 3352–3354; and Andrew Tayler, "GOP Pet Projects Give Boost to Shaky Incumbents," *Congressional Quarterly Weekly Report,* August 3, 1996, 2169–2173.

43. Paul R. Abramson, John H. Aldrich, and David W. Rohde, *Change and Continuity in the 2004 Elections* (Washington, DC: CQ Press, 2006), chap. 10.

44. David Rohde, *Parties and Leaders in the Postreform House* (Chicago: University of Chicago Press, 1991); Gary Cox and Mathew McCubbins, *Setting the Agenda* (New York: Cambridge University Press, 2005).

45. Karen Foerstel, "Campaign Finance Passage Ends a Political Odyssey," *CQ Weekly,* March 23, 2002, 800.

46. Donna Cassate, "'Independent Groups' Ads Increasingly Steer Campaigns," *Congressional Quarterly Weekly Report,* May 2, 1998, 1114.

47. Associated Press, "New Congress to Look More Like Real America," November 5, 2004.

48. Carol Swain, *Black Faces, Black Interests: The Representation of African Americans in Congress* (Cambridge, MA: Harvard University Press, 1993).

49. For a thoughtful treatment of these and related issues, see Jane Mansbridge, "In

Defense of Descriptive Representation," working paper, Harvard University, 1997.

50. Library of Congress–Election Archive.

51. "Americans Rate Their Society and Chart Its Values," *The Public Perspective,* February/March 1997, 25

52. See Charles Cameron, David Epstein, and Sharyn O'Halloran, "Do Majority-Minority Districts Maximize Substantive Black Representation in Congress?" *American Political Science Review* 90 (1996): 794–812.

53. David Lublin and D. Stephen Voss, "The Missing Middle," *Journal of Politics* 65 (February, 2003): 227–237; Lublin and Voss, "Racial Redistricting and Realignment in Southern State Legislatures," *American Journal of Political Science* 44 (October, 2000): 792–810; Lublin and Voss, "Boll-Weevil Blues," *American Review of Politics* 22 (Fall/Winter, 2000).

54. Juliana Gurenwald, "Incumbents Survive Redistricting," *Congressional Quarterly Weekly Report,* November 9, 1996, 3229; D. Stephen Voss and David Lublin, "Black Incumbents, White Districts: An Appraisal of the 1996 Congressional Elections," *American Politics Research* 29 (March, 2001): 141–182.

55. Lee Sigelman and Susan Welch, *Black Americans' Views of Racial Inequality* (Cambridge, England: Cambridge University Press, 1991).

56. Donald Kinder and Lynn Sanders, *Divided by Color* (Chicago: University of Chicago Press, 1996).

57. Former Representative Mike Espy (D-MS), who harbored gubernatorial or senatorial ambitions, openly espoused such beliefs. More recently, the relatively moderate record of Representative Harold Ford (D-TN) has been explained by reference to his interest in being Tennessee's first black governor or senator. Nancy Zuckerbrod, "Tennessee Democrat Has His Sights Set High," *USA Today,* March 27, 2000: 29A.

58. Writing about politics in New Haven, in the 1950s, an old-style machine city, Dahl observed that African Americans were much better represented in government jobs and political offices than in the private sector. See Robert Dahl, *Who Governs* (New Haven, CT: Yale University Press, 1961), p. 294.

59. Quoted in George Hager and David Cloud, "Democrats Tie Their Fate to Clinton's Budget Bill," *Congressional Quarterly Weekly Report,* August 7, 1993, 2123.

60. Martha Angle, "Tallying Up the Thank-Yous," *Congressional Quarterly Weekly Report,* May 29, 1993, 1344.

61. Hager and Cloud, "Democrats Tie Their Fate," pp. 2125, 2127.

CHAPTER 12

1. Kate O'Beirne, "Introducing Pork-Barrel Homeland Security: A Little Here, a Lot There," *National Review*, August 11, 2003.

2. Veronique de Rugy, "Homeland Security Pork," *Washington Times*, August 1, 2005.

3. These and other examples appear in Rich Lowry, "Homeland Pork," *National Review Online*, July 19, 2005; JoAnn Wypijewski, "Homeland Security on the Range," *MotherJones.com*, March/April, 2006; and Veronique de Rugy and Nick Gillespie, "America's Fleecing in the Name of Security," *SFGate.com*, February 19, 2006.

4. O'Beirne, "Introducing Pork-Barrel Homeland Security."

5. Speaker Thomas Reed, as quoted in Neil McNeil, *Forge of Democracy* (New York: McKay, 1963).

6. David Mayhew, *Congress: The Electoral Connection* (New Haven, CT: Yale University Press, 1974), pp. 81–82; and John Aldrich, *Why Parties?* (Chicago: University of Chicago Press, 1995).

7. Richard Fenno, *The United States Senate: A Bicameral Perspective* (Washington, DC: American Enterprise Institute, 1982).

8. "Voting Participation: House," *Congressional Quarterly Weekly Report*, January 27, 1996, 256.

9. Nelson Polsby, Miriam Gallagher, and Barry Rundquist, "The Growth of the Seniority System in the U.S. House of Representatives," *American Political Science Review* 63 (1969): 787–807. For a partial dissent, see Keith Krehbiel and Alan Wiseman, "Joseph Cannon: Majoritarian from Illinois," *Legislative Studies Quarterly* 26 (2001): 357–389.

10. Polsby, Gallagher, and Rundquist, "The Growth of the Seniority System."

11. Charles Jones, "Joseph G. Cannon and Howard W. Smith: An Essay on the Limits of Leadership in the House of Representatives," *Journal of Politics* 30 (1968): 617–646.

12. Ibid.

13. Jackie Koszczuk, "For Embattled GOP Leaders, Season of Discontent," *Congressional Quarterly Weekly Report*, July 20, 1996, 2019–2023; and Jackie Koszczuk, "Unpopular, Yet Still Powerful, Gingrich Faces a Critical Pass," *Congressional Quarterly Weekly Report*, September 14, 1996, 2573–2579.

14. Barbara Sinclair, *Majority Leadership in the U.S. House* (Baltimore, MD: Johns Hopkins University Press, 1983).

15. For a full discussion, see Steven S. Smith and Marcus Flathman, "Managing the Senate Floor: Complex Unanimous Consent Agreements Since the 1950s," *Legislative Studies Quarterly* 14 (1989): 349–374.

16. Keith Krehbiel, "Where's the Party?" *British Journal of Political Science* 23 (1993): 235–266; and James Snyder and Tim Groseclose, "Estimating Party Influence in Congressional Roll-Call Voting," *American Journal of Political Science* 44 (2000): 193–211.

17. David Rohde, *Parties and Leaders in the Postreform House* (Chicago: University of Chicago Press, 1991).

18. Barbara Sinclair, *Legislators, Leaders, and Lawmaking: The U.S. House of Representatives in the Postreform Era* (Baltimore, MD: Johns Hopkins University Press, 1995).

19. Gary Cox and Mathew McCubbins, *Legislative Leviathan* (Berkeley, CA: University of California Press, 1993), especially chap. 2.

20. Ibid. chap. 5.

21. Jim Drinkard, "Confident Candidates Share Campaign Wealth," *USA Today*, April 19, 2000: 10A.

22. Gerald Gamm and Kenneth Shepsle, "Emergence of Legislative Institutions: Standing Committees in the House and Senate, 1810–1825," *Legislative Studies Quarterly* 14 (1989): 39–66; and Joseph Cooper, *The Origins of the Standing Committees and the Development of the Modern House* (Houston, TX: Rice University Studies, 1970).

23. Richard Fenno, *Congressmen in Committees* (Boston: Little, Brown, 1973), p. 172.

24. Karen Foerstel, "Gingrich Flexes His Power in Picking Panel Chiefs," *Congressional Quarterly Weekly Report*, November 19, 1994, 3326.

25. Mark Ferber, "The Formation of the Democratic Study Group," in *Congressional Behavior*, ed. Nelson Polsby (New York: Random House, 1971), pp. 249–267.

26. Norman Ornstein, "Causes and Consequences of Congressional Change: Subcommittee Reforms in the House of Representatives, 1970–1973," in *Congress in Change,* ed. Norman Orstein (New York: Praeger, 1975), pp. 88–114; and Roger Davidson and Walter Oleszek, *Congress Against Itself* (Bloomington: Indiana University Press, 1977).

27. Lawrence C. Dodd and Richard L. Schott, *Congress and the Administrative State* (New York: John Wiley, 1979), p. 124; and Roger H. Davidson and Walter J. Oleszek, *Congress and Its Members*, 2nd ed. (Washington, DC: CQ Press, 1985), pp. 228–230.

28. John Ferejohn, *Pork Barrel Politics* (Stanford, CA: Stanford University Press, 1974); and R. Douglas Arnold, *Congress and the Bureaucracy* (New Haven, CT: Yale University Press, 1979).

29. Barry Weingast and William Marshall, "The Industrial Organization of Congress," *Journal of Political Economy* 91 (1988): 132–163.

30. Keith Krehbiel, *Information and Legislative Organization* (Ann Arbor: University of Michigan Press, 1991).

31. Gary W. Cox and Mathew D. McCubbins, *Setting the Agenda: Responsible Party Government in the U.S. House of Representatives* (New York: Cambridge University Press, 2005).

32. Norman Ornstein, Thomas Mann, and Michael Malbin, *Vital Statistics on Congress: 1999–2000* (Washington, DC: American Enterprise Institution Press, 2001), see especially chap. 4.

33. David King, *Turf Wars: How Congressional Committees Claim Jurisdiction* (Chicago: University of Chicago Press, 1997).

34. Alan Ota, "Caucuses Bring New Muscle to Legislative Battlefield," *CQ Weekly*, September 27, 2003, 2334–2341; and "Caucuses and Their Members Make Up a Large Contingent," *CQ Weekly*, September 27, 2003, 2379–2388.

35. The most comprehensive study to date is Susan Webb Hammond, *Congressional Caucuses in National Policy Making* (Baltimore, MD: Johns Hopkins University Press, 2001).

36. Jeffrey Talbert, Bryan Jones, and Frank Baumgartner, "Nonlegislative Hearings and Policy Change in Congress," *American Journal of Political Science* 39 (1995): 391–392.

37. For a detailed study of how and why individual members participate at these various stages of the legislative process, see Richard Hall, *Participation in Congress* (New Haven, CT: Yale University Press, 1996).

38. On the conference committee in recent years, see Stephen Van Beek, *Post-Passage Politics: Bicameral Relations in Congress* (Pittsburgh: University of Pittsburgh Press, 1995).

39. Richard Munson, *The Cardinals of Capitol Hill* (New York: Grove Press, 1993).

40. Quoted in Stephen Skowronek, *The Politics Presidents Make* (Cambridge, MA: Harvard University Press, 1993), p. 389.

41. Diana Evans, "Policy and Pork: The Use of Pork Barrel Projects to Build Policy Coalitions in the House of Representatives," *American Journal of Political Science* 38 (1994): 894–917.

42. Harrison Donnelly, "Reagan Opposition Threatens EDA Development

Program," *Congressional Quarterly Weekly Report* 40 (1982): 2295–2296.

43. Chuck Henning, *The Wit and Wisdom of Politics* (Golden, CO: Fulcrum, 1992), p. 39.

44. For institutional comparisons, see John Hibbing and Elizabeth Theiss-Morse, *Congress as Public Enemy* (New York: Cambridge University Press, 1995), chap. 2.

45. Kelly Patterson and David Magleby, "Trends: Public Support for Congress," *Public Opinion Quarterly* 56 (1992): 539–551.

46. Glenn Parker and Roger Davidson, "Why Do Americans Love Their Congressmen So Much More Than Their Congress?" *Legislative Studies Quarterly* 4 (1979): 52–61.

47. Richard Fenno, "If, As Ralph Nader Says, Congress is the 'Broken Branch,' How Come We Love Our Congressmen So Much?" in *Congress in Change*, ed. Norman Ornstein (New York: Praeger, 1975), pp. 277–287.

CHAPTER 13

1. "President Bush Delivers State of the Union Address," www.whitehouse.gov/news/releases/2006/01/20060131-10.html, accessed March 15, 2006.

2. President George W. Bush, "Remarks Following a Tour of United Solar Ovonic in Auburn Hills, Michigan," February 20, 2006, *Weekly Compilation of Presidential Documents*, week ending Friday, February 24, 2006, pp. 296–297.

3. Paul Blustein, "Some in Congress Object to Arab Port Operator," *Washington Post*, February 17, 2006: A11.

4. *CQ Weekly*, Vote Studies, various years.

5. Dan Froomkin, "When the Trust is Gone," *WashingtonPost.com*, February 22, 2006, www.washingtonpost.com/wp-dyn/content/blog/2006/02/22/BL2006022201449.html, accessed March 15, 2006.

6. "President Addresses National Newspaper Conference," www.whitehouse.gov/news/releases/2006/03/20060310-2.html, accessed March 15, 2006.

7. Elisabeth Bumiller and David E. Sanger, "Bush is Business as Usual Despite Party Blunders," *New York Times*, March 12, 2006: 20.

8. John F. Harris, "Both Sides Frustrated as Budget Wars End," *Washington Post*, November 15, 1999: A1.

9. George W. Bush, State of the Union Address, January 28, 2003, Washington, DC: White House Office of the Press Secretary, www.whitehouse.gov/news/releases/2003/01/20030128-19.html, accessed January 8, 2004.

10. Jonathan Weisman, "Thomas Questions Dividend Tax Cuts," *Washington Post*, January 28, 2003: A4.

11. Terry Moe, "The Politicized Presidency," in *The New Direction in American Politics*, ed. John Chubb and Paul E. Peterson (Washington, DC: The Brookings Institution, 1985).

12. Mark Peterson, *Legislating Together: The White House and Capitol Hill from Eisenhower to Reagan* (Cambridge, MA: Harvard University Press, 1990), chap.6; and Jon R. Bond and Richard Fleisher, *The President in the Legislative Arena* (Chicago: University of Chicago Press, 1990), chap. 4; Steven A Shull and Thomas C. Shaw, "Determinants of presidents' legislative support in the House, 1949–1995," *Social Science Journal*, 39 (3): 381–398.

13. Judy Keen, "Bush Isn't on the Ballot, But His Influence Is," *USA Today*, April 29, 2002: 7A.

14. National Public Radio transcript, "Talk of the Nation," host: Neal Conan, October 19, 2005.

15. Haynes Johnson and David Broder, *The System: The American Way of Politics at the Breaking Point* (Boston: Little, Brown, 1996).

16. Peterson, *Legislating Together*, p. 157.

17. Charles O. Jones, "Campaigning to Govern: The Clinton Style," in *The Clinton Presidency: First Appraisals*, ed. Colin Campbell and Bert A. Rockman (Chatham, NJ: Chatham House, 1996), p. 16. Also see Michael L. Mezey, *Congress, the President and Public Policy* (Boulder, CO: Westview, 1989).

18. As quoted in Chuck Henning, *The Wit and Wisdom of Politics: Expanded Edition* (Golden, CO: Fulcrum Publishing, 1992), p. 240.

19. Jack Nelson, "Angry Clinton Rebukes His Whitewater Critics," *Los Angeles Times*, December 21, 1995: A1.

20. Richard E. Neustadt, *Presidential Power and the Modern Presidents* (New York: Free Press, 1990), p. 29.

21. Benjamin Ginsberg and Martin Shefter, *Politics by Other Means: The Declining Importance of Elections in America* (New York: Basic Books, 1990).

22. Daniel Stid, *The Statesmanship of Woodrow Wilson: Responsible Government Under the Constitution* (Lawrence, KS: University Press of Kansas, 1998), chap. 6.

23. Jeffrey Tulis, *The Rhetorical Presidency* (Princeton, NJ: Princeton University Press, 1987), p. 91.

24. Thomas Bailey, *The American Pageant* (Boston: D.C. Heath, 1956), p. 669.

25. Samuel Kernell, *Going Public* (Washington, DC: CQ Press, 1986).

26. Inaugural Address, January 20, 1961, as quoted in *Bartlett's Familiar Quotations*,

Revised and Enlarged, 15th ed. (Boston, MA: Little, Brown, 1980), p. 890.

27. Neustadt, *Presidential Power*, p. 274.

28. Henning, *Wit and Wisdom of Politics*, p. 240.

29. Norman C. Thomas, Joseph A. Pika, and Richard A. Watson, *The Politics of the Presidency*, 3rd ed. (Washington, DC: CQ Press, 1993), p. 204.

30. Office of the Clerk, U.S. House of Representatives, "Presidential Vetoes, 1789–2001," http://clerkweb.house.gov/histrecs/househis/lists/vetoes.htm, accessed April 21, 2002.

31. Senate Library under the Direction of Walter J. Stewart, Secretary of the Senate, *Presidential Vetoes, 1789–1988*, S. Pub. 102-12, Washington, DC: U.S. Government Printing Office, 1992; Senate Library under the Direction of Jeri Thomson, Secretary of the Senate, *Presidential Vetoes, 1989–2000*, S. Pub. 107-10, Washington, DC: U.S. Government Printing Office, 2001.

32. Nick Anderson "Deal on Media Could Bring Passage of Spending Bill," *Los Angeles Times*, November 25, 2003: 23; Bill Miller, "Senators Take Up Homeland Security; Bush Strengthens Veto Threat," *Washington Post*, September 5, 2002: A29.

33. "Bush Signs Patriot Act Extension, Military Bill," *Los Angeles Times*, December 31, 2005: A20.

34. Adam Nagourney, "Budget Restraint Emerges as a G.O.P. Theme for 2008," *New York Times*, March 13, 2006: 18.

35. As quoted in James P. Pfiffner, *The Modern Presidency* (New York: St. Martin's, 1994), p. 114.

36. John Hart, *The Presidential Branch: From Washington to Clinton*, 2nd ed. (Chatham, NJ: Chatham House, 1995), pp. 26–30.

37. See Matthew Dickinson, *Bitter Harvest: FDR, Presidential Power, and the Growth of the Presidential Branch* (New York: Cambridge University Press, 1997).

38. Harold W. Stanley and Richard Niemi, *Vital Statistics on American Politics 1999–2000* (Washington, DC: CQ Press, 1999), pp. 250–251; and Office of Personnel Management, *Federal Civilian Workforce Statistics: Employment and Trends*.

39. Paul Quirk, "Presidential Competence," in *The Presidency and the Political System*, 4th ed., ed. Michael Nelson (Washington, DC: CQ Press, 1994), pp. 171–221; and John P. Burke, *The Institutional Presidency* (Baltimore, MD: Johns Hopkins University Press, 1992), pp. 40–42.

40. Colin Campbell, "Management in a Sandbox," in Colin Campbell and Bert A. Rockman, *The Clinton Presidency: First*

Appraisals (Chatham, NJ: Chatham House, 1996), p. 60.

41. Charles O. Jones, "Campaigning to Govern: The Clinton Style," in Campbell and Rockman, *The Clinton Presidency*, p. 16.

42. Terry Moe, "The Politicized Presidency"; and Andrew Rudalevige, "The President's Program and the Politicized Presidency," paper presented at the Annual Meeting of the American Political Science Association, Atlanta, Georgia, September 2–5, 1999.

43. Bruce E. Altshuler, *LBJ and the Polls* (Gainesville: University of Florida Press, 1990); and Lawrence R. Jacobs, "The Recoil Effect: Public Opinion in the U.S. and Britain," *Comparative Politics* 24 (1992): 199–217.

44. *Wall Street Journal*, December 22, 1993: A4.

45. Peter Baker, "Senior White House Staff May be Wearing Down," *Washington Post*, March 13, 2006: A4.

46. Jack Mitchell, *Executive Privilege: Two Centuries of White House Scandals* (New York: Hippocrene Books, 1992), pp. 89–90.

47. John Farrell, "Embattled Security Official Quits, Calls Getting FBI Files a 'Mistake,'" *Boston Globe*, June 27, 1996: 12.

48. Richard Berke, "Bush Is Providing Corporate Model for White House," *New York Times*, March 11, 2001: 1.

49. John W. Kingdon, *Agendas, Alternatives and Public Policies* (Boston: Little, Brown, 1981).

50. Tulis, *Rhetorical Presidency*, chap. 3.

51. Ibid.

52. Harry McPherson, *A Political Education* (Boston: Little, Brown, 1972), p. 268, as quoted in Paul C. Light, *The President's Agenda: Domestic Policy Choice from Kennedy to Reagan* (Baltimore, MD: Johns Hopkins University Press, 1991), p. 13.

53. Dana Milbank and Ellen Nakashima, "Bush Team Has 'Right' Credentials; Conservative Picks Seen Eclipsing Even Reagan's," *Washington Post*, March 25, 2001: A1.

54. Stephen Hess, *Organizing the Presidency* (Washington, DC: The Brookings Institution, 1988), pp. 11–18.

55. Richard Brody, *Assessing the President: The Media, Elite Opinion and Public Support* (Stanford, CA: Stanford University Press, 1991), p. 40.

56. Rockman, "Leadership Style and the Clinton Presidency," in Campbell and Rockman, *The Clinton Presidency*, p. 334.

57. Paul West, "Behind Bush's Low Key Style Is a Blueprint Drafted Well in Advance," *Baltimore Sun*, April 25, 2001: A8.

58. Rep. Robert Matsui (D-CA), quoted in David Westphal, "High Marks for a Solid Start," *Minneapolis Star Tribune*, April 29, 2001: 8A.

59. Walter Bagehot, *The English Constitution* (London: Fantana, 1993).

60. Gerald F. Seis, "Soul on High: Clinton Strikes Deeper Chords," *Wall Street Journal*, December 15, 1993.

61. Elisabeth Bumiller with David E. Sanger, "A Day of Terror: The President," *New York Times*, September 12, 2001: A1.

62. Lou Cannon, *President Reagan: The Role of a Lifetime* (New York: Simon & Schuster, 1991), p. 25.

63. Doris Kearns Goodwin, *No Ordinary Time: Franklin and Eleanor Roosevelt: The Home Front in World War II* (New York: Simon & Schuster, 1994).

64. Laurence McQuillan, "Laura Bush's Travel Agenda: Education First Lady Heads to California to Promote Teaching Careers," *USA Today*, March 22, 2001: 12A.

65. Henning, *Wit and Wisdom of Politics*, p. 261.

66. Paul C. Light, *Vice Presidential Power* (Baltimore, MD: Johns Hopkins University Press, 1984), p. 258.

67. Sidney Milkis, *The President and the Parties: The Transformation of the American Party System Since the New Deal* (New York: Oxford University Press, 1993), p. 81.

68. Theodore Sorensen, as quoted in M. Miller, *Lyndon: An Oral Biography* (New York: Putnam, 1980), p. 254.

69. Adam Nagourney, "A Partner with Contrasts That Complement," *New York Times*, July 7, 2004: A1.

70. Peter Baker of the *Washington Post*, quoted in Greg Mitchell, "More Questions Raised about Delay in Reporting Cheney Misfire," *editorandpublisher.com*, www.editorandpublisher.com/eandp/news/article_display.jsp?vnu_content_id=1001995719, accessed April 8, 2006.

71. Stephen Skowronek, *The Politics Presidents Make: Leadership from John Adams to George Bush* (Cambridge, MA: Harvard University Press, 1993), p. 250.

72. As quoted in James L. Sundquist, *The Decline and Resurgence of Congress* (Washington, DC: The Brookings Institution, 1981), p. 31.

73. *United States v. Belmont*, 301 U.S. 324 (1936); Harold Bruff and Peter Shane, *The Law of Presidential Powers: Cases and Materials* (Durham, NC: Carolina Academic Press, 1988), p. 88; and Joseph Paige, *The Law Nobody Knows: Enlargement of the Constitution—Treaties and Executive Orders* (New York: Vantage Press, 1977), p. 63.

74. William Howell, "The President's Powers of Unilateral Action: The Strategic Advantages of Acting Alone" (Ph.D. diss., Stanford University, 1999).

75. Louis Fisher, *Constitutional Conflicts Between Congress and the President*, 3rd ed., rev. (Lawrence: University of Kansas, 1991), p. 154.

76. *United States v. Nixon*, 418 U.S. 683, 709 (1974).

77. Michael Doyle, "U.S. Sues U.S. Over Cheney Files," *Chicago Sun-Times*, February 24, 2001: 21.

78. Mike Allen, "Bush Issues Pardons to Seven in First Exercise of Clemency Power," *Washington Post*, December 24, 2002: A2.

79. The man who cast the decisive vote provided subject matter for John F. Kennedy's *Profiles in Courage* (New York: Harper & Row, 1964).

80. *Washington Post*/ABC News Poll, January 28–30, 1999.

81. Robert J. Spitzer, "Clinton's Impeachment Will Have Few Consequences for the Presidency," *PS: Political Science and Politics* 32:3 (September 1999): 541–545.

82. Harvey Mansfield, Jr., *Taming the Prince: The Ambivalence of Modern Executive Power* (New York: Free Press, 1989); and James McPherson, *The Battle Cry of Freedom: The Civil War Era* (New York: Oxford University Press, 1988), pp. 264–275, 505.

83. *Wall Street Journal*, December 22, 1993: A1.

84. Neustadt, *Presidential Power*, chap. 4.

85. Henning, *Wit and Wisdom of Politics*, p. 219.

86. As quoted in Henning, *Wit and Wisdom of Politics*, p. 222.

87. The effect of time on presidential support is stressed by Paul Brace and Barbara Hinckley, "The Structure of Presidential Approval: Constraints Within and Across Presidencies," *Journal of Politics* 53 (November 1991): 993–1017; and by John Mueller, "Presidential Popularity from Truman to Johnson," *American Political Science Review* (March 1970): 18–24. For contrasting views, which stress events rather than time, see Brody, *Assessing the President;* and Samuel Kernell, "Explaining Presidential Popularity," *American Political Science Review* (June 1978): 506–522. Also see Michael MacKuen, "Political Drama, Economic Conditions, and the Dynamic of Public Popularity," *American Journal of Political Science* (May 1983): 165–192; Charles Ostrom and Dennis Simon, "Promise and Performance: A Dynamic Model of Presidential Popularity," *American Political Science Review* (June 1985): 334–358; and James Stimson, "Public Support for American

Presidents," *Public Opinion Quarterly* (1976): 401–421.

88. Paul Brace and Barbara Hinckley, *Follow the Leader: Opinion Polls and the Modern Presidents* (New York: Basic Books, 1992), p. 33, Figure 2.3.

89. Samuel Kernell, *Going Public*, 2nd ed. (Washington, DC: CQ Press, 1993), chap. 5.

90. Anthony Stephen King, *Running Scared: Why America's Politicians Campaign Too Much and Govern Too Little* (New York: Free Press, 1997).

91. "Los Angeles Times Interview: Clinton Sees 'A Lot of Insecurity in This Country,'" *Los Angeles Times*, December 5, 1993: A38.

92. "Bush Twin Gets Maximum Fine, License Penalty," *Houston Chronicle*, July 7, 2001: A29.

93. George C. Edwards III, *At the Margins: Presidential Leadership of Congress* (New Haven, CT: Yale University Press, 1989) pp. 120–124; Calvin Mouw and Michael MacKuen, "The Strategic Configuration, Political Influence, and Presidential Power in Congress" (paper prepared for the annual meeting of the Midwest Political Science Association, Chicago, 1989); and Terry Sullivan, "Headcounts, Expectations and Presidential Coalitions in Congress," *American Journal of Political Science* 32 (1988): 567–589.

94. James Barber, *The Presidential Character: Predicting Performance in the White House* (Englewood Cliffs, NJ: Prentice-Hall, 1972).

95. For criticism of Barber's analysis, see Michael Nelson, "The Psychological Presidency," in *The Presidency and the Political System*, 4th ed., ed. Michael Nelson (Washington, DC: CQ Press, 1994), pp. 198–224; Alexander George, "Assessing Presidential Character," *World Politics* 26 (January 1974): 234–282; Jeffrey Tulis, "On Presidential Character," in *The Presidency in the Constitutional Order*, ed. Jeffrey Tulis and Joseph M. Bessette (Baton Rouge: Louisiana State University Press, 1981); and Erwin C. Hargrove, "Presidential Personality and Leadership Style," in *Researching the Presidency: Vital Questions, New Approaches*, ed. George C. Edwards III, John H. Kessel, and Bert A. Rockman (Pittsburgh, PA: Pittsburgh University Press, 1993), pp. 93–98.

96. Fred Greenstein, *The Hidden-Hand Presidency: Eisenhower as Leader* (New York: Basic Books, 1982).

97. Charles O. Jones, "The Separated Presidency—Making It Work in Contemporary Politics," in *The New American Political System*, 2nd version, ed. Anthony King (Washington, DC: American Enterprise Institute, 1990), p. 24.

98. Stephen Skowronek, *The Politics Presidents Make.*

99. Henning, *Wit and Wisdom of Politics*, p. 92.

100. Editorial, "George 'McKinley' Bush?" *Pittsburgh Post Gazette*, April 2, 2002: A-17.

CHAPTER 14

1. John Donnelly, "U.S. Security Aspects Familiar to Some," *Boston Globe*, September 12, 2001: A9.

2. *Road Map for National Security: Imperative for Change*, the Phase III report of the United States Commission on National Security for the 21st Century, February 15, 2001, p. 15.

3. Richard Simon and Charles Piller, "Security Chief Must Battle Bureaucracy," *Los Angeles Times*, October 8, 2001: A9.

4. Alison Mitchell, "Dispute Erupts on Ridge's Needs for His Job," *New York Times*, November 4, 2001: B7.

5. James Gerstenzong, "Response to Terror: Bush Proposes a Cabinet-Level Homeland Security Department," *Los Angeles Times*, June 7, 2002: 1.

6. *New York Times*, September 9, 1993: D20.

7. Committee on Government Reform and Oversight, U.S. House of Representatives, *U.S. Government Policy and Supporting Positions ("Plum Book")* (Washington, DC: U.S. Government Printing Office, 1996).

8. Because the dividing line between independent agencies and government corporations is sometimes difficult to pinpoint, these numbers are necessarily inexact. General Accounting Office, *Government Corporations: Profiles of Existing Government Corporations* (GAO/GGD-96-14) (Washington, DC: General Accounting Office, 1995).

9. Martha Derthick, *Agency Under Stress: The Social Security Administration in American Government* (Washington, DC: The Brookings Institution, 1990).

10. Max Weber, *Essays in Sociology* (New York: Oxford University Press, 1958); and Max Weber, *Economy and Society* (Berkeley: University of California Press, 1978).

11. James Q. Wilson, "The Bureaucracy Problem," *The Public Interest* (Winter 1967): 3–9.

12. Michael Lipsky, *Street-Level Bureaucracy: Dilemmas of the Individual in Public Services* (New York: Russell Sage, 1980).

13. Ibid.

14. Tony Perry, "Forest Service Official Defends Cedar Fire Response," *Los Angeles Times*, November 8, 2003: B14.

15. William A. Niskanen, *Bureaucracy and Representative Government* (Chicago: Aldine-Atherton, 1971), chaps. 2–4.

16. Aaron Wildavsky, *The New Politics of the Budgetary Process* (Boston: Little, Brown, 1988), pp. 84–85.

17. Graham Allison, *Essence of Decision: Explaining the Cuban Missile Crisis* (Boston: Little, Brown, 1971), chap. 3.

18. Tom McGinty and Dan Fagin, "One Tangled Web; Experts Agree: Nation's Electric System Aging, Byzantine," *Newsday*, November 17, 2003, A6.

19. Barton Gellman and Dana Millbank, "Blackout Causes Mass Disruption; Millions Struggle Without Power from N.Y. to Toronto to Detroit," *Washington Post*, August 15, 2003: A1.

20. Laurence J. Peter, as quoted in Chuck Henning, *The Wit and Wisdom of Politics: Expanded Edition* (Golden, CO: Fulcrum Publishing, 1992), p. 16.

21. Steve Berry, Mitchell Landsberg, and Doug Smith, "A New View of High-Rise Firefighting," *Los Angeles Times*, September 24, 2001: A1.

22. Kaufman, *Red Tape*, p. 434.

23. Jay Tokasz, "The I.R.S. Moves Rapidly to Process New Charities," *New York Times*, November 12, 2001: G12.

24. Deborah Solomon and Siobhan Hughes, "SEC Relaxes Rules in Storm Zone," *Wall Street Journal*, September 6, 2005: A12.

25. Lucius Wilmerding as quoted in Herman Finer, "Better Government Personnel," *Political Science Quarterly* 50, 4 (1936): 577.

26. Stanley Elkins and Eric McKitrick, *The Age of Federalism* (New York: Oxford University Press, 1993), p. 170.

27. James Young, *The Washington Community 1800–1828* (New York: Harcourt, 1966), pp. 49, 23.

28. Robert V. Remini, *The Life of Andrew Jackson* (New York: Harper & Row, 1988), p. 185.

29. John Bartlett, *Familiar Quotations: Revised and Enlarged*, 15th ed. (Boston: Little, Brown, 1980), p. 455.

30. Seymour J. Mandelbaum, *Boss Tweed's New York* (New York: Wiley, 1965).

31. As quoted in Henning, *Wit and Wisdom of Politics*, p. 11.

32. A. James Reichley, *The Life of the Parties* (New York: Free Press, 1992), pp. 157–158.

33. William L. Riordon, *Plunkitt of Tammany Hall: A Series of Plain Talks on Very Practical Politics* (New York: E. P. Dutton, 1963), p. 3.

34. Eugene Kennedy, *Hurrah! The Life and Times of Mayor Richard J. Daley* (New

York: Viking, 1978), pp. 255, 274.

35. Robert Dahl, *Who Governs?* (New Haven, CT: Yale University Press, 1961); Raymond E. Wolfinger, *The Politics of Progress* (Englewood Cliffs, NJ: Prentice-Hall, 1974), chap. 4; Edward Banfield and James Q. Wilson, *City Politics* (New York: Random House, 1963); and Robert K. Merton, *Social Theory and Social Structure* (Glencoe, IL: Free Press, 1957), pp. 71–81.

36. Quoted in Reichley, *Life of the Parties,* p. 212.

37. Paul E. Peterson, *The Politics of School Reform, 1870–1940* (Chicago: University of Chicago Press, 1985), pp. 86–87.

38. Rufus P. Browning, Dale Rogers Marshall, and David H. Tabb, *Protest Is Not Enough: The Struggle of Blacks and Hispanics for Equality in Urban Politics* (Berkeley: University of California Press, 1984), chap. 5.

39. Alben W. Barkley, vice president of the United States from 1949 to 1953, as quoted in Henning, *Wit and Wisdom of Politics,* p. 17.

40. 2004 National Election Study, University of Michigan, www.umich.edu/~nes/nesguide/toptable/tab5a_3.htm, accessed March 29, 2006.

41. FOX News/Opinion Dynamics Poll, May 26, 2000, question ID USODFOX. 052600, R45L.

42. Paul Light, *Thickening Government* (Washington, DC: The Brookings Institution, 1995), p. 9, Table 1-2; Paul Light, "The Changing Shape of Government," Brookings Institution Policy Brief 45 (Washington, DC: The Brookings Institution, February 1999), p. 1; and "Urgent Business for America: Revitalizing the Federal Government for the 21st Century," Report of the National Commission on the Public Service (the "Volcker Commission"), January 2003, p. 18.

43. G. Calvin MacKenzie, "The Presidential Appointment Process: Historical Development, Contemporary Operations, Current Issues" (background paper for the Twentieth Century Fund Panel on Presidential Appointments, March 1, 1994), p. 1.

44. "Urgent Business for America: Revitalizing the Federal Government for the 21st Century," Report of the National Commission on the Public Service (the "Volcker Commission"), January 2003, p. 1.

45. As quoted in G. Calvin MacKenzie, *The In-and-Outers: Presidential Appointees and Transient Government in Washington* (Baltimore, MD: Johns Hopkins University Press, 1987).

46. Haynes Johnson and David Broder, *The System: The American Way of Politics at the Breaking Point* (Boston: Little, Brown, 1996).

47. *Wall Street Journal,* February 9, 1994: 1.

48. Council for Excellence in Government survey, March 2004, reprinted in Partnership for Public Service, "Poll Watch: Public Opinion on Public Service," PPS-05-03, May 2, 2005, www.ourpublicservice. org/usr_doc/PPS-05-03.pdf, accessed March 29, 2006.

49. Lyn Ragsdale, "Studying the Presidency: Why Presidents Need Political Scientists," in *The Presidency and the Political System,* 5th ed., ed. Michael Nelson (Washington, DC: CQ Press, 1998), p. 50.

50. Thomas E. Cronin, *The State of the Presidency,* 2nd ed. (Boston: Little, Brown, 1980).

51. Jefferson Cohen, *The Politics of the U.S. Cabinet* (Pittsburgh, PA: University of Pittsburgh Press, 1988).

52. Judy Keen, "Bush, Lay Kept Emotional Distance," *USA Today,* February 26, 2002: 6A; Joseph Kahn, "Contract Offers Look at How Global Played Influence Game," *New York Times,* February 28, 2002: C1.

53. Michael E. Kanell, "Business Scandals: Bush Official Seeks 'Severe' Action," *Atlanta Journal Constitution,* July 12, 2002: 5D.

54. Kermit Gordon, *Reflections on Spending* (Washington, DC: The Brookings Institution, 1967), p. 15.

55. Marver H. Bernstein, *Regulating Business by Independent Commission* (Princeton, NJ: Princeton University Press, 1955); Harold Seidman, *Politics, Position and Power: The Dynamics of Federal Organization,* 2nd ed. (New York: Oxford University Press, 1975); George J. Stigler, "The Theory of Economic Regulation," *Bell Journal of Economics and Management Science* 2 (Spring 1971): 3–21; Terry Moe, "Regulatory Performance and Presidential Administration," *American Journal of Political Science* 16 (May 1982): 197–224; B. R. Weingast and M. J. Moran, "Bureaucratic Discretion or Congressional Control? Regulatory Policymaking by the Federal Trade Commission," *Journal of Political Economy* 91: 5 (1983): 765–800; and B. R. Weingast, "The Congressional-Bureaucratic System: A Principal–Agent Perspective (with Application to the SEC)," *Public Choice* 44: 1 (1984): 147–191.

56. Stephen Labaton, "Exemption Won in '97 Set Stage for Enron Woes," *New York Times,* January 23, 2002: A1.

57. Herbert Kaufman, *The Administrative Behavior of Federal Bureau Chiefs,* p. 183, n. 8.

58. Hugh Heclo, "OMB and the Presidency—the Problem of 'Neutral Competence,'" *Public Interest* 38 (Winter 1975): 80–98; and Karen Hult, "Advising the President," in George C. Edwards, John H. Kessel, and Bert A. Rockman, *Researching the Presidency: Vital Questions, New Approaches*

(Pittsburgh, PA: University of Pittsburgh Press, 1992), p. 126.

59. Richard W. Stevenson, "Bush's Budget Director Girds for a Tough Year," *New York Times,* December 31, 2001: p. A8; Esther Schrader and Janet Hook, "Bush's $87 Billion Request Detailed; Most of the Funding Sought by the White House Would Go to Iraq Military Operations," *Los Angeles Times,* September 18, 2003: A10.

60. Karen Masterson, "Defense Budget Flap Delays Funds for War," *Houston Chronicle,* November 24, 2001: p. A1; and Nick Anderson, "Senate OKs Defense Bill Without NY, Domestic Security Extras," *Los Angeles Times,* December 8, 2001: A27.

61. Johnson and Broder, *The System,* p. 116.

62. David R. Francis, "Medicare Reform Carries Huge Fiscal Toll," *Christian Science Monitor,* October 17, 2003: 5.

63. Johnson and Broder, *The System,* p. 397.

64. Derthick, *Agency Under Stress,* p. 200.

65. *Staffing a New Presidential Administration: A Guide to Personnel Appointments in a Presidential Transition* (Washington, DC: The Presidential Appointee Initiative, a project of the Brookings Institution funded by the Pew Charitable Trusts), November 2000.

66. Frederic Ogg and P. Orman Ray, *Introduction to American Government,* 10th ed. (New York: Appleton-Century-Crofts, 1951), p. 405.

67. Jim VandeHei and Colum Lynch, "Bush Names Bolton U.N. Ambassador in Recess Appointment," *Washington Post,* August 2, 2005: A1.

68. David King, "The Nature of Congressional Committee Jurisdictions," *American Political Science Review* 88 (March 1995): 48–62.

69. See *New York Times,* September 5, 1993: Sec. I, 39.

70. Paul Light, quoted in Janet Hook, "Turf Battles Could Snag Bush's Security Proposal," *New York Times,* June 15, 2002: A18.

71. Richard W. Stevenson, "Breaking Up Is Hard; Merging Is Harder," *New York Times,* June 23, 2002: Sec. 4, 3.

72. James Q. Wilson, *Bureaucracy: What Government Agencies Do and Why They Do It* (New York: Basic Books, 1989), pp. 295–314; and Ezra N. Suleiman, *Politics, Power and Bureaucracy in France: The Administrative Elite* (Princeton, NJ: Princeton University Press, 1974).

73. T. J. Pempel, "The Bureaucratization of Policymaking in Postwar Japan," *American*

Journal of Political Science 18 (November 1974): 64. See also, Michio Muramatsu and Ellis S. Krauss, "Bureaucrats and Politicians in Policymaking: The Case of Japan," *American Political Science Review* 78, 1 (March 1984): 126–146.

74. R. Shep Melnick, *Regulation and the Courts: The Case of the Clean Air Act* (Washington, DC: The Brookings Institution, 1983).

75. David Epstein and Sharyn O'Halloran, *Delegating Powers: A Transaction Cost Politics Approach to Policy Making under Separate Powers* (New York: Cambridge University Press, 1999), Figure 5.9, p. 116.

76. Dick Kirschten, "Slicing the Turf," *Government Executive*, April 1999.

77. Robert L. Park, director of the Washington office of the American Physical Society, as quoted in Graeme Browing, "Fiscal Fission," *National Journal* (June 8, 1996): 1259.

78. Graeme Browning, "Fiscal Fission," p. 1259; and Jeffrey Brainard and Ron Southwick, "A Record Year at the Federal Trough," *Chronicle of Higher Education*, August 10, 2001, 20. See also James D. Savage, *Funding Science in America: Congress, Universities and the Politics of the Academic Pork Barrel* (New York: Cambridge University Press, 1999).

79. Isaiah Poole, "Marathon Conference Clears Highway Bill," *CQ Weekly*, July 29, 2005, 02114.

80. Kathryn A. Wolfe, "Coburn Sets off Earmark Battle," *CQ Weekly*, October 21, 2005, 02854.

81. Ibid.

82. Bill McAllister, "Byrd's Big Prize: Bringing Home the FBI," *Washington Post*, March 13, 1991:A1.

83. Office of Senator Robert C. Byrd, News Release, "Byrd Funding for WVU Homeland Defense Effort Now Law," December 14, 2001.

84. Joel Aberbach, *Keeping a Watchful Eye* (Washington, DC: The Brookings Institution, 1990), p. 38; Policy Agendas Project, University of Washington, www.policyagendas.org, hearings data.

85. Policy Agendas Project.

86. Matthew McCubbins and Thomas Schwartz, "Congressional Oversight Overlooked: Police Patrols vs. Fire Alarms," *American Journal of Political Science* 28: 1 (February 1984): 165–179.

87. Joel Aberbach and Bert Rockman, *In the Web of Politics: Three Decades of the U.S. Federal Executive* (Washington, DC: The Brookings Institution, 2000), p. 121.

88. Grant McConnell, *Private Power and American Democracy* (New York: Knopf, 1966); Theodore Lowi, *The End of Liberalism*, 2nd ed. (New York: Norton, 1979); and Mark P.

Petracca, ed., *The Politics of Interests: Interest Groups Transformed* (Boulder, CO: Westview, 1992).

89. Joel Aberbach, *Keeping a Watchful Eye*, pp. 162–166.

90. Graeme Browning, "Fiscal Fission," p. 1260.

91. "Public Broadcasting Develops Dialogue with House GOP," *Congressional Quarterly Weekly Report*, March 23, 1996, 791.

92. Hugh Heclo, "Issue Networks and the Executive Establishment," in *The New American Political System*, ed. Anthony King (Washington, DC: American Enterprise Institute, 1978), pp. 87–124.

93. John E. Chubb, *Interest Groups and the Bureaucracy* (Stanford, CA: Stanford University Press, 1983); John Chubb "U.S. Energy Policy: A Problem of Delegation," in *Can the Government Govern?*, ed. John Chubb and Paul E. Peterson (Washington, DC: The Brookings Institution, 1989); Seong-Ho Lim, "Changing Jurisdictional Boundaries in Congressional Oversight of Nuclear Energy Regulation: Impact of Public Salience" (paper presented before the annual meeting of the American Political Science Association, 1992); and Frank R. Baumgartner and Bryan D. Jones, "Agenda Dynamics and Policy Subsystems," *Journal of Politics* 53 (November 1991): 1044–1074.

94. Bill Lambrecht, "Industries Have Pumped Millions Into Energy Bill," *St. Louis Post-Dispatch*, December 7, 2003: A1.

95. Paul E. Peterson, Barry G. Rabe, and Kenneth K. Wong, *When Federalism Works* (Washington, DC: The Brookings Institution, 1986), chap. 8; John J. Harrigan, *Political Change in the Metropolis*, 2nd ed. (Boston: Little, Brown, 1981), pp. 267–268, 350–351; and Rochelle L. Stanfield, "Communities Reborn," *National Journal* (June 22, 1966): 1371.

96. John Dilulio, *No Escape: The Future of American Corrections* (New York: Basic Books, 1991), pp. 19–26.

97. James A. Morone, *Democratic Wish: Popular Participation and the Limits of American Government* (New York: Basic Books, 1990).

98. Francis Rourke, "Executive Secrecy: Change and Continuity," in Rourke, *Bureaucratic Power in National Policy Making*, pp. 536–537.

99. Todd Purdom and Alison Mitchell, "Bush, Angered by Leaks, Duels with Congress," *New York Times*, October 10, 2001: A1.

100. Robert Turner, quoted in Warren Richey, "Tribunals on Trial," *Christian Science Monitor*, December 14, 2001: 1.

101. John Mintz and Susan Schmidt,

"'Dirty Bomb' Was Major New Year's Worry," *Washington Post*, January 7, 2004: A1.

102. Department of Defense Personnel Security Research Center poll, cited in *Secrecy & Government Bulletin* 48 (May 1995) (Washington, DC: Federation of American Scientists).

103. Martin Halstuk, "New Privacy Policy Hinders Public's Right to Know," *Los Angeles Times*, November 19, 2001: part 2, 11.

104. Jeffrey Birnbaum, Eileen Gunn, et al., "Unbelievable! The Mess at the IRS *Is* Worse Than You Think," *Fortune*, April 13, 1998.

105. Ibid.

106. Ibid.

107. Albert B. Crenshaw, "Witnesses Say IRS Agent Tried to Frame Ex-Senator," *Washington Post*, May 1, 1998: A1.

108. Albert B. Crenshaw, "IRS Overhaul Set for Passage; Measure Gives Taxpayers New Rights, Includes Capital Gains Break," *Washington Post*, June 25, 1998: A1.

109. Jonathan Weisman, "GAO Finds Increases in Tax Evasion; Report Says IRS Needs More Resources," *Washington Post*, December 19, 2003: E1.

110. Matthew McCubbins and Thomas Schwartz, "Congressional Oversight Overlooked: Police Patrols vs. Fire Alarms," *American Journal of Political Science* 28:1 (February 1984): 165–179.

111. Martha Derthick, *Agency Under Stress*, p. 87.

112. Christopher Lee, "Federal Workforce Is Largest Since 1990," *Washington Post*, September 5, 2003: A19.

113. Christopher Lee, "Federal Case; Government Workers Protest Outsourcing," *Washington Post*, May 21, 2003: A31; Christopher Lee, "Outsourcing Shield Weakened; Appeals Rights Stripped as Worker Raises Are Approved," *Washington Post*, November 26, 2003: A23.

114. Blaine Harden, "Cuts Sap Morale of Parks Employees; Many Fear Losing Jobs to Outsourcing," *Washington Post*, June 10, 2003: A19.

115. Paul Light, "To Restore and Renew: Now is the Time to Rebuild the Federal Public Service," *Government Executive*, November 2001: 32–47.

116. Former Bureau of the Budget director Kermit Gordon, as quoted in Kaufman, *Administrative Behavior*, p. 443.

117. Paul J. Quirk, "Food and Drug Administration," in James Q. Wilson, *The Politics of Regulation* (New York: Basic Books, 1980), p. 199.

118. Terry Moe, "The Politics of Bureaucratic Structure," in John E. Chubb and

Paul E. Peterson, *Can the Government Govern?* (Washington, DC: The Brookings Institution, 1988).

119. Brian Hassel, "Charter Schools: Designed to Fail?" (Ph.D. diss., John F. Kennedy School of Government, Harvard University, 1997); Carolyn M. Hoxby and Jonah Rockoff, "Findings from the City of Big Shoulders," *Education Next*, Fall 2005, www.educationnext.org/20054/52.html, accessed April 29, 2006; Robert Bifulco and Helen F. Ladd, "Results from the Tar Heel State," *Education Next*, Fall 2005, www.educationnext.org/20054/60.html, accessed April 29, 2006.

120. Robert L. Kahn, Barbara A. Gutek, Eugenia Barton, and Daniel Katz, "Americans Love Their Bureaucrats," *Psychology Today* (1975), as reprinted in Rourke, *Bureaucratic Power in National Policy Making*, p. 290.

121. John Clayton Thomas and Gloria Streib, "The New Face of Government: Citizen-Initiated Contacts in the Era of E-Government," *Journal of Public Administration Research and Theory*, 13:1 (January 2003): 92.

122. James H. Boren, quoted in Antony Jay, *The Oxford Dictionary of Political Quotations*, (New York: Oxford University Press, 2001), p. 48.

123. Charles Lindblom, "The Science of 'Muddling Through,'" *Public Administration Review* XIX (Spring 1959): 79–88.

124. Herbert Kaufman, *The Forest Ranger: A Study in Administrative Behavior* (Baltimore, MD: Johns Hopkins University Press, 1960). For recent confirmations of this analysis, see Warren Wolfe, "A Milestone for the BWCA: 25 Years of Nature and Fighting," *Minneapolis Star Tribune*, October 11, 2003: 1A; Charles Seabrook, "Forest Use Rules May Relax; Logging Expected to Increase," *Atlanta Journal-Constitution*, November 28, 2002: 3A; Glen Martin, "Cattlemen Prod Forest Service; Federal Land Use Policies to Come Under Review, Again," *San Francisco Chronicle*, July 5, 2002: A3; Jim Robbins, "Logging Plan for West's Burned Forests Incites a Debate," *New York Times*, July 22, 2001: 23; Douglas Jehl, "Forest Officials Address Unusual Uses of Land," *New York Times*, July 5, 2001: A12.

CHAPTER 15

1. "The Second Bush-Kerry Presidential Debate," Washington University, St. Louis, MO, October 8, 2004, Transcript from Commission on Presidential Debates, www.debates.org/pages/trans2004c.html, accessed April 29, 2006.

2. Robin Toner, "After a Brief Shock, Advocates Quickly Mobilize," *New York Times*,

July 2, 2005: A2.

3. Douglas Jehl, "At White House, Surprise is Borne out in Name Only," *New York Times*, July 2, 2005: A2.

4. Peter Baker and Jo Becker, "Court Watchers are Resigned to Wait," *Washington Post*, July 9, 2005: A7.

5. Dahlia Lithwick, "Confirmation Report: Oh the Humanity!" Slate.com, September 14, 2005, http://slate.msn.com/?id=2126131&entry/2126220/nav=tap1/, accessed September 15, 2005.

6. For example, Gallup/CNN/*USA Today* poll, September 16–18, 2005: 60 percent support confirmation.

7. Carolyn Lochhead, "Key Senator Backs Roberts – Focus Turns to Next Pick," *San Francisco Chronicle*, September 22, 2005: A1.

8. Charles Babington and Peter Baker, "Roberts Confirmed as 17th Chief Justice," *Washington Post*, September 30, 2005: A1.

9. Calculated by authors from Richard Y. Schlauffer, Robert C. LaFountain, Neal B Kauder, and Shauna M. Strickland, *Examining the Work of State Courts, 2004: A National Perspective From the Court Statistics Project* (Williamsburg, VA: National Center for State Courts, 2005), p. 14, and Judicial Conference of the United States, "Judicial Facts and Figures," www.uscourts.gov/judicialfactsfigures/contents.html, accessed April 22, 2006, Table 4.1. Most recent data available are from 2003. Total state cases: 100.1 million; total federal court cases: 323,604.

10. Commission to Promote Public Confidence in Judicial Elections, *Final Report to the Chief Judge of the State of New York* (New York: Fordham University School of Law, February 6, 2006), pp. 6–7.

11. *2005 Annual Report: Georgia Courts*, Judicial Council of Georgia, Administrative Office of the Courts, Atlanta, GA, 2005.

12. "The Texas Judicial System," Texas Judiciary Online, www.courts.state.tx.us/, accessed April 22, 2006, 15.

13. Melinda Gann Hall, "Justices as Representatives: Elections and Judicial Politics in the American States," *American Politics Quarterly* 23 (October 1995): 485–503.

14. Henry R. Glick, "Courts: Politics and the Judicial Process," in Virginia Gray and Russell L. Hanson, Eds. *Politics in the American States: A Comparative Analysis*, 8th ed. (Washington, DC: CQ Press, 2004), p. 240.

15. John Gibeaut, "Bench Battle: Trial Judges Often Keep their Seats Without Facing Election," *ABA Journal* (August 2000): 42.

16. Seth S. Anderson, director, American Judicature Society, Hunter Center for Judicial Selection, quoted in Gibeaut, ibid.

17. Don L. Horn, quoted in Gibeaut, ibid.

18. Jamie B. W. Stecher, "Democratic and Republican Justice: Judicial Decision Making in Five State Supreme Courts," *Columbia Journal of Law and Social Problems* 13 (1977): 137–181.

19. Zach Patton, "Robe Warriors," *Governing*, March 2006, 34.

20. Professor Anthony Champagne, quoted in Jerry Crimmins, "Experts: Negative Ads Erode Confidence in Judges," *Chicago Daily Law Bulletin*, November 9, 2001: 1.

21. Henning, *Wit and Wisdom*, p. 108.

22. Los Angeles County District Attorney's Office, http://da.co.la.ca.us/oview.htm, accessed April 23, 2006.

23. Robert A. Carp, Ronald Stidham, and Kenneth L. Manning, *Judicial Process in America*, 6th ed. (Washington, DC: CQ Press, 2004), p. 100.

24. "Investigate, Then Prosecute; Bungled Lewis Trial: Atlanta Prosecutors, Police Rushed to Indict Before They Had All the Evidence," *Baltimore Sun*, June 14, 2000: 22A.

25. Cynthia Tucker, "Murder Acquittals: Running for Glory, Fulton DA Fumbles," *Atlanta Constitution*, June 14, 2000: 14A.

26. Alexander Hamilton, James Madison, and John Jay, *The Federalist Papers* (New York: Bantam Books, 1982 [1787]), "Federalist 78," p. 393.

27. American Judicature Society, www.ajs.org/cji/cji_impeachment.asp, accessed February 7, 2004.

28. Ibid.

29. William Rehnquist, *2002 Year-End Report on the Federal Judiciary* (Washington, DC: U.S. Supreme Court, January 1, 2003), p. 2.

30. Richard A. Posner, *The Federal Courts: Challenge and Reform* (Cambridge, MA: Harvard University Press, 1996), pp. 29–33.

31. Henning, *The Wit and Wisdom of Politics: Expanded Edition* (Golden, CO: Fulcrum Publishing, 1992), p. 250.

32. Robert G. McCloskey, *The American Supreme Court, Third Edition* (Chicago: University of Chicago Press, 2000), p. 8.

33. U.S. Constitution, Article 3, Section 2.

34. Clarence Thomas, "Be Not Afraid," speech at the American Enterprise Institute, Washington, DC, February 13, 2001, www.aei.org/news/newsID.15211/news_detail.asp, accessed February 7, 2004.

35. Ibid.

36. *Lochner v. New York*, 195 U.S. 45 (1905).

37. William J. Brennan, Jr. "The Constitution of the United States; Contemporary Ratification," in David

O'Brien, ed., *Judges on Judging: Views from the Bench* (Chatham, NJ: Chatham House, 1997), p. 204.

38. Ibid.

39. *Beauharnais v. Illinois*, 343 U.S. 250 (1952).

40. *Kelo v. New London*, 04-108 (2005).

41. Ibid.

42. *Dred Scott v. Sandford*, 19. How. 393 (1857).

43. See, for example, Abraham Lincoln's comments in Robert W. Johannsen, ed., *The Lincoln-Douglas Debates* (New York: Oxford University Press, 1965), pp. 14–21.

44. *Lochner v. New York*, 198 U.S. 45 (1905). Ellipses deleted from excerpt.

45. *Schechter Poultry Corp. v. United States*, 295 U.S. 495 (1935).

46. John Agresto, *The Supreme Court and Constitutional Democracy* (Ithaca, NY: Cornell University Press, 1984), p. 163.

47. Congressional Research Service, Library of Congress, *The Constitution of the United States of America: Analysis and Interpretation, 2004 Supplement* (Washington, DC: Government Printing Office, 2004).

48. Excerpted with ellipses deleted. Robert A. Dahl, "Decision-Making in a Democracy: The Supreme Court as a National Policy-Maker," *Journal of Public Law* 6 (Fall 1957): 293–294. See also Richard Y. Funston, "The Supreme Court and Critical Elections," *American Political Science Review* 69 (1975): 795–811.

49. James A. Stimson, Michael B. Mackuen, and Robert S. Erikson, "Dynamic Representation," *American Political Science Review* 89 (September 1995): 555. Also see William Mishler and Reginald S. Sheehan, "The Supreme Court as a Counter-Majoritarian Institution? The Impact of Public Opinion on Supreme Court Decisions," *American Political Science Review* 87 (1993): 87–101; and Helmut Norpoth and Jeffery Segal, "Popular Influence on Supreme Court Decisions," *American Political Science Review* 88 (September 1994): 711–724.

50. Whittington, Keith E., "'Interpose Your Friendly Hand': Political Supports for the Exercise of Judicial Review by the United States Supreme Court," *American Political Science Review* 99:4 (November 2005): 583–596.

51. John C. Jeffries, Jr., *Justice Lewis F. Powell, Jr.: A Biography* (New York: Scribner, 1994), p. 248.

52. George L. Haskins and Herbert A. Johnson, *History of the Supreme Court of the United States, Vol. 2, Foundations of Power: John Marshall 1801–15* (New York: Macmillan, 1981) p. 33.

53. David O'Brien, "Background Paper," in Twentieth Century Fund, *Judicial Roulette* (New York: Priority Press, 1988), p. 37; Sheldon Goldman, "Unpicking Pickering in 2002: Some Thoughts on the Politics of Lower Federal Court Selection and Confirmation," *U.C. Davis Law Review*, 36:695 (February 2003): 707.

54. Craig Gilbert, "Supreme Duty for Two Senators; Kohl, Feingold will scrutinize nominee; is ideology 'relevant'?," *Milwaukee Journal Sentinel*, online edition, July 8, 2005, www.jsonline.com/news/nat/jul05/339807.asp, accessed July 9, 2005.

55. Linda Greenhouse, "Rehnquist Sees a Loss of Prospective Judges," *New York Times*, January 1, 2002: A18.

56. Lyle Denniston, "Court Nominee Withdraws in Senate Battle, Democrats Prevail by Way of Filibuster," *Boston Globe*, September 5, 2003: A2.

57. Robert A. Carp and Ronald Stidham, *The Federal Courts*, 2nd ed. (Washington, DC: CQ Press, 1991), p. 116; and *U.S. News & World Report*, May 26, 1997, 24.

58. Richard A. Serrano, "Alito's Sole Trial Before a Jury was A Gamble that Paid Off," *Los Angeles Times*, November 14, 2005: A11.

59. *Martin v. Hunter's Lessee*, 14 U.S. (1 Wheat.) 304 (1816).

60. As quoted in C. Herman Pritchett, *The American Constitution* (New York: McGraw-Hill, 1959), pp. 65, 215.

61. Congressional Research Service, Library of Congress, *The Constitution of the United States of America: Analysis and Interpretation, 2004 Supplement* (Washington, DC: U.S. Government Printing Office, 2004). (Note: State and local laws held preempted by federal laws not included in the figure reported.)

62. Pritchett, *The American Constitution* (New York: McGraw-Hill, 1959), p. 134.

63. Henning, *Wit and Wisdom*, p. 187.

64. *In re Chapman*, 16 U.S. 661 (1897).

65. Linda Greenhouse, "Legacy of a Term," *New York Times*, July 3, 1996: A1.

66. Linda Greenhouse, "Roberts Is at Court's Helm, but He Isn't Yet in Control," *New York Times*, July 2, 2006: 1.

67. As quoted in Henning, *Wit and Wisdom*, p. 107.

68. Carl B. Swisher, *American Constitutional Development*, 2nd ed. (Boston: Houghton Mifflin, 1954), pp. 1075–1079.

69. Paul Simon, *Advice and Consent* (Washington, D.C.: National Press Books, 1992), p. 275.

70. Henry J. Abraham, *Justices and Presidents: A Political History of Appointments to the Supreme Court*, 3rd ed. (New York: Oxford University Press, 1992).

71. The term *stealth nominee* was coined by Alabama Senator Howell Heflin during nomination hearings for Justice Souter. See Ruth Marcus and Michael Isikoff, "Souter Declines Comment on Abortion," *Washington Post*, September 14, 1990: A1.

72. Twentieth Century Fund, *Judicial Roulette* (New York: Priority Press, 1988), pp. 10–11.

73. Jonathan Swift, *Gulliver's Travels* (New York: Penguin, 2003 [1726]), p. 230.

74. *Parts and Electric Motors v. Sterling Electric*, 866 F 2d 288 (1988).

75. Hart Pomerantz, as quoted in Henning, *Wit and Wisdom*, p. 250.

76. H. W. Perry, Jr., *Deciding to Decide: Agenda Setting in the United States Supreme Court* (Cambridge, MA: Harvard University Press, 1991), p. 27.

77. See "Judicial Business of the United States Courts, 2001," Washington, DC: Administrative Office of the U.S. Courts, 2001, Table A-1.

78. Ibid., pp. 218–219.

79. Ibid., p. 99.

80. Address of Chief Justice Vinson before the American Bar Association, September 7, 1949, as quoted in Perry, *Deciding to Decide*, p. 36.

81. *Zelman v. Simmons-Harris*, No. 00-1751 (2002).

82. Jeffries, *Justice Lewis R. Powell, Jr.*, p. 248.

83. Bernard Schwartz, *A History of the Supreme Court* (New York: Oxford University Press, 1993), chap. 13.

84. Linda Cohen and Matthew Spitzer, "The Government Litigant Advantage: Implications for the Law," *Florida State University Law Review* 28 (Fall 2000): 391.

85. Scigliano, *Supreme Court and the Presidency*, p. 162.

86. Jeffrey A. Segal, "*Amicus Curiae* Briefs by the Solicitor General During the Warren and Burger Courts: A Research Note," *Western Political Quarterly* 41 (March 1988): 135–144.

87. Joan Biskupic and Elder Witt, *Guide to the U.S. Supreme Court*, 3rd ed., vol. II, (Washington, DC: Congressional Quarterly Press, 1997), p. 832.

88. Perry, *Deciding to Decide*, p. 71.

89. Perry, *Deciding to Decide*; and Schwartz, *History of the Supreme Court*, chap. 16.

90. Biskupic and Witt, *Guide to the U.S. Supreme Court*, p. 828.

91. As quoted in Henning, *Wit and Wisdom*, p. 106.

92. Jeffries, *Justice Lewis F. Powell, Jr.*, p. 247.

93. Ibid., pp. 245–247.

94. *Harris v. Forklift*, 508 U.S. 938 (1993).

95. Lawrence Sirovich, "A Pattern Analysis of the Second Rehnquist U.S. Supreme Court," *Proceedings of the National Academy of Sciences*, 100 (13) 7432-7437 (at p. 7435).

96. Jeffrey A. Segal and Albert D. Cover, "Ideological Values and the Votes of U.S. Supreme Court Justices," *American Political Science Review* 83 (June 1989): 557–565.

97. Henning, *Wit and Wisdom*, p. 250.

98. As quoted by Austin Ranney, "Peltason Created a New Way to Look at What Judges Do," *Public Affairs Report, Institute of Governmental Studies* 36:6 (November 1995): 7.

99. Excerpted with ellipses deleted. "Federalist 2," edited, and with introduction, by Jacob E. Cooke (Middletown, CT: Wesleyan University Press, 1961), pp. 522–523.

100. Pritchett, *American Constitution*, p. 99.

101. Robert H. Birkby, "The Supreme Court and the Bible Belt: Tennessee Reaction to the 'Shempp Decision,'" *Midwest Journal of Political Science* 10 (August 1966), as reprinted in *The Impact of Supreme Court Decisions*, ed. Theodore L. Becker and Malcolm M. Feeley (New York: Oxford University Press, 1973), p. 114.

102. James Sterngold, "Overhaul of Prison Health System Delayed," *San Francisco Chronicle*, November 3, 2005: B1.

103. Steven Lee Myers, "U.S. Judge Upsets Rules to Control How Jails Are Run," *New York Times*, July 24, 1996: B2.

104. Abram Chayes, "The Role of the Judge in Public Law Litigation," *Harvard Law Review* 89 (May 1976): 1281–1316.

105. Alexis de Tocqueville, *Democracy in America*, ed. J. P. Mayer (New York: Harper, 1988), p. 270.

106. R. Shep Melnick, *Between the Lines* (Washington, DC: The Brookings Institution, 1994), p. 149.

107. Myron Levin and Henry Weinstein, "Big Tobacco Must Pay Damages in Florida Case," *Los Angeles Times*, April 8, 2000: A1.

108. Jerry Hirsch, "Talks to Settle Suit Against Enron, Others, Fail," *Los Angeles Times*, May 2, 2002: part 3, 3.

109. Dirk Johnson, "City of Deep Pockets," *Newsweek*, December 15, 2003, 45.

CHAPTER 16

1. Kevin Whitelaw and Chitra Ragavan, "A Good Spy is Hard to Find," *U.S. News & World Report*, November 22, 2004: 59.

2. Patrick Radden Keefe, "Can Network Theory Thwart Terrorists?" *New York Times Magazine*, March 12, 2006: 16.

3. James Bamford, *Body of Secrets: Anatomy of the Ultra-Secret National Security Agency* (New York: Random House, 2001), pp. 428–429.

4. James Risen and Eric Lichtblau, "Bush Lets U.S. Spy on Callers Without Courts," *New York Times*, December 16, 2005: 1; Brian Ross, "NSA Whistleblower Alleges Illegal Spying," *ABCNews.com*, January 10, 2006, http://abcnews.go.com/WNT/Investigation/story?id=1491889, accessed May 13, 2006.

5. Eric Lichtblau and Adam Liptak, "Bush and His Senior Aides Press On in Legal Defense for Wiretapping Program," *New York Times*, January 28, 2006: 13.

6. Leslie Cauley, "NSA Has Massive Database of Americans' Phone Calls; 3 Telecoms Help Government Collect Billions of Domestic Records," *USA Today*, May 11, 2006: 1A.

7. Richard A. Posner, "Our Intelligence Quotient," *Wall Street Journal*, May 15, 2006: A14.

8. Richard A. Falkenrath, "The Right Call on Phone Records," *Washington Post*, May 13, 2006: A17.

9. Greg Miller, "New Furor over NSA Phone Logs," *Los Angeles Times*, May 12, 2006: A1.

10. Paul Taylor, "Qwest Snubbed 'Illegal' Call for Details of Phone Records," *Financial Times*, May 13, 2006: 1.

11. Richard Sisk, "They Know Who We're Calling," *New York Daily News*, May 12, 2006: 7.

12. CNN Poll, May 16–17, 2006 (54% approve); CBS News Poll, May 16–17, 2006 (51% approve); FOX News Poll, May 16–18, 2006 (52% approve).

13. Richard Sisk, "They Know Who We're Calling," *New York Daily News*, May 12, 2006: 7.

14. Henry Steele Commager, ed., *Documents of American History*, 6th ed. (New York: Appleton-Century-Crofts, 1958), pp. 125–126. Also see Willi Paul Adams, *The First American Constitutions: Republican Ideology and the Making of the State Constitutions in the Revolutionary Era* (Chapel Hill: University of North Carolina Press, 1980).

15. Charles R. Ritcheson, "'Loyalist Influence' on British Policy Toward the United States After the American Revolution," *Eighteenth Century Studies* 7:1 (Autumn 1973): 1–17. See also Paul A. Smith, "The American Loyalists: Notes on Their Organization and Numerical Strength," *William and Mary Quarterly*, 25:2 (April 1968): 259–277.

16. Arthur M. Schlesinger, *Prelude to Independence: The Newspaper War on Britain, 1764–1776* (New York: Alfred Knopf, 1958), pp. 297–298.

17. Ibid., p. 299.

18. Michael W. McConnell, "Establishment and Disestablishment at the Founding, Part I, Establishment of Religion," 44 *William and Mary Law Review* 2105 (April 2003): 2157–2159.

19. *Barron v. Baltimore*, 1833, as quoted in C. Herman Pritchett, *Constitutional Civil Liberties* (Englewood Cliffs, NJ: Prentice-Hall, 1984), p. 6.

20. Robert G. McCloskey, revised by Sanford Levinson, *The American Supreme Court*, 3rd ed. (Chicago: University of Chicago Press, 2000), p. 80.

21. *Palko v. Connecticut*, 302 U.S. 319 (1937).

22. *United States v. Miller*, 307 U.S. 174 (1939)

23. Alexander Hamilton, James Madison, and John Jay, "Federalist 10," *The Federalist Papers* (New York: Bantam Books, 1982 [1787–1788]), pp. 45–46.

24. John Emerich Edward Dalberg-Acton, *The History of Freedom, and Other Essays*, eds. John Neville Figgis and Reginald Vere Laurence (Freeport, NY: Books for Libraries Press, 1967), p. 97.

25. John Stuart Mill, *On Liberty* (New York: Norton, 1859/1975), p. 36.

26. David M. Rabban, *Free Speech in Its Forgotten Years* (New York: Cambridge University Press, 1997), p. 193.

27. Robert G. McCloskey, *The American Supreme Court* (Chicago: University of Chicago Press, 1960), p. 224.

28. Quoted in Robert Goldstein, *Political Repression in Modern America: 1870 to the Present* (New York: Schenkman, 1978), p. 565.

29. *Schenck v. United States*, 249 U.S. 47 (1919).

30. *Abrams v. United States*, 250 U.S. 616 (1919).

31. *Stromberg v. California*, 283 U.S. 359 (1931).

32. Goldstein, *Political Repression*, p. 262.

33. *Chaplinsky v. New Hampshire*, 315 U.S. 568 (1942).

34. As quoted in C. Herman Pritchett, *The American Constitution*, 3rd ed. (New York: McGraw-Hill, 1969), p. 375.

35. John Mueller, "Trends in Political Tolerance," *Public Opinion Quarterly* 52:1 (Spring 1988): 1–25; and National Opinion Research Center, General Social Survey 1975, 2004.

36. *United States v. Carolene Products Co.*, 304 U.S. 144 (1938).

37. George Anastaplo, as quoted in

Goldstein, *Political Repression*, p. 532.

38. *Papish v. Board of Curators of the University of Missouri*, 410 U.S. 667 (1973).

39. Robert Goldstein, *Saving "Old Glory": The History of the Desecration Controversy* (Boulder, CO: Westview, 1995).

40. *Texas v. Johnson*, 491 U.S. 397 (1989).

41. Ibid.

42. *United States v. Eichman*, 496 U.S. 310, (1990).

43. *R. A. V. v. City of St. Paul, Minnesota*, 112 S Ct. 2541 (1992).

44. Schlesinger, *Prelude to Independence*, pp. 64–65.

45. *Near v. Minnesota*, 283 U.S. 697 (1931).

46. Jonathan Krim, "Congress Acts to Curb Offensive Programs; Senate Panel Proposes Stiff Fines, Delaying Media Consolidation," *Washington Post*, March 10, 2004: E1.

47. Frank Ahrens, "The Price for On-Air Indecency Goes Up," *Washington Post*, June 8, 2006: D1.

48. *NAACP v. Alabama*, 357 U.S. 449 (1958).

49. *Boy Scouts of America v. Dale*, 530 U.S. 640 (2000).

50. *Miller v. California*, 413 U.S. 15 (1973).

51. Linda Greenhouse, "Court, 9–0, Upholds State Laws Prohibiting Assisted Suicide, Protects Speech on Internet," *New York Times*, June 27, 1997: A1.

52. *Ashcroft v. American Civil Liberties Union*, 00-1293 (2003).

53. Anthony Lewis, *Make No Law: The Sullivan Case and the First Amendment* (New York: Random House, 1992).

54. Felicity Barringer, "Appeals Court Rejects Damages Against ABC in Food Lion Case," *New York Times*, October 21, 1999: 1.

55. As quoted in Charles L. Glenn, Jr., *The Myth of the Common School* (Amherst, MA: University of Massachusetts Press, 1987), p. 84.

56. Diane Ravitch, *The Great School Wars: New York City, 1805–1973* (New York: Basic Books, 1974); and Paul E. Peterson, *The Politics of School Reform, 1870–1940* (Chicago: University of Chicago Press, 1985).

57. *Meek v. Pittenger*, 421 U.S. 349 (1975).

58. *Engel v. Vitale*, 370 U.S. 421 (1962); *School District of Abington Township v. Schempp*, 374 U.S. 273 (1963); and *Wallace v. Jaffree*, 472 U.S. 38 (1985).

59. *Board of Education v. Mergens*, 496 U.S. 226 (1990); see also *Good News Club v. Milford Central School*, 99–2036 (2001).

60. *Mitchell v. Helms*, 98–1648 (2000).

61. *Agostini v. Felton*, 96–552 (1997).

62. *Meyer v. Nebraska*, 262 U.S. 399 (1923). See also *Pierce v. Society of Sisters*, 268 U.S. 510 (1925).

63. *Wisconsin v. Yoder*, 406 U.S. 205 (1972).

64. *Church of the Lukumi Bablu Aye v. City of Hialeah*, 508 U.S. 520 (1993).

65. *Employment Division, Oregon Department of Human Resources v. Smith*, 494 U.S. 872 (1990).

66. Paul E. Peterson, "The New Politics of Choice," in *Learning from the Past*, eds. Diane Ravitch and Maris Vinovskis (Baltimore, MD: Johns Hopkins University Press, 1995).

67. Publius Syrus, as quoted in John Bartlett, *Familiar Quotations*, p. 111.

68. *Olmstead v. United States*, 277 U.S. 438 (1927).

69. *National Crime Victimization Survey: Criminal Victimization, 2004*, U.S. Department of Justice, Bureau of Justice Statistics, September, 2005, p. 1.

70. Senator Joe Biden, as quoted in Chuck Henning, *The Wit and Wisdom of Politics: Expanded Edition* (Golden, CO: Fulcrum Publishing, 1992), p. 47.

71. Justice Potter Stewart, quoted in Bernard Schwartz, *A History of the Supreme Court* (New York: Oxford, 1993), p. 264.

72. Bernard Schwartz, *A History of the Supreme Court* (New York: Oxford, 1993), p. 263.

73. *Chimel v. California*, 395 U.S. 752 (1969).

74. *Mapp v. Ohio*, 167 U.S. 643 (1961).

75. Ibid.

76. *United States v. Leon*, 468 U.S. 897 (1984).

77. Joan Biskupic, "Police May Stop, Frisk Those Who Flee at Sight of Officer," *Washington Post*, January 13, 2000: A10.

78. *Dickerson v. United States*, 99–5525 (2000).

79. Pritchett, *Constitutional Civil Liberties*, p. 78.

80. *Sheppard v. Maxwell*, 384 U.S. 333 (1966).

81. *Nebraska Press Association v. Stuart*, 427 U.S. 539 (1976).

82. Lisa J. McIntyre, *The Public Defender: The Practice of Law in the Shadows of Repute* (Chicago: University of Chicago Press, 1987), p. 162.

83. Robert B. Spangenberg, Marea L. Beeman, and James Downing, "State and County Expenditures for Indigent Defense Services in Fiscal Year 2002" (West Newton, MA: Report prepared for the American Bar Association, September 2003).

84. Jonathan D. Casper, *American Criminal Justice: The Defendant's Perspective* (Englewood Cliffs, NJ: Prentice-Hall, 1972), p. 101.

85. *U.S. v. Lanza*, 260 U.S. 377 (1922).

86. *Hamdi v. Rumsfeld*, 03-6696 (2004); *Rumsfeld v. Padilla*, 03-1027 (2004); *Rasul v. Bush*, 03-334 (2004).

87. Casper, *American Criminal Justice*; and Jerome Skolnick, *Justice Without Trial* (New York: Wiley, 1966).

88. *Santobello v. New York* (1971), as quoted in Lawrence M. Friedman, *Crime and Punishment in American History* (New York: Basic Books, 1993), p. 392.

89. Keith Bradsher, "Boy Who Killed Gets Seven Years; Judge Says Law Is Too Harsh," *New York Times*, January 14, 2000: A1.

90. Robert H. Bork, "Neutral Principles and Some First Amendment Problems," *Indiana Law Journal* 47 (1971): 8.

91. *Griswold v. Connecticut*, 381 U.S. 479 (1965).

92. Ibid.

93. *Lawrence v. Texas*, 02-102 (1993).

94. The Gallup Poll: "Social and Economic Indicators—Homosexual Relations," www.gallup.com/poll/topics/homosexual.asp, accessed February 18, 2002.

95. *Harris v. McRae*, 448 U.S. 297 (1980).

96. *Webster v. Reproductive Health Services*, 492 U.S. 490 (1989).

97. *Planned Parenthood v. Casey*, 112 S Ct 291 (1992).

98. *Planned Parenthood of Southeastern Pennsylvania v. Casey*, 505 U.S. 833 (1992).

99. David Streitfeld and Charles Pillar, "Big Brother Finds Ally in Once-Wary High-Tech," *Los Angeles Times*, January 19, 2002: A1.

100. "Feds, States Work Toward 'National' Driver's License; Plan Is to Improve Existing ID Systems," *San Diego Union Tribune*, January 8, 2002: A7.

101. Streitfeld and Piller, "Big Brother Finds Ally."

102. Ibid.

103. Sonia Arrison, "New Anti-Terrorism Law Goes Too Far," *San Diego Union Tribune*, October 31, 2001: B9.

104. *Kyllo v. United States*, 99–8508 (2001).

CHAPTER 17

1. Stephanie Stoughton, "Fighting Terror, Security vs. Discrimination; Fliers See Bias as Pilots Move to Bump Them," *Boston Globe*, November 11, 2001: A1.

2. American Civil Liberties Union of Northern California, "Caught in the Backlash: Arshad Chowdhury, Pittsburgh, Pennsylvania," www.aclunc.org/911/backlash/chowdhury.html, accessed May 20, 2006.

3. Harriet Chiang, "ACLU sues airlines for discrimination after September 11," *San Francisco Chronicle*, June 5, 2002: A16.

4. American Civil Liberties Union of Northern California, "Caught in the Backlash: Arshad Chowdhury, Pittsburgh, Pennsylvania," www.aclunc.org/911/backlash/chowdhury.html, accessed May 20, 2006.

5. Andrew C. McCarthy, "Garden State Variety Profiling Hysteria," National Review Online, www.defenddemocracy.org//in_the_media/in_the_media_show.htm?doc_id=302808, accessed May 20, 2006.

6. Gallup Poll, June 9–30, 2004.

7. Patrick Driscoll, "Air Travelers: Behaviors can get you singled out," *San Antonio Express News*, December 31, 2005: 1B.

8. Driscoll.

9. Terese Loeb Kreuzer, "Now I Lay Me Down to Sleep, in a Pod, at the Airport," *New York Times*, April 12, 2005: C6.

10. Ruth Bader Ginsburg, "Employment of the Constitution to Advance the Equal Status of Men and Women," in *The Constitutional Bases of Political and Social Change in the United States*, ed. Shlomo Slonim (New York: Praeger, 1990), p. 188.

11. Martin Luther King, Jr., "Civil Right No. 1: The Right to Vote," in *A Testament of Hope: The Essential Writings and Speeches of Martin Luther King, Jr.*, ed. James M. Washington (New York: HarperCollins, 1986), p. 188.

12. John Agresto, *The Supreme Court and Constitutional Democracy* (Ithaca, NY: Cornell University Press, 1984), p. 27. Ellipses deleted.

13. Philip Converse, "The Nature of Belief Systems in Mass Publics," in David E. Apter, *Ideology and Discontent* (New York: Free Press, 1964), pp. 206–261.

14. John D. Hicks, *The American Nation* (Cambridge, MA: Riverside Press, 1949), p. 21.

15. Eric Foner, *A Short History of Reconstruction* (New York: Harper, 1990).

16. Eric Foner, *Reconstruction, 1863–1877* (New York: Harper & Row, 1988), pp. 425–444.

17. Ibid, p. 428.

18. Richard M. Valelly, "National Parties and Racial Disfranchisement," in *Classifying by Race*, ed. Paul E. Peterson (Princeton, NJ: Princeton University Press, 1995), pp. 188–216.

19. U.S. Commission on Civil Rights, *Report of the Commission on Civil Rights* (Washington, DC: Government Printing Office, 1959), p. 32. Ellipses deleted.

20. V. O. Key, Jr., *Southern Politics* (New York: Random House, 1949).

21. J. Morgan Kousser, *The Shaping of Southern Politics: Suffrage Restriction and the Establishment of the One-Party South, 1880–1910* (New Haven, CT: Yale University Press, 1974), p. 61.

22. Leon F. Litwack, *Trouble in Mind: Black Southerners in the Age of Jim Crow* (New York: Knopf, 1998), p. 229.

23. *Civil Rights Cases*, 109 U.S. 3 (1883).

24. The majority opinion in the Civil Rights Cases suggested that states could ban discrimination in public accommodations, however, and many did so in the 1880s, especially in the North. See Donald G. Nieman, *Promises to Keep: African Americans and the Constitutional Order, 1776 to the Present* (New York: Oxford University Press, 1991), pp. 103–104.

25. *Plessy v. Ferguson*, 163 U.S. 537 (1896).

26. Ibid.

27. Nieman, p. 110.

28. Edward Banfield and James Q. Wilson, *City Politics* (New York: Vintage Books, 1963); and James Q. Wilson, *Negro Politics* (New York: Free Press, 1960). For caveats, see Steven P. Erie, *Rainbow's End: Irish-Americans and the Dilemmas of Urban Machine Politics, 1840–1985* (Berkeley: University of California Press, 1990).

29. Richard A. Keiser, *Subordination or Empowerment? African American Leadership and the Struggle for Urban Political Power* (New York: Oxford University Press, 1997), p. 27.

30. Harold Gosnell, *Negro Politicians* [1935] (Chicago: University of Chicago Press, 1967); Thomas M. Guterbock, *Machine Politics in Transition* (Chicago: University of Chicago Press, 1980); and Ira Katznelson, *Black Men, White Cities* (Chicago: University of Chicago Press, 1976).

31. Oscar DePriest, also of Chicago, had served three terms in the House from 1929 to 1933. As the only African American in Congress at the time, he was a source of inspiration for many blacks—and a point of controversy for some white politicians. See David S. Day, "Herbert Hoover and Racial Politics: The DePriest Incident," *Journal of Negro History* 65:1 (Winter 1980): 6–17.

32. David McCullough, *Truman* (New York: Simon & Schuster, 1992), pp. 586–590; and Patricia Gurin, Shirley Hatchett, and James S. Jackson, *Hope and Independence: Blacks' Response to Electoral and Party Politics* (New York: Russell Sage, 1989), pp. 36–38.

33. Gerald N. Rosenberg, *The Hollow Hope: Can Courts Bring About Social Change?* (Chicago: University of Chicago Press, 1991), p. 61.

34. Nieman, pp. 139–40.

35. Hugo Black (1937), Felix Frankfurter (1939), William Douglas (1939), Frank Murphy (1940), and Wiley Rutledge (1943). See Nieman, p. 142.

36. *Smith v. Allwright*, 321 U.S. 649 (1944).

37. *Shelley v. Kraemer*, 334 U.S. 1 (1948).

38. *Cumming v. Richmond County Board of Education*, 357 U.S. 528 (1899).

39. *Missouri ex rel. Gaines v. Canada*, 305 U.S. 337 (1938).

40. *Sweatt v. Painter*, 339 U.S. 629 (1950).

41. *Brown v. Board of Education*, 347 U.S. 483 (1954).

42. *Brown v. Board of Education*, 347 U.S. 483 (1954), note 11. The citation of six psychological and sociological studies in this note led Herbert Garfinkel to charge that the Court was making decisions on the basis of sociology, not law. "Social Science Evidence and the School Segregation Cases," *Journal of Politics* 21 (February 1959): 37–59. Kenneth B. Clar, "Effect of Prejudice and Discrimination on Personality Development" (Midcentury White House Conference on Children and Youth 1950, as cited in note 11 to *Brown*).

43. *San Antonio School District v. Rodriguez*, 411 U.S. 1 (1973). Similar reasoning can be found in *Cooper v. Aaron*, 358 U.S. 1 (1958).

44. A. Leon Higginbotham, Jr., *Shades of Freedom: Racial Politics and Presumptions of the American Legal Process* (New York: Oxford University Press, 1996).

45. A. D. Morris, *Origins of the Civil Rights Movement: Black Communities Organizing for Change* (New York: Free Press, 1984).

46. Ibid., pp. 51–63.

47. Martin Luther King, Jr., "Walk for Freedom," in *A Testament of Hope: The Essential Writings and Speeches of Martin Luther King, Jr.*, ed. James M. Washington (New York: HarperCollins, 1986), p. 83.

48. Michael Lipsky, "Protest as a Political Resource," *American Political Science Review* LXII (December 1968): 1144–1158.

49. University of Georgia, Carl Vinson Institute of Government, "Historical Documents Related to Georgia," www.cviog.uga.edu/Projects/gainfo/gahisdoc.htm, accessed April 6, 2000.

50. Rosenberg, *The Hollow Hope*, p. 50.

51. Taylor Branch, *Parting the Waters: America in the King Years 1954–63* (New York: Simon & Schuster, 1988), p. 375.

52. Martin Luther King, Jr., "I Have a Dream," in *A Testament of Hope: The Essential Writings and Speeches of Martin Luther King, Jr.*, ed. James M. Washington (New York: HarperCollins, 1986), p. 219.

53. Gerald D. Jaynes and Robin M. Williams, Jr., eds., *A Common Destiny: Blacks*

and *American Society* (Washington, DC: National Academy Press, 1989), p. 224.

54. Gerald N. Rosenberg, *The Hollow Hope: Can Courts Bring About Social Change?* (Chicago: University of Chicago Press, 1991), Table 2.1, p. 50.

55. Patricia Gurin, Shirley Hatchett, and James S. Jackson, *Hope and Independence: Blacks' Response to Electoral and Party Politics* (New York: Russell Sage, 1989), pp. 42–49.

56. Jaynes and Williams, *A Common Destiny*, p. 233.

57. Joint Center for Political and Economic Studies, *Focus* (Washington, DC: Joint Center for Political and Economic Studies 1993); and David A. Bositis, *Black Elected Officials: A Statistical Summary, 2001* (Washington, DC: Joint Center for Political and Economic Studies, 2003), p. 5.

58. William J. Grimshaw, *Bitter Fruit: Black Politics and the Chicago Machine, 1931–1991* (Chicago: University of Chicago Press, 1992).

59. Gary Orfield, *The Reconstruction of Southern Education: The Schools and the 1964 Civil Rights Act* (New York: Wiley, 1969); Gary Orfield, *Must We Bus?* (Washington, DC, The Brookings Institution, 1978); and Jennifer Hochschild, *The New American Dilemma* (New Haven, CT: Yale University Press, 1984).

60. Taylor Branch, *Pillar of Fire: America in the King Years 1963–65* (New York: Simon & Schuster, 1998), p. 549.

61. Katherine Tate, *From Protest to Politics* (Cambridge, MA: Harvard University Press, 1993), chap. 8; see also Edward G. Carmines and James A. Stimson, *Issue Evolution: Race and the Transformation of American Politics* (Princeton, NJ: Princeton University Press, 1989).

62. *Milliken v. Bradley*, I 418 U.S. 717 (1974); 433 U.S. 267 (1977).

63. *Regents of the University of California v. Bakke*, 438 U.S. 265 (1978).

64. *Grutter v. Bollinger*, No. 02-241 (2003).

65. Ibid.

66. *Gratz v. Bollinger*, No. 02-516 (2003).

67. *Grutter v. Bollinger*, No. 02-241 (2003).

68. Linda Greenhouse, "Justices Back Affirmative Action by 5 to 4, But Wider Vote Bans a Racial Point System," *New York Times*, June 24, 2003: A1.

69. U.S. Bureau of the Census, *Statistical Abstract of the United States, 2006*, Table 696.

70. U.S. Bureau of the Census, *Statistical Abstract of the United States, 2006*, Table 576, 578.

71. U.S. Bureau of the Census, *Statistical*

Abstract of the United States, 2006, Tables 81 and 104.

72. Jennifer L. Hochschild, *Facing Up to the American Dream: Race, Class, and the Soul of the Nation* (Princeton, NJ: Princeton University Press, 1995).

73. Jaynes and Williams, *A Common Destiny*, p. 313.

74. U.S. Bureau of the Census, *Statistical Abstract of the United States, 2006*, Table 214.

75. U.S. Department of Education, National Center for Education Statistics, *Digest of Education Statistics, 2004*, http://nces.ed.gov/programs/digest/d04/index.asp, accessed May 20, 2006, Table 120.

76. United States Bureau of the Census, *Statistical Abstract of the United States, 2006*, Table 693; U.S. Bureau of the Census, Current Population Survey, *Annual Demographic Survey, March Supplement*, 2005, Table POV01.

77. U.S. Census Bureau 2005 Population Estimates, www.census.gov/popest/ estimates.php Table 3, accessed May 20, 2006.

78. Tony Affigne, "Latino Politics in the United States: An Introduction," *PS: Political Science and Politics*, 33:3 (September 2000): 523–527, Table 3.

79. National Election Studies, 2004 data for blacks; for Latinos, figure based on 2005 National Latino Survey, The Latino Coalition, www.thelatinocoalition.com/surveysandpolls.htm accessed May 20, 2006, those who answered "don't vote" excluded from analysis.

80. Tyche Hendricks, "Parade, Enthusiastic Crowd Celebrate Cesar Chavez Day," *San Francisco Chronicle*, April 1, 2001: A18.

81. *Lau v. Nichols*, 414 U.S. 563 (1974).

82. Bernard Grofman, Lisa Handley, and Richard G. Niemi, *Minority Representation and the Quest for Voting Equality* (New York: Cambridge University Press, 1992), pp. 16–25; also see Thomas Weyr, *Hispanic U.S.A.: Breaking the Melting Pot* (New York: Harper, 1959); and Peter Skerry, *Mexican Americans: The Ambivalent Minority* (New York: Free Press, 1993).

83. Daron Shaw, Rodolfo O. de la Garza, and Jongho Lee, "Examining Latino Turnout in 1996: A Three State, Validated Survey Approach," *American Journal of Political Science* 44:2 (April 2000): 332–340.

84. Steven Greenhouse, "About Face; Guess Who's Embracing Immigrants Now?" *New York Times*, March 5, 2000: D4.

85. Matthew Dowd, "Doing the Latin Swing; Latino Voters Are the Soccer Moms of the New Decade," *Weekly Standard*, December 3, 2001: 20.

86. James G. Gimpel, "Q: Is the GOP Outreach to Latinos Likely to Succeed?"

Insight on the News, October 15, 2001, 41.

87. Frank del Olmo, "On the Road to Latino Votes," *Los Angeles Times*, August 19, 2001: M5; Ricardo Alonso-Zaldivar, "Bush Would Open U.S. to Guest Workers," *Los Angeles Times*, January 8, 2004: A1.

88. U.S. Census Bureau 2005 Population Estimates, www.census.gov/popest/estimates.php, Table 3, accessed May 20, 2006; U.S. Bureau of the Census, Statistical Abstract of the United States, 2006, Table 43.

89. Stanley Karnow and Nancy Yoshihara, *Asian Americans in Transition* (New York: Asia Society, 1992).

90. Don Nakanishi, "Beyond Electoral Politics: Renewing a Search for a Paradigm of Asian Pacific American Politics," in *Asian Americans and Politics: Perspectives, Experiences, Prospects*, ed. Gordon H. Chang (Washington, DC: Woodrow Wilson Center Press, 2001), pp. 102–129; and William Schneider, "Asian Americans Will Matter More," *National Journal* (August 14, 1999): 2398.

91. Amit R. Paley, "A Date with Tradition: Chinese New Year Ushers in Quest for Official Holiday Recognition," *Washington Post*, January 29, 2006: C1; Errol Louis, "Strength in Numbers: John Liu galvanizes the city's Asian community to quash bias," *New York Daily News*, May 16, 2006: 31.

92. Robert Goldstein, *Political Repression in Modern America: 1870 to the Present* (New York: Schenkman, 1978), pp. 266–267.

93. *Korematsu v. United States*, 323 U.S. 244 (1944).

94. Nakanishi, p. 121.

95. Angelo Ancheta, *Race, Rights, and the Asian-American Experience* (New Brunswick, NJ: Rutgers University Press, 1997).

96. Timothy Cook, "The Empirical Study of Lesbian, Gay, and Bisexual Politics: Assessing the First Wave of Research," *American Political Science Review* 93:3 (September 1999): 679.

97. Shawn Zeller, "Gay Rites: Giving to Democrats," *National Journal* (May 8, 1999): 1241.

98. Donald P. Haider-Markel, "Creating Change—Holding the Line: Agenda Setting on Lesbian and Gay Issues at the National Level," in *Gays and Lesbians in the Democratic Process: Public Policy, Public Opinion, and Political Representation*, eds. Ellen D. B. Riggle and Barry Tadlock (New York: Columbia University Press, 1999), pp. 242–268.

99. Data from the Gay and Lesbian Victory Fund, www.victoryfund.org, accessed May 20, 2006.

100. Deb Price, "Gays Need Democrats to Win 2000 Elections," *Detroit News*, November 1, 1999: A7; and Human Rights

Campaign, www.hrc.org, accessed May 20, 2006.

101. Dean E. Murphey, "San Francisco Mayor Exults in Move on Gay Marriage," *New York Times*, February 19, 2004: A14.

102. Gregory B. Lewis and Marc Rogers, "Does the Public Support Equal Employment Rights for Gays and Lesbians?" in *Gays and Lesbians in the Democratic Process: Public Policy, Public Opinion, and Political Representation*, eds. Ellen D. B. Riggle and Barry Tadlock (New York: Columbia University Press, 1999), pp. 118–145; Steven H. Haeberle, "Gay and Lesbian Rights: Emerging Trends in Public Opinion and Voting Behavior," in Riggle and Tadlock, eds., *Gays and Lesbians in the Democratic Process*, pp. 145–169; and *Newsweek* Poll February 7, 2004 (Princeton Survey Research Associates, question USPSRNEW.020704, R14A).

103. Human Rights Campaign, www. hrc.org, accessed May 20, 2006.

104. Scott Helman, "Tactics Honed as Debate Nears on Banning Gay Marriage," *Boston Globe*, May 18, 2006: B1.

105. Vine Deloria, Jr., "The Distinctive Status of Indian Rights," in *The Plains Indians of the Twentieth Century*, ed. Peter Iverson (Norman: University of Oklahoma Press, 1985), p. 241.

106. Ibid., pp. 237–248.

107. U.S. Census, *Poverty in the United States: 2000,* Current Population Reports P60-214, September 2001, p. 7, Table B.

108. Toby Harnden, "Choctaws Take Their Slice of the American Pie," *London Daily Telegraph*, September 2, 2000: 15.

109. Deloria, "The Distinctive Status of Indian Rights," p. 237.

110. Agresto, *The Supreme Court and Constitutional Democracy*, pp. 148–149.

111. Theda Skocpol, *Protecting Soldiers and Mothers: The Political Origins of Social Policy in the United States* (Cambridge, MA: Harvard University Press, 1992); and Sara Evans, *Personal Politics: The Roots of Women's Liberation in the Civil Rights Movement and the New Left* (New York: Knopf, 1979).

112. As late as 1975 Gallup polls showed 74 percent favored "a constitutional amendment which would give women equal rights and equal responsibilities." (Gallup Poll, October 18–21, 1975).

113. Nancy McGlen and Karen O'Conner, *Women's Rights: The Struggle for Equality in the Nineteenth and Twentieth Centuries* (New York: Praeger, 1983), chap. 9.

114. Jane J. Mansbridge, *Why We Lost the ERA* (Chicago: University of Chicago Press, 1986).

115. Ruth B. Mandel, "The Political Woman," in *American Women in the Nineties: Today's Critical Issues*, ed. Sherri Matteo (Boston: Northeastern University Press, 1993), pp. 34–65.

116. *Hoyt v. Florida*, 368 U.S. 57 (1961).

117. *Craig v. Boren*, 429 U.S. 190 (1976).

118. Ginsburg, *Employment of the Constitution*, p. 191.

119. Mary Delach Leonard, "Should Women be in Combat?" *St. Louis Post Dispatch*, July 10, 2005: A1.

120. *Rostker v. Goldberg*, 453 U.S. 65 (1981).

121. Mansbridge, *Why We Lost the ERA*, chap. 7; Gallup Poll cited in Leonard.

122. *Watson v. Fort Worth Bank & Trust*, 487 U.S. 997–999; *New York City Transit Authority v. Beazer*, 440 U.S. at 587, no. 31; and *Griggs v. Duke Power*, 401 U.S. at 432.

123. *Wards Cove v. Antonio*, 490 U.S. 642 (1989).

124. *Meritor Savings Bank v. Vinson*, 477 U.S. 57 (1986).

125. Catherine S. Manegold, "Women Advance in Politics by Evolution, Not Revolution," *New York Times*, October 21, 1992: A1.

126. *Harris v. Forklift Systems*, 510 U.S. 77 (1993).

127. "Hillary's Class," *Frontline* (PBS television broadcast, No. 15, 1994), as cited in Karla Cooper-Boggs, "The Link Between Private and Public Single-Sex Colleges: Will Wellesley Stand or Fall with the Citadel?," *Indiana Law Review* 29 (1995): 137.

128. Cooper-Boggs, "The Link Between Private and Public Single-Sex Colleges," p. 135.

129. "Bush Aims to Ease Coeducation Rules for Public Schools," *Los Angeles Times*, March 4, 2004: A9.

130. *United States v. Virginia*, 116 S Ct. 2264 (1966).

131. United States General Accounting Office, *Women in Management: Analysis of Selected Data from the Current Population Survey*, GAO-02-156 (September 2001).

132. Robin Toner, "Welfare Chief Is Hoping to Promote Marriage," *New York Times*, February 19, 2002: A1.

133. White House Office, "Fulfilling America's Promise to Americans with Disabilities," www.whitehouse.gov/news/freedominitiative/freedominitiative.html, accessed May 20, 2006.

134. Laura Trupin, Dorothy P. Rice, and Wendy Max, *Medical Expenditures for People with Disabilities in the United States, 1987* (Washington, DC: U.S. Department of Education, National Institute on Disability and Rehabilitation Research, 1995), Table G (figures updated for 1993 and adjusted for inflation to 2002 dollars).

135. Robert A. Katzman, *Institutional Disability: The Saga of Transportation Policy for the Disabled* (Washington, DC: The Brookings Institution, 1986).

136. Frederick J. Weintraub, ed., *Public Policy and the Education of Exceptional Children* (Washington, DC: Council for Exceptional Children, 1976).

137. Paul E. Peterson, "Background Paper," in Twentieth Century Fund, *Making the Grade: Report of the Twentieth Century Fund Task Force on Federal Elementary and Secondary Education Policy* (New York: Twentieth Century Fund, 1983), chap. 5.

138. Linda Greenhouse, "Justices Hear an Argument for Not Hiring the Disabled," *New York Times*, February 28, 2002: A22.

139. *Alabama v. Garrett*, 99–1240 (2001).

140. *Toyota Motor Manufacturing, Kentucky, Inc. v. Williams*, 00-1089 (2002).

141. Gerry Dulac, "Happy for Martin, Unhappy with Ruling," *Pittsburgh Post-Gazette*, May 30, 2001: A8.

142. Rufus Browning, Dale Rogers Marshall, and David H. Tabb, *Protest Is Not Enough: The Struggle of Blacks and Hispanics for Equality in Urban Politics* (Berkeley: University of California Press, 1984).

CHAPTER 18

1. Jonathan Weisman, "Deficit Projections Soar with Bush Stimulus Plan; Economists Say a Record Shortfall is Likely," *Washington Post*, January 10, 2003: A1.

2. "President Delivers 'State of the Union'" (The White House: Washington DC, January 28, 2003), www.whitehouse .gov/news/releases/2003/01/20030128-19.html, accessed March 30, 2004.

3. Dan Freedman, "Bush Drug Plan Blasted; Groups Say Changes Would Gut Medicare," *Milwaukee Journal Sentinel*, January 30, 2003: 2A.

4. Carolyn Lochhead, "Medicare Bill Gives GOP Win on Dems' Turf," *San Francisco Chronicle*, November 26, 2003: A4.

5. Robert J. McCarthy, "Clinton Calls for Changes in Drug Plan," *Buffalo News*, January 23, 2006: B1; Robert Pear, "In Medicare Debate, Massaging the Facts," *New York Times*, May 23, 2006: A4.

6. Vicki Kemper, "Secrecy Probed in Medicare Plan Cost Estimates," *Los Angeles Times*, March 20, 2004: p. A24; Joseph Antos, "Medicare and the Prescription Drug Benefit: Increased Pressure for Reform," Testimony before the United States Senate, Committee on Homeland Security and Governmental

Affairs, Subcommittee on Federal Financial Management, Government Information, and International Security, September 22, 2005.

7. John Kingdon, *Agenda, Alternatives and Public Policies* (Boston: Little, Brown, 1984); and Paul Light, *The President's Agenda* (Baltimore, MD: Johns Hopkins University Press, 1991).

8. Arthur Maass, *Congress and the Common Good* (New York: Basic Books, 1983).

9. Eugene Bardach, *The Implementation Game,* 4th ed. (Cambridge, MA: M.I.T. Press, 1982); and Jeffrey L. Pressman and Aaron Wildavsky, *Implementation,* 3rd ed. (Berkeley: University of California Press, 1984).

10. Thomas R. Dye, *Politics, Economics and the Public: Policy Outcomes in the American States* (Chicago: Rand McNally, 1966).

11. U.S. Department of Health and Human Services, Office of Family Assistance, "TANF Recipients —Through September 2005, As of March 7, 2006," www.acf.dhhs.gov/programs/ofa/caseload/2005/4qrtrecipients.htm, accessed May 25, 2006; U. S. Department of Health and Human Services, Office of Family Assistance, "Temporary Assistance for Needy Families (TANF), Percent of Total Population 1960–1999" www.acf.dhhs.gov/news/stats/6097rf.htm, accessed May 25, 2006.

12. Ibid.

13. Jonathan Weisman, "Budget Cuts Pass by a Slim Margin; Poor, Elderly, and Students to Feel the Pinch," *Washington Post,* February 2, 2006: A1.

14. Lee Rainwater and Timothy M. Smeeding, "Doing Poorly: The Real Income of American Children in a Comparative Perspective," Maxwell School of Citizenship and Public Affairs, Syracuse University, Syracuse, NY, August 1995, Working Paper No. 127; and United Nations Children's Fund (UNICEF), "Child Poverty in Rich Countries 2005" *Innocenti Report Card No. 6,* UNICEF Innocenti Research Centre, Florence, Italy, 2005.

15. Neil Howe and Richard Jackson, *Entitlements and the Aging of America* (Washington, DC; National Taxpayers Union Foundation, 2001).

16. United States Bureau of the Census, International Data Base, www.census.gov/ipc/www/idbnew.html, accessed May 26, 2006, Table 10; CIA World Factbook 2006, www.cia.gov/cia/publications/factbook/index.html, accessed May 26, 2006. Infant mortality data are from 2006; GDP data from 2005.

17. Ibid., Chart 4-27, comment.

18. Congressional Budget Office, *Federal Spending on the Elderly and Children,* Summer 2000 (Washington, DC: U.S. Government Printing Office), p. 2; Isabel Sawhill, Senior Fellow and Director, Economic Studies, The Brookings Institution, "Domestic Entitlements and the Federal Budget," Testimony Before the Committee on the Budget, United States House of Representatives, February 15, 2006, Figure 3.

19. Thomas A. Bailey, *The American Pageant: A History of the Republic* (Boston: D.C. Heath, 1956), p. 840. See also Daniel J.B. Mitchell, "Townsend and Roosevelt: Lessons from the Struggle for Elderly Income Support," *Labor History,* 42:3 (August 2001), pp. 255–276. The figure is in 2005 dollars—the amount was $200 in 1934dollars.

20. Martha Derthick, *Policymaking for Social Security* (Washington, DC: The Brookings Institution, 1979); and Theda Skocpol, *Protecting Soldiers and Mothers: The Politics of Social Provision in the United States* (Cambridge, MA: Harvard University Press, 1993).

21. "Life Expectancy for Social Security," Social Security Administration, www.ssa.gov/history/lifeexpect.html, accessed May 26, 2006; U.S. Department of Health and Human Services, National Center for Health Statistics, *Health, United States, 2005, With Chartbook on Trends in the Health of Americans,* National Center for Health Statistics, 2005, Table 27.

22. R. Kent Weaver, *Automatic Government: The Politics of Indexation* (Washington, DC: The Brookings Institution, 1988).

23. Orlo Nichols, Michael Clingman, and Alice Wade, *Internal Real Rates of Return Under the OASDI Program for Hypothetical Workers,* Social Security Administration, Office of the Chief Actuary (Baltimore, MD: March 2005) Table 1.

24. *Boston Globe,* December 27, 1994: 70.

25. As quoted in Chuck Henning, *Wit and Wisdom of Politics,* expanded ed. (Golden, CO: Fulcrum, 1992), p. 252.

26. *Strengthening Social Security and Creating Personal Wealth for All Americans,* Report of the President's Commission on Social Security, December 21, 2001, p. 8.

27. As quoted in Henning, *Wit and Wisdom of Politics,* p. 95.

28. Larry Lipman, "Social Security Overhaul Fizzles," *Atlanta Journal-Constitution,* January 15, 2006: 1B.

29. *Budget of the United States Government, Fiscal Year 2007, Historical Tables* (Washington, DC: Office of Management and Budget, 2006), Table 16.1, p. 317 (figures in constant 2005 dollars).

30. U.S. Bureau of the Census, *Voting and Registration in the Election of November 2000,* February 2002, Table C, p. 12; U.S. Bureau of the Census, *Voting and Registration in the Election of November 2004,* March 2006, Table B, p. 4.

31. U.S. Bureau of the Census, *Voting and Registration in the Election of November 2000,* February 2002, Table B, p. 6.

32. Susan A. MacManus, with Patricia A. Turner, *Young v. Old: Generational Combat in the 21st Century* (Boulder, CO: Westview, 1996), pp. 60, 141.

33. *AARP Annual Report,* 2002, p. 5.

34. Employment and volunteer figures: "AARP: Making the Most of Life After 50," www.aarp.org/leadership/Articles/a2003-01-13-aarphistory.html, accessed March 30, 2004; Expenditure figures: AARP Annual Report, 2004, p. 27.

35. Robert Rector, *Welfare Reform* (Washington, DC: Heritage Foundation, 1996).

36. Michael Lipsky, *Street Level Bureaucracy* (New York: Russell Sage Foundation, 1980); and Theda Skocpol, "Targeting within Universalism: Politically Viable Policies to Combat Poverty in the United States," in *The Urban Underclass,* ed. Christopher Jencks and Paul E. Peterson (Washington, DC: The Brookings Institution, 1991), pp. 411–436.

37. Mark Nord, Margaret Andrews, and Steven Carlson, *Household Food Security in the United States, 2004,* (Washington, DC: United States Department of Agriculture, Economic Research Service, October 2005), p. 28 (2004 figure in 2005 dollars).

38. Internal Revenue Service, "2005 1040A Instructions," Earned Income Credit (EIC) Table, pp. 52–58.

39. *SSI Annual Statistical Report, 2004* (Washington, DC: Social Security Administration, September 2005), p. i.

40. This program is now known as the Housing Choice Voucher Program; see www.hud.gov.

41. Office of Management and Budget, "Budget for Fiscal Year 2007, Historical Tables," Table 16.1, p. 317 (both figures in 2005 dollars).

42. Percentage of monies going for services to the elderly in fiscal year 1993. Marilyn Werber Serafini, "Pinching Pennies," *National Journal* 27:37 (September 16, 1995): 2273. Also see Mark Rom, "Health and Welfare in the American States," in *Politics in the American States,* 6th ed., eds. Virginia Gray and Herbert Jacob (Washington, DC: CQ Press, 1995).

43. Paul E. Peterson, "An Immodest Proposal," *Daedalus* 121 (Fall 1992): 151–174.

44. U.S. House of Representatives, Committee on Ways and Means, *Overview of*

Entitlement Programs: Background Material and Data on Programs Within the Jurisdiction of the Committee on Ways and Means (otherwise known as the 2004 Green Book) (Washington, DC: U.S. Government Printing Office, 2004), Table I-5, p. I-9. All subsequent references to this document in this chapter will be simply to the Green Book. They refer to the 2004 edition.

45. Green Book, Table I-5, p. I-9.

46. *Changes in Participation in Means-Tested Programs* (Washington, DC: Congressional Budget Office, April 20, 2005), p. 6.

47. Joe Garofoli, "Food Stamp Hurdles; For Many, the Hassle Outweighs the Benefits," *San Francisco Chronicle*, February 8, 2002: A21.

48. U.S. Department of Health and Human Services, Office of Family Assistance, *Temporary Assistance for Needy Families (TANF), Sixth Annual Report to Congress*, November 2004, Table C, p. I-11.

49. Gene Falk, "Temporary Assistance for Needy Families (TANF): Its Role in Response to the Effects of Hurricane Katrina," CRS Report for Congress, September 16, 2005.

50. Paul E. Peterson and Mark Rom, *Welfare Magnets: A New Case for a National Standard* (Washington, DC: The Brookings Institution, 1990).

51. Rules vary widely by state. See U.S. Department of Health and Human Services, Office of Family Assistance, *Temporary Assistance to Needy Families, Sixth Annual Report to Congress*, November 2004, Table 12:6, pp. XII-12 and XII-13.

52. Ibid., Table 12:5, pp. XII-9, XII-10, & XII-11.

53. Testimony of Mark H. Greenberg, senior staff attorney, Center for Law and Social Policy, Human Resources Subcommittee, House Committee on Ways and Means, March 7, 2002.

54. "Social Security Penalty on Earnings Is Repealed," *Los Angeles Times*, April 8, 2000: A14.

55. Skocpol, *Protecting Soldiers and Mothers*.

56. Mary Jo Bane and Lawrence M. Mead, *Lifting Up the Poor: A Dialogue on Religion, Poverty, and Welfare Reform* (Washington, DC: Brookings Institution Press, 2003), p. 67.

57. *Statistical Abstract of the United States, 2006*, Table 53.

58. Poverty rate for married couple households: 5.4 percent; for female-headed households: 28 percent. *Statistical Abstract of the United States, 2006*, Table 699.

59. *Statistical Abstract of the United States, 2006*, Table 1319.

60. William J. Wilson, *The Truly*

Disadvantaged: The Inner City, the Underclass, and Public Policy (Chicago: University of Chicago Press, 1987).

61. U.S. Bureau of the Census, *Current Population Survey, 2000,* Historical Tables, Table A-3; U.S. Census Bureau, "Educational Attainment in the United States: 2004, Detailed Tables" (PPL-169), www.census.gov/population/www/socdemo/education/cps2004.html, accessed May 31, 2006, Table 8.

62. 2004 IRS Form 990, available via www.guidestar.org, accessed June 1, 2006.

63. Associations Unlimited, 2002.

64. Henry J. Kaiser Family Survey, October, 2005; NBS News/*Wall Street Journal* Poll, April 28, 1995.

65. "About FRC" www.frc.org/get.cfm?c=HISTORY_ABOUT, accessed June 8, 2006.

66. Jeff Shear, "The Credit Card," *National Journal* 27:32 (August 12, 1995): 2056–2058; and Marilyn W. Serafini, "Turning Up the Heat," *National Journal* 27:32 (August 12, 1995): 2051–2055.

67. Paul E. Peterson, "Background Paper," in Twentieth Century Fund Task Force on Federal Elementary and Secondary Education Policy, *Making the Grade* (New York: Twentieth Century Fund, 1983); and *Digest of Education Statistics, 2000*, National Center for Education Statistics, March 2000, Table 158.

68. "Land Ordinance of 1785," in *Documents of American History*, 6th ed., ed. Henry S. Commager (New York: Appleton-Century-Crofts, 1958), p. 124.

69. Charles L. Glenn, Jr., *The Myth of the Common School* (Amherst: University of Massachusetts Press, 1987); Diane Ravitch, *The Great School Wars: New York City, 1805–1973* (New York: Basic Books, 1974); David Tyack and Elizabeth Hansot, *Managers of Virtue: Public School Leadership in America, 1820–1980* (New York: Basic Books, 1982); and Paul E. Peterson, *The Politics of School Reform, 1870–1940* (Chicago: University of Chicago Press, 1985).

70. Caroline Hoxby, "What Has Changed and What Has Not," in Paul E. Peterson, Ed. *Our Schools and Our Future* (Stanford, CA: Hoover Institution Press, 2003), pp. 101–102.

71. Author's calculation, based on *Digest of Education Statistics, 2000*, National Center for Education Statistics, March 2000, Table 75; and *Statistical Abstract of the United States, 2001*, Table 647. Average teacher salaries compared with national per capita personal income, 1970–1999.

72. Eric A Hanushek, "School Resources and Student Performance," in *Does*

Money Matter? The Effect of School Resources on Student Achievement and Adult Success, ed. Gary Burtless (Washington, DC: The Brookings Institution, 1996), pp. 43–73.

73. The Gallup Organization, Roper Center for Public Opinion Research Database, Question ID Numbers USGALLUP. 870.Q005A; USGALLUP. 99JNE25R11E, USGALLUP.03JNE09, R02H.

74. David K. Kirkpatrick, *Choice in Schooling: A Case for Tuition Vouchers* (Chicago: Loyola University Press, 1990); and Terry Moe, ed., *Private Vouchers* (Stanford, CA: Hoover Institution Press, 1995).

75. William H. Clune and John F. Witte, eds., *Choice and Control in American Education*, vols. I and II (New York: Falmer Pres, 1990); and Henig, *Rethinking School Choice*.

76. Diane Ravitch, *National Standards in American Education: A Citizen's Guide* (Washington, DC: The Brookings Institution, 1995).

77. John Kerry, "Education Trust Fund," Remarks at Thomas Jefferson High School, Council Bluffs, IA, November 25, 2003, www.johnkerry.com, accessed March 31, 2004.

78. Peter W. Cookson, Jr., *School Choice: The Struggle for the Soul of American Education* (New Haven, CT: Yale University Press, 1994); Carnegie Foundation for the Advancement of Teaching, *School Choice* (Princeton, NJ: Carnegie Foundation, 1992); Larry V. Hedges and Rob Greenwald, "Have Times Changed? The Relation Between School Resources and Student Performances," in *Does Money Matter? The Effect of School Resources on Student Achievement and Adult Success*, ed. Gary Burtless (Washington, DC: The Brookings Institution, 1996), pp. 74–92; Amy Gutmann, *Democratic Education* (Princeton, NJ: Princeton University Press, 1987); and Jeffrey Henig, *Rethinking School Choice: Limits of the Market Metaphor* (Princeton, NJ: Princeton University Press, 1994).

79. *Statistical Abstract of the United States, 2001*, Tables 119 and 640.

80. U.S. Department of Education, National Center for Education Statistics, *Digest of Education Statistics, 2000*, May 2001, Tables 158, p. 175; 412, p. 469; and *Statistical Abstract of the United States, 2001*, Table 640.

81. James Peyser and Robert Costrell, "Exploring the Costs of Accountability: Claims That The No Child Left Behind Act Represents An Unfunded Mandate Wilt Under Close Scrutiny," *Education Next* (Spring 2004): 22–29; Paul E. Peterson and Martin R. West, "The Contentious 'No Child' Law II: Money Has *Not* Been Left Behind," *Education Week*, March 17, 2004, www.edweek.org,

accessed April 10, 2004; Paul E. Peterson and Martin R. West, *No Child Left Behind? The Politics and Practice of School Accountability* (Washington, DC: Brookings Institution Press, 2003).

82. Eric A. Hanushek, "The Economics of Schooling: Production and Efficiency in Public Schools," *Journal of Economic Literature* 24 (September 1986): 1141–1177.

83. Sandra Blakeslee, "Expert Warned that Mad Cow Was Imminent," *New York Times*, December 25, 2003: A1.

84. Joe Ruff, "Mad Cow's Rarity Could Cut Testing," *Omaha World-Herald*, April 29, 2006, 1A.

85. Denise Grady, "U.S. Issues Safety Rules to Protect Food From Mad Cow Disease," *New York Times*, December 31, 2003: A1.

86. Craig Petersen, *Business and Government*, 2nd ed. (New York: Harper & Row, 1985), p. 173.

87. *Heart of Atlanta Motel v. United States*, 322 U.S. 533 (1964); and *United States v. South-Eastern Underwriters Association*, 322 U.S. 533 (1944).

88. Jonathan Krim, "Judge Accepts Settlement in Microsoft Case," *Washington Post*, November 2, 2002: A1; Jim Puzzanghera, "Keeping Software Giant on Watch," *Los Angeles Times*, May 13, 2006: C1.

89. Gregg Easterbrook, *A Moment on the Earth: The Coming Age of Environmental Optimism* (New York: Penguin, 1995), p. xv. For a more pessimistic view, see Paul R. Ehrlich and Anne H. Ehrlich, *Betrayal of Science and Reason: How Anti-Environmental Rhetoric Threatens Our Future* (Washington, DC: Island Press, 1996).

90. Murray Weidenbaum, "Government Power and Business Performance," in *The United States in the 1980s*, eds. Peter Duignan and Alvin Rabushka (Stanford, CA: Hoover Institution Press, 1990), pp. 197–220.

91. Douglas Jehl, "National Parks Will Ban Recreation Snowmobiling; A Further Curb on the Use of Public Lands," *New York Times*, April 27, 2000: A14.

92. T. R. Reid, "For Snowmobiles, An Uncertain Fate," *Washington Post*, March 15, 2004: A23.

93. Ibid.

94. Jim Robbins, "Gone! Snowmobile Herds and Tourists," *New York Times*, February 28, 2006: A3.

95. Clair Wilcox, *Public Policies Toward Business*, 4th ed. (Homewood, IL: Irwin, 1971), p. 589.

96. Marc K. Landy, Marc J. Roberts, and Stephen R. Thomas, *The Environmental Protection Agency: Asking the Wrong Questions from Nixon to Clinton*, expanded ed. (New York: Oxford University Press, 1994).

97. Ibid.

98. Ibid., p. 290.

99. Kenneth Meier, *Regulation: Politics, Bureaucracy, and Economics* (New York: St. Martin's, 1985).

100. Charles Seabrook, "Eagle Delisting a Bit Premature?," *Atlanta Journal-Constitution*, February 26, 2006: 7MS.

101. Martha Derthick and Paul Quirk, *The Politics of Deregulation* (Washington, DC: The Brookings Institution, 1985); and Mark C. Rom, *Public Spirit in the Thrift Tragedy* (Pittsburgh, PA: University of Pittsburgh Press, 1996).

102. Hardaway, "Transportation Deregulation," p. 143. Another view is given by Paul Dempsey, "The State of the Airline, Airport and Aviation Industries," *Transportation Law Journal* 129 (1992): 130–200.

103. David Monk, "The Lessons of Airline Regulation and Deregulation: Will We Make the Same Mistakes in Space?" *Journal of Air Law and Commerce* 57:3 (Spring 1992): 715–753.

104. See, for example, Dennis Carlton and William Landes, "Benefits and Costs of Airline Mergers: A Case Study," *Bell Journal of Economics and Management Science* 65:11 (1982): 65–83.

105. Kelly Yamanouchi, "Deregulator Eyes Airlines' Evolution," *Denver Post*, February 18, 2006: C1.

CHAPTER 19

1. United States Bureau of the Census, *Statistical Abstract of the United States, 2001*, Table 643; and *Statistical Abstract of the United States, 1999*, Table 1434.

2. United States Bureau of the Census, *Statistical Abstract of the United States, 1999*, Table 1430; and "Hot Jobs Market Fuels Consumer Confidence," *Los Angeles Times*, May 31, 2000: C1.

3. United States Bureau of the Census, *Statistical Abstract of the United States, 1999*, Table 1436.

4. Anne E. Kornblut and Sue Kirchhoff, "It Could Be Worse . . . But as Economy Stumbles and Voters Lose Confidence, the Bush Administration Could Be in Political Peril—Making Republicans Worry and Giving Democrats an Opportunity," *Boston Globe*, July 8, 2001: E1.

5. Frank Bruni, "Bush Says Rebate Isn't a Substitute for His Tax Plan," *New York Times*, March 28, 2001: A1.

6. Byron York, "Bush by the (Poll) Numbers: How Does He Stand, and What's He Doing?" *National Review*, August 6, 2001, 15.

7. See, for example: Pew Research Center Survey, January 4–8, 2006.

8. Michael Evans, "What Happened to the Recovery?" *Industry Week*, June 2002, 88.

9. Authors' calculations based on the Standard & Poor's 500 composite index. For historical data on this index, see U.S. Census Bureau, *Statistical Abstract of the United States: 1999*, Table 1436, p. 883.

10. "U.S. Theatrical Market: 2005 Statistics," Motion Picture Association Worldwide Market Research, 2006, p. 25.

11. P. J. Huffstutter, "Buyout Feels to Them Like Being Sold Out," *Los Angeles Times*, March 23, 2006: A23.

12. A. W. Phillips, "The Relationship Between Unemployment and the Rate of Change of Money Wage Rates in the United Kingdom 1862–1957," *Economica* 25 (1958): 283–299.

13. Morris Fiorina, "Elections and Economics in the 1980s," in *Politics and Economics in the 1980s*, ed. Alberto Alesina and Geoffrey Carliner (Chicago: University of Chicago Press, 1991), pp. 17–38.

14. John Mueller, *Wars, Presidents, and Public Opinion* (New York: Wiley, 1973); and Douglas Hibbs, *The American Political Economy* (Cambridge, MA: Harvard University Press, 1987), chap. 5.

15. For a summary of the relevant literature, see Fiorina, "Elections and Economics in the 1980s."

16. Morris Fiorina, *Retrospective Voting in American National Elections* (New Haven, CT: Yale University Press, 1981), pp. 164–167.

17. Office of Management and Budget, *Budget of the United States Government, Fiscal Year 2007*, Historical Tables, Table 1.4 (Washington, DC: Office of Management and Budget, 2006); U.S. Department of Commerce, Bureau of Economic Analysis, National Income and Product Accounts, www.bea.gov/bea/dn1.htm, accessed June 12, 2006.

18. Office of Management and Budget, *Budget of the United States Government, Fiscal Year 2007*, Historical Tables (Washington, DC: Office of Management and Budget, 2006), Tables 8.1, 8.4 and 8.5.

19. Paul Peretz, *The Political Economy of Inflation in the United States* (Chicago: University of Chicago, Press, 1983), p. 42.

20. Ibid.

21. "The Genie in the Wings," *The Economist*, June 8, 2002.

22. George W. Bush, State of The Union Address, January 28, 2003, www.whitehouse.gov/news/releases/2003/01/20030128-19.html, accessed April 1, 2004.

23. Paul Krugman, *Peddling Prosperity* (New York: Norton, 1994), chaps. 3 and 6.

24. M. Kathryn Eickhoff, Office of Management and Budget, quoted in Peter T. Kilborn, "A $2 Trillion National Debt: Not Just Another Milestone," *New York Times*, September 15, 1985: 1.

25. Office of Management and Budget, *Budget of the United States Government, Fiscal Year 2007*, Historical Tables, Table 1.1, p. 22.

26. Gallup-CNN-*USA Today* Poll, May 30, 2002, question ID USGALLUP. G02MY28, R07J.

27. Louis Uchitelle, "Ideas and Trends: The Bondholders Are Winning: Why America Won't Boom," *New York Times*, June 12, 1994: D4.

28. For a general discussion, see Steven Sheffrin, *Rational Expectations* (London: Cambridge University Press, 1983).

29. Joseph H. Carter, *Never Met a Man I Didn't Like: The Life and Writings of Will Rogers* (New York: Avon Books, 1991), p. 250.

30. Jennifer Hughes, "Fed Chief Regrets 'Lapse in Judgment' at Dinner," *Financial Times*, May 24, 2006: 10.

31. *Annual Report: Budget Review, 2006* (Washington, DC: Board of Governors of the Federal Reserve System, 2006), p. 1.

32. *88th Annual Report* (Washington, DC: Board of Governors of the Federal Reserve System, 2001), p. 383.

33. William Greider, *Secrets of the Temple: How the Federal Reserve Runs the Country* (New York: Simon & Schuster, 1987).

34. Schrage, Michael, "It's Time to Put a Transaction Tax on Credit Card Purchases," *Washington Post*, October 17, 1990: F3.

35. John Wooley, *Monetary Politics: The Federal Reserve and the Politics of Monetary Policy* (New York: Cambridge University Press, 1984).

36. Alberto Alesina, "Macroeconomics and Politics," in *NBER Macroeconomics Annual, 1988*, ed. Stanley Fischer (Cambridge, MA: MIT Press, 1988), pp. 13–52.

37. Douglas Hibbs, "The Dynamics of Political Support for American Presidents Among Occupational and Partisan Groups," *American Journal of Political Science* 26 (1982): 312–332.

38. Douglas Hibbs, "The Partisan Model of Macroeconomic Cycles: More Theory and Evidence for the United States," *Economics and Politics* 6 (1994): 1–23.

39. Edward Tufte, *Political Control of the Economy* (Princeton, NJ: Princeton University Press, 1978), chap. 2.

40. James Harding, "America's Battleground: Insecurity over Jobs Fuels Voters' Passions in the Election's Crucial Swing States," *Financial Times*, March 11, 2004: 19.

41. America Votes, 2004: U.S. President, National Exit Poll, www.cnn.com/ELECTION/2004/pages/results/states/US/P/00/epolls.0.html, accessed June 13, 2006.

42. GDP grew slightly more than 3 percent in nonelection years, and slightly more than 4 percent in presidential election years from 1960 to 2001. Analysis by authors of data from U.S. Department of Commerce, Bureau of Economic Analysis, National Accounts Data.

43. Donald Kettl, *Leadership at the Fed* (New Haven, CT: Yale University Press, 1986).

44. "Steady Greenspan; Clinton Plays It Safe on Choice of Fed Chief," *San Diego Union-Tribune*, February 26, 1996: B4.

45. David Bradford, *Untangling the Income Tax* (Cambridge, MA: Harvard University Press, 1986).

46. Calculated by the authors from U.S. Bureau of the Census, *Statistical Abstract of the United States, 1999*, Tables 1434 and 1443.

47. Daniel J. Parks with Bill Swindell, "Tax Debate Assured a Long Life As Bush, GOP Press for New Cuts," *CQ Weekly*, June 2, 2001, 1308–1309.

48. Richard W. Stevenson, "Republicans Can't Match Bush's Plan for Tax Cuts," *New York Times*, March 16, 2000: A18. www.johnkerry.com/issues/economy/index.html, accessed April 1, 2004.

49. Figures on tax expenditures for this and the following tax preferences are drawn from the *Budget of the United States Government, Fiscal Year 2007* (Washington, DC: Office of Management and Budget, 2006), Analytical Perspectives, Table 19-1. College tuition tax credit figures include the Lifetime Learning Tax Credit, the HOPE Tax Credit, exclusion of scholarship and fellowship income, deductibility of student loan interest, deduction for higher education expenses, state prepaid tuition plans, and exclusion of interest on student loan bonds. Charitable contribution figures include charitable contributions to educational and health institutions. Figures are estimates for 2005.

50. William C. Mitchell and Michael Munger, "Economic Models of Interest Groups: An Introductory Survey," *American Journal of Political Science* 35:2 (May 1991): 512–546.

51. Howard Schuman, *Politics and the Budget*, 3rd ed. (Englewood Cliffs, NJ: Prentice-Hall, 1992), p. 121.

52. Democratic National Committee, "Bush Tax Bill Leaves the Middle Class Behind," www.dnc.org/a/2006/05/bush_tax_bill_l.php, May 18, 2006, accessed June 13, 2006.

53. Larry Bartels, "Homer Gets a Tax Cut: Inequality and Public Policy in the American Mind," *Perspectives on Politics* 3:1 (March 2005): 15–31.

54. The specific statistic in the text is for a family of four with median income. Reductions were similar for both higher- and lower-income families. C. Eugene Searle, *The Tax Decade* (Washington, DC: Urban Institute Press, 1985).

55. The intellectual basis of such proposals is usually credited to Robert Hall and Alvin Rabushka, *The Flat Tax* (Stanford, CA: Hoover Institution Press, 1985).

56. Internal Revenue Service, "Taxpayers Receiving Assistance, Paid and Unpaid, Specified Tax Years 1990–2004," *SOI Bulletin*, Winter 2005–2006, Table 1 and Table 26.

57. J. Scott Moody, Wendy P. Warcholik, and Scott Hodge, "The Cost of Tax Compliance" (Washington, DC: Tax Foundation, December 2005).

58. *Central Government Debt: Statistical Yearbook 1994–2003, 2005 Edition*, Paris, France: Organisation for Economic Cooperation and Development, 2005; U.S. Bureau of the Census, *Statistical Abstract of the United States, 1999*, Table 1372.

59. *Comparative Civilian Labor Force Statistics, 10 Countries, 1960–2005*, United States (Washington, DC: Department of Labor, Bureau of Labor Statistics, April 5, 2006), Table B.

60. "Judgement Day," *The Economist*, February 18, 1995, 49–51.

61. Study by the McKinsey Global Institute summarized in "How Regulation Kills New Jobs," *The Economist*, November 19, 1994, 78; "Economy Producing Mostly Bad Jobs? Not So Fast," Annenberg Political Fact Check, Annenberg Public Policy Center, University of Pennsylvania, July 9, 2004, www.factcheck.org, accessed August 25, 2004.

62. *Statistical Abstract of the United States, 2006*, Table 608.

63. U.S. Bureau of the Census, *Statistical Abstract of the United States, 1999*, Tables 1432 and 1442.

64. *Statistical Abstract of the United States, 2006*, Table 606.

65. *Digital Economy 2002* (Washington, DC: U.S. Department of Commerce, Economics and Statistics Administration, June 2002), Figure 2.8; World Telecommunication Indicators Database, (Geneva, Switzerland: International Telecommunications Union, 2006), www.itu.int/ITU-D/ict/publications/world/world.html, accessed June 13, 2006.

66. Arthur S. Alderson, Jason Beckfield, and Francois Nielson, "Exactly How Has Income Inequality Changed? Patterns of

Distributional Change in Core Societies," Luxembourg Income Study, Working Paper No. 422, May 2005; United States Bureau of the Census, Historical Income Tables – Income Inequality, www.census.gov/hhes/income/histinc/ie6.html, accessed June 13, 2006.

67. For a critical survey, see Krugman, *Peddling Prosperity*, chap. 5.

CHAPTER 20

1. James M. Lindsay, quoted in John Donnelly, "Campaign 2000: The Issues; Foreign Policy is Pushed onto Center Stage," *Boston Globe*, October 7, 2000: A6.

2. Joseph Cirincione, quoted in Steve Goldstein, "Campaigns Drop Foreign Policy Issues; Bush, Gore put Focus on Topics at Home," *Milwaukee Journal-Sentinel*, October 8, 2000: 23A.

3. Goldstein, p. 23A.

4. *National Security Strategy of the United States of America* (Washington, DC: The White House, September 2002), p. 6.

5. Ivo H. Daalder and James M. Lindsay, *America Unbound: The Bush Revolution in Foreign Policy* (Washington, DC: Brookings Institution Press, 2003).

6. Aaron Wildavsky, "The Two Presidencies," in Steven A. Shull, *The Two Presidencies: A Quarter Century Assessment* (Chicago: Nelson Hall, 1991 [1965]), pp. 11–25.

7. Alexander Hamilton, *The Federalist Papers, No. 70* (Baltimore, MD: Johns Hopkins University Press, 1981), p. 199.

8. Chuck Henning, *The Wit and Wisdom of Politics: Expanded Edition* (Golden, CO: Fulcrum, 1992), p. 56.

9. Wildavksy, "The Two Presidencies," p. 15.

10. John E. Mueller, *War, Presidents and Public Opinion* (New York: Wiley, 1973); and Gary King and Lyn Ragsdale, *The Elusive Executive: Discovering Statistical Patterns in the Presidency* (Washington, DC: CQ Press, 1988).

11. Mueller, *War, Presidents and Public Opinion*.

12. Linda Feldman, "Candidates Want Bush's Cash, Sans Bush," *Christian Science Monitor*, March 28, 2006: 3.

13. Richard Stevenson, "White House Says Prisoner Policy Set Humane Tone," *New York Times*, June 23, 2004: A1.

14. Doyle McManus and James Gerstenzang, "The Conflict in Iraq: Bush Delivers the News, with a Sobering Warning," *Los Angeles Times*, June 9, 2006: A1.

15. Wildavksy, "The Two Presidencies," p. 16.

16. James Baker, III, with Thomas M. DeFrank, *The Politics of Diplomacy: Revolution, War, and Peace, 1989–1992* (New York: Putnam, 1995), p. 116.

17. Wildavksy, "The Two Presidencies," p. 17.

18. Barry M. Blechman, *The Politics of National Security: Congress and U.S. Defense Policy* (New York: Oxford University Press, 1990); Duane M. Oldfield and Aaron Wildavsky, "Reconsidering the Two Presidencies," in *The Two Presidencies: A Quarter Century Assessment,* ed. Steve A. Shull (Chicago: Nelson-Hall, 1991), pp. 181–190; Thomas Franck and Edward Weisband, *Foreign Policy by Congress* (New York: Oxford University Press, 1979); Thomas E. Mann, ed., *A Question of Balance: The President, the Congress and Foreign Policy* (Washington, DC: The Brookings Institution, 1990); and Stephen R. Weissman, *A Culture of Deference: Congress's Failure of Leadership in Foreign Policy* (New York: Basic Books, 1955).

19. Hamilton, "Federalist 2," ellipses deleted.

20. Speech before the House of Representatives, March 7, 1800, as quoted in *Marbury v. Madison*, 5 U.S. (1 Cranch) 137 (1803).

21. As quoted in Henning, *The Wit and Wisdom of Politics*, p. 240.

22. *U.S. v. Curtiss Wright Export Corporation*, 299 U.S. 304 (1936).

23. *Youngstown Sheet & Tube Co. v. Sawyer*, 343 U.S. 579 (1952).

24. Harold Hongju Koh, *The National Security Constitution: Sharing Power After the Iran-Contra Affair* (New Haven, CT: Yale University Press, 1990); Gordon Silverstein, "Judicial Expansion of Presidential Power," in Paul E. Peterson, ed. *The President, Congress, and the Making of Foreign Policy* (Norman, OK: Oklahoma University Press, 1994), pp. 23–48; and Gordon Silverstein, *The Imbalance of Powers: Constitutional Interpretation and the Making of American Foreign Policy* (New York: Oxford University Press, 1996).

25. Joint Resolution of Congress, H.J. RES 1145, August 7, 1964.

26. Louis Fisher and David Gray Adler, "The War Powers Resolution: Time to Say Goodbye," *Political Science Quarterly* 113:3: 1–20.

27. "A joint resolution to authorize the use of United States Armed Forces against those responsible for the recent attacks launched against the United States," Public Law 107-40, September 18, 2001.

28. "A joint resolution to authorize the use of United States Armed Forces against Iraq," Public Law 107-243, October 16, 2002.

29. United States Senate, "Treaties," www.senate.gov/artandhistory/history/common/briefing/Treaties.htm, accessed June 20, 2006.

30. *United States v. Belmont*, 301 U.S. 324 (1937).

31. Ann Devroy, "Pact Reached to Dismantle Ukraine's Nuclear Force; Detailed Plan to Be Signed Friday, Clinton Announces," *Washington Post*, January 11, 1994: A1.

32. NSC-68, "United States Objectives and Programs for National Security," National Security Council, April 14, 1950.

33. Ibid.

34. George F. Kennan, "The Sources of Soviet Conduct," *Foreign Affairs* 25 (July 1947): 566–582.

35. White House National Security Council, "The National Security Strategy of the United States of America," September, 2002.

36. National Commission on Terrorist Attacks Against the United States, "Staff Statement 17: Improvising a Homeland Defense" (Washington, DC: June 17, 2004), p. 28.

37. George Marshall, secretary of state under Harry Truman, as quoted in Alexander De Conde, "George C. Marshall," in *An Uncertain Tradition: American Secretaries of State in the Twentieth Century,* ed. Norman A. Graebner (New York: McGraw Hill, 1961), p. 252.

38. Henning, *The Wit and Wisdom of Politics*, p. 69.

39. Ibid., p. 68.

40. Norman A. Graebner, "Dean G. Acheson," in *An Uncertain Tradition: American Secretaries of State in the Twentieth Century,* ed. Norman A. Graebner (New York: McGraw Hill, 1961), p. 13.

41. Don Van Natta, Jr., "President Rewards 43 Members of Fund-Raising Club with Prominent Posts," *New York Times*, March 6, 2002.

42. Barry Rubin, *Secrets of State: The State Department and the Struggle Over U.S. Foreign Policy* (New York: Oxford University Press, 1985), p. 64.

43. Stephen Holmes, "What Russia Teaches Us Now; How Weak States Threaten Freedom," *The American Prospect*, July-August 1997, 30.

44. General Omar Bradley, Chair of Joint Chiefs, Testimony to the Committee on Armed Services, House of Representatives, October 19, 1949, as quoted in John Bartlett, *Familiar Quotations* (Boston: Little, Brown, 1980), p. 824.

45. These points are taken from an insightful analysis of the way in which the Bush Administration changed U. S. counterterrorism

policy. See Abraham D. Sofaer, "The 'War' on Terrorism: Doctrinal Foundations," Hoover Institution, March 2002.

46. James R. Locher III, "Taking Stock of Goldwater-Nichols," *Joint Forces Quarterly* (Autumn 1996): 19-17.

47. Donald H. Rumsfeld, "Defense for the 21st Century," *Washington Post*, May 22, 2003: A35.

48. Michael R. Gordon and Bernard E. Trainor, *Cobra II: The Inside Story of the Invasion and Occupation of Iraq* (New York: Random House, 2006), p. 4.

49. Barbara Slavin and Dave Moniz, "How Peace in Iraq Became So Elusive," *USA Today*, July 22, 2003: 1A.

50. Loch K. Johnson, *America's Secret Power: The CIA in a Democratic Society* (New York: Oxford University Press, 1989), pp. 12, 43.

51. Ibid., chap. 2.

52. "Testing Intelligence," *Economist*, October 6, 2001.

53. Ibid.

54. Rubin, *Secrets of State*, p. 50.

55. Speech at the Constitutional Convention, as quoted in Hans J. Morgenthau, *Politics Among Nations*, 4th ed. (New York: Knopf, 1966), p. 12.

56. Speech in Philadelphia, February 22, 1861, as quoted in Morgenthau, *Politics Among Nations*, p. 35.

57. Steve Chapman, "Should We Be in the Balkans Forever?" TownHall.com Columnists, October 26, 2000. Available at www.townhall.com.

58. George W. Bush, "Remarks by the President on Iraq and the War on Terror," United States Army War College, Carlisle, PA, May 24, 2004.

59. Al Gore, "Our Founders and the Unbalance of Power," Remarks to the American Constitution Society for Law and Policy, June 24, 2004.

60. Ivo H. Daalder and James M. Lindsay, *America Unbound: The Bush Revolution in Foreign Policy* (Washington DC: Brookings Institution Press, 2003), chap. 1.

61. For a useful discussion of the "Bush Doctrine" see Robert Jervis, *American Foreign Policy in a New Era* (New York: Routledge, 2005).

62. Robert Keohane, *After Hegemony: Cooperation and Discord in the World Political Economy* (Princeton, NJ: Princeton University Press, 1984).

63. Morgenthau, *Politics Among Nations*; Kenneth N. Waltz, *Theory of International Politics* (New York: McGraw Hill, 1979); John J. Mearscheimer, "Back to the Future: Instability in Europe After the Cold War," *International Security* 15:1 (Summer 1990): 5–56; and Samuel Huntington, *The Clash of Civilizations* (New York: Simon & Schuster, 1996).

64. Joel R. Paul, "The Geopolitical Constitution: Executive Expediency and Executive Agreements," *California Law Review* 86:671 (July 1998): 749–752.

65. Marcus Noland, "Learning to Love the WTO," *Foreign Affairs*, September-October 1999, 78.

66. "Reactions," *Seattle Times*, December 1, 1999: A17.

67. Robert Matthew and Neil King, Jr., "Imposing Steel Tariffs, Bush Buys Some Time for Troubled Industry," *Wall Street Journal*, March 6, 2002: 1.

Name Index

SUBJECT INDEX

Pages numbers followed by an *f, t,* or *b*
indicate figures, tables, and boxed
material.

A

Abolitionist movement, 186
Abortion
  morality and legality in debate on, 134
  original intent and, 432
  partial-birth, 134
  privacy rights and, 481–483
  public opinion on, 133–135
  Roe v. Wade, 133, 432, 481
Abrams v. United States, 465
Abstentions, 160*b*
Abu Ghraib, 248, 263, 578
Administration, defined, 367
Administrative discretion, 392–393
Advanced Energy Initiative, 358
Advertising, radio, 239
Advice and consent, 41
Advocacy ads, 194
Affirmative action, 505–506
Affirmative action redistricting, 327
Afghanistan, 92, 574, 591
AFL-CIO, 535
African Americans. *See also* Civil rights;
    Racial minorities
  in Congress, 326–327
  in government workforce, 398*f*
  individualistic values of, 108*f*
  Jim Crow laws and, 495–496
  majority-minority districts and,
    326–327
  post-Civil War restrictions on,
    494–496
  in segregated schools, 505*f*
  spoils system and, 398
  voter participation by, 504*f*
  voter turnout by, 163*f*
  voting rights for, 152
Age
  in voter turnout, 164
  in voting franchise, 152
Agencies, 391
Agenda setting, 522
Agostini v. Felton, 472
Agriculture
  grape boycott, 508
  iron triangles in, 199
  mad cow disease, 539–540

in populism rise, 218
Shays's Rebellion, 35
subsidies for votes, 2
Aid to Families with Dependent
    Children (AFDC), 77
AIDS, 417
Air America, 254*b*
Air pollution, 542
Airline Deregulation Act, 546
Airline industry deregulation, 545–546
Al Jazeera, 258*b*
al Qaeda, 376, 479, 591
Alien and Sedition Act, 66
Ambassadors, 587–588
American Association of Retired Persons
    (AARP), 181, 187, 529–530
American creed, 104
American exceptionalism, 5–6
American Federation of Teachers, 539
American Indian Religious Freedom
    Resolution, 512
American people. *See also* United States
  civic republicanism of, 104
  colonial immigration, 95–96
  exceptions to general principles
    of, 142*f*
  individualism of, 105–107
  as joiners, 179*t*
  liberalism of, 103–104
  news sources relied on by, 244–247
  political attitudes of, 94–95
  positivism of, 110
  religious attitudes of, 109–112
  self-reliance of, 113
  as self-selected, 114
Americans with disabilities, 516–518
Americans With Disabilities Act, 71, 517
Amish, 472, 473
Animal sacrifice, 473
Annapolis Convention, 37
Anti-federalism, definition of, 27
Anti-Federalist-Federalist debate,
    44–46, 63
Anti-Saloon League, 192
Appeal, 446
Appeals courts, 438
Appropriations Committee, 340
Appropriations process, 347
Approval ratings, 379–380
Arab Americans, 92. *See also* Muslims
Aristocracy, 8–9

Armed Forces. *See* Military
Articles of Confederation, 34–36, 40*t*
Asian American civil rights, 509–510
Assemblies
  colonial, 28
  in unitary government, 62*b*
Associate justices, 447
Authorization process, 347

B

Baby boomers, 527
Bad tendency test, 463–464
Bakke decision, 506
Balancing doctrine, 466–467
Barron v. Baltimore, 460
"Battle for Seattle," 197*b*
Bay of Pigs, 593
Beltway insiders, 379
Benton v. Maryland, 479
Berlin Wall, 586
Bicameralism
  description of, 334
  in Virginia Plan, 38
Bilingual education, 509
Bill markup, 346
Bill of Rights. *See also* Civil liberties
  civil liberties protected by, 44, 45*t*
  death penalty and, 54
  initial neglect of, 43–44
  origins of, 459–460
  pre-Civil War application of, 460–461
  selective incorporation of, 462
  state government and, 461–462
Bipartisan Campaign Reform Act
    (BCRA), 283, 323
Bipolar world, 586
Black codes, 494
Blame avoidance, 544
Bloc voting, 326
Block grants, 76–79, 80*b*
Blogosphere, 243
Boat people, 114
Bork, Robert, 444, 480
Borking, 444
Boston News-Letter, 235
Boston Tea Party, 30
Bovine spongiform encephalopathy,
    539–540
Bowers v. Hardwick, 481
Boy Scouts of America v. Dale, 469
Briefs, 449

PHOTO CREDITS